Psychology
Boundaries and Frontiers

Psychology *Boundaries and Frontiers*

WILLIAM BUSKIST
AUBURN UNIVERSITY

DAVID W. GERBING
PORTLAND STATE UNIVERSITY

HarperCollins*Publishers*

For Connie,
and for Gordon and Marilynn

Credit lines for photos, illustrations, and other copyrighted materials appearing in this book are in the *Acknowledgments* section beginning on page A-1. This section is to be considered an extension of the copyright page.

Library of Congress Cataloging-in-Publication Data
Buskist, William.
  Psychology : boundaries and frontiers / William Buskist, David W. Gerbing.
    p. cm.
  ISBN 0-673-38023-8 : $31.00
    1. Psychobiology. 2. Psychology. I. Gerbing, David W. II. Title.
QP360.B86 1990   89-29896
150'.1'574—dc20   CIP

3456—VHJ—959493929190

Preface

We believe that the introductory psychology course can be one of the most important and interesting classes for students during their undergraduate careers. The course can challenge their intellectual curiosity, pique their personal interest in both the basic and applied dimensions of psychology, and satisfy their demand for a clear, coherent, and current account of the field. It is with these considerations in mind that we conceived and wrote *Psychology: Boundaries and Frontiers.*

In keeping with these considerations, we had three overarching goals. The first has been to portray psychology as a dynamic discipline essential to understanding human behavior, both at the level of the individual and at broader sociocultural levels. Within this framework, we strive to provide a broad perspective of biology's relationship to psychology. We do not limit our discussions of biological variables to only physiological ones, though; throughout the book we discuss the important roles of evolutionary and genetic factors in shaping our actions. This strategy allows us to place behavior in its proper context: in terms of the interaction of environmental and biological variables.

Our second and perhaps most important goal has been to convey to students that psychology is a research-based endeavor, and throughout the text we try to reinforce the importance of this by pointing up examples of important experiments and studies. By drawing on its broad data base, psychology has provided society with many useful insights into human behavior. However, it still has a long way to go to offer a complete explanation of our thoughts and actions. To highlight psychology's future challenges, we conclude each chapter with a special *Boundaries and Frontiers* section that explores particularly problematic or unanswered research questions. While these questions represent clear boundaries in our understanding of human behavior, they also serve as frontiers for further exploration and discovery. In some instances, the *Boundaries and Frontiers* sections are presented in terms of focused issues and problems that need to be addressed, and in other cases, they are presented more philosophically. We hope students will appreciate the frankness with which we discuss psychology's accomplishments and admit its limitations. More importantly, we hope they will be stimulated to think critically about the challenges that psychology's boundaries and frontiers pose for current and future generations of psychologists.

Our final goal has been to write a book with simple but effective pedagogy: to introduce a point, explain it, and then summarize and extend that explanation in terms of other, related points. In each chapter, readers will consistently find the same pedagogical structure:

- A *Chapter Preview* highlights the major points that will be featured in the chapter.
- Call-out quotes identify and reinforce important concepts.
- Frequent in-text summaries actively review major points and concepts, relating them to the proverbial "big picture" of psychology.
- A *Concept Summary*, written in essay-question form and page-referenced, prompts students to review the major points made within the chapter. (Answers to these questions are provided in the *Instructor's Manual.*)

- A *Key Terms and Concepts* listing provides an expanded definition and explanation of the most important terms and ideas in the chapter. (A page-referenced glossary comprised of key terms and concepts from all chapters is also found at the end of the book.)

The *Chapter Previews, Concept Summaries,* and *Key Terms and Concepts* sections are each organized around the first-level headings from the body of the chapter. This format is intended to help students understand, during review, the context in which major points were presented and developed.

ORGANIZATION OF THE BOOK

As will become apparent when you turn to the *Table of Contents*, in many ways the organization of this book is unique, both within and across chapters. Chapter 2, **Research Methods in Psychology,** is positioned early in the text to highlight the importance of scientific methodology in the discipline. The next chapter, **Evolution, Heredity, and Behavior,** is also positioned early in the text to make clear to students the interaction of ultimate and proximate variables in determining behavior, and to reflect psychology's increasing awareness that behavior is influenced by both classes of variables. In Chapter 4, **Biopsychology and Consciousness,** we discuss the structures and functions of the brain and nervous system using changes in consciousness, particularly drug abuse and sleep, as organizing themes. Because many teachers of introductory psychology focus on visual processes in their treatment of sensation and perception, we discuss basic principles of sensation and perception and visual processes together in Chapter 5, **Sensation and Perception: Basic Principles and Visual Processes.** Next, in Chapter 6, **Sensation and Perception: Audition, the Somatosenses, Smell, and Taste,** we discuss sensation and perception in terms of the other senses. This organization allows instructors to cover basic principles and vision, or basic principles and all senses, without having to skip around a single chapter or even two chapters to do so. Chapter 7, **Learning and Behavior Analysis,** begins rather than ends (like most other introductory texts) with a discussion of the biological bases of learning. This tack allows students to understand from the start of the chapter the importance of genetic and environmental variables and their interaction in determining an organism's ability to learn.

A unique combination of theoretical and topical approaches is used to examine developmental psychology. Chapter 11, **Life-Span Developmental Psychology,** includes both a discussion of traditional theories of development and a topical overview of the important events and processes that characterize each of the major phases of the life span. In the following chapter, **Gender Development and Sexual Behavior,** the importance of gender is highlighted within the context of development and its implications for sexual behavior and orientation. The final chapter, **Life-Style, Health, and Survival,** is perhaps the most unique in the text. Cast in the backdrop of cultural evolution, this chapter examines how important behavioral changes, and not just technological changes, are critical to improving personal health, quality of life, and the quality of our environment.

In sum, we have organized the context of the book according to a single theme: function. We view psychology as an empirical discipline that seeks to understand how the interaction of biological and environmental variables influences behavior. Accordingly, we have positioned chapters on research methods and heredity early to give students the perspective they need to understand and evaluate the material in the remaining chapters. Likewise, our goal in organizing the contents of individual chapters has been to maximize their usefulness in engendering student comprehension. After all, it makes sense, at least from the standpoint of enhancing student interest, to discuss well-established psychological principles within the framework of current cultural problems such as drug abuse and the threatened environment. Thus, a secondary goal driving how we organized the book has been to write a text whose organization could incorporate the relevance of psychology to everyday life in the 1990s.

TEXT FEATURES

The three goals described above have provided the framework for the content of each of the book's eighteen chapters. Consider some of the text's features within the context of these goals.

Goal 1: To portray psychology as a dynamic discipline essential to understanding human behavior. Chapter 1 provides the historical context for understanding the different perspectives from which psychologists and others have viewed human behavior. Chapters 3 and 4 highlight the rapidly burgeoning view that human behavior is a function of both biological and environmental variables and their interaction. Chapter 3 focuses on evolutionary and hereditary influences on behavior, and Chapter 4 explores the approaches that neuroscientists are currently using to unravel the mysteries of how the brain and nervous system affect behavior. In Chapter 12, the interaction of biological variables and the sociocultural context within which each of us matures from child to adult is discussed. Chapter 17 returns to the topic of evolutionary influences as they relate to social psychology. Chapter 18 then uses the theme of cultural evolution to explore how our modern day life-styles threaten the quality of the environment in which we live and how that environment, in turn, influences our quality of life.

Goal 2: To convey to students that psychology is a research-based endeavor. The prevailing theme of Chapter 2 is that research is the source of psychological knowledge. Both group and single-subject research approaches as well as correlational approaches are examined. Also included is an extended discussion of ethical issues in both human and animal research. The important relationship between theory and research is present in every chapter of the book. Consider the following examples. In Chapter 7, the research that led to the formulation of the Rescorla-Wagner Model of classical conditioning is discussed. The heart of Chapter 8 lies in a discussion of the research that led to the development of both the three-component and the levels of processing models of memory, as well as recent research that calls for modification of these models. Chapter 9 is organized around the computational metaphor, which serves as the basis for understanding information processing theory and the kinds of research that it has generated.

Goal 3: To write a book with simple but effective pedagogy. In addition to the specific pedagogical features mentioned above, each chapter is written as a narrative that invites students to participate in a scholarly journey through the myriad avenues of psychological research and theory. Chapter introductions are designed to pique students' intellectual curiosity. For example, Chapter 3 begins by piecing together the personal and scientific circumstances that led Charles Darwin to develop his theory of evolution.

To introduce the important distinction between sensation and perception, Chapter 5 begins with an account of Helen Keller's experience at the water pump, when she first became aware of her own thoughts. Chapter 12 opens with an engaging comparison of cultural variables that influence sexual behavior, and Chapter 13 begins with a compelling historical overview of the social and cultural influences that led to the development of intelligence testing.

Beyond chapter introductions, the use of examples can be a critical component of effective pedagogy, and we have tried to use ones that will enhance student understanding of the concepts being discussed. For example, synaptic transmission is discussed within the context of drug use and its effects on behavior (Chapter 4). The basics of research methodology are illustrated in a discussion of SAT scores (Chapter 2). Psychology's contribution to our understanding of motivation is presented in terms of the high-interest topics of eating and aggression (Chapter 10). To demonstrate how computers can be used to model human thinking, we discuss expert systems (Chapter 9). We use the example of sound waves coming from a stereo system to help students understand how sound is "heard" in the cortex (Chapter 6). And individual case studies highlight how the symptoms of psychological disorders can disrupt even the routine matters of everyday life (Chapter 15).

We want students to come away from their introductory psychology course with the idea that psychology has much to contribute to our understanding of the circumstances in which life places us. At the very least, we hope students emerge from the course with an appreciation for the practical as well as the theoretical side of our discipline. If there is any one message that we are trying to convey to students about psychology, it is this: If we are to explain the past and control our future, we need to understand how biological and environmental forces interact to influence behavior. As teachers, it is important that we provide our students with the means to understand their behavior and its potential effects on the world. Perhaps the best we can do is to teach them that many of the solutions to personal and even global problems are behavioral ones and not technological ones.

THE ANCILLARY PROGRAM

As experienced teachers of introductory psychology, we believe that the ancillary package is critical to the success of the textbook, both in terms of helping the instructor teach psychology and in terms of helping the student learn it. As such, accompanying *Boundaries and Frontiers* is an extensive set of supplementary aids to help both teacher and student get the most from their experience with the introductory psychology course. To ensure that the materials in the ancillary package accurately reflect the content of the text, one of the text authors has been closely involved with outlining and writing the ancillaries.

For the Student

The *Study Guide*, prepared by William O. Dwyer (Memphis State University) and William Buskist, contains practical exercises to help students understand the material presented in each chapter. The study guide is divided into two parts. The first provides advice pertaining to developing sound study habits. The second provides chapter study exercises, including a list of student mastery objectives, a matching exercise for key terms and concepts, a fill-in-the-blank review, a writing-to-learn exercise comprised of short-answer essay questions, and a multiple-choice quiz taken directly from the test item file (these items are identified in the test item file).

A computerized self-diagnostic tutorial, called *Star*, by Charles G. Halcomb (Texas Tech University) is also available to students. This exciting program offers students the opportunity to test their knowledge of chapter concepts through simulated chapter tests, mid-terms, and final exams. As students answer the questions, they are graded immediately on their responses and given advice on where to turn in the text for further information.

Students will also find SIMLABS, a unique computer-simulated series of classic experiments and demonstrations, useful in their studies. Students who have access to a microcomputer can work through and analyze problems, experimental questions, and research.

With each new copy of the text, students will also receive Scott, Foresman/Little Brown's highly touted special edition of *Time* Magazine. This edition provides a historical look at the coverage of psychology in *Time* from 1923 to 1988.

For the Instructor

The Ory Testing Program, prepared by William Buskist and John Ory, contains over 1500 multiple-choice questions that have been screened by a field-tested system that guarantees quality and consistency. These questions include those that are conceptual, factual, and applied. Each question is referenced to the page in the text where the correct answer can be found. Questions marked with an asterisk appear in the *Study Guide. The Ory Testing Program* is available on *TestMaster*, a user-friendly test generator compatable with both IBM and Apple formats. *The Ory Testing Program* is also available in printed form.

The *Instructor's Resource Manual*, prepared by William Buskist and David L. Morgan (Indiana University Southeast), is organized into three parts. The first includes general information about the pedagogical features of the text; how to organize the introductory class taking into consideration class size, orientation of the course, and so forth; and a listing of the overhead transparencies and video materials that are available to teachers using our text. The second part deals with the information provided in each chapter of the text and includes a list of student mastery objectives, a timeline representing key advances and discoveries, a suggested lecture outline, answers to the concept summary questions that appear in the text, a biographical sketch of key researchers, and suggested films. The final section contains handouts that may be xeroxed and distributed to students.

A handsome set of four-color transparencies taken from illustrations in the text is also available, as is a set of generic transparencies relevant to the introductory course. Available, too, is a *Videotape Library* comprised of VHS tapes ranging from 15 to 30 minutes in length; the tapes are offered on loan to users of *Boundaries and Frontiers.*

Perhaps the most useful teaching innovation to come along in many years is *The Psychology Encyclopedia*, a laser disk program that contains images from a wide array of transparencies, slides, films, and videotapes. The laser disk is easy to use and is operated by remote control. The laser disk provides immediate and random access to the images. *The Psychology Encyclopedia* has been revised for 1990 and now contains original footage from Pavlov's laboratory, recreations of Thorndike's and Harlow's discoveries, excerpts from "One Flew Over the Cuckoo's Nest," and recent news footage of important world events, as well as numerous new still images.

ACKNOWLEDGMENTS

Although only two names appear on the cover of this book, a large number of other people contributed significantly to the content and quality of it. Without their contributions of time, effort, constructive criticism, and plain common sense, *Boundaries and Frontiers* would be a far less substantive and appealing book. We are speaking, of course, of the Scott, Foresman/Little, Brown editorial staff, who worked behind the scenes developing and honing our rough manuscript into clear and readable prose, and of the many reviewers who gave generously of their time and expertise to read and comment on both early and final drafts of the book. From the start our goals were clear, but determining how to execute them well required both editorial development and market input at each stage of what turned out to be a minimum of three (and in some cases four) drafts of each chapter before we and our publisher were satisfied that the end product was what professors teaching the course would like to see in a new text for the introductory market.

At Scott, Foresman/Little, Brown, we are especially indebted to Scott Hardy, editorial vice-president, who persuaded both of us to write this text. His thoughtful advice kept us focused on the goals and blueprint we originally set forth in our prospectus. We are also indebted to Joanne M. Tinsley, who is arguably one of the best developmental editors in college publishing. Her constant and thoughtful attention to all aspects of the development of this project are reflected on each and every page of the text. Paula Fitzpatrick also assisted with the developmental editing of a couple of chapters, and Iris Ganz, program secretary, proved an invaluable resource in keeping track of the commentary of over 80 reviewers. Project editor Jan Mauer carefully copyedited the manuscript and skillfully oversaw the book through the entire production process. She was assisted by Ginny Guerrant, Mary Lenart, and Kathy Crabtree, all of whom helped considerably with the myriad details of project editing. Debbie Costello is responsible for the elegant and functional design of the book, including the artwork that so nicely reflects many of important issues we addressed in the book. The visual appeal of the book is also enhanced by the photographs selected by Sandy Schneider. Acquisitions editor Don Hull coordinated the *Boundaries and Frontiers* ancillary package and contributed no small amount of enthusiasm during all phases of the project. And marketing manager Otis Taylor has contributed much—with more to come, no doubt—to the marketing of this text. To each of these people, we offer our appreciation for a job done well.

The chapter reviewers for *Boundaries and Frontiers* were selected not only on the basis of their expertise in particular subdisciplines of psychology, but also on the basis of their interest in the teaching of psychology. As a result, we think we have written a book that is not only accurate and current in research and theory, but also one that is pedagogically sound and appealing to teachers and students who take learning seriously. We extend out gratitude and indebtedness to our reviewers:

Stephan Ahadi	*University of Illinois, Champaign-Urbana*
Jack B. Arnold	*Saint Mary's College of California*
Lewis Barker	*Baylor University*
John B. Best	*Eastern Illinois University*
Tom Brothen	*University of Minnesota*
Tom H. Carr	*Michigan State University*
Edward J. Clemmer	*Emerson College*
Richard T. Colgan	*Bridgewater State College*
Charles E. Collyer	*University of Rhode Island*
Richard B. Day	*McMaster University*

William O. Dwyer	*Memphis State University*
Norman S. Endler	*York University*
Claire Etaugh	*Bradley University*
Hiram E. Fitzgerald	*Michigan State University*
Paul W. Foos	*Florida International University*
Robert J. Gregory	*University of Idaho*
Richard A. Griggs	*University of Florida*
Charles G. Halcomb	*Texas Tech University*
Ralph W. Hansen	*Augustana College*
Myra Heinrich	*Mesa College*
Wendy L. Hill	*Lafayette College*
Sandra Holmes	*University of Wisconsin, Stevens Point*
James J. Johnson	*Illinois State University*
James H. Korn	*Saint Louis University*
Carlton Lints	*Northern Illinois University*
Vance E. Maloney	*Taylor University*
M. Jackson Marr	*Georgia Institute of Technology*
John A. McNulty	*Dalhousie University*
Harold L. Miller, Jr.	*Brigham Young University*
Richard Miller	*Western Kentucky University*
John M. Morgan	*Humboldt State University*
Edward K. Morris	*University of Kansas*
Steve A. Nida	*Franklin University*
R. W. Payne	*University of Victoria*
Michael Perone	*West Virginia University*
Nancy A. Perrin	*Portland State University*
Robert W. Proctor	*Purdue University*
Kathryn Rileigh	*Pembroke State University*
Brendan G. Rule	*University of Alberta*
Dave Schneider	*Rice University*
David A. Shroeder	*University of Arkansas*
Brent D. Slife	*Baylor University*
Judith Stein	*Le Moyne College*
Joseph J. Tecce	*Boston College*
Barbara Wanchisen	*Baldwin-Wallace College*
Michael G. Weiss	*California State University, San Bernardino*
Shelly L. Williams	*Washington and Jefferson College*
Dale Wise	*San Jose State University*
Edwin S. Zolik	*De Paul University*

In the early stages of the project, a number of colleagues responded to a survey based on the prospectus and the general orientation we had in mind for the book. These individuals responded enthusiastically to the survey and their comments helped us refine our goals and plans for the book. We are thankful to them for their advice:

Denise L. Bachara	*Macomb Community College, South*
Irwin Badin	*Montclair State College*
Elliott Bonem	*Eastern Michigan University*
Richard Bowen	*Loyola University*
Thomas P. Cox	*Black Hills State College*
Mary Dudley	*Howard College*
Barry Fish	*Eastern Michigan University*
Stanley Fitch	*El Camino College*
John Foust	*Parkland College*
Kenneth M. Froemke	*Bryan College*
Richard Halverson	*Luther College*
Michael J. Kiphart	*St. Mary's College of Maryland*

Pete Kolesnik	*El Camino College*
Ben Knox	*Northeast Alabama State Junior College*
Don Lehr	*SUNY, Fredonia*
John M. Lembo	*Millersville University*
Willie J. Manning	*Clayton State College*
John M. Morgan	*Humboldt State University*
Frank S. Murray	*Randolph Macon Woman's College*
Daniel Nelson	*Siena College*
Ray Paloutzian	*Westmont College*
Wayne Poniewaz	*University of Arkansas, Monticello*
Kathryn K. Rileigh	*Pembroke State University*
James Schaffer	*Thiel College*
Brent D. Slife	*Baylor University*
Randolph A. Smith	*Quachita Baptist University*
Josh Weinstein	*Humboldt State University*
Shelly L. Williams	*Washington and Jefferson College*
James D. Wynne	*York College, CUNY*
E. Yeterian	*Colby College*
Michael J. Zeller	*Mankato State University*

We wish to thank our colleagues closer to home who generously lent us moral support as well as provided an ample dose of perspective on the role of textbook writing. Deserving special mention are Jim Patton and Bud Barker at Baylor University, both of whom provided the initial impetus for undertaking this project; their understanding of the integration of the biological perspective throughout all of psychology provided the intellectual spark with which this project began. We would like to thank too, Hal Miller, Dave Morgan, and Josh Gerow for their extended input and advice as this book evolved. Also, Steve Bailey's guidance and encouragement throughout this project has been greatly valued. Although originally trained as an engineer, his comprehensive knowledge of psychology and his friendship often provided the energy to continue onward. At Auburn University, special thanks to Peter Harzem, Chris Newland, Bill Hopkins, Richard DeGrandpre, and Dudley Terrell for their support of the project and to Linda Weil for her expert secretarial assistance.

Most importantly, we thank our families for their patience and understanding during what appeared to be an endless project. Connie Buskist and Monica Gerbing—along with Tara, Colin, Caden, Kyle, and Cale Buskist and Bradley Gerbing—deserve heartfelt thanks.

B.B.
D.G.

Contents in Brief

Contents

5 Sensation and Perception: Basic Principles and Visual Processes   *147*

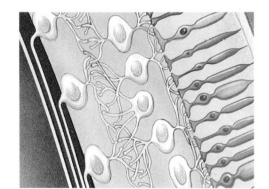

6 Sensation and Perception: Audition, The Somatosenses, Smell, and Taste   *191*

7 *Learning and Behavior Analysis*   225

8 *Memory*   265

9 Thinking and Language 295

10 Motivation and Emotion 331

11 Life-Span Development   *375*

12 Gender Development and Sexual Behavior   *421*

13 Intelligence   459

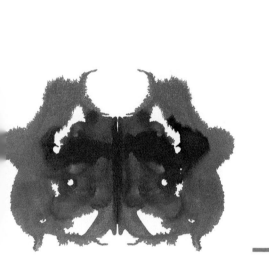

16 Therapy *567*

17 Social Psychology *601*

18 *Life-Style, Health, and Survival*   *637*

For the Student: A User's Guide

What we store in long-term memory is the meaning of stimuli . . .

Welcome to introductory psychology. Like your instructor, we are happy that you have decided to take this psychology course. Whether your interest is to discover what exactly it is that psychologists do, to learn about people and why they behave like they do, or just to use up some elective credit taking an interesting course, we are determined to help you meet your goals. We have tried to write *Psychology: Boundaries and Frontiers* with you in mind. That is why we have built into this book so many features to help you study. Here is what you need to know about the organization of this book to make the best use of your study time for this course.

Each chapter is organized around the same basic structure:

1. Each chapter begins with a *Chapter Preview* that summarizes the most important points of the chapter. The *Chapter Preview* is organized around the major headings in the chapter.
2. Within the chapter, key terms and concepts appear in **boldface** type.
3. Call-out quotes also appear throughout the chapter to underscore important points and concepts in the chapter.
4. Within the chapter, major points and concepts are summarized frequently. These summaries are designed to help you gain a perspective of how those points and concepts are related to each other.
5. At the end of the chapter is a *Concept Summary* that contains a number of open-ended questions as well as the page numbers indicating where within the chapter you can find the answer (your instructor has been given the answers to these questions).
6. Also found at the end of the chapter is a listing of *Key Terms and Concepts,* which provides an expanded definition of all **boldfaced** terms in the chapter.

At right is a sample chapter opener spread. The Chapter Preview section on the right gives students a concise outline of chapter highlights.

A sample Concept Summary and Key Terms and Concepts section is shown above. These sections help students review important points at the end of each chapter.

7. Following the *Key Terms and Concepts* listing is a section entitled *Additional Sources of Information*, which identifies specific articles and books that you may consult should you desire more information on particular topics discussed in the chapter.

Although there are a number of ways that you might use these features to help you study, here is our suggestion. First, read the *Chapter Preview* to gain a sense of the major points of the chapter. Next, read the *Concept Summary*. This will help you focus more clearly on the points mentioned in the *Chapter Preview*. Now read the chapter, but don't try to read it all at once. Instead, read it section by section, stopping occasionally for breaks and to refer back to the *Concept Summary*. (You may wish to highlight with a marker the answers to the *Concept Summary* questions.) Once you have read the entire chapter, review the *Key Terms and Concepts* at the end of the chapter. Doing so will reinforce your ability to recognize and understand the important points of the chapter.

Following this routine will give you a firm grasp of the material in the chapter and will help you identify points in the chapter that need further review before you take a quiz or an examination. You may also find the *Study Guide* that accompanies the text to be helpful in your study of psychology. The *Study Guide* is designed to help you become even more familiar with the contents of the book; it contains matching, fill-in-the-blank, and short-answer essay questions, as well as multiple-choice questions derived from your instructor's test item bank.

Like most texts, *Boundaries and Frontiers* also contains a glossary of key terms, complete subject and name indexes, and references following the last chapter. Consulting these sources is useful when you wish to locate or identify a term or researcher in the main text quickly, or when you wish to locate the original source of information upon which we based a specific discussion.

Shrinkwrapped with your new copy of *Boundaries and Frontiers* was a copy of a special of *Time* magazine dedicated to its coverage of psychology during the 65-year period, 1923–1988. This supplement was provided to you not because it would help you score higher grades—although it may—but rather, because we think it will stimulate your interest in psychology, both as a science and a profession.

We wish you the very best of success with your psychology course this term. We hope that *Boundaries and Frontiers* stimulates your interest and intellectual curiosity in psychology. If you have comments about the book to which you would like us to respond or suggestions that might help us improve the book in later editions, please write us in care of the publisher:

Scott, Foresman and Company
1900 East Lake Avenue
Glenview, IL 60025
Attn: Social and Life Sciences
      Higher Education Division

1 Introduction to Psychology

1

The purpose of this book is to introduce you to the science of psychology. What is psychology? What do psychologists do? You may be surprised and, we hope, fascinated by the answers to these questions. Our aim in writing this text is to introduce you to the exciting and rather challenging nature of psychology's quest: to understand the actions, the desires, and the thoughts of human beings. As we will see, psychologists study many different animals such as chimpanzees, white rats, pigeons, and even goldfish, but the emphasis is on people.

THE SCOPE OF PSYCHOLOGY

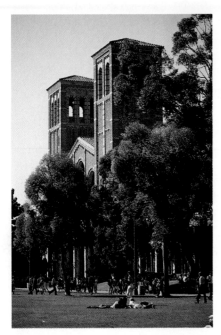

Behavior refers to actions that can be directly observed, such as these college students walking to class.

Psychology is the scientific study of the behavior and cognitive processes of individual organisms. The goal of psychology is to describe, understand, predict, and control behavior. To properly introduce you to psychology requires the entire book, but we will begin with a brief explanation of a few key terms followed by some examples. An organism, of course, is a person or animal. **Behavior** refers to the actions of organisms that can be directly observed by others. Walking to class is an observable behavior. So is talking to a friend and taking notes in your psychology class.

Psychologists also study cognitive processes (or cognition for short). **Cognitive processes** refer to unobservable mental activities such as thinking, feeling, sensing, and perceiving. Thinking about walking to class is *not* an observable behavior because another person cannot see your thoughts. Because cognitive processes cannot be observed directly, psychologists must study them by making inferences from observable behavior—what someone says and does. Only by studying behavior can the psychologist learn what someone is thinking, feeling, sensing, or perceiving.

Some cognitive processes such as memories and desires are particularly difficult to study. These memories and desires may influence our actions, thoughts, and feelings, but they do so without our conscious awareness.

Psychologists study both behavior and cognition. They study observable behavior by viewing it directly. Cognition is studied by making inferences from observable behavior. In essence, psychologists are interested in systematically uncovering functional relationships between behavior and other variables, which could also be behavioral. Psychologists study these topics within the context of teaching, research, business, athletics, medicine, government, and, of course, therapy for the treatment of psychological problems.

Most psychologists are genuinely interested in understanding human behavior at home, at work, and at play, and in finding solutions to human problems. A quick glance at the rest of this text will provide you with a glimpse of the specific topics that psychologists study: human development, sexual behavior, thinking, motivation, emotion, social relationships, perception, language, stress, and so on. Psychology's broad scope is reflected in the diversity of its subject matter. Consider, for example, some of the questions that psychologists are addressing today.

- To what extent is our behavior determined by hereditary factors, by environmental factors, or by their interaction?
- How do alcohol and other drugs affect the brain and nervous system?
- How do our perceptions influence what we can learn about our environment?
- Can viewing violent actions on television or in movies contribute to a person becoming aggressive in real life?

- What factors contribute to the development of eating disorders, such as anorexia nervosa and bulimia?
- How and to what extent do reward and punishment influence learning and behavior?
- How is memory related to the physical structure of the brain?
- What cognitive processes are involved in decision making? Are human thought processes analogous to the way computers process information?
- As we grow older and mature, what sorts of physical, cognitive, personality, social, and sexual changes might we expect to experience?
- Is dreaming reflective of our innermost desires and fears?
- How successfully do intelligence tests measure intelligence? Why do people's intelligence and other personality characteristics differ?
- Does stress have harmful effects on the body as well as the mind?
- What causes schizophrenia—a chemical imbalance in the brain? Stress? Can schizophrenia be inherited?
- What is an effective treatment for depression?
- Why are some people helpful to those in need while others are not?
- What factors determine when and with whom we fall in love?

n the midst of all this diversity you might be able to detect a single common thread—the behavior of individual organisms . . .

In the midst of all this diversity you might be able to detect a single common thread—the behavior of individual organisms—that unites these questions of how those organisms learn, think, act, perceive, and interact with their environment and with other organisms. The organism might be a fish, a rat, a pigeon, or a chimpanzee. More often than not, however, the organism is a human being.

THE BEGINNINGS OF PSYCHOLOGY

Imagine for a moment the difficulties that the first pioneers of psychology must have faced. There were no departments of psychology, there were no psychology textbooks, and believe it or not, there were not even any psychology professors! Where would you start? What would you study? Who would you study? Not surprisingly, early psychologists developed several different schools of philosophical thought on what constituted the proper subject matter for psychology. Other psychologists then aligned themselves with these schools, which are summarized in Table 1.1 and are discussed next.

TABLE 1.1. *The five early schools of psychology.*

SCHOOL	A MAJOR FIGURE	TIME OF EMERGENCE	EMPHASIS
Structuralism	Wilhelm Wundt	1880	Structure of the mind
Functionalism	William James	1880	Function of the mind
Behaviorism	John Watson	1910	Observable behavior
Gestalt theory	Wolfgang Köhler	1910	Organization of the mind
Psychoanalysis	Sigmund Freud	1900	Unconscious motivation

Structuralism

Psychology emerged as a new scientific discipline in Germany at the research laboratory of Wilhelm Wundt (1832–1920). Wundt was the first person to identify himself as a psychologist, and he established the first psychological laboratory in 1879. Wundt interpreted psychology as the study of the mind and its structure, and in so doing participated in another first; he founded the first school of psychology. He believed that the human mind was another part of the body, and as such, that it could be studied scientifically by analyzing its components. This approach soon became known as **structuralism.**

Structuralists believed the primary objective of psychology was to study directly the basic elements of conscious experience—sensations (such as sights, sounds, smells), images (memory), and emotions (such as love, hate, joy, and sorrow). Their goal was to identify and then see how these basic elements combined with each other to create different forms of conscious experience. Structuralists examined their subject matter subjectively through **introspection,** a highly disciplined self-analysis of conscious experiences. Structuralists trained themselves as well as their subjects to describe accurately the sensations, images, and emotions they experienced as they were stimulated by carefully selected stimuli, for example, a light or a sound.

Wilhelm Wundt (middle) and associates in the lab.

Suppose you were a structuralist. You might look in your refrigerator and see a lemon. How would you explain this experience? You would realize that this image of a lemon that your brain has constructed is based on its component properties, such as the form, size, and color of the actual lemon. You would try to understand how the more complex perception of the lemon is related to these more basic components; that is, how the brain assembles all of these parts into the experience of seeing the lemon as a complete object.

Wundt's theories have not had much impact upon modern American psychology, partly because of the development of other schools of psychology, especially behaviorism, and partly because Americans turned away from Germanic influences following the onset of World War I. Wundt's influence, however, was great as he established the first psychological laboratory and taught over 24,000 students during his long career (Fancher, 1979).

Functionalism

Other early psychologists believed that the structuralist's definition of psychology was too restrictive. They believed that many psychological processes could not be meaningfully broken down into more basic components. William James (1842–1910), a prominent American psychologist, for example, often referred to the active and fluid nature of psychological processes and the stream of consciousness (James, 1890).

James' ideas formed the basis for a school called **functionalism,** which stressed that the mind functions to aid the organism in adjusting to changes in its environment. The *function* of the mind rather than its structure was of paramount interest. Influenced by Charles Darwin's theory of evolution, functionalists were basically interested in studying the function of cognitive processes in aiding the survival of both human and nonhuman organisms. Although some functionalists used introspection as their primary analytical tool, others directly observed behavior as a means for studying conscious experience. Hence, functionalism broadened the scope of psychology to include the study of behavior as well as the study of cognitive processes.

*Above left: William
James. Above right:
Wolfgang Köhler.
Right: John B.
Watson.*

Gestalt Psychology

Unlike the other early schools of psychology, **Gestalt psychology** focused on describing the *organization* of cognitive processes. Gestalt is a German word that roughly translates into "form" or "overall shape." Like the functionalists, Gestalt psychologists were not interested in breaking down conscious experience into its component parts; rather, Gestalt psychologists analyzed consciousness as a unified process. Gestalt psychologists, such as Wolfgang Köhler (1887–1967), were particularly influential in studying perceptual processes.

One problem that fascinated early Gestalt psychologists was based on the then recent invention of motion pictures. How is it that we perceive motion as a unified process when viewing a motion picture? In essence, the motion picture is composed of nothing but a series of individual still photographs running in rapid succession through the projector. Yet in some way, the perception of motion is something more than the sum of the information provided by each individual frame. According to Gestalt psychologists, our perception of continuous motion is formed by the way that the mind actively organizes the pattern of changing photographs, constructing the illusion of continuity from the sequence of individual photographs. Studying how the mind creatively organizes pieces of information into unified wholes, or gestalts, was the core of Gestalt psychology.

Early Behaviorism

The school of psychology known as **behaviorism** argued that observable behavior and not cognitive processes were the proper subject matter for psychology. Early behaviorists such as John Watson (1878–1958) even went so far as to reject the introspective method in its entirety, avoiding all references to consciousness and mental experience. To Watson (1913), the matter was a closed case. He felt that "Introspection forms no essential part of its methods, nor is the scientific value of its data dependent upon the readiness with which they lend themselves to interpretation in terms of consciousness" (p. 158).

Of all the early schools of psychology, behaviorism, by far, had the greatest influence on the development of the emerging science of psychology. As we soon see, this influence continues to the extent that a modified form of behaviorism is one of the major forces in contemporary psychology.

O*f all the early schools of psychology,
behaviorism, by far, had the greatest
influence on the development of the emerging
science of psychology.*

*Although a motion picture is
composed of a series of individual still
photographs, our minds organize the
individual frames to construct an
illusion of continuity.*

Sigmund Freud

Early Psychoanalysis

The school of **psychoanalysis** was founded on the theory that human behavior and personality development is due primarily to unconscious motivations, those feelings, desires, and wishes that are blocked from our conscious awareness. Psychoanalysts such as Sigmund Freud (1856–1939) conducted detailed studies of the lives and experiences of individuals for the purpose of diagnosing and treating abnormal behavior such as hysteria and anxiety. Freud and his students believed that the unconscious contains numerous anxiety provoking wishes and desires that influence our conscious thoughts and actions. Using techniques such as analyzing dreams and studying slips of speech, psychoanalysts believed they could open a window and peer into the unconscious regions of the human mind.

CURRENT PERSPECTIVES IN PSYCHOLOGY

Although they do not exist as separate schools in modern psychology, the early schools of psychology have left an important mark on modern psychology. Together, they defined psychology's boundaries and frontiers, endowing us with a broadly defined and unexplored agenda for research, theory building, and speculation. Vestiges of the early schools can be found in the five major perspectives present in modern psychology. In fact, two of these current perspectives—the behavioral and the psychodynamic perspectives—trace their beginnings directly to the corresponding early schools.

These five contemporary perspectives are described briefly below and are summarized in Table 1.2. As you read about each perspective, keep in mind that when a psychologist adopts a particular perspective to guide his or her work, the perspective serves as a lens by which the entire subject matter of psychology is viewed. Just as the world looks different when you are wearing green-tinted glasses than when you are wearing rose-colored glasses, the world of psychology looks different depending on the perspective from which it is viewed.

TABLE 1.2. *The five perspectives of contemporary psychology.*

PERSPECTIVE	SUBJECT MATTER	RESEARCH METHODS
Behavioral	How behavior is changed under different conditions with an emphasis on learning	Objective measures of behavior; experimentation
Biological	The study of the effects of genetics, brain structure, chemistry, and hormones on behavior and cognition	Physiological measures of brain functioning; chemistry of brain processes and hormones
Cognitive	Mental processes such as thinking, sensing, and perceiving	Objective measures of behavior; experiments from which mental processing is inferred
Psychodynamic	The influence of unconscious motivations on behavior and cognition	Analysis of the fears, desires, and memories that are not consciously recognized by a person who is often a patient undergoing therapy
Social	Social interaction	Objective measures of behavior; experiments that involve the real or implied presence of others

Far right: B. F. Skinner constructing a scale model of a Skinner box. Right: Michael Gazzaniga.

The Behavioral Perspective

> The environment acts in an inconspicuous way: it does not push or pull, it *selects.* . . . It is now clear that we must take into account what the environment does to an organism not only before but after it responds. Behavior is shaped and maintained by its consequences.
>
> B. F. Skinner, 1971
> *Beyond Freedom and Dignity*

Psychologists working from the **behavioral perspective** are primarily interested in studying how different aspects of the environment affect behavior, either alone or in conjunction with biological variables. Behavioral psychologists may study the relation between behavior and the environment in the laboratory or in applied settings such as schools, homes, and businesses. They are particularly interested in the relation between behavior and its consequences. Some behavior might lead to pleasant outcomes. For example, studying hard can lead to good grades, which can lead to acceptance into medical school. Other behavior might lead to less desirable outcomes. Ignoring studies and skipping class leads to poor grades. This link between behavior and its consequences is at the core of behavior analysis, the branch of modern psychology that endorses the principles of behaviorism.

The Biological Perspective

> Understanding the brain's relation to basic issues of human nature raises some deep questions about knowledge of structure and function of that particular piece of biological tissue.
>
> Michael S. Gazzaniga, 1985
> *The Social Brain*

Psychologists working from the **biological perspective** study how genetic, physiological, and other biological processes influence behavior. They are interested in problems such as genetic influences on learning, brain structure and function, and how drugs and other chemicals affect our behavior, our thoughts, and our emotions. Biopsychologists search for the biological bases of behavior and cognition. Three interrelated versions of the biological perspective are explored in this text: the evolutionary basis of behavior is the study of how heredity and genetics affect behavior; neuroscience involves the study of the brain and nervous system and their concerted influence on behavior; and ethology is the study of behavior as it occurs in the natural world, particularly among nonhuman species.

Right: A researcher observes rats' behavior after they are given a drug that destroys a portion of their brains. Psychologists of the biological perspective study how such biological changes affect behavior and cognition. Below: Ulric Neisser.

The biological basis of psychology has been part of psychological theory and research from the beginning. Indeed, both Wundt and Freud began their careers as physiologists before establishing their respective schools of psychology, and Watson's doctoral thesis focused on the physical structure of the brains of young rats (Fancher, 1979). Within the last few decades, however, psychology and related sciences have placed a new emphasis on biology, creating what some refer to as a "biological revolution." Advances in technology have provided psychologists and other scientists with new tools for investigating the biological underpinnings of behavior and cognition. As we'll see, deft use of these tools has led to many significant discoveries ranging from better understanding the genetics of inheritance to better understanding the chemical structure of the brain and nervous system.

The Cognitive Perspective

> Cognition is the activity of knowing: the acquisition, organization, and use of knowledge. It is something that organisms do and in particular something that people do. For this reason the study of cognition is a part of psychology, and theories of cognition are psychological theories.
>
> Ulric Neisser, 1976
> *Cognition and Reality*

Psychologists who are primarily interested in studying how people sense, perceive, think, remember, solve complex problems, use language, and, in general, process information about their environments, generally work from the **cognitive perspective.** Although a distant cousin of this perspective is Wundt's structuralism, the cognitive perspective did not become a powerful force in psychology until the 1960s. By the 1970s, the "cognitive revolution" in psychology was well under way.

Cognitive psychologists assume that the brain forms, stores, retrieves, and modifies images and other internal representations of the external world. These representations, which are inferred to exist on the basis of an individual's observable behavior, result from a blend of one's life experiences. Moreover, these representations are constantly undergoing change as new experiences modify them.

Cognitive psychologists explain mental processes on the basis of these representations. Using computer programs as an analogy, these psychologists usually focus on studying the "software" of the mind rather than its underlying "hardware." In fact, many cognitive psychologists, such as Herbert Simon (who was awarded a Nobel prize in 1978 for his research on human cognition), develop computer models of human cognition.

The Psychodynamic Perspective

> The unconscious is the true psychical reality; in its innermost nature it is as much unknown to us as the reality of the external world.
>
> Sigmund Freud, 1900
> *The Interpretation of Dreams*

Sigmund Freud founded the early psychological school of psychoanalysis that emphasized the unconscious determinants of behavioral processes in human life, an emphasis that continues to be central to the work of many contemporary psychoanalysts. Unconscious motivations, fears, and desires continue to be essential to some theories of personality and in some types of therapy. Enough has changed from Freud's early work, however, that the intellectual descendants of Freud work from what is now called the **psychodynamic perspective.**

Freud had, for example, originally constructed an elaborate theory of the development of personality that was strongly based on unconscious sexual motivation. Without discounting all of this early work, most modern psychologists reject many of the details of this theory. The emphasis on sexual motivation continues to be important but not paramount. The psychodynamic perspective also incorporates other elements of modern psychology such as the insights gleaned from the study of conscious cognitive processes (Horowitz, 1988).

The Social Perspective

> One cannot describe or deduce the facts of competition and cooperation, of leadership and submission if one does not observe them; language and law cannot be studied in a "generalized, human, normal, adult" mind purified of social experience . . . . It follows that a general psychology, to be adequate, must extend the observation of psychological processes to social conditions.
>
> Solomon Asch, 1952
> *Social Psychology*

Psychoanalysis began here in Sigmund Freud's office. To help his patients relax, Freud had them lie on this couch and talk about themselves and their feelings while he sat out of view.

According to the social psychology perspective, the way these children play and interact shapes their behavior, attitudes, and thinking.

Some psychologists are primarily interested in the role of the social environment in influencing and changing our lives. We live our lives around other people, and we derive large measures of satisfaction, and sometimes frustration, from these people. We influence and are influenced by other people to a profound degree. Our families, our teachers, our friends, and our enemies have strong influences on our lives, and in turn, we also influence them. Consider for a moment, how your parents have influenced your thinking and behavior. Imagine, too, how different their lives would be had you not been born.

According to the **social perspective,** other people in our social environment shape an individual's behavior, attitudes, and thinking. An entire subfield of psychology, social psychology, is dedicated to this study, though other psychologists also use the social perspective. For example, psychologists interested in how children develop and mature might study a young child as he or she interacts with others.

Comparing the Perspectives

As you might expect, each of these different perspectives provides a unique framework from which to understand behavior and cognition, and from which to use psychology to help solve some of the problems that people face in their day-to-day lives. To illustrate how these five perspectives guide the understanding and interpretation of psychology, suppose that five psychologists—a neuroscientist, a behavioral psychologist, a cognitive psychologist, a psychodynamic psychologist, and a social psychologist— have been hired as consultants by a research firm to study cigarette smoking. Their task is to study the smoking behavior of several individuals to determine the factors that influence smoking.

Each psychologist would probably describe the patterns in the same general fashion, carefully documenting such information as the kind of cigarette each person smokes, how many cigarettes each person smokes a day, and the time of day each cigarette is smoked. However, merely describing behavior is not the same as explaining it. Explanation requires that the factors controlling the behavior be identified and manipulated. Description is only the first step in a scientific analysis. Thus, each psychologist's interpretation will be colored by his or her theoretical orientation; that is, the perspective that he or she has adopted.

Merely describing behavior is not the same as explaining it. Explanation requires that the factors controlling the behavior be identified and manipulated.

Examples of these analyses of smoking follow. This is a hypothetical example that we use to clarify some of the distinctions between the different perspectives. However, in real life these distinctions may not always be as clear-cut as they are presented here.

■ The neuroscientist would likely focus on the physiological effects of smoking, including the chemical influences of nicotine on the brain and nervous system. For example, some or all of the smokers may be addicted to the nicotine contained in cigarette smoke.

■ The behavioral psychologist would focus on the environmental conditions under which smoking occurs. For example, is the frequency of cigarette smoking higher during periods of stress than at other times? Do these people smoke more cigarettes than usual when they drink alcoholic beverages?

■ The cognitive psychologist would probably be interested in the individual's perception of himself or herself as a smoker and the thoughts and perceptions that precede and accompany smoking.

■ The psychodynamic psychologist might focus on the early childhood and social experiences of each person. Do these people smoke because they have an unconscious desire for oral stimulation?

■ The social psychologist might seek to understand smoking from the individual's interaction with other individuals. How do peers influence a person's decision whether or not to start smoking? Do these people smoke more or less when in the presence of others? Do they smoke more or less in the presence of particular kinds of people?

We are biological organisms who think and behave within a social environment.

Keep in mind that these five different types of explanations complement one another in our understanding of behavior. For the still emerging science of psychology, arriving at a truly complete understanding of human behavior requires an integration of all five perspectives. We are biological organisms who think and behave within a social environment. This theme provides the backdrop for exploring and explaining issues in contemporary psychology.

A complete theoretical integration of these perspectives is not yet possible at this stage in the history of psychology. However, throughout this text, we have attempted to explain psychology in terms of these biological, cognitive, behavioral, psychodynamic, and social factors that influence our thoughts and actions. In Table 1.3 we present a road map of where you will find these perspectives emphasized throughout the text. Some of the chapters concentrate primarily on a single perspective, though several of the perspectives can usually be found throughout each chapter.

TABLE 1.3. *A roadmap of the contemporary psychological perspectives in this text.*

CONTENT		PERSPECTIVES	
		Primary	*Others*
Chapter 1	Introduction to Psychology	All	
Chapter 2	Research Methods in Psychology	All	
Chapter 3	Evolution, Heredity, and Behavior	Biological	Social
Chapter 4	Biopsychology and Consciousness	Biological	Behavioral, Cognitive
Chapter 5	Sensation and Perception: Basic Principles and Visual Processes	Biological	Cognitive
Chapter 6	Sensation and Perception: Audition, the Somatosenses, Smell, and Taste	Biological	Cognitive
Chapter 7	Learning and Behavior Analysis	Behavioral	Biological
Chapter 8	Memory	Cognitive	
Chapter 9	Thinking and Language	Cognitive	
Chapter 10	Motivation and Emotion	Biological	Behavioral, Social
Chapter 11	Lifespan Development	Biological	Social
Chapter 12	Gender Development and Sexual Behavior	Cognitive	Behavioral, Social
Chapter 13	Intelligence	Cognitive	Social
Chapter 14	Personality	Cognitive	Social
Chapter 15	Psychological Disorders	All	
Chapter 16	Therapy	All	
Chapter 17	Social Psychology	Social	
Chapter 18	Life Style, Health, and Survival	All	

Psychology can also be broadly viewed in terms of what individual psychologists actually do rather than by the general perspective from which they identify themselves. Two general areas of employment for psychologists can be identified. **Research psychologists** primarily conduct psychological research; **practitioner psychologists** primarily offer psychological services such as counseling and therapy to the public. Some psychologists are exclusively researchers, some are exclusively practitioners, and some are both. Many university and college professors, for example, conduct research in addition to providing psychological services.

Research Psychologists

Research psychologists typically hold a Ph.D. degree, the Doctor of Philosophy. Someone who has earned the Ph.D. degree has received intensive instruction in the conduct of scientific research. Research psychologists study experimental questions in one of psychology's many subfields and have conducted at least one original and thorough research project, the doctoral dissertation.

Research psychologists are interested in a variety of questions about psychological phenomena. The questions may be as basic as, "What are the physical changes in the brain that result from learning?" or as applied as, "What is an effective method for teaching children problem-solving skills?" Some researchers seek answers to questions that may not have any immediate applicability to improving the quality of life, while others seek immediate answers to specific problems such as obesity, improving memory, and treating depression.

About one-third of all psychologists work in colleges or universities where they are involved in some combination of research and teaching (Stapp & Fulcher, 1981; Howard et al., 1986). Naturally many of these psychologists are employed in departments of psychology, but psychologists are also found in departments of communication, management, marketing, and sociology; schools of education; and in professional programs such as schools of law, medicine, and public health.

> The goal of the research psychologist is to produce new knowledge about human behavior and cognition . . .

The goal of the research psychologist is to produce new knowledge about human behavior and cognition and to develop theories that explain and integrate this knowledge. These same psychologists also train new generations of psychologists to conduct thoughtful and carefully planned research. While at work, research psychologists are most likely to be found in the laboratory or in other research settings, such as the workplace or public schools, designing and conducting studies with humans or animals. When not in the lab, research psychologists are often found in their offices preparing a written account of their work for publication in a scientific journal. For research psychologists, journal publications are the chief means of communicating their work to other scientists. Table 1.4 lists 14 prominent research journals in psychology.

Broadly speaking, research psychologists fall into four basic research specialities or subfields: experimental, developmental, personality, and social psychology. Research psychologists who study basic behavioral and cognitive processes such as sensation, perception, motivation, emotion, learning, memory, and problem solving are called experimental psychologists. Experimental psychologists provide teachers and practitioners alike

TABLE 1.4.   *Some major journals in research psychology.*

JOURNAL	PERSPECTIVES
1. *Behavioral Neuroscience*	Biological, Behavioral, Cognitive
2. *Physiology and Behavior*	Biological, Behavioral
3. *Journal of Experimental Psychology*	Behavioral, Cognitive
4. *Journal of Consulting and Clinical Psychology*	Behavioral, Cognitive
5. *Behavioral and Brain Sciences*	Biological, Behavioral, Cognitive
6. *Journal of the Experimental Analysis of Behavior*	Behavioral, Biological
7. *Memory and Cognition*	Cognitive
8. *Animal Learning and Behavior*	Biological, Behavioral, Cognitive
9. *Cognitive Psychology*	Cognitive
10. *Developmental Psychology*	Social, Biological, Cognitive
11. *Abnormal Psychology*	Behavioral, Cognitive
12. *Journal of Personality and Social Psychology*	Social, Cognitive
13. *Journal of Applied Behavior Analysis*	Behavioral

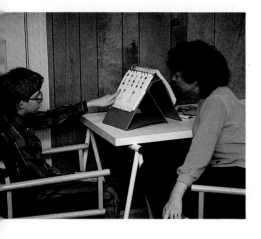

Personality psychologists use methods such as intelligence testing to identify people's cognitive and behavioral differences in order to study personality and its causes.

with data and theories regarding the behavior of many different organisms. Experimental psychologists conduct much of their research within the psychological laboratory, but they also conduct research in more natural settings such as the classroom and workplace.

Developmental psychologists study the psychological processes during growth and change as organisms mature from conception to death. These psychologists design studies and formulate theories that attempt to explain developmental processes as diverse as gender identity, language acquisition, and puberty. In the past, developmental psychologists concentrated their research efforts on understanding developmental processes in young people. More recently, they have broadened their research agenda to include the study of developmental changes over the entire life span.

Personality psychologists study the ways that people are different from one another. Intelligence, impulsiveness, creativity, shyness, anxiety, and happiness are just a few examples of some of the attributes in which people differ. In other words, personality psychologists are most interested in those personality characteristics that make each of us unique. Personality psychologists study their subject matter by first identifying cognitive and behavioral differences among people. These differences lead to theories about personality and its causes, which in turn, lead to research.

Social psychologists study how people interact with each other as well as how people are affected by changes in social environments. Social psychologists might study issues like cooperation and competition, attitude development and change, conformity and compliance, obedience, group behavior, persuasion, attraction, love, the effect of group influences on emotion, and our memory of social events. Thus, in studying individual behavior in social contexts, social psychologists fill an important gap between psychology—the study of individual behavior—and sociology—the study of society.

TABLE 1.5.	Psychology employment settings and subfields (Stapp, Tucker, & VandenBos, 1985).	
SPECIALTY		PERCENT
I. Subfields		
1. Clinical and counseling		51.1
2. School/education		19.4
3. Experimental		6.7
4. Developmental, social, and personality		6.7
5. Measurement		1.9
6. Industrial/organizational		5.7
7. Other		8.5
		100.0
II. Employment Settings		
1. Colleges and universities		26.7
2. Private practice		17.5
3. Clinical and counseling centers		16.0
4. School and education		14.9
5. Business and government		12.2
6. Hospitals		8.9
7. Medical schools		2.6
8. Not specified		1.2
		100.0

Practitioner Psychologists

While many psychologists are engaged primarily in conducting research, even more psychologists work as practitioners. Table 1.5 compares the primary employment settings for both research and practitioner psychologists. Most practitioner psychologists have earned the traditional Ph.D. degree, though some have earned the Psy.D. (Doctor of Psychology) degree, which was first offered by universities in the 1960s. The Psy.D. degree indicates that its holder has been trained primarily in the *practice* of psychology, usually in the context of mental health. Because the emphasis is on application, training for the Psy.D. degree requires less focus on research methods and analysis and more hands on training for treating psychological problems. People who hold a master's degree in psychology can also practice psychology and treat patients. However, in some cases, their educational background limits the extent of service they can provide to the public. People who graduate with bachelor's degrees in psychology are able to work as practitioner psychologists as well, especially as counselors. Often people with bachelor's or master's degrees in psychology work under the supervision of a licensed clinical psychologist.

Practitioner psychologists work in many different areas of our society. The primary subfields of psychology occupied by practitioner psychologists include clinical psychology, industrial/organizational psychology, and school and educational psychology. Each of these subfields is briefly discussed below, though as you can see from Table 1.5, there are far more clinical psychologists than there are other types of psychological practitioners, and clinical psychology is the only specialty area discussed in more detail later in the text.

Clinical Psychology. **Clinical psychologists** are concerned with the origins and treatment of psychological problems. They specialize in therapy or therapy-related research. In addition to having earned a Ph.D. or Psy.D. degree, clinical psychologists also must obtain a license before they can legally treat individuals with psychological problems. To qualify for this license, psychologists must obtain special training in clinical techniques, including a year of providing treatment under the supervision of experienced clinical psychologists, and earning a passing score on a test designed to measure general knowledge of the field.

Because clinical psychologists provide treatment for psychological problems, they are sometimes called health-care providers. Another type of health-care provider in the field of psychology is the counseling psychologist, who usually deals with issues and problems less severe than those dealt with by clinical psychologists, though the responsibilities of clinical and counseling psychologists overlap. But where a clinical psychologist would treat psychological problems, a counseling psychologist might provide guidance for students choosing a career or help resolve family difficulties.

Although clinical psychologists are health-care providers, they are *not* psychiatrists. Though the roles of clinical psychologists and psychiatrists often overlap considerably, **psychiatrists** have earned an M.D. or the Doctor of Medicine degree. Psychiatrists may prescribe drugs for the treatment of psychological disorders and admit patients to hospitals. Because clinical psychologists are not medical doctors, they cannot write prescriptions or admit patients, but clinical psychologists usually have more training in psychology than do psychiatrists. Both clinical psychologists and psychiatrists treat psychological problems such as mild depression, shyness, irrational fears, and more severe disturbances that might require hospitalization, such as serious depression and schizophrenia.

At this family counseling session, a counseling psychologist helps a father and his daughters work through their problems.

Psychologists in the Workplace and School. Psychologists can be found applying their skills in settings other than those providing health care. Practitioner psychologists are also found in the workplace and in schools. Industrial/organizational psychologists (or simply I/O psychologists) apply psychological principles to a variety of employment-related problems encountered in the workplace. Working in government, business, and industry, I/O psychologists conduct surveys about job satisfaction, screen personnel during the hiring process, and recommend changes in the work environment that will lead to increased worker efficiency or improved relations between employees and management.

Engineering psychologists help manufacturers design new products to make them safer and easier to use. For example, engineering psychologists help design the cockpits of commercial and military jets so that large amounts of information are presented to the flight crew in a form that can be understood and properly interpreted in a short period of time. Consumer psychologists help design marketing strategies based on their knowledge of consumer purchasing habits and study the reactions of consumers to new products.

For the most part, school psychologists work with students in primary and secondary schools. Their job is to study the intellectual and personality characteristics of individual students to help them maximize their success in school. School psychologists might recommend changes in class placement, new or different study programs, specialized tutoring, or they might refer someone with serious problems to a physician or clinical psychologist for further help.

Educational psychologists typically work in colleges and universities. They may conduct research on how to improve student performance in the classroom or how to increase teaching effectiveness. Educational psychologists also write many of the standardized tests that are administered to students in all levels of the school system.

The Complementary Roles of Science and Practice

Today psychologists are scientists, practitioners, or both. This change of emphasis can be seen by the changing memberships of the original organization of American psychologists, the American Psychological Association or APA. Founded in 1892 with 26 charter members, the APA had grown to about 1,000 members by 1929 and in 1980 had well over 50,000 members (Hilgard, 1987). Although from 1900 onward, Freud and his students of psychoanalysis were pursuing the clinical aspects of psychology, their work was not considered to be part of psychology, and for the first few decades, membership in the APA was restricted to researchers only. As the organization grew, however, the membership requirements were gradually changed to permit practitioner psychologists to also become members. Now, according to the APA membership roster, members registered as research psychologists are in the minority. The majority of doctorates awarded to new psychologists are awarded to those who become primarily practitioners (Howard et al., 1986).

Because of the APA's changing emphasis, on August 12, 1988 research psychologists formed a new organization called the American Psychological Society, or APS. The bylaws of the APS require that all members be scientists, as was the case with the original APA. The formation of the APS demonstrates the increasing distinction between research psychologists and practitioner psychologists.

> **Today psychologists are scientists, practitioners, or both.**

Why has this distinction between psychological research and psychological practice evolved? One reason is that despite all the gains and accomplishments of research psychology, there still remains a large gap between our formal, scientific knowledge and the complexities of daily life. Thus, although clinical psychologists are guided by the knowledge gained from psychological science, the manner in which they actually treat psychological problems involves a considerable amount of judgment and intuition. Clinical psychologists must sometimes confront the problems of their clients with less than a perfect theoretical understanding of these problems.

Consider, for example, something as complex and important to our lives as marriage. Most people get married and enter that marriage with the belief that it will succeed. Yet somehow, up to half of all marriages fail. Although psychological tests and guidance are available for exploring compatibility between prospective partners, no psychologist or anyone else is currently able to predict with reasonable accuracy the success of a particular relationship. In addition to all of the outside factors that influence the success and stability of a relationship, no one is able to explain precisely all of the psychological factors that contribute to the success or failure of that marriage. An equation to predict such results would have to include such variables as personality characteristics, emotions, intelligence, sensitivity, feelings of self-esteem and competency, sexual attraction and satisfaction, friendship, and dependence. This equation would also have to account for the complex ways in which people grow psychologically throughout their lives with changing interests and competencies.

TABLE 1.6. *A comparison of research and clinical psychology.*

	RESEARCH PSYCHOLOGY	CLINICAL PSYCHOLOGY
Objective	Produce new knowledge and develop scientific theories	Directly confront the complexities of daily life and treat the resultant problems
Advantage	Precision and control; rigor	Help people cope with the problems and stresses of day-to-day life
Disadvantage	Like all sciences, some research is narrowly focused and of primary interest only to other researchers	Lack of precision and control; speculation is often required without precise scientific guidance
Employment	Highly competitive, often with many more applicants than openings	Openings in a wide variety of settings from private practice to university settings
Education	Ph.D.	Ph.D. or Psy.D.

The complementary roles of research and practitioner psychology are shown in Table 1.6. The goal of psychology in general is to provide a more complete scientific explanation of all aspects of our lives. In the meantime, clinical psychology will, by necessity, rely at least in part on intuition. Thus, as you read this text, you will probably learn many valuable things that may help you understand yourself. At the same time, though, remember that the information that we present to you has definite boundaries formed by gaps in our current knowledge of human behavior—gaps that future research psychologists will begin to fill.

BOUNDARIES AND FRONTIERS

Psychologists often take it for granted that their work contributes to our understanding of human nature and to improving our quality of life. To be sure, almost all people who become psychologists have a keen interest in people and believe that their work will add to the existing body of knowledge about human thought and action. You might wonder, though, as you begin your study of psychology, exactly how studying psychology can benefit you. Besides getting a grade out of the course this term, how can the study of psychology help you develop a better understanding of your own behavior and thinking?

Before going on to study the next chapter, take a few minutes to browse through the rest of the book. By doing so, you will begin to get an idea of some of the things you will learn about psychology and how psychology can help you in understanding everyday life. For example, if you turn to Chapter 4, Biopsychology and Consciousness, you will see how your nervous system makes it possible for you to interact with the environment; you will also see how drugs affect your nervous system to produce changes in different states of consciousness. Turning to Chapter 10, Motivation and Emotion, you will learn how the interaction of physiological, behavioral, social, and cognitive factors influence your eating habits, including what you eat and when you eat it. In that chapter, you can also learn about some of the variables that influence aggression, including how watching violence on television can lead to aggressive behavior. Turning to Chapters 13 and 14, Intelligence and Personality respectively, you will see in detail some of the ways in which you might differ from your fellow human beings, and some of the reasons why those differences exist. In Chapter 17 you will learn about the different meanings of those often spoken but almost as often misinterpreted words, "I love you." Finally, if you peruse Chapter 18, Lifestyle, Health, and Survival, you will learn how stress can affect you, both physically and psychologically. You will also learn some of the strategies that other people have found effective for coping with the stress of daily life.

Browsing through the text will also show you that psychology is a young and changing science, and that we don't have all the answers to humanity's many problems. Psychology is only beginning to understand the intricate web of human emotions and experiences that accent each of our lives. Answers to many interesting psychological questions remain to be discovered, and many important questions have not yet been asked. The many unanswered questions represent clear boundaries in our understanding of life. Such boundaries, when viewed in another light, are actually frontiers—thresholds of knowledge and understanding that beckon psychologists to explore and discover.

Although you will learn much of personal and intellectual interest from studying psychology, you can also learn important things about people from reading good novels or studying the great works of art. In some ways the typical novel provides a more interesting narrative of the passions and dramas of life than does psychology. Novels are full of love, intrigue, sex, and in general, all the colors and shades of human experience. So why study psychology? The answer is simple: because novels cannot explain behavior; they can only document it. It is up to psychologists to do the explaining in terms of developing theories of human behavior that can be tested with scientific methods.

CONCEPT SUMMARY

THE SCOPE OF PSYCHOLOGY

- What is psychology? How are cognitive processes different from behavior? (p. 2)
- What are some of the phenomena that psychologists study? (pp. 2–3)

THE BEGINNINGS OF PSYCHOLOGY

- What was structuralism? What kinds of research methods did structuralists apply to their subject matter? (p. 4)
- What was functionalism? How did it differ from structuralism and Gestalt psychology? (pp. 4–5)
- How did early behaviorism differ from early psychoanalysis? (pp. 5–6)

CURRENT PERSPECTIVES IN PSYCHOLOGY

- What are the five major perspectives found in psychol-

ogy today? How might advocates of each perspective attempt to study the influences that lead people to drink alcoholic beverages in excess? (pp. 6–11)

PSYCHOLOGY—RESEARCH AND PRACTICE

- What is the difference between a research psychologist and a practitioner psychologist? (p. 12)
- What are the four major subfields of research psychology? What differences exist among the subfields? (pp. 12–14)
- What are some of the activities in which a clinical psychologist might engage? What kinds of psychologists are found in the workplace and in school settings? (pp. 15–16)
- In what ways are the roles of research and practitioner psychologists complementary? (pp. 16–17)

KEY TERMS AND CONCEPTS

THE SCOPE OF PSYCHOLOGY

Psychology The scientific study of the behavior and cognitive processes of individual organisms. (p. 2)

Behavior The actions of organisms that can be observed directly by others. Such actions are sometimes referred to as "observable behavior." (p. 2)

Cognitive Processes Unobservable mental activities such as thinking, sensing, and perceiving. (p. 2)

THE BEGINNINGS OF PSYCHOLOGY

Structuralism The school of psychology founded by Wilhelm Wundt that emphasized the structure of the mind as being the appropriate subject matter for psychology. (p. 4)

Introspection The method used by structuralists for the self-analysis of one's conscious experiences. The method involves learning how to describe precisely sensations, images, and emotions caused by simple stimuli such as lights and sounds. (p. 4)

Functionalism The school of psychology founded by William James that studied the mind's role in helping organisms adapt to their environment. (p. 4)

Gestalt Psychology The school of psychology that studied the organization of cognitive processes, particularly perceptual processes. (p. 5)

Behaviorism The school of psychology often associated with John B. Watson, who argued that observable and not mental processes were the proper subject matter of psychology. (p. 5)

Psychoanalysis The school of psychology founded by Sigmund Freud that portrays human behavior and personality development as due primarily to unconscious motivations and desires. (p. 6)

CURRENT PERSPECTIVES IN PSYCHOLOGY

Behavioral Perspective A current view in psychology based partially on the view of early behaviorists that behavior is caused by environmental variables and their interaction with biological ones. (p. 7)

Biological Perspective A current view in psychology that behavior is influenced by genetic, physiological, and other biological processes. (p. 7)

Cognitive Perspective A current view in psychology that emphasizes the study of how organisms process information about their environment (sensing, perceiving, thinking, remembering, and so on). (p. 8)

Psychodynamic Perspective A current view in psychology based on the earlier work of Freud and his followers that focuses on the unconscious determinants of behavior and mental processes. (p. 9)

Social Perspective A current view in psychology emphasizing the role that our social environment plays in shaping our behavior, attitudes, and thinking. (p. 10)

PSYCHOLOGY—RESEARCH AND PRACTICE

Research Psychologist A psychologist, generally a Ph.D., who conducts psychological research. Research psychologists may work in laboratory settings or in more naturalistic settings such as schools or the workplace. (p. 12)

Practitioner Psychologist A psychologist who provides psychological services, such as counseling or therapy, to the public. Practitioners may hold either the Ph.D. or the Psy.D. degree. Some practitioners, especially those in academic settings, may conduct research as well as practice. (p. 12)

Clinical Psychologist A practitioner psychologist who specializes in therapy and/or therapy-related research. (p. 15)

Psychiatrist A person with an M. D. degree who treats those with psychological problems. Clinical psychologists receive more training in psychology and psychological research than psychiatrists do, but psychiatrists can prescribe drugs as a means of therapy while clinical psychologists cannot. (p. 15)

ADDITIONAL SOURCES OF INFORMATION

American Psychological Association. (1986). *Careers in psychology.* Washington: American Psychological Association. This pamphlet provides useful information about the different subfields of psychology and the different employment opportunities for people interested in becoming psychologists. You can receive a free copy of the booklet by writing directly to:

> The American Psychological Association
> 1200 Seventeenth Street, NW
> Washington, DC 20036.

The psychology department at your school probably has a chapter of the National Honor Society for psychology majors, Psi Chi. You may wish to consult a member of Psi Chi about opportunities to participate in informative and interesting activities such as conferences and tours of mental health facilities with psychology majors.

Hilgard, E. R. (1988). *Fifty years of psychology: Essays in honor of Floyd Ruch.* Glenview, IL: Scott, Foresman. This little book is a concise and very readable summary of the history of several of psychology's major subfields.

Hilgard, E. R. (1987). *Psychology in America: A historical perspective.* San Diego: Harcourt Brace Jovanovich. A highly interesting and thorough overview of the major developments in psychology's growth as a scientific force in the United States. In addition to documenting the important events that shaped psychology into its present form, this book also contains brief biographies of the major contributors to twentieth century psychology.

2 Research Methods in Psychology

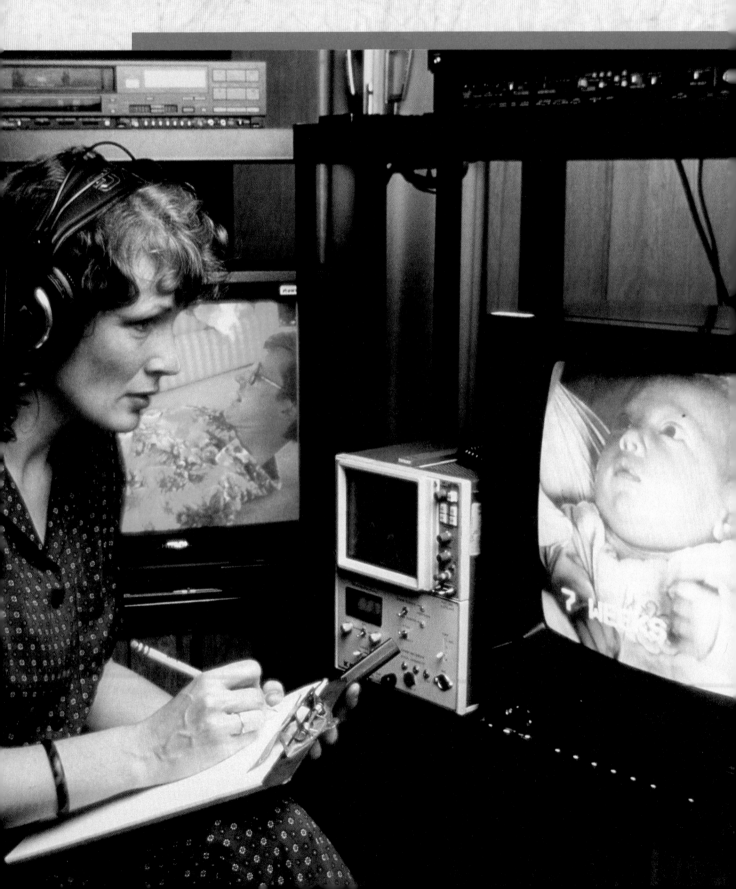

THE NATURE OF SCIENTIFIC KNOWLEDGE *(22–29)*

Scientific Knowledge is Empirical Knowledge
Relationships Among Variables: Correlation and Prediction
Hypotheses and Theory

Scientific knowledge is empirical knowledge. The purpose of psychological research is to reveal the relationship between certain kinds of variables and behavior. Scientific questions about these relationships are called hypotheses. Two kinds of hypotheses, relational and causal, correspond to two different kinds of research, purely observational and experimental.

OBSERVATIONAL RESEARCH *(29–34)*

Self-Report   Naturalistic Observation   Case Studies
A Limitation of Observational Research

Observational research is most appropriate for testing hypotheses that do not specify cause and effect relationships. In this case, researchers are passive observers of behavior; that is, they do not manipulate the circumstances under which behavior occurs.

EXPERIMENTAL RESEARCH *(34–42)*

The Experiment   Single-Subject Research
Potential Pitfalls of Experimental Research

In experimental research, the researcher systematically changes the circumstances in which behavior occurs and then observes the effect of this change on behavior. This deliberate and controlled change means that experimental research is better suited than purely observational research for testing causal hypotheses.

ANALYZING DATA *(42–51)*

Descriptive Statistics   Correlation and Prediction Revisited
Inferential Statistics

The strength of the observed relationships between variables are analyzed with statistics. Some statistics are used to describe the results of a research study, and other kinds of statistics allow the researcher to generalize his or her results beyond the context of a single study to an entire population.

ETHICS IN PSYCHOLOGICAL RESEARCH *(51–54)*

Ethics and the Use of Animals   Ethics and the Use of Human Subjects

Psychological research should be conducted with certain ethical considerations in mind. Foremost among these is safeguarding the well-being of subjects, regardless of whether they are animals or people.

Some time this term you will probably have the opportunity to serve as a participant in a psychological research study. A lab assistant will come to your class, describe the study, and pass around a sign-up sheet for you to leave your name and phone number if you are interested in participating. Let's imagine that you decide to volunteer—after all, you will be receiving extra credit for your time, and you are interested in getting an inside look at a real psychology experiment. Several days later, you get a call from the lab assistant who asks you to report to the laboratory of Dr. Gregory Zilstein tomorrow afternoon.

When you show up at the lab, you are led into a small room and asked to sit with the other volunteers but asked not to talk to any of them. Your attention is drawn to the front of the room, where you see a chair, complete with leather straps, and several large pieces of electrical equipment.

Soon after you are seated, Dr. Zilstein enters the room. Dr. Zilstein explains that the purpose of the experiment is to study the effects of electric shock on learning. You begin to wonder whether or not you did the right thing when you volunteered to participate: the thought of being shocked is more than a little frightening. Dr. Zilstein goes on to describe the effects of the shocks: they will hurt and they will be intense, although he promises that they will not cause any permanent tissue damage. Your heart begins to pound and you can feel yourself sweating.

Could such a study actually happen? Not only could the study happen, but it did happen, although no one was actually shocked (Schachter, 1959). The participants—the subjects—were simply told that they were to be shocked for the purpose of studying their reactions. Although it was conducted over 30 years ago, the study is interesting not only for the findings it yielded but also for the ethical questions it raises. Is it ethical to deceive subjects? Is it ethical to make people anxious and uncomfortable? We will address these questions and tell you the actual purpose and results of this study later in this chapter. First, however, let's discuss the means by which scientists, particularly psychologists, answer questions about behavior.

Most of us are not asked to explain to others how we gained our understanding of the world. Even if asked, we probably could not say how we know what we know. Scientists, however, are held accountable for the methods they use to understand the world and must explain not only what they know, but also how they arrived at that knowledge. Our society places high value on scientific knowledge and consequently expects scientists to make their findings and methods public for inspection. If a scientist's methods are sloppy or suspicious, then his or her findings may be also. Of course, if a scientist's methods are sound, then his or her findings are also generally considered sound.

In this chapter, we will discuss the methods that psychologists use to study behavior. We will begin by discussing different types of knowledge, focusing upon the unique aspects of scientific knowledge and will then discuss the different methods that psychologists use in their research. We will see that sometimes behavior is studied through purely observational means and at other times it is studied by manipulating different aspects of the environment. How psychologists use statistics to analyze their research data is also discussed. The chapter closes with an overview of the ethical concerns that psychologists must consider in their research.

THE NATURE OF SCIENTIFIC KNOWLEDGE

Our knowledge of the world comes in many forms. One kind of knowledge is mathematical knowledge, which is obtained solely by reasoning from basic assumptions to conclusions. The traditional tools of the mathematician have been paper and pencil and logic (in these modern times a com-

We learn about the world we live in through various types of knowledge, such as mathematical knowledge, which allows us to calculate and explore our surroundings, and artistic knowledge, which allows us to express and appreciate creativity.

puter can also be helpful). By beginning with certain assumptions such as the existence of real numbers and given basic operations such as addition and multiplication, mathematicians have been able to develop complex systems of mathematics, such as geometry, algebra, and calculus. These systems have been incredibly useful in helping us adapt and explore our world. For example, our knowledge of mathematics has helped us learn to build things from houses to cars to space shuttles.

Another kind of knowledge is religious knowledge, which may include accepting on faith various beliefs about the nature of the universe and the history of life, and moral guidelines and values for living life. The source of much religious knowledge is believed to be divine inspiration. Other types of religious knowledge are derived from interpretation and analysis of the writings of religious thinkers.

Knowledge is also found in the arts and humanities. Literature, painting, theater, and music communicate artistic knowledge primarily through emotion. You gain such knowledge by reading a novel or seeing a painting that makes you *feel* different about yourself or the world, even though you may not be able to express these feelings. After watching a movie or seeing a play you might smile, shed a tear, or even feel a sense of enlightenment.

Scientific Knowledge is Empirical Knowledge

Although all these kinds of knowledge are useful in one way or another, none of them is scientific knowledge. Science is characterized by the pursuit of **empirical knowledge**, which is knowledge obtained from carefully observing and measuring behavior under highly controlled conditions. Our observations provide the **data** or information about the aspect or aspects of the behavior under study. Observing a rat run a maze and recording its speed, observing the number of times a child solves problems correctly, and observing and measuring the biochemical processes involved in brain functioning, are all forms of empirical knowledge. Let's look at a specific example.

Careful observation and measurement of behavior under controlled conditions allows researchers to gain scientific knowledge about this rat as it runs a maze.

Suppose a psychologist wishes to know how aggressive someone is. The psychologist might observe the person's actions directly, watching him or her interact with others. Observing behavior may also include observing people's reports of their own behavior, so the psychologist might ask the person directly if he or she is aggressive. The question could be asked verbally, or it could be asked in questionnaire form where the person is asked to agree or disagree with statements such as "I feel like hitting someone when things don't go my way." If the psychologist is a neuroscientist, then he or she might study the role that the brain or biochemistry might play in aggressive behavior.

Of course, psychologists do more than just collect data. Psychologists also theorize about the nature of things that cannot be observed directly. What causes aggression—perhaps anger? Although aggression is an observable behavior, its underlying cause may not be. The psychologist cannot observe anger directly because it is an emotion and not a concrete, physical thing. So then, how can the psychologist tell if anger causes aggression? One way would be to induce anger in someone and then observe whether or not they become aggressive. But how do we know that someone is angry in the first place? The key is that some characteristics of anger are observable. You cannot see anger itself, but you can see the behavioral expression of anger; people behave differently when they are angry than they do when they are not angry. Angry people may have grimaces on their faces, and if they are particularly angry, they may raise their voices. So, based on our observation of a person's actions, we typically infer the cause of those actions. If we see a person grimace or raise his voice and at the same time act aggressively, we have some basis for speculating that aggression may be related to anger.

Thus, psychologists sometimes use empirical knowledge to make inferences about causes of behavior that are not directly observable. This is an important point because much human behavior would seem to be influenced by factors that cannot be observed directly such as thoughts, emotions, and perceptions. However, and this is part of what keeps psychology a lively science, different psychologists will often draw different inferences from the same body of empirical knowledge.

Empirical Knowledge and Falsifiability. Because the inferences that scientists make are based on empirical knowledge, they are falsifiable. That is, if an inference is actually false, then theoretically it should be possible to demonstrate it to be false (Popper, 1959). The ability to find errors and problems in your own or someone else's research is thus a crucial aspect of science.

Measurement is the key to establishing **falsifiability**; that is, to proving that a statement of inference is false. Regardless of whether the measurements involve a psychologist observing a person's behavior directly, a person reporting on his or her own behavior, or a scientist recording some biological characteristic of a person, the measurements are based on behavior that can be observed by others. If one psychologist believes that another's study is in error, then he or she can personally repeat the study taking a new measurement of the behavior under study. If the study was done correctly the first time—that is, if the methodology was sound, the second psychologist should be able to reproduce the original results. If the methodology was flawed, then the second psychologist will obtain different data. Falsifiability, then, is an important characteristic of scientific research. Let's look at an example.

In the late 1950s, a group of researchers reported that they had discovered the cause of schizophrenia, a psychological disorder characterized by disorganized thinking, inappropriate emotions, and distorted perceptions (Heath and others, 1957, 1959). They found that taraxein, a protein found in the blood of schizophrenics but not in normal people, produced schizophrenia. When normal people were injected with taraxein they showed schizophrenic-like symptoms. In contrast, when other normal people were injected with saline, a nonactive substance, such symptoms did not appear.

Because schizophrenia is so prevalent (the majority of people hospitalized for psychological disorders are suffering from schizophrenia) and because its effects on people are so devastating, the possible discovery of the cause of the disorder was important news in psychological and medical communities. Not surprisingly, other researchers were interested in looking more closely at the methods used by Heath and in replicating his study. However, even when researchers in other laboratories meticulously followed Heath's methods, they could not reproduce his results (Abramson, 1959; Siegal and others, 1959). How could researchers in one lab produce positive evidence that taraxein causes schizophrenia and researchers in other laboratories produce negative results? To answer that question, we need to look more closely at flaws in the methods Heath used to measure the effects of taraxein.

f one psychologist believes that another's study is in error, then he or she can personally repeat the study taking a new measurement of the behavior under study.

As it turned out, some subjects in Heath's studies knew that they were participating in a study about schizophrenia and probably also knew that they were receiving special treatment. They may have acted schizophrenically, not because of the injection of taraxein they received but because they thought that that was how they were supposed to act.

There were also other problems. The people giving the injections were the same people who observed and recorded the behavior of the subjects. Knowing which subjects were injected with taraxein and which were injected with saline may have biased the researchers' observation and interpretation of the subjects' behavior. Researchers who replicated Heath's studies but who also took steps to safeguard that neither experimenters nor subjects knew about the contents of the injections did not replicate Heath's findings.

Thus, Heath's research was proven wrong because the conclusions he drew from his experiments were falsifiable. He concluded that schizophrenia is caused by taraxein. Other researchers examined his methods and findings with the opposite conclusion in mind: schizophrenia may not be caused by taraxein. In the end they turned out to be right simply because the methods Heath used did not provide for the proper measurement of his subjects' behavior.

Variables. Many of the factors that psychologists and other scientists study vary from one instance to the next. Some of these factors are individuals' characteristics. Think of all the ways you can describe a person. Some of these observable characteristics are physical: height, blood type, eye color, and gender. Other characteristics are psychological: fear, intelligence, willingness to lie, and shyness. People's behavior also varies based on circumstances. For example, your behavior is affected by whether other people are around, who those people are, and what your relationship is with those people. All of the ways in which organisms and circumstances can differ are called **variables** because their level or degree can vary from one organism or circumstance to the next. Thus, a variable can be a characteristic of the person or the environment. The level or degree of a variable is referred to as its **value.** For example, intelligence is a characteristic that varies from one person to the next, so it is a variable. If Sara scores 130 on an intelligence test then the value of Sara's intelligence variable is 130.

In sum, psychologists are interested in asking questions that can be answered with empirical knowledge, and empirical knowledge is obtained by measuring observable behavior. Since measuring behavior involves determining the value of some variable or variables that are observed to change across people and across situations, the issue we will turn to now is the psychologist's purpose in measuring variables.

Relationships Among Variables: Correlation and Prediction

Psychologists are interested in knowing how variables of psychological interest are related to each other and in explaining how these relationships occur. The statistical term used to describe the degree of relationship between two variables is **correlation**. Closely related to the concept of correlation is **prediction**, which is the ability to foretell the value of one variable when the value of the other variable is known. Variables that are related are said to be correlated because the value of one variable can be predicted from the value of the other. Let's look at an example of how correlation and prediction are used by psychologists (and others) to understand behavior.

Before you applied to college, you probably took the Scholastic Aptitude Test (SAT), which, as you know, is a test used by college admissions officers to learn if applicants have the educational qualifications for college-level work. The test is used because researchers have found that SAT scores are correlated with college grade point average (GPA). Generally speaking, students with high SAT scores have higher GPAs than students with low SAT scores. Because of this correlation, admissions officers are able to predict how well a student will do in college on the basis of his or her SAT score. Look closely at Table 2.1. For each of 10 college students we have two measurements: each person's SAT score from his or her senior year in high school, and each person's college GPA. As you can see, Joanne has a high score on the SAT

P

sychologists are interested in knowing how variables of psychological interest are related to each other . . .

TABLE 2.1.	Comparison of SAT scores and GPAs for 10 college freshmen.	
NAME	*SAT SCORE*	*FRESHMAN GPA*
Joanne	1300	3.8
Scott	900	1.8
Mary	1180	2.1
Bess	1240	3.8
Tom	1040	3.4
Joe	985	2.5
Ruth	1040	2.3
Alex	1160	2.7
Sally	1140	3.3
Jane	1080	3.5

(1300) and a relatively high GPA (3.8). Scott, on the other hand, has a low SAT (900) score and a low GPA (1.8). It appears that, in general, high SAT scores go with high GPAs and low scores go with low grades. Because this relationship between the two variables continues to be true for much larger groups of students, college admissions officers can use an individual applicant's high school SAT score to predict how well the applicant will do at that particular college before the student is ever admitted! If the predicted score was too low, then the applicant might not be admitted to the college. If the predicted score was very high, then not only would the applicant be admitted, but he or she might also be awarded an academic scholarship or invited to join the college's honors program.

To say that two variables are correlated does not necessarily mean they are causally related to each other. In fact, two variables can be correlated but not causally related. We would not say, for example, that high (or low) SAT scores cause high (or low) GPAs. In addition to scholastic aptitude, an individual's GPA is influenced by a host of other variables such as homesickness, interest in classes, hours spent studying, ability to write, willingness to participate in class discussion, and so on. Thus, like Jane (Table 2.1), a student may have a fairly low SAT score but do very well in school. Or like Mary, a student with a high SAT may do poorly in class. Whatever the reason, both of these students' actual college GPAs was different than the GPA that would be predicted on the basis of the individual SAT scores alone. In both cases, we would be correct in saying that variables other than their SAT score are more highly correlated with their GPA. We will learn more about the important differences between correlation and causation throughout the chapter.

Hypotheses and Theory

In their search to understand how behavioral variables are affected by other variables, psychologists are guided by hypotheses that suggest how variables are related and how they might go about discovering those relationships. Consider, for the example, the statement that "fear causes affiliation." This statement implies that fear and affiliation are correlated variables and is an example of a **hypothesis**, a proposed relationship between two or more variables that can be tested empirically. In this case, the higher the fear, the stronger the tendency to affiliate. Evidence regarding the validity of the hypothesis is an objective of any scientific study.

Often the truth of a hypothesis is tested within the broader context of a theory. In fact, hypotheses are often derived from a theory. For psychologists, a **theory** is a set of statements that attempts to explain relationships that may exist between behavior and other variables. Theories are, therefore, more general than hypotheses, and in fact, can be made up of many hypotheses. For example, a theory of affiliation might be made up of several hypotheses about the variables that affect affiliation. In addition to the hypothesis that fear causes affiliation, we might have other hypotheses such as: "uncertainty causes affiliation" or "common goals cause affiliation." Hypotheses are formulated to be consistent with a particular theory, so if the hypothesis is shown to be correct, evidence is obtained for the theory. Likewise, if the hypothesis is shown to be incorrect, evidence is obtained against the theory. A very simple theory explaining why fear causes affiliation is that fear is modulated by the presence of others who may offer protection and comfort. That is, when individuals are fearful, they seek others for help. Theories may also be very complex as indicated by Freud's elaborate theory of personality and its development, a topic that we will study in the personality chapter.

Hypotheses can be classified in two ways. Some hypotheses are referred to as **causal hypotheses** because they specify that one variable causes the other. Causal hypotheses not only specify a relationship between the variables of interest, but they also account for the existence of the relationship in terms of cause and effect. The causal hypothesis regarding fear and affiliation states that fear and affiliation are related because fear causes affiliation.

In science, as in life in general, a specification of causality is usually considered one of the most powerful forms of knowledge. For example, if the "fear causes affiliation" hypothesis is correct, then we have accounted for at least one of the reasons why people affiliate. For any one individual, changes in the value of the variable "fear" cause changes in that person's value of the variable "affiliation." In particular, fear and affiliation would be correlated because increasing the level of fear leads to a corresponding increase in the level of affiliation. Fearful people affiliate more than those who are not fearful.

A scary roller coaster ride may not seem so awful if it is shared with a friend. This may explain the theory of why fear causes affiliation. Fear is modulated by the presence of others who may offer protection and comfort.

The other type of hypothesis is called a **relational hypothesis** in which two or more variables are specified to be related but none of the variables can be found to cause the other variables. An example of a relational hypothesis is, "On average, the higher an individual's SAT score is the higher that individual's GPA will be." A relational hypothesis does not explain a relationship, but it does specify that a relationship exists. In this case, the hypothesis only states that SAT scores and GPA are related; it does not specify why. Relational hypotheses provide information about a relationship between variables, but not as much information as is provided by causal hypotheses. Only causal hypotheses attempt to explain *why* the variables are related.

In sum, psychologists devise theories to account for how different kinds of variables affect behavior. Specific theoretical statements called hypotheses specify the nature of the relationship that may exist. Relational hypotheses state only that such a relationship exists; causal hypotheses state that changes in one variable produce a corresponding change in another variable. The purpose of psychological research is to test hypotheses regarding the relationships between behavior and other variables. As we will see, observational research is best used to test relational hypotheses, and experimental research is more appropriate for testing causal hypotheses.

> *The purpose of psychological research is to test hypotheses regarding the relationships between behavior and other variables.*

OBSERVATIONAL RESEARCH

Many psychological studies are designed merely to observe the existing relationships among variables. In **observational research**, the psychologist observes and measures the variables of interest without attempting to influence the values of the variables or to intervene in any other way. Because of the passive nature of the observation in this type of study, observational studies are sometimes more formally referred to as passive–observational research (Cook & Campbell, 1979). And, as we noted above, observational studies are best suited for testing relational hypotheses.

As an example of the type of question that would be investigated with an observational study, consider the relationship between two variables we have already discussed: SAT scores and college GPA. To see if a relationship between these variables exists, we simply need to gather data—SAT and GPA scores for, say, 200 students. Once these data are in hand, we would perform a statistical test of these data. The test would give us a numerical measure of the degree of relationship that exists between the two variables. Note that we would do nothing to alter the environment or the people whose SAT scores and GPAs we have used. The main function of observational studies, then, is to gather data.

There are several special techniques that psychologists use to observe behavior, including self-reports, naturalistic observation, and case studies. Let's take a closer look at each technique.

Self-Report

The data for many psychological studies are obtained through **self-report**, a technique in which people provide information about themselves—age, gender, feelings, beliefs, evaluations, or interests—to the researcher. These kinds of studies are aimed chiefly at discovering people's attitudes about particular topics or at understanding behavior that is not easily observed under normal circumstances. For example, psychologists have hypotheses and theories about variables that affect human sexual behavior, even though observing it directly is a difficult matter. Most people consider sex a private act and would find it distracting, if not unethical, to have a group of psychologists intruding upon their intimacy. But many people are willing to kiss and tell, so to speak, and as a result, the self-report has been one of the most useful tools for studying variables related to human sexual behavior (Kinsey, 1948; Hunt, 1974).

One way of collecting self-report data is through a **questionnaire**, a series of written questions specifically designed to address a particular topic. A questionnaire may be administered to one person at a time, or several hundred may be handed out simultaneously to a large group of people. Or the questionnaire could be mailed to hundreds of people, whose names were taken from a magazine subscription list or a telephone book.

The questionnaire is a good way to collect large quantities of self-report data in a short period of time. However, it does not allow the researcher to alter the line of questioning during the course of the study. That is, there are some cases in which the researcher may wish to ask a particular subject different questions based on his or her answers to earlier questions. In this case, the interview is the more appropriate method of collecting self-report data. In the **interview**, a researcher requires subjects to respond verbally to questions. The researcher then records the subject's answers either in written form or on video.

What is done with the data collected from questionnaires and interviews? They are usually analyzed for content and specific answers about one variable are examined for their correlation to specific answers about other variables.

Questionnaires and interviews are just two of the many ways researchers can obtain data for psychological studies. These methods are also referred to as self-reports.

In any self-report study, it is important that the researchers not influence the value of the variables that they are studying. To safeguard against doing just that, researchers using questionnaires and interviews typically try to have all subjects provide their self-reports under the same conditions. Self-reports can be biased by a number of factors, including time allowed to respond to the questionnaire or interview, whether the researcher is male or female and kind or rude, time of day, and whether the conditions are warm and comfortable or cold and uncomfortable.

Another means of preventing unwanted influences from biasing self-report data involves the way in which the researcher selects subjects for the study. The researcher should select a group of subjects that will be more or less representative of all those people about whose behavior the researcher wishes to test a hypothesis. For example, if we wished to study the relationship between early family life and the tendency to become an aggressive adult, we would not interview only people who are in prison for committing violent crimes but people who have never been imprisoned as well. We would also want to interview a larger and more heterogeneous group that included people of both sexes, different religions and subcultures, different socioeconomic levels, different ages, and so forth.

The main advantage of the self-report method is convenience. One of the easiest ways of collecting data is simply to have people tell you what it is that you wish to know. However, people do not always respond accurately to questions, and some people may deliberately lie to provide a favorable impression of themselves to the researcher. A more fundamental problem is that people often are unable to report on what they did or would do in certain situations. That is, people are not always very good at describing their own behavior. Can you, for example, describe how you felt just before the last time you became aggressive? How you would act if the person sitting next to you in your psychology class had a seizure? (And if you could describe what you would do in that situation, would your answer match what you would actually do in such a situation?) One way to sidestep these problems is simply to observe people or animals as they behave naturally without asking them to fill out a questionnaire or interviewing them.

Naturalistic Observation

Another form of observational research is called **naturalistic observation**. In this type of research, data are gathered by observing behavior as it occurs naturally. Individuals are observed in the context of their normal daily routine, often without any awareness of being part of a psychological study. People ride the subway home, sit in movie theaters, walk down the street holding hands, shop for food, work in offices and factories, play with their children, and participate in sports. With the proper training, psychologists can observe and measure all of these individual behaviors as they occur naturally, without changing or influencing those who are being observed.

Naturalistic observation is also ideal for studying the behavior of animals. As we will see in the chapter on learning, psychologists have learned a good deal about how animals behave in the wild simply because scientists have carefully observed their actions and the circumstances under which they have occurred. Consider chimpanzees, for example. Chimpanzee behavior may be observed and relevant aspects systematically recorded, as was done in the classic study by Jane Goodall (1971). Day after day for over a decade Goodall studied chimpanzees in their natural East African environment, slowly and painstakingly gaining their confidence and trust. Her remarkable observations uncovered a wealth of valuable information about chimpanzee life in the wild. She discovered that they have a complex social structure organized by dominance hierarchies with those higher in the hierarchy having more social power than those lower in the hierarchy. She also found that chimpanzees have the ability to make and use tools. Perhaps most importantly, she showed that mother and child form close bonds and that bonds are also formed in the development of friendships. From our view, the important thing to remember about Goodall's work is that she made insightful discoveries about the chimpanzee without attempting to change the conditions under which they lived and played.

Naturalistic observation is an excellent way to study animal behavior. Here, Jane Goodall, a primate specialist, observes a group of chimpanzees to gain information about chimpanzee life in the wild.

Naturalistic observation can even be conducted in the laboratory because naturalistic settings can be arranged for that purpose. For example, children might be allowed to play freely with each other or with toys while a developmental psychologist observes them from behind a one-way mirror. The observer might record the number and kind of interactions that the children have with each other. In this case, the observer might also videotape the children. That way he or she can check the observations against a permanent record of the children's interactions and study the verbal interactions of the children.

To become skilled in the naturalistic observation of behavior, whether in or out of the laboratory, requires extensive training and practice. Observers are trained to notice and record certain behaviors. Accurately measuring behaviors such as facial expressions, loudness of the voice, and touch is a more difficult task than might be first presumed. Although naturalistic observation requires such training, it has two advantages over the self-report. First, naturalistic observation is more objective than the self-report because researchers rely on their own observations rather than subjects' self-descriptions of behavior. And second, naturalistic observation involves the study of ongoing behavior rather than verbal descriptions of past behavior or estimates of future behavior. Naturalistic observation is an effective means of collecting behavioral data, but there are also other methods of observation. We turn now to a discussion of one such observational tool—the case study.

Case Studies

The **case study** is an intensive investigation of a single individual or a small group of individuals over an extended period of time based on the use of observational techniques. Instead of asking people to fill out questionnaires or observing several people interact, the case study examines one individual in depth, usually through analysis of that individual's self-reports. Although a case study involves only a single individual, its purpose is the same as studies that involve many individuals: to discover psychological relationships and processes that apply to people in general. The case study is particularly useful in clinical psychology, where therapists attempt to understand and modify individuals' thinking or behavior.

Perhaps the most famous advocate of the case study approach is Sigmund Freud. Freud developed an extensive theory of personality based on the role of the unconscious by studying the case histories of only a small number of people. By carefully noting his patients' psychological reactions to various events in their lives, he developed hypotheses about personality functioning that he generalized to all people.

Another well-known application of the case study method was by a Swiss developmental psychologist, Jean Piaget, whose work we will study in Chapter 11. Piaget formed general theories of the development of children's cognitive abilities largely from an intensive, detailed study of his own children. By watching his own children grow and mature, Piaget learned general principles that he then applied to understanding the cognitive development of all children.

Freud's and Piaget's work illustrates the primary advantage of a case study. The intensive study of one or just a few people provides considerable depth to the analysis of behavior. The researcher may eventually observe relationships that would otherwise have gone unnoticed without the intensive observation of just a few people. However, any hypotheses or theories that are constructed from the case study are eventually tested with research that examines the behavior of many individuals.

A Limitation of Observational Research

To conclude from an observational study that two variables are related provides useful information about the variables. To say that the variables are related because one causes the other provides additional information because this new information explains *why* the variables are related. Unfortunately, as we have said, we cannot conclude that a causal relationship exists by simply observing the relationship. That is, given only the information that two variables are correlated, we cannot correctly infer that one variable causes the other. This is sometimes a particularly vexing problem because people often tend to make this inference from observational data, especially if the inference fits with their particular theory or simply if it sounds good.

W*e cannot conclude that a causal relationship exists by simply observing the relationship.*

Consider the following example. Recently a reputable newspaper reported that a survey of married couples found a definite relationship between the success of the marriage and the number of close friends each spouse had outside of the marriage. The headline for the article read: "Close friendships can strengthen your marriage." What was the problem with this headline? A causal inference had inappropriately been made from observational data because observational data by themselves cannot establish causality. Another rival hypothesis may explain this correlation equally well.

One possible rival hypothesis might be that some third variable is causing the correlation of the other two variables. Perhaps a general characteristic such as "niceness" or "friendliness" leads to both successful marriages and close friendships outside of marriage. Maybe people who have lots of friends to begin with are the same people who have successful marriages; loners and brooders may not make good friends in or out of marriages. From this third-variable hypothesis it also follows that we would expect to observe a correlation between "number of close friends" and "marital success."

Our point is that each of these rival hypotheses is consistent with the data in the sense that each hypothesis explains the observed correlation equally well. Both hypotheses lead to exactly the same conclusion: the number of close friends is correlated with success in marriage. However, each of these hypotheses is relational not causal, which means that they

FIGURE 2.1
Rival hypotheses specifying potential patterns of causality that explain the observed correlation between the variables X and Y.

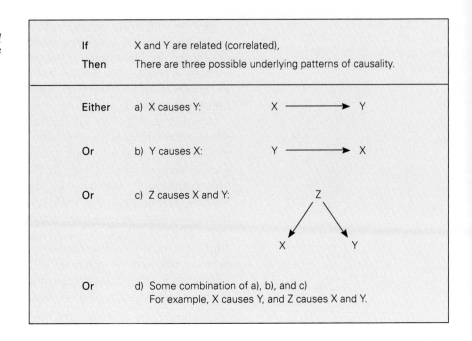

cannot shed any light on what actually causes a happy marriage. A relational hypothesis only suggests a cause; it cannot unequivocally isolate the cause. The three primary rival hypotheses that explain a correlation from an observational study are listed in Figure 2.1.

If causal explanations are difficult to infer from observational studies alone, then another methodology is needed, one that more readily permits causal inference. This methodology is the experiment, our next topic.

EXPERIMENTAL RESEARCH

An **experiment** is a research method in which the investigator manipulates certain variables and measures their effects on other variables. The variable that is manipulated is called the **independent variable** and the variable that is measured is called the **dependent variable**. That is, experiments are conducted to determine the effect of the independent variable on the dependent variable. In psychological research, the dependent variable is always behavior and the independent variable is always a variable hypothesized to influence behavior. Of the different methodologies available to psychologists, the experiment provides the best basis for inferring cause-and-effect from an observed relation between two variables. Unfortunately, because of ethical considerations and the kind of hypothesis being tested, it is not always possible for psychologists to conduct experiments. But when possible and practical, experiments are almost always preferred over observational studies.

The Experiment

In both observational research and experimental research, the researcher observes relationships among variables. The characteristic that distinguishes an experiment from an observational study is systematic control over variables. In contrast to the passive nature of observational research, the researcher actively manipulates the value of the independent variable in an experiment. To illustrate this difference, let's consider the "fear causes affiliation" hypothesis once again.

In an observational study, the researcher could recruit a group of subjects, measure the level of fear for each person, and then measure the degree to which each person affiliates with others. In this case, the researcher would simply measure the values of two variables, fear and affiliation; no attempt would be made to manipulate the values of either variable.

Manipulating Variables. In an experiment the researcher could study the same two variables but in a very different manner. In this case, the researcher might first divide a group of people into two smaller groups of approximately equal size and then manipulate the environment of just one of the groups, the high-fear group, in such a way that they would experience fear. The environment for the people in the other group would be arranged so that they experienced little fear (low-fear group). After the manipulation, the experimenter would measure and compare the degree to which people in each group affiliate with other people. If the high-fear group had a much higher average affiliation score than the average for the low-fear group, the experimenter would conclude that fear caused affiliation.

This experimental procedure is outlined in Figure 2.2. This experiment was, in fact, conducted by Stanley Schachter (1959), and was discussed in part at the beginning of this chapter. Subjects in the experiment were seated in small groups in a room that contained a variety of electrical equipment. The experimenter introduced himself as Dr. Gregory Zilstein, a scientist from the Department of Neurology and Psychiatry. Dr. Zilstein explained that the purpose of the experiment was to study the effects of electric shock that were to be administered to the subjects. For subjects in the high-fear group, Dr. Zilstein described the effects of the shocks in frightening terms. The subjects were told that the shocks would hurt and would be intense, although they would not cause any permanent damage. Subjects in the low-fear group heard a much less threatening description of what they were about to experience: they were told that the shocks would not be painful, and that they would only be felt as a tickle or a tingle.

After his description of the experiment, Dr. Zilstein told the subjects that there would be a ten-minute delay while he set up the equipment. He explained to the subjects that they might like to wait in a more comfortable setting, either alone or with other people. Each subject was then given a brief questionnaire on which to indicate his or her preference. The responses to this questionnaire constituted the data, the measure of affil-

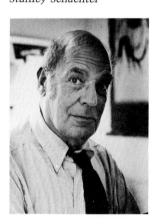

Stanley Schachter

FIGURE 2.2
Outline of the fear–affiliation study. Fear is the independent variable, the variable that is manipulated, and the tendency to affiliate is the dependent variable, the variable that is measured.

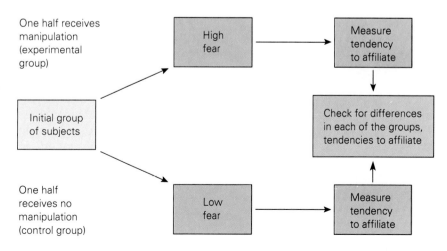

	PERCENTAGE CHOOSING		
Condition	Together	Don't Care	Alone
High Fear	62.5	28.1	9.4
Low Fear	33.0	60.0	7.0

TABLE 2.2. *Results of Schachter's (1959) experiment showing the effect of fear on affiliation.*

iation. As shown in Table 2.2 Schachter's (1959) results supported the hypothesis. Sixty-two percent of the subjects in the high-fear group preferred to wait with other people compared to only 33 percent of the subjects in the low-fear group. From this experimental study, Schachter (1959) concluded that fear causes affiliation.

The experiment described above was relatively uncomplicated. There were two variables of interest, the independent variable, fear, and the dependent variable, affiliation. In this study, the independent variable had two possible values: low fear or high fear. The experimenter assigned one of these values to each subject by assigning the subject to the high- or low-fear group. The outcome of the experiment was assessed by measuring the value of the dependent variable, affiliation, for each subject. High fear results in higher affiliation tendencies than does low fear. In any experiment, a change in the value of the independent variable is hypothesized to "cause" a corresponding change in the value of the dependent variable. If the value of the dependent variable tends to change across the levels of the independent variable, then the conclusion is usually that the differences are attributable to differences in the level of the independent variable. For example, subjects in the high-fear group, on average, tended to have a higher affiliation score, so the hypothesis was supported.

Experimental and Control Groups. Of course, people are different. As you can see from Table 2.2, some of the people in the low-fear condition preferred to affiliate, some of the people in the high-fear condition preferred to be alone, and some people in both groups didn't care whether they waited alone or with someone else. As is true of almost any experiment, scores on the dependent variable are potentially due to many different conditions and characteristics of the subjects. The results of an experiment, however, are *averaged*, and the average difference across the two groups demonstrated that a higher level of fear tends to increase the affiliation score, which leads to the inference that fear causes affiliation.

An important feature of an experiment is that subjects are randomly assigned to the different groups. **Random assignment** means that each subject is assigned to a group on the basis of chance alone. Randomly assigning subjects to different groups minimizes differences that may have existed among subjects prior to the experiment. For example, perhaps some subjects in Schachter's experiment had experience with electric shock prior to meeting Dr. Zilstein. Such experience may have led these subjects to be more or less fearful of electric shock than other subjects. However, randomly assigning subjects to groups reduces the likelihood that all of these preexposed subjects would be assigned to one group and thereby bias the results. The purpose of random assignment is to equate both groups on important variables that might influence the results of the experiment.

The group that is exposed to the independent variable, in this case the high-fear group, is called the **experimental group**. The group that receives less or no exposure to the independent variable, in this case the low-fear group, is called the **control group**. To demonstrate the existence of a causal relationship, the scores on the dependent variable for the experimental group are compared to the corresponding scores for the control group. If the independent variable does not affect behavior, then the measure of the dependent variable, affiliation, should yield about the same values for both the high- and low-fear groups. In other words, the measure of the dependent variable for the control group represents a standard against which the value of the dependent variable for the experimental group is compared. Only if the values of the dependent variable in the two groups differ by a reasonably wide margin can researchers conclude that the independent variable affected the dependent variable.

Before the manipulation of the independent variable occurs, there should be, on the average, no differences between the groups on any variable. That is, the groups should have approximately the same average intelligence, the same average height, the same average level of personality variables (such as shyness), the same average need for affiliation, and the same average level of fear. Of course, the averages across the groups will not be exact, but they should be approximately equal for any variable that

In any experiment, a change in the value of the independent variable is hypothesized to "cause" a corresponding change in the value of the dependent variable.

the experimenter wishes to consider. The key point of an experiment is that if there are no average differences between the groups before the manipulation, but there is after the manipulation, then the independent variable has caused a change in the dependent variable. Thus, if the underlying causal hypothesis is correct, the values of the dependent variable can be predicted from the values of the independent variable—that is, the two variables are related, in this case, causally.

For example, prior to the experiment, subjects in the high-fear group should not be, on average, any smarter or more shy or more fearful than subjects in the low-fear group. But after the manipulation, there should be one crucial difference between the groups: the subjects in the high-fear group should be more affiliative than the subjects in the low-fear group. Thus, with everything else held constant, an increase in fear should usually lead to an increase in affiliation.

The study described here is the simplest possible experiment: one independent variable with only two levels—high and low fear—and one dependent variable—affiliation. The key concepts underlying the experiment are summarized in Table 2.3. These basic concepts also apply to more complex

TABLE 2.3. *The key concepts of an experiment.*

CONCEPT	DEFINITION
Manipulation	The fundamental characteristic of an experiment is that the researcher actively manipulates the value of at least one variable to determine its effect on another variable.
Independent Variable	Changes in this variable are hypothesized to cause changes in the dependent variable. Each level of the independent variable corresponds to a single group of subjects.
Experimental Group	The experimental group is comprised of those subjects who are exposed to some value of the independent variable.
Control Group	The control group is comprised of those subjects who are either not exposed to the independent variable or who are exposed to a low value of the independent variable.
Dependent Variable	This variable is hypothesized to be an "effect;" that is, it is dependent on the assigned value of the independent variable.
Random Assignment	The group that each subject is assigned to is determined by a random procedure so that, on the average, the groups do not differ in any systematic way before the manipulation of the independent variable.

experiments, such as those that involve several independent variables. However, remember this: the essence of any psychological experiment, no matter how complex, is that for one group of subjects the independent variable is manipulated and its effects on behavior measured. These measurements are then compared to the behavior of a different group of similar subjects who were not exposed to the same level of independent variable.

Single-Subject Research

Experiments that use groups of subjects are the most common means of conducting psychological experiments. However, some psychologists, such as those who study learning or treat people for specific behavioral problems, use **single-subject research** methods in which experiments are conducted using only one or a few subjects. Advocates of the single-subject approach argue that the group approach, which is based on the comparison of group averages, masks important information about the behavior of individual subjects (Sidman, 1960; Johnston & Pennypacker, 1980). For example, the results of Schachter's (1959) study concerning fear and affiliation provided only the average response of the subjects; it tells us nothing about each individual subject's behavior. In the high-fear condition, it is possible that subjects who showed a large affiliation response and those who showed a smaller affiliation response were influenced by the experimental situation differently. But why? We can't answer that question because Schachter did not analyze the behavior of individual subjects. Single-subject research could provide an answer to that question by focusing on these kinds of individual differences.

The logic underlying most single-subject experimental research is similar to the logic of experimental research with groups of subjects: to manipulate the independent variable and measure its effects on the dependent variable. In experimental research with groups of subjects, the subjects in the control group are observed with little or no manipulation of the independent variable. The scores on the dependent variable of these control group subjects are then compared to the scores of the subjects in the experimental group. In single-subject experimental research, each subject serves as his or her own control.

n single-subject experimental research, each subject serves as his or her own control.

How can a subject serve as his or her own control? First, the behavior of interest—the dependent variable, is measured over several sessions or days during a **baseline condition** in which there is no manipulation. Second, the independent variable is manipulated and its effects on the subject's behavior is measured over several sessions or days that constitute the **treatment condition**. Next, the subject is reexposed to the baseline condition: the experimenter stops manipulating the independent variable, but the subject's behavior is again monitored for several sessions. Finally, the subject is reexposed to the treatment condition for several sessions. The experimenter assesses the effects of the independent variable on the dependent variable by comparing the subject's behavior during the treatment and baseline conditions.

As an example of single-subject research in which the independent variable of interest can be manipulated several times, let's suppose that we are interested in assessing the effect of alcohol on a driver's reaction time. We have the necessary equipment for measuring an individual's reaction time. To test reaction time, the subject will be asked to step on a brake pedal with his or her right foot as quickly as possible in response to a brief flash of a red light. Our equipment will automatically record the amount of time that elapses between the onset of the red light and the subject's foot contact with the brake pedal.

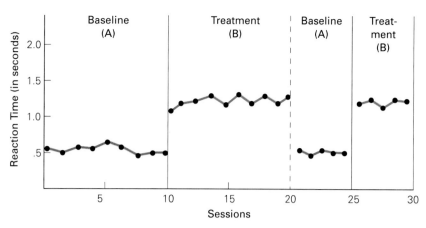

FIGURE 2.3
The results of a single-subject experiment.

During the first baseline condition, we would take several measurements of the subject's reaction time under normal circumstances, that is, when our subject is sober. Once our subject's reaction time has stabilized (is about the same from one session to the next), we introduce him or her to a treatment condition in which we permit our subject to consume, say, 3 ounces of alcohol 15 minutes prior to being placed in the reaction time situation. We find that our subject's reaction time has increased relative to the baseline condition, and we attribute the slower reaction time to consumption of the alcohol. To ensure that our finding was, in fact, due to the effects of alcohol and not to other variables, we once more expose our subject to the original baseline and treatment conditions. During the second baseline condition we find that the subject's reaction time was very similar to that during the first baseline condition and during the second treatment condition we also find that our subject's reaction time increases. The results of our hypothetical single-subject experiment are shown in Figure 2.3.

This alternating sequence of baseline and treatment conditions is referred to as an ABAB design (A for baseline and B for treatment). Only if there is a noticeable change in the subject's behavior during the treatment condition relative to the baseline condition is the independent variable said to have an effect. Thus, an important difference between single-subject research and group research is the basis by which the relevant comparisons are made. For single-subject research, comparisons are made between the same subject's behavior under two different conditions. For group research, comparisons are made between groups of subjects under different conditions. Another important difference is that in group research, the experimenter generally only measures the dependent variable once, whereas in single-subject research, the dependent variable is measured many times. Thus, in single-subject research, the dependent variable under both baseline and treatment conditions is more closely monitored.

Single-subject research does have a drawback because it takes a good deal of time to conduct. Some single-subject experiments can last for months. In contrast, group research involving an experimental and a control group usually can be conducted more quickly, which saves time and money.

Actually, any kind of experimental research can have problems that lead to incorrect conclusions about the relationship between the independent and dependent variables. Let's take a closer look at these problems and how they can be sidestepped.

Potential Pitfalls of Experimental Research

As we have said, the inference of causality is stronger from a properly conducted experiment than from an observational study. The advantage of the experiment is that it allows the active manipulation of the independent variable. By manipulating the independent variable, many rival hypotheses can be eliminated from an experiment that cannot be eliminated by the use of observational research. Unfortunately, even with an experiment not all rival hypotheses are always eliminated. Three factors — confounding variables, experimenter expectancies, and demand characteristics — can affect experimental findings, leading the researcher to the wrong conclusion.

Confounding Variables. Variables other than the independent variable that can systematically influence the value of the dependent variable are called **confounding variables.** An experimenter does not manipulate a confounding variable; rather he or she has overlooked its presence in the experiment, and so, failed to control its potential effects on the dependent variable. If an experiment contains confounding variables, any differences between the experimental and control groups on the measures of the dependent variable cannot be attributed solely to the effect of the independent variable.

For example, let's assume that instead of randomly assigning subjects to high- and low-fear conditions, Schachter had allowed subjects to sign up for either a morning or afternoon time to participate in his study. Then suppose that he assigned subjects who signed up for the morning time to the high-fear group and those who signed up for an afternoon time to the low-fear group. Can you see the potential problem here? The problem is that after the manipulation, the subjects differ on at least two variables: fear, and preference for sign-up times. The preference for a sign-up time may seem trivial, but often such apparently trivial considerations are later shown to also influence the dependent variable.

What if consistent differences exist between those who volunteer for morning activities and those who volunteer for afternoon activities? Perhaps, and this is purely hypothetical, morning people are more outgoing than afternoon people, who tend to be shy. If so, how are the data from Schachter's experiment to be interpreted? Did subjects in the high-fear group affiliate more than subjects in the low-fear group because they were fearful or because they were more outgoing from the start? Fortunately, Schachter controlled for this possible confounding variable by randomly assigning subjects to groups, and so, ensured that both groups presumably had roughly equal numbers of outgoing and shy subjects.

Experimenter Expectancy. Another factor that can influence experimental findings follows from the fact that psychologists are people and people often find what they expect to find. Experimenters generally work long and hard to develop their hypotheses and to design and set up the experiment to test them. In some cases, expectations of what the results should be may influence the outcome of an experiment. How can an experimenter's expectations produce such an effect? The experimenter may inadvertently communicate his or her expectations to the subject who, in turn, may act in a way that fulfills these expectations. This effect is called **experimenter expectancy**. This effect may also occur when an experimenter "sees" only what he expects to see and unintentionally overlooks other findings.

Robert Rosenthal has convincingly demonstrated the extent to which experimenter expectancy may influence the outcome of an experiment. For example, Rosenthal & Fode (1963) conducted a study in which students trained rats to run a maze. The independent variable had two levels: half of the students were told that they had dumb rats and the other half were told they had smart rats. In fact, there were no differences between the abilities of the rats in the two groups. However, on average, the smart rats learned to run the maze in less time than did the dumb rats. Thus, the only factor that could account for the differences in performance between the rats in the two different groups was not the ability of the rats, but the expectations the student trainers had of the rats' ability. Such expectations caused the students with the smart rats to take better care of their animals, which in turn, affected their rats' performance in the maze.

Rosenthal (1966) also demonstrated that elementary school teachers may be influenced in the same way. Teachers were told that some of their students were particularly bright, when, in fact, these "bright" students were selected at random from the class. At the end of the school year, teachers tended to rate these "bright" students as being happier, more interested, and more curious than the rest of the students. Today this study would be considered unethical and, therefore, would probably not be conducted.

In psychological research, a standard method to control experimenter expectancy is the double blind procedure. Ordinarily, the subject does not know if he or she is in the experimental group or the control group, and maybe the subject does not even know the purpose of the study. In a **double-blind** study, neither the subjects nor the person conducting the experiment know the purpose of the study or to which group subjects are assigned. Thus, in a double-blind study, the person conducting the experiment (usually an assistant to the experimenter) cannot convey an expectancy to the subjects.

Demand Characteristics. Experimenter expectancy occurs when the experimenter unintentionally communicates his or her expectancies to the subject, and the subject then behaves in a manner consistent with the expectancy. A related threat to the integrity of an experiment is actually a variety of problems that are collectively referred to as demand characteristics. **Demand characteristics** are factors in an experiment that cause subjects to behave in a manner consistent with what they believe the study is about. Regardless of how the experimenter wants the study to turn out, the subject may try to figure out the underlying hypothesis of the experiment and then respond accordingly.

A well-known example of how demand characteristics may unintentionally bias the results of an experiment is a study concerning worker productivity done in an industrial plant in Hawthorne, Illinois. In this study, the researchers wanted to determine how different environmental variables such as the amount of lighting and the number of hours employees had to work affected overall production. The independent variables in this experiment were the environmental variables, and the dependent variable was employee performance. The surprising result was that no matter what the researchers did, production increased. This result was true even when the manipulation should have reduced productivity, such as when lighting was reduced to well below normal levels. In other words, because the subjects knew they were being studied, they behaved differently than they would have otherwise. In effect, the characteristics of the study demanded that the workers increase their productivity.

In sum, we have learned that psychologists conduct two different kinds of research: observational and experimental. Observational research involves the researcher merely observing and recording behavior; no manipulation of variables is involved. Experimental research involves the experimenter actively manipulating the independent variable and measuring the effect of this manipulation on the dependent variable. To conclude that the independent variable and the dependent variable are causally related requires that two conditions be met: first, manipulating the independent variable produces changes in the dependent variable; second, the experimenter must control for confounding variables—experimenter expectancy and demand characteristics—thereby eliminating the rival hypothesis that might explain the causal relationship between the independent and dependent variables. In general, experimental research is preferred to observational research because only experimental research is useful in establishing cause and effect relationships. Observational research can only produce results that indicate the degree to which variables are correlated.

Now that we know something about how psychological research is conducted, let's take a look at how data from that research is analyzed.

ANALYZING DATA

An observational study or an experiment is not over when the last questionnaire has been passed out or after the last subject has been exposed to the independent variable. In fact, for the researcher, the really interesting part of the study—analyzing the results of the study—is just beginning. Why is analyzing data so interesting for researchers? The answer is because this is when they find out whether or not their hypothesis is correct; it is the time when the data "talk," so to speak, about the degree of relationship between the variables of interest. Up to the time the data are analyzed, the researcher only has a hunch as to whether or not there exists a relationship between variables. Analyzing the data, in essence, removes the mystery. For most researchers, analyzing data is probably the most exciting part of their work.

One of the main tools used by psychologists to analyze data is **statistics**, which are used for two purposes. First, they are used to simply describe the data. And second, they are used to assess the degree to which one variable was affected by another variable and not by chance. Accordingly, there are two kinds of statistics: descriptive statistics and inferential statistics. **Descriptive statistics** are those used to describe a particular set of data. As we shall see, inferential statistics also describe a particular set of data, but

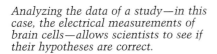

Analyzing the data of a study—in this case, the electrical measurements of brain cells—allows scientists to see if their hypotheses are correct.

TABLE 2.4.	*Frequency distribution of test scores.*
SCORE %	FREQUENCY
100	0
95	1
90	3
85	4
80	14
75	20
70	21
65	15
60	9
55	4
50	0
45	0
40	1

NOTE: All scores between 92.5% and 97.5% are listed as 95%, all scores between 87.5% and 92.5% are listed as 90%, and so on.

in addition, they are used to make general statements about that data set to some aspect of real life. Next we will discuss descriptive statistics, correlation, and inferential statistics.

Descriptive Statistics

In attempting to test hypotheses regarding the relations between variables, psychologists encounter two problems. They need a way to describe the values that different subjects have for a specified variable, and they need a way to describe the relationship between that variable and one or more other variables. These needs are met, in part, by descriptive statistics. Let's look at how descriptive statistics can be applied to a variable near and dear to you: test performance.

After your first psychology test, two questions you might ask are, "How well did I do?" and "How well did the class as a whole do?" The variable of interest is the first test score. Statistically, the values of this variable can be described in several different ways to answer your questions. We will look at four possibilities—frequency distributions, the mean, the median, and the standard deviation—each of which tells us something different about that first test score.

Frequency Distribution. To summarize the performance of an entire class on the first test, your instructor could construct a **frequency distribution**, which is a listing of all the possible values of the variable and how many subjects actually obtained each of these values. In this case, the variable is test performance and the subjects are the students who took the exam. (For our example, we assumed that 92 people took the test, and that the test had 20 questions worth five points each.)

Frequency distributions can be depicted as tables or graphs. An example of the tabular format is shown in Table 2.4. Along the left side of the table the possible scores are listed, and to the right, is listed how frequently each of those scores was obtained by students taking the test. This shows us immediately that most students obtained a score between 65 and 80. Considerably fewer students scored in the 90s or below 60.

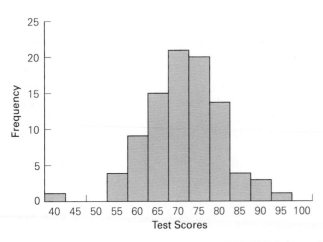 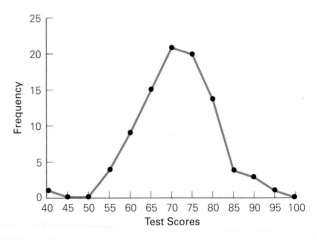

FIGURE 2.4a and FIGURE 2.4b
Left: A histogram of the test scores based on the data given in Table 2.4. Right: A frequency polygon of the test scores based on the data given in Table 2.4.

A frequency distribution is displayed graphically as either a histogram, shown in Figure 2.4a, or as a frequency polygon, shown in Figure 2.4b. Both of these figures depict the test score data shown in Table 2.4. A histogram represents each possible value of a variable by a single bar, which is centered over the value of interest. The height of this bar corresponds to the frequency of subjects who obtained the value. As you can see from Figure 2.4b, the frequency polygon communicates the same information as a histogram. Instead of using bars, however, a frequency polygon represents each value of the variable by a single point centered over the value of interest. Adjacent points are then joined by straight lines.

As you can see, frequency distributions quickly tell us about the pattern and range of values for a variable. But they are cumbersome to talk about because they contain so many numbers. In addition, they do not give us much specific information about the distribution of values. To do that, we have to do some calculations of the data. Two of the more important statistical calculations that can be performed are the mean and median. Each of these descriptive statistics provides a summary of important characteristics of a distribution of scores with just a single number.

The Mean and the Median. A frequency distribution, whether presented as a table or a graph, conveniently displays the entire distribution of test score data. However, sometimes we wish to *summarize* important characteristics of these scores with just a few numbers. For example, one question you might ask of the distribution of scores for the first test is, "How did the class as a whole perform on the test?"

One way to find out how the class did as a whole on the test would be to calculate the arithmetic average or **mean** of the test scores. As you may already know, the mean of a distribution is computed by adding all of the scores in the distribution and then dividing by the total number of scores. For example, suppose that four students took a make-up exam for the first psychology test. These four test scores were 95, 85, 75, and 60. To compute the mean of these scores first add the scores.

$$95 + 85 + 75 + 60 = 315$$

Then divide the total by four.

$$315 \div 4 = 78.75$$

Note that the mean, 78.75, is not any one of the four values of the distribution of make-up exam scores. The mean, then, represents the middle of the distribution of scores.

The middle of a distribution can also be defined by its **median**, the number above and below which 50 percent of the scores in the distribution fall. The median of the distribution of four test scores in the example above is 80. Two scores, 95 and 85, are above 80, and two scores, 75 and 60, are below 80. Note that the median, like the mean, does not have to be a value in the distribution. By convention, if the number of scores in the distribution is an even number such as four, the median is defined as the average of the two numbers closest to the middle. In this example, the median, which is defined as the average of 85 and 75, is 80. If the number of scores in a distribution is an odd number, then the actual score that divides the distribution into equal halves is considered the median. For example, if five students had made up the test and their scores were 100, 90, 85, 75, and 55, respectively, the median would be the middle number, 85.

When a distribution of scores is such that one or a few of the scores are substantially different from the rest of the scores, researchers will often use the median in place of the mean to summarize the data. They do so, quite simply, because the median in this case presents a more accurate summary of the data. To illustrate this, consider the following scenario: most of a group of people living in an area of a city might have modest incomes, but one person might be wealthy. In this situation, the mean would poorly represent the income of the typical person living in this area because it would be inflated greatly by the income of the one wealthy person. Suppose the incomes of the five people were as follows:

$20,000 $25,000 $30,000 $31,000 $1,000,000

The mean of these numbers is $221,200, but the median is more representative of the typical person, being only $30,000. Thus the mean can be a deceiving statistic if you don't know something about the variability of values in a distribution, our next topic.

Standard Deviation.   Variability is a fact of life. The fact that people differ on the values of a large number of psychological variables is at the heart of psychology; that is, much of psychology is devoted to explaining these differences. Accordingly, another important descriptive statistic of a distribution of scores is their variability.

If some people scored high on a test and some scored low, then the scores are spread out across a wide range of possible values. An example of such a distribution has already been given:

95, 85, 75, and 60.

If everyone in the class has almost the same test score, then the distribution of scores on the first test has little variability, such as in the following scores:

81, 80, 78, and 76.

Note that both of these distributions of four values have the same mean, 78.75. Their variability is, however, quite different. Because the scores are so close to one another in value in the second distribution, this distribution has less variability of scores than does the first distribution. In the first distribution the range of scores falls between 60 and 95, whereas in the second distribution the range of scores falls between 76 and 81.

The descriptive statistic that expresses the amount of variability among scores in a frequency distribution is called the **standard deviation (SD)**. The standard deviation for the first set of test scores is 14.64; it is only 2.29 for the second set. A precise definition and a computational formula for the standard deviation are best left to statistics texts, but the underlying concept is straightforward. The standard deviation is based on the distance of each score from the mean; it can be thought of as the typical distance of a score from the mean. If all the scores are bunched up around the mean so that everyone gets about the same grade on the test, then the standard deviation of the test scores will be small, as in 2.29, for the second distribution. On the other hand, if some people score much higher than the mean and others score much lower, then the scores will tend to be further from the mean. Thus, the standard deviation will also be higher, as shown by the first distribution with a standard deviation of 14.64.

Frequency distributions, means, medians, and standard deviations are used to describe important characteristics of a single set of scores obtained for a single variable such as test scores. The importance of these statistics is demonstrated by their ability to summarize large amounts of data; they have been used to summarize the results of almost all of the hundreds of thousands of psychological studies that have been conducted. Descriptive statistics also provide us information about the degree of relationships that might exist between variables. That kind of information is usually obtained by analyzing the correlation between variables.

Correlation and Prediction Revisited

We learned earlier that variables can be related—as the value of one variable changes, so may the value of the other variable. In other words, some variables "go together" in such a manner that the value of one variable can be predicted if the value of the other variable is known. In this way, the variables are said to be correlated. Recall, for example, the way in which SAT scores and college GPA are related: in general, the larger the value of SAT, the larger the value of the college GPA. These variables are said to be correlated because one variable could be predicted from the other. Let's take a closer look at how psychologists use statistics to analyze correlation.

One of the first things that a psychologist might do to analyze the correlation between two variables is to graph the data in a **scatter plot**, a two-dimensional graph used to display the degree of correlation between two variables. The scatter plot provides a common sense, understandable basis for showing a relationship. One variable in a scatter plot is represented by the horizontal axis and the other variable is represented by the vertical axis, and each point represents the two scores for a single person. In addition to a table (Table 2.1), the relationship between SAT and college GPA can be shown in a scatter plot (see Figure 2.5a). SAT scores are plotted along the horizontal axis and GPA scores are plotted along the vertical axis.

The essence of any relationship between two variables is predictability.

The complete data set consists of the SAT scores and GPAs of ten people, so the scatter plot constructed from the information in Table 2.1 and Figure 2.5a contains the same information presented in two different ways: in a table and in a graph, respectively.

To construct a scatter plot, we begin by listing the range of values for one of the variables along the horizontal axis and the range of values for the other variable along the vertical axis. To plot a point, take the two scores from a single person and find the corresponding point on the graph (see Figure 2.5b). For example, to plot the point that corresponds to Joanne's score, note that Joanne scored 1300 on the SAT. Find 1300 on the horizontal axis and draw a vertical line to it. Joanne's GPA was 3.8, so find this value on the vertical axis, and draw a horizontal line to it. As shown in

FIGURE 2.5a
Right: Scatter plot of SAT scores and GPAs from the data given in Table 2.1.

FIGURE 2.5b
Below left: Plotting the point of Joanne's SAT and GPA scores given in Table 2.1.

FIGURE 2.5c
Below right: Scatter plot of SAT score and freshman GPA score with regression line indicating a positive relationship.

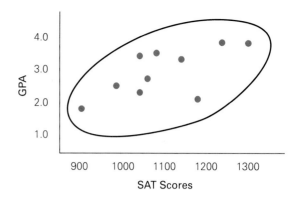

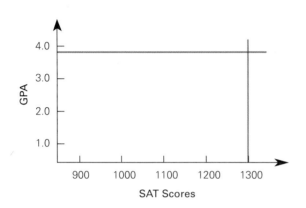

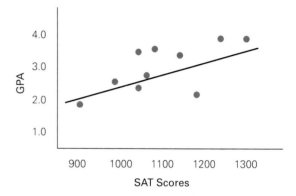

Figure 2.5b, the point in the scatter plot that corresponds to Joanne's score is at the intersection of the two lines. The complete scatter plot is constructed when the points for all subjects have been plotted.

Remember that the essence of any relationship between two variables is predictability. Knowing the applicant's SAT score before he or she was admitted to college would allow a useful, though not perfect, prediction to be made of the applicant's *eventual* GPA if admitted. Looking at the complete scatter plot, especially after enclosing the ten points within an ellipse, you can perhaps more easily visualize the relationship between SAT scores and GPA upon which this prediction is based: people with low SAT scores *tend* to have low college GPAs, and people with high SAT scores *tend* to have high GPAs.

Graphically, the predictability inherent in a relationship is shown by the amount of "scatter" in the scatter plot. The scatter of the points in a scatter plot becomes more apparent when a diagonal line is drawn through the middle of the scatter plot, as shown in Figure 2.5c. The **regression line** is a line drawn through the points in a scatter plot that allows researchers to predict the value of one variable when given the value of the other variable. In the case of SAT scores and college GPA, the regression line shows that these variables are positively correlated because as the value of one increases, so does the value of the other. The predicted GPA is obtained from this line (or from the equation for this line). Thus, by knowing a person's SAT score, the college GPA can be predicted by locating the corresponding point on the regression line for GPA. That is, for any given SAT score, a corresponding point on the regression line can be found that is the predicted GPA. Using more advanced statistical techniques, the regression line relating SAT scores to college GPA or any other variables for any number of people can be found.

Of course, the regression line used here is based on only ten people and so is presented for illustrative purposes only. In real life, a college admis-

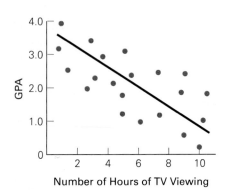

FIGURE 2.6
Scatter plot of GPA score and hours of TV viewing with regression line indicating a negative relationship.

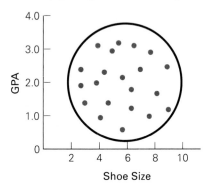

FIGURE 2.7
Scatter plot of GPA score and shoe size indicating no correlation.

sions officer would compute the regression line from the SAT scores and GPAs of hundreds and probably thousands of students already enrolled in the college and would use additional variables such as high school GPA, to further increase the accuracy of prediction. On average, the more relevant information the admissions officer has regarding the applicant's qualifications and interests, the smaller the difference between the applicant's predicted GPA and actual GPA will be.

SAT scores and college GPA are positively correlated. When two variables are positively correlated, as the values of one of these variables increases, the values of the other variable tend to increase as well. In general, the larger the SAT score, the larger the GPA.

The correlation between two variables may also be negative. As an example of this type of relationship, let's use the variables "the number of hours spent watching TV" and "college GPA." The more a student watches TV, the more likely that his or her college GPA will be low. Here large values of TV watching are associated with small values of GPA. In negatively correlated relationships, the value of one variable becomes smaller as the value of the other variable becomes larger. The scatter plot and regression line for a negative relationship are shown in Figure 2.6.

Some variables, such as GPA and shoe size, are not related at all. If someone knew your shoe size, he or she would have no more information about your GPA than someone who did not know your shoe size. GPA cannot be predicted from shoe size, so GPA and shoe size are *not* correlated. The scatter plot for two uncorrelated variables has no tilt, indicating the lack of either a positive or negative relationship. An example of such a scatter plot is shown in Figure 2.7. High values for one variable are paired with both high and low values for the second variable. A person with a high GPA is just as likely to have a large shoe size as a small shoe size. Similarly, low values for one variable are paired with both high and low values for the second variable.

The amount of correlation, that is, the strength of the relationship between variables, is expressed statistically by the **correlation coefficient**. A strong relationship means that the value of one variable can be accurately predicted from the value of the other variable. The strongest possible correlation occurs when knowledge of the value of one variable for a single person allows perfect prediction of the value of the second variable. For example, if SAT and GPA were perfectly related, then an admissions officer who knew an applicant's SAT score could perfectly predict the applicant's GPA if he or she was to be admitted to the university. In the case of perfect prediction, there would be no "scatter" around the regression line in the scatter plot because all of the data points would fall on the regression line, indicating that everyone with the same SAT score would obtain exactly the same GPA after they were admitted to the university. Unfortunately, perfect prediction does not very often occur in real life. And when it does, it is usually for trivial relationships, such as predicting someone's weight when you know his or her height.

The correlation coefficient is a number that ranges from −1 to +1. The direction of the relationship is given by the sign of the correlation coefficient; positive correlations have a positive sign and negative correlations have a negative sign. The sign itself has nothing to do with the strength of a relationship, which is given by the size (absolute value or magnitude) of the correlation. The closer the correlation is to −1 or to +1, the stronger is the relationship between the two variables. Thus, a correlation of −1 or +1 represents a perfect relationship; that is, perfect predictability. The correlation coefficient for variables that are not related is zero or close to zero. A strong negative relationship, with a correlation of −.85, is stronger than a weak positive relationship, with a correlation of .20.

Let's return to our example of the relation between SAT scores and college GPA. As mentioned previously, colleges correlate SAT scores and GPAs from students already in college to obtain predictions of incoming student GPAs from SAT scores. The College Board (1984) reports a typical correlation of SAT with GPA of .42 with some correlations as high as .57 or more. In the example illustrated in Figure 2.5a, the correlation of SAT scores and GPAs is .61. All of these correlations represent relationships of moderate strength and reasonable predictability.

In sum, the degree to which two variables may be related can be graphically depicted in a scatter plot. By looking at the direction of the tilt of the regression line of the scatter plot, researchers can get a rough estimation of whether the variables are positively or negatively correlated or not correlated. The degree to which two variables are correlated is expressed in terms of the correlation coefficient, which may range from -1, indicating a strong negative correlation to $+1$, indicating a strong positive relationship.

Inferential Statistics

So far, we have discussed data analysis solely in terms of descriptive statistics, which are used to summarize particular characteristics of the data. However, psychologists usually wish to not only describe the data that they have collected in their research, but also to generalize their results to a larger group of individuals. The larger group of individuals to which research results are generalized is called a **population**. In some research the population includes all college age females or all blue collar workers. In other studies the population may be all pregnant women or all people living in a particular culture. Of course, it is impossible to observe all members of a population, so researchers work with a **sample** or a representative subset of the population for their study.

One example of the distinction between population and sample that is familiar to most of us is the polling that occurs before presidential elections. Pollsters are interested in knowing how many people who intend to vote will vote for a particular candidate. The problem is that it is impossible, or at least impractical, to ask all of the millions of people who will vote which candidate will receive their vote. The solution is to take a sample of only a few thousand voters. By asking just these people how they intend to vote, a reasonable guess can be obtained as to how many of the millions of actual voters will vote for a particular candidate.

In order to generalize their research results to a larger population, psychologists collect data from a sample or representative subset of their study population.

Psychologists face the same challenge in their research. It is impossible, for example, to investigate the memory capabilities of all people or to investigate the mental distortions of all people institutionalized for severe mental and psychological problems. Instead, psychologists select samples of these large populations, conduct their studies, analyze their data, and then generalize their results to the full populations. To make these generalizations, psychologists once again rely on statistics—not the statistics that describe the data, such as the mean or correlation, but inferential statistics, which allow inferences to be made about the population as a whole given the specific sample of data collected from that population. Based on the computation of these statistics from a sample of data, **inferential statistics** provide a means for the psychologist to make inferences about the complete population. In order to make generalizations from their data, however, psychologists must do more than simply calculate descriptive statistics. Before making generalizations, psychologists want to know what the likelihood is that their results were due to their manipulation of the independent variable and not to chance. That is, psychologists want to know whether they would obtain similar results if they were to conduct their experiment again.

To illustrate the basis for inferential statistics, consider a study that consists of polling in presidential elections. Suppose that 55 percent of the voters voted for Candidate A in the election. Of course, before the election, the pollsters do not know voting results, so they select samples of voters to estimate how many people will vote for Candidate A. The pollster collects one sample to estimate the general voting trend in the entire population. If everyone could be polled, 55 percent of the population would have voted for Candidate A, but by chance, one sample of several thousand voters drawn by one pollster might yield a result of 53.2 percent, while another sample drawn by a different pollster might yield 56.9 percent, and yet a third pollster might yield a result as small as 49.8 percent.

What is of interest to the pollsters is the overall trend that 55 percent of the population voted for one candidate. The problem the researcher (in this case, the pollster) faces is that the results computed from any one sample are always due in part to chance. The key point to note here is that although the true value in the population is actually 55 percent, the pollsters will probably observe a slightly different percentage of voters voting for Candidate A in almost every sample. Because chance always influences the results of any one sample, the exact results of any one study will differ from the exact results obtained from repeating the study with another sample. The overall trend in the population, however, will remain relatively stable in all samples drawn from that population.

Inferential statistics provide researchers a method for seeing how representative the sample result is of the entire population. The pollster could, for example, use inferential statistics to estimate the error in the population percentage he or she computed. The first pollster may have obtained a sample value of 53.2 percent, but because of chance influences in any one sample, he or she knows that the true population value is not exactly equal to 53.2 percent. After applying inferential statistics, the pollster would be able to say something like, "The actual number of people voting for Candidate A is likely to be within three percentage points of 53.2 percent."

Another example of the use of inferential statistics is from Schachter's (1959) experiment that investigated the relationship between fear and affiliation. Almost two-thirds (62.5 percent) of Schachter's subjects in the high-fear condition wished to affiliate with others, but only one-third (33 percent) of the low-fear subjects wished to do so (see Table 2.2). If the study were to be repeated, the influence of chance on any one sample means that the exact percentages of 62.5 percent and 33 percent would probably not be obtained. Schachter had to decide if his results indicating a large difference in affiliation would generalize to the population as a whole, or if they were a fluke. Perhaps if the study were repeated, the percentages would be 50 percent and 50 percent. Or if his results were indicative of a general trend, he would probably once again obtain a large difference, perhaps as large as 65 percent and 35 percent.

So Schachter observed a large difference between the means of the dependent variable, affiliation, across the experimental and control groups. The question answered by inferential statistics is, "Does this difference found in one sample exist as a general trend in the population?" He concluded that if the study were to be repeated, approximately the same results would be obtained. That is, the large difference in means is representative of the entire population. The experiment's conclusion that fear causes affiliation applies not only to most of Schachter's subjects, but also to most people in general.

Inferential statistics allow the psychologist to conclude with a reasonable degree of confidence whether the results of a study are indicative of a hypothesized general trend in the population as a whole. If the general trend exists, the researcher knows in advance that the obtained results based on a single sample would be replicated without actually having to go to the trouble of repeating the study. Relationships that generalize to real life, such as those demonstrated by the large difference in affiliation across the experimental and control groups in Schachter's study, are said to be **statistically significant**. Thus, whenever the psychologist wishes to generalize his or her results beyond the confines of a single study and sample, as is usually the case, inferential statistics are used to test a given result for statistical significance. If the obtained results based on one sample are statistically significant, the researcher is confident that his or her specific results generalize to the entire population of interest.

> *Inferential statistics allow the psychologist to conclude with a reasonable degree of confidence whether the results of a study are indicative of a . . . general trend in the population . . .*

ETHICS IN PSYCHOLOGICAL RESEARCH

Psychological research with both humans and nonhuman animals often raises important ethical issues—issues that concern moral principles and values and questions of right and wrong. For instance, do researchers have the right to inflict physical harm or psychological stress on their subjects? Is it right to deceive subjects in an experiment for the purpose of finding out how they would behave under certain conditions? Because psychologists study living organisms, they have special responsibilities to treat their subjects with respect, dignity, and concern for their physical and psychological safety.

To guide psychological researchers in the fulfillment of their responsibilities, the American Psychological Association (APA) has established a set of guidelines for the treatment of both human and other animal subjects and expects all psychologists to adhere to these guidelines. In this section, we will look at the ethics involved in psychological research, starting with ethical treatment of animal subjects.

Ethics and the Use of Animals

Psychology has a long tradition of using animals as subjects in its research. Most studies involving animals use rats, mice, or birds. These animals are exposed to a wide variety of independent variables, including some that might seem rather harsh: food or water deprivation, electric shock, high or

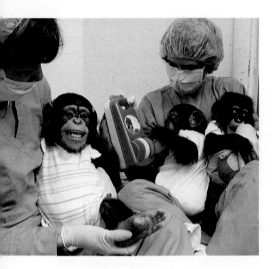

Animals have always been a part of psychological research. Psychological researchers have an ethical responsibility to treat their subjects with respect, dignity, and concern for their physical and psychological safety.

low temperatures, and isolation, to name just a few. What is the purpose of exposing animals to these sorts of aversive variables? Sometimes it is to understand nothing more than how these variables influence learning and behavior; that is, how these animals adapt to changes in their environments. Many other times, the purpose is to gain knowledge that can be applied either to help the animal species under study or to help our own species. For example, from psychological research with animals have come discoveries that have led to breakthroughs in understanding and treating psychological disorders, improving methods for teaching basic skills to developmentally delayed people, and developing effective coping skills for dealing with stress, anxiety, and fear.

You may ask what could be wrong with conducting research that has these sorts of benefits. Some argue that it is morally and ethically wrong to place the welfare of humans above that of animal subjects. In essence, they argue that animals, like people, have rights to well-being and comfort and that those rights are violated when animals are subjected to research, psychological or otherwise.

Is it morally right that animals should suffer so that we can benefit? After considering the question carefully, most psychologists would answer yes to this question. The main reason for this answer involves the historical precedent animal research has set for discovering cures to human ailments. Consider, for example, Louis Pasteur's research with dogs that led to the development of a vaccine against rabies, or Jonas Salk's work with mice that led to the development of a vaccine against polio. In other words, in the past, animal research benefitted humans tremendously, and we can expect that future animal research will yield similar breakthroughs in the treatment of neurological and psychological disorders for which, currently, there are no cures.

However, most psychologists look with disdain upon research that involves needless suffering of animal subjects. In conducting research with animals, the APA urges psychologists to take every precaution against causing their subjects undue discomfort, illness, and pain. The only case in which any pain or stress is allowed is when no other possible alternative is available and the goal of the research is justified by its potential scientific, educational, or applied value. In fact, most universities have established ethics committees for the express purpose of carefully reviewing research proposals of its faculty to help protect animal subjects from experiencing undue stress or harm during the course of research. Moreover, most universities even have a committee that from time to time conducts surprise inspections of animal facilities to ensure that animals' day-to-day living conditions are adequate.

Ethics committees, then, have been established to discourage inhumane treatment of laboratory animals. Although this is not a perfect solution to the problem of animal abuse, it is nonetheless a positive step toward enhancing the quality of care and treatment of animals used for scientific research.

Ethics and the Use of Human Subjects

Let's suppose that you actually had been a subject in Dr. Gregory Zilstein's experiment. Recall that as a subject, you would have been told that you were going to receive a shock—either an intense shock or a very mild shock. Was Dr. Zilstein's research ethical? Was it right to put you and the other subjects under such stress (fear of being shocked)? Was it ethical for him to deceive you and the other subjects (everyone was told they were going to experience shock, although nobody actually did)? These are examples of the kinds of ethical questions that can arise in human research.

It is interesting to consider these questions both from the perspective of the researcher and from that of the subject. On one hand, the researcher views the research as important and valuable and so is willing to deceive subjects or place them under stress when necessary. Unfortunately, in some cases, researchers can become so personally involved with their research that they cannot always objectively see whether or not such procedures are actually necessary to accomplish the goals of the research. From the subject's point of view, more may be entailed in the research than receiving extra credit in exchange for participation—after all, he or she is the one who may be deceived, and he or she may become vulnerable to certain risks including experiencing needless psychological stress or harm.

It is from these two perspectives that the APA developed its ten "Ethical Principles in the Conduct of Research with Human Participants" (June, 1981). These guidelines urge all psychologists conducting human research to pay particular attention to treating their subjects with due respect and consideration. Let's take a closer look at four of the more important guidelines.

One APA guideline urges researchers not to coerce potential subjects into participating in research. This means, for example, that your instructor cannot require you to participate as a subject in psychological research as a condition of completing the class. Researchers must give all potential participants every opportunity to decline or withdraw from research, without fear of punishment for doing so.

A second APA principle requires that researchers obtain the informed consent of potential subjects prior to their participation in the research. **Informed consent** is a written statement provided to potential subjects by the researcher that discloses those aspects of the research that might affect their willingness to participate in the study. Informed consent constitutes a contract between subject and researcher. It states the requirements of the subject's participation during the course of the study, and the kind of compensation (usually extra class credit) provided by the researcher to the subject for that participation. The subject reads the informed consent statement and signs it, as does the researcher.

nformed consent constitutes a contract between subject and researcher.

Often the design of a study requires that the subjects not be aware of the true nature of the research. As we have seen, knowing the purpose of the experiment may bias subjects' responses so that they behave in a manner that supports the researcher's hypothesis simply because they are aware of the purpose of the study. Such behavior renders the study's methods useless and the research is of no scientific value. Thus, in some studies some kind of deception is necessary to protect the integrity of the research. According to the APA, this deception is justified as long as the researcher satisfies the following conditions:

- The participant is provided with a sufficient explanation of this action as soon as the research is completed.
- The deception does not otherwise psychologically or physically harm potential subjects.
- The dignity of the subjects is maintained.

In short, informed consent requires that potential subjects understand exactly what is expected of them during the course of the research, and that the investigator protects participants from physical and psychological discomfort, harm, and danger. Obviously the matter of psychological harm, discomfort, and danger are more difficult to assess and anticipate than are physical problems. For some subjects, simply being involved in an experiment, no matter how straightforward it is, can be stressful. The point is that if stress or danger is possible, the participant must be so informed, and every step must be taken to minimize these negative effects.

A third APA guideline concerns **confidentiality** or the privacy of the subject's participation in research. This guideline specifies that all assurances must be taken that the subject's participation in the study will remain confidential, and these assurances must be explained to the subject. In no case is it justified to identify individual participants, or the nature of their behavior, in a research study. If there is any chance that anyone else other than the researchers themselves may have access to the data, then this possibility must be discussed with subjects before they provide informed consent to participate in the study.

A fourth APA guideline and one of the most important aspects of any psychological research involving human subjects is embodied in the ethical principle concerning debriefing. **Debriefing** is the procedure of fully informing subjects of the true nature and purpose of the research after all the data have been collected. Debriefing is usually the last contact that subjects and researchers have with each other. Its purpose is educational as well as ethical: subjects are not only informed of the nature of the study, but they may also be told why the study was conducted and what scientific value the results represent. If there is concern that other potential subjects may learn of the nature of the research before the project is completed, debriefing may be delayed. But in doing so the investigator must take special care that no damaging consequences arise from postponing the debriefing.

In developing ethical guidelines for psychological research with human subjects, the APA has attempted to balance the researchers' rights to discover new knowledge with the well-being of the subjects in such research. Indeed, in virtually every case in which these ethical guidelines are applied, the basic task is to weigh any risk to the participant against the potential benefits to be derived from the research to be undertaken. These decisions are to be considered and made during the planning stage of research before the research is actually begun.

BOUNDARIES AND FRONTIERS

There are three primary ways to study human behavior. The first is to apply our findings from studying the behavior of animals to the behavior of humans. Historically, that kind of research has been a valuable tool in understanding basic principles of human behavior. However, generalizations from animal research can only go so far in helping us understand ourselves. After all, we are different both biologically and intellectually from the animals used in psychology experiments. So, studying animal behavior, although useful and interesting in its own right, is limited in what it can tell us about the causes of our own behavior.

The second way to study human behavior is to simply ask people why they do what they do. Why did you do that? How often do you do that? Do you think you will ever do that again? As we have seen, there are problems with this approach, too. People do not always tell the truth when it comes to their own behavior. Sometimes they cannot remember what they did, and at other times, they simply do not know why they did what they did. Despite these sorts of problems, the self-report is a very popular research tool in psychology today. Why? Probably because it is such an easy way of gathering information about human behavior. Nonetheless, this approach to studying human behavior can only provide hints at causal relationships. It cannot with any certainty, identify causal relationships.

The third way to study human behavior, as you by now know, is through experimentation—manipulate the value of an independent variable of interest and then measure changes in the dependent variable of interest. If a psychologist wants to understand how different variables cause changes in human behavior, his or her best bet is to conduct the proper experiment. Experiments are not as simple to conduct as self-report studies, but they provide more reliable information about behavior.

But experimentation, too, has its problems. Perhaps the most pressing problem is that many important psychological questions cannot ethically be addressed by experiments. Child abuse, rape, sexual behavior, happiness in marriage, and success as a mother or father, are important issues in psychology today, yet none can be studied by conducting an experiment. So what are researchers to do? In this case, the best they can do is use a self-report procedure, but as we have just seen, that, too, has its problems.

The message here is plain to see: our knowledge of human behavior is constrained by the methods of psychological science. For some research questions (such as What causes child abuse?), there is simply no good way, at present, to find a reliable and sound answer. That fact is a constraint under which all psychological researchers must work. But as you will see throughout the book, every boundary is also a frontier. Part of the challenge of being a research psychologist involves developing new methods for investigating the important and often pressing behavioral issues of our time. Indeed, the reward of being a research psychologist lies not only in discovering the answer to a question, but also in devising the methods that made the discovery possible.

CONCEPT SUMMARY

THE NATURE OF SCIENTIFIC KNOWLEDGE

- How does scientific knowledge differ from other kinds of knowledge? (pp. 22–24)
- What is empirical knowledge? (p. 23)
- What is the role of falsifiability in testing scientific knowledge? (pp. 25–26)
- How are correlation and prediction related? (pp. 26–27)
- What is the difference between a hypothesis and a theory? (pp. 27–29)
- How do causal hypotheses differ from relational hypotheses? (pp. 28–29)

OBSERVATIONAL RESEARCH

- What are the basic features of observational research? (p. 29)
- What is a self-report? What are its advantages and disadvantages? How do questionnaires differ from interviews as tools for gathering self-report information? (pp. 29–30)
- How do case studies differ from naturalistic observation? (pp. 31–33)

- What is a major limitation of observational research? (pp. 33–34)

EXPERIMENTAL RESEARCH

- What is the purpose of experimental research? How does it differ from observational research? (p. 34)
- What are the basic features of an experiment (explain the role of independent and dependent variables, random assignment, and experimental and control groups)? (pp. 34–38)
- What are the basic features of single-subject research? What are the advantages and disadvantages of such research? (pp. 38–39)
- How can confounding variables, experimenter expectancy, and demand characteristics each influence the outcome of an experiment? How can the double-blind procedure help prevent experimenter expectancy? (pp. 40–42)

ANALYZING DATA

- What is the difference between descriptive and inferential statistics? (pp. 42–51)

- What is a frequency distribution and how is one constructed? In what ways can the data contained in a frequency distribution be displayed? (pp. 43–44)
- What sorts of information do the mean, median, and standard deviation provide a researcher about a frequency distribution? (pp. 44–46)
- How are scatter plots useful in showing correlation between two variables? What is the purpose of drawing a regression line on a scatter plot? (pp. 46–49)
- What are the important features of the correlation coefficient? (pp. 48–49)
- What is the difference between a population and a sample? What role do inferential statistics play in relating data that has been gathered from a sample to a population? (pp. 49–50)

ETHICS IN PSYCHOLOGICAL RESEARCH

- Why has the APA established a set of ethical guidelines to be followed in conducting psychological research? (pp. 51–54)
- From the APA's point of view, under what conditions is it justifiable to place animal subjects under stress? (pp. 52–54)
- What role do informed consent and debriefing play in safeguarding the well-being of human subjects in psychological research? (pp. 53–54)

KEY TERMS AND CONCEPTS

THE NATURE OF SCIENTIFIC KNOWLEDGE

Empirical Knowledge   Knowledge that is obtained from carefully observing and measuring behavior under highly controlled conditions. (p. 23)

Data   Scientific information usually obtained by numeric measurement. (p. 23)

Falsifiability   The ability to prove that a statement of inference is false. Falsifiability is a key to testing hypotheses. (p. 25)

Variables   Any characteristics of organisms or the environment that vary from one instance to the next. (p. 26)

Value   The level or degree of a variable. (p. 26)

Correlation   The statistical term used to describe the degree of relationship between two or more variables. Variables that are related are said to be correlated because the value of one variable can be predicted from the value of the other. (p. 26)

Prediction   The ability to foretell the value of one variable from the value of another variable. (p. 26)

Hypothesis   A proposed relationship between two or more variables that can be tested empirically. Evidence regarding the truth of a hypothesis is an objective of any scientific study. (p. 27)

Theory   A set of statements that attempts to explain relationships that may exist between behavior and other variables. (p. 28)

Causal Hypotheses   Hypotheses that specify that one variable causes the other. Causal hypotheses not only specify a relationship between the variables of interest, but they also account for the existence of the relationship in terms of cause and effect. (p. 28)

Relational Hypotheses   Hypotheses that specify that two or more variables are related, but none of the variables can be specified to cause the other variables. (p. 29)

OBSERVATIONAL RESEARCH

Observational Research   Research in which the psychologist observes and measures the variables of interest without attempting to influence the values of the variables, or to intervene in any other way. Observational research is mainly concerned with testing relational hypotheses. (p. 29)

Self-Report   A technique in which people provide subjective information about themselves—feelings, beliefs, evaluations, or interests—to the researcher. (p. 29)

Questionnaire   A self-report technique in which a series of written questions specifically designed to address a particular topic are given to a subject to answer. (p. 30)

Interview   A self-report procedure in which the researcher requires subjects to respond verbally to questions. The researcher then records the subject's answers either in written form or on video. (p. 30)

Naturalistic Observation   A type of research in which data are gathered by observing behavior as it naturally occurs. Individuals are observed in the context of their normal daily routine, often without any awareness of being part of a psychological study. (p. 31)

Case Study   An intensive investigation of a single individual over an extended period of time based on the use of observational techniques. (p. 32)

EXPERIMENTAL RESEARCH

Experiment   A research method in which the investigator manipulates certain variables and measures their effects on other variables. Experiments are conducted to determine the effect of the independent variable on the dependent variable. (p. 34)

Independent Variable   The variable that is manipulated in an experiment. In psychological research, the independent variable is always a variable hypothesized to influence behavior. (p. 34)

Dependent Variable   The variable that is measured in an experiment. In psychological research, the dependent variable is always behavior. (p. 34)

Random Assignment   An experimental procedure in which each subject is assigned to a group on the basis of chance alone. Randomly assigning subjects to different groups minimizes differences that may have existed among subjects prior to the experiment. (p. 36)

Experimental Group   The group of subjects in an experiment that is exposed to the independent variable. (p. 36)

Control Group The group of subjects in an experiment that is either not exposed to the independent variable or is exposed to a lesser value of the independent variable relative to the experimental group. (p. 36)

Single-Subject Research A type of research in which experiments are conducted using only one or a few subjects. (p. 38)

Baseline Condition The part of an experiment in which the independent variable is not manipulated, but the dependent variable is measured over several sessions or days. (p. 38)

Treatment Condition The part of an experiment in which the independent variable is manipulated and its effects on the subject's behavior is measured over several sessions or days. (p. 38)

Confounding Variables Variables other than the independent variable that can influence the value of the dependent variable. (p. 40)

Experimenter Expectancy An experimenter's inadvertent communication of his or her expectations to the subject, which may influence the subject's behavior. (p. 40)

Double-Blind An experimental procedure for controlling experimenter expectancy in which neither the person conducting the experiment nor the subjects know the purpose of the study or to which group subjects are assigned. (p. 41)

Demand Characteristics Factors in an experiment that cause subjects to behave in a manner consistent with what they believe the study is about. (p. 41)

ANALYZING DATA

Descriptive Statistics Statistics used to describe a particular set of data such as the mean, median, and standard deviation. (p. 42)

Frequency Distribution A listing or graph of all the possible values of a variable, and how many subjects actually obtained each of these values. (p. 43)

Mean The average of a distribution is computed by adding all of the scores in the distribution and then dividing by the total number of scores. (p. 44)

Median The number above and below which 50 percent of the scores in the distribution fall. (p. 45)

Standard Deviation A descriptive statistic that expresses the amount of variability among scores in a frequency distribution. (p. 45)

Scatter Plot A two-dimensional graph used to display the degree of correlation between two variables. (p. 46)

Regression Line The line drawn through the points in a scatter plot that allows researchers to predict the value of one variable when given the value of the other variable. (p. 47)

Correlation Coefficient A statistical expression of the amount of correlation between two variables, with a value that ranges from -1 to $+1$. The direction of the relationship is given by the sign of the correlation coefficient; positive correlations have a positive sign and negative correlations have a negative sign. (p. 48)

Population A large group of individuals to which researchers generalize their results. (p. 49)

Sample A representative subset of a population. (p. 49)

Inferential Statistics The kind of statistical analyses that allow the researcher to make informed estimates about characteristics of the complete population from the values of statistics computed from a single sample of data. (p. 50)

Statistically Significant A term used in inferential statistics to indicate that results from a study are generalizable to an entire population of individuals. (p. 51)

ETHICS IN PSYCHOLOGICAL RESEARCH

Informed Consent A written statement provided to potential subjects by the researcher that discloses those aspects of the research that might affect their willingness to participate in the study. In essence, informed consent constitutes a contract between subject and researcher. (p. 53)

Confidentiality The privacy of the subject's participation in research. (p. 54)

Debriefing A procedure of fully informing subjects of the true nature and purpose of the research after all the data have been collected. (p. 54)

ADDITIONAL SOURCES OF INFORMATION

McCain, G., & Segal, E. M. (1982). *The game of science* (4th ed.). Monterey, CA: Brooks/Cole. This entertaining book presents the human side of science. The excitement of scientific research, the place of science within our culture, and common misunderstandings of science are all discussed.

Stanovich, K. E. (1986). *How to think straight about psychology.* Glenview, IL: Scott, Foresman. Many of the issues discussed in this chapter are explored in more detail in this small book. If you are thinking of continuing your study of psychology, reading this book would provide you with a more in-depth understanding of the science of psychology and its methods. The writing style is engaging and the material is presented clearly.

Kiess, H. O., & Bloomquist, D. W. (1985). *Psychological research methods.* Boston: Allyn & Bacon. This textbook is one of many excellent junior- or senior-level texts designed for specific courses in the methods of psychology. As such, much of this text is technical, particularly the sections on statistics. Nonetheless, looking at this or similar books would provide you with a more in-depth overview of psychological methods than we could provide in this chapter.

3 Evolution, Heredity, and Behavior

Heredity and environment interact to influence our behavior. Psychologists seek to understand these influences by studying both ultimate causes, historical conditions that have slowly shaped the behavior of our species over generations, and proximate causes, which are events in the immediate environment that affect behavior.

CHARLES DARWIN—A BIOGRAPHICAL SKETCH
(61–64)

Youth and Early Adulthood   Development of Darwin's Theory

Our understanding of ultimate causes of behavior stems largely from Darwin's theory of evolution by natural selection, which he developed from studying natural history. Natural selection is the tendency of organisms to reproduce differentially; that is, within a species, some animals will produce more offspring than others.

NATURAL SELECTION AND EVOLUTION   *(64–71)*

Natural Selection   A Brief Sketch of Human Evolution
Selection Pressures in Human Evolution

Natural selection is the basic means by which evolution proceeds. Natural selection works because individual organisms vary in physical and behavioral traits, and because these traits have a genetic basis. Over time, competition for food and other resources allows only individuals with the most adaptive physical and behavioral characteristics to survive and pass on their traits. Two key traits that aided the evolution of our species were the ability to walk upright and the enlargement of the brain.

HEREDITY AND GENETICS
(71–81)

Basic Principles of Genetics   Heredity   Genetic Disorders

Our physical traits and behavior are partially determined by our genetic endowment: genes define the boundaries by which we can be influenced by environmental factors. However, in many cases, the complementary roles of heredity and environment are so intertwined that their separate influences on behavior are difficult to assess clearly.

SOCIOBIOLOGY   *(81–86)*

The Problem of Altruism   Reciprocal Altruism   Criticisms of Sociobiology

Sociobiology represents the extension of Darwin's work to human affairs. The key to understanding sociobiology is understanding the evolution of altruism—how could natural selection possibly favor behavior that benefits others while endangering the life of the altruist? Sociobiology's answer is that individuals are likely to help only those with whom they share genes or those who might be in a position to reciprocate. Many psychologists, though, argue that altruism is a learned behavior rather than an inherited one.

. . . From my early youth I have had the strongest desire to understand and explain whatever I observed—that is, to group all facts under some general laws. . . . Therefore, my success as a man of science, whatever this may have amounted to, has been determined, as far as I can judge, by complex and diversified mental qualities and conditions. Of these, the most important have been—the love of science—unbounded patience in long reflecting over any subject—industry in observing and collecting facts—and a fair share of invention and common sense. With such moderate abilities as I possess, it is truly surprising that I should have influenced to a considerable extent the belief of scientific men on some important points.

Charles Darwin
(from *The Autobiography of Charles Darwin*
1887, pp. 67–71)

These are humble words from a man who has influenced and changed the course of scientific thinking and research more than any individual since Copernicus, who in 1543 proposed that the sun, not the earth, was at the universe's center. Darwin, of course, contributed to our understanding of **biological evolution**, the theory that over time, organisms originate and become adapted to their environment by biological means. Ernst Mayr (1978), an influential biologist of our era, has noted that Darwin's theory, although "modified and explicated by the science of genetics stands today as the general theory of life."

The importance and scope of Darwin's theory transcends the biological sciences and extends to the social sciences, particularly psychology. Psychology's ambitious task, given the backdrop of biological diversity, is to develop general laws that explain the behavior of organisms, especially humans. Understanding evolutionary processes allows psychologists to understand behavior in terms of its possible origins and adaptive significance as well as its causes and functions in everyday life.

Both biologists who study evolutionary processes and psychologists have the same purpose: to study and understand behavior. They go about their tasks differently, however. For example, consider how each might go about studying human learning. The biologist might be interested in discovering how past environmental conditions favored learning as the chief means of human adaptation over genetically controlled behavior patterns, which are the chief means by which most other animals adapt to their environment. A psychologist, on the other hand, might be interested in how variables in the immediate environment such as intelligence, sensation and perception, and previous experience influence our ability to learn. That is, evolutionary biologists piece together the puzzle of behavior from a very broad perspective. They are interested in **ultimate causes** of behavior: evolutionary events and conditions that have slowly shaped some of the behavior of our species over generations. Ultimate causes are best understood through studying evolutionary processes. Psychologists, on the other hand, most often study behavior in terms of **proximate causes** or events and conditions in the immediate environment that affect behavior. Such causes are best understood by manipulating certain aspects of that environment and then observing the effect on behavior.

For at least two reasons psychologists have become increasingly aware that ultimate causes of behavior are related to proximate ones. First, understanding how our species adapted to the environment through evolution partially accounts for how an individual adapts to his or her own particular environment through learning. That is, by understanding the adaptation of the species through the long-term process of evolution, psychologists are able to develop a more thorough understanding of our ability to adapt to changes in our immediate environment (Skinner, 1987).

A second reason for studying the relation between ultimate and proximate causes is to provide a useful means of better understanding the ways in which heredity and environment together shape and influence our behavior and cognition. To understand the present we must understand the past—both the history of the individual and the history of the entire species. We behave in the ways we do both because we are members of the human species, an ultimate cause, and because we have learned to act in special ways, a proximate cause. Thus, biology and environment both contribute to our personal development.

We will begin this chapter by piecing together the events that led to Darwin's formulation of evolution via natural selection and by outlining the essential features of his theory. Next, we will discuss general principles of heredity and genetics, the basic means by which biological and, in many cases, behavioral characteristics are passed from one generation to the next. Finally, we will examine sociobiology, a recently established branch of biology that seeks to identify and understand evolutionary influences on social behavior.

CHARLES DARWIN—A BIOGRAPHICAL SKETCH

The story of how Charles Darwin developed his ideas points up the mix of hard work, sheer intellect, and plain good fortune that often underlies scientific discovery. In fact, Darwin is an excellent example of how observation and experimentation, together with careful weaving of theory to fact, can lead to important scientific breakthroughs.

Youth and Early Adulthood

Darwin's experiences and habits as a young man bore a direct and profound influence on his later work as a scientist. As a youth, Darwin possessed a driving curiosity for natural history and literature and reeled in the pleasure he derived from understanding any complex subject or thing. He was given to long solitary walks, reading, and collecting things such as rocks, minerals, plants, and bugs.

After graduating in theology from Christ's College in 1831, Darwin was introduced to Captain Robert Fitz-Roy, who was looking for a young man to serve as a naturalist and traveling companion, without pay, on board the five-year voyage of the H. M. S. *Beagle*, a ten-gun brig converted to an ocean-going research vessel. The *Beagle's* mission was to explore and survey the coast of South America and to make longitudinal measurements worldwide. Darwin was anxious to volunteer but his father was strongly

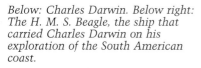

Below: Charles Darwin. Below right: The H. M. S. Beagle, the ship that carried Charles Darwin on his exploration of the South American coast.

opposed. (Can you imagine being a college graduate nowadays and still having to obey your parents' wishes for your career?) Fortunately for Darwin, his father appended his refusal with a challenge, "If you can find any man of common sense who advises you to go I will give my consent." Darwin recounts the story in his autobiography: "On the very next morning I went to Maer . . . and whilst out shooting my uncle sent for me offering to drive me over to Shrewsbury to talk with my father, as my uncle thought it wise that I should accept the offer. My father always maintained that he was one of the most sensible men in the world, and he at once consented in the kindest manner" (Darwin, 1887, p. 36).

Darwin then went to London to meet Fitz-Roy and make arrangements for the voyage. Darwin was to learn later that Fitz-Roy nearly rejected him because of the shape of his nose! Fitz-Roy believed that he could judge a person's character by the shape of one's nose. Fitz-Roy suspected that anyone with a nose like Darwin's could not "possess sufficient energy and determination for the voyage." In the end though, the Darwin family's aristocratic standing and Charles' references convinced Fitz-Roy to allow Darwin aboard (Engel, 1962; Gould, 1977). Darwin later noted, "But I think he was afterwards well satisfied that my nose had spoken falsely" (Darwin, 1887, p. 36).

The *Beagle* departed England on December 27, 1831. On board, Darwin made the best of difficult circumstances. He was plagued by seasickness the entire trip. He and Fitz-Roy had frequent and sometimes heated disagreements over, among other things, slavery (Fitz-Roy favored slavery, Darwin did not), politics (Fitz-Roy was a zealous Tory and Darwin was a devoted Whig), and Darwin's penchant for collecting things.

Nonetheless, Darwin went about his business. He hiked hundreds of miles inland, often jeopardizing his life, to observe the flora and fauna of South America, Australia, South Africa, and the islands of the Pacific, South Atlantic, and Indian oceans. In addition, he took copious notes on the geology of each country he visited. These notes served as the basis of three books he would later write on geology. Darwin spent the majority of the voyage, however, doing what he enjoyed most—collecting. During his five years at sea, he collected creatures and objects of every sort—marine animals, reptiles, amphibians, land mammals, birds, insects, plants, rocks, minerals, fossils, and sea shells. These specimens, which were sent back to England at various stages of the voyage, were examined by naturalists from all over Europe. Darwin later noted that the experiences he had while on board the *Beagle* were among the most important in his life and noted ". . . yet it depended upon so small a circumstance as my uncle offering to drive me thirty miles to Shrewsbury (to talk to my father), which few uncles would have done, and on such a trifle as the shape of my nose . . ." (Darwin, 1887, p. 38).

Darwin later noted that the experiences he had while on board the Beagle *were among the most important in his life . . .*

Development of Darwin's Theory

Darwin did not form his theory of evolution while aboard the *Beagle*. Although impressed by the tremendous amount of diversity among seemingly related animals, he believed in creationism, the view that the species were nonevolving. At this point in his life, he only flirted with the possibility that species might undergo evolutionary change. For example, during his visit to the Galapagos Islands, Darwin discovered that the mockingbirds on some islands were distinguishable from those that inhabited the other islands. Darwin considered two explanations that might account for the variety of mockingbirds. Either the differences represented only minor variations on a common theme, a view that was consistent with nineteenth century creationism, or the differences represented separate species

Varieties of pigeons. (a) The wild rock pigeon is believed to be the ancestor of each of the other breeds of pigeons shown here. (b) Frillback. (c) Satinette oriental frill. (d) English pouter. (e) Pomeranian pouter. (f) Carrier. (g) Fantail.

Based on photographs in W. W. Levi, The Pigeon, Levi Publishing Co., 1957.

of mockingbirds, each specially adapted to the specific conditions present on the different islands, an evolutionary view. Darwin rejected the evolutionary view while still at sea (Gould, 1985).

Upon his return home in 1836, Darwin continued to marvel at the variety of ways animals and plants become adapted to their environments. He sifted through his collections, often calling on specialists to help him examine his specimens and interpret his findings. He became interested in **artificial selection**, a procedure in which animals are deliberately mated to produce offspring who possess particularly desirable characteristics. For example, if a rancher wishes to develop cattle that yield the largest steaks possible, then he or she might selectively breed those cattle that currently yield the largest steaks. That is, the rancher will survey the available breeding stock and allow only the "beefiest" to reproduce. If this process is repeated over many generations, most of some future generation of cattle will be beefier than the majority of those in the original population assuming, of course, that beefiness is inherited. Darwin, himself, experimented with artificial breeding in pigeons (see Figure 3.1).

As a result of his systematic inquiry into the origin of species, his views on selection began to change. Specifically, he began to wonder whether or not there might be some process in nature that corresponds to the role that humans play when they artificially breed animals. In his own words:

> . . . without any theory [I] collected facts on a wholesale scale, more especially with domesticated productions, by printed enquiries, by conversation with skillful breeders and gardeners, and by extensive reading . . . (and) soon perceived that selection was the keystone of man's success in making useful races of animals and plants. But how selection could be applied to organisms living in a state of nature remained for some time a mystery to me. (Darwin, 1887, p. 53)

The seeds of a great idea were thus sown, but it would be another year and a half before Darwin's intensive study of plant and animal domestication would bear fruit. Many of the great mysteries of nature unveil themselves to human understanding under rather surprising circumstances. Darwin's insight into the driving force of evolution was no exception, as he seized the idea while doing some leisurely reading. Darwin recalls the event in his autobiography:

> I happened to read for amusement Malthus on *Population*, and being well prepared to appreciate the struggle for existence which everywhere goes on from long continued observation of plants and animals, it at once struck me that under these circumstances favourable variations would tend to be preserved, and unfavourable ones to be destroyed. The result would be the formation of a new species. (Darwin, 1887, p. 54)

What struck Darwin was the idea of **natural selection** or the tendency of organisms to reproduce differently: within any given species, some animals, the survivors, will produce more offspring than others of the same species. Darwin was well aware of the significance of his discovery but did not publish his theory until twenty years later. Why? Among other things, he devoted a considerable amount of time to gathering supportive evidence. Darwin was sensitive to the philosophical and religious implications of his theory and took great pains to develop a clear, coherent, and accurate case for his views. He examined and reexamined his specimens, carefully studied current research and theory in the natural sciences, conducted his own research on artificial selection, and perhaps most importantly, tested his ideas out on his closest colleagues.

A. R. Wallace

Darwin might have been even slower in publishing his theory had it not been for an intriguing coincidence. In 1858, he received a manuscript from Alfred Russell Wallace outlining a theory of natural selection identical to his own. What was he to do? If he published his theory now, it would look like he had stolen the idea from Wallace; if he didn't publish, his twenty years of painstaking toil would be for naught. He presented the dilemma to his colleagues. They suggested that he and Wallace make a joint presentation of their separate works before a learned society—the Linnean Society—so that each might lay equal claim to the theory of natural selection. This was done, and a year later Darwin published his abstract, which we know today as *The Origin of Species*. The book sold out on its first day of publication and has been selling steadily ever since.

NATURAL SELECTION AND EVOLUTION

Darwin's theory of evolution has four basic premises (Mayr, 1978). First, the world's animal and plant communities are dynamic, not static; that is, they change over time with new forms originating and others becoming extinct. Second, the evolutionary process is gradual and continuous; new species tend to arise not through sudden and dramatic environmental changes, but through slow and steady environmental changes that gradually "perfect" each animal to its surroundings. Third, organisms descended from a common ancestor. Any particular group of organisms, for example, birds, descended from an original and common ancestor. Over time, selective pressures have resulted in the formation of different species of animals, each specifically adapted to an ecological niche, a particular set of environmental circumstances. The fourth and final component of Darwin's theory is natural selection, which we will discuss fully in a moment. Many modern biologists still support these premises, although recently some doubt has been cast on the gradual nature of evolutionary change;

evolutionary change may occur more abruptly than Darwin believed (Gould, 1982; Gould & Eldridge, 1977).

Natural Selection

In general, the essence of Malthus' essay was that the earth's food supply grows more slowly than do populations of living things. The resulting scarcity of food produces competition among animals, with the less-abled losing the struggle for life. For example, wolves who are fleet-of-foot are better able to chase and eventually capture prey than their slower packmates. Fast wolves will, therefore, tend to outlive and outreproduce slower wolves (Figure 3.2). If the tendency to run fast is part of a wolf's genetic endowment, then it will be passed on to the wolf's offspring, which, of course, will afford them a better chance of catching prey, living longer lives, and producing offspring of their own.

Suppose that a particular pair of wolves was able to reproduce without limit. If each of their offspring were to do the same and the pattern continued for several generations, it would not be too long before the world would be overpopulated with wolves. The crucial point, however, is that the size of animal populations remains relatively stable over long periods of time. Thus, there must be some selection process that holds reproductive capability in check. That process is, of course, natural selection. A dramatic example is provided by elephant seals (Le Boeuf, 1974). Male seals compete with other males in vicious battles for the opportunity to mate. Generally only the older, more experienced males win these battles, with the major spoil of war being female companionship, for females will not choose to mate with losers.

The relative ability of an individual to produce offspring defines the individual's **personal fitness**, which is measured in terms of **reproductive success** or the number of viable offspring (those capable of becoming sexually mature adults) one produces relative to the number of viable offspring produced by other individuals of the same species. Contrary to popular interpretation, survival of the fittest does not always mean survival of

FIGURE 3.2

Natural selection at work. Wolves that are fast will be more adept at escaping predators, capturing game, and reproducing successfully than their slower packmates. Because of the selective advantage that running confers upon a wolf's survival and reproductive success, the genotype for running speed will be passed on to and will increase in frequency across future generations.

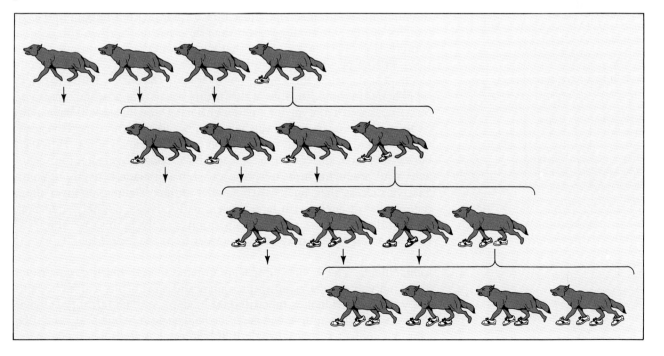

the most physically fit or of the strongest. There are many factors that contribute to the maximization of personal fitness. In humans, for example, charm, intelligence, and wealth sometimes play an important role in an individual's ability to attract a suitable mate. The evolutionary "bottom line" is not physical strength but reproductive success. Physical strength is only one factor that might, in some circumstances, contribute to reproductive success.

Why are some individuals more reproductively successful than others? The answer to this question is because of variation and competition, two important aspects of natural selection. Let's look at each.

Variation. **Variation** includes the differences we find across individuals of any given species in terms of their biological characteristics (size, strength, physiology) and psychological characteristics (intelligence, sociability, behavior). Some bald eagles are better at catching field mice than other bald eagles, and some cotton tail rabbits blend in with their surroundings better than other cotton tails, and so on. Variation exists at two levels. First, an organism's genetic make up—its **genotype**—typically differs from that of other species' members. Second, an organism's physical appearance and behavior—its **phenotype**—varies from individual to individual. Every individual's phenotype is the result of the interaction between its genotype and the environment. In essence, the genotype determines the extent to which the environment can influence an organism's development and behavior. For instance, identical twins have exactly the same genotype. If they are separated at birth and raised in different nutritional environments, they will likely show differences in phenotypes, with the twin receiving the better nutrition possessing, for example, greater height and physical strength. In other words, an organism's genotype establishes the range within which the phenotype might vary. Of course, even when identical twins are reared together, they have different interactions with the environment, and so, develop different phenotypes.

Thus, phenotypes and their underlying genotypes may or may not be selected, depending on any particular advantage they confer upon the organism in adapting to its environment. For instance, the genotype of some buck mule deer may, under favorable environmental conditions, allow them to grow a larger than average set of antlers. If large antlers aid the buck in self-defense and allow him to mate with a larger number of females during the rutting season than do other bucks, then the gene or combination of genes (genotype) that give rise to the large antlers (phenotype) will be passed on to the buck's male offspring. Does, like female elephant seals, select their mates on the basis of the buck's ability to defeat other bucks in the skirmishes of the rutting season. Suppose too, that some bucks possess a genotype for smaller antlers. These bucks will have a difficult time finding mates; nevertheless, a few will find mates and the genotype for small antlers will be passed on to their male offspring. However, bucks with large antlers will be selected for mating by a greater number of does, thus producing more offspring and showing a greater degree of reproductive success than bucks with smaller antlers (Figure 3.3). Over time, the number of bucks with large antlers will increase, possibly squeezing small antlered bucks out of the competition entirely. In this case, the genotype for small antlers may even disappear from the gene pool.

Competition. The second dimension of natural selection is **competition**. Since individuals of a given species share the same ecological niche with every other individual, competition for food, mates, and territory is inevitable. Every fish captured and eaten by bald eagle A is one that cannot be captured and eaten by bald eagle B. If bald eagle A finds a suitable mate,

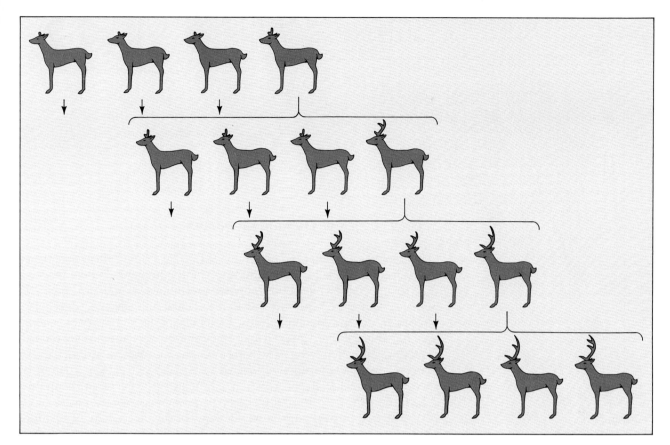

FIGURE 3.3
Natural selection in buck mule deer. Since large antlers give bucks an advantage in self-defense and reproduction, the genotype for large antlers will be passed on to male offspring.

then there is one less potential mate in the population from which bald eagle B may select, and so forth (Salthe, 1972).

Competition can also occur when members of different species compete for similar ecological resources such as food and territory. For example, yellow-headed blackbirds and red-winged blackbirds compete for similar foodstuffs and exclude each other from their respective breeding territories. Such competition does not usually involve competition for mates (for example, yellow-headed blackbirds do not attempt to court red-winged blackbirds and vice versa). However, interspecies competition does indirectly influence reproductive success, since an animal's ability to find and court a suitable mate is partially dependent upon staking out and defending a territory that has an adequate food supply. Thus, the probability of a yellow-headed blackbird finding a mate and successfully rearing a family is dependent upon not only its success in competing against other yellow-headed blackbirds for mates, food, and property, but also its success in competing against red-winged blackbirds for food and property.

In summary, natural selection is based on reproductive success; typically, only the fittest organisms find mates and successfully rear offspring. Natural selection works because the individual members of any species vary phenotypically, and because the phenotype has a genetic basis, or genotype, which may be passed on from one generation to the next. Over time, competition for food and other resources will allow only the best-adapted phenotypes (and their corresponding genotypes) to survive, thereby producing evolutionary change. We now turn to a discussion of how these concepts apply to the evolution of our own species and its behavior.

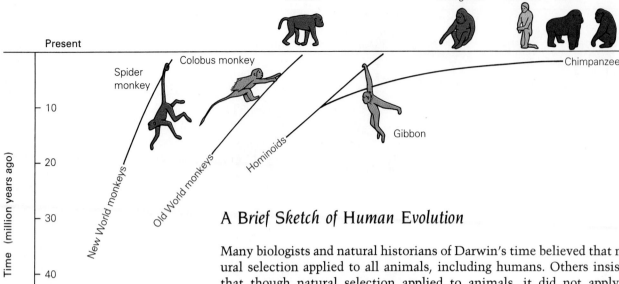

Baboon **Orangutan** **Human** **Gorilla**

Present

Spider
monkey

Colobus monkey

Chimpanzee

Gibbon

New World monkeys

Old World monkeys

Hominoids

Time (million years ago)

10

20

30

40

50

60

FIGURE 3.4
*The ancestral line of humans and
related primates.*

A Brief Sketch of Human Evolution

Many biologists and natural historians of Darwin's time believed that natural selection applied to all animals, including humans. Others insisted that though natural selection applied to animals, it did not apply to humans. However, both the fossil record and the recently developed molecular biological techniques used to compare the similarity of genetic material among different species, strongly suggest that humans are related to other mammalian forms. The gorilla and the chimpanzee are our closest living relatives, and together we appear to have descended from a common ancestor (Figure 3.4). Reconstruction of human evolution is a difficult job, something akin to assembling a giant jigsaw puzzle whose pieces have been scattered throughout the world. Some of the pieces may be lost forever; others have become damaged beyond recognition; and those few that are found force continual reinterpretation of how the other pieces might fit the puzzle. In short, our past will likely always remain a mystery. At best, all we can do is to make an educated guess about the evolution and lifestyles of our ancestors.

The earliest humans have been labeled *Homo habilis* (literally, "handy man"). There is some doubt regarding the origin of this line. Some researchers believe that *Homo habilis* descended from *Australopithecus*, a creature who lived in Africa about 2 to 3 million years ago. Other researchers believe *Homo habilis* coexisted with *Australopithecus*. *Homo habilis*, like *Australopithecus*, was small, probably only about 1.3 meters tall and about 40 kilograms in weight and was bipedal (able to walk upright on two feet). Unlike *Australopithecus*, *Homo habilis* had a larger brain and powerful hands that were well-suited to making and using simple stone tools. Hence, the name "handy man." It is easy to see why natural selection favored such traits, for surely they helped these early humans adapt to the environment in terms of catching and preparing food, making weapons for protection, and creating shelter against the elements.

About 1.6 million years ago, *Homo habilis* was succeeded by *Homo erectus* ("upright man"). *Homo erectus* had a much larger brain than *Homo habilis* and lived a more complex and varied life style. *Homo erectus* was the first of our early ancestors to establish regular base camps. These camps probably served as a center for social activities such as the preparation and eating of food. *Homo erectus* was a creative and skilled toolmaker whose primary tool was a tear-drop shaped hand ax made from better quality rock types than the simple tools of *Homo habilis*. Evidence is clear that *Homo erectus* was a successful big game hunter. *Homo erectus* also discovered and used fire. Fire enabled these early humans to heat and soften food, remain warm in cold weather, and protect themselves against predators.

The use of fire, coupled with their social nature and ability to walk upright and successfully hunt big game, allowed *Homo erectus* to explore and eventually settle new and probably hostile environments. *Homo erectus* not only extended its territory to other parts of Africa but to Europe and Asia as well.

The earliest known *Homo sapiens* ("intelligent man"), *Homo sapiens neanderthalensis*, lived throughout Europe and Central Asia. Neanderthals constructed small huts from bones and animal skins and sometimes burned bones as fuel. They were skilled big game hunters, toolmakers, and clothiers and were the first humans to adopt rituals for burial. For example, in one archaeological find in France, a teenage boy was buried as if sleeping on his right side. A pile of flints formed a pillow under his head and a stone ax was positioned near his hand. Many other such burial sites have been unearthed, indicating that Neanderthals possessed cultural traditions not previously found in the prehistoric record (Lewin, 1984).

Neanderthals had thicker bones, and larger teeth than early *Homo sapiens sapiens*, or modern humans. Scientists believed that the two *Homo sapiens* lines overlapped each other with the Neanderthals originating about 150,000 years ago and becoming extinct about 35,000 years ago, and *Homo sapiens sapiens* arising between 100,000 and 40,000 years ago. There are three theories regarding the origin of modern humans. The first theory suggests that modern humans from an isolated population, perhaps from Africa, spread throughout Eurasia replacing the Neanderthals through fierce competition for resources and possibly, war. The second theory suggests that the Neanderthals simply represented a transitional state between *Homo erectus* and modern humans. The third theory combines these two models and suggests that an isolated form of modern *sapiens* migrated throughout Eurasia and interbred extensively with local populations of Neanderthals, eventually resulting in the complete ascendancy of *Homo sapiens sapiens*. Figure 3.5 shows the time frame involved in the evolution of our species along with the major adaptations that made our evolution possible.

R*econstruction of human evolution is a difficult job, something akin to assembling a giant jigsaw puzzle whose pieces have been scattered throughout the world.*

Recently, scientists from the University of California, Berkeley and Emory University in Georgia believe that they have discovered the genetic path that leads to "Eve," as they call her. Eve was not discovered by traditional "stones and bones" anthropologists in their search for ancient fossils and human remains—that is, we have no physical evidence at hand. Instead, anthropologists who specialize in molecular biology and work almost exclusively in indoor laboratories have analyzed biological materials from living women known to have ancestors originating in Africa, Asia, or Europe. They have uncovered a genetic path that they say points "to a single woman from whom we are all descended" (Tierney, Wright, & Springen, 1988). The path is marked by a special kind of genetic substance that is inherited only from mothers, making it possible to trace the maternal family line. These researchers theorize that Eve was a muscular and probably African woman who lived about 200,000 years ago and who, quite literally, is the biological mother of the 5 billion humans living today. In essence, she is the one common ancestor all humans have in their family trees. These researchers are quick to note that their Eve was not the first or only woman on earth during the period in which she was alive; however, for some unknown reason, she was more successful reproductively than other females of the era. We should add one final point: The "Eve theory" is very new, and although interesting, remains speculative until further evidence is collected.

Selection Pressures in Human Evolution

The remarkable success of the human family in adapting to various and changing ecological niches stems from natural selection favoring two important developments in human evolution: bipedalism and encephalization (see Figure 3.5). **Bipedalism** refers to the ability to move about the environment on two feet. **Encephalization** refers to increases in brain size. As the human brain became larger, more of its volume became devoted to abstract thinking, reasoning, and other complex cognitive functions. Over time, the interaction of bipedalism and encephalization permitted humans to exploit new environments and establish what might be called the hallmark of human existence—civilization.

Humans' ability to walk upright not only allowed greater mobility in moving about the environment, but it also freed the hands for grabbing, holding, and throwing objects. The ability to grasp objects, in combination with an expanding capacity for learning and remembering new skills, led to advances in toolmaking and hunting. Humans who were able to fashion and use tools for hunting and self-defense lived longer and produced more offspring than their less resourceful counterparts. Ultimately, natural selection permitted only the more intelligent bipeds to survive.

The increased life span of humans resulted in the gradual accumulation of wisdom as the older members of early human communities began to share their knowledge and experiences with younger members. Although the fossil record cannot document the advent of language, we can be sure that those who were able to communicate with others through language or art had a distinct evolutionary advantage over those who could not. Milford Wolpoff (1980) speculates that the *Australopithecines* may have had a primitive language system, and Alexander Marshack (1976) reckons that the Neanderthals had an advanced form of language about 100,000 years ago. (Written language is believed to have originated about 3600 B.C.)

Language originated and subsequently evolved because of its immensely practical consequences (Skinner, 1986). Language not only provided a simple means of warning others of danger but also afforded members of local communities a means of learning ancestral lore and tradition as well as relaying important information to others such as the location of a good hunting spot or instructions on how to craft an ax. Perhaps most importantly, language reinforced the already strong social tendencies of early

FIGURE 3.5

Major milestones in human evolution. The ability to walk upright freed the hands for tool use and other manipulative skills. Increased brain size brought with it increased intelligence. These two factors combined probably contributed significantly to all other major events in human evolution.

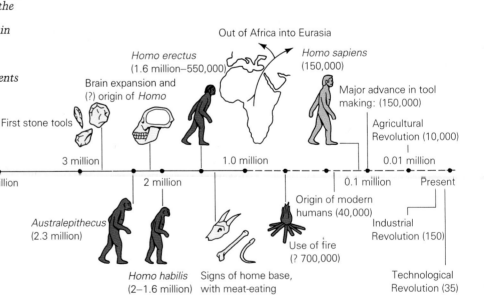

Over time, the interaction of bipedalism and encephalization permitted humans to exploit new environments and establish what might be called the hallmark of human existence – civilization.

humans. It is not difficult to imagine a group of early humans sitting around a camp fire eating the catch of the day and enjoying simple, although primitive, conversation. There is little doubt that language contributed to the development and maintenance of strong bonds between individuals, families, and tribes in primitive societies. Indeed, language is the foundation upon which all human cultures are built.

As cultures continued to develop, humans gained further advantage in controlling and modifying their environments. The same intellectual resourcefulness that permitted early humans to discover and use fire and to invent useful tools prompted the agricultural revolution of 10,000 years ago, the industrial revolution of 150 years ago and the technological revolution that began only 40 years ago with the invention of the computer. **Cultural evolution**, or the adaptive changes of cultures to recurrent environmental pressures over time, is possible only because humans have been genetically endowed with a capacity for learning. In other words, every generation of ancient humans did not have to rediscover fire or reinvent the wheel. Instead, each succeeding generation found new and better ways to use the discoveries and knowledge of past generations. Fire came to be used for preparing foods and hardening metals as well as to warm the body; the invention of the wheel led to the invention of the axle and later, the design of simple carts for hauling wood, crops, and other supplies. Language became the chief means of passing on such knowledge from one generation to the next. Cultural evolution is faster than biological evolution, thus allowing us to make very rapid adjustments to unpleasant environmental conditions. Advances in medicine, for example, have allowed us to control life threatening diseases such as polio, small pox, malaria, syphilis, rabies, tetanus, scurvy, typhoid fever, and diptheria. (It would take hundreds of thousands of years, maybe even millions, to evolve humans that are immune to disease.)

In summary, selective pressures favored the evolution of people who were bipedal and intelligent. These characteristics allowed our ancestors to interact increasingly with one another as well as to explore and settle new environments. These same characteristics have been passed down from generation to generation over millions of years to us. Although the environment in which we live is drastically different from that in which our early progenitors took their first steps and thought their first thoughts and spoke their first words, bipedalism and encephalization permit us similar adaptive benefits, and more. The pleasures derived from appreciating literature, music, art, and science are a direct consequence of the evolutionary pressures placed upon the first humans in their struggle for survival. This is perhaps why psychologists are so interested in evolutionary processes in general and in human evolution in particular. Both reveal the possible circumstances under which adaptive behavior first emerged and those conditions that have been important for the continued expression of adaptive behavior down to the present time.

HEREDITY AND GENETICS

Darwin's research unveiled the process of natural selection, an important boundary in our understanding of life. The same research pointed up new frontiers for exploration and experimentation. One of the most important of these frontiers was genetics, the study of heredity. Although Darwin had built a strong case for natural selection, he could not account for a key tenet of his theory—inheritance. He knew that individual differences occurred within a given species and that those differences were subject to natural selection, but what he didn't know was how adaptations were passed from parent to offspring. Six years after *The Origin of Species* was published, Gregor Mendel, an Austrian monk, led the scientific community to the correct answer—genes. Ironically, Mendel's research went unnoticed for 35 years (probably because he held no scientific credentials) before it was rediscovered and applied to understanding the transmission of inherited traits.

Basic Principles of Genetics

Psychologists are interested in genetics because at least part of our behavior is influenced by those factors that we have inherited biologically from our mothers and fathers. In this section we will discuss briefly the basic principles of genetics.

The Organization of Genetic Material. Every living thing contains genetic material in each of its cells. With very few exceptions, this material consists of the nucleic acid known as **DNA** (deoxyribonucleic acid). Each molecule of DNA is organized into small units called **genes**, which communicate and convert the information needed to synthesize proteins found in cells. Genes are the basic units of heredity; through coded instructions contained in DNA, they direct the biological and physical development of all living things. Genes regulate the metabolic activities of cells and regulate physiological processes; they also control the biological basis and expression of phenotypes or physical traits such as eye color, height, and so on. Genes are found on **chromosomes**, the rodlike structures found in the nuclei of living cells. We inherit 23 chromosomes from each of our parents, giving us 46 chromosomes in each cell. Given that each chromosome may contain thousands of genes, the union of an ovum with a sperm will produce one of over several billion possible gene combinations, leaving very little mystery as to why no two people, except identical twins, are exactly alike.

One pair of chromosomes, the **sex chromosomes**, contain the instructional code for the development of male or female sex characteristics. Mothers always donate an X chromosome but fathers may contribute either an X or a Y chromosome to this pair. If the chromosomes match (two X chromosomes), the developing embryo is a female, otherwise, it is a male (one X chromosome and one Y chromosome).

Determination of Phenotypic Traits. Phenotypic traits are determined by the interaction of genes on complementary pairs of chromosomes. In other words, more than a single gene comprises a genotype for any particular phenotype. Recall, too, that the environment interacts with the genotype

Below left: Female chromosomes.
Below right: Male chromosomes.

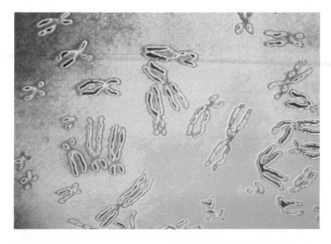

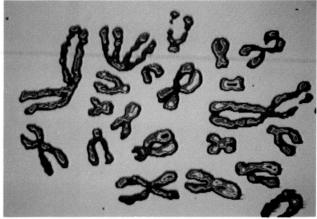

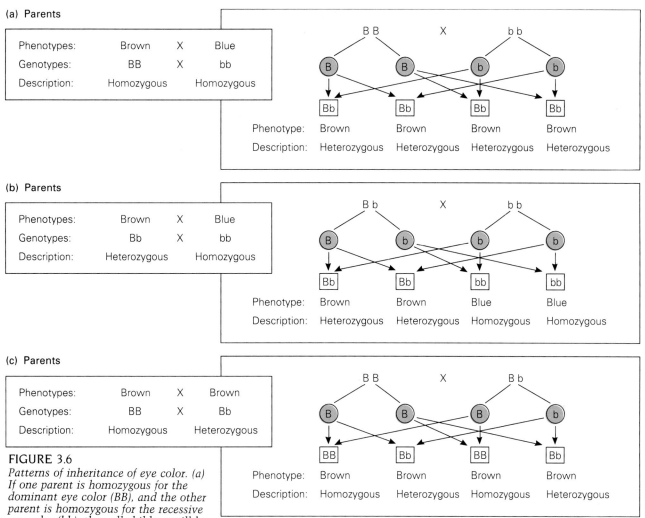

(a) Parents

Phenotypes:	Brown	X	Blue
Genotypes:	BB	X	bb
Description:	Homozygous		Homozygous

B B   X   b b

	B	B	b	b

	Bb	Bb	Bb	Bb
Phenotype:	Brown	Brown	Brown	Brown
Description:	Heterozygous	Heterozygous	Heterozygous	Heterozygous

(b) Parents

Phenotypes:	Brown	X	Blue
Genotypes:	Bb	X	bb
Description:	Heterozygous		Homozygous

B b   X   b b

	B	b	b	b

	Bb	Bb	bb	bb
Phenotype:	Brown	Brown	Blue	Blue
Description:	Heterozygous	Heterozygous	Homozygous	Homozygous

(c) Parents

Phenotypes:	Brown	X	Brown
Genotypes:	BB	X	Bb
Description:	Homozygous		Heterozygous

FIGURE 3.6

Patterns of inheritance of eye color. (a) If one parent is homozygous for the dominant eye color (BB), and the other parent is homozygous for the recessive eye color (bb), then all children will be heterozygous for eye color (Bb) and will have brown eyes. (b) If one parent is heterozygous (Bb), and the other parent is homozygous recessive (bb), then their children have a 50 percent chance of being either heterozygous (brown eyes) or homozygous recessive (blue eyes). (c) If one parent is homozygous dominant (BB) and the other parent is heterozygous (Bb), then 50 percent of their children will be homozygous for the dominant eye color (BB) and will have brown eyes, 50 percent will be heterozygous (Bb) for the trait and will have brown eyes.

B B   X   B b

	B	B	B	b

	BB	Bb	BB	Bb
Phenotype:	Brown	Brown	Brown	Brown
Description:	Homozygous	Heterozygous	Homozygous	Heterozygous

SOURCE: William S. Klug and Michael R. Cummings, *Concepts of Genetics,* Second Edition. Glenview, Illinois: Scott, Foresman and Company, 1986.

in determining phenotype. In some cases traits are influenced by the interaction of only a single pair of genes. In other cases traits are said to be polygenic; that is, they are determined by more than a single pair of genes. Mendel established the basic principles of inheritance by studying the interaction of pairs of genes. Although Mendel studied traits such as tall/dwarf stems and round/wrinkled seeds in garden peas, we will use eye color, blood characteristics, and baldness to demonstrate his basic findings of trait inheritance in humans.

If each parent contributes to their child an identical gene for eye color, the gene combination is said to be homozygous. However, if each parent contributes a different gene, the gene combination is said to be heterozygous. When the gene combination is heterozygous, the phenotype is controlled by the dominant gene. For example, when a child inherits the gene for brown eye color (dominant) from one parent and the gene for blue eye color (recessive) from the other parent, the child will have brown eyes because the dominant gene determines how much of a certain pigment will be present in the iris. The blue eye color controlled by the recessive gene is not expressed. Only if the child inherits homozygous recessive genes for eye color will she have blue eyes. Inheritance of homozygous dominant genes will result in brown eyes (see Figure 3.6). Other eye colors such as hazel or black are produced when other genes influence the dominant brown gene to code for more (black) or less (hazel) pigment in the iris.

Heredity and Genetics **73**

Pattern baldness is a trait caused by sex-influenced genes.

| | PHENOTYPE | |
| TABLE 3.1. *Sex-influenced inheritance of male pattern baldness.* | | |
GENOTYPE	♀	♂
BB	Bald	Bald
Bb	Not bald	Bald
bb	Not bald	Not bald

Sex Influences on Heredity. The sex of an individual plays a crucial role in influencing the expression of certain traits. A good example is hemophilia, excessive bleeding from even the most minor of injuries. Normal people will develop blood clotting in the first few minutes after sustaining a cut; hemophiliacs may require 30 minutes or sometimes even hours before the blood oozing from a cut begins to clot. Hemophilia is caused by a recessive gene on the X chromosome that fails to produce the necessary protein for normal blood clotting. Because females have two X chromosomes they can carry the gene for hemophilia but still have normal blood clotting if one of the two genes is normal. Males, however, have only a single X chromosome and will have hemophilia if they receive the recessive gene from their mothers.

The gene for hemophilia is an example of sex-linked genes, so named because this gene resides only on the sex chromosomes (in the case of hemophilia, the X chromosome). Another class of genes related to sex are sex-limited genes, which influence, among other things, the development of secondary sex characteristics such as body hair. Although both sexes may carry these genes on any chromosome, the phenotype is expressed in only one sex, hence the term, sex-limited. For example, the genes for facial hair are generally expressed only in males.

There also are sex-related genes that express themselves in both sexes, although the phenotype appears more frequently in one sex than in the other. These genes are called sex-influenced genes because they are dominant in one sex and recessive in the other. For example, pattern baldness (thin hair across the top of the head) develops in men if they inherit one gene for the trait whereas women suffer from pattern baldness only if they inherit both genes for the trait (Table 3.1).

Mutations and Chromosomal Aberrations. Changes in genetic material arise from two sources, mutations and chromosomal aberrations. **Mutations** involve accidental alterations in the DNA code within a single gene. Mutations can be either spontaneous and occur naturally or they can be the result of man-made factors such as high-energy radiation.

Hemophilia is one of the most famous examples of mutation in humans. Although hemophilia has appeared many times in human history, no other case of hemophilia has had as far-reaching effects as the spontaneous hemophiliac mutation that was passed among the royal families of nineteenth century Europe. Through pedigree analysis (tracing hemophilia through genealogical lines) researchers have discovered that this particular mutant gene arose with Queen Victoria (1819–1901), since she was the first in her family line to bear affected children, two female carriers and an afflicted son (Figure 3.7). The aristocratic tradition that nobility marry only other nobility caused the mutant gene to spread rapidly throughout the royal families.

The second type of genetic change, **chromosomal aberration,** involves either the rearrangement of genes within or between cells or a change in the total number of chromosomes. An example of a disorder caused by a chromosomal aberration, in this case the partial deletion of the genetic material in one member of chromosome pair #5, is cri-du-chat syndrome. Infants with this syndrome have gastrointestinal and cardiac problems, are severely mentally retarded, and emit crying sounds that resemble the mewing of a cat (hence, its name, "cry of the cat"). In general, the severity of the syndrome appears to be related directly to the amount of genetic material missing. Psychologists and developmental disability specialists have discovered that early special education training permits many individuals suffering from this syndrome to learn rudimentary self-care and communication skills. This fact highlights an important point about genetics and behavior: even behavior that has a genetic basis can usually be modified to some extent through training or experience. It also points out the potential usefulness of an interdisciplinary approach to studying behavior. Geneticists and other biologists may provide their expertise at identifying and explaining the role of evolution and heredity in influencing behavior; psychologists may provide theirs in terms of controlling and changing behavior so that it is expressed most adaptively with respect to a given social environment.

Heredity

Reflect for a few moments on the personal qualities that make you unique—your personality, your physical attributes, your athletic abilities. Do you know anyone who is exactly like you? Unless you have an identical twin, your answer must be an unqualified "no." However, you probably

FIGURE 3.7

Pedigree analysis of the inheritance of hemophilia in European royal families. The gene for hemophilia likely originated with Queen Victoria of England or one of her close ancestors. She was the first woman in the English royal family to bear an afflicted son or a carrier daughter.

SOURCE: *Genetics: A Survey of the Principles of Heredity,* Fourth Edition, by A. M. Winchester (Boston: Houghton Mifflin Company, 1972). Reprinted by permission of the author.

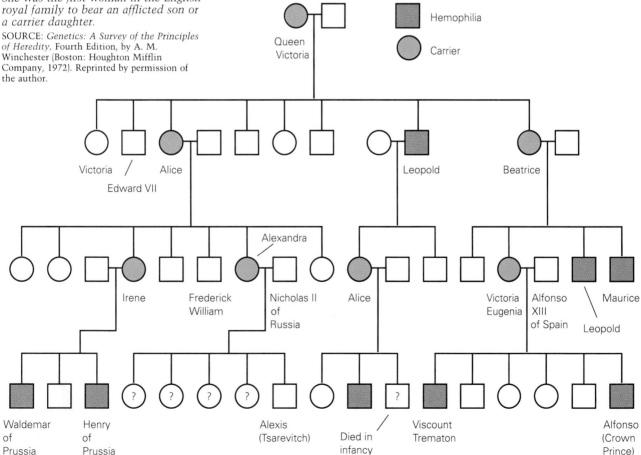

share many similarities with your parents and maybe even some of your friends. Nevertheless, subtle differences remain. You may have your mother's smile but do you also have her sense of humor? Heredity certainly accounts for many of these kinds of similarities and differences but personal experiences and environmental factors also play an important role.

Gene-Environment Interaction. Historically, the extent to which genetic and environmental factors separately influence the expression of human traits has been a topic of considerable controversy among psychologists. This controversy is most obvious in the "nature-nurture debate" that has often surfaced when psychologists of different persuasions debate origins of behavior. Psychologists defending the nature side of the issue contend that most, if not all, of our behavior is inherited. Those psychologists arguing the nurture position adopt the opposite stance and feel our behavior is learned. However, recall that the genotype determines the extent to which the environment can influence behavior. Because environmental effects depend upon one's genetic endowment, it is unlikely that either factor alone determines who or what we ultimately become. In many instances the complementary roles of heredity and environment are so intertwined that their individual contributions to behavior and cognition cannot be separated.

t is our genetic structure that determines whether we will develop into human beings rather than into lizards or aardvarks.

It is clear that our genes play a major role in our lives, since it is our genetic structure that determines whether we will develop into human beings rather than into lizards or aardvarks. On the other hand, it is obvious that the environment also plays a critical role in shaping our lives, since our personal experience always influences our behavior in educational, social, and career settings.

The interaction of genetic and environmental factors in determining trait expression is made clear in the case of dermatographia, an inherited disorder in which genetic factors permit the skin to react to surface pressure (Figure 3.8). Although the disorder is due to a genetic defect, without the environmental factor of pressure, the trait—welting of the skin—cannot be expressed. Even in cases where expression of behavior or physical traits are more strongly determined by genetic factors, the environment may still exert a modest influence. Recall, for example, that individuals afflicted with cri-du-chat syndrome may learn simple adaptive skills provided they are given special education training early in life.

FIGURE 3.8
Dermatographia is a genetic defect that requires environmental interaction for the trait to be expressed. People suffering from the disorder develop welts in response to surface pressure on their skin.

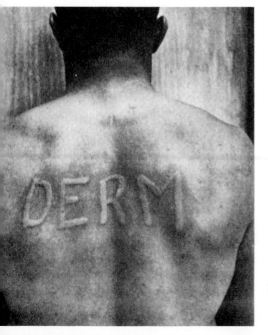

Heritability. Because each of us is born into different environmental circumstances with a unique combination of genetic instructions, we differ from one another along a considerable number of dimensions. Consider, for instance, your psychology classmates. They come in different sizes and shapes, vary in personality and intelligence, and possess unequal artistic and athletic abilities. To what extent are differences in intelligence, for example, attributable to heredity or to environmental influences? Had all your classmates been reared in identical environments (which, in reality, is impossible), we could be assured that any differences between them would necessarily be due to genetic factors. Conversely, if all your classmates had come from the same fertilized egg (also an impossibility) but were subsequently raised in different environments, the resulting differences in intelligence would necessarily be due to only environmental factors. In the first case, the heritability for intelligence would be very high; in the latter case, it would be very low. **Heritability** is a technical term developed by geneticists to refer to the amount of variability in a trait in a given population that is due to genetic factors. The more that a trait in a given population of individuals is influenced by genetic factors, the greater its heritability is.

TABLE 3.2.	A comparison of concordance for various traits between monozygotic (MZ) and dizygotic (DZ) twins.	
	CONCORDANCE	
TRAIT	MZ	DZ
Blood types	100%	66%
Eye color	99	28
Mental retardation	97	37
Measles	95	87
Idiopathic epilepsy	72	15
Schizophrenia	69	10
Diabetes	65	18
Identical allergy	59	5
Tuberculosis	57	23

SOURCE: Derived from various sources.

This does not mean, however, that highly heritable traits may not be modified by environmental circumstances. For example, although intelligence is believed to have a strong genetic component (Bouchard & McGue, 1981), underprivileged children may not express their intellectual talents as they might under more favorable environmental conditions. As we shall see in the chapter on intelligence, intelligence is to some extent modifiable.

Heritability is sometimes confused with inheritance, the tendency of a given trait to be passed from parent to individual offspring. Heritability does not apply to individuals, it pertains only to the variation of a trait across a specific population at a particular point in time. Thus, we must be cautious when making statements regarding the differential contribution of genetics and environment to our physical, intellectual, and behavioral development.

Assessing Genetic Influences. There are two barriers to studying directly the effects of heredity on trait expression in humans. First, ethical considerations prevent psychologists and geneticists, in the manner of a true experiment, from manipulating one's genetic history or restricting the type of environment in which one is reared. Second, in many cases, the enormous variability in human environments—from the garbage-strewn streets of urban slums to the neatly landscaped private drives of the rich and famous—effectively masks any correlation that might exist between genetics and trait expression across populations. Psychologists have been able to effectively side step these barriers by taking advantage of an important quirk in nature—multiple births, and in particular, twins. Identical or **monozygotic twins** (MZ twins) arise from a single fertilized ovum (egg), called a zygote, that splits into two genetically identical cells. Fraternal or **dizygotic twins** (DZ twins) develop from the separate fertilization of two ova. DZ twins share the same degree of genetic relatedness as any two nontwin siblings. Many psychologists reason that since MZ twins have identical genotypes, they should be more similar to one another in terms of their psychological phenotypes, for example, personality, intelligence, and behavior than DZ twins or nontwin siblings.

Concordance research supports this line of thinking. Twins are concordant for a trait if either both or neither express it, and they are discordant if only one of them shows it. If concordance values of any given trait are substantially higher for MZ twins than DZ twins, we have good reason to believe that heredity is involved in the expression of the trait. Table 3.2 compares concordance values for several traits between MZ and DZ twins.

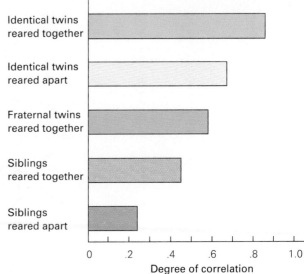

FIGURE 3.9

Above left: Both genetic and environmental similarities contribute to the high correlation of IQ scores between identical twins. Above right: The correlations between IQ test performance and genetic relatedness. Individuals who share a greater number of genes, such as identical twins, tend to perform more similarly on IQ tests than do individuals who share fewer genes, such as fraternal twins. Rearing individuals together in similar environments regardless of the degree of genetic relatedness also increases the likelihood that those people will perform similarly on IQ tests.

Klug and Cummings (1986) note that concordance data must be interpreted cautiously. High concordance values with only MZ twins are likely to lead us to believe that a strong genetic component is involved. This is especially true with a trait such as blood type, which has a concordance value of 100 percent. Clearly though, the same argument cannot be made for a temporary characteristic such as measles. In this case, a high concordance value means only that the characteristic is due to a common variable in the environment in which both twins are reared, a virus. That the concordance values for measles are high for both types of twins substantiates the environment's role in expression of this characteristic. Thus, it is critical that concordance values for both MZ and DZ twins be compared. For any trait, high MZ and low DZ concordance values support the case for a genetic component (for example, eye color and mental retardation).

Further evidence for genetic influences on trait expression comes from an extensive analysis of the heredity and intelligence literature conducted by psychologists Thomas Bouchard and Matthew McGue (1981). Bouchard and McGue analyzed over one hundred published reports on the correlation between genetic relatedness and IQ (one measure of intelligence) and discovered that MZ twins showed more similarity in their IQ scores than other siblings, including DZ twins. Figure 3.9 shows that the correlation of IQ scores for MZ twins reared together is about 30 percent higher than that of DZ twins raised together and about 40 percent higher than that of siblings reared together.

If intelligence were due entirely to genetic factors, however, there should be no difference between the correlation values of IQ scores of MZ twins reared together and MZ twins reared apart. Clearly, Bouchard and McGue's data indicate otherwise; there is a 19 percent difference between the correlation values for these two groups and a 21 percent difference between nontwin siblings reared together and nontwin siblings reared apart. The moral here is clear: in some cases such as intelligence, arguments attributing trait expression exclusively to heredity or the environment are most likely bad arguments.

Genetic Disorders

Many genes affect an organism's viability, or ability to survive. These "killer" genes are quite common. On the average, we each carry the equivalent of two to four of them. Fortunately, these lethal genes are typically recessive ones, and there are so many different types of them that most partners do not carry the same ones. When a child inherits the dominant healthy gene from one parent and the recessive lethal gene from the other, the destructive effects of the lethal gene are generally not expressed. A few genetic disorders, such as Huntington's chorea, result from a dominant gene, however. Different lethal genes express themselves at different times in the life span. In some cases, the fetus aborts before the woman is even aware that she is pregnant. In other instances, the baby is stillborn. In still other cases, the deadly effects of lethal genes are not expressed until middle age.

Types of Genetic Disorders. In addition to hemophilia and cri-du-chat syndrome that were already discussed, there are a number of other human genetic disorders. Here are several of the more common ones that impair mental functioning and behavior, and so, are of special interest to psychologists.

Down's syndrome is caused by a chromosomal aberration resulting in an extra 21st chromosome. People with Down's syndrome are generally short in stature with broad skulls and round faces, and they suffer impairment in physical, psychomotor, and cognitive development. About 15 percent of children born with this condition die before their first birthday, usually from heart and respiratory complications. The frequency of Down's syndrome increases with the age of the mother—40 percent of all Down's syndrome children are born to women over 40 years of age. To a lesser extent, the age of the father also increases the possibility of Down's syndrome. Although people with Down's syndrome are mentally retarded, special educational training permits many of them to hold jobs involving simple tasks such as sorting. The average life expectancy of a person with Down's syndrome is about 20 years.

Huntington's chorea does not emerge until the afflicted person is between 30 and 40 years of age and is caused by a dominant lethal gene. Before the onset of this disease, an individual may be healthy and happy in every respect. After onset, however, the individual experiences slow but progressive mental and physical deterioration, including loss of coordination and motor ability. Death generally occurs 5 to 15 years after onset.

Individuals with **phenylketonuria** (PKU) are unable to break down phenylalanine, an amino acid found in many high protein foods. As a result, blood levels of phenylalanine increase, causing severe brain damage and mental retardation. PKU is one of the many diseases that infants are routinely tested for before they leave the hospital. Infants diagnosed as having PKU are placed on a low-phenylalanine diet shortly after birth. In some instances children may be taken off the diet at about 6 or 7 years of age.

It was once believed that males with **XYY syndrome**, that is, an extra Y chromosome, were predisposed to violence and aggression. The most famous case was that of Richard Speck, who murdered eight nurses in Chicago in the 1960s. Chromosomal tests conducted subsequently on other males institutionalized for similar violent crimes revealed that a number of them were XYY. However, surveys of the general male population have shown that XYY is common, occurring about once in every 1,000 male births. Only a small percentage of these persons, though, are ever institutionalized for violent acts.

People with Down's syndrome generally exhibit distinct physical characteristics and have a shortened life span.

Genetic Counseling and Gene Therapy.

About three percent of all prospective parents face the risk of having a child with a genetic disorder (Klug & Cummings, 1986). Combined, genetic diseases are the leading cause of death in children and adolescents. Couples who are concerned about the possibility that they may have genetically defective children often seek genetic counseling, which can serve three major functions. First, parents may learn their probability of having a child with a genetic disorder. Second, the parent may receive educational training regarding the particular genetic disorder with which their child might be afflicted. Third, genetic counselors may recommend that pregnant women, especially those over 35, or those whose family pedigrees reveal a genetic problem, undergo a prenatal screening procedure to detect any genetic defects in the fetus. The most common prenatal detection method is amniocentesis, which involves removal and examination of the fetal cells found in the amniotic fluid that surrounds the developing fetus. In addition to discovering genetic defects, amniocentesis will also reveal to parents the sex of their unborn child.

The purpose of genetic counseling is to provide parents with objective information with which to make rational decisions about having a child. In cases where the probability of having a genetically defective child is high and the woman is not pregnant, the couple must decide whether or not to have a child. On the other hand, if the woman is in the early stages of pregnancy with a genetically defective child, the couple must decide whether or not to abort the pregnancy. The latter situation is particularly difficult as it involves sensitive moral and personal issues.

Recent advances in genetic research may soon make possible gene therapy or the replacement of defective genes with ones that work properly. The discovery of a class of enzymes that splits DNA at specific sites has permitted researchers to recombine DNA molecules and synthesize new forms of the genetic code. Genetic engineering, as this work is now called, is having a considerable impact on current medical and disease control practices. Genetic engineering is used to manufacture human insulin and clinical testing of gene products is possible. Testing is currently underway on products such as proteins used in the treatment of hemophilia, enzymes used to dissolve blood clots, human growth hormone, and vaccines used against infectious diseases.

In July 1978, Louise Brown, the first "test tube" baby was born. The test tube or *in vitro* fertilization technique involves transferring an ovum from a female to a nutrient culture where it is mixed with the sperm of the husband or other donor. Once fertilized, the ovum is implanted into the woman's uterus. This technique is now commonly used to treat cases in which blockage in the female reproductive system prevents normal (*in vivo*) fertilization of the ovum. *In vitro* fertilization techniques have been used to transfer genetic information from one species to another. In one instance, mouse zygotes were injected with a copy of a human growth hormone gene (Klug & Cummings, 1986). These mice grew to twice their normal size and passed the gene on to their offspring. This procedure is important because it may eventually allow us to transfer a copy of a genetic code, say for normal blood clotting, from a healthy individual to a sick one. It may also lead to the copying of psychologically significant genetic codes, such as those related to intelligence, happiness, or friendliness.

Genetic engineering is currently on the threshold of an era of advances in medical knowledge and technology whose scope and importance can only be compared to the industrial revolution of the past century. There can be no doubt that genetic engineering will soon affect our lives in significant ways. From having healthier children to living longer ourselves, the prospects are indeed promising. Some people, however, believe that

Louise Brown, the world's first test tube baby, was born in 1978 and is shown here at age 3.

human society may pay a high price for such promises. They argue that genetic engineering may, quite accidently, unleash pathogenic organisms that cause widespread and uncontrollable plagues. Others fear that such technology, if placed into the wrong hands, could result in political tampering of the human gene pool in an attempt to better the human race. These issues, along with debate over whether genetic engineering should be used only to repair defective genes or to create new and more powerful genes, are not soon to be resolved. The current sentiment among most scientists and politicians, however, is that genetic engineering is proceeding safely and securely and is well worth the inherent risks involved.

SOCIOBIOLOGY

Sociobiology is the study of the genetic bases of social behavior. Sociobiologists are interested in understanding the evolutionary roots of our modern-day social actions and in doing so, they study many of the same behaviors that have traditionally fallen into psychology's domain. Our capacity to learn about our environments and to use language, our sexual behavior and strategies in mate selection, as well as personality characteristics like aggression, gregariousness, and selfishness are just a few of the many psychological phenomena that sociobiologists study. Sociobiology, then, represents something of an interface between psychology and the biological sciences. In essence, it is the extension of Darwin's work to human affairs. For this reason alone, psychologists are paying attention to sociobiology. Sociobiological theory offers psychologists a novel framework from which to cast some of their research questions. For example, in Chapter 10, we will learn how psychologists study environmental factors that influence aggression; sociobiologists attempt to explain the genetic and evolutionary basis for aggression. In Chapter 12 we will study the psychological variables that influence our sexual behavior; sociobiologists attempt to account for how and why we evolved sensitivity to these factors. Not all psychologists or all biologists, though, are ardent supporters of sociobiology. As we will see, many critics think that sociobiology is too simplistic and that its emphasis on genetic determinants of behavior is inadequate to explain the subtle complexities of human behavior and learning.

Sociobiology, . . . in essence . . . is the extension of Darwin's work to human affairs.

The Problem of Altruism

The essential key to understanding sociobiology is understanding **altruism**, the unselfish concern of one individual for the welfare of another. Examples of altruistic behavior abound in our culture, and in their most extreme form are represented when one person risks his or her life to save that of another. Examples of altruism are not limited to our species; in fact, they are quite common throughout the animal kingdom. Consider, for example, the honey bee that sacrifices its life on behalf of its hivemates by stinging an intruder, or the rodent who gives an alarm call, thereby drawing the predator's attention to itself and increasing its chances of being captured. In each case, the altruist's chances of survival and reproductive success are lowered while those of the other individuals are raised.

You can probably guess how psychologists might explain altruistic behavior in humans. They would look for proximate causes—environmental influences such as parental training, special instruction (like a Red Cross lifesaving class), and other learning experiences that may predispose people to respond positively to emergency situations. The sociobiologist,

Above left: Humans are not the only species to exhibit altruism. This arctic ground squirrel sounds a warning call to notify other squirrels of danger. Above right: This soldier shows the most extreme form of altruism. Caught in enemy crossfire, he risks his life to try to help a wounded comrade.

on the other hand, would look to ultimate causes, in particular, natural selection, to explain altruistic behavior. In short, sociobiologists maintain that natural selection has favored the evolution of organisms that show altruistic tendencies.

However, there is a problem here. Recall that natural selection favors those phenotypic traits that help an organism adapt to its environment and maximize reproductive success. How could natural selection possibly favor behavior that appears to benefit the reproductive success of others while distinctly decreasing that of one's own? How could altruistic behavior have evolved since it is, by definition, less adaptive than selfish or competitive behavior?

The answers to these questions were developed in a series of important mathematical papers written between 1964 and 1970 by geneticist William D. Hamilton (e.g., 1964, 1970). Hamilton's breakthrough stemmed from examining natural selection from a novel perspective—from the gene's viewpoint, rather than from the organism's. (You should realize that genes, of course, do not really have viewpoints, because they are not conscious entities.) The essence of his argument is that natural selection does not favor mere personal fitness (one's own reproductive success) but rather **inclusive fitness**, or the reproductive success of all those who share the same genes. Altruistic acts are generally aimed at individuals who share some of the altruist's genes, such as parents, brothers, sisters, grandparents, grandchildren, and under certain conditions, distant relatives. The closer the relatives, the larger the probability that they carry the same gene. Such biologic favoritism toward relatives is referred to as **kin selection** (Maynard Smith, 1964). Thus, under similar conditions, we would expect a sister to behave more altruistically toward her brother, with whom she shares half of her genes than toward a cousin, with whom she shares only one-eighth of her genes. The message here is clear: under the proper circumstances, individuals behave altruistically toward others with whom they share a genetic history, with the willingness to do so decreasing as the relative becomes more distant. In this view, altruism is not necessarily a conscious act, but rather an act driven by a biological prompt, which has been favored by natural selection. Natural selection would favor this kind of altruism simply because organisms who share genes also help each other survive, which, of course, is highly adaptive. Research with animals supports this prediction (Barash, 1982).

Parenting is a special case of kin selection and an important contributor to one's survival and reproductive success. Reflect for a few moments on the altruistic behavior of your parents, beginning with the large investment of time and metabolic energy that your mother expended on you while she was pregnant with you, through the present time, during which both of your parents have most likely sacrificed time, emotional resources, personal opportunities, and a good deal of hard-earned cash on your rearing and education. What has been the purpose of their labors? Probably nothing short of providing you with at least the same, if not better, opportunities for success than they had. In the short run, their altruistic actions have promoted your continued survival; in the long run, these same actions increase the likelihood that you, too, will become a parent and they, grandparents. Such cycles continue according to biological schedule, generation after generation barring unforeseen calamities. In the words of sociobiologist David Barash:

> It is obvious why genes for parenting have been selected: All living things are the offspring of parents who themselves were parents! It is a guaranteed, unbroken line stretching back into time. [Genes] that inclined their bearers to be less successful parents left fewer copies of themselves than did those [genes] that were more successful. Hence living things make other living things called offspring, because that is how their genes get passed into the next generation. . . . As Samuel Butler first said, "A hen is an egg's way of making more eggs" (Barash, pp. 69–70, 1982).

What is at stake, of course, is not the survival of individual organisms but the survival of the individual genes carried by those organisms. Hamilton's insightful contribution to sociobiological theory was to show that altruistic behavior has a genetically selfish basis. According to this view, an organism is used by the gene to make more genes (Dawkins, 1976). In other words, genes allow organisms to maximize their inclusive fitness through altruistic behavior directed at other organisms sharing the same genes. This is the genes' way of assuring themselves longevity. You carry copies of genes that have been in your family line for thousands of years and probably longer. When the opportunity presents itself, you will most likely carry on the tradition, projecting your biological dowry into yet another generation. But you didn't reach sexual maturity totally on your own; the unselfish concern for your welfare by your parents, brothers and/ or sisters, grandparents, and perhaps an aunt or uncle, has contributed to your chances of being reproductively successful, and thus, to the genes' (unconscious) bid for immortality. Genes that are not projected into the next generation will simply disappear.

Reciprocal Altruism

Kin selection accounts for altruism toward relatives, but what about altruism directed toward nonrelatives? Do sociobiologists have an explanation for a person's altruistic actions toward a friend or acquaintance? According to Robert Trivers (1971), the answer is yes. This kind of altruism, referred to as **reciprocal altruism**, is the expression of a crude biological version of the Golden Rule: the likelihood of "your doing unto others as you would have them do unto you" increases with your certainty that they might, should circumstances be reversed, reciprocate aid to you or your kin. Thus, according to sociobiological theory, reciprocal altruism is a second means by which we might maximize our personal fitness.

Certain practical conditions must be satisfied before reciprocity is likely. First, giving aid must carry with it low risk to the altruist but a high benefit for the recipient. In other words, altruists behave as if they have calculated a cost–benefit ratio for their action—the lower the cost and the greater the benefit, the more likely the altruistic act. Second, there must be a good chance that the situation could be reversed—will the altruist ever be in a position to benefit from similar action on the part of the original recipient? If not, the chances of altruism are lowered. And third, the recipient must be able to recognize the altruist. We are more likely to render assistance to people we are most familiar with and in situations where personal risk is less than the benefit.

Imagine yourself as the hero (or heel) in the followng scenario: You are the only uninjured member of several persons involved in a light plane crash high in the Uintah mountains in northern Utah. Two people are dead, but your sister and her friend, whom you don't know very well, are alive although both are badly injured. Without immediate medical attention, both will likely die. You can only carry one of them down the mountain and into the small town below. Whom do you help—your sister or her friend? Most likely you would help your sister, a choice consistent with the concept of kin selection. Now suppose we alter the scenario slightly. Instead of having to choose between saving your sister's life or saving her friend's life, the choice is to save either a friend or a stranger. Whom would you help this time? Most likely you would choose your friend—a response consistent with reciprocal altruism. Why? According to the idea of reciprocal altruism, because your friend is more likely than the stranger to be in a future position to come to your aid or to the aid of one of your relatives. What if the choice you faced was which of two strangers to help? In this case, sociobiological theory predicts that you would save the person most like yourself.

What about psychological theory? How would a psychologist explain your behavior? As we saw earlier for kin selection, psychologists would probably make the same predictions as would sociobiologists for each of the cases, but for different reasons. Psychologists would point to more immediate explanations, such as the degree of familiarity you have with each person, your experiences in observing altruistic role models, or the influence of parental or religious training in coming to the aid of others. Remember, an important difference between sociobiological and psychological theories is that the latter focuses on proximate causes—events in the immediate environment that may influence a particular action—while the former focuses on ultimate causes—the evolutionary significance of those events in the history of the species, in this case, humans.

An important difference between sociobiological and psychological theories is that the latter focuses on proximate causes . . . while the former focuses on ultimate causes . . .

Interestingly, some biologists agree more with psychological theory that sees altruism as learned, than with sociobiological theory that sees altruism as genetically acquired. For instance, Steven Jay Gould, a Harvard biologist, believes that altruism is a set of learned behaviors that are passed from one generation to the next through cultural means such as books, stories, and so forth. Thus, for nonhuman animals, altruism has a very strong genetic basis, but for humans, altruism may be more learned than genetic. Perhaps the best way to view the basis of altruism in humans is to say that the human gene pool makes learning possible, but what will be learned is left to the interaction of the organism with its environment. This view would account for the wide variety of altruistic as well as non-altruistic behaviors common to human cultures.

In addition to altruism, sociobiologists have used the concept of reproductive success to account for the evolution of many other kinds of social behavior, including courtship, friendship, cooperation and competition, and parenting, to name just a few (Wilson, 1975, 1978). Keep in mind that sociobiologists consider any and all of an individual's behavior to have consequences for its reproductive success. In this view, natural selection favors behavior, social or otherwise, that aids the organism in adapting to its environment and selects against behavior that is not adaptive. Adaptive behavior provides opportunities for greater reproductive success, which in turn, enhances the probability for the underlying (and adaptive) genotype to be passed on to future generations.

Criticisms of Sociobiology

We have seen that sociobiology embodies the extension of evolutionary theory and genetics to the study and explanation of social behavior. Research supports many of the predictions of sociobiological theory, particularly with nonhuman animals (Barash, 1982). Nonetheless, sociobiology has been the center of a fierce scientific controversy ever since E. O. Wilson published his *Sociobiology: The New Synthesis* in 1975, the discipline's official birth date. (Wilson is considered by many researchers to be the "father" of sociobiology.) Although Wilson's work, which is based chiefly on studies of nonhuman animal behavior, has generated an enormous outpouring of scientific research, it has also roused a number of serious charges (Montagu, 1980). Wilson's *On Human Nature* (1978), which extended sociobiological theory to human affairs, ignited even more criticism. Most of the criticism focuses on the extension of the theory to human behavior. In this section we will briefly review these criticisms as well as sociobiology's rebuttal.

Some critics argue that the technological innovations spawned through cultural evolution have rendered the sociobiological account of human behavior irrelevant. They point out that since the environment we now live in is so vastly different from the one in which we evolved, cultural evolution not biological evolution exerts the selective pressures by which human behavior is shaped. In short, natural selection no longer exerts any control over human evolution. Sociobiologists agree that cultural practices play a tremendous role in shaping human behavior today, but they also argue that natural selection favored the particular phenotypes (and their underlying genotypes) that made such culture possible. Therefore, sociobiologists argue that understanding natural selection and its role in human evolution is critical to understanding how both human culture and human behavior evolved.

Another criticism of sociobiology is that it draws simplistic analogies between research done with nonhuman animals and human behavior. This criticism maintains that we cannot learn anything important about human social behavior based on research with nonhumans. In turn, sociobiologists argue that our understanding of human genetics and physiology is a direct result of research with nonhuman animals and that advances in understanding human behavior are likely to follow a similar avenue.

Sociobiology is also criticized for explaining human social behavior only in terms of genetic determinants and ignoring environmental factors such as experiential and cultural influences. Sociobiologists point out that genes and environmental factors interact to produce any given phenotype. They stress that genes only endow organisms with a behavioral capacity; it is the environment that selects and maintains a specific repertoire of responses.

The most resounding criticism of sociobiology is not a scientific one, but a political one. Opponents of sociobiology argue that it sanctions superiority of one group over another, be it a race, a gender, or a political organization. After all, they argue, if one group of individuals is genetically superior to another, then there are "natural" grounds for justifying the "survival of the fittest" and one group's unethical and immoral domination of another. An example is Hitler's quest for world domination in the name of Aryan superiority. Sociobiologists flatly deny such allegations and argue that it is the critics and not they who have confused the term "natural" with the terms "good" and "superior." When scientists study AIDS (Acquired Immunodeficiency Syndrome), they do so to understand its characteristics and effects, not to condone it (see Barash, 1982). Likewise, sociobiologists contend they study the biological bases of social behavior only to understand it further, not to find justification for particular cultural practices and customs. Wilson has articulated eloquently the sociobiological defense:

> The purpose of sociobiology is not to make crude comparisons between animal species or between animals and men. . . . Its purpose is to develop general laws of the evolution and biology of social behavior, which might then be extended in a disinterested manner to the study of human beings. In the same way that biologists have learned about heredity from the study of fruit flies and the little bacterium *E. coli* and applied the principle to human heredity, we expect to extend such general principles of sociobiology as can be devised to assist in the explanation of human behavior. . . . The evidence is very strong that there does exist a human biogram, a pattern of potentials built into the heredity of the species as a whole. In some cases we vary very little. . . . *Homo sapiens* share with other social mammals a tendency toward male dominance systems, a sexual division of labor, prolonged maternal care, and an extended socialization of the young based in good part on social play. It is vital not to misconstrue the political implications of such generalizations. To devise a naturalistic description of human social behavior is to note a set of facts for further investigation, not to pass a value judgment or to deny that a great deal of the behavior can be deliberately changed if individual societies wish. . . . Human behavior is dominated by culture in the sense that the greater part, perhaps all, of the variation between societies is based on differences in cultural experiences. But this is not to say that human beings are infinitely plastic. Even during periods of relative isolation human societies did not drift apart in the manner of stars in an expanding universe. . . . To understand the evolutionary history . . . is to understand in a deeper manner the construction of human nature, to learn what we really are and not just what we hope we are, as viewed through the various prisms of our mythologies.
>
> (Wilson, pp. xiv–xv.
> in Barash, 1982)

Sociobiology is likely to remain a controversial field of study for many years. In forming your own views and opinions on sociobiology, or on any topic, be sure to review carefully the evidence and consider the arguments of both sides.

BOUNDARIES AND FRONTIERS

Why do we behave as we do? How is it that we are capable of learning so much about our world, or for that matter, how is it that we can learn anything at all? Historically, psychology has provided us two answers. Strictly biologically minded psychologists once argued that we are genetically programmed to behave the way we do and learn the things we learn. In short, these persons held that nature, not nurture, determined behavior. Environmentally oriented psychologists argued the other side of the coin, namely, that nurture not nature shapes human action. The "nature versus nurture" debate characterized the early days of psychology and can, in fact, still be heard today. Fortunately, however, research in evolutionary theory, genetics, and psychology has shown modern psychologists quite convincingly that human behavior results from a mixture of both nature and nurture. While some researchers may argue that a certain behavior is more or less influenced by either of these factors, the important point is that many psychological researchers now appreciate the fact that the dependent variable in which they are most interested—behavior—is sensitive to independent variables that may be either nature-based, nurture-based, or some combination of the two.

The real advantage of this relatively new perspective is that psychologists can view behavior from a broader perspective than that of their predecessors. Now, instead of studying behavior or searching for solutions to specific psychological problems such as schizophrenia from only a single view, we ask questions about *both* ultimate and proximate causes: Does schizophrenia have a biological basis? Does schizophrenia tend to run in families? Are certain environmental conditions more conducive to the development of schizophrenic symptoms than others? How do environmental factors interact with biological ones to determine if and when schizophrenic symptoms first appear? Once a person becomes afflicted by the disorder, should he or she be treated with drugs, therapy, or a combination of the two?

An important boundary in psychology, as any other field, is the field of vision through which its subject matter is viewed. Approaching the study of behavior from only one perspective is something akin to viewing a rainbow through a high-powered telescope—you may have a particularly good view of one small part of the rainbow, but you lose the bigger picture of the entire rainbow. Likewise, approaching the study of behavior with both nature and nurture in mind permits a more complete picture of behavior and its causes than does approaching behavior from either perspective alone. With the broader view come new research questions, new frontiers that await exploration.

These frontiers permeate psychology and fuel our curiosity about our own actions and thoughts. From the study of intelligence to the study of obesity, from the study of consciousness to the study of abnormal behavior, questions about how our genetic makeup interacts with environmental variables to determine our behavior provide fertile ground for new research. The remainder of this book tells the story of how psychologists, biologists, and others—cultural anthropologists, linguists, neuroscientists, and philosophers—are working together in discovering and exploring the frontiers of human behavior.

CONCEPT SUMMARY

- What are the differences between ultimate and proximate causes of behavior? (p. 60)
- How can understanding ultimate causes of behavior help us to understand proximate causes? (pp. 60–61)

CHARLES DARWIN—A BIOGRAPHICAL SKETCH

- How did Darwin's experiences as a youth influence his work on board the H. M. S. *Beagle*? (pp. 61–62)

- Describe how Darwin's interest in artificial selection influenced his thinking about natural selection. What insight did his reading of Malthus give him into natural selection? (pp. 63–64)

NATURAL SELECTION AND EVOLUTION

- How do variation and competition influence one's reproductive success? (pp. 66–70)
- What is the relationship between genotype and phenotype? (p. 66)

- In what ways did the successive lines of our ancient ancestors differ from one another? (pp. 68–71)
- What is so significant about bipedalism and encephalization in human evolution? What factors made cultural evolution possible? (pp. 70–71)

HEREDITY AND GENETICS

- How do genes influence phenotypic traits? What is the relationship between sex and phenotypic traits? (pp. 72–74)
- In what ways do heredity and environment interact to influence phenotypic traits and behavior? What methods are used to study such interaction? (pp. 76–78)
- What is the basis of a genetic disorder (give examples)?

How can gene counseling and gene therapy help people who fear that their children may suffer from a genetic disorder? (pp. 79–81)

SOCIOBIOLOGY

- Why is understanding altruism the key to understanding sociobiology? (pp. 81–83)
- How does inclusive fitness differ from personal fitness? How does inclusive fitness relate to kin selection? (pp. 82–83)
- How does reciprocal altruism explain altruism toward nonrelatives? (pp. 83–85)
- What are the criticisms of sociobiology (give examples)? What are sociobiologists' responses to these criticisms? (pp. 85–86)

KEY TERMS AND CONCEPTS

Biological Evolution   The theory that, over time, organisms originate and become adapted to their environment by biological means. (p. 60)

Ultimate Causes   Evolutionary conditions and processes that have slowly shaped behavior of our species over generations. (p. 60)

Proximate Causes   Events and conditions in the immediate environment that affect behavior. (p. 60)

CHARLES DARWIN–A BIOGRAPHICAL SKETCH

Artificial Selection   A procedure in which animals are deliberately mated to produce offspring that possess particularly desirable characteristics. (p. 63)

Natural Selection   The tendency of organisms to reproduce differentially, which is caused by differences among them. Within any given species, some animals, "the survivors," will produce more offspring than other animals. (p. 64)

NATURAL SELECTION AND EVOLUTION

Personal Fitness   The relative ability of an individual to produce offspring. (p. 65)

Reproductive Success   The number of viable offspring one produces relative to the number of viable offspring produced by other individuals of the same species. (p. 65)

Variation   The differences found across individuals of any given species in terms of their biological characteristics (size, strength, physiology) and psychological characteristics (intelligence, sociability, behavior). (p. 66)

Genotype   An organism's genetic makeup. (p. 66)

Phenotype   The outward expression of an organism's genotype; an organism's physical appearance and behavior. (p. 66)

Competition   A striving or vying with others who share the same ecological niche for food, mates, and territory. (p. 66)

Bipedalism   The ability to move about the environment on two feet. (p. 70)

Encephalization   Increases in brain size. (p. 70)

Cultural Evolution   The adaptive changes of cultures to recurrent environmental pressures over time. Cultural evolution is possible only because humans have been genetically endowed with a capacity for learning. (p. 71)

HEREDITY AND GENETICS

DNA   Deoxyribonucleic acid. Genetic material found in the cells of most living things. (p. 72)

Genes   The small units of DNA that are located on chromosomes. (p. 72)

Chromosomes   The rodlike structures found in the nuclei of living cells that contain genes. (p. 72)

Sex Chromosomes   The chromosomes containing the instructional code for the development of male or female sex characteristics. (p. 72)

Mutation   An accidental alteration in the DNA code within a single gene. Mutations can either be spontaneous and occur naturally or they can be the result of man-made factors such as high energy radiation. (p. 74)

Chromosomal Aberration   The rearrangement of genes within or between cells or a change in the total number of chromosomes. (p. 74)

Heritability   The amount of variability in a trait in a given population at a given time that is due to genetic factors. (p. 76)

Monozygotic Twins   Identical twins. Monozygotic twins develop from a single fertilized ovum (egg), called a zygote, which has split into two genetically identical cells. (p. 77)

Dizygotic Twins   Fraternal twins. Dizygotic twins develop from the separate fertilization of two ova. (p. 77)

Down's Syndrome   A genetic disorder caused by a chromosomal aberration resulting in an extra 21st chromosome. People with Down's syndrome are generally short in stature with broad skulls and round faces, and they suffer impairment in physical, psychomotor, and cognitive development. (p. 79)

Huntington's Chorea A genetic disorder caused by a dominant lethal gene in which a person experiences slow but progressive mental and physical deterioration. (p. 79)

Phenylketonuria (PKU) A genetic disorder characterized by the inability to break down phenylalanine, an amino acid found in many high protein foods. As a result, blood levels of phenylalanine increase, causing severe brain damage and mental retardation. (p. 79)

XYY Syndrome A genetic disorder in which an individual has an extra Y chromosome. At one time psychologists believed that XYY syndrome predisposed its sufferers to violence and aggression. (p. 79)

SOCIOBIOLOGY

Sociobiology The study of the genetic bases of social behavior. (p. 81)

Altruism The unselfish concern of one individual for the welfare of another. (p. 81)

Inclusive Fitness The reproductive success of all those who share common genes. (p. 82)

Kin Selection A type of selection process that favors altruistic acts aimed at individuals who share some of the altruist's genes, such as parents, brothers, sisters, grandparents, grandchildren, and under certain conditions, distant relatives. (p. 82)

Reciprocal Altruism A kind of altruism in which people behave altruistically toward another because they are confident that such acts will be reciprocated toward either them or their kin. (p. 83)

ADDITIONAL SOURCES OF INFORMATION

Darwin, C. (1869). *The origin of species by means of natural selection.* London: Murray. This book contains the full argument that Darwin garnered in defense of evolution by natural selection. For serious students of evolutionary theory, reading this book is a must.

Dawkins, R. (1986). *The blind watchmaker.* New York: Norton. This book addresses many common misconceptions and erroneous beliefs that people have regarding Darwin's theory.

Gould, S. J. (1977). *Ever since Darwin: Reflections in natural history.* New York: Norton.

Gould, S. J. (1980). *The panda's thumb: More reflections in natural history.* New York: Norton. These two books are collections of Gould's essays written originally for the magazine, *Natural History.* Evolution, the history of evolutionary biology, and biological determinism are the common threads running through both books.

Klug, W. S., & Cummings, M. R. (1986). *Concepts of genetics.* Glenview, IL: Scott, Foresman. A very good introductory presentation of the basic principles of genetics.

Wilson, E. O. (1975). *Sociobiology: The new synthesis.* Cambridge: Harvard University Press. This well-written and engaging graduate-level text represents the evolutionary argument for the biological basis of social behavior. The last chapter contains applications of the theory to humans.

4 Biopsychology and Consciousness

Randy felt tense. His breathing was rushed, his palms were sweaty and his heart was pounding so fast that he felt like it was going to leap through his chest. His hands and fingers formed deep impressions in the arm rests of the leather chair in which he was sitting.

"How's your molar, Randy? Are you going to let me fix that cavity this time?" inquired Dr. Tinsley.

"The tooth has been fine, really. It hasn't bothered me at all. Why don't you just clean my teeth today, and we'll wait and see what happens," Randy said hopefully.

Dr. Tinsley knew exactly what would happen. The cavity would get bigger, maybe abscess, and then Randy would be back, in terrible pain, begging to have the tooth fixed.

"I'd better have a look just to make sure. Open up."

Randy opened his mouth, ever so slowly, his eyes firmly closed. Randy believed that if he didn't see the dental instruments entering his mouth, the pain wouldn't be so bad.

"Mmmm. . . . It's not a very big cavity, but it's definitely a cavity, Randy," she said after examining the tooth. "We can have it drilled and filled in no time. Let's go ahead and take care of it today."

"Okay," Randy gave in. "Just make sure you give me plenty of novocaine. I don't want to feel anything."

Randy opened wide for the second time. Dr. Tinsley swabbed the gum beside the molar with a cherry-flavored medicine to help prevent Randy from feeling the sting of the hypodermic. Randy winced a little as she sank the needle into the gum. Accustomed to such reactions, Dr. Tinsley continued to release the pain blocker until the syringe was empty.

"That should numb up your tooth pretty well. I'll be back in a few minutes," she said as she left the suite.

Randy gave a sigh of relief. For the first time since he sat down he relaxed his grip on the arm rests. His breathing slowed down and he felt reprieved, like he had just made the game-winning basket as time ran out on the clock. He sat alone in the suite as the lower right side of his mouth slowly fell asleep.

"I'm back," Dr. Tinsley said cheerfully. "Is your mouth numb yet?"

Randy sat up in the chair. "She's back already," he thought. Some of his nervousness returned. "It feels numb, sort of," replied Randy as he closed his eyes. "Are you sure you used enough novocaine?"

"I think so, but if you feel any pain, let me know and I'll give you some more." She sat down on the swivel stool next to Randy and reached for the drill.

"Okay, Randy, let's take care of that tooth," she said, as she positioned Randy's head into the proper angle and adjusted herself slightly on the stool.

Opening his mouth reluctantly, he sank his fingers deep into the arm rests. He tensed every muscle in his frame, preparing himself for the rush of excruciating pain that he expected to shoot through his mouth at any moment.

Dr. Tinsley revved the drill for a moment and then set it in motion against the decayed surface of the tooth. It dug easily into the soft decay, making a shrill, shrieking sound as she deftly maneuvered it deeper into the cavity.

Randy felt the rough vibration of the instrument against the tooth. He was breathing heavily again and his forehead began to hurt because of the force with which he was keeping his eyes shut. Time stood still. "It's only supposed to be a small cavity—how much longer is she going to take?" he thought. Then, it happened. The moment he had been waiting for became the present.

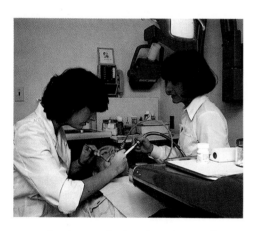

Anxiety-producing situations such as a visit to the dentist affect our behavior and experiences.

"I'm finished," she said. "All that's left now is to place the filling."

Randy released his grip on the chair and opened his eyes.

Such anxiety-filled experiences are not all that uncommon. Their uniqueness is derived from their context—in the example above, from a visit to the dentist's office. Regardless of their context, our individual experiences, good, bad, or otherwise, constitute our actions and emotions and provide substance and texture to our lives. For the most part we take these things for granted, seldom questioning how we are able to act and react, and experience the myriad of sensations, from ticklishness to pain, that form the colors and shades of life. These questions of how and why we act and react lie at the very heart of **biopsychology**, the study of the nervous system and its relation to behavior. Biopsychologists, or neuroscientists as they are called, attempt to understand our actions and thoughts in terms of underlying physiological processes occurring in the nervous system.

Questions of how and why we act and react lie at the very heart of biopsychology . . .

Let's go back to Randy for a moment. What did his nervous system have to do with what he experienced in Dr. Tinsley's office? That is a pretty tough question to answer if you are not aware of the important relationship between our nervous system, our conscious experience of the world, and our behavior. (That is what we will read about in this chapter.) The answer, in general terms, might be something like this:

■ A portion of Randy's nervous system, the autonomic nervous system, directed his body to increase perspiration, breathing, and heart rate in response to the stress of visiting the dentist. His endocrine system pumped the hormone, adrenalin, into his bloodstream, which also caused Randy to feel physiologically aroused.

■ An area in the left side of Randy's brain allowed him to understand the words Dr. Tinsley spoke to him and another area on the same side of the brain allowed him to generate speech in response to her remarks and questions.

■ The chemical messengers in Randy's nervous system relayed information about vibration, pain, and auditory and visual stimulation to his spinal cord and brain. In the brain this information was interpreted, probably in the context of stored memories about previous visits to the dentist's office. That interpretation contributed to Randy's anxiety.

■ Drugs, such as novocaine, change how the chemical messengers of the nervous system relay their messages. Thus Randy's ability to sense and perceive pain was altered. (Although he was expecting to feel pain, he never did. Without the novocaine, though, he probably would have.)

In short, Randy's nervous system had *everything* to do with his experience at the dentist's office. Indeed, neuroscientists see the nervous system as the basis for our interaction with the environment. They believe that understanding the nervous system is fundamental to understanding human experience and behavior. According to this view, our thoughts and behavior—that is, our *psychology*—are to a large extent determined by our nervous system and other aspects of our physiology—that is, our *biology*. Thus, by learning more about our biology, especially the nervous system, neuroscientists are able to learn more about our psychology.

One final example will reinforce the importance of our biology in determining our behavior. Imagine a person who is not able to sense pain—he or she will have very different experiences with objects such as hot stoves, dentists' drills, and razor blades than a person with a fully functioning nervous system. Most people think that their lives would be much better if they didn't experience pain. But would it really be a better life? Despite the billions of dollars we spend each year on "pain relief," pain serves a very useful function: it directs our actions away from potentially damaging, even fatal, stimuli. Think of the disastrous consequences that might result from not sensing that you had been leaning against a hot stove for several seconds or from not knowing that you had been bitten by a poisonous snake. Not feeling pain does not mean that you are impervious to bodily damage; a defective nervous system is a threat to life.

In this chapter we will study the structures of the nervous system and their functions in regulating our emotions, cognitions, and behavior. We will look especially at the neuron, the basic unit of the nervous system, and at its interactions with other neurons. Next, we will describe how the endocrine system influences our psychology through its secretion of hormones. Last, we will look at the brain's role in regulating nervous system activity and consciousness.

THE NERVOUS SYSTEM

The nervous system is made up of billions of nerve cells called **neurons** that relay information to and from the brain by chemical and electrical means. Although some animals such as fish and birds have nervous systems that continue to produce new neurons over their life span, humans and other primates are born with all the neurons they will ever possess. Each day thousands of neurons die within us; fortunately, though, the large number of neurons we have at birth keeps us supplied with all we will ever need to function properly.

Each day thousands of neurons die within us . . .

A second type of cell, found in even greater numbers than the neuron, is the **glial cell**. The term, glial, stems from the Greek word for glue, *glia*. This may give you a hint as to an important role played by glial cells—they bind neurons together, although not so close that they actually touch one another. Glial cells also serve several other functions critical to the normal operation of neurons: they supply nutrients to neurons, aid in the repair of damaged neurons, dispose of neuronal waste products, and help protect neurons from potentially damaging substances in the blood. It is best to think of glial cells as playing a supporting role in the smooth functioning of the nervous system, for as we shall soon see, the neuron is the real star of the show.

FIGURE 4.1
The organization of the human nervous system.

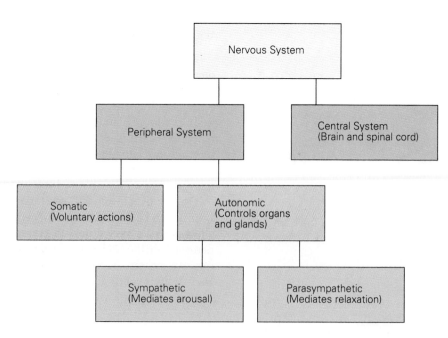

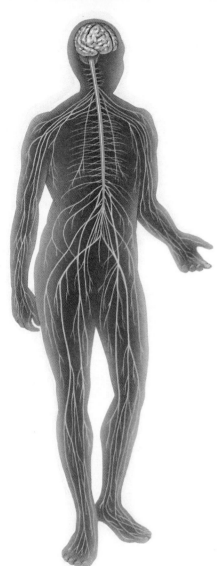

FIGURE 4.2
The peripheral nervous system. The spinal cord links the motor and sensory nerves of the peripheral nervous system with the brain.

The nervous system consists of two major subsystems of neurons, the **central nervous system** (CNS) and the **peripheral nervous system** (PNS) (see Figure 4.1). The CNS includes all of the neurons in the brain and spinal cord; the PNS consists of the neurons that connect the CNS to other parts of the body (see Figure 4.2).

The PNS is further subdivided into the somatic and autonomic nervous systems. The **somatic nervous system** controls the actions of the skeletal muscles, the muscles involved in voluntary movements. For example, if you highlight an important passage in this book, your somatic system controls the movement. Neurons in your fingers, hand, and arm transmit signals to the CNS regarding the position and movement of the muscles used in highlighting. In turn, neurons in the CNS transmit signals to those muscles, stimulating your fingers, hand, and arm to move or to stop.

The **autonomic nervous system** controls bodily processes over which you generally exert no conscious control, such as heart rate, respiration, and digestion. The autonomic system links the CNS to the body's glands and internal organs, and it is further divided into sympathetic and parasympathetic nervous systems. The **sympathetic nervous system** is activated in stressful or emergency situations. If suddenly you become frightened or alarmed, the sympathetic system increases your heart rate and breathing, slows down digestion, increases blood sugar levels and, in general, increases your alertness. The **parasympathetic nervous system** on the other hand, takes control after stressful or emergency situations are over, functioning to calm you down by slowing heart rate and respiration, and lowering blood sugar levels.

The major components of the autonomic nervous system and their functions are summarized in Figure 4.3. Let us now turn to a discussion of the neuron.

The Neuron

Neurons differ in size, shape and function, but they are similar in their basic structure (see Figure 4.4). Neurons are comprised of five basic parts—the cell body, the dendrites, the axon, the axon terminals, and the terminal buttons (see Figure 4.5). The **cell body** contains the nucleus and other structures that control the moment-to-moment functioning of the cell. Jutting out from the cell body are **dendrites**—tiny, treelike projections that, along with the cell body, receive nerve impulses from neighboring neurons or receptors.

Once received, these impulses are transmitted to other neurons, glands, or muscles via the **axon**, a pipelike fiber projecting from the cell body to the axon terminals. Axons range in length from less than a millimeter to more than a meter. The speed with which axons relay their messages ranges from 2 to 200 miles per hour and basically depends on the neuron's diameter: the fatter an axon, the faster it sends information. Another factor that determines how fast the axon sends information is whether or not it is surrounded by a fatty substance called the **myelin sheath**, which insulates and protects the neuron. The myelin sheath is actually made up of specialized glial cells that wrap themselves around axons. The smooth surface of the sheath is divided into small segments of myelin separated by small gaps between glial cells. Myelinated axons relay messages about ten times faster than nonmyelinated axons because the impulse jumps from gap to gap instead of covering the entire surface of the neuron. Each axon has several thin **axon terminals** at its tip. At the end of each axon terminal is a **terminal button**. It is through the terminal buttons that a neuron actually stimulates an adjacent neuron, gland, or muscle.

There are three general types of neurons. **Sensory neurons** transmit information from receptors to the brain and spinal cord. Receptors are

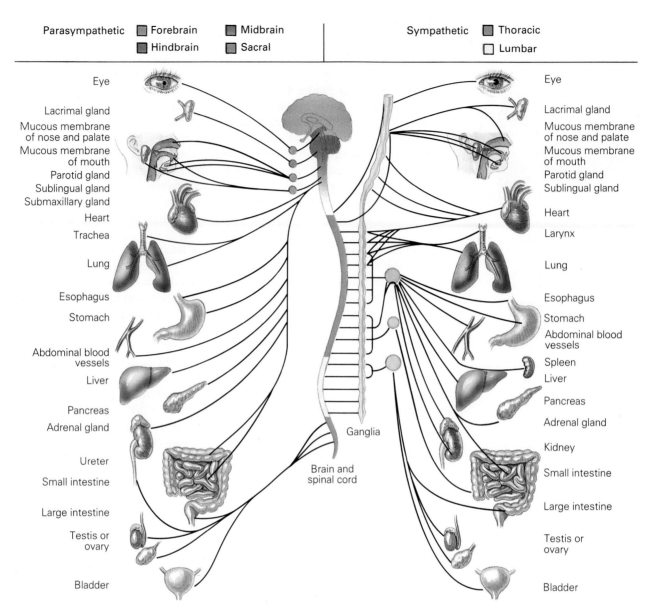

Eye

Lacrimal gland

Mucous membrane
of nose and palate

Mucous membrane
of mouth

Parotid gland

Sublingual gland

Submaxillary gland

Heart

Trachea

Lung

Esophagus

Stomach

Abdominal blood
vessels

Liver

Pancreas

Adrenal gland

Ureter

Small intestine

Large intestine

Testis or
ovary

Bladder

Ganglia

Brain and
spinal cord

Eye

Lacrimal gland

Mucous membrane
of nose and palate

Mucous membrane
of mouth

Parotid gland

Sublingual gland

Heart

Larynx

Lung

Esophagus

Stomach

Abdominal blood
vessels

Spleen

Liver

Pancreas

Adrenal gland

Kidney

Small intestine

Large intestine

Testis or
ovary

Bladder

FIGURE 4.3

*The autonomic nervous system. The
sympathetic system, which is active
during times of arousal and stress is
shown at left, and the parasympathetic
system, which is active during normal,
nonstressful activities is shown at
right. The nerves of the sympathetic
system are linked to the spinal cord
through chain ganglia, or nerve
bundles, which lie just outside the
spinal cord.*

highly specialized cells that translate physical energy from the environment into the electrochemical language of the nervous system. Other neurons called **motor neurons** transmit signals from the brain or spinal cord to
the effectors, the body's muscles and glands. The last group of neurons,
association neurons, is found only in the brain and spinal cord, where they
receive impulses from sensory neurons and convey these impulses to other
association neurons or to motor neurons.

In the simplest arrangement of neurons, one association neuron may
link a single sensory neuron with a single motor neuron. Consider, for
example, the pain reflex (see Figure 4.6). Stepping on a nail or other sharp
object stimulates pain receptors near the skin's surface and initiates neural
activity that is relayed by a sensory neuron to an association neuron in the
spinal cord. In turn, the association neuron stimulates muscles in the foot
via a motor neuron, instantaneously causing the foot to pull away from the
nail. Interestingly, the reflex is executed before the brain has time to interpret the neural activity as pain. Sensory information involved in this particular reflex must travel via the spinal cord to the brain before the pain is
actually felt.

The Nerve Impulse

When we speak of information being received by the dendrites or being sent along the axon to the terminal buttons, we are referring to the **nerve impulse** (or **action potential**), a change in the chemical composition and electrical status of the neuron. The nerve impulse, then, is actually an electrochemical code that provides the means for neurons to exchange information within the nervous system. The key to understanding the nerve impulse is to understand the remarkable properties of the neuron's membrane.

A neuron, like other cells, has a thin membrane that is selectively permeable to different kinds of ions, which are electrically charged chemical particles. The membrane allows some, but not all, ions to pass freely in and out of the neuron through pores called ion channels. Specifically, the membrane allows positively charged potassium (K+) ions to pass freely in and out of the neuron, but it prevents positively charged sodium (NA+) ions from entering. The membrane also prevents negatively charged protein ions from leaving the cell. Because the membrane forces more negative ions to accumulate on the inside of the neuron, the inside of the neuron is slightly more negatively charged than the outside. Batteries work on the same principle, except with larger charges. When the neuron is not transmitting impulses, this difference in potential is referred to as the **resting potential** because the neuron is inactive but has the potential or energy necessary to transmit an impulse (just like a battery). If we were to measure the electrical potential of the inside of the neuron relative to the outside, we would see that its resting potential is, in fact, slightly negative, -70 millivolts.

When one of the dendrites of a neuron is stimulated by the terminal button of an adjacent neuron, there is a change in the electrical potential across the receiving neuron's membrane at the point of stimulation. This change then alters the permeability of the membrane and permits positively charged sodium ions to rush into the neuron and potassium ions to exit the neuron. In a matter of just a few milliseconds, a wave of electrochemical changes passes through the cell body and along the axon. The neuron is no longer resting; rather, it is propagating the action potential— the inside of the neuron is now positively charged relative to the outside.

FIGURE 4.4
The different sizes and shapes of neurons.

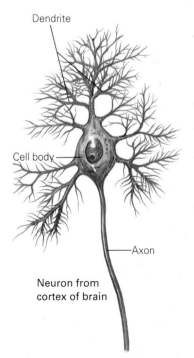

Dendrite

Cell body

Axon

Neuron from
cortex of brain

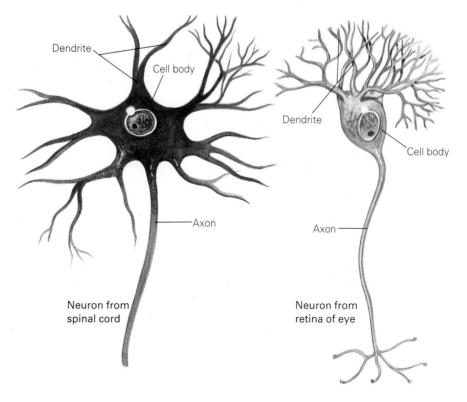

Dendrite

Cell body

Axon

Neuron from
spinal cord

Dendrite

Cell body

Axon

Neuron from
retina of eye

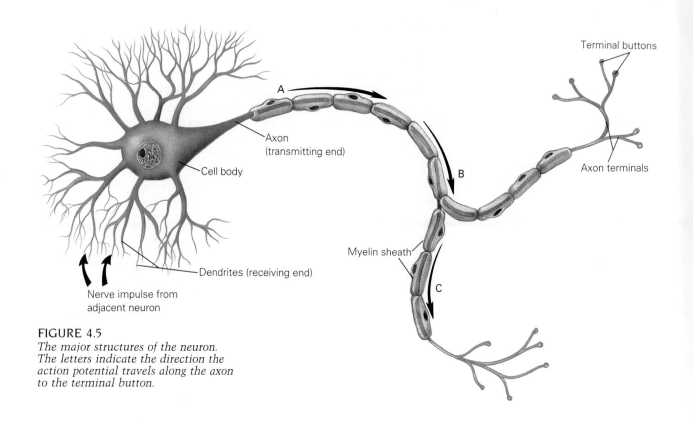

FIGURE 4.5
The major structures of the neuron. The letters indicate the direction the action potential travels along the axon to the terminal button.

Neuroscientists often refer to nerve impulses as action potentials because of this rapidly spreading change in electrical potential. The generation of the action potential at various points along the axon is shown in Figure 4.7.

It is important to keep in mind that an action potential is not affected by the intensity with which the dendrite or cell body was stimulated. In other words, once the action potential begins, it travels down the axon at the same speed, regardless of the amount of stimulation that initiated it. In this respect, the action potential is similar to a bullet leaving a gun. Regardless of how hard the trigger is pulled beyond a minimum level, the speed of the bullet leaving the gun is the same; pulling the trigger harder will not affect the bullet's speed. Likewise, all that is necessary for the generation of the action potential is stimulation of the dendrite beyond some minimum value; once that value is exceeded, the intensity of the stimulation is irrelevant. For this reason, the action potential is said to be governed by the all-or-none principle, which states that increases in stimulation beyond a certain point do not affect the speed of the action potential. However, the intensity of stimulation *does* directly affect the frequency of the action potential. In general, the greater the intensity, the more frequently an action potential may be generated.

Action potentials are very short-lived, lasting only for a millisecond or so (see Figure 4.8.) When the inside of the neuron reaches about +50 millivolts, the action potential is over and the neuron enters a very brief recovery period called the **refractory period,** during which its membrane cannot be stimulated to generate another nerve impulse. During the refractory period, the channels through which sodium ions were entering the neuron close. The return to resting potential is further hastened by the potassium reentering the neuron until the resting potential (−70 millivolts) is restored. Thus, in about three or four milliseconds, a neuron may fire and reset itself so that it is able to fire again. In fact, at any given moment you probably have several million neurons firing and resetting themselves simultaneously, although not in any special order—a truly awe-inspiring thought which, of course, just generates more action potentials!

Synaptic Transmission

Thus far we have seen how the action potential is generated within individual neurons. In this section we will discuss how the information contained in the action potential is transmitted from one neuron to another.

Synapses are junctions where two neurons meet one another. Most neurons do not actually touch one another; rather, there is a very small (measured in billionths of a meter) fluid-filled gap called the **synaptic cleft** that separates the terminal buttons of one neuron from the adjacent surface of a cell body or dendrite. Neural messages must cross the synaptic cleft for one neuron (the presynaptic neuron) to "communicate" with another (the postsynaptic neuron). The discovery of how the nerve impulse crosses the synaptic cleft represents one of the most important and exciting biopsychological breakthroughs of the 20th century. It has allowed researchers to study how drugs and other chemicals affect synaptic transmission, and this has led to breakthroughs in drug therapy for psychological disorders such as schizophrenia and depression.

FIGURE 4.6
The role of sensory, motor, and association neurons in a simple reflex.

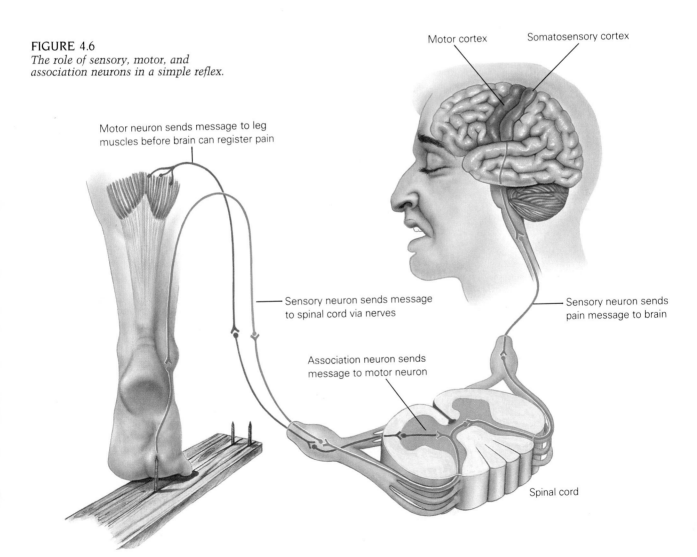

Motor neuron sends message to leg muscles before brain can register pain

Motor cortex

Somatosensory cortex

Sensory neuron sends message to spinal cord via nerves

Sensory neuron sends pain message to brain

Association neuron sends message to motor neuron

Spinal cord

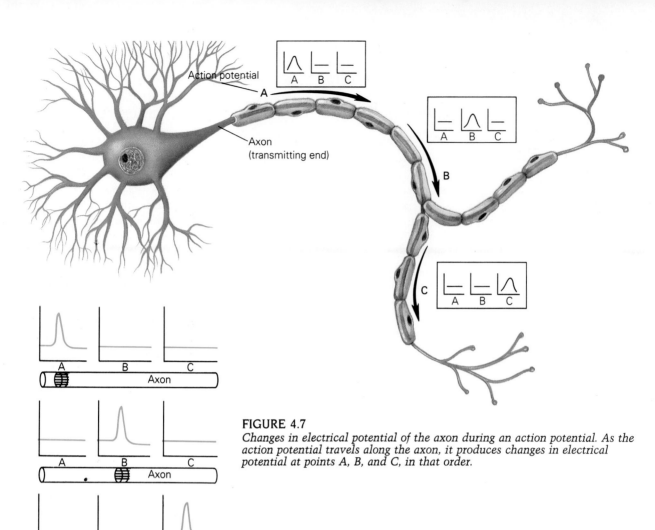

Action potential

Axon
(transmitting end)

A

B

C

Axon

Axon

Axon

Direction of impulse

FIGURE 4.7
Changes in electrical potential of the axon during an action potential. As the action potential travels along the axon, it produces changes in electrical potential at points A, B, and C, in that order.

Synaptic transmission is the dispatching of information from one neuron across the synaptic cleft to another. Like the generation of the nerve impulse itself, synaptic transmission occurs electrochemically. The basic process involves four steps (see Figure 4.9):

1. When an action potential within a neuron reaches the axon terminal, it stimulates tiny saclike structures called **synaptic vesicles** stored in the terminal button to move toward and fuse with the interior surface of the terminal button. The synaptic vesicles are filled with chemical messengers called **neurotransmitters.** The function of neurotransmitters is to change the resting potential of a postsynaptic neuron.

2. Once fused with the surface of the terminal button, the synaptic vesicles rupture, spilling their contents into the synaptic cleft.

3. The neurotransmitter molecules diffuse quickly across the synaptic cleft to the postsynaptic neuron.

4. Once across the synaptic cleft, neurotransmitter molecules attach themselves to receptor molecules embedded in the membrane of the postsynaptic neuron, similar to how a key fits a lock (see Figure 4.10). If the receptor molecule does not already contain a neurotransmitter molecule and if the shape of the neurotransmitter molecule matches the shape of the receptor molecule the neurotransmitter may alter the resting potential of the postsynaptic neuron.

A neurotransmitter may affect the resting potential of the receiving neuron in two ways. First, some neurotransmitters are excitatory and increase the permeability of the postsynaptic neuron's membrane to sodium, making the generation of an action potential more likely. Second, other neu-

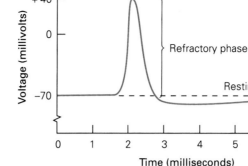

FIGURE 4.8
Time course and changes in electrical potential of the action potential. During the refractory period, which lasts for only a millisecond, the neuron cannot be stimulated. It is during the refractory period that the balance between ions inside and outside of the cell is restored.

rotransmitters are inhibitory and, therefore, produce the opposite effect—they cause the inside of the neuron to become more negative, making the generation of an action potential less likely.

The response of the postsynaptic neuron is determined collectively by all of the stimulation that reaches it. The generation of a nerve impulse within the postsynaptic neuron occurs if it receives sufficiently more excitatory messages than inhibitory messages from other neurons. In a sense, synaptic transmission of nerve impulses follows the parliamentary procedure of majority vote. If the majority of synaptic connections are excitatory, the postsynaptic neuron generates a nerve impulse; otherwise, it may remain at resting potential, or if the connections are primarily inhibitory, it may become more negatively charged.

Please note that it is very easy to become confused when we talk of stimulating a neuron. When one neuron stimulates another, it may do so by either exciting it or inhibiting it. The word "stimulation" in this case simply means that one neuron has been acted upon by another neuron. One neuron may stimulate another to release an inhibitory neurotransmitter. Thus, to neuroscientists, stimulating a neuron does not mean the same thing as exciting it.

FIGURE 4.9
Synaptic transmission.

(a)

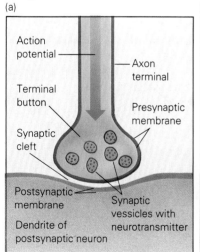

Action potential stimulates synaptic vessicles to move toward and fuse with the terminal button.

(b)

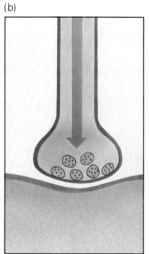

Synaptic vessicles fuse with the interior surface of the terminal button.

(c)

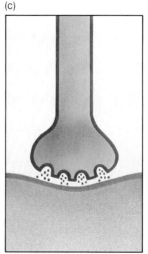

Synaptic vessicles rupture, releasing neurotransmitters across the synaptic cleft.

(d)

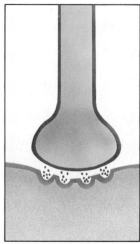

Neurotransmitters make contact with receptor molecules in the membrane of the postsynaptic neuron.

A single synaptic transmission, from the time that the neurotransmitters are released from the presynaptic neuron to their contact with the receptor molecules embedded in the postsynaptic neuron, occurs very rapidly—in less than a millisecond. If the transmission were any longer, the nervous system would lose precise control over the transfer of nerve impulses between neurons and the result would be garbled transmissions, and ultimately, disorganized behavior. Timing, then, is of the essence. Two processes, reuptake and degradation, are responsible for controlling the duration of the synaptic transmission. **Reuptake** involves the absorption of neurotransmitter molecules by terminal buttons of the presynaptic neuron almost immediately after they are released. Neurotransmitter molecules not quick enough to make it to the postsynaptic neuron are simply recycled; that is, they are taken back into the presynaptic neuron, repackaged in new synaptic vesicles, and used again. Neurotransmitters can also be destroyed by enzymes in the membrane of postsynaptic neurons, a process known as **degradation.** As we will see later, drugs and other chemicals interfere with synaptic transmission by disrupting the processes that control its otherwise clockworklike timing.

FIGURE 4.10
The synapse. Neurotransmitters from the presynaptic neuron cross the cleft and stimulate the postsynaptic neuron at specific receptor sites.

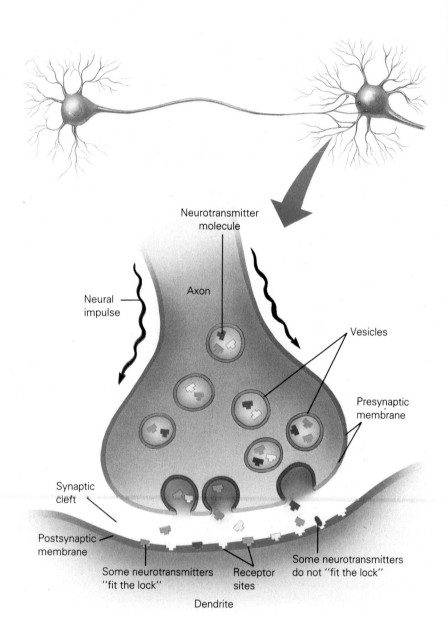

Neurotransmitter molecule

Neural impulse

Axon

Vesicles

Presynaptic membrane

Synaptic cleft

Postsynaptic membrane

Some neurotransmitters "fit the lock"

Receptor sites

Some neurotransmitters do not "fit the lock"

Dendrite

Neurotransmitters

In 1921 the Austrian physiologist Otto Loewi produced the first compelling experimental evidence that neurons secrete the chemical substances that we now call neurotransmitters. His experiment, which is said to have stemmed from a dream, was very simple. Loewi was interested in determining how the vagus nerve, a bundle of axons whose cell bodies are located in the brain and whose terminal buttons form synapses with the heart and other organs, slowed the beating of frog hearts. Loewi placed two frog hearts and their accompanying vagus nerves in separate containers filled with saline solution (salt water). Both hearts were intact and still beating. Next, he electrically stimulated the vagus nerve connected to one of the hearts and, as he expected, the rate of beating of that heart decreased. While stimulating that heart, he gathered some of the surrounding saline solution. After the heart had returned to its normal resting state, he injected the saline solution directly into the heart; its rate of beating slowed down. On the other hand, when he injected the saline solution surrounding the nonstimulated heart and vagus nerve into the heart, it did not have any effect. Loewi correctly concluded that stimulation of the vagus nerve results in the release of a chemical substance that decreases heart rate. We now know that this chemical substance is acetylcholine, a neurotransmitter that we will learn more about in just a moment.

In the years since Loewi's discovery, over sixty neurotransmitters have been discovered. Neuroscientists have also discovered that certain diseases and many of the substances people eat, drink, inject, or otherwise consume, affect neurotransmitters and their ability to transmit nerve impulses. In addition to studying the structure and function of the different neurotransmitters, scientists are also mapping the brain in an attempt to identify the pathways that different neurotransmitters use in transmitting their electrochemical messages. This is no easy task if only because neurotransmitters are so widely dispersed throughout the brain. The brain is actually a vast and complex web of neural circuits, bustling with momentary changes in electrical activity mediated by a variety of neurotransmitters. We will discuss six of the better understood neurotransmitters: acetylcholine, norepinephrine, dopamine, GABA, serotonin, and enkephalins.

Acetylcholine, or ACh for short, is perhaps the most common neurotransmitter in the nervous system. It is found in the brain, spinal cord, and synapses between neurons and skeletal muscles. ACh appears to produce excitatory effects in the brain and spinal cord and inhibitory effects in organs such as the heart.

Once ACh has exerted its effects on the postsynaptic membrane, it is usually degraded by an enzyme, acetylcholine esterase (AChE), present in the synaptic cleft. Several drugs have been discovered that increase ACh activity in the nervous system by inhibiting AChE. Such drugs are logically called AChE inhibitors. Such drug action may produce corresponding changes in behavior, most of which are not desirable. For example, malathion, a pesticide commonly used by farmers and home owners in residential areas, may temporarily cause hallucinations, feelings of confusion and irritability, and decreases in cognitive and motor abilities.

A variety of poisonous substances affect the action of ACh. For example, curare, a paralytic drug first discovered by South American Indians, prevents ACh from establishing contact with receptor molecules of postsynaptic neurons in the respiratory system. A person poisoned with curare will die of suffocation if not placed on artificial respiration until the effect of the drug wears off. Botulinum toxin, a substance produced from improperly canning foods, prevents release of ACh from presynaptic neurons and can also cause death by suffocation. On the other hand, nerve gases exert their deadly effects by enhancing the ACh's effects on postsynaptic neurons, thereby producing massive convulsions in the respiratory system.

Acetylcholine also plays a role in learning and memory and has been implicated as a cause of memory loss observed in people suffering from Alzheimer's disease, a progressive brain disorder affecting mostly the elderly. People who die from this disease have less than half as much acetylcholine in their brains as healthy people.

Norepinephrine (NE) and **dopamine** (DA) are two neurotransmitters that belong to a group of chemically similar compounds known as catecholamines. Norepinephrine is primarily an excitatory neurotransmitter found in the brain and spinal cord. Because people suffering from psychological depression often have low levels of this neurotransmitter, researchers believe that NE's chief function is to mediate moods. Drugs that affect NE will also affect an individual's emotional disposition. For example, lithium, a drug often prescribed for persons suffering from the psychological disorder known as manic-depression, hastens the reuptake of NE, thereby decreasing an individual's mood level during the mania phase of the disorder. (Mania refers to an affective disorder in which a person's behavior may be characterized by euphoria, excessive talkativeness, impaired judgment and sometimes delusions of grandeur.) On the other hand, drugs such as cocaine, which increase the release of norepinephrine, give rise to feelings of alertness, self-confidence, and vigor.

Dopamine is also an excitatory neurotransmitter. Brain researchers believe that dopamine plays a role in the regulation of movement, cognition, and emotion. For example, increased activity of dopamine receptors produces some of the symptoms of schizophrenia, a disorder characterized by disorganized thinking, hallucinations, and inappropriate displays of emotion. On the other hand, too little activity among dopamine neurons results in disturbances of movement, such as tremors, and inability to walk at a normal pace. These symptoms are found in persons suffering from Parkinson's disease, who, not surprisingly, have extremely low levels of dopamine in their brains. Although many forms of schizophrenia are commonly treated with drugs, you can easily see one potential problem: a drug that reduces dopamine to extremely low levels can produce the symptoms of Parkinson's disease. We will learn more about dopamine's role in schizophrenia and Parkinson's disease later.

GABA (gamma-amino butyric acid) is the main inhibitory neurotransmitter found in the brain. In essence, GABA keeps the excitatory activities of the brain in check; without GABA the brain would be overrun with excitatory neural impulses, which would lead to convulsions and seizures. GABA, or more precisely, lack of GABA, has been implicated in some forms of epilepsy, a nervous system disorder that involves symptoms ranging from sleepiness to seizures. Tetanus, a disease that may result from being bitten by a wild animal or by cutting oneself on rusty metal, is caused by bacteria that inhibit the terminal buttons' release of GABA into the synaptic cleft, which, in turn, produces rigidity of movement and convulsions. Similarly, anxiety appears to be caused by too much excitatory synaptic transmission in the brain. Valium and other antianxiety drugs facilitate GABA neurons by increasing synaptic transmission of GABA and inhibiting excitatory neurons, which reduces tension. Interestingly, researchers have recently discovered that if GABA receptors are blocked, the effects of antianxiety drugs are reduced. This discovery is important because of its clinical implications—blocking GABA receptors may reverse the intoxicating and sometimes lethal consequences of abusing antianxiety drugs (Julien, 1988).

Distance runners often experience "runner's high," which may be due to the release of enkephalins.

Serotonin is also an inhibitory neurotransmitter found in the brain and spinal cord that plays an important role in the brain's control of sleep and arousal, body temperature, and sensory and perceptual functions. Drugs that block the brain's production of serotonin produce insomnia; drugs that aid production of serotonin have the opposite effect: they cause sleep. Because some hallucinogenic drugs such as LSD are chemically similar to serotonin, some brain researchers believe that such drugs interfere with normal functioning of serotonin in neurons.

Enkephalins are a class of neurotransmitters that appear to be involved in the body's ability to tolerate and mediate pain (Watkins & Mayer, 1982). Enkephalins are found in amino acid chains known as endorphins that are stored in the pituitary gland of the brain. They are sometimes referred to as the "body's natural painkillers" because their effects are very similar to the effects of narcotics such as morphine, a widely used (and sometimes abused) painkiller. Morphine and other opiates exert their analgesic effects because they bind to the same receptor sites to which these natural compounds bind (Snyder, 1984). Enkephalins appear to play a role in pain reduction procedures such as acupuncture, the Chinese art of inserting needles in strategic spots of the body to eliminate the sensation of pain. Apparently, acupuncture stimulates the release of enkephalins in the brain, thereby reducing feelings of pain. Drugs, such as nalaxone, which reduce the effectiveness of acupuncture, also inhibit enkephalin-containing neurons (Mayer, Price, & Rafii, 1977). Enkephalins are also thought to be responsible for the so-called "runner's high" that some runners experience during and immediately after a hard run (Colt, Wardlaw, & Frantz, 1981). Solid experimental evidence for this effect, however, has yet to be gathered.

DRUGS AND CONSCIOUS EXPERIENCE

Almost everybody is a drug user. We take a few aspirin or acetominophen to relieve a headache or a muscular pain; we request novocaine or nitrous oxide to prevent the pain that may result from having a tooth drilled or extracted; and we use stronger drugs like percodan or demerol when suffering from more intense pain. Some people take drugs to fall asleep, others take drugs to stay awake. We also use drugs, most often alcohol, in social situations to relax or to just have "a good time." Fifty million Americans use tobacco products which, as you probably know, contain the drug nicotine. Even more of us use coffee, tea, and cola beverages, which, as you also probably know, contain caffeine. All of these drugs in some way affect the normal operation of the central nervous system, particularly synaptic transmission. This is important from a psychological point of view because whenever normal synaptic transmission is altered, so is behavior. This fact permits neuroscientists to induce changes in the nervous system with drugs to study the resulting changes in behavior.

Drugs in some way affect the normal operation of the central nervous system, particularly synaptic transmission . . . whenever normal synaptic transmission is altered, so is behavior.

Of particular interest to neuroscientists are the **psychoactive drugs**, those drugs that affect our behavior, perceptions, arousal level, emotional status, and ability to think clearly. Indeed, people use, often illegally, these kinds of drugs because of the pleasurable and sometimes dramatic changes in subjective experience they induce. In this section, we examine how drugs affect the central nervous system, and subsequently, our conscious experience of the world.

The Nature of Addiction

To say that a person is addicted to a psychoactive drug generally means two things. First, it means that his or her nervous system has developed a tolerance to the drug. And second, it means that he or she has become physically dependent on drugs. **Tolerance** simply means that the neurons in the central nervous system respond progressively less and less to the drug. In other words, larger doses of the drug are required to produce the same effects on the nervous system that smaller doses produced earlier. **Physical dependence** refers to the fact that the neurons in the nervous system now require the drug to function normally. Without the drug, the individual will experience withdrawal symptoms, which may include trembling, perspiration, nausea, headaches, and depending upon the drug, even death.

Initially, psychoactive drugs are used because of their intensely pleasurable effects. However, as tolerance and physical dependence develop with continued use of the drug, the frequency and severity of withdrawal symptoms also increase. Now, the addict uses the drug both to induce a high and to avoid the physical pain and stress of withdrawal. Addiction to many psychoactive drugs may also involve **psychological dependence**, an all-consuming craving to use the drug for its euphoric effects. The drug becomes the center of the person's life, forcing the individual to restructure his or her life-style around both obtaining and using the drug—and all because of the manner in which the CNS is influenced by chemical properties of the drug. Drug abuse will be discussed in Chapter 18.

Exactly how do psychoactive drugs affect the CNS? Psychoactive drugs exert much of their influence at synapses. Recall that the synapse plays the key role in the transmission of messages between neurons. Neurotransmitters from the presynaptic neuron must cross the synaptic cleft and fit into the receptor molecules of the postsynaptic neuron like a key fits into a lock to transmit successfully their messages. Psychoactive drugs meddle with this process by enhancing or hampering its execution in any one of several ways:

- Stimulating or retarding the release of neurotransmitters from the synaptic vesicles.
- Slowing down or speeding up reuptake of the neurotransmitter.
- Slowing down or speeding up degradation of the neurotransmitter.
- Mimicking the effects of the neurotransmitter.
- Occupying receptor molecules, thereby blocking the neurotransmitter from binding with receptor molecules of the postsynaptic neuron.

Any of these changes in synaptic transmission will affect conscious experience. However, exactly how a drug will affect an individual's conscious experience and behavior is a different matter. There seems to be a number of factors other than the psychoactive chemical in a particular drug that influences that drug's psychological effects. These factors include body size and metabolism (the process by which the body converts food to energy) of the individual user, dosage of the drug, the immediate context in which the drug is used, how long and in what quantities an individual has been using the drug, whether the drug is smoked, snorted, injected, or consumed orally, and the individual's expectations of the drug's effects. Thus, drug effects may vary widely from person to person and from context to context not because of any specific properties of the drug itself, but because of individual differences among drug users and the conditions under which they take the drug.

D*rug effects may vary widely from person to person and from context to context . . .*

TABLE 4.1.	*Classification of drugs.*

Drugs are classified into five categories depending upon their effect on the nervous system or usefulness in treating psychological disorders. Representative drugs from each class are listed.

1. Central Nervous System Depressants
   Barbiturates
   Long-acting: phenobarbital (Luminal)
   Intermediate-acting: amobarbital (Amytal)
   Short-acting: phenobarbital (Nembutal), secobarbital (Seconal)
   Ultrashort-acting: pentothal (Thiopental)
   Antianxiety agents
   Meprobamate (Miltown, Equanil)
   Chlordiazepoxide (Librium)
   Diazepam (Valium)
   Others
   Ethyl alcohol

2. Behavioral Stimulants and Convulsants
   Amphetamines: (Benzedrine, Dexedrine, Methedrine)
   Cocaine
   Convulsants: strychnine
   Caffeine
   Nicotine

3. Narcotic Analgesics: Opiates
   Opium, heroin, morphine, codeine (Numorphan, Dilaudid, Percodan, Demerol)

4. Antipsychotic Agents
   Phenothiazines: chlorpromazine (Thorazine)
   Reserpine (Serpasil)
   Lithium

5. Psychedelics and Hallucinogens
   LSD (lysergic acid diethylamide)
   Mescaline
   Cannabis, marijuana, hashish, tetrahydrocannabinol

Adapted from Julien, 1988.

Classes of Psychoactive Drugs

Psychoactive drugs are classified according to the manner in which they influence the central nervous system. Table 4.1 lists the five classes of psychoactive drugs and gives representative examples of each. With the exception of caffeine and nicotine, the drugs discussed below are illegal. All of them can have damaging effects on the nervous system.

We now turn to a discussion of how each of the different classes of psychoactive drugs affect central nervous system activity and subsequently, behavior.

Stimulants. **Stimulants** are drugs that stimulate CNS activity by increasing the amount of neuronal activity that normally occurs in the brain. Behaviorally, stimulants increase arousal and physical activity, decrease fatigue and appetite, and elevate mood. Some stimulants like caffeine and nicotine produce relatively minor behavioral changes; others such as amphetamines (speed) and cocaine produce more dramatic changes in behavior. Let's look at each of these drugs in more detail.

Amphetamines. Amphetamines are synthetic drugs. They were first produced in laboratories around the turn of the century but did not become widely available to the public (mainly for medical purposes) until the

1930s. Structurally, amphetamines, sometimes referred to as "speed" or "uppers," are similar to norepinephrine and mimic the effect of this neurotransmitter on the central nervous system. In other words, neurons generally affected by norepinephrine are now even more likely to be affected. Amphetamines also increase norepinephrine levels in the brain. Both effects produce elevations in mood as well as loss of appetite, increases in energy, alertness, and confidence. No wonder that amphetamines and chemically related drugs were once marketed widely as appetite suppressants and "energy pills."

Regular use of amphetamines may result in both physical and psychological dependence. The euphoric effects following intake of amphetamines sometimes produce a compulsion to continue to use the drug. Withdrawal from amphetamines causes fatigue, increased appetite, and often deep emotional depression. The appetite-suppressing effects of the drug are subject to tolerance, which explains why amphetamines are not effective in helping to maintain long-term weight loss. Users also develop tolerance to the euphoric effects of amphetamines very quickly.

People who take large doses of amphetamines intravenously often experience dramatic changes in consciousness and behavior, including delusions, hallucinations, paranoia, aggressive and antisocial behavior, confused thinking, and compulsive repetition of insignificant behaviors. In addition, users who habitually take large doses often neglect their physical health and suffer from poor nutrition, insomnia, chronic weight loss, and infections.

Cocaine. Cocaine is derived from the leaves of the coca trees native to Bolivia, Colombia, and Peru. Natives of these countries often chew the leaves to induce euphoria and increase stamina. In Western countries, cocaine is most often used in a powdered form produced by mashing the leaves and extracting the drug. Users prefer the powdered form because it is absorbed directly into the bloodstream when inhaled or snorted, thus producing a more intense rush of euphoria than is possible by chewing the leaves. Cocaine was one of the ingredients in the original formula for a popular soft drink; the leaves, *minus the cocaine*, are still used today as a flavoring for the soft drink.

Cocaine exerts its intense euphoric effects by stimulating dopamine activity at synapses in the brain and peripheral nervous system. It does so by blocking the reuptake of dopamine by presynaptic neurons, allowing more dopamine to remain in the synaptic cleft, which binds quickly with postsynaptic receptor sites. Psychologically, the high produced by cocaine is nearly identical to that produced by amphetamines and includes heightened mental awareness, decreased fatigue, and increased feelings of well-being and euphoria.

Sigmund Freud, the father of psychoanalysis, once described cocaine as a "magical" drug, and argued its usefulness in relieving depression and tiredness. Freud, himself, used small doses of the drug to treat his own depression and described its effects as exhilarating. Freud was so taken by cocaine's effects on his behavior that in 1884 he published the first of several papers on cocaine and its euphoric properties. At that time, of course, neither Freud nor any one else could foresee that abuse of cocaine would become a widespread social, medical, and economic problem.

Regular users of cocaine develop a tolerance for the drug's effects, and habitually heavy users may suffer withdrawal symptoms, chiefly depression, soon after the drug's effects wear off. When taken in large doses, the cocaine can produce hallucinations, including the sensation that insects are crawling under one's skin.

Top left: Although caffeine and nicotine are widely consumed substances, they are drugs and have powerful effects on the central nervous system and heart. Right: Cocaine and crack can produce euphoric effects but can also produce hallucinations when taken in large doses. Regular users develop a tolerance to the drug and must consume increasingly larger doses to produce the same effects.

Several years ago, a modified and much less expensive form of cocaine known as "crack" became popular. Crack is sold in crystalline form and produces a quicker and more intense high than cocaine. With cocaine there is a several minute delay between snorting it and experiencing a 15 to 20 minute rush of euphoria; but smoking crack produces an almost instantaneous and extremely intense although shorter-lived high. Its greater punch, combined with its lower price tag, has made crack an extremely popular drug of abuse on the streets of most of our nation's cities.

Caffeine. Caffeine is one of the most widely consumed drugs in the world today. Consumption of caffeine in the United States is estimated to be about 15 million pounds a year (Julien, 1988). In addition to coffee and tea, it can also be found in chocolate and cocoa. A 5-ounce cup of coffee has between 100 and 150 milligrams of caffeine, and a 12-ounce cola drink contains between 35 and 55 milligrams. Some candy bars contain as much as 25 milligrams of the drug per ounce.

Of importance to psychologists is the finding that caffeine causes neurons in the brain to become more active, increasing arousal, mental alertness, and wakefulness and thereby permits sustained intellectual efforts and improved psychomotor performance. When consumed in large amounts, for example, ten cups of coffee or thirty cola drinks a day, arousal may take the form of anxiety, agitation, and even muscular tremors.

Interestingly, although caffeine increases the flow of blood to the heart and increases the heart's overall output of blood, it decreases the amount of blood flowing to the brain. This latter fact is the reason why caffeine is sometimes recommended for relief of migraine headaches and hypertensive headaches (those caused by high blood pressure).

In small doses, caffeine does not appear to be addictive; tolerance and physical dependence are unlikely. However, tolerance and physical dependence may develop after prolonged use of large doses of the drug. For example, someone who drinks more than four or five cups of coffee per day is likely to experience withdrawal symptoms—headaches, nausea and irritability—for the first few days after abruptly quitting coffee drinking.

Nicotine. After caffeine, nicotine is perhaps the most widely used drug in the world today. Nicotine exerts powerful effects on the central nervous system and heart apparently by stimulating postsynaptic surfaces receptive to acetylcholine. Such stimulation results in increased heart rate and blood pressure, changes in hormones released by the pituitary gland, and the release of adrenalin from the adrenal glands. In some doses, nicotine can cause tremors, and in large doses, it can lead to convulsions.

Nicotine is an addictive drug that causes both physiological and psychological dependence. Cigarette smoking is a very tough habit to break because the smoker becomes physically dependent upon the nicotine and psychologically dependent upon the behaviors associated with smoking. People who attempt to quit smoking often suffer from withdrawal symptoms that include headaches, insomnia, and irritability. These symptoms are usually quite prolonged and are often inducement enough for the person to start smoking again. Indeed, of the nation's millions of smokers, over 60 percent have tried to quit smoking at least once. In a recent report on smoking, C. Everett Koop, Surgeon General of the United States, warned that the nicotine contained in cigarette smoke is as addictive as cocaine and heroin.

In addition to being addictive, nicotine also poses serious health risks for people who smoke, especially those who smoke cigarettes. Cigarette smokers face increased risks of suffering from emphysema, heart diseases, and cancer of the lung, mouth, throat, larynx, pancreas, and bladder. Lung cancer induced by cigarette smoking alone claims about 92,000 lives annually in the United States. Over 300,000 persons die annually from illnesses related to cigarette smoking. One writer has even gone so far to state that a person's lifetime is shortened by 14 minutes each time he or she smokes a cigarette (Julien, 1988).

Nicotine alone, though, cannot be blamed for the health risks posed by cigarette smoking. Rather, these risks are caused by the nicotine combining with other toxic substances, such as carbon monoxide and tars in cigarette smoke. For example, while nicotine causes an increase in heart rate, the carbon monoxide in smoke deprives the heart of the oxygen needed to perform its work properly. Thus, the smoker's heart undergoes an unnatural stress because it is working harder with fewer nutrients than normal. Over a period of years, the continual stress weakens a smoker's heart, making it more susceptible to disease than the heart of a nonsmoker.

Many smokers believe that they can diminish the health risks posed by their habit by switching to low nicotine cigarettes. Unfortunately, this strategy is undermined by the fact that smokers develop a tolerance to nicotine and typically smoke more cigarettes to make up for the decreased nicotine content of their new brand.

Depressants. **Depressants** are drugs that depress the nervous system by slowing down its activities. Their general effect is to depress the activity of neurons. Inhibition of neural activity may range from relief from anxiety at low doses to complete sedation at higher doses. Two extensively used depressants are alcohol and barbiturates (downers).

Alcohol. Alcohol is nonselective in its effects on the central nervous system, which means that it depresses the activity of neurons in all regions of the brain. Interestingly, alcohol was once thought to be a stimulant because persons under the influence of the drug often say and do things that they would normally not say or do when sober. However, these behavioral changes appear to be due mostly to depression of neural circuits that usually inhibit behavior. This example underscores an important point about drug classification: drugs are classified as depressants or stimulants not because of their effects on behavior but because of their effects on nervous system activity. That is, stimulants speed up nervous system activity and depressants slow it down.

You are probably already familiar with some of the behavioral effects associated with consuming alcohol. Because neuronal activity of the brain becomes depressed when moderate to heavy amounts of alcohol are consumed, individuals become more relaxed, more outgoing, show impaired motor coordination, and have difficulty thinking clearly. As more alcohol is consumed, neuronal activity in the brain is depressed further, producing distortions in perception, slurred speech, memory loss, impaired judgment and incredibly poor control over body movement. Unconsciousness and death may result from ingesting extremely large amounts of alcohol over a relatively short period of time.

Once ingested, alcohol is rapidly absorbed from the stomach and intestinal tract. Because alcohol is a tiny, fat and water soluble molecule, it is quickly and evenly distributed throughout the body via the circulatory system. However, blood alcohol levels may be affected by body weight and muscularity. Generally speaking, an obese or muscular individual would have to consume more alcohol than a slender person to produce the same level of intoxication. In addition, regardless of body characteristics, blood levels of alcohol increase more slowly in people who drink on a full stomach than in those with little or no food in their stomachs. Food in the stomach dilutes the alcohol and impairs absorption of the drug through the gastrointestinal tract. The moral here is plain to see: drinking on a full stomach reduces the inebriating effects of alcohol.

Inebriation is related to the manner in which alcohol is metabolized by the body. Unlike most drugs, alcohol is metabolized by the liver at a constant rate regardless of how much alcohol has been consumed. For example, in one hour the body will metabolize 12 ounces of beer or 1 ounce of 80-100 proof liquor. Hence, if you consume more than 12 ounces of beer or 1 ounce of liquor per hour, your blood alcohol level rises and you become intoxicated. When blood alcohol levels reach 0.3 to 0.4 percent, you lose consciousness, and at 0.5 percent, neurons in the brain that control the respiratory and circulatory systems become completely depressed and stop functioning, causing death. (Driving under the influence is defined by most states as a blood alcohol level greater than 0.1 percent.)

Alcohol is the most widely used and abused of all depressant drugs, and with the exception of nicotine, is the cause of the most serious drug problem in the world today. Although moderate drinkers develop little or no tolerance to alcohol, people who regularly consume large quantities of alcohol usually develop a tolerance. Heavy drinkers often suffer the "DTs"—delirium tremens—a pattern of withdrawal symptoms including trembling, hallucinations, sleeplessness, irritability, and confusion when they attempt to "dry out." In many cases, alcoholics become so physically dependent upon the drug that abrupt cessation of drinking produces convulsions and sometimes death. Interestingly, an individual's tendency to become an alcoholic may have a genetic basis. Vaillant and Milofsky (1982) in a long-term study of adopted boys, found that boys who were closely related to alcoholics had a greater tendency to become alcoholics themselves, despite the fact that their adoptive parents were nonalcoholics. In a more recent study of adopted children, Cloninger (1987) found that children of alcoholic parents adopted at birth into normal (nonalcoholic) homes were about four times more likely to abuse alcohol than other adopted children whose biological parents were nonalcoholics.

Recently, researchers have found that women who drink moderate to heavy quantities of alcohol during their pregnancies do so at the risk of giving birth to children suffering from symptoms of fetal alcohol syndrome

Despite the stimulation some people claim to experience while drinking alcohol, it is a depressant that slows nervous system activity.

Psychedelics can produce intense visual hallucinations such as the ones shown in this piece of artwork painted by a Huichol Indian under the influence of the drug peyote.

(Clarren & Smith, 1978). In this case, alcohol crosses the placental barrier and retards the development of the fetus' nervous system. This syndrome is characterized by decreased birth weight and physical malformations, and is the third leading cause of birth defects involving mental retardation. Ironically, it is also preventable: if a woman does not drink alcohol during her pregnancy, there is no possibility that she will give birth to a child with fetal alcohol syndrome.

Barbiturates. Clinically, barbiturates are used to reduce anxiety and to induce muscle relaxation and sleep. They exert their calming effects by depressing the activities of neurons along pathways in the brain that control arousal and wakefulness. The psychological effects resulting from barbiturate consumption are similar to and sometimes indistinguishable from those characteristic of drunkenness. Regular use of barbiturates can induce both tolerance and physical and psychological dependence. In fact, even when taken in low doses, serious withdrawal symptoms may result when use of the drug is halted abruptly.

An important property of depressants is that their effects are additive. If two depressant compounds are ingested within a short time of each other, the sedative effects of the second drug would be added to those of the first. Thus, the behavioral effects of drinking may be compounded by taking a barbiturate or two. Such additive effects can be lethal if large doses of barbiturates are consumed following a period of heavy drinking (or vice versa). Accidental or premeditated overdoses of depressants and alcohol are not uncommon. So, if you generally take sedatives to help you sleep at night, *do not* use them when you have been drinking.

Psychedelics. **Psychedelics** are drugs that produce dramatic changes in consciousness including distorted or intense sensory experiences characterized by vivid auditory and visual hallucinations. The term, "psychedelic," means mind expanding. Many psychedelics are naturally occurring substances whose effects on consciousness have been described as magical, mystical, and even spiritual. For these reasons, this class of drugs has been long used in religious and mystical ceremonies. Psychedelics became popular among the "hip generation" of the 1960s and 1970s, who used the drugs to enhance their perception. Users feel that psychedelic drugs heighten sensory experiences, permitting even the slightest changes in sensory stimulation to be interpreted as having great significance and profound personal meaning. Three of the most widely used psychedelic drugs are LSD (lysergic acid diethylamide), phencyclidine (PCP), and marijuana.

LSD. LSD is a synthetic drug that was first produced in the laboratory of Swiss pharmacologist, Albert Hofmann, in 1938. It is derived from a fungus that grows on rye, a grain common to the United States and Europe. LSD is an immensely powerful drug; a very small dose is capable of inducing remarkable changes in consciousness. After accidentally consuming some LSD and subsequently experiencing a change of consciousness, Hofmann conducted an experiment on himself with the drug. Under controlled conditions he orally ingested only .25 milligrams (a milligram equals one thousandth of a gram) of the drug. What follows is his description of the experience:

> After 40 minutes, I noted the following symptoms in my laboratory journal: slight giddiness, restlessness, difficulty in concentrating, visual disturbances, laughing. . . . Later: I lost all count of time. I noticed with dismay that my environment was undergoing progressive changes. My visual field wavered and everything appeared deformed as in a faulty mirror. Space and

time became more and more disorganized and I was overcome by a fear that I was going out of my mind. The worst part of it being that I was clearly aware of my condition. My power of observation was unimpaired. . . . Occasionally, I felt as if I were out of my body. I thought I had died. . . . It was particularly striking how acoustic perceptions, such as the noise of water rushing from a tap or the spoken word, were transformed into optical illusions.

(Hofmann, quoted in Julien, 1988, p. 180)

We now know that the dose of LSD ingested by Hofmann was much greater than needed to induce psychedelic effects; ingesting as little as 25 micrograms (one-millionth of an ounce) of the drug will produce psychedelic changes in consciousness. Once ingested, LSD acts rapidly and its effects last up to 12 hours.

LSD blocks serotonin receptors of neurons found in the lower part of the brain. Thus, neurons usually inhibited by serotonin-producing neurons are "emancipated" and become hyperactive, giving rise to vivid sensory experiences similar to those experienced by Hofmann. Although tolerance to the drug develops rapidly, physical dependence does not develop, and psychological dependence develops only occasionally. Most persons who quit LSD do so on their own because they are either bored with it or because they want to switch to other less powerful psychedelics. Nonetheless, just because dependence on LSD does not occur, it is still a potentially dangerous drug. LSD can induce disorientation, confusion, panic reactions, and sometimes terrifying sensory experiences. These effects can be so powerful that they overpower one's ability to adequately cope with the experience. Frequently, an LSD "trip" will induce psychotic behavior. Such behavior often requires long-term therapy and sometimes hospitalization.

Phencyclidine. PCP, or angel dust as it is often referred to on the street, was first synthesized in the late 1950s but did not become a common recreational drug until the late 1960s and 1970s. PCP was originally used as an anesthetic until patients reported experiencing serious side effects such as confusion, disorientation, and amnesia for recent events. On the street, PCP may be taken orally, intravenously, snorted, or smoked. Its long-lasting psychedelic effects include feelings of disassociation from one's immediate surroundings, delusions, distorted perception of time and spatial events, and euphoria. Heavy PCP users sometimes behave violently, even psychotically, under the influence of the drug and occasionally suffer periods of stupor and coma lasting up to four hours. Prolonged use of the drug may permanently impair learning and memory abilities (Kolb & Brody, 1982). Because PCP is an analgesic (pain killer) and makes its users disoriented, people under its influence are prone to injuries, usually self-inflicted, some of which are fatal (Cravey, Reed, & Ragle, 1979). Overdoses of PCP shut down the respiratory system, causing death. Clearly, PCP is an extremely dangerous drug.

The specific means by which PCP affects the nervous system are not well understood. However, the drug does seem to increase the activity of dopamine, serotonin, and norepinephrine neurons in the brain. PCP also has been found to bind with opiate receptors located in the areas of the brain involved with motivation and emotion (Zukin & Zukin, 1983).

Marijuana. Marijuana is a natural substance found in *cannabis sativa,* a hemp plant that can be grown in both temperate and tropical climates. The active chemical in marijuana is THC (Δ^9-tetrahydrocannabinol), which is found in its greatest concentrations in the resin derived from the flowers and leaves of the female plant. Marijuana is usually smoked but also may be eaten.

In the early parts of this century, marijuana was used primarily by people of lower socioeconomic status and by members of certain subcultures, particularly avant garde artists and musicians living in metropolitan areas. Until the late 1950s, marijuana was portrayed as a sinister drug that transformed its users into heroin addicts and/or aggressive and insane criminals. Then in the 1960s and 1970s, perhaps because of the changing social and political climate in the United States, marijuana became a popular recreational drug. Marijuana use peaked in the late 1970s and has been declining steadily ever since.

Marijuana produces different psychological effects in its users depending upon the dosage consumed. At low doses, its effects resemble those of the depressant drugs, producing sedativelike effects. At moderate to high doses, the sedative effects of the drug are intensified and involve distortions in sensation, perception, and emotion. At extremely high doses, the effects of the drug resemble those of the psychedelics, inducing hallucinations, increased sensory perception, paranoia, confusion, delusions, and euphoria.

Although the pharmacological and physiological effects have been studied intensively with both animal and human subjects, little is known about the precise manner in which THC affects the central nervous system. We know that THC causes increases in blood pressure and pulse rate, decreases body temperature, slows reflexes, and impairs memory. However, precisely how THC affects the neurotransmitter systems involved with these bodily functions remains to be discovered. Although occasional use of marijuana does not lead to tolerance or physical dependence to THC, prolonged use of high doses does. Withdrawal symptoms include trembling, chills, agitation, weight loss, and insomnia.

Perhaps the greatest concerns that our society has expressed about the long-term effects of chronic marijuana use are the decreased motivation levels induced by the drug and the potential for brain damage. To date, however, researchers have not been able to discover any permanent, irreversible brain damage caused by chronic use of marijuana (Jaffe, 1985). It is true, though, that repeated use of the drug over long periods of time may contribute to what has become known as the amotivational syndrome, a pattern of behavior characterized by lack of ambition, apathy, and emotional and intellectual dullness. This problem is particularly distressing because many teenagers regularly use marijuana during a period of their lives when they are learning coping, goal setting, and social skills and making decisions that will affect the rest of their lives. Most researchers believe, however, that marijuana is not the only factor involved in the amotivational syndrome among young people. Some teenagers who use marijuana may show signs characteristic of the syndrome before ever using the drug; personal experiences common to adolescence such as stress and peer pressure may also contribute to the syndrome (Cohen, 1981; Jaffe, 1985).

Narcotics. **Narcotics** include the opiates, opium and morphine, which are naturally occurring substances derived from the opium poppy. Heroin, another very well known opiate, is not a natural derivative of the poppy plant; rather it is synthesized by chemically modifying morphine. (The chemist who first produced aspirin was the same person who first synthesized heroin.) This modification process produces a drug that is about three times as powerful as the original substance. Stimulation of neurons containing opiate receptors produces analgesia, or the reduction of pain; therefore, morphine and other opiates are widely used as painkillers. In fact, few other compounds are as effective analgesics as the opiates. Narcotics also produce significant, and often intensely pleasurable, elevations in mood, which accounts for their widespread recreational use. Although heroin is the most widely used narcotic among opiate addicts, its effects on the nervous system are similar to those of morphine because the brain converts heroin into a chemical structure nearly identical to that of morphine. Morphine is perhaps the best understood of the opiate drugs, and so we shall focus on this drug in our discussion of the biological and psychological effects of narcotics.

Morphine and the other opiates resemble the enkephalins in their chemical structure and, as mentioned earlier, have a special affinity for receptor sites normally occupied by these "naturally occurring opiates." The pain killing effects of morphine are caused by morphine binding to receptor sites in pathways in the brain and spinal cord that transmit sensory information about painful stimulation. Interestingly, morphine does not appear to impair nerve impulses of afferent neurons laden with information about pain; instead, morphine simply dulls the individual's perception or awareness of the pain.

The effects of consuming morphine and depressants are additive and in some cases, fatal. For example, a person who ingests morphine and later consumes several alcoholic drinks or takes a sleeping pill will experience lower respiration, possibly leading to coma and death. Accidental deaths following this scenario are not uncommon.

By itself, morphine is a potent suppressor of respiration. It does so by binding with opiate receptors in the brain that regulate breathing. At very high doses, morphine can inhibit breathing completely, causing death. Lesser side effects of chronic morphine use include nausea, vomiting, and drowsiness. For habitual users, morphine-induced euphoria seems to far outweigh these negative side effects, leading them to become psychologically dependent upon the drug.

Tolerance to the euphoric properties of morphine varies with both dose and frequency of use. When the drug is used infrequently and in low to moderate doses, tolerance usually does not develop. However, with regular use, tolerance develops rapidly, causing the user to sometimes ingest large quantities of the drug for the desired effect. When tolerance develops to one opiate, cross-tolerance develops to the other opiates. For example, if a person develops tolerance to morphine, he or she will also develop a tolerance to other opiates such as codeine and heroin.

With regular use of morphine also comes physical dependence. (Recall that physical dependence means that neurons are dependent upon a drug or other chemical to maintain their day-to-day functioning.) Abrupt withdrawal of the drug produces a variety of unpleasant and sometimes dramatic physical consequences including bodily aches and pains, fever, chills, retching and vomiting, cramping, diarrhea, and increased respiration. The severity of these symptoms depends upon the length of time the drug has been used as well as the dosage and frequency of use.

The personal consequences of becoming addicted to morphine or heroin, like any other drug, are both profound and sad. Tolerance to morphine demands that the individual use larger and larger doses of the drug to avoid withdrawal symptoms and to maintain a desired level of euphoria. As tolerance levels rise so does the cost of supporting a narcotics habit, which in the case of heroin, can cost from $100 to $500 a day. Most addicts, many of whom are only adolescents, do not have the kind of income that can easily accommodate such a habit; many resort to criminal activities to foot the bill. Even for wealthy people, tolerance and physical dependence demands changes in work habits, social patterns, and life-style, to keep their habit secret from friends, business associates, and law enforcement officials.

Once more, we see that drugs, simply by the way they affect our nervous system and thereby alter our conscious perception of the world, can exert powerful and dramatic control over behavior.

Heroin addicts are often treated with methadone, an addictive drug that can be prescribed legally. Methadone, like heroin, stimulates the brain's opiate receptors, thereby satisfying the addict's physical craving for the drug without producing the euphoria. Over time, the addict is gradually weaned from the drug, reducing the likelihood of withdrawal symptoms even further. Because methadone is both legal and less expensive than heroin, addicts are not forced to resort to crime to finance their addiction. Although methadone therapy has helped many heroin addicts "kick the habit," it is not a guaranteed cure. Probably because they enjoy the psychological high that heroin produces, some addicts take heroin in between methadone treatments; others abandon therapy completely and return to using heroin.

THE ENDOCRINE SYSTEM

The nervous system transmits its electrochemical messages with dazzling speed. Physical stimulation of a receptor—a pain receptor in the toe, for example—produces nerve impulses that are transmitted to the CNS which, in turn, transmits its own chemical message to the muscles in the leg, foot, and toe, causing them to react to the pain, all in less than a second. Our bodies also possess a slower acting communication network, the **endocrine system**, which is composed of endocrine glands. These glands stimulate other glands, muscles, and organs via **hormones**, chemical substances that they secrete directly into the bloodstream (see Figure 4.11). Once secreted into the bloodstream, a hormone travels through the body until it reaches its target cell. Special receptors in the target cell recognize only the hormone molecules designated to act on that cell. These receptors retrieve the hormone molecules from the bloodstream and transport them into the cell.

The pituitary gland, sometimes referred to as the "master gland" because it appears to control the secretory processes of the other endocrine glands, is a small pea-shaped structure located at the base of the brain that secretes a number of different kinds of hormones. Hormones released by this gland are involved in a number of important physiological processes including body growth, production of ova in females, and production of sperm in males. In stressful situations, neurons in the sympathetic nervous system stimulate specific endocrine glands to secrete hormones that increase or decrease heart rate, respiration, and sweating.

A *slower acting communication network is the endocrine system . . .*

Other important endocrine glands include the thyroid gland, the adrenal glands, and the sex glands. The thyroid gland is located in the neck on both sides of the throat and secretes thyroxin, a hormone that plays a critical role in regulating metabolism. If too little thyroxin is secreted, metabolism is slowed down, a condition known as hypothyroidism. People with this disorder generally suffer from obesity, and reduced heart rate, body temperature, and perspiration. Common complaints include a lack of energy and feeling rundown. When the thyroid secretes too much thyroxin, a disorder known as hyperthyroidism occurs. Symptoms of hyperthyroidism include weight loss, and elevated levels of body temperature, perspiration, heart rate, and arousal.

The adrenals are glands situated just above the kidneys. Each adrenal gland is divided into two sections, an inner region called the adrenal medulla and an outer region known as the adrenal cortex. The adrenal

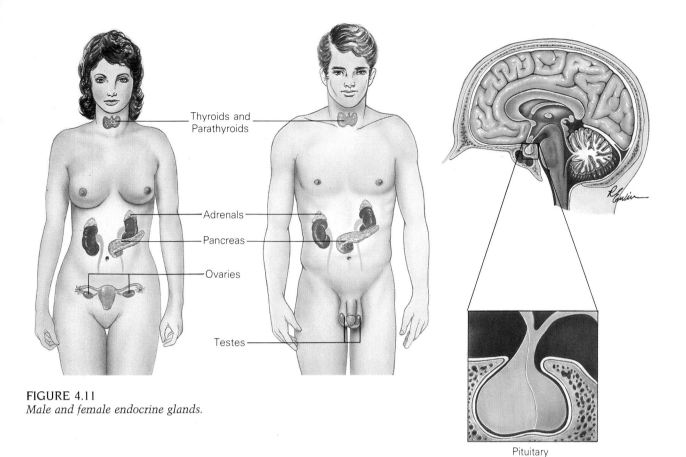

Thyroids and Parathyroids

Adrenals

Pancreas

Ovaries

Testes

Pituitary

FIGURE 4.11
Male and female endocrine glands.

medulla secretes adrenalin, which, as you probably know, plays a key role in the body's ability to deal with stress. Under conditions of high stress, such as might occur when you are threatened with physical danger, your adrenal medulla kicks in and secretes adrenalin into your bloodstream. In turn, elevated levels of adrenalin cause respiration, heart rate, and blood pressure to increase, extra glucose (sugar) to be released into the bloodstream, and an increase in blood flow to the skeletal muscles. These physiological activities permit us to run faster, jump higher, and, in general, to be stronger physically, than under everyday conditions.

The adrenal cortex produces a number of hormones that appear to control blood sugar levels as well as the supply of water and minerals to different parts of the body. Androgens, sometimes referred to as the male hormones, are also secreted by the adrenal cortex. These hormones function chiefly to stimulate changes in the voice, growth of muscle, and the growth of facial and chest hair.

The sex glands, the ovaries in women and the gonads in males, secrete hormones that also stimulate sexual development and differentiation. We will discuss the role of these glands in greater detail in Chapter 12, Gender Development and Sexual Behavior.

Despite the large difference in speed of communication, the nervous system and endocrine systems share an important characteristic: they both relay chemical messages between the cells and structures of the body. Neurotransmitters from one neuron excite or inhibit adjacent neurons; hormones from endocrine glands influence certain target organs. In fact, some chemical substances, for example norepinephrine, act as both neurotransmitters and hormones, depending upon the type of cell from which they are secreted.

THE BRAIN

Our discussion of biopsychology thus far leaves us with one inescapable conclusion: our conscious experiences of the world—seeing, hearing, thinking, and remembering—are embedded in our nervous systems. A little over a century ago, one of the most hotly debated topics among physiologists was whether or not these kinds of conscious experiences were controlled by specific areas of the brain. The debate inspired a long line of research that has yet to come to an end. One of the most important results of this research is the finding that neurons in the brain are organized into highly specialized units called nuclei, each of which do appear to play critical roles in controlling different kinds of behavior. Some nuclei regulate sleep and arousal, others are involved in eating and thirst, memory, aggression, or sexual behavior, to name just a few. Specifically, how are such behaviors controlled by the brain and by which parts? That is the main question we will address in the remainder of the chapter. However, first let's see how neuroscientists study the brain and its relation to behavior.

Studying the Brain

Looking at the brain's exterior with the naked eye, we would not be able to tell much about its organization or function, since with only a few exceptions, one part of its surface looks pretty much like any other part. Actually, this three pound mass of wrinkled gray tissue looks rather like an oversized walnut. Opening the brain by simply splitting it in half down the middle would provide us with a better, although still rough, idea of the brain's overall structure. We would first be struck by the brain's symmetry, that is, both halves of the brain appear identical. Looking closely at either half, we would see that the large wrinkled section surrounds several smaller odd-shaped structures (see Figure 4.12). Beyond this point, however, we would be hard pressed to describe further the brain's organization. We must rely on the sophisticated research methods of the neuroscientist to supply the details overlooked by the naked eye.

The first modern attempts at studying the brain were not very sophisticated. Soon after the turn of the nineteenth century, a Viennese physician named Franz Gall (1758–1828) speculated that different regions of the brain had different functions. Recalling that a number of his boyhood friends who had very good memories also had protruding eyes, Gall reasoned that the front of the brain must be involved in memory, for what

FIGURE 4.12
The human brain. The two hemispheres of the brain appear symmetrical to the naked eye.

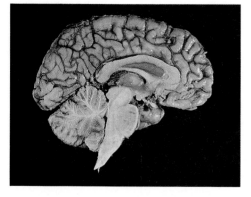

Top and side views of the brain.

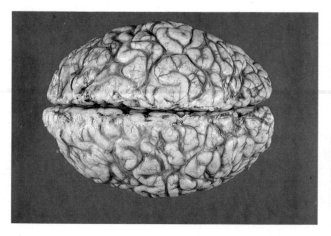
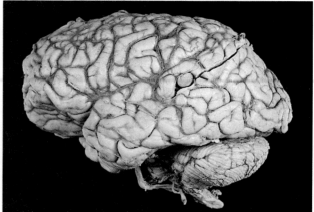

FIGURE 4.13
A phrenological map of the functions of the human brain. According to phrenologists, the shape of an individual's skull revealed his or her special talents and abilities. Although incorrect, phrenology stimulated interest in the relationship between the brain and behavior.

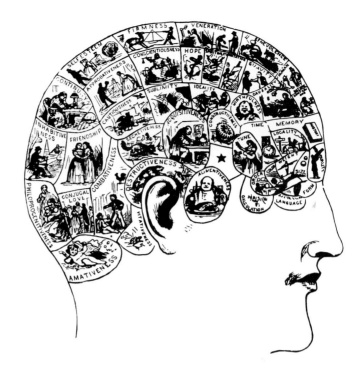

else, but an overdevelopment of this part of the brain could cause the eyes to bulge so? This logic soon led him to the compelling conclusion that other irregularities in the head's shape must be representative of other abilities. In a short time, Gall and his students proceeded to map the brain and its functions by "reading" the bumps on people's heads, a procedure they called phrenology (see Figure 4.13). Although phrenology became something of a fad in both Europe and the United States, scientists soon realized that the geography of the head had little to do with the brain's role in regulating behavior and cognitive processes. Nonetheless, Gall's emphasis on phrenology and his belief that certain abilities are localized in specific brain regions stimulated other researchers to continue their study of brain function. A logical way to proceed was to study the effects of brain damage and injury on behavior.

Brain Damage and Injury. In truth, people had been observing the effects of brain disease and damage on behavior long before Gall hatched the idea of phrenology. However, it has been only since about the time of Gall's work that people started to document carefully those effects. A classic example is found in the work of Paul Broca (1824–1880), the great nineteenth century French neurosurgeon who, among other things, studied individuals who had lost the ability to speak. His first patient, a man named "Tan" (so named because that was the only word he could speak) died of an infection shortly after coming under Broca's care. Broca's autopsy of Tan revealed severe damage to the front left part of the brain. Over the next few years Broca examined eight more patients with speech disorders and found damage to the front part of the brain in each case.

Broca's strategy in studying brain function was to work backwards. He started with the result, in this case, a speech deficit, and from there searched for irregularities in brain structures that might be associated with the disorder. Broca's discovery of the "speech center" soon prompted other researchers to study the nervous systems of individuals with injured or damaged brains. Their studies have uncovered much of what we know today about the relationship between brain structures and their functions.

TABLE 4.2. *Nervous system disorders.*

NAME	SYMPTOMS	NEURONAL BASES	TREATMENT	OTHER INFORMATION
Alzheimer's disease	Memory and cognitive impairment; massive mental deterioration	Deterioration of neurons secreting acetylcholine in the hippocampus	None	Possibly genetically based; can lead to death
Huntington's chorea	Progressive mental deterioration beginning in a person's 30s or 40s; loss of control of movement	Degeneration of GABA neurons in brain region controlling movement	None	Definitely genetically based
Parkinson's disease	Progressive mental deterioration; eventual total loss of control over initiating and sustaining movement	Degeneration of neurons secreting dopamine in deep brain region	L-dopa, a substance the brain converts to dopamine; fetal cells	L-dopa only retards the disease and does not cure it. A person suffering from Parkinson's disease eventually dies
Schizophrenia	Disturbance of thought, attention, perception, emotions, and behavior	Overproduction of dopamine	Chlorpromize; psychotherapy	Over reduction of dopamine produces Parkinson-like symptoms
Multiple sclerosis	Progressive deterioration of cognitive function from ages 20–30 onward; loss of muscular control; sensory deficit	Destruction of myelin sheath surrounding axons in brain	None	Myelin sheaths are destroyed by body's own immune system

A variety of brain disorders, most of which are lethal, can be traced to malfunctions in synaptic transmission in the brain. These malfunctions produce profound behavioral changes in individuals suffering from them, including loss of memory and motor control, and disorganized and confused thinking. By carefully studying these disorders, neuroscientists, neurosurgeons, and other brain researchers have provided valuable insight into the symptoms, neuronal basis, and, in some cases, successful treatment approaches. Table 4.2 summarizes these findings for several brain disorders.

Lesions. Studying and understanding the effects of brain damage that result from accident, injury, or disease is difficult because the researcher cannot detect the extent or location of the damage. To sidestep this problem, modern neuroscientists may intentionally **lesion**, or cut, specific parts of the brain in nonhuman subjects. Lesions may be produced with pinpoint accuracy by surgically removing or severing brain tissue and by chemically or electrically destroying brain tissue. Lesioning research has been important in identifying brain regions involved with eating, drinking, and with emotional and aggressive behavior.

Producing lesions in the brain is not only a useful means for discovering how the brain works, but it is also effective for treating certain brain disorders. Consider for example, how neurosurgeons sometimes treat severe cases of epilepsy, a brain disorder characterized by seizures. They sever the neurons that connect the two sides of the brain, thus preventing the spread of seizure-producing neural activity from one side of the brain to the other.

Electrical Recording and Stimulation. As you will recall, neurons are sensitive to electrically charged chemical particles (ions) that trigger the release of neurotransmitters. This means that brain activities are partially electrical in nature. Neuroscientists have discovered that they can monitor the electrical activity of the brain in two ways. First, by inserting very small ultrasensitive recording electrodes into the brain, neuroscientists can detect minute electrical changes within a single neuron. This procedure, referred to as single unit recording, was the means by which our understanding of the nerve impulse and synaptic transmission was derived. These electrodes are so sensitive to changes in a neuron's electrical potential that it is possible in some cases to trace the flow of information through the brain triggered by a flash of light, a sound, or a stimulus applied to the skin.

Second, neuroscientists use the electroencephalograph to detect larger patterns of electrical activity, particularly patterns present on the brain's surface. The electroencephalograph works by attaching large, round electrodes to an individual's scalp. These electrodes feed information about the brain's electrical activity into the electroencephalograph which, in turn, produces an **electroencephalogram** or **EEG,** an amplified tracing of the brain's electrical activity. The EEG is useful in helping neuroscientists study gross electrical changes in the brain while a person is asleep or aroused. The EEG in Figure 4.14 shows the difference in the electrical activity of the brain during different kinds of arousal. EEGs are also useful to physicians in the diagnosis of disorders such as epilepsy. By recording the electrical activity in specific brain regions, doctors are able to locate the source of epileptic seizures and study the disorder's spread to other parts of the brain, allowing them to plan surgical interventions more efficiently.

Neuroscientists not only have the technical sophistication to record the electrical activity of the brain, but they also can electrically stimulate specific regions of the brain to study how such stimulation affects behavior and mental processes. Electrical stimulation involves implanting an electrode, in this case a very fine wire through which mild electric current can be passed in the brain, to alter the electrical activity of small regions of the

The electroencephalograph, or EEG, is a device that measures the electrical activity of the brain.

FIGURE 4.14
EEG patterns during different stages of arousal in humans.

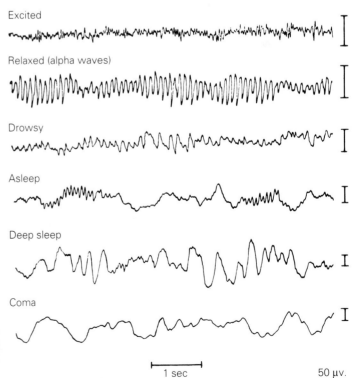

brain. In essence, electrical stimulation of the brain can be used to simulate the way in which the brain's own electrical activities might affect behavior. Neuroscientists today use electrical stimulation to study numerous kinds of cognitive activities and behavior including memory, eating, drinking, sleeping, aggression, and emotional arousal.

Brain Scans. Without a doubt the most exciting recent technological breakthrough in studying the brain is the invention of computer driven devices that scan the brain. For example, the CAT (computed axial tomography) scan takes X-ray photographs of the brain structures from a number of different angles. The photographs are then fed into a computer where they are integrated into three-dimensional representations of the brain from which specific structures can be examined for damage (see Figure 4.15a).

More recently, scientists have developed two other kinds of brain scanners. The PET (positron-emission tomography) scan monitors the functions and activities of different regions of the brain, tracing each region's consumption of glucose, a sugar that is the brain's main energy source. The more active the region, the more glucose consumed. The PET scan procedure involves two steps. First, a radioactive form of glucose is injected into the brain. The PET scanner is then used to locate and measure the distribution of the radioactive glucose in the brain. Depending upon the activity in which a person is engaging—singing, sewing, reading, and so on—the image of the brain on the computer monitor will "glow" in different areas. This indicates which part of the brain is active during a particular activity. On the other hand, damaged areas, such as those affected by a stroke or epilepsy appear dully illuminated. Dead areas show up as very dark patches (see Figure 4.15b).

MRI (magnetic resonance imaging) involves placing the person to be examined into a strong magnetic field. The magnetic field causes the atoms in each part of the brain to vibrate. Specially designed radio receivers controlled by computers detect the vibrations and allow researchers to diagram the brain. The atoms of the various brain structures are affected by the MRI differentially, allowing researchers to discriminate between brain structures as well as between healthy and damaged tissue (see Figure 4.15c).

Technological advances such as single unit recording and brain scanning have allowed us to uncover many of the secrets of the brain's role in regulating our behavior and mental processes. Within the span of 150 years, researchers have gone from reading bumps on the head to observing the electrical activity of single neurons to producing three-dimensional photographs of living brain tissue. It seems very likely that within our lifetime we will progress even further in our understanding of the brain and its relation to behavior. But before we get too far ahead of ourselves, let's discuss what we already know about this relationship.

Structures and Functions of the Brain

The key to understanding the structure of the brain is understanding that the brain is the result of many millions of years of evolution. By examining the brains of rats, chimpanzees, and finally humans, a particular pattern emerges. What has happened is that the more advanced brains have parts of the more primitive brains embedded within them. Apparently, new brain structures have not replaced the more primitive structures, but rather have supplemented them. The original structures have remained basically intact but are now surrounded by new ones. For example, our brains have the added capability for abstract thinking, but the brain structures that

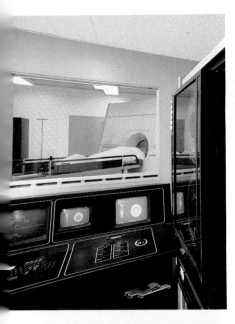

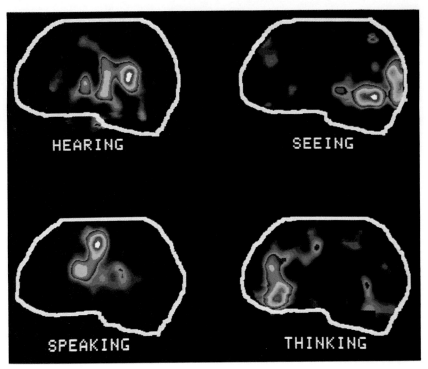

HEARING

SEEING

SPEAKING

THINKING

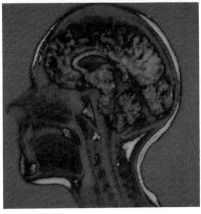

FIGURE 4.15
Computer brain scanning devices like the CAT scan (top left), PET scan (right), and MRI (bottom left), have allowed researchers to examine the brain's structure and study how the brain affects human behavior and mental processes.

control the more fundamental processes such as respiration and emotion were well developed before humans evolved and even before mammals walked the face of the earth.

Before discussing the brain's major structures and their functions, a caveat is in order. It would be very easy to discuss the brain as if each of its structures were separate and distinct entities that serve as independent centers for certain types of actions such as aggression, emotion, eating, drinking, and so on. Nothing could be further from the truth, however. The brain, if nothing else, is an incredibly intricate network of neurons linking the structures in one region to those in another and thus far, biopsychological research has not shown any one brain structure to have complete and total control over any given behavior. Rather, each structure in the brain is merely an important component in a larger and integrated system. With that in mind, let's look at the three major sections of the brain: the central core, the limbic system, and the cerebral cortex (see Figure 4.16).

The Central Core. From an evolutionary perspective, the **central core** is the oldest part of the human brain. The central core forms most of the brain stem, the point where the spinal cord enters the skull, thus linking the brain's higher regions with the major neural pathways of the body. It is comprised of the medulla, pons, cerebellum, thalamus, and the reticular formation (see Figure 4.17). The **medulla** is positioned at the very bottom of the brain and is actually an enlargement of the top of the spinal cord. The medulla is involved with the control of autonomic processes such as breathing, swallowing, digestion, and heartbeat. An injury to the medulla can disrupt, sometimes fatally, these basic life processes. The medulla also marks the spot where axons ascending from the spinal cord and descending from the brain cross over so that the right side of the brain is connected to the left side of the body and the left side of the brain is connected to the right side of the body. This crossing over of nerve fibers plays an important role in brain functioning, as we shall see later.

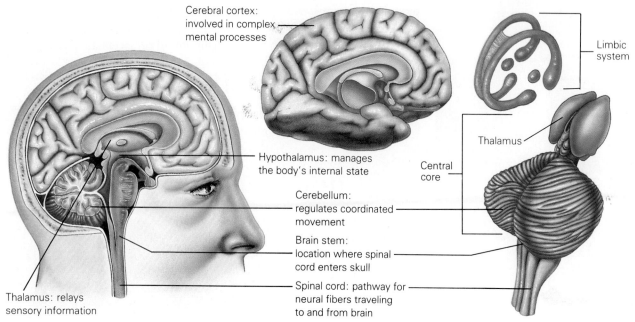

Cerebral cortex: involved in complex mental processes

Limbic system

Hypothalamus: manages the body's internal state

Thalamus

Central core

Cerebellum: regulates coordinated movement

Brain stem: location where spinal cord enters skull

Spinal cord: pathway for neural fibers traveling to and from brain

Thalamus: relays sensory information

FIGURE 4.16
The central core, limbic system, and cerebral cortex are the three major divisions of the brain.

Atop the medulla is a structure called the **pons**, which is involved with arousal and dreaming. The pons actually coordinates incoming sensory signals from the spinal cord and face, directing them to the proper area of the brain, and in turn, directs motor signals from the brain to the body. Directly behind and slightly above the medulla is a small wrinkled structure known as the **cerebellum**. To many researchers, the cerebellum looks like a miniature brain. In fact, cerebellum means "little brain." The cerebellum's chief function is to regulate coordinated movement. Higher regions of the brain may initiate movements but their smooth execution is largely engineered by the cerebellum. A person who receives a blow to the back of the head and suffers damage to the cerebellum as a result, has difficulty executing even the simplest of movements. Behavior that was once effortless and smooth becomes rigid and jerky, requiring intense concentration to complete.

Directly above the pons and medulla at the exact center of the brain are a pair of egg-shaped structures called the **thalamus**. Incoming sensory information involving vision, audition (hearing), taste, and touch is channeled to the thalamus, where it is then relayed to higher regions (the cortex) of the brain. The thalamus also mediates some of the brain's messages to the body, routing them through the cerebellum and medulla. Damage to the thalamus hinders the smooth relaying of information from brain to the body and vice versa.

Within the brainstem lies a diffuse, interconnected network of neurons referred to as the **reticular formation**. This fingerlike structure extends from the lower tip of the medulla through the thalamus, and plays a role in sleep and arousal. Electrically stimulating the reticular formation will cause a sleeping animal (cat or dog) to wake up and an otherwise alert animal to fall asleep. Massive damage to the reticular formation can cause the animal to fall into a coma from which it will never awake. Together with the cerebral cortex, the reticular formation also plays a role in attention. Your ability to focus attention on this sentence without being distracted by events occurring around you (the distant sound of a TV, radio, or someone's voice) is due partially to your reticular formation's ability to filter out certain sensory information from your conscious awareness.

The Limbic System. Enveloping the central core is the **limbic system**, a group of structures involved primarily with motivation, emotion, and memory. Although the central core is present in all vertebrate animals, the limbic system is only fully developed in mammals. Reptiles, for instance, do not have well developed limbic systems. The limbic system thus appears to have evolved more recently than the central core. The components of the limbic system include the amygdala, the hypothalamus, and the hippocampus (see Figure 4.18).

The **amygdala**, two roundish structures located in the center of the brain, is involved in the control of aggressive behavior. In the late 1930s two researchers, Heinrich Kluver and Paul Bucy, discovered that lesioning the amygdala produces sedative effects—otherwise ill-natured and fearless rhesus monkeys were transformed into agreeable and tranquil creatures. Just as amazing were Wood's (1956) results: wild rats trapped in Baltimore sewers were tame enough to be carried around in the experimenter's shirt pocket after destruction of their amygdalas.

Other studies, however, showed that destruction of the amygdala can have serious side effects. Schreiner and Kling (1953) lesioned the amygdala of a cat and later observed deviations in normal feline sexual behavior. The cat attempted to mate with a dog in one situation and a chicken in another. Kling (1972) later examined the effects of lesioning the amygdala on the behavior of monkeys living in the wild. He trapped several monkeys and performed a lesion on some of them. The remainder of the monkeys served as the control group and received a "sham" treatment—experiencing the same general treatment as the other captured monkeys (capture, anesthesia, surgery, recovery) except for the destruction of their amygdalas. When released back into the wild, the control animals soon resumed normal activities within their troops. The monkeys with lesioned amygdalas fared worse. They were unable to understand other monkeys' social signals. In

FIGURE 4.17
The primary structures of the central core, the group of brain structures involved basically with autonomic functions such as respiration, arousal, heartbeat, balance, and so on.

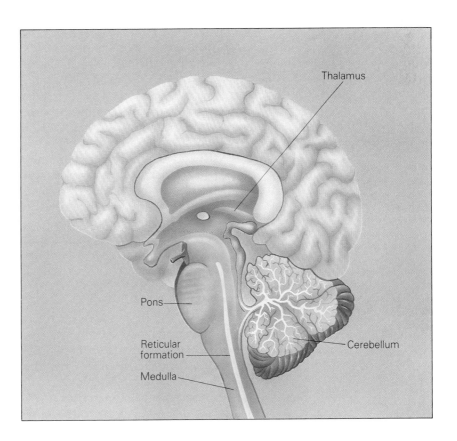

FIGURE 4.18
The primary structures of the limbic system, the group of brain structures involved in motivated behavior and emotion.

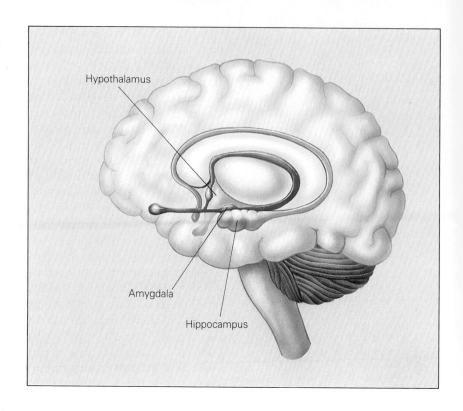

some cases, a potential mate would show sexual interest in them, only to have the offer spurned. In other cases, they would fail to show submissive gestures to the dominant monkey which, of course, resulted in vicious and bloody fights. Thus, in addition to its involvement with controlling aggressive behavior, the amygdala may also be involved in the understanding of and response to social signals.

The **hypothalamus** is a very small structure that lies below (hypo) the thalamus. Despite its size, the hypothalamus plays a critical role in regulating bodily processes. Hunger, thirst, body temperature, and sexual arousal are each regulated by different parts of the hypothalamus. Destruction of the hypothalamus interferes with the brain's ability to regulate these processes. The hypothalamus also monitors and controls the activity of the pituitary gland which, in turn, regulates the hormonal secretions of the endocrine system. In short, the primary function of the hypothalamus is to maintain a balanced internal state. The hypothalamus is sensitive to even minor deviations in normal bodily processes. When it detects an imbalance, for example if we are too hot or too cold, it initiates a series of events that attempts to restore internal equilibrium: when we are too hot, signals from the hypothalamus cause us to perspire, and when we are too cool, signals from the hypothalamus cause our blood vessels to constrict and our bodies to shiver.

Researchers have discovered that mild electrical stimulation of a particular region of the hypothalamus is highly pleasurable to some animals. Actually this discovery was something of an accident. In 1954, two young researchers at McGill University in Montreal, James Olds and Peter Milner, implanted electrodes into what they thought was the reticular formation of a rat. Their objective was to study the effects of electrical stimulation on learning. With the electrode embedded firmly in the rat's skull, Olds and Milner let the rat roam free in a large table top enclosure. Every time the rat entered a particular corner of the enclosure, they stimulated it, expecting that it would soon learn to avoid that corner (they had assumed that the stimulation would be unpleasant, leading the rat to avoid the corner with which the electrical stimulation was associated). Much to their surprise, the rat kept returning to the same corner! An autopsy of the rat revealed that Olds and Milner had implanted the electrode in the septal region of the limbic system and not the reticular formation.

Their curiosity piqued, Olds and Milner next carefully designed a series of experiments that allowed rats to stimulate (electrically) themselves on demand. They placed rats who had electrodes implanted in the septal region in small chambers containing only one lever. By pressing the lever, each rat could stimulate itself with a brief jolt of electrical current (see Figure 4.19). The rats soon learned to press the bar at a blistering pace of 6,000 to 7,000 times per hour! Further experiments revealed that rats would go without food and water for the opportunity to obtain electrical stimulation; hungry rats would even cross an electrified grid floor to obtain electrical stimulation but not to obtain food (Olds, 1958).

FIGURE 4.19
Studies by Olds and Milner have shown that electrical stimulation of certain areas of the brain in rats produces pleasure and can be reinforcing.

While researchers agree that the hypothalamus plays an important role in mediating pleasure, they also agree that other structures are also involved. The hypothalamus is linked to several other limbic system structures that, when electrically stimulated, also produce pleasurable consequences (Olds & Forbes, 1981). Thus, it is perhaps more accurate to describe the hypothalamus as a vital link in a chain of structures that mediate pleasure as well as other processes. We will learn in Chapter 10, Motivation and Emotion, that although the hypothalamus plays an important role in regulating hunger, other factors are also critically involved.

Do humans find electrical stimulation of the hypothalamus as pleasurable as the rats in Olds and Milner's experiments? Apparently not, for most humans report that while the stimulation is mildly pleasant, they are not willing to work as hard as rats to initiate it. Nonetheless, Olds and Milner's research gives us good reason to speculate that somewhere in the human brain there may be a network of structures that together play a central role in the mediation of pleasure.

The largest structure in the limbic system, the **hippocampus**, plays a crucial role in memory. Damage to the hippocampus results in anterograde amnesia, the inability to remember new information. But there is an interesting twist to this finding. Researchers have shown that people with damage to the hippocampus can still learn new skills and information, they simply don't remember having learned it. For example, in one study, subjects with anterograde amnesia were trained to read words reflected in a mirror (Cohen & Squire, 1980). Over a three-day period, the subjects showed improvement in the task, a surprising result given the fact that some of Cohen and Squire's subjects could not recall their previous day's experience with the task! Such findings have led both Cohen (1984) and Squire (1982) to suggest that the hippocampus is important not for remembering how to execute a response but, instead for recalling that it has, in fact, been executed. The role of the hippocampus in memory will be discussed in greater detail in Chapter 8.

The Cerebral Cortex. We often tout our intelligence as being superior to that of animals, and it is often said that the ability to manipulate symbols or use language is a distinctively human quality. Roughly speaking, other animals eat, drink, sleep, reproduce, fight, and flee from danger in a manner similar to humans. But when it comes to problem solving, planning for future events, making decisions, and reasoning abstractly, we stand apart from the other creatures on the planet.

The biological reason for our humanness lies within the cerebral cortex . . .

The biological reason for our humanness lies within the **cerebral cortex**, the large, convoluted mass of brain tissue located just beneath the skull. This structure, which is the most recent achievement of brain evolution, is involved in complex mental processes such as reasoning and decision making. As we compare the brains of animals capable of increasingly complex behavior, we note two very important differences (see Figure 4.20). First, the amount of cortex relative to the central core and the limbic system is greater in animals capable of more complex behavior. Second, the cortex becomes increasingly wrinkled in these animals. For example, the cerebral cortex of the cat is small and relatively smooth while the cerebral cortex of a human is large and wrinkled. The wrinkles or convolutions of the cerebral cortex provide more surface area than would a smooth covering over the cortex. Other than the cerebral cortex, the rest of our brain is very similar to other mammals, which accounts for why our self-preservation and reproductive behavior may be similar to theirs.

A deep fissure running from front to rear divides the cortex into right and left hemispheres (see Figure 4.21). The hemispheres are roughly symmetrical. In general, each hemisphere receives sensory information from and directs the muscular actions of the opposite side of the body. The left hemisphere controls spontaneous speaking and writing, and memory of numbers and words; it coordinates complex sequences of movements, and is involved in feelings of anxiety and positive emotions. The right hemisphere is involved with recognition of faces, memory related to shapes and music, and it directs negative emotions and overall emotional responsiveness.

Each hemisphere is divided into four regions or lobes (see Figure 4.21). The frontal lobe is located immediately behind the forehead. The parietal lobe, which is located atop the head about midway back, is separated from the frontal lobe by the central fissure. The temporal lobe is located on either side of the head and is separated from the frontal and parietal lobes by the lateral fissure. The occipital lobe is located at the very back of the head. In our study of the cortex, it will be helpful to keep in mind that each lobe is not a sovereign region that acts independently of the other lobes of the brain. Rather, many higher cognitive processes stem from the complex interaction of neurons located in each lobe.

Neuroscientists have been very successful in mapping out each lobe in terms of its specific functions. That is, different parts of the cortex have been discovered to have distinct functions. Three different functional areas have been mapped: the motor area, the sensory areas, and the association areas.

FIGURE 4.20
An organism higher on the evolutionary ladder, such as a human, has a larger cerebral cortex with more convolutions than an animal lower on the evolutionary ladder.

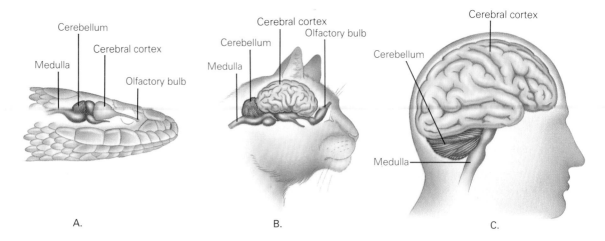

A.

B.

C.

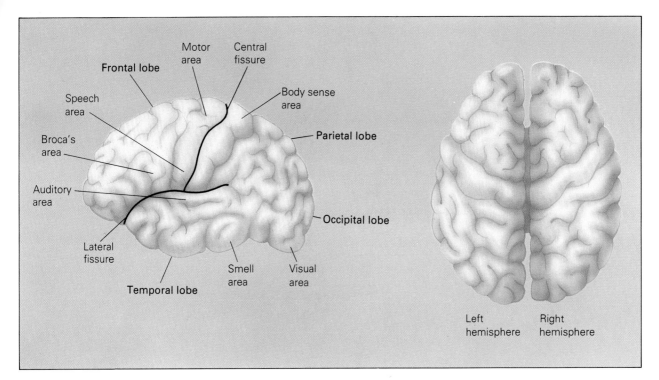

FIGURE 4.21
The cerebral cortex is comprised of two hemispheres, each of which contains four lobes. Each lobe is associated with different sensory or motor functions.

The **motor area** is located in the portion of the frontal lobe closest to the central fissure and is the part of the cortex that controls voluntary movement by sending nerve impulses to the skeletal muscles. The fact that voluntary movements of the body are under direct control of the cortex was discovered by two German physiologists, Gustav Fritsch and Eduard Hitzig (1870), over 100 years ago. While examining the brain of an anesthetized dog, they showed that electrically stimulating a specific region of the cortex (the motor area) resulted in movements in various parts of their subject's body. Fritsch and Hitzig also noted that stimulating the left motor cortex produced movement in the right side of the body and that stimulating the right motor cortex produced movement in the left side of the body. A little more than seventy years later, the Canadian neurosurgeon Wilder Penfield, made similar observations while exploring the brains of human patients suffering from seizures (Penfield, 1975). Penfield's carefully devised and precisely executed explorations revealed that stimulation of specific sections of the motor cortex produced movement in a corresponding body part, with each hemisphere governing movement on the opposite side of the body.

Penfield's work is noteworthy because it revealed that body parts that are involved in finely tuned movement such as the lips, tongue, and fingers are represented in the brain by larger cortical areas than are body parts involved with gross movement such as the shoulder and buttocks (see Figure 4.22a). These findings make good sense, if only because we depend upon our fingers and mouth for so much of our daily activities, particularly in using tools and language. (You might recall from the previous chapter that tool use and language played essential roles in the evolution of our species.)

Each sensory area corresponds to a specific sense: sensory signals from the receptors are routed to different parts of the cortex, depending upon the kind of information they contain. For example, visual information is sent to the occipital lobe and auditory information is sent to the temporal lobes.

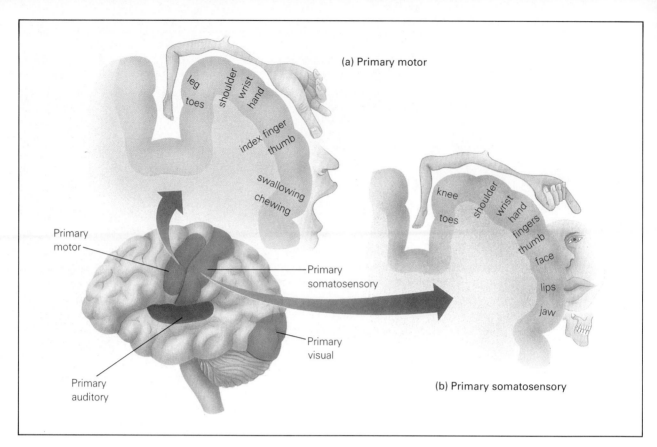

(a) Primary motor

Primary motor

Primary somatosensory

Primary visual

Primary auditory

(b) Primary somatosensory

FIGURE 4.22
The sensitivity of different body regions as represented in the motor and somatosensory areas of the brain. The larger the body part is drawn, the greater its representation in the brain, and consequently, the greater the brain's control over its movement (motor functions) or its sensitivity to environmental stimulation (sensory functions).

What does the cortex do with the sensory information it receives? To answer that question, let's take a close look at the somatosensory areas.

Lying in the parietal lobes, just behind the central fissure is the **somatosensory area**, the portion of the cortex devoted to the sensations of warmth, cold, pain, touch, and bodily movement. Electrical stimulation of this part of the cortex often produces tingling sensations, and to a lesser extent, sensations of warmth, cold and bodily movement in various regions on the *opposite* side of the body depending, of course, upon which hemisphere of the somatosensory area is stimulated. Similar to the motor cortex, the somatosensory cortex represents body parts disproportionately. In this case, the most sensitive areas of the body, for example the lips and fingers, are allotted the greatest amount of cortical space (see Figure 4.22b).

As you are reading this page, nerve impulses from the receptors in each of your eyes are being transmitted to a region in the back of each occipital lobe known as the visual area. Once there, these impulses are translated into the images we see. Figure 4.23 illustrates the neural pathways that link each eye to the visual cortex. Stimuli in the *left* visual field stimulate receptors in the *right* half of each eye; light waves from stimuli in the *right* visual field stimulate receptors in the *left* half of each eye. Nerve impulses leaving the eye travel along the optic nerve to a junction called the optic chiasma, where they are projected to the visual cortex. Notice that neural fibers from the right side of each eye are projected to the right hemisphere and that those from the left side of each eye are projected to the left hemisphere. Damage to the visual area in either occipital lobe produces blind spots in the *opposite* visual field. For example, an injury to the visual area in the right occipital lobe will result in blind spots in the left visual field. Of course, damage to the entire visual cortex often produces complete blindness.

Although the auditory area is located in the temporal lobe of both hemispheres, the parts of it that specialize in the production and comprehension of language are generally found only in the left hemisphere. This is particularly true of right-handed people. For some reason, however, the language abilities of some left-handed people are controlled by the right hemisphere or by both hemispheres.

Our understanding of the function of these language centers is a direct result of two early researchers' search for the biological basis of a disorder called aphasia, which is an impairment of language use. Paul Broca's autopsy of Tan in 1861 revealed damage to an area in the frontal lobe of the left hemisphere now known as **Broca's area** (see Figures 4.24a–b). Broca's area, then, is critical in the production of speech. Recall that Tan had difficulty expressing words—he was only able to utter the word "tan." In 1874, Carl Wernicke, a German physiologist, discovered that damage to a different area in the temporal lobe of the left hemisphere, now referred to as **Wernicke's area**, resulted in a different form of aphasia (see Figures 4.24a–b). In this case, individuals utter strings of words that do not make any sense. For example, when asked to describe a picture of two boys stealing some cookies behind their mother's back, one patient with damage to Wernicke's area replied, "Mother is away here working her work to get her better, but when she's looking the two boys looking in the other part. She's working another time." (Geschwind, 1979, p. 111). People with extensive damage to Wernicke's area cannot use or comprehend meaningful language, even single words.

FIGURE 4.23
The neural pathways for visual information in humans. Light enters the eye and stimulates receptor cells in the retina. From the retina, visual information travels to the thalamus via the optic nerve. From the thalamus, visual information is projected to the visual cortex, which is located in the occipital lobe.

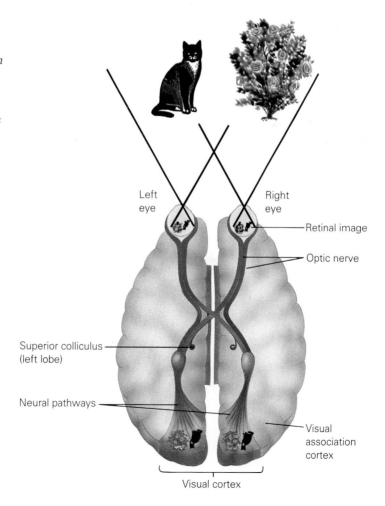

Left eye

Right eye

Retinal image

Optic nerve

Superior colliculus
(left lobe)

Neural pathways

Visual association cortex

Visual cortex

By piecing together Broca's work with his own, Wernicke developed a model of the brain's role in the generation of the spoken word that is still widely accepted today (see Figure 4.24a). The model, which is a prime example of how the interplay of neurons in different areas of the cortex is translated into actual behavior, can be summarized as follows:

1. Speech originates in Wernicke's area. It is here that words are strung into meaningful sentences.
2. The word or sentence is relayed to Broca's area via nerve impulses that travel along nerve fibers linking the two areas.
3. In turn, nerve impulses are transmitted from Broca's area to the section of the motor cortex involved with muscular movements of the face, lips, tongue, and larynx.

More recently, researchers have discovered that a third area of the left hemisphere, the angular gyrus, is also involved with language use, particularly reading aloud. Reading a passage aloud, whether from a billboard or from one of Shakespeare's sonnets, stimulates the visual area of the cortex where the neural impulses of the letters and words are relayed to the angular gyrus. There the nerve impulses are transmitted to Wernicke's area (see Figure 4.24b). From this point on, the sequence of events that lead to actually speaking the passage follows the outlined steps above (Geschwind, 1979).

Only a relatively small portion of the cerebral cortex is devoted to receiving sensory information and initiating motor responses. The remainder of the cortex, the **association areas**, are devoted to the so-called higher cognitive processes of humans, for example, planning, and decision making. Supporting evidence for this point has been derived from two sources. First, a comparison of the human cortex with that of different animals reveals an interesting anatomical difference: as the behavioral complexity of the animal increases, so does the proportion of the cerebral cortex devoted to association areas (see Figure 4.25). Another way of putting it is to say that animals such as the rat have more of their cortex occupied by sensory and motor areas than do more complex animals such as monkeys and humans.

Second, although damage to the association areas in the frontal lobes does not interfere with the ability to solve problems or satisfactorily complete other intellectual tasks, it does disrupt an individual's ability to use language, formulate plans, and make simple judgments. For example, a person with frontal lobe damage may still be able to learn and remember the directions to your house but may lack the ability to make plans to

FIGURE 4.24

Left: The neural events involved in hearing a spoken word and then speaking that word. Neural impulses from the cochlea are channeled to the primary auditory area. In Wernike's area, the acoustical code of the word is deciphered and relayed to Broca's area. Neural impulses from Broca's area are sent to the motor cortex, which stimulates the tongue, lips, and larynx to generate a spoken word. Right: Neural impulses from the retina are sent to the primary visual area and angular gyrus. The angular gyrus compares the visual code for the word with the acoustical code stored in Wernike's area. When the acoustical code is located, the meaning of the word is known. The events involved in speaking the word are then the same as those already described.

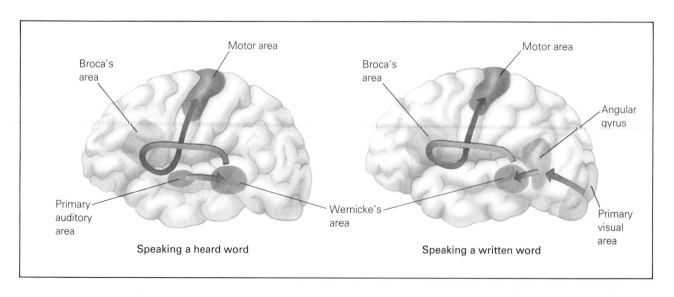

Broca's area · Motor area · Primary auditory area · Speaking a heard word

Broca's area · Motor area · Angular gyrus · Wernicke's area · Primary visual area · Speaking a written word

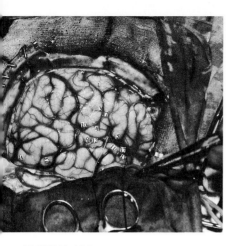

FIGURE 4.25
The exposed cortex of a human patient with association areas labeled.

come visit you sometime. Damage to the association areas in the rear of the brain may impair an individual's ability to recognize or discriminate forms and to locate objects in the environment.

Keep in mind that learning and memory do not seem to be localized in any particular spot in the brain. Rather, learning and memory appear to be the result of the brain's complex neural interplay of its various areas permitting integration of our daily sensory and motor experiences. In a very real sense, learning and memory are not *things* that exist in and of themselves. They cannot be located in the same way that one locates a parked car or a pair of glasses. Indeed, after reflecting upon his lifetime search for the biological seat of learning, the noted neuroscientist Karl Lashley once remarked, "I sometimes feel, in reviewing the evidence for the memory trace, that the necessary conclusion is that learning just is not possible" (Lashley, 1950, pp. 477–478).

THE BRAIN AND CONSCIOUSNESS

Let's summarize what we have learned about the cerebral cortex to this point. We know that:

- The cortex is divided into left and right hemispheres that appear to be mirror images of each other.
- Each hemisphere receives sensory information from, and controls the muscular actions of, the *opposite* side of the body.
- The cortex plays a crucial role in higher mental functions including language use, processing and integration of sensory information, planning, decision making, and reasoning.
- Damage to particular regions of the cortex may impair one or more of these functions.
- The left hemisphere controls both the production and comprehension of speech. Damage to it often results in aphasia, or impaired use or understanding of spoken or written language.

Our summary reveals that, so far, the left hemisphere seems to play a greater role in cognitive activities than does the right hemisphere. We have not learned much about the right hemisphere other than that it seems to control the muscular actions of the left side of the body. What about the right hemisphere? Is it involved with important cognitive functions as is the left hemisphere?

One thing that we do know about the right hemisphere is that damage to it does not seem to catastrophically impair mental functioning like damage to the left hemisphere can. For this reason, the left hemisphere was once considered to be superior to the right hemisphere. In fact, researchers often referred to the left hemisphere as the dominant hemisphere and to its idle twin as the subordinate hemisphere. If, in fact, the left hemisphere shoulders the bulk of the intellectual work load, what is the function of the right hemisphere? And why do we have two hemispheres if one appears to be sufficient?

The Split Brain

Devising and conducting an experiment to test the question of why we have two hemispheres has intrigued researchers as far back as the 1800s when Gustav Fechner first proposed splitting the two hemispheres so that the independent functions of each might be studied. Dividing the brain in two, though, seemed like a wild idea in Fechner's time. Neuroscientist Roger Sperry and his students, driven by the same kind of intellectual

Left: Gustav Fechner. Right: Roger Sperry.

curiosity but armed with the sophisticated surgical technology of the twentieth century, made Fechner's experiment a reality. In 1983, Sperry was awarded the Nobel Prize for his split-brain research. Let's pick up the story in 1961.

That was the year that two brain surgeons, Philip Vogel and Joseph Bogen hypothesized that massive epileptic seizures first started in one hemisphere and then spread to the other hemisphere via the **corpus callosum**, a large bundle of axons that connects the two hemispheres (see Figure 4.26). They reasoned that disconnecting the two hemispheres by severing the corpus callosum might lessen the severity of the seizures by limiting them to only one hemisphere. They tried the procedure, and their reasoning turned out to be correct (Bogen & Vogel, 1962). Not only did the seizures become less severe, they also became less frequent. Moreover, there seemed to be no aftereffects of the surgery. Splitting the brain by cutting the corpus callosum did not appear to disrupt patients' intellectual functioning or alter their personalities.

The opportunity to study the neuropsychological effects of corpus callosum surgery on Vogel and Bogen's patients fell to Sperry who had a long standing interest in lateralization, or the separate functions of each hemisphere. In fact, it was Sperry who pioneered the use of split-brain techniques to study lateralization in nonhuman animals. From his research with cats and monkeys, Sperry knew that split-brain surgery had subtle effects on cognitive functioning. His task with Vogel and Bogen's patients was to develop a series of experiments that would reveal similar effects, if any, in human subjects. Thus, the stage was set for Sperry to develop an ingenious program of research that would, over the course of two decades, uncover several of the brain's best kept secrets (Sperry, 1968, 1982). Let's take a closer look at that research.

One of Sperry's first observations with split-brain subjects gave him a clue that humans, like his animal subjects, were psychologically affected by split-brain surgery. He had instructed patients to close their eyes. Next, he touched a spot on their left arms. He then asked the subjects to point, with their right hand, to the spot on their arm he had touched. His results may surprise you—none of the subjects could carry out his request!

Sperry's next experiments were designed to explain this curious result and were based on his knowledge of lateralization. Consider Sperry's knowledge base. Sperry was well aware of the following: in most people language is controlled by the left hemisphere; the right hemisphere controls muscular movement on the left side of the body, and the left hemisphere similarly controls the right side; and stimulation from the right half of the visual field is received initially only by the left hemisphere. Just the opposite is true for the left half of the visual field—stimulation from it is received initially only by the right hemisphere (review Figure 4.23).

For people with intact brains, information about the stimulation received by the right hemisphere is quickly routed to the left hemisphere via the corpus callosum. Sperry, of course, wanted to know what happens in a patient whose corpus callosum has been severed. He reasoned that by flashing a word or picture into either the patient's right or left visual field, he could examine the different responses of either hemisphere.

In one study, patients stared at a point on a screen situated immediately before them (Gazzaniga, 1967). He then flashed the word "HEART" on the screen such that "HE" was located in the patient's left visual field and "ART" was located in the right visual field. He first asked the patients to say what they saw. The patients replied "ART." He next asked the patients to point with their left hand to the word they had seen. Subjects pointed to "HE." Apparently neither hemisphere had "seen" the same word! How did Sperry explain these results? Examine Figure 4.27. When the word "HEART" was momentarily flashed on the screen, only "ART" was

FIGURE 4.26

The corpus callosum is comprised of millions of axons that connect the right and left hemispheres. In essence, the corpus callosum is a "communication bridge" over which information can be passed between hemispheres. Severing the corpus callosum interrupts permanently the flow of neural information between hemispheres.

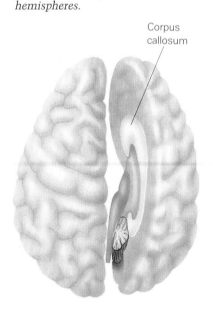

Corpus callosum

FIGURE 4.27

Crossing over of visual information. Visual stimulation from the left visual field strikes the right half of each retina and is projected to the right hemisphere. Visual stimulation from the right visual field strikes the left half of each retina and is projected to the left hemisphere. This information is then integrated by the brain. In Sperry's experiments, severing the corpus callosum interfered with this integration. Although his patients had seen "HE ART" they could only verbally report that they had seen "ART." Why? Because without a corpus callosum, neural information regarding "HE," which was projected to the right hemisphere could not be relayed to the language area of the brain, which is located in the left hemisphere.

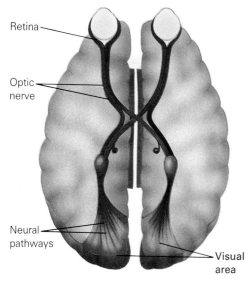

received by the patients' left hemispheres, since that is where information from the right visual field is received by the brain. Because the language area is also located in the left hemisphere, the patients had no difficulty reporting what their left hemisphere had seen. What happened in the patients' right hemispheres is quite different. This hemisphere can neither provide a verbal description nor relay the information (HE) to the left hemisphere. Thus the brain cannot integrate "HE" and "ART" into a single word—"HEART." However, patients are able to point to the word "HE" with their left hands, and so nonverbally report what their right hemisphere saw, because the right hemisphere controls the movement of the left side of the body.

These and other experiments demonstrated that the right hemisphere can interpret and respond to simple verbal requests and plays an important role in the integration of visual information (Sperry, 1982). Other experiments have shown that the right hemisphere is actually superior to the left at spatial relations and recognizing faces. For example, when a drawing is momentarily flashed to both hemispheres, and the patient is asked to copy it twice—once using each hand—the left hand's version (controlled by the right hemisphere) is better than the right hand's version (controlled by the left hemisphere) (see Figure 4.28).

So, as it turns out the right hemisphere is not actually as subordinate to the left hemisphere as neuroscientists once thought. In fact, more recent researchers, stimulated by Sperry's work, have shown that the right hemisphere shoulders cognitive responsibilities that are just as important to our day-to-day functioning as those controlled by the left hemisphere (Springer & Deutsch, 1985). While the left hemisphere is involved with language, analytical, and mathematical abilities, the right hemisphere is involved with symbolic reasoning, spatial abilities, and artistic abilities. Thus, our ability to be amused by a good joke and to repeat the joke later on resides in the left hemisphere, but our ability to solve a mathematical equation or to sketch a house or a horse or anything else resides in our right hemisphere.

We must remember, though, that only split-brain patients have "separate" hemispheres that can function independently of each other. For people with healthy brains, the hemispheres work together to process, integrate, and respond to information supplied to the brain by the senses. That is, our stream of consciousness—our sensation and perception of the world—is a matter of the right and left hemispheres working together. For instance, running into your psychology professor and saying, "Hi," to him or her involves the right hemisphere recognizing that person (identifying and integrating facial features and body characteristics) as your professor and relaying that information via the corpus callosum to Wernicke's area in the left hemisphere where language is initiated.

The cerebral hemispheres are "on duty" 24 hours a day, bustling with electrical activity even while we sleep. However, the nature of the electrical activity changes over the course of each day and is related to our overall level of arousal or how awake we feel. It is easy to understand why the brain's electrical activity fluctuates while we are awake; after all, the stimulation it receives varies tremendously over the course of a day. But to what stimulation is the brain responding when we sleep? What keeps the cerebral hemisphere so busy after we've gone to bed? Because we spend such a significant amount of time sleeping, and because sleep represents such a dramatic change in consciousness from wakefulness, many neuroscientists are keenly interested in discovering what goes on in the brain during sleep. The ultimate goal of these researchers is to discover the relationship between electrical activity in the brain and changes in consciousness. In the next section we discuss what neuroscientists have learned about this relationship.

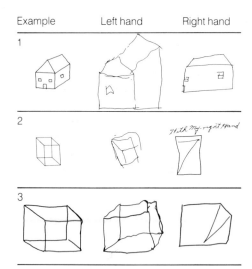

Example	Left hand	Right hand

1

2

With my right Hand

3

FIGURE 4.28
The right hemisphere and spatial ability. A split brain patient was asked to draw the objects shown in the far left column using first one hand and then the other. Although right-handed, this patient's drawings, which were done with the left hand, better represent the spatial relations in the example than those done with the right hand. Apparently, for this person like for most of us, spatial abilities are represented in the right hemisphere.

The Sleeping Brain

Humans, like most other animals, are not active all the time; we typically spend some portion of each day, usually when it is dark, asleep. The human body seems to have its own biological clock that regulates intervals of activity and rest over approximately each 24-hour period. This clock is often referred to as a **circadian rhythm**, a cycle in the physiological activity of the nervous system. Interestingly, sleep is not the only aspect of biological functioning that adheres to a circadian rhythm. Metabolism, body temperature, urine production, and secretion of some hormones also ebb and flow with the passing of each day. Metabolism and body temperature, for instance, peak during the daylight hours and decrease during the night.

Circadian Rhythms. There is little doubt that our individual circadian rhythms affect us psychologically. We are more aware, better able to learn and retain information, and more effective in dealing with stress at some times of the day rather than others. Some people are said to be morning people because they do their best work early in the day, while other people are said to be night people—they do their best work late at night and sometimes into the wee parts of the morning. The point is that our behavior is affected by circadian rhythms, and although each of our circadian rhythms is controlled by internal processes, changes in the environment can throw the cycle off schedule. For instance, if you were to be placed in an environment in which you had no way of telling time or when it was day or night, your cycle would tend to be about 25 hours long rather than 24. Persons blind since birth, for example, tend to have cycles lasting about 25 hours. We also know that emotional and intellectual stress as well as physical exertion produce changes in the body's biological rhythms, and so affect our behavior. For example, pulling an "all nighter" can disrupt a person's circadian rhythm for one or two days—he or she may tend to feel tired, sluggish, and want to sleep during the day as well as during the night.

Similar symptoms, although they are often more long-lasting, characterize jet lag, a phenomenon that often occurs when we travel by air through several time zones. Jet lag is caused by an inconsistency between the body's circadian rhythm for sleep and the day/night cycle of a new environment. For example, suppose you lived in Honolulu and were used to going to bed at 10:00 p.m. and rising at 6:00 a.m. If you were to travel to New York City, which is six time zones away, you would want to go to bed about 4:00 a.m. and get up at noon. Of course, this schedule does not match the work and leisure schedules of (most) Big Apple residents, some of whom you depend upon for activities during your stay, so you would try to adjust your biological clock to the new environment. This would mean, of course, that you would attempt to get to bed around 4:00 p.m. and get up at midnight, Honolulu time! Obviously, you would probably not sleep very well; you would probably feel tired when you get up, and in general, act sluggish. Jet lag can disrupt circadian rhythms so much that many businesses will not permit their executives to perform their duties on foreign soil until they have had an adequate amount of time to adjust to the new time zone.

Two factors—number of time zones crossed and direction of travel—seem to be critical in determining jet lag's effect. Apparently, our biological clocks have more difficulty in adjusting to decreases in time than to increases, for eastbound travelers tend to experience greater jet lag than westbound travelers. Keep in mind that as you travel westward, day breaks later than usual but as you head eastward, dawn comes earlier than usual. There is probably no way to prevent jet lag when you cross several time zones. Give yourself three or four days to adjust your circadian rhythm to the new time scale before doing any serious work or play.

The Stages of Sleep.   Whether in Honolulu, New York City or anywhere else, our sleep is characterized by distinct stages that wax and wane over time. If we were to simply watch a person sleeping, we would probably be unable to distinguish one stage from the next. But if we attach electrodes from an EEG to the person's scalp, the stages, as represented by different kinds of electrical activity in the brain, would become evident. There are five different stages of sleep. Figure 4.29 shows sample EEG characteristics from each of them. As you can see from looking at this figure, brain waves, that is, patterns of electrical activity, change along two dimensions as a person sinks deeper and deeper into sleep during the first four stages. First, amplitude or the height of the wave increases, reflecting an increase in the voltage of the wave; second, the frequency (as measured in cycles per second, or cps) of the wave first increases and then decreases, reflecting an overall decrease in the speed of the wave.

While you are wide awake, your brain waves travel at a rate of about 14 or more cps. If you were to relax and close your eyes, the rate decreases to between 8 to 12 cps. These waves are called alpha waves. As you fade away into Stage 1 sleep, you become more relaxed, the amplitude of brain waves is reduced, and the speed of the waves decreases to between 3 and 7 cps. In Stage 2, relaxation continues, and the EEG is marked by spindles, brief bursts of electrical activity ranging from 12 to 16 cps. Stages 3 and 4, the two deepest stages of sleep, are characterized by delta waves—very slow waves ranging from 1 to 2 cps. People in these two stages are very difficult to awaken, although familiar stimuli such as a baby crying or a child calling their name will arouse them. Decreases in breathing, body temperature, and pulse rate, as well as relaxation of the musculature, are also present in these deeper stages of sleep. Interestingly, the amount of time a person spends in Stage 3 and 4 sleep seems to be a function of how long the person has been awake: generally, the longer a person has been awake, the more time the person spends in Stage 3 and 4 sleep.

During the fifth stage of sleep, the sleeper's eyes move rapidly back and forth; this is called rapid eye movement or **REM sleep**, and it is during this stage of sleep that dreaming most frequently occurs (Aserinsky & Kleitman, 1953). EEGs recorded during this stage look similar to those observed during Stage 1 sleep, but as we shall soon see, other characteristics of REM sleep are very different. For obvious reasons, the first four stages of sleep are often collectively referred to as nonREM sleep.

During the night, we cycle through the stages of sleep, with the first four stages of sleep lasting about 90 minutes followed by 10 to 15 minutes of REM sleep. Depending upon how long one sleeps, the number of cycles may vary, ranging from four to six cycles during an eight-hour sleeping period. The ratio of REM sleep to nonREM sleep increases during the night, with the amount of time spent in Stages 3 and 4 decreasing and the amount of time spent in REM sleep increasing (see Figure 4.30).

Specific sleep patterns vary from one person to the next according to age (see Figure 4.31). To the relief of many a parent, newborn infants may sleep up to two-thirds of the day, spending up to eight hours in REM sleep. The typical five-year-old spends about eleven hours asleep with only a little more than two hours of it spent in REM sleep. Adolescents get by on about eight to nine hours with about two hours of REM sleep. The elderly sleep only about six hours a night, with less than an hour's worth of REM sleep. The predominance of REM sleep in younger persons may play a role in the development of the nervous system, with progressively less REM sleep needed to stimulate the nervous system as the individual ages (Groves & Rebec, 1988).

FIGURE 4.29
EEG patterns representative of the different stages of sleep.

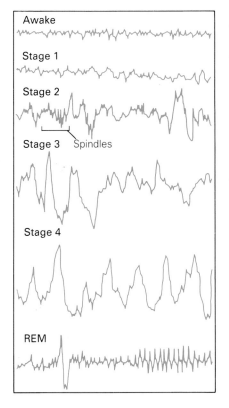

Awake

Stage 1

Stage 2

Stage 3   Spindles

Stage 4

REM

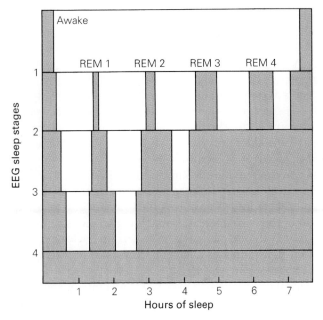
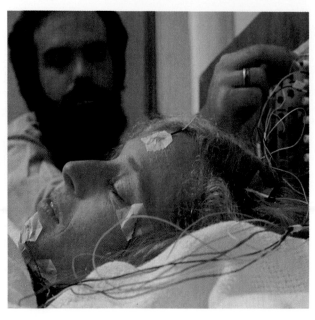

FIGURE 4.30
Left: The sleep cycle during the course of a single night's sleep.
Right: Subjects in sleep labs provide scientists with information about humans during sleep. By hooking the subjects to EEGs, scientists can study the activity of the brain during sleep.

Why Do We Need Sleep? Although science has yielded much information about the electrophysiology and stages of sleep, researchers are less certain of exactly why we sleep. From an evolutionary perspective, nature may have favored those animals who were able to conserve energy at times when energy expenditure was likely to be wasted. For most, although not all animals, foraging and food gathering, courtship, and home building are activities difficult to pursue in darkness.

On a more proximate level, though, sleep seems to serve a restorative function. That is, without sleep, our energy levels wane and, in general, we may feel physically and psychologically tired. After we sleep, we generally feel refreshed and considerably more energetic. What researchers do not know, however, is *how* sleeping rejuvenates us. One way that researchers have attempted to understand the need for sleep is by conducting sleep deprivation experiments: preventing subjects from falling asleep and noting the effects on their performance of simple behavioral and cognitive tasks.

After we sleep, we . . . feel refreshed . . . . What researchers do not know, however, is how sleeping rejuvenates us.

Contrary to what you might expect, such studies have shown that sleep deprivation, even for prolonged periods, has no major effects on our bodies and minds other than to produce drowsiness, a strong desire to sleep, and an increased tendency to doze off easily (Dement, 1978). Even people kept awake for two days or longer show only minor changes in attention and perception (Webb, 1975, 1982). Studies in which people were kept awake for longer periods also have not shown sleep deprivation to have major effects on behavioral and cognitive functioning (Gulevich, Dement, & Johnson, 1966). On the other hand, you know from personal experience that sleep deprivation does produce some minor changes in your behavior. After a night without much sleep you might become less vigilant, not remember things as well, and perhaps you might even become more irritable than normal. This is one instance where research does not confirm everyday experience.

FIGURE 4.31

Changes in sleep patterns across the life span. As we grow older, we not only tend to spend less time sleeping, we also tend to spend less time in REM sleep. We spend less time in nonREM sleep as well, but the decrease is not as steep.

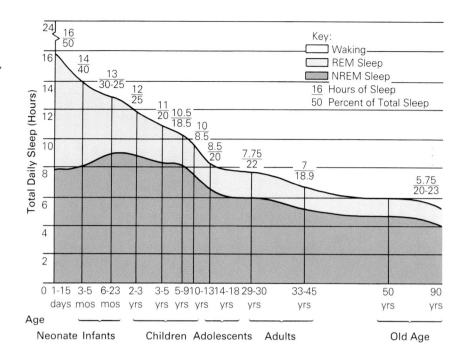

Although all of us are motivated to sleep, not all of us sleep equally well. Some people have difficulty falling asleep or staying asleep; others have irresistible urges to sleep in the middle of the day; still others awake from their sleep screaming in terror for reasons they cannot identify. Sleep disorders are described in Table 4.3.

The Mysteries of REM Sleep. Imagine yourself in the following situation. You show up at the laboratory of a sleep researcher as a volunteer to participate in a sleep study. You are escorted to a cot upon which you will spend the night sleeping. The research assistant attaches electrodes from an EEG to your scalp and near your eyes. Despite the awkwardness of the situation you manage to drift off to sleep easily. So far, so good. However, when the research assistant notices that you have fallen into REM sleep, she awakens you and asks for a report on your "mental activity." What do you think you would say? Could you describe what was going on inside your head at the very moment you were awakened? If you are like most people, you would most likely report that you were dreaming, and you could describe your dream in some detail.

Suppose the research assistant continues to awaken you every time you enter REM sleep. Do your responses continue to be coherent in both style and content? Again, if you are like most of us, it is harder and harder to arouse you as you are denied, time and again, access to REM sleep. In fact, you might have to be removed physically from bed, and held upright before you finally awaken and give your report. If denied access to REM sleep long enough, your entire sleep cycle will be disrupted and you will enter REM sleep more frequently. If you remain as a subject in the research for several days and are consistently awakened every time you enter REM sleep, you will enter REM sleep so frequently that the research assistant will have little to do during the night other than to wake you!

Actually the experiment in which you just served as a fictitious subject was conducted about thirty years ago by William Dement (1960). He found that when he finally let his subjects sleep through the night, the amount of time they spent in REM sleep was double that of a normal night's sleep.

William Dement

TABLE 4.3. *Sleep disorders.*

NAME	SYMPTOMS	NEURONAL BASES	TREATMENT	OTHER INFORMATION
Insomnia	Inability to fall or stay asleep	A number of factors that produce arousal of the nervous system	Relaxation therapy, depressants, or antianxiety drugs	Insomnia affects 6 percent of males and 18 percent of females (Kripket, Gillin, 1988)
Narcolepsy	Falling sound asleep in the middle of daily activities; sudden muscle relaxation	Unknown	Drug therapy	Ranges from mild—the person falls asleep for a few seconds—to severe—the person falls asleep for a long period
Sleep apnea	Breathing suddenly stops while asleep	Neurons involved in respiration malfunction; neurons controlling windpipe aperture cause it to relax and close	Drug therapy	Most common in middle-age, overweight males
Sleepwalking	Sit up, walk, or perform other activities while still asleep	Unknown	Psychotherapy	Common in childhood and adolescence; incidence decreases with age
Night terrors	Wake up in middle of night frightened, sometimes screaming; source of fear is not usually identifiable	Unknown	Psychotherapy	Not the same as dreams; night terrors occur in stage 4 sleep; dreams occur most often in REM sleep

This phenomenon is now referred to as REM rebound. Sleepers awakened an equal number of times during nonREM sleep did not show any rebound effect when allowed to sleep through the night.

Although the brain attempts to compensate for decreases in REM sleep, sleep researchers are not sure of the significance of REM sleep for everyday functioning. However, levels of REM sleep do appear to be correlated with everyday events. For example, stressful or novel events during periods of wakefulness tend to increase the amount of time spent in REM sleep (Luce, 1971). Likewise, the amount of time spent in REM sleep can produce changes in wakeful behavior. For example, Dement (1969) showed that long-term deprivation of sleep in cats produces increased sexual behavior. Such findings may indicate that REM sleep is one way that the nervous system adjusts to changes in life events.

REM Sleep as Paradoxical Sleep. REM sleep is accompanied by physiological changes that, interestingly enough, resemble those of an otherwise alert individual. For example, the electrical activity of the brain during REM sleep resembles that of a wide-awake person (compare the top EEG record with the bottom EEG record in Figure 4.30). Activity of the autonomic nervous system also increases during REM sleep; breathing, pulse rate, and blood pressure fluctuate between high and low levels. In males, the penis usually becomes erect, and in females, there is increased lubrication and blood flow in the vagina. (Such sexual arousal does not appear to be correlated with the content of dreams experienced during REM sleep, however.) Despite this heightened physiological activity, the muscles of the body are deeply relaxed; the sleeper does not react to touch or sound, and is generally very difficult to wake. For this reason, REM sleep has been sometimes referred to as paradoxical sleep.

Dreaming represents one of the great unsolved mysteries of the brain: researchers do not yet know why people dream, why they dream about the things they do, or what brain systems are involved in dream production. But, of course, this does not mean that we know absolutely nothing about the nature of dreaming. For instance:

■ Although not all of us recall our dreams in the morning, all of us dream. Apparently, some people can just recall their dreams better than others. A major factor influencing people's ability to recall dreams is distraction upon awakening. Distractions that occur in a wakeful period immediately following dreaming may interfere with memory consolidation for those dreams (Koulack & Goodenough, 1976).

■ Although dreaming occurs during both REM and nonREM sleep, it is more common during REM sleep. In fact, a sleeper awakened during REM sleep almost always reports a dream, whereas a sleeper awakened during non-REM sleep reports a dream only about a third of the time. Dream quality also differs during the two kinds of sleep. Dreams that occur during REM sleep are highly visually stimulating and are often illogical, even bizarre. Dreams occurring during nonREM sleep are considerably more mundane, and appear to be related to normal everyday thinking.

■ Dreams occur in real time. That is, the events depicted in dreams last neither longer nor shorter than those events would last during a period of wakefulness. For example, in one study, Dement and Wolpert (1958) awoke subjects during REM sleep and asked them to act out the activity in their dreams. The length of time subjects took to act out the dream was roughly the same length of the REM period in which the dream took place.

■ People can be trained to recognize when they are dreaming and, to a limited extent, to control the content of their dreams. Recognizing that you are aware of your own dreaming is like being a spectator at a sporting event: you do not interrupt the natural rhythm of activity. For example, if, just before you go to sleep tonight, you focus on a particular topic or event that you wish to dream about, you may, in fact, experience at least one dream in which it is present (Cartwright, 1974). Whether or not you recall it, of course, is another matter. Your chances of remembering the dream will be increased if you can persuade a roommate or friend to first carefully watch you for signs of REM sleep and then to wake you.

■ Dreams, even the most bizarre ones, seem to be related to the same needs, desires, hopes, and aspirations that we experience during waking hours. In other words, the personality of the sleeper during a dream is consistent with his or her actual personality in real life (Hall & Nordby, 1973).

Our understanding of sleeping and dreaming is still far from being complete. Although we know that both sleeping and dreaming involve changes in the electrical activity of the brain's billions of neurons, we are not sure of the precise nature of those changes, or exactly how they produce such dramatic effects on consciousness. Thus, sleep and dream research represents one of psychology's great unsolved puzzles.

BOUNDARIES AND FRONTIERS

Our survey of the nervous system has been an interesting and eventful one. We have learned that the nervous system, considering all of its many structures, which collectively is comprised of billions of individual neurons, serves as the seat of consciousness. More than merely reacting to changes in environmental stimulation, the nervous system defines aspects of the environment to which organisms are sensitive, and conversely, those to which they are not sensitive. In short, our nervous systems define the

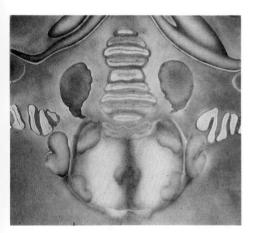

A research subject who works on brain tissue sections during the day painted this picture illustrating the content of his dream.

boundaries of conscious experience. An intact nervous system adapts well to the environment and reacts normally to change, and conscious experience is marked by stability and predictability. A damaged nervous system or one that has been assaulted by drugs or is otherwise plagued by chemical imbalances adapts poorly to the environment, responds abnormally to change, and is considerably less stable in controlling behavior patterns.

Psychology's quest for complete understanding of the nervous system, from its physical composition to its interaction with the environment, has been driven by two important goals: 1) a desire to identify and understand the biopsychological correlates of human action, particularly cognition and learning, and 2) a desire to understand the biopsychological causes of abnormal human behavior and develop cures for such problems. But regardless of science's motivation for studying the nervous system, the major obstacles to such study remain the same, namely, technological limitations in identifying and discriminating its myriad chemical and physical components. Biopsychology has become and will continue to become "high tech" in its approaches to understanding the nervous system.

Inevitably, though, biopsychological research raises ethical and moral questions, some of which have profound implications for society as a whole. Animal activists argue that it is inhumane to damage the nervous systems of nonhuman animals for any reason, let alone to understand better the human nervous system. Some have called for an end to any kind of animal experimentation. Researchers counter that such research is not only necessary to develop a better understanding of the human nervous system, but also that such research is essential to developing effective treatments for people and nonhuman animals with damaged nervous systems.

Most people believe that science has a moral responsibility to improve the human condition, particularly when it comes to suffering. But do we have the right to inflict pain and suffering on so-called lower life forms to meet that responsibility? Science's retort to this question is "Yes," if only because such research has proved so effective and so safe in benefiting members of our own species in the past.

Perhaps a more intriguing question is posed by the philosophy that most, if not all, human problems (drug abuse for example) can be abated through technological means. Are the best solutions to such problems always technological ones? Consider the following scenario: An individual goes to a bar, gets roaring drunk, then takes a pill that sobers him up almost immediately and drives home safely. This seems like a rather sane solution to the problem of drunk driving, especially when one considers the tremendous human toll taken by drunk driving and the fact that we already rely on pills to help us in so many other ways.

The problem is that a technological solution to this case does nothing to help the individual learn self-control with alcohol. Indeed, the mere knowledge that by taking a pill one can become sober may be viewed by some people as license to drink more frequently and to drink in larger quantities. You may say, "So what's the harm?" The harm is that other problems associated with drinking may be overlooked. Problems involving aggressive and abusive behavior brought on by drunkenness, physical problems caused by the toxic effects of alcohol on the body, and problems with lost productivity would still remain. Because alcohol impairs judgment and thinking, we must also raise the question of whether a drunk individual will have the desire or even remember to take the pill!

The history of biopsychological research over the last 100 years has shown that the mysteries of the brain can be unravelled technologically. However, those very same advances present our species with some very difficult questions about our morality and about scientific and societal decision making.

CONCEPT SUMMARY

THE NERVOUS SYSTEM

- What is a neuron and how does it differ from a glial cell? (p. 94)
- What are the major components of the nervous system and how do they differ from each other? (pp. 94–95)
- What roles do sensory, motor, and association neurons play in the nervous system? (pp. 95–96)
- How is a nerve impulse or action potential generated? What is a refractory period? (pp. 97–99)
- What is the role of neurotransmitters in synaptic transmission? How do reuptake and degradation affect synaptic transmission? (pp. 99–102)
- Six different neurotransmitters were described in the chapter. What are the different ways in which each affect our behavior? (pp. 103–105)

DRUGS AND CONSCIOUS EXPERIENCE

- What does it mean to say that a person is addicted to a psychoactive drug? What are the ways in which such drugs affect synaptic transmission? (p. 106)
- What are the different classes of psychoactive drugs and how do they differ in their effects on behavior (give examples)? (pp. 107–116)

THE ENDOCRINE SYSTEM

- How does the endocrine system differ from the central nervous system? (pp. 116–117)
- What are the major endocrine glands and what are their functions? (pp. 116–117)

THE BRAIN

- What kind of methods are used by neuroscientists to study the brain? Are some of these methods more useful than others in terms of what neuroscientists can learn about the brain? (pp. 118–122)
- In what ways are the structures of the central core (medulla, pons, cerebellum, thalamus, and reticular formation) related to behavior? (pp. 123–124)
- In what ways are the structures of the limbic system (amygdala, hypothalamus, and hippocampus) related to behavior? (pp. 125–127)
- What is the cerebral cortex? What are the functions of the different areas of the cerebral cortex? (pp. 122–133)
- What is the importance of Broca and Wernicke's work to our understanding of the brain's role in language? (pp. 131–132)

THE BRAIN AND CONSCIOUSNESS

- What are the implications of Sperry's research for understanding consciousness? What does Sperry's work tell us about lateralization? (pp. 133–135)
- How do circadian rhythms affect behavior? (pp. 136–137)
- Describe the sleep cycle. How do the stages of sleep differ from one another? (p. 137)
- Why do we need sleep? (pp. 138–139)
- What is REM sleep and why is it often referred to as paradoxical sleep? (pp. 139–140)

KEY TERMS AND CONCEPTS

Biopsychology The study of the nervous system and its relation to behavior. (p. 93)

THE NERVOUS SYSTEM

Neurons The basic unit of the nervous system. Neurons relay information to and from the brain by chemical and electrical means. (p. 94)

Glial Cell A cell in the nervous system that binds neurons together, although not so close that they actually touch one another. Glial cells also perform other supportive functions such as supplying nutrients to neurons and aiding in the repair of damaged neurons located outside the nervous system. (p. 94)

Central Nervous System The network of neurons in the brain and spinal cord. (p. 95)

Peripheral Nervous System The network of neurons that connect the central nervous system to other parts of the body. (p. 95)

Somatic Nervous System The part of the peripheral nervous system that controls the actions of the skeletal muscles, the muscles involved in voluntary movements. (p. 95)

Autonomic Nervous System The part of the peripheral nervous system that controls bodily processes over which we generally exert no conscious control, such as heart rate, respiration, and digestion. (p. 95)

Sympathetic Nervous System The part of the autonomic nervous system that speeds up nervous system activities in stressful or emergency situations. (p. 95)

Parasympathetic Nervous System The part of the autonomic nervous system that is in control after stressful or emergency situations are over, functioning to slow down nervous system activities. (p. 95)

Cell Body The part of the neuron that contains the nucleus and other structures that control the moment-to-moment functioning of the cell. (p. 95)

Dendrites Tiny, treelike projections jutting out from the cell body that receive nerve impulses from neighboring neurons or receptors. (p. 95)

Axon The long pipelike fiber projecting from the cell body to the axon terminals that transmits messages to other neurons, glands, or muscles. (p. 95)

Myelin Sheath A fatty substance that insulates and protects the neuron. The myelin sheath is actually made up of specialized glial cells that wrap themselves around axons. (p. 95)

Axon Terminal The part of the neuron that connects the axon to the terminal buttons. (p. 95)

Terminal Button The part of the neuron that releases neurotransmitters. It is through terminal buttons that the neuron actually stimulates an adjacent neuron, gland, or muscle. (p. 95)

Sensory Neuron A neuron that transmits nerve impulses from the receptors to the brain and spinal cord. (p. 95)

Motor Neuron A neuron that transmits signals from the brain or spinal cord to the body's muscles and glands. (p. 96)

Association Neuron A neuron found only in the brain and spinal cord that receives nerve impulses from sensory neurons and conveys these impulses to other association neurons or to motor neurons. (p. 96)

Nerve Impulse or **Action Potential** The electrochemical code that provides the means for neurons to exchange information within the nervous system. (p. 97)

Resting Potential The electrical potential (−70 millivolts) of the neuron when it is not transmitting a nerve impulse. (p. 97)

Refractory Period A very brief recovery period just after the neuron has stimulated another neuron, in which its membrane cannot be stimulated to generate another nerve impulse. (p. 98)

Synapse Junctions where two neurons meet, but do not actually establish contact with one another. (p. 99)

Synaptic Cleft The very small fluid-filled gap that separates the terminal buttons of one neuron from the adjacent surface of a cell body or dendrite. (p. 99)

Synaptic Transmission The electrochemical process by which one neuron stimulates another. (p. 100)

Synaptic Vesicles Tiny saclike structures found in the terminal button that contain neurotransmitters. (p. 100)

Neurotransmitters Chemical substances that transmit neural impulses between neurons. When released from the terminal buttons, they cross the synaptic cleft and attach themselves to receptor molecules in the postsynaptic neuron, and thereby alter its resting potential. (p. 100)

Reuptake The absorption of neurotransmitter molecules by terminal buttons of the presynaptic neuron. (p. 102)

Degradation The process by which neurotransmitters are destroyed by enzymes in the synaptic cleft. (p. 102)

Acetylcholine A neurotransmitter found in the brain, where it is involved in learning and memory, and in the spinal cord and body, where it is involved in the control of the skeletal muscles and organs. (p. 103)

Norepinephrine A neurotransmitter that is involved in the regulation of mood. Decreases in norepinephrine are related to depression; increases of it are related to feelings of vigor and self-confidence. (p. 104)

Dopamine A neurotransmitter that plays a role in brain regulation of movement, cognition, and emotion. Extremely high levels of dopamine produce symptoms of schizophrenia; extremely low levels of it produce symptoms of Parkinson's disease. (p. 104)

GABA (gamma-amino butyric acid) The main inhibitory neurotransmitter found in the brain. Without GABA the brain would be overrun with excitatory neural impulses, which would lead to convulsions and seizures. A lack of GABA has been implicated in some forms of epilepsy. (p. 104)

Serotonin An inhibitory neurotransmitter found in the brain and spinal cord, which plays an important role in the brain's control of sleep and arousal, body temperature, and sensory and perceptual functions. (p. 105)

Enkephalins A class of neurotransmitters that appear to be involved in the body's ability to tolerate and mediate pain. (p. 105)

DRUGS AND CONSCIOUS EXPERIENCE

Psychoactive Drugs Those drugs that affect our behavior, perceptions, arousal level, emotional status, and ability to think clearly. (p. 105)

Tolerance The physical condition in which neurons in the central nervous system respond progressively less and less to a drug. Larger doses of the drug are required to produce the same effects on the nervous system that smaller doses produced earlier. (p. 106)

Physical Dependence The phenomenon in which the neurons in the nervous system require the drug to function normally. Without the drug, the individual will experience withdrawal symptoms, which may include trembling, perspiration, nausea, headaches, and depending upon the drug, even death. (p. 106)

Psychological Dependence An all-consuming craving to use a psychoactive drug for its euphoric effects. (p. 106)

Stimulants Psychoactive drugs that speed up the nervous system's activities, producing increases in arousal and mood. (p. 107)

Depressants Psychoactive drugs that slow down the nervous system's activities, producing drowsiness and sedation. (p. 110)

Psychedelics Psychoactive drugs that produce dramatic changes in consciousness including hallucinations and enhanced perception. (p. 112)

Narcotics Psychoactive drugs such as morphine and heroin that produce analgesia or pain reduction. (p. 114)

THE ENDOCRINE SYSTEM

Endocrine System A slow acting communication network, composed of endocrine glands. These glands stimulate other glands and organs via hormones. (p. 116)

Hormones Chemical substances such as adrenalin that are secreted directly into the bloodstream by endocrine glands. Hormones stimulate glands, muscles, and internal organs. (p. 116)

THE BRAIN

Lesion A cut produced with pinpoint accuracy by surgically removing or severing brain tissue or by chemically or electrically destroying brain tissue. (p. 120)

Electroencephalogram (EEG) An amplified tracing or recording of the brain's electrical activity. The EEG is useful in helping neuroscientists study gross electrical changes in the brain while a person is asleep or aroused. (p. 121)

Central Core The portion of the brain comprised of the medulla, pons, cerebellum, thalamus, and reticular formation. From an evolutionary perspective, the central core is the oldest part of the human brain, and its functions include regulating autonomic processes such as respiration and pulse. (p. 123)

Medulla A structure positioned at the very bottom of the brain involved with the control of autonomic processes such as breathing, swallowing, digestion, and heartbeat. (p. 123)

Pons A structure just above the medulla that is involved with arousal and dreaming. (p. 124)

Cerebellum A structure located just behind and slightly above the medulla that is involved in the regulation of coordinated movement. (p. 124)

Thalamus The structure of the central core that relays sensory information to the cerebral cortex. (p. 124)

Reticular Formation A fingerlike network of neurons found in the central core that extends from the lower tip of the medulla through the thalamus and that plays a role in sleep and arousal. (p. 124)

Limbic System A group of structures, including the amygdala, the hypothalamus, and the hippocampus, which envelop the central core and are involved primarily with motivation, emotion, and memory. (p. 125)

Amygdala The structure in the limbic system that is involved with the control of aggression. (p. 125)

Hypothalamus The structure in the limbic system located directly below the thalamus. Different parts of the hypothalamus are involved in the control of hunger, thirst, body temperature, and sexual arousal. The hypothalamus also monitors and controls the activity of the pituitary gland. In essence the hypothalamus manages the body's internal state. (p. 126)

Hippocampus The structure of the limbic system that plays a crucial role in memory. (p. 127)

Cerebral Cortex The large convoluted mass of brain tissue located just beneath the skull. The structure, which is the most recent achievement of brain evolution, is involved in complex cognitive processes such as reasoning and decision-making. (p. 127)

Motor Area The region of the cerebral cortex located in the portion of the frontal lobe closest to the central fissure that controls voluntary movement by sending nerve impulses to skeletal muscles. (p. 129)

Somatosensory Areas The region of the cerebral cortex lying in the parietal lobes just behind the central fissure, that is involved in the ability to sense warmth, cold, pain, touch, and bodily movement. (p. 130)

Broca's Area The portion of the frontal lobe that is involved in the motor production of speech. (p. 131)

Wernicke's Area The portion of the temporal lobe that is involved with initiation and understanding of meaningful speech. (p. 131)

Association Areas The portion of the cerebral cortex that is devoted to the so-called higher mental processes including planning, and decision making. (p. 132)

THE BRAIN AND CONSCIOUSNESS

Corpus Callosum A large cable of axons that connects the two hemispheres of the brain. (p. 134)

Circadian Rhythm The cycle of activities of the nervous system. Circadian rhythms wax and wane over the course of each 24-hour period. (p. 136)

REM Sleep The stage of sleep characterized by rapid eye movements and dreaming. (p. 137)

ADDITIONAL SOURCES OF INFORMATION

Carlson, N. R. (1986). *Physiology of behavior* (3rd ed.) Boston: Allyn and Bacon. This well written and elaborately illustrated book is the standard undergraduate text in biopsychology today.

Gazzaniga, M. S. (1988). *Mind matters: How the mind and brain interact to create our conscious lives.* Boston: Houghton Mifflin. Written by one of the pioneers of split-brain research, this lively book is the story of the chemical basis of our conscious experience.

Julien, R. (1988). *A primer of drug action.* (2nd ed.) New York: Freeman. This paperback is a useful source of recent information about the physical and psychological effects of most common drugs.

Restak, R. M. (1984). *The brain.* New York: Bantam. This popular book served as the basis of the PBS series also called *The Brain.*

5 Sensation and Perception: Basic Principles and Visual Processes

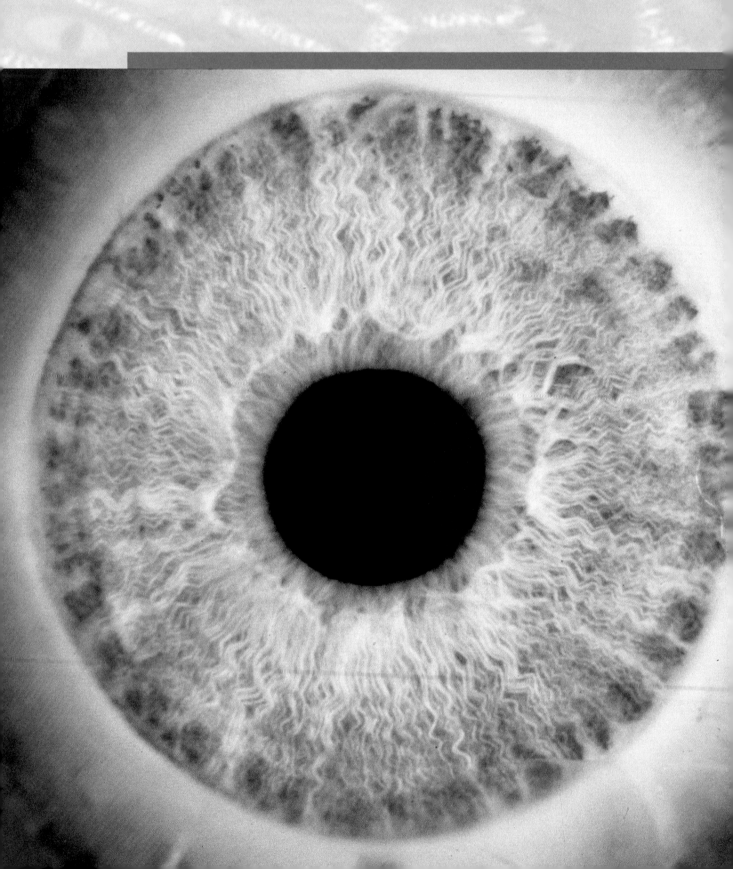

Sensations are immediate and simple experiences that are caused by physical stimuli. Perceptions are the processes by which the brain organizes and interprets sensations. Perception, then, is dependent upon sensation.

BASIC PRINCIPLES OF SENSATION *(150–155)*

Absolute Thresholds   Signal Detection Theory   Difference Thresholds

Sensation involves being able to detect both the presence of a stimulus and changes in the stimulus. These kinds of thresholds are influenced by two variables: our ability to detect a stimulus against background noise accurately, and our tendency to detect the presence or absence of a stimulus whether or not we actually were stimulated.

VISION–SENSORY PROCESSES *(155–169)*

*The Nature of Light   The Eye   From the Retina to the Brain
Neural Processing of Visual Information   Light Adaptation
Brightness Contrast   Color Vision*

Light waves vary along three physical dimensions with each having a psychological counterpart: wavelength and hue, amplitude and brightness, and purity and saturation. The sensation of seeing is caused by light stimulating receptors found in the retina. These receptors convert light into neural signals that are then relayed to the brain. Specialized neurons in the brain respond to visual stimulation on the basis of its physical features.

VISION–PERCEPTUAL PROCESSES *(170–185)*

*Perceptual Organization   Perceptual Constancies   Illusions
Perception and Attention   Pattern Recognition*

Our brains organize sensations in such a manner that we are able to locate and recognize objects in the environment and detect the movement of those objects. However, we are capable of perceiving only those objects to which we attend, and at best, we can only attend to one source of stimulation at a time. Perception is not entirely innate; we can learn to perceive.

Every June the townspeople of Tuscumbia, Alabama gather at a local park to honor their famous native daughter, Helen Keller (1880–1968). The "Helen Keller Festival" attracts tourists and admirers from across the country. Many people travel great distances to join Tuscumbians in paying tribute to a person whose life bespoke only the best qualities of human nature: courage, faith, patience, and charity. Helen Keller's lifelong struggle to overcome the debilitating effects of a childhood illness that left her both deaf and blind is truly an inspirational story (Keller, 1904). But the details of one of her childhood experiences hold special significance for students of psychology, namely, her discovery that she could "see" and "hear" the world through her hands and fingers.

Helen Keller was born a bright and healthy baby. By the time she was six months old she could imitate many of the words and short phrases spoken to her. She walked her first steps on her first birthday. She delighted her parents with her games and affectionate manners. In short, she held all the promise of any normally developing infant. All that changed when, on a chilly February day, nineteen-month-old Helen was overcome by scarlet fever. The illness was severe—the family physician told her parents that Helen would not live. Then, as suddenly as it had come, the illness disappeared. Her parents' exuberance over her remarkable recovery was short-lived, however. The day after the crisis was over Mrs. Keller discovered the permanent effects of the illness. While bathing Helen, Mrs. Keller noticed that Helen's eyes did not close when she passed her hands in front of them. "Her mother screamed in horror, but Helen could not hear it" (Harrity & Martin, 1962).

Without sight and hearing, how would Helen learn about the world? Could she, in fact, learn about the world? Even simple communication was laborious. Unable to hear, Helen's speech development came to an abrupt halt. When she wanted ice cream, she pretended to shiver; to request bread, she imitated the motions of cutting bread and spreading butter. She often screamed and pounded the floor when she failed to make someone understand what she wanted.

For five long years, the Kellers struggled to raise Helen on their own, ever hopeful that they might ease their daughter's plight. When Helen was seven, her parents arranged for a teacher, Anne Sullivan, to live with them and to teach Helen a manual alphabet. Helen and Anne's first few interactions were not positive. On one occasion, Anne gave Helen a doll which Helen promptly dashed against the floor shattering it into tiny fragments. It was at this point that Helen's life was about to take a dramatic turn. In her own words:

The blindness and deafness that afflicted Helen Keller early in her life did not hinder her drive to learn or her work on behalf of others like herself.

I felt my teacher sweep the fragments to one side of the hearth, and I had a sense of satisfaction that the cause of my discomfort was removed. She brought me my hat, and I knew that I was going out into the warm sunshine. This thought, if a wordless sensation may be called a thought, made me hop and skip with pleasure.

We walked down the path to the well-house, attracted by the fragrance of the honeysuckle with which it was covered. Some one was drawing water and my teacher placed my hand under the spout. As the cool stream gushed over one hand she spelled into the other the word water, first slowly, then rapidly. I stood still, my whole attention fixed upon the motions of her fingers. Suddenly I felt a misty consciousness as of something forgotten—a thrill of returning thought; and somehow the mystery of language was revealed to me. I knew then that "w-a-t-e-r" meant the wonderful cool something that was flowing over my hand.

I left the well-house eager to learn. As we returned to the house every object seemed to quiver with life. That was because I saw everything with the strange new sight that had come to me. . . . It would have been difficult to find a happier child than I was as I lay in my crib at the close of that eventful day and lived over the joys it had brought me, and for the first time longed for a new day to come.

(Keller, 1904, pp. 23–24)

The experience at the well-house changed Helen's view of the world and brought one extraordinary change to her life: she became intensely determined to learn everything possible about her environment. Her passion for learning is reflected in her many accomplishments. Helen graduated *cum laude* from Radcliffe College in 1904, where she acquired a sound reading knowledge of Greek, Latin, German, and French. Her autobiography, *The Story of My Life*, was published while she was still in college. She championed several causes including women's suffrage and education for the handicapped. She devoted the bulk of her adult life to raising money for the American Foundation for the Blind. And once within a span of three years, Helen gave over 250 public addresses on the needs of the blind (she had, by this time, learned to speak). In short, Helen accomplished more in her life without sight and hearing than do most people who have normal sensory capacities. Granted, Helen never saw a sunset or heard a bird sing, but she did learn about and interact with the world through touch and came to have an understanding of reality somewhat similar to the one you and I have.

The Helen Keller story points up the distinction between **sensation**, immediate and simple experiences caused by physical stimuli, and **perception**, the processes by which the brain organizes and interprets sensations. What we know about the world depends wholly on the information gathered by our senses and channeled into our brains. Without sensation, there is little, if anything, for our brains to organize and interpret. How might Helen's life have been different had she also lost her sense of touch? Through touch one can sense and perceive shape, size, and movement. It also provides for an effective, albeit crude, means of communication. In terms of learning, taste and smell are poor substitutes for vision, audition, and touch, so it is unlikely that Helen would have learned significant things about her world despite the fact that her brain had the potential to do so.

For the brain to organize and interpret information about the world, such information must first have a means of entering the brain. In other words, our perception of the world is, to a large extent, dependent upon sensation. Our abilities to sense the world play a critical role in what we learn about the world and how we communicate with others. Sensation and perception thus influence both our thinking and our behavior, and so, are important topics for psychology.

O*ur perception of the world is, to a large extent, dependent upon sensation.*

Our discussion of sensation and perception begins with an overview of the general characteristics and measurement of sensation. Next, we discuss the sensory and perceptual processes underlying vision. Hearing (audition), smell (olfaction), and the other senses are discussed in Chapter 6. By keeping in mind the story of Helen Keller as you read these two chapters, you will appreciate the important role the senses play in our learning about the world. Without sensation there is no way of knowing about our physical environment, and so, no way to perceive or appreciate its beauty or its dangers.

Johannes Müller

Some of the earliest psychological research, conducted during the mid-nineteenth century, was aimed at understanding the physiological processes involved in sensation. As we have learned in earlier chapters, the language of the brain and central nervous system is expressed in terms of neural signals. Yet our external environment is a world of matter and physical energies that are *not* neural signals.

Like most animals, we have the extraordinary ability to convert the physical energies of the external world into neural signals that often correspond to subjective experiences. Different patterns of neural signals can produce different subjective experiences. A tree falls somewhere in the forest producing a pattern of sound waves. If we are present, the sound waves strike the sound organs of the ear and the pattern of waves is captured and translated into a pattern of neural signals. Upon reaching the brain, the pattern of neural signals is subjectively experienced as a sound—perhaps a loud, cracking crash, or as a soft, sweeping thud.

Broadly speaking, sensory psychologists are interested in two fundamental questions: (1) How does the nervous system convert physical energy from the environment, such as light and sound waves, into neural signals that the brain can understand? and (2) What is the relation between changes in physical stimulation and a person's subjective experience?

To answer the first question, sensory psychologists study the manner in which different forms of energy stimulate sensory organs (eyes, ears, nose, skin, and tongue). In 1838 Johannes Müller theorized that sensory experiences are dependent on the sensory organ that is stimulated. The eye is sensitive only to light, the ear responds only to movements of molecules in the air, the skin is sensitive to changes in temperature and pressure, and the tongue and nose respond only to chemical stimulation. Research has shown Müller's doctrine of specific nerve energies to be essentially correct. Each sensory organ has highly specialized receptor cells that perform one basic function: **transduction**, which is the conversion of physical energy into nerve impulses. These neural impulses are then relayed from the peripheral nervous system to the brain where they are interpreted as light, sound, warmth (or cold), pain, taste, or smell. Each sensory organ differs from the others with respect to both the specific physiological processes involved in transduction and the neural pathway linking receptors to the brain. We will discuss these physiological processes and pathways in turn as we discuss each sensory organ.

To answer the second question (What is the relation between subjective experience and changes in physical stimulation?), sensory psychologists must be able to measure both the intensity or magnitude of physical stimuli and an individual's subjective reaction to physical stimulation. To do so, psychologists measure two kinds of sensory thresholds—absolute thresholds and difference thresholds. Psychologists are interested in thresholds if only to learn the minimal amounts of stimulation necessary to produce a sensation or a change in behavior.

Absolute Thresholds

What is the least amount of light you can see in an otherwise dark room? What is the faintest sound you can hear in an otherwise silent environment? These questions concern your ability to detect stimulation, specifically the minimum amount of physical energy required to produce a sensation. Because we can only sometimes detect the presence of particular stimulus magnitudes, the **absolute threshold** for any sensory modality is arbitrarily defined as the value at which the stimulus is detected 50 percent of the time. Absolute thresholds may vary considerably from person to person. Factors such as arousal level, physical condition, and experience can affect our sensitivity to physical stimulation. Most people in an alert state, however, are fairly sensitive to detecting the presence of stimuli in their environments. For example, most people have absolute thresholds that would permit them to:

- See a single candle flame 30 miles away on a clear, dark night;
- Hear the ticking of a watch worn by a friend who is standing 20 feet away in a quiet room;
- Taste the sweetness of a solution in which one teaspoon of sugar has been dissolved in two gallons of water;
- Smell the fragance of a single drop of perfume that has been diffused into the entire volume of a three-room apartment;
- Feel the wing of a bee fall upon their cheek from less than one-half inch (from Galanter, 1962).

The absolute threshold, then, is the smallest magnitude of a stimulus that we can detect from the absence of that stimulus. Very intense stimuli can be detected virtually all of the time and very weak stimuli are almost always not detected. In between lies a fuzzy area in which we may not be sure whether we detected a stimulus.

Absolute thresholds are typically measured by asking alert, healthy subjects to respond to the presence or absence of a particular stimulus in a stimulus detection task. For example, most of us have had our hearing evaluated by listening to a series of tones. The tones vary in loudness and are presented one at a time in random order. Recall that your task was to report whether you heard each of the tones. Each tone was presented several times, and the percentage of your "yes" responses was calculated for each level of stimulus magnitude, in this case, loudness. These results can then be summarized in terms of a psychophysical function or a graph in which the percentage of "yes" responses are plotted as a function of stimulus magnitude. Figure 5.1 shows a hypothetical but typical psychophysical function in which the absolute threshold is four units.

For each of our senses, the corresponding psychophysical function is nearly always an S-shaped curve, indicating that the percentage of yes responses increases gradually as the stimulus magnitude increases. Very low stimulus magnitudes are not detected and slightly larger stimulus magnitudes are detected only a very small percentage of the time. However, as the stimulus magnitude increases, so does our ability to detect the presence of the stimulus. From a psychological perspective, psychophysical functions are important because they show us just how sensitive we are to the presence (or absence) of environmental stimulation, and therefore, how likely we are to respond to such stimulation.

The absolute threshold specifies the minimum amount of stimulation required to detect a given stimulus (that is, for transduction to occur). But what about stimuli that impinge upon our receptors and yet go undetected—might they not affect our behavior nevertheless? This question has been at the heart of research investigating subliminal stimulation; that is, stimulation below threshold. As you may know, in the late 1940s and early 1950s, cinema operators announced they could increase their sales of popcorn and soda by simply flashing invisible or subliminal messages on the screen to "eat popcorn" and "drink soda." Other entrepreneurs using subliminal techniques would have us believe that we could learn French, reduce hypertension, or improve our self-concept while we sleep.

FIGURE 5.1

The absolute threshold represents the minimum amount of stimulation required to detect the presence of a stimulus. Shown here is a hypothetical psychophysical function in which the absolute threshold is four units.

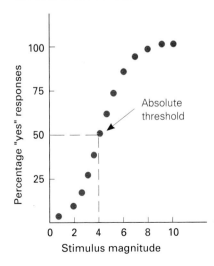

Psychological research supports the idea that behavior can be influenced by subliminal stimulation, although probably not to the degree suggested by advertisers and entrepreneurs. For example, in one study, college students were shown a series of geometric patterns, one at a time for 0.001 second each —just long enough for the subjects to see only a flash, but not the actual patterns (Kunst-Wilson & Zajonc, 1980). Later, when students were allowed to view these figures along with others they had not seen before, they reported a greater preference for the subliminal patterns, even though they were not consciously aware of having seen some of the figures previously. A replication of this study with a different set of college students produced similar results (Seamon, Brody, & Kauff, 1983). So far, however, psychologists have shown only that subliminal stimulation affects human behavior under controlled laboratory conditions; no evidence currently exists that shows subliminal messages affect our behavior in everyday life (Moore, 1985; Vokey and Read, 1985). Indeed, the more intense the stimulus, the greater the likelihood of it influencing behavior, and subliminal messages are just not that intense. Thus, the smell and sight of freshly buttered popcorn is more likely a greater inducement for us to buy popcorn than are subliminal messages on the movie screen that secretly command us to do so.

Signal Detection Theory

The absolute threshold would appear to represent a clear line of demarcation between sensitivity and insensitivity. Do such absolute thresholds actually exist? Many sensory psychologists would argue no, such things do not exist. Why? There are three reasons. First, take another look at the psychophysical function shown in Figure 5.1. The transition from not detecting stimuli to detecting weak stimuli is gradual, not abrupt, as one might expect if indeed the absolute threshold was a distinct boundary. Second, psychological factors such as experience and expectations can influence our ability to detect or not detect a stimulus. Thus, detecting a stimulus depends on factors other than on its presence or absence. A third problem involves **response bias**, the tendency of an individual to detect or report the presence or absence of a stimulus, whether or not he or she was actually stimulated. Consider two real life examples of such a tendency:

t is late evening and you have just finished watching a frightening horror movie . . .

- It is late evening and you have just finished watching a frightening horror movie on television (the movie was a graphic portrayal of a vampire attacking innocent college students while they slept). You are alone in your apartment. You're having difficulty falling asleep: you hear sounds in the apartment that you do not usually hear at night—and you interpret them as the noises of an intruder. The creaking of the floor sounds like approaching footsteps and the wind blowing against your window sounds like someone trying to enter your bedroom.
- You are administering a hearing test to a child. The child raises her thumb every time she detects a tone. Unbeknownst to you, the child is afraid she will have to wear a hearing aid. She does her best to indicate to you that she has perfect hearing—she raises her thumb even on those occasions when she is not sure that a tone has been presented.

In other words, absolute thresholds can often be distorted by our individual circumstances; our expectations, experiences, and desires lead to response bias. Because of the smooth, gradual change in the psychophysical function for absolute thresholds and response bias, signal detection theorists do not employ the concept of absolute threshold to explain sensation and perception.

Response

		Yes	No
Signal condition	Signal On	Hit	Miss
	Signal Off	False alarm	Correct rejection

FIGURE 5.2
The four possible outcomes for any trial in a signal detection experiment.

FIGURE 5.3
Results from two hypothetical subjects in a signal detection experiment. Compared to Annette, Sam was more likely to report the presence of a stimulus but less likely to report its absence. These results reflect differences in subjects' response biases.

Sam's Response

		Yes	No
Signal condition	Signal On	45	5
	Signal Off	20	30

Annette's Response

		Yes	No
Signal condition	Signal On	29	21
	Signal Off	4	46

Signal detection theory attempts to address these problems by assuming that detection of any stimulus is a matter of distinguishing that stimulus from all other stimuli in the sensory world (Tanner & Swets, 1954; Green & Swets, 1966). It further assumes that sensation is due to a combination of response bias and the subject's sensitivity or ability to detect accurately a stimulus against background noise. The stimulus to be detected is called the signal; all other stimulation is called noise. Noise is a part of virtually all sensation and is due, in part, to random patterns of neural activity. In determining whether or not a stimulus is present, an observer must decide if the stimulation in the sensory system is due to the signal or to noise.

Here is how the typical signal detection experiment is organized: The researcher alternates trials in which a weak stimulus is presented (called signal trials) with trials in which no stimulus is presented (called catch trials). On each trial, the subject is required to respond either "yes" if he or she detects a signal or "no" if he or she does not detect a signal. Considering the stimulus condition (stimulus present or absent) in combination with the response given by the observer ("yes" or "no"), there are four possible outcomes for every trial in a signal detection experiment (see Figure 5.2):

1. *Hit:* A signal is present and the observer responds "yes."
2. *Miss:* A signal is present and the observer responds "no."
3. *False alarm:* A signal is absent and the observer responds "yes."
4. *Correct rejection:* A signal is absent and the observer responds "no."

The main purpose of any signal detection experiment is to measure the subject's sensitivity taking response bias into account. Thus, the subject's main task is to discriminate between a genuine stimulus and noise. Often, however, the observer is unsure whether a stimulus was presented, so he or she must guess. The guess is made on the basis of the observer's **response criterion**, the level of sensation above which he or she will report detecting a stimulus and below which he or she will report not detecting a stimulus. On catch trials, the noise alone may be sufficient to exceed the subject's criterion, and the subject may commit a false alarm, reporting the presence of a stimulus when, in fact, no stimulus was presented. On the other hand, the noise may be sufficiently low that when a weak stimulus is presented, the sum of signal plus noise is below criterion and the subject commits a miss, reporting the absence of stimulus, when in fact, a stimulus was presented.

Personal factors such as an observer's desires and expectations often influence or bias his or her response criteria. Some observers will tend to report detecting more signals than are actually presented. These observers will have a high hit rate but also a high false alarm rate. On the other hand, other observers will tend to report fewer signals than are actually presented and thus have lower hit and false alarm rates than their more responsive counterparts. By statistically manipulating the four outcomes of a signal detection experiment, sensory psychologists can determine the relative contributions of sensitivity and response biases to observers' reports regarding the presence or absence of signals. Figure 5.3 gives the results from two hypothetical observers participating in a signal detection experiment involving auditory stimulation. Sam and Annette each have 75 correct responses (hits plus correct rejections). However, notice the difference between Sam and Annette in terms of the number of misses and false alarms—Sam has 5 and 20, respectively; Annette has 21 and 4, respectively. Based purely on the number of correct responses (hits plus correct rejections), we might conclude that Sam and Annette are equally sensitive to auditory signals. However, examining the overall pattern of responses for both observers, we see that they each had different response criteria, and hence, different response biases. Compared to Annette, Sam was more likely to report the presence of a stimulus, but less likely to report its absence. Such findings have implications for how people make decisions. After all, the possible outcomes of any yes–no decision neatly fall into the categories hit, miss, false alarm and correct rejection. Whether you are a physician deciding what to make of a small light speck on a lung X-ray (Should you operate or not?), or a college student trying to interpret the warm smile of a member of the opposite sex (Should you ask that person for a date?), signal detection theory is useful in describing decision outcomes and their possible consequences. Signal detection theory predicts, in both cases, that factors other than the signals themselves will figure in the decision. The physician must consider the seriousness of the illness and the consequences for performing a potentially needless operation. The student might take into consideration past success in asking people out and the attractiveness of the person.

Difference Thresholds

Ernst Weber

The absolute threshold defines our ability to detect the presence or absence of a stimulus. We also have the ability to discriminate the differences between stimuli (two sounds, two lights, two tastes, and so on). The **difference threshold** is defined as the minimal change in stimulation that can be reliably detected 50 percent of the time. The study of difference thresholds differs from the study of absolute thresholds in two ways. First, observers are presented pairs of stimuli during each trial rather than a single stimulus. Second, observers are asked whether the two stimuli are the same or different rather than whether a stimulus is present or not. Over a series of many trials, one stimulus, called the reference stimulus, is held constant while the second stimulus is increased or decreased. For example, suppose we are interested in detecting the difference threshold for visual brightness. We might begin the experiment by showing an observer two lights, both 100 watts. Next, we would keep the reference stimulus at 100 watts but change the wattage (although technically we would really be changing it in terms of lumens, the unit of luminosity) of the other stimulus to, say, 101 watts. Over a series of trials, we would continue to manipulate the size of the second stimulus (100 watts, 101.1 watts, 101.2 watts and so forth) until we found the exact point at which the observer recognized the two stimuli as being different 50 percent of the time. This value is called the **just noticeable difference** (jnd).

Let's assume that we found the jnd in our experiment to be about 1.7 watts. Can we conclude that the jnd for visual brightness in all cases is 1.7 watts? For example, would our observer be able to distinguish a 300 watt light from a 301.7 watt light? According to Ernst Weber (1795–1878), the first person to note the relationship between the size of the reference stimulus and the size of the jnd, the answer is no. Why? Because it is the *relative* difference between stimuli and not the *absolute* difference that determines our ability to discriminate between them. In other words, our ability to discriminate between two stimuli depends upon the size of the reference stimulus: the greater the magnitude of the reference stimulus, the larger the change in intensity needed to produce a jnd. According to Weber, the ratio of jnd to the reference stimulus is a constant value. This relationship is now referred to as **Weber's law**, and the size of the constant value is referred to as **Weber's fraction**. For example, Weber's fraction for visual brightness is 1/60. Thus, with a reference stimulus of 300 watts, we would have to increase (or decrease) the size of the comparison stimulus by 5 watts (1/60 × 300 watts = 5 watts) instead of 1.7 watts for our observers to report a jnd.

TABLE 5.1.	*Common constant values for the Weber Fraction*
SENSE	*WEBER FRACTION ($\Delta I/I$)*
Vision (brightness, white light)	1/60
Kinesthesis (lifted weights)	1/50
Pain (thermally aroused on skin)	1/30
Audition (tone of middle pitch and moderate loudness)	1/10
Pressure (cutaneous pressure)	1/7
Smell (odor of India rubber)	1/4
Taste (table salt)	1/3

The Weber fraction is the proportional amount of increase in intensity needed to produce a just noticeable difference (jnd). The smaller the fraction, the less change is necessary to produce a jnd. Thus, less than a 2 percent change in white light is needed to be detectable, while a 25 percent difference is needed in the smell of India rubber for it to be noticed.
From Schiffman (1976)

The value of Weber's fraction varies, depending on the particular stimulus under study (see Table 5.1). Weber's law is useful because it allows sensory psychologists to compare directly the differences in sensitivity of the sensory modalities, and therefore, determine which modalities are more likely to influence our behavior. If Weber's fraction is small, the sensitivity of the sensory modality is great—proportionally little must be added (or subtracted) to the reference stimulus for us to detect a difference. Just the opposite is true for large Weber fractions: proportionally more must be added (or subtracted) to the reference stimulus for us to detect a difference. For example, suppose we wish to know whether our eyes are more sensitive to stimulation than our ears. The answer is given in Table 5.1: Weber's fraction is smaller for visual brightness (1/60) than for loudness (1/10). This means, other things being equal, that we are more sensitive to small changes in visual stimulation than in auditory stimulation.

The absolute threshold represents the minimum amount of stimulation necessary to detect a stimulus and the difference threshold represents the amount of stimulation necessary to detect a change in stimulation. Signal detection theory is based on the idea that psychological factors such as experience and expectations influence an individual's absolute threshold and response bias and so, his or her response criterion. We turn now to a discussion of the sensory processes involved in vision.

VISION—SENSORY PROCESSES

If we were to characterize each of our senses as windows through which we look upon the world, vision would not only be the largest window, but also the window with the grandest view. We gather most of our information about the world through our eyes, and we think and reason about the world largely through the visual symbols and images that we manipulate with our brains. Vision is tremendously helpful to us in moving about the world. Humans and other animals with good vision have the ability to maneuver through complex mazes—in our case, for example, bumper-to-bumper traffic at rush hour. Changing lanes, avoiding fender-benders, and in general, watching out for the other guy (including those who give speeding tickets) is a responsibility left largely to our eyes. In short, the ability to see provides us with an incredibly effective means of adapting to our environment.

Our study of vision begins with a discussion of the nature of the visual stimulus—light. We will then discuss the structure of the eye and its function as a receptor and transducer of light. We will also discuss the characteristics of visual sensitivity and how the brain analyzes and interprets the visual information it receives from the eye. We will conclude with a discussion of color vision.

The Nature of Light

Our eyes respond to light, which is electromagnetic energy in the form of light waves. When we see an object, what we are actually seeing is the object in the medium of light waves reflected from that object's surface. The electromagnetic spectrum, shown in Figure 5.4 encompasses the various forms of electromagnetic energy ranging from rather long waves such as television and radio waves to very short ones such as X-rays. We are blind to all energy waves but light, which comprises only a tiny band of the electromagnetic spectrum. And we can see only those wavelengths that fall between 380 and 760 nanometers (nm) (a nanometer is equal to one billionth of a meter).

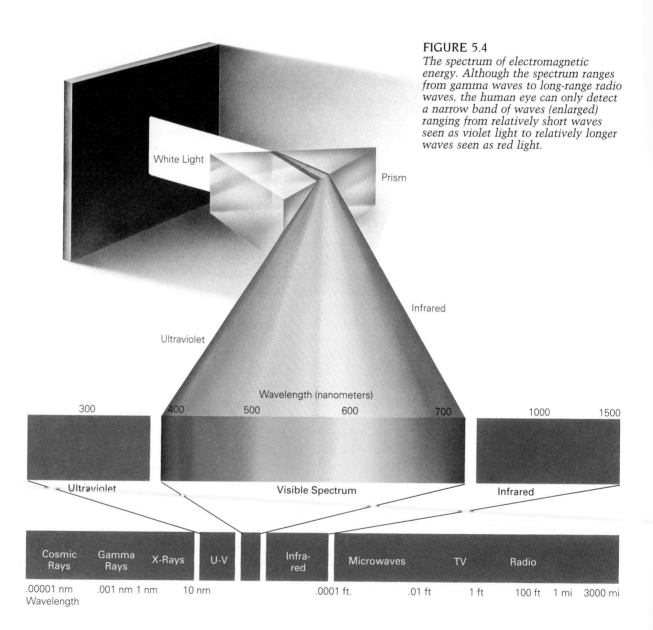

FIGURE 5.4
The spectrum of electromagnetic energy. Although the spectrum ranges from gamma waves to long-range radio waves, the human eye can only detect a narrow band of waves (enlarged) ranging from relatively short waves seen as violet light to relatively longer waves seen as red light.

Our sensory experiences with light are determined by three important physical characteristics of light waves: wavelength, amplitude, and purity. However, we experience or see these characteristics of light primarily in terms of its hue or color, its brightness, and its saturation. In other words, each physical characteristic has a psychological counterpart: wavelength and hue; amplitude and brightness; and purity and saturation.

Wavelength is the distance from one wave crest to the next. Different wavelengths are seen as different colors. Short wavelengths (400 to about 480 nm) are seen as violets and blues, intermediate wavelengths (500 to about 620 nm) as greens and yellows, and long wavelengths (650 to about 760 nm) as oranges and reds (see Figure 5.4). Remember that these colors or **hues** are the psychological counterpart of wavelength.

Amplitude is the height of each wave and represents the number of quanta or particles of light emitted from a source over a given unit of time. The amplitude of light corresponds to a different psychological property of light, **brightness**. As amplitude increases, the brighter the light appears.

Purity is the number of wavelengths that constitute a light. Psychologically, the purity of a light corresponds to its colorfulness or **saturation**. A light comprised of only one wavelength, say violet (400 nm), is seen as a pure or saturated color. As other wavelengths are combined with the violet (white, for example), the color appears less pure (in this instance, lavender). Most of the colors we see are comprised of mixtures of various wavelengths.

In sum, the three physical properties of lightwaves correspond to three psychological properties of light. Wavelength gives rise to hue; amplitude gives rise to brightness; and purity gives rise to saturation.

The Eye

Right now you are reading. Seeing the words, like seeing anything, involves two separate processes, both of which are performed by your eyes. First, certain structures gather light waves reflecting from the page's surface and focus them to a spot at the very back of your eyes. Second, once there, the waves are converted from electromagnetic energy to nerve impulses that are then relayed to the brain. Interpreting or perceiving what you see does not take place in the eye, but rather in the brain. Damage to the structures of the eye will hinder visual information from reaching the brain, and so, interfere with perception. For this reason, understanding how the eye works is important to understanding how we perceive our world.

Structures and Functions of the Eye. To understand the operation of the eye, let's trace a beam of light as it passes through the front of the eye to the **retina**, the thin layer of receptors that lines the interior of the back of the eye (see Figure 5.5). Light enters the eye through the **cornea**, the transparent, fluid-filled cover at the front of the eye that aids in bending or refracting lightwaves entering the eye. Next, light passes through an opening called the **pupil**. The size of the pupil is controlled by the **iris**, a small group of muscles that contracts or relaxes in response to the amount of light passing through the cornea. In dimly lit environments the iris relaxes so that the pupil can let available light into the eye. In bright light, just the opposite occurs: the iris contracts, the pupil becomes smaller, and less light enters the eye. The iris is also pigmented, giving the eye its color.

Once a light wave passes through the cornea, it is bent, passes through the pupil, and strikes the **lens**, a transparent structure that changes shape depending upon whether we are viewing objects close up or far away. The shape of the lens is controlled by a group of muscles attached to the top and bottom of the lens. As these muscles contract (when viewing objects close

FIGURE 5.5

The human eye. Light waves reflected from objects pass through the cornea, pupil, and lens before striking the retina. The image of objects on the retina is reversed and upside down because light waves travel in straight lines. Thus, light waves reflected off the top of objects are projected onto the bottom of the retina and light waves reflected off the bottom of objects are projected onto the top of the retina. The brain compensates for this rearrangement so that we see the object as it really is.

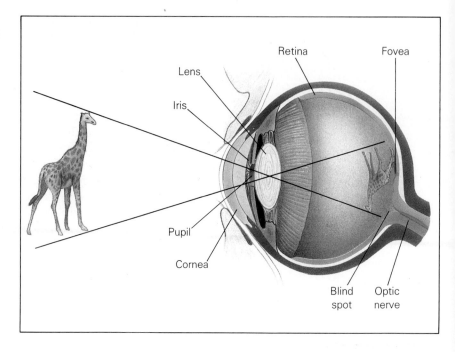

up) or relax (when viewing distant objects), the lens bulges or narrows, respectively. This process, referred to as **accommodation**, permits the lens to focus incoming light waves at a single point on the retina. Light waves from the top of the object are focused at the bottom of the image on the retina, and light waves from the left side of the object are focused on the right side of the image on the retina. In other words, the retinal image of the object being viewed is inverted and reversed (see Figure 5.5). The brain compensates for this rearrangement so that we see the object as it actually is.

Accommodation occurs automatically—without conscious effort. The muscles constantly adjust the lens' shape to keep images focused sharply on the retina. When viewing objects close up, however, accommodation has a definite limit. Try the following demonstration. Hold your pen (or pencil) at an arm's distance from your eyes. Now gradually move it toward your face. As the pen approaches, there will be a point, called the near point, at which the lens cannot bring the pen into focus. The distance of the near point increases with one's age. The near point for most college-age people is about 10 cm. By the time an individual is 40 years old, the near point is about 23 cm, and at 60, it is about 100 cm. Most of us will not experience problems with accommodation until we are in our mid- to late 40s. Around this age, accommodation decreases rapidly, causing the near point to increase beyond a comfortable reading distance. What causes such increases in the near point? Advancing age affects the lens in two ways: the lens hardens, causing it to become less flexible, and the muscles controlling the lens weaken, so accommodative ability is decreased. Fortunately, this problem can be remedied with corrective lenses (bifocals) that help the eye focus light onto the retina.

In sum, the cornea, pupil, iris, and lens perform two functions: (1) they gather light, and (2) they focus it on the retina. Once light reaches the retina, a series of important physiological events takes place. These events, like those just discussed are not, in themselves, important psychologically. However, keep in mind that such physiological processes are necessary for normal everyday functioning. So, if a problem arises in getting visual information from the eye to the brain, as was the case with Helen Keller, our perception of the world becomes distorted, if not destroyed. That, of course, is psychologically significant for the simple reason that our behavior is affected. Let's turn now to a closer look at the eye.

The Retina.   The retina (from the Latin word *rete* meaning "net," which it resembles) contains approximately 126 million photoreceptors—nerve cells sensitive to light (see Figure 5.6). These photoreceptors transduce light into neural impulses. Specifically, light striking the photoreceptors initiates a chemical reaction that generates neural impulses carrying visual information from the eye to the visual cortex. There are two kinds of receptor cells in the retina, **rods** and **cones**. Each human eye contains about 120 million rods but only about 6 million cones.

Rods are light-sensitive receptors found throughout the retina except in the fovea. Rods have a lower absolute threshold than cones for the detection of light. Hence, rods are more useful in twilight and cones are more useful in day vision and in other highly illuminated settings.

Cones are found primarily in the center of the retina, although some may be found in the retina's outer region or periphery. About 50,000 cones are jam-packed into the **fovea**, a tiny area (about one square millimeter) in the center of the retina directly in back of the pupil. Our vision is sharpest when the objects we view are focused on the fovea. In fact, though you may

FIGURE 5.6
Retinal processing of light waves. Light waves striking the retina are transduced by the rods and cones. Neural impulses generated by transduction travel to bipolar cells and then to ganglion cells, whose axons form the optic nerve.

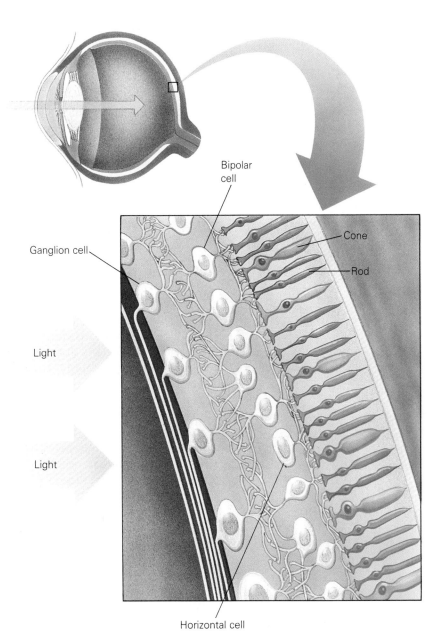

A scanning electromicrograph of the retina's two types of receptors, rods and cones.

FIGURE 5.7

(a) A person with normal vision sees both close and distant objects clearly. (b) In nearsighted vision, the person sees close objects clearly while distant objects appear blurry. (c) A farsighted person sees distant objects clearly while close objects appear blurry.

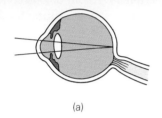

(a)

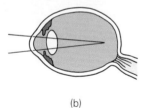

(b)

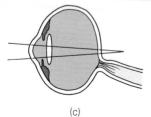

(c)

not have noticed it, when you wish to examine an object closely you move your eyes until the image of that object focuses on the fovea. Our perception of color and our sensitivity to subtle differences between colors is influenced by the cones. Unlike rods, cones are not very sensitive to low-intensity light, a fact that accounts for our poor perception of color in dimly lit settings.

The neural responses generated when light strikes rods and cones are channeled to other kinds of neurons in the retina on their way to the brain (see Figure 5.6). Light striking receptor cells in the retina's periphery generates an action potential that first goes to bipolar cells and then to ganglion cells. Many receptor cells are connected to a single bipolar cell and, in turn, many bipolar cells are connected to a single ganglion cell. Because there are fewer bipolar and ganglion cells than receptors in the retina's periphery, action potentials from the latter are combined, a process referred to as spatial summation. Since there are about 126 million receptors and only about one million ganglion cells, signals from about 126 receptors, on average, converge upon each ganglion cell. However, there is no summation in the fovea; the cones located in the fovea have a direct connection to the bipolar and ganglion cells. Visual detail that is normally lost during summation, is preserved in foveal vision. This explains why foveal vision is sharper than peripheral vision. To demonstrate the differences in sharpness between foveal and peripheral vision, look directly at any word in the center portion of this paragraph. Notice that words close to the center are clear, but that words a centimeter or so away appear fuzzy.

The Retina and Visual Acuity. **Visual acuity**, or keenness of vision, is affected by the locations on the retina on which images fall. As we have just seen, acuity is greatest for images that are focused on the fovea. Actually, visual acuity is a measure of spatial resolution or one's ability to see patterns such as printed words or billboards and road signs. When a person visits an eye doctor, one of the first tasks he or she is asked to perform is to look at a chart in which the size of printed letters becomes progressively smaller with each line. A person with average visual acuity or 20/20 vision can correctly identify, from a distance of 20 feet, the letters that the average person can read accurately at 20 feet. A person who can correctly identify letters half of the size of the 20/20 line from 20 feet is said to have 20/10 vision. Similarly, a person with 20/40 vision can see clearly from 20 feet what the average person can see clearly from 40 feet. Hence, the smaller the second number, the better is the visual acuity.

Poor visual acuity is caused by structural problems with the eye. Normally the lens focuses the images squarely on the retina. But if the eyeball is misshaped, the image will be focused elsewhere and vision will be blurred (see Figure 5.7). If the distance between the lens and retina is longer than normal, light is focused in front of the retina, a problem referred to as **myopia**, or nearsightedness. On the other hand, if the distance between the lens and retina is shorter than normal, just the opposite occurs: light is focused behind the retina, a condition known as **hyperopia** or farsightedness. People who are nearsighted can see close objects well, but distant objects appear fuzzy; farsighted people can see distant objects clearly, but close objects appear fuzzy.

A common problem that interferes with the ability to see patterns clearly is **astigmatism**, or defects in the spherical shape of the cornea. When the cornea is misshaped, visual images are not focused equally on different parts of the retina. Although almost everyone's corneas are misshaped, only those whose corneas are highly irregular will have blurred vision. Prescription lenses can eliminate the blur. Do you have a vision

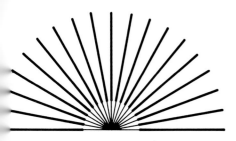

FIGURE 5.8

Do you have a problem with vision due to astigmatism? To find out, stare at the center dot. To people without astigmatism, all of the black bars look equally black. To people with astigmatism, some of the bars look lighter than others. If you wear glasses or contact lenses, test yourself with and without wearing them.

problem due to astigmatism? To test yourself, stare at the dot shown in Figure 5.8 (do not look directly at the black bars). If you wear glasses or contacts, try the test with and without them. To people without astigmatism, all of the black bars look equally dark. But people with astigmatism typically report that some of the black bars look lighter than the others.

With advancing age visual acuity generally decreases. Age-related problems such as decreases in the lens' accommodative ability, cataracts (clouding of the lens), and shrinking of the pupil can produce gradual, dramatic decreases in our ability to see detail. For example, individuals at age 65 require about three times as much light to detect the same amount of brightness in their environments as they did when they were about 20 years of age (Kline & Schieber, 1985).

Myopia, hyperopia, and astigmatism can affect our ability to read, to write, and to negotiate through traffic, as well as a multitude of other behaviors in which we routinely engage. Once again, we can see how important sensation is to our perception and interaction with the environment. If sensation (in this case visual sensation) is impaired, our behavior is likewise impaired. After all, it is difficult to respond to a stimulus when you can't see it or at least can't see it clearly enough to recognize it.

From the Retina to the Brain

Look again at Figure 5.6; focus on the illustration on the right (the structure of the retina). Do you notice anything surprising? You would think that the rods and cones would be the first layer of the retina struck by incoming light waves. In fact, they are the last layer. Light rays must pass through the bipolar and ganglion layers before striking the receptor cells. How then are we able to see anything at all? Fortunately, bipolar and ganglion cells are semitransparent, allowing most of the light rays through to the retina.

The bipolar and ganglion cells link the rods and cones with the nerve fibers (the axons of ganglion cells) that make up the **optic nerve**. The optic nerve, in turn, links the retina with structures in the brain that react to neural impulses laden with visual information. The optic nerve exits the back of the eye, creating a hole in our vision known as the **blind spot**. The blind spot is located just below and to the side of the fovea and contains no rods or cones; hence, this part of the retina is not sensitive to light or color. Finding your blind spot is quite easy. Hold your book at an arm's distance away from your face, close your left eye, and fixate on the cat shown in Figure 5.9. Now slowly move the book toward you. You will find that you will be able to see the dog to the right of the cat in the periphery of your vision; however, when the book is about 20 to 25 centimeters away, the dog will disappear. The disappearance is caused by the dog's image falling on the blind spot. Moving the book closer or farther away will cause the image of the dog to reappear. The psychological significance of the blind spot is that most of us are not aware that it exists because the brain fills in the blind spot with information perceived from the entire visual field.

The brain, specifically the visual cortex, is the ultimate destination for impulses carrying visual information. Figure 5.10 shows the major neural pathway linking the retina to the visual cortex. Some nerve fibers from the

FIGURE 5.9

Locating the blind spot. Hold your book about an arm's length away from your face. Close your left eye and fixate on the cat. Slowly move the book closer. You should be able to see the dog with your peripheral vision. However, when the book is about 20 to 25 centimeters away, the dog will disappear. Magic? No—the disappearance of the dog is caused by its image falling on the blind spot. Moving the book closer or farther away will cause the dog to reappear.

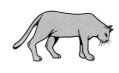

FIGURE 5.10
The pathways for visual information in humans. Neurons from the left side of each retina transmit visual information to the left side of the visual cortex. Neurons from the right side of the retina transmit visual information to the right side of the visual cortex. Notice that the neurons leaving the inner portion of each retina cross over and travel to the opposite side of the visual cortex.

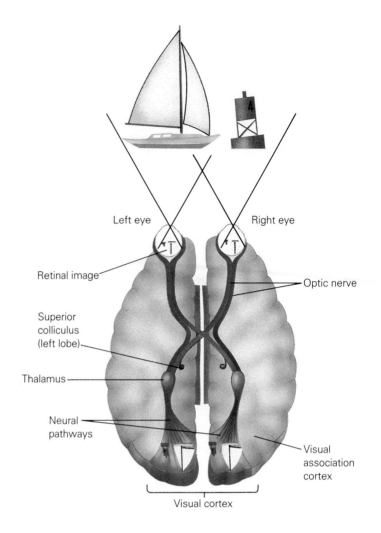

inner portion of each retina (closest to the nose) leave the retina, cross over to the opposite side of the brain, and wind up at either superior colliculus, a cluster of neurons involved with visual attention, localization of visual stimulation, and control of eye movements. However, a larger number of nerve fibers emanating from both sides of the retina go to the thalamus. There the nerve fibers synapse with neurons from other brain regions before projecting to the visual cortex. As we will soon see, neurons in the visual cortex process visual information. These cells recognize and respond to specific types of visual stimulation from the environment and define our perception of color, shape, size, depth, and movement. Before considering the role of the visual cortex further, let's recap what we have learned about the visual pathways so far:

- Electromagnetic energy in the form of light enters the eye through the cornea, passes through the pupil, and strikes the lens.
- The lens and the cornea bend the light and direct it toward the retina.
- Photoreceptors in the retina—the rods and cones—react to light chemically, thereby generating a nerve impulse.
- Nerve impulses exit the retina via the bipolar and ganglion cells. The axons of the ganglion cells form the optic nerve, along which nerve impulses travel to either the superior colliculi or to the thalamus. Nerve fibers from the inner portion of the retina cross over, carrying nerve impulses to the opposite side of the brain.
- From the thalamus, nerve fibers carrying visual information project to the visual cortex.

Neural Processing of Visual Information

Vision is an active, not a passive process. The visual system actively responds to and changes optic nerve signals at strategic points along the visual pathway, particularly in the visual cortex. Neurons in the visual cortex are excited by particular patterns of light, such as lines and angles of different sizes and shapes. Hence, cortical neurons are often referred to as **feature detectors**.

Feature detectors were identified through a classic series of experiments conducted by David Hubel and Torsten Weisel (1959, 1963, 1968). Their procedure for identifying the detectors—single-cell recording—was simple, yet elegant: an anesthetized animal, usually a cat or monkey, was placed before a projection screen. The electrical activity of specific neurons in the visual cortex was recorded as visual stimuli and were projected onto the screen. For example, lines of different angles were presented in various parts of the screen. Some neurons were found to increase their rates of firing while other neurons were found to decrease their firing rate. In either case, the stimulus that produced the largest change in a given neuron's firing rate was considered to be that stimulus to which a particular cell was most sensitive. By recording the electrical activity of the visual cortex, Hubel and Weisel discovered three types of neurons in the visual cortex, each of which is selectively responsive to particular features of any given visual stimulus:

- *Simple cells* respond to lines, such as thin bars of light oriented in a particular direction and location.
- *Complex cells*, like simple cells, respond maximally to bars of light oriented in a particular direction. Unlike simple cells, however, complex cells also respond to moving visual stimuli, particularly if the visual stimulus is moving in a certain direction. Simple cells respond maximally only to stimuli in particular locations; complex cells respond to stimuli that move.
- *Hypercomplex cells* fire in response to a moving line or corner of specific length moving in a particular direction.

Simple, complex, and hypercomplex cells are called feature detectors because they respond best to the elementary features (lines, angles, and corners) of simple visual stimuli. More recent research has shown that feature detectors may respond to more complex features of visual stimuli, such as changes in light intensity patterns (DeValois & DeValois, 1975; Shapley & Lennie, 1985). Thus, feature detectors appear to be the basis by which animals recognize visual stimuli.

Visual information about the environment stimulates receptors in the eye which, in turn, generate neural impulses. These impulses contain details about shape, size, movement, and orientation of visual stimuli that are analyzed by the neurons of the visual cortex. There, the visual stimulus is "seen" so to speak, and recognized as a familiar or unfamiliar object. Thus, embedded within the visual cortex, lies the psychological explanation for our ability to see: specialized neurons that respond to specific features of visual stimuli.

Left: David Hubel. Right: Torsten Weisel.

Light Adaptation

On any given day, most of us will experience environments that differ in terms of illumination. Consider, for example, two parts of our daily routine, getting out of bed and going to bed. You hobble out of bed at 6:00 a.m. and shuffle to the bathroom. Your bedroom is dark except for the dim light from your alarm clock. As you reach for the light switch with one hand, you shield your eyes from the bright lights with the other. After a minute or so, your eyes become adjusted to the lights and you are able to see. At bedtime, of course, just the opposite occurs: After you turn off your bedroom light, you can hardly see the foot of your bed, let alone the dresser across the room. Gradually, however, your ability to see in the dark increases. Fifteen minutes or so after going to bed, you can now make out most, if not all, of the objects in your room (assuming, of course, you are still awake!). The process of our eyes adapting to increasing luminance levels is called **light adaptation**, while adapting to decreasing luminance levels is called **dark adaptation**. Light adaptation is a more rapid process than dark adaptation.

The course of adapting to decreasing illumination is shown in Figure 5.11. The y-axis represents the absolute threshold for detecting light, and the x-axis represents time in the dark. Dark adaptation is marked by decreases in the absolute threshold for detecting light and is essentially a two step process. The two steps correspond to the different rates at which the cones and rods adapt to decreases in illumination. The cones adapt first, requiring about 10 to 15 minutes to reach their maximal sensitivity. The rods adapt much more slowly, taking about 30 to 40 minutes. You may recall that our twilight vision is primarily regulated by the rods. Now you know the reason why—rods have a much lower absolute threshold for light than do cones.

Brightness Contrast

Examine Figure 5.12 for a moment. As you scan this figure from left to right, notice that the center gray patches appear lighter as the background becomes darker. What is unique about this figure is that the center patches are exactly the same shade of gray. This effect, called **brightness contrast**, increases as the intensity between contrasting regions increases and is due, physiologically, to a process known as lateral inhibition. In essence, neurons in one area of the retina stimulated by an intense light tend to inhibit those in neighboring regions. As a general rule, the lighter the background relative to the center region, the greater the lateral inhibition effect. Psychologically, objects appear lighter or darker depending upon the brightness of the background.

FIGURE 5.11
Dark adaptation is a two-step process. First, the cones adapt, requiring about 10 to 15 minutes to reach their maximal sensitivity. The rods require about 30 minutes to adapt.

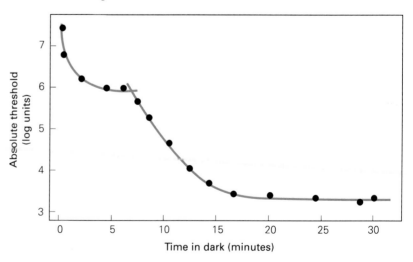

FIGURE 5.12
Brightness contrast. Although the gray squares are identical in brightness, they appear lighter or darker, depending upon the relative darkness of the background squares.

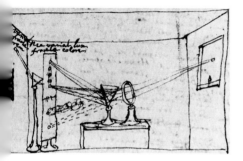

Newton's sketch of his prism experiment in which he discovered that white light is composed of all other spectral colors. His sketch shows how sunlight hits the prism and bends to form a spectrum.

Color Vision

We have already noted three important properties of light: wavelength, amplitude, and purity. Recall that wavelength corresponds to hue or color, amplitude to brightness, and purity to saturation. Our perception of color is a result of the interaction of these properties and is reflected in how we sometimes describe the appearance of different color shades: deep blue (a highly saturated blue), baby blue (a highly unsaturated blue), bright blue (an intense blue), dull blue, and so forth. Unfortunately, our everyday descriptions of color do little to explain precisely how we see color. To do that, we must consider two things: first, the composition of sunlight or other ordinary white light, and second, the ability of objects to reflect some wavelengths but not others.

Seeing Color. To understand the nature of sunlight, let's go back about three centuries to the year 1704. That was the year that Sir Isaac Newton (1642–1727) conducted a simple but ingenious prism experiment in his room at Cambridge University in England. When Newton positioned a prism so that sunlight entering the room through a small hole in a shutter struck it, he noticed that light leaving the prism formed a spectrum of colors, an artificial rainbow, so to speak. In other words, by refracting or bending the white light with the prism, Newton discovered that white light, which is not part of the spectrum, is composed of all the wavelengths of the spectrum. Newton also showed that the spectral colors could be recombined into white light again by placing a lens behind the prism. The rainbow struck the lens and emerged on the opposite side of the lens as white light.

So what gives an object its color when illuminated by sunlight or other white light? Why is an orange orange but a lemon yellow? These questions lead us to the fact that objects do not reflect all wavelengths contained in white light equally—they reflect some but absorb others. The wavelength or combination of wavelengths reflected by an object determines our perception of its color (see Table 5.2). Thus, an orange appears orange because it reflects long and a few medium wavelengths but absorbs all others while a lemon appears yellow because it reflects both long and medium wavelengths. The difference in apparent color between an orange and a lemon is in the amount of medium wavelengths (green) that each reflects.

There are some objects, though, that do not reflect wavelengths selectively; rather, they reflect all wavelengths about equally. Black objects reflect about 5 percent of all wavelengths, and white objects reflect about 80 percent of all wavelengths. So, whether we see an object as black or white depends upon the total amount of light it reflects.

TABLE 5.2.	Relationship between color perceived and wavelengths reflected

PREDOMINANT WAVELENGTHS REFLECTED	PERCEIVED COLOR
Short	blue
Medium	green
Long	red
Long and medium	yellow
Long and a little medium	orange
Long and short	purple
Long, medium, and short	white

From Goldstein (1984)

Color Blindness. People with normal color vision are able to discriminate one wavelength from another, for example, red from green. Others, however, cannot. When asked to match different wavelengths of light to different mixtures of four primary colors (red, green, blue, and yellow), these individuals often respond unusually. Some match mixtures of only two primary colors to all wavelengths. They often can distinguish between blue and yellow but confuse red with green. Only a few people have the opposite problem—confusing blue and yellow while discriminating red and green. Still other people match wavelengths to color mixtures on the basis of brightness and not color. In other words, they will say a wavelength and mixture match as long as the two appear equally bright.

People who cannot discriminate one wavelength from another are considered to be color-blind. Color blindness is a genetic disorder that is transmitted from parent to offspring through a recessive gene on the X chromosome. Thus, more men (about 6 percent of all males) than women (less than 1 percent of all females) are color-blind. The recessive gene may influence either the functioning of the cones or the processes higher in the visual pathway.

However, most color-blind people learn to function very well in a world that, to the rest of us at least, is so resplendent with color. In fact, some color-blind people may never discover that they see the world differently than other people simply because they have learned to match color names with objects so well: green grass, blue ocean, red blood, and so on. Color-blind people also learn to name colors on the basis of their brightness. Thus, one shade of grey may be called red, another green, and yet another blue.

As you might suspect, such learned abilities make it difficult to detect whether or not an individual is genuinely color-blind. Determining color blindness is accomplished with special tests that eliminate brightness and contextual cues. A sample from one test, the Ishihani test, is illustrated in Figure 5.13.

The Color Circle. The spectral colors present in white light are often described by using the color circle. The color circle is created by placing similar colors next to one another in precisely the same way they appear in the spectrum. Take a close look at Figure 5.14. Notice that the four so-called primary colors, red, yellow, green, and blue are equidistant from each other. Primary colors cannot be created by mixing other colors. The other colors are not considered to be primary colors because they can be created by combining two primary colors. Both shades of purple shown on the color circle are called nonspectrum colors because they do not occur naturally in the spectrum; rather, they are formed by different combinations of red and blue. Many colors, for example, brown, gold, silver, and pink, are not found on the color circle for a similar reason: they represent a blending of two or more spectral colors.

Colors that are opposite one another on the color circle are called **complementary colors.** The center of the circle is gray because when any set of complementary colors is mixed in the correct proportion the result will be either white or gray, a balanced mixture of wavelengths (and therein lies the explanation of Newton's finding).

Seeing color is a psychological phenomenon. The color we call an object is literally a reflection of light waves from that object; the cones in our retinas are differentially sensitive to the reflected lightwaves. We turn now to a discussion of the two seemingly contrary theories of color vision, the trichromatic and the opponent-process theories, each of which attempts to explain how our visual system "sees" color.

Theories of Color Vision. In 1802, long before cones were known to exist, Thomas Young (1773–1829) proposed that the typical human eye has color receptors sensitive to the primary colors of red, green, and blue. Stimulation of any one of these receptors produces the sensation of the corresponding color. He suggested that the creation of other colors, such as purple and orange for example, involved interaction of the three different receptors. In 1857, Hermann von Helmholtz (1821–1894) refined Young's ideas and the theory came to be known as the **trichromatic theory.**

In Young and Helmholtz's day, the trichromatic theory was simply a good guess as to how the human visual system might operate to produce the psychological sensation of color. Neither the research methodology nor the technology was available to study the human visual system directly. However, modern sensory psychologists with their sophisticated gadgetry and research designs, have gathered substantial support for the trichromatic theory. We have data that confirm that the human eye has three

FIGURE 5.13
The Ishihani color blindness test. To identify the number in this plate, a person must be able to discriminate hues or colors. A person who cannot discriminate red-green colors cannot identify the number. People with normal color vision will see the number 26.

FIGURE 5.14
The color circle.

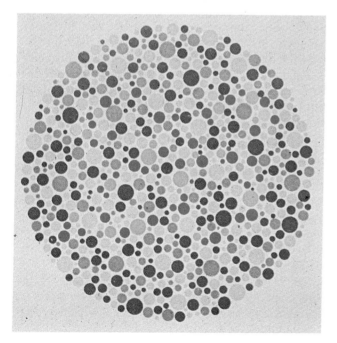

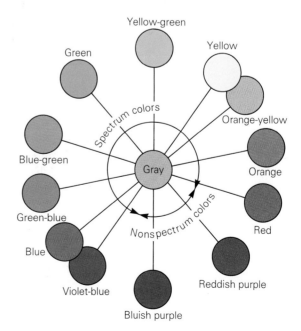

different cone systems, each of which is maximally sensitive to a distinct set of wavelengths: 435 nm (blue), 535 nm (green), and 765 nm (red). That is, each cone system is stimulated by wavelengths to which they are specifically tuned (Dartnell, Bowmaker, & Mollon, 1983). Each cone system also is stimulated by a wide range of other wavelengths. For instance, a short wavelength cone responds maximally to wavelengths of 435 nm but also responds with less intensity to other wavelengths. The closer those other wavelengths are to 435 nm, the stronger the cone's response. Our perception of nonprimary colors thus appears to be the result of the relative level of neural activity occurring at any given time in the three cone systems.

Unfortunately, trichromatic theory could not explain other aspects of color vision. Two dimensions of color vision posed particularly thorny problems. First, why do color-blind people fail to discriminate pairs of colors—red and green or blue and yellow? Second, why does staring at one hue, such as blue, produce a negative afterimage in its complementary color, yellow? (To experience a negative afterimage, try the demonstration illustrated in Figure 5.15.)

Hermann von Helmholtz

In an attempt to address these and other deficiencies in the Young-Helmholtz theory, Ewald Hering (1834–1918) proposed the **opponent-process theory** in 1878. Hering held there were three sets of color-sensitive receptors in the visual system: one set for red and green, another for blue and yellow, and the third for black and white.

According to Hering, the members of each set work in opposition to each other through neural inhibition (hence, the name, opponent-process). For example, if a long wavelength excites the red component of the red-green set, the red component, in turn, inhibits the green component. Similarly, if medium wavelengths stimulate the green component, the red component becomes inhibited. The perception of color depends upon the interaction of the red-green and blue-yellow sets. Stimulation of components in the black-white set affects only the brightness or darkness of a hue, not the hue itself.

Suppose light containing two wavelengths, one short (blue) and the other long (red), strike your eye. What color might Professor Hering say that you would see and why? The answer is violet, because it is a combination of blue and red. The short wavelength in the light will stimulate the blue component, which, in turn, will inhibit its opposing component, yellow. The long wavelength will excite the red component, thereby inhibiting its opposing component, green. On the other hand, had the light that struck your eyes been white light, you would not have perceived any color. Professor Hering's explanation: since white light contains all spectral colors in equal amounts, each color receptor component is stimulated equally, cancelling out neural signals from each other.

Hering's opponent-process theory clearly accounts for why color-blind people confuse red and green or blue and yellow. In either case, the particular receptor system is simply not functioning properly. How, though, can the opponent-process theory account for negative afterimages?

If you have not yet experienced the negative afterimage produced by observing the flag in Figure 5.15, now is a good time to do so. If you have, go back and try it again, if only to refresh your memory. By staring at the white spot for 30 seconds or more, you fatigue the green, yellow and black components of the three receptor systems. When you move your eyes to the white surface, the light it reflects stimulates the components of the red-green, blue-yellow and black-white sets equally. However, because the green, black, and yellow components are fatigued, they cannot respond as intensely as their respective antagonists (red, white, and blue), giving rise to the faint image of "Old Glory."

FIGURE 5.15
Negative afterimage. To see a negative afterimage, stare at the dot on the flag for 30 seconds and then stare at the center of a sheet of white paper or a blank wall. You should see the afterimage of the flag.

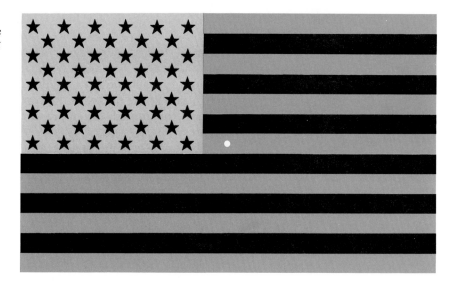

For several decades, the trichromatic and opponent-process theories remained poised against one another. Each theory could account for some aspects of color vision but not for others. Modern sensory psychologists, most notably Leo Hurvich and Dorthea Jameson (Hurvich, 1981) believe that the best way to explain color vision is to combine the two theories. They proposed that a trichromatic or three-color mechanism operating at the level of the cones, and an opponent-process four-color mechanism operating higher in the visual pathway each contribute to our ability to see color (Hurvich & Jameson, 1957). The discovery of color-opponent cells in the retina (at the level of ganglion cells) (Hurvich & Jameson, 1974) and in the thalamus (DeValois & Jacobs, 1984) provides support for Hurvich and Jameson's theory. Opponent cells in the thalamus are excited by one set of wavelengths and inhibited by a different set. For example, one cell is excited by red and inhibited by green while another set is excited by green and inhibited by red. Another set of cells function similarly but for blue and yellow, and still another set for black and white.

In sum, Young and Helmholtz' trichromatic theory held that we see color because our eyes have color receptors sensitive to the primary colors of red, green, and blue and that other colors are seen when these receptors interact. On the other hand, Hering's opponent-process theory argued that we see color because our eyes have three sets of color-sensitive receptors: one set for red and green, another for blue and yellow, and the third for black and white. Modern psychological research has shown that both theories are right, but that neither theory alone could fully account for color vision. Hurvich and Jameson suggested, and recent research has shown, that combining both theories produces a better account of color vision.

Although sensations arise at the moment light strikes the rods and cones, it is not until those sensations are interpreted by the brain that we are capable of perceiving.

The eye is truly a remarkable structure. It provides the means by which physical energy in the form of light is transduced to the electrochemical language understood by the nervous system. But as we have hinted, more than just the eye is involved in seeing. Without the visual cortex to interpret neural messages from the eye, there would be no perception. Although sensations arise at the moment light strikes the rods and cones, it is not until those sensations are interpreted by the brain that we are capable of perceiving. Let's take a closer look at the perceptual processes involved in seeing.

FIGURE 5.16
Can you identify the figure in this picture? See Figure 5.17 for a clue.

VISION—PERCEPTUAL PROCESSES

Examine, for a minute, Figure 5.16. What do you see? Unless you have seen this photo before you probably are not quite sure what you see. The best you can probably do is to say that you see black and white patches. But look again at the photo. In the very center is a dog, a dalmatian, with its nose to the ground. If you are having difficulty seeing the dog, look at Figure 5.17.

This exercise—interpreting vague stimulus information—is a reminder of the distinction we made earlier between **sensation,** immediate and simple experiences caused by physical stimuli, and **perception,** the processes by which the brain organizes and interprets sensations. As you were looking at Figure 5.16, your visual system was working just the way it was supposed to: the black and white patches in the photo were detected by your retinas, and information about the size and shape of the patches was relayed to your brain. Nonetheless, you weren't able, at least at first, to make any sense of the photo because your brain was unable to recognize or organize the patches into a meaningful form. Normally, we recognize an object as soon as we look at it, but in this instance, there was probably a noticeable delay between first looking at the photo and then seeing the dalmatian.

Perceiving an object as what it really is, a dog or a cat, an apple or an orange, a truck or a car, and so on, is easy enough; we don't think about it or plan it, we just do it automatically. However, explaining perception is an entirely different matter. The heart of the problem is this: Any object in the environment, the **distal stimulus,** can be known to us only through its image on the retina, the **proximal stimulus,** an image that is only two-dimensional and is always changing. The size of the proximal stimulus changes as we move toward or away from the distal stimulus and changes its position on the retina as we change our viewing angle. Under normal conditions, we quickly recognize a dog as a dalmatian whether we are looking at it from 2 feet or from 20 feet, whether we are moving or stationary, and whether we are viewing it from above, below, or the side, despite the fact that, in each case, the proximal stimulus changes. How do we manage to perceive the constant properties of the dog when its image upon our retinas keeps changing? Cast in more general terms, this question echos the central problem of visual perception: How are organisms able to perceive the constant properties of an object when the proximal stimulus keeps changing? In order to answer this question, we first examine how our perceptions are organized and then explain how perceptions remain constant while proximal stimuli change. As we shall see, in many instances,

FIGURE 5.17
The figure in 5.16 is a dalmatian. Look at Figure 5.16 again and see how much easier it is now to identify the figure.

FIGURE 5.18
Recognition or form perception.

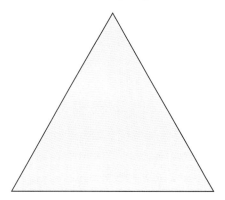

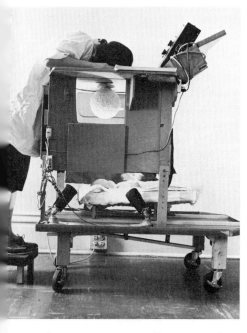

The Fantz apparatus allows researchers to study an infant's visual preferences.

the brain's organization and interpretation of sensations produced by proximal stimuli appears to account for perceptual constancy.

Perceptual Organization

Sensations are caused by your sensory system being stimulated by objects and events in your environment. Your brain, in turn, organizes sensations in such a way that you can locate and recognize objects and events in the environment and detect action or movement of those objects. Understanding perceptual organization, then, is a matter of understanding how we perceive form, depth, and motion.

Recognition—Form Perception. Soon after the turn of the century, a number of German scientists calling themselves Gestalt psychologists argued that humans have an inborn tendency to organize the individual elements of any visual scene into a well-organized whole or gestalt. They further argued that the key to understanding perception was to identify the relations among various parts of a stimulus. We simply do not perceive a triangle, for example, as consisting of three separate lines; rather, we perceive the relation among the three lines. When asked what object we see in Figure 5.18, we automatically reply, "a triangle," which in this case means three equal sized line segments connected in such a way that they form three equal angles. In short, we perceive objects as well-organized configurations or gestalts rather than as the sum of their individual parts. That is, an equilateral triangle is more than just adding together three lines: it is a matter of how those lines are organized, physically and perceptually.

Modern research has shown that form perception may indeed be part of our genetic endowment. Newborns prefer viewing complex figures to simple ones (Fantz, 1961), and they tend to scan specific features of objects, such as edges and contours that define form, rather than scanning them randomly (Haith, 1980). More importantly, newborns prefer looking at forms that resemble the human face to looking at other forms (Fantz, 1961, 1970). That infants have built-in tendencies to perceive facelike patterns makes good psychological sense. After all, infancy is an intense period of immaturity in which the newborn's very survival may depend upon its ability to recognize familiar faces, particularly those of its parents.

Two Gestalt principles, the figure-ground relation and perceptual grouping, are still used today in describing how we organize our perceptions of the world.

Figure-Ground Relationship. Our perception of any object depends upon our ability to recognize it as an entity, called a figure, distinct from its surroundings, called the ground. For obvious reasons, the relationship between the figure and the ground is called the **figure-ground relationship.** We recognize the white area in Figure 5.19 as the figure because it appears as a well-organized configuration, a pine tree. We perceive the dark area as the ground because it is relatively formless and appears to continue behind the figure.

Distinguishing between figure and ground is the job of the perceptual system, independent of the object or objects being viewed. The job is not always an easy one, as the reversible figure shown in Figure 5.20 demonstrates. A reversible figure allows the viewer to perceive either of two figure-ground relations, in this case, a white vase against a dark background or two silhouetted faces against a white background. That is, the same distal stimulus often gives rise to different perceptions depending upon how the brain organizes the sensations arising from the proximal stimulus. Organizing the sensations one way, we see the vase; organizing them another way, we see the two silhouettes.

FIGURE 5.19
The figure-ground relationship. We recognize the white area as a figure because it appears as a well-organized configuration—a pine tree. We perceive the dark area as the ground because it is relatively formless and appears to continue behind the figure.

FIGURE 5.20
A reversible figure. Whether you perceive this figure as a white vase against a darker background or two silhouetted faces against a lighter background depends upon how your brain organizes sensations produced by the proximal stimulus.

Perceptual Grouping. Once a figure is discriminated from the ground, the next step in perception is to organize the figure into a meaningful pattern or shape. Gestalt psychologists refer to the perceptual system's tendency to impose organization upon figures as **perceptual grouping.** Max Wertheimer (1880–1943), an important figure in the Gestalt movement, argued that perceptual grouping could be described in terms of several basic rules of perceptual organization. Underlying each of these rules is the principle that the whole is greater than the sum of its parts. Consider, for example, four of these rules:

Proximity. Objects that are near to each other tend to be grouped together, perceptually. For example, the six objects below will generally be perceived as three pairs of triangles rather than as six individual triangles.

Similarity. We also tend to group objects according to their similarity to each other. In the drawings below, we group triangles with triangles and squares with squares. Consequently, we perceive the left panel to be arranged according to rows and the right panel according to columns.

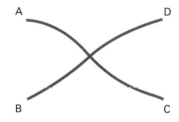

A   D

B   C

FIGURE 5.21
Good continuation. We tend to perceive objects as being constructed of smooth continuous features rather than discontinuous ones. Therefore, line segments A and C appear to be connected as do line segments B and D.

Good Continuation. Other things being equal, we tend to perceive objects as being constructed of smooth, continuous features rather than discontinuous ones. Thus, in Figure 5.21 we perceive line segment A linked with C and B with D rather than A with D and B with C. Good continuation is the perceptual process that makes camouflage possible.

Closure. We tend to complete objects that have spaces or gaps in them. By filling in the gaps we see a dog in Figure 5.16. The change of background makes it easier for us to immediately recognize the figure as a dalmatian simply because there are now fewer gaps for our visual system to fill in.

A special form of closure gives rise to the subjective contours illusion. Subjective contours are shapes that are seen, when in fact they do not physically exist. A good example is shown in Figure 5.22. Notice that the white triangle appears brighter than the white background. The contour of the white triangle, although visible, is not physically real. We "see" the white triangle because our perceptual systems complete the lines originating from each of the black circles. Cover the black circles and the white triangle disappears.

Location–Depth Perception. Visually locating objects in the environment is often a matter of gauging their distance from us or other objects, a process referred to as **depth perception**. Perception of depth is a rather amazing phenomenon: we perceive the world in three dimensions—height, width, and depth—despite the fact that the surface of our retinas is only two dimensional (height and width). But how can a two-dimensional surface represent three-dimensional scenes? The answer involves the idea of **depth cues**, which are aspects of any stimulus situation that indicate how far an object is from the observer or other objects. These cues fall into two categories: binocular (two eyes) and monocular (one eye).

Binocular Cues. Try the following experiment. Hold a pencil or similar object at an arm's distance from your face. Gradually move the object toward you until it touches your nose. When you do this, your eyes rotate inward until they eventually cross. The tendency of the eyes to turn inward when viewing nearby objects is called **convergence**, and it is one binocular cue to depth. Our eyes converge naturally on any object we view. However, when our eyes converge on nearby objects, the angle between them is greater than when they converge on objects farther way.

Many sensory psychologists believe that convergence is a depth cue because it is positively correlated with the distance between us and any object we view: the closer the object, the greater the convergence. However, convergence is only useful for gauging the distance of objects up to about 10 meters away (Hochberg, 1971). The degree of convergence does not change very much when you shift your focus from an object 30 meters away to an object 20 meters away. In contrast, shifting your focus from an object 10 meters away to one a meter away produces changes in the amount of convergence. And it is usually more important to be able to judge distance accurately within an arm's length than it is to judge distance 30 meters away.

Because our eyes are about 7 cm apart, they each see the world from a slightly different angle. When we focus on an object in the environment, the eyes are positioned in slightly different locations, causing slightly different images of objects to be cast on different parts of each retina, giving rise to the binocular cue of **binocular disparity**. Binocular disparity is useful in judging the relative depth of objects up to about 20 feet away. We are not usually aware of binocular disparity because the brain combines information from both eyes into a single, coherent picture of the world.

You can easily demonstrate binocular disparity for yourself. Hold your right index finger about 30 centimeters from your eyes. If possible, hold your finger so that it covers up the edge of a painting or other wall ornament. While focusing on the finger, keep your right eye open but close your left eye. Next, do just the opposite: keep your left eye open but close your right eye. Did your finger appear to move back and forth against the background? Now move your finger to about an inch from your eye and repeat the procedure for opening and closing your eyes. Did your finger appear to move more this time than when it was held at arms length? This demonstrates an important aspect of binocular disparity: it becomes greater the closer the object is to the observer.

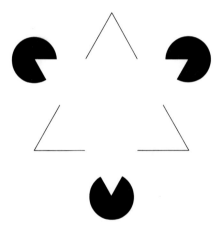

FIGURE 5.22
Subject contours. The contour of the white triangle, although visible, is an illusion. We perceive the triangle because our perceptual systems complete the lines that start from each of the black circles.

Monocular cues. Top to bottom: interposition, linear perspective, relative size, texture gradient, and aerial perspective. Right: motion parallax.

Monocular Cues. Binocular cues alone, though, cannot account for our ability to perceive depth. Three-dimensional vision is possible even if we use only one eye to view the world. Indeed, people blind in one eye since birth can easily perceive depth. Obviously monocular cues or depth cues involving the image cast upon one retina only help us perceive depth. Six monocular cues are listed below.

- **Interposition** If object A partially blocks our view of object B, we perceive object A as being closer than object B.
- **Linear Perspective** As parallel lines recede, they appear to converge on a vanishing point somewhere in the distance, creating the impression of depth.
- **Relative Size** The larger the image cast upon the retina by an object, the closer the object appears to be.
- **Texture Gradient** Objects that are larger and coarser appear closer than objects that are smaller and smoother.
- **Aerial Perspective** Objects far off in the distance appear hazy and less distinct than nearby objects.
- **Motion Parallax** Nearby objects appear to race by while distant objects appear to move slowly. As an example, consider driving down an open stretch of freeway. Trees, billboards, and other objects close to the road seem to speed by us but farmhouses and other objects far off the road only seem to creep by us.

Monocular cues, with the exception of motion parallax, are sometimes called pictorial cues because artists use them to represent three dimensional scenes on their two dimensional canvases. In fact, artists were using monocular cues in their work many centuries before psychologists started to study perception systematically.

Is depth perception innate? Like form perception, depth perception seems to be a part of our native endowment. Richard Walk and Eleanor Gibson (1961) have shown that human infants as young as 6 months old can perceive depth. Gibson was first struck with the idea to study depth perception in infants while enjoying a view from the rim of the Grand Canyon. She became curious as to whether an infant peering over the edge

Fixation point

Direction of passenger's motion

Motion parallax

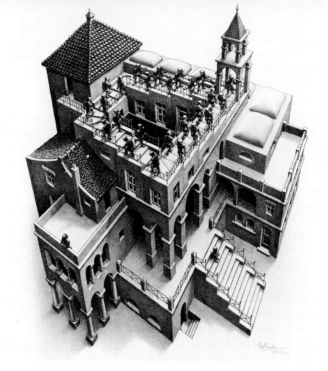

Artists can render objects three dimensionally as in this drawing by M. C. Escher, which uses monocular or pictorial cues.

An infant crawls reluctantly across the "deep side" of the visual cliff toward his mother.

would perceive the danger and retreat. When she returned to her laboratory at Cornell University in New York, she and Walk designed and constructed the visual cliff, an apparatus that simulates a steep precipice yet is completely safe. The visual cliff is actually a large glass table, about three feet high, that is divided into two segments. On the "shallow side," a checkerboard pattern is attached directly to the underside of the glass. On the "deep side," this pattern is placed on the floor. Gibson and Walk placed infants on the edge of the cliff and had their mothers call to them. When a mother called from the shallow side, the infant crawled directly to her. However, most infants were reluctant to crawl out on to the glass covering the apparent drop-off when beckoned by their mothers from the deep side.

Of course, these results do not show that depth perception in humans is innate. It might be argued that by the time infants are old enough to crawl, they have had plenty of visual experience and have likely learned to use some of the cues discussed above to gauging depth. (Regrettably, isolating innate factors in human depth perception is problematic if only because infants must be mature enough to give the researcher some indication that they can, in fact, perceive depth, as in Walk and Gibson's study in which crawling to one side of the visual cliff or the other was taken as evidence of depth perception.) On the other hand, psychologists can study depth perception in other species in which motor coordination develops soon after birth. For example, lambs and goats tested as soon as they were able to stand never ventured onto the deep side of the cliff. Likewise, chicks less than twenty-four hours old behaved similarly. At the very least, the ability to perceive depth appears to be present at very early ages in many species.

The ability to perceive depth allows us to comprehend psychologically the three dimensional nature of our world. Without this ability, we would not be able to judge the distances of objects from us, making it impossible to perform simple activities such as playing catch, let alone complex activities such as driving a car. But depth perception is not the only perceptual skill that we need to engage in these sorts of behavior. We must also be able to perceive motion.

FIGURE 5.23

Stroboscopic movement occurs when several lights are flashed one after another in the darkness, creating an illusion of continuous movement.

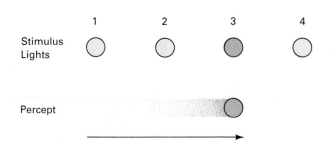

Action–Motion Perception. Many major league pitchers can throw a baseball toward home plate in excess of 90 miles per hour. At that speed, it takes only a fraction of a second for the ball to travel the 60 feet 6 inches separating the pitcher's mound from home plate. To even the best batters, the ball appears as little more than a blur the size of an aspirin. Yet remarkably, they hit the ball consistently and sometimes for great distances. How is it that a batter can see the ball as it speeds toward him? Or for that matter, how is it that a spectator in the stands can see the ball as it is thrown or hit? More generally, how do we detect movement? The most obvious answer is through movement of the proximal stimulus across the retina. This answer, although true, is only partially correct, for we sometimes see movement even when the proximal stimulus does not move across the retina. A classic example is the illusion called **stroboscopic movement**.

Stroboscopic movement is produced easily by flashing a light in darkness and then several milliseconds later, flashing a second identical light in a slightly different location (Figure 5.23). The light will appear to move from the first location to the second, although it does not actually move between the two locations. Stroboscopic movement is the basic principle behind motion pictures, in which slightly different still photographs are flashed on the screen at the rate of 24 frames per second. When the timing between light flashes is just right, stroboscopic movement is indistinguishable from real movement. When the timing is off, as in very early moving pictures where the frame rate was only 16 per second, movement appears rigid and jerky. Thus, the relative change in position of objects over time is an important cue for the perception of movement. Stroboscopic movement is an example of apparent movement, the illusion of movement when motionless stimuli are manipulated to simulate the changes that occur in real movement.

Most movement we perceive, however, is not illusory. To the batter standing at home plate, the 90 mph plus fastball is very real, and to pedestrians crossing a busy street, oncoming vehicles are not imaginary. Although any moving object we perceive casts an image that traverses our retinas, perceiving movement is more complicated than merely "seeing" movements of objects as they are projected on the retina because natural movements of our eyes can also cause the proximal stimulus to move. Thus, displacement of proximal stimuli may occur because the object has moved or because the eye has moved, or because of some combination of both. How then can we judge whether or not something is actually moving?

Many perception experts agree that the brain must in some way compensate for movements of the proximal stimulus produced by natural eye movements. When your eyes scan a stationary object, your brain adjusts for such movement; although the proximal stimulus moves, you perceive the object as staying put. When you scan a moving object, your brain similarly adjusts for natural eye movements, permitting you to perceive the object as moving due only to environmental causes.

FIGURE 5.24

Lightness constancy. The lump of coal appears to be equally black even though it is viewed under two different levels of illumination.

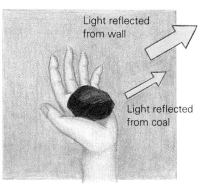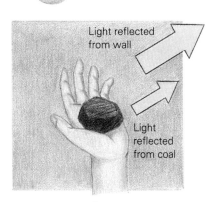

a   b

FIGURE 5.26

Size constancy. We perceive the man on the right side of the photo to be normal size because he is at a distance. In reality, the size of the image he casts on our retinas is identical to the size of the tiny image shown at far left.

Perceptual Constancies

We can readily recognize and locate objects in our environment and can discern their movement. We also manage one other remarkable perceptual feat—perceiving objects as possessing certain stable features such as lightness, size, and shape, despite changes in their appearances. This ability is termed **perceptual constancy**. What is so remarkable about perceptual constancy? Precisely this: Psychologically, our perception of objects remains constant although the conditions under which we view them may change. A mountain appears large whether viewed from the plains or from the foothills, the moon appears round whether observed at its zenith or along the horizon, and the grass appears green whether viewed in the bright sunlight of mid-day or in the dimness of twilight. In more technical jargon, the same object may cast different images upon our retinas without disrupting our perception of that object. Although our sensory world is ever changing, our perception of it, in terms of lightness, color, shape, and size, remains relatively constant. Examples of lightness, shape, and size constancies are shown in Figures 5.24 to 5.26.

Illusions

Illusions are misperceptions of real objects or events. Physical illusions such as seeing a break in a pencil where it sticks out of the water (Figure 5.27) are caused by distortions in the stimulus image cast upon our retinas. Perceptual illusions such as the moon illusion (Figure 5.28) are caused by miscues in our visual system. Perceptual illusions have fascinated psychologists for several decades simply because they represent ways in which the

FIGURE 5.25

Shape constancy. We perceive the door as having a constant shape despite changes in the image it casts upon our retinas when it is opened at various angles.

Vision—Perceptual Processes **177**

FIGURE 5.27
Physical illusion. Physical illusions are caused by distortions in the stimulus image cast upon our retinas. Is the pencil really divided?

FIGURE 5.28
The moon illusion. The moon appears much larger on the horizon than it does when it is directly overhead.

perceptual system can be misled. Over 200 perceptual illusions have been discovered (Gillam, 1980). Two well-known illusions, the Muller-Lyer illusion and the Ames Room are shown in Figures 5.29 and 5.30, respectively.

Perception and Attention

In any visual scene, some objects or events are more likely to capture our attention than others. Attention is the focusing or concentrating of psychological activity on a specific object. When we look at a work of art, we focus more on the figure than the background; when we watch a sporting event such as a football game, we notice the actions of the player with the ball more than we do the actions of the other players; when we read, we focus on only a few words at a time and not on all the words on the entire page. In other words, visual perception is selective: we tend to perceive only that portion of the visual scene to which we direct our attention. Likewise, we generally attend to only those things we wish to perceive.

Attention is an important part of visual perception because of the way in which our retinas are constructed. We see clearly only that part of the visual scene cast upon our foveas. Thus, we must direct our foveas to that part of the scene we wish to see clearly. Although we can still see the rest of the scene in our peripheral vision, we focus our attention on the object we are looking directly at. For example, when we read, only a few words are in focus at a time because that is as many as we can see clearly with our foveas. And although we see the remainder of the words, they are blurry because they fall upon our retina's periphery.

The ability to perceive only one visual stimulus while ignoring others is referred to as **selective looking**. Consider the following experiment. An observer is shown two superimposed films, one of three people playing catch with a round ball and the other of a handslapping game (Figure 5.31). Every time the ball is passed the observer is to press a button with his or her right hand and every time one player successfully slapped the other's hand the observer is to press a second button with the other hand. Based on what you know about attention, do you think that our observer could follow both games at once? If your answer is no, you are absolutely right. In fact, this very experiment was performed by Ulric Neisser and Robert Becklen in 1975. When their subjects were asked to monitor one game at a time, they had little difficulty in doing so. But when asked to monitor both games at once, subjects' performances deteriorated markedly. Error rates for not pressing the button when they should have were nearly eight times higher than when monitoring one game at a time.

FIGURE 5.29
The Muller-Lyer illusion. The vertical lines in the left panel appear to be unequal, but in fact, they are the same length. The illusion is caused by the fact that we tend to perceive the lines as three-dimensional objects with corners (see right panel). The vertical lines that look like the inside corner of a room appear larger and, therefore, farther away.

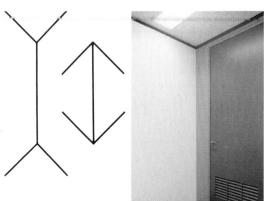

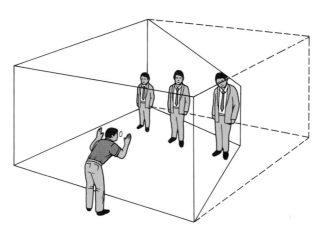

FIGURE 5.30

The Ames Room. In this illusion, the person on the right side of the room appears to be much larger than the person on the left, when actually, both people are the same size. The illusion occurs because the room looks like a normal rectangle but is actually constructed of nonrectangular surfaces with odd angles in depth and height.

In more recent studies, Neisser (1979) and Becklen and Cervone (1983) required subjects to view a short film of three men in black T-shirts passing a basketball superimposed over a film of three other men in white T-shirts also passing a basketball. Subjects were asked to monitor the game by pressing a button every time the black-shirted men tossed the ball. About halfway through viewing, a third film was projected onto the screen: a young woman carrying an umbrella walked through the game (Figure 5.32). Did subjects see the woman? No, subjects perceived only the ball-tossing. In fact, when the film was replayed and the woman pointed out to them, subjects were surprised. Like subjects in the Neisser and Becklen experiment, these subjects had selectively perceived only one aspect of the visual scene. Visual perception appears to be organized so that, psychologically, we can only easily attend to one source of stimulation at a time, and therefore, we perceive little or nothing from the unattended sources of stimulation.

Although we can attend to only one stimulus at a time, our visual system is bombarded by many stimuli. As we walk through a shopping mall or along side a busy street, we are confronted with a vast array of stimuli. Yet only a few stimuli catch our eye. Why do we pay attention to some stimuli and ignore others? Although the answer to this question will vary from one person to the next because of differences in individual interests, motivation, and emotionality, there are several specific features of stimuli that are sure attention-grabbers (Wilding, 1983). Novel stimuli, those that are different or unusual are likely to attract attention. You are more likely to notice a Rolls Royce cruising down the road than you are a new subcompact. Size, color, and movement are also powerful determinants of attention.

FIGURE 5.31

The stimulus arrangement used by Neisser and Becklin (1974). The videotape of the hand-slapping game (a) was superimposed on a videotape of three people playing catch (b). The result is shown in (c).

(a)　　　　　　　　(b)　　　　　　　　(c)

Pattern Recognition

We see clearly only those objects to which we attend. But attention itself does not permit us to recognize objects. Once we have located an object in space and determined its shape and whether or not it is moving, how do we manage to recognize what kind of thing that object is? To recognize an object means that it can be correctly identified either in general terms such as "That is a car" or in specific terms, such as "That is a BMW." Like other aspects of perception, recognition is an ability most of us take for granted until we mistake one object for another. Most of us have had the embarrassing experiencing of mistaking one person for another. We greet or wave to an individual we "recognize" as a friend, only to learn shortly afterward that that person was not who we thought he or she was. In some instances, the consequences of mistaken identity are more serious, as when an innocent person is imprisoned for the crime of a guilty person because eye witnesses have mistaken one person for the other (see Figure 5.33).

FIGURE 5.33
A case of mistaken identity. The man on the left was imprisoned for 5 years for a crime committed by the man on the right.

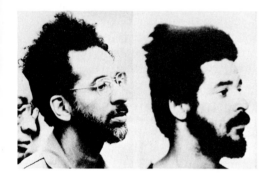

Precisely how we recognize patterns and why we sometimes make recognition errors have been issues of considerable interest to psychologists. Recognizing patterns depends on the manner in which our brains analyze features of patterns, a process called feature analysis.

Feature Analysis. As its name implies, **feature analysis** involves recognition of an object based on the distinctive characteristics or components that, because of the specific manner in which they are arranged, define it. Consider, for example, the letters of the alphabet. Letters are composed of lines of various lengths and orientations, angles, curves, intersections, and so on. Specific combinations of these features produce patterns that distinguish one letter from the others. Our recognition of any of the 26 letters of the alphabet depends upon our ability to detect and recognize each letter's distinctive characteristics.

The most popular version of feature analysis theory was developed in 1959 by Oliver Selfridge and elaborated by Peter Lindsay and Donald Norman (1977). According to Selfridge, pattern recognition involves four progressive stages:

Stage 1: Detecting the pattern of stimulation;
Stage 2: Disassembling the pattern into its component parts;
Stage 3: Comparing the component features with information (a "feature list") stored in visual memory;
Stage 4: Deciding: correct recognition of the pattern.

Figure 5.34 illustrates the process by which this model of feature analysis explains the recognition of the letter *R*. In the first stage, the image of the object's pattern is detected by the rods and cones. Stage two involves the brain disassembling the pattern into its constituent parts, perhaps by

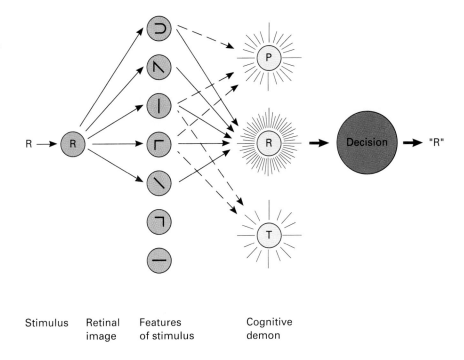

Stimulus	Retinal image	Features of stimulus	Cognitive demon

specialized cells in the visual cortex. Notice that the *R* shares features in common with other letters such as *P* and *T*. In stage three, features of the pattern generate neural excitement proportional to their similarity to those represented in a feature list stored in memory. In this case, the features present in the *R* more closely resemble the comparison features of an *R* than those of the *P* or a *T* represented in memory. The final stage involves correctly identifying the pattern as being characteristic of a specific object on the basis of the amount of neural excitation present in stage three. The decision that the stimulus pattern is characteristic of an *R* is based solely on the amount of neural excitation in the previous stage.

Context and Perceptual Set. Feature analysis theory has been an attractive explanation of human pattern recognition for two reasons. First, its components can be linked to specific physiological processes in the brain (recall Hubel and Weisel's discovery of feature detectors in the visual cortex). Second, it lends itself well to computer simulation. As we shall see, though, the theory is not without its shortcomings. An important criticism of feature analysis is that it ignores the role that context can play in pattern recognition. By context we mean the conditions under which an object or event is perceived. Context is anything that helps us identify an object other than the object itself. The way we often express our failure to recognize objects and events testifies to the role of context in pattern recognition. For example, we often hear expressions like "I didn't recognize you with your glasses on," or "I didn't recognize you in that Porsche. I am so accustomed to seeing you in that old tank you used to drive."

Contextual cues to recognition are particularly important when an object is ambiguous. Examine Figure 5.35. Do you recognize the scribble in the top line as the letters, *I* and *S* or as the numbers, 1 and 5? Given the right context you might interpret it as either. When you read the middle line of Figure 5.35, you interpret the scribble as an *I* and an *S*, because it appears with letters of the alphabet. But you interpret the identical scribble in the bottom line as a 1 and a 5 because it appears with numbers.

FIGURE 5.35

The effect of context on recognition. In each line, we recognize the S as a number or letter depending upon contextual cues. (After Goldstein, Sensation and Perception, second edition, 1984.)

IS

THE CAT IS MINE

14, 15, 16

When objects, even familiar ones, appear in novel contexts, recognition becomes difficult, if not impossible, as Irving Biederman (1981) discovered in his simple but telling experiment on pattern recognition. Subjects in this experiment were shown a series of scenes in rapid succession. For each scene, Biederman first told subjects which part of the scene to look at and then asked them to identify an object located at a particular position in the scene. For example, subjects were asked to identify the fire hydrant in the scene shown in Figure 5.36. Biederman found that subjects made more identification errors when the hydrant was located in a strange place (on top of the mailbox) than when it was located in its usual place (on the sidewalk), even though subjects were told before each scene exactly where to direct their attention. Subjects knew from previous experience where to find fire hydrants, but in this instance that knowledge interfered with their ability to recognize the object on top of the mailbox as a hydrant.

Biederman's results make good psychological sense when we consider the difficulties we sometimes have recognizing some people outside of their usual context. For example, although you see your psychology professor at the podium several days a week, you would probably have at least a little trouble recognizing him or her clad in the latest ski wear on the ski slope or in faded blue jeans and a T-shirt at a rock concert. Most students don't expect to see their professors in the mountains or at a concert, but they do expect to see them on campus and perhaps occasionally around town.

The tendency of a person's expectations to influence his or her perception is called **perceptual set**. The term *set* refers to the notion that we are sometimes predisposed to process sensory information. Look at the picture of the old woman shown in Figure 5.37. Notice her large nose and tightly drawn lips and how her chin appears to be tucked into her coat. Stop! Suppose we tell you that this is a picture of a young woman: the old woman's lips form the young woman's neckband; the old woman's nose forms the young woman's chin; the old woman's left eye forms the young

FIGURE 5.36

The stimulus arrangement used by Biederman (1981). When shown this picture, subjects were asked to locate the fire hydrant. Subjects had difficulty performing this simple task because of their knowledge of where fire hydrants are usually located.

FIGURE 5.37

The effects of perceptual set on recognition. Is the woman shown in this picture young or old? Actually, this is an ambiguous figure. Depending on which features of the picture you focus on, the figure may be perceived as either an old woman or a young woman.

woman's left ear. To be sure, this ambiguous figure can be perceived as either an old woman or a young woman, depending on which features of the picture you focus your attention on. However, the initial information we gave you (about the old woman) should have been sufficient for you to develop a perceptual set or expectation that would cause you to see an old woman when you looked at the picture. And as a result, you likely ignored information in the picture about the young woman.

Learned Factors in Pattern Recognition. We know that our abilities to perceive form and depth mature at an early age, and we also know that we are born with highly specialized cells (feature detectors) that respond to specific features of objects in our environments. On the other hand, we also know that our perception of the world can be changed by new and different experiences. In this section, we discuss such changes in terms of restricted sensory experience, perceptual adaptation, and perceptual learning.

How important are early visual experiences to the development of normal vision? Such a question, although important, is difficult to answer directly if only because ethical considerations prevent psychologists from devising experiments that purposely deprive a human being of his or her sight. Rather, psychologists have had to rely on natural experiments on people who were born blind (usually due to cataracts) or whose vision has been surgically corrected to answer that question (Gregory, 1978).

People born with cataracts can see only diffused patterns of light; they have virtually no visual acuity. When the cataracts are removed surgically, these persons can discriminate figure-ground relationships and see color, but they can not recognize the shape and form of objects. In fact, some of these people may never learn to recognize objects. Interestingly, if we restrict the vision of an adult by covering one or both eyes with a patch for several weeks, vision will not be impaired when the patch is removed. Apparently, the abilities to distinguish figure from ground and to *see* color are part of our native endowment, but the ability to *perceive* shape and form require early visual experience.

The ability to perceive shape and form requires early visual experiences.

Research with animals also testifies to the importance of early experience in visual perception. In a classic study, Colin Blakemore and Grahame Cooper (1970) placed visually inexperienced kittens in an environment of all vertical stripes or all horizontal stripes for five hours each day. During the remaining nineteen hours, the kittens were placed in completely darkened environments. When Blakemore and Cooper later tested the sensitivity of the cortical neurons in each kitten's visual cortex to vertical and horizontal stimuli, they found that the cortical neurons of kittens reared in the all-vertical environment responded maximally to vertical stimuli and that the cortical neurons of kittens reared in the all-horizontal responded mostly to horizontal stimuli. Thus the kittens' early visual experience seemed to determine the features to which their cortical cells were maximally responsive. Even though feature detectors are present at or soon after birth, they seem to rely on early visual experiences for their final development. In other words, early visual experience has profound effects on visual perception.

Although our early visual experiences can shape our perception of the world, their effects need not be permanent. Visual perception is modifiable. Consider, for example, the clever work of George Stratton (1865–1957), the first known human to experience a right side up retinal image. Stratton (1897) devised and wore an optical device that shifted right to left and inverted up to down. At first, Stratton was confused. Walking across a room became akin to navigating through an obstacle course. Eating

We learn to perceive according to our own interests and needs. For example, most of us may not be able to make the fine distinction between different species of birds that experienced bird watchers can.

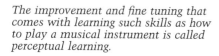

The improvement and fine tuning that comes with learning such skills as how to play a musical instrument is called perceptual learning.

required concentrated effort. Even learning to do very simple things such as reaching upward to pick an object off the floor and to turn right to go left was not easy. Nonetheless Stratton's tenacity prevailed, and after eight days his behavior finally adapted to his new perception of the world. He no longer tripped over objects and could easily reach in the right direction for things he wanted to grasp. When Stratton removed the device, he had only minor problems in readjusting to his old perception of the world. In sum, Stratton learned to adjust his behavior to changes in his perception of the world.

It is also possible to learn how to perceive. Each of us knows people who appear to have extremely keen vision; they seem able to see things that we cannot. For example, to most of us one sparrow looks pretty much like any other sparrow or, for that matter, any small bird. However, an avid bird watcher can accurately identify any of the many species of sparrow and tell you with just a glance whether it is male or female, or juvenile or adult. But the ability to distinguish objects from one another is not usually due to one person naturally having keener vision than another. Rather, each of us learns to perceive the environment in ways that fit our interests and needs.

Any change in a person's perceptual skills due to learning is referred to as **perceptual learning.** Eleanor Gibson and her colleagues have studied perceptual learning and have noted an important change in perceptual ability that is brought about through such learning (Gibson, 1969). Over time, larger and larger quantities of information are extracted from the environment. In essence, we learn to "see" features of our environment that we once overlooked. Thus, perceptual learning results in an increased economy of information being extracted. With practice, we learn to make accurate and increasingly finer discriminations in shorter and shorter periods of time. Consider some of the skills you have learned in your lifetime, perhaps driving a car, playing a musical instrument, or playing a sport. You may recall how, at least at first, learning was difficult because there seemed to be so many things to pay attention to. Gradually, however, you mastered the task and now it seems almost second nature to you. This is

the kind of economy to which Gibson referred: you learned which features of the task to pay attention to and which features could be ignored.

Bottom-Up and Top-Down Processing.   Clearly, pattern recognition occurs at two different levels. Feature analysis is often labeled **bottom-up processing,** because processing of the pattern begins at the level of the receptors and proceeds in an orderly fashion through specialized neurons in the visual cortex. However, information processing can occur in reverse order: in many cases, a person's knowledge of the world influences which features of a pattern will be detected and recognized. This kind of information processing is often referred to as **top-down processing** because processing of the pattern begins with the higher levels of abstract thinking directing receptors to attend to particular features of the pattern. If pattern recognition were a matter of only bottom-up processing, we would necessarily have to attend to every feature of each object in our environment. Processing that amount of information would place tremendous demands upon our sensory-perceptual system. Think of how difficult reading even a single sentence would become if you had to attend to and analyze the four or five features of each letter of each word. Top-down processing, however, allows us to draw on our previous perceptual experiences and enables us at times to disregard some features of an object without detracting from our understanding of it. For example, consider the statement, "Sally got in her car and put the in the ignition." Our knowledge of driving and cars allows us to provide the missing word, *key,* almost before we finish reading the sentence. Even if the sentence was complete, we would not need to devote much attention to the word *key* to understand Sally's action. Perhaps the best way to view pattern recognition is as a combination of both kinds of information processing. In some cases, top-down processing determines which features of an object will undergo bottom-up processing and in others, bottom-up processing detects the important features of an object which direct future top-down processing.

In conclusion, our ability to recognize patterns seems to be the result of an interaction of natural and learned abilities. On one hand, we are born with the basic physiological hardware we need for perceiving the world; on the other hand, our experiences with the environment determine the development of that hardware and the features of objects to which we attend.

BOUNDARIES AND FRONTIERS

The scientific study of sensation and perception represents one of the oldest areas of psychology. Although studied formally after Wilhelm Wundt established his laboratory in Leipzig, Germany in 1879, questions about sensation and perception have been posed at least since the time of the ancient Greeks. At first these questions were of the form, "How is knowledge acquired?" and "What role do the senses play in acquiring knowledge?" But the Greeks and other early philosophers had no way of looking inside the body and brain for an answer; intense and often eloquent debate was their only avenue toward an answer. Later, with the invention of what, by today's standards, are crude surgical instruments, these questions focused on the physiological basis of sensation. Modern sensory psychologists, armed with sophisticated gadgetry that allows them to eavesdrop on the activity of individual neurons in the brain and central nervous system, have pursued the latter question with remarkable success. For example, we know a great deal about the eye and how its specialized cells, the rods and cones, convert electromagnetic energy in the form of light waves into neural impulses. We also know the route these impulses take to their final destination, the visual cortex. Such knowledge has had tremendous applied value for both psychologists and others. We now understand many visual disorders, such as myopia and hyperopia, and how to treat them.

But while sensations can be traced to specific neural pathways linking a given sensory system with the brain, perception seems rather more elusive. Perception cannot be reduced to an aggregate of sensations, for to perceive something is more than to merely sense something. A perception places sensory information into a context, one that takes into account previous experiences as well as present environmental conditions. Understanding perception, then, must go beyond an understanding of sensation.

Therein lies the challenge facing modern sensory and perceptual psychologists. Questions such as "How does perception affect the acquisition and uses of knowledge?," "How do sensory and perceptual processes influence each other?," and "How does perception affect motivation, learning, thinking, and social interaction (and vice versa)?" have, to a large extent, broadened the scope of questions raised earlier. They do, in a sense, take us beyond the boundaries of the questions faced by early sensory psychology, and so, become the frontiers for modern research.

CONCEPT SUMMARY

- What is the difference between sensation and perception? (p. 149)

BASIC PRINCIPLES OF SENSATION

- What is an absolute threshold? Describe its typical psychophysical function. (pp. 150–152)
- What are the major tenets of signal detection theory? How do sensitivity and response bias influence an individual's absolute threshold? (pp. 152–154)
- What is a difference threshold and how does it differ from an absolute threshold? (pp. 154–155)
- Why is Weber's function useful in comparing difference thresholds for the various sensory modalities? (pp. 154–155)

VISION–SENSORY PROCESSES

- What are the psychological counterparts to a light's wavelength, amplitude, and purity? (pp. 156–157)
- What happens to light as it passes through the structures of the eye? (pp. 157–160)
- What is the role of the rods and cones in responding to visual stimulation? (pp. 159–160)
- What factors affect visual acuity? (pp. 160–161)
- What is the brain's role in responding to visual stimulation? What are feature detectors? (pp. 161–163)

- How do our eyes adapt to light? (pp. 163–164)
- What is the relationship between lateral inhibition and brightness contrast? (p. 164)
- How do we see color? What are the important differences between the trichromatic and opponent-process theories of color vision? What have Hurvich and Jameson contributed to applying these theories to understanding color vision? (pp. 165–167)

VISION–PERCEPTUAL PROCESSES

- What is the relationship between distal and proximal stimuli? (p. 170)
- What were the contributions of the Gestalt psychologists to our understanding of form perception? (pp. 171–173)
- By what means are we able to perceive depth? Describe both monocular and binocular depth cues. (pp. 173–175)
- What cues do we use to perceive motion? (p. 176)
- How can our perceptions of objects remain constant even when the conditions under which we view them change? (pp. 177–178)
- What is the relationship between visual perception and attention? (pp. 178–179)
- By what means do we perceive patterns of visual stimulation? Is it an innate or a learned ability? What role does feature analysis play in pattern recognition? (pp. 180–185)

KEY TERMS AND CONCEPTS

Sensation Immediate and simple experiences caused by physical stimuli. (p. 149)

Perception The processes by which the brain organizes and interprets sensations. (p. 149)

BASIC PRINCIPLES OF SENSATION

Transduction The conversion of physical energy into nerve impulses. (p. 150)

Absolute Threshold The value at which a stimulus is detected 50 percent of the time. (p. 151)

Response Bias The tendency of an individual to detect or report the presence or absence of a stimulus whether or not he or she was actually stimulated. (p. 152)

Signal Detection Theory The theory that detection of any stimulus is a matter of distinguishing that stimulus from all other stimuli in the sensory world. (p. 153)

Response Criterion In a signal detection experiment, the level of sensation above which an individual will report detecting a stimulus and below which he or she will report not detecting a stimulus. (p. 153)

Difference Threshold The minimal change in stimulation that can be reliably detected 50 percent of the time. (p. 154)

Just Noticeable Difference (jnd) The exact point at which an observer can recognize two stimuli as being different 50 percent of the time. The jnd is the unit of measurement for studying difference thresholds. (p. 154)

Weber's Law The law that holds that our ability to discriminate between two stimulus magnitudes is a constant ratio of the reference stimulus: the larger the reference stimulus, the larger the change in intensity needed to produce a jnd. The size of this constant ratio is referred to as Weber's fraction. (p. 154)

Weber's Fraction The size or value, expressed as a constant, of the ratio of jnd to the reference stimulus. For example, Weber's fraction for visual brightness is 1/60. (p. 154)

VISION—SENSORY PROCESSES

Wavelength The distance from one wave crest to the next. Different wavelengths are seen as different hues or colors. (p. 157)

Hue The psychological counterpart of a wavelength, often called color. (p. 157)

Amplitude The height of each light wave. The amplitude of a light wave determines a different psychological property of light, brightness. (p. 157)

Brightness The psychological counterpart to amplitude. As amplitude changes, so does brightness: the larger the amplitude, the brighter the light appears. (p. 157)

Purity The number of wavelengths that constitute a light. Psychologically, the purity of a light determines its colorfulness or saturation. (p. 157)

Saturation The psychological counterpart to purity. As the number of wavelengths in light increases, its saturation decreases. (p. 157)

Retina The thin layer of receptors, rods and cones, that lines the interior of the back of the eye. (p. 157)

Cornea The transparent fluid filled cover at the front of the eye through which light enters the eye. (p. 157)

Pupil The opening, surrounded by the iris, that controls the amount of light entering the eye. (p. 157)

Iris A small muscle that contracts or relaxes in response to the amount of light passing through the cornea. (p. 157)

Lens A transparent structure within the eye that changes shape depending upon whether we are viewing objects close up or far away, permitting light to be focused on the retina. (p. 157)

Accommodation The process by which the lens focuses light on the retina: as muscles contract (when viewing objects close up) or relax (when viewing distant objects), the lens bulges or narrows, respectively. (p. 158)

Rods Light-sensitive receptors that are found throughout the retina except in the fovea. (p. 159)

Cones Color-sensitive receptors found primarily in the fovea, although some may be found in the retina's outer region or periphery. (p. 159)

Fovea A tiny area (about one square millimeter) in the center of the retina, containing only cones. The fovea is located directly behind the pupil. (p. 160)

Visual Acuity Our keenness of vision. Visual acuity is affected by the locations on the retina upon which images fall. Acuity is greatest for images that are focused on the fovea. (p. 160)

Myopia A visual disorder, also known as nearsightedness, in which the distance between the lens and retina is longer than normal, causing light to be focused in front of the retina. People who are nearsighted can see close objects well but distant objects appear fuzzy. (p. 160)

Hyperopia A visual disorder, also called farsightedness, in which the distance between the lens and retina is shorter than normal, causing light to be focused behind the retina. Farsighted people can see distant objects clearly, but close objects appear fuzzy. (p. 160)

Astigmatism A visual disorder caused by defects in the spherical shape of the cornea. When the cornea is misshaped, visual images are not focused equally on different parts of the retina. (p. 160)

Optic Nerve The bundle of nerve fibers (the axons of ganglion cells) that make up the pathway leading from the retina to structures in the brain that react to neural impulses laden with visual information. (p. 161)

Blind Spot The point on the retina at which the optic nerve exits the back of the eye, creating a hole in our vision. The blind spot is located just below the fovea and contains no rods or cones; hence, this part of the retina is not sensitive to light. (p. 161)

Feature Detectors Neurons in the visual cortex are excited by particular patterns of light, such as lines and angles of different sizes and shapes. Examples of feature detectors are simple, complex, and hypercomplex cells. (p. 163)

Light Adaptation The process of our eyes adapting to increasing levels of illumination. Our eyes adapt to increases in illumination more rapidly than to decreases. (p. 164)

Dark Adaptation The process of our eyes adapting to decreasing levels of illumination. (p. 164)

Brightness Contrast The phenomenon in which a color appears brighter as the background becomes darker. The degree of brightness contrast increases as the intensity of the difference between contrasting regions increases, and is due, physiologically, to a process known as lateral inhibition. (p. 164)

Complementary Colors Pairs of primary colors (red and green or yellow and blue) that produce a white or gray when mixed together. (p. 167)

Trichromatic Theory The theory proposed by Young and Helmholtz that the typical human eye has color receptors sensitive to the primary colors of red, green, and blue. Stimulation of any one of these receptors produces the sensation of the corresponding color. The creation of other colors, such as orange and brown, involves interaction of the three different receptors. (p. 167)

Opponent-Process Theory Hering's theory that there are three sets of color-sensitive receptors in the visual system: one set for red and green, another for blue and yellow and the third for black and white. Members of each set work in opposition to each other through neural inhibition. (p. 168)

VISION—PERCEPTUAL PROCESSES

Distal Stimulus Any object in the environment that can be known to us only through its image on the retina, the proximal stimulus. (p. 170)

Proximal Stimulus The two-dimensional and ever changing image of the distal stimulus as it appears on the retina. The size of the proximal stimulus changes as we move toward or away from the distal stimulus and changes its position on the retina as we change our viewing angle. (p. 170)

Figure-Ground Relationship An organizational principle of Gestalt psychology describing our tendency to perceive some objects, called figures, as standing out from their surroundings, called the ground. (p. 171)

Perceptual Grouping A second organizational principle of Gestalt psychology that describes our ability to organize the figure into a meaningful pattern or shape. (p. 172)

Proximity A principle of perceptual grouping in which objects near one another tend to be perceived as a group. (p. 172)

Similarity A principle of perceptual grouping in which objects that look alike tend to be perceived as a group. (p. 172)

Good Continuation A principle of perceptual grouping in which objects are perceived to be constructed of smooth continuous features rather than discontinuous ones. Objects can be camouflaged by using good continuation. (p. 172)

Closure A principle of perceptual grouping in which an object tends to be perceived as a whole even though a part of it is missing. Perceptually, we tend to complete objects that have spaces or gaps in them. (p. 172)

Depth Perception The ability to judge the distance of objects from us or other objects. Perception of depth is a rather amazing phenomenon because we can perceive the world in three dimensions—height, width, and depth—despite the fact that the surface of our retinas is only two dimensional (height and width). (p. 173)

Depth Cues Those aspects of any stimulus situation that indicate how far an object is from the observer or other objects. (p. 173)

Convergence The binocular cue in which the eyes tend to turn inward when viewing nearby objects. Our eyes naturally converge on any object we view. However, when our eyes converge on nearby objects, the angle between them is greater than when they converge on objects farther away. (p. 173)

Binocular Disparity A binocular cue produced because the eyes are positioned in slightly different locations, causing slightly different images of objects to be cast upon each retina. (p. 173)

Interposition The monocular cue produced when one object partially blocks our view of another object, causing the first object to appear closer. (p. 174)

Linear Perspective The monocular cue produced by receding parallel lines, which gives the appearance that the lines converge on a vanishing point somewhere in the distance, creating the perception of depth. (p. 174)

Relative Size The monocular cue in which large objects appear closer than small objects because they cast larger images upon the retina. (p. 174)

Texture Gradient The monocular cue in which objects that are larger and coarser appear closer than objects that are smaller and smoother. (p. 174)

Aerial Perspective The monocular cue in which objects far off in the distance appear hazy and less distinct than nearby objects. (p. 174)

Motion Parallax The monocular cue in which nearby objects appear to race by while distant objects appear to move slowly. (p. 174)

Stroboscopic Movement A form of apparent movement that can be produced by flashing a light in darkness and then several milliseconds later, flashing a second identical light in a slightly different location. (p. 175)

Perceptual Constancy Our ability to perceive objects as possessing certain stable features, including lightness, size, and shape, despite changes in the conditions under which we view those objects. (p. 177)

Illusions Misperceptions of real objects or events. Physical illusions are caused by distortions in the stimulus image cast upon our retinas. Perceptual illusions are caused by miscues in our visual system. (p. 177)

Selective Looking The ability to perceive only one visual stimulus while ignoring others. (p. 178)

Feature Analysis The recognition of an object based on the distinctive characteristics or components that, because of the specific manner in which they are arranged, define it that object. (p. 180)

Perceptual Set The tendency of a person's expectations to influence his or her perception. (p. 182)

Perceptual Learning Increases in a person's perceptual skills due to learning. (p. 184)

Bottom-Up Processing Processing of a pattern that begins at the level of the receptors and proceeds in an orderly fashion through specialized cells in the visual cortex. (p. 185)

Top-Down Processing Processing of a pattern that begins with the higher brain centers directing receptors to attend to particular features of the pattern. (p. 185)

ADDITIONAL SOURCES OF INFORMATION

Goldstein, E. B. (1989). *Sensation and perception.* Belmont, CA: Wadsworth. A very good and current introductory text on sensation and perception. The first ten chapters discuss various topics related to vision, including perceptual development and clinical aspects of vision. The book contains many good demonstrations and illustrations of visual processes.

Hubel, D. H., & Weisel, T. N. (1979). Brain mechanisms of vision. *Scientific American, 241,* 150–161. An excellent summary of the way the neurons in the visual cortex detect and process information by the Nobel Prize winners who conducted the research.

Rock, I. (1986). The description and analysis of object and event perception. In K. Boff, K. Kaufman, & J. Thomas (Eds.), *Handbook of perception and performance.* New York: Wiley. An excellent, but sophisticated discussion of theories of visual illusion.

Vokey, J. R., & Read, J. D. (1985). Subliminal messages: Between the devil and the media. *American Psychologist, 40,* 1231–1239. A very good summary of the evidence for and against subliminal perception.

6 Sensation and Perception: Audition, the Somatosenses, Smell, and Taste

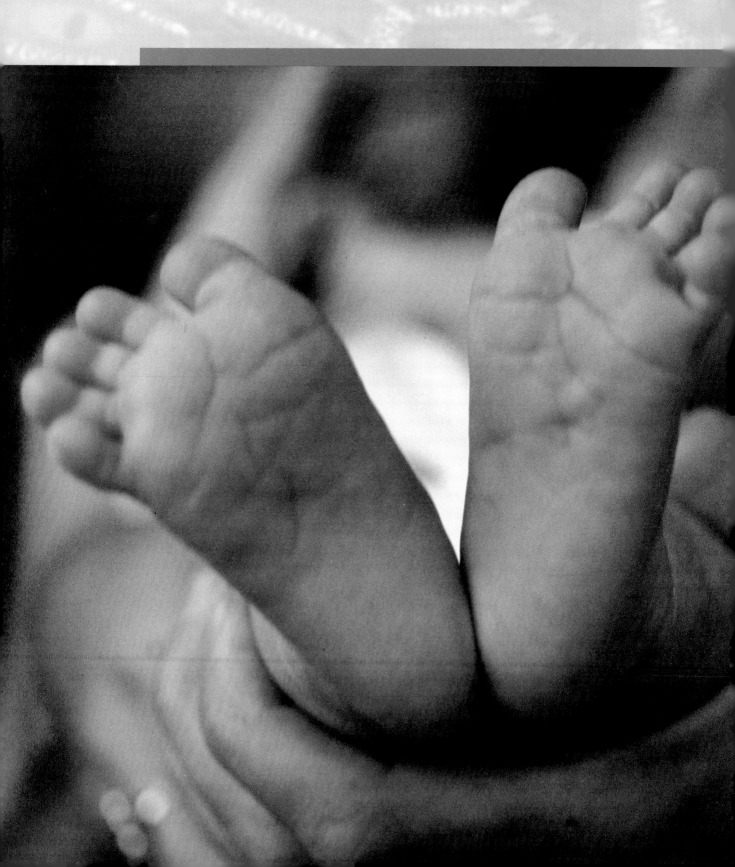

AUDITION: SENSORY AND PERCEPTUAL PROCESSES
(192–203)

The Nature of Sound   The Ear   From Cochlea to Brain
Neural Processing of Sound   Locating Sound   Selective Attention
Hearing Impairment

The three physical characteristics of sound each correspond to a different psychological experience: amplitude corresponds to loudness, frequency to pitch, and purity to timbre. The sensation of hearing is caused by variations of air pressure striking the ear drum, which in turn, initiates a series of events that eventually stimulates receptors found deep within the ear. These receptors send neural impulses regarding the different properties of sound waves to the brain. The brain interprets these signals in terms of loudness, pitch, and the location from which the sound is emanating.

THE SOMATOSENSORY SYSTEM *(204–212)*

The Skin Senses   Kinesthesis and Equilibrium

The somatosensory system involves our ability to sense pressure, temperature, pain, body position, movement, and balance. Pressure, temperature, and pain are sometimes referred to as the skin senses because physical contact with the skin gives rise to one or more of these sensations. Our bodies readily adapt to changes in pressure and temperature but not to changes in pain, particularly if it is intense. A prominent theory of pain—the gate-control theory—holds that both psychological factors, such as expectations, and physiological factors, such as the interplay of certain nerve fibers, influence our perception of pain.

The kinesthetic system, whose receptors reside in joints and deep muscles, senses the location, movement, and posture of the muscles and skeletal joints. The vestibular system responds to changes in our equilibrium or balance.

THE CHEMICAL SENSES: SMELL AND TASTE *(212–220)*

Smell   Taste

Our senses of smell and taste respond to chemical stimulation. Our understanding of smell lags behind that of the other senses because we are unsure of the physical properties of smell that correspond to our perception of odor. We do know, though, that odor molecules stimulate receptors found deep inside the nose, which then send neural messages to the brain. Thresholds for smell vary from odor to odor and from person to person. However, all of us can learn to recognize different odors through practice.

Many sensory psychologists believe that taste can be divided into four different categories: bitter, sweet, sour, and salty. The receptors for taste are found in the taste buds located on the tongue and in the mouth. Women outperform men in tests of both taste and odor recognition. Our sensitivity to a substance's taste is influenced by both temperature and texture, but especially by odor.

So far, our discussion of sensation and perception has focused primarily on the visual system. You may be wondering why we have devoted an entire chapter to vision while devoting only a few pages to each of the other senses. Our appropriation of space in this manner does not reflect a bias we have for vision and against the other senses. Rather, it reflects psychology's progress in studying and understanding the senses: Vision has been the object of long and intensive research; the other senses have not received the same kind of scrutiny. In short, we simply know more about vision than we do about any of the other senses.

One thing we do know about all of the senses, however, is that many of the general principles of sensory and perceptual processing involved in vision apply to all of the other senses. We have seen that physical energy in the form of light is converted to neural impulses by receptor cells in the eye, the rods and cones. We have also learned that these neural impulses are sent via the optic nerve to the brain where they are analyzed and interpreted by specialized neurons in the visual cortex called feature detectors. Each of our sensory modalities follows a similar mode of operation: Specialized receptor cells first convert a particular form of physical energy into neural impulses; these impulses are then channeled to a specific region of the brain where they are analyzed and interpreted. In other words, regardless of the sensory modality, sensation always originates at the level of the receptors, and perception always originates at the level of the brain.

Our objective in this chapter is to provide you with the important details of these processes for each of the other senses. We will begin by discussing audition, or the sense of hearing. Following our study of the ear, we will describe the somatic or bodily senses that register pressure, temperature, and pain. We will also discuss kinesthesis and equilibrium, two closely related sensory systems that inform us of our bodily movement and orientation in space respectively. Finally, we will look at our senses of smell and taste, both of which respond to chemical stimulation.

AUDITION: SENSORY AND PERCEPTUAL PROCESSES

After vision, we depend principally upon our sense of hearing to provide us with sensory information about the world. Hearing is essential to much human communication and social interaction, and in all cultures including your own, hearing is central to transmitting knowledge. For example, classroom instruction from kindergarten to college is centered on our ability to hear the teacher's voice. Before we can understand the information being taught, we must first hear what the teacher is saying. Hearing also allows us to be informed about danger. In fact, sometimes we hear danger before we see it: the rattle of a well-camouflaged rattlesnake along side a hiking trail, the growling of a dog that is quickly approaching from behind, the honking of a car horn. But our ability to hear is also important to us for reasons other than its practical and survival value. Sound adds an important psychological dimension to our everyday lives: we rely upon our ears to enjoy much of the aesthetic side of life. From the pounding of the ocean surf against the shore to the gentle lapping of waves at a lake's side, from the first words of a child to the laughter of friends, sounds give us pleasure and enjoyment. Surely, you are atune to particular sounds that are especially pleasing to you. Take a moment to reflect upon them. How would the quality of your life be different if you were no longer able to hear them?

Our study of the auditory system begins with a brief description of the nature of sound. We will then discuss how the structure of the ear and brain are designed to detect and process the physical properties of sound. Later, we will explore the perceptual processes involved in hearing.

The Nature of Sound

The physical stimuli that we perceive as sound are actually minute variations in air pressure caused by the vibrations of objects. For example, when a violinist moves his or her bow across the strings of a violin, the strings vibrate back and forth. The vibration causes alternating patterns of tiny increases and decreases in air pressure. When the strings move toward your ear, they compress the air molecules, creating a region of high air pressure; when the strings move away from your ear, a partial vacuum is created, decreasing the density of molecules near the strings and resulting in a region of low pressure. Drawing the bow across the violin's string only once causes it to vibrate hundreds of times a second and produces a **sound wave**, an alternating pattern of high and low pressure that travels through the air at approximately 740 miles per hour (the speed of sound). Sound waves, like the ripples produced when a stone is dropped into a calm body of water, travel outward in all directions from their source (see Figure 6.1).

When sound waves strike your ear, they cause your eardrum to vibrate in synchrony with the variations in air pressure, which in turn initiates a vibratory pattern in three tiny bones located in the middle part of your ear. The vibratory pattern is then transmitted to the innermost part of your ear and eventually to your brain where the pattern is experienced as sound. As with light waves, however, not all sound waves are created equal; what you hear depends upon the specific characteristics of the particular sound wave reaching your ear.

Like light waves, sound waves vary along three dimensions: amplitude, wave frequency, and purity, which we will discuss below (see Table 6.1). Each of these physical properties corresponds roughly to a psychological property of sound: amplitude corresponds to loudness, wave frequency to pitch, and purity to timbre.

As the sound wave travels past a fixed point such as a stationary person's ear, the air pressure around the ear alternatively increases and decreases over time. Graphing this cyclical change leads to the classic wave pattern shown in Figure 6.2a with air pressure represented on the vertical axis and time on the horizontal axis. As you can see from this figure, the peak represents the highest level of air pressure and the trough represents the lowest level of air pressure.

The difference between the high and low pressure levels of a sound wave is called **amplitude**. The amplitude of sound waves gives rise to the psychological experience of **loudness**. The more intense the vibration of the violin string or any object, the greater the amplitude, and to some extent, the louder the psychological experience of the sound (see Figure 6.2b).

FIGURE 6.1

The sound waves produced by vibrating violin strings. The dark areas represent areas of low air pressure and the light areas between them represent areas of high pressure.

TABLE 6.1 *Properties of sound.*

PHYSICAL PROPERTIES	PSYCHOLOGICAL PROPERTIES
Frequency (wavelength)	Pitch
Amplitude	Loudness
Complexity (purity)	Timbre

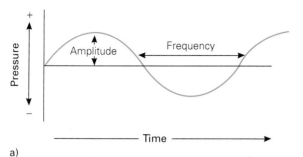

a)

FIGURE 6.2
The characteristics of a sound wave determines loudness and pitch. The height of the sound wave represents amplitude and determines our perception of loudness. The frequency or number of times per second that the wave completes one cycle represents pitch. In (a), the sound would be soft and low pitched. In (b), the sound would be loud and high pitched.

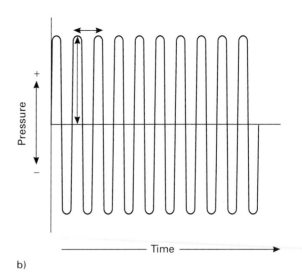

b)

FIGURE 6.3
The decibel scale measures a sound's loudness. Zero decibels represents the threshold for hearing—the softest sound that can be heard.

Humans are sensitive to a wide range of sound amplitudes. In fact, if we were any more sensitive to sound, we would be able to hear the sound of blood flowing through veins close to our ears as well as random collisions of air molecules (Groves & Rebec, 1987). Amplitude (and loudness) is measured according to the **decibel** (dB) scale (so named after Alexander Graham Bell) with zero decibels representing the absolute threshold for normal hearing. (Recall that the absolute threshold is the value of a stimulus at which it is detected fifty percent of the time.)

How sensitive is the human ear to changes in sound amplitude? The answer is very sensitive. According to S. S. Stevens (1955), perceived loudness doubles with every 10 decibel increase in amplitude. Figure 6.3 gives decibel measurements of several common sounds as well as the danger levels for hearing loss due to exposure to loud sounds.

The second dimension of a sound wave, **wave frequency**, refers to how quickly variations in air pressure occur. One variation, the change from high pressure to low pressure and back again, is one cycle. Sound wavelengths are measured in terms of their frequency, the number of cycles per second. The frequency of a sound wave is expressed in units called **hertz** (Hz), with one Hz equivalent to one cycle per second.

The frequency of a sound wave primarily determines the psychological quality known as perceived **pitch**. As a rule, the higher the frequency, the higher the pitch. Pitch, then, is related to whether a sound is heard as low (bass) or high (treble). Under optimal conditions, humans can hear tones ranging from 20 to 20,000 Hz. As we age, however, our sensitivity to pitch declines, especially for frequencies greater than 10,000 Hz. Figure 6.4 compares the range of sound frequencies to which humans and several other animals are sensitive. At low frequencies, we can pretty much hold our own, but at very high frequencies, we tend to fare relatively poorly. Even a mouse can hear sounds that we cannot.

The third dimension of sound is **purity**, or the mixture of sound waves that make up a sound. Just as pure light is rare, so is pure sound. In other words, most of the sounds we hear are composed of a mixture of different frequencies. A pure sound is one in which sound waves are vibrating at exactly the same frequency. A sound's purity corresponds to the psychological experience of **timbre**; that is, a sound's clarity.

Although a sound wave's amplitude and frequency are correlated with the sound's loudness and pitch respectively, the relation is imperfect. For example, our perception of a sound's loudness generally depends upon the duration, and to some extent, the pitch of a sound. Long lasting sounds seem louder than brief sounds, and up to a point, the higher the pitch, the louder the sound. Likewise, our perception of a sound's pitch is determined at least partially by its loudness. The pitch of pure tones, such as those produced by striking a tuning fork against a surface, are enhanced by increasing loudness: low tones appear lower and high tones appear higher with increasing loudness levels.

In sum, the three psychological qualities of sound, loudness, pitch, and timbre, correspond roughly to three physical qualities of sound waves: amplitude, frequency, and purity respectively. A sound's psychological qualities interact to influence our perception of sound: pitch is enhanced by increasing loudness and the higher the pitch (and the greater its duration), the louder the sound.

The Ear

To understand how the ear and brain work together to hear sound, let's trace a series of sound waves as they leave your stereo system's speakers and enter your ears. The physiological process of hearing sound is the same whether you are listening to Beethoven's Ninth Symphony, Whitney Houston or Van Halen. But as you shall see, your enjoyment of sound depends to a large extent upon your previous experiences with similar sounds—a matter more of perception than sensation.

Vibrations coming from your stereo's speakers broadcast sound waves through the air. If you adjust the volume on your stereo high enough, you can actually feel the floor vibrating; softer levels of sound produce vibrations that only your ears can detect. On their way to becoming transformed into neural impulses, vibrations pass through three aptly named sections of the ear: the outer ear, which includes the pinna, auditory canal, and tympanic membrane; the middle ear, which includes the ossicles and the oval window; and the inner ear, which includes the basilar membrane and the hair cells (see Figure 6.5a). We will discuss each of these sections in order.

FIGURE 6.4
Hearing differences among species.

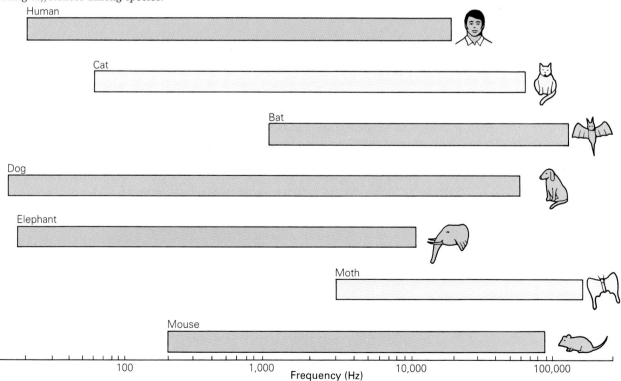

Frequency (Hz)

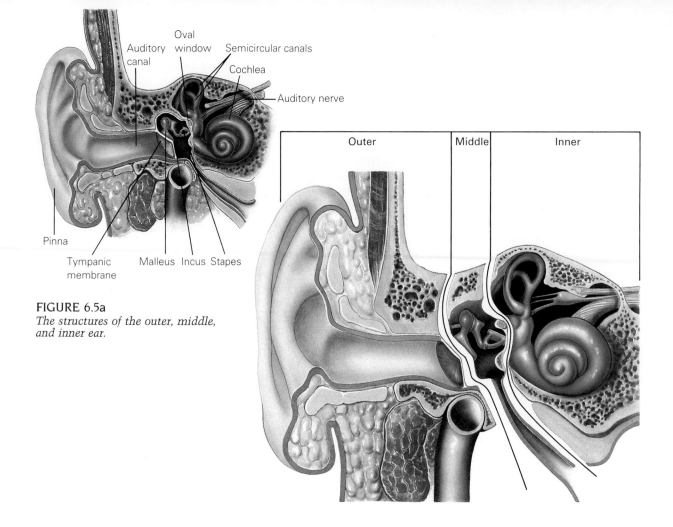

Auditory
canal

Oval
window

Semicircular canals

Cochlea

Auditory nerve

Pinna

Tympanic
membrane

Malleus Incus Stapes

Outer

Middle

Inner

FIGURE 6.5a
*The structures of the outer, middle,
and inner ear.*

The Outer Ear. The sound waves emanating from your stereo speakers first strike the visible part of the ear, the **pinna**. Although we generally consider this part of the ear a useful device from which to suspend earrings and support eyeglasses, it actually has a more important function, which is to collect and funnel sound waves deeper into the ear. Some animals such as dogs and cats can move their pinnae to catch sound waves, enabling them to locate accurately sources of sound. Though some of us might be able to wiggle our ears, our pinnae are not flexible enough to help us localize sound with precision akin to that of the family pet. Sound waves enter the ear through the **auditory canal**, a 3-cm-long recess that connects the pinna with the **tympanic membrane**. Also known as the eardrum, the tympanic membrane is a thin, conically shaped membrane separating the inner and outer ears that vibrates when struck by sound waves. The auditory canal appears to serve two functions. First, it protects the tympanic membrane from being struck by large and potentially damaging objects. (You may recall your family physician warning you as a child: "Don't stick anything smaller than your elbow into your ear!") Second, it directs sound waves toward the tympanic membrane.

The Middle Ear. Located just behind the tympanic membrane are the three smallest bones in the human body, the malleus, the incus, and the stapes. These three bones, known collectively as the **ossicles**, serve a dual function: They amplify and transmit the vibrations of the tympanic membrane to another membrane, the **oval window**, which divides the middle ear from the inner ear. Understanding how the ossicles transmit the vibrations of the tympanic membrane is straightforward. The malleus is attached to the tympanic membrane, and thus, vibrates whenever the tympanic membrane vibrates. Vibrations of the malleus cause the incus to vibrate, which in turn, causes the stapes, the bone connected to the oval window, to also vibrate. Understanding how the ossicles amplify the vibrations of the tympanic membrane is almost as easy. The area of the tympanic membrane is about seventeen times that of the stapes. When vibrations from the larger surface are focused onto the smaller surface, the pressure from the vibrations is amplified about twenty-fold. Thus, the ossicles may convert moderately weak stimuli acting upon the tympanic membrane into much stronger ones that exert pressure on the oval window. In other words, it is here in the middle ear that the vibrations produced by sound waves striking the tympanic membrane are amplified. If this is a difficult concept for you to grasp, consider the following analogy. A 100-pound woman wearing spiked heels with a surface area of one square centimeter can produce a pressure of over 100,000 pounds per square foot by placing all of her weight on one heel (Goldstein, 1989).

The Inner Ear. The structures of the inner ear perform the task of transduction. Recall that transduction is the process by which sensory receptors convert physical energy into neural impulses. In this case, the structures of the inner ear transform the mechanical vibrations produced by the ossicles into neural impulses that are channeled to the brain via the auditory nerve. Here's how they do it:

The movement of the oval window sets in motion the fluid in the **cochlea**, a bony, coiled chamber that houses the auditory receptors (see Figure 6.5a). It is important to note that the cochlear fluid is a poor conductor of sound waves. That is why the amplification processes of the middle ear are so important. Without benefit of amplification, that is, if sound waves were to pass directly from the air to the cochlear fluid, only a very small percentage of sound waves would be detected and our sense of hearing would be too impaired to be a very useful means of gathering information about the world (Durrant & Lovrinic, 1977).

The motion of the cochlear fluid initiates a wavelike pattern of movement along the **basilar membrane**, a structure that runs nearly the entire length of the cochlea and functionally divides the cochlea into upper and lower divisions. Embedded in the basilar membrane are the auditory receptors, the **hair cells** (see Figure 6.5b). Whenever the basilar membrane vibrates, it forces the hair cells upward against another membrane, bending

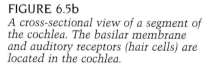

FIGURE 6.5b
A cross-sectional view of a segment of the cochlea. The basilar membrane and auditory receptors (hair cells) are located in the cochlea.

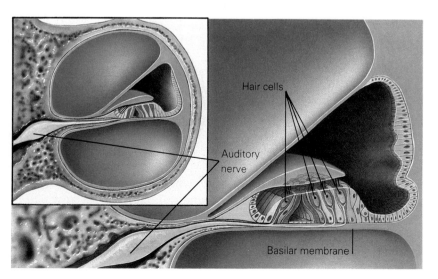

them in a shearing motion. Deformations of the hair cells in this manner produce neural responses that are channeled to the brain via the **auditory nerve**. Individual neurons making up the auditory nerve synapse with different sections of the basilar membrane (and so, different hair cells) and respond to different sound frequencies.

Before tracing the final leg of the sound waves' journey from your stereo speakers to your brain, let's briefly recap what we have learned about sound and hearing.

■ Sound waves produced by vibrations of objects in the environment strike the outer ear. The pinna gathers these sound waves and funnels them down the external auditory canal toward the tympanic membrane. The tympanic membrane vibrates when struck by the sound waves.

■ The ossicles, three bones that bridge the gap between the outer and inner ears, vibrate whenever the tympanic membrane vibrates. In addition, the ossicles amplify the vibrations of the larger tympanic membrane and concentrates them onto the smaller oval window.

■ In turn, the vibrations of the oval window force the cochlear fluid along the basilar membrane, pushing the hair cells upward against another membrane. The shearing action produces neural impulses that are transmitted to the brain. It is here in the heart of the inner ear that physical energy is converted into the electrochemical language that the brain will interpret as the psychological experience of sound.

From Cochlea to Brain

Figure 6.6 diagrams the neural pathway linking the ear with the brain. After exiting each cochlea, nerve impulses laden with auditory information (regarding the sound waves coming from your stereo speakers) first synapse in their respective cochlear nuclei. The cochlear nuclei are tiny bundles of neurons located in the lower back portion of the brain. The auditory system, like the visual system, has a means by which information is transmitted to both sides of the brain. Each of the cochlear nuclei send neural impulses to structures on both sides of the brain called the superior olives. The main function of the superior olives is to compare and integrate auditory information from both ears. From each superior olive, information is relayed to a nucleus of cells located in the thalamus. In turn, the thalamus relays the information to the auditory cortex. Thus it is deep within the brain that the sound waves leaving your stereo speakers are finally "heard" as music.

t is deep within the brain that sound waves leaving your stereo speakers are finally "heard" as music.

Neural Processing of Sound

Thus far we have concentrated on the physiological structures involved in hearing. We have seen how sound is transmitted from the outer ear to the inner ear and how the cochlea transduces sound waves to neural impulses. But how are these processes related to *psychological* aspects of hearing? More specifically, how do these physiological processes register sound qualities, particularly loudness and pitch?

Most sensory psychologists agree that a sound's loudness is determined by two physiological factors: the number of hair cells stimulated by a sound wave and the rate at which those hair cells fire in response to stimulation. High amplitude sounds produce greater movement in the tympanic membrane, ossicles, cochlear fluid, and basilar membrane than low amplitude sounds, inducing hair cells to fire at greater rates and in greater numbers.

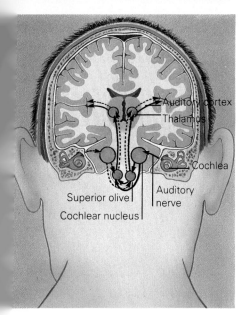

FIGURE 6.6
The neural pathway leading from the ear to the auditory cortex.

Understanding pitch is a bit more complex. Recall that a sound wave's frequency is the physical characteristic of sound that corresponds to the psychological quality of pitch. Recall, too, that our perception of pitch is determined largely by a sound wave's frequency. Casting the puzzle of pitch perception in more concrete terms, we might then ask the following question: How can the shearing of the hair cells lodged between the two membranes account for our uncanny perceptual ability to distinguish among these sorts of sound nuances? (Incidentally, without this ability, all sound would be perceived as the same pitch and we would live in a world where all music would be heard as the same note.)

Over the past century, two theories, the place theory and the frequency theory, have arisen as the preeminent accounts of pitch perception. Both theories propose mechanisms by which a given sound frequency is registered according to the firing pattern of neurons along the auditory pathway. But as we shall soon see, neither theory can account wholly for our ability to hear pitch. Rather, hearing pitch appears to depend upon the joint influence of mechanisms described by both theories.

Place Theory. In 1863 Herman von Helmholtz, advocate of the trichromatic theory of color vision (Chapter 5), proposed the **place theory** of pitch, which stated that the basilar membrane is composed of independent nerve fibers, each sensitive to a different sound frequency. According to Helmholtz, the brain interprets stimulation from different parts of the basilar membrane as different tones. Stimulation of nerve fibers along one end of the membrane leads to the sensation of low pitches, whereas stimulation of fibers at the other end of the membrane produces sensations of high pitches.

Twentieth-century research has shown that Helmholtz's theory is partially correct. Stimulation of different regions of the basilar membrane does, in fact, produce sensations of different pitches. High frequencies stimulate portions of the membrane closest to the oval window, while low frequencies stimulate regions near the far end of the membrane. Very low frequencies, however, do not seem to be localized; rather, they cause the entire membrane to vibrate (for example, von Bekesy, 1960).

Frequency Theory. The second major theory of pitch perception, **frequency theory**, was first advanced by the English physicist William Rutherford (1886) and is based on the idea that the entire basilar membrane vibrates in synchrony with the frequency of sound waves striking the ear. These vibrations are then transduced to an equivalent number of neural impulses that are channeled to the brain. For example, striking a middle C on the piano produces a 256 Hz sound wave. When this sound wave strikes the ear, it causes the basilar membrane to vibrate 256 times per second. In turn, this causes the hair cells and auditory neurons embedded in the basilar membrane to fire at exactly the same rate. Thus, according to frequency theory, the rate of neural firing in the ear corresponds directly to the frequency of the sound wave.

The major shortcoming of the frequency theory is that neurons cannot fire faster than 1,000 times per second, which suggests that auditory neurons cannot respond to sound frequencies greater than 1,000 Hz. However, recall that we can hear frequencies up to 20,000 Hz. If the frequency theory is correct, how can we possibly hear such high frequency tones? An idea proposed in 1937 by Wever and Bray, seems to resolve this dilemma partially. These researchers believed that one group of hair cells fires while another group rests. Wever and Bray called this the **volley principle** because it reminded them of the manner in which groups of soldiers alternated their musket fire during the Revolutionary War. While one group was reloading their weapons, another would fire, and vice versa. For example, the ear could detect a 5,000 Hz tone if each of 10 hair cells fired 500 times a second, a rate well within the ability of most receptors. However, the volley principle, and hence the frequency theory, cannot explain how frequencies greater than 5,000 Hz are heard.

Neither theory alone, then, can account wholly for the range of sound frequencies that we are able to hear. Most contemporary sensory psychologists believe that when combined, both theories might explain hearing. Low frequencies (those below 1,000 Hz) are registered by the frequency of neural firing of the hair cells and higher frequencies (those above 5,000 Hz) are registered according to the place of stimulation along the basilar membrane. Intermediate sound frequencies (approximately 1,000 to 5,000 Hz) are likely encoded by mechanisms described by both theories (Green, 1976). In essence, our ability to hear sound is based on the way different sound wave frequencies are transduced by the nervous system.

Locating Sound

Besides discriminating a sound's pitch and loudness, we can generally locate its source with reasonable accuracy. That is, we are pretty good at judging both the direction and relative distance from which a sound originates. Recall that for visually locating objects we use both monocular and binocular cues. Likewise for hearing, we use monaural (one-ear) and binaural (two-ear) cues in locating sound.

Monaural Cues. Monaural cues are useful mainly for judging relative distance and movement of a sound-emitting object. One such cue is the amplitude or loudness of sound waves striking the ear. As sound waves travel over long distances, they tend to decrease in amplitude partially because they are absorbed by objects in the environment. Generally speaking, the louder the sound, the closer its source. When the loudness of a sound changes, we perceive its distance from us to be changing. If a sound's loudness increases, we perceive its source to be moving closer to us, and if it decreases, we perceive its source to be moving away from us. This is precisely what we experience when we are waiting to cross a busy street. Moving vehicles sound louder as they approach and softer as they recede.

A second monaural cue to the changing position of moving objects is the **Doppler effect**, or the changes in pitch emanating from a sound-emitting object moving relative to a listener. For example, suppose you are driving to school and you hear the siren of a police car approaching you from the rear. As the vehicle approaches you, the shrillness of its siren increases, almost to the point where you experience pain in your ears; but once it passes you and recedes into the distance (You were lucky this time!), the shrillness seems to fade. Such changes in our psychological perception of pitch are due to changes in the physical relation among sound waves emit-

FIGURE 6.7
The Doppler effect. Sound waves emanating from a moving object tend to cluster in front of the object.

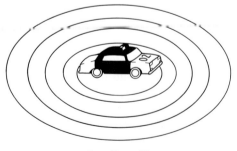

Standing still

Moving left to right

ted from moving objects. As an object moves, it emits sound waves that are projected only slightly ahead of itself. As a result, the sound waves tend to cluster just in front of the object, meaning that the distance between these sound waves is decreased (see Figure 6.7). As you may recall from our discussion on the nature of sound, the shorter the distance between sound waves, the higher the frequency, and to a listener, the higher the pitch. Just the opposite occurs once the sound-emitting object has passed: The distance between sound waves increases, frequency decreases, and to a listener, the pitch decreases.

The so-called sonic boom produced by jet airplanes and other objects that travel faster than the speed of sound waves is related to the Doppler effect. In this case though, the sound waves join together behind the moving object, creating a single, large sound wave that is perceived by a listener as an extremely loud thunder clap.

Binaural Cues. Although we can detect a sound's pitch and loudness using only one ear, locating its origin precisely requires us to use both ears. An important binaural cue for judging sound location is the time difference between sound waves reaching both ears. Depending upon the location of their source, sound waves reach each ear at slightly different times. Figure 6.8 illustrates this principle. Notice that when a sound comes from a source directly in front of or directly behind the listener, the distance the sound waves must travel to each ear is the same. (This is why in some instances, such as when a person directly behind you calls your name, you have difficulty at first telling whether the caller is in front or in back of you.) However, when sound waves originate from a source to the side of the listener, the sound waves must travel farther to reach one ear than the other and so do not reach both ears simultaneously. In this case, the sound waves reach the left ear a fraction of a second before reaching the right ear. This time difference, although only a few microseconds (1 microsecond equals one-millionth of a second), is enough to cue us to a sound's location. Our response to sounds coming from positions on either side of our bodies may be to turn our heads toward the source so it comes in line with our foveal vision.

A second important binaural cue to sound localization is the difference in intensity between sound waves reaching each ear. In Figure 6.8, the sound waves originating from C not only reach the two ears at different times, they also reach the ears at different intensities. The ear closest to the sound source always experiences slightly more intense sound waves. In addition, the head serves as a barrier that reduces sound wave intensity reaching the ear farther away from the sound. For example, your head reduces the intensity of sound waves traveling from a source located on your right side to your left ear.

Thus, we gauge the location of a sound source on the basis of two binaural cues: the ear closest to the sound source always receives sound waves first, and those waves received by the closer ear are always slightly more intense than those received by the farther ear. As you may recall from our discussion of the auditory pathway, the brain structures involved in comparing and integrating information from the ears are the superior olives (see Figure 6.6). In all likelihood, the superior olives analyze incoming auditory stimulation in terms of these two binaural cues and, therefore, play an important role in our ability to locate sound sources.

Locating a sound source is of tremendous adaptive significance for getting along in the world. Answering a phone, responding to a child's cry, and reacting to the call of "Heads up" or "Hey you," depends as much on locating the sound as it does on hearing it. Just imagine hearing a cry for help but not being able to tell where it is coming from. In such a case, you would be helpless.

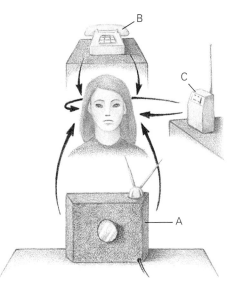

FIGURE 6.8
Localizing sound. An important binaural cue for judging a sound's location is the time difference between when sound waves reach each ear. Depending on a sound's location, sound waves reach each ear at slightly different times.

Selective Attention

You may recall from the previous chapter that visual perception appears to be organized so that we can only attend primarily to one source of visual stimulation at time. We perceive little, if anything, from unattended sources of visual stimulation. Auditory perception appears to be organized similarly. Consider, for example, the auditory stimulation you encounter at a party. If you were to sit in a corner and simply listen without focus to the sounds of the party, what you would hear is a mixture of talking, laughing, doors opening and closing, ice jiggling in glasses, and music. Yet if you were to engage in a conversation with someone at the party, you would be able to ignore all of these sounds and hear clearly only the voice of the person with whom you are conversing without much effort. The ability to perceive only one auditory stimulus while ignoring others is called **selective listening**.

Although selective listening has obvious adaptive value (we can concentrate on one auditory stimulus without being distracted by others), it can at times be a hindrance. Let's go back to the party. Suppose you find yourself as listener in one conversation but want to listen to the conversation going on just behind you. It is impossible to listen to both simultaneously, so you switch back and forth between conversations, hoping that the person talking to you doesn't realize that you are not devoting all of your attention to him or her. You do fine until the person talking to you asks you a question or makes a statement to which he or she expects a reply. Now you are stuck in an embarrassing situation simply because your auditory system can only process a limited amount of auditory stimulation at one time. In fact, selective attention is sometimes referred to as the "cocktail party phenomenon."

Psychologists have studied the cocktail party phenomenon in the laboratory using dichotic listening tasks. This task requires a person to listen to two tape recorded spoken messages simultaneously; one message is presented to the left ear and the other message is presented to the right ear. The person is asked to attend to only one of the messages by repeating aloud that message exactly as he or she hears it. This technique of following only one of the messages, commonly known as shadowing, was developed in 1953 by Colin Cherry as a part of his now classic study of selective listening. Cherry's subjects wore headphones that presented a different message to each ear, and they were asked to shadow one of the messages. His subjects noticed very little about the unattended message. Indeed, Cherry found that his subjects were unaware of the unattended message even when it was switched to a different language or contained backward speech. Subsequent research in dichotic listening has revealed only three major exceptions to Cherry's results. Subjects can sometimes notice the unattended message when the voice reading it is switched from male to female (Cherry & Taylor, 1954), when it contains the listener's name (Moray, 1959), or when it is switched to the other ear.

Thus, in hearing as in vision, we typically attend selectively to only one stimulus at a time and consequently perceive little, if any, information from unattended stimuli. The psychological moral is clear. We can only direct our attention, and thus, our behavior, to one source of stimulation at a time.

Hearing Impairment

Imagine a world in which your ability to hear was partially or completely impaired. This is probably a difficult task simply because you are so accustomed to hearing. About 25 million Americans understand exactly what life is like to have less than perfect hearing, for they are hearing impaired—

Selective listening, also called the "cocktail party phenomenon," refers to an individual's ability to focus on only one auditory stimulus at a time. A party demonstrates this idea quite well in that no matter how hard a person tries to engage in one conversation while listening to another, it is impossible for his or her auditory system to process both conversations.

they cannot hear with the same kind of acuity as the rest of us. Any measurable decrease in sensitivity to sound is called hearing loss. Hearing impairments stem from a variety of causes ranging from genetic defects to exposure to loud noises. Failure to diagnose hearing impairments, particularly in young children, can have devastating psychological, educational, and social effects. Deficient hearing can interfere with a child's ability to learn to speak and understand language, as well as with other skills generally taught in grammar school.

There are two major forms of hearing loss—conduction hearing loss and nerve hearing loss. **Conduction hearing loss** refers to the obstruction or destruction of the conductive structures of the ear, specifically, the external auditory canal, tympanic membrane, and ossicles. The excessive buildup of ear wax and puncturing of the tympanic membrane are two common and nonpermanent causes of conduction hearing loss. **Nerve hearing loss** refers to decreases in hearing ability resulting from damage to the neural structures involved in transmitting auditory information from the cochlea to the brain, including the hair cells, basilar membrane, and the auditory nerve. "Noise pollution" or exposure to extremely loud sounds such as those from jet engines, factory machinery, and even loud music can produce nerve hearing loss (Figure 6.3). The intensive vibration of cochlear fluid caused by high amplitude sound waves may be sufficient enough to dislodge the hair cells embedded in the basilar membrane, causing irreversible deafness to sound frequencies in that particular range.

Hearing aids may not benefit people suffering from nerve hearing loss. If all hair cells are destroyed, the person is deaf. Without receptors, there is no means by which auditory information can be transmitted to the brain. Advances in audition-related computer technology, however, may yield a device that will restore hearing, if only partially, to the deaf. In fact, remarkable progress in this line of research has already been made. An "electronic ear" or cochlear implant has been developed recently that converts sound waves to electrical impulses, which are then channeled directly to the auditory nerve, detouring the hair cells completely (Schmeck, 1984; Loeb, 1985). At present, however, cochlear implants lack the sophistication necessary to restore normal hearing, particularly for speech. However, they do provide for some sound detection, and thereby allow deaf people to experience a welcome relief to the monotony of silence—noise.

Hopefully, in the future we will see technological advances that will produce cochlear implants that will come closer to providing or restoring normal hearing in the deaf. Imagine the kinds of psychological changes that such advances will bring to the deaf. Hearing plays an important role in learning, in communicating, and in socializing, and therefore, in forming relationships with others.

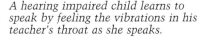

A hearing impaired child learns to speak by feeling the vibrations in his teacher's throat as she speaks.

THE SOMATOSENSORY SYSTEM

The **somatosensory system** includes our ability to sense pressure, temperature, pain, and kinesthesis and equilibrium (our sense of balance, body position, and movement). For discussion purposes, we have divided the somatosensory system into two broad categories: the skin senses (pressure, temperature, and pain) and kinesthesis and equilibrium (balance, body position and movement).

The Skin Senses

Our skin is perhaps the most versatile of all human sensory organs. It certainly is the largest. A six-foot-tall person has approximately 3,000 square inches of skin (Schiffman, 1976). Your skin serves a variety of important functions. Its supple exterior retains body fluids, gives shape to your skeleton and viscera, helps regulate inner body temperature, protects us from the harmful rays of the sun, wards off bacteria, helps regulate blood pressure, and, in many cases, even repairs itself when punctured, torn, or ripped. In addition to these functions, our skin also performs one other important (and psychological) duty: it keeps us informed about environmental stimuli contacting our bodies.

Embedded throughout your skin are nerve fibers that convey information about changes in pressure and temperature and painful stimuli to your brain. A widely held theory of how receptors encode different kinds of somatic qualities was proposed in 1962 by Ronald Melzack and Patrick Wall. They argued that nerve fibers differ from one another; they also proposed that somatic qualities are encoded according to the firing pattern of many nerve fibers. For example, we may sense cold when nerve fibers fire in a particular pattern and feel warmth when they fire in a different kind of pattern. Melzack and Wall developed their theory to account for the perception of pain, and we will discuss their theory in detail in the section on pain.

Although our understanding of the skin's encoding of sensory information is largely theoretical, our understanding of the neural pathways by which neural impulses travel from nerve fibers in the skin to the brain is more certain. We know, for example, that there are three such neural pathways, each of which originates in the spinal cord. One pathway has large nerve fibers that relay neural impulses very rapidly. The other two pathways have smaller nerve fibers that relay neural impulses more slowly. The first system also differs from the other two systems in that it carries information about the specific location of somatic stimulation whereas the neural fibers of the two other systems do not encode location information so precisely.

In addition to having a common origin in the spinal cord, the three systems have two other commonalities. First, the somatosensory cortex is the ultimate destination of somatosensory information, regardless of the part of the body from which it originates. The somatosensory cortex is located in the parietal lobes just behind the central fissure (see Figure 4.21 page 129). You may recall from our discussion of the brain in Chapter 4 that the somatosensory cortex represents body areas in proportion to their sensitivity; the more sensitive the body part, the larger the amount of space representing that area in the somatosensory cortex.

Second, in all three systems, neural impulses carrying somatosensory information from one side of the brain are channeled to the opposite side of the brain. For example, an itch on your right arm would be registered in the somatosensory cortex in your left hemisphere.

In general, the somatosenses, like all the senses, have one thing in common: they each provide physical feedback that can motivate behavior.

The sensation of pressure can range from light and pleasant, such as a spouse's gentle touch, to forceful and unpleasant, such as one football player tackling another.

When we are too cold, we put on more clothes, throw an extra log on the fire, or raise the thermostat. When in pain, we take an aspirin or other pain reliever, or we go to the doctor. In essence, our senses provide the brain with information that allows us to adapt our behavior to changes in environmental stimulation.

Now that we have a general knowledge of how our somatosensory systems operate, we are ready to consider the distinct skin senses of pressure, temperature, and pain.

Pressure. The sensation produced by any contact of an object with the skin is pressure. Sometimes the contact may be light and pleasant, such as a lover's caress, while at other times, it may be more forceful and unpleasant, such as someone pushing you while you are in line.

The physiological basis for the sensation of pressure is the **Pacinian corpuscle**, a nerve ending that responds to touch and vibration. When pressure is applied to or removed from the skin, Pacinian corpuscles become excited, sending impulses toward the somatosensory cortex via one of the three neural pathways described previously. However, Pacinian corpuscles do not respond to constant pressure. For example, they become excited when someone first grasps or lets go of your hand, but they do not respond to the stimulation in between, as when you are holding hands with a friend.

We can measure our sensitivity to touch by using a two-point discrimination threshold, the smallest distance between two points on the skin's surface that can be perceived as two distinct points. To determine this threshold, the researcher gently touches a person with both arms of a set of calipers and then asks him or her to report whether the resulting sensation is felt at one or two points on the skin's surface (see Figure 6.9). The distance between the arms of the calipers can be adjusted narrower or wider. The closer the arms of the calipers are when the person reports feeling two distinct sensations, the greater the sensitivity of that area of skin. As Figure 6.10 shows, the two-point discrimination threshold varies considerably across the surface of our bodies. In general, our hands, fingers, and face are more sensitive to touch than other regions of the body, particularly the legs, arms, and trunk.

FIGURE 6.9

The two-point discrimination threshold method. The closer the arms of the calipers when the individual reports feeling two distinct sensations, the greater the sensitivity of that portion of the skin.

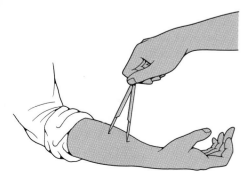

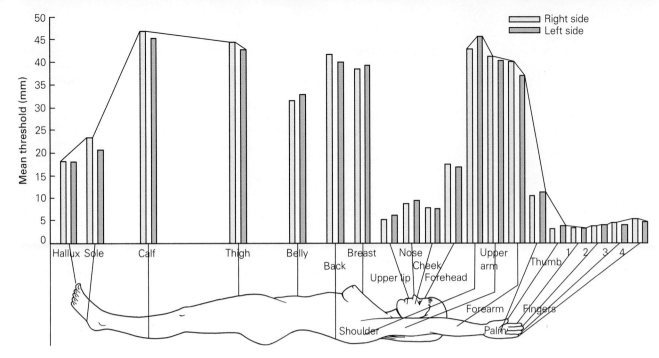

FIGURE 6.10
Variations in the two-point discrimination threshold. For both men and women, the two-point discrimination threshold varies considerably across body parts.
From *The Skin Senses*, compiled and edited by Dan R. Kenshalo. Copyright © 1968 by Charles C. Thomas, Publisher. Courtesy of Charles C. Thomas, Publisher, Springfield, Illinois.

Jumping into a swimming pool illustrates two points about temperature. Initially, the water feels cold, and the body becomes cold, showing we are sensitive to change in temperature. After staying in the water awhile, the water feels comfortable, and the body adjusts to the change.

You may think that the areas of your body most sensitive to pressure have more Pacinian corpuscles than do less sensitive regions, but this is not so. Why do different body regions vary in their sensitivity to pressure? The reason involves the way in which different body areas are represented in the cerebral cortex. You may recall from Chapter 4 that sensitive areas like the hands, fingers, and face are better represented than relatively less sensitive areas, like the legs, arm, and trunk.

Temperature. Most of us have had an experience similar to the following one: It is a fairly warm day, and a friend has invited you over for a swim in her pool. When you arrive at her house she is already in the pool and obviously enjoying herself. The first thing you ask her is, "How's the water?" She replies, "It's perfect! Jump in!" Despite her enthusiasm, you venture cautiously toward the water, dipping in only your big toe to check the accuracy of her report. As soon as your toe hits the water, goose bumps arise from every pore in your body. She coaxes you, though, saying that it's not really too bad once you get used to it. But, taking the slow approach, you adapt yourself to the water gradually—first your toes, then your foot, and so on, slowly adjusting each part of your body to the cold water until you are totally submerged except for your head. No sooner have you gotten used to the water than another friend, clad in his bathing suit, shows up at poolside. "How's the water?" he inquires naively. Your response—"Perfect, dive in!"

This example highlights two important points about temperature that most of us are well aware of from personal experience. First, our bodies are sensitive to changes in temperature, and second, within limits, our bodies can adapt to those changes. What our experience doesn't always tell us is why we are sensitive to changes in temperature and how we adjust to those changes. The purpose of this section is to discuss these two issues.

In general, most people find a surrounding air temperature of about 22° centigrade (72° F) to be most comfortable. As you might guess, the greater the deviation from this temperature, colder or warmer, the more uncomfortable people become. Our sensitivity to such deviations is not a single process, however. Rather, two separate temperature systems appear to be at work, one for cold and one for warmth (Dallenbach, 1927).

When the warm and cold receptors in any specific region of skin are stimulated simultaneously, we experience, oddly enough, the sensation of hotness. Consider the following sensory illusion (see Figure 6.11). Two tubes, one containing ice-cold water and the other containing warm water are coiled together. If you were to touch either tube independently of the other, you would, of course, experience the expected sensation of either coldness or warmth. Suppose, though, that you grasp both tubes with one hand. Would you experience cold on one part of your hand and warmth on another? You would experience neither sensation. Rather, you would feel a sharp burning sensation, much like you would if you were to place the palm of your hand on a candle's flame. Indeed, the pain would be so intense that you would not be able to hold the tubes in your hand for much longer than a second or so. Such demonstrations have led sensory psychologists to believe that hot stimuli activate both warm and cold receptors.

We can, though, adapt to changes in temperature. The normal temperature of the surface of our skin is about 33°C (92°F). This temperature is referred to as physiological zero, because if an object of this same temperature were pressed against your skin, you would feel neither warmth nor coldness. All you would feel is the pressure of the object against your skin. In other words, we experience the sensation of warmth or coldness only when temperatures in our surrounding environment deviate from physiological zero.

To a certain degree, we can adapt to deviations in temperature from physiological zero. Our morning shower first feels hot, then merely warm; our dive in the lake first feels cold, then invigorating. Most people can adapt totally to changes in skin temperature ranging between 29°C and 37°C (84°F to 99°F) (Kenshalo, 1971). Temperatures that fall outside of this range, however, will continue to feel warm, cold, or hot, regardless of how long our skin is exposed to them.

Pain. Extreme temperatures, whether they are experienced by spilling scalding water on yourself or by grasping an ice cube with your bare hand, are not only perceived as hot or cold but are painful as well. Of course, many other kinds of stimulation are also perceived as painful. Stepping on a tack, hitting your head on a low overhang, biting your lip, and dropping a bowling ball on your foot are just a few experiences that we might describe as painful.

Despite our efforts to avoid situations associated with pain-producing stimuli and the billions of dollars spent each year on remedies to eliminate or reduce pain, pain itself has undeniably important survival value: it warns us that we have encountered a harmful, even life-threatening stimulus, and often prompts us to withdraw from the pain-producing elements of the situation. Although you may think that a life without pain might be enviable, it certainly is not desirable. People who suffer from pain perception disorders in which they cannot sense pain have been known to bite off their fingers or their tongues by accident and have suffered ruptured appendixes and broken bones without realizing it (Sternbach, 1978). Such damage to the body can result in death if not treated with proper medical care. But if an injury doesn't hurt, what, if anything, would cause you to protect yourself from further damage or to seek medical care? Clearly, pain plays a critical role in helping us survive.

Pain has two basic components, one biological and the other psychological. Both components influence our **pain threshold**, the lowest level of stimulation at which pain is sensed.

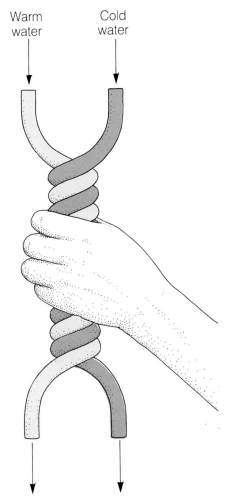

FIGURE 6.11
A sensory illusion of heat. When two pipes—one containing cold water and the other warm water—are braided together, a person touching the pipes will feel an illusion of heat. The perceived heat coming from the pipes is so great that a person could not touch them for more than a second or so.

Warm water   Cold water

The biological component of pain is the actual sensation of hurting. One factor that can influence this component is the physical condition of pain receptors, which are nerve endings that lie next to the skin. If the receptors are not working properly or if they have been deadened with anesthesia, the pain threshold is reduced, and sensations of pain are decreased or even eliminated. Another important factor is the intensity of the pain-provoking stimulus. In general, the more intense the stimulus, the greater the chances that the pain threshold will be exceeded. Being pinched hurts more than being tickled, and a lover's hug is more pleasant than a bear hug.

The psychological component involves our emotional reaction to both the sensation of pain and potentially painful situations. Emotional states can raise or lower pain thresholds, depending upon the situation. Soldiers in combat and people in intense athletic competition have been known to sustain sizeable injuries while in the throes of battle, only to discover afterward that they were, in fact, injured. In everyday life, however, just the opposite seems to occur: our emotional state often lowers, not raises, the pain threshold. Consider having a tooth drilled by your dentist. If you are like most people, you feel a bit nervous while waiting for the dentist to begin work on your tooth. Even though you have received an ample dose of novocaine, which should give you some relief from pain, every muscle in your body is braced for the pain that you "know" is coming. Even the slightest pain in the tooth elicits your grimmest wince. Simply put, our expectation of pain can sometimes lower our threshold for pain. At the very least, expecting that something will be painful seems to increase the likelihood that we will interpret it as painful. Pain thresholds vary from person to person, though, and largely because of differences in emotional states. That is, individual differences in emotions give rise to individual differences in the ability to tolerate pain.

Psychologically, pain signals us that we are in trouble physically and prompts us to seek relief. This makes sense because we do not readily adapt to pain, especially intense pain. We never quite seem to get used to a toothache or a stomachache no matter how long we experience them. We are likely to experience as much pain from a toothache after 5 hours as we do after 15 minutes. On the other hand, we are able to adapt, within limits, to less intense pain such as that produced by a pinprick or putting your hand in mildly hot water.

Thus, although pain thresholds vary considerably from one person to the next, adaptation to pain does not. Most people find it difficult to adjust to intense pain, regardless of their pain thresholds, and therein lies the motivation to seek pain relief.

The most influential theory of pain perception, the **gate-control theory**, was proposed by Melzack and Wall in 1965. According to these theorists, our perception of pain is determined by psychological factors as well as by the extent of bodily injury, and involves the interplay of the nerve fibers that carry information about pain to the brain (see Figure 6.12). The gist of the theory can be stated as follows: Both the large, fast fibers and the small, slow fibers of the peripheral nervous system send information about painful stimulation to a neural "gate" located in the spinal cord. This gate regulates the flow of neural information traveling from pain receptors in the skin and muscles to the brain. Neural impulses passed along by the large fibers serve to close the gate while neural impulses carried by the small fibers tend to open the gate. Messages from the brain can also cause the gate to close. Melzack (1973) believes that various and ever-changing emotional states can influence the ability to sense pain. In certain life-threatening situations, signals from the brain may close the gate, reducing

Our expectation of pain can sometimes lower our threshold for pain.

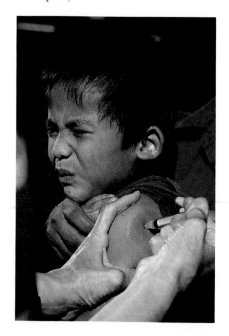

The expectation of pain, such as this boy's anticipation of receiving a vaccination, can often lower the threshold for pain. As a result, he grimaces and interprets the shot as more painful.

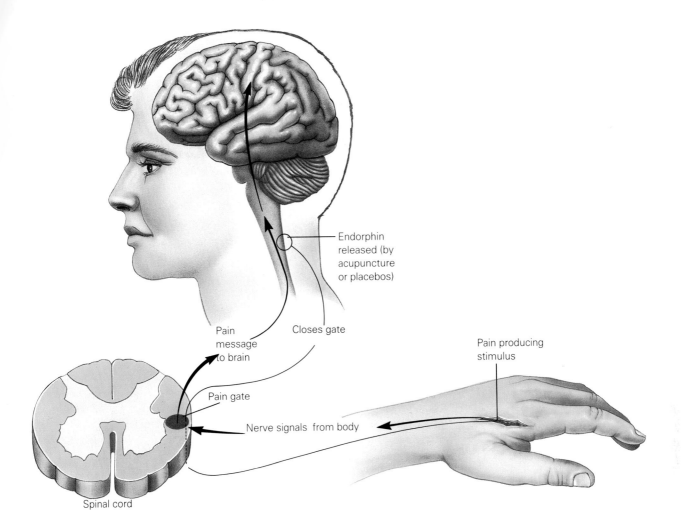

Endorphin
released (by
acupuncture
or placebos)

Pain
message
to brain

Closes gate

Pain producing
stimulus

Pain gate

Nerve signals from body

Spinal cord

FIGURE 6.12
The gate-control theory of pain.

or eliminating the sensation of pain, and allowing the individual to perform his or her task without distraction. As mentioned previously though, failure to notice the pain, at least in some cases, may increase the extent of bodily injury.

If gate-control theory is correct, our awareness of pain is a matter of whether the gate is open or closed. Thus, the key task before Melzack and other pain researchers subscribing to gate-control theory has been to explain those factors that may control the gate (Sherrick & Cholewiak, 1986). Let's briefly examine two such factors.

■ Counterirritation. On some occasions scratching or rubbing the skin near an injury may reduce pain intensity. To reduce their patients' awareness of the sting of a novocaine-filled hypodermic needle, dentists will often vigorously rub the area on the gums into which the needle is inserted. Likewise, rubbing the spot on your head that you just banged on a low overhang reduces the feeling of pain. According to gate-control theory, counterirritation is effective in reducing pain because it stimulates neurons to close the gate, thereby preventing messages laden with pain information from reaching the brain.

■ Analgesia. Pain relievers, such as aspirin, are common means of reducing pain. Psychologists believe that these substances stimulate the release of endorphins in the brain. Endorphins, as you may recall from Chapter 4, are naturally occurring opiates that are normally released in the brain during periods of pain or intense physical stress. If gate-control theory is correct, endorphins exert their analgesic effects by stimulating neurons that descend from the brain to close the gate. That is, signals from the brain, in addition to those from pain receptors on the skin's surface, can exert control over the gate (Frederickson & Geary, 1982).

Other methods of pain relief such as placebos and acupuncture also appear to involve endorphin control over the gate. A **placebo** is any substance that an individual *believes* to have certain properties, including inducement of pain relief, when in fact, it does not. The belief is sometimes all that is needed. People given a pill containing nothing but inert substances and perhaps a little sugar often report a reduction in pain shortly after the pill is consumed. The pain may have a known biological basis such as a gunshot wound, yet the psychological effect of believing in a placebo can make the pain recede. The reduction in pain appears to be genuine, but how can this be?

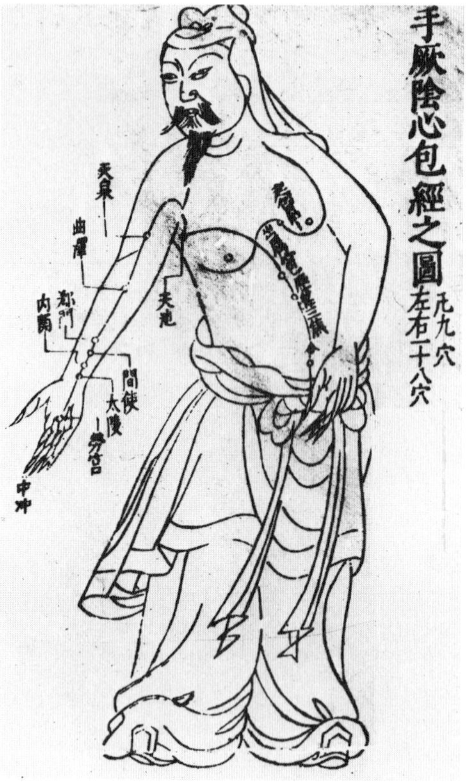

The answer to this question addresses the mind–body problem that has fascinated philosophers and scientists for centuries. The issue underlying the mind–body problem is how psychological events such as thought and emotion interact with biological and physiological events such as the release of neurotransmitters. Research into the understanding of how placebos work has provided some of the first suggestions as to how this interaction occurs.

Pharmacological research has shown that placebos exert their effects via endorphins. For example, nalaxone, a chemical that blocks the action of endorphins when injected into the brain, also reduces the analgesic effects of placebos (Watkins & Mayer, 1982). Somehow then, the *belief* that the pill contains pain relievers leads to the release of endorphins, which has analgesic properties.

Another phenomenon that involves the interaction of mind and body is **acupuncture**, a procedure of pain reduction developed by the Chinese in which small needles are inserted into the body at strategic spots (see Figure 6.13). Often the needles are twisted, heated, or charged with a small electrical current. The analgesic effects of acupuncture are so powerful that in many cases, patients treated with this procedure undergo major surgery while fully conscious. Not surprisingly, the main evidence linking acupuncture with endorphin control of the spinal gate also involves nalaxone. When injected into the brain, nalaxone reduces the analgesic effects of acupuncture.

Although acupuncture has been practiced by the Chinese for over 2,000 years, it has not yet become a popular means of controlling pain in most western cultures. In fact, many people are skeptical about the procedure's analgesic effects. Psychologically, it is difficult for many people to truly believe that sticking little needles into different body parts will actually reduce pain. Research on acupuncture, however, has shown that the procedure does reduce pain. Consider, for example, the research of Chapman, Wilson, & Gehring (1976). Each subject in this study first received electrical stimulation to a single tooth. Subjects reported the stimulation as painful, similar to that experienced while having a tooth drilled. Subjects were then divided into three groups. The first group underwent acupuncture: electrically charged needles were inserted between the thumb and index finger of each subject, a spot believed to play a role in the relief of dental pain. A second group also underwent acupuncture, but the needles were inserted in a location not considered to be related to relief of dental pain. A third group served as a control and underwent no acupuncture therapy. Subjects in each group then received electrical stimulation a second time. Subjects receiving acupuncture treatment between the thumb and index finger reported feeling much less dental pain when given electrical stimulation a second time than subjects in the other two groups. In short, acupuncture appears to have merit as a means of pain relief.

FIGURE 6.13
A diagram of the strategic spots used in acupuncture.

Kinesthesis and Equilibrium

Two distinct sensory systems, the kinesthetic and vestibular systems inform us of the position, orientation, and movement of our bodies in space. They allow us to know, for example, whether we are standing, sitting, or lying down, stationary or moving, upright or bent over, and so on.

The **kinesthetic system** senses the location, movement, and posture of the skeletal joints and muscles. The physiological basis for kinesthesis is nerve endings embedded in joints and deep muscles. Whenever we move—whether it is simply raising the hand to answer a question in class or the relatively more complex movements involved in running a pass pattern in a game of touch football—the corresponding joints and connective tendons and muscles exert pressure on these receptors, which in turn, send nerve impulses to the brain.

The **vestibular system** controls our sense of equilibrium or balance. The vestibular apparatus located in the inner ear just above the cochlea contains three **semicircular canals**, which in turn, contain receptors sensitive to changes in body orientation (see Figure 6.14). The semicircular canals are filled with a viscous fluid that moves whenever the head is rotated. Such movement causes the fluid to bend hair cells located within the canals, which, in turn, gives rise to nerve impulses.

The vestibular system is stimulated by the natural, active movement of the body—starting, stopping, and changing direction. Passive movement, such as traveling in a plane or bus at a constant speed, does not stimulate the vestibular system. Thus, in these cases, the hair cells in the vestibular system are not stimulated and we do not experience movement. The only way we can tell whether or not we are moving is by looking out the window and experiencing motion parallax. In other words, it is acceleration and deceleration, not motion per se, that matter.

FIGURE 6.14
The vestibular system. The vestibular apparatus, located just above the cochlea, contains the semicircular canals that, in turn, contain receptors sensitive to change in body orientation.

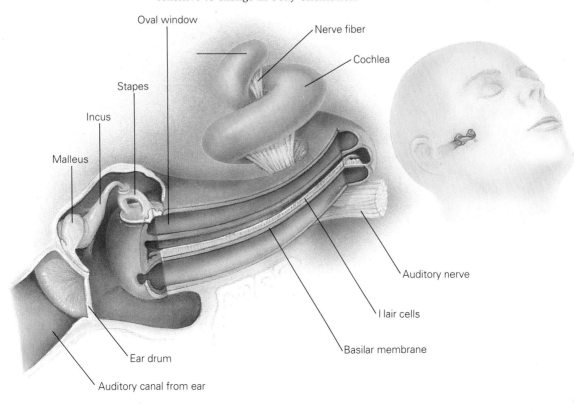

Vestibular sacs in the inner ear working in conjunction with the eyes enable the baseball player pictured here to keep his eyes on the ball while he is moving.

Some kinds of stimulation of the vestibular system, such as that produced by flying in turbulence or by being onboard a ship in rough waters, may produce **motion sickness**, a distressing physical condition characterized by nausea, dizziness, and sometimes vomiting. Factors such as visual disorientation, rank odors, heat, and emotional anxiety may increase a passenger's likelihood of suffering motion sickness in a moving vehicle (Schiffman, 1976). Motion sickness is more likely to occur during passive than active movement. Hence, passengers in moving vehicles have a greater chance of experiencing motion sickness than do drivers or pilots who can control the movement of their vehicles. Fortunately, many people who must travel eventually become accustomed to the kinds of movements that give rise to motion sickness. Others who find that experience does not help may take medication that retards the symptoms of motion sickness.

Located just below the semicircular canals in the inner ear is a second set of receptors, the **vestibular sacs**, which plays an important role in helping the head maintain its proper upright orientation. In addition, the vestibular sacs also help us to see clearly as we move through space. For example, suppose you are running after a pop fly ball. Each stride jostles your head a bit, yet you are able to keep your eyes focused squarely on the ball. How is it that you manage to "keep your eye on the ball"? Nerve impulses from the vestibular sacs stimulate the eyes to move reflexively in a direction exactly opposite and equal to the movement of the head. Damage to the vestibular sacs may interfere with this reflex to the point that afflicted individuals cannot see clearly when they are moving.

Whether you are walking, running, or standing still, your brain receives feedback from the kinesthetic and vestibular systems about the position, orientation, or movement of your body. Thus, like the skin senses, they provide the brain with critical information that helps you adapt your behavior to changes in environmental stimulation.

THE CHEMICAL SENSES: SMELL AND TASTE

Freshly baked chocolate chip cookies. Just reading those words is enough to bring to mind their scrumptious aroma and mouth-watering taste. Psychologically, our enjoyment of eating chocolate chip cookies, or any food for that matter, results from the interaction of smell and taste.

Smell and taste have two important characteristics in common. First, both are responses to chemical stimulation. Receptors in our noses respond to airborne chemicals and taste buds are sensitive to chemicals that dissolve in saliva. Second, both senses readily adapt to stimulation. You probably cannot smell the cologne or aftershave you put on this morning, and if you can, it is probably not as intense as it was when you first took the cap off the bottle. You have probably also noticed that the fourth or fifth chocolate chip cookie you consume is not nearly as delicious as the first one.

Despite these similarities, smell and taste are generally studied as distinct sensory processes. Our discussion of them will follow suit. We begin with our sense of smell, which is also referred to as olfaction.

Smell

Although our sense of smell is not quite as good as that of other animals such as dogs, we are quite sensitive to odors in our immediate environments. For example, we can smell the fragrance of a single drop of perfume that has been diffused into the volume of a three room apartment. Because of its sensitivity, our sense of smell has survival value. Under normal circumstances, we can smell smoke before fire reaches us, spoiled food before we consume it, and gas leaks before they reach deadly levels. Smell also has special aesthetic value as testified to by the amount of money we spend on pleasant smelling colognes and perfumes. Let's see how odors stimulate the receptors in the nose.

The Nature of Smell. Our understanding of the olfactory system lags behind our understanding of other sensory systems. An important part of the problem is that sensory psychologists have not yet identified the specific physical properties of smell stimuli that correspond to our perception of specific odors. As you may recall from our discussion of some of the other senses, manipulations of certain physical properties of sensory stimuli produce corresponding changes in perception. For example, changing the wavelength of visual stimuli changes our perception of color. Likewise, changing the frequency of auditory stimuli changes our perception of pitch. But what are the physical properties of smell stimuli that must be changed before we notice a difference in our perception of an odor? Until researchers can answer that question, that is, until researchers discover a physical property of smell stimuli that is analogous to wavelength or frequency, our understanding of smell will remain incomplete.

One early theory of smell focused on a classification system that involved six basic odors (Henning, 1916). Another theory was based on the premise that odors could be classified according to the similarity of their molecular structure (Amoore, 1970). Both of these classification schemes appear to be too simplistic. Many researchers find it impossible to classify odor using only six or seven odors (Cain, 1978). Other researchers have found no relation between an actual odor molecule's shape and its odor. For example, Schiffman (1974) found that subjects in her study often judged stimuli with similar molecular configurations as having very different odors. Thus, discovering the physical basis for olfactory stimulation still remains the most important research question before modern smell researchers.

When we are smelling an aromatic flower, we are responding to chemical stimulation. Like the sense of taste, the sense of smell, or olfaction, adapts to stimulation. Therefore, the aroma of the flowers lessens after a time.

The Nose. Although we have not determined the physical means by which odors stimulate the nose, we do know the basic features of the human olfactory system (Figure 6.15). Each time you inhale, air is channeled into the **nasal cavity**, the hollow portion of each nostril. Air can also reach the nasal cavity through the back of the throat. Odor receptors are located in the **olfactory mucosa**, which is at the top of the nasal cavity just beneath the base of the brain. One researcher (Mozel, 1969) estimates that only about two percent of the molecules entering the nose on a given breath ever reach the olfactory receptors. The remainder of the molecules are absorbed by the lining of the lower nasal cavity, which has no receptors. The mucosa in the human nose contain about 10 million receptors. In contrast, a typical dog's nose contains about 200 million olfactory receptors, which helps show why dogs have a better sense of smell than humans do.

When struck by molecules, the olfactory receptors generate neural impulses that travel along their axons to the **olfactory bulb**, an enlarged bundle of neural tissue located in the brain just above the bone separating the brain from the olfactory mucosa. From the olfactory bulb, neural information regarding smell is sent to various areas of the brain, where it is interpreted. These areas include the hypothalamus and amygdala (which as you will recall, are involved in eating, drinking, and sexual behavior), the thalamus (where information from the other senses is also sent), and the frontal lobe.

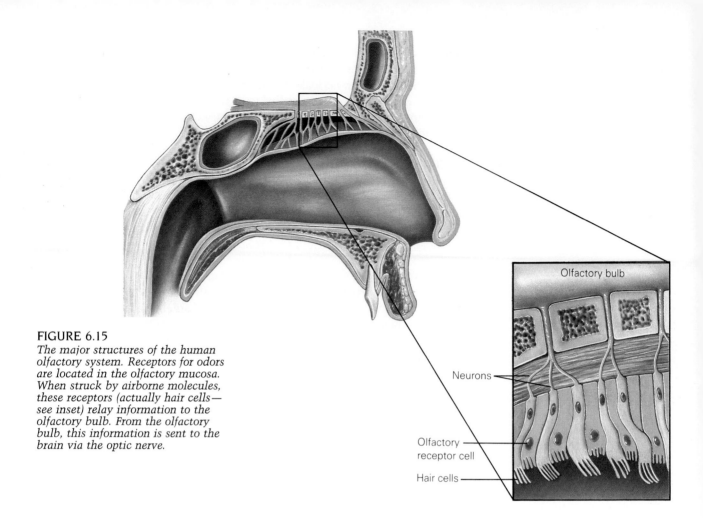

FIGURE 6.15
The major structures of the human olfactory system. Receptors for odors are located in the olfactory mucosa. When struck by airborne molecules, these receptors (actually hair cells— see inset) relay information to the olfactory bulb. From the olfactory bulb, this information is sent to the brain via the optic nerve.

Olfactory bulb

Neurons

Olfactory receptor cell

Hair cells

Olfactory Thresholds and Adaptation. Our sensitivity to smell depends on a number of factors. Obviously, our absolute threshold for smell varies from odor to odor. We can detect some odors, such as that of ethyl mercaptan (the chemical added to natural gas, which has no odor of its own), in quantities as minute as 1 part per 50 billion parts air. Other odors, such as those from ether or carbon monoxide, require considerably stronger concentrations before we can detect their presence.

Sensitivity to smell varies from person to person too. William Cain, an expert on human olfaction, suggests that the absolute threshold for smell varies about 100 fold (Cain, 1978). This means that an individual with a particularly keen nose might be able to detect .01 milligram of a substance per unit of air while a person with a very poor sense of smell would require an entire milligram of the substance per unit of air before he or she could detect its presence. Cain believes that differences in the size and wetness of people's nasal cavities may account for such individual differences in smell. His theory is the bigger and wetter the nostrils, the lower the absolute threshold.

S

ensitivity to smell varies from person to person . . .

Although most of us are pretty good at detecting the presence or absence of an odor, our ability to distinguish between concentrations of odors leaves something to be desired. In laboratory conditions, two concentrations of the same substance must differ by about 7 percent (depending upon the substance) for a difference between the concentrations to be noticed (Cain, 1977). In real life, the difference must be substantially greater— about 20 to 30 percent (Matlin, 1983). At least part of the reason for our difficulty in detecting differences between two concentrations of the same odor is attributable to the conditions under which we normally smell. Usually more than one odor is in the air, and often we just are not paying attention to the odors around us.

You may reason that you can smell an odor better if you inhale more deeply than usual. After all, the greater the number of odor vapors that you can take in, the more odor molecules there will be to stimulate olfactory receptors, and the stronger the smell, right? Wrong. A study by Teghtsoonian and colleagues (1978) has shown that our judgments of odor intensity are not affected by depth of breathing. Subjects were first trained to inhale at two different depths, with one inhalation twice as deep as the other. Next, subjects smelled different odors using shallow or deep breathing. After each breath, subjects judged the perceived intensity of the odor. Although deep breaths would seem likely to take in twice as many odorous molecules as shallow breath, subjects reported little, and sometimes, no differences in perceived odor intensity between the two breathing styles.

One final point about difference thresholds is worth making. As you are well aware from everyday experience, prolonged exposure to an odor decreases your sensitivity to that odor. Laboratory studies have shown, however, that regardless of how long we breathe an odor, we never become completely insensitive to it. Rather, at the lowest point, the perceived intensity of a strong odor falls to about 30 percent of its original value (Cain, 1978). If you first adapt to a strong odor though, it may be impossible to detect a weaker concentration of that same odor.

This latter idea lies at the heart of **cross-adaptation**, the decrease in sensitivity to one odor because of exposure to a different odor. Odors that are similar are more susceptible to cross-adaptation than odors that are very different. Try the following demonstration (Sekuler & Blake, 1985). First, take the cap off a bottle of cologne and sniff it long enough to recognize its smell. Next, hold an open can of instant coffee close to your nose until your nose becomes adapted to its smell. Then take a quick smell of the cologne again. The fragrance of the cologne should be just as intense as the first time you smelled it. Repeat the procedure, substituting a bar of soap for the coffee. Now you should find that the cologne's fragrance is markedly less strong. The reason: your sensitivity to the cologne has become cross-adapted to the smell of the soap.

Gourmet chefs and discriminating cooks have long understood some of the practical problems posed by cross-adaptation. The enjoyment of multicourse meals is often affected by the sequence of courses. For example, if the flavor of the main course is determined by a subtle trace of garlic, then the salad should not be seasoned with strong onion or garlic.

Recognizing Odors. Just because a person can detect an odor or discriminate between two different odors does not necessarily mean that he or she can also recognize that odor. Identifying a smell requires that a person equate a smell with a specific verbal label, and this is a more difficult task than one would think. For example, if you were asked to identify an object's odor without being able to see or touch the object, how well do you think you would do? If you are like most subjects who have participated in these kinds of studies, you would do pretty well at recognizing the smells of familiar objects such as coffee, paint, and bananas, but you would fare considerably worse when asked to recognize the smells of less familiar objects such as crayons, ham, and sawdust. In fact in one study (Desor & Beauchamp, 1974), fewer than 20 percent of the subjects were able to identify accurately these and other unfamiliar smells. In some cases, you may be familiar with an odor, but not familiar enough with it to give it a name. This problem has been called the "tip of the nose" phenomenon (Lawless & Engen, 1977).

Fortunately, odor recognition is a skill that improves quickly with practice. Regardless of the amount of practice, though, females have proven to be more sensitive to smell than males. For example, Cain (1982) asked male and female undergraduates to identify eighty common odorous substances. Every subject was exposed to each substance several times and received feedback concerning the accuracy of their verbal responses on each trial. Although all subjects improved with practice, females were more accurate than males in correctly identifying the odor of over 81 percent of the substances.

Interestingly, most people are very accurate without practice at recognizing sex-related odors. Most people can distinguish their own body odor from that of another person. They can also accurately identify the sex of another person if first given the opportunity to smell that person's body odor. Let's consider some of the empirical evidence supporting these statements.

Perhaps the most famous study of the human ability to recognize sex-related odors is the "dirty T-shirt" study conducted by British psychologist Mark Russell in 1976. Twenty-nine undergraduates were instructed to first bathe with clear water and then to wear the same T-shirt for a 24 hour period during which they were not to use deodorants or perfumes. Russell then collected the T-shirts and placed each in its own container. In the next phase of the study, Russell asked his subjects to serve beyond the call of duty—he had each subject smell three dirty T-shirts: their own T-shirt, a T-shirt worn by an unknown female, and a T-shirt worn by an unknown male. Twenty-two of the twenty-nine subjects were able to correctly identify their own dirty T-shirt! Even more impressive is Russell's finding that the same number of subjects were able to tell which of the remaining two T-shirts had been worn by a female and which had been worn by a male. Subjects described the smell of T-shirts worn by females as "sweet" and those worn by males as "musky."

A later study by Patricia Wallace (1977) showed that college students could discriminate females from males by merely sniffing a person's hand. Wallace first blindfolded her subjects and then asked them to smell the hands of males and females whose hands had been washed and covered with a plastic glove (to induce sweating) prior to the experimental session. Subjects made accurate discriminations in over 80 percent of the trials with females outperforming males.

In sum, even though many people are not very accurate at recognizing unfamiliar odors, they do improve with practice. However, even without practice, people are very accurate at recognizing gender-related odors. Although smell is not as useful to us as vision or hearing, it is nonetheless adaptive. We have a very keen sense of smell when it comes to identifying the odor of spoiled food, ethyl mercaptan, or other odors associated with danger. We also easily recognize odors associated with pleasant experiences, such as freshly baked bread, or a cologne or perfume.

Taste

Taste refers only to those sensations produced when chemical molecules stimulate the receptor cells found in the mouth. Our enjoyment of food, whether it is the appetizer, main course, or dessert, is based largely on its flavor. To most sensory psychologists, **flavor** refers not only to a food or drink's taste but also its consistency, temperature, texture, and smell (Gibson, 1966). Do you prefer your steak well-done or rare, tough or tender? How about your coffee—do you prefer it hot, lukewarm, or cold? And as any good chef knows, the taste of food is often influenced by other factors such as appearance (chefs call it "presentation").

Of all the components of flavor, taste has been the subject of the most research. Taste is considered one of the basic senses while the other components of flavor, for example, temperature and texture, seem to be related to the skin senses, which we have already discussed. For these reasons, this section of the chapter is concerned primarily with taste. Let's begin by taking a look at the nature of taste.

The Nature of Taste. We taste only those substances that can be dissolved in saliva. If you put your tongue on a clean fork or spoon, or on a clean glass or plate, you would not experience the sensation of taste simply because these materials cannot be dissolved in saliva. The stimulus for taste, then, is any substance that is soluble.

Many sensory psychologists believe there are four basic classes of taste stimuli: sweet, sour, salty, and bitter. Others, like Schiffman, believe that there are seven primary tastes and not four (she adds alkaline, sulfurous, and fatty to her list) and has obtained some empirical evidence to support her position (Schiffman & Dackis, 1975). Based on studies in which people were asked to evaluate complex taste solutions (solutions formed by combining the four taste qualities), Erickson argues that we do not perceive complex tastes solely in terms of their primary qualities, but rather that complex tastes have their own distinct characteristics, which are often different from their individual component tastes (Erickson, 1982).

Nonetheless, the four-taste classification system remains the predominant model of taste for two very good reasons. First, researchers have discovered that substances belonging to the same taste class are similar molecularly (Beidler, 1978). For example, any two sweet substances are likely to have similar molecular structures. Second, receptors on the tongue appear to be sensitive to sweet, sour, salty, and bitter tastes (Collings, 1974).

The Taste System. If you were to stick out your tongue while looking at yourself in a mirror, you would notice that it is covered with thousands of tiny bumps. These bumps, called **papillae**, are lined with the **taste buds**, which house the actual receptors for taste (see Figure 6.16). To a lesser extent, taste buds are also found on the roof of the mouth, inside the cheeks, and in the throat. You may have noticed that when food or other taste-evoking substances are placed directly onto the center of your tongue, you experience little, if any, sensation of taste. That is because the papillae in the center of your tongue have no taste buds; only those near the periphery of your tongue have taste buds (see Figure 6.16). Among papillae that contain taste buds, some may house as few as one or two or as many as several hundred (Bradley, 1979).

The life of a taste bud spans about ten days (Beidler & Smallman, 1965). They are constantly dying and being replaced by new ones. The rate at which the number of taste buds wax and wane, however, varies depending on a person's age. When you were a child, the total number of taste buds in your mouth increased steadily to a total of about 10,000. When you approach age 40, more taste buds will die than will be replaced (Cowart, 1981), and as a result, your sensitivity to taste may be dulled (Schiffman, 1983).

Although papillae can be seen easily with the naked eye, taste buds cannot. Each individual taste bud houses an average of about fifty receptor cells (see Figure 6.17) (Sekular & Blake, 1985). Notice that the receptor cells appear to cling together like a clump of bananas. At the top of the clump are thin, threadlike fibers that extend outside of the taste bud and make contact with chemical substances in the saliva. When stimulated, the receptor cells undergo a change in electrical potential, triggering a neural impulse that eventually reaches nuclei in the brain.

FIGURE 6.16

The human taste system. The bumps on the tongue are called papillae and are lined with taste buds, which house the taste receptors.

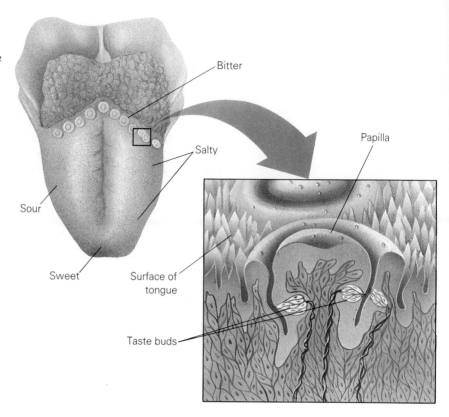

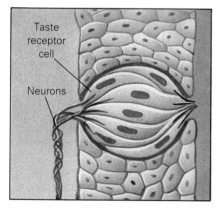

FIGURE 6.17

A single taste bud. A taste bud houses on average about fifty receptor cells.

Not all taste buds on the tongue respond to the same kinds of chemical stimulation. In fact, as Virginia Collings (1974) has shown, the tongue can be divided into four taste regions, with each region being sensitive only to sweet, sour, salty, or bitter flavors.

Under carefully controlled conditions, Collings placed tiny strips of paper soaked in weak taste solutions on specific regions of each of her subjects' tongues or on other parts of the mouth. Once subjects tasted the solution-soaked paper, they pointed to a card that identified the flavor as being sweet, sour, salty, or bitter. Collings repeated the procedure until subjects had an opportunity to respond to each taste several times, allowing her to map the taste regions of the tongue. Her subjects reported that sweet and salty tastes were experienced when papers soaked in these solutions were placed on the front of the tongue. Papers soaked in the sour solution evoked the greatest response when placed on the sides of the tongue. Papers soaked in the bitter solution evoked the greatest response when placed upon the back of the tongue.

Since the purpose of Collings' research was to examine the tongue's sensitivity to weak taste solutions, we must add two qualifying statements about her results. First, different taste sensations can be elicited by placing different solutions on an individual taste bud, indicating that perhaps taste quality is encoded by particular patterns of stimulation across taste buds (Pfaffman, 1955). Second, any of the four taste qualities can be elicited when a strong taste solution is applied to areas of the tongue that house taste buds. Thus, if a very sour solution were applied to the front of your tongue, you would probably experience a sour taste, despite the fact that this area of your tongue is not especially sensitive to that taste. Collings' work is important because it demonstrated that the different regions of the tongue are *not* equally sensitive to the four taste qualities.

Taste Thresholds and Adaptation. Some people have an astonishing sense of taste. For example, experienced wine tasters have been known not only to identify a wine's name and the date when it was bottled with a single taste, but also the vineyard in which the grapes used in the wine were grown! Most of us, however, have a less discriminating sense of taste. Like smell, our recognition threshold for taste is much higher than our detection threshold for taste. That is, we may be able to taste a substance but not to name it, particularly if the taste solution is a weak one. Incidentally, as with odor recognition, women outperform men in tests of taste identification (Meiselman & Dzendolet, 1967).

An important variable in influencing our sensitivity to taste is the temperature of the substance being tasted. Consider, for example, how temperature affects the taste of wine. Chilling a wine, particularly if it is a less expensive wine, will conceal any sour, sweet, or bitter tastes it may have. By contrast, serving the wine at room temperature allows these aspects of the wine to be tasted. Figure 6.18 illustrates how each of the four basic tastes are influenced by changes in temperature. We seem to be most sensitive to tastes when substances or solutions are served at temperatures near room temperature (McBurney, 1978). However, each taste is affected differently by changes in temperature. Increasing a sweet substance's temperature to between 25°C and 30°C increases its sweetness; beyond this point however, temperature diminishes sweetness. Increasing the temperature of a substance much beyond room temperature will also detract from any bitter or salty quality it may possess. Changing the temperature of sour substances only slightly affects its taste: a tart lemon meringue pie is going to taste sour whether it is warm or cold.

As we noted in the section on smell, a substance's flavor is affected by its odor. In the taste laboratory, Mozel and colleagues (1969) have demonstrated just how important odor is to our ability to identify tastes. Subjects in the experiment were asked to identify twenty-one common substances by name under two different conditions. In one condition, the smell of the substances was prevented from reaching olfactory mucosa, while in the other, subjects could smell the aroma of the substances freely. When subjects were prevented from smelling the substance dropped onto their

FIGURE 6.18
The effect of temperature on changes in each of the four tastes.

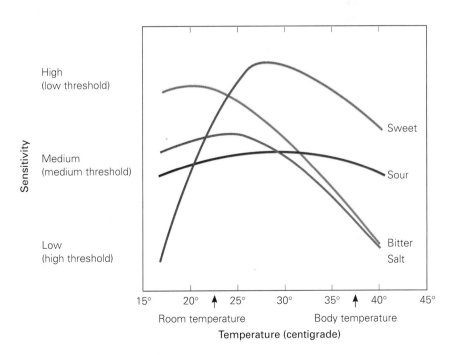

tongues, their ability to identify the taste of that substance correctly was reduced dramatically. Indeed, without being able to smell them, some substances could not be correctly identified. On the other hand, when subjects could smell the odor of each substance, their accuracy in identifying the substances increased markedly.

Like smell, we readily adapt to taste. The last forkful of a salad covered with oil and vinegar dressing does not seem as bitter as the first one; the first bite of ham may seem considerably more salty than the last bite; and the last bite of key lime pie may not taste quite as sour as the first bite. That is, our sensitivity to taste is diminished by prior exposure to the same substance. Our sense of taste also cross adapts: adaptation to one taste raises the adaptation threshold to a second, similar substance.

In conclusion, taste buds located in the papillae of the tongue house the receptors for taste. We seem to be especially sensitive to four basic tastes: bitter, sweet, sour, and salty. Our sensitivity to any taste is influenced mainly by temperature and odor. The receptors in our taste buds adapt to flavor depending upon prior exposure to that substance, and adaptation to one flavor will produce adaptation to other similar flavors. Taste also serves an adaptive function: it alerts us to which substances are safe to eat and which are not.

BOUNDARIES AND FRONTIERS

Nature has endowed us with remarkable means with which to learn about the world. Everything we know about the world we know through our senses. (Can you think of something that you know that you have not learned through one of your senses?) Our behavior and thinking, that is, our actions and reactions to objects and events in the world, are guided by information received by the brain through the senses. The senses, then, represent an indispensable means of adapting to the environment.

But why aren't we even better adapted to the environment? Why can't we hear as well as the mouse, smell as well as the dog, or detect insects and other small moving objects the way bats can? Why didn't nature endow us with these kinds of sensory abilities?

There are two ways to answer the last question. The first involves sensory abilities that weren't favored by natural selection, probably because they never existed in our ancestors. The second involves intelligence, which has been favored by natural selection, and our ability to better use sensory information.

In order for natural selection to favor a trait such as a sense, it must, of course, exist. In our evolutionary past, the genetic code for such increased sensory capacity may never have existed. If the code didn't exist, there could be no corresponding phenotype or outward expression of the genetic code, and so, nothing upon which natural selection could act. That is, our ancestors probably never possessed any extraordinary sensory abilities that could be passed on via genes to future generations.

However, as we learned in Chapter 3, natural selection favored increases in brain size in the evolution of our early ancestors. Individuals with large brains tended to leave more offspring than individuals with smaller brains, and eventually, only humans with large brains existed. Most of the increase in brain size involved expansion of the cerebral cortex, which as we have seen in the last two chapters, is the final destination of nerve impulses carrying sensory information. As you may recall from Chapter 4, the cortex not only receives sensory information, it also integrates that information with other information from past experiences stored in memory. Thus, combined with other adaptations, such as the ability to grasp objects with our hands and the ability to walk upright, we have the capacity to use sensory information to act upon the world in ways that no other organism can. The mouse may hear better than we hear and is clearly adapted to its environment, but we have the ability to use auditory information in ways that the mouse can't, and in so doing, are highly adapted to our environment. Thus, we may not be able to hear like the mouse, or smell as well as the dog, or detect small moving objects like the bat can, but because we *are* able to use sensory information in more sophisticated ways than other organisms can, we can fashion our environment to better suit or stimulate the sensory abilities we do have. In essence, what we lack in sensory capacity, we make up for in intellectual capacity.

Consider just a few of the many ways we manipulate the environment to benefit our sensory abilities:

- We use electricity to light our environment and help us to see objects that would otherwise be impossible to see clearly, and we decorate our homes and workplaces with colors that are pleasing to the eye.
- We build stereo systems to enhance the sound of music and speech.
- We adjust climate control systems to heat or cool our homes and workplaces.
- We build rides at amusement parks that stimulate the vestibular system.
- We use perfumes and colognes that have alluring fragrances.
- We season foods to enhance their flavor.

In short, compared to other animals we possess only modest sensory abilities. However, we have an adaptive advantage over other animals: our relatively greater intellectual capacity allows us to use sensory information in ways that other animals cannot.

One important boundary and frontier of our knowledge of the sensory world is to discover ways to help those with sensory deficits adapt better to their world. As you know, defects in any sensory modality result in a loss of certain kinds of knowledge about the world and, therefore, diminish quality of life. Recall the story of Helen Keller presented at the outset of Chapter 5. Although she could not see or hear, she was able to learn about the world through use of her other senses, particularly touch (pressure). Still, despite her accomplishments, Helen Keller did not know the world like people who see and hear normally.

Thus an important and inviting research question lies before sensory psychologists and others in related fields: how can we manipulate the environment to enable those with sensory deficits to come to know the world as the rest of us know it?

CONCEPT SUMMARY

AUDITION: SENSORY AND PERCEPTUAL PROCESSES

- What are the psychological counterparts to a sound wave's wavelength, amplitude, and purity? (pp. 193–195)
- How do the structures of the outer and inner ear respond to stimulation by sound waves? (pp. 195–198)
- Where in the ear are sound waves converted to nerve impulses? How are sound waves transduced? (pp. 197–198)
- How are we able to perceive loudness? Pitch? (pp. 198–200)
- How does the Doppler effect cue us to a sound's location? (pp. 200–201)
- How do binaural cues help in locating sounds? Describe two binaural cues. (p. 201)
- What is the relationship between auditory perception and attention? What is the cocktail party phenomenon? (p. 202)
- What is the difference between conduction hearing loss and nerve hearing loss? (pp. 202–203)

THE SOMATOSENSORY SYSTEM

- How is somatosensory information encoded, and how does such information get from the receptors to the brain? (pp. 204–205)
- What is the physiological basis for sensing pressure? How sensitive to pressure are we? (pp. 205–206)
- How sensitive are we to changes in temperature? To what extent can we adapt to changes in temperature? (pp. 206–207)
- In what sense is the ability to sense pain adaptive? (pp. 207–208)
- How do psychological factors influence pain thresholds and the perception of pain? (p. 208)
- How does the gate-control theory of pain account for the perception of pain? (pp. 208–210)
- What are the differences between the kinesthetic and the vestibular senses? (pp. 211–212)

THE CHEMICAL SENSES: SMELL AND TASTE

- Why do we understand less about smell than about the other senses? How are odors best classified? (pp. 212–213)
- How does the nose convert olfactory stimulation into nerve impulses? (p. 213)
- What factors influence olfactory thresholds and adaptation? (pp. 214–215)
- How good are people at recognizing odors? What is the relationship between odor recognition and practice? (pp. 215–216)
- What is the stimulus for taste? How are tastes classified? (pp. 216–217)
- How is chemical stimulation of the taste buds converted to nerve impulses? (pp. 217–218)
- How does temperature and odor affect taste thresholds? What is the relationship between prolonged exposure to a flavor and taste adaptation? (pp. 219–220)

KEY TERMS AND CONCEPTS

AUDITION: SENSORY AND PERCEPTUAL PROCESSES

Sound Wave An alternating pattern of high and low air pressure caused by vibrating objects. (p. 193)

Amplitude The difference between the high and low pressure levels of a sound wave. Graphically, amplitude is represented by the height of the wave. (p. 193)

Loudness The psychological counterpart to amplitude. The more intense the vibration, the greater the amplitude, and to some extent, the louder the psychological experience of the sound. (p. 193)

Decibel (dB) The unit of measurement for studying a sound wave's amplitude and loudness. (p. 194)

Wave Frequency The speed with which variations (from high to low) in air pressure occur. (p. 194)

Hertz (Hz) The unit of measurement for studying a sound wave's frequency and pitch. (p. 194)

Pitch The psychological quality of sound corresponding to wave frequency. (p. 194)

Purity The mixture of sound waves that make up a sound. (p. 194)

Timbre The psychological quality corresponding to a sound's clarity. (p. 194)

Pinna The visible part of the ear. (p. 196)

Auditory Canal The tubelike structure connecting the pinna with the tympanic membrane and through which sound waves enter the ear. (p. 196)

Tympanic Membrane A thin, conically shaped membrane separating the outer and middle ears that vibrates when struck by sound waves. The tympanic membrane is also known as the ear drum. (p. 196)

Ossicles Three bones (the malleus, incus and stapes) that amplify and transmit the vibrations of the tympanic membrane to the oval window. (p. 196)

Oval Window The membrane dividing the inner and middle ears that vibrates when stimulated by the ossicles. (p. 196)

Cochlea A bony, coiled, fluid-filled chamber in the inner ear that houses the auditory receptors. (p. 197)

Basilar Membrane A structure that runs nearly the entire length of the cochlea and functionally divides the cochlea into upper and lower divisions. The hair cells are embedded in the basilar membrane. (p. 197)

Hair Cells The auditory receptors. Whenever the basilar membrane vibrates, it forces the hair cells upward against another membrane, bending them in a shearing motion. Deformations of the hair cells in this manner produce neural impulses that relay information to the brain. (p. 197)

Auditory Nerve The bundle of neurons along which auditory information from the hair cells to the brain is channeled. (p. 198)

Place Theory The theory proposed by von Helmholtz stating that the basilar membrane is composed of independent nerve fibers, each sensitive to a different sound frequency, and so also sensitive to pitch. (p. 199)

Frequency Theory The theory of pitch that proposes that the entire basilar membrane vibrates in synchrony with the frequency of sound waves striking the ear. These vibrations are then transduced to an equivalent number of neural impulses that are channeled to the brain. (p. 199)

Volley Principle The idea that the hair cells in the cochlea alternately fire and rest. This principle was developed to account for hearing sound wave frequencies above 1,000 Hz. (p. 199)

Doppler Effect The changes in pitch emanating from a sound-emitting object moving relative to a listener. (p. 200)

Selective Listening The ability to perceive only one auditory stimulus at a time. (p. 202)

Conduction Hearing Loss The obstruction or destruction of the conductive structures of the ear, specifically, the external auditory canal, tympanic membrane, and ossicles. (p. 203)

Nerve Hearing Loss Decreases in hearing ability resulting from damage to the neural structures involved in transmitting auditory information from the cochlea to the brain, including the hair cells, basilar membrane, and the auditory nerve. (p. 203)

THE SOMATOSENSORY SYSTEM

Somatosensory System Our sense of pressure, temperature, pain, balance, and equilibrium. (p. 204)

Pacinian Corpuscle A nerve ending that responds to touch and vibration. (p. 205)

Pain Threshold The lowest level of stimulation at which pain is sensed. (p. 207)

Gate-Control Theory A theory stating that our perception of pain is determined by the interplay of the nerve fibers that carry information about pain to the brain. Large, fast fibers close a neural gate through which information about pain must pass on its way to the brain. Small, slow fibers open the gate. (p. 208)

Placebo Any substance that an individual believes to contain pain-relieving ingredients, when in fact, it does not. (p. 210)

Acupuncture A procedure of pain reduction in which small needles are inserted into the body at strategic spots. (p. 210)

Kinesthetic System Our sense of the location, movement, and posture of the skeletal joints and muscles. (p. 211)

Vestibular System Our sense of equilibrium or balance. (p. 211)

Semicircular Canals The structure in the inner ear that contains receptors sensitive to changes in body orientation. The semicircular canals are filled with a viscous fluid that moves whenever the head is rotated. (p. 211)

Motion Sickness The nausea and dizziness caused by some kinds of stimulation of the vestibular system, such as that sometimes experienced by flying in turbulence or by being onboard a ship in rough waters. (p. 212)

Vestibular Sacs A set of receptors located just below the semicircular canals, that plays a critical role in maintaining the head in its proper upright orientation. (p. 212)

THE CHEMICAL SENSES: SMELL AND TASTE

Nasal Cavity The hollow portion of each nostril. (p. 213)

Olfactory Mucosa The part of the nose located at the top of the nasal cavity just beneath the base of the brain that contains odor receptors. (p. 213)

Olfactory Bulb An enlarged bundle of neural tissue located just above the bone separating the brain from the olfactory mucosa that sends neural information about smell to various regions of the brain. (p. 213)

Cross-Adaptation The decrease in sensitivity to one odor because of exposure to a different, but similar, odor. (p. 215)

Taste The sensation produced by chemical molecules stimulating receptor cells found in the mouth. (p. 216)

Flavor A food or drink's taste, consistency, temperature, texture, and smell. (p, 216)

Papillae The tiny bumps on the tongue that are lined with taste buds. (p. 217)

Taste Buds The parts of the papillae that house the receptors for taste. (p. 217)

ADDITIONAL SOURCES OF INFORMATION

Goldstein, E. B. (1989). *Sensation and perception* (3rd ed.). Belmont, CA: Wadsworth. A very good and current introductory text on sensation and perception. The last five chapters discuss hearing, the somatosensory system, and smell and taste.

Pfaff, D. W. (Ed.). (1985). *Taste, olfaction and the central nervous system.* New York: Rockefeller University Press. A graduate-level account of recent research in the chemical senses.

Boff, K. R., Kaufman, L., Thomas, J. L. (Eds.). (1986). *Handbook of perception and human performance.* Hillsdale, NJ: Erlbaum. This volume is part of an edited series of very prestigious books dealing with the operation of each of our sensory and perceptual systems. The book is sophisticated reading but represents state-of-the-art research in sensation and perception.

7 Learning and Behavior Analysis

Learning is a relatively permanent change in behavior based on experience. Psychologists study the relationship between learning and behavior by manipulating environmental variables. However, the extent to which behavior can be modified by experience is constrained by genetic factors.

LEARNING: OPEN AND CLOSED GENETIC PROGRAMS *(227–232)*

Fixed-Action Patterns   Imprinting

Across species, the capacity to learn from experience varies along a continuum. Organisms with open genetic programs have a greater potential for behavior modification through experience than do those with closed genetic programs. Fixed-action patterns and imprinting are two kinds of species-specific behavior whose expression is influenced by environmental variables.

LEARNING AND THE ANALYSIS OF BEHAVIOR *(232–233)*

In general, open genetic programs provide for two types of learning, classical conditioning and operant conditioning. While ethologists seek to understand the adaptive significance and evolutionary history of learning and behavior within species, behavior analysts attempt to uncover general laws of learning that describe behavior across species. Accordingly, behavior analysts study environmental variables that influence behavior.

CLASSICAL CONDITIONING *(233–245)*

*Pavlov's Serendipitous Discovery   The Importance of Pavlov's Work
Basic Principles   What Is Learned in Classical Conditioning?*

In classical conditioning, the organism's behavior, the conditioned response (CR), is elicited by one stimulus, the conditioned stimulus (CS), which predicts the occurrence of another stimulus, the unconditioned stimulus (UCS). The basic principles of classical conditioning include acquisition of the CR, extinction of the CR, spontaneous recovery of the CR after its extinction, stimulus generalization of the CR to other stimuli, and discrimination of a CS from other stimuli. Through classical conditioning, animals learn how well the CS predicts the occurrence of the UCS.

OPERANT CONDITIONING *(245–259)*

*The Law of Effect   Skinner and Operant Behavior
The Three-Term Contingency   Reinforcement and Punishment
The Analysis of Human Behavior*

In operant conditioning, the organism's behavior is modified by the consequences of that behavior. This is called the law of effect. Reinforcement strengthens or increases the frequency of a behavior and punishment weakens or decreases the frequency of a behavior. Generally speaking, operant behavior occurs only in the presence of a discriminative stimulus because, in the past, such behavior has been reinforced in the presence of that stimulus. Through reinforcement and punishment, operant behavior can be shaped, extinguished, generalized to other discriminative stimuli, or trained to occur only in the presence of certain stimuli. Recent operant research involving humans has focused on the effects of instructions or rules on behavior and stimulus equivalence.

If there is one topic in psychology with which you are familiar, it is surely learning. After all, we humans spend much of our time learning. As children, we learned such things as how to walk, how to talk, and how to interact with other people. As teenagers, we learned about world history, math, literature, and many other topics. And as adults, we continue to learn: in college, on the job, and at our hobbies. With that much experience as a learner, you might suppose that by now you would know quite a bit, if not everything about learning. But could you define learning precisely or describe different kinds of learning correctly? Probably not, for often our experience teaches us only that we have learned something and not how we have learned it. For example, can you explain how you learned to solve algebra or calculus problems, or even how you learned to read and write?

Understand what learning involves is complicated because there appear to be so many different kinds of learning. Consider the following examples:

■ Immediately after birth, ducklings incubated in the laboratory will follow the first large moving object they see, regardless of whether the object happens to be their mother, a human being, a dog, or a wooden decoy. If there is a delay of say even 24 hours between when a duckling hatches and when it sees a large moving object, the duckling will not follow the object.

■ A hungry pigeon is placed in a laboratory apparatus containing a green light and a red light. Grain is given to the bird after it pecks the green light but not after it pecks the red light. Soon the bird pecks only the green light.

■ After drinking a saccharin-flavored solution, a laboratory rat is injected with a nonlethal dose of poison and becomes ill. Later, the rat will not drink the saccharin solution although it will drink other flavored solutions.

■ A young Japanese macaque rinses sweet potatoes and wheat that researchers have scattered on a sandy beach in the ocean. Soon, other young macaques are doing likewise. Within a decade, 66 percent of the macaques in the troop are washing their food in the ocean before eating it.

■ A 2-year-old boy watches his mother apply deodorant to her underarms. He says "Me! Me!" while pointing to his armpits. His mother hands him the deodorant, after which he awkwardly applies it to his own underarms.

These examples are useful not only because they show the variety of circumstances under which learning has occurred, but also because they point up a characteristic of all learning: it seems to involve observable changes in an organism's behavior due to experience.

The common element of all types of learning is that it always involves observable changes in behavior due to experience. For example, shortly after hatching, ducklings (left) will follow the first large moving object they see, which may or may not be their mother. Researchers observed that after a young Japanese macaque (right) began washing the food it was given, more than half of the other macaques in that group began displaying the same behavior.

Learning can be defined as a relatively permanent change in behavior based on experience. Learning cannot be observed directly; typically, it is inferred from changes in behavior. Behavioral change or performance is not itself learning—it merely reflects the possibility that learning has occurred. We also must be careful not to infer from this definition that changes in behavior always reflect learning. Consider, for example, how your behavior changes according to whether you are drowsy or wide awake. Your level of arousal may determine how well you perform on an examination, or the skill with which you operate an automobile, but it certainly would be incorrect to say that these kinds of changes in your behavior reflect learning. Changes in behavior that result from fatigue, ingestion of drugs, or certain emotional problems are not necessarily evidence of learning.

*B*ehavioral change or performance is not itself learning—it merely reflects the possibility that learning has occurred.

Likewise, learning may occur even without noticeable change in observable behavior. In some cases learning is not apparent, at least right away, from changes in our observable behavior. In other cases, we may never have the opportunity to demonstrate what we have learned. For example, although you may have received training in how to change a flat tire in a driver's education class, your behavior will not likely be noticeably different unless you have the opportunity to change a flat tire. In still other cases, you may not be sufficiently motivated to demonstrate things you have learned. This is the case when a teacher poses a question to the class and you know the answer but you do not answer because you don't feel like raising your hand or because you get nervous when speaking in front of others.

As you can see, learning and behavior are closely related. In fact, for psychologists, it is rare to speak of one without also speaking of the other. Psychologists study the relationship between learning and behavior by manipulating environmental variables; that is, experience. We will see, though, that the extent to which changes in the environment can affect behavior is limited by certain biological constraints. In this chapter, we discuss learning in terms of both biological and environmental factors. We will start with an overview of biological influences on learning. Next, we will discuss classical and operant conditioning, the major forms of learning studied by psychologists this century. Simply put, both classical and operant conditioning involve changes in behavior due to exposure to certain kinds of relationships between or among stimuli in the environment. Psychologists who study learning attempt to discover general principles of behavior by identifying commonalities in the learning process across a wide variety of species. Finally, we will consider briefly cognitive approaches to the study of learning.

LEARNING: OPEN AND CLOSED GENETIC PROGRAMS

How can we know that changes in behavior are due to learning and not genetic or biological factors? How can we be sure that ducklings are not genetically "preprogrammed" to follow the first large moving object they see or that a child applying deodorant does not have an innate tendency to imitate actions in which he or she sees others engaged?

These sorts of questions lie at the heart of much of the research on the psychology of learning that has been conducted since the turn of this century. Early researchers aligned themselves with one of two distinct schools of thought. One school held that most behavior is a result of **instinct;** that is, it is due to inborn or genetically determined factors. Some researchers,

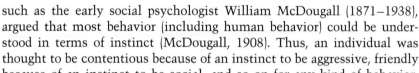

Closed Genetic
Program

Open Genetic
Program

grasshopper   frog   rat   dog   monkey   human

low   high

Capacity for learning

FIGURE 7.1
The continuum of genetic systems. The capacity for learning varies along a continuum with one end anchored by animals with little capacity for learning (closed genetic program) and the other end anchored by animals with great capacity for learning (open genetic program).

such as the early social psychologist William McDougall (1871–1938), argued that most behavior (including human behavior) could be understood in terms of instinct (McDougall, 1908). Thus, an individual was thought to be contentious because of an instinct to be aggressive, friendly because of an instinct to be social, and so on for any kind of behavior. Those in the other school, led by behaviorist John B. Watson (1878–1958), argued that labeling a behavior as instinctive does little to explain the origins of that behavior, for as you already know, describing or naming a behavior is not the same as explaining it (Watson & McDougall, 1929). Instead, Watson and his colleagues argued that most behavior is learned and that psychologists should look solely to the organism's environment for explanations of behavior.

Psychological research conducted over the last three decades has not provided equivocal support for either McDougall's or Watson's position; rather, in many instances, changes in behavior seem to reflect the *interplay* of both genetic and environmental factors. Many modern researchers believe that behavior is more or less shaped by the continual interaction of an organism's genetic endowment with the environment (Fantino & Logan, 1979). Ernst Mayr, an eminent biologist of our time, has provided a useful conceptual framework for describing how these two factors interact to determine how and what organisms may learn (Mayr, 1974). In essence, he believes that that type of **genetic program**, that is the genetic instructions an organism inherits at birth, determines the extent to which that organism's behavior may be changed through interaction with the environment. Across species, the capacity to learn varies along a continuum that has organisms with closed genetic programs at one end and organisms with open genetic programs at the other end (see Figure 7.1). Closed genetic programs allow for relatively little learning. Organisms with closed programs, such as insects and some reptiles, generally have short life spans, mature quickly, and receive little or no parental care. Many such animals behave reflexively like the stimulus-response operation of the keys on your computer keyboard or typewriter. At birth, these animals are genetically predisposed to respond in a certain way in a particular situation each and every time that that particular situation presents itself. Experience has virtually no opportunity to leave its mark on the behavior of animals with closed programs. In short, these animals learn relatively little about their environment.

On the other hand, organisms with open genetic programs, such as some mammals and most primates, generally have much longer life spans and extended periods of immaturity and parental care. For these organisms, experience can leave an indelible impression upon behavior, allowing for a great deal of learning to take place. Learning provides the means by which organisms with open genetic programs adapt to a wide range of environments. Consider the organism with the most open genetic program—the human being. People can live in the city or country, in the tropics or in the arctic, and can learn Swahili, English, or Pascal (a computer language). In

William McDougall

between closed and open genetic programs is a vast middle ground made up of various combinations of these two types of programs, partially explaining why different organisms learn different amounts about their environments.

In this view, learning is an inherited capacity for an organism's behavior to be modified through interaction with the environment. An organism's "genetic blueprint" essentially determines its capacity to learn. Some animals, like insects, do not have genes that allow their behavior to be changed much as a result of experience. Others, like you and I, have different genes that allow our behavior to be modified by interactions with the environment. We can read, write, and drive automobiles due, in part, to genetics and in part to living in a culture where such activities are valued. Had we grown up elsewhere, such as in the Australian outback, we may not have learned these skills, despite having the genetic potential to do so.

A

n organism's "genetic blueprint" essentially determines its capacity to learn.

Behavior, then, differs from species to species depending upon the species' genetic endowment and environment. Behavior that is common to a given species is called **species-typical behavior** and is studied mainly by ethologists, scientists trained to study animal behavior as it occurs in natural habitats. Let's examine some contributions made to the psychology of learning.

Fixed-Action Patterns

Imagine yourself in a pet store. After admiring the puppies and kittens your interest is captured by the iridescent blue and red coloring of several small fish kept in separate bowls next to the larger and more populated fish tanks. Thinking that a couple of these fish would look great in your aquarium at home, you ask the clerk for assistance. She is glad to help, and while carefully removing each fish and putting it into a separate plastic bag, she tells you that you are purchasing male fish of the species *Betta splendens.* At home, you put the bags into the water to allow the fish to adapt to the water temperature in their new home. As you watch the fish, you notice that each time the two bags are close together, both fish appear to deepen in color and fly into a rage, darting toward each other with fins erect. What the salesperson failed to tell you was that *Betta splendens* are more commonly known as Siamese fighting fish! Now with your interest piqued by their aggressive behavior, you move the plastic bags to opposite corners of the aquarium, and notice immediately that both fish calm down. When you move the bags close together again, the fish again become pugnacious. You repeat this procedure several times, observing that both fish are only aggressive when they have a clear view of one another. To confirm your observations, you decide to conduct one further experiment. You reason that if the presence of another Siamese fighting fish is the cause of each fish's aggressive actions, then perhaps seeing its own image in a mirror would be a sufficient stimulus to provoke the behavior in the fish. Accordingly, you let one of the fish into the aquarium, and a few minutes later submerge a mirror into the tank. Each time the fish sees its image reflected, it attacks the image.

What your simple experiments have revealed is an example of what ethologists call a **fixed-action pattern**, a species-typical behavior characterized by a highly stereotyped pattern of responses. Fixed-action patterns are often displayed uniformly across all species members, but in the case of *Betta splendens,* the pattern of aggression is seen only among males. Fixed-action patterns appear to be an innate response to a specific environmental stimulus, referred to as a **sign stimulus**. Ethologists have speculated that

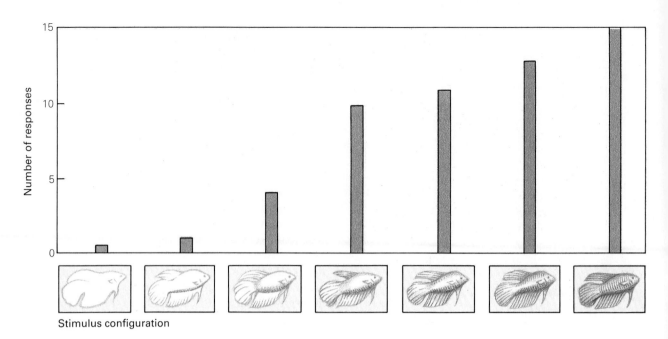

FIGURE 7.2

Results of the Thompson and Sturm (1965) experiment. This figure shows the number of times in 16 trials that each model elicited an aggressive response from a male Betta. *As the models became more lifelike, they elicited attack more frequently.*

After Thompson and Sturm, 1965.

FIGURE 7.3

Egg-rolling behavior in the graylag goose. This behavior is an example of a fixed-action pattern: once elicited by the egg (the sign stimulus), the retrieval responses continue without further environmental stimulation.

the sign stimulus activates a sequence of behavioral responses, which in the case of the male *Betta*, results in aggression.

Your experiments showed that the male *Betta* responds to a visual stimulus, whether it be another male *Betta* or its own reflected image. What your experiments failed to show, however, was the particular component of the stimulus that elicited the aggressive behavior. To which aspect of the visual stimulus do male *Bettas* respond?

To answer this question, Thompson and Sturm (1965) exposed male *Bettas* to a series of models of the male Siamese fighting fish, each model looking progressively more like an actual male *Betta* in terms of its coloration. Figure 7.2 shows the number of times out of sixteen trials that the model elicited an attack from the actual *Betta*. As the models became more true-to-life, they elicited more attacks. In short, the sign stimulus that elicited aggressive behavior in the male Siamese fighting fish is the color pattern of a second male Siamese fighting fish.

Another example of a fixed-action pattern is the egg-rolling behavior of the graylag goose (Lorenz & Tinbergen, 1938). Presented with an egg outside of its nest, a graylag goose will extend its bill just beyond the egg and pull it toward the nest with the underside of the bill (see Figure 7.3). In this case, the sign stimulus is the shape of the egg, and the fixed-action is the pattern of responses involved in rolling the egg back into the nest. Interestingly, if the egg is removed after the goose has started rolling it toward the nest, the rolling behavior continues, as if the egg were still there. Thus, once elicited by the sign stimulus, the fixed-action pattern continues without further environmental stimulation. A graylag goose will roll any object that looks like an egg into its nest, including eggs that are several times larger than the typical goose egg.

Fixed-action patterns are typical of animals possessing primarily closed genetic programs. The male Siamese fighting fish and the graylag goose are just two examples of creatures born with genetically predetermined responses to specific environmental stimuli. Neither species has the capacity to learn much about its environment, yet both species are deftly adapted to certain critical and very specific conditions of their respective environments (see Table 7.1). The male *Betta* responds aggressively to another male *Betta* only because it has inherited naturally selected genetic instructions from ancestors who behaved similarly; the graylag goose retrieves eggs for the same reason. No learning is involved. For both creatures, such a genetic instruction provides successful adaptation to the environment because they live in environments similar to their ancestors; if their environments were to change drastically, their respective fixed-action patterns might no longer be adaptive. Only animals with a capacity for learning seem able to adapt to environmental change. We turn now to a discussion of simple learning, imprinting.

Imprinting

Ethologists have also studied imprinting, a type of learning that forms the basis for a young animal's social attachments to an adult member of the same species, usually its mother. More specifically, **imprinting** is a form of learning that occurs only during some restricted period in an organism's life. The restricted period itself is called the **critical period.**

Although he did not discover imprinting, Konrad Lorenz, the famous Austrian ethologist, was among the first to study it carefully. Lorenz (1952, 1970) knew that the young of some species of waterfowl, such as ducks and geese, usually begin to tag behind their mothers within a day of hatching, a behavioral pattern that continues until the young birds are about a month old. Lorenz discovered that these baby birds would tag behind any large moving object (even a cardboard box moved by ropes and pulleys) so long as they were exposed to that object sometime during their first day of life. When Lorenz himself reared a brood of goslings, they soon learned to follow him when he was walking or swimming, in the same way they would follow their own mother. Lorenz also showed that if these kinds of baby birds do not see a large moving object in their immediate environment during the critical period within the first day after hatching, they do not learn to follow any object.

The "following" response appears to be of social significance to these young birds: the birds become socially attached to the specific moving object they are following. Of course in the natural environment, the first large moving object that young birds see is generally their mother, and as a result, they eventually court appropriate sexual partners a year or so later. If the birds do not see, and consequently do not follow, an adult female of their species (or any other large moving object) during the critical period, imprinting cannot occur, and as a result, appropriate courtship behavior fails to emerge at the time of sexual maturity. On one occasion, Lorenz found a young bird and took it home to raise by hand. Several months later, when the bird reached sexual maturity, it began courting Lorenz.

According to Eckhard Hess (1959), another well-known ethologist, the critical period during imprinting is bounded by two maturational processes, motor coordination and fear. First, immediately after hatching, the

| | Stimuli, response patterns, and adaptive significance of behavior in the Siamese |
| TABLE 7.1. | fighting fish and the graylag goose. |

BEHAVIOR	SIGN STIMULUS	FIXED-ACTION PATTERN	ADAPTIVE CONSEQUENCE
Aggressive action	Color pattern of another male Siamese fighting fish	Attack	Protects territory and mate
Egg retrieval	Egg outside of nest	Retrieve egg	Helps ensure birth of offspring

Konrad Lorenz, pictured here with a brood of goslings, discovered that during the critical period of imprinting, the young birds would follow any large object, including Lorenz himself. He further concluded that if the birds were not exposed to a large moving object during the critical period, they did not learn to follow any object.

baby bird is very clumsy. If exposed to a moving object too soon, it will not have the coordination to keep pace with the object and so imprinting is unlikely to occur. Second, near the end of its first day of life, the baby bird becomes fearful of unfamiliar aspects of its environment, including those that are large and moving. If the baby bird does not imprint to an object during the critical period, its increasing fearfulness of novel objects will prevent imprinting from ever occurring.

The kind of learning involved in imprinting provides adaptability that fixed-action patterns do not. If following in ducklings were part of a fixed-action pattern and not constrained by the critical period, ducklings might indiscriminately follow every large moving object with which they came into contact. The duckling's evolutionary heritage and immediate environment compel it to become attached to an object that provides nourishment and protection. In nature, that object is likely to be its mother. If the duckling does not become so attached, its fitness and chances of survival are slim.

You may have noted that fixed-action patterns seem to fit the definition of "instinct" given earlier. However, the term "instinct" is not used very often today, probably because of its overuse by early psychologists. Nonetheless, ethologists have renewed scholarly interest in instinctual behavior because they have systematically sought to understand the variables that control it and have opted not to label all behavior as simply "instinctive" or "innate" as did McDougall and his colleagues.

Imprinting, although also a kind of species-typical behavior, is a type of learning. Imprinting is a change in behavior that results from an organism's experience with its environment. It is considered a species-typical behavior because the exact nature of imprinting depends upon the species' genetics as well as the peculiarities of that species' environment.

The discovery of fixed-action patterns and imprinting were important because they taught us how different species have adapted to their idiosyncratic environments and about behavior in general. Behavior, whether species-typical or learned, is due to the expression of genetic instructions in an environment. As Whalen (1971) so aptly put it, "genes without environments would not yield organisms, much less behaving organisms" (p. 57). Thus, the nature-nurture controversy, which so often reared its head in earlier chapters, is clearly founded on oversight, for neither component by itself ever determines behavior.

LEARNING AND THE ANALYSIS OF BEHAVIOR

Species-typical behavior is a clear example of how nature can exert tight genetic control over behavior. At birth, organisms are given either a prepackaged set of responses that manifest themselves only in the presence of highly specific environmental stimuli (fixed-action patterns) or a capacity to learn under very specific and time-limited conditions (imprinting). Nature, of course, also endows many organisms with more open-ended capacities for learning. This greater capacity for learning, though, is no more or less a product of a genetic endowment than imprinting. In other words, the capacity to learn always bears a direct connection to an animal's genetic program. The main behavioral difference between animals with closed genetic programs and those with open ones is that open genetic programs allow for relatively more learning. Animals that inherit open genetic programs inherit a capacity for learning; that is, sensitivity to the eliciting properties of stimuli as well as sensitivity to be affected by the consequences of their behavior.

Historically, psychologists have been interested in two forms of learning, classical conditioning and operant conditioning. In classical conditioning, the organism's behavior is elicited by one stimulus that predicts another; in operant conditioning the organism's behavior is modified by its consequences, some pleasant, others aversive.

Psychologists who have studied these forms of learning have been traditionally referred to as behaviorists, although today many such psychologists prefer to be called behavior analysts. Behavior analysts approach the study of learning with a very different view of behavior than do ethologists. Ethologists, as we have just seen, approach their work from an evolutionary perspective and so, tend to emphasize the adaptive significance and evolutionary history of behavior and learning *within* species. Behavior analysts tend to approach their work from an environmental perspective and emphasize the generality of basic principles of learning and behavior *across* species. In other words, unlike ethologists, behavior analysts attempt to discover general laws of learning by identifying commonalities in the learning process across a variety of species. Historically, behavior analysts have based their work on three general assumptions.

> *Behavior analysts emphasize that what organisms inherit is not an innate tendency to behave in a certain fashion, but rather a capacity to be affected by the consequences of their behavior.*

1. Although all organisms are first and foremost biological creatures, learning is a function of the characteristics of environmental settings. Like ethologists, behavior analysts hold that all organisms and their behaviors are products of natural selection. However, behavior analysts emphasize that what organisms inherit is not an innate tendency to behave in a certain fashion, but rather a capacity to be affected by the consequences of their behavior (Skinner, 1974).

2. Learning, regardless of its complexity, is due to either classical conditioning, operant conditioning, or both. The simple associations learned through conditioning represent the foundation upon which subsequent, and generally more complex, learning rests. Indeed, differences in the complexity of learning are assumed to be attributable to the number and sequence of simple associations to be learned. For example, although they are similar skills, learning to drive an automobile with a standard transmission is more difficult than learning to drive one with an automatic transmission simply because of the greater number and particular sequence of actions that must be learned.

3. Learning in all animal species, including humans, can be more or less described by the same "laws of learning." Hence, the way humans learn to avoid an unpleasant stimulus in everyday life appears to be similar to that by which a rat learns to avoid electric shock in a laboratory experiment. Based on this assumption, behavior analysts traditionally have chosen to conduct most of their experimental research with nonhuman organisms that can be controlled more easily in the laboratory environment.

With these assumptions in mind let's turn now to a discussion of classical conditioning.

CLASSICAL CONDITIONING

In December of 1904, the Russian physiologist Ivan Pavlov (1849–1936), was awarded the Nobel Prize in physiology/medicine for his work on the digestive system. Invited to Stockholm to receive the award and to deliver an acceptance speech, the 55-year-old Pavlov did not speak of his pioneering work on digestion (Babkin, 1949). Instead, his address, entitled "The

First Sure Steps Along the Path of a New Investigation," focused on his more recent work involving conditioned reflexes, or "involuntary" responses. Pavlov's new line of research was to take him far from the research for which he was awarded the Nobel Prize, but today he is better remembered for his work in psychology than in physiology. Interestingly enough, though, it was while studying the digestive system that Pavlov stumbled upon the phenomenon that was to make him one of the most famous psychologists of all time. Let's pick up Pavlov's story as it unfolded nearly ninety years ago.

Pavlov's Serendipitous Discovery

Pavlov's chief ambition as a physiologist was to discover the neural mechanisms that controlled glandular secretions during digestion. He carefully measured the quantity and chemical composition of these secretions as well as their sequence during the course of a meal. It was while conducting routine studies of salivation in dogs that Pavlov's interest in digestive processes became forever sidetracked.

Pavlov's research strategy was to study salivary processes in individual dogs over several test sessions. Each trial consisted of first placing dry food powder inside the dog's mouth and then collecting the saliva. All went according to plan until the dogs became experienced subjects. After several sessions of testing, the dogs began salivating *before* being fed. They usually began salivating as soon as they saw the laboratory assistant enter the room with the food powder. What Pavlov discovered was a simple form of learning in which two stimuli or events become associated. In this case, the dogs associated the appearance of the laboratory assistant with food.

Rather than ignoring this phenomenon or even treating it as a confounding variable that needed to be controlled, Pavlov designed systematic experiments to discover exactly why his subjects were salivating before being given the opportunity to ingest the food powder. Pavlov suspected that salivation might be triggered by stimuli that were initially neutral; that is, unrelated to eating. Somehow, these neutral stimuli came to control what is normally a natural reflexive behavior. After all, salivation is not a natural reaction to stimuli usually unrelated to eating. Pavlov's new chief ambition was to understand the variables that controlled this unexpected behavior.

Pavlov's basic research strategy was to manipulate the various components of a simple experimental procedure. An inexperienced dog was placed in a harness similar to the one shown in Figure 7.4 and was given small bits of food powder every so often. Just prior to placing the food powder in the dog's mouth, Pavlov sounded a buzzer or some other auditory stimulus. At first, the dog showed only a startled response to the sound and perked up its ears and turned its head toward the sound. The dog salivated only when the food powder was placed in its mouth. But after only a dozen or so pairings of the buzzer and food powder, the dog began to salivate at the sound of the buzzer. Placing the food powder in the dog's mouth was no longer necessary to elicit salivation; the sound by itself elicited salivation. Thus, Pavlov showed that a neutral stimulus, when associated with a different but more significant stimulus (in this case the food powder), can come to elicit what would appear to be a similar response to the original reflex. Today this learning process is referred to as **classical (or Pavlovian) conditioning.**

Figure 7.5 illustrates the basic components of the classical conditioning procedure. For dogs and many other animals, salivation facilitates digestion. Presumably, an adaptively significant behavior is to salivate first before ingesting the food. The result is that reflexive salivation to food has

FIGURE 7.4

The experimental apparatus used in a Pavlovian experiment. To study classical conditioning, Pavlov placed dogs in restraining harnesses and isolated them in large chambers.

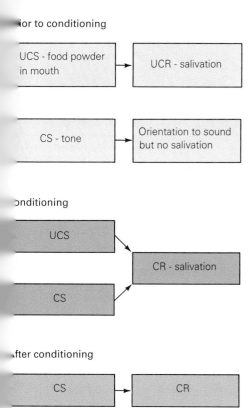

FIGURE 7.5

Basic components of the classical conditioning procedure. Prior to conditioning, the UCS but not the CS elicits a response (the UCR). During conditioning, the CS is presented in conjunction with the CS. Once conditioning is completed, the CS alone elicits a response (the CR).

been naturally selected to become a part of the genetic endowment of the species. A stimulus such as food that naturally elicits reflexive behavior such as salivation is called the **unconditional stimulus (UCS)**. The reflexive behavior itself is called the **unconditional response (UCR).**

Dogs, however, possess relatively open genetic programs so that any one particular dog may have its behavior modified through interactions with the idiosyncrasies of its environment; that is, the dog's behavior can be conditioned. If, for a particular dog, a bell signals food, then the bell may also come to elicit salivation through classical conditioning. For a different dog, the sound of an electric can opener may reliably precede food, and so, that stimulus may come to elicit salivation. Any neutral stimulus paired with the unconditional stimulus that eventually elicits a response is called a **conditional stimulus (CS).** When the reflexive behavior is elicited by the conditional stimulus, it is referred to as a **conditional response (CR).** In the case of Pavlov's dogs, food powder served as the unconditional stimulus, eliciting salivation, the unconditional response. When Pavlov first paired the sound of the buzzer with the meat powder, the dogs did not salivate to the sound; the sound was merely a neutral stimulus and not a CS. With repeated pairings of this sort, however, the sound became a CS, reliably eliciting the salivary CR.

In sum, Pavlov's experiments demonstrated conclusively that an innate reflexive behavior can be elicited by novel stimuli. Thus, a response that is naturally under the control of appropriate environmental stimuli, such as food in the mouth, can also come to be controlled by other kinds of stimuli that may bear no such natural relation to it.

The Importance of Pavlov's Work

Pavlov's discovery and subsequent research would have been of only minor significance if the phenomenon of classical conditioning were limited to dogs salivating to buzzers and metronomes under laboratory conditions. However, classical conditioning has been shown to have a broad scope outside the laboratory, and Pavlov's ideas have had a profound influence on psychology.

In addition to dogs, a number of other animals including fish, pigeons, cats, octopi, and humans have been shown to be capable of learning simple associations between stimuli via classical conditioning. As you might imagine from a list of species this diverse, a variety of different kinds of responses have been shown to be subject to classical conditioning. Table 7.2 provides examples of some of these responses as well as the species in which they were conditioned.

Classical conditioning has also been shown to play a role in the development of certain emotional responses such as fear and anxiety. This discovery is of particular importance in helping us understand how such behavior might develop in humans. For example, fear conditioning is easily produced in dogs under the following experimental conditions. Every so often the dog is given a brief electric shock. The dog reacts by quivering and whimpering. Each shock is preceded by a green light, which at first may be considered a neutral stimulus because it does not elicit any reaction from the dog during the early part of the experiment. However, with repeated pairings of the light and the shock, the light alone elicits quivering and whimpering from the dog. The light has been transformed from a neutral stimulus to a conditional stimulus through classical conditioning, eliciting fear reactions from the dog.

The early behaviorist, John Watson, used a similar procedure to produce a conditional fear response in an infant, "Little Albert." Each time Little Albert touched a white rat (CS), a bell was struck with a hammer (UCS).

TABLE 7.2.	Reflexes that can be classically conditioned.	

SPECIES	CONDITIONED RESPONSE
Blow fly	Feeding movements
Sea anenomes	Swimming movements
Fish	Feeding movements
Pigeons	Feeding movements
Rabbits	Eyelid blinking
Dogs	Salivation
	Fear
Humans	GSR*
	Salivation
	Eyelid blinking
	Respiration changes
	Fear

* The GSR, galvanic skin resistance, is a measure of the skin's ability to impede conductance of electricity.

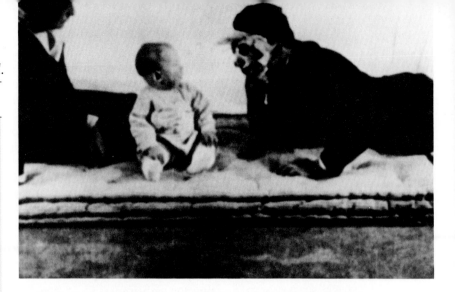

Early behaviorist John Watson applied Pavlov's theories of classical conditioning to his experiments with infant "Little Albert." Watson, pictured here in a mask, was able to elicit a conditioned response from the infant to many different objects.
Courtesy of Professor Benjamin Harris.

The fear of open places leads agoraphobics to avoid all contact with the outside world. Standing among the people on this busy street corner would produce great anxiety for a person suffering from agoraphobia.

After only several trials, Little Albert cried (CR) each time he saw the rat. His fear of the white rat generalized to other objects, including white rabbits.

Your own personal experiences are no doubt full of examples of classical conditioning. The scent of a special perfume, the memory of a favorite song, the sight of a particular article of clothing, and the sight of an insect or snake are but a few of the neutral stimuli that may become transformed into conditional stimuli, eliciting a conditional response on your part. Many people suffer from phobias, which are intense or excessive fears of objects, events, or places. For example, some people suffer from agoraphobia, a fear of open places. Agoraphobics, who are afraid to venture outside for a walk or a trip to the supermarket, are literally captives of their own homes. While this fear sounds odd, even silly, it can incapacitate those who suffer from it. According to the classical conditioning perspective, this phobia develops presumably while the individual is a child or adolescent because of an unpleasant experience, perhaps in a park or other public place. Stimuli associated with being out of doors have become conditional stimuli, eliciting fear and anxiety in the agoraphobic. One treatment for agoraphobia is to expose the sufferer to open places (the conditional stimulus) gradually and repeatedly without the unpleasant experience (the unconditional stimuli) present. Chapters 16 and 17 discuss phobias and their treatment in more detail.

Basic Principles

Pavlov's research soon led to the discovery of several interesting conditioning phenomena that still bear the names he gave them over sixty years ago (for example, Pavlov, 1927). These include acquisition, extinction, spontaneous recovery, stimulus generalization, and discrimination. Let's take a closer look at each of these.

Acquisition. In laboratory experiments, a single pairing of the CS with the UCS is not usually sufficient to elicit a CR. Only with repeated CS-UCS pairings does conditional responding gradually appear (although there are important exceptions, as we shall discuss below). The portion of a classical conditioning experiment in which a conditional response first appears and increases in frequency or strength is referred to as **acquisition**. The left side of Figure 7.6 shows a learning curve, which in this case is the course of acquisition of a conditional eyeblink response in human subjects. In this experiment, a tone (the CS) was paired with a puff of air into the eye (the UCS). Conditioning was measured by the percentage of trials in which conditional eyeblinks (the CR) occurred. Note that at the experiment's outset, the tone elicited very few conditional eyeblinks. During the first 50 trials, the percentage of conditional eyeblinks increased rapidly but then tapered off. The portion of the curve showing the maximum level of responding that is gradually reached after repeated exposure to CS-UCS pairings is termed the asymptote. For subjects in this experiment, the asymptote of conditional eyeblink responding was between 50 and 60 percent of the trials.

Two factors that influence the strength of the conditional response are the intensity of the UCS and the temporal relationship between the CS and UCS. The intensity of the UCS can also determine how quickly the CR will be acquired: more intense UCSs often produce more rapid learning. For example, fear conditioning in rats is faster with higher levels of shock than with lower levels (Annau & Kamin, 1961). Salivary conditioning in dogs is faster when larger amounts of food are used (Wagner, Siegal, Thomas, & Ellison, 1964). The intensity of the UCS determines both the speed of conditioning and the maximum or asymptotic level of the conditioned response.

Generally speaking, the more intense the UCS, the stronger the CR. Look at the middle panel of Figure 7.6. After experiencing 100 trials of conditioning, Subject 1 was exposed to a less intense puff of air while Subject 2 continued to be exposed to the same UCS intensity used during the first 100 trials. You can see clearly that the percentage of CRs elicited from Subject 1 decreased soon after the intensity of the air puff was decreased and leveled off at about 35 percent. This value represents the asymptotic level of conditioned responding that can be maintained by the weaker UCS.

The second factor affecting the acquisition of the conditioned response is the timing of the CS and UCS. A variety of temporal relationships can exist between the CS and the UCS, but we will discuss the most com-

FIGURE 7.6

Acquisition and extinction of a conditioned response. The left panel shows the learning curve for acquisition of a conditioned eyeblink response in human subjects. The middle panel shows a decrease in the percentage of CRs (eyeblinks) elicited by the UCS (tone) when its intensity was reduced. The right panel shows the extinction curve produced when the UCS (tone) was no longer presented with the CS (airpuff). Without the UCS, the CS eventually fails to elicit the CR altogether.

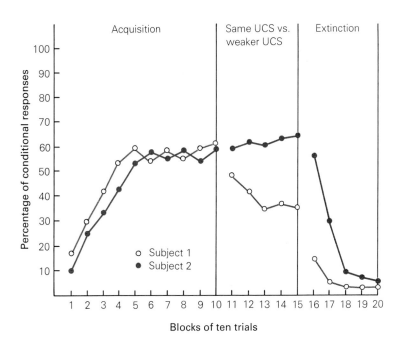

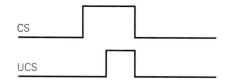

FIGURE 7.7
Delay conditioning. Delay conditioning produces the quickest and most powerful classical conditioning.

FIGURE 7.8
Stimulus generalization in classical conditioning. Zero represents the CS to which subjects were originally trained, positive numbers represent increasingly higher pitched stimuli, and negative numbers represent increasingly lower pitched stimuli. The degree of generalization decreases as training and test stimuli become increasingly dissimilar.

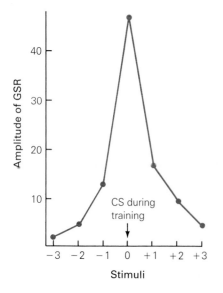

monly used one, delay conditioning (see Figure 7.7). In **delay conditioning**, the CS begins shortly before the UCS. From Figure 7.7 you can see that the UCS begins while the CS is still present and that both stimuli terminate at the same time. Delay conditioning produces the quickest and most powerful conditioning. In his experiments with salivary conditioning, Pavlov found that one-half second was the optimal delay between the onset of the CS and the onset of the UCS. With longer delays between the CS and UCS, conditioning proceeds less rapidly and is usually weaker.

Extinction. Assuming that a response has been conditioned, what would happen to that response if the UCS no longer followed the CS? This procedure, which Pavlov referred to as **extinction**, results in eventual elimination of the conditional response. Let's return to our conditional eyeblink response and suppose that after we manipulate the intensity of the UCS, we do not present the UCS (the puff of air) to either subject. We do, however, continue to present the CS (the tone) to both subjects. The third panel of Figure 7.6 shows the results of our extinction procedure. For both subjects, conditional eyeblink responses decrease until eventually the CS fails to elicit them altogether. (Note, though, that extinction occurs more rapidly for Subject 1, indicating that the course of extinction is affected by the UCS intensity.) Thus, once conditional responses are formed, they do not necessarily remain a part of the organism's behavior.

Spontaneous Recovery. Once a CR has been extinguished, it may not disappear from the organism's behavior permanently. Pavlov demonstrated that after conditional responding had been extinguished, the response would often suddenly reappear on the next CS presentation following a "time-out" from the experimental procedure. Pavlov referred to this impromptu reappearance of the conditional response as **spontaneous recovery**. Although the CS elicits fewer and fewer responses over the course of extinction, some conditional responding will occur during the early portion of each session but not in later trials. Thus, after the first day of extinction, we might think the conditional response has been eliminated completely. Nevertheless, it will reappear in the early parts of the next several sessions, until finally it is eliminated altogether. However, if the spontaneous recovery of the conditional response were to be followed by the consistent presentations of UCS, it would become, in effect, reinstated. This "relearning" would be quicker than the original learning.

Stimulus Generalization and Discrimination. Once a response has been conditioned to a particular CS, other similar stimuli will also elicit that response, despite never having been explicitly paired with the UCS. The more closely other stimuli resemble the CS, the more conditional responses they will elicit. This phenomenon, called **generalization**, explains why many organisms respond to unfamiliar stimuli that resemble familiar ones. Figure 7.8 shows the results of an experiment with human subjects involving the conditioning of an emotional response, the galvanic skin response (GSR), to a tone when electrical shock was used as the UCS (Hovland, 1937). The GSR is a measure of change in the electrical activity of the skin. During the training phase of this experiment, the tone reliably elicited an increase in subjects' GSR. In the experimental phase, subjects were exposed to seven different tones, but in each case, without presentation of the UCS (extinction). One tone was the same one used during training, three tones were higher than the training tone, and three were lower. GSRs were elicited by each of the seven stimuli, with the size of the GSR being positively correlated to its similarity to the CS used during the training phase.

It makes good sense that responses generalize to stimuli that closely resemble certain CSs. The cat that doesn't avoid dogs resembling the very first one that chased it up a tree, or the person who doesn't avoid snakes that look and sound like the rattler that recently bit him certainly are not behaving adaptively. On the other hand, it would be maladaptive for the cat to climb a tree every time it saw a creature that looked like a dog or for a human to become frightened of all snakes. Fortunately, nature has also endowed many organisms with the capacity to respond to some but not other similar stimuli. This phenomenon, called **discrimination**, is the opposite of generalization and involves distinguishing one stimulus from another. In an experiment, discrimination is conditioned by using two CSs during training. On some trials, one CS always precedes the UCS. On other trials, the other CS is never followed by the UCS. For example, suppose we train subjects to blink to a low tone but not to a high tone. During training, we regularly deliver a puff of air to the subject during each trial in which a low tone is sounded, but on trials in which a higher tone is sounded no air puff is presented. At first, increased amounts of blinking are observed on both kinds of trials (generalization). Gradually, however, fewer and fewer increases in blinking occur on high tone trials; eye blinks are elicited only on low tone trials.

Thus, generalization and discrimination are opposite sides of the same coin. Generalization occurs when responses are elicited by stimuli that resemble the CS, even though those stimuli have never been explicitly paired with the UCS. Discrimination involves responding only to the stimuli that are followed by the UCS.

In sum, Pavlov's research is important because it showed that the way in which the relationship between the CS and UCS is arranged determines the nature of the CR. Acquisition of the CR is influenced by the intensity of the UCS and the temporal relationship of the CS and UCS. Extinction of the conditioned response occurs when the CS is no longer followed by the UCS. However, the CR may show spontaneous recovery at the very beginning of sessions following extinction. Generalization occurs when stimuli similar to the CS used in training elicit the CR. Discrimination occurs when the CS is the only stimulus to elicit the CR.

What Is Learned in Classical Conditioning?

We have just seen that by tinkering with the basic classical conditioning procedure, Pavlov discovered several different ways in which CS-UCS pairings can develop control over an organism's behavior. But why does such control develop in the first place? What is it about the CS-UCS relation that produces a conditional response?

Contiguity or Contingency? Pavlov believed that the answer to these questions rested solely on the temporal relation between the CS and the UCS. From his vantage, the CS becomes associated with the UCS because of contiguity, that is, because CS and UCS occurred close together in time. Pavlov felt that an association between almost any two stimuli could be conditioned as long as the CS occurred shortly before the UCS. Pavlov's view was widely accepted, although not unchallenged, for the forty years that followed the publication of his most important work, *Conditioned Reflexes* (Pavlov, 1927).

In the late 1960s and early 1970s, a series of important experiments and theoretical breakthroughs forged by Robert Rescorla and Allen Wagner of Yale University, and Leon Kamin, then at McMaster University in Canada, changed our view of classical conditioning. In essence, their studies have shown that the ability of a CS to predict the UCS reliably rather than mere

Discrimination is the opposite of generalization and means that one stimulus may be distinguished from another. For example, a person may not fear all dogs despite a bad experience with one.

he ability of a CS to predict the UCS reliably . . . is the critical factor in classical conditioning.

temporal contiguity between the CS and UCS, is the critical factor in classical conditioning. In other words, a contingency (in this case, a CS that reliably predicts the UCS) and not contiguity (closeness in time) between the CS and UCS is the key factor in classical conditioning. A contingency exists any time that the CS provides systematic or reliable information about the occurrence of the UCS. When the probability of the occurrence of the UCS is equally likely in both the presence or absence of the CS, no conditioning occurs. An example may help illustrate the crux of this account, which has become the most widely accepted view of classical conditioning among contemporary psychologists.

Imagine yourself as the subject in a classical conditioning demonstration involving a tone as the CS, a puff of air into your left eye as the UCS, and the eyeblink as the conditional response. Your psychology professor asks you to come to the front of the class and seats you in a comfortable chair. Every so often, a tone comes on for a second or two. Following the tone, a brief but strong puff of air strikes your eye. You blink each time the puff of air strikes your eye. Soon though, you begin to blink during the tone, before the puff of air reaches your eye! But now consider all of the other stimuli in the classroom—your teacher explaining to the class what you are experiencing as the subject, your classmates' remarks and questions, squeaks from students shifting in their chairs, and so on. Why do you not become conditioned to blink in response to any of these stimuli? Why do you come to blink only during the tone? After all, some of these stimuli do occur at the same time as the puff of air. Rescorla and Wagner's answer is simple: among the stimuli present in the room during the demonstration, only the tone reliably predicts the puff of air; each of the other stimuli are poor forecasters of the UCS. The lesson to be learned from this example is that the so-called neutral stimulus is a reliable predictor of the UCS, and therefore, it becomes associated with the UCS when the following two conditions are satisfied:

1. The CS occurs prior to the presentation of the UCS;
2. The CS does not occur when the UCS is not presented.

In other words, classical conditioning occurs only when the presentation of the UCS is dependent or contingent upon the occurrence of the CS. This is just another way of saying what we have said before: The key factor in classical conditioning is the ability of the CS to predict reliably the presentation of the UCS.

A number of studies have supported Rescorla's contingency account of classical conditioning. We will briefly examine one conducted by Rescorla himself (Rescorla, 1966).

FIGURE 7.9
Shuttle box for dogs. In Rescorla's research, the frequency of jumping over the barrier was used as an index of fear conditioning. The more frequently the dog jumped the barrier, the greater the degree of fear conditioning.

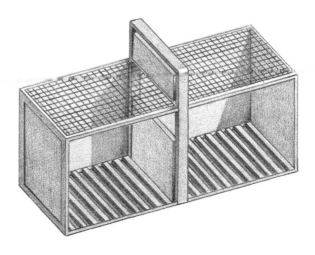

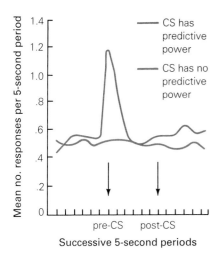

FIGURE 7.10
The role of contingency in classical conditioning. Dogs exposed to the contingent CS-UCS relation showed much higher rates of jumping than did dogs exposed to the contiguous but noncontingent CS-UCS relation. The arrow indicates introduction of the tone during the test period.

Experimental group	Control group
	Phase 1.
	Training
CS$_1$	
UCS → CR	
CS$_1$	CS$_1$
CS$_2$	CS$_2$
UCS → CR	UCS → CR
	Phase 2.
	Testing
CS$_1$ → CR	CS$_1$ → CR
CS$_2$ → No CR	CS$_2$ → CR

CS$_1$ = tone   CS$_2$ = light

FIGURE 7.11
The procedure used in Kamin's blocking experiment. For subjects in the experimental group, conditioning to the tone (CS$_1$) during Phase 1 blocked conditioning to the light (CS$_2$) during Phase 2. Because subjects in the control group did not experience conditioning to the tone (CS$_1$) alone during Phase 1, there is conditioning to the light (CS$_2$) during Phase 1.

Rescorla first trained dogs to jump a barrier in a shuttlebox to avoid occasional, unsignaled electric shock (see Figure 7.9). Dogs were shocked unpredictably and without warning every several seconds or so. By jumping the barrier, dogs could postpone delivery of the shock. Rescorla used the response of jumping over the barrier as an index of fear conditioning: the more frequently the dogs jumped the barrier, the greater the degree of fear conditioning.

Once the dogs had learned to jump the barrier consistently, they were exposed to one of two different CS-UCS (tone-shock) arrangements for eliciting conditioned fear responses (jumping the barrier).

Group 1 (Random): CSs and UCSs were arranged randomly and independently of each other. This meant that the CS had virtually no predictive power since shock was as likely to occur in the absence of the tones as it was in the presence of the tones.

Group 2 (Contingency): CSs and UCSs were arranged so that shock always followed the tone. In other words, shock was confined to the period of time shortly after the tone was turned off; the tone was a reliable predictor of the occurrence of shock.

Next, the dogs were again required to jump the barrier in the shuttle box to avoid shock. This time, however, the tone used in the classical conditioning procedure was sounded occasionally during the task. If fear had been conditioned to the tone, then dogs should increase their rate of jumping during the tone to avoid the shock. Rescorla reasoned that if the fear conditioning depended only upon temporal contiguity, then both groups of dogs should show about the same amount of conditioned fear and, therefore, have the same rate of jumping relative to baseline training. But if fear conditioning was dependent upon contingency, then the results should be very different because there was a contingent relation between the tone and shock only for dogs in Group 2. Only dogs in Group 2 should show signs of any fear conditioning and therefore an increase in their rate of jumping.

Figure 7.10 shows that Rescorla's results supported his theory: dogs exposed to the contingent CS-UCS relation showed higher rates of jumping than did dogs exposed to the contiguous but noncontingent CS-UCS relation. It appears that Pavlov's account of the critical factor necessary for classical conditioning to occur, contiguity, was incorrect. Rescorla's work demonstrated, quite conclusively, that contingency, and not contiguity alone, is the essential factor involved in classical conditioning.

Blocking. We have just seen that contingency is necessary for classical conditioning to occur, but will a contingent CS-UCS relation alone result in conditioned responding? Consider the following experiment conducted by Leon Kamin in 1969 (see Figure 7.11). One group of rats, the experimental group, was first trained under a conditioned fear procedure with a tone as the CS, shock as the UCS, and a lever press as the CR. Next, a second CS, a light, was added to the conditioning procedure so that now the UCS was preceded by the tone and a light. A second group of rats, the control group, was trained only with the compound stimuli of tone plus light paired with shock. Both groups of rats were subsequently tested for fear conditioning (amount of responding) to the tone alone and to the light alone. In essence, Kamin wanted to know whether previous training with the tone would interfere with subsequent fear conditioning to the light in experimental animals.

The results? Both the tone alone and the light alone elicited conditional fear responses from rats in the control group. For rats in the experimental group, however, only the tone alone elicited conditional fear responses; these rats showed no conditional fear responses to presentations of the light alone. If contingency was the only critical factor necessary to produce classical conditioning, shouldn't presentations of either the tone alone and light alone have elicited conditioned responding from both groups of rats? The answer, of course, is yes, which means we now need an explanation for Kamin's results. A good first clue, at least on the surface, is that for rats in the experimental group, the presentation of the tone at the beginning of the experiment seemed to obstruct or block the subsequent association of the light with shock. In fact, the ability of one CS to obstruct conditioning to a subsequent CS because of an organism's previous conditioning experience is commonly referred to as **blocking**. But to give a more detailed account of Kamin's results, we need to discuss the Rescorla-Wagner model of classical conditioning (Rescorla & Wagner, 1972).

The Rescorla-Wagner Model. To explain how the Rescorla-Wagner model accounts for blocking involving two CSs, we first need to explain how it accounts for classical conditioning involving only a single CS. Rescorla and Wagner make two assumptions about classical conditioning involving a single CS (actually, their model is based on several more assumptions; but for our purposes, we need discuss only two of these):

1. Classical conditioning produces changes in the associative strength between a given CS and a given UCS. **Associative strength** is the correlation between the CS and UCS, or the degree to which the CS reliably signals the UCS. In effect, classical conditioning produces positive changes (increases) in associative strength. (By this definition, extinction produces negative changes).

2. Any UCS can support only a given amount of conditioning. Recall that the maximum level of conditioning that can occur between a given CS and a given UCS is called the asymptotic level of learning.

To illustrate this point, consider Figure 7.12, which shows a typical learning curve derived from a classical conditioning experiment. The darkened triangles below the curve represent the increases in associative strength, or the amount of learning that takes place with each CS-UCS pairing. Notice that with each pairing, the increase in associative strength becomes smaller. At first, when the associative strength is low, there remains much to be learned and increases in associative strength with each CS-UCS pairing are relatively large. With continued CS-UCS pairings, however, the increases in associative strength become smaller and relatively little is learned during each CS-UCS pairing as associative strength approaches the asymptotic level. However, to explain classical conditioning using two CSs, and therefore, Kamin's blocking effect, Rescorla and Wagner made another assumption.

The total associative strength of two CSs is equal to the sum of the associative strengths of each CS. When two CSs are used, we learn how well each CS in the compound predicts the UCS.

Figure 7.13 illustrates how the Rescorla-Wagner model explains Kamin's results. Let's start with the experimental group (left panel). In the first phase of the experiment, rats were given only tone-shock pairings. In line with Rescorla and Wagner's assumptions, the associative strength of the tone increased, reaching a maximal level in which CRs were elicited reliably from the rats. In the second phase, rats were exposed to the compound of tone and light paired with shock. But because the UCS had already reached a maximal level of conditioning in phase one of the experiment, little associative strength became linked with the light, resulting in only a few responses to the light when it was presented without the tone. Therefore, little was learned about the light as a predictor of the shock.

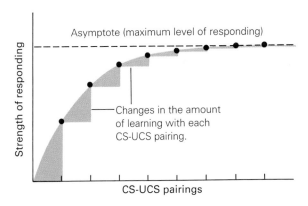

FIGURE 7.12
Above: A typical learning curve from a classical conditioning experiment. The darkened triangles below the curve represent increases in associative strength or the amount of learning that takes place with each CS-UCS pairing. With repeated CS-UCS pairings, the amount of learning in each trial decreases.

FIGURE 7.13
Right: The Rescorla-Wagner account of blocking. These graphs show the amount of conditioning that accrues to both the tone (CS_1) and the light (CS_2) during training and test phases of a hypothetical blocking experiment.

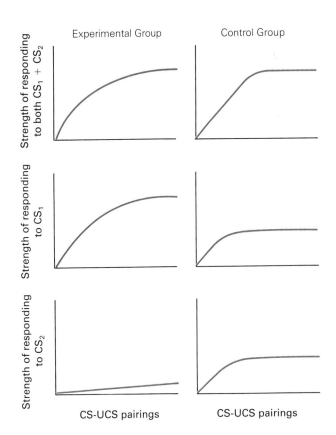

For the control group (right panel), which never experienced the tone or light alone during the training phases, both the tone and the light received equal amounts of conditioning. Both stimuli had the same associative strength and, therefore, elicited the same amount of responding when later presented individually. In this case, both the tone and the light reliably signaled the shock. The difference between the two groups of rats was simply that the experimental group had had previous experience with tone-shock pairings. This experience, though, was sufficient to prevent any associative strength from accruing to the light, thus, preventing the light from serving as a predictor of shock.

So, what is learned in classical conditioning? The Rescorla-Wagner model tells us that in classical conditioning, organisms learn how well the CS predicts the occurrence of the UCS. In cases where two CSs are involved, the CS that better predicts the presentation of the UCS will gain more associative strength and will more reliably elicit responses. If both CSs predict the presentation of the UCS equally well, then equal amounts of associative strength accrue to each CS.

Taste-Aversion Learning. At about the same time Rescorla was designing and conducting experiments to test his ideas on the contiguity-contingency issue, another group of researchers led by John Garcia among others, was investigating a very different but equally fascinating area of classical conditioning—taste-aversion learning. Taste-aversion learning refers to the association of a substance's flavor with an illness caused by eating that substance. The organism thereafter avoids substances with that or a similar flavor. You have probably eaten foods that have made you sick and now avoid them on the basis of their flavor alone.

The study of taste-aversion learning is important not only because it is a real-life phenomenon that many of us experience, but also because it has taught psychologists about the kinds of relationships that can exist

TABLE 7.3. *Garcia and Koelling's experimental design.*

GROUP	CS	UCS
1	Tasty water	Illness
2	Tasty water	Pain (Electric shock)
3	Bright-noisy water	Illness
4	Bright-noisy water	Pain (Electric shock)

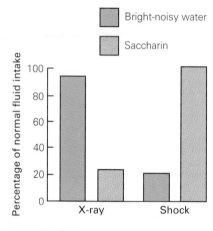

FIGURE 7.14
Results of Garcia and Koelling's (1966) experiment. Rats avoided the saccharin water only when it predicted illness and avoided the "bright-noisy" water only when it predicted electric shock. These results underscore the inborn bias rats have to associate particular stimuli cues with particular consequences.

between certain CSs and certain UCSs. At one time, many learning psychologists believed nearly any stimulus (CS—flavors, lights, noises) could be paired with nearly any event (UCS—illness, fear) to produce nearly any conditional response. However, in a now classic experiment, Garcia and his colleague, Robert A. Koelling, showed that in some cases, conditioning and learning definitely do not involve arbitrary relations among CSs, UCSs, and responding.

In the first phase of their experiment, Garcia and Koelling (1966) permitted rats to drink saccharin flavored water from a tube. Each lick from the tube produced three CSs: taste, noise, and bright lights. This phase ensured that rats were equally familiar with each of the CSs. In the next phase, the rats were divided into different groups with each group experiencing either "bright-noisy" water or "tasty" water. Each CS was paired with either illness (induced by radiation treatment or poison) or electric shock. Thus, Garcia and Koelling's experimental design involved four treatment conditions and four different groups of rats (see Table 7.3).

Following several trials of this procedure, the amount of water consumed by the rats was measured and compared against the amount of water consumed normally by the rats (see Figure 7.14). Basically, Garcia and Koelling found that a rat can learn the association between flavor and illness but not between flavor and pain produced by electric shock. Likewise, the rat can learn to associate noise and sounds with shock-induced pain but not with illness. Thus, classical conditioning seems to be constrained at least in some cases by the kinds of stimuli being paired. Some CS-UCS combinations will produce conditioning and others will not. Garcia later showed that if there was a delay of several hours between when a rat tasted a substance's flavor and when the rat became ill, the rat still developed a taste aversion to that food. This finding was surprising because conditioning involving long CS-UCS delays (in this case, a very long delay) generally produces poorer learning than does conditioning involving shorter CS-UCS delays. In taste-aversion learning though, the UCS does not have to immediately follow the CS for learning to occur.

The generality of the phenomenon discovered by Garcia and Koelling was verified by the fact that other animals, including birds, free-ranging carnivores, and humans also show taste-aversion learning. Bobwhite quail have been shown to avoid water that has been paired with illness, although visual cues (the color of the water) proved to be much more salient than taste cues (Wilcoxon, Dragoin, & Kral, 1971). Coyotes have been observed to develop a taste aversion to meats laced with an illness-inducing agent (Gustavson, Garcia, & Hankins, 1974). This finding has considerable potential in controlling livestock predation without killing the predator.

Many psychologists have interpreted the results of taste-aversion studies to mean that organisms have a genetic bias toward responding to certain stimuli in certain contexts. Taste-aversion learning would seem to involve components of both closed and open genetic programs. On one hand, the tendency to associate certain CSs with certain UCSs is probably genetically determined and so is controlled by a closed genetic program.

On the other hand, the specific flavor that is associated with illness is defined totally by experience. Presumably, any flavor can become associated with an illness. That is why taste-aversions are considered to be learned rather than genetically based behaviors.

Garcia and Koelling's findings provide a compelling rationale for why rats have been so successful in foiling humankind's best efforts to exterminate them. Consider the rat in its natural environment. It is familiar with the food sources in its territory. When introduced to a new food, say a plate of poisoned meat, the rat eats but a tiny sample, just enough to taste it. If the rat later becomes ill, it avoids foods with that taste. The association between taste and illness requires only one pairing to become a part of the rat's behavioral pattern. The rat will avoid foods that make it ill and consume foods that are safe. And so rats survive handily, exquisitely adapted to the environment they share with us.

In sum, through classical conditioning animals learn that certain stimuli, CSs, reliably predict the presentation of other stimuli, UCSs. If the UCS does not regularly follow the CS, classical conditioning does not occur or occurs only weakly. In taste-aversion learning, organisms learn that a substance's flavor predicts illness, and as a result, substances with that flavor are avoided.

OPERANT CONDITIONING

In classical conditioning, the UCS is presented independently of the organism's response. Consider again Pavlov's dogs. During classical conditioning, the food powder is presented regardless of whether the dogs salivate or not. The dogs' responses have absolutely no effect on the presentation of food. Imagine that in addition to getting the dogs to salivate, Pavlov also had been interested in teaching his subjects to perform tricks. Would he have been able to train his dogs successfully to roll over or to speak in the same way he trained them to salivate to a tone? The answer is no, simply because in classical conditioning there is no relation between these actions and food. In other words, obtaining food is not a consequence of the dog's behavior. From the dogs' point of view, why perform the act when the food is free? But suppose that Pavlov had modified his procedure. Suppose he had withheld the food powder until the dogs performed the trick or at least performed an action that approximated the trick. Would the result be any different? The answer is yes, because now delivery of the food is dependent upon performance of the trick. From the dogs' point of view, food is delivered only after the performance of the required behavior. With continued practice, the dogs would soon perform the trick reliably upon command, and often for rewards substantially different than food; a few kind words or a pat on the head would also do.

Modifying an organism's behavior by manipulating the consequences of that behavior is called **operant (or instrumental) conditioning**, and is another form of learning. Responses learned through operant conditioning are called operants because they operate on, or change, the environment. The essence of operant conditioning is that behavior is affected by its consequences. In the case of teaching a dog a trick, the dog's response produces a reward such as food or approval. In other words, an action (the performance of the trick) produces a change in the environment (the delivery of the reward). Pavlov never did teach his dogs any tricks, nor did he conduct any research into operant conditioning, at least so far as the recorded history of psychology reports. The formal discovery of operant conditioning was made in the basement of a house in Cambridge, Massachusetts by a 24-year-old man who would later become one of this century's most influential educational psychologists, Edward L. Thorndike (1874–1949).

The Law of Effect

As a graduate student at Harvard University in 1898, Thorndike had become interested in how domesticated animals like cats solve simple problems. Thorndike's research design was simple involving essentially only three steps:

1. He placed a hungry animal (a cat) inside a "puzzle box," like the one shown in Figure 7.15. To escape the box, the animal had to perform some mechanical task such as stepping on a treadle that would open the door. Once outside the box, the animal was given a small portion of food and then put back into the box for another trial.
2. On each trial, Thorndike measured the amount of time the animal used to solve the problem and escape the box.
3. Thorndike repeated steps 1 and 2 until the animal had mastered the task.

Figure 7.15 illustrates the general finding of Thorndike's experiments. On early trials, Thorndike's subjects required several minutes to escape the box, but as training progressed, each cat took less time to escape until finally it was able to flee the box almost immediately. As the number of trials increased, the time to escape the box decreased. Thorndike also observed that during early trials, each cat engaged in a variety of actions irrelevant to the response required for escape. The cats meowed, hissed, and bit and scratched the interior walls of the box. Once they emitted the correct response though, these kinds of behavior gradually disappeared until the cats made only the response leading to escape.

Had you observed Thorndike's cats escaping the box, you probably would have said that they had learned the task well. You might even have been tempted to say that the cats behaved rationally, as if they had used some sort of mental reasoning to solve the problem. But look again at the learning curve shown in Figure 7.15b. The curve decreases gradually not sharply as you might have expected if the cat had suddenly "discovered" the solution to the problem at some point in the experiment. This fact led Thorndike to offer a very different interpretation. Thorndike proposed that at the experiment's outset, the cat engages in a variety of different kinds of actions to escape the box—meowing, scratching, pacing, and so on. Eventually, the cat emits a response that produces a positive outcome. According to Thorndike, this outcome has the effect of strengthening the response

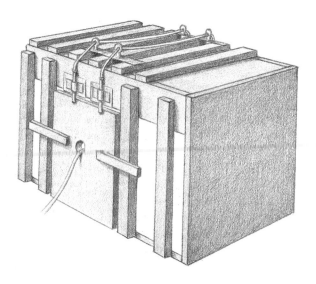

FIGURE 7.15
Thorndike's puzzle box. With repeated trials, cats learned to unlock the door and push it open to escape. The graph shows the time required by one of Thorndike's cats to escape from the puzzle box. After Thorndike, 1898.

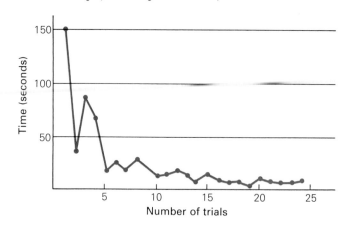

that produced it, increasing the likelihood that that response will occur more often than other kinds of responses on subsequent trials. Thorndike called this relation between a response and its consequences the **law of effect**. In his own words:

> Of several responses made to the same situation, those which are accompanied or closely followed by satisfaction to the animal will, other things being equal, be more formally connected with the situation, so that, when it recurs, they will be more likely to recur. . . . (1911, p. 244)

Over many trials, responses that produce positive outcomes tend to be repeated. The law of effect, then, is analogous to the concept of natural selection, a point made by Thorndike himself. Whereas natural selection determines which members of a species will survive to reproduce, the law of effect determines which responses will survive and become part of the organism's behavioral repertoire. As Skinner (1981) said, it is a sort of selection by consequences. The ability to adjust behavior to fit particular changes in the environment is highly adaptive and is characteristic of organisms possessing open genetic programs. The more open the genetic program, the greater the organism's capacity for behavior modification by interaction with the environment. As Thorndike so aptly wrote, "He who learns and runs away, will live to learn another day" (Thorndike, 1899, p. 91).

Whereas natural selection determines which members of a species will survive to reproduce, the law of effect determines which responses will survive . . .

The impact of Thorndike's formulation of the law of effect upon the early development of psychology as a science would be difficult to overstate. In particular, it affected research in the psychology of learning in one very important way—it stimulated an enormous number of experimental studies aimed at understanding behavior-environment interactions, a line of research that is still very much alive today. Nowhere is this effect more evident than in the work of B. F. Skinner, to whose research we now turn.

Skinner and Operant Behavior

Although Thorndike discovered the law of effect, it was another Harvard psychologist, Burrhus Frederic Skinner (b. 1904), who championed the laboratory study of the law of effect and who advocated the application of behavior analysis and its methods to solving human problems (Skinner, 1953, 1971; Mazur, 1986). He devised rigorous laboratory methods for studying behavior, invented laboratory apparatus and methods for observing it, and created his own philosophy for interpreting it (Bolles, 1979). Moreover, he has written several books for the general public, including a novel showing how his discoveries might be used for the betterment of society (Skinner, 1948).

Although Skinner has made many contributions to behavior analysis, one merits special attention here. Skinner invented the **operant chamber**, an apparatus in which an animal's behavior can be easily observed, and manipulated, and automatically recorded (see Figure 7.16). Behavior analysts who study human behavior use specially modified operant chambers suitable to the unique characteristics of their subjects. In this example, points (as in a video game) or points exchangeable for money can be given for responding instead of using food (Galizio & Buskist, 1988).

Behavior analysts are primarily interested in manipulating environmental events to determine their effects on response rate, the number of responses emitted over a given unit of time. Events that increase response rate are said to strengthen responding; events that decrease response rate are said to weaken responding. The behavior of subjects in the operant

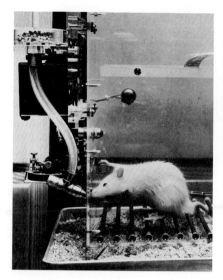

FIGURE 7.17
The cumulative recorder provides a continuous record of an organism's responding in an operant chamber. Each lever press moves the pen, and each reinforcer delivery is indicated by a "blip."

chamber, then, is measured in terms of its rate of response, or the number of times the subject responds per unit of time (usually minutes). To record response rate, Skinner devised the cumulative recorder, a mechanical device that records each response as it occurs in time (see Figure 7.17).

Skinner's ideas have spawned an abundance of research in the 50 years since the publication of his first book, *The Behavior of Organisms* (1938). Skinner's discoveries have led to two distinct but not unrelated paths in psychological research. Many researchers strive to understand basic behavioral processes through laboratory research, an avenue of research that has come to be known as the experimental analysis of behavior. An even larger number of researchers though, have chosen to apply the findings and basic principles first discovered in the laboratory to understanding and treating human behavioral problems, an avenue of research and treatment that has come to be called applied behavior analysis (Epling and Pierce 1988). In the remainder of this chapter we will be concerned primarily with the experimental analysis of behavior.

The invention of the operant chamber and the cumulative recorder represented a clear advance over Thorndike's research methods simply because subjects could (1) emit responses freely over an extended time period and (2) be studied for long periods of time without the interference produced by the experimenter handling or otherwise interacting with them between trials. Under highly controlled conditions such as these, behavior analysts have been able to discover and investigate a wide range of important behavioral principles. It is to these principles that we now turn.

The Three-Term Contingency

Behavior does not occur in a vacuum; certain environmental events usually precede and follow behavior. Consider, for example, answering the telephone. The phone rings, you pick it up and say, "Hello" into the mouthpiece, and someone on the other end of the phone begins to speak. How many times have you picked up a telephone when it was not ringing and said, "Hello"? That would be an absurd thing to do simply because there is no one on the other end of the phone. Certainly your roommates would think you were very odd for behaving this way. We answer the phone (the behavioral event) only when it rings (the preceding event) because in the past, someone has been at the other end of the line with whom to talk (the following event). Skinner referred formally to the rela-

FIGURE 7.18
The three-term contingency.

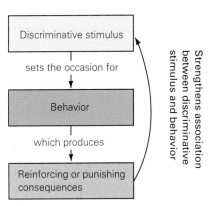

tionship among these three events as the **three-term contingency** and described its components as follows (see Figure 7.18):

■ The preceding event, the **discriminative stimulus**, "sets the occasion" for responding, because in the past, the response has produced certain consequences in the presence of that particular stimulus (if the phone rings, we are likely to answer it because in the past, doing so has produced a specific, and in this case, favorable consequence). Discriminative stimuli are not to be confused with CSs. CSs, as you recall, signal the presentation of the UCS. Discriminative stimuli do not signal other stimuli; rather in their presence, responding is likely to have some effect on the environment. Remember that in classical conditioning, behavior has no such effect.

■ The behavioral event or the response itself (in this case, picking up the phone and saying, "Hello").

■ The following event, or the consequence, is dependent on the response (the speaking of the person on the other end of the phone).

In other words, operant behavior generally occurs in the presence of certain stimuli and is always followed by certain consequences. More specifically, in the presence of discriminative stimuli, a consequence will occur if and only if an operant response occurs.

Acquiring a Response: Shaping. How does a discriminative stimulus come to control responding? How does an organism learn the relation among its behavior, discriminative stimuli, and consequences? In short, how is behavior acquired? Most behavior is acquired gradually through the organism's interaction with reinforcing and punishing events in its environment. In fact, Skinner developed a technique for teaching new behavior to his subjects. This technique is called **shaping.** Shaping involves reinforcing any behavior that successively approximates the desired reponse. Suppose we want to train a pigeon to peck a colored disk in an operant chamber. Although the bird has pecked many objects in its lifetime, it has never pecked a disk before. Thus, when the bird is first placed in the operant chamber, it is not likely to peck the disk even once on its own. Shaping is a means by which we can train the bird to peck.

Before we can shape disk pecking, we must limit the bird's access to food to ensure that food will be a rewarding stimulus for the behavior we want to shape. We then train the bird to eat grain from the food hopper in the operant chamber. Once the bird is hungry and has learned where it can obtain food in the chamber, we are ready to begin shaping the desired response. Now we make the food dependent upon certain aspects of the bird's behavior. We start by giving the bird grain for just facing in the direction of the disk. Next, we withhold food until the bird moves toward the disk, giving the bird grain only as it moves closer and closer to the disk until finally its beak makes contact with it. Soon we have a bird that performs rather like Thorndike's cats. It emits primarily the same response time and time again in the presence of the disk. Once the bird has learned to eat from the hopper, a skilled pigeon trainer can shape the bird to peck the disk in less than an hour's time.

In sum, shaping is a means by which organisms can be trained to make responses that will be reinforced in the presence of a discriminative stimulus. In the case of the pigeon, the disk pecking (behavior) is reinforced with food (the consequence) in the presence of the colored disk (discriminative stimulus).

Shaping has been shown to have many practical applications. Pigeons have even been trained to navigate guided missiles and spot people lost at sea. Animals such as dogs and monkeys have been trained to help humans perform everyday tasks through the use of shaping procedures. Young children and developmentally delayed individuals have been trained via shap-

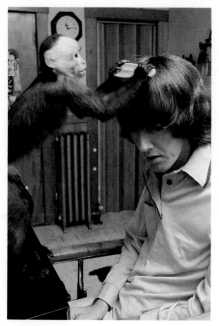

One practical application of shaping is training animals to help people with everyday tasks. Pictured above is a monkey helping a handicapped person.

ing procedures to cooperate with one another in classroom situations and to perform self-help skills such as proper toilet use, dressing, and grooming. Skills such as riding a bike, or catching a baseball, or making a bed are all ones that usually are acquired through shaping. After all, when a child learns these skills, he or she first learns behaviors that only approximate the final level of skill he or she will eventually obtain. Shaping, then, is an example of a psychological principle discovered in the laboratory that has been shown to have widespread application in everyday life.

Generalization and Discrimination. Recall that in classical conditioning generalization means that stimuli resembling the CS to which the UCS had been conditioned originally also elicits the CR. In operant conditioning, **generalization** means something slightly different. Once a response has been reinforced in the presence of a discriminative stimulus, other similar stimuli may also serve as discriminative stimuli for the same response. Those stimuli will also set the occasion for the animals to respond.

In operant conditioning as in classical conditioning, generalization can be reduced through discrimination training. You may remember that in classical conditioning discrimination means that CRs occur only to certain CSs and not to other similar stimuli. In operant conditioning, **discrimination** means that responding occurs in the presence of only certain kinds of discriminative stimuli—those associated with reinforcement. Responding does not occur in the presence of discriminative stimuli associated with extinction (nonreinforcement of operant responding). Let's return to the pigeon lab for an example. Suppose we wish to train a bird to peck a yellow disk but not a green one. To do so, all we have to do is to reward pecking when the disk is yellow and not reward pecking when the disk is green; pecking produces food only when the disk is yellow. At first, our pigeon is likely to peck either disk; with a bit of experience though, the pigeon will respond only to the yellow disk.

While generalization and discrimination are produced in the controlled atmosphere of the laboratory, they are also apparent in everyday life. For example, we learn:

- to stop our vehicle when the traffic light is red but to continue moving the vehicle when the traffic light is green (discrimination).
- to sit quietly in our seats during class examinations, while our instructor is lecturing, during church services, during theatrical presentations, and so on (generalization).
- to raise our hands before speaking in class but not before speaking on other occasions such as parties or while talking to a friend (discrimination).
- to put our feet up on our desk, our own coffee table, on our parents' coffee table (generalization) but not on our grandparents' coffee table (discrimination).

Discriminative stimuli can exert powerful control over responding because of their association with the consequences of such responding. In or out of the laboratory, such control is always dependent on the relationship that exists among components of the three-term contingency.

Reinforcement and Punishment

As you have probably surmised on your own, manipulating the different kinds of relationships that can exist among components of the three-term contingency is the primary means by which behavior analysts study behavior-environment interactions. Of the three elements, the consequences of behavior is the most frequently manipulated variable. In general, behavior analysts can arrange four different kinds of consequences to be dependent on the operant responding of their subjects. Note that these consequences are always defined in terms of their effect upon responding:

1. **Positive reinforcer:** Any stimulus or event that, when made dependent upon a response, increases the frequency of that response over time. The delivery of a positive reinforcer following a response is called positive reinforcement. For pigeons, receiving a bit of food is a reinforcer for disk pecking. For humans, receipt of money or a few words of praise can positively reinforce work-related behavior.

2. **Negative reinforcer:** Any stimulus or event that, when removed, reduced, or prevented following a response, increases the frequency of that response over time. The withdrawing of a negative reinforcer following a response is called negative reinforcement. For example, the response of taking an aspirin when you have a headache is negatively reinforced by pain relief. Obeying the speed limit is also an example of a behavior that is negatively reinforced.

WARNING: It is very easy to confuse positive and negative reinforcement. Remembering the following rule will help you keep the two straight: Both positive and negative reinforcement increase the likelihood that a given response will occur again. However, positive reinforcement involves the presentation of a stimulus whereas negative reinforcement involves the removal, reduction, or prevention of a stimulus.

3. **Extinction:** Any procedure in which a reinforcer is no longer presented following a response. Behavior that is no longer reinforced decreases in frequency. Such behavior is said to extinguish because it no longer produces a reinforcer. A pigeon whose disk pecking has been reinforced previously with food will eventually stop pecking completely when the food reinforcers are no longer delivered. Suppose you were to deposit money into a soda pop machine but receive no soda pop. How long would you continue to put money into the machine? One interesting effect of extinction is that variability in behavior temporarily increases soon after the extinction procedure begins. The soda pop example illustrates this point well. When the machine is working properly, your behavior is simple: You drop a few coins into the machine, push a button, and remove your soda pop. But what happens when the machine isn't working, when it "eats" your money, so to speak? Now your behavior changes some: You may press the button associated with your choice of soda pop a little harder and move the coin return lever up and down several times. If these responses fail, you may emit other behaviors such as hitting or pushing the machine, and maybe uttering a few expletives. Eventually, these responses decrease and you walk away from the mechanical bandit. We see then, that extinction initially produces an increase in other behavior and then a decrease in the operant behavior.

4. **Punisher:** Any stimulus or event that, when it occurs following a response, decreases the frequency of that response. The delivery of a punisher following a response is called punishment. Parents often punish the behavior of their children through scoldings and loss of special privileges.

WARNING: It is also very easy to confuse punishment with negative reinforcement. Punishment and negative reinforcement are closely related concepts. They are, in a sense, opposite sides of the same coin. On the one side, if a stimulus is delivered to an organism and the behavior that caused delivery of that stimulus decreases, then punishment is said to occur (for example, a child is scolded for writing on the wall and subsequently she stops writing on the wall). On the other side, if the delivery of the stimulus is prevented or postponed and the behavior that prevented or postponed the delivery of that stimulus increases, negative reinforcement is said to occur. By definition,

By definition, punishment involves the delivery of a punisher following a response. An example is a parent scolding a child for behaving a certain way.

negative reinforcement always entails avoidance of, or escape from, a stimulus that is otherwise punishing. In any potentially aversive situation, the organism has only two response choices. It can either behave in a manner that results in delivery of the aversive stimulus (punishment), or it can behave in a manner that results in avoidance of or escape from the aversive stimulus (negative reinforcement).

Behavior analysts restrict the use of the terms reinforcement, extinction, and punishment to describe only environmental operations and their effects on the behavior of organisms. Behavior, not the organism, is said to be reinforced, extinguished, or punished.

Schedules of Reinforcement. Your own experience has no doubt taught you that there is not always a one-to-one correlation between your behavior and its consequences. Sometimes your behavior is reinforced by its consequences and sometimes it is not. Dialing the telephone sometimes results in a busy signal, sometimes in no answer, and sometimes in the expected, "Hello." Sometimes you get away with exceeding the posted speed limit on the interstate and sometimes you do not. Depending upon the activity, reinforcement and punishment often vary in frequency over time. To study the effects of variations in the frequency of reinforcement on behavior, behavior analysts have devised schedules of reinforcement that specify the conditions that must be satisfied before an organism's responding is reinforced (Ferster & Skinner, 1957). These conditions are usually based on the passage of time, the number of responses emitted by the subject, or some combination of time and responses.

Broadly speaking, reinforcement delivery can occur continuously or intermittently. With a **continuous reinforcement schedule**, each response is reinforced. Putting your money into a soda pop machine and pressing a particular button is usually reinforced with delivery of the soda pop. In contrast, with **intermittent reinforcement schedules**, responding is only occasionally reinforced. Not surprisingly, intermittent schedules affect behavior differently than do continuous schedules. This finding was first demonstrated when Skinner was low on food supplies for his rats and he attempted to conserve food pellets by occasionally reinforcing his subjects' responses with food instead of after every response (Skinner, 1956). Skinner discovered that this procedure had two outcomes. First, it increased the longevity of his food supply. Second, compared to continuous reinforcement it produced large amounts of responding in his subjects. He also later found that during extinction conditions, rats whose responding was reinforced intermittently emitted a greater number of responses before extinction than did rats whose responding had been reinforced continuously. That is, training under the intermittent schedule had made rats' responding more resistant to extinction, or more durable than responding under the continuous reinforcement schedule.

Skinner's discovery of the effectiveness of intermittent reinforcement in maintaining behavior has stimulated an enormous amount of laboratory research on the effects of different schedules of reinforcement on both animal and human behavior. Four kinds of intermittent schedules, the so-called simple schedules, have received the most experimental attention. These schedules were created by combining fixed or variable delivery of reinforcement with response-based or interval-based (time-based, only one response required) criteria for reinforcement. Hence, their names: fixed-ratio, variable-ratio, fixed-interval, and variable-interval schedules of reinforcement. That these four schedules have different effects on behavior is evidenced by the fact that the same animal will produce a different pattern of responding under each schedule as shown in Figure 7.19. Let's look at these schedules more closely.

FIGURE 7.19
Different patterns of responding under different schedules of reinforcement.

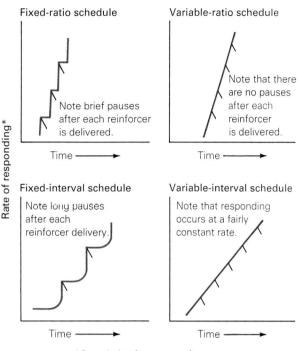

1. **Fixed-ratio (FR) Schedules.** These schedules require that reinforcement be delivered only after the organism has emitted a fixed number of responses. Thus, in an FR 5 schedule, every fifth response is reinforced. As you might expect, FR schedules produce high rates of responding since the rate of reinforcement is directly correlated with the amount of responding. The greater the number of responses emitted by the organism, the greater the number of reinforcers it receives. Animals working under FR schedules characteristically pause briefly after reinforcement but then respond rapidly until the next reinforcer is delivered.

2. **Variable-ratio (VR) Schedules.** The response requirement for reinforcement in VR schedules varies from one reinforcer delivery to the next. For example, in a VR 100 schedule, the reinforcer may be delivered after 80 responses one time, after 120 responses the next time, and after 100 responses the next time. In other words, in a VR 100 schedule, the average number of responses necessary to produce a reinforcer is 100. VR schedules produce higher rates of responding than do FR schedules; they also produce behavior that is highly resistant to extinction.

3. **Fixed-interval (FI) Schedules.** With these schedules, only the first response that occurs after a fixed amount of time has elapsed is reinforced. For example, in an FI 30-second schedule, the first response after each 30 second interval (following the previous reinforcer delivery) is reinforced. All other responses have no effect on reinforcer delivery. For many animals, FI schedules produce a response pattern that is said to be "scalloped": immediately after reinforcement, there is no responding; there is a post-reinforcement pause in responding. As time passes though, responding gradually increases right up to the point of the next reinforcer delivery.

4. **Variable-interval (VI) Schedules.** Like VR schedules, the response requirement for reinforcement in VI schedules varies from one reinforcer delivery to the next. Unlike VR schedules, the criteria for reinforcer delivery is more time-based than response-based. For instance, in a VI one-minute schedule, responses are reinforced on the average of every one minute since the previous reinforcer delivery. Some reinforcers are delivered after short intervals and some after long intervals, thereby producing a moderate, steady rate

Operant Conditioning **253**

of responding. Behavior conditioned under VI schedules, like that conditioned under VR schedules, is highly resistant to extinction.

While it is tempting to look for these kinds of schedules of reinforcement operating in everyday life, they are more likely to be found in the highly controlled conditions of the laboratory than in the much less rigid environments of home, office, or shop. Nature, it seems, does not parcel out its reinforcers in neat little packages that arrive according to one specific schedule (Crossman, 1983). For example, although most people receive a paycheck after fixed intervals of time, they generally do not pause before continuing with their work. Too many other factors such as peer pressure, natural enjoyment of work, and fear of being fired, make it unlikely that a "post-reinforcement pause" will occur following receipt of the paycheck (reinforcement). Even behavior analysts do not raise their children or shape their colleagues to emit behavior according to the stringent criteria of reinforcement schedules ("I'll smile at her every third time she says 'Hi' to me" or "Sorry, son, but I can't talk to you until you study your math for another two minutes").

Nonetheless, schedules of reinforcement have been tremendously useful tools to behavior analysts in understanding how environmental events affect behavior. In their experiments, behavior analysts typically first train a subject under a particular schedule of reinforcement until its behavior is consistent. As you may recall from Chapter 2, this phase of the experiment serves as a baseline condition against which the experimenter can assess the effects of independent variables introduced in a subsequent (treatment) condition. Some environmental event such as a drug is present in the latter but not the former condition, although the same schedule of reinforcement is used in both conditions. The independent variable, in this case the drug, is said to affect behavior if and only if that behavior is observed to be different under the two conditions. For an example, let's look at an actual study.

Grove and Thompson (1970) were interested in understanding exactly when, for how long, and in what way, pentobarbital, a barbiturate commonly used as a sedative, affects behavior. They first trained rats to respond under a FR 120 schedule of food reinforcement. When behavior during baseline was consistent, rats were injected with a certain dosage of the drug and its effects on FR performance were observed. This sequence of

A conditioned reinforcer attains its reinforcing properties by associating with primary reinforcers. An award is an example of a conditioned reinforcer. The award itself may not be worth a lot, but it can reinforce and strengthen other responses.

baseline-treatment conditions was repeated for three different levels of the drug. Grove and Thompson found a dose-dependent effect of the drug: as drug dosage increased, behavior was increasingly disrupted and response rate decreased. In this experiment, the time course of the drug's action as well as the drug's behavioral effects were revealed by the disruption of rats' baseline responding. Such research has been useful to scientists and pharmaceutical companies in understanding how drugs influence behavior.

In sum, reinforcement schedules specify the relationship between behavior and reinforcement. Schedules differ in terms of whether reinforcement is arranged according to number of responses (FR and VR schedules) or the passage of time, although one response is still required for reinforcement, (FI and VI schedules). Schedules of reinforcement are useful because they represent tools by which the effects of environmental variables on behavior can be studied.

Conditioned Reinforcement.

Up to now, we have discussed reinforcement mainly in terms of primary reinforcers, biologically significant stimuli such as food and painful events. But as you know from personal experience, behavior can also be successfully reinforced with a wide variety of other stimuli—money, a smile, a hug, kind words, a pat on the back, and prizes and awards. These stimuli acquire their reinforcing properties through association with primary reinforcers, and are referred to as **conditioned reinforcers**. Because it can be exchanged for so many different kinds of primary reinforcers in our society, money is by far the most common conditioned reinforcer among humans. That money is truly a conditioned reinforcer can be demonstrated by asking yourself a simple question. Would you continue to work for money if it were no longer exchangeable for food, drink, shelter, medical services, and other necessities of life?

An important function of conditioned reinforcers is to bridge the temporal gap between behavior and receipt of a primary reinforcer. Consider the following classic experiment (Wolfe, 1936). A chimpanzee was trained to make a response to obtain a poker chip that could later be inserted into a "chimp-o-mat," producing a primary reinforcer, a grape (see Figure 7.20). In effect, through its association with the grapes, the poker chip had become a conditioned reinforcer; responding was effectively maintained when it was reinforced with the poker chip. When a delay was introduced between earning the chip and the chance to exchange it for the grape, the chip maintained its conditioned reinforcing properties. However, when a comparable delay was introduced between the time the chip was inserted into the "chimp-o-mat" and delivery of the grape, the chimp no longer worked as consistently to acquire the chips.

Conditioned reinforcement is also the principle upon which token economies are based. A token economy is a system used in some mental institutions as well as in classrooms to successfully engender desired behavior (Kazdin, 1983). For example, in institutions residents might be given small plastic tokens, which are later exchangeable for different goods and services, dependent upon execution of desired behavior such as proper self-care or positive social interaction. In the classroom, tokens that are later exchangeable for snack items and school supplies may be earned by students who behave appropriately.

Aversive Control of Behavior.

Your own experience has probably taught you that punishment can be as effective, if not more effective than positive reinforcement in producing behavior change. Such aversive control of behavior seems to permeate every nook and cranny of society. From the spankings given to naughty toddlers and the fines given for exceeding the posted speed limits on our highways and interstates, to assigning students

FIGURE 7.20
Conditioned reinforcement. Tokens, such as plastic disks, can serve as conditioned reinforcers for animals, including humans. In this picture, a chimpanzee is shown depositing a token that produces a primary reinforcer, food.

Punishment in our society takes many forms. One of the most common is issuing a ticket to someone violating a traffic law. As with other forms of punishment, it is hoped that the undesirable behavior stops altogether or is at least reduced.

poor grades, and imprisoning felons for criminal deeds, our society uses punishment to attempt to control the behavior of its citizens. The aversive control of behavior is so common for two main reasons. First, it can be highly effective in inducing behavior change, producing nearly immediate results. The parent who spanks a child for misbehaving sees an abrupt halt of the misdeed; a person given a stiff fine for running a stop sign is likely, at least for a short while, to heed the sign's instruction. Interestingly, the very effectiveness of punishment as a means of behavior change can serve as a relatively immediate reinforcer for the person who is doing the punishing.

Second, in many cases, society cannot control the positive reinforcers that shape and maintain the behavior of its members. However, society can control the aversive stimuli that can be used to punish misconduct. For example, while society has no control over the kinds of stimuli that positively reinforce robbery (money, power), society does control the stimuli for punishing such behavior (fines, community service, imprisonment). Although your driver's education instructor probably complimented you on obeying road signs, when was the last time your behavior was positively reinforced for obeying the posted speed limit or coming to a full stop at a stop sign? Your answer, of course, is never because in this case the police do not possess stimuli that can be used to positively reinforce behavior; but they do, as your experience has probably taught you, possess stimuli that can be used to punish or negatively reinforce behavior.

Although punishment is effective in reducing and even eliminating undesirable behavior, it can also produce several extremely negative side effects:

- Unrestrained use of physical force by a punisher may cause serious bodily injury to the person being punished (for example, child abuse).
- Negative associations become attached to people meting out punishers; punishment often induces fear, hostility, and other undesirable emotions in people receiving punishment. It may even result in retaliation against the punisher.
- Through punishment, the organism learns only which response not to emit; punishment does not necessarily involve teaching the organism desirable responses.

In sum, punishment is a widely used means for attempting to control behavior. It is a popular method because it produces almost immediate changes in behavior and society has better control over aversive stimuli than positively reinforcing stimuli. Nonetheless, the use of punishment can and does have serious drawbacks.

The Analysis of Human Behavior

As we mentioned earlier, most behavior analysts have studied human behavior only indirectly, preferring to study the behavior of nonhuman animals in the laboratory first and then to generalize or apply their findings to everyday human behavior (for example, Skinner, 1953). Over the past twenty years though, this emphasis has changed considerably. Although there is still plenty of research being conducted using nonhumans, behavior analysts have become increasingly interested in studying behavior that is unique to humans, such as certain social and verbal behavior (Hake, 1982). In this section, we briefly describe two current areas of operant research involving human behavior: instructional control of behavior and stimulus equivalence.

Instructional Control of Behavior. A unique aspect of human behavior is that it can be influenced not only by reinforcement but also by the interactions of reinforcement with rules; that is, verbal descriptions of the relation between behavior and reinforcement. In fact, much of our everyday behavior involves following rules of one sort or another. Cooking from a recipe, following directions to a friend's house, and obeying the speed limit are common examples of how behavior can be influenced by rules. Because rules are so common and have the potential to influence our behavior in almost any situation, behavior analysts are interested in learning more about how rules and reinforcement interact.

One way to investigate this interaction is to give subjects rules that are false; that is, rules that are inaccurate descriptions of the behavior required for reinforcement (Baron & Galizio, 1983; Galizio, 1979). In such experiments, subjects may behave in accordance with either the rule or the reinforcement requirement, depending upon whether or not rules directly contradict the reinforcement schedule in effect. For example, in one study (Buskist & Miller, 1986), subjects were told that the schedule in effect was an FI 15-second schedule, when in fact, it was an FI 30-second schedule. At first, subjects responded according to the instructions, emitting one response about every 15 seconds. However, because the rule directly contradicted the reinforcement schedule, they soon learned to emit a response about once every 30 seconds. In essence, these subjects abandoned the rule in favor of the reinforcement contingency. Another group of subjects was told the truth about the schedule in effect and responded accordingly. A third group of subjects was exposed to the FI 30-second schedule but was told that the schedule in effect was a FI 60-second schedule. The rule given to these subjects was ambiguous but not false—it did not directly contradict the reinforcement contingency: one response every 60 seconds would still produce a reinforcer. These subjects never learned to respond according to the actual schedule. The point is that rules can be influential in controlling behavior not only when they are true, but also when they are ambiguous. The problem, of course, is that ambiguous instructions often lead to inefficient behavior. For example, subjects given the FI 60-second instruction earned fewer reinforcers by following the instruction (less than one reinforcer per minute) than they would have had they responded according to the FI 30-second schedule (two reinforcers per minute).

Other researchers have shown that subjects sometimes generate their own rules about the relationship between their behavior and its consequences (Lowe, 1979). Such "self instructions" as the experimenter-provided instructions described above, can influence responding (Matthews, Catania, & Shimoff, 1985). Some researchers, such as Fergus Lowe, maintain that language, specifically our ability to describe verbally the relationship between our behavior and its consequences, is a critical factor

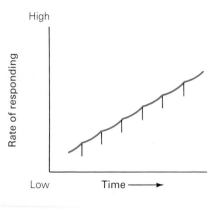

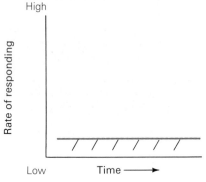

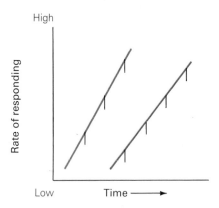

FIGURE 7.21
Typical cumulative records of human responding under a fixed-interval schedule of reinforcement. Some humans respond in a scalloped pattern (top), others respond at a very slow rate (middle), and still others respond at a high rate (bottom).

in why humans respond differently from animals when placed under similar reinforcement contingencies (for example, Lowe, Beasty, & Bentall, 1983). As you may recall, when exposed to FI schedules, animals do not respond immediately after reinforcement. As time passes though, responding gradually increases until the next reinforcer is delivered. Humans, however, respond either very slowly, emitting only one or two responses per reinforcer, or very rapidly, emitting many responses per reinforcer (see Figure 7.21). Those subjects who respond slowly often describe the schedule as time-based, which it is, and they respond accordingly. Those who respond rapidly characteristically describe the schedule as response-(ratio) based, which it is not, but they respond according to their description. Thus, language may indeed exert control over one's own behavior. The extent to which language and behavior interact is the subject of intense ongoing experimental and theoretical work (Hayes, 1989).

Stimulus Equivalence. Probably the "hottest" area of current operant research with humans is stimulus equivalence, which refers to the emergence of novel behavior without direct reinforcement of that behavior (Sidman & Tailby, 1982; Sidman & de Rose, 1989). The experiments designed to study stimulus equivalence are extremely complex, so we will not describe them in detail here. Instead, let us give you a brief overview.

Suppose that you were asked to learn the relationship among a group of symbols, let's say, A, B, and C. Suppose further that after some training without reinforcement, you discovered that A = B and B = C. How then would you respond to the following question: Does A = C? You would probably reason that if A = B and B = C, then A too, is equal to C. But notice that you were never trained or received any direct reinforcement for learning that A = C. Rather, the equivalent relationship between the two stimuli (A and C) emerged from your previous learning; hence, the term, stimulus equivalence. In order for stimulus equivalence to emerge, certain relationships about A and B must first be learned. Specifically, one must learn that A = A, A = B and B = A and B = C and C = B. Without such training, stimulus equivalence (A = C) does not emerge.

Stimulus equivalence is an important area of research because it represents the way we learn to use and understand symbols such as language. For example, let A represent a picture of a dog, B represent the spoken word, *dog*, and C represent the printed word, *dog*. Suppose we teach a child to point to the picture of the dog (A; A = A) when we speak the word, *dog* (B). In this case, the child learns A = B and that B = A. Next, suppose that we teach the child to say the word, *dog* (B) when we point to the printed word, *dog* (C). Here, the child learns that B = C and that C = B. What we are really interested in, though, is whether or not the child will have learned that the picture of the dog (A) is equivalent to, or means the same thing as, the printed word, *dog* (C) (see Figure 7.22). Research shows that this is precisely what children learn under these circumstances, even though the equivalent relationship, A = C, has not been directly trained (Sidman & Tailby, 1982). Rather, it emerged as a consequence of the child's learning history.

Current research into stimulus equivalence focuses on two issues: how it develops, especially in young children and the developmentally delayed (Devany, et al., 1986), and whether it is unique to humans (McIntyre et al., 1987; Hayes, 1989). Understanding how stimulus equivalence develops is likely to lead to a better understanding of language development. Currently, though, researchers are not sure if stimulus equivalence is a cause or an effect of language (McIntyre, et al., 1989). The problem is akin to the

Training A = B

B = C

Test A = C?

FIGURE 7.22
Stimulus equivalence.

familiar chicken and the egg question (Which came first, the chicken or the egg?): Which comes first, stimulus equivalence or language? The second issue is interesting because stimulus equivalence may represent a fundamental difference between other species and us. The capacity to learn stimulus equivalence, like the capacity to learn language, may be one that is most fully realized in our species.

BOUNDARIES AND FRONTIERS

The success of behavior analysis in discovering laws of learning that accurately describe and predict behavior across species and across experimental settings is one of psychology's foremost achievements. These laws are not only valued for their theoretical elegance, but also for their practical utility in understanding behavior in everyday life such as child rearing, weight control, and improving academic performance. But as your experience with previous chapters has demonstrated, few if any, approaches or perspectives in psychology go unchallenged. Such is also the case with behavior analysis. From early in this century to about the mid-1960s the behavioral approach dominated studies of learning and behavior. Gradually though, some researchers became dissatisfied with the behavioral approach and its strict emphasis on environmental determinants of learning. Many psychologists believed that thoughts, perceptions, emotions, and so on, are important causes of behavior. As a result, their research has focused on understanding cognition, or the mental processes by which organisms acquire and store information about their environment and how that information is subsequently used to make plans and solve problems. Thus, if you were to tour your school's experimental psychology laboratory, you would likely find one group of psychologists studying the relation between an organism's behavior and its environment, and another group studying the relation between an organism's mental processes and its behavior. Although we will discuss cognitive psychology in detail in the next two chapters, we include here a hint of how it has challenged the behavior-analytic view of learning.

Cognitive psychologists believe that organisms mentally process information about their environments (Neisser, 1967). Thus, in the cognitive view, behavior is not due solely to environmental causes, but rather it has an internal cause: processing information about the environment, storing it in memory, and then manipulating that information until a solution is found. Cognitive psychologists hold that the extent to which an organism can learn about its environment depends upon three things: its capacity to form mental representations of its environment, its ability to manipulate those representations, and its ability to implement the results of such manipulations as it interacts with the environment.

The cognitive perspective has been nurtured by metaphors inspired by recent advances in computer technology. Like computers, organisms and humans in particular are said to process information by encoding and storing it in memory and retrieving it from memory when necessary. In short, people are said to form and then operate on internal representations of environmental stimuli in the same way that computers operate on inputs. Based on this view, the brain is analogous to the computer and learning is analogous to the means by which the computer generates outputs (solves problems) based on the operations it performs on inputs (information about the environment).

Behavior analysts counterargue that there is no solid evidence that such internal representations actually exist. They accuse cognitive psychologists of talking about "internal surrogates" of the real world as if they actually exist, when in fact, they are simply hypothetical constructs (Skinner, 1978). After all, no one has ever directly observed an internal representation; the very best that we can do is to observe behavior directly and then make inferences about what cognitive processes seem to be responsible for the behavior, a point also held by cognitive psychologists. But it is these very inferences about cognition to which behavior analysts take exception. Since we cannot gather direct evidence that such things exist, how can we be sure that we are not on a wild goose chase, looking for and talking about things that do not exist? Behavior analysts do believe that such events as thoughts exist, but they do not view them as causes of behavior; instead thoughts are viewed as another instance of behavior that is influenced by environmental variables.

The debate between cognitive psychologists and behavior analysts has been and will continue to be a lively one. If nothing else, cognitive psychology has exposed the boundaries of the behavior analytic position (its emphasis on only observable behavior) and defined new frontiers in need of exploration (cognitive processes). The debate has been a useful one, with both behavior analysts and cognitive psychologists designing research and conducting experiments to bolster their respective positions. This chapter has given you an overview of the behavior analytic position and the research that supports it. The next two chapters will fill you in on the important work of today's cognitive psychologists.

CONCEPT SUMMARY

LEARNING: OPEN AND CLOSED GENETIC PROGRAMS

- What are the important differences between open and closed genetic programs? (pp. 227–229)
- How do fixed-action patterns differ from imprinting? (pp. 229–232)
- Why is the critical period an important feature of imprinting? (pp. 231–232)

LEARNING AND THE ANALYSIS OF BEHAVIOR

- How do ethologists and behavior analysts differ in their approach to studying learning and behavior? (pp. 232–233)
- Upon what assumptions do behavior analysts base their approach to studying learning and behavior? (pp. 232–233)

CLASSICAL CONDITIONING

- In what sense was Pavlov's work serendipitous? (pp. 234–235)
- What are the four basic components of the classical conditioning procedure and how do they differ from one another? (pp. 234–235)
- Of what value is classical conditioning to understanding human behavior? (pp. 235–236)
- What is acquisition? What two factors are important in the acquisition of the conditional response? How does acquisition differ from extinction? (pp. 236–238)
- Under what conditions does spontaneous recovery occur? (p. 238)
- What are the important differences between stimulus generalization and discrimination? (pp. 238–239)
- What is learned in classical conditioning? (pp. 239–240)
- What is blocking? How does the Rescorla-Wagner model explain blocking? (pp. 241–242)

OPERANT CONDITIONING

- How did Thorndike's research lead to his discovery of the law of effect? (pp. 246–247)
- In what way is the law of effect like natural selection? (pp. 246–247)
- In terms of the analysis of behavior, what advantages does the operant chamber have over Thorndike's puzzle box? (p. 248)
- How does the three-term contingency explain the relation among discriminative stimuli, behavior, and consequences? (pp. 248–249)
- How would one go about shaping an operant response in, say, a pigeon? (pp. 249–250)
- In operant conditioning, what do the terms generalization and discrimination mean? How does the operant interpretation of these terms differ from that of classical conditioning? (pp. 250, 238–239)
- What is the difference between positive reinforcement and negative reinforcement? What is the difference between negative reinforcement and punishment? (pp. 251–252)
- What are the basic characteristics of the four main types of reinforcement schedules? (pp. 252–255)
- What is the role of conditioned reinforcement in a token economy? (p. 255)
- How does society use the aversive control of behavior to help keep law and order? What are the advantages and disadvantages of using punishment to control behavior? (pp. 255–256)
- How can instructions or rules influence behavior? What is stimulus equivalence? (pp. 257–258)
- In terms of the study of learning, what are the important ways that cognitive psychology differs from behavior analysis? (pp. 258–259)

KEY TERMS AND CONCEPTS

Learning A relatively permanent change in behavior based on experience. (p. 227)

LEARNING: OPEN AND CLOSED GENETIC PROGRAMS

Instinct Inborn or genetically-determined factors, which, in the earlier days of psychology, were believed by some to be the major determinants of behavior. (p. 227)

Genetic Program The genetic instructions an organism inherits at birth. The genetic program determines the extent to which behavior may be changed through interaction with the environment. Some genetic programs are said to be closed programs because they do not permit much learning; in this case, experience has little or no effect on behavior. Other programs are said to be open programs because they permit relatively more learning to occur. (p. 228)

Species-typical Behavior Behavior that is common to a given species. Species-typical behavior is studied mainly by ethologists, people who study animal behavior as it occurs in natural habitats. (p. 229)

Fixed-action Pattern A species-typical behavior characterized by highly stereotyped pattern of responses. Fixed-action patterns are elicited by specific environmental stimuli called sign stimuli. (p. 229)

Sign Stimulus Stimulus that elicit fixed-action patterns. (p. 229)

Imprinting A form of learning that occurs only during some restricted period in an organism's life. Imprinting is the basis for the formation of social attachment between recently born animals and an adult member of the same species (usually the mother). (p. 231)

Critical Period The period of time during which imprinting can occur. Imprinting cannot occur once the critical period has passed. (p. 231)

CLASSICAL CONDITIONING

Classical (or Pavlovian) Conditioning The form of learning in which one stimulus or event predicts another stimulus or event. (p. 234)

Unconditional Stimulus (UCS) In classical conditioning, any stimulus, such as food, that naturally elicits a reflexive response, such as salivation. (p. 235)

Unconditional Response (UCR) In classical conditioning, the response, such as salivation, that is naturally elicited by the unconditional stimulus. (p. 235)

Conditional Stimulus (CS) In classical conditioning, any neutral stimulus paired with the unconditional stimulus that eventually elicits a response. (p. 235)

Conditional Response (CR) In classical conditioning, the reflex or response elicited by the conditional stimulus. (p. 235)

Acquisition The portion of a classical conditioning experiment in which a conditional response first appears and increases in frequency or strength. (p. 236)

Delay Conditioning The relationship between the CS and UCS in which the CS begins shortly before the UCS. Specifically, the UCS begins while the CS is still present and both stimuli terminate at the same time. Delay conditioning produces the quickest and most powerful conditioning. (p. 238)

Extinction In classical conditioning, the procedure of no longer presenting the UCS after the CS to the subject after conditioning of a response. Extinction results in the eventual elimination of the conditional response.

In operant conditioning, **extinction** is any procedure in which a reinforcer is no longer presented following a response. Behavior that is no longer reinforced decreases in frequency until it stops occurring altogether. (p. 238)

Spontaneous Recovery The reemergence of the conditional response after it has been extinguished. In other words, once the conditional response has been extinguished, it may not disappear from the organism's behavior permanently. Pavlov demonstrated that after conditional responding had been extinguished, the response would often suddenly reappear on the CS presentation following a "time-out" from the extinction procedure. (p. 238)

Generalization In classical conditioning, conditional responses elicited by stimuli that resemble the CS used in training. In other words, once a response has been conditioned to a particular CS, other similar stimuli will also elicit that response, despite never having been explicitly paired with the UCS. The more closely that other stimuli resemble the CS, the more conditional responses they will elicit. (p. 238)

In operant conditioning, **generalization** means something slightly different. Once a response has been reinforced in the presence of a discriminative stimulus, other similar stimuli may also serve as discriminative stimuli for the same response. That is, those stimuli will set the occasion for a response to be entitled. (p. 250)

Discrimination In classical conditioning, distinguishing one stimulus from another. Organisms learn to respond to some but not other stimuli. Responses are elicited by the CS because they are followed by the UCS; other stimuli do not elicit the responding because they are never followed by the UCS. (p. 239)

In operant conditioning, **discrimination** means that responding occurs in the presence of only certain kinds of discriminative stimuli—those associated with reinforcement. Responding does not occur in the presence of discriminative stimuli associated with extinction (nonreinforcement of operant responding). (p. 250)

Blocking The ability of one CS to obstruct or block conditioning to a subsequent CS because of an organism's previous conditioning experience. (p. 242)

Rescorla-Wagner Model A current and widely held view of classical conditioning that accounts for blocking. For our purposes, the model is based on two assumptions. First, classical conditioning produces changes in the associative strength between a given CS and a given UCS. Second, a given UCS can support only a certain amount of conditioning. (p. 242)

Associative Strength The correlation between the CS and UCS, or the degree to which the CS reliably predicts the UCS. In effect, classical conditioning produces positive changes (increases) in associative strength and extinction produces negative changes (decreases). (p. 242)

OPERANT CONDITIONING

Operant (or Instrumental) Conditioning A form of learning in which behavior is affected by the consequences it produces. Reinforcing a behavior strengthens it, whereas punishing a behavior weakens it. (p. 245)

Law of Effect Thorndike's description of operant conditioning: The effects that behavior has on the environment determine whether or not that behavior is likely to be repeated. (p. 247)

Operant Chamber An apparatus in which an animal's operant behavior can be easily observed, manipulated, and automatically recorded. (p. 247)

Three-term Contingency The relationship among discriminative stimuli, behavior, and the consequences of that behavior. (p. 249)

Discriminative Stimulus In operant conditioning, the preceding event or stimulus that sets the occasion for responding because in the past, that behavior has produced certain consequences in the presence of that particular stimulus. (p. 249)

Shaping Reinforcing any behavior that successfully approximates the desired response until that response is acquired. (p. 249)

Positive Reinforcer Any stimulus or event that, when it follows a response, increases the frequency of that response over time. The delivery of a positive reinforcer following a response is called positive reinforcement. (p. 251)

Negative Reinforcer Any stimulus or event that, when removed, reduced, or prevented following a response, increases the frequency of that response over time. The procedure of withdrawing, removing or reducing stimulus is called negative reinforcement. (p. 251)

Punisher Any stimulus or event that, when it occurs following a response, decreases the frequency of that response. The delivery of a punisher following a response is called punishment. (p. 251)

Continuous Reinforcement Schedule A reinforcement schedule in which a reinforcer is arranged for each response. In other words, each response is reinforced. (p. 252)

Intermittent Reinforcement Schedules Reinforcement schedules in which responses are only occasionally reinforced. Compared to continuous schedules, intermittent schedules produce responding that is more resistant to extinction. (p. 252)

Fixed-ratio (FR) Schedules These schedules require that reinforcement be delivered only after the organism has emitted a fixed number of responses. (p. 253)

Variable-ratio (VR) Schedules Reinforcement schedules in which the response requirement for reinforcement varies from one reinforcer delivery to the next. (p. 253)

Fixed-interval (FI) Schedules These schedules require that reinforcement be delivered only if a response occurs after a fixed amount of time has elapsed since delivery of the previous reinforcer. (p. 253)

Variable-interval (VI) Schedules These schedules require that responses be reinforced only after varying amounts of time have elapsed between reinforcer deliveries. (p. 253)

Conditioned Reinforcers Stimuli and events that acquire their reinforcing properties through their association with primary reinforcers. (p. 255)

ADDITIONAL SOURCES OF INFORMATION

Catania, A. C. (1985). *Learning.* Englewood Cliffs, NJ: Prentice-Hall.

Mazur, J. E. (1986). *Learning and behavior.* Englewood Cliffs, NJ: Prentice-Hall. Both of these books were written for the upper-division course in behavior analysis, and both are excellent sources of additional information about the topics discussed in this chapter. Both texts have superb overviews of classical and operant conditioning and are up-to-date on current research and theoretical positions in behavior analysis. Be prepared, though, because both books are very technical in presenting the basic principles of conditioning.

Skinner, B. F. (1953). *Science and human behavior.* New York: The Free Press. This book, although originally published over 35 years ago, is still a valuable interpretation of the behavior analytic position. The basic principles of operant conditioning and their application to understanding a wide range of behaviors are explained interestingly and clearly. This book is an excellent choice if you wish to know more about Skinner's view of psychology.

Skinner, B. F. (1987). *Upon further reflection.* Englewood Cliffs, NJ: Prentice-Hall. This little book is an anthology of Skinner's recent thoughts. In the preface, Skinner notes that the book is committed to the "... experimental analysis of behavior and its use in the interpretation of human affairs." Topics discussed range from why we are not acting to save the world to cognitive science to behaviorism to education. This book, too, is thought provoking and clearly written.

8 Memory

HOW PSYCHOLOGISTS VIEW MEMORY *(267–278)*

*The Three-Component Model   The Levels of Processing Model
Modification of the Models*

Cognitive psychologists sometimes view memory as a process, sometimes as a place, and sometimes as a thing. The three-component model of memory postulates that we have not one, but three types of memory: sensory, short-term, and long-term. Each component operates differently in its capacity, the length of time it holds information, and how it encodes. The levels of processing model proposes that memory cannot be broken down into individual components, but rather that memory is wholly a matter of processing information. The deeper the level at which information is processed, the better it is remembered. Both models have been challenged and modified, but neither has been abandoned.

PROCESSING AND FORGETTING INFORMATION: ENCODING, STORAGE, AND RETRIEVAL *(278–288)*

Encoding   Storage   Retrieval

Memory involves the processes of encoding, storage, and retrieval. Encoding is a matter of putting information into memory, either automatically or with effort, and how we encode information affects our ability to retrieve it later. Once formed, memories are stored more or less permanently. Retrieval is enhanced by specific retrieval cues and impaired by new information interfering with recall of old information or by old information interfering with recall of new information. Retrieval may also sometimes be more a matter of reconstructing memories than recalling events as they actually happened.

BIOLOGICAL BASES OF MEMORY *(288–290)*

Insights from the Study of Amnesia   Insights at the Neural Level

The brain's role in memory has been investigated by studying people with amnesia as well as by studying learning in simple animals like the marine slug, *Aplysia*. From studies of amnesiacs, neuroscientists have learned that the hippocampus plays an important role in our ability to form memories. From studies of *Aplysia*, neuroscientists have learned that formation of memories involves changes in the nervous system at the neural level.

Although he is perhaps the most famous subject ever to participate in memory research, he is known to the psychological community only by his initials, "H.M." (Corkin, 1984; Milner, 1966, 1970; Scoville & Milner, 1957). And although he is famous for his involvement with memory research, H.M. is not famous for his ability to remember things. Indeed, he is famous for his *inability* to remember things, particularly recent events. In psychology as in other disciplines, we often learn more by studying things when they are not working well than when they are working well. That is the reason why H.M. is so well-known among memory researchers. By studying his inability to remember the recent past, psychologists have been able to learn how important memory is in our day-to-day lives.

Let's pick up H.M.'s story where it began in 1953. That was the year that H.M., then 27, underwent a radical surgical procedure in an attempt to reduce the number and severity of his epileptic seizures. The surgery was a last resort—no other treatment had worked. Although the surgery was successful in reducing H.M.'s seizures, during the course of the surgery his hippocampus was damaged: nearly two-thirds of it was removed. The hippocampus, you will remember, is a small structure in the limbic system (see Figure 8.1).

H.M.'s surgery probably saved his life, but there were some side effects, including a lessening of sexual interests and a peculiar lack of taste perception. The most devastating side effect, though, was on H.M.'s memory. He could remember well almost all of the events and experiences that had been stored in his memory *before* the surgery. But his memory for experiences that occurred *after* the surgery seemed to be limited to those that occurred within the previous 30 seconds or so. For almost 40 years, H.M. has been without a recent past. Although he may see a doctor four or five times a day, every day for two weeks, for H.M., each meeting is an introduction to someone new. He can read and reread magazines and newspapers, but he has no memory of the previous reading—there is no old news. Although H.M.'s general intellectual skills were undiminished by the operation, he simply cannot remember anything new for more than a few seconds at a time.

Like H.M., our learning would be of little value if everything we learn had to be relearned constantly. Unlike H.M., we can take advantage of **memory**, the cognitive processes of encoding, storing, and retrieving information (see Figure 8.2). **Encoding** refers to the active process of putting stimuli into a form that can be used by our memory system. Simply put, encoding is a matter of placing information into memory. **Storage** refers to the process of maintaining information in memory, and **retrieval** refers to the active processes of locating and using stored information.

Without memory, each of our experiences would have to be treated anew. Our memories provide us with a record, imperfect as it may be, of our life's experiences. Take away memory and one loses the sense of self. H.M.'s record of his life experiences hasn't changed since 1953, and so neither has his conception of who he is. In short, H.M. has ceased to change or grow and experience life like the rest of us can and will because he has no memory for recent events.

Our goal in this chapter is to help you understand memory—what it is, how it works, and why it sometimes doesn't work. Because memory is part of the domain of cognitive psychology, we will focus primarily on cognitive theory and research in our discussion. We will begin by taking a close look at how cognitive psychologists have defined and characterized memory. Next, we will examine the memory processes introduced above: encoding, storage, and retrieval. Finally, we will explore the biological basis of memory.

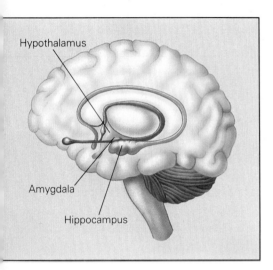

FIGURE 8.1
The primary structures of the limbic system.

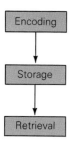

FIGURE 8.2
The three cognitive processes involved in memory. Encoding is the conversion of stimuli into a form that can be understood by the memory system. Once encoded, information is said to be stored or maintained within the memory system for future use. Retrieval is the process of locating and using stored information.

HOW PSYCHOLOGISTS VIEW MEMORY

Cognitive psychologists generally view memory as a process. Everyday experience suggests another possibility. We often treat memory as if it were a location or a place where we put information to be retrieved for later use. We hear someone talk about putting a fact into memory, or when struggling to recall an answer to a test question, having trouble getting it out of memory. The implication with such usage is that memory is a place, presumably in the brain, into which information can be put and from which information can later be retrieved. We also sometimes refer to memory as something that one can have as in "I have a vivid memory of that afternoon." As it happens, cognitive psychologists too sometimes think of memory as a place or a thing as well as a process. How can memory be both a process and a place or a thing? How can cognitive psychologists hold both views? To answer these questions, we need to discuss the two major models of memory, the three-component model and the levels of processing model.

Before we start our discussion of these models, you should know that cognitive psychology's vision of memory and how it works has changed considerably over the past twenty-five years. It wasn't until the mid-1960s that cognitive psychologists began to propose models or theories of how human memory might work. It was from this effort and this research that the three-component and levels of processing models emerged. Both models consider memory as a process involving encoding, storage, and retrieval. They differ, though, as to whether memory is also a place or a thing. We cannot say that there is agreement on which of the two models of memory is the best. But we can say that both models have made significant contributions to our understanding of memory, and that both have been strongly challenged. One well-known theorist and researcher, Endel Tulving, has gone so far as to suggest that about the only thing that we may be truly certain of regarding memory is that most of our present assumptions are wrong and will be replaced by better ones (Tulving, 1985). But for now, let's consider the two models and why they have been useful in understanding memory.

The Three-Component Model

By 1970, a number of cognitive psychologists had challenged the previously common notion that memory was a single, unified structure into which information was encoded, stored, and later retrieved. The complexity of memory functioning suggested that there might be different types of memory (Broadbent, 1958; Hebb, 1949; Miller, 1956; Waugh & Norman, 1965). The most influential model was one that proposed that memory is comprised of three components. This model was developed by Richard Atkinson and Richard Shiffrin (1968, 1971). Theirs is a **three-component model,** which postulates a sensory register (or store) that "picks up" and briefly holds stimuli from the environment, a short-term store of limited capacity, and a long-term store where information is kept with some permanency (see Figure 8.3). The basic idea of this model is that we have not one but three types of memory: sensory, short-term, and long-term. Atkinson and Shiffrin also argued that each component of our memory system operates differently in its capacity, the length of time each holds information, and the form or code each uses to hold information. Let's look more closely at each of these components and the empirical evidence that supports their existence.

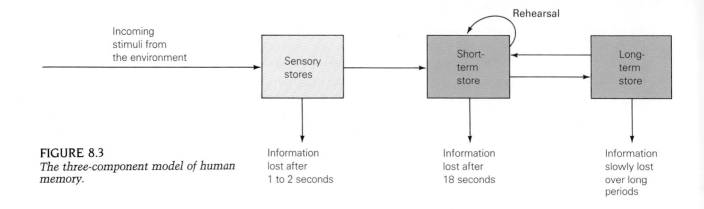

FIGURE 8.3
The three-component model of human memory.

The figure shows: Incoming stimuli from the environment → Sensory stores → Short-term store (with Rehearsal loop) ↔ Long-term store. Information lost after 1 to 2 seconds (Sensory stores); Information lost after 18 seconds (Short-term store); Information slowly lost over long periods (Long-term store).

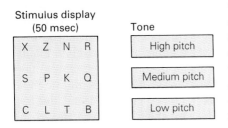

Stimulus display (50 msec)

X	Z	N	R
S	P	K	Q
C	L	T	B

Tone
High pitch
Medium pitch
Low pitch

FIGURE 8.4
The critical features of the experiment designed by Sperling to study sensory memory.

SOURCE: George Sperling, The information available in brief visual presentations. *Psychological Monographs, 74,* 1960, p. 3.

The Sensory Register. The three-component model begins with a basic assumption with which most cognitive psychologists agree: information first enters our memory through our senses. Once our sensory systems are stimulated, some sort of record of the stimulation is made within memory. The initial record is made in the **sensory register,** a memory component in which the physical features of a stimulus are stored for extremely brief durations (see Figure 8.3).

By proposing a sensory register, Atkinson and Shiffrin were making a place in their model for data of the sort that George Sperling had reported nearly a decade earlier (Averbach & Sperling, 1961; Sperling, 1960, 1963). Sperling conducted a series of experiments in which arrays of consonants and numbers were shown to subjects for very brief periods of time. For example, subjects might see a matrix of randomly chosen consonants such as the one in Figure 8.4. The matrix would be visible for only a fraction of a second (usually 50 milliseconds or one-twentieth of a second). Even after such a brief exposure, subjects recognized that the stimulus display contained consonants, but they could recall less than half of them (about 4 or 5). If subjects were told *before* the matrix was presented to concentrate on only the top row or the bottom row, they showed little difficulty in recalling all four of the items presented there.

The critical features of Sperling's experiment required subjects to view the matrix for its 50 ms exposure, and then report the items in one of the three rows. However, subjects did not know which row they were to recall until *after* the matrix left the screen. The row they were to recall was signaled by different tones. If they heard a high-pitched tone, they were to report the consonants in the top row of the matrix. A low tone signaled that they were to recall the bottom row of consonants, and a tone of middle pitch signaled subjects to recall the consonants in the middle row.

Sperling wanted to learn whether subjects' recall of any row of the matrix would be influenced by the length of time between the disappearance of the visual display and the sounding of the tone. In other words, would delaying the tone affect subjects' accuracy in recalling the row of consonants signaled by that tone? The results showed that if the tone was presented within a fraction of a second of the visual stimuli, recall was nearly perfect. If, however the tone was delayed as much as one second, the subjects' performance dropped significantly (see Figure 8.5).

Sperling made the following interpretation of his results: Because subjects did not know which row they were to recall until the tone sounded, *all* of the items in the visual matrix must have been available to them in their sensory memories when the tone was presented. After all, the items were no longer in view. They were no longer "out there" in the environment to be read and reported. They must be somewhere in the subject. All of the items must be stored in the subjects' sensory registers, available for inspection and recall. Once the tone informed them which row they were to report, they could scan the matrix in their sensory registers, find the appropriate row, and recall the consonants found there. After doing so, the remaining consonants were no longer available for the subjects to recall.

Subsequent research has confirmed the presence of a sensory register for visually presented materials (Averbach & Coriell, 1961; Haber & Standing, 1969; Rumelhart, 1970). The visual register appears to have a rather large capacity (at least 25 unrelated items) and a very short duration (clearly less than one second). A similar register also has been reported for auditory stimuli (Crowder, 1971; Darwin, Turvey, & Crowder, 1972), except that auditory signals seem to last for between three and ten seconds in that sensory register (Cowan, 1984).

What does Sperling's research mean? It means that we have a component in our memory system, the sensory register, that can hold large amounts of incoming stimulus material for very brief durations. This component seems to have little practical use in and of itself. The three-component model, however, proposes that it is while information is held briefly in the sensory register that we take the opportunity to attend selectively to some portion of that information, thereby moving it along to the next component in the system: our short-term store.

The Short-Term Store. The capacity of the **short-term store** or short-term memory is limited because we have only a limited attention span. The duration of storage within this component is also thought to be severely limited. Here we'll review two of the classic experiments that support the reality of a short-term store.

Lloyd Peterson and Margaret Peterson (1959) presented subjects with a three-consonant stimulus, such as *JRG*. Not surprisingly, they found that with rehearsal, subjects could easily recall this stimulus 30 seconds later. But what if subjects were prevented from rehearsing the three consonants? Suppose that after being presented with *JRG*, subjects were required to count rapidly out loud backward by threes from a three-digit number they were given immediately after the consonants. A subject is presented with *JRG* and then *397* and has to count out loud, "397 . . . 394 . . . 391 . . . 388 . . . 385," and so on until the subject receives a signal to recall the string of three consonants. As you might suspect, the accuracy of the subject's recall is determined in large measure by the length of the interval between presentation of the consonants and when recall is requested (see Figure 8.6). When rehearsal is disrupted by the backward counting—which

FIGURE 8.5
Results of Sperling's (1960) study showing the total number of characters that subjects could report as a function of the number of seconds the partial report cue was delayed.

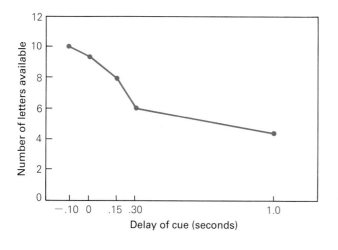

FIGURE 8.6
Percent correct in the recall of the stimulus as a function of the duration of the distractor activity in the Brown-Peterson task (Peterson & Peterson, 1959).

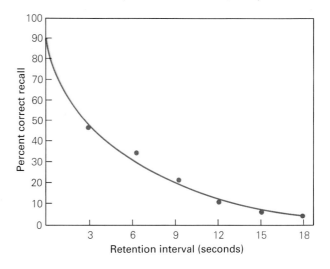

Students in a class lecture can hold several single concepts or chunks of information from that lecture in short-term store at once.

Short-term store allows us to recall a small bit of information, such as a phone number, for a short period of time.

requires considerable attention—the consonants remain accessible in memory for only a few seconds. After a 15- to 18-second delay between the presentation of the consonants and the recall signal, recall drops to near zero. So, for now we can conclude that once attended to, stimuli remain in short-term store for less than 20 seconds unless they are rehearsed further. What about the capacity of this short-term component of memory? How many items can it hold?

The capacity of the short-term store is about seven, plus or minus two units; that is, between five and nine items. This estimate comes from a classic paper by one of the pioneers of cognitive psychology, George Miller, who was commenting on our limits of processing information (Miller, 1956). As we will see, determining just what is meant by an "item" is a critical issue, but for now, we can say that the capacity of the short-term store is limited to 7±2 randomly presented letters, digits, or simple words.

We seldom have much difficulty attending to and remembering a five-digit ZIP Code or a seven-digit phone number. What about this string of letters: T W A A I D S C I A F B I L R I G D N A Y O B? These twenty-three letters are well beyond the capacity of anyone's short-term memory store, unless or until they are reordered into more meaningful items: TWA, AIDS, CIA, FBI, and BOY AND GIRL (spelled backwards). Now we can argue that we are only dealing with about seven items or chunks of information, which is well within the limits of short-term memory. In this context, **chunk** becomes a technical term meaning the representation of a single, meaningful concept or idea, and we may properly say that the capacity of the short-term store is 7±2 chunks of information.

The short-term store has two other additional features. First, information can enter short-term memory from two directions: from either the sensory register or from the long-term store. In fact, the long-term store is involved in the transference of information into short-term store from both directions. In Figure 8.3 this feature is represented by arrows pointing to the short-term store from both directions. For example, when we are asked to multiply 7 times 19, information about the request enters our short-term store from our sensory register. Actually performing the task, however, requires that we retrieve some information from long-term store. What does *multiply* mean? What is a 7 or a *19*? How does one multiply two numbers? At the moment of the request, such information is not being furnished through our senses, but it is available from our long-term store. Notice the implication here that information is not recalled directly from long-term storage. It is first moved, or returned, to the short-term store and then reported as recall.

A second feature of the short-term store is that information is encoded into it acoustically. This means that no matter how information from the environment is furnished to us—whether it enters the nervous system through our eyes, ears, skin, nose, or mouth—it is processed in the short-term store as if it were spoken. In a sense, we describe the sensation we are experiencing to ourselves. Consider as evidence for this idea research studies that show that when errors are made in retrieving items from short-term store, those errors tend to be acoustic ones. For example, when subjects were shown (visually) a series of letters and then asked to recall them while they are still in short-term store, subjects were more likely to confuse a stimulus such as *C* with *Z* or *P*, which both sound like *C*, rather than with *O*, which looks much more like the letter to be recalled but doesn't sound like it (Baddeley, 1966; Conrad, 1964; Wickelgren, 1965).

In sum, information from the environment enters the sensory store where it is held only briefly. If not attended to, this information is lost. If attended to, it is encoded acoustically and moved into the short-term store. Up to 7 ± 2 chunks of information can be held in the short-term store at any one time and for up to about 20 seconds if not practiced or otherwise learned. If practiced, information is moved to the third and final component of the model, the long-term store.

The Long-Term Store. Long-term memory or the **long-term store** of our memory system is memory as we generally think of it—the storehouse in which information is represented in a permanent or nearly permanent basis. The three-component model proposes that much of the information in the long-term store gets there through active processes such as learning, practice, and rehearsal. In fact, rehearsal is a means by which information is "driven" or moved through the entire memory system. The model also postulates that some information can pass into long-term store simply by being maintained in the short-term store long enough. Atkinson and Shiffrin proposed that the long-term store has a virtually unlimited capacity; that is, there seems to be no limit to the amount of information we can store away in our long-term memories.

According to the three-component model, information is held in each of the three memory stores in different forms. The sensory register maintains information in the form in which it is presented. The short-term store recodes information and holds it in an acoustic form. And the model proposes that information in long-term store is encoded mainly semantically, that is, according to its meaning. In other words, what we store in long-term memory is the meaning of stimuli as we understand it. For example, you may hold in your long-term store an idea akin to "long-term store = the meaning of things," without ever hearing or seeing that particular phrase.

What we store in long-term memory is the meaning of stimuli . . .

Empirical support for this idea again comes from the analysis of errors made in recall. For example, suppose subjects are asked to learn a list of common words presented to them visually one at a time, and much later, they are asked to recall that list. If the word *boat* were on the list but not recalled, we are more apt to find someone erroneously recalling the word *ship* (about the same meaning) than the word *coat* (which sounds more like *boat*) or *boar* (which looks more like *boat*) (Baddeley & Dale, 1966; Sachs, 1967).

Episodic memory

Semantic memory

Procedural memory

FIGURE 8.7
Long-term store contains episodic, semantic, and procedural memory. Episodic memory is our store for personal experiences; semantic memory is our store for data, facts, and information; procedural memory is our store for our knowledge of learned behaviors.

Within the long-term store there appear to be different kinds of memory, and the long-term store can be subdivided on the basis of the types of information stored in it. Although not a part of the original three-component model, Endel Tulving (1972, 1983) proposed that within the long-term store, a distinction can be made between episodic memory and semantic memory (see Figure 8.7). **Episodic memory** provides us with a record of our life's experiences. Events stored there are quite literally autobiographical. Your recollections of your first kiss, your last visit to the dentist, and your arrival at college are all found in your episodic memory. **Semantic memory,** on the other hand, is your long-term store of data, facts, and information, including your vocabulary. Your knowledge of what psychology is, how psychology is defined, and the five different perspectives found in modern psychology (biological, behavioral, cognitive, psychodynamic, and social) are each part of your semantic memory. (If they are not, you should go back and review Chapter 1!) But recalling where you were (the library, your dorm room) when you first studied that information is part of your episodic memory.

Tulving (1985, 1986) has recently proposed a third type of memory in the long-term store, which he calls procedural memory. **Procedural memory** is where our knowledge of simple learned associations, and as the name implies, our knowledge of how to perform well-learned habits is stored. For example, the rules that govern the use of our social interactions and the skills involved in riding a bicycle are stored in procedural memory.

So what do we have so far? We have a model that is essentially structural in nature and that proposes that memory is made up of the following set of three components through which information passes: from the sensory register to the short-term store, and ultimately to the long-term store. With each passage, the information is recoded from its original form into an acoustic code and then into a semantic code. We'll return to this three-component model shortly, but now let's examine another model that, to a large extent, developed as an alternative point of view.

The Levels of Processing Model

A number of psychologists take issue with the proposal that memory could be broken down into individual components or separate stores. For them, memory is simply memory and it has no components, no parts, and no structures. To them, what matters most is the level or degree to which information is processed into memory. The clearest articulation of this model was presented by Fergus Craik and Robert Lockhart (1972; see also Cermack & Craik, 1979; Craik, 1970). According to this model, called the **levels of processing model,** our focus should be not on memory structures but on the degree to which information in memory has been cognitively processed. The key feature of the levels of processing model is the extent to which an individual becomes cognitively involved with incoming information.

According to this model, memory is similar to the long-term store of a component model. Memory is proposed to have a boundless capacity and can hold information for a virtually limitless period of time. But at any one moment, we can access and process only a small sample of the information that is stored in our memories. We can choose and control the extent to which we process information that is coming into our memories or process information that is already stored there. Thus, if the levels of processing model of memory is an accurate one, our memory skills would be limited by our ability or willingness to process information. Let's look at this hypothesis more closely.

Above left: We recall facts, data, and such information as the vocabulary we need to spell words from our semantic memories. Above right: Memories of meaningful life events, such as a person's wedding are stored in episodic memory.

A central issue in the levels of processing model of memory is the distinction made between maintenance rehearsal and elaborative rehearsal (see Figure 8.8). By **maintenance rehearsal,** Craik and Lockhart mean the rote repetition of information, perhaps just by repeating a given item over and over again. By **elaborative rehearsal** they mean processing material more deeply: forming associations, attending to the meaning of the material, thinking about it, and so on. Simply repeating the syllables *nu-ka, nu-ka, nu-ka* to yourself over and over again is unlikely to enhance your memory of the syllables. But when you recognize the sounds as the same as those in the word *canoe,* the stimuli can be processed more meaningfully. Maintenance and elaborative rehearsal were not meant to define distinct types of rehearsal but rather to indicate extremes of processing, from shallow (maintenance) to deep (elaborative). According to the model, the deeper the processing of information, the more durable and more easily accessible the memory for that information. Likewise, the shallower the processing of information, the more fragile and less accessible the memory for that information. From a practical point of view, you are more likely to remember information for a test by processing it deeply or meaningfully. Simply glossing over the material to be tested won't do. Remembering it well requires studying.

FIGURE 8.8

Maintenance and elaborative rehearsal. Maintenance rehearsal involves rote repetition of information; it is a relatively shallow means of processing information. Elaborative rehearsal involves attending more carefully to the information; it is a relatively deep means of processing information. In this figure, which strategy is more likely to be a better means of remembering and understanding the processes involved in memory?

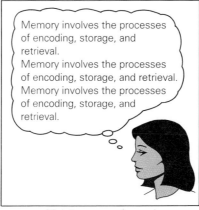

Memory involves the processes of encoding, storage, and retrieval.
Memory involves the processes of encoding, storage, and retrieval.
Memory involves the processes of encoding, storage, and retrieval.

Maintenance rehearsal

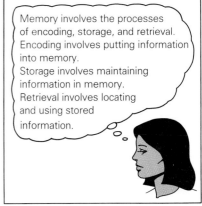

Memory involves the processes of encoding, storage, and retrieval.
Encoding involves putting information into memory.
Storage involves maintaining information in memory.
Retrieval involves locating and using stored information.

Elaborative rehearsal

Let's examine two typical experiments of the sort that support the levels of processing model. In one experiment (Craik & Tulving, 1975), subjects were asked to make a judgment about a word they had not yet been shown. Some of the judgments had to do with the physical characteristics of the word ("Is the word in capital letters?"). Some dealt with how the word would sound if spoken ("Does the word rhyme with clip?"). Still other judgments had to do with whether or not the word would fit in a sentence ("Does the word fit the sentence, 'The men crossed the ocean in a small _____ without sails.'?"). *After* they were asked one of these types of questions, they were shown a target word such as *SHIP*. Subjects were to respond with a simple "Yes" or "No." Now making these judgments was easy. The most important part of the experiment came after the subjects made judgments about many words. They were given a surprise recognition test to see how many of the target words they remembered. Subjects remembered nearly 80 percent of the words for which they had made semantic judgments (Does it fit a sentence?), only 50 percent of the words for which they had made a rhyming decision, and fewer than 20 percent of the words for which they had made a judgment in terms of physical features. Craik and Tulving interpreted these results in terms of the levels of processing model. The more work or elaboration on the stimulus words the subjects had to put into performing the initial task, the better they remembered the words. The semantic judgments required that words be processed at a deeper level than did the other kinds of judgments. In short, information is remembered best if it is processed at a deep level.

Another experiment also conducted by Craik (Craik & Watkins, 1973) supports the notion that it is the nature of rehearsal (level of processing) rather than the amount of rehearsal (amount of processing) that determines long-term retention of information. Subjects were presented with twelve lists of words each containing twelve items. They were told to practice the words on the list because they were to be tested later on their recall of the words. Craik and Watkins asked subjects to rehearse the lists out loud so that they could record the number of times each list was rehearsed. However, Craik and Watkins emphasized to their subjects that the last four words of each list were of prime importance and that no matter what else, every effort should be made to remember the last four words on the list. Quite predictably, when recall was tested soon after a list was presented, subjects remembered the last four words from the list almost perfectly. Subjects' recall was also tested a second time. When all twelve lists had been presented and recall had been tested for each list, subjects were asked to recall for the final time as many words as they could from the 144 words they had seen during the course of the experiment. Figure 8.9 compares the results of these two tests. In this test, words that had occupied the last four positions on the twelve lists were *not* recalled any more frequently than words from any other position on the lists (see Figure 8.9). Why? Because apparently, subjects used maintenance rehearsal, mere rote repetition of those words to memorize them. So, although these words at the ends of the lists clearly had been rehearsed to a greater degree than any other words (which did help when recall followed soon after the presentation of the list), that rehearsal proved to be insufficient for the subjects to process the words deeply enough to remember them any better than the other words when the final recall was requested.

If nothing else, the basic thrust of this approach to memory should sound reasonable to you. As a student, you are required to recall large amounts of information at several critical times during the term. There is some intuitive appeal for a model of memory proposing that the more you elaborate on information and the more you work with material, the deeper it will be processed into your memory and the more likely you will be able

FIGURE 8.9
Results of Craik and Watkin's (1973) study. Maintenance rehearsal helped subjects recall the last four words in the lists, but it did not help them recall those words when tested at a later time.

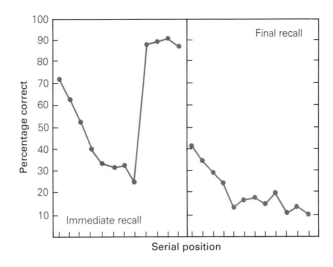

to recall it at the critical time. The moral here is obvious: to remember information well, it must be processed at a deep level.

Now that we've briefly outlined the essential properties of the two major models of human memory systems, let's look at some of the research that these approaches have stimulated.

Modification of the Models

As we learned in Chapter 2, one criterion for evaluating the worth of a theory or a model is the extent to which it stimulates further research. On this criterion, it is clear that both the Atkinson/Shiffrin three-component model and the Craik/Lockhart levels of processing model have been major successes. Although a theory may stimulate research, that research may not always support that theory. Over the last two decades, research data have accumulated that challenge some of the basic premises of both models. Neither model has, in any sense, been proven wrong. What has happened, though, is that both models have been modified. Specifically, those aspects of the models that fit with the new research findings have been retained, while other aspects have been modified to accommodate new data. In this section we'll explore just a few of the challenges to both models of memory (see Table 8.1). We'll start with the notion of the sensory register.

Today, most cognitive psychologists agree that human memory includes a component something like the sensory register proposed by Atkinson and Shiffrin and demonstrated in experiments by Sperling. The major points of controversy center on the encoding process by which information is held in the sensory register, and whether this register is of any practical importance.

The three-component model proposed that stimuli are held in the sensory register in the same form in which they are presented. Visually presented stimuli (such as those used by Sperling) form a type of visual record called an "icon" (Neisser, 1967), while sounds are recorded in an auditory code called an "echo." The three-component model held that storage in the sensory register is so primitive and so cursory, that no manipulation of incoming stimuli is possible. However, Philip Merikle (1980) has shown, with a simple change in Sperling's basic experimental procedure, that the information in the sensory register may be sensitive to apparently "higher" cognitive processes. Among other things, Merikle found that if a matrix of digits and letters is flashed briefly before subjects, they are just as accurate

TABLE 8.1.	Criticisms of the three-component and levels of processing models of memory.

THREE-COMPONENT MODEL	LEVELS OF PROCESSING MODEL
1. The sensory registers may not be a separate component of memory; they may be influenced by other components.	1. Nonsemantic as well as semantic cues may aid retrieval of information from memory.
2. Some information in short-term store may be encoded semantically rather than acoustically.	2. There is no reliable means to control the level at which subjects in memory research process information.
3. The capacity of the short-term store may be larger than 7 ± 2 items depending upon how a chunk is defined.	

in responding to a cue to "recall the digits" as they are when responding to a cue to "recall the top line." So what is the significance of this finding? Merikle argues that if items in the sensory register are there in physical, unanalyzable form only, subjects could not "know" which were letters and which were digits. That sort of information, which is not inherent in the display itself, but in the nature of the items within the display, is stored much deeper in the subjects' memory. Thus, the sensory register appears not to be a separate and distinct component of memory after all. It may respond to information according to other kinds of information already stored in other components of the memory system.

More recently, Haber (1983) made a compelling, though largely logical and nonempirical, argument that we should not agonize to any great degree over the presence or the nature of the sensory register. A critical point he makes is that evidence for a sensory register has been found only under artificial laboratory conditions, which may mean that it is not likely to be relevant to memory processing in the real world. The sensory register may simply be an artifact of the psychology laboratory.

What about the short-term store and long-term store as separate components of a memory system? The three-component model proposes a short-term store of limited capacity (7±2 chunks), limited duration (less than 20 seconds), with information acoustically coded within it. The long-term store is seen as a nearly permanent and boundless storehouse of information coded semantically or in terms of its meaning to the individual.

Let's deal first with the acoustic coding proposal. Data continue to support the idea that information held for relatively brief periods are typically encoded in terms of their sounds. Considerable evidence has accumulated, however, that suggests that at least some semantic coding is possible in the short-term store. Consider, for example, the work of Shulman (1971, 1972). Subjects saw a list of ten words. Immediately afterward, they were shown another (probe) word and asked whether or not it was in the list they had just seen. When the probe word was not in the list but was a synonym for one of the words in the list, subjects often replied that yes, the word was in the list they had just seen. To make that sort of mistake, subjects must have stored the list in some semantic, meaningful way and not just in terms of how the words sounded.

Difficulties with the notion of acoustically encoding information into short-term store also arise when we try to account for some now classic data first reported by Bousfield in 1953. If a list of words (different nouns, for example) is presented to subjects in a random order, we would find that their immediate recall of the list is not random. Rather, their recall would reflect **category clustering** or the recalling of words according to semantic categories. For example, given a list that begins, *France, blue, golf, yellow, Edward, tennis, red, George, hockey, green . . . ,"* subjects cluster their recall into categories, something like: *"green, red, blue . . . tennis, golf, hockey . . . George, Edward,"* and so on. Recall involving category clustering, as you can see, is based on the meaning of the items held in the short-term store, not on their acoustic properties.

Yet another problem with the three-component model has to do with the capacity of the short-term store. We've noted that short-term store is said to hold between five and nine chunks of information, where a chunk is defined as a meaningful unit of information. This is all well and good until we begin to consider the realistic nature of what a chunk can be. Research evidence and our own experience tells us that the capacity of the short-term store is indeed about seven randomly presented letters. But we can also easily hold seven randomly presented three-letter words in the short-term store. In this case, the capacity of the short-term store seems to be twenty-one letters. Might we not also be able to hold in the short-term stores three simple concepts such as months of the year, days of the week, and seasons of the year? Now we've got "January, February, . . . Monday, Tuesday, . . . Summer, Fall, . . ." or twenty-three words and nearly 150 letters. Clearly, there are limits to the amount of information with which we can sensibly deal in active consciousness, and "7±2 chunks" may be as reasonable an estimate as any other. The problem is, however, that the terms, *chunk* and *capacity* are very imprecise ones when describing the properties of the short-term store. Short-term store, then, may have a greater capacity than the three-component model originally proposed.

The problems we've raised so far all deal with the three-component model of memory. But the levels of processing model has not gone without its share of criticism. For one thing, there is evidence that sometimes retrieval from memory can be enhanced more by nonsemantic cues than by semantic cues. Suppose that we show you a list of words and then ask you to recall words from the list. Suppose further that we help you out by providing cues to remind you of some of the words. Suppose one of the words is *scissors.* A cue such as __ *issors* is likely to be much more helpful than telling you that one of the words on the list is something we can use to cut paper (after Nelson & McEvoy, 1979).

A second problem with the levels of processing model involves coming to grips with exactly what is meant by terms such as *elaboration* or *depth of processing.* No matter what we may ask a subject to do when we present a stimulus (for example, "Count the letters."), we have no way of knowing what else the subject may be doing that may aid retrieval of that item on a subsequent test of recall. In other words, it is difficult for researchers to control the depth to which a subject processes information, because they have no way of peering into his or her head and knowing exactly how the information is being manipulated. For each of us, our memory, its processes, and its contents are private. Memory simply is not an observable phenomenon.

Before we take a different approach to understanding memory processes, let's summarize what we've covered so far. We've examined two models of human memory. The three-component model focuses on memory structures, calling for a separate sensory register, a short-term store, and a long-term store. The levels of processing model suggests that what matters most is the extent or depth to which materials are processed, but that there are limits on how much information we can process in a given period of time. Both of these models have been challenged and modified, but neither has been abandoned. Let's now return to our original definition of memory and concentrate more fully on the interrelated processes of encoding, storage, and retrieval. In the next section, we will highlight more practical applications of what cognitive psychology has learned about human memory.

PROCESSING AND FORGETTING INFORMATION: ENCODING, STORAGE, AND RETRIEVAL

Today, cognitive psychologists think of memory as a matter of processing information, whether it is into different stores or at different levels. Both the three-component and the levels of processing models assume that information is encoded, stored, and retrieved. The phrase "processing information" is a metaphor borrowed from computer science. A metaphor, as you probably know, is a means of comparison in which a phrase is used to describe an object or event figuratively. Common phrases such as "the autumn of one's life" and "food for thought" are examples of metaphors. We humans do not really process information exactly like the computer does, but from a theoretical viewpoint, cognitive psychologists have found it useful to compare such processes as how we sense, perceive, and think to the way a computer functions. Information processing, then, affords cognitive psychologists a framework from which to study memory and other cognitive processes.

The processing of information that is accomplished by our memories is sensibly continuous—we can't easily tell when or how information is put into storage, held there, or when or how it is brought forth from storage. Clearly, the processes of encoding, storage, and retrieval are interrelated and work together. Knowing how information will be retrieved from storage guides our strategies for encoding. (You study differently for a multiple-choice exam than you do for an essay exam.) Our ability to retrieve specific aspects of a stimulus is influenced by how we encode it in the first place. (You will do better on a test if you study the material meaningfully as opposed to superficially.) For sake of clarity as well as to see what further insights we might gain about memory, we will discuss encoding, storage, and retrieval separately.

Encoding

As we have said now a number of times, encoding basically involves getting material into memory. More than that, how we encode information is likely to affect our ability to retrieve information later. We have already seen that to some degree, encoding information involves our paying attention. We've also seen that if we can make material more meaningful during encoding, we may decrease the likelihood of forgetting that information later. Let's consider these two issues further.

Automatic Versus Effortful Processing. Psychologists (and educators) have long known that the retrieval of information is enhanced by the extent to which one practices or rehearses that information. Practicing rehearsing information is called **effortful processing.** You, too, from your experience as a student know this to be true: the more you study, the more you concentrate on your studying, and the more likely you will do well on a classroom exam.

Your own experience also tells you that you have stored away in your memory information that you know you never rehearsed in the first place. Somehow, without any effort on your part, information gets encoded into

Students who concentrate on their studies and rehearse the material they are learning will be able to retrieve that information more easily on a test or in class.

your memory. Such observations have led psychologists to suggest that, indeed, some information is encoded automatically. This sort of memory encoding is called **automatic processing,** and refers to the formation of memories of events and experiences with little or no attention or effort (Hasher & Zacks, 1979; Posner & Snyder, 1975; Shiffrin & Schneider, 1977).

The sorts of information that seem to be processed automatically tend to be related directly to frequency (How many times have you read the word *encode* today?), time (When did you meet your best friend for the first time?), place (Where in the textbook is the graph of Sperling's data located?), and significance (the Alaskan oil spill). Automatic processing, then, allows us to learn with relative ease, which, of course, makes life a lot less taxing than if everything that we learned had to first be processed effortfully. Unfortunately, and perhaps because of the complexity of the material, textbook learning is effortful, not automatic.

Meaningful Elaboration. When encoding is not automatic, it is said to be effortful, where the most useful effort involves our attempt to make new or difficult material meaningful. (This is the process that Atkinson and Shiffrin called "elaboration.")

There are two conclusions that we offer at the outset concerning elaborative encoding. First, it seems quite clear that with regard to rehearsal, more is better than less.

The second conclusion concerns **encoding specificity,** the principle that *how* we encode information may determine our ability to retrieve it later. For example, suppose that someone reads you a list of words you are to recall at some later, unspecified time. The list contains the word *beet,* along with a number of terms related to music such as *melody, tune,* and *jazz.* When asked if the list contained the names of any vegetables, you may report that it did not, because you encoded *beet* as *beat* and never thought of the red, tuberous vegetable while you were rehearsing the list (Flexser & Tulving, 1978). Retrieving information from memory, then, is related to how that information is encoded.

List to be remembered:
   cheese   milk   eggs   taco sauce   lettuce

  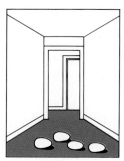  

FIGURE 8.10
The method of loci. Items to be remembered are visualized in certain well-known locations.

A number of experiments have made the point that the meaningful elaboration of information during encoding is helpful and probably necessary for the formation of useful memories. Imagine, for example, trying to remember the following passage:

> With hocked gems financing him, our hero bravely defied all scornful laughter that tried to prevent his scheme. "Your eyes deceive," he had said, "An egg, not a table correctly typifies this unexplored planet." Now three sturdy sisters sought proof. Forging along, sometimes through calm vastness, yet more often over turbulent peaks and valleys, days became weeks as many doubters spread fearful rumors about the edge. At last from nowhere welcomed winged creatures appeared, signifying momentous success.

How do you think you would have done on this task—could you have remembered this passage very well? Probably not, for it is a strangely worded paragraph. However, what if, *before* you read the paragraph, you were told that it had a title: "Columbus Discovers America"? Do you think you might have encoded the story differently and so, improved your recall? This is exactly what happened to subjects who were asked to do so in an experiment (Dooling & Lachman, 1971). But, if subjects were given a title like this one *after* they had read and processed the story, recall was not improved (Bransford & Johnson, 1972). Apparently, the time to make information meaningful is when it is being encoded.

Is there a "best" way to encode information? Many memory experts argue that encoding information through visual imagery has a very positive effect on retrieval. Forming visual images is considered a different process than attempting to make new material meaningful by forming semantic or verbal associations (Paivio, 1969). Some words evoke visual images more readily than do others. The image-producing value of words can be rated. Words of high imagery value, such as *balloon* and *rainbow*, are much easier to recall than are words of low-imagery value, such as *session* or *treason*. This is true even for words rated to be equally meaningful (Paivio, 1986).

Improving Memory. Visual images can be used to encode information, and this forms the basis of **mnemonic devices**, which are special techniques or strategies consciously employed in an attempt to improve memory. Some helpful hints for improving memory are purely semantic in nature, such as Bower and Clark's narrative chaining technique (1969). The idea here is that when faced with having to remember a series of apparently

List to be remembered:
cheese   milk   eggs   taco sauce   lettuce

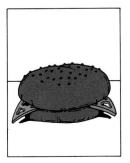    

FIGURE 8.11
The peg-word method. Items to be remembered are associated with nouns that rhyme with numbers.

unrelated terms, memory is enhanced if the terms can be woven into a meaningful story during encoding or rehearsal. But most mnemonic devices involve encoding with visual imagery.

How is visual imagery used in mnemonic devices? The basic idea is to form a visual image of the material to be remembered, tying that image whenever possible to something commonplace and readily available in memory. A classic example is the method of loci (see Figure 8.10). Suppose you wish to remember a short shopping list without writing it down. Your list consists of the following five items: cheese, milk, eggs, taco sauce, and lettuce. First, think of a familiar location, perhaps your house. Next, mentally "walk" through your house, visually "placing" different items from your list at locations or loci in the house: a package of cheese is hanging from the doorknob on the back door, milk is dripping from the kitchen faucet, eggs are lying on the floor of the hall, a bottle of taco sauce is in the easy chair, and the lettuce is on the sofa. Then, in the store, you mentally retrace your path through the house and note what you have "stored" at the different loci. Any familiar location will do the trick, as long as you can visually imagine the items to be remembered in the various "landmarks."

A similar technique is called the peg-word method (Miller, Galanter & Pribram, 1960). As with the method of loci, the goal here is to visually associate the new with the familiar (see Figure 8.11). In the peg-word method, the familiar material is a set of "mental pegs" that you already have in memory. One example of these pegs is to take the numbers from one to ten and rhyme each number with a peg word, for example, one is a bun, two is a shoe, three is a tree, four is a door, five is a hive, and so forth. Now returning to your grocery list, you imagine the package of cheese in a hamburger bun, a shoe full of milk, eggs dangling from a tree, taco sauce on a door, and the lettuce on top of a bee hive. In the grocery store, you review each of the peg words in order and recall the item visually associated with it. At first, these techniques may seem a bit silly, but there is ample research data suggesting that they do, in fact, work (Marshark, Richman, Yuille, & Hunt, 1987).

In summary, the two most important things to remember about encoding is (1) that it is the means by which information is placed into memory, and (2) the deeper you process information during encoding, the more likely that you will be able to recall that information. Mnemonic devices or strategies that aid the encoding process through visual imagery are useful in improving memory for some information, particularly lists. Now that we've seen how encoding influences memory processing, let's consider the nature of memory storage.

Storage

There are three important issues to discuss regarding memory storage. (1) In what form are memories stored? This issue relates to encoding or forming memory codes for incoming information. We've already mentioned this point, noting that we seem to store memories using a variety of different representations, including visual, auditory, and semantic codes. (2) What are the physiological bases of memory storage? That is, what parts of the brain are involved in storing information, and how is the nervous system changed when memories are processed? These are questions we'll examine in the last section of the chapter. (3) Once memories are formed, for how long will they remain in storage? Let's turn to this question now.

The first thing to consider is how we can approach the question empirically. Is the permanency of memory a phenomenon that lends itself to scientific scrutiny? Only with great difficulty. Just think about how difficult it is to demonstrate that a memory even exists. An individual may claim to have no recollection of a past event. "If it happened, I don't remember it," he or she may say. Perhaps the event never really occurred. Perhaps it did, but the person is lying. Perhaps the experience was never encoded into memory in the first place. Perhaps a memory was formed, but somehow it decayed and faded away. Perhaps the event was encoded into memory and is still stored there, but at least for the moment, it cannot be retrieved. To say the least, understanding the storage of memories is no simple task.

Be that as it may, once again our own experiences as well as research data both suggest that some memories seem to last for a very long time indeed. Actually, the first experiment to determine the duration of memory was reported by Herman Ebbinghaus in 1885. Ebbinghaus memorized a list of thirteen nonsense syllables (such as *dax*, *wuj*, *lep*, and *pib*). He then assessed how long it took to relearn a list after intervals of differing length (from a few minutes up to 31 days). Ebbinghaus found that much of what he learned was lost very quickly—within a day or two—but even after 31 days, he could still recall some of the original information (see Figure 8.12).

Most psychologists agree that once memories are formed, many, but not all, are stored permanently (Loftus & Loftus, 1980). Some memories, such as flashbulb memories—extremely lucid recollections of important

Hermann Ebbinghaus

FIGURE 8.12
The Ebbinghaus (1885) forgetting curve.

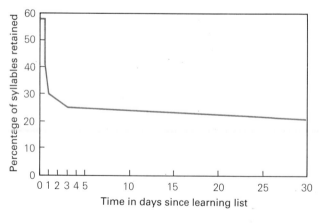

FIGURE 8.13
The forgetting curve for Spanish vocabulary (Bahrick, 1984).

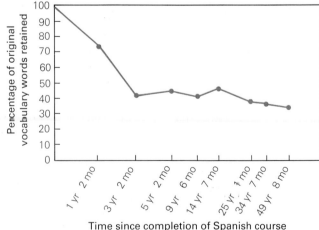

Vivid memories of important events like where you were when the space shuttle Challenger *exploded are not easily forgotten.*

events—are remarkably durable. Can you recall where you were and what you were doing when you learned of the explosion of the space shuttle *Challenger*? Many people can. Other kinds of memories, though, are not so resilient and are forgotten in time.

Although his research does not directly address the issue of permanence, some recent studies by Harry Bahrick and his associates are at least helpful in understanding the difficulty of studying permanence of memory (Bahrick, 1983, 1984a, 1984b; Bahrick, Bahrick, & Wittlinger, 1975).

Bahrick used a cross-sectional approach in his research. That is, he tested the memories of people of different ages, all of whom had accumulated similar information at different times in their past. For example, Bahrick has been interested in his subjects' ability to recall the names and faces of high school classmates, Spanish learned in high school or college, or significant aspects of a small town in which all the subjects had been raised.

The tests of memory were given to everyone in the study at about the same time. Obviously though, the retention intervals involved for the older subjects were much longer than were those for the younger subjects. Bahrick found that his subjects remembered considerable amounts of information without further use, elaboration, or rehearsal even almost fifty years after learning. In fact, retention scores showed little decline for the period between 3 years after learning and nearly 50 years after learning (see Figure 8.13). About the only factor that significantly affected subjects' recall ability was the degree to which the original material was learned (which shows us once again the importance of initial encoding).

We must view these data cautiously, however. They may tell us more about retrieval of information than they do about storage of information. That is, some of the items that subjects attempted to recall but couldn't still may have been stored in memory but just couldn't be retrieved. Thus, for information that is not practiced or otherwise rehearsed elaborately, as in Bahrick's research, the problem may not so much be a matter of storage but of retrieval. Let's look more closely at retrieval.

Researchers have found that there is little decline in recall of things like the names and faces of our high school classmates even 50 years after learning occurred.

Retrieval

Recall that retrieval is the active process of extracting information out of memory. For example, if asked the simple question, "What is the capital of the United States?" you somehow retrieve that information from your long-term store. Before the question was posed, you probably were not consciously thinking about Washington, D.C., but because in the past the answer was learned and stored in memory, you were able to respond correctly. Essentially, retrieving the name is a matter of transferring that information from long-term store to short-term store. This is true for nearly all instances of retrieval.

So to start, we assume that the information one is trying to retrieve is, in fact, stored in memory in the first place. Up to now, we have spoken of retrieval only generally. Now it is time to concentrate on those variables that seem to most strongly influence retrieval. We'll focus on three issues: the role of retrieval cues, retrieval as a process of reconstruction, and interference and retrieval. Beginning with retrieval cues, we'll look at each of these variables in turn.

Retrieval Cues. Our retrieval of information from memory may be influenced greatly by how we are asked the question. If we were to ask you to name one thing that you had to eat yesterday, you might not even understand what it was we were asking. The more we can tell you about what it is that we want you to recall (the more retrieval cues we provide) the more likely it is that you will remember and name what we have in mind. "You know. It was at breakfast. You had some juice, eggs, and what else?" If you still don't recall, we could provide even more cues: "Come now; it's made from bread, is rather crunchy on the outside, and you covered it with grape jelly." Well, by now we've provided you with so many cues you can hardly fail to recall that you had toast for breakfast.

Which question is more difficult?

(1) What is the name of a psychologist associated with classical conditioning?

(2) Who is the Russian Nobel Prize-winning physiologist who studied the salivation reflex in dogs, and who we best associate with classical conditioning?

What we know about retrieval cues tells us that the second question should be much easier to answer than the first. Why? Because the first question could be answered a number of different ways since there are a number of different psychologists associated with classical conditioning, including Ivan Pavlov and Robert Rescorla (Chapter 7). The second question offers more retrieval cues (Russian, Nobel Prize winner, salivation in dogs), removing any ambiguity regarding the correct answer (Tulving & Osler, 1968).

As you might guess, the usefulness of retrieval cues often depends on encoding specificity or how the material to be retrieved was originally encoded. Encoding specificity is quite general in its impact on retrieval. In one rather strange example, skilled scuba divers served as subjects and learned a list of words either submerged under the water or on land (Godden & Baddeley, 1975). Their ability to recall the lists were later tested in either the same or a different environment. That's right, the variable of interest in this study was where subjects learned the list: in or out of the water. The results showed that when lists were learned under water, they were recalled much better under water than on dry land, and lists learned on land were recalled better on land than in the water. The context in which information is learned or processed influences our ability to retrieve that information. Do you know the implication for studying? To improve recall of material to be tested, perhaps the best study technique is to review that material under conditions similar to those during the test.

Empirical evidence also suggests that memory is better when the subject's mental or emotional state at retrieval matches the emotional state at encoding, a phenomenon called **state-dependent memory.** Usually, the mood of the subject is manipulated experimentally by hypnosis (Bower, 1981), or through drug-induced changes in consciousness (Eich, Weingartner, Stillman, & Gillin, 1975). Next, the subject is given a list of items to memorize. Later when the subject may or may not be experiencing the same or a similar mental or emotional state, he or she is asked to recall the items on the list. As we have mentioned already, retrieval is typically best when the subject's mood or emotional state at retrieval matches what it was during encoding of the original items.

Thus, retrieval cues may take different forms ranging from semantic materials associated with the items to be recalled to the emotional state of the subject during encoding. Remember, too, that retrieval cues are the basis for the mnemonic devices that we discussed earlier. The moral here is this: Retrieval cues play an important role in remembering.

Retrieval as a Reconstructive Process. Regardless of our ability to use retrieval cues to prompt recall, our ability to remember is less than perfect even at its best. Certain details are left out, other details are embellished, and yet others may be added, simply to make the story better. Remembering is not always a matter of retrieval; sometimes it is a reconstructive process. This observation carries with it serious implications. Although research on memory as an actively reconstructive process has had a long history in psychology dating back to studies by Sir Frederic Bartlett (1932), current interest has been triggered by concerns over the practical matters of eyewitness testimony (Wells & Loftus, 1979). Let's look at two examples of the more recent work in this area.

R*emembering is not always a matter of retrieval, sometimes it is a reconstructive process.*

In one study conducted by Elizabeth Loftus and her colleagues (Loftus, Miller, & Burns, 1978), subjects were shown a series of slides of what appeared to be a real traffic accident. One of the slides showed a red automobile stopped at a stop sign. After viewing all the slides, half the subjects were asked a few questions, including, "Did another car pass the red car when it was parked at the yield sign?" Other subjects were asked about the red car being passed while at the stop sign. Later, all subjects were shown two slides, one with the car parked at a yield sign, and one with the car parked at a stop sign. Their task was simply to identify the slide that was in the original set. Subjects who had been asked the yield sign question made nearly twice the number of errors as those who had been asked the stop sign question. In other words, the subjects' memory of what they saw was influenced by a subsequent question they had been asked (Loftus, Miller, & Burns, 1978). In fact, memory of the slide had been reconstructed based on that question.

Loftus' work has implications for evaluating eyewitness testimony. Consider an even more telling study (Loftus & Palmer, 1974). Subjects saw a film clip of an auto accident and were then questioned as if they were eyewitnesses to the accident. Half of the subjects were asked, "How fast were the cars going when they hit each other?" The other half were asked, "How fast were the cars going when they smashed into each other?" Several days later, both groups of subjects were asked whether they recalled seeing broken glass at the scene of the accident. More subjects who had been asked about the cars smashing into each other than subjects asked about the cars hitting each other remembered the broken glass. Interestingly, the film clip showed no broken glass! According to Loftus, these subjects' reconstruction of the accident was influenced by the question posed afterwards: two cars smashing into each other connotes more damage, including broken glass, than does two cars hitting each other. Our reconstruction of past events, then, can be influenced by subsequent experiences.

A different task was used by Spiro (1980). In this study, subjects were first asked to read either of two presumably true stories about a couple engaged to be married—Bob and Margie. In both stories, Bob does not want to have children, and although reluctant at first to share his feelings with Margie, he finally does so. In one version of the story, Margie does not want to have children either, but in the second version she is horrified, because having a family has long been one of her dearest dreams. After the subjects read their version of the story, the experimenter casually mentioned that the story is true, and then added that either a) Bob and Margie are now happily married, or b) they broke up and never saw each other again. This added piece of information was consistent with the story for some subjects and inconsistent for others. Recall of the original story was then tested at intervals of two days, three weeks, and six weeks. After three weeks had passed, the reconstructive nature of memory was evident. Subjects who had received consistent information after they read the story made significantly fewer errors in their recall. Those subjects who were told inconsistent information after reading the story often changed the facts of the story to help explain the inconsistency between the story and what they had been told later about Bob and Margie. For example, if the story claimed that Bob did not want children, but the subject was told that the couple was now happily married, the subject was likely to "remember" that in the story, Bob changed his mind after talking with Margie. In the original story, though, Bob never changed his mind!

So, sometimes we remember things accurately and other times we remember them differently than they really occurred. At still other times, and despite trying our hardest, we simply can't recall those things at all. In this case, cognitive psychologists suspect that interference may be the culprit in forgetting. Let's now consider how the interfering presence of other memories "get in the way" of our ability to retrieve information from

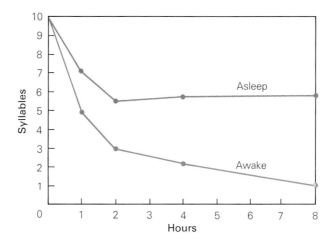

memory. (Notice how we have switched now to the mode of discussing memories as if they were events or objects, "things" that interfere with each other rather than a process.)

Retrieval and Interference. That the formation of some memories may interfere with the retrieval of others is a near classic assumption in psychology. Data can be traced to an early study by Jenkins and Dallenbach (1924), who discovered that people are less likely to remember information after an interval of wakefulness than after an interval of sleep, presumably because of new memories that are formed when one is awake (see Figure 8.14).

Subsequent research soon showed that there are two types of interference with retrieval. Sometimes we experience **retroactive interference.** That is, when we try to retrieve information, other information, which we have learned more recently, interferes. The top panel in Figure 8.15 diagrams how retroactive interference occurs. You now may have difficulty recalling some of the details of Chapter 3 because you have probably studied at least two or three of the subsequent chapters. You also probably have a hard time recalling the presents you received on your seventh birthday because you have had a number of birthdays since. If your seventh birthday had been just yesterday, you would likely demonstrate perfect recall. When the memories that interfere with retrieval are formed *after* the learning that is being tested, we have retroactive interference.

At other times retrieval is impaired by **proactive interference,** in which our ability to recall new information is reduced because of information we have learned previously (see Figure 8.15 bottom panel). Let's assume you took a Spanish class for two years in high school, and that you are now taking a French class in college. You find that some of the knowledge and study skills from your high school class are beneficial. But almost as often, you discover that when you try to recall some French, Spanish pops up instead. This is interference, and because the interfering learning took place *before* the learning that is being tested, it is called proactive interference. Indeed, one reason that you may not be able to recall with certainty what birthday presents you received last year is that you have had so many birthdays before.

As reasonable and intuitive as the principle of interference may be, it has not gone unchallenged by today's cognitive psychologists. No one refutes the basic reality of interference as a variable that can and does influence retrieval. The issue now largely revolves around the kinds of information and memory tasks that are most susceptible to interference

FIGURE 8.15

*Retroactive and proactive
interference.*

Retroactive Interference

Group	Initial Learning	Retention Interval	Retention Test
Experimental	Learn A	Learn B	Recall A
Control	Learn A		Recall A

Proactive Interference

Group	Initial Learning	Retention Interval	Retention Test
Experimental	Learn A Learn B		Recall B
Control	Learn B		Recall B

effects. Specifically, the kinds of recall tasks subjects are asked to perform in the laboratory are affected by interference, although in real life situations, such effects may not be so powerful. It seems, for example, that meaningful prose such as that you might find in novels is very resistant to interference. In the lab, however, interference is most often demonstrated in tasks involving unrelated words and nonsense syllables (Anderson & Myrow, 1971).

In sum, retrieval is the process of getting information out of memory and into our conscious awareness. Retrieval is enhanced by cues that clue people to different kinds of information stored in their memories. Sometimes though, what we remember isn't exactly accurate: that is, sometimes retrieval is a reconstructive process, especially in those situations where we are asked to recall specific aspects of past events. Finally, retrieval can be impaired by two types of interference: retroactive, in which new information interferes with retrieval of previously learned information, and proactive, in which previously learned information interferes with retrieval of more recently learned information.

Up to this point, we have been using the language of the cognitive psychologist and talking about memory metaphorically in information processing terms used to describe the operation of computers (encoding, storage, and retrieval). In the last section of this chapter, we'll look at memory from an entirely different and more concrete perspective. We turn now to an exploration of the biological bases of memory.

BIOLOGICAL BASES OF MEMORY

Common sense tells us that memory processing occurs in our brains. Stimuli from the environment that are above some threshold level activate neurons in our sense organs. Neural impulses race from receptor sites, from neuron to neuron, from synapse to synapse, to the brain. There, changes are made in the neural substrate that somehow represent the formation of a new memory. With recollection or retrieval, that change in brain structure or function is somehow re-experienced. This is easy to say and to express in theoretical generalities but difficult to support with evidence. Where in the brain does memory happen? How are experiences recorded in the brain? How are stored events re-experienced? We are still far from having clear answers to questions like these. But neuroscientists have learned a great deal about the brain's role in memory, and in this section, we'll review some of what they have discovered.

Insights from the Study of Amnesia

Amnesia is the profound loss of once-demonstrated memory skills. It occurs in two major forms. **Retrograde amnesia** refers to a loss of the ability to retrieve memories of one's past, particularly episodic memories or memories involving one's personal experiences. Retrograde amnesia may cover only limited segments of one's past. For example, someone may lose their memory of everything that happened to them between the ages of eleven and fourteen. Sometimes the forgetting is complete and all memories up to a certain point in time are lost.

Psychologists have found it more useful to study the memory skills of people suffering from **anterograde amnesia,** a condition in which the person can remember events from before a certain time but has difficulty forming memories of events that occur after that time. H.M., to whom you were introduced at the beginning of the chapter, suffered from anterograde amnesia caused by surgical damage to his hippocampus. Recall that H.M. can remember events in his life that occurred prior to surgery, but he cannot remember experiences that he has had after the surgery. Consider, for example, H.M.'s doomed attempt to recall the number 584 (Milner, 1970).

People who have difficulty recalling past personal experiences may be suffering from retrograde amnesia.

Thus he was able to retain the number 584 for at least 15 minutes, by continuously working out elaborate mnemonic schemes. When asked how he had been able to retain the number for so long, he replied: "It's easy. You just remember 8, subtract it from 17 and it leaves 9. Divide 9 in half and you get 5 and 4, and there you are: 584. Easy." A minute or two later, H.M. was unable to recall either the number 584 or any of the associated complex train of thought; in fact, he did not know that he had been given a number to remember because in the meantime the examiner had introduced a new topic.

A couple of things seem clear from the study of H.M. over the years. The hippocampus is not involved in the retrieval of memories made long ago but is crucial in the formation of new memories. By now you know not to accept such bold statements without some reservation. In fact, recent evidence suggests that H.M. does demonstrate some degree of retrograde amnesia as well as anterograde amnesia, so his problems are more than just a matter of an inability to consolidate new experiences into long-term store (Corkin, 1984). It is also true that animals whose hippocampal regions are lesioned do not always show the types of amnesic effects one might expect on the basis of H.M.'s experience (for example, Squire, 1987). So while the hippocampus seems to play an important role in forming new memories, that role is not yet clearly understood.

As it happens, there *are* some new experiences that people with anterograde amnesia—including H.M.—can remember beyond just a few seconds (Mishkin & Appenzeller, 1987; Squire, 1982). Those experiences involve learning to perform a task, like navigating your way through a maze, or writing legibly while watching what you are doing in a mirror. When H.M. is given daily practice on these kinds of tasks, he shows absolutely no recollection of ever having tried such a thing before. But, as he continues his daily practice, his performance on the task shows definite improvement—as if something about doing the task is retained in procedural memory. Current thinking is that information of a procedural sort (remembering *how* to do something) is processed differently from information of a declarative sort (remembering that in fact, you did it). The former may somehow bypass the hippocampus on its way to being stored.

FIGURE 8.16
Aplysia *is a marine snail with a simple nervous system, which makes it an ideal subject for research investigating the biological bases of learning. Kandel and Schwartz (1982) found that classical conditioning of the gill withdrawal reflex produces increases in the amount of serotonin released by particular neurons located in the siphon.*

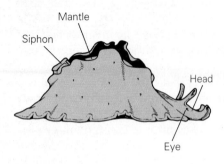

Mantle

Siphon

Head

Eye

F*ormation of memories involves a change in the nervous system at the level of the neuron.*

Memory occurs in the brain, and the hippocampus appears to be the structure that plays an important role in the encoding of long-term memories. Surely though, memory processes must be operating at a more fundamental level than specific brain structures. Next, we'll look at what occurs in individual neurons and synapses during the encoding, storage, and retrieval of information.

Insights at the Neural Level

When studying memory at the level of the individual neuron, neuroscientists have been drawn to consider the synapse as the most likely site of structural or chemical change. Why? Because, as you may recall from Chapter 4, the synapse is the place in the nervous system where information is exchanged between neurons. Unfortunately, studying changes within the nervous system of a living human is difficult, if only because of the sheer number of neurons and synapses. Fortunately, there are a number of more primitive creatures whose nervous systems are smaller and less complex and whose basic neural structure and function is similar to ours. By studying the changes that learning produces in simpler but similar nervous systems, neuroscientists make generalizations as to how memories might be formed within our own nervous system.

Because its nervous system is made up of only about 20,000 neurons, the *Aplysia*, a small snail-like creature (actually it's a slug) is a favorite organism for such studies (see Figure 8.16). In addition, the *Aplysia* is quite capable of learning and remembering simple behaviors (Kandel & Schwartz, 1982). Of particular interest to Kandel and Schwartz was the *Aplysia*'s gill-withdrawal reflex (the withdrawal of the gills in response to water movement). Using electric shock as the unconditional stimulus, Kandel and Schwartz classically conditioned the gill-withdrawal reflex. They were not interested in merely discovering if *Aplysia* were capable of simple learning. What they wanted to discover was whether or not learning is accompanied by corresponding chemical changes in the animal's nervous system. And that is exactly what they found: conditioning the gill-withdrawal reflex produced changes in the amount of neurotransmitter substance produced and released by sensory neurons in the animal's siphon. After conditioning, measurably more serotonin was released at certain synapses than before conditioning. When drugs were later used to block the effects of the serotonin release, the snail seemed to "forget" what it had learned. Thus, it is possible that forming memories is largely a matter of creating neural pathways throughout areas of the brain by increasing the production of serotonin at synapses along those pathways.

Other researchers agree that experience forms a record in the nervous system at the level of the synapse, but they argue that it is the postsynaptic membrane that is most affected. What matters, these researchers claim, is not the release of more neurotransmitters (a presynaptic phenomenon) but physical changes—often simply increases—in the available receptor sites on the postsynaptic side of the synapse (Lynch & Baudry, 1984). When synapses in some particular neural circuit are used, and reused, more and more receptor sites are created. When this circuit is stimulated again, the neural pathway most likely to be taken will be the one taken before where more receptor sites are now available.

Whether or not the formation of new memories is influenced more by presynaptic or postsynaptic activities, the important thing for you to remember is that formation of memories involves a change in the nervous system at the level of the neuron.

BOUNDARIES AND FRONTIERS

That memories are formed at the level of the neuron is a profoundly important discovery if only because of the doors it opens for future research. At present, our understanding of the biology of memory is bounded by our understanding of neurotransmission. But as neuroscientists push back those boundaries, we are likely to uncover more specific information about the biochemical basis of memory. That kind of knowledge—how neurotransmitters influence receptor sites during learning—is likely to lead to the development of drugs and physical therapies that restore memories to the absentminded and enhance memory in the rest of us.

In reality, some of those boundaries have already begun to give way, and neuroscientists are developing technologies that have already proved to be clinically successful in improving memory in certain populations of people. Although serotonin is involved in memory of the gill-withdrawal reflex in the marine snail, *Aplysia*, acetylcholine seems to be the neurotransmitter involved in some memory processes in humans. For example, acetylcholine appears to be involved in Alzheimer's disease, which affects mainly older people and involves a progressive deterioration of mental functioning, especially memory. People suffering from this disease have been found to have low levels of acetylcholine in their brains. The obvious research question that this finding raises is whether increases of the level of acetylcholine in the brain will improve memory for Alzheimer's patients.

Research on drugs and other chemicals that might enhance memory is not far enough along to ensure their safe use and the degree and permanancy of their effects on improving memory. Clearly though, the discovery of the biochemical basis of memory represents an important frontier in memory research and is one that has tremendous potential for broadening learning and cognitive functioning for many people.

Discovering that a drug or family of drugs enhances memory does not necessarily mean that we understand how memories are formed or that we are sure of the biological underpinnings of memory. In fact, knowing that a drug has a particular effect on behavior doesn't necessarily entail understanding how that drug works within the nervous system. (Recall that observing a behavior is, though, the first step toward an explanation of behavior). To develop an understanding of the biological basis of memory means that more research like Kandel's is necessary. Kandel's breakthrough in revealing the role of neurotransmitters in memory inspires a whole new set of research questions. Kandel himself has raised several interesting problems in need of solution (Kandel & Schwartz. 1982). What kinds of changes within cells explain the long-term store of information? Do memory processes involve specific genes? Is the biochemistry of memory related only to synaptic activity or are other neuronal processes involved? To these questions we can add a few of our own. What biochemical differences exist between short-term and long-term store of information? What synaptic changes occur during retrieval, that is, during recollection of a past event? How does elaboration or rehearsal of information affect the kind and degree of synaptic activity?

These are important questions because they represent unambiguous boundaries in our knowledge of learning and memory. Answering them will not only be of scientific value, but also of applied value as well. Once the biological basis of memory is understood, psychologists may be able to develop broad-based programs for enhancing memory and treating psychological disorders, like Alzheimer's disease, that involve memory deficits. To be sure, these questions and others similar to them are at the frontier of today's biopsychological research in learning and memory.

CONCEPT SUMMARY

HOW PSYCHOLOGISTS VIEW MEMORY

- Is memory considered to be a process, place, or event? Why? (pp. 267–270)
- What are the functions of each component in the three-component model of memory? (pp. 268–272)
- How does Sperling's research provide evidence for the existence of the sensory register? (pp. 268–269)
- In terms of capacity and permanence, how does the long-term store differ from the short-term store? (pp. 269–272)
- What kinds of memories are kept in the long-term store? (pp. 271–272)
- What are the main differences between the three-component model and the levels of processing model? (pp. 268–275)
- How does rehearsal affect our ability to remember? (pp. 273–275)
- In what ways have the three-component and levels of processing models been modified by recent research findings? (pp. 275–278)

PROCESSING INFORMATION: ENCODING, STORAGE, AND RETRIEVAL

- To cognitive psychologists, what does it mean to say that "information is processed"? (p. 278)

- What role does encoding play in the formation of memories? (pp. 278–280)
- How does the principle of encoding specificity influence memory? (pp. 279–280)
- What is the role of visual imagery in mnemonic devices? How does the method of loci differ from the peg-word method? (pp. 280–281)
- What difficulties are encountered when one tries to study storage of memories? (p. 282)
- Once stored, how permanent are memories? (pp. 282–283)
- What is the role of retrieval cues in recall? (pp. 284–285)
- In what sense is memory sometimes said to be reconstructed? (pp. 285–287)
- How is retrieval affected by interference? (pp. 287–288)

BIOLOGICAL BASES OF MEMORY

- What have studies of amnesia told us about the biological bases of memory? Specifically, what have memory researchers learned about the role of the brain through studying H.M. and his inability to recall recent events? (pp. 288–289)
- What did Kandel and Schwartz's study of *Aplysia* tell us about the relationship between the formation of memories and changes in the nervous system? (p. 290)

KEY TERMS AND CONCEPTS

HOW PSYCHOLOGISTS VIEW MEMORY

Memory The cognitive processes of encoding, storing, and retrieving information. (p. 266)

Encoding The active process of putting stimuli into a form that can be used by our memory system. Encoding is simply a matter of placing information into memory. (p. 266)

Storage The process of maintaining information in memory for future use. (p. 266)

Retrieval The active processes of locating and using stored information. (p. 266)

Three-component Model The model of memory proposed by Atkinson and Shiffrin, which postulates a sensory register (or store) that "picks up" and briefly holds stimuli from the environment, a short-term store of limited capacity and a long-term store where information is kept with some permanency. (p. 267)

Sensory Register The first component of the three-component model in which the physical features of a stimulus are stored for extremely brief durations. (p. 268)

Short-term Store The second component of the three-component model. This store has a limited capacity (7 ± 2 chunks of information) and limited duration (less than 20 seconds). Information that enters short-term store is encoded acoustically. (p. 269)

Chunk The representation in memory of a single, meaningful concept. (p. 270)

Long-term Store The third component of the three-component model in which information is represented on a permanent or nearly permanent basis. (p. 271)

Episodic Memory A type of memory found in long-term store that serves as a record of our life's experiences. Events stored there are quite literally autobiographical. (p. 272)

Semantic Memory A type of memory found in long-term store that houses data, facts, and other information, including your vocabulary. (p. 272)

Procedural Memory The portion of long-term store where our knowledge of simple learned associations and our knowledge of how to perform well-learned habits is stored. (p. 272)

Levels of Processing Model   A model of memory based on the work of Craik and Lockhart, which holds that memory is information processing. The deeper or more meaningfully that information is processed, the better our memory of that information. This model also proposes that memory has a boundless capacity and that it can hold information indefinitely. (p. 272)

Maintenance Rehearsal   The rote repetition of a given rehearsal strategy, perhaps just by repeating a given item over and over again. (p. 273)

Elaborative Rehearsal   The processing of information on a deeper or more meaningful level, such as forming associations, attending to the meaning of the material, thinking about it, and so on. (p. 273)

Category Clustering   The recalling of words according to semantic categories. (p. 277)

PROCESSING INFORMATION: ENCODING, STORAGE, AND RETRIEVAL

Effortful Processing   Practicing or rehearsing information. (p. 278)

Automatic Processing   The formation of memories or events and experiences with little or no attention or effort. (p. 279)

Encoding Specificity   The principle that how we encode information may determine our ability to retrieve it later. (p. 279)

Mnemonic Devices   Special techniques or strategies consciously employed in an attempt to improve memory. (p. 280)

State-dependent Memory   The tendency to recall information better when the subject's mental or emotional state at retrieval matches that during encoding. (p. 285)

Retroactive Interference   The kind of interference in recall that is caused when recently learned information disrupts our ability to remember older information. (p. 287)

Proactive Interference   The kind of interference in recall that is caused when previously learned information disrupts our ability to remember newer information. (p. 287)

PHYSIOLOGICAL BASIS OF MEMORY

Amnesia   The profound loss of once-demonstrated memory skills. It occurs in two major forms, retrograde amnesia and anterograde amnesia. (p. 289)

Retrograde Amnesia   The loss of the ability to retrieve memories of one's past, particularly episodic memories or memories involving personal experiences. (p. 289)

Anterograde Amnesia   A condition in which the person can remember events from before a certain time but has difficulty forming memories of events that occur after that time. H.M., to whom you were introduced at the beginning of the chapter, suffered from anterograde amnesia caused by surgical damage to his hippocampus. (p. 289)

ADDITIONAL SOURCES OF INFORMATION

Ashcraft, M. H. (1989). *Human memory and cognition.* Glenview, IL: Scott, Foresman. This upper-level undergraduate text is a well written and thoughtful consideration of memory and its processes. The book's discussion of memory is placed in the larger context of cognitive psychology, so you can expect to find coverage of several other topics as well, especially language, decision making, reasoning, and problem solving (all topics we discuss in the next chapter).

Cermack, L. S. (1975). *Improving your memory.* New York: Norton. Although dated, this book serves as one of
the better sources of information on learning to use mnemonic devices.

Neisser, U. (1982). *Memory observed: Remembering in natural contexts.* San Francisco: Freeman. This interesting book discusses people's abilities to recall events in their own lives and in terms of their own experiences. Included in the book is John Dean's recollection of events involved in the Watergate break-in as given in testimony before a congressional committee and compared to the Nixon tapes. (Although Dean's testimony captured the essence of Watergate, his memory of the exact details was poor.)

9 Thinking and Language

INFORMATION, SYMBOLS, AND CONCEPTS *(296–304)*

The Computational Metaphor   Organizing Knowledge with Concepts

The way computers process information provides a useful analogy for studying human thinking. According to this analogy, human cognition involves computational processing of symbols.

REASONING *(304–308)*

Deductive Reasoning   Inductive Reasoning

One of the fundamental types of thinking is reasoning. There are two types of reasoning: deductive and inductive. Deductive reasoning is used to describe knowledge that necessarily follows from the truth of our observations of the world around us, whereas inductive reasoning provides the basis for discovering new knowledge from our observations.

PROBLEM SOLVING *(308–317)*

Algorithms and Heuristics   Heuristic Strategies Based on Induction
Heuristics and Expertise   Biases in the Use of Heuristics
Thinking and Fixation

Problems are solved by two major methods: algorithms and heuristics. Humans typically use heuristics and computers have traditionally been programmed to solve problems with algorithms. Two important problem solving heuristics are forward and backward chaining. Other important heuristics are availability and representativeness, both of which are sometimes used incorrectly. Fixation can inhibit problem solving, but restructuring the problem representation can lead to a solution.

LANGUAGE *(317–325)*

Characteristics of Language   The Structure of Language
Language Development   Nonhuman Communication

Characteristics of language include displacement and productivity. Most children learn language by the age of two. The language learned probably does not dramatically affect the development of other cognitive processes. Chimpanzees and other primates have more language ability than previously realized, though their language abilities are rudimentary compared to humans.

Without a doubt, the pinnacle of human evolution is the brain. The brain, specifically, the cerebral cortex, has been a major force in our success in adapting to our environment. Although other species no doubt have the capacity for thinking, only in our species does this capacity appear to be highly developed. No other species has been shown to have the same penchant for thinking and language that we do. We will study these two topics in this chapter. It is our goal to help you to understand thinking and language as psychological processes or activities in which we engage and whose consequences affect our behavior. Although these topics have fascinated philosophers and scientists for centuries, only recently have the tools of psychology been applied to the study of thinking and language. The result has been incredible. The knowledge psychologists and other scientists have gained from studying human cognition has the potential for ultimately changing our world as dramatically as did the inventions of the airplane, television, and controlled nuclear fission. For example, the more we learn about how we think, the more we learn about ourselves, and the better we will be able to build "brains" for machines. What this means is that as our knowledge of cognitive processes increases, the age of robotics nears. Robots that look, act, or think like human beings might still be science fiction, but some of the information presented in this chapter is already serving as a basis for these developments.

How could knowledge about the human thought processes possibly be changing our world so? A leading cause of change is the development and continued refinement of the computer, and it is the computer that is playing a surprisingly important role in the study of thinking. Consider the assessment of one expert (Pylyshyn, 1984), who argues that advances in computer technology are demonstrating that we are a "sibling of the computer" just as conclusions from biological science provide evidence that we are "the nephew or niece of the great ape." Of course in many ways we are very different from chimpanzees and computers, but the similarities between humans and chimps and between humans and computers should not be overlooked as we study the cognitive processes of thinking and language. We have explored some of the biological and psychological similarities between humans and other primates in earlier chapters. In this chapter, our study of human cognition will lead us to focus on some of the similarities between humans and computers—similarities that will probably grow as computer technology becomes even more sophisticated.

Now, some basic terminology. **Cognition** refers to the full range of mental activities used to represent and process knowledge; it includes perception, memory, thought, and the use of language. The study of cognition is interdisciplinary—just as biopsychology shares advances with other disciplines such as biology and physiology, cognitive psychology benefits from and shares advances with related disciplines such as computer science and linguistics. For the last several decades the cognitive perspective has been so thoroughly integrated with psychology that the study of cognition is being pursued in almost all areas of psychological research.

We have already discussed some cognitive processes in the chapters on perception and memory. Our study of thinking here is divided into two major topics: reasoning and problem solving. The remainder of the chapter covers communicating with others through the use of language.

INFORMATION, SYMBOLS, AND CONCEPTS

Deciding the best way to study cognition is not an easy task. Scientific questions are investigated empirically, yet how can cognitive processes be studied empirically when they cannot be observed directly? As we saw in Chapter 1, the discipline of psychology was founded by those who sought

According to the computational metaphor, human cognition is computation. We can gain insight into the way humans process information by looking at the way computers process information.

to study cognition by introspection, and yet their approach was a scientific dead-end. Having people try to describe the details of their own sensations and other conscious experiences yielded few scientific advances. Often subjects had difficulty repeating the same experience, and the subjective nature of the reports meant that they could not be verified by others (Watson, 1913).

Modern cognitive psychology, on the other hand, depends heavily on the study of information processing. Today, cognitive processes such as perceiving, remembering, thinking, and using language are conceived as nothing more or less than the processing of information. **Information processing** refers to the way that knowledge is represented and processed, which provides the basis for the cognitive perspective in modern psychological research and theory (Lachman, Lachman, & Butterfield, 1979; Boden, 1988).

The Computational Metaphor

Cognitive psychologists have also noted many useful parallels between the ways in which humans and computers process information. Cognitive psychologists have found that the way a computer processes information provides a useful metaphor for the study of human cognitive processes. (A metaphor is a means of comparison in which a phrase is used to describe an object or event figuratively. For example, we might say, "Our dreams are castles in the air," or "Life is a constant battle"). A metaphor, then, is a figure of speech in which one thing is understood in terms of another thing. Indeed, this metaphor has become a central theme of contemporary cognitive psychology.

Computers process information by running computer programs, which are sets of instructions processed by the computer for carrying out specified procedures. There are computer programs that find the mean of a set of numbers, draw a conclusion from a set of facts, or scan the environment to recognize specific objects. Similarly, when you find the mean of a set of numbers, draw a conclusion, or locate a familiar object, you are invoking cognitive processes that can be considered a type of computation. Using a computer program as a metaphor for human cognition is called the **computational metaphor** (Newell & Simon, 1972; Simon 1980). The essence of the computational metaphor is straightforward: cognition is computation. A perception, a thought, or a memory is viewed as an outcome of a computational process.

> The essence of the computational metaphor is straightforward: cognition is computation.

To illustrate the similarity in how people and machines process information, consider a task that both humans and computers can accomplish: adding a list of numbers. According to the computational metaphor, studying how humans add a list of numbers is like studying how the computer adds a list of numbers. No one claims that humans and computers have exactly the same program to accomplish this task, but there are some important similarities. Both humans and computers have to store knowledge regarding the meaning of summation and the meaning of numbers. Further, both humans and computers have a method of running the summation program to achieve the desired result. For humans, the method involves following the rules of addition learned in grade school; for the computer the method involves following the program written in a special code (binary code) by a computer programmer.

In essence, machines are capable of processing information in ways similar to though not the same as our own cognition. According to this perspective, cognitive processes such as perceiving the world around us, thinking about the world, and remembering information are like computer programs that run according to a set of directions. The task of understanding human cognition is similar to discovering how a computer has been programmed. The basis of all intelligent systems, human or machine, is the processing of information, whether this is accomplished by silicon computer circuits or by networks of neurons.

Although biological intelligence has evolved over millions of years, the intelligence exhibited by machines, known as artificial intelligence, is just now beginning to evolve. The importance of artificial intelligence to cognitive psychology is that we cannot build machines to process information without first understanding how knowledge can be represented and processed. The premier example of knowledge processing is the human brain. Artificial intelligence is of central importance to cognitive psychology because programming a machine to process information becomes a way that theories of human information processing can be tested. Just as mathematics provides an abstract language for much of science in general, artificial intelligence provides an abstract language for understanding and expressing theories of human cognition. When people write computer programs to store knowledge or to scan the environment and recognize objects, they may also be testing theories of information processing in humans.

The processing of information also includes the representation of information, or encoding. Specifically, information must be encoded into the language of the cognitive system. One important way in which this encoding is accomplished is with **symbols**, or mental constructions that represent an event or object. For example, the word *telephone* can represent an actual telephone. The word is a symbol for the actual object. The symbol can be manipulated in a variety of ways by the human information processor just like a functioning computer program can manipulate numbers or other symbols. For example, we can use *telephone* as a noun as in, "Please answer the telephone," or as a verb as in, "I will telephone you tonight."

An information processor, human or machine, builds symbolic representations that are then manipulated in various ways. To think is to process symbols. Using language involves symbols to communicate with others. Symbol manipulation is the key to the computational metaphor: both people and computer programs process information by manipulating symbols. One of the most basic assumptions made by cognitive psychologists is that understanding how people manipulate symbols is crucial to understanding human behavior. To understand why people do what they do, the cognitive psychologist seeks to discover their understanding of the world.

We need to organize and structure our knowledge of this world in order to understand its complexity. We do so by creating and using concepts, our next topic.

Organizing Knowledge with Concepts

At this very moment you are probably sitting in a chair. You have seen many different chairs, and each chair is in some way unique. A wooden rocking chair is different from an overstuffed recliner, which is different from a baby's highchair. Yet you can recognize instantly thousands of different objects that you have never seen before as being chairs.

A **concept** is a grouping of similar objects, events, or people into categories. Concepts allow us to simplify our symbolic representation of the world by organizing our knowledge; they serve as building blocks. The concept of "trout" falls within the higher concept of "fish," which falls within an even higher concept of "things that live in the water." Without concepts, our ability to use language, to reason and solve problems, and to

Concepts allow us to make general groupings of similar objects, events, or people. For example, the concept of vegetable does not refer to one specific vegetable, but to a whole group.

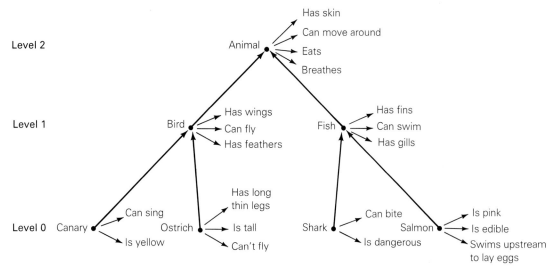

FIGURE 9.1
Hierarchically organized structure of concepts (Collins & Quillian, 1969).

perceive things would become overwhelmed by countless details. By providing a framework for organization, concepts play a central role in defining the realities of our everyday life, how we perceive the world around us, and how we relate to others.

Concepts then, represent abstractions. Concepts describe a general set of characteristics or relationships without limiting the description to any particular instance. The concept of *chair* does not refer to any one particular chair, but is a general symbol for an entire class of objects.

Organization of Concepts. Some concepts are more abstract than others, and concepts can be related in terms of their levels of abstraction. For example, all chairs represent a more abstract concept called furniture. These different levels of abstraction provide a way for us to organize concepts in relation to each other in our semantic memories, our stored knowledge of the world. Concepts seem to be organized according to a hierarchical structure, a series of concepts nested within other concepts. In other words, our organization of knowledge appears to be arranged in a manner that reflects the interrelationships among concepts.

As illustrated by the hierarchical structure that appears in Figure 9.1, all canaries are members of the more abstract category of birds, and all birds are members of the more abstract category of animals. Canaries, birds, and animals then, are hierarchically related concepts. Likewise, all sharks are fish and all fish are animals. According to this hierarchical structure, any characteristic of an animal, such as "eats," is also a property of all birds and all canaries.

The hypothesis that knowledge is organized according to a hierarchy of concepts is an interesting idea, but how can it be tested empirically? An answer to this question was provided by a clever experiment conducted by Allan Collins and Ross Quillian in 1969.

Collins and Quillian hypothesized that within a hierarchy, the more distant the concepts, the more time required to process information about the concepts. The hypothesized hierarchy they tested is presented in Figure 9.1. The distance in the hierarchy between two concepts is based, in part, on the levels of these concepts within the hierarchy. For example, because a canary is yellow, the information "is yellow" is at the same level in the hierarchy as "canary"; it is zero levels away. The information "has

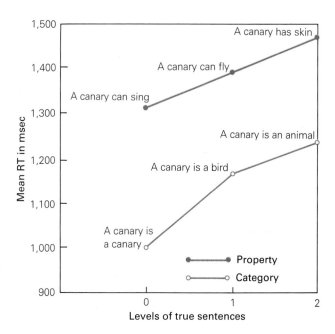

FIGURE 9.2
Subjects' reaction times to statements about concepts (Collins & Quillian, 1969).

wings" is stored one level away from "canary" because that is a characteristic of the more abstract category of birds. And the information "eats" is stored two levels away because it is a property of the even more abstract category of animals.

The information in this hierarchy was presented to the subjects via a series of two kinds of simple statements. One kind of statement involved two categories such as "A canary is a bird" or "A canary is a shark." Alternatively, each statement listed a potential characteristic of a concept such as "A canary is yellow" or "A canary is dangerous." The subject's task was to answer true or false to each statement. The dependent variable was reaction time, the time that elapsed between the presentation of the stimulus (the statement) and the response (the true or false). That is, Collins and Quillian attempted to measure directly an important property of the human information processing system—the amount of time required for processing a specific task. In this case, the time required to evaluate the truth of each statement was measured.

The initial results of the study confirmed Collins and Quillian's hypothesis. As shown in Figure 9.2, reaction time increased depending upon which level in the hierarchy the statement represented. The average reaction time to the statement *A canary is an animal,* was over 1200 milliseconds, but the reaction time to *A canary is a canary* was only about 1000 milliseconds. Similarly, for the statements that express the attributes of concepts, the reaction time to *A canary has skin* was longer than the reaction time to *A canary can fly*

Collins and Quillian's (1969) conclusions have since been modified. Cognitive psychologists now believe that the hierarchies of concepts tend to be more complex than a simple tree structure (Conrad, 1972; Collins & Loftus, 1975). However, the importance of the Collins and Quillian study extends beyond the precise details of their results. This study was a landmark because it was among the first to demonstrate that properties of the human information processing system, such as reaction time, can be measured directly.

Cognitive Economy Concepts may be stored hierarchically, but what level of abstraction in the hierarchy is used to classify an object? If you see a chair, do you think of the chair as a recliner chair, a chair, a piece of furniture, or a nonliving thing? Each of these concepts is unique, so a detailed classification system would assign each object to its own category, and each category might be defined in considerable detail. For example, the category may be faded green recliner chairs that have a stain in the upper-right-hand corner of the right arm rest and that squeak slightly when you sit in them. For most purposes, though, you would probably employ a more general category. The question is, how general would that category be?

The problem with organizing objects and events into abstract categories is that for each additional level of abstraction, some information about the original objects and events is lost. For example, classifying two different chairs into the same general "chair" category would lose the unique properties of each chair. Classification of objects into successively more general categories results in the loss of even more information. For example, the category "nonliving things" is quite large and includes not only all chairs, but also objects as diverse as cars, clothing, and houses.

So why classify? As we have seen, the use of concepts provides us with a more organized picture of the world and frees us from always concentrating on the unique features of each stimulus we encounter. When representing objects in terms of concepts, there is a tradeoff of generality and loss of detail for specificity and too much detail.

Our cognitive processing system handles this tradeoff by using basic level categories. The level of abstraction for an object that provides sufficient detail with minimal processing represents a compromise between too much and too little information (Rosch, 1977). Given the different levels of abstraction by which we classify objects, the desirable level of abstraction is the one that provides the most information with the least cognitive effort. Minimizing the amount of effort and time required in processing stimuli is called **cognitive economy**.

How can these basic level categories that we use to classify objects be uncovered? An answer to this question was provided by Eleanor Rosch and her colleagues (1976) who had subjects list all of the attributes they could think of in 90 seconds for each of the following three levels of concepts: furniture, chair, and kitchen chair. Subjects tended to list only a small number of attributes for the furniture category. These attributes included phrases such as "belongs inside house." But many more attributes were listed for the chair category, such as "has legs," and "is used to sit on." Only a relatively small number of additional attributes were listed for the kitchen chair category.

For this set of hierarchically ordered concepts, chair represents the basic level because it is the highest level in the hierarchy for which a relatively large list of attributes can be produced. Concepts higher in the hierarchy, such as furniture, are too abstract to generate many attributes readily. Concepts lower in the hierarchy, such as kitchen chair, provide more detail than provided by the basic level category, but not much more detail. By classifying something into a basic level category, we can obtain the largest number of characteristics of that object with the least cognitive effort. Cognitive economy is an extremely efficient means by which to process information.

Meaning of Concepts. We have seen that concepts are related to one another through hierarchies and we have seen how these hierarchical relationships can be used to process information efficiently. Another issue that has intrigued cognitive psychologists is just how a single concept is represented symbolically in semantic memory. How is the meaning of particular concepts represented?

One possibility endorsed by psychologists for many decades is that a concept is stored as a list of characteristics that define the concept (Smith, 1988). For example, what is a bachelor? The definition must have three characteristics: unmarried, male, and adult. All bachelors must be unmarried, they must be male, and they must be of marriageable age. And, if anyone has all three of these characteristics then he is a bachelor.

Listing defining characteristics to determine relationships between concepts works for some concepts but not for others. Consider the concept "bird." What are the defining features of a bird? You could list a variety of features including, lays eggs, flies, and has feathers. But some species of birds do not fly, some do not lay eggs, and if you plucked all of the feathers off some unlucky bird, would it no longer be a bird? A problem with representing concepts in terms of defining characteristics becomes clear: There is no list of characteristics that will always apply to each instance of the category. Thus, our cognitive processing system cannot possibly represent concepts in terms of these kinds of lists. Otherwise, we would not be able to recognize the featherless bird as a bird.

As an alternative to using defining characteristics, Rosch (1977) maintained that concepts are represented in terms of **prototypes**, a set of characteristics that apply to the most representative or typical member of the category but that do not necessarily apply to all instances. Try this. Relax for a moment and imagine a bird. What bird comes to mind? When asked to name a specific bird most people think of a robin (Malt & Smith, 1984). A robin is a prototypic bird because it is described by the prototype for a bird. It has feathers, flies, lays eggs, sings, and so on. You probably did not think of a penguin because although penguins have feathers and lay eggs, they do not fly or sing. Empirical support for how representative robins and penguins are of the bird category is found in Table 9.1. Robins are rated as typical of birds with a 6.89 rating on a 7 point scale, but penguins only receive a 2.63 rating (Malt & Smith, 1984).

According to the prototype theory of concept representation, we classify new objects and events in terms of their similarity to our prototypes. Similarity appears to be the basis for how concepts are organized in semantic memory. One consequence of this representation is that the more similar

TABLE 9.1	Typical ratings for different classes of birds by subjects in the Malt & Smith (1984) study.

BIRDS	RATING
robin	6.89
bluebird	6.42
seagull	6.26
swallow	6.16
falcon	5.74
mockingbird	5.47
starling	5.16
owl	5.00
vulture	4.48
sandpiper	4.47
chicken	3.95
flamingo	3.37
albatross	3.32
penguin	2.63
bat	1.53

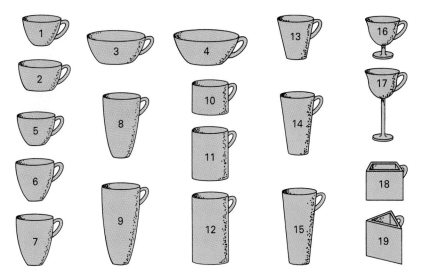

FIGURE 9.3
Fuzzy concept boundaries: When is a cup not a cup? (Hunt, 1982).

an object is to the prototype, the faster it should be categorized. Pretend for a moment that you look out the window and see a bird that you have never before seen. If the bird resembles a robin, you should immediately recognize the animal as a bird. On the other hand, if the bird is a penguin, classification is not so straightforward, and so presumably it would require more cognitive processing time. To test this idea empirically, subjects were presented stimuli, such as pictures of various birds (Smith, Shoben, & Rips, 1974). The dependent variable of interest was the time it took subjects to recognize each stimulus. Indeed, the reaction time to the question, "Is a robin a bird?" was considerably faster than the reaction time to, "Is a penguin a bird?"

Representing concepts in terms of prototypes instead of defining characteristics means that a concept need not have a fixed, rigid definition. Membership in a category is not all or nothing. Instead, similar concepts are often called "fuzzy" because the boundaries that separate them may not be well-defined (Smith, 1988; Zadeh, 1965). An illustration of a fuzzy concept is a series of objects whose similarity can be varied systematically such as the cups, vases, and bowls shown in Figure 9.3. The question is, "When is a cup a cup, and not a vase or a bowl?" Object number 5 is clearly a cup, but is number 3 a cup or a bowl? Is number 7 a cup or a vase? As you can see, the boundaries separating a cup from a vase or a bowl are not clear-cut. Objects are classified according to the prototype to which they are most similar, but judgments about similarity may vary from situation to situation, so objects that are close to a boundary may be classified differently at different times. Today you might consider object number 3 in Figure 9.3 to be a cup, but tomorrow you might classify it as a bowl. Your classification of an object may depend on the purpose for which you use it.

In sum, our ability to process information can be understood by comparing it to how a computer processes information. Human cognition is like computer computation. Therefore, studying cognition is like trying to understand how a computer program works, but without actually being able to see the program itself. Our knowledge of the world is represented by symbols for concepts that are stored in semantic memory. Concepts are organized hierarchically, and each concept appears to be represented in memory in terms of its prototype.

Reasoning involves examining a set of facts from an object or situation and drawing conclusions from those facts. Here, two anatomy students examine a human skull to help them understand how various parts of the body are constructed and fit together.

Now that we have described the information processing approach that defines the cognitive psychology perspective, we are ready to focus on the analysis of a rather important activity that uses these concepts: thinking. We will begin by discussing reasoning and follow with an overview of problem solving.

REASONING

All of us think, but what is thinking? The information processing approach to cognition provides us with a basis for viewing thinking as a form of computation that is not necessarily restricted to humans. **Thinking** is the manipulation or construction and modification of internal symbolic representations. Thinking involves a series of processes that cannot be observed directly by psychologists or anyone else.

Reasoning is the process of drawing conclusions from a set of facts. If you know that your friend likes the same kind of restaurants that you like, and if your friend says that a new restaurant that just opened serves very good food, then from these facts, you may conclude that you would also probably like the new restaurant. No one said directly that you would like the restaurant, and you haven't yet sampled its cuisine. Instead, your evaluation of the new restaurant was formed by reasoning from the information given.

Psychologists want to understand the processes by which people reason, and how accurately they reason. Arriving at a conclusion by reasoning from the given facts leads to a natural question: How do we know if our conclusions are justified by the information given? That is, how can we distinguish good reasoning from bad reasoning?

When psychologists study how people reason, they can evaluate the actual performance of our own mental processing capability by comparing our conclusions to the logically correct conclusions. As we shall see, the findings regarding the reasoning capabilities of humans are often interesting but not always reassuring. Two important reasoning strategies exist: deduction and induction.

Deductive Reasoning

In **deductive reasoning** we are given two or more statements and then form a conclusion that is intended to follow logically from those statements. A deductive reasoning problem can be expressed as an argument in which two statements called premises are given, and a third statement, the conclusion, is derived by reasoning from the premises. One of the more well-known illustrations of deductive reasoning is:

> *If* all people are mortal,
> *and if* Socrates is a person,
> *then* Socrates is mortal.

In this example, the premises are the first two statements of the argument from which the conclusion regarding Socrates' mortality follows.

This argument leads to a deductively valid conclusion because the conclusion necessarily follows from the premises. Deductively valid arguments are logically related and are correct in the sense that if the premises are true, then the conclusion is guaranteed to be true.

Now consider a different argument. Suppose that someone adamantly claimed that "All people are mortal" and that "Socrates is a person" but concluded that "Socrates is not mortal." This conclusion does not follow from these premises. The fact that you immediately recognize the invalidity of this conclusion indicates that deductive reasoning is a fundamental part of our reasoning ability (Rips, 1988). The ability to reason deductively is crucial to our day-to-day functioning. Deduction allows us to plan for the future, solve problems, and answer questions by reasoning based on information stored in memory.

Sometimes though, a person's preexisting knowledge and beliefs can lead him or her to draw an invalid conclusion. An example of this is the **belief-bias effect**, a situation in which people often evaluate the validity of a conclusion on the basis of what they believe instead of from a logical analysis of the premises. This effect is particularly true for invalid arguments that have believable conclusions (Evans, Barston, & Pollard, 1983). The following argument illustrates the belief-bias effect.

> *If* all people who believe in democracy
>   believe in free speech,
> *and if* Nazis do not believe in democracy,
> *then* Nazis do not believe in free speech.

When many people first encounter this argument, they believe that the conclusion is valid. A reason for this belief is that the conclusion, "Nazis do not believe in free speech," is true. Yet the argument itself is deductively *invalid* because the conclusion does not follow logically from the premises.

The first premise only makes an assertion about people who believe in democracy. It says nothing about those who do not believe in democracy. Yet the second premise specifically states that Nazis do not believe in democracy. Thus, these two premises are not interrelated logically, so the conclusion does not follow from the premises. The conclusion happens to be true, but it is not true because of the truth of the two premises.

Deduction allows us to plan for the future, solve problems, and answer questions . . .

Consider another invalid argument.

> *If* all students have brains,
> *and if* dogs are not students,
> *then* dogs do not have brains.

Once again, the first premise makes an assertion that is unrelated to the assertion of the second premise. The only difference from this example and the Nazi example is that in this case, the conclusion is clearly false, making the invalidity of the argument more apparent.

Because of the belief-bias effect, when someone believes that a conclusion is true, he or she is likely to also believe that the conclusion is valid. Do you see the problem? What happens when your beliefs are actually false, but you believe they are true? You might use reasoning to justify your belief, but at the same time, you would be more susceptible to accepting an invalid conclusion as supporting your argument. Your belief in the false conclusion has misled you to justify this belief on the basis of incorrect reasoning.

In sum, deductive reasoning involves arriving at a conclusion that logically follows from the premises. The belief-bias effect occurs when preexisting knowledge or beliefs cause people to draw a conclusion that is not related logically to the premises. Now we turn to another kind of reasoning, inductive reasoning.

Inductive Reasoning

Consider the following argument. As you read it, think about how it differs from arguments involving deductive reasoning.

> *If* the sun rose in the eastern sky fifty years ago,
> *and if* the sun rose in the eastern sky last month,
> *and if* the sun rose in the eastern sky yesterday,
> *then* the sun will rise in the eastern sky tomorrow.

Although this conclusion would seem to be sensible, this is not a deductively valid argument because the truth of the premises does not absolutely guarantee the truth of the conclusion. After all, it is possible (although not likely) that some solar catastrophe will result in the sun fizzling out before morning. Another way to say this is that the conclusion of this argument is not implied by the truth of the premises, but instead is rendered likely by or is generalized from, the truth of the premises. Because the premises are true, we may be 99.9999999 percent sure that the sun is going to rise tomorrow morning in the east, but we can not be absolutely certain.

Arguments of this nature are examples of inductive reasoning. Reasoning that generalizes our knowledge beyond the known facts is called **inductive reasoning**. In deductive reasoning, the conclusion of a valid deductive argument must necessarily follow from the premises. In inductive reasoning, we generalize from the known to the unknown, but we can never be certain that the generalization is correct (Hunt, 1982). True premises of an inductive argument never absolutely guarantee the truth of the conclusion; inductive conclusions only reflect degrees of likelihood and are qualified by terms such as "maybe" or "likely" or perhaps with probabilities.

An argument such as the rising sun example is not deductively valid, but because the premises provide good evidence for the conclusion, the argument is said to be inductively strong (Skyrms, 1966). Other inductive arguments, such as the following, are weaker.

> *If* Hank flunked two classes last term,
> *and if* Hank is chairman of his fraternity's social
>   committee next semester,
> *and if* Hank has a new girlfriend,
> *then* Hank will flunk more classes next term.

We would say that it is likely that Hank will flunk more classes next term, but Hank might surprise everyone and pass. The conclusion is probably justified, but the justification is not as strong as the conclusion of the rising sun example. In fact, we can say that the conclusions from the Hank example are inductively weak.

Inductive reasoning, then, provides a means for reasoning in situations in which we cannot be certain of the outcome. It provides a means for discovering new information and going beyond what is known. When we

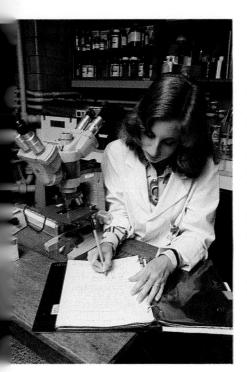

Inductive reasoning involves generalizing from the known to the unknown. It is a very valuable form of reasoning and is used in situations, such as scientific experimentation, where the outcome is uncertain.

see the sun rise in the east every morning, we have observed a regularity that we generalize to the next morning; we expect the sun to rise. Understanding inductive reasoning is important because many scientific discoveries, as well as our own personal discoveries about the world in which we live are based on inductive reasoning. Whenever we formulate a rule based on regularities that we observe in the world around us, we are reasoning inductively. These rules can be stated as hypotheses. The conclusion that "Tomorrow the sun will rise" is a hypothesis about the position of the sun. Another example of inductive reasoning would be the hypothesis that we forgot to put the yeast in the bread batter when, unlike all the other times we've baked bread, the bread failed to rise.

How effective are people at reasoning inductively? As we shall see, people do not always use inductive reasoning as efficiently as they might. As an example, consider a study of how people generate and test hypotheses (Wason, 1968). The subjects' task was to discover a rule that described a series of three digits. The experimenter began by presenting the triplet, *2, 4, 6,* and then telling the subject that these numbers conformed to a rule. The subject then generated another triplet of his or her own choosing, and the experimenter told the subject whether or not the new numbers matched the rule. Whenever he or she wished, the subject guessed at what the rule might be (for example, "Start with any number and add two each time," or "Three consecutive even numbers"). Each time a proposed rule was suggested, the experimenter told the subject whether or not the rule was correct. Because the first hypotheses formed by the subjects were usually wrong, this process was repeated until the subject succeeded in guessing the rule correctly or gave up.

So what was the rule waiting to be discovered? It was simple: the numbers were listed in increasing order of magnitude. Yet despite the simplicity of the underlying rule, subjects often had great difficulty discovering it. Why? Because almost all of the sequences of three numbers provided by the subjects were *consistent* with their particular hypothesis at the time the numbers were generated. Very few subjects ever tested their rule by providing numbers that were *contrary* to the hypothesis.

For example, if the subject's rule was to add two to each successive number, the rule was tested by generating triplets such as *9–11–13, 44–46–48,* and *20–22–24.* After each of these three sequences, the experimenter informed the subject that the sequence conformed to the correct rule, but when the subject guessed what the rule might be, hypotheses were usually wrong. The subject might then formulate a new hypothesis such as "The middle number is the average of the other two numbers" and provide triplets such as *20–25–30* and *80–90–100.* Again, the hypothesis was tested only by providing instances that were consistent with the rule. Disconfirming instances such as *100, 90, 80* were almost never given. Some subjects even became upset when their numbers continued to conform to the rule, yet their hypotheses were incorrect.

This study was replicated with different subjects and different types of tasks (for example, Mynatt, Doherty, & Tweney, 1978) and always with the same result. When we try to find out if our beliefs about the world are correct, we find it much easier to search for instances that confirm our beliefs than to search for evidence that falsifies what we believe; this tendency is called a **confirmation bias.** We apparently do not like to be wrong, even if being wrong a few times helps us ultimately to be correct. Although searching only for confirming evidence works well enough in some situations, often the better and more efficient method for testing and revising hypotheses is to seek confirming *and* disconfirming instances of a hypothesis. As the study described above demonstrated, many confirmations cannot prove that the hypothesis is correct, but one disconfirmation can show that it is incorrect. Applying this lesson would improve not only the performance of the subjects trying to guess the rule about the triplets, but it would help all of us as we use inductive reasoning to figure out the rules and regularities of our lives and the world within which we live. In psychology, as in all sciences, research is designed to test theories by setting up experimental conditions that will disconfirm hypotheses related to theory.

In sum, inductive reasoning involves the generalization of information and knowledge beyond a set of premises. The validity of a conclusion is made more or less likely, but is not guaranteed, by the validity of the premise. Although the best way to test hypotheses is to conduct experiments that have the potential to disconfirm them, most people tend to search for results that confirm their hypotheses. We turn now to a different kind of reasoning ability, problem solving.

PROBLEM SOLVING

A **problem** is a situation in which there is a goal that is not immediately obtainable. The problems that we are interested in are those that require thinking to derive a solution for obtaining the goal. The problem solver has to process information to figure out how to arrive at the solution.

Algorithms and Heuristics

Two different strategies can be used to solve problems: algorithms and heuristics. An **algorithm** is a completely specified, step-by-step set of rules for solving a problem. For example, how is the mean of a set of numbers calculated? The following two-step algorithm solves this problem:

1. Add all the numbers in the set.
2. Divide the result from the first step by the total number of numbers in the set.

Or, suppose you know of a party Friday night, but you don't know how to find the house in which the party is being held. From a friend you receive directions, which can be stated in the form of an algorithm:

1. From where you are standing, go three blocks past the stoplight up ahead.
2. Turn right.
3. Go to the second house on the left.

As you can see, algorithms are sets of precise, mechanical rules. If the algorithm is correct, and if it is followed correctly, then it will provide the correct solution to a problem.

The mechanical nature of algorithms means that they are well-suited to being programmed into a computer. Most of the problems that we attempt to solve in our day-to-day lives, however, are not solved by algorithms. More often, we encounter problems that must be solved in the context of uncertainty. These are problems for which we do not have all of the information, for which we are not certain of the truth of our premises, and for which we must use inductive reasoning to solve. Remember, using inductive reasoning means that the truth of our conclusions is likely but not guaranteed. Problem solving, then, requires more flexible strategies than those provided by a rigid algorithm. These solutions range from the mundane (Is it safe to cross the street now?) to the more weighty (Which college should I attend? or Which person should I marry?).

To solve these types of problems, people use intuitive strategies called **heuristics**, which are simple, informal rules of thumb or general guidelines. A heuristic is a "seat of the pants" approach that usually works well; however, even if the heuristic is appropriate to the problem at hand and is applied correctly, it is not guaranteed to provide the correct answer. When you chose a university or college, your judgment regarding the best school for you may have been little more than an intelligent guess. Nonetheless, to make your decision, you probably relied upon heuristics such as, "Choose a school that is close to home, but not too close, that has a friendly atmosphere, and good academics." Using heuristics in the presence of so many unknowns often helps us make better decisions than we would by relying only on more rigid algorithms.

Let's contrast algorithms and heuristics by showing how the two methods can be used to solve a problem. Consider, for example, playing a game of chess against a computer. The software used to instruct the computer how to play chess is based on algorithms that analyze all possible moves and countermoves that could be made by the opponent. More complex software might also evaluate each move that could be made in response to each countermove, though the number of possibilities grows so quickly that even the most powerful computers can only "look ahead" a relatively small number of moves. The move that offers the most benefits calculated according to precise formulas is then chosen as the next move.

Humans, on the other hand, use heuristics as well as algorithms to play chess (de Groot, 1965). They recognize patterns from previous games, work to control the center of the board, develop tactics such as bluffing, and are able to shift strategies as the game progresses. Players apply all these guidelines to choose their moves. The strategies are complex, and lack precision, which means that they are not easily programmed for a computer. But when an expert chess player applies these heuristics with skill, they may provide a better solution than that provided by a computer using the algorithmic approach.

Today, the best humans still beat the best machines. The most powerful chess programs, however, are becoming more powerful. The key is that we are learning how to program computers to use heuristics to solve problems instead of relying solely upon algorithms. The result is that the way computers process information is beginning to more closely resemble human thought. We will discuss this development in a later section, but first we will examine some specific heuristic problem-solving strategies based on inductive reasoning.

Chess players rely on both heuristics and algorithms to play the game. Because of their ability to use these strategies, players can successfully beat even the most well-programmed computers at chess.

Heuristic Strategies Based On Induction

To show how we use reasoning to solve some types of problems, we need to first express a problem as a set of premises followed by the likely conclusion. To illustrate, suppose that your younger brother Tommy is sick and you want to find out what is wrong with him. The evidence that you have to work from is that Tommy has a runny nose and he sneezes a lot. From this evidence you might use the following inductive argument, which is part of your long-term memory, to hypothesize that Tommy probably has a cold.

> *If* Tommy has a runny nose,
> *and if* Tommy sneezes a lot,
> *then* Tommy likely has a cold.

Within the context of problem solving it is often useful to think of each premise as a piece of evidence and the conclusion as a hypothesis that we are attempting to verify or reject. We will see, however, that problems in real life are often so complex that their solutions require reasoning based on not just one inductive argument, but on an entire spectrum of arguments. The problem solver searches for the solution by using a heuristic strategy that involves relating a broad mosaic of inductive arguments into an overall pattern (Newell & Simon, 1972; Lesgold, 1988).

To illustrate one of these search strategies, consider the following perhaps all-too-familiar problem (Van Horn, 1986). On your way to school or work one morning, you discover that your car will not start. Why? The first thing that you might do is observe whether the engine turns over or if there is complete silence when you turn the key in the ignition. If the engine turns over, then you might check the gas gauge. If there is enough gas, then you might check for loose wires. If you find that your distributor cap is loose, then you would tighten the cap and attempt to restart the engine. If the engine starts, your problem has been diagnosed and solved.

This particular troubleshooting strategy is called **forward chaining**, a heuristic problem-solving procedure in which the problem solver reasons forward from the evidence to a solution by selecting the best out of many possible actions, observing what happens, and then, depending on the result, repeating the process by taking another action. Forward chaining is also sometimes called "bottom up" or "data driven" reasoning because the strategy begins at the bottom with the data provided by the situation. The strategy is then to narrow down the range of possible solutions and move forward to the solution by chaining together a set of premises and conclusions.

Forward chaining, then, is a problem-solving strategy that starts from the evidence, reasoning forward to the hypothesis or likely solution. Another problem-solving strategy works in the opposite direction, reasoning from the hypothesis to the evidence. **Backward chaining** is a heuristic problem-solving procedure in which the problem solver begins with a likely hypothesis and then searches for evidence that confirms or disproves the hypothesis. Backward chaining is also sometimes called "top down" or "goal driven" reasoning because it starts at the top with the hypothesis or likely solution and searches for evidence that supports the hypothesis.

An example of backward chaining is the strategy a detective might use in solving a murder. The detective begins with a list of the most likely suspects (hypotheses) and evaluates the evidence for and against each one to see which hypothesis best matches the available data.

The first hypothesis might be: "The butler did it." If he has no motive and a good alibi, that is, if the evidence does not match the hypothesis for this case, then this hypothesis is ruled out. Simply put, the argument is weak inductively:

> *If* the butler has no motive,
> *and if* the butler has a good alibi,
> *then* the butler likely committed the murder.

Did the victim's business partner do it? Upon the victim's death, the partner assumes full control of the company, so a potential motive has been established. Other evidence is also produced. For example, the business partner has been linked to the murder weapon. The hypothesis looks like:

> *If* the business partner profits from the victim's death,
> *and if* the business partner is linked to the murder weapon,
> *then* the business partner likely committed the murder.

This hypothesis is strong inductively because the evidence given in the premise supports the argument.

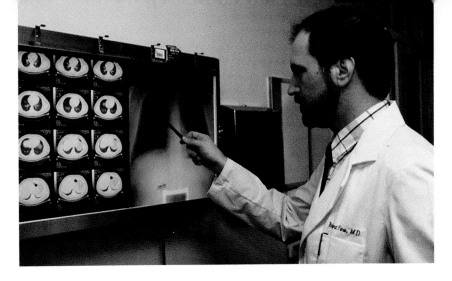

An expert is someone whose knowledge combined with an ability to use heuristics enables him or her to solve problems that an untrained person could not solve. For example, a physician who specialized in a specific area of medicine is considered an expert.

All of us use the heuristic problem-solving strategies of forward and backward chaining, but some people apply these information processing strategies more effectively than others. We turn now to the topic of expertise.

Heuristics and Expertise

Some people, through years of training and experience, have become so successful at solving some types of problems that they have become experts in a particular area. Experts possess a broad base of knowledge and an ability to apply heuristics in ways that allow them to solve problems that an untrained person could not. By studying how experts apply their knowledge to solve problems, cognitive scientists have uncovered principles of reasoning that apply to a variety of problem-solving situations.

Examples of expertise can be found in almost any profession. Experts using heuristics save lives, discover new scientific principles, and run successful businesses. The physician who specializes in infectious blood diseases can observe a variety of patient symptoms such as lethargy and persistent headaches as well as reams of data from diagnostic testing. Applying heuristics to this knowledge base, the physician might conclude that the patient probably is suffering from meningitis caused by a particular strain of bacteria. An expert geologist may study detailed observations of the rock types and formations over an area of many square miles and decide that one particular location shows promise for yielding a commercially viable copper deposit.

The practical problem of relying on these kinds of specialized problem-solving abilities is the short supply of expertise. Expertise is a knowledge-intensive skill that usually requires years of schooling and on-the-job experience to develop.

Why then, don't experts write down details of their expertise? The difficulty in providing these details reflects the fundamental difference between algorithms and heuristics (Van Horn, 1986; Lesgold, 1988). The explicit step-by-step nature of the algorithm means that the person using an algorithm to solve a problem can probably explain to others how he or she arrived at a decision. But experts usually rely not on the precise application of the algorithm, but on the seat-of-the-pants thinking of the heuristic. The use of heuristics is often so complex and so vaguely defined that even experts cannot easily provide a simple description of what they have learned over a period of years; no simple how-to manual can substitute for expertise. When asked how a solution was reached (Hunt, 1982), the expert's response may be something like, "It just came to me."

In trying to understand the underlying processes of heuristic thinking, and in trying to provide a means for dealing with the short supply of expertise, cognitive psychologists and other cognitive scientists have been learning how to program computers to reason heuristically. The natural question to ask is, "Can a computer program be developed that could replace, or at least assist, an expert?" The product of this question is one of the first practical applications of artificial intelligence: the development of expert systems. An **expert system** is a computer program that, like a human expert, uses heuristics and knowledge about the world to solve problems.

Both of the previously introduced examples of experts, the physician and the geologist, are in actuality represented not only by people but also by computer programs. *Mycin*, one of the first large-scale expert systems, was developed at the Stanford Medical Center during the mid-1970s to assist in the diagnosis of infectious blood diseases. *Prospector* is an expert system for locating mineral deposits. Other expert systems have been designed to make decisions that help guide America's space shuttle through reentry and landing, free oil drilling bits that become stuck thousands of feet below the surface, and evaluate the suitability of a loan applicant (Van Horn, 1986).

Expert systems are designed to mimic the heuristic problem-solving process of human experts. How do expert systems work? Knowledge is stored in expert systems in the form of inductive arguments of the type we have seen in this chapter, except that the conclusion is expressed in terms of a specific probability. For example, the infectious disease expert system *Mycin* has hundreds of rules that are simply more complex and technical versions of, *If* Tommy has a runny nose, *and if* Tommy sneezes a lot, *then* there is a 60 percent probability that Tommy has a cold. These inductive arguments are the knowledge base for the system.

How does the expert system apply its knowledge to the details of a particular situation and arrive at an answer? Given the specifics of a particular problem, the expert system uses the same heuristic problem-solving strategies used by human problem solvers—forward and backward chaining. The problem solving strategy as it is represented by the computer program is called the inference engine. And just as humans can use the same strategy to solve different types of problems, different expert systems can be created by providing different knowledge bases for the same inference engine. The inference engine provides the framework for thinking, and the knowledge base provides the knowledge upon which the inference engine operates.

Heuristics . . . can sometimes be applied incorrectly and can lead to erroneous conclusions.

Currently the best expert systems can do almost as well as the corresponding human expert and often much better than someone who is trained to do the job but who is not an expert. Although expert systems are not yet good enough to replace the human expert, they do serve as a knowledgeable assistant. As cognitive scientists understand more about how humans make judgments, and as computer technology becomes more powerful, expert systems will probably become a more integrated part of our society.

Although heuristics are generally useful in solving problems, they can sometimes be applied incorrectly and can lead to erroneous conclusions. Next we discuss some ways in which heuristics may be misused.

Biases in the Use of Heuristics

The good news is that the unsystematic type of "educated guess" provided by heuristics helps us simplify complex tasks and solve problems for which we cannot be sure that our conclusions are correct. Heuristics are often efficient, practical, and effective. The bad news is that they may also be used inappropriately. Several researchers, particularly Amos Tversky and Daniel Kahneman, have demonstrated that people sometimes misuse heuristics in systematic, predictable ways. The result is that in some situations, people—both novices and experts alike—are biased toward making notoriously poor judgments. Of the many such biases that have been discovered, we will discuss two, the misuse of the "availability" and the "representative" heuristics.

The Availability Heuristic. Those who direct educational campaigns warning against the effects of drunken driving have learned an important fact about the ways in which people process information. Instead of providing tables and graphs of statistical data, most such campaigns now focus on displaying vivid photographs or video clips that graphically portray the injury that can result from accidents caused by drunken driving. The information portrayed by these images tends to leave an impression that is more readily accessible to cognitive processing than does the information conveyed by statistics.

In general, things that are familiar, recent, and emotional all tend to be more readily recalled and tend to have a stronger impact on our thinking and behavior than do other kinds of information. The greater availability of this type of information also tends to influence the way in which we solve problems. When solving a problem, we may rely primarily on information that is most readily available (Tversky & Kahneman, 1973). This problem solving approach has been coined the **availability heuristic,** and it has been applied most often to problems that involve estimating the frequencies of specific events. For example, one way to estimate the divorce rate is to recall how many of your acquaintances have been divorced. If two or three of your friends have been divorced recently, you are likely to judge the divorce rate to be high. Available information can be useful in helping us make decisions effectively and solve problems correctly—but not necessarily. The indiscriminate use of the availability heuristic is likely to result in misleading and biased solutions.

An example of the bias that can result from the availability heuristic was demonstrated by Tversky and Kahneman (1973) in the "famous name" study. Subjects listened to long lists of names played through a tape recorder and then were asked to remember how many male and female names were on each of the lists. The list of male and female names was 50/50, but the names for the women were well-known and the names for the men were not as well-known. When subjects were asked to recall as many of the names as possible after hearing the list read to them, most subjects (57 out of 86) recalled more names of the famous than the names of the not-so-famous. The famous names were more "available" to the subjects than the not-so-famous names. However, the interesting result of this study was that when subjects were asked to remember the number of men compared to the number of women on the lists, most subjects (80 out of 99) erroneously judged women to have been more frequently listed than men. When new lists were devised in which the men were famous and the women were not well-known, subjects tended to believe mistakenly that many more male names than female names were on the list. Thus, the more available information led subjects to overestimate the number of names of the sex with the more well-known names. Availability distorted judgment.

The Representativeness Heuristic. A second type of bias in the use of heuristics is illustrated by the following problem constructed by Tversky and Kahneman (1982):

FEELING NO PAIN

IF YOU DRINK, DON'T DRIVE.

An effective use of the availability heuristic occurs in educational campaigns such as the one above aimed at discouraging drinking and driving. Rather than listing statistics, a graphic photograph depicting the results of drunken driving is used. The image tends to leave a more lasting impression than would the statistical data.

We hold images of certain roles and professions that help us categorize people. The image of a man cooking dinner for his family every night does not fit the image of a homemaker, which many people, using the representativeness heuristic, typically associate with a woman.

Steve is very shy and withdrawn, invariably helpful, but with little interest in people, or in the world of reality. A meek and tidy soul, he has a need for order and structure, and a passion for detail. Would you guess that Steve is a farmer, salesman, airline pilot, librarian, or a physician?

What is your answer? Does a salesman fit your image of those who have a need for order and structure? Who is likely to be the more meek and tidy, a farmer, an airline pilot, or a librarian?

If you answered this question like most people, your answer depended on the degree to which this description of Steve matches your concept of each profession. People use the **representativeness heuristic** when an object is classified into the category to which it appears to be the most similar (Tversky & Kahneman, 1973). For example, how typical is Steve of people who are placed in your category of "librarian." Applying this heuristic, the more closely Steve resembles your knowledge of a typical librarian, the more probable it is that you think Steve is a librarian.

Often this heuristic works just fine. What is wrong with this strategy of classifying on the basis of representativeness? The problem is that in other situations, some important factors are ignored. An example is the failure to consider the base rate, the probability that a person or object is in a particular group without knowledge of any specific information about that person or object. If there are ten times as many farmers as there are librarians, then the probability that any one individual is a farmer is ten times the probability that he or she is a librarian.

When you classify Steve you should consider more than just the representativeness of Steve's personality to each of the different categories—you should also consider base rate. It may be true that Steve fits your image of the typical librarian, but it is also true that at least some farmers are meek and tidy, have a need for order and structure, and have a passion for detail. If farmers outnumber librarians by a large number, it may be more likely that Steve is a farmer instead of a librarian. Even after the particulars of the case are introduced, the base rate information that was known before the case was presented should also be considered in making the classification.

Another instance of bias that can result from the indiscriminate use of the representativeness heuristic pertains to gambling (Tversky & Kahneman, 1971). If the red and black outcomes of the spin of a roulette wheel are equally likely, then a representative sample that results from multiple spins of the roulette wheel will consist of about half red and half black outcomes. For large samples consisting of outcomes of hundreds of spins, the proportion of red and black outcomes will be almost exactly 50/50. For a small sample of only several spins, though, an unrepresentative ratio of red and black outcomes is likely to occur. The **gambler's fallacy** is the mistaken belief that the outcome of the next chance event will be to ensure representativeness, such as when he or she bets heavily on a black because the previous five spins resulted in five reds. The problem for the gambler is that the probability of a black on any single spin is always the same: one-half. The roulette wheel does not have a memory; it does not know that the previous five outcomes were red and it doesn't "try" for a black on the sixth spin. Yet gamblers often act as if the roulette wheel was a conscious being that was trying to generate representative outcomes in small samples.

Errors in everyday thinking are not limited to those involving inappropriate use of heuristics. Sometimes we begin our analysis of a problem from the wrong perspective. We turn next to a discussion of this kind of problem in thinking and some of the ways we can improve our thinking.

FIGURE 9.4 (a)
The nine-dot problem.

URE 9.5
chain problem.

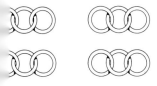

problem: If opening a link costs 2 cents and
sing a link costs 3 cents, how can these four
ces of chain be linked together to form a
sed ring for only 15 cents?

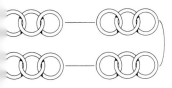

First attempt at solving the problem: Linking
ain ends of each piece together to form a closed
cle. This procedure is not correct because it
sts 20 cents.

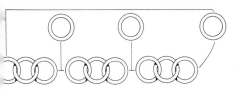

ne solution: Breaking up one of the pieces of
ain and then using the individual links to tie
gether the remaining links. This procedure
osts only 15 cents.

Thinking and Fixation

Consider the nine dots in Figure 9.4a. Do you think you could connect all of the dots with four continuous lines without ever lifting your pencil or pen off the paper? Go ahead and try solving this problem before you see the anwer in Figure 9.4b.

If you tried to solve the nine-dot problem like most people, your solution illustrates an important characteristic of problem solving: the way in which we initially view a problem often determines the quality of the solution. The wrong starting point may lead to a dead end; the right starting point may invoke a heuristic search strategy that leads directly to the correct solution (Lesgold, 1988).

The difficulty here involves our initial perception of the problem. Once a problem is represented in a certain way, we may have trouble cognitively finding a new perspective from which to view the problem. This tendency to view a problem solely in one particular way is called a **fixation**. Most people approach the nine-dot problem with a fixation of drawing lines within the boundaries of the square. Staying within the lines was not a statement of the original problem as you can see from Figure 9.4b. The solution requires that some of the lines extend outside of the square. Once such a fixation is broken, the solution is obvious, as is the impossibility of obtaining the solution under the old perspective.

Another example in which fixation is a barrier to effective problem solving is a **mental set**, the tendency to repeat the type of solutions that have worked in the past, even when a different approach would be more effective. Viewing a problem only one way can often be beneficial; otherwise each time we encounter a similar problem, we could not apply what we have learned previously. The difficulty, of course, is that sometimes these past successes interfere with devising solutions to new and different problems.

To illustrate mental set, consider the following problem (see Figure 9.5a). You have four pieces of chain, and each piece is made up of three links. The problem is to link all four pieces into a single closed ring with the following restrictions. The local craftsman charges 2 cents to open a link and 3 cents to close a link, and you only have 15 cents. Before reading on, try to solve the problem. Most of us have experience in putting together chains such as this. We have strung together a chain of paper clips, or decorated the Christmas tree with a paper chain, or put back together a necklace that had begun to fall apart, so at first glance, this problem seems straightforward. The difficulty in solving this particular problem is that the way we have approached similar problems in the past no longer applies (see Figure 9.5b). If we simply unfasten one of the links on each of the four pieces of chain and then hook all of the open links together, we will have spent 20 cents: four openings at 2 cents each and four closings at 3 cents each. The key to the solution is to overcome the initial mental set and approach the problem in a novel way (see Figure 9.5c). Instead of unfastening one link on each piece, unfasten all of the links on one of the four pieces and then use these three unattached pieces to chain together the remaining three pieces. With this technique, only three openings and closings are required. The total cost: exactly 15 cents.

Another example of fixation is provided by **functional fixedness**, the tendency to limit possible solutions by using objects only in the way that they have been used traditionally. Finding the solution to a problem may require using objects in creative and innovative ways—ways in which they are not typically used. The classic illustration of functional fixedness is from an experiment by Gestalt psychologist Karl Duncker (1945). As illustrated in Figure 9.6a, Duncker gave each subject some tacks, some

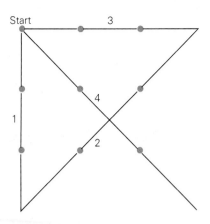

FIGURE 9.4 (b)
The solution to the nine-dot problem.

Start   3

1

4

2

FIGURE 9.6 (a)
The candlestick problem. The materials provided.

matches, three candles, and three small boxes. The problem was to find a way to mount the candles on a wall and then light them. Each subject worked alone. Before you continue, take a look at Figure 9.6a and see if you can solve this problem.

Before attempting the solution, each subject was randomly assigned to an experimental or control group. In the control group, the boxes were laid out on a table as separate items. In the experimental group, the boxes were used as containers so that the tacks, matches, and candles were in their respective boxes. Subjects in the control group had a much higher success rate in solving the problem than those in the experimental group. The solution is not obvious because the tacks are not thick enough to go through the candle and into the wall. The key to solving the problem, then, was to recognize that one of the boxes could be used as a platform on which to mount the candles (see Figure 9.6b). When the boxes were used as containers, subjects had difficulty seeing that the three boxes could be used as anything but containers. They could not break this fixation. Duncker not only demonstrated functional fixedness in the laboratory, he also demonstrated that the way in which a problem is presented can foster efficient or inefficient ways for solving the problem.

We have seen that fixating on an inappropriate initial representation of a problem may hinder or even prevent solving the problem. Obtaining the solution requires breaking free of the fixation by gaining a fresh perspective and creatively restructuring the initial perceptions. For example, a dime may be used as a screwdriver to loosen or tighten a screw, or a necktie or scarf can be used as tourniquet to lessen the bleeding from an injury. Sometimes this restructuring is accomplished by a sudden flash of understanding called **insight**, where all of the pieces of a problem suddenly fit together and the solution becomes clear.

One of the first psychologists to study insight was the Gestalt psychologist, Wolfgang Köhler (1887–1968). At the outbreak of World War I, Köhler, a German, became stranded on a remote African island. Köhler devoted his stay on the island to studying the problem-solving abilities of the chimpanzees living there. Köhler presented the chimps with different problems and watched as they attempted to solve each problem. As shown in Figure 9.7, a typical problem involved hanging something particularly desirable, such as a banana, out of reach of the chimp. In one setting, three or four boxes were also in the enclosed area with the chimp. The solution to the problem was to stack the boxes and then climb on top to get the banana.

Most of Köhler's chimps were not only able to solve this problem successfully, but they also apparently did so insightfully. The typical chimp would first try to reach the banana by jumping. Failing at that, the chimp would often act perplexed, mull around the cage, perhaps toy with the boxes. Suddenly the chimp would stop, visually scan the area, stack the boxes on top of each other, climb to the top, and grab the banana.

The perceptual restructuring of a problem afforded by insight is an important aspect of **creativity,** the generation of novel, useful solutions. Another aspect of a creative solution is often a time lag between the initial attempts to solve the problem and the solution itself. Insight into a problem may occur *after* the person has stopped thinking consciously about potential solutions, a phenomenon called **incubation**. Although experimental verification of incubation is difficult, many examples of the role insight can play in scientific discovery have been documented extensively (Rothenberg, 1979). The scientist may be relaxing without thinking actively about the problem for hours or even days. Suddenly, while vacationing, sleeping, or traveling, the solution becomes clear. For example, the scientist who had discovered the circular form of a chemical structure called benzene attributes his discovery to a dream in which a snake formed

FIGURE 9.7
*This chimpanzee uses insight to find a
way to reach the banana.*

a circle by biting its own tail. Awaking, he quickly worked out the implications of his dream, and found that the circular structure best accounted for the previously unexplained data.

What accounts for incubation? One explanation is that the initial representation of the problem may have been inappropriate, and this representation may become even more constricting as the person continued to work intensely on the problem. However, after attending to other matters, the initial representation may fade, and the problem can then be examined in different ways, and a creative, fresh perspective may emerge.

In summary, we have now discussed the topic of problem solving, covering heuristic search strategies for generating solutions and the initial representation of the problem from which the search strategy proceeds. We have also seen that problem solving can be studied within the context of the computational metaphor because problem solving is information processing. Indeed, when the specific nature of the information processing can be specified, as it is with forward and backward chaining and inductive arguments, the heuristics used by the human problem solver can be programmed into the computer. Remember, though, that heuristics, such as the availability and representative heuristics, can be misused and so can lead to incorrect thinking. Likewise, solutions to problems are sometimes deterred by fixedness and mental set, both of which are created by our initial perception of the problem. Cognition entails more than just problem-solving abilities. It also involves the ability to use and to understand language, the topic of the next section.

FIGURE 9.6 (b)
*The solution to the candlestick
problem.*

LANGUAGE

One of the most impressive human cognitive abilities is **language**—a written or spoken system of symbol manipulation that we use to represent and communicate our thoughts to others. As we will see, there is some evidence that other animals such as chimpanzees have rudimentary language abilities, but even if we consider these abilities to be language, they are strikingly simple compared to the richness and complexity of the languages produced by human beings. Only people can read a book, write a letter, or tell their children about good and bad.

The study of language is central to cognitive psychology because language represents the pinnacle of our ability to manipulate symbols. In the words of Noam Chomsky, an influential language scholar, "Anyone concerned with the study of human nature and human capacities must somehow come to grips with the fact that all normal humans acquire language" (1972, p. 66). Of course, languages differ from one another to the extent that people who do not understand a particular language cannot understand someone speaking that language, but all languages have some basic, universal properties in common. The search for these properties is one approach that psychologists use to study cognition.

Characteristics of Language

Perhaps the most fundamental characteristic of language is that it is meaningful. When we communicate to others our primary goal is to communicate meaning. The purpose of using language is to affect the behavior of the listener or reader (Hormann, 1986). Utterances from a simple, "Look behind the desk" to the more profound, "I love you," are intended to change some aspect of the other person's awareness and perception of the world. Ultimately, almost all questions about the way in which we use language concern, at some level, the way that meaning is communicated and understood.

> *The purpose of using language is to affect the behavior of the listener or reader.*

A second characteristic of language is that it is symbolic; that is, we have the ability to symbolize objects and events that are not immediately present. Without this ability, we would be forever trapped in the world of the here and now, experiencing the world only on the basis of immediate sensations. By using symbols, the young child is able to think and talk about mother even when mother is away. With symbols, we can plan for the future and reflect upon the past, we can imagine, and we can dream. Symbols also provide the basis for a crucial accomplishment of our species, the ability to transmit information from one generation to the next. Because of this remarkable ability, much of our learning begins not from scratch, but from the accumulated knowledge of previous generations.

A third characteristic of language is that most of its symbols are arbitrary; that is, they have no intrinsic relationship to the object they symbolize. The word *buzz* may indeed resemble the actual buzzing noise of a bee, but most words in human languages are like the English word *father*. Neither the written word *father*, nor the sound of that word when pronounced, is logically or physically related to the person of father. Because the symbols of human language are arbitrary, almost all of the words for *father* in the thousands of different human languages past and present differ from one another. Despite these wide differences, each speaker of a particular language recognizes and uses the word for *father* in that language. We say *my father* and the French say *mon pere*, but both refer to a person's father.

A fourth characteristic of human language is that it is productive—we have the ability to create new sentences we've never before encountered. Not only do we generate these expressions effortlessly, but other people can also understand and respond to them as well. For example, have you ever heard anyone say, "My goodness, my psychology class is such a thrill that I feel like using the money I was going to spend on my new stereo system to make a donation to the university above and beyond my tuition." Do you understand this sentence well enough to provide a response?

In sum, language is meaningful, symbolic, arbitrary, and productive. To use language is to be creative and to generate sentences that you have never before seen or heard. To understand how such creativity is possible, we need to understand some of the rules that allow us to generate and understand the language. These rules, and other basic structures of language, are the subject of the next section.

The Structure of Language

Language is a marvelous mixture of freedom and constraint. We can express countless ideas and feelings with language, but these expressions do not communicate meaning to other people unless they are grammatical. A surprising aspect of language use is that all of us have mastered the basic rules of our language, yet most of us are unable to state precisely these rules. We use language effortlessly and accurately without being aware of the rules.

One set of rules for a spoken language governs how we understand sounds. Every sound uttered differs in some way from every other sound. We only hear a limited number of sounds when listening to any spoken language, so we must group similar sounds into the same category and then perceive these similar sounds as the "same" sound. The smallest unit of sound that can be heard is called a **phoneme**. Any word can be broken down into separate phonemes. For example the word *beat* consists of three phonemes: the *b* sound, the long *e* sound designated by the letters *ea* , and the *t* sound. Note that the same letter can designate different phonemes depending on the context in which the letter is used. All long and short vowels, such as the *a* in *bake* and *bat* are examples of different phonemes represented by the same letter.

To use a spoken language we must be able to generate the sounds of the language, and we must understand these sounds when we listen to others speak. Together, all known spoken languages use a total of about 200 phonemes, but each language uses only a fraction of this total (Ashcraft, 1989). For example, combinations of the 26 letters of the English alphabet correspond to about 44 phonemes in the English language. Some languages such as Hawaiian use 15 or fewer phonemes. This is why the Hawaiian traveler (or resident) soon learns to pronounce most Hawaiian words; they use only five vowels and seven consonants, all of which appear in the following words: Honolulu, Kukuiolono, Hanapepe, Waininiua, and Mahukona.

The purpose of spoken language is to communicate, so the phonemes of a language singly or in groups must communicate meaning. Although some individual phonemes by themselves convey meaning, such as the word *I*, the smallest unit of meaning in language, the **morpheme**, usually represents a combination of phonemes. Sometimes a morpheme may be the complete word, such as *chair*, or the morpheme may be a prefix or suffix that is grouped with other morphemes to form a more complex word. For example, the morpheme *s* indicates a plural and the morpheme *pre* indicates before. The word *chairs*, then, consists of two separate morphemes: *chair* and *s*. The English language has about 90,000 morphemes, of which the average English speaker uses about 50,000.

To represent and communicate more complex meaning than that conveyed by the individual morpheme, morphemes are grouped into words which, in turn, are grouped into phrases and sentences. These groupings are far from arbitrary, though. Instead, the form of each coherent sentence we write or speak is organized according to well-defined rules that specify how the words of a sentence should be arranged. Collectively, these rules are called the **syntax** of language. We immediately and effortlessly recognize violations of syntax even though few of us can precisely state these rules.

Although evidence shows that some animals have basic language skills, the unique ability to read, write, and converse in rich and complex languages belongs to human beings.

The syntax of our language is so well-defined that it can be recognized even in sentences that have no meaning. Consider the following example of correct syntax: *Colorless green ideas sleep furiously.* A meaningless sentence, to be sure, but you immediately recognize it as a grammatically correct sentence. Contrast this sentence with the following: *Furiously sleep ideas green colorless.* This second sentence is meaningless too, but it is also ungrammatical—it simply does not conform to the structure of how words are grouped together to make sentences in our language.

Proper syntax produces sentences that can be understood in terms of what is called **surface structure**—the organization of sentences in terms of component phrases as they are actually spoken or read (Chomsky, 1965). Simple sentences such as, *The boys saw Mary,* consist of only two phrases, a noun phrase, *The boys,* and a verb phrase, *saw Mary.* More complex sentences are described by correspondingly complex phrases.

These various elements of language—phonemes, morphemes, words, phrases, and sentences—can be organized into a hierarchical system as shown in Figure 9.8 for the sentence *The boys saw Mary.* At the bottom level of the hierarchy are individual sounds for spoken language and letters for written language. Letters are grouped together into syllables, which are then grouped into words. Words, in turn, are grouped together to form phrases, and then sentences. At this point, this hierarchy can be extended beyond that shown in Figure 9.8. Sentences are arranged to form paragraphs, and paragraphs are chained together to form complete stories or texts.

The use of phonemes, morphemes, words, phrases, and sentences is an essential part of language, but psychologists are primarily interested in the cognitive processing that underlies language use. One psychological implication of surface structure pertaining to spoken language is that it provides the basis for perceiving the spoken sentence. Specifically, regardless of how a sentence is actually spoken, we tend to perceive pauses at the boundaries that separate phrases, such as between the noun phrase *the boys* and the verb phrase *saw Mary.*

To show this, Fodor and Bever (1965) tape-recorded a variety of sentences and then randomly superimposed a series of clicks over the original sentences. The words of a sentence such as *The boys saw Mary* were presented to one ear of a subject at the same rate with the same acoustic break between each pair of words in the series. While each subject heard the sentence in one ear, a click played in his or her other ear. Although this click could have appeared anywhere in the sentence, the result was that

FIGURE 9.8
The hierarchical structure of a sentence.

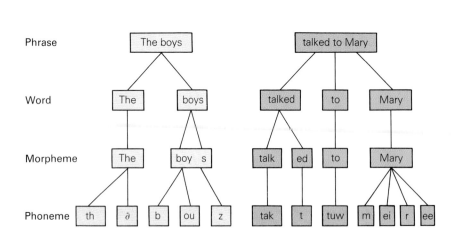

Some people are cleaning the machines.

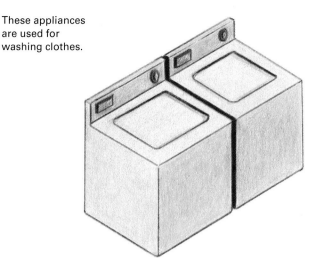

These appliances are used for washing clothes.

FIGURE 9.9
Two interpretations of the sentence They are washing machines.

regardless of where the clicks did occur, subjects tended to "hear" them at the phrase boundaries.

Why would the listener tend to hear clicks at boundaries regardless of where the clicks actually occurred? Because in spoken language, the perception of brief pauses at the boundaries between the phrases of a sentence allows the listener to easily comprehend the intended meaning of individual phrases.

The importance of the organization of a sentence according to its surface structure is that this organization provides the listener with clues as to the meaning of the sentence. The surface structure alone, however, does not convey the meaning of a sentence, as can be seen by analyzing ambiguous sentences, sentences that can be interpreted in more than one way. For example, consider the meaning of the following sentence: *They are washing machines.* This ambiguous sentence could refer to one of two possible meanings (see Figure 9.9): (1) some people are cleaning the machines, or, (2) those machines are used to wash clothes. In the first interpretation, the word *washing* in the original sentence is a verb; it designates what the people are doing. In the second interpretation, *washing* is an adjective, describing what kind of machines are being discussed.

The sentence *They are washing machines* shows that different meanings can underlie the same set of words. Yet, in other sentences, we can completely rescramble the words without changing the meaning. For example, *The cat ate the food* and *The food was eaten by the cat* have different surface structures, but they convey the same meaning. How do we recognize the common meaning underlying these two sentences? The answer to this question involves the deep structure of the sentences. **Deep structure** refers to the meaning of the sentence. The fact that we view these sentences as more or less synonymous implies that we cognitively process them at a deeper level of organization that underlies their surface expressions.

Consider the meaning of the following sentence, *Visiting relatives can be a pain.* Does this sentence refer to the relatives who are visiting you, or does it refer to you visiting the relatives? As with the washing machines sentence, we again have two different meanings that underlie the same sentence. The surface structure that corresponds to these two meanings are identical: a noun phrase, *visiting relatives,* followed by a verb phrase, *can be a pain.* These two meanings, then, can only be distinguished at the level of the deep structure. In order to generate or comprehend the meaning of any sentence, we must cognitively process the sentence at the level of deep structure. Although the specific nature of this processing awaits clarification from further research, in general, two different transformations must change two distinct meanings into the same surface structure.

To understand how we use language, then, we need to understand two different ways of processing information cognitively. One way is at the level of the surface structure of a sentence, which refers to how the sentence is actually expressed. This expression can be understood in terms of a hierarchical structure beginning with the phrases, the words, the morphemes, and finally the phonemes. In addition to the surface structure, we also process information in terms of its deep structure, or the underlying meaning of the sentence. We turn now to a discussion of how we acquire language.

Language Development

Throughout your life you have learned a wide variety of skills, but nothing you have ever learned is more remarkable than learning language. Not only did you memorize the meanings of thousands of words, but you also learned the complex syntax of this language, which for most of you is English. And to master language, you didn't have to be a genius, apply much conscious effort, receive formal training, or put in years of practice. One of the most distinguishing characteristics of our species is that most children begin to use language spontaneously sometime during their second year. How can we describe the early speech of the child, and how can we account for how it occurs?

The very first sounds recognizable as an early form of speech is the babbling of the 3- or 4-month old infant. All infants capable of speech babble, even those who are deaf (Fromkin & Rodman, 1983). These babbles represent a wide range of the 200 or so phonemes that people can produce, though usually not all of the phonemes in any one language appear in the babbling (Oller et al., 1976). In other words, early babbling seems to consist of phonemes that are not part of any particular language, including the language of those who are raising the child. As the child approaches one year of age, only the phonemes of the language he or she regularly hears begin to be used, so the babbling gradually begin to resemble the sounds of that language.

Early babbling by 3- or 4-month-old infants consists of phonemes that are not necessarily part of a specific language. When children approach one year of age, babbling starts to resemble the sounds of the language they hear and eventually will be using.

Around one year of age the child begins to understand that specific sounds can have specific meanings. At this time the child also begins to say single words, the first of which for English speaking children are usually the words *mama* and *dada*. For several months or so thereafter the young child builds a vocabulary of about 50 single words, most of which describe things of interest in his or her environment, such as a favorite toy or a friendly sister or brother. Sometimes though, these words are used to convey meanings more complex than that ordinarily attached to a single word, particularly when used with pointing and other gestures. For example, the young child pointing toward his or her mother and saying, *"Mama, mama,"* may be asking his mother to pick him or her up—a request considerably more detailed than the literal interpretation of the word *mama*.

Usually a few months before the second birthday, the young child graduates to using primitive sentences that consist of two-word phrases such as *more milk* and *tummy hurt*. This speech is often called **telegraphic speech** because the phrases resemble those sent in a telegram in which the sender is charged by the word, so he or she attempts to be as brief as possible. Most of these two-word phrases consist of words that emphasize content such as *tummy* and words that directly describe the content such as *hurt* (Brown, 1973). This emphasis on content, however, depends to some extent on the specific language being learned. Children learning some languages that differ greatly from English, however, might also use words in their telegraphic speech that do not refer to content, such as the words that mean *will* and *to* (Slobin, 1985).

By 2½ years, the child's grasp of language is developing rapidly. At this point the complexity of language usage quickly explodes to include three- and four-word sentences, and soon, the child is speaking full-length sentences. The speed at which children acquire language is phenomenal.

How is language acquired? Although the answer to this question is still sketchy, there are several different theories of language acquisition (Rice, 1989). For much of this century, the behaviorist explanation of language acquisition prevailed. The most influential statement of this position was made by B. F. Skinner (1957), who used the basic principles of operant conditioning to explain how language is acquired. Skinner treated the development of language as he treated the development of behavior in general: it is the product of learning. Behavior is shaped through successive approximations and differential reinforcement. For Skinner, the key to language learning is the same as the key to any kind of learning—reinforcement. For example, as the child begins to learn how to say a new word such as *airplane*, parents reinforce utterances that only they could recognize as referring to *airplane*. As learning proceeds, however, parents and others reward the child for successively better pronunciations. Over time, the child's behavior is gradually shaped until everyone can recognize his or her pronunciation of *airplane*.

Without denying the importance of reinforcement in language learning development, most psychologists today argue that learning principles alone cannot account for this language acquisition. Today, psychologists tend to advocate an interactionist position (Bohannon & Warren-Leubecker, 1985; Ashcraft, 1989). Psychologists generally agree that we cannot fully understand language acquisition until we are able to understand its biological basis, its environmental basis, and the way in which biology and the environment interact to influence this development. Without both the inherited structure of the brain that provides the physical capacity for language processing, and the experience of interacting with others in an environment rich in language usage, this extraordinary cognitive ability would simply not develop.

We have seen that the use of language is not only universal, but that similar patterns of language acquisition exist around the world. Yet, the specific content and syntax of two different human languages can be dramatically different. The question explored in the next section is whether other animals are capable of language.

Nonhuman Communication

Recall that in Chapter 4 we learned about the physiological basis of language. Briefly, language use and comprehension are under the control of two brain structures, Broca's area and Wernicke's area. For most people, these structures are located in the left hemisphere. Recall, too, that the evolution of the brain, particularly the brain structures involved in higher cognitive processes, is an important distinction between our species and others with whom we share the planet. The effects of brain evolution on behavior are perhaps most apparent in the area of language.

The chasm between our language use and that of other species is so large that many scientists argue that the simpler communication systems of nonhuman animals do not qualify as even a simple language. However, this chasm has been narrowed during the last few decades as we have learned more about animal behavior. Since the late 1960s researchers have shown that some primates, primarily chimpanzees and gorillas, have learned some impressive language-like skills.

The issue of whether chimps and gorillas have learned a language that indeed resembles a human language has proved to be difficult to answer. One problem is the difficulty of defining language precisely. When one researcher claimed that an animal had learned to use language, another would add another criterion to the definition of language. Today, researchers are less concerned with whether animals are capable of learning a humanlike language, and instead focus on understanding animals' cognitive capacities in their own right (Roitblat, 1987).

The first attempts at teaching language to animals were failures because researchers tried to teach chimpanzees to speak. In two different studies (Hayes, 1952; Kellogg & Kellogg, 1933), chimpanzees were raised as if they were human children. The Kelloggs went so far as to raise a chimp along with their young son. After many years of training, the chimps were able to speak only a few words, and these words were barely recognizable to anyone other than those who raised the animal. Only later did researchers realize that the reason for the chimps' poor language performance was the inability of their vocal tracts to produce the phonemes of the English language.

Chimpanzee language use studies produced more successful results when researchers selected a nonverbal means of expression, particularly one suited to the chimp's high level of manual dexterity. The issue of interest is not whether a chimp can vocalize human speech, but what the capacity of the chimpanzee's cognitive processing ability is. Beatrice and Allen Gardner (1969) chose to teach their chimp Washoe a simplified version of the American Sign Language or ASL, the sign language used by deaf people in North America. The Gardners raised Washoe from about her first birthday in 1966, and spent part of almost every day with her for several years. When around Washoe, the Gardners even communicated between themselves in ASL. After seven months, Washoe had learned only four signs, but then the number of signs she learned increased rapidly until after 51 months of training her vocabulary grew to 132 signs. Washoe was also able to combine signs to form simple phrases such as *Washoe sorry* and *Out open please hurry* (Gardner & Gardner, 1971). Some of the phrases were even her own constructions. After learning how to sign for the verb *open* she signed *Open faucet* when she wanted a drink.

FIGURE 9.10
Koko the gorilla listens to her trainer, Penny Patterson, read the story of the three little kittens who lost their mittens. Koko signs the word bad *when she hears that the mother cat is angry and the kittens are crying.*

Since the work of the Gardners, a variety of animal language teaching projects have been conducted. Roger Fouts, who worked with the Gardners for many years with Washoe, has shown that chimps will use ASL to communicate with each other (Fouts, 1973). Not only do chimps who know elements of ASL send messages to each other, but a young chimp who spends some of her time with Washoe has been observed learning the signs directly from her (Fouts, Hirsch, & Fouts, 1983).

Many researchers have focused on teaching ASL to chimpanzees, while others have taught different languages or used different species. David and Ann Premack (1972) trained a chimp named Sarah to manipulate small plastic tokens that symbolized different words and relations. Sarah learned to form sentences by arranging the tokens into a column on a board. In one impressive demonstration, Sarah performed some elementary symbol manipulation. In this plastic token language a blue plastic triangle represented an apple. When asked to choose the symbols that describe the color and shape of the blue plastic triangle, Sarah chose the tokens that represent "red" and "round," indicating that she could use the symbol of a blue plastic triangle to represent a red, round apple. Premack (1983) has even argued that chimps who learn a language are able to solve certain types of problems that other chimps cannot solve.

The animal that has acquired the largest vocabulary is a gorilla named Koko, who has learned about 800 ASL signs (Patterson & Linden, 1981). Trained by Penny Patterson since her birth, Koko has become adept at forming phrases from ASL signs as shown in Figure 9.10, and apparently of even thinking in terms of the signs. She uses signs to express her mood (happy or sad), has told a lie when she tried to hide the fact that she broke a toy, and refers to both past and future events. Not only is Koko's use of language characterized by properties of human language, but some of the intentions that she communicates are similar to those communicated by human language, such as emotion and lying.

Can nonhuman primates use language in the same sense that humans can use language? These animals have certainly not matched the language abilities of people. However, they have been shown to manipulate symbols to represent objects, events, and relations. This, of course, means that these animals are capable of processing information cognitively. The extent to which these animals can think and process information is an issue that awaits further research.

BOUNDARIES AND FRONTIERS

A major theme of this chapter has been that cognitive processes are computational processes. According to this computational metaphor, cognitive processes resemble functioning computer programs, because they both appear to process information similarly. Recent research is extending this metaphor beyond information processing (the software) to the hardware itself, the computer. The hardware on which the programs of human cognition run is the most profound biological system that we know of—the human brain.

The field of study that attempts to understand the relationship between human cognition and the organization and functioning of the brain is called *neurocognition*. The goal of this field is to understand the biological bases of cognitive processes. Consistent with the computational metaphor, one way in which neurocognition is studied is to design the physical structure of machines to resemble the physical structure of neural circuits within the brain in some ways. Instead of programming the cognitive processing directly, as with expert systems, some research in neurocognition tests theories of the functioning of the human brain by building machines to mimic its physical activities. Cognitive processing should then emerge as a consequence of the physical structure and operation of this machine, just as human cognitive processing emerges from the interplay of billions of neurons within the human brain.

The computers with which researchers in neurocognition work are not those that closely resemble ordinary computers of the early 1990s. Almost all computers built today, whether relatively small, inexpensive microcomputers or large, multi-million dollar mainframe computers, process information serially. The instructions contained in computer programs must be arranged and processed in order, one after the other. The computers of interest to those studying neurocognition are parallel processors, which may have thousands of individual processing units all working simultaneously and in concert to form a vast network of neuronlike connections. A parallel processing computer is much more similar to the human brain than is a serial processing computer (Anderson, 1983). To emphasize this similarity, these new machines are often called neural networks. As is true of individual neurons within the brain, all of the individual processing units in the neural network are capable of simultaneous action.

The principle that underlies the construction of neural networks is called collective action. The primary point of collective action is the same principle of Gestalt theory we discussed in Chapter 5: the behavior of the overall system often cannot be easily predicted from the behavior of its constituent parts. New properties emerge from specific configurations of components. Instead of following the traditional information processing approach to cognition, in which cognitive processes were broken down into components such as rules and operations, these scientists, who call themselves connectionists, focus on these emergent properties of brain functioning.

To illustrate collective action, consider an example provided by the physicist John Hopefield (1986, p. 24).

> Suppose you put two molecules in a box. Every once in a while they collide. . . . If we put 10 or even 1,000 more molecules in the box, all we get is more collisions. If we put a billion billion molecules in the box, there's a new phenomenon—sound waves. There was nothing in the behavior of two molecules in the box, or 10 or 1,000 molecules, that would suggest to you that a billion billion molecules would be able to produce sound waves. Sound waves are a collective phenomenon.

Connectionists argue that the same phenomenon can be applied to neurons. Properties emerge from the workings of thousands or billions of neurons that are not predictable from the properties of individual neurons. One such property, the connectionists maintain, is human thought.

Where do the blueprints from these machines come from? One approach is to build (or simulate) machines that directly mimic aspects of the nervous systems of very primitive animals, such as those that are found in the *Aplysia* discussed in the previous chapter. The goal, then, is to map the pattern of neuronal activity that underlies specific tasks (Gluck & Thompson, 1987). At present, learning how the activities of billions of neurons are coordinated to regulate and define mental processing is well beyond the technology and theory of contemporary neurocognition and cognitive psychology. It may be possible, however, to learn some basic principles of neural functioning in relation to cognitive processing from the study of primitive nervous systems, again applying the principles of collective action.

If this code is deciphered, progress toward understanding the biological basis of cognition could increase considerably. Roughly similar to the plight of those who first learned to translate ancient Egyptian hieroglyphics, once a few basic principles and words of the language of the nervous system are deciphered, the rest of the deciphering proceeds much easier.

As we have seen, researchers in the field of neurocognition are taking the beginning steps for exploring the relationship between the human brain and cognitive process. Many of them are using computers not just to process their data but as models of the brain and cognitive processing as well. The success of this task will not be known for some time, and the research will likely continue well into the next century. Without question, neurocognition represents one of the most exciting frontiers in cognitive psychology.

CONCEPT SUMMARY

INFORMATION, CONCEPTS, AND SYMBOLS

- What is the computational metaphor? How does this metaphor influence psychologists in their study of thinking? (pp. 297–298)
- What is the role of symbols in information processing? (p. 298)
- What does it mean to say that concepts are organized hierarchically? (pp. 298–301)
- In terms of concepts, what is a prototype? (pp. 302–303)

REASONING

- How does inductive reasoning differ from deductive reasoning? (pp. 304–308)
- How does the belief-bias effect influence deductive reasoning? (pp. 305–306)
- How does confirmation bias influence our ability to draw inductively valid conclusions? (pp. 307–308)

PROBLEM SOLVING

- How do heuristics differ from algorithms? (pp. 308–309)
- How do expert systems work? (pp. 311–312)
- How can availability and representativeness heuristics be misused? (pp. 312–314)
- In what ways might people become "fixated" in their thinking? (pp. 315–316)

LANGUAGE

- What are the characteristics of language? (pp. 318–319)
- How is language structured? What is the difference between surface and deep structure? (pp. 319–322)
- How is language acquired? (pp. 322–324)
- Do animals other than humans possess language capacity? Explain. (pp. 324–325)

KEY TERMS AND CONCEPTS

INFORMATION, SYMBOLS, AND CONCEPTS

Cognition The full range of mental activities used to represent and process knowledge, including perception, memory, thought, and the use of language. (p. 296)

Information Processing The way that knowledge is represented and processed. (p. 297)

Computational Metaphor The metaphor used by cognitive psychologists that likens human cognition to a computer program. Cognition is computation. (p. 297)

Symbol A mental construction that stands for or represents something else. (p. 298)

Concept A grouping of similar objects, events, or people into categories. (p. 298)

Cognitive Economy The minimization of the amount of effort and time required in the processing of stimuli. (p. 301)

Prototypes A set of characteristics that apply to the most representative or typical member of the category but not necessarily to all instances. (p. 302)

REASONING

Thinking The manipulation or construction and modification of internal symbolic representations. (p. 304)

Reasoning The process of drawing conclusions from a set of facts. (p. 304)

Deductive Reasoning A form of reasoning in which a conclusion is implied by two or more statements. (p. 304)

Belief-bias Effect The improper evaluation of the validity of a conclusion on the basis of what is believed to be true instead of from a logical analysis of the premises. (p. 305)

Inductive Reasoning Reasoning that extends our knowledge beyond the known facts. (p. 306)

Confirmation bias People's tendency to search for instances that confirm our beliefs rather than to search for evidence that falsifies what we believe. (p. 307)

PROBLEM SOLVING

Problem A situation in which there is a goal that is not immediately obtainable. Problem solving involves processing information about that situation. (p. 308)

Algorithm A completely specified, step-by-step set of rules for solving a problem. (p. 308)

Heuristics Intuitive strategies for solving problems that use simple informal rules of thumb or general guidelines. (p. 309)

Forward Chaining A heuristic problem-solving procedure that involves selecting the best out of many possible actions, observing what happens, and then, depending on the result, repeating the process by taking another action. (p. 310)

Backward Chaining A heuristic problem-solving procedure that begins with a potential solution called the hypothesis and searches for evidence that explains the hypothesis. (p. 310)

Expert System A computer program that, like a human expert, uses heuristics and knowledge about the world to solve problems. (p. 312)

Availability Heuristic A heuristic for judging frequencies that relies primarily on the importance of the information that is most readily and easily available to the person solving the problem. (p. 313)

Representativeness Heuristic A heuristic in which people classify an object into the category to which it appears to be the most similar. (p. 314)

Gambler's Fallacy A mistaken belief that the outcome of the next chance event is predicted on the basis of representativeness. (p. 314)

Fixation The tendency to view a problem solely in one particular way. (p. 315)

Mental Set An example of a fixation. The tendency to repeat the type of solutions that have worked in the past. (p. 315)

Functional Fixedness An example of a fixation. The tendency to limit possible solutions by using objects only in the way that they have been traditionally used. (p. 315)

Insight The sudden flash of understanding, where all of the pieces of a problem suddenly fit together and the solution becomes clear. (p. 316)

Creativity The generation of novel and useful solutions to problems. (p. 316)

Incubation The development of insight into a problem only *after* a person has stopped consciously thinking about potential solutions. (p. 316)

LANGUAGE

Language A written or spoken system of symbol manipulation that is used to represent and communicate our thoughts to others. (p. 317)

Phoneme The smallest unit of sound that can be heard. (p. 319)

Morpheme The smallest unit of meaning in language. (p. 319)

Syntax The well-defined rules that specify how the words of a sentence should be arranged. (p. 319)

Surface Structure The organization of a sentence in terms of its component phrases as it is actually spoken or read. (p. 320)

Deep Structure The structure underlying a sentence that is directly related to the meaning of the sentence. (p. 321)

Telegraphic Speech A form of early speech in which a young child uses short, two-word phrases resembling those sent in a telegram. (p. 323)

ADDITIONAL SOURCES OF INFORMATION

Ashcraft, M. H. (1989). *Human memory and cognition.* Glenview, IL: Scott, Foresman. A recent, thorough, and readable text that explores each of the major areas of cognition.

Gardner, H. (1985). *The mind's new science: A history of the cognitive revolution.* New York: Basic Books. A fascinating account of the history of cognitive science. Well-written and documented, this book explains the major issues of cognitive science from a historical perspective.

Kahneman, D., Slovic, P., & Tversky, A., (Eds.). (1982). *Judgment under uncertainty: Heuristics and biases.* New York: Cambridge University Press. This is the classic summary of work in the biases of heuristics up until the early 1980s. Although written for a professional audience, much of the material should be accessible to the undergraduate.

Simons, G. (1986). *Is man a robot?* New York: Wiley. As computer technology and cognitive science progress, people are becoming better at building robots that perform human functions. Simons turns the question around, and provocatively stretches the computational metaphor to its limit, asking if humans are robots.

Sternberg, R. J., & Smith, E. E. (1988). *The psychology of human thought.* New York: Cambridge University Press. An edited text that surveys the field of cognition. Each chapter is written by an expert in the specific topic area of the chapter.

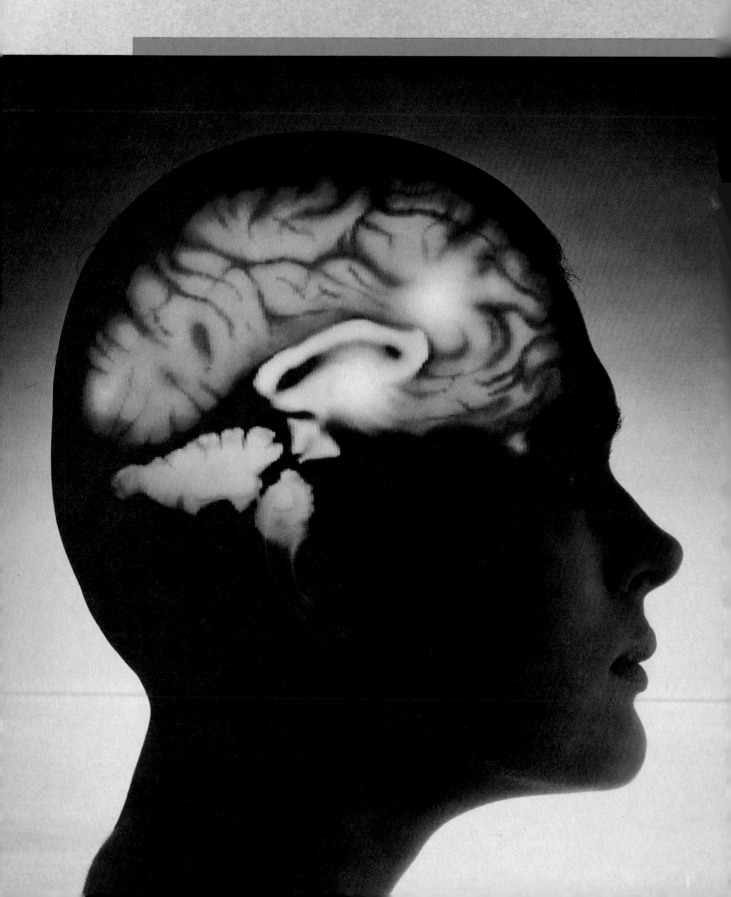

Motivation involves three major aspects of behavior: the initiation and orientation of a behavior toward a goal, the intensity of a behavior, and the cessation of a behavior.

MOTIVATION *(332–334)*

Motivation is viewed as an intervening variable that cannot be observed directly. Since intervening variables cannot be seen or manipulated directly, their existence is inferred based on changes in an individual's observable behavior. Intervening variables are believed to be either genetic, learned, or a combination of heredity and learning.

GENERAL THEORIES OF MOTIVATION
(335–345)

Instinct Theory   Drive Theory   Need Theories   Optimal-Arousal Theory
Opponent-Process Theory   Incentive and Expectancy Theories

Psychologists do not agree on which motivational concepts and theories best explain behavior. Instinct theory, in its original form, was based on the misguided idea that all behavior is genetically preprogrammed. Some theories like drive, optimal-arousal, and opponent-process are based to different extents on homeostasis, the idea that our bodies seek a balance in certain internal states. Other theories are based on the concept of need as well as homeostasis. We have certain physiological and psychological needs that, when left unsatisfied, impel us to action until they are satisfied. Incentive and expectancy theories do not involve either need or homeostasis. Rather, they stress that the role of rewards and our expectations about them determine motivation.

MOTIVATION FOR EATING *(345–353)*

Internal Signals for Hunger   External Signals for Hunger
The Brain and Eating: Is There a Control Center?   Obesity: The Facts and the Likely Causes   Eating Disorders: Anorexia Nervosa and Bulimia

Eating is correlated with both internal and external signals. The hypothalamus and other brain structures also play an important role in motivating eating. A high number of fat cells, high set point, sensitivity to external food cues, and disinhibition and stress are correlated with overeating and obesity. Anorexia nervosa and bulimia are two common eating disorders in females that apparently are triggered by social pressures to maintain a thin figure.

MOTIVATION FOR AGGRESSION
(353–358)

Instinct Theories   Physiological Factors in Aggression   Frustration and Aggression   Arousal and Aggression   Social Learning Theory and Aggression

Psychologists have several theories to explain aggression. Instinct theory holds that aggression is an innate response. Other theories claim that the brain, particularly the amygdala, triggers aggressive behavior. The frustration-aggression hypothesis holds that aggression results when progress toward a goal is hindered. Aggression may also stem from physical arousal, such as that caused by exercise. According to social learning theory, people may learn to behave aggressively by observing the reinforcement of aggressive behavior in other people.

EATING, AGGRESSION, AND MOTIVATION *(359)*

Although our understanding of eating and aggression is far from complete, we do know that both are likely due to the interaction of biology and learning. By better understanding how these factors interact, we will not only learn more about motivation, but we will also be able to develop interventions to modify maladaptive patterns of eating and aggression.

EMOTION *(359–370)*

Classifying Emotion   The Facial Expressions of Emotion
The Physiology of Emotion   Theories of Emotion

Emotion has four components: a particular affect or feeling, physiological arousal, cognitive appraisal, and behavioral reaction. Plutchik's emotion solid represents a classification system for emotion. Darwin's work, along with the recent work of Ekman, shows that facial expressions accompanying emotion have a strong biological basis. Regardless of cultural background, people tend to link particular facial expressions with particular emotions. Although the brain exerts some control over emotion, our experience of emotion is also due to direct environmental stimulation of the autonomic nervous system. Theories of emotion attempt to explain specifically how physiological arousal, emotion-eliciting stimuli, behavioral expression, cognition, and previous experience interact to produce emotions.

■ The date is July 18, 1984. The place is San Ysidro, California. After telling his wife that he is "going hunting for humans," James Huberty, 41, walks into a busy McDonald's restaurant carrying a 9mm Uzi semiautomatic rifle, a 9mm pistol, and a shotgun. Less than 90 minutes later, 21 people lay dead, 19 wounded. Among the dead: an 8-month old baby, an 11-year-old boy who aspired to be the world's greatest guitar player, a 24-year-old pregnant woman who had three sons, and a retired couple only a few months away from their fiftieth anniversary. El asesino (the assassin), as Huberty came to be referred to by the people of San Ysidro, was himself killed, picked off by a dead-eyed SWAT sniper from atop a neighboring building.

■ The date is now. The place is the community in which you live. Susan, a 19-year-old college student, is on her knees, her face lowered into a toilet. She has just finished eating and is now forcing herself to vomit. Oddly enough, she is not ill. You see, hers was not a normal meal. She consumed a carton of eggs, a liter of soft drink, a double batch of homemade chocolate-chip cookies, and an entire bag of potato chips. Two days from now she will go on another eating binge but will purge herself this time by taking several strong laxatives instead of vomiting. In fact, during the next month, Susan will "binge and purge" at least a dozen times.

The people in these examples are interesting to us because their behavior is out of the ordinary. Although eating disorders are actually quite common in our society, not many of us know people who suffer from them. Huberty's cruelty and bizarreness stun us. We want to know more about these people and others like them. Why did Huberty murder those helpless people? Why would anyone eat so much and then throw it all up?

In this chapter we consider the topic of motivation, the area of psychology that deals with such "why" questions. All psychologists must understand motivation in order to understand behavior.

MOTIVATION

The term *motivation* stems from the Latin word, *movere*, which means "to move." What sorts of things can move behavior, so to speak? What causes you to do the things you do? **Motivation** may be defined broadly as the cause of behavior. In particular, it is concerned with three major aspects of behavior:

- the initiation and orientation of a behavior toward a specific goal
- the intensity or strength of a behavior
- the cessation of behavior

Traditionally, psychologists have approached questions about motivation from two different perspectives. One holds that motivation is comprised of different drives that arise from within us. These internal drives may be either temporary, like the hunger drive that motivates us to eat every now and then, or permanent and stable, like our tendencies to be friendly, aggressive, or loving. We often think of the latter kinds of drives as reflective of our disposition or personality.

FIGURE 10.1
The hypothesized causal relationship between intervening variables and behavior. In this chapter, we discuss seven different kinds of intervening variables.

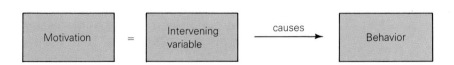

Whether we are doing a Tyrolian traverse high above the ground or dancing in a ballet, we are driven or motivated to perform these tasks. Biological, environmental, cognitive, and social factors are all at work to determine our varying behaviors.

The other perspective holds that motivation is caused by forces in the environment, that is, from the goals and rewards that we obtain as a result of our actions. Psychologists refer to these external drives as incentives or reinforcements. In general, people act to obtain pleasant or good incentives and to avoid or escape negative or unpleasant ones.

The one thing that both perspectives have in common is that they view motivation as an **intervening variable,** a hypothetical variable believed to cause behavior (see Figure 10.1). This means that motivational variables can be neither seen nor touched; rather, they are inferred on the basis of observable behavior. For instance, when we observe a girl ask her father for lunch, we say that she must be hungry. In this case, hunger is the intervening variable, and we might say that hunger is the girl's motive for asking her father for food. We cannot see hunger, but we infer it based on the girl's question. We might make the same inference if we were to see the girl go to the refrigerator or to the food cupboard, or ask her dad to take her for pizza (see Figure 10.2). One thing we know for sure though, is that when the girl becomes hungry, food becomes reinforcing. Any behavior she emits that produces food will tend to be repeated under similar circumstances when she is hungry again.

As we have seen in earlier chapters, psychologists tend to look at behavior as being due to either heredity or environmental factors. This is an important consideration when we look at motivation as well. Some actions like eating, drinking, and sex come naturally to us, but at the same time, many of the foods we like and the sorts of sexual activities we find pleasurable are surely learned. Our carnivorous tendencies are due to our biological past, but one's preferences for steak over chicken or well-done over rare are learned. Likewise, our tendency to engage in procreative activities has a genetic basis, but the kinds of activities that we enjoy most reflect our unique sexual experiences. By postulating different intervening variables, psychologists use the motivational concepts to link different stimuli with different responses.

Our experiences seem to be the result of a complex interplay of biological, environmental, cognitive, and social factors.

It should be clear by now that understanding motivation is not an easy task. Any given behavior is not usually determined by one factor alone. Instead, our experiences seem to be the result of a complex interplay of biological, environmental, cognitive, and social factors. Examining behav-

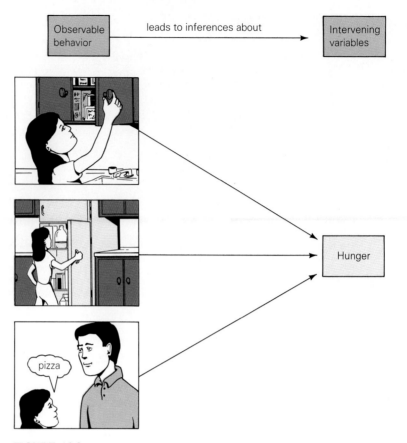

FIGURE 10.2
The nature of intervening variables. Intervening variables are not things that can be observed directly. Rather, they are inferred on the basis of observable behavior.

ior for any one of these factors alone falls short of capturing the richness of human experience. In other words, a complete understanding of motivation means that we must study behavior from more than a single perspective.

One additional factor we must consider when we study motivation is the significance of emotions in determining behavior. Our behavior always seems to have an emotional component. Our successes are accompanied with happiness and joy, our failures with frustration and disappointment. Somewhere in between lie emotions such as hope, anticipation, fear, and anxiety. An important issue we will address in this chapter is whether emotions are a cause or a by-product of behavior.

We will apply the basic concepts of motivation to understanding two very different kinds of action—eating and aggression—each of which was represented in our opening examples. Our selection of these topics was not arbitrary. We chose eating because it is an aspect of our existence that is necessary for survival. Understanding eating involves understanding related physiological processes, the cognitive and social cues that often accompany eating and eating disorders, and the consequences of eating. We chose aggression because it represents the darker side of our existence, a side that most of us wish to avoid but to which we occasionally succumb.

We turn now to an overview of theories of motivation. We then discuss eating and aggression. Next, we introduce you to the basic principles of emotion and apply them, in conjunction with the basic principles of motivation, to understanding behavior.

Psychologists do not agree on which motivational concepts and theories best explain behavior. Theories of motivation are usually developed with a single perspective in mind. For example, a cognitive psychologist might develop a theory that explains motivation from purely a cognitive point of view, overlooking other factors that might also be useful for understanding a given action. As you study the theories of motivation presented below, keep this point in mind. Doing so will help you see the shortcomings of each theory and will give you an idea of the difficulties different psychologists have run into in attempting to understand motivation.

Instinct Theory

At the turn of the century, some psychologists subscribed to **instinct theory,** the view that all behavior is motivated by instincts, which are innate or genetically determined tendencies to perform certain acts or respond in particular ways. In essence, instinctive behavior is any action that is not learned. Early use of instinct as a motivational concept finds its roots in Darwin's theory of evolution by natural selection. As you may recall, Darwin argued that animal behavior was instinctive. He felt that animals' abilities to find and court mates, defend territories, forage for food, and so on, were patterns of behavior inherited from their parents. Following Darwin's lead, several psychologists proposed that humans, too, are motivated by instincts.

William James (1890), one of the early leaders of American psychology, argued that humans are strongly guided by instincts, among them rivalry, sympathy, curiosity, and parental love. William McDougall (1908), perhaps the most ardent advocate of early instinct theory, held that there were at least ten human instincts, and that they formed the basis for all human behavior. Sigmund Freud, on the other hand, argued that only two classes of instincts were necessary to explain human action, eros, life instincts, and thanatos, death instincts. To Freud, eros involved both hunger and sexual instincts, and thanatos involved self-destructive instincts.

But these early instinct theories had problems. Unlike Darwin's theory, these arguments for instinct were not supported with data. For example, instincts were proposed for almost every kind of human action, and thus, merely described behavior rather than explained it. Consider the circularity of McDougall's idea of pugnacity, the instinct to behave aggressively. How do we know that humans are pugnacious? Because we observe them behaving aggressively. Why are they aggressive? Because of their pugnacious instinct. Instinct theory simply could not account for the wide variety of behaviors that humans were capable of learning. It seems unlikely for example, that people are born with instincts for writing or doing arithmetic. Instinct theory also fell victim to the growing popularity of behaviorism, which convinced many psychologists of that era that behavior can only be explained by observable causes, not unobservable ones such as instinct.

Instinct theory, though in a new form, is still used by ethologists. They have found the concept of instinct useful to explain the occurrence of universal response patterns in a given species that are elicited only in the presence of highly specific environmental stimuli. These response patterns, which have been shaped by natural selection over the course of evolution, are the fixed-action patterns that we discussed in Chapter 7. Ethologists have sought to establish the biological basis of fixed-action patterns by studying animal behavior under natural conditions. An example of an instinctive behavior, in this case, the zigzag or mating dance of the three-spine stickleback, is shown in Figure 10.3.

FIGURE 10.3
The zig-zag or mating dance of the three-spined stickleback. Each part of the dance is stimulated by the specific actions of each fish.

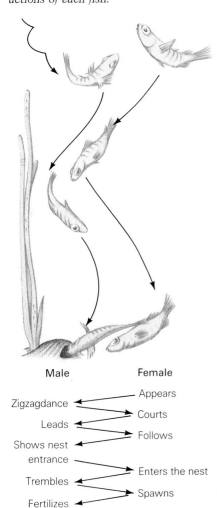

Drive Theory

Once the pitfalls of early instinct theory were realized, drive theory, another biologically based theory, became the dominant view of motivation. Drive theory stimulated a good deal of behavioral research during the 1940s and 1950s and is often associated with Clark Hull (1884–1952), the Yale University psychologist (for example, Hull, 1943).

Drive theory is based upon the idea of **homeostasis,** the tendency for all animals to strive to maintain certain internal bodily states at constant levels (Cannon, 1932). At one time or another, however, an internal state may be thrown out of balance because a basic biological need goes unsatisfied. The unsatisfied need creates a state of internal tension or arousal called a **drive.** For example, when we have gone for a long period without eating, we usually feel hungry. Hunger may be viewed as a drive state caused by food deprivation that motivates organisms to seek food. In this drive state, the behavior of the organism becomes goal oriented, and the organism attempts to re-establish homeostasis either by eliminating or reducing the drive state. Thus, when we are hungry, we forage for food. We are motivated to seek food in order to satisfy or reduce the drive (see Figure 10.4). According to Hull, behavior that successfully reduces the drive is reinforced: it is strengthened, and so is likely to be repeated any time that particular drive is present. Behavior that fails to reduce the drive is weakened and is unlikely to occur again in that particular drive state.

Drive theorists argued that there were two kinds of drives, primary drives and secondary (or acquired) drives. **Primary drives** arise from physiological needs and do not involve learning. Primary drives serve as the motivators that impel us to seek food when we are hungry, to drink when we are thirsty, and to seek warmth when we are cold. **Secondary drives** are those brought about through experience; they are learned drives believed to underlie psychological motives such as acquiring wealth, desiring affiliation, seeking approval from parents and significant others, and so on. Drive theorists believe that such drives are acquired through their association with primary drives. For example, through experience we learn that money can buy food, drink, shelter, and other things that may satisfy biological needs. The need for money to buy these things (as well as other things) creates, through learning, a secondary drive.

Primary drives arise from physiological needs and are not learned. Seeking a drink of water to quench our thirst or huddling in a blanket to keep warm are examples of satisfying primary drives.

FIGURE 10.4

Drive theory. According to drive theory, we are motivated to behave in order to satisfy or reduce drives that arise from within us.

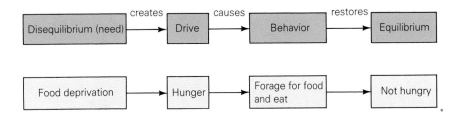

Like instinct theory, drive theory also has problems—some behaviors seem to be directed at increasing, not decreasing drive. For instance, rats will learn to make responses that permit them to initiate, but not finish, sexual intercourse with female rats (Sheffield, Wulff, & Backer, 1951). If you have ever sky dived, water or snow skied, or even watched a horror movie, you know very well that the tremendous changes in physiological and emotional arousal involved in these kinds of activities can be very enjoyable, even thrilling. Yet, these behaviors do not reduce any drive. Why not, then, postulate the existence of additional drives that account for such behaviors? The answer is because then we run into the same problem as the instinct theorists did, namely, a long list of drives (or instincts) that describe, not explain, behavior.

A second problem with drive theory is that some kinds of behavior simply do not reduce drive. For example, hungry flies will eat saccharin, which, because it is a nonnutritive substance, cannot reduce the so-called hunger drive (Sheffield & Roby, 1950). Likewise, people adrift at sea without fresh water will sometimes drink salt water, which cannot quench their thirst.

Despite these problems, concepts developed by drive theorists, such as need and homeostasis, have proved to be useful ways of thinking about motivation. Drive theory has played an enormously important role in the history of psychology if for no other reason than it provided us with a reasonable starting point at which to begin asking questions about motivation. As you will soon see, many of the concepts first developed by drive theorists have been incorporated into other theories of motivation, although in different forms and under different names.

> *rive theory . . . provided us with a reasonable starting point at which to begin asking questions about motivation.*

Need Theories

The concepts of need and homeostasis formed the cornerstones of Abraham Maslow's (1943, 1970) theory of motivation. Maslow held that both biological and psychological needs are inborn and can be powerful motivators of behavior. As a humanistic psychologist, Maslow believed that each individual's goal is to reach his or her potential. He argued that in order to reach such a goal, people must first satisfy several more basic needs. These needs are the same for everyone and are arranged in a hierarchical order (see Figure 10.5).

Maslow's Hierarchy of Needs.   Actually, Maslow argued that our motivation for different activities passes through seven stages, with entrance to subsequent stages dependent upon satisfying the needs present in previous stages. In toto, these stages are referred to as **Maslow's hierarchy.** Although these needs are inborn, we learn to satisfy them by means taught to us by our family and culture. That may be one reason we don't all like the same kinds of food, drink, and clothing styles.

Abraham Maslow

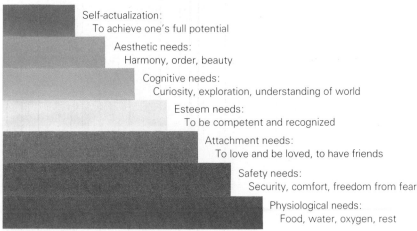

FIGURE 10.5
Maslow's hierarchy of needs. According to Maslow, the goal of every individual is to become self-actualized. In order to reach that goal, individuals must first satisfy several basic needs.

Our most basic needs are physiological, the need for food, water, oxygen, rest, and so on. Until these needs are met, we cannot be motivated by needs found in the next (or any other) stage. Why worry about love and esteem if our stomachs are empty and our throats are parched? However, if we are reasonably well-fed and do not want for either air or rest, we find ourselves motivated by safety needs, including the need for security and comfort, as well as for peace and freedom from fear. Once the basic survival and safety needs are met, we can become motivated by attachment needs, the need to love and be loved, to have friends, and to be a friend. You are probably beginning to get the picture—we are motivated by needs higher in the hierarchy only after lower needs are satisfied. If we are able to lead a life in which we have been able to provide ourselves with food and shelter and surround ourselves with loved ones and peace, we are free to pursue **self-actualization,** or achievement of our greatest potential as humans, whatever that potential might be. Maslow believed that self-actualized people are recognized by their unique qualities, including self-awareness, creativity, spontaneity, and willingness to accept change and confront challenges. Who might we consider to have reached this level of personal development? Maslow considered people such as Albert Einstein, Eleanor Roosevelt, and Henry David Thoreau to be self-actualized. And if Maslow were alive today, he would surely include Mother Teresa and Martin Luther King on his list.

According to Maslow's hierarchy, once we satisfy our basic needs in life, we move on to pursue self-actualization. Albert Einstein was among the people Maslow considered to be self-actualized or as having reached his greatest personal potential. Mother Teresa is another example of someone who has attained self-actualization.

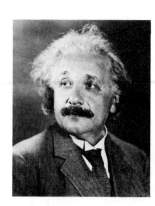

Maslow's hierarchical scheme has powerful intuitive appeal and has had considerable influence on the development of psychological therapies for helping people better their lives. Nonetheless, real life suggests that some people are able to satisfy needs of later stages before satisfying those at earlier stages: people have been known to sacrifice satisfaction of their own physiological and safety needs for the sake of love and friendship. For example, parents may go without food to have enough to give their children, and soldiers put their lives in jeopardy to protect the lives of their compatriots. Perhaps a more serious criticism of Maslow's theory is that it has not been confirmed by research; its terms and concepts have proved too vague to be tested adequately through rigorous experimentation.

The Need for Achievement, Affiliation, and Power. Another need theory proposed by personality theorist Henry Murray (b. 1893) in 1938 has fared the test of time much better than Maslow's theory. Murray believed that human motivation is comprised of a variety of psychosocial needs (see Table 10.1). In describing these needs, Murray was careful to distinguish between biologically based motives and psychologically based motives. This distinction provided fertile ground for new research into human motivation (Hilgard, 1987). Chief among Murray's needs was the **need for achievement (nAch),** the motivation to meet or surpass performance standards or to accomplish difficult tasks. Murray not only laid the conceptual background for the study of this need, but he also advocated a method for its study, a projective test called the thematic apperception test (TAT). The TAT is a personality test that requires the subject to write short stories about several ambiguous figures. The stories are then scored according to a set of objective criteria indicative of themes such as success, goal setting,

TABLE 10.1.	A Sample of Henry Murray's List of Psychosocial Needs
NEED	*DESCRIPTION*
Achievement	To overcome obstacles, to exercise power, to strive to do something difficult as well and as quickly as possible.
Acquisition	To gain possessions and property. To grasp, snatch, or steal things. To bargain or gamble. To work for money or goods.
Affiliation	To form friendships and associations. To greet, join, and live with others. To cooperate and converse sociably with others. To love. To join groups.
Cognizance	To explore (moving and touching). To ask questions. To satisfy curiousity. To look, listen, inspect. To read and seek knowledge.
Defendance	To defend oneself against blame or belittlement. To justify one's actions. To offer extenuations, explanations, and excuses. To resist "probing."
Deference	To admire and willingly follow a superior allied other. To cooperate with a leader. To serve gladly.
Nurturance	To nourish, aid, or protect a helpless other. To express sympathy. To "mother" a child.
Play	To relax, amuse oneself, seek diversion and entertainment. To "have fun," to play games. To laugh, joke, and be merry. To avoid serious tension.
Recognition	To excite praise and commendation. To demand respect. To boast and exhibit one's accomplishments. To seek distinction, social prestige, honours or high office.
Succorance	To seek aid, protection, or sympathy. To cry for help. To plead for mercy. To adhere to an affectionate, nurturant parent. To be dependent.

or attempting difficult tasks. The main idea behind the TAT is that subjects will project themes from their own lives into their interpretation of the ambiguous figures.

Following on the heels of Murray's work, David McClelland and his colleagues have studied the origins of achievement motivation and its prevalence across different societies extensively (McClelland, 1985; McClelland et al., 1976). McClelland's research methods were similar to Murray's. He showed his subjects different pictures and asked them to write stories about what they thought the pictures portrayed (see Figure 10.6). McClelland found that the themes of many of these stories were achievement-oriented, focusing on an individual attempting to obtain a particular goal. Depending on whether the subjects in the stories obtained their goals, their emotions were described as happy or sad, elated or depressed.

Researchers, though, have not been satisfied with learning only what people say about achievement, they have also sought to demonstrate whether or not their behaviors would actually reflect nAch. Experiments that have addressed this issue typically involve first judging subjects as being high or low in nAch on the basis of their stories. Next, subjects are given tasks in which the degree of difficulty can be manipulated experimentally. High achievers prefer tasks in which success is not guaranteed but which are also not so difficult that there is no chance for success. However, people high in nAch persist longer at impossible tasks than do people low in nAch when both are led to believe that the task is difficult. High achievers also accept personal responsibility for success or failure in accomplishing tasks and prefer immediate feedback as to how they are performing at the tasks (for a review, see McClelland, 1985).

McClelland has also tried to understand the origins of achievement motivation, particularly in terms of parental and cultural influences. His research in this area has lead him to study parent-child interactions and cultural practices in a number of different nations. Several of his more important and interesting findings are listed below.

- Achievement motivation is usually acquired in early childhood. Children high in nAch generally have parents who encourage them in positive ways to succeed at difficult tasks and who reward them for their successes. These children usually also have parents who have encouraged them to be creative in finding ways to accomplish difficult goals rather than urging them to quit.
- Parents who place emphasis on achievement and success in school or at work tend to have children with the same kinds of values.
- Cultures that have strong economies generally have folktales and childrens' storybooks containing themes relating to achievement, such as hard work and productivity.
- Cultures in which there is civil unrest, such as labor strikes and political protests, tend to have young people high in nAch. One reason for this finding may be that in some countries, there is little or no opportunity for those high in nAch to achieve.

In addition to the need for achievement, two other powerful motivators of human behavior appear to be the **need for affiliation**—the need to form friendships and associations with others, and the **need for power**—the need to be in control of events, resources, or other people, usually for your own advantage. As you might expect, these two motives are incompatible; it is unusual to find a person with both a high need for affiliation and a high need for power. People with a strong need for power have a strong desire to be respected, if not revered, and they tend to view others as subordinates. While these people may be voted by their colleagues as "most likely to

FIGURE 10.6
An example of the kinds of ambiguous figures used by McClelland.

In forming friendships and associations with others we are demonstrating the need for affiliation, another motivator of human behavior.

succeed" they probably would not also be voted as "most well-liked." People with a strong need for affiliation, on the other hand, desire to be with other people, but not necessarily as a "superior."

Need theory as envisioned and developed by Murray and McClelland has been successful in terms of generating research aimed at better understanding human social behavior. Nonetheless, the theory is still incomplete. Perhaps its most critical deficit is its lack of a biological basis. As McClelland (1985) admits, we do not understand the physiological basis for motives relating to achievement, affiliation, and power. In his own words:

> Clearly, what is needed is a much better way of determining what natural incentives exist for the human species, how they produce different types of affective arousal represented by varying profiles of hormone release, and how specific types of arousal form the basis for developing major motive systems through cognitive development and . . . learning. Working out these relationships is a problem of the greatest importance to understanding the nature of human motives. . . . (1985, p. 602)

Optimal-Arousal Theory

Recall that a serious drawback to drive theory was that it could not account for behaviors that actually increased drives. The **optimal-arousal theory** of motivation maintains exactly the opposite: all organisms behave to maintain an optimal level of arousal (Berlyne, 1971). If you are bored, you find something fun or interesting or exciting to do; if you are worn out, you might prefer to take a nap. According to Berlyne, our desire to engage in arousal-producing activities is motivated by the difference between our actual arousal level, or our current level of arousal, and our optimal arousal level, or the level of arousal necessary for us to function at an efficient level. If there is no difference between the actual and optimal arousal levels, an individual is functioning efficiently; but if an individual's actual arousal level is less than his or her optimal arousal level, then he or she is motivated to increase it. What happens if the actual arousal level is greater than the optimal arousal level? Berlyne's answer is that the individual is motivated to reduce his or her actual arousal level and so seeks rest or solitude. In Berlyne's view, then, people may be motivated to either increase or decrease their arousal level, depending upon its relation to the optimal arousal level (see Figure 10.7).

FIGURE 10.7

Berlyne's optimal-arousal theory. According to this theory, people are motivated to change actual-arousal level depending upon its relationship to optimal-arousal level.

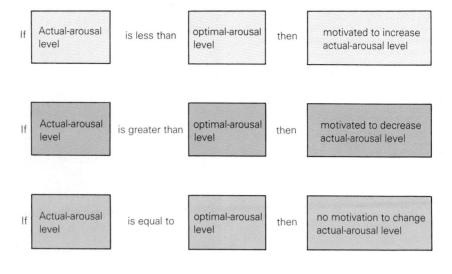

If | Actual-arousal level | is less than | optimal-arousal level | then | motivated to increase actual-arousal level

If | Actual-arousal level | is greater than | optimal-arousal level | then | motivated to decrease actual-arousal level

If | Actual-arousal level | is equal to | optimal-arousal level | then | no motivation to change actual-arousal level

What the optimal-arousal theory doesn't tell us, however, is what determines people's actual and optimal-arousal levels in the first place. People vary tremendously in the amounts and kinds of arousal they seek. Some, like race car drivers or mountain climbers, seek and enjoy high levels of arousal (Zuckerman, 1980). Others prefer more mundane and less dangerous activities like reading, sewing, or table tennis. One point of which motivational researchers are sure, though, is that there is an optimal level of arousal necessary for optimal performance of any task. Too little arousal or too much arousal interferes with performance. For example, if you are either indifferent or too anxious about how you might do on your next psychology exam, you are likely to do poorly on it. An intermediate level of arousal will produce the best results. This relation, shown in Figure 10.8, is known as the **Yerkes-Dodson law,** in honor of its formulators (Yerkes & Dodson, 1908).

Opponent-Process Theory

Imagine yourself in the door of an airplane flying 3000 feet above earth; on your back is a parachute. You are about to jump out of the plane and float to the ground below. What do you suppose you would be feeling at this moment? You are probably highly aroused—your knees feel weak, your breathing is rushed, and your palms are sweaty. You sense a hollowness in your stomach. Suddenly, your instructor gently nudges you from the plane. Your chute opens, you are bucked upward for a few seconds, and you feel a tremendous sense of relief. Once safely on the ground, you feel incredibly elated. "What a rush," you think to yourself. "Maybe I'll do this again!"

What has happened here? At one point, you are terrified, and then a few minutes later, you are ecstatic and consider putting yourself into the same situation again. According to motivational theorist Richard Solomon, the elation you experienced after the jump compensated for the anxiety you felt just before the jump. Solomon's basic point, as expressed in his **opponent-process theory**, is that for every emotional experience there is an opposite emotional experience that maintains an equilibrium between opposing emotional and motivational states. Thus, we are motivated to maintain a relatively stable emotional state. The opponent emotion that develops in response to the initial emotion may persist longer than the

A parachutist's initial feelings of anxiety, fear, and weakness, followed by relief and the strong desire to jump again are explained in Richard Solomon's opponent-process theory. The theory states that for every emotional experience there is an opposite emotional experience that maintains an equilibrium between emotional and motivational states.

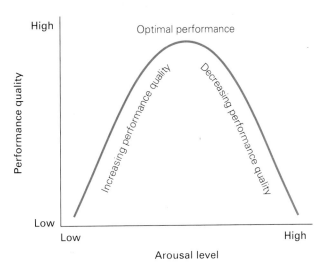

High ┤   Optimal performance

Increasing performance quality

Decreasing performance quality

Performance quality

Low ┤

Low   High

Arousal level

FIGURE 10.8
The Yerkes-Dodson Law. Extremely low or high levels of arousal lead to poor quality of performance. An intermediate level of arousal produces optimal performance.

initial emotion, thereby reducing the strength of the first emotion. Hence, your fear of parachuting will diminish with every jump, but your elation with each safe landing will persist. This is exactly what happens with people who actually do parachute or who engage in other high arousal activities, such as drug use (Solomon, 1980; Solomon & Corbitt, 1974). Opponent processes also work in reverse: pleasant emotional experiences such as a drug high will be followed by an emotional letdown which, in turn, motivates drug users to seek the high again.

Like optimal-arousal theory, opponent-process theory does not account for why people initially engage in different behaviors. For example, what causes a person to sky dive the first time? It would seem unlikely that people are motivated to sky dive or engage in other high-arousal activities initially because they have recently experienced an opposite emotion or motivational state. Opponent-process theory, then, may account for only the maintenance of such arousal-producing behaviors and not their initiation.

Incentive and Expectancy Theories

You have probably noticed that the instinct, drive, need, optimal-arousal, and opponent-process theories are similar in that they emphasize internal processes that "push" people to act in some way. In contrast, **incentive theory** embodies the idea that external events, such as goals or incentives, motivate or "pull" us to behave. Incentive theory focuses on behavior-environment interactions rather than on physiology-behavior interactions. It is an attempt to account for learned motivation.

Incentive theory holds that both positive and negative incentives motivate our behavior. That is, we either act to obtain a pleasurable outcome (positive reinforcers) or act to avoid or escape a negative outcome (negative reinforcers). For example, ask yourself why you study for an exam. Is it to earn a good grade or to avoid getting a bad one? In either case, the behavior—reading and studying—is the same, but the motivation is surely different. Incentive theory, then, emphasizes the role of learning in understanding motivated behavior and has some immediate practical implications for explaining an enormous variety of everyday actions. For example, positive incentives like money and praise or negative incentives like fines and physical punishment are used to motivate salespeople to work harder, children to take baths and clean up their rooms, students to study for exams, and so on. Our society, and most others, tends to use more negative incentives than positive ones to control the behavior of its citizens. Consider the last time a police officer pulled you over while you were obeying the speed limit and handed you money or said, "Hey, we just wanted to let you know that you are doing a great job driving. Keep up the good work!"

Incentives may not always serve as good motivators, however. Lepper and Greene (1978) argue that incentives can sometimes undermine behaviors that are intrinsically motivated, such as reading, drawing, and singing. That is, we perform some behaviors simply for their own sake; they are intrinsically rewarding and no extrinsic incentive is needed to induce us to perform them. Deci and Ryan (1980) defined **intrinsic motivation** as "the need for competence and self-determination." When people are given external rewards like money for performing an intrinsically motivating task, such as completing a puzzle, they begin to lose interest in the task, and will, in fact, stop working on it (Deci & Ryan, 1980; Lepper, Greene, & Nisbett, 1973).

Expectancy theory, a variant of incentive theory, holds that an incentive by itself is not the most important factor underlying motivation. Rather, it is the individual's anticipation or expectancy of the reward that motivates behavior. Why do you study? An expectancy theorist would answer, "Because by doing so you expect to get a good grade and avoid a bad grade." What led you to this conclusion? The expectancy theorist would answer, "Because your past experiences with studying have taught you that such behavior usually pays off; it is this past experience that gives rise to your expectation." Thus, expectancy theorists argue that incentives affect more than our behavior; they affect our beliefs and expectations.

We have looked briefly at seven theories of motivation: instinct, drive, need, optimal-arousal, opponent-process, incentive, and expectancy. Instinct theory, in its original form, was based on the misguided idea that all behavior is genetically preprogrammed; that is, motivation is entirely innate. Some theories like the drive, arousal, and opponent-process theories are based to different extents on homeostasis, the idea that our bodies seek a balance or equilibrium in certain of its internal states. Other theories, such as Maslow's hierarchy, are based on the concept of need as well as homeostasis: we have certain physiological and psychological needs that, when unsatisfied, impel us to action until they are satisfied. Incentive

TABLE 10.2. *Seven theories of motivation.*

THEORY	BEHAVIOR MOTIVATED BY
Instinct	Innate factors
Drive	Physiological factors operating to maintain homeostasis
Need	Either physiological or learned needs or both
Optimal-arousal	Learned factors to maintain optimum level of arousal
Opponent-process	Learned factors to maintain or balance emotional state
Incentive	Reinforcers and punishers; we seek reinforcers and avoid punishers
Expectancy	The expectancy that behavior will produce a certain outcome

and expectancy theories do not involve either the concept of need or homeostasis; rather, they stress the role of rewards and our expectations about them as being the chief determinants of motivation. To help make these kinds of distinctions among theories of motivation clearer, we have summarized the major feature of each theory in Table 10.2.

You should know that no one of these theories on its own can account completely for all human motivation and emotion. To even begin to fully explain behavior, we must borrow ideas from each theory. Need, drive, homeostasis, incentives, expectations, and arousal each are likely to play a role in motivated behavior. As examples, we first turn to a discussion of eating, and next, to aggression.

MOTIVATION FOR EATING

Our need for food is clear: we become hungry when we do not eat for a while; if we go too long without eating, we die. Surely, homeostasis is involved in our motivation for eating, for the primary effect of eating is to supply the body with the nutrients necessary for the operation of internal systems that maintain life. Researchers who study eating, though, are interested in learning about the specific processes involved in homeostatic control of eating. In this section, we will provide answers to three questions researchers have asked about eating:

- What initiates eating and what stops it?
- What is obesity and what are its causes?
- What motivational factors underlie eating disorders?

Internal Signals for Hunger

Walter Cannon

To detect its need for food, an organism must have some way of monitoring the nutrient supply within the body. Likewise, an organism must be able to tell when it has consumed enough nutrients. We can generally tell when we are hungry because our stomachs may growl or rumble a bit, a signal that may motivate us to seek food. But are signals from the stomach truly the instigators of eating? How would one answer such a question?

Nearly eighty years ago, Walter Cannon, a champion of the homeostatic theory of motivation had an interesting idea: he persuaded a student named Washburn to swallow a deflated balloon. The balloon was attached to a device that measured the pressure of stomach contractions against the balloon when it was inflated. Washburn only reported feelings of hunger when the device showed his stomach to be contracting; from this, Cannon concluded such contractions were involved in hunger (Cannon & Washburn, 1912).

Cannon's finding, though, has been shown to be only partially accurate. Humans who have had their stomachs removed due to cancer or other illnesses, still report feelings of hunger when they have not eaten for a while (Inglefinger, 1944; Janowitz & Grossman, 1950). Thus, it appears that "hunger detractors" must reside somewhere else besides the stomach.

Other researchers proposed that changes in the levels of blood sugar or glucose may initiate and terminate eating (Mayer, 1955). (Glucose is the major energy source used by the body to supply the energy demands of its various tissues.) When we have not eaten for a while, blood sugar levels are low, and we are motivated to find and eat food. On the other hand, when blood sugar levels are high, we generally become less interested in food and stop eating. The liver appears to be the organ responsible for monitoring blood sugar levels. When glucose levels are low, it sends a signal to the hypothalamus, and foraging or eating is initiated. When glucose levels are high, a different signal is sent to the hypothalamus, and the organism stops eating (Friedman & Stricker, 1976). However, the brain appears to be capable of monitoring blood sugar levels even when the pathway between the liver and hypothalamus is severed (Granneman & Friedman, 1980).

Thus, it does not appear that either stomach contractions or changes in blood sugar levels are involved directly with the regulation of hunger. These findings suggest two other possibilities. First, external factors may play a role in the control of eating, and second, the brain, particularly the hypothalamus, may somehow monitor and integrate both internal and external signals to regulate food intake. Let's look briefly at both of these possibilities, starting first with incentives or external signals for hunger.

External Signals for Hunger

Not all signals for eating arise within the body. As you know, a food's palatability, along with its smell and texture, play an important role in eating. Under normal circumstances, people simply do not eat things that they do not like. In many cases, our dietary preferences are influenced by the culture we live in and by the types of food resources available. For example, do you prefer steak to crickets, salad to seaweed, a candy bar to a root or tuber? Sure, you do, but be assured that people in some cultures prefer, in each case, the latter choice.

That we learn which foods to eat, of course, implies that we also learn which foods not to eat. Recall, for example, the phenomenon of taste-aversion learning that we discussed in Chapter 7. After becoming ill due to eating a particular food, people and other animals typically do not eat that food again, at least for a short while after becoming sick. Why? Because psychologically, the taste of the food has become associated with the illness. Some taste-aversions are powerful enough to induce wretching at the sight of the food associated with the illness or to cause avoidance of that food over several years.

External cues can also interact with biological processes to produce eating. In one study, Judith Rodin (1984) asked subjects to fast for eighteen hours and then to report to her lab for a blood test and lunch. During the blood tests, Rodin found that the insulin levels of her subjects rose when steaks, fresh off the grill, were brought into the room. As insulin levels rose, subjects reported increased feelings of hunger. Presumably, insulin levels rose at the sight and smell of the steaks for the same reason that these cues often produce salivation: these cues are naturally associated with food (they are unconditional stimuli). Both insulin production and salivation help prepare the body to digest the food about to be consumed.

Rodin has also produced evidence suggesting that the foods we eat affect insulin levels, and thus, our metabolism and feelings of hunger (Rodin, 1985). In essence, she argues that eating high calorie foods actually produces a greater appetite than eating lower calorie foods. Here is her reasoning.

When insulin is present in the blood, blood sugar levels decline and when insulin is absent, as in the case of diabetes, blood sugar levels remain high. Recall, too, that high blood sugar levels contribute to our feelings of being "full." Foods high in glucose, the kind of sugar found in candy bars and other confections, produce dramatic increases in insulin and large decreases in blood sugar levels. Fructose, on the other hand, the kind of sugar found in fruits, produces a smaller increase in insulin and a less dramatic decline in blood sugar levels. The message here is clear: An afternoon snack of a candy bar, which not only has more calories than a banana or an orange but will also produce more insulin, may give you a larger appetite at suppertime.

The Brain and Eating: Is There a Control Center?

We know from studying Chapter 4 that the brain plays a major role in more or less regulating different behaviors. Eating is no exception. Today, the hypothalamus is acknowledged to play a major role in the control of hunger as well as other homeostatic processes (Grossman, 1979).

In the 1940s and 1950s, research with rats implicated two specific parts of the hypothalamus as being control centers for eating. One area, the **lateral hypothalamus** or **LH**, was believed to function as the on switch for feeding, because when stimulated chemically or electrically, it induces foraging and eating. The other area, known as the **ventromedial hypothalamus** or **VMH**, was thought to be the off switch for eating because, when stimulated, eating stops. These findings led researchers to propose the **dual center theory of eating,** the idea that the LH and VMH work in concert to control eating.

Evidence for the dual center theory has been supported from research conducted in Philip Teitelbaum's laboratory, which showed that when the LH was destroyed, animals refused to eat. These animals would have starved to death, had researchers not force-fed them (Teitelbaum & Stellar, 1954). Animals will learn to eat again, especially when given moistened chocolate-chip cookies or eggnog (Teitelbaum & Epstein, 1962). However, their body weight did not return to normal; rather it was maintained at a much lower level. Destruction of the VMH has the opposite effect, producing overeating and maintenance of body weight at a much higher level than normal (see Figure 10.9). Some animals with VMH lesions may eat so much that their weight can triple (Teitelbaum, 1955).

Enmeshed in the dual center theory of eating is the notion of **setpoint** or maintenance level for the body's fat reserves or body weight. The hypothalamus as a homeostatic mechanism, determines this set point (Keesey & Powley, 1975; Nisbett, 1972). If an organism's fat reserves fall below the set point value, it will eat voraciously until the set point is reached; if its fat reserves exceed the set point value, then the animal decreases its food intake until the set point is restored. Destruction of either the LH or VMH would seem to prevent the hypothalamus from receiving signals from the body and so, may alter the set point. Hence, the set point may be elevated when the VMH is destroyed, causing the animal to eat more and eventually maintain its body weight at a higher level. Likewise, the set point may be lowered by destruction of the LH, causing the animal to eat less and maintain its body weight at a lower level than normal.

Although the hypothalamus plays a major role in controlling eating, current researchers believe that other brain structures must also be involved. In other words, rather than viewing the LH and VMH as the "on" and "off" centers for eating, researchers believe that both are part of a larger and more integrated homeostatic system (Grossman, 1979). Evidence for this newer view comes from further studies of VMH-lesioned animals. For instance, VMH-lesioned rats do not eat voraciously for the rest of their lives. After about three weeks they eat only slightly larger meals than normal animals. Interestingly, even if they consume an identical amount of food as normal animals, they gain more weight, suggesting that lesions may also affect the body's ability to metabolize food (Stricker & Zigmond, 1976). VMH animals become finicky eaters and will not overeat unless the food is particularly tasty; when food is adulterated with quinine, they actually eat less (Weingarten, 1982; Teitelbaum, 1955). It seems unlikely that

FIGURE 10.9
Rats whose ventromedial hypothalamus has been lesioned will overeat and gain an enormous amount of weight.

Obese individuals not only face the emotional and social repercussions of being overweight, but important physical side effects as well.

animals would reduce food intake levels and become finicky eaters if the VMH was truly the sole "off" center for eating.

Neuroscientists have not yet discovered all of the brain structures involved in the homeostatic system that regulates eating, and they do not know precisely how the system works. From our view, it would seem that the cerebral cortex must somehow play a role in eating behaviors, since this structure is responsible for higher mental processes, some of which are likely involved with making conscious decisions regarding when, what, where, and how much to eat.

Obesity: The Facts and the Likely Causes

If eating were only a matter of replenishing the body's nutritional stores, eating would be very different than we know it to be. We would probably only eat when we were hungry, and then we would only eat those foods highest in nutritional value. Likewise, none of us would overeat. We would stop eating when the brain received signals from the body that its nutritional requirements had been realized, and we would only eat again when the brain was informed that nutritional stores were getting low. The fact is, though, that many of us eat when we aren't hungry, and some of us overeat and become fat, even to the point of obesity. **Obesity** is defined by many psychologists and health researchers as a body weight 20 percent in excess of that considered average for a given height.

Obesity can have tremendously negative personal and social consequences (Wadden & Strunkard, 1985). Obese people can be extremely self-conscious of the negative way in which their weight is perceived by others, especially in a society that places importance on being thin and physically fit. From grammar school to the workplace, obese individuals are often the target of "fat jokes," prejudice, and ridicule. To some, obese people are gluttons, unable to resist even the smallest temptation to eat. To others, obese people are just plain physically unattractive. Many of us might wish to have the humor or income of a John Candy or Rosanne Barr, but few of us would want to have their physiques. The result can be a disastrous combination of a highly negative self-concept and a low self-esteem.

Obesity can also pose a threat to one's health, including increased risk of diabetes, high blood pressure, and heart disease (Kolata, 1985). Even obese children face increased health risks; obese children as young as four years old have been found to have high blood pressure (Epstein & Wing, 1987). The threat to health, together with the psychological side effects of being overweight, has caused millions of Americans to wage war on their weight, an effort that has been costly in terms of both time and money. In fact, for some, there seems to be no limit to their desire to be slim, a fact that allows them to fall prey to food fads and lose-weight-quick schemes. The point is that obesity and body size have captured nearly everyone's attention, and the fascination is likely to continue, if not increase.

The risk of an obese child becoming an obese adult increases with age (Epstein & Wing, 1987) and may be caused by poor eating habits and lack of exercise. In contrast to normal adults, obese adults tend to have very different eating patterns. For example, obese people:

- generally consume more calories than the body can use;
- are finicky eaters—they eat large quantities of foods they like but much less of foods they don't like (Nisbett, 1968);
- seem to be more sensitive to external cues related to eating such as time of day and the sight, smell, and taste of foods (Rodin, 1973, 1980; Schachter & Rodin, 1974);
- eat less food if they must expend effort in preparing the food for consumption (Schachter & Friedman, 1974).

The important question is what triggers these kinds of eating patterns? So far, researchers have four leads: fat cells, set points, external cues, and disinhibition and stress.

Fat Cells. Our fatness or our leanness is determined by the number and size of fat cells in our bodies. The total number of fat cells a person has may be determined by genetic factors, early childhood eating patterns, or their combination (Collip, 1980; Sjostrom, 1980). Obese people have about three times more fat cells than normal people have (Hirsch & Knittle, 1970). Dieting, no matter how intense or sustained, will reduce the size, but not the number of fat cells. As if this were not enough bad news, these shrunken fat cells may send signals to the brain requesting reinforcement, leaving the dieter with a continual urge to eat. For an obese person, the urge to eat is one temptation that is irresistible. Thus, once fat, the body strives to stay fat. The ability to lose weight and not gain it back is not easy, as the following study showed (Johnson & Drenick, 1977). Over 200 people who had lost weight during a 2-month period were followed over the next 10 years. After 3 years, less than 50 percent of the subjects had managed to keep the weight off; after 10 years, the percentage had dropped to less than 10 percent.

*D**ieting . . . will reduce the size, but not the number, of fat cells.*

Set Point. Some people may be obese and others normal because of differences in their set point for body weight. According to the idea of homeostasis, the body strives to maintain the set point. It can do so in two ways: by taking in more or less food or by changing its rate of metabolism—the rate at which it uses food as energy. In fact, studies of dieters have shown that these two factors may work in concert (Keesey & Powley, 1986). When a dieter begins to eat less food than is needed to maintain the set point, the body automatically compensates by burning fewer calories (if a person were to begin eating more food than is required by the set point to maintain a particular body weight, the body would counter by burning more calories). Thus, this theory too, is the bearer of bad news for obese people. A person may launch a successful diet but will also have the urge to eat because of the body and brain's tendency to re-establish the body weight dictated by the set-point (Nisbett, 1972). Even if the dieter resists the temptation to eat, the body would slow down its use of fuel, making weight loss seem slow.

Although researchers believe that early eating experiences can determine a person's set point, evidence also exists that genetic factors are involved. In one study (Strunkard, 1986), adopted children were discovered to have body weights more similar to their natural parents than their adoptive parents. Corroborative evidence also comes from twin studies: identical twins reared apart are more likely to have similar body weights than nonidentical twins reared apart (Bray, 1981).

External Cues. The fact that obese subjects are more sensitive than normal subjects to external cues related to eating suggests that such cues override internal, bodily cues for hunger. However, researchers are not sure whether heightened sensitivity to external cues is a cause or an effect of obesity (Nisbett, 1972; Rodin, 1980). It may be that obese people are driven to eat not because they have a heightened awareness of food and food cues, but because they are simply more aware of food and food cues in the environment because of their drive to eat. In either case, conclusive evidence has yet to be gathered.

Disinhibition and Stress. Interestingly, people who are concerned with their body weight and restricting their eating are more likely than others to eat larger quantities of food once they have started eating. That is, eating food, especially that which is considered "off-limits," may disinhibit an otherwise inhibited (dieting) eater. (A disinhibitor negates or undoes the effects of an inhibitor.) Consider the following experiment (Herman & Mack, 1975). Subjects were brought into the laboratory to participate in what they were led to believe was an experiment on taste perception. Some subjects were required to taste 8 or 16 ounces of a milkshake. Next, they were left alone to judge the taste of ice cream, with no restriction placed on the amount that they might "sample." The real object of the experiment was, of course, to see how much ice cream subjects would eat. See Figure 10.10 for the results. Intuitively, you might think that the more milk shake consumed prior to the taste-testing of ice cream, the less ice cream would be consumed. Restrained eaters, subjects who before the experiment had indicated that they were dieting or were concerned with their body weight did just the opposite: the more milk shake they drank, the more ice cream they ate. Only unrestrained subjects (those who had not expressed such concerns) sampled the ice cream according to logic. Why didn't the restrained eaters eat as little as the unrestrained eaters? Herman and Mack's conclusion: because prior exposure to the milk shake weakened or disinhibited the restraints these subjects had for eating. Once they started eating, they couldn't hold back. This experiment is a classic example of the "Oh, what the hell—I've blown my diet this far, why not go all the way" phenomenon (Herman & Mack, 1975).

Likewise, stress or anxiety may cause would-be dieters to break their diets, even if only temporarily. When placed under stressful conditions in the laboratory, obese subjects will consume more food than normal subjects (Slochower, 1976). In fact, normal subjects eat less food under these circumstances relative to nonstressful conditions. Stress, then, appears to act as a disinhibitor in obese people; under stress, obese people find it difficult to inhibit or restrain their eating. From a learning perspective, eating may reduce stress and so, be negatively reinforced.

So far, we have given you only the bad news that for many people maintaining a desirable body weight is a constant battle, if only because of the way our brains and bodies regulate food intake. The inertia of homeostasis is a difficult force from which to break free. We have also hinted that losing

FIGURE 10.10

Disinhibition in restrained eaters. In Herman and Mack's study, restrained and unrestrained eaters consumed either zero, one, or two milkshakes prior to judging the taste of ice cream (of which they could eat as much as they liked). Restrained eaters ate more ice cream after drinking one or more milkshakes; unrestrained eaters ate less ice cream after drinking one or more milkshakes.

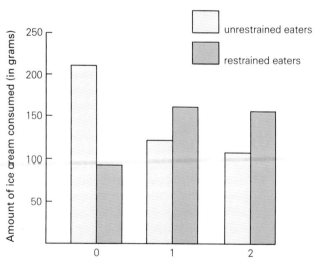

TABLE 10.3. *How to keep weight off.*

1. *Eat small nutritious meals.* Many people who diet feel that they must deprive themselves of food to lose weight. A better way to diet is to eat small nutritious meals when hungry. Doing so maintains a supply of nutrients to the body. The key is to avoid eating high calorie foods.

2. *Avoid falling prey to food cues that tempt you when you are not truly hungry.* We are sometimes tempted to eat when we smell or see particularly tempting foods. Keep tempting foods out of your house or apartment; if possible, avoid routes to school or work on which bakeries and fast food restaurants are located. The golden arches can do more than satisfy an appetite—they can create one.

3. *Eat low-calorie, high fiber foods and exercise regularly.* Weight regulation is a matter of two basic factors: the amount of calories consumed, and the amount of calories burned up. To lose weight, then, one can either take in fewer calories, burn up more calories, or even better, do both. For every 3500 calories you trim from your diet, you can lose up to one pound. That means by cutting 250 calories a day, you can lose about a pound a week. Substituting low-cal foods for foods higher in calories is a good way to reduce your daily caloric consumption, and regular exercise is a tremendous way to burn excess fat. Moreover, regular exercise not only helps shrink fat cells, it also enhances muscle tone, makes us feel more energetic and healthier, and increases metabolism.

4. *Once you go on a diet, stay on it.* The yo-yo dieter, the person who is on then off a diet, is fighting a losing battle. If your weight is greater after binging than before, you may have actually produced new fat cells. Remember, once you have a fat cell, it stays with you forever. The best you can do is shrink it. But here's the really bad news for the yo-yo dieter: our bodies adjust to changes in body weight by speeding up or slowing down metabolism. With continual changes in body weight, the body reduces its metabolism to compensate for dieting, making weight reduction even tougher (Polivy & Herman, 1985).

weight or maintaining a weight below your body's normal set point can be problematic. Now it's time for some good news: Whether we are slim and wish to stay that way or whether we are overweight and wish to lose weight, weight regulation is a skill that, for many of us, can be learned. At the same time, it should be realized that there is no single, easy formula for weight regulation and maintenance. The research we have reviewed suggests that the steps shown in Table 10.3 can be helpful in keeping weight off permanently.

Dieting and weight regulation is not a goal that can be accomplished over the short run. For this reason, food fads and lose-weight-quick schemes are bound to fail. If you want to lose weight, plan on changing your eating habits and exercise patterns permanently. No other plan will succeed in keeping your weight at a stable level for any appreciable length of time. The key to losing weight permanently can be summed up in seven words: take in fewer calories than you burn.

Eating Disorders: Anorexia Nervosa and Bulimia

In addition to obesity, problems with the motivational system regulating eating can result in other eating disorders. Two of the more serious eating disorders are anorexia nervosa and bulimia. People with **anorexia nervosa** are generally young women between the ages of 15 and 30 who have a pathological fear of weight gain and are obsessed with not eating, and so, refuse to eat. As a result, weight loss can be dramatic, causing damage to the brain and heart, even to the point of death (Davis, 1986; Eisner, 1985; Treichel, 1982).

Although anorexia nervosa was observed as early as 1689, and has long been considered a rare disease, its incidence appears to be increasing in cultures such as ours that place psychological pressure on women to have thin, shapely figures. For example, seldom do we see an overweight woman pose for a magazine, television, or billboard ad for a product other than "full body" fashions. It is true that our culture's definition of female attractiveness has changed dramatically, with the emphasis on narrower waist lines, over the last several decades. Not surprisingly, women most vulnerable to anorexia nervosa include models and dancers, people who must

The effects of anorexia nervosa are dramatic and can be fatal as evidenced by singer Karen Carpenter, pictured here, who died in 1983 from complications brought on by years of living with this eating disorder.

stay thin to stay working. About 10 percent of anorexics have mothers who, themselves, are highly weight conscious.

Here are some of the signals present in anorexic people:

- refusal to eat food
- developing rituals with food such as dividing it into different patterns on the plate, cutting it into very small pieces, or playing with it
- overexercising or making exercise a rule before eating
- unusually high intake of diet beverages
- increased tendency to avoid social interaction, especially with friends and family
- wearing baggy clothes (to prevent detection of weight loss)

Anorexia nervosa is curable, particularly if it is treated in its early stages. Treatment may involve hospitalization and forced feeding in extreme cases, but only therapy in others. In severe cases, though, treatment does not always help: about 25 percent of those suffering from it do not benefit at all, 50 percent remain susceptible and about 25 percent are completely cured.

Bulimia is a disorder in which people eat enormous quantities of food and then either force themselves to regurgitate or use laxatives to rid their bodies of the food. Susan, the woman in our opening example for this chapter, is a bulimic. Bulimics also tend to be women who frequently binge-purge several times a week, although some bulimics may binge and purge several times a day. About half of all bulimics also suffer from anorexia nervosa.

Because bulimics eliminate most of the food they ingest soon after eating, they often suffer from malnutrition, dehydration, and intestinal and throat irritations. In addition, they may sustain heart, kidney, and liver damage, and tooth decay caused by stomach acids. Like anorexics, bulimics are obsessed with thinness and so, also possess a poor sense of their own body size. Both anorexics and bulimics tend to view themselves as fat, even when the reflection in the mirror or the needle on the bathroom scale indicates otherwise. Therapy can help these individuals to develop proper eating habits, but the very nature of the disorder makes it embarrassing for people with anorexia nervosa or bulimia to admit it publically. Recently, antidepressants have been shown to be effective in treating bulimia; unfortunately these drugs appear to work only over the short run, with relapse rates being high when the drug is no longer used (Mitchell, 1988).

Society's emphasis on thinness as shown in fashion magazines and other media is an influencing factor for many people suffering from eating disorders. In turn, both anorexics and bulimics grow to have a distorted view of themselves.

In summary, both anorexics and bulimics have a psychologically distorted perception of their body size. Behaviors aimed at reducing weight are likely motivated by an abnormal perception of personal and societal pressures to have and maintain a thin and trim figure.

MOTIVATION FOR AGGRESSION

Aggression is any action, verbal or physical, that is intended to harm another individual. Although aggression can be defensive, our concern here will be understanding aggression that is seemingly unprovoked—of the sort demonstrated by James Huberty, in our opening example, when he shot those people at McDonald's. The reasons for defensive aggression, such as protecting yourself from a mugger, are obvious, but the reasons for aggression like Huberty's are not. For that reason, psychologists find the study of unprovoked aggression an important area for research. So, in this text, the word aggression refers to nondefensive aggression.

Although we have a need to eat, none of us would say that we have a need to be aggressive, in the sense that without such, we would perish. It seems wrong, even immoral, to say that James Huberty had a need to kill. Yet, like eating, aggression seems to be a motivated act. But if not a need, then what motivates aggressive behavior? In this section, we will review the major psychological theories regarding the motivation for aggression.

Instinct Theories

Although no longer widely accepted as explanations of human aggression, two theories of aggression follow the early lead of instinct theory and view aggressive actions as being motivated by instinct. According to psychodynamic theory, aggression is due to pent-up energy that accumulates slowly until it reaches the point that it must be released; it is rather like spontaneous combustion. Freud called the release of pent-up energy **catharsis** and believed that many cultural and social activities provide socially acceptable means of expressing aggressive instincts. Two cathartic outlets are displacement and sublimation. In displacement, aggressive tendencies are channeled toward objects other than the original source that arouses your aggression. Thus, after a long day at school, you may have built up aggressive energy toward one of your teachers, let's say your psychology professor. That night, you verbally abuse a friend whose mannerisms resemble those of your teacher (using him as a substitute for your professor), providing the cathartic outlet for your anger at your unsuspecting psychology professor. In sublimation, aggressive tendencies are transformed into socially acceptable activities, such as athletic or academic endeavors. For example, your pent-up aggression toward your professor may be transformed into studying extra hard for your next exam in his or her class. Displacement and sublimation, in Freud's view, are two outlets that fulfill our instinct to be aggressive.

The second instinct-based theory, advocated by ethologist Konrad Lorenz (1966), holds that the expression of our aggressive instinct is generally preceded by a specific stimulus in the environment; without the stimulus, aggression simply cannot occur. The stimulus, called a sign stimulus, elicits a species-typical response. As we learned in Chapter 7, such patterns of aggression are characterized by stereotypical and ritualistic behavior and are common in the animal world. Evidence that such patterns are indeed innate comes from studies in which animals are raised

Evidence suggests that in the animal world certain patterns of aggression are innate. The instinct theory as applied to humans, however, is not as clear.

in total isolation (so as to prevent learning an action by observing it being performed by others) but show an aggressive response typical of their species when presented with the sign stimulus for the first time.

The ethological account is also supported by evidence showing that aggressive tendencies can be inherited. For example, K. Lagerspetz (1979) wanted to know if aggressive tendencies could be artificially selected. Accordingly, she bred each of two different groups of mice for 25 generations. Aggressive mice were bred with each other and mice that were extremely pacific were bred with each other. At the end of her experiment, she had one group of animals that were so vicious that they would aggress immediately when given the opportunity. The other group was so docile that they could not be provoked, no matter what she did to them. Lagerspetz not only demonstrated that aggressive tendencies have a genetic basis, but also that docile characteristics do as well.

In terms of human aggression, instinct theory, both from the ethological and the psychodynamic perspectives comes up short: it cannot explain our ability to learn when and how to be aggressive. For example, through experience people learn that some means of aggression are more effective than others: many cases of human aggression occur after dark with a gun, instead of during broad daylight without a weapon. Instinct theory also does not take into consideration the physiological factors that have been discovered to play a role in aggression. It is to these factors that we now turn.

Physiological Factors in Aggression

As with motivation for eating, we know that physiological variables play an important role in motivation for aggression. We know, for example, that rabies, a viral disease that attacks the brain, produces intensely aggressive behavior in diseased animals. One area of the brain attacked by rabies is the amygdala, which, as you may recall from Chapter 4, is part of the limbic system, an area of the brain thought to play a leading role in emotion.

Damaging the amygdala seems to interfere with the responses to specific kinds of environmental stimulation. For example, male cats with lesioned amygdalas show indiscriminate sexual behavior and will mount other male cats, monkeys, and even chickens (Schreiner & Kling, 1953). A more telling result comes from a well-known experiment that investigated the effects of damaging the amygdala on the social dominance order of a troop of eight monkeys (Rosvold, Mirsky, & Pribram, 1954). In monkeys as well as many other animal species, social rank is held in check by the aggressive behavior of the dominant animals. The researchers hypothesized that lesioning the amygdala of the troop's leaders would change the dominance ranking within the troop. These researchers first lesioned the amygdala of the top-ranking and most aggressive monkey in the troop. He immediately became the lowest ranked monkey in the troop—even the previously lowest ranked monkey in the troop attacked him fearlessly. Next, the researchers lesioned the amygdala of the remaining most aggressive monkey, and then the next one, and so on, and they, too, became submissive and cowardly. In this experiment, then, damaging the amygdala had profound effects on the social structure of the troop.

The amygdala may also play an important role in aggression in humans. As an example, consider the following true story (Mark & Ervin, 1970). As a young woman, Julia was prone to sudden outbursts of violent behavior including baring her teeth and clenching her fists. One time her violent behavior went further, while in a restroom in a theater she stabbed a woman. (The woman lived because, after stabbing her, Julia's screams attracted the attention of help.) An electrophysiological analysis of Julia's

Acts of aggression often result from frustration. When a given goal is blocked in some way, we become frustrated; as frustration builds, so does the aggressive response.

brain showed abnormal patterns of electrical activity in the amygdala just prior to episodes of violent behavior. In an attempt to reduce her aggressive behavior, Julia later underwent psychosurgery in which her amygdala was destroyed. The surgery was a success: Julia demonstrated markedly fewer episodes of aggressive behavior afterwards.

Physiological evidence from both animals and humans also suggests that the neurotransmitter serotonin may be involved in aggressive behavior. Amphetamine and testosterone, which block the release of serotonin, also increase the likelihood of aggressive behavior in both animals and humans (Essman & Essman, 1981; Valzelli, 1981; Valzelli, Bernasconi, & Garattini, 1981). People who attempt suicide by violent means have also been found to have depressed levels of serotonin (Brown, et al., 1982).

A mphetamine and testosterone . . . increase the likelihood of aggressive behavior in both animals and humans.

Frustration and Aggression

When a goal is blocked or progress toward a goal is hindered in some way, we become frustrated; we may also become aggressive. Some researchers believe that aggression is caused by frustration. More specifically, they view aggression as a learned response that may be produced when attempts at fulfilling biologically or socially important needs such as food and water or attention and recognition are impeded. The more intense the frustration, the greater the aggressive response.

The idea that frustration leads to aggression, first expressed by Dollard, Doob, Miller, Mowrer, & Sears (1939), stimulated a good deal of research, most of which has shown that frustration and aggression do, in fact, seem to be related (Barker, Demo, & Lewin, 1941). Some studies have indicated, however, that frustration may not always lead to aggression (Gentry, 1970) and that aggression, as we will see below, may have other causes (Zillman, 1978, 1982).

One alternative view of the relationship between frustration and aggression has been proposed by social psychologist Leonard Berkowitz (1980), who believes that frustration does not produce aggression per se but rather a readiness to act—in this case, to aggress—if conditions are just right. In order for frustration to produce aggressive behavior, particular environmental cues must be present, such as those associated with the frustrating situation or with aggression. Thus, aggression may not always be premeditated; it may occur in response to particular cues in the environment.

To test this idea, Berkowitz conducted the following study. Subjects were first criticized harshly by a confederate for their inability to complete a simple laboratory task—this constituted "frustration." Subjects then viewed a movie in which Kirk Douglas was physically beaten and were then given the opportunity to administer electric shocks to the confederate, although they had not been previously informed of this opportunity. Some of the subjects had been told that the confederate's name was Bob; others were told that his name was Kirk. Subjects delivered higher intensity shocks to Kirk than Bob (of course, the subjects were unaware that shocks were not actually administered to the confederate). Berkowitz explained these results by reasoning that subjects were primed by their earlier frustration, and then the name "Kirk" had become associated with aggression in the film, and thus, served as an aggression-eliciting cue.

It also is possible that frustration produces the tendency to aggress, but that environmental factors, such as learning and experience override such tendencies, thereby inhibiting the expression of aggression. Consider the child who, although provoked by his younger brother, waits until his parents leave the room before retaliating. Fear of punishment or retaliation is one reason why many people may choose nonaggressive rather than aggressive means for resolving their differences with others. In other cases, we may find scapegoating a more appropriate response: We "take out our frustrations" on an object or person unable to retaliate. A child, angry because she must take a nap, may strike or talk abusively to her doll or stuffed animal rather than talking back to her parents because, in the past, her parents have punished her for such behavior.

Arousal and Aggression

According to one theory, the fighting that we see so often during sporting events may result from the arousal that is created by physical exercise. Players' initial excitement can then turn into aggressive behavior.

Another view of the relation between emotions and aggression is embodied in Dolf Zillman's (1978, 1982) notion of transfer of excitation in which arousal from one source, such as physical exercise, can be transferred to other behavior, such as aggressing. This may be the reason why fights are common during sporting events—arousal from watching competition and physical exertion essentially disposes individuals to behave aggressively when the opportunity arises. Consider an example from the laboratory. Subjects exercised hard for two minutes. Afterwards, some subjects were verbally insulted; others were not. When subjects were given the opportunity to deliver electrical shocks to another person, only those who were insulted did so (Zillman, Katcher, & Milavsky, 1972). Zillman has more recently argued that excitation (arousal) depends upon cognition to determine whether or not the individual becomes aggressive (Zillman, 1988). That is, the cognitive appraisal of the individual's circumstances may or may not lead to excitation (and aggression). If the individual perceives that his or her well-being is in danger, excitement leading to aggression is a likely possibility. Another possibility is flight or escape from the situation, if the individual also perceives that aggression on his or her part will not be effective.

Social Learning Theory and Aggression

Social learning theorists like Albert Bandura believe that much, if not all, human aggression is learned (Bandura, 1973, 1977). According to Bandura, two factors are important in learning to behave aggressively: imitation and reinforcement. Let's take a look at one of Bandura's studies, the now classic Bobo doll experiment.

Preschool children were shown films in which an adult either sat calmly beside the Bobo doll or struck it (see Figure 10.11). The children

FIGURE 10.11
Social learning theory and aggression. To see whether behavior can be learned through imitation, Albert Bandura first allowed young children to watch an adult model strike an inflated Bobo doll. Later, when given the opportunity, these children showed similar aggressive behavior toward the doll (Bandura, Ross, & Ross, 1963).

were later put in the room with the doll and allowed to play with it. Those who had observed the aggressive adult were more likely to strike the doll (Bandura, Ross, & Ross, 1963). In this case, children imitated the aggressive act, even though the model's behavior was not explicitly reinforced. Bandura later showed that children who observed reinforcement of a model's aggressive behavior were even more likely to behave aggressively toward the Bobo doll than children who observed a model whose behavior was either not reinforced or punished (Bandura, 1965). How did Bandura explain this finding? In short, he argued that children's aggressive behavior resulted from vicarious learning, that is, they learned the relationship between behavior and its consequences by observing others. In other words, people may learn to behave aggressively (or not) simply because they have observed the reinforcement (or punishment) of aggressive behavior in other people. Through such learning, children come to expect that they will receive rewards for behaving aggressively. Likewise, if people observe a model performing a kind act and receiving a reward, they will then expect kindness on their part to produce similar favorable outcomes (for example, Mussen & Eisenberg, 1977).

If children will imitate filmed models in the laboratory, will they also imitate actors on television and in movies? This question lies at the heart of an enormous amount of research spawned in part by Bandura's research and in part by the concerns of parents and others about the effects of television violence on the behavior of young people. It is not unreasonable to suspect that television exerts some effect on behavior, especially given the amount of time many of us spend watching it. In 1987, for example, the average 12-year-old watched about four hours of television a day (Liebert & Sprafkin, 1988). One group of researchers has gone so far as to say that, all things considered, the average child spends more time watching TV than sitting in the classroom (Liebert & Poulos, 1975). By the time the average child is 15, he or she will have witnessed thousands of shootings, not to mention countless numbers of fistfights, muggings, stabbings, and rapes.

On average, in most countries there are about five to six violent acts per hour shown on prime time television (Cumberbatch, Jones, & Lee, 1988).

But let's get back to the question: Does watching television violence increase aggressive behavior in viewers? Both laboratory and field studies have shown that the answer is unquestionably "Yes." Consider some of the evidence.

- In a laboratory study, children who watched a violent clip of the TV show "The Untouchables" behaved more aggressively during a later play period than children who watched a nonviolent clip of athletic competition (Liebert & Baron, 1972).
- Children who viewed several movies with aggressive themes were more likely to behave aggressively toward other children than children who viewed an equal number of movies with nonaggressive themes (Leyens et al., 1975).
- In a longitudinal study, teenagers who watched more aggression on TV were judged more aggressive than a similar group who had watched less TV violence. These same children—the more aggressive ones—were also more likely to be convicted of a serious crime by the time they were 30-years-old than were their less aggressive counterparts (Eron & Huesmann, 1984).
- Children who viewed aggression were less likely to break up a fight between younger children than were children who did not view aggression (Drabman & Thomas, 1974).

As you might expect, critics of this research have argued that there is no convincing evidence that watching violence on TV contributes to increased viewer violence. You may wonder how anyone could conclude that watching violence on TV could contribute to anything but increased aggressive behavior. The argument that viewing violence on TV does not contribute to aggression in viewers, hinges on two basic points worth discussing because they highlight the limitations of scientific research in making accurate generalizations about life in the real world (for a review, see Stipp & Milavsky, 1988).

- Point 1: Many studies of TV-induced aggression take place in the artificial confines of the laboratory. People don't generally watch TV under such highly controlled conditions, and most may not have the opportunity to behave aggressively right after watching a violent TV show. The research would have us believe that immediately after watching a violent TV show, the viewer will go out and kill someone or, at the very least, beat someone up. Why doesn't that happen more often—why aren't more TV viewers muggers, rapists, or murderers?
- Point 2: Since most studies of TV-induced violence are correlational, they do not establish a cause-and-effect relationship between TV viewing and aggression. Just because a person watched large amounts of violence on TV does not mean that he or she will later commit a violent crime as the result. Violence could occur for other reasons, such as parental or peer influences, or the need for money. What about those people who commit crimes but have never watched a TV program, violent or otherwise?

The first point questions the applicability of results produced under unnatural viewing conditions. The second points up the fact of poor control over confounding variables in field research and the Achilles heel of all correlational research—it cannot determine cause-and-effect relationships. These points, of course, do not mean that there is no relation between TV viewing and aggressive behavior; they simply indicate that science may not presently have the means for convincingly demonstrating that relation.

What does the study of eating and aggression tell us about motivation? We have learned that both eating and aggression can be the result of a number of different factors. We know that genetic and physiological factors can be involved, and that both eating and aggression can be turned on and off by electrically stimulating or lesioning particular areas of the brain. We also know that eating and aggression can be modified through learning. Eating, aggression, or any other motivated behavior is likely due to the interaction of both biology and learning. For example, even when we are prompted by physiological signals, such as a rumble in our stomachs or low blood sugar, we may feel hungry but postpone eating. It may not be time for dinner, or we might be on a diet. Likewise we may desire to strike or verbally abuse someone, but resist.

So what can we say about the reasons why people eat or behave aggressively? In short, what can we say about motivation?

In essence, understanding motivation is a matter of understanding circumstance, which puts psychologists in a position to do two things. First, they should understand the circumstances, both biological and environmental, surrounding and affecting behavior. Second, where appropriate, they should intervene and change those circumstances, thereby changing

n essence, understanding motivation is a matter of understanding circumstance . . .

behavior. For example, by understanding the circumstances that cause anorexia nervosa, psychologists can devise therapies to alter the anorexic's dietary habits. As the circumstances differ from anorexic to anorexic, so will the therapy used to treat the problem.

As you no doubt have surmised, psychology does not have all the answers to motivational questions. Our understanding of eating and aggression is, at this point, far from complete. For example, we don't really know why James Huberty went on his killing spree. We know that he did not have a tumor on or near his amygdala, so we cannot conclude that mass murderers are driven to kill because of an abnormality in that brain site. We also know that he had poor social skills, but most people with poor social skills do not wind up killers. He remarked to his wife before leaving home that "society had their chance." What did that mean? What interaction had he had with society that led him to make that remark? Did his gripe with society lead him, armed, to McDonald's? If so, why? These are the kinds of important real-life questions that keep psychologists involved in research.

There can be little doubt that we are motivated to act, but our actions, regardless of their causes, comprise only a part of our life's experience. Another perhaps equally important part, is made up of emotions. We feel joy at our successes, disappointment in our failures, love and respect for our friends and family, contempt for those we distrust, frustration at those who get in our way, happiness when things are going our way, anger at those who hurt us, and sympathy for those who suffer. We are never without emotion; we are never truly numb to the experience of life.

EMOTION

We generally think of **emotions** as moods or feelings; that is, felt internal conditions that change from time to time largely as a function of things that happen to us. From a psychological perspective, emotions entail four components (Frijda, 1988):

- a particular affect or feeling to which we generally give labels, such as happiness, joy, fear, or envy

- physiological arousal, bodily changes mediated largely by the limbic system and autonomic nervous system
- cognitive appraisal, or an interpretation of the immediate environmental situation
- behavioral reaction, the overt expression of the emotion

Because emotions can be a product of our behavior, they can sometimes serve as a motivator.

Emotions are related to motivation in at least three ways. First, because emotions can be a product of our behavior, they can sometimes serve as a motivator, such as when our behavior brings about a particularly pleasing emotional state or when we act to avoid or escape a particularly negative one. Second, emotions sometimes serve as signals that tell us when to do or to refrain from doing things. Third, emotions generally accompany our actions.

Emotion and motivation don't always go together, however, for emotions may occur in the absence of motivation. Emotions can be produced by changes in the environment that we may have no conscious control over, such as when we learn of the death of a close friend.

We will look now at how different emotions are classified. Then we discuss the facial expression of emotion and the biological bases of emotion. We conclude by discussing theories of emotion.

Classifying Emotion

Like other scientists, psychologists are trained to be pigeonholers: they strive to fit their subject matter into neat and unambiguous categories that distinguish one kind of psychological event from others. Classification makes it easier to see possible relationships among events, and to devise research. So it is with the psychology of emotion. But where would a psychologist start? How can sadness be distinguished from grief, disgust from loathing, or shame from humiliation? The classification scheme has to take into consideration the following facts about emotions:

- they vary in their intensity (really happy to sort of happy);
- they range from positive to negative (love and joy to hate and sadness);
- they differ in their purity ("Primary" emotions, like grief and ecstasy are pure in contrast to "mixed" emotions, which are blends of other emotions. Jealousy, for example, is considered by some psychologists to be a blend of love and anger.);
- they exist in opposites (love vs. hate, or joy vs. sadness).

The range of emotions we can experience is broad and includes everything from the happiness we express for a team's victory to the sadness children feel when they are denied something they've had their heart set on.

FIGURE 10.12
Plutchik's emotion solid.

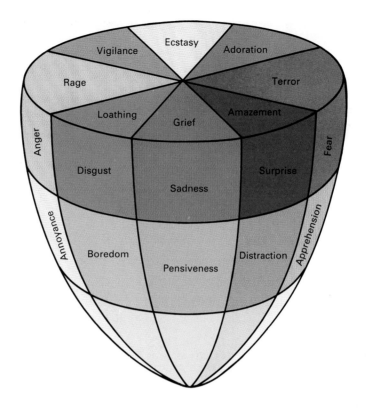

A classification system that is popular among emotion researchers, shown as an "emotion solid" in Figure 10.12, has been devised by Robert Plutchik (1980, 1984). Similar emotions are placed next to each other and opposite emotions are placed opposite one another. The combination of two primary emotions forms a mixed emotion. Acceptance and joy, for example, combine to form the feeling of love; disgust and anger blend to form contempt. The eight primary emotions (anger, disgust, sadness, surprise, fear, acceptance, joy, and anticipation) are shown on the vertical face of the solid, with the most intense emotions placed at the top of the solid and the least intense placed near the bottom. For example, amazement is the more intense form of surprise, and distraction the less intense form. The solid's shape represents the idea that as emotions become less intense, they also become less discriminable from one another.

Plutchik's concept of emotions is based on his idea that emotions, like physical characteristics and behavior, are a product of natural selection. Emotions are biologically based adaptions that aid the organism in responding to particular environmental stimuli. Further, Plutchik argues that emotions have evolved in a number of other animals besides humans, and that despite various forms of behavioral expression in different species, there are certain common emotional patterns that can be identified across species. For example, when confronted with a threat, say an attacker, "a deer may run from it, a bird may fly from it and a fish may swim from it," but the underlying emotional pattern is the same—in this case, it is probably fear (Plutchik, 1980).

In developing his emotional solid, Plutchik studied how people use words to describe emotions (1980). He wanted to know how people in ordinary life classify emotions—which emotions are similar, which are different? The emotional solid, then, represents how we generally think about the relationships among different emotions. He first asked subjects to place words describing different emotions at some point along a seven-

	HAPPINESS	DISGUST	SURPRISE	SADNESS	ANGER	FEAR
United States (N = 99)	97%	92%	95%	84%	67%	85%
Brazil (N = 40)	95%	97%	87%	59%	90%	67%
Chile (N = 119)	95%	92%	93%	88%	94%	68%
Argentina (N = 168)	98%	92%	95%	78%	90%	54%
Japan (N = 29)	100%	90%	100%	62%	90%	66%

FIGURE 10.13

Photos showing people displaying these facial expressions were shown to college students in five different countries. The students were asked to name the emotion displayed in each photograph. The percentage of students who correctly associated the photos with the specific emotion is shown.

point scale that varied in dimensions such as weak-strong, good-bad, and high-low. He next asked subjects to rate emotions in their similarity to the subjective experiences of anger, sadness, and acceptance. His results showed that people tend to cluster their emotions along the dimensions represented by the emotion solid. In other words, the emotion solid represents the possible relationships that may exist among various emotions.

The Facial Expressions of Emotion

Charles Darwin was among the first to study facial expression of emotions. In his 1872 book, *The Expression of the Emotions in Man and Animals*, he argued that facial expressions evolved because they aided the organism in adapting to its environment, particularly to its social environment. For example, an animal that fails to recognize a particular facial expression of a more dominant member of its species may be attacked. Research with rhesus monkeys supports this idea. In one study (Sackett, 1966), infant rhesus monkeys were separated from their mothers at birth and reared so that they never saw or heard another monkey. When shown a photograph of an adult male baring its teeth, the isolate immediately got on all fours and raised its buttocks, a sign of subordination. In many species, communication involving facial expression and other bodily changes have become ritualized and integrated into a larger pattern of behavior, such as courtship and mating rituals (Huxley, 1923).

Darwin's ideas lay largely dormant for nearly a century until psychologists became interested in emotional expression across human cultures. People throughout the world, regardless of their cultural and social backgrounds, are able to recognize and agree upon the kinds of emotions conveyed by facial expressions. For example, Ekman & Friesman (1971) asked college students in five different countries to match the name of an emotion written in their native tongues with photographs expressing six different primary emotions. (The photographs used and the degree of agreement among cultures are presented in Figure 10.13.) The high degree of agreement means that regardless of cultural background, specific facial expressions are linked to specific emotions. Such findings suggest that facial expression of emotion has a strong biological basis.

In the attempt to ensure that such findings were not due to factors such as mass media influence, Ekman and his colleagues went to New Guinea to study emotionality in members of an aboriginal tribe known as the Fore (Ekman, Sorenson & Friesen, 1969; Ekman & Friesen, 1971). The members of the tribe had never been exposed to mass media and few had ever seen people other than those in their tribe. Ekman told stories to the Fore, translated into their native language, that were designed to elicit emotions like happiness or sadness. He then asked them to match the different stories to photographs of Caucasians whose faces expressed different emotions. With the exception of confusing the facial expression of fear with that of surprise, the Fore subjects accurately matched the photographs to the stories. Ekman also asked the Fore to express different emotions facially. Again, with the exception of fear and surprise, their facial expressions showed universal agreement with the way those emotions are facially expressed in other countries. Lest you think recognition of facial expressions is a trivial feat, consider that the muscles in the human face can produce 6000 to 7000 different expressions (Izard, 1971). Ekman has argued that the only way to interpret the universality of particular emotions with certain facial expressions is to point to an evolutionary basis for facial expression of emotion (Ekman, 1980).

According to Carroll Izard (1977), the movement and positioning of our facial muscles not only expresses our feelings but also contributes to them. This idea, known as the **facial feedback hypothesis,** holds that feedback from our facial muscles helps us experience emotion by providing us information about the emotion being experienced. Break into a big grin right now. Do you feel any different than you did the moment before? Now grit your teeth. Do you feel any different than you did when smiling? One study has shown that just by changing facial expression, different patterns of physiological arousal may be produced (Ekman, Levenson, & Friesen, 1983). Thus, an emotional expression is not produced by physiological arousal alone, but rather emotional expression contributes to the feeling of physiological arousal.

The Physiology of Emotion

Suppose that you are walking home alone. The street is quiet and unusually dark. You get an eerie feeling, a premonition that something bad is about to happen; you begin to walk a little faster, hoping to get to your house safely. Suddenly, a man brandishing a large knife steps out of the darkness. As he does, he raises the weapon above his head and brings it toward you. To say that you are scared at this moment is an understatement. What you are feeling is pure terror, a major part of which stems from the responses of your autonomic nervous system (ANS) and endocrine system to the situation. All emotions have a physiological component.

The Role of the Autonomic Nervous System. Recall from Chapter 4 that the ANS is comprised of two parts, the parasympathetic nervous system and the sympathetic nervous system. As you began your walk home, the parasympathetic nervous system was working to maintain your body in its normal, relaxed state.

That all changed, however, when you first sensed that something was not quite right. Under the control of the sympathetic nervous system, your body automatically underwent a number of internal changes:

- your respiration and heart rate increased
- your digestion came to a standstill as blood was now directed toward your brain and limbs
- your blood-sugar levels rose
- epinephrine (adrenalin) was pumped into your bloodstream
- you began to perspire
- your pupils became dialated

These internal reactions were intensified as soon as you saw the attacker. All of these changes have one very important effect: they mobilize physiological resources preparing you for "fight or flight." Increases in heart rate and blood sugar provide your muscles with increased energy supplies; increasing respiration provides more oxygen; digestion stops, conserving energy and directing blood flow to the brain and limbs.

The main role of the endocrine system during times of stress is to secrete the hormones adrenalin (epinephrine) and noradrenalin (norepinephrine) into the blood via the adrenal glands. Both hormones increase emotional arousal—in this case, feeling scared; adrenalin also increases heart rate.

Changes in physiological activity can be used to measure emotions. In fact, lie detection is based on the theory that changes in physiological arousal reveal a person's true feelings. These changes can be measured by a polygraph, a device that simultaneously records and measures respiration, pulse rate, blood pressure, muscle tension, and the skin's conductance of minute amounts of electrical current (the skin's resistance to conductance is decreased by perspiration).

Can a person's physiological responses really reveal his or her true feelings? Is the polygraph an accurate and reliable detector of truth-telling? The answer to these questions depends on whom you ask. Some researchers believe that the polygraph is accurate in detecting lies about 90 percent of the time (Raskin & Podlesny, 1979), while others claim this figure is more like 50 percent (Lykken, 1979). One thing is certain though, the use of the polygraph to detect deception is widespread by police departments, security firms, and some businesses (at present 23 states, and many branches of the federal government use the polygraph regularly). Nevertheless, both the American Psychological Association and the British Psychological Society have expressed serious reservations about the polygraph (Abeles, 1985; British Psychological Society, 1986). Among the most serious concerns is the possibility of a false positive: falsely accusing an innocent person.

The Role of the Brain. Your emotional responses are mediated by the limbic system, which also plays a central role in motivation. We know, for example, that electrical stimulation of the hypothalamus can provoke attack in animals. The kind of attack, as well as the degree of emotion expressed, seems to be affected by the hypothalamic region that is stimulated (Flynn et al., 1970). Stimulate the lateral hypothalamus in a cat and it will deliberately stalk its prey and then quickly attack. Stimulate the medial hypothalamus, and the cat will arch its back, flash its teeth, and hiss and growl; but it will actually attack its prey only after repeated stimulation.

We learned earlier that the amygdala plays an important role in mediating emotions. Recall that removal of the amygdala has a taming effect on animals. Recall also that research has shown that another area of the lim-

A polygraph, as pictured here, records and measures certain vital signs, respiration, muscle tension, and the skin's conductance of very small amounts of electrical current. The accuracy of the device in lie-detection is the subject of controversy, though it remains widely used by some businesses and the police.

bic system, the septal area, also plays a role in emotion. In 1954, James Olds and Peter Milner implanted electrodes into the septal region of rats. The investigators then put the animals into an operant chamber, and gave them a brief burst of electrical current every time they pressed a lever. Much to Olds and Milner's surprise, the rats continued to press the lever. Some rats continued to press the lever at extremely high rates over prolonged periods, leading the researchers to label the septal area a "pleasure center."

Even though Olds and Milner's research reveals that brain structures are involved in emotional behavior, we still know too little about the brain to make unequivocal statements about which part of the brain controls specific emotions. The highly integrated nature of the brain's neural circuitry makes it unlikely that every emotion or behavior is tied to a specific brain center.

Theories of Emotion

The brain's complexity has not deterred psychologists from theorizing about where emotions come from and the internal mechanisms that may control their ebb and flow. A credible theory of emotion must, among other things, explain specifically how physiological arousal, emotion-eliciting stimuli, behavioral expression, cognition, and previous experience interact to give rise to emotions. We may ask questions like "Which comes first, physiological arousal or emotion?" or "Did you become physiologically aroused because you were afraid or were you afraid because you became physiologically aroused?" Questions of this nature have ignited an "emotional" debate that has continued in psychology for nearly a century.

The James-Lange and Cannon-Bard Theories. One of the first theories of emotion dates back to the late 1800s when the American psychologist, William James, and a Danish physiologist, Carl Lange, independently hypothesized that physiological arousal precedes the experiencing of an emotion. This idea, known as the **James-Lange theory,** would explain your terror in the earlier example as the result of your perception of your heart racing and your breathing becoming short. In James' own words: " . . . bodily changes follow perception of the exciting fact. . . . our feeling of the

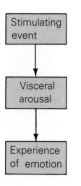

FIGURE 10.14
*The James-Lange theory of emotion.
According to this theory, events in the
environment stimulate visceral
arousal, which in turn, gives rise to the
experience of emotion.*

same changes as they occur *IS* the emotion. . . ." (James, 1890, p. 449).
According to this view, we first perceive a stimulus, which induces a particular pattern of physiological arousal, which is then interpreted as a specific emotion (see Figure 10.14.)

The James-Lange theory was the dominant view of emotion until 1927 when Walter Cannon published a harsh critique of the theory (Cannon, 1927). Cannon faulted the theory saying that because internal organs are only sparsely supplied with nerves, physiological arousal—increases in heart rate, breathing, and so on —occur too slowly to produce the spontaneity of emotion. Cannon also believed that different emotions do not seem to correspond to a unique pattern of physiological arousal. He believed that instead, most emotions seem to entail a similar pattern of physiological arousal. Cannon argued that emotions are in no way dependent upon a preceding change in physiological arousal.

A fellow physiologist, Philip Bard (1928), proposed that the ANS has nothing directly to do with the experience of emotion; rather, emotion-provoking stimuli are transmitted to the thalamus, which then relays the information about emotion simultaneously to the cortex and to the ANS. This view of emotions, now referred to as the **Cannon-Bard theory,** holds that the experiencing of both physiological arousal and emotion are controlled by the brain. Emotionality and physiological arousal are independent of each other: your heart races and your breathing becomes short at the same time you feel afraid (see Figure 10.15).

Which theory has turned out to be the most accurate? To answer this question, let's review some of the research findings in terms of three key issues.

- Which part of the brain is involved with emotion?
- Are distinct patterns of physiological arousal linked to the experiencing of different emotions?
- Would we be able to experience emotion if the brain were unable to sense physiological arousal of the internal organs?

On the first point, you already know that the Cannon-Bard theory missed the mark in terms of the brain center involved with emotion. The hypothalamus and limbic system, and not the thalamus as Cannon and Bard argued, are the brain regions that play the major role in emotion.

The second point requires a little more critical thinking. If the James-Lange theory is correct, different patterns of physiological arousal should be positively correlated with different kinds of emotions. If the Cannon-Bard theory is correct, the pattern of physiological arousal should be the same for all emotions. In actuality, some patterns of emotion can be linked to distinct patterns of physiological arousal, adding another point in James-Lange's favor. Ekman et al. (1983) have shown that when people experience anger, blood flow is directed to the hands and feet, but when a person is experiencing fear, blood flow is directed away from the hands and feet. The James-Lange theory is also supported by another study (Schwartz, Weinberger, & Singer, 1981) that showed that heart rate and systolic blood pressure (blood pressure during heartbeats) are higher for negative emotions like anger, fear, and sadness than for positive emotions like happiness.

Recall too, Izard's facial feedback hypothesis and Eckman's work, which supports Izard's hypothesis: as the position of the facial muscles changes so does physiological arousal emanating from the muscles and the kind of emotion experienced. The James-Lange theory would predict such results.

The third issue also has been resolved in favor of the James-Lange theory. According to James-Lange, we must be able to sense physiological arousal in order to experience emotion. Cannon-Bard disagrees because, in

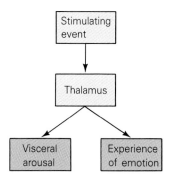

FIGURE 10.15
The Cannon-Bard theory of emotion. According to this theory, events in the environment stimulate the thalamus, which in turn, simultaneously produces visceral arousal and the experience of emotion.

their view, physiological arousal occurs independently of emotion. This disagreement was resolved partially in favor of James-Lange when George Hohmann (1966) showed that people with severed spinal cords experienced different degrees of emotion, depending upon how high in the spinal cord the damage occurred. Hohmann interviewed 25 veterans who had suffered spinal cord injuries during World War II. Veterans who experienced damage to the lower parts of the spinal cord and could not feel sensations in their legs reported that they were able to experience emotion to about the same degree as before their injuries. Veterans whose spinal damage was as high as the neck could not feel sensations arising from their legs, arms, or torso; they also reported emotions lacked the intensity they had before their injuries. Interestingly, veterans with upper spinal damage reported that they could still act emotionally but that they did not feel the same degree of intensity. Here is one example:

> I say I am afraid, like when I'm going into a real stiff exam at school, but I don't really feel afraid, not all tense and shaky, with that hollow feeling in my stomach, like I used to. (quoted in Schachter, 1975, p. 558)

Two-Factor Theory of Emotion. Although the research we just reviewed supports the James-Lange theory, the Cannon-Bard theory seems to have been right about one thing: the brain plays a role in our emotional experience.

Suppose you recognized the man with the knife as your practical joker roommate? Would your emotional reaction be any different? Would you have felt relief (or anger) rather than fear? Most modern psychologists would say that your emotional reaction would be different based on your cognitive appraisal of the situation. In the one case, you perceive danger, in the second relief. In other words, your ability to recognize the man as your roommate, who is a practical joker, changes your subjective reaction. You are still highly physiologically aroused, but you no longer view it as fear.

With this view, two factors would appear to be involved in emotion: physiological arousal and cognition. Physiological arousal in conjunction with a cognitive interpretation of the environmental situation producing the arousal *is* emotion. If this is true, the kind of emotion experienced should depend upon how we interpret the situation producing the arousal, even if the underlying pattern of physiological arousal is similar from one situation to the next (see Figure 10.16). This theory is called the **two-factor theory of emotion.** A critical test of this theory came in 1962 in an experiment carried out by Stanley Schachter and Jerome Singer.

FIGURE 10.16
The Two-factor theory of emotion. According to this theory, environmental events simultaneously stimulate both visceral arousal and cognitive appraisal of the context of those events. These two factors produce the experience of emotion.

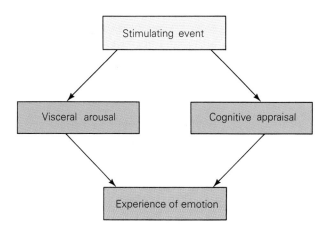

Subjects in this experiment were college males who were led to believe that they were participating in an experiment dealing with the effects of vitamin supplements on vision. They were asked if they minded receiving an injection of suproxin. Suproxin was not really a vitamin supplement, rather it was either a placebo or adrenalin (epinephrine). Subjects who received the adrenalin injection soon experienced tremors, palpitations, and slightly increased breathing. Subjects given the placebo had no physiological reaction. After receiving an injection, all subjects except those given the placebo were given one of three different kinds of information about the side effects of suproxin.

- *Informed:* Some subjects were told to expect temporary tremors, palpitations, and increased breathing, so these subjects had a complete explanation of their physiological arousal.
- *Uninformed:* Some subjects were not given any information about the drug's side effects.
- *Misinformed:* Some subjects were told that the drug would make them feel numb, itchy, and possibly give them a slight headache.

Schachter and Singer believed that informed subjects, who already knew why they were feeling what they were feeling, would need no further explanation of their heightened arousal. By contrast, the uninformed and misinformed subjects would not have any clue to their arousal and would be expected to seek an appropriate explanation.

Thus, the critical question was: Would uninformed and misinformed subjects, in comparison to informed subjects, interpret their feelings in a manner consistent with their social environment? To answer that question, each subject was placed in the company of a confederate whom the experimenters had trained to act either euphorically or angrily. No misinformed subjects were exposed to confederates who acted angrily. Thus, Schachter and Singer's experiment involved seven different groups of subjects:

Anger Condition	Euphoria Condition
Informed	Informed
Uninformed	Uninformed
Uninformed	Misinformed
Placebo	Placebo

True to the researchers' expectations, the uninformed and misinformed subjects behaved either more euphorically or angrily than informed subjects, depending upon the social context in which they had been placed (see Figure 10.17.) Schachter and Singer concluded, then, that subjects interpreted feelings of physiological arousal in terms of the situation.

Schachter and Singer's research may be of only limited value in helping to understand emotion in everyday life, however. One reason is that subjects given only a placebo were affected by the confederate's behavior, although not to the same degree as subjects in the other groups. However, because their emotional ratings were consistently greater than informed subjects, it is difficult to evaluate clearly subjects' states of physiological arousal, which, of course, puts Schachter and Singer's theoretical edifice on shaky ground. A second reason is that their findings have been difficult to replicate (Marshall & Zimbardo, 1979; Reisenzein, 1983). In an extensive review of the literature aimed at evaluating two-factor theory, Reisenzein found no research that supported the idea that experiencing emotion depended upon first being physiologically aroused. He pointed out, for instance, that drugs that block sympathetic arousal do not generally prevent people from experiencing some kinds of emotion, such as anxiety or anger, under laboratory conditions. It would appear, then, that the first factor in the two-factor theory, physiological arousal, is less important in our experiencing of emotion than Schachter and Singer's findings suggest.

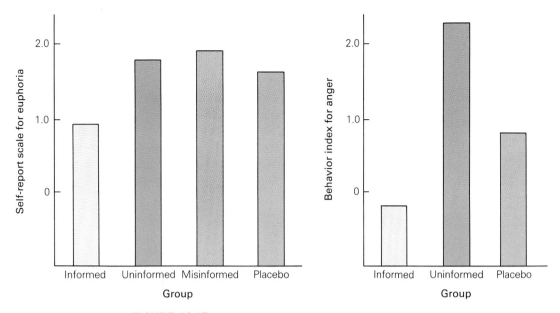

FIGURE 10.17
The results of Schachter and Singer's experiment. For both the euphoria and anger data, larger numbers indicate greater emotional levels, that is, the happier or angrier the subjects reported feeling. Based on Schachter, 1975.

However, the second factor, cognition, appears to play an important role, and is the focus of two more recently developed theoretical views of emotion.

Cognition Then Emotion or Emotion Then Cognition? The current debate in the psychology of emotion, like previous debates, focuses on the sequence of events involved in experiencing emotion. Robert Zajonc, a psychologist at the University of Michigan, believes that emotion precedes cognition; Richard Lazarus at the University of California, Berkeley, believes that Zajonc has things backwards and that cognition comes before emotion.

Zajonc (1980, 1984) argues that in many instances our emotions occur before we have had time to appraise the situation cognitively. We do think about things, but only after we have reacted emotionally to them. Everyday experience would seem to confirm this idea. How many times have you said something or reacted with like or dislike to a person, place, or thing without first thinking about it? In support of his position, Zajonc cites evidence from laboratory studies in which subjects were first very briefly exposed to a stimulus such as music (Wilson, 1979) or geometric shapes (Kunst-Wilson & Zajonc, 1980). Next, subjects were presented with these stimuli and others like them and asked to identify the stimuli that had been presented previously. Subjects generally were unable to make this distinction. But when asked which stimuli they liked better, they almost always reported the ones that had been presented previously even though they had no recollection of seeing them before. So, Zajonc contends, emotional behavior is not premeditated.

Lazarus (1982, 1984) argues that cognition precedes emotion. He contends that the laboratory studies cited above did not involve real life kinds of emotion. After all, how we react to the people and events in our lives is a far cry from how we react to music and geometrical shapes presented to us under artificial conditions. He agrees with Zajonc that long and drawn out thinking is not necessary for emotion. Instead, he suggests that emotions are based on quick, sometimes instantaneous cognitive appraisals of situations that can occur simultaneously with emotion. The speed with which we think about situations is hastened by previous experience with similar situations. The debate sparked between the James-Lange and Cannon-Bard theories is still with us today, although it involves slightly different ideas and different players. The question of which comes first, cognition or emotion, is an important one, since an answer to it would tell us the extent to which emotions and thinking are related. Cognitions and emotions do not appear spontaneously, however. Rather, they are caused. They are prompted by our experience, our recollection of memories, and by changes in our environment, which leaves unanswered larger and perhaps more important questions. Can we, by controlling the environment, also control our cognitions and our emotions? To what extent do cognition and environmental factors interact to determine motivational and emotional states?

BOUNDARIES AND FRONTIERS

Motivation and emotion, of course, are the raw materials from which human nature is made. Human nature probably has not changed very much in recent evolutionary history, say in the last 2500 years or so. People are still motivated to eat and sleep, make love and war, and get emotional about it at the same time, for most, if not all, of the same reasons as they were back then. Even tremendous advances in science, technology, and medicine have left human nature essentially unchanged. At the very least, human nature is resilient stuff. Fortunately, our understanding of human nature has not been so impervious to change. We have seen that our understanding of human nature has changed enormously since James, McDougall, Freud, Cannon, and others first began theorizing about motivation and emotion. The clearest lesson we have learned about motivation and emotion is that both are determined by a complex interplay of physiological, cognitive, social, and behavioral factors specific to each individual. Because the strength of these factors and their degree of interplay can differ from individual to individual, individuals themselves differ.

Early psychologists like James and McDougall knew that human motivation and emotion were influenced by the interaction of physiological, cognitive, social, and environmental factors, but they had no way to know either how or to what extent they interacted with one another. Their ability to understand motivation and emotion, that is, to know themselves, was bounded by their ability to conduct scientific investigations—they simply did not have available the kinds of sophisticated gadgetry and experimental techniques necessary to manipulate and measure precisely the subject matter. Such technology and methods have allowed modern psychologists to discover and study some of the physiological substrates of motivation and emotion and to complete research that teases apart some of the roles that cognition and physiological, social, and environmental factors play. Clearly, though, there remain frontiers. We don't know, for instance, how these factors and their interaction change over life's course. Presumably, James Huberty was as cute, warm, and loving a baby as any of the rest of us—how did he become transformed into a mass murderer? On the other hand, as a child, Mother Teresa probably misbehaved (like all of us), yet she went on to lead the kind of noble and virtuous life about which most of us can only dream. Hers, too, was not likely a change that occurred overnight. In other words, experiences earlier in life are as much a part of the context for present motivation and emotion as our physiology or cognition, yet scientifically we know little about their roles in influencing motivation and emotion later in life.

Hundreds of narrower and more specific questions about motivation and emotion remain unanswered. In addition, we have seen that psychological research often raises as many questions about motivation and emotion as it answers, providing still more frontiers to be explored and understood.

CONCEPT SUMMARY

MOTIVATION

- What are the three aspects of behavior with which the study of motivation is concerned? (p. 332)
- What are the main differences between theories that emphasize internal drives as motivators and those that emphasize goals and rewards as motivators? (pp. 332–333)
- What is the relationship between an intervening variable and observable behavior? (pp. 333–334)

GENERAL THEORIES OF MOTIVATION

- What is the important difference between the instinct theories of James and McDougall and newer ones proposed by ethologists? (p. 335)
- How is the concept of homeostasis related to the idea that organisms are motivated to eliminate or reduce drives? (p. 336)
- Why is Maslow's theory intuitively appealing? What are its shortcomings? (pp. 337–339)
- How has McClelland's research extended Henry Murray's work on achievement motivation? What important findings has McClelland's research revealed? (pp. 339–341)
- How does optimal-arousal theory differ from opponent-process theory? (pp. 341–343)
- Is there an optimal level of arousal in terms of behavioral performance? Explain. (pp. 342–343)
- What are the major differences between incentive and expectancy theories? (pp. 343–345)

MOTIVATION FOR EATING

- What initiates eating and what stops it? What roles do internal and external signals and the brain play in eating? (pp. 345–347)
- To what physiological process does the term set point refer? (pp. 347–348)
- What are the likely causes of obesity? (pp. 348–351)
- What steps can one take to prevent becoming obese? (p. 351)
- What motivational factors are related to anorexia nervosa and bulimia? (pp. 351–353)

MOTIVATION FOR AGGRESSION

- What role do catharsis, displacement, and sublimation play in Freud's (instinctive) theory of aggression? (p. 353)
- What sort of research evidence supports the idea that aggression may have a genetic basis? (p. 354)
- What role does the amygdala play in aggressive behavior? (pp. 354–355)
- What is the relation between frustration and aggression? (pp. 355–356)
- How might "transfer of excitation" result in aggressive behavior? (p. 356)
- According to Bandura, how are aggressive behaviors learned? (pp. 356–358)
- To what extent can watching violence on television lead to aggressive behavior? (p. 358)
- What does the study of eating and aggression tell us about motivation? (p. 359)

EMOTION

- What are the four components to any emotion? (p. 360)
- What is the emotion solid? From which perspective does Plutchik view his work? Explain. Would Ekman agree with that perspective? Why? (pp. 361–362)
- What basis does Ekman have for arguing that the relation between emotion and its expression is universal? (pp. 362–363)
- According to Izard, how does the facial expression of emotion contribute to our feeling of the physiological component of emotion? (p. 363)
- What contributions do the autonomic nervous system and brain make to the experiencing of emotion? (pp. 363–365)
- How does the two-factor theory of emotion differ from the James-Lange and Cannon-Bard theories of emotion? (pp. 365–369)
- In what sense does the debate between Zajonc and Lazarus represent a continuation of the debate sparked earlier by the James-Lange and Cannon-Bard theories? (pp. 369–370)

KEY TERMS AND CONCEPTS

MOTIVATION

Motivation The causes of behavior, particularly as they influence the initiation and cessation of behavior, and the intensity or strength of behavior. (p. 332)

Intervening Variable Any hypothetical variable believed to cause behavior. (p. 333)

GENERAL THEORIES OF MOTIVATION

Instinct Theory The view, popular at the turn of the century, that all behavior is motivated by instinct, innate or genetically determined tendencies to perform certain acts or respond in particular ways. (p. 335)

Homeostasis The tendency for all animals to strive to maintain internal bodily states at a constant level. (p. 336)

Drive A state of internal tension or arousal caused by an unsatisfied need. The unsatisfied need usually results from deprivation of biologically relevant resources such as food and water. There are two kinds of drives, primary and secondary. (p. 336)

Primary Drives Drives that arise from physiological needs and do not involve learning. Primary drives serve as the motivators that impel us to seek food when hungry, to drink when thirsty, and to seek warmth when we are cold. (p. 336)

Secondary Drives Drives that are brought about through experience. They are learned drives believed to underlie psychological motives such as acquiring wealth, desiring affiliation, seeking approval from parents and significant others, and so on. Drive theorists believed that secondary drives are acquired through their association with primary drives. (p. 336)

Maslow's Hierarchy Abraham Maslow's idea that our motivation for different activities passes through several hierarchical stages, with entrance to subsequent stages depending upon satisfying the needs in previous stages. (p. 337)

Self-actualization The achievement of our greatest potential as human beings, whatever that might be. Maslow believed that self-actualized people are recognized by their unique qualities, among them self-awareness, creativity, spontaneity, and their willingness to accept change and confront challenges. (p. 338)

Need for Achievement (n Ach) The motivation to meet or surpass performance standards or to accomplish difficult tasks. (p. 339)

Need for Affiliation The motivation to form friendships and associations with others. (p. 340)

Need for Power The motivation to be in control of events, resources or other people, usually for your own advantage. (p. 340)

Optimal-Arousal Theory The view that all organisms are motivated to maintain an optimal level of arousal. (p. 341)

Yerkes-Dodson Law The inverted U-shaped relationship between performance and arousal: for any task to be performed there is an optimal level of arousal necessary for optimal performance. Too little arousal or too much arousal interferes with performance. (p. 342)

Opponent-process Theory Richard Solomon's theory that for every emotional experience there is an opposite emotional experience that maintains our emotional and motivational levels at some homeostatic level. (p. 342)

Incentive Theory The theory that external events, such as goals or incentives, motivate or "pull" us to behave. Incentive theory focuses on behavior-environment interactions rather than on physiology-behavior interactions as do the drive and need theories of motivation. (p. 343)

Intrinsic Motivation The need for competence and self-determination. (p. 344)

Expectancy Theory The theory that an individual's anticipation or expectancy of the reward motivates his or her behavior. (p. 344)

MOTIVATION FOR EATING

Lateral Hypothalamus (LH) The brain region believed to function as the "on switch" for feeding, because when stimulated chemically or electrically, it induces foraging and eating. (p. 347)

Ventromedial Hypothalamus (VMH) The brain region thought to be the "off switch" for eating because, when stimulated, eating stops. (p. 347)

Dual Center Theory of Eating The idea that the lateral hypothalamus and ventromedial hypothalamus work in concert to control eating. (p. 347)

Setpoint The idea that the hypothalamus, functioning as a homeostatic mechanism, sets a level, probably based on the combination of body weight, blood sugar levels, and metabolism, that determines when and how much an animal will eat. (p. 347)

Obesity A body weight 20 percent in excess of that considered average for a given height. (p. 348)

Anorexia Nervosa An eating disorder, characterized by a pathological fear of weight gain, an obsession with not eating food, and a refusal to eat. Anorexics are typically women between the ages of 15 and 30. (p. 351)

Bulimia An eating disorder in which people eat enormous quantities of food and then either force themselves to regurgitate or use laxatives to rid their bodies of the food. (p. 352)

MOTIVATION FOR AGGRESSION

Aggression Any action, verbal or physical, that is intended to harm another individual. (p. 353)

Catharsis Freud's term to describe the process in which pent-up energy is released or purged. Displacement and sublimation may provide such an outlet. (p. 353)

EMOTION

Emotions Moods or feelings. Felt internal conditions that change from time to time largely as a function of things that happen to us. (p. 359)

Facial Feedback Hypothesis The idea that feedback from our facial muscles helps us experience emotion by providing us with information about the emotion. (p. 363)

James-Lange Theory The idea that physiological arousal precedes the experiencing of an emotion.(p. 365)

Cannon-Bard Theory The theory that the experiencing of emotion and the experiencing of physiological arousal are controlled by the brain and are independent of each other. (p. 366)

Two-factor Theory of Emotion The theory that two factors are involved in emotion: physiological arousal and cognition. Emotion is the combination of physiological arousal and a cognitive interpretation of the environmental situation producing the arousal. (p. 367)

ADDITIONAL SOURCES OF INFORMATION

Izard, C. E., Kagan, J., & Zajonc, R. B. (Eds.) (1984). *Emotions, cognition, and behavior.* Cambridge, England: Cambridge University Press. This graduate-level text surveys recent research conducted by the leading psychologists in the areas of emotion and cognition.

James, W. (1890). *Principles of psychology.* New York: Holt. Although now 100 years old, this classic text contains James' views regarding motivation, emotion, and many other dimensions of modern psychology.

Logue, A. W. (1986). *The psychology of eating and drinking.* New York: Freeman. This book is an excellent review of eating, drinking, and associated disorders. Its coverage of obesity and eating disorders is particularly well done.

McClelland, D. C. (1985). *Human motivation.* Glenview, IL: Scott, Foresman. Written by one of the leading researchers in the field, this text offers a top-notch review of achievement motivation and its development.

Petri, H. L. (1986). *Motivation: Theory and research* (2nd ed). Belmont, CA: Wadsworth. This book is widely used in undergraduate classes in motivation. It has excellent coverage of the major aspects of motivation as well as their relation to emotion.

Helen Burke stepped out of her car and walked slowly across the thick carpet of grass. The bright April sun felt warm and made her feel happy. In her hand she carried a vase of freshly picked lilies. She gently set the vase before the tombstone and then sat down in the grass.

She and Bob had been married 40 years before he died in a car accident on this day three years ago. Visiting the grave always brought a flood of memories to her mind, and sometimes she would come here just for that reason. She thought mostly about her marriage and family. She felt good about herself: she had a sense of satisfaction about the successes in her life, she had come to understand the disappointments, and she accepted the fact that she, too, would die. She had virtually no feelings of despair about her life.

A young couple strolling hand-in-hand down the road alongside the cemetery caught Helen's eye. She recalled when Bob and she first fell in love. They were only kids in high school then. "What a great time of life that was. We had no responsibilities, and we talked and laughed and dreamed about growing old together," she thought. The good times really stood out, but then she recalled the more trying times and the changes that growing up forced upon her. It seemed like just yesterday that her friends were convincing her to do one thing while her parents pressured her to do another. She remembered, too, how difficult it was for her to decide where to go to college, and whether to stay with Bob or to date other boys. "All in all," she thought to herself, "I made the right decisions."

She continued to reminisce; her thoughts turned to her children, Anne and Mark, and the things they did as children. She remembered how much they used to like to be with her, and how they would cry when she left them with a sitter, or even sometimes with Bob. "What a contrast with when they were teenagers and were so independent, they didn't really want to be with me much," she thought. She remembered, too, one of her husband's favorite tricks with the kids. When they were little, Mark had to have everything that Anne had, especially when it came to snacks. If Mark didn't get his way, he would throw a temper tantrum until he either got what he wanted or fell asleep. Bob, though, would see that Mark and Anne were treated fairly. One time, Anne was given two cookies and Mark only one. Mark threw a tantrum and demanded that he have two cookies also. Not wanting to give Mark two cookies, Bob simply took Mark's cookie, broke it in half, and gave the two halves to him. Mark took the two halves, stopped his crying, and remarked to his sister that he now had two cookies, too.

Helen heard a car pull up behind hers. She turned around and saw that it was her daughter, Anne, now 35, and her two granddaughters, 4-year-old Emma and 6-year-old Kimberly. She thought for a moment how much of herself she saw in Anne. She was captured by the idea that her life was a cycle, and that that cycle was repeating itself in Anne, and that in not too long, it would repeat itself in Emma and Kimberly, too. "Oh, the details are different, of course, but the general pattern is the same," she reflected. "How much they have to look forward to."

"We thought we'd find you here, Mom," Anne called. "How are you feeling?"

"I feel wonderful," Helen said. "I was just thinking about you. How's everybody?"

"We're doing just fine, aren't we girls?" Anne asked while looking at her daughters. The girls, happy to see Grandma, were already running at top speed toward her. They quickly wrapped themselves around her legs, each chanting, "Kiss me first, Grandma, kiss me first!" Helen bent over and hugged them both, planting a kiss first on Kimberly's head and then on Emma's. The children smiled, kissed her in return, and then ran up ahead, toward their grandfather's grave.

By looking at the generations in our family, we can see the cycles of human development. Not only do we grow older, but we grow and change personally, intellectually, and socially as well.

TABLE 11.1. *Phases of the life-span.*

PHASE	APPROXIMATE AGE	HIGHLIGHTS
1. Prenatal	Conception through birth	Rapid physical development of both nervous system and body
2. Infancy	Birth to 1½ years	Motor development; attachment to primary caregiver
3. Childhood	1½ years to 12 years	Increasing ability to think logically and reason abstractly; refinement of motor skills; peer influences
4. Adolescence	13 years to about 20 years	Thinking and reasoning become more adultlike; identity crises; continued peer influences
5. Adulthood	20 years to 65 years	Stability and then decrease in physical abilities, love, marriage, career
6. Old age	65 years and older to death	Reflect upon life's work and accomplishments; physical health deteriorates; prepare for death; death

Anne put her arm through her mother's and together they walked toward the grave.

"They sure love you, Mom. I wish Dad was still alive to see them growing up." Anne smiled and said, "Do you remember that old cookie trick Dad used to pull on Mark? Well, it still works. Emma falls for it every time!" They both laughed.

THE LIFE-SPAN PERSPECTIVE

Helen's thoughts and reminiscences reflect the major theme of this chapter: human development over the life span. Human development can be viewed as a cycle of changes that each of us experiences during our lives. We can see different parts of the cycle by looking at our grandparents, our parents, our friends, and our children. At one time, psychologists emphasized development as it occurred at life's outset, namely infancy and childhood. But as psychologists have learned more about development, it has become obvious that developmental processes do not stop with childhood. Growing older is not simply a matter of aging, but of growing and changing personally, intellectually, and socially as well (see Table 11.1). **Life-span developmental psychology** is the area of psychology that focuses on these processes and the patterns of change that occur within an individual over his or her life span. Psychologists who study life-span development are interested in learning more about how and why these processes and changes occur.

The essence of life is development and change.

Development is inevitable. Indeed, the essence of life is development and change. Each one of us shares similar developmental experiences that help bond us as friends, colleagues, and human beings. This is particularly true of individuals of the same sex and culture. In general, we all learn how to walk and talk at about the same time and in the same sequence. We all experience puberty at about the same time, and beyond that, the aging process is accompanied by fairly predictable changes. This does not mean, though, that we are not each unique. If experience teaches us anything, it surely has shown that people differ. What causes these differences? One of the goals of this chapter is to show you that, although the overall process of development is pretty much the same for each one of us, our individual life experiences accent our development, and so contribute to the rather idiosyncratic patterns of thinking and behaving that psychologists call personalities. In a way, our individual development is like a signature: most of us learn to write at about the same time, but each of our signatures is truly distinct.

Developmental psychologists, then, study both the similarities and differences among people as they develop and change over the course of their lives. In this chapter, we are interested in when and how these similarities and differences occur. You will not only be given psychological explanations for many of the changes that you have experienced so far, but you will also be given a preview and account of the developmental changes yet to come. We will present the major theories of development and discuss each of the major periods of development: prenatal development, infancy, childhood, adolescence, adulthood, and old age. First let's briefly discuss two major questions in developmental psychology and the means by which psychologists study developmental processes.

Two Questions in Life-Span Development

It may well be that we are born able to live a thousand different lives, but it is no less true that we die having lived just one.

(David Barash, 1979, p.1)

Each of us has the potential to be a unique person, extraordinarily different from others in the way we act, the way we think, and the way we lead our lives. But the underlying factor that gives us that potential is something that we share with every other member of our species. Whether we ultimately become a politician, an athlete, a banker, a scholar, or whatever, we will experience similar developmental processes. Keeping in mind that there seems to be no limit to the number of different courses and changes of direction that life can take, the central question in which developmental psychologists are interested is this: What directs the developmental process? Finding an answer to that question has required that developmental psychologists wrestle with two important questions. First, to what degree do heredity and environment influence development (Plomin, 1987), and second, is development a continuous or discontinuous process? Let's look at each issue more closely.

By now you are well aware that both heredity and environment play an important role in development. For example, when identical twins are adopted into different families, their rates of physical growth, food preferences, selection of friends, hobbies, and academic performance are similar (Bouchard, 1981). Other studies have shown that simply by improving social conditions, dramatic developmental changes may take place. For example, while living in an understaffed orphanage where their interaction with humans was minimal, two little girls were found to be developmentally delayed and labeled as unadoptable. However, several months after being transferred to another institution with a more homelike atmosphere, both girls showed tremendous changes. They were more alert and active and approached normal intellectual development for their age (Skeels, 1966).

As you may recall, the genetic program or genotype that people inherit at birth determines the extent to which the environment can influence the development of the phenotype, or the individual's physical, cognitive, and behavioral characteristics. It is helpful to think of the genotype as a capacity that might be realized if the environment is favorable: the genotype endows individuals with an indefinite spectrum of possible phenotypes, but the environment aids in determining the extent to which those phenotypes eventually develop (Platt & Sanislow, 1988).

The second issue facing developmental psychologists is the manner and pace with which development occurs. Simply put, is development a gradual and continuous process or is it discontinuous and marked by distinct stages involving clear and abrupt transitions between stages? Clearly, we personally experience development as continuous. In general, psychologists who emphasize biological factors in development tend to view it as a discontinuous process; those who emphasize the role of experience in development tend to view it as a continuous process. As you can see, the continuous-discontinuous question is related to the heredity-environment question. Development is not likely to be either wholly continuous or discontinuous because heredity and environment interact. In this chapter, we discuss both sides of this question in detail.

Approaches to Studying Changes Over the Life Span

Development is difficult to research because the phenomena under study change over the entire life span, which is such a very long period of time. For developmental psychologists, this means that their research must include a method for comparing and contrasting people at different points in their development. Two different research approaches are useful to accomplish this task: the cross-sectional approach and the longitudinal approach. The rationale behind both approaches is outlined in Figure 11.1.

The Cross-Sectional Approach. The **cross-sectional approach** enables psychologists to test or observe differences in various groups of individuals of various ages simultaneously. Each group is called a **cohort**, that is, people born in the same year or time period. For example, the people born in 1972 represent the 1972 cohort. In cross-sectional research, different cohorts are compared on variables hypothesized to influence development.

These comparisons make it possible to determine the differences that exist among cohorts, as well as to make general inferences about developmental processes across the life span. For example, suppose we wish to

FIGURE 11.1

A comparison of the cross-sectional and longitudinal approaches to researching life-span development. In a cross-sectional study of development between the ages of 5 and 15, groups of 5-, 10-, and 15-year-olds would be compared at the same time on different variables. In a longitudinal study of the same age range, the same group of individuals would be compared at ages 5, 10, and 15 years. The longitudinal study would take 10 years to complete; the cross-sectional study could be completed in the same year it was started.

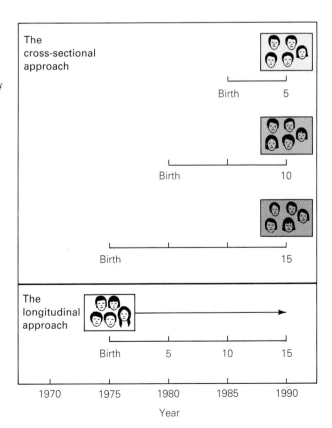

TABLE 11.2. *Advantages and disadvantages of cross-sectional and longitudinal approaches.*

APPROACH	ADVANTAGES	DISADVANTAGES
Cross-sectional	Provides a general overview of developmental processes	Does not provide information about the stability of developmental changes over time
	Quick and relatively inexpensive to conduct	Cannot control for cohort effects
Longitudinal	Provides a direct comparison of developmental changes within individuals	Requires much time to conduct
	Provides information about how behavior at an earlier time affects development changes at a later time	Is costly to conduct
	Provides information about the stability of developmental changes over time	Potential loss of subjects due to death and relocation
	Control for cohort effects	

discover how intelligence differs across the life span. Using a cross-sectional approach, we might give several different cohorts (1952, 1962, and 1972) an intelligence test. Once the subjects in each cohort complete the test, we would compare the results, and then draw general conclusions from our findings. This study has actually been conducted (Schaie, 1975), and the results showed that younger people (ages 25 to 35) performed better on selected intelligence measures than did middle-aged and elderly people.

The main advantage of the cross-sectional approach is that it provides the researcher with a general overview of the developmental process being studied (see Table 11.2). It also has the advantage of being a quick and inexpensive way to conduct developmental research, since it can be carried out over a relatively brief period of time. Nonetheless, the cross-sectional approach has several drawbacks, not the least of which is that it does not provide information about developmental differences among individuals. It also does not inform us if those developmental differences are stable; that is, whether the behavior observed at one time will remain the same when observed at a later time. The most serious shortcoming of the cross-sectional approach is that it cannot take into account the fact that cohorts differ in terms of the time period in which they were reared, and thus, in terms of the environmental factors that have influenced their development. Being an 18-year-old in 1969 at the height of the Vietnam War and civil protests against the war, is a very different experience from being a 18-year-old in 1990, which may be described as a much more peaceful time.

Consider an example. During the 46-year period between 1932 and 1978, the average IQ score of Americans on two IQ tests, the Stanford-Binet and the Wechsler tests, increased an average of nearly 14 points (Flynn, 1984). Does this mean that during this period, the native intelligence of each cohort (generation) of Americans was increasing? Probably not. An alternative interpretation might point out that during this time period more and more Americans were going to college, nutrition and health care improved, and television viewing and exposure to information via mass media were becoming common. In other words, cultural experiences change across generations and may affect development. To sidestep this sort of problem, many developmental researchers turn to the longitudinal approach.

The Longitudinal Approach. The **longitudinal approach** involves repeated observation or testing of the same cohort over an extended time period. The exact period of time and the amount of time in between testing or observation may vary from study to study and depend on the developmental process under investigation. For example, if we are interested only in cognitive development in children, we might follow a cohort of children, carefully monitoring their intellectual progression from infancy to adolescence. However, if we are interested in cognitive development as it occurs over the life span, we would not end our observations there; rather, we would study the same cohort from infancy through old age. In contrast to cross-sectional studies on the development of intelligence, longitudinal studies have shown that middle-aged adults perform better on IQ tests than they did as young adults (Eichorn, Hunt, & Honzik, 1981).

Compared to the cross-sectional approach, the longitudinal approach has three advantages (see Table 11.2). First, because repeated measures of each subject's development are studied, it permits a direct comparison of developmental processes within individuals over time. Second, longitudinal studies are helpful in identifying behaviors occurring at one time that contribute to the development of other behaviors occurring at a later time. Third, they are useful in determining the stability of behavior over time.

The longitudinal approach, however, also has several drawbacks. The most serious problem is the fact that it requires so much time and money to conduct. After all, following a large cohort over a long time period in which its members may have relocated to far away places, requires a tremendous investment of both time and money (and a good deal of patience on the part of the investigator). In very long-term longitudinal studies there is also another problem: loss of subjects due to death and change of address. Moreover, it is nearly impossible for any one investigator to collect data across the entire life span of a cohort. For example, if a researcher in her 30s begins collecting data on a cohort of infants, those individuals will themselves be only in their 30s when she reaches retirement age! For these reasons, longitudinal studies are often limited to about five years in length.

Both cross-sectional and longitudinal approaches emphasize the passing of time in determining developmental changes. Time, however, is not a variable that can be manipulated. Neither psychologists nor anyone else has the ability to speed up or slow down time so that its effects on development can be investigated. As time passes, people mature into adults. Time has little to do with that process, however. Rather, variables such as genotype, nutrition, and the social environment affect development. Developmental changes are coincidental with time, but not because of time.

Despite their drawbacks, both cross-sectional and longitudinal approaches have identified major developmental milestones through which each of us pass on the way to old age. Both kinds of studies have also been instrumental in the formation of theories of human development, the topic of the next section.

THEORIES OF DEVELOPMENT

Recall that theories serve two functions. First, they help researchers pose questions about the subject matter in which they are interested. Second, they provide a framework or perspective from which to interpret research findings. Theories in psychology, then, influence the way people's behavior is perceived.

There are many important theories of development, each of which focuses on particular aspects of development. In this section, we look at three theories: Jean Piaget's theory of cognitive development, Lawrence Kohlberg's theory of moral development, and Erik Erikson's theory of psychosocial development.

Piaget's Theory of Cognitive Development

Jean Piaget

Cognitive development refers to the series of progressive intellectual changes that we experience as we come to more fully know and understand the world. Cognitive development is actually concerned with those aspects of intelligence that allow us to reason logically, think abstractly, solve problems, remember events in the past, and be creative. The most influential theory of cognitive development was proposed by the famous Swiss biologist, psychologist, and philosopher, Jean Piaget (1896–1980).

Piaget interviewed and observed hundreds of children of different ages, including his own, noting carefully the ways in which their knowledge of the world was constructed (Piaget, 1952). He would often present his subjects with specific problems to solve. His major finding was that, on their way to becoming adults, children progress through a series of qualitatively distinct intellectual periods (Piaget & Inhelder, 1969). Each period is characterized by the particular way in which information is used to construct a knowledge base of the world. Cognitive development, from Piaget's view, involves not merely accumulating more and more information about the world as we grow older, but rather organizing and using that information in different ways to make sense of the world. In other words, children undergo an orderly series of developmental changes until finally they reach the same general way of learning about the world as do adults.

Piaget believed that children form **schemes,** or organized mental representations of the world based on their experiences, and that these schemes function as the basis for understanding current and future experiences. A child's current view of the world is based on a perspective created by his or her previous experiences. For example, a child is said to have a "grasping scheme" when she is able to grasp a rattle in her hand. Once she has learned how to grasp a rattle, she can then use the same scheme to grasp other objects. She has acquired a "picking up scheme" when she is able to actually lift the rattle from a surface. Individual schemes such as these generally become integrated into larger schemes that manifest themselves when the child is able to grasp the object and pick it up in one smooth action. According to Piaget, integration of schemes helps children adapt to the environment. To survive, the child's schemes adjust constantly to environmental changes.

Below left: According to Piaget, children form schemes, such as grasping objects, which become the basis for understanding current and future experiences. Below right: The process of accommodation can produce new schemes or change existing ones. An infant's sucking scheme may change when she puts a flower in her mouth and discovers that the taste is unpleasant.

TABLE 11.3.	The four periods of Piaget's theory of cognitive development.	
PERIOD	APPROXIMATE AGE	MAJOR FEATURES
Sensorimotor	Birth to 2 years	Object permanence; deferred imitation; rudimentary symbolic thinking
Preoperational	2 to 6 or 7 years	Increased ability to think symbolically and logically; egocentrism; cannot yet master conservation problems
Concrete operational	6 or 7 years to 11 years	Can master conservation problems; can understand categorization; cannot think abstractly; decrease in egocentric thinking
Formal operational	11 years upward	Can think abstractly and hypothetically

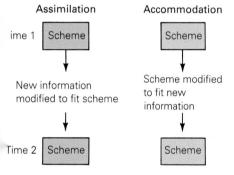

FIGURE 11.2
Assimilation and accommodation. In assimilation, new information about the world is incorporated into existing schemes. In accommodation, schemes are changed to fit new information.

Adaptation is based on two processes that Piaget referred to as assimilation and accommodation. **Assimilation** is the process by which new information about the world is modified to fit existing schemes. For example, when a child moves a wooden block along a surface while making the rumbling sound of an engine, he has assimilated the wooden block into his scheme of a car. On the other hand, **accommodation** is the process by which old schemes are changed by new experiences. Accommodation produces either new schemes or changes in existing ones. An infant with a sucking scheme may quickly modify the scheme when she puts a bar of soap or a stick of deodorant in her mouth. The unpleasant taste of these objects will cause accommodation in the existing sucking scheme so that in the future, she will discriminate among objects that she wants in her mouth and those that she doesn't (see Figure 11.2).

Piaget believed that assimilation and accommodation work in concert to help us adapt to changes in our environment across four distinct periods of cognitive development, which are outlined in Table 11.3. Each period essentially involves a reorganization and reinterpretation of knowledge acquired in previous periods. Although all people progress through these periods in the same order, they may do so at slightly different ages, depending upon, for example, the environment in which they live. A child whose parents and siblings read to him and encourage him to learn his *ABCs* and to count is likely to progress faster than children who do not have the same kinds of experiences. Interestingly, the first three periods formulated by Piaget are relatively universal in describing cognitive development. People in all cultures appear to progress through these periods in the same order and at about the same ages. As we will see, there is more variation in the fourth period. Let's look at each period in detail.

The Sensorimotor Period. In the **sensorimotor period,** which lasts from birth to about 2 years of age, infants learn about the world through their sensory experiences and motor activities. They begin to explore and understand their world only through direct contact and manipulation of the objects in the immediate environment.

Up to the time they are about a month old, infants experience the world through their reflexes, involuntary actions initiated by environmental stimulation. For example, the sucking reflex is caused by an object (a nipple, a finger, a rattle) contacting the area around the mouth. Infants quickly learn to orchestrate their reflexes, enabling them to better explore objects with which they come into contact. For example, a 4-month-old infant will look (and even smile) at a mobile suspended above his head; he may also move his hand toward the dangling objects, alternating grasping and letting them go. He will also move his head in the direction of sounds emanating from the mobile.

During the early stages of the sensorimotor period, infants react reflexively to stimuli in their environments, such as the movement and sounds from this mobile.

During the next two months, infants explore their world by pulling and pushing objects, shaking them, and placing them in their mouths. Such exploration is haphazard at first, as when the infant is surprised by the sound made by banging a rattle against the side of the crib. Such sounds apparently please infants, though, because they continue to bang the rattle against the crib, a sign that their behavior, even at this early point in life, is susceptible to operant conditioning—banging the rattle against the crib is reinforced by the sound it produces.

At around the age of 8 to 12 months, infants make an important discovery: they learn that an object does not cease to exist when it is removed from sight. For example, if we were to allow a 6-month-old infant to play with an interesting toy and then hide it, perhaps by putting it under or behind a blanket while he watches, he would behave as if it ceased to exist. Performing this experiment with a typical 12-month-old infant produces the opposite result: she will search behind the blanket for the toy! The idea that objects do not disappear when they are out of sight is called **object permanence.** At about the same time, infants also develop a crude sense of cause and effect. In essence, babies at this age are able to realize that certain actions, like crying, lead to certain effects, like mom or dad giving them attention. This development, in combination with object permanence, allows babies to predict events that occur within a short time span. Consider the game of peek-a-boo. The baby laughs because he or she knows that you are soon to pop out from behind the blanket and say, "Peek-a-Boo."

Near the end of the sensorimotor period, two other important developments take place. First, the infant develops the capacity to imitate actions that he or she has seen others perform in the past. Piaget believed that such behavior, which he referred to as **deferred imitation,** is the result of the child's new ability to form mental representations of actions that he or she has observed. These representations may then be recalled at a later time to direct particular imitative actions and symbolic play. Pretending to feed a doll or change its diapers or taking a stuffed animal for a walk are common examples of the 2-year-old child's imitative activities.

Second, as having an imagination demonstrates, 2-year-old children begin to think symbolically; they are now capable of forming cognitive

Older infants have developed the concept of object permanence. The infant sees the toy, and when it is out of view, realizes that it is still there and crawls to get it.

FIGURE 11.3
The conservation principle.

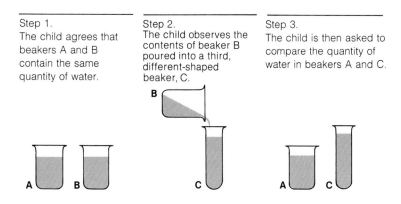

Step 1.
The child agrees that beakers A and B contain the same quantity of water.

Step 2.
The child observes the contents of beaker B poured into a third, different-shaped beaker, C.

Step 3.
The child is then asked to compare the quantity of water in beakers A and C.

representations of objects in the real world. They are able to use words to represent objects such as mom and dad. This is a very important developmental step because these kinds of cognitive skills are useful in communicating more effectively with others.

In sum, the first two years of life, referred to by Piaget as the sensorimotor period, are marked by an orderly progression of increasingly complex cognitive development, including reflexive behavior, object permanence, a rough approximation of cause and effect, imitating the actions of others, and finally, symbolic thinking. Reaching these developmental milestones prepares the child for the events that occur in the second period in Piaget's theory, the preoperational period.

The Preoperational Period. The **preoperational period** represents a four- to five-year period of transition (from ages 2 to about 6 or 7) between first being able to think symbolically and then being able to think logically. During this period, children progress rapidly in their understanding, use, and integration of symbols. Their vocabulary increases at a quick pace, and they become increasingly capable of stringing words together in meaningful sentences. They also begin to role play extensively, assuming such roles as a school teacher, doctor, nurse, police officer, firefighter, and mother and father.

Part of a child's rapidly developing activities during the preoperational period include a tendency to role play, imitating familiar adult roles.

There are two ways in which preoperational children's cognitive skills differ from those of older children. First, preoperational children are **egocentric,** or self-centered in their perspective of the world. They are unable to see the world from any point of view but their own. A 3-year-old child may run to a corner, turn his back to you and cover his eyes, in the attempt to hide during a game of hide and seek, not realizing that he is still in plain view. The preoperational child's egocentric nature is also evidenced by his or her speech. For example, a 4-year-old may be with a room full of people but talk only to his "horsey."

A second way in which the preoperational child's thinking differs from that of older children involves the principle of **conservation,** understanding that specific properties of objects—height, weight, volume, length, width—remain the same despite apparent changes in the shape or arrangement of those objects. Do you recall the "cookie trick" from the beginning of this chapter? A 4-year-old child believed he had two cookies when he had a single cookie that had been cut in half. Preoperational children do not understand conservation.

An illustration of the conservation principle is shown in Figure 11.3. A child is first shown two physically identical beakers that contain equal amounts of colored water. When asked how much water is in each beaker, the child responds, "The same amount." Next, the water from one of the beakers is emptied into a third beaker, which is both taller and thinner

Theories of Development   **385**

FIGURE 11.4
Conservation of number and length.

A

When shown A, the child agrees that both columns contain the same number of pennies.

B

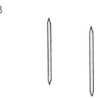

When shown B, in which one column has been made physically shorter, the child is asked whether both columns contain the same number of pennies and says that the left column has more pennies.

A

When shown A, child agrees that both toothpicks are the same length.

B

When shown B, in which one toothpick is physically moved below the other, the child is asked if both toothpicks are the same length and answers no.

than the other two beakers. When asked if the two beakers contain the same or different amounts of water, the child typically responds that the taller beaker contains more water. Piaget's explanation for this result is that preoperational children think about the world largely in terms of what they see. Because the water level in the tall beaker is higher than that of the other beaker, they say that the tall beaker contains more water. To Piaget, conservation, like object permanence and deferred imitation, represents a developmental milestone in the child's increasing ability to understand the world.

The Concrete Operational Period. Entering Piaget's third period of cognitive development (roughly ages 7 to 11), the **concrete operational period,** is heralded by the child's ability to master the conservation principle and other logical concepts. Concrete operational children understand that pouring water into the taller, thinner beaker does not change its volume. When pressed to explain their answer, these children explain, "The skinnier bottle just makes it look like it has more water than the other bottle." Children also learn conservation concepts such as that of number and length (Figure 11.4). Central to the concrete operational child's learning to conserve is the idea of reversibility, or the reversal of operations. For example, he or she realizes that if water from the taller beaker were to be poured into the original beaker, it would contain the same amount of water as before.

During this period, children also begin to understand other logical concepts, such as categorization. For example, children realize that dogs and cats are animals, blue and yellow are colors, and that their father is a son and a husband. With the development of logical reasoning, children begin to view themselves less egocentrically. Now, at least to a greater extent than during the previous two periods, children are able to understand perspectives other than just their own.

Despite their expanding ability to reason logically and to take into consideration the perspectives of others, concrete operational children still have not matured completely in their intellectual development. The concrete operational child is able to reason logically about objects and events only so long as he or she is able to view them or see them manipulated. That is the reason that their ability to reason is said to be concrete. They can perform cognitive operations on only tangible things; they do not yet have the ability to think abstractly or hypothetically. According to Piaget, it is during the next, and last, period of cognitive development that children begin to develop these cognitive abilities, and therefore, the capacity to think and reason like adults.

Formal Operational Period. During the **formal operational period,** which begins at about age 11, children first become capable of more formal kinds of thinking involving abstract concepts such as freedom and love. They also begin to understand that under different conditions, their thinking and behavior can have different consequences. They can now think and reason about hypothetical objects and events. As evidence that children think differently as they progress through the different periods of cognitive development consider the answers that my children gave to the following question.

If you were to go to the moon today, what would it be like? Their answers:

> Caden (age 7, but still preoperational because he cannot solve the water conservation problem): "I don't know, what do you think?"

> Colin (age 9, concrete operational because he easily solves the water conservation problem): "I don't know because I've never been to the moon."

> Tara (age 11, early formal operational): "It would be cold, dark, scary, and lonely, if I were there by myself."

Notice the difference between Colin's and Tara's answers. Colin doesn't know the answer to the question because he's never been there before, a clear indication of concrete operational thinking; but Tara, obviously more formal operational in her reasoning, can imagine what it's like, partly because she has learned something about the moon in school (it's "cold and dark") and partly because she can hypothetically place herself on the moon and imagine that it's also a lonely and scary place. In short, the thinking of children in the formal operational stage is not limited to concrete operations. Instead, their thinking is marked by the ability to reason in abstract terms and hypothetical constructs.

The thinking of children in the formal operational stage is . . . . marked by the ability to reason in abstract terms and hypothetical constructs.

Although Piaget held that there are four periods of cognitive development, not all people reach the formal operational period, even as physically mature adults. In some cases, adults show formal operational thought only in their area of training or expertise. Thus, a mechanic may be able to think abstractly while repairing an engine but not while solving math or physics problems, or a physicist may be able to reason abstractly when solving physics problems but not while reading poetry. However, once an individual reaches that level of thinking, he or she will always, except in the case of a physical accident or injury, perform intellectually at that level (Piaget, 1972).

Reactions to Piaget's Theory. Piaget's theory has had an enormously positive impact on stimulating interest and research in developmental psychology. More specifically, his theory has provided conceptually rich and empirically testable hypotheses about the nature of cognitive development. As you may recall from Chapter 2, the hallmark of a good theory is that it must be empirically testable and so, subject to disproof. How has Piaget's theory stood empirical testing? Very well. Today, psychologists support Piaget's general findings, and his terminology is still used to describe how cognitive development occurs.

However, recent research has shown that Piaget may have erred in at least one respect: he may have underestimated the intellectual competency of children (Gelman & Baillargeon, 1983). For example, Piaget argued that preoperational children cannot master conservation tasks. As it turns out, though, some preoperational children can be taught to understand and demonstrate mastery of conservation (Gelman, 1969). How could Piaget have overlooked such a possibility? Probably because of his methodology. Recall that in his research he relied heavily on children's responses to his questions and on their physical demonstrations of concepts. Other researchers who have used the same basic method but rephrased questions to make them more understandable or conducted demonstrations differently have shown that preoperational children are more cognitively skilled than Piaget thought. Likewise, the physical demands of the experimental task may also affect the results. For example, in a study of object permanence, Rader and his colleagues (1979) found that infants were better able to uncover a hidden object (a set of plastic keys) when the barrier was a piece of paper than when the barrier was a larger and heavier piece of cloth. Thus, had the cloth only been used, the researchers might have erroneously concluded that their subjects were not able to master object permanence.

Kohlberg's Theory of Moral Development

Piaget's work not only provided insight into how children develop cognitively, it also stimulated other researchers to think about other kinds of development in terms of periods or stages. One such researcher was Lawrence Kohlberg (1927–1987), who developed a theory of moral development.

Moral development refers to the development of a person's thoughts and actions regarding right and wrong. In Kohlberg's view, an individual's sense of right and wrong changes as he or she matures from childhood into adolescence and then into adulthood. Kohlberg believed that moral development was positively correlated with cognitive development (Kohlberg, 1981, 1984). The greater an individual's moral development, the greater the individual's cognitive development. Kohlberg viewed moral development as being characterized by three levels and seven stages (see Table 11.4).

In Kohlberg's Theory of Moral Development, children progress from having a selfish motivation for being nice to others to an attitude in which they want to share and help others because it is the right thing to do.

The Preconventional Level. During the first level of moral development, the **preconventional level,** children tend to think solely in terms of the immediate consequences of their behavior. Their moral reasoning is centered on obtaining rewards and avoiding punishment. As you might imagine, children of this age show almost complete obedience to authority. The preconventional level has two stages. In *Stage 1*, children are "good boys and girls" because they fear being punished for being "bad." They act selfishly and are unable to take into consideration the interests and intentions of others. In *Stage 2*, children still look after their own interests first, but they are sometimes willing to be kind to others only because they want others to be kind to them. For example, a child will share a toy with another child if he or she believes that the other child will share a toy in return. Thus, morality in this stage is characterized by a "If you'll be nice to me, I'll be nice to you" attitude rather than on mutual respect or consideration.

TABLE 11.4.	Levels and stages of Kohlberg's theory of moral reasoning.
LEVEL AND STAGE	*HIGHLIGHTS*
Preconventional	
Stage 1: Fear of punishment	Avoidance of punishment
Stage 2: Guarded reciprocity	Egocentric perspective; will share with others only if others share with them
Conventional	
Stage 3: Seek approval from others	Morality based on whether others will approve
Stage 4: Law and order	Rules and laws define morality
Postconventional	
Stage 5: Social contracts	Obey societal rules for the common good
Stage 6: Universal ethical principle	Self-selection of personal values
Stage 7: Cosmic orientation	Adoption of values that transcend societal values and norms

The Conventional Level. In the second level of moral development, the **conventional level,** children's moral reasoning becomes subject to conformity. Their sense of right and wrong and their actions toward others are based largely on whether, from their point of view, others will approve of their intentions and behaviors. In *Stage 3,* children are able to understand the intentions underlying actions and want approval from others. In *Stage 4,* children begin to understand "law and order." They adhere to rules and regulations not only because they believe that doing so will bring approval from others but also because they believe that rules define morality.

The Postconventional Level. The last level of moral development, the **postconventional level,** involves the development of personal values of morality and contains three stages. In *Stage 5,* people view laws as serving the public interest and are willing to enter into a "social contract" and abide by society's rules for the common good. However, at this stage, people also realize that sometimes laws are not effective but that they should be obeyed anyway to benefit society as a whole. People who attain *Stage 6* think and act in terms of universal ethical principles such as "reverence for life" and "goodness." Moral development in this stage is characterized by self-selected values that help us make decisions and interact with others. At this stage, people who believe certain laws to be ineffective or unjust work to have them changed. In *Stage 7,* the "Cosmic orientation stage," individuals adopt values that transcend society's values and norms. This stage represents the zenith of moral development; Kohlberg believed that only a very few people, such as Eleanor Roosevelt and Albert Schweitzer, have ever reached this stage.

Kohlberg believed that people generally do not function totally within one stage. Rather, they may function largely within one stage but also in other stages. A person may, for example, reason at *Stage 4* in most settings but at *Stage 3* in others. Kohlberg also believed that not all people reach the postconventional level of moral reasoning (*Stages 5, 6, and 7*).

Kohlberg's procedure for studying moral development was simple: subjects were posed with moral dilemmas to which they had to provide a verbal solution. For example, a certain man's wife has cancer. A drug exists that may cure the woman, but it is in the possession of a druggist who wants more money for it than the man can afford. Should he steal the drug so he can help save his wife? The problem here is the difference between

Kohlberg's final stage of moral development is achieved by only those few individuals, such as Eleanor Roosevelt and Albert Schweitzer, who developed morals and values above and beyond those of normal society.

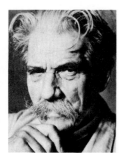

saying and doing. Do subjects' verbal responses correspond to how they might actually behave when faced with a real moral dilemma? Kohlberg argued that moral reasoning is indeed related to behavior. His research has demonstrated that junior high school students who reasoned at the Stage 5 level of morality were less likely to cheat on exams or in games than were adolescents who reasoned at lower levels (Krebs & Kohlberg, 1973). Delinquent adolescents have also been shown to be more likely than nondelinquents to show lower levels of moral reasoning (Blasi, 1980). But the relationship between saying and doing appears to be equivocal. Situational factors, such as social pressure to conform and personal costs, can help determine the degree to which an individual's moral reasoning corresponds to his or her actions (Maccoby, 1980). Thus, people might say they would not cheat on an exam, but if their passing the class hangs on the outcome of that exam, cheating might occur.

Reactions to Kohlberg's Theory. Kohlberg's theory has not been accepted universally. Two aspects of the theory appear problematic. First, his theory is based largely on research conducted with male subjects. At least one psychologist, Carol Gilligan (1982), has argued that gender differences in moral reasoning exist. Because of the way they are generally reared in our culture, females tend to view moral issues in terms of their effects on interpersonal relationships and males tend to view them in terms of their own personal interests. Females also work toward establishing and maintaining harmony in relationships whereas males tend more toward protection of individual rights. In Gilligan's view, neither perspective is better than the other, but both perspectives do exist and therefore should not be neglected. However, recent reviews of the moral reasoning research reporting that males and females of similar ages and educational backgrounds do not differ in their moral reasoning calls into question Gilligan's view (Bebeau & Brabeck, 1987). Clearly, this issue is in need of further research before it can be put to rest.

A second problem with Kohlberg's theory involves his basic premise that justice is the ultimate good, which, of course, was a value judgment on his part. Value judgments are not data-based; rather, they are based on an opinion or a point of view. You may not hold the point of view, and that may influence your thinking and behavior in certain situations. Arguably, there are also other "ultimate goods" upon which people might base their values and behavior, such as charity, mercy, and retribution.

TABLE 11.5. *Erikson's eight stages of psychosocial development.*

| PERIOD | CONFLICT | OUTCOME | |
		POSITIVE RESOLUTION	NEGATIVE RESOLUTION
Childhood	Trust vs. mistrust Autonomy vs. self-doubt Initiative vs. guilt Competence vs. inferiority	Trust, security, confidence, independence, curiosity, competence, industry	Insecurity, doubt, guilt, low self-esteem, sense of failure
Adolescence	Identity vs. role confusion	Strong sense of self-identity	Weak sense of self
Adulthood	Intimacy vs. isolation	Capacity to develop deep and meaningful relationships and	Isolating unhappiness
	Generativity vs. stagnation	care for others; consideration for future generations;	Selfishness, stagnancy
	Integrity vs. despair	personal sense of worth and satisfaction	Sense of failure and regret

Despite these criticisms, Kohlberg's work has stimulated theoretical and empirical interest in morality and moral development. The idea that moral reasoning progresses through different stages as individuals mature has some empirical support (Colby et al., 1983). As with Piaget, Kohlberg's theory is a cognitive one. Both theories focus on peoples' abilities to think and reason about problems confronting them. Another well-known developmental theory, Erikson's theory of psychosocial development, also has a cognitive flavor, but it has an emphasis on social development (Erikson, 1963). Unlike Piaget's theory, which emphasizes intellectual development, or Kohlberg's theory, which centers on moral development, Erikson's theory focuses on the way in which people resolve psychosocial conflicts at critical periods in their lives.

Erikson's Theory of Psychosocial Development

Erik Erikson

Children whose parents provide all the basic needs and loving care will learn to trust their caregivers. This trust will help them develop positive attitudes towards others later in life.

Erik Erikson (b. 1902) is a psychoanalyst who was trained by Freud's daughter, Anna. In addition to bringing a psychoanalytic perspective to the study of development, Erikson was also interested in cultural differences in human development. Most of his research was conducted with children, whom he observed playing with tiny figures of humans and animals. Both his background in psychoanalysis and cultural differences greatly influenced his views of psychosocial development.

Erikson, like many other developmental psychologists, believes that human development proceeds according to a biologically determined agenda called the **epigenetic principle,** which has two components. First, development is influenced by biological factors that exert their influence at critical points during the individual's maturation. According to Erikson, these critical points always involve some sort of psychosocial conflict. Second, the environment or culture in which one lives provides the context in which the individual resolves the conflict.

From Erikson's perspective, the manner in which these conflicts are resolved determines the nature of development. In fact, according to Erikson, the resolution of these conflicts is development. If the conflict is resolved positively, the outcome is a healthy one; if the conflict is resolved negatively, the outcome is unhealthy. The resolution of one conflict sets the stage for the way in which the next conflict is handled. Erikson believes that human development bridges the entire life span and involves eight conflicts or stages (see Table 11.5). Let's take a closer look at these stages.

Psychosocial Development in Childhood.
According to Erikson, childhood is accompanied by four conflicts. The first one, *trust versus mistrust,* occurs in the first year of life and involves the manner in which care is provided for the child. If the child is cared for lovingly and all her needs (food, water, warmth, and physical contact) are met, she develops trust in her caregivers. If these needs go unsatisfied, trust does not develop. Erikson believes this stage is especially important in an individual's psychosocial development because, in his view, trust is the key factor in determining our attitude toward others and toward life.

The second conflict that takes place between the ages of 1 and 3 is *autonomy versus shame or doubt.* As children begin exploring their world and learning to do things, such as walking, eating, and talking, they either develop confidence in their abilities or shame and doubt. If parents gently encourage children to do things they are capable of, or if they are rewarded for their successes, they will develop confidence in themselves. However, if a child is not permitted to do things himself, if he is rushed into doing something that he cannot do, or if he is scolded for his failures, he will develop shame and doubt.

Erikson's third stage, *initiative versus guilt*, occurs between the ages of 3 and 6, and is similar to the second stage. During this stage, children are usually capable of formulating questions and ideas about their immediate environment. They are also generally interested in exerting their independence. If parents encourage their child's curiosity about the world, then she will develop a sense of initiative. If she is punished for her curiosity, or her questions are ignored, guilt may develop, which may then lead to low self-esteem.

By the time children reach middle childhood (ages 7 to 11), they have learned to read, write, solve simple arithmetic problems, and interact socially with others outside their immediate families. These skills are generally valued by others, and so mastering them leaves children with a sense of competence, productiveness, and industry. However, if children fail to master these skills or are compared unfavorably with other children who are more competent, they will develop a sense of failure and inferiority.

If Erikson is right about the kinds of issues with which children must deal, then parenting plays a critical role in early development. From Erikson's perspective, parents who provide a supportive and positive environment for their children are likely to have children who are trusting, independent, and competent. Parents who are less supportive or who react negatively toward their children's strivings and accomplishments are likely to have children who mistrust others, who are dependent on others, and who have low self-esteem.

Psychosocial Development in Adolescence. During adolescence, teenagers are faced with the important task of deciding on what to do with their lives. Decisions about a career and personal life-style, including sexual, moral, and political issues, are the preeminent issues during this stage of life, which is called the *identity versus role confusion* stage. If adolescents are able to develop a plan for accomplishing career and personal goals and to decide to which social and cultural groups they belong, then a personal identity has been formed. Failure to form an identity leaves the teenager confused about his or her role in life.

Psychosocial Development in Adulthood. Acquiring an identity prepares the teenager to deal with the psychosocial conflicts that occur in adulthood. The first conflict of adulthood (Stage 6) is called *intimacy versus isolation* because the individual is faced with either developing deep and meaningful relationships with others or becoming a loner. Developing intimate relationships depends on one's ability to make and keep commitments to others, be they friends or lovers. Some people, perhaps because they never formed an identity during adolescence, are unable to make or keep such commitments. As a result, they become isolated and often unhappy.

The second conflict (Stage 7) that adults face is whether they will become productive people capable of giving of their time and talents to others, or totally absorbed in their own lives, selfishly satisfying their own needs without regard to others. Erikson called this the *generativity versus stagnation* stage. If adults can find meaning in their work and family and are able and willing to share their talents with others, then they have resolved the conflict positively. However, if they cannot, they become stagnant.

The eighth and final stage of development is *integrity versus despair*. It is probably not hard for you to imagine what this stage concerns simply because no doubt you have periodically reviewed the direction your life has gone and decided whether you wanted it to continue in that direction.

Such evaluation is similar to what happens in this stage, except that now there is a life spanning several decades of which to make sense. If an individual looks back and is able to see meaning in his or her existence, then that individual is filled with a sense of worth and integrity. If the individual looks back and sees goals not accomplished and personal promises not kept, he or she is left with a feeling of failure and despair. Certainly, the way in which conflicts were resolved, if they were resolved, in the earlier stages of development plays a central role in weighing the value of one's life.

In sum, Erikson's theory focuses on the different conflicts that arise during the course of one's life. According to Erikson, an individual develops into either a psychologically healthy, happy, and productive person or a psychologically unhealthy, unhappy, and unproductive person, depending on how the conflicts are resolved.

There is general consensus among psychologists that Erikson's theory is a useful one. As we will see later, empirical evidence supports the existence of some of Erikson's stages (Marcia, 1967; Levinson, 1978). (We will also later see that Erikson's theory is not without its critics.) Erikson's main contribution to the study of human development was the idea that development occurs across the life span. Today, largely because of Erikson's work, most psychologists view development as an ongoing process that is halted only by death. Psychological growth, as your grandparents can well assure you, is lifelong.

As we shall see, though, in life-span developmental psychology, the focus is not on any one theory of development but on the unique processes that influence physical, cognitive, and social development. It is to these processes that we turn for the balance of this chapter.

DEVELOPMENT AND THE LIFE CYCLE

W*e can cast development into a larger perspective by focusing on the interaction of the different systems that affect the course of development.*

Although we will undergo Piaget's periods of cognitive development, Kohlberg's levels of moral development, and Erikson's stages of psychosocial development, human development is much more complex than what these three theories might lead us to believe. Even if they were to be combined, these theories would still fall far short of giving us a full account of development, for other psychologists have revealed a broader vista of human ontogeny. We can cast development into a larger perspective by focusing on the interaction of the different systems that affect the course of development.

Figure 11.5 portrays such a systems approach. Normative prenatal variables are those that direct the course of prenatal development. They include hormonal influences and the nutrition of the mother. Normative

FIGURE 11.5
The interaction of three systems that influence the nature of life-span development.

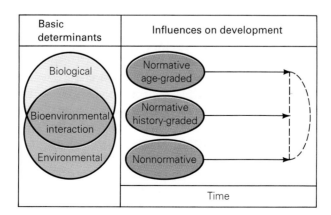

age-graded variables are biological and environmental variables that vary with age. They include biological processes such as motor development and environmental processes such as socialization in family, school, and work. Normative history-graded variables are those common to a specific culture at a specific time. These, too, may be either biological (epidemics, such as AIDS) or environmental (political decisions, war). Nonnormative variables are those that are significant but not to all individuals (breaking a bone, suffering from an illness, marriage, divorce, or unhappiness with work). These four kinds of variables may affect individuals at different points in their development. For example, age-graded variables mainly affect people at either end of the life cycle—children and the aged. History-graded and nonnormative variables exert their effects mainly during early and middle adulthood. As we shall see, research in these areas follows suit. Psychologists interested in child development and old age study chiefly age-graded variables whereas psychologists interested in adulthood focus largely on history-graded and nonnormative variables. With this in mind, let's turn to understanding physical, cognitive, and social development across the life span, starting with prenatal development and ending with old age.

PRENATAL DEVELOPMENT

The 9 months between conception and birth is called the **prenatal period.** Actually, the length of a normal pregnancy is 266 days or 38 weeks. The prenatal period can be divided into three developmental stages: the ovum, the embryo, and the fetal stages.

During the **ovum stage,** which lasts about 2 weeks, the zygote divides many times, and the internal organs begin to form. By the end of the first week, the fertilized ovum contains about 100 cells. At about this time, many of the cells are arranged in two layers, one for the skin, hair, nervous system, and sensory organs, and the other for the digestive and respiratory systems and glands. Near the end of the ovum stage, a third layer of cells, those that will eventually develop into the circulatory and excretory systems and muscles, appears.

The second stage of prenatal development, the **embryonic stage,** begins at about 2 weeks and ends about 8 weeks after conception. During this stage, development occurs at an incredible pace. In just a month after conception, the heart has begun to beat, the tiny brain has started to function, and most of the major body structures are beginning to form. By the end of the embryonic stage the major features that define the human body—the hands, shoulders, head, eyes, fingers—are discernable. Behaviorally, the embryo can react reflexively to stimulation. For example, if the mouth is stimulated, the embryo moves its upper body and neck.

Just a month after conception, the heart has begun to beat, the tiny brain has started to function, and most of the major body structures are beginning to form.

The embryonic stage is also noteworthy because it is during this period that the embryo is most susceptible to teratogens, or agents such as alcohol or nicotine, which cause birth defects. We will learn shortly how some teratogens affect embryonic development.

The final stage of the prenatal development is the **fetal stage,** which lasts about 7 months. The fetal stage officially begins with the appearance of bone cells and ends with birth. At the end of the second month of pregnancy, the fetus is about 1½ inches long and weighs about 1 ounce. By the end of the third month, development of major organs is completed, and the bones and muscles are beginning to develop. The fetus is about 3 inches long and weighs about 3 ounces. The fetus may show some movement, especially kicking.

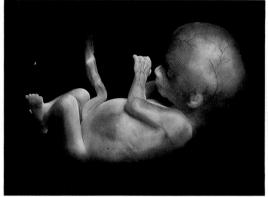

This 6-week-old human embryo and 14-week-old fetus show the rapid pace at which physical development occurs during the embryonic stage of prenatal development.

By the end of the fourth month, the fetus is about 6 inches long and weighs about 6 ounces. By the beginning of the fifth month, the fetus is sleeping and waking regularly. Fetal movements also become strong enough to be felt by the mother and the heartbeat is strong enough to be heard through a stethoscope. During the sixth month, the fetus is now over a foot long and weighs about 1½ pounds. The seventh month is a critical month because, if the baby is born prematurely at this point, it has a fair chance of surviving. However, keep in mind that fetuses mature at different rates, meaning that some 7-month-old fetuses may be mature enough to survive while others may not.

During the last 2 months of prenatal development, the fetus gains weight rapidly at the rate of about ½ pound per week. Much of this weight gain is due to the growth of fatty tissue. On average, the fetus is about 20 inches long and weighs about 7 pounds at the end of this period. At this point, the fetus is ready for birth.

Threats to Normal Prenatal Development

The prenatal environment is a fragile one; under normal conditions it provides just the right supply of nutrients to the fetus, and provides it with warmth and comfort. Probably the single most important factor in the fetus' development is the mother's diet. The mother's consumption of food is the fetus' only source of nutrition. If the mother is extremely malnourished, the fetus' nervous system develops abnormally, and it may be born mentally retarded.

Beyond diet, teratogens such as drugs or other chemicals, radiation poisoning, or diseases can also cause birth defects. Psychologists are primarily interested in how drugs affect the fetus, because taking drugs is a behavior that is directly under the control of the mother, while exposure to disease and radiation poisoning may not be. Over-the-counter drugs, like aspirin and antibiotics, especially when taken in large quantities over long periods, can produce defects in the fetus. For example, tetracycline, a common antibiotic, can cause irregularities in the bones and discoloration of the teeth (they may yellow). Tranquilizers may produce a cleft palate. More powerful drugs, like heroin and cocaine, have more dramatic effects. For example, if a pregnant woman is addicted to heroin, her baby is likely to be born addicted to the drug. The baby will show withdrawal symptoms, such as hyperactivity, irritability, and tremors. The symptoms make the baby harder to care for, which, in turn, makes the psychological bonding between mother and baby difficult. In such cases, both mother and infant may pay the price for the mother's behavioral problems. And a steep price it is—addiction, motherly neglect, and in some cases, permanent brain damage.

This anti-smoking ad targets its message at pregnant women. Smoking has many harmful effects on the health of the unborn child and increases the risk of miscarriage and premature birth.

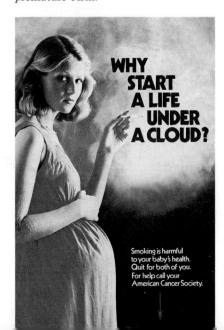

WHY START A LIFE UNDER A CLOUD?

Smoking is harmful to your baby's health. Quit for both of you. For help call your American Cancer Society.

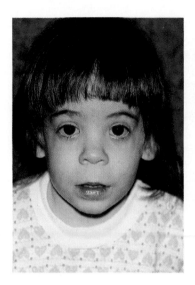

Heavy drinking during pregnancy may cause a baby to be born with Fetal Alcohol Syndrome. Side effects of FAS include stunted infant growth and internal and external physical deformations.

A pregnant woman's cigarette smoking is another behavior that can affect the fetus. The carbon monoxide contained in cigarette smoke reduces the supply of oxygen to the fetus. Reduced oxygen levels are particularly harmful to the fetus during the last half of pregnancy when the fetus is developing most rapidly and its oxygen demand is greatest. The main effects of the mother's cigarette smoking are increased rate of miscarriages, low birthweight babies, and increased chance of premature birth.

Although a woman's regular use of any psychoactive drug during her pregnancy is likely to have harmful effects on the fetus, psychologists and other researchers have been especially interested in the prenatal effects of alcohol. Heavy use of alcohol by pregnant women has notable and serious negative effects on their babies. Collectively, these effects are known as the **fetal alcohol syndrome (FAS)** and include both pre- and postnatal growth deficits, deformations of the eyes and mouth, brain and central nervous system abnormalities, and deformation of the heart. The likelihood of stunted growth is doubled if a woman drinks and quadrupled if she smokes and drinks. Such effects are permanent. Even if children with FAS are reared in a healthy environment with regular, nutritious meals, their physical and intellectual development falls short of that of normal children (Hanson, Jones, & Smith, 1976).

In sum, the three stages of prenatal development span the time between conception and birth. In just 9 months, the zygote is transformed from a single cell, void of human resemblance, into a fully developed fetus, complete with physical features that look much like yours and mine, except in miniature. Normal fetal development can be disrupted by the presence of teratogens, which can cause mental retardation and physical deformation. One especially well-studied teratogen is alcohol, which when abused by a pregnant woman can lead to fetal alcohol syndrome.

INFANCY AND CHILDHOOD

Infancy is considered to be the period of development that spans from birth to about 2 years of age. Childhood is the period between infancy to the teenage years. Infants, as you know, are extremely dependent on others for life-sustaining support such as food, shelter, warmth, and attention. But infants, though largely helpless, are not merely passive consumers of parental attention and affection. Rather, they are prepared to learn about the world. They are born with the physiological hardware that makes behavioral, cognitive, and social development possible.

All newborns have plenty of reflexes. Reflexes, as you may recall, are unlearned responses to specific environmental stimuli. Newborns enter the world preprogrammed to respond to particular stimuli in particular ways. These reflexes help newborns survive their first several months in the world. For example, consider the *rooting* and *sucking reflexes.* When an object touches a new newborn's cheek, he or she will turn toward the object and attempt to suck; when an object is put into the baby's mouth, he or she will begin to suck. Babies are also born with a *grasping* or *palmar reflex*, which is the response of grasping an object placed in the palm of the hand. Another important reflex is the *rage reflex.* If a cloth is placed over a baby's head so that it interferes with breathing, he or she will begin to cry and struggle. Infants, then, are born prepared to eat (sucking reflex), cling (grasping reflex) and to fight for air, if necessary (rage reflex).

Most reflexes disappear within 3 to 4 months after birth. They are replaced by voluntary actions that the baby has learned through experience with the environment. For example, infant behavior can be classically conditioned. In one study (Lipsitt & Kaye, 1964), a tone served as the conditioned stimulus, a rubber nipple served as the unconditioned stimulus, and the sucking reflex served as the unconditioned response. After repeated pairings of the tone and nipple, the tone alone elicited the sucking response. Infant behavior has also been shown to be susceptible to operant conditioning (Butterfield & Siperstein, 1972). In this study, sucking on a nipple was reinforced with music; as long as the baby sucked, music was played. When this was reversed and sucking led to the music being turned off, the babies stopped sucking. Infants less than 3 days old can also imitate facial gestures (Meltzoff & Moore, 1983).

Our point here is twofold. First, babies are born with a set of behavioral responses called reflexes that help them adapt to the world. Second, these reflexes are soon replaced with learned behaviors that permit infants to become even more adapted to the world. That infant behavior can be classically and operantly conditioned demonstrates that infants can benefit from experience. This is important because, as you already know, learning allows organisms to adapt to a wider variety of environmental conditions than does purely reflexive behavior.

Physical Development

Two important and related variables can help explain the newborn's growing capacity for learning: development of the brain and nervous system, and the increasing ability to move about the environment. Let's look at these two variables more closely.

Brain Development. At birth, the newborn's brain weighs only a third as much as an adult's brain. At the end of two years of life, the infant's brain will weigh almost 75 percent of that of an adult. Much of the weight gain is due to three factors. First, axons of brain neurons become enveloped in myelin. Myelin, as you might recall from Chapter 4, is important because it is critical to the rapid transmission of nerve impulses along the axon. Without myelin, the brain would not function normally; synaptic transmission would be garbled and the growing infant's behavior would be disorganized. Second, the number of synapses among brain neurons increases rapidly. Although the infant has all of the brain neurons that he or she will ever have, the extent of their synaptic connections increases dramatically in the first two years after birth. Third, the cerebral cortex develops. During the first month of life, the motor area of the cerebral cortex begins to function, and by the third month, the sensory area has developed to the point that the newborn can now coordinate actions in response to stimuli; for example, the newborn can now reach for an object at which he or she is looking.

As we learned in Chapter 5, experience is necessary for the brain and nervous system to develop normally. Recall the classic work of Colin Blakemore and Grahame Cooper (1970) who demonstrated the importance of early visual stimulation on perception. Visually inexperienced kittens were placed in an environment of all vertical stripes or all horizontal stripes for 5 hours each day. During the remaining 19 hours, the kittens were placed in completely darkened environments. When the sensitivity of the neurons in each kitten's visual cortex to vertical and horizontal stimuli were later tested, the cortical neurons of kittens reared in the all-vertical environment responded mostly to vertical stimuli, and the cortical neurons of kittens reared in the all-horizontal environment responded mostly to horizontal stimuli. Thus, neurons in the visual cortex rely on early visual experiences for development. For a review of other aspects of perceptual development, refer to Chapters 5 and 6.

Motor Development. One of the pleasures of being a parent is being able to watch your child change from a virtually helpless infant to a curious and ever-energetic child. To be sure, there is one developmental milestone that all parents await with great anticipation and not a little trepidation: their child's first step. Motor development, or the infant's ability to move about its environment, unfolds in a systematic fashion for nearly all infants during their first year of life and includes the following steps: lifting their heads while laying on their stomachs, rolling from stomach to back, sitting, standing, crawling, assisted walking, and finally unassisted walking (see Figure 11.6). Motor development is aided by the maturation of the infant's arm and leg muscles. The first few steps, though wobbly and uncoordinated, transform with time and practice into a more confident and determined waddle.

Motor development is guided by three basic principles of growth.

The **cephalocaudal principle.** Body growth proceeds from head to torso to feet; control over the upper body takes place before control over the lower body. This principle helps explain why babies are able to use their arms and hands in moving about the environment before they are able to use their feet.

The **proximodistal principle.** Development of the internal organs and torso occurs faster than development of the hands and feet. This principle partially accounts for the fact that infants gain control over their arms before their hands and gain control of their hands before their fingers.

The **mass to specific principle.** Control over large groups of muscles that are used in gross body movements develops faster than control over smaller groups of muscles that are used in finer movements. This principle accounts for the fact that infants and young children are not very deft when drawing or scribbling. However, as the nervous system develops, so does control over the small groups of muscles involved in coordinated movement of the fingers.

In sum, at birth the infant relies largely on its reflexes to interact with the world. These reflexes are useful in helping the baby locate and grasp objects and to eat. As the number of synapses increases and the cortex develops, so does the infant's ability to learn and to move about its environment. Physical growth and maturation proceed along specific lines, with development of the upper body parts occurring before development of the lower body parts, internal organs and control of the torso developing before the extremities, and control of large muscle groups occurring before control of smaller muscle groups. As the infant's physical abilities are developing so are its cognitive abilities, which is the topic of our next section.

During the first year of life, an infant's motor skills develop from movement while lying down to sitting, crawling, standing, and finally walking.

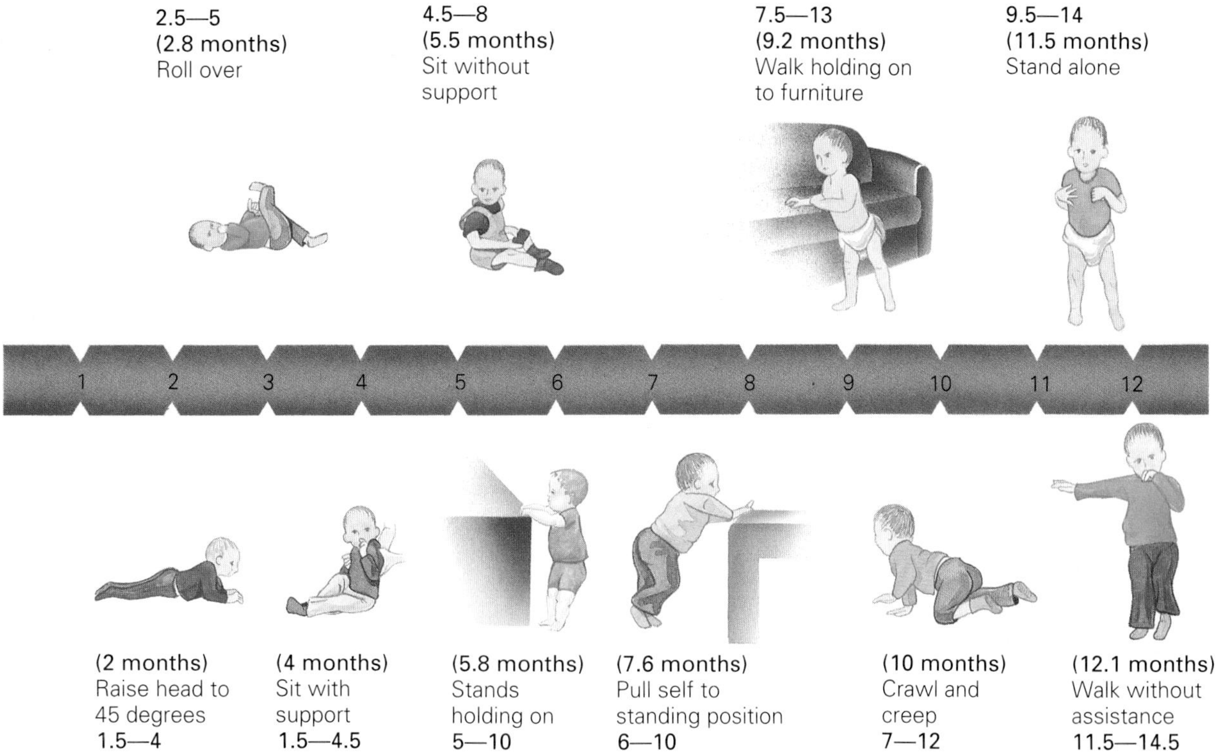

| 2.5—5 (2.8 months) Roll over | 4.5—8 (5.5 months) Sit without support | 7.5—13 (9.2 months) Walk holding on to furniture | 9.5—14 (11.5 months) Stand alone |

| (2 months) Raise head to 45 degrees 1.5—4 | (4 months) Sit with support 1.5—4.5 | (5.8 months) Stands holding on 5—10 | (7.6 months) Pull self to standing position 6—10 | (10 months) Crawl and creep 7—12 | (12.1 months) Walk without assistance 11.5—14.5 |

FIGURE 11.6

The average age and variations around that average for the major milestones in motor development in children. (After Frankenburg & Dodds, 1967; Shirley, 1931).

Cognitive Development

As Piaget observed, infancy is a period in which the newborn rapidly develops sensory and motor skills that are useful in exploring the environment. Piaget also noted that near the end of infancy, the child also acquires object permanency. One other important cognitive skill also develops in infancy and childhood—memory.

Research in infant memory has emphasized both recognition and recall. As you will recall from Chapter 8, recognition involves the ability to select a correct answer from among a group of responses, and recall involves providing a correct answer with only a few or no prompts. Infants are very good at recognition tasks, especially faces. For example, if first allowed to see pictures of their mothers, they are able to distinguish them later from pictures of other people (Barrera & Maurer, 1981). Even when given only 2 minutes to observe a face, 5- to 6-month-old infants are able to recognize it 2 weeks later (Fagan, 1973).

Recall seems to emerge as a new cognitive skill in infants at about the age of 8 months (Brody, 1981). Over time, the infant is able to recall information after longer and longer delays between first being exposed to that information and later being prompted to recall it. Recall would seem to be important to the development of object permanence, which does not occur until the infant is about 8 months old. By the time children are between 3 and 7 years old, they can recall short lists (up to five items), as long as the items in the list are made meaningful (Istomina, 1975).

As children approach adolescence, their powers of recognition and recall increase dramatically, partly because of the emphasis placed on rote learning in school. Prior to adolescence, children also become aware of their own memory (called metamemory) and cognitive processes. **Metacognition** refers to self-awareness of one's cognitive processes. Becoming aware of one's own memory and cognitive processes is important because doing so means that individuals have the ability to distinguish what they can remember from what they can't remember and what they know from what they don't know. An important aspect of becoming intellectually competent involves being able to understand what you don't know and devising ways to satisfy that deficiency. If researchers can discover how children come to understand their own cognitive processes, they might be able to implement ways to help them study better.

Social Development

That infants can remember faces is testimony to their emerging social nature. To be sure, infants use their developing cognitive skills to interact socially with others. What kinds of social behavior do infants show? How do social experiences affect development of an infant's personality? These two questions have guided research into the social development of infants.

What has emerged from this research is a fascinating account of the important and complex social experiences of infants. The most important type of social behavior, **attachment,** is the social and emotional bond between infant and caregiver that spans both time and space. Attachment is not only the first social relationship that infants experience, but it is also the first loving relationship that they experience.

Attachment is not only the first social relationship that infants experience, but it is also the first loving relationship that they experience.

Attachment. Attachment is not unique to humans. Other animals, including waterfowl, sheep, cows, and monkeys show bonding between infant and caregiver. (You may recall the imprinting of young waterfowl on their mothers that we read about in Chapter 7). According to theorist John Bowlby (1969), attachment is a part of many organisms' native endowment. Babies are born prepared to become attached to their primary caregivers, which, in most cases, are their mothers. Attachment appears to be a behavior pattern that is necessary for normal development (Ainsworth, 1974; Bowlby, 1969, 1973). However, although attachment appears to be an inherited disposition, infants do not have a natural inclination to become attached to any one specific adult. Rather, the specific person to whom the baby becomes attached is determined through learning; the individual who serves as the infant's primary caregiver is usually the object of the attachment.

Attachment partially reveals itself in two specific forms of infant behavior: stranger anxiety and separation anxiety. **Stranger anxiety,** which usually appears in infants between the ages of 6 and 12 months, consists of wariness and sometimes fearful responses, such as crying and clinging to their caregivers in the presence of strangers. Male strangers generate the most anxiety in infants and child strangers generate the least anxiety, while female strangers generate an intermediate amount of anxiety (Lewis & Brooks-Gunn, 1972; Skarin, 1977). Stranger anxiety can be reduced and even eliminated under certain conditions. For example, if the infant is in familiar surroundings with its mother, such as at home, and the mother acts friendly toward the stranger, the infant is likely to show less anxiety in the presence of the stranger than he or she would if the surroundings were unfamiliar or if the mother was unfriendly toward the stranger (Rheingold & Eckerman, 1973).

Separation anxiety is a set of fearful responses, such as crying, arousal, and clinging to the caregiver when the caregiver attempts to leave the infant's presence. Separation anxiety differs from stranger anxiety in two ways: time of emergence and the conditions under which the fear responses occur. It first appears in infants when they are about 8 to 9 months old and climaxes at about 12 to 16 months. Some children, though, continue to show separation anxiety when they are 2 and 3 years old. Like stranger anxiety, separation anxiety can occur under different conditions with different degrees of intensity. For example, if an infant is used to being left in a certain environment, say a day care center or at a relative's house, he may show little or no separation anxiety (Maccoby, 1980). The same holds true for situations in which the infant is left with a sibling or other familiar person (Bowlby, 1969). However, if the same infant is left in an unfamiliar setting with unfamiliar people, he is likely to show separation anxiety (Bowlby, 1982). Thus, familiarity with settings and people plays a crucial role in determining the extent to which an infant will show separation anxiety. Remember that the more familiar the infant is with a given setting or person, the less likely she is to show separation anxiety when her caregiver leaves (Rheingold, 1985). Familiarity, then, at least for infants, breeds attachment.

Development of Attachment. An important question to ask about attachment is how it develops. If we know the answer to that question, we might be able to discover ways to strengthen the parent-child bond and enhance infant social development. Interestingly, one answer to that question was discovered with rhesus monkeys, not humans.

Harry Harlow (1905–1981), a well-known animal psychologist at the University of Wisconsin at Madison, wanted to know whether parental nourishment or physical contact serves as the basis for attachment. To find out, he first separated infant monkeys from their mothers. Next, he provided each infant monkey with two different "surrogate mothers" (see Figure 11.7). Both were actually wire cylinders with wooden heads. One was bare and the other was covered with foam rubber and terry cloth. Either surrogate could be outfitted with a bottle to provide nourishment to the infant. Harlow used the amount of time the infants spent with each surrogate as a measure of preference. Which one did the infants prefer? Infants preferred the terry cloth one even when only the surrogate providing nourishment was the bare wire one (Harlow, 1958).

FIGURE 11.7
The surrogate mothers used in Harlow's study (1958) of attachment. Infant monkeys preferred the terry cloth surrogate mother even when only the wire surrogate provided nourishment.

Later studies with his wife, Margaret, (Harlow & Harlow, 1962) and others (Harlow & Suomi, 1970) showed that infant monkeys preferred warm surrogates or rocking surrogates to ones that were cold or stationary, respectively. Thus, for monkeys, attachment depends more on physical contact with a comfortable or warm or stimulating caregiver than it does on nourishment alone. In other words, simply meeting an infant's needs, in this case, nourishment, is not sufficient for the infant to develop a bond with its caregiver. A lesson we might take from the Harlows' work is that physical contact—hugging, cuddling, holding—establishes the basis for the emotional and social bond that develops between parent and child; feeding merely provides the opportunity for such contact.

Human infants develop attachment to the caregiver whether they are breast or bottle fed (Ferguson, Horwood, & Shannon, 1987) or whether the caregiver is male or female (Lamb, 1979). The quality of attachment depends on the amount of time and the quality of interaction caregivers have with infants. As we shall see next, the more time that a caregiver spends holding, caressing, and playing with an infant, the stronger and more secure the attachment.

Secure and Insecure Attachment. One research method to study attachment in human infants is the "strange situation" developed by Mary Ainsworth (Ainsworth & Wittig, 1969). In the strange situation, an infant is introduced to an unfamiliar setting and his or her behavioral reactions to several separations and reunions with the mother can be observed. By observing a large number of infants and their reactions, researchers have discovered two distinct types of attachment. **Secure attachment** is the kind of attachment in which infants will use their mothers as a base for exploring a new environment. They will venture out from her to explore but will return periodically. Securely attached infants do become upset when their mothers leave the room, but they greet them happily when they return. The other kind of attachment, **insecure attachment,** is very different. In this case, the infant is reluctant to explore a new environment, and is likely to cling to the mother in the presence of strangers. They become quite upset when the mother leaves and remain distressed even upon her return. An infant can be so insecurely attached that he or she becomes avoidant of the mother on her return, preferring a stranger for attention and comfort. From an evolutionary perspective, it would seem that secure attachment is more adaptive than insecure attachment. However, as Michael Lamb and his colleagues (1984) have pointed out, it is unlikely that there is only one pattern of parent-offspring interaction that is adaptive. Rather, secure and insecure attachment may both represent adaptive changes on the part of the infant to different modes of parental care or different environmental circumstances. That is, given the differences in childrearing and home environments, both secure and insecure attachment may be different but equally adaptive paths to maturity.

Research indicates that attachment bears a strong relationship to the kind of personality the infant possesses later in life. Compared to insecurely attached infants, securely attached infants are

- more positive and resolute when given demanding tasks as 2- to 3½-year-olds (Sroufe, 1978; Sroufe, Fox, & Pancake, 1983),
- interact more quickly and skillfully with strangers at 3 years of age (Lutkenhaus, Grossman, & Grossman, 1985),
- receive more positive feedback from their peers when they are 3 years old (Jacobson & Wille, 1986), and are
- more friendly and cooperative with their mothers and peers (Londorville & Main, 1981; Pastor, 1981).

Hence, in our present culture, secure attachment would seem to be more adaptive in terms of getting along with both peers and adults than insecure attachment. Whether these two kinds of attachment are similar in terms of helping the infant develop into a reproductively successful adult as suggested by Lamb is a question in need of further research.

Attachment and Parent-Child Interaction. The upshot of attachment research is plain to see: securely attached infants appear to develop into children with a higher level of social competency than do insecurely attached children. How can parents foster secure attachment in their children? Answers to this question have been provided by research focusing on patterns of parent-child interaction. For example, Ainsworth, Bell, & Slayton (1971) found that mothers of securely attached infants were more accepting than mothers of insecurely attached infants. Mothers of securely attached infants will hold, caress, and cuddle their babies. Mothers of insecurely attached infants may kiss their babies but do not otherwise encourage physical contact. Likewise, infants whose mothers are sensitive to their actions and respond accordingly are generally more securely attached than infants whose mothers attend to them inconsistently (Ainsworth, 1979).

Responsive mothers, those who have securely attached infants, are different in other respects from nonresponsive mothers, those who have insecurely attached infants. Responsive mothers seem to have more positive and realistic expectations of parenting and adjust easily to the role of mother; nonresponsive mothers often have negative and unrealistic expectations (Maccoby & Martin, 1983; Wise & Grossman, 1980). Unrealistic expectations include thinking that parenting is easy, that infants will sleep through the night, and that children will always be obedient to requests. As you probably know, these truly are unrealistic expectations; infants and children just don't always behave along these lines.

The caregiver is not the only variable in the childrearing equation, though; we must also consider the infant's contribution to that relationship. One important factor influencing infants' ability to elicit positive responses from their caregivers is their temperament. Infants who are happy and generally well-behaved elicit positive responses from their caregivers, while infants who are irritable and unhappy elicit negative responses (Dunn, 1981; Donovan, Leavitt, & Balling, 1978). Note, however, that parental reaction to a baby's behavior will affect, to some degree, the continued development of the infant's temperament (see Figure 11.8). Nature may provide the infant with its initial set of responses to the world, but how that world reacts to those responses will determine whether or not the infant's behavior is reinforced or extinguished (Kaplan, 1988).

Might attachment also be impeded by factors such as deprivation by a caregiver or inconsistent caregiving? Most psychologists who have studied the effects of nonparental day care on infant and child development feel that attachment is not adversely affected as long as the day care is high-quality (a low child-to-caregiver ratio in a setting that is verbally and socially stimulating) (Scarr & Weinberg, 1986).

Approaches to Childrearing. What was your home life like as a child? Did your parents establish rules and expect you to obey them, or did they let you do as you pleased whenever you pleased? Psychologists have found that whether parents establish rules, and how they enforce those rules affects the social development of their children (Baumrind, 1983; Buri, Louiselle, Misukanis, & Mueller, 1988).

In general, parents seem to adopt one of three approaches in raising their children: authoritarian, permissive, or authoritative (Baumrind, 1983).

FIGURE 11.8
The interactive nature of infant and parent behavior. The infant's temperament may influence his or her parents' reaction, which may in turn, reinforce or extinguish particular aspects of the infant's temperament.

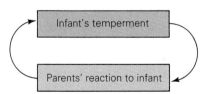

Authoritarian parents establish firm rules and expect them to be obeyed without question. Disobedience is met with punishment. **Permissive parents** adopt the opposite strategy: few rules are imposed on the children, and parents do little to influence the behavior of their children. **Authoritative parents** also establish rules and enforce them, but not merely through punishment. Instead, authoritative parents seek to explain the relationship between the rules and punishment. In addition, authoritative parents foster independence in their children by encouraging them to learn why family rules exist. In authoritative homes, allowances are also made for exceptions to the rules. Rules are established not as absolute or inflexible laws, but rather as general behavioral guidelines that take the child into consideration.

Let's suppose a 10-year-old boy has just broken a glass vase by accidentally hitting it with a ball. How would the three kinds of parents react to the child? That reaction might go something like this:

Authoritarian parents: "You know better than that! Don't you ever play with a ball in the house again. Now go to your bedroom and don't come out until I tell you to."

Permissive parents: "Well, don't worry about it. These things happen; it was an accident."

Authoritative parents: "You know better than that—you agreed not to play with the ball in the house. Now you know exactly why we made that rule. Go get the broom and the dust pan and clean up this mess. When you finish, go to your bedroom and wait for me. I want to talk to you some more about what you just did."

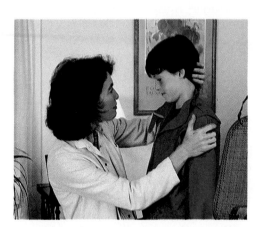

The style of childrearing a parent uses plays a major role in the type of person that child develops into.

Not surprisingly, authoritarian parents tend to have children who are more unhappy and distrustful than children of permissive or authoritative parents. You may think that children of permissive parents are most likely to be self-reliant and curious. Not so. In fact, they appear to be the least self-reliant and explorative. Why? Probably because they never received parental encouragement and guidance for developing these sorts of behaviors. Rather, they are left on their own without benefit of learning directly from an adult's experience and without the guidance needed to learn self-control. Authoritative parents raise their children in an environment in which individuality and personal responsibility are encouraged, and so they tend to produce children who are self-controlled, independent, and socially competent. Psychologically then, the key to raising happy and independent children is an open line of communication between parent and child.

Parenting style alone, though, does not determine the course of a child's social development. Granted, the quality of the home environment is likely to be a critical factor influencing children's social actions and personality. However, it is also likely that personality has a genetic component, which means that children inherit a part of their disposition from their parents. In addition, other factors, such as the environment outside the home, may exert at least some influence on the developing child. Children's attitudes and behaviors may be changed by the different kinds of people they encounter as they become involved in school and other activities. They may, for example, have an authoritative physical education instructor, or a permissive home room teacher, or an authoritarian piano teacher. Interaction with peers helps children learn social skills, understand social events, and obtain information about school, community, and athletic events, and become involved in group activities. These sorts of events are important in preparing children for future social interaction during adolescence and adulthood (Rubin, 1980; Hartup, 1979).

As children mature, so do their cognitive and social skills. By age 12, a child is able to think logically and to view the world from another person's perspective. Children are also at the stage of moral development where they are beginning to seek the approval of others, including people outside the home. As we shall see, children's cognitive and social development continues to change during adolescence.

ADOLESCENCE

Adolescence is the period of life spanning the teenage years. Its beginning is heralded by the onset of **puberty,** the sudden maturation of the genitalia that endows each of us with the capacity for sexual reproduction. Girls generally begin puberty between the ages of 8 and 12, nearly two years, on average, before boys. In both sexes the onset of puberty is due to the influence exerted by two brain structures, the hypothalamus and the pituitary gland, over the gonads (testes in males and ovaries in females). The major physical changes that occur during adolescence are related to puberty. Because puberty plays such an important role in physical development and gender-related behavior, we will discuss it in greater detail in the next chapter, Gender Development and Sexual Behavior.

The end of adolescence is difficult to judge because the line between adolescence and young adulthood is fuzzy—there are no physical changes that mark this transition. State governments, of course, have laws declaring that a person is an adult at age 18 or 21, but as most people know, the beginning of adulthood cannot be pinpointed with that kind of accuracy. Most psychologists generally agree that adolescents become adults when they have become emotionally and socially independent of their parents. And for most people, this is a gradual process.

The physical changes that transform children into adolescents and then into adults are accompanied by changes in cognition and social behavior. In general, adolescents are able to reason in ways that children cannot. Their metacognition, or self-awareness of their own ways of thinking, enables them to develop values and set personal goals for themselves. These values and goals influence their interactions with others. Just as importantly, adolescents are able to backtrack in their thinking, allowing them to understand the logical development of their thoughts, values, and goals.

Cognitive Development

Recall that from Piaget's perspective, older children have only limited reasoning abilities relative to adults. This part of childhood (ages 7 to 11) is called the concrete operational stage because children can only reason in concrete terms. They are able to reason deductively and solve conservation problems correctly, but they can neither solve hypothetical problems very well nor truly understand abstract concepts like social equality, freedom, and love. However, between the ages of about 12 to 15, the cognitive abilities of the individual go through their final qualitative stage, the formal operational period. Now the child is able to think more like an adult. Abstract thinking and the ability to use inductive reasoning to solve complex problems emerge as hallmarks of adolescent cognition. Not until adolescence are individuals able to think abstractly about intellectual matters and moral issues.

A*bstract thinking and the ability to use inductive reasoning to solve complex problems emerge as hallmarks of adolescent cognition.*

Although adolescents begin to think more like adults, they still tend to be egocentric and naive in some of their thoughts. Consider, for example, the **personal fable,** the belief that what you are thinking and feeling is completely new and unique and has never before been experienced by anyone else (Elkind & Bowen, 1979). Personal fables tend to center on the unique experiences of the individual. For example, on more than one occasion, an adolescent has been heard to remark to his or her parents, "You have no idea how hard school really is. You don't know what it's like to be in class all day studying, and then come home and do homework." As adolescents think about their experiences, they develop the belief that they alone have the privilege or misfortune of experiencing some event. As the formal operations stage continues, adolescents mature in their thinking, and they gradually learn that many of their experiences are not so unique after all. The journey from adolescence to adulthood is filled with such insights.

Social Development

Most psychologists agree with Erikson that the major task facing the adolescent is to develop a personal identity. To a teenager, developing a sense of identity must be something like a very complicated juggling act. Somehow he or she must balance past experiences and family and peer relationships with expectations and plans for the kind of adult he or she expects to become. Erikson, as you recall, believed that during adolescence, teenagers face an identity crisis from which they will emerge either with a clear sense of self or confused about who they are and where they are going. For adolescents, the goal of the teenage years is, in everyday language, to "find yourself." In Erikson's view, the goal is to achieve an identity.

Erikson's theory of adolescent development has been extended and researched extensively by James Marcia (1967, 1980). Marcia argued that establishing an identity involves two components, crisis and commitment. A **crisis** is a period during which the adolescent struggles intellectually to resolve issues related to personal values and goals. For example, the teenager who questions the religious and moral values of his or her parents is experiencing a crisis. **Commitment** is a decision based on consideration of alternative goals and values that leads to a specific course of action; the teenager is committed to thinking and acting in a manner consistent with how the crisis has been resolved. For instance, the teenager who decides to go to the same church as her parents and who adopts their views of morality is said to be committed to those beliefs. In this case, she also is said to identify with those beliefs.

Marcia hypothesized that adolescents experience different degrees of crisis and commitment. Some adolescents never experience crises, and others do, but they never resolve them. In trying to make sense of the different ways in which adolescents experience the identity crisis, Marcia developed four possibilities, which he called identity statuses (see Figure 11.9).

Adolescents who experience a crisis in their values or goals, consider alternative resolutions to that crisis, and are committed to a course of action based on personal values are said to be *identity achievers*. Adolescents who experience a crisis but do not resolve that crisis, and thus, do not become committed, are called *moratoriums*. Teenagers who have not experienced a crisis but who are nonetheless committed are said to be *foreclosures*. Foreclosures are typically adolescents who identify strongly with people such as their parents, and as result, never consider alternatives to that identity. They have, in Marcia's view, foreclosed their identity. Adolescents who do not experience a crisis and who do not become committed are referred to as *identity diffusions*. Erikson would probably have considered these individuals as identity confused.

Marcia's research has shown that adolescents move in and out of the different stages as they experience new situations and crises; a teenager does not necessarily move progressively from one status to another. For example, after considerable thinking about whether to major in business or

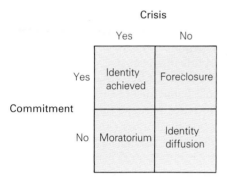

FIGURE 11.9
Marcia's four identity statuses.

engineering, a college student may decide to go into engineering because she thinks she will like the work and make enough money to do the kinds of things she wants to do with her life. In terms of this important decision, she has become an identity achiever. However, upon taking several engineering courses, she decides she doesn't really like engineering after all and now must decide whether to keep her major or change it to business or some other field. Since she is now no longer committed, she is in moratorium.

Marcia's research is important for two reasons. First, it shows that most adolescents do, indeed, experience crises in their search for an identity. Second, it shows the teenager's psychological reaction to a crisis depends upon the point in time during which he or she is dealing with the crisis. That there are four possible avenues that can be involved in the process of resolving a crisis testifies to the complexity of "finding oneself." Perhaps the real point of Marcia's work is that by discovering the kinds of crises a teenager is experiencing and how he or she is dealing with them, we can better understand adolescents' thinking and behavior.

Marcia's work, then, buttresses Erikson's view of adolescence. Erikson's theory would have us believe that adolescents are searching for an identity of their own; that is, one independent of their parents and others. However, as Carol Gilligan (1982) contends, this is likely to be more true for boys than girls. Her point is that girls more so than boys seek to develop close relationships with others. In her view, a girl's search for identity is strongly influenced by the desire to be involved in close relationships with others.

Gilligan's point is a good one simply because it reinforces the idea that the adolescent's search for an identity does not occur in a vacuum. Rather, the search is enmeshed in a social context that may influence how a teenager responds to a crisis. Two of the most important sets of actors in that social context are the adolescent's parents and peers.

Most teenagers report that they generally have a good relationship with their parents and agree with their parents on educational and career goals and values regarding social, political, and religious issues (Steinberg, 1987; Gallatin, 1980). Teenagers who are raised in homes with supportive parents with whom they can communicate openly and without fear of condemnation for their values and ambitions tend to develop a clear sense of independence and personal identity (Grotevant & Cooper, 1985).

The influence of peers in the lives of most adolescents is greatest on issues related to life-style (Britton, 1963, 1966). When it comes to making decisions about which record album or jeans to buy, adolescents tend to go along with their peers rather than with their parents. Decisions concerning how to spend leisure time, the circle of friends with which to associate, and whether or not to use drugs are also adolescent choices influenced more by peers than by parents. When is peer influence strongest? Research on this question shows that peer influence increases steadily during late childhood

Above: Teenagers whose parents are supportive and maintain an open line of communication are usually happier and more well adjusted. Right: Peers have a strong influence on a child's life-style decisions during adolescence.

(from about ages 8 to 11), peaks during early adolescence (from about ages 13 to 15) and declines steadily thereafter (Berndt, 1979).

In sum, the adolescent's search for an identity is a social process—one in which teenagers actively attempt to resolve crises dealing with personal values and future expectations within the context of family and friends. As Marcia showed, resolving crises is not an easy task, and once a crisis is resolved, it is not necessarily resolved permanently. Indeed, many adolescent crises, such as career and dating decisions, spill over into adulthood. The questions of "Who am I?" and "Where am I going?" are never fully answered in adolescence simply because human development does not end there. In fact, adulthood brings with it a whole new set of crises that shape our identities. From a life-span developmental perspective, adulthood—the subject to which we now turn—is the discovery of new identities and refinement and extension of the ones we formed as adolescents.

ADULTHOOD AND OLD AGE

Most psychologists view the transition from adolescence to young adulthood as beginning in the late teen years, plus or minus a year or so depending upon the individual life experiences of the particular adolescent. The developmental changes that take place during adulthood are not as dramatic or obvious as those that occur during childhood and adolescence, but nonetheless, they are real. And these changes are not hastened by age itself, but rather by the kinds of life experiences that typically accompany growing older. Our experiences determine when and whom we marry, how we raise our children, how much wisdom we amass, how healthy we are, and so on.

Physical Changes

As we grow older, there is one set of changes that we are assured of experiencing—physical changes. Our physical abilities peak around age 30 and decline gradually thereafter. By maintaining a well-balanced diet, exercising regularly, and not smoking, drinking, or using drugs, we can, in large measure, help our bodies maintain some of their physical vigor even into old age. This is not to say that through diet and exercise a 70-year-old person can feel and look like a 25-year-old. But if we don't eat well and exercise regularly, we will have less physical energy and poorer muscle tone than if we did do these things. And apparently staying in shape as a younger adult pays off in one's later years. Older people who were physically fit as younger adults are generally in better health and feel better about themselves than those who were not (Perlmutter & Hall, 1985).

Unfortunately though, eating and exercising are not panaceas for the physical changes that accompany aging. People in their 50s and 60s often experience the following physical changes:

- decreases in visual acuity, loss in ability to perceive depth
- decreases in hearing
- decreases in sensitivity to tastes and smells
- decreases in reaction time, agility, and physical mobility
- decreases in physical strength

Of course, all individuals do not experience these physical changes at the same age or to the same extent. These sorts of changes, though, do cause middle-aged individuals and the elderly to worry about their health. In addition to sensory losses, chances of suffering from a heart attack or cancer increase with age. Among people over 65, heart disease is related to

Although a gradual decline in physical ability usually accompanies aging, older adults who are physically active can maintain good health.

The memory loss and decline in thought processes caused by advanced Alzheimer's disease leaves many older adults disoriented and unaware of their surroundings.

40 percent of all deaths, and cancer is the second leading cause of death.

In terms of psychological health, dementia (the loss of intellectual ability) affects many people later in life. **Alzheimer's disease,** a well-known form of dementia, strikes over 100,000 individuals each year. The disease generally afflicts those who are in their 40s and older, eventually killing them. Typically, thinking, language skills, and especially memory deteriorate as the disease progresses. The disease leaves its victims confused, disoriented, and intellectually bereft. Middle-aged individuals may experience gradual mental deterioration for 10 to 20 years before they die; older individuals will experience a more rapid intellectual decline and die sooner, sometimes as soon as 3 years after onset of the disease (Butler & Lewis, 1982).

Researchers have two leads as to the possible causes of Alzheimer's disease. First, geneticists have discovered that defects in the twenty-first chromosome cause at least one kind of Alzheimer's disease (Selkoe, 1989). Second, reduced levels of brain acetylcholine are common in Alzheimer's patients (Gottfries, 1985). Unfortunately, a treatment for the disease does not presently exist. However, with continued research into the biological basis of this disorder, the outlook for a cure brightens.

Cognitive Development

What about cognitive development during adulthood and old age—does it, like physical development, peak during young adulthood and then decline with age? Developmental psychologists have generally used two different approaches to study the relationship between aging and cognition. The first is to compare the performances of younger and older adults on cognitive tasks such as memory tasks. The second approach is to look at changes in intelligence as measured using different kinds of intelligence tests. Both kinds of studies show that as we age, our cognitive abilities do decline, but not as precipitously as you might think.

For example, in a 21-year longitudinal study of changes in adult memory, K. Warner Schaie (1980) investigated subjects' ability to recognize and recall words. The results, depicted in Figure 11.10, showed that adult sub-

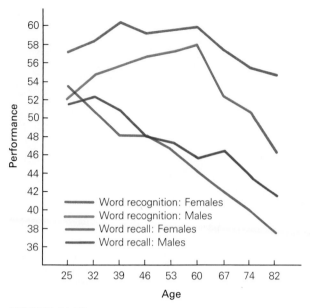

FIGURE 11.10
A longitudinal study of changes in adult ability for word recognition and recall over 21 years. With age, ability for word recall decreased faster than word recognition.

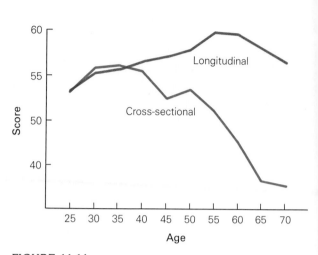

FIGURE 11.11
A comparison of cross-sectional and longitudinal data concerning changes in verbal ability. In contrast to the cross-sectional data, the longitudinal data show that verbal ability increased gradually to about age 55 and then decreased gradually.

jects' ability to *recognize* words actually increased slightly up to about age 60 and declined slightly thereafter. (Note, too, that females at all ages outperformed males at word recognition.) In contrast, adults' ability to *recall* words decreased at a moderate pace from age 25 onward. Schaie has suggested that these results might be interpreted to mean that older people benefit more from retrieval cues found in recognition tasks than do younger persons (Schaie & Willis, 1986).

How can we explain the decrease in memory associated with aging? Developmental psychologists believe most of the difficulties associated with memory and aging are due to problems with either encoding or retrieving information (Poon, 1985). In other words, as we age, entering information into long-term memory and accessing that information is not accomplished as efficiently and accurately as it was when we were younger. Understanding the exact nature of encoding and retrieval problems, though, awaits future research.

If memory shows wear with age, one might reasonably suspect that intelligence, too, would show a similar decline with age. This was once thought to be true based on results from cross-sectional studies. Today, however, we know that this is not the case, largely due to the work of Schaie and his colleagues, who compared results from a cross-sectional approach with results from a longitudinal approach. For example, look at Figure 11.11, which shows performance on a verbal abilities subsection of an intelligence test plotted as a function of age. (Here "verbal abilities" means verbal meaning, or the ability to understand ideas represented by words.) The data collected using the cross-sectional approach show that intelligence scores decrease with age and rather precipitously so after age 50. The data collected using the longitudinal method paint a very different picture: scores increase until about age 55 and then decline gradually afterward. What accounts for these differences? Recall that earlier in the chapter we discussed a problem with cross-sectional studies, namely, they do not take into consideration the fact that the people being tested are not the same age and were reared in different time periods. Thus, one explanation for these disparate results is that older people did not have the same educational and career opportunities as their younger counterparts taking the test may have had. The longitudinal method takes this possibility into consideration by testing the same people at regular intervals spanning many years. In doing so, it gives a more accurate picture of the relationship between age and intelligence.

Data from other researchers suggest that these results hold for only the kinds of intelligence measured by general IQ tests (Horn, 1970, 1982). For example, Horn showed that intelligence actually comes in two varieties, crystallized and fluid, and that younger and older people differ markedly with respect to them. **Crystallized intelligence** is intelligence that reflects both formal education and the "seat of the pants" learning that comes in everyday life. Crystallized intelligence thus reflects knowledge of the world as well as wisdom. **Fluid intelligence** is intelligence that reflects our native capacity for reasoning, problem solving, and remembering. It is not related to one's education and life experiences. Instead, it represents the brain's ability to process information and generate an intelligent response. As Figure 11.12 shows, older people do better than younger people on tests of crystallized intelligence, but worse on tests of fluid intelligence. Why doesn't age affect both kinds of intelligence similarly? According to Horn, the decrease in fluid intelligence with age is caused by progressive deterioration of brain structures involved with information processing. Crystallized intelligence, because it represents already processed information, does not require the nervous system to process new information for its expression.

Social Development

Recall that Erikson believes that the adult years consist of three psychosocial stages: intimacy versus isolation, during which people succeed or fail in loving others; generativity versus stagnation, during which an individual either withdraws inwardly and concentrates on his or her problems or reaches out to help and care for others and their problems; and integrity versus despair, during which life is reviewed with either a sense of satisfaction or with despair.

FIGURE 11.12
Comparison of different cohorts on tests of generalized, fluid, and crystallized intelligence. Older people perform better on tests of crystallized intelligence than do younger people, but worse on tests of fluid intelligence.

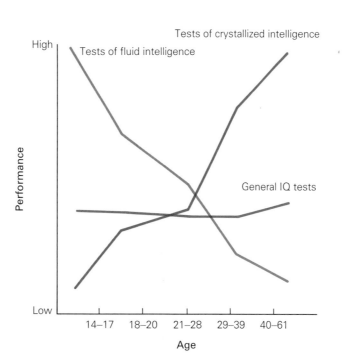

*S*uccess in love and work is the yardstick by which life satisfaction is measured.

Passing through these stages, whether successfully or unsuccessfully, occurs against the backdrop of what many developmental psychologists consider to be the two most important aspects of adult life: love and work. For most of us falling in love with someone is more than just a compelling feeling of wanting to spend time with that person. It often brings with it major life responsibilities, such as marriage and children. Work, too, is more than just a way to pass time. It involves setting and achieving goals related to income, status among peers, and accomplishment outside the family. Work does not have to entail personal material benefits; one can work for causes such as raising money to help fight childhood diseases or protecting the environment. For most adults, overall satisfaction with life reflects the degree to which they have been successful in marriage, rearing a family, and achieving goals. In other words, success in love and work is the yardstick by which life satisfaction is measured. With this in mind, let's look briefly at how love and work ebb and flow over the course of adult development.

Marriage and Family. For 95 percent of adults under 40 falling in love with someone results in marriage (Bureau of the Census, 1987). Newlyweds are generally very happy with their marriage, and seem to become even happier when children enter the picture (Rollins & Feldman, 1970). However, as children begin to demand more of the parents' time and emotional resources, couples report increasing unhappiness in marriage. Generally speaking, mothers assume more responsibility than fathers for the day-to-day care of children (Parke & Tinsley, 1981). As a result, they spend more time doing housework and less time talking to their husbands (Peskin, 1982; Udry, 1974), which places a considerable strain on the couple's marital happiness. However, if husband and wife can find time together in the evenings, and if the husband is able to help with the children, the stress of adapting to family life is lessened (Daniels & Weingarten, 1982).

As children grow older and become self-sufficient in caring for themselves, the day-to-day burdens of raising a family taper off, and husbands and wives are able to spend more time with each other. However, adolescent children pose new problems for their parents: they may question parental views and authority, and their burgeoning social agenda can put a wrinkle in their parents' personal and social calendar. For many parents, rearing adolescent children, particularly the time just prior to their leaving home, represents the low point of marital happiness (Rollins & Feldman, 1970).

Generally speaking, once a family's youngest child has left the home, marital happiness increases and continues to do so through the remainder of the couple's life together. It was once thought that the "empty nest" posed problems for the middle-aged couple, particularly for the mother, who defined her role solely around her children. Although parents may miss the daily contact with their children and knowing what is going on in their children's lives, they also feel happy that a major responsibility of life has been completed successfully, namely, raising self-reliant children who become responsible members of the culture. Just as importantly, the couple now has time for each other and the freedom to pursue their own hobbies and personal goals. It may be true, as one bumper sticker says, that "An empty nest is a happy nest." Psychological research tends to support this statement. In one study, only 6 percent of empty nest couples reported that life prior to their last child leaving home was better than their empty nest experience. Over 50 percent of the couples interviewed said their lives were better now than before their children left home (Deutscher, 1968; Neugarten, 1974).

As children grow up and leave home, older adults are once again free to pursue their own interests and goals and have time for activities together.

Work. The task of raising a family is balanced with one or both parents having a career. In fact, events that occur in the workplace can often affect the quality of home life for better or for worse. A promotion and a salary increase can mean that a family can do things together that they couldn't do before—they can now afford to pursue a new hobby or travel together. Working long hours to get that raise, however, can decrease the amount of time that a couple can spend together or with their children.

With the dramatic increase in women entering the work force in the past 20 years, many psychologists have focused their research efforts on understanding dual-earner marriages, or those in which the husband works full time and the wife works full or part-time (Pleck & Staines, 1982). Compared to single-earner families, dual-earner families generally have a better standard of living in terms of material possessions and saving money for their children's education and their own retirement (Rapoport & Rapoport, 1980). Another important benefit accrues especially to the wife: she is able to achieve recognition outside of the home. Most husbands in dual-earner marriages support their wives working. In addition, they find their wives more interesting, more essential, and more helpful as partners in marriage (Schaie & Willis, 1986).

But all is not bliss for dual-earner marriages. If both partners are working, who manages domestic household duties and takes care of the children? In most cases, the woman still does, which often means she has two roles, one as mother and the other as wage earner. Apparently, a husband's support of his wife's working does not always go as far as actually physically helping out at home. However, husbands who believe strongly in equality for women are especially likely to pitch in at home (Bird, Bird, & Scruggs, 1984).

Death. The final event in life is death. Death is a biological and social event—family and friends are emotionally affected by the death of a loved one. Although death may claim a life at any time, most people die when they are old. One question developmental psychologists have asked about death and dying among the elderly is: How do old people view the inevitability of their own deaths?

At one time or another, most of us contemplate our own death. Some of us may contemplate it more than others, but to be sure, the thought of death crosses our minds at least occasionally. As you might expect, elderly people contemplate their deaths more often than do younger adults. Generally speaking, elderly people fear death less than their younger counterparts (Kalish, 1976). Why? No one knows for sure, but one tentative explanation may be that older people have had more time to review their pasts and plan for their futures knowing that death may be close at hand. Thus, they are able to prepare themselves psychologically (and financially) for their death.

Contemplating and preparing for your own death, though, is not like knowing that you are actually dying. The changes in attitude that terminally ill people undergo have been studied by Elisabeth Kübler-Ross (1969, 1981). After interviewing hundreds of dying people, she concluded that they experience five distinct phases of psychologically coping with their own deaths. The first stage is *denial.* When terminally ill people learn of their condition they simply deny it. *Anger* comes next; now they resent the certainty of death. In the third stage, *bargaining,* individuals attempt to negotiate their fate with God or others, pleading that their lives might be spared. While bargaining, they gradually begin to realize that they are, in fact, going to die. This leads to *depression,* the fourth stage, which is characterized by a sense of hopelessness and loss. The fifth and final stage, *acceptance,* is marked by a peaceful resignation to the facts.

Kübler-Ross' work points up the psychological factors involved in the dying process and has provided an initial theory about how the dying come to grips with their fate. Her work, though, has not been accepted uncritically. As several researchers have pointed out (for example, Kastenbaum, 1981), Kübler-Ross' research was not scientific. Her method for interviewing her subjects was unsystematic, and her results were largely anecdotal. Moreover, of the five stages, denial is the only one that appears to be universal. Apparently, not all terminally ill people have the same psychological response to the knowledge that they may soon die.

However, despite its flaws, Kübler-Ross' work is important because it has prompted an awareness, both scientific and public, of the plight of the dying. The scientific response to this prompting has been, as anyone would predict, to conduct more research. Hopefully, this research will provide us all with a better and more compassionate understanding of what the terminally ill experience. The public response has involved the attempt to provide the dying with support for both them and their families through hospice services. In the past, hospices were places where strangers and pilgrims could find rest and shelter. Today, hospices are special facilities that provide medical and psychological support for the dying and their families. In cases where the dying person wishes to die at home, hospice volunteers work in that setting. The primary functions of the hospice services are twofold: to provide relief from pain and to allow the person to die with dignity. No attempt is made to prolong life through technology if doing so would diminish the self-respect of the dying person and his or her loved ones. To die with dignity is perhaps to die the best death possible, for the dying and his or her loved ones are able to experience for the last time together, reverence for the life experience.

BOUNDARIES AND FRONTIERS

It is an understatement to say that life-span development is an enigmatic process. The complex interaction of genetic, physiological, social, and cultural factors underlying human development means that development is not a unitary process, or even due to two or three variables. Matters are made even more complicated when we consider that, although certain aspects of development are the same for all of us, experience leaves its own indelible mark on who and what we ultimately become. That means that there are as many permutations of the developmental process as there are human beings. Thus, it is also an understatement to say that much remains to be learned about how we humans grow and change.

The logical questions to ask here are: What things don't we know about human development? What barriers stand in the way of understanding human development better? Certainly, researchers such as Piaget, Kohlberg, Erikson, Bowlby, Harlow, and Ainsworth have endowed us with fertile theory and sound empirical findings with which to approach these questions, especially as they apply to understanding development in childhood and adolescence. However, the range of questions to be addressed in development is broader than those encountered in youth. Of increasing concern to developmental psychologists as well as to the public in general is finding answers to developmental questions that are related to old age.

The current interest in researching developmental issues involved in old age is driven primarily by practical concerns, although there are also interesting theoretical issues tied to understanding developmental changes during this phase of life. The major practical concern is this: More and more people are living longer, which means that older people make up a larger segment of society than ever before. Today, the median age of Americans is approximately 33; by the year 2000, the median age is estimated to be just over 36, and by the year 2025, the estimated median age of Americans will be 40 (U.S. Bureau of the Census, 1982). However, the increasing number of elderly people is not the problem. The problem is that society may not be prepared to integrate the growing number of elderly people into active and meaningful social roles. Consider, for example, that presently about 12 percent of our population is over 65; by the year 2030 it is estimated that that figure will nearly double (U.S. Bureau of the Census, 1982). In absolute terms, there is likely to be more than 50 million people over the age of 65 in 2030. Because opportunities for making meaningful social contributions may be limited, many of these 50 million people are likely to experience substantial psychological problems in adjusting to life after retirement.

Let's consider the burgeoning elderly population in light of the two questions posed above. First, what things don't we know about developmental changes in older people? What sorts of information about the developmental changes that occur late in life would be useful for us to help the elderly play active and meaningful social roles? Perhaps the most significant frontier for us to explore is the intellectual capacities of the elderly. We know that intellectual decline with age is not inevitable, but we do not know the determinants of maintaining a stable level of intellectual functioning during old age. Discovering those determinants would be useful to many people who will be 65 or older in 2030. They might be able to control those determinants to combat intellectual decline. Having and maintaining a sharp mind is a cornerstone (along with good health) for being socially active.

A second important frontier for psychologists to explore is social psychological in nature, namely, the role that family, friends, and others play in determining an elderly person's ability to cope successfully with life changes (Rodin, 1987). This is a particularly relevant question for the baby boomers (those born in the 20 years following World War II) because when they retire, they will have fewer supportive family members than preceding generations of retirees (due to the fact that family size among baby boomers is smaller than that among preceding generations). In addition, because the generations following the baby boomers are smaller in numbers, the social security base that provides financial support for retirees will be relatively small. In other words, as the number of people drawing social security increases, the number of people contributing to that financial reserve will be decreasing. Thus, the baby boom cohort will likely rely on support systems that provide financial as well as social support. One important outcome from research in this area is likely to be strategies for helping elderly people develop new social support systems and improve existing ones.

Now, for the second question: What barriers (or boundaries) stand in the way of conducting research related to the elderly? Although there are many impediments to conducting research on aging, let us mention two of the more important ones here. First, compared to researchers who use children or adolescents or college students as subjects, those who use elderly people have a more difficult time obtaining subjects. Children, adolescents, and college students can be found in large numbers at central locations, and often in samples that are representative of the population. The elderly are more dispersed and often separated by financial barriers. Some are found in "missions," some in the streets of urban areas, others in nursing homes, and almost always in relatively small numbers. Although this should not prevent research on aging from being conducted, it does pose logistical and practical problems that are often decisive in, for example, the topics chosen for graduate student thesis and dissertation research. Unless researchers are enmeshed in aging research while they are graduate students, the chances that they will devote their careers to that endeavor are slim.

The second barrier, myths about aging, does not impede aging research being conducted so much as it does the dissemination of the results of such research to the public. Even scientifically sound research has difficulty overcoming the inertia of everyday misconceptions of the elderly and their abilities. Here are a few such myths (Schaie & Willis, 1986):

- Elderly people become senile sooner or later.
- The majority of people age 65 and older are unhealthy.
- Elderly people cannot benefit from education.
- Elderly people rarely produce significant works of art, science, or scholarship.

These myths, and others like them, cast the elderly in a negative light that can prevent older people from being included in many important societal roles. The elderly have been and continue to be deprived of educational, recreational, and employment opportunities on the basis of their age alone, regardless of their actual abilities. Only by debunking myths about aging and putting the correct information in the hands of responsible public officials and private business people can discrimination against the elderly be ultimately arrested. In other words, scientific research should influence public policy and employment-related decisions with respect to issues in aging.

So-called retired people represent a tremendous national resource, a reservoir of accumulated knowledge, expertise, and labor. It is our belief that psychological research into aging can and will eventually reveal the depths of this reservoir and open up new avenues for the elderly to contribute to the well-being of our culture.

CONCEPT SUMMARY

THE LIFE-SPAN PERSPECTIVE

- What is life-span developmental psychology? What do developmental psychologists study? (pp. 377–378)
- How do developmental psychologists view the heredity versus environment issue? (pp. 378–379)
- Is development a continuous or discontinuous process? Explain. (pp. 378–379)
- How does the cross-sectional approach to studying development differ from the longitudinal approach? (pp. 379–381)

THEORIES OF DEVELOPMENT

- According to Piaget, what role do schemes play in development? How are schemes modified by accommodation and assimilation? (pp. 382–383)
- What are Piaget's four stages of cognitive development? How do they differ from one another? (pp. 383–387)
- What is symbolic thinking? What role does it play in a child's ability to understand the world? (pp. 384–385)
- What is conservation? When does a child master this

principle? How is the concept of reversibility related to conservation? (pp. 385–386)
- What sorts of criticisms have been levied against Piaget's theory? (pp. 387–388)
- What are Kohlberg's three levels of moral development? How do they differ from one another? (pp. 388–390)
- Is moral reasoning related to moral behavior? Explain. (pp. 389–390)
- How have critics responded to Kohlberg's theory? (pp. 390–391)
- According to Erikson, what are psychosocial conflicts? What role do they play in development? (p. 391)
- What are the psychosocial conflicts encountered in childhood, in adolescence, and adulthood? Describe each of them. (pp. 391–393)

DEVELOPMENT AND THE LIFE CYCLE

- How do normative age-graded and history-graded variables interact with each other and with nonnormative variables to influence development? (pp. 393–394)

PRENATAL DEVELOPMENT

- What are the three stages of prenatal development? What important developmental events occur in each stage? (pp. 394–395)
- What sorts of threats do teratogens pose for the fetus? (pp. 394–396)
- What are the causes and consequences of fetal alcohol syndrome? (p. 396)

INFANCY AND CHILDHOOD

- By what means do babies become adapted to their environments? (pp. 396–397)
- What changes does the brain undergo during infancy? (p. 397)
- What are the three major principles involved in motor development? Explain each of them. (pp. 398–399)
- Why is metacognition an important factor in development? (p. 400)
- How does attachment develop? Is attachment a biologically based or experientially based set of behaviors?

Explain the differences between secure and insecure attachment. (pp. 400–403)

ADOLESCENCE

- What are the high points of cognitive development during adolescence? (pp. 405–406)
- How has Marcia's research supported Erikson's ideas about adolescent identity? (pp. 406–408)

ADULTHOOD AND OLD AGE

- What sorts of physical changes accompany aging? What is Alzheimer's disease? (pp. 408–409)
- Do changes in cognition parallel the course of physical changes for adults? Explain. What is the difference between crystallized intelligence and fluid intelligence? (pp. 409–411)
- How is the relationship between a husband and wife affected by having children and by career decisions? (pp. 412–413)
- What did Kübler-Ross find in her research on how the terminally ill face death? Why has her work been important? (pp. 413–414)

KEY TERMS AND CONCEPTS

THE LIFE-SPAN PERSPECTIVE

Life-span Developmental Psychology   The study of the processes and patterns of change that occur within individuals over the life span. (p. 377)

Cross-sectional Approach   A research design used to test or observe different individuals of various ages at the same point in time. (p. 379)

Cohorts   The people born in the same year or time period. For example, the people born in 1985 represent the 1985 cohort. The concept of cohort is used to distinguish among groups of people according to their year or time of birth. (p. 379)

Longitudinal Approach   A research design involving repeated observation or testing of the same group of people over an extended period of time. (p. 380)

THEORIES OF DEVELOPMENT

Schemes   Mental representations of the world based on previous experiences. Schemes function as the basis for understanding current and future experiences. (p. 382)

Assimilation   The process by which new information about the world is modified to fit existing schemes. (p. 383)

Accommodation   The process by which existing schemes are modified or changed by new experiences. (p. 383)

Sensorimotor Period   This stage, the first in Piaget's theory of cognitive development, is marked by an orderly progression of increasingly complex cognitive development: reflexive behavior, object permanence, a rough approxi-

mation of cause and effect, imitating the actions of others, and finally, symbolic thinking. (p. 383)

Object Permanence   The idea that objects do not disappear when they are removed from sight. (p. 384)

Deferred Imitation   The result of the child's new ability to form mental representations of actions that he or she has observed, which then may be recalled at a later point to direct particular imitative actions. (p. 384)

Preoperational Period   The second of Piaget's four stages, which represents a 4- to 5-year period of transition (from age 2 to about 6 or 7) between first being able to think symbolically and then being able to think logically. During this stage, children's vocabulary increases at a quick pace, and they become increasingly capable of stringing words together in meaningful sentences. (p. 385)

Egocentric   Self-centeredness, which is a characteristic of preoperational children: they are unable to see the world from any point of view but their own. (p. 385)

Conservation   The understanding that specific properties of objects (height, weight, volume, length, width) remain the same despite apparent changes in the shape or arrangement of those objects. (p. 385)

Concrete Operational Period   Piaget's third stage of cognitive development (roughly ages 7 to 11), in which children develop the ability to understand the conservation principle and other logical concepts, such as categorization. (p. 386)

Formal Operational Period   The fourth and final of Piaget's stages, which begins roughly at about age 11. During this stage, individuals first become capable of more formal kinds of abstract thinking and hypothetical reasoning. (p. 387)

417

Moral Development The development of a person's thoughts and actions regarding right and wrong. In Kohlberg's view, an individual's sense of right and wrong changes as he or she mature into an adolescent and then into an adult. (p. 388)

Preconventional Level The first level in Kohlberg's theory of moral development during which children tend to think solely in terms of the immediate consequences of their behavior. The preconventional level has two stages. In Stage 1, children act selfishly and are unable to take into consideration the interests and intentions of others. In Stage 2, children still look after their own interests first, but are sometimes willing to be kind to others, but only because they want others to be kind to them. (p. 388)

Conventional Level The second level in Kohlberg's theory of moral development during which children's moral reasoning becomes subject to conformity. This level also contains two stages. In Stage 3, children are able to understand the intentions that underlie actions and desire approval from others. In Stage 4, children begin to understand law and order. (p. 389)

Postconventional Level The last level of moral development in Kohlberg's theory. This level is concerned mainly with the development of personal values of morality and contains three stages. In Stage 5, people view laws as serving the public interest and are willing to enter into a "social contract" and abide by society's rules for the common good. In Stage 6, people think and act in terms of universal ethical principles such as "reverence for life" and "goodness." In Stage 7, the "cosmic orientation stage," individuals adopt values that transcend society's values and norms. This stage represents the zenith of moral development. (p. 389)

Epigenetic Principle The idea that human development proceeds according to a biologically determined agenda based on two factors, biology and culture. Biological factors exert their influence at critical points (conflicts) during the individual's maturation; the culture in which one lives provides the context in which the individual resolves the conflict. (p. 391)

PRENATAL DEVELOPMENT

Prenatal Period The 9 months between conception and birth. Actually, the length of a normal pregnancy is 266 days or 38 weeks. The prenatal period can be divided into three developmental stages: the ovum, the embryo, and the fetal stages. (p. 394)

Ovum Stage The first of the three stages of prenatal development during which the zygote divides many times and the internal organs begin to form. (p. 394)

Embryonic Stage The second stage of prenatal development, during which the heart begins to beat, the brain starts to function, and most of the major body structures begin to form. This period begins 2 weeks and ends about 8 weeks after conception. (p. 394)

Fetal Stage The third and final stage of prenatal development. This stage lasts for about 7 months, beginning with the appearance of bone and ending with birth. (p. 394)

Fetal Alcohol Syndrome (FAS) The several serious side-effects produced by a pregnant woman's heavy consumption of alcohol on her fetus. These effects include: both pre- and postnatal growth deficits, deformations of the eyes and mouth, brain and central nervous system abnormalities, and deformation of the heart. (p. 396)

INFANCY AND CHILDHOOD

Cephalocaudal Principle The idea that growth of the body proceeds from head to torso to feet; control over the upper body takes place before control over the lower body. This principle helps explain why babies are able to use their arms and hands in moving about the environment before they are able to walk. (p. 398)

Proximodistal Principle The idea that development of the internal organs and torso occurs faster than development of the hands and feet. This principle partially accounts for the fact that infants gain control over their arms before their hands and gain control of their hands before their fingers. (p. 398)

Mass to Specific Principle The idea that control over large groups of muscles that are used in gross body movements develop faster than control over smaller groups of muscles that are used in finer movements. This principle accounts for the fact that infants and young children are not very deft when drawing or scribbling. However, as the nervous system develops, so does control over the small groups of muscles involved in control of the fingers. (p. 398)

Metacognition Self-awareness of one's cognitive processes. Becoming aware of one's own memory and cognitive processes is important because doing so means that individuals have the ability to distinguish what they can remember from what they can't and what they know from what they don't know. (p. 400)

Attachment A social and emotional bond between infant and caregiver that spans both time and space. Attachment is not only the first social relationship that infants experience, it is also, in essence, the first loving relationship that they experience. (p. 400)

Stranger Anxiety A set of fearful responses in infants, such as crying and clinging to their caregiver, in the presence of strangers. Stranger anxiety usually appears in infants between the ages of six and twelve months. (p. 400)

Separation Anxiety A set of fearful responses in infants, such as crying and clinging to their caregivers, when the caregiver attempts to leave the infant's presence. Separation anxiety first appears in infants when they are about 8- to 9-months old and climaxes at about 12 to 16 months. (p. 400)

Secure Attachment A kind of attachment in which infants will use their mothers as a "base" for exploring a new environment. They will venture out from her to explore a strange situation but return periodically. Securely attached infants do become upset when their mothers leave the room, but greet her happily when she returns. (p. 402)

Insecure Attachment A kind of attachment in which an infant is reluctant to explore a new environment, and is likely to cling to the mother in the presence of strangers. He becomes quite upset when the mother leaves, and will remain distressed even upon her return. An infant may be so insecurely attached that he avoids his mother upon her return, preferring a stranger for attention and comfort. (p. 402)

Authoritarian Parents Those who establish firm rules for their children and expect them to be obeyed without question. Disobedience is met with punishment rather than understanding or reasoning. (p. 404)

Permissive Parents Those who establish few rules and who do little to influence the behavior of their children. (p. 404)

Authoritative Parents Those who establish rules and enforce them, but not through punishment alone. Authoritative parents seek to explain the relationship between rules and punishment to their children. In addition, authoritative parents foster independence in their children by encouraging them to know and understand why family rules exist. (p. 404)

Adolescence The period of life spanning the teenage years. It begins with puberty and ends with the establishment of emotional and social independence from parents. (p. 405)

Puberty The sudden maturation of the genitalia that endows each of us with the capacity for sexual reproduction. (p. 405)

Personal Fable The belief that what one thinks and feels is completely new and unique and never before experienced by anyone else. Personal fables tend to center on personal experiences of the individual. (p. 405)

Crisis According to Marcia, a period during which the adolescent struggles intellectually to resolve issues related to personal values and goals. (p. 406)

Commitment According to Marcia, a decision based on consideration of alternative goals and values that leads to a specific course of action—the teenager is "committed" to thinking and acting in a manner consistent with how the crisis has been resolved. (p. 406)

ADULTHOOD AND OLD AGE

Alzheimer's Disease A form of dementia or loss of intellectual ability that affects many people later in life. The disease generally afflicts those who are in their 40s and older, eventually killing them. Typically, thinking, language skills, and especially memory, deteriorate as the disease progresses. (p. 409)

Crystallized Intelligence A kind of intelligence that reflects both formal education and the "seat of the pants" learning that comes in everyday life. Crystallized intelligence reflects knowledge of the world as well as wisdom. (p. 411)

Fluid Intelligence A kind of intelligence that reflects our native capacity for reasoning, problem solving, and remembering. It is not related to one's education and life experiences. Instead, it represents the brain's ability to process information and generate an intelligent response. (p. 411)

ADDITIONAL SOURCES OF INFORMATION

Fitzgerald, H. E., & Walraven, M. G. (1989). *Annual editions: Human development.* Guilford, CT: Duskin. This anthology contains recent popular articles written on a variety of topics related to life-span development including genetic and prenatal influences on development, the role of the brain in childhood development, cultural influences on development, and the effects of loneliness and depression on development.

Kegan, R. (1982). *The evolving self: Problem and process in human development.* Cambridge, MA: Harvard University Press. In this book, Harvard psychologist Robert Kegan combines the views of Piaget, Kohlberg, and Erikson into a new theory of personality and social development. Kegan focuses on how people strive cognitively to make sense of the culture in which they live. Accordingly, he touches upon intellectual, moral, social, and personal issues with which people must deal to become fully psychologically developed individuals.

Kaplan, P. S. (1988). *The human odyssey: Life-span development.* St. Paul, MN: West. A competent and current survey of life-span development.

Schaie, W. K., & Willis, S. L. (1986). *Adult development and learning* (2nd ed.). Boston: Little, Brown. A well-written and thorough introduction to the major issues in studying adult development.

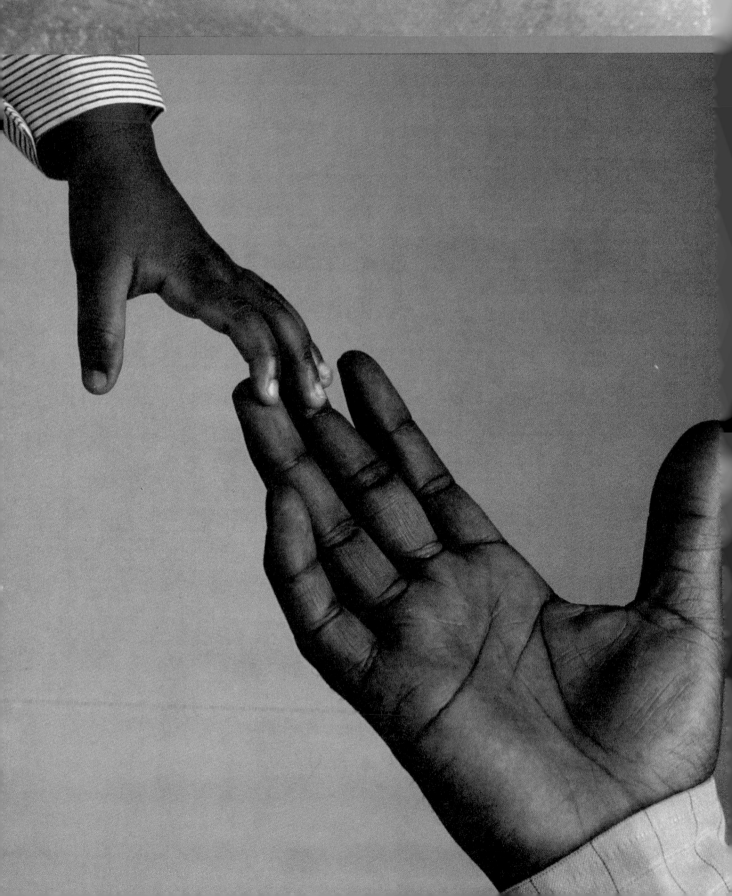

12 Gender Development and Sexual Behavior

Imagine for a few moments how different your life might be if you had been reared in another culture: your language, food, and clothing styles would all differ from that to which you are accustomed. One other aspect of your life that might also be different is your sexual behavior. Suppose, for example, that you had been reared in Inis Beag, a tiny island off the coast of Ireland. From an early age you would have been taught that any sexual activity, particularly sexual intercourse, is repugnant and to be shunned (Messenger, 1972). Adults of both sexes have little understanding of sexual matters, including menstruation, sexual arousal, and conception. Women regard sexual intercourse as a necessary evil and men regard it as being hazardous to their health. Nudity is avoided at all times. Even on those rare occasions when a couple engages in sexual intercourse, both people remain in their underwear. Orgasms among Inis Beag women are virtually unknown, and when they do occur, they are considered abnormal. It is clear that had you grown up on this island, your sexual attitudes and behavior would be quite conservative.

On the other hand, suppose that you had grown up as a Mangaian (Mangaia is one of the Cook Islands of the South Pacific). Early in your teenage years you would have received extensive instruction in sexual matters from an "expert" (Marshall, 1972). Experienced men tutor boys as to how to stimulate the breasts and genitalia of their partners, including how to bring a woman to orgasm several times before reaching their own climaxes. Next, each boy receives "hands on" experience with an older woman who further refines his sexual prowess. Sex education for Mangaian girls follows a similar agenda. Each girl is first trained by an experienced female and then is permitted to apply her newly acquired knowledge with an experienced man. With their training complete, Mangaian teenagers actively pursue members of the opposite sex (with parental blessings), engaging in sexual intercourse daily. Had you been born and raised a Mangaian, your sex life would have been extremely active.

The culture one lives in plays an influential role in determining one's sexual attitudes and behavior: the people of Inis Beag go to great lengths to repress sexual knowledge and behavior; the Mangaians go to great lengths to promote the same. While both perspectives may be found in North America, your own sexual attitudes and experiences probably fall somewhere between these two extremes. The point is that sexual behavior is a major focal point of life. Our own culture is no exception. Witness the tremendous amount of time, money, and nervous energy that we devote to developing and maintaining our sexual attractiveness and dating, the sexual lures with which advertisers bait their products, the multi-billion dollar pornography industry, and the universal importance of marriage and child-rearing.

An important cultural factor influencing sexual behavior, as well as other behaviors is **gender**, or the individual qualities of a person that a given culture uses to define that person as a male or female. Although a person's biological sex, as specified by the sex chromosomes (XX—female or XY—male), is often a critical component of gender, in some instances, a person's gender may or may not be the same as his or her biological sex. For example, some individuals, referred to as hermaphrodites, are genetically one sex, but due to physiological problems during prenatal development, possess the genitalia of the opposite sex. That is, genetically, a person may be a female, but possess the genitalia of a male. If this person is reared in a manner consistent with physical appearance (is given a boy's name, is dressed like a boy, is referred to as a boy, and so on) we would say that that person's sex is female but gender is male. Thus, although gender is influenced by biological variables, it is also influenced by psychological variables. For that reason, the words "gender" and "biological sex" are not

As with other cultures, sexual behavior is an important focal point of life in our culture. The amount of time, money, and energy expended on dating alone illustrates this point.

synonymous. This is an important distinction: remembering it will help you to better understand the contributions of biological and psychological variables to gender.

In this chapter, we focus on two topics: gender development and sexual behavior. Because gender is determined by both biological and psychological factors, we will discuss the role that each plays in gender development. Next, we will look at how natural selection has favored different kinds of sexual behavior for males and females. We will learn, surprisingly, that men and women often differ greatly in their sexual attitudes and behavior. We also describe sexual arousal and sexual dysfunctions. We conclude the chapter by considering sexual attitudes and behavior in our country and some of the important psychological factors that influence their expression.

THE BIOLOGY OF GENDER DEVELOPMENT

Fertilization, the union of a sperm and ovum resulting in conception, sets in motion a series of truly remarkable events. The genetic makeup of the fertilized ovum, or zygote, whether the sex chromosomes it carries are XX or XY, determines the sexual anatomy and physiology of the fetus long before it is born. Further developmental processes occur during puberty. As we will see, the outcome of these processes has profound psychological implications for an individual's sexual attitudes and behavior.

Prenatal Contributions

Early in the prenatal period, the embryo is sexually undifferentiated. The internal genitalia contain a pair of gonads (sex cells). Between 5 and 12 weeks after conception, the gonads begin to develop into either testes, the male sex glands that produce sperm, or ovaries, the female sex glands that produce ova. Once the gonads differentiate, a process determined completely by the presence or absence of the Y sex chromosome (XY for male and XX for female), the sex chromosomes exert no further control over sexual differentiation (Money & Ehrhardt, 1972). Further sexual differentiation is controlled by hormones, highly specialized chemical substances secreted by the glands of the body's endocrine system, in this case, the testes and ovaries. The testes produce androgens, the most important of which is testosterone, and the ovaries produce estrogens. Both male and female fetuses produce testosterone, but the male fetus produces more than the female fetus.

Prenatal sexual differentiation generally occurs 5 to 7 weeks after conception in males, and usually 11 to 12 weeks in females. In males, secretion of androgens causes internal male genitalia to form. In females, the relative absence of androgens results in the formation of the internal female genitalia. By the fourth prenatal month the external genitalia of the fetus is generally developed enough to reveal its sex. If testes of the prenatal male fail to develop or otherwise malfunction, secretion of androgens is retarded, causing internal female genitalia to develop. Only if androgen is present will male sexual differentiation take place.

What happens if female fetuses are exposed to androgens? The answer lies in a particular quirk in the prenatal development of some female fetuses known as adrenogenital syndrome. This disorder occurs when the adrenal glands secrete considerable amounts of androgens causing masculinization of the external genitalia of female fetuses. Does androgen affect more than just development of the external genitalia? Does it also affect behavior—will androgenized females behave in masculine ways? The

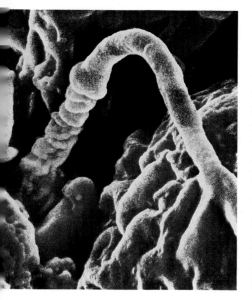

Of the many sperm that are ejaculated, only one can fertilize an egg. Shown here is a sperm penetrating an egg's plasma membrane.

answers have been provided by John Money, who studied the interests of females who either suffered from adrenogenital syndrome or who had been inadvertently exposed to an androgen-like hormone (a drug given to their mothers to prevent miscarriage) and so had become androgenized. Money found that compared to control groups of normal girls, androgenized females preferred playing with boys rather than girls, preferred vigorous athletic activities to less vigorous ones, and considered themselves to be tomboys (Money & Ehrhardt, 1972). Although Money's findings are intriguing, you should be a bit cautious in accepting them. Perhaps parental reaction helped shape their daughter's masculine attitudes and behavior. Thus, the question of whether exposure to androgens causes some females to acquire masculine characteristics remains open.

In sum, one's biological sex is determined well before birth and according to the presence or absence of androgens. If androgens are present, male genitalia develop, otherwise, female genitalia develop. We now turn to a discussion of biological factors that affect gender during puberty.

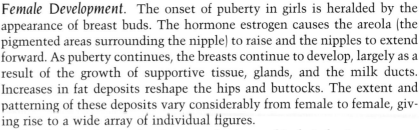

B *iological sex is determined well before birth and according to the presence or absence of androgens.*

Puberty

Each of us embarks upon adulthood in our own way and in our own time. Becoming sexually mature is not something that we choose to do, nor is it something that we can put off, even though we may not be quite ready for it. **Puberty**, as you may recall from the last chapter, is the sudden growth and maturation of the genitalia that endows each of us with the capacity for sexual reproduction. It is an awkward stage of life for most of us. We seem to be not quite finished with the pleasures and delights of childhood before we find ourselves capable of producing children of our own.

Girls generally begin puberty between the ages of 8 and 12, nearly two years, on average, before boys. In both sexes, the onset of puberty is due to the influence that two brain structures, the hypothalamus and pituitary gland, exert over the gonads (testes in males and ovaries in females). The hypothalamus stimulates the pituitary gland to produce two hormones, **follicle-stimulating hormone (FSH)** and **luteinizing hormone (LH)**. In males, FSH stimulates the manufacture of sperm and LH stimulates production of testosterone by the testes. In females, FSH prepares the ovaries for ovulation and LH stimulates ovulation, the monthly release of mature ova from the ovaries, one at a time. Because these hormones affect males and females differently, we will discuss male and female development separately. The pubertal changes for both sexes are summarized in Table 12.1.

The transition from childhood to adulthood progresses a little differently in everyone and is an equally awkward time for both boys and girls. The onset of puberty for girls generally occurs 2 years before it begins for boys.

Female Development. The onset of puberty in girls is heralded by the appearance of breast buds. The hormone estrogen causes the areola (the pigmented areas surrounding the nipple) to raise and the nipples to extend forward. As puberty continues, the breasts continue to develop, largely as a result of the growth of supportive tissue, glands, and the milk ducts. Increases in fat deposits reshape the hips and buttocks. The extent and patterning of these deposits vary considerably from female to female, giving rise to a wide array of individual figures.

Shortly after breast development begins, pubic hair begins to grow. About two years later, axillary (underarm) hair appears. Between the ages of 9 and 14, girls experience a tremendous growth spurt. The female growth spurt generally ends before the male growth spurt (see Figure 12.1).

TABLE 12.1. *Some physical changes in males and females during puberty.*

| | GIRLS | | | BOYS | |
Characteristic	Age of first appearance (years)	Major hormonal influence	Characteristic	Age of first appearance (years)	Major hormonal influence
1. Growth of breasts	8–13	Pituitary growth hormone, estrogens, progesterone	1. Growth of testes	10–13.5	Pituitary growth hormone, testosterone
2. Growth of pubic hair	8–14	Adrenal androgens	2. Growth of pubic hair	10–15	Testosterone
3. Body growth	9.5–14.5	Pituitary growth hormone, androgens, estrogens	3. Body growth	10.5–16	Pituitary growth hormone, testosterone
4. Menarche	10–16.5	FSH, LH, estrogens, progesterone	4. Growth of penis	11–14.5	Testosterone
			5. Change in voice (growth of larynx)	About the same time as penis growth	Testosterone
5. Underarm hair	About two years after pubic hair	Androgens	6. Facial and underarm hair	About two years after pubic hair	Testosterone

After B. Goldstein, (1976) *Introduction to human sexuality* New York McGraw-Hill, pp. 80–81.

While the girl's physical appearance is undergoing significant change, her reproductive system is also developing rapidly. Estrogen causes the ovaries to enlarge and other genital structures to mature. Internally, the uterus (the cavity where the fetus grows) enlarges, as do the cervix (the lower part of the uterus), fallopian tubes (the tubes running between the uterus and ovary through which ova are transported), and the vagina (the cylindrical cavity through which the baby passes during birth). Externally, the labia minora (the inner lips surrounding the vaginal opening) and labia majora (the tissue that surrounds the vaginal opening and inner lips) thicken. Androgens produced by the adrenal glands cause the clitoris to enlarge and become more sensitive to tactile stimulation. The clitoris is a highly sensitive organ located in front of and just above the vaginal opening that develops from the same type of embryonic tissue as the penis.

At about age 13, girls experience **menarche**, their first menstruation. Menstruation is the result of monthly fluctuations of sex hormones that regulate ovulation. If an ovum is not fertilized, the tissues and substances lining the uterine wall that would support the developing fetus had fertilization occurred, are shed through the vagina.

Psychologically, menarche is an extremely important event in the lives of young girls. If girls are not prepared for menarche, the event is marked by surprise and possibly negative reactions such as shame and embarrassment. If a girl is properly informed about the significant life transition that menarche represents, her reaction is more likely to be positive with feelings of pride, excitement, and an increased sense of womanliness (Greif & Ulman, 1982; Woods, Dery, & Most, 1983). Soon after menarche, girls begin to view themselves as young women and behave with increasing independence from their parents.

In the United States as well as in other countries, the average age at which girls experience menarche has been declining steadily. For example, in 1920, the average age of menarche for American girls was about 14 years;

by 1960, the average had dropped to less than 13 years. At present, the trend has appeared to level off at around 12-1/2 years. The age at which menstruation begins varies from girl to girl. It is not uncommon for menarche to appear as early as age 10 or as late as 17.

What factors control the onset of menarche? One theory, the percent of body fat hypothesis (Fishman, 1980; Frisch & McArthur, 1974), suggests that the percentage of body fat must reach a certain level for menarche to occur and remain at or above that level for menstruation to continue. Hence, girls low in body fat may experience menarche later than girls high in body fat. This hypothesis may also account for the cessation of menstruation in female distance runners and women who suffer from anorexia nervosa. Once the percentage of body fat falls below some critical level, the menstrual cycle is interrupted and will not begin again until the percentage of body fat exceeds that level.

A woman's sexual desire has been shown to be positively correlated with characteristics of the menstrual cycle, particularly increases in body temperature. In one study (Stanislaw & Rice, 1988), over a thousand women recorded their level of sexual desire, body temperature, frequency of sexual intercourse, and their menstrual cycle daily for two years. About 57 percent of the women reported increases in sexual desire a few days prior to increases in their body temperature. Women had sexual intercourse more often during periods of sexual desire than periods during which sexual desire was not reported. This is an interesting finding because this is when ovulation usually begins; ovulation, of course, is the point in the menstrual cycle during which fertilization may occur. As the researchers suggested, this finding raises the possibility that both psychological (sexual desire) and biological (ovulation) aspects of sexual behavior are controlled by a common hormonal process.

In sum, menarche represents an important transitional stage in female gender development. Menarche signals the beginning of a female's sexual maturity; in some girls, menarche may be accompanied by psychological

FIGURE 12.1
Growth patterns for males and females. The female growth spurt begins before the male growth spurt.

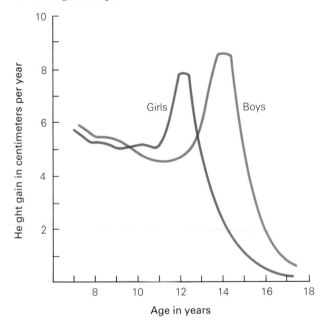

changes concerning femininity as they attempt to deal with the physical changes they are experiencing. As we shall see next, male sexual development involves a very different series of events.

Male Development.   For boys, the hormonal changes that herald the onset of sexual maturity generally begin between the ages of 10 and 11. FSH and LH stimulate the testes to produce testosterone, the hormone that is chiefly responsible for pubertal changes in males. The first sign of puberty is growth of the penis, testes, and scrotum. About two years later, pubic hair appears. Facial and underarm hair do not generally appear until about age 15 or 16.

Between the ages of 13 and 14, several important developments occur. First, the testes have now nearly doubled in size and are producing large amounts of testosterone. In turn, testosterone begins to stimulate growth of both internal and external genitalia, including the penis, testes, seminal vesicles (the two sacs that contribute fluids that help activate sperm), and the prostate (the gland that secretes most of the substances contained in semen, the fluid ejaculated from the penis during orgasm). Second, the growth spurt, also stimulated by increased testosterone levels, begins. The male growth spurt may continue until the male is in his late teens (see Figure 12.1). Third, testosterone stimulates growth of the larynx (the "voice box") causing the voice to deepen. Boys castrated before puberty will have high pitched voices for the rest of their lives. (During the height of great European choirs in the eighteenth century, boys with particularly fine sopranic voices were castrated so they would sing this way throughout their lives.) Fourth and perhaps most important, the prostate begins to produce enough fluids for males to become capable of ejaculation. Although males at this age are now able to experience both orgasm and ejaculation, they are not generally fertile until a year or so later when FSH begins to stimulate production of mature sperm. Although boys do not experience an equivalent to menarche, they do occasionally have a nocturnal emission or wet dream, which has a similiar psychological significance. Wet dreams involve the ejaculation of seminal fluids during dreams involving sexual content. If uninformed about wet dreams, the boy may find the ejaculation unusual or even worry about whether he is ill (Masters, Johnson, & Kolodny, 1988).

Biological Changes in Later Life

Under normal circumstances and barring pregnancy, women, on average, menstruate monthly until they are around 47 years of age. At about this time, women experience dramatic physical changes. The ovaries become less responsive to FSH and ovulation becomes irregular. Eventually, the ovaries stop functioning altogether resulting in infertility and the end of the menstrual cycle. The cessation of the menstrual cycle is known as **menopause**. Menopause is accompanied by decreased estrogen and progesterone production, which in turn, causes specific physical changes. Reduction of estrogen causes the vaginal walls to become thinner and lose their elasticity, and the mucous membranes in the vaginal walls dry up, reducing lubrication during sexual arousal. Either of these vaginal changes may cause pain during sexual intercourse. The labia become rigid, and the breasts lose their firmness. Many women also experience "hot flashes," a sudden sensation of heat spreading rapidly over the body. Reddening of the skin and severe perspiration often accompany these flashes. Hot flashes may last for only a few seconds or up to a half hour, and may occur only occasionally or several times a day.

Menopause represents a major transitional period in every woman's life and is sometimes accompanied by psychological changes, including depression, anxiety, irritability, and sadness about the inevitable end of the child bearing years. There is some question, however, as to whether this period of life is any more psychologically difficult than the other phases of a woman's life, including puberty (Neugarten & Kraines, 1965). Some women, in fact, show renewed sexual vitality after menopause and an increased capacity for orgasm (Hallstrom, 1979; Starr & Weiner, 1981).

Males do not experience a physiological equivalent to the female menopause, although they may experience physiological difficulties in sexual arousal. By middle age, many males require more time to get an erection while being sexually stimulated. Some middle-aged men, perhaps as many as 35 percent (Russman, 1980) become impotent—they are unable to have or maintain an erection at least 25 percent of the time they wish to have one (Masters & Johnson, 1970). Unlike the production of ova in females, the production of sperm remains fairly constant over most of a male's lifetime, decreasing only slightly with age. Even in very old age men may still be fertile.

Biology and Gender in Perspective

There can be little doubt that biological factors play a major role in determining gender: our biological sex is determined by the sex chromosomes that we inherit from our parents. Gender, the social category of male or female, is almost always determined by biological sex, and for the majority of people, that means that gender matches biological sex. The chromosomes exert their masculizing or feminizing effects by coding for hormones that influence the development of physical characteristics during prenatal development. But biology alone does not determine the extent to which an individual develops masculine or feminine qualities. Once the baby is born, a variety of environmental factors play host to gender development; experience augments and extends the process of gender development initiated 9 months before by the union of the egg and sperm. Let's look now at the role of experience in gender development.

PSYCHOLOGICAL ASPECTS OF GENDER DEVELOPMENT

FIGURE 12.2
Is this baby a boy or a girl?

Look carefully at the infant shown in Figure 12.2. Can you tell if it is a boy or a girl? Suppose we gave you a hint—this infant is aggressive, moody, likes balls, and is stubborn. On the other hand, suppose we said that this infant likes dolls, is very sweet, and smiles a lot. In the first case, you would probably say that the infant is a boy, and in the second case, a girl. Why? Because these are the kinds of differences in personality and behavior we expect of males and females, respectively. In other words, we tend to form stereotyped ideas, based on our personal experiences with members of both sexes, of what it means to be a boy or a girl, and a man or a woman.

Suppose that in reality, the infant in the photo is a girl. How will she come to view herself? Will she apply the same stereotypes to herself? Although biologically she is a female, to what degree will she view herself as a female? Will her private sense of her own gender match the expectations others hold for her?

This example points up the complex interplay of biological, personal, and cultural factors that influence how we and others come to view our sexuality. Psychologists who study this developmental process have found

Gender roles today and our views of them have changed significantly from the way they were 30 years ago. Society's expectations of a woman's place being at home is no longer the case, since many women are pursuing careers outside the home and in areas formerly dominated by men, such as construction. Similarly, more men are participating in domestic roles.

it useful to distinguish among three concepts: gender identity, gender typing, and gender roles.

Gender identity is the individual's private sense of being a male or female. In most cases, one's gender identity matches one's biological sex. The learning of the attitudes and behaviors appropriate to their gender identity is called **gender typing**. Cultural expectations about the ways in which men and women should think and behave are referred to as **gender roles**. Let's take a closer look at each of these concepts, starting with gender roles.

Gender Roles

Gender roles constitute a cultural reaction to the biological sex of an individual. A given culture expects biological males to behave in masculine ways and biological females to behave in feminine ways. Exactly what is meant by "masculine" and "feminine" varies from culture to culture. In most aboriginal cultures, men do the hunting and protect the tribe; women tend children and gather nongame food. In more sophisticated cultures like ours, men and women may both pursue political or professional careers, although more women than men tend children. Notions of femininity and masculinity have also changed with time—a point that underscores the social nature of gender development. For example, 30 years ago, women in the United States were expected to stay at home and take care of various "domestic duties." Now in the 1990s, despite the fact that many women still occupy this role, cultural expectations of the woman's (and the man's) place in the home and workplace have changed. A greater percentage of women than ever before are pursuing professional careers (Astin, 1987), and more men are participating in domestic roles (Pleck, 1987).

Even for individuals, gender roles may change from time to time, depending on the circumstances. For example, consider a widely cited study conducted by Mark Zanna and Susan Pack (1975). Female undergraduates were asked to describe themselves on questionnaires that included both stereotypical feminine and masculine traits. Once the questionnaires were completed, the women were divided into two groups. The first group was told that they were going to be introduced to a tall, attractive, "unattached" male who has a car and is interested in meeting women. The second group was told that they were going to be introduced to a short, young male who has a girlfriend and no car. Next, half of the women in each group were told that the male had traditional gender role expectations for women, such as "home-oriented" and "emotional." The remaining subjects in both groups were told that the male had nonstereotypical views of female gender roles, such as independence, competitiveness, and ambitiousness. The women were then asked to rate their traits for a second time and to take an aptitude test of their general cognitive abilities; they were told that the male would be given the results of the questionnaire and aptitude test. What Zanna and Pack wanted to know was whether their subjects would describe themselves differently the second time, given the information about the male.

Zanna and Pack's results supported the hypothesis that individuals will adjust their descriptions of their gender roles to fit the situation. The group of women who were told that they would meet the attractive male with stereotypical female values modified their self-ratings to appear more traditional. The other group of women who were told they would meet either an attractive male with nontraditional values or the unattractive male made fewer alterations in their self-ratings. How did the women compare in terms of their performance on the aptitude tests? The women who were led to believe they were going to meet an attractive male with traditional values performed worse than did the other women. The researchers attributed this finding to the idea that the women who were to meet the attractive male wanted to appear nonthreatening. Zanna and Pack's research points out that our beliefs about what others expect of us may alter the kind of situational gender roles we adopt. Indeed, one recent theory of gender proposes that gender-related behaviors may be the product of a dynamic and complex interaction of situational variables, individual goals, and others' expectations (Deaux & Major, 1987).

But how do we learn which gender roles to adopt in the first place? The few crosscultural comparisons given above, along with Zanna and Pack's study, suggest that people learn and adopt gender roles because of the way they are socialized. To better understand how socialization processes influence gender role development, we need to take a closer look at gender identity and gender typing.

Gender Identity and Gender Typing

Most psychologists agree that gender identity is determined by the time one is 3 or 4 years old, and once determined, it is difficult to change (Doyle, 1985). Likewise, most researchers agree that gender identity is probably due more to social factors than to biological factors (Ehrhardt & Meyer-Bahlburg, 1981). Generally speaking, if children are reared as females, they will identify themselves as females and adopt female gender roles. Similarly, children will identify themselves as males if they are reared as males and adopt male gender roles.

Most psychologists agree that gender identity is determined by the time one is 3 to 4 years old, and once determined, it is difficult to change.

A child is almost always assigned a gender on the basis of his or her biological sex. Recall though, that due to hormonal imbalances, some children are born with ambiguous-looking genitalia (that is, on the basis of physical appearances alone, accurate judgment of biological sex is unclear). How do these children develop their gender identities? Like normal children, gender identity is based on the social assignment to one category or the other. This is true even if the assigned gender is opposite that specified

Children are gender typed at an early age by various parts of our culture, including home, school, and the media. All of these factors work together to influence children. Girls playing dress up and boys playing with trucks are examples of traditional gender roles that children have adopted throughout the years.

by the sex chromosomes (Ehrhardt & Money, 1967). For example, a child who is genetically a female but reared as a male, will generally adopt the identity of a male, which means that social and psychological factors can, in some situations, override the contributions of biology to gender role development.

Early in childhood we are gender typed: we learn attitudes and behaviors that are more or less consistent with our gender identities. Who says which attitudes and behaviors are appropriate to one gender or the other? Generally, the culture in which one is reared. For most of us, the major institutions involved in this socialization process are home, school, and the media. Parents' views on what they consider to be appropriate gender-related behavior and values influence the gender roles adopted by their children (Repetti, 1984). In school, the books from which children learn to read may be biased toward traditional gender roles for boys and girls (Women on Words and Images, 1972). Mere common sense tells us that many television programs and commercials portray males and females in certain gender roles: some women swoon over the scent of their dishwasher detergent, others direct board meetings; some men debate the qualities of beer and others change diapers. Portrayals of men and women in these roles may or may not reinforce the kinds of gender-related attitudes and behaviors that children learn at home and in school.

Some people do not develop a gender identity that is consistent with either their biological gender or their assigned gender. For instance, a man may feel that he is actually a woman trapped in a man's body, or a woman may feel that she is actually a man trapped in a woman's body. A person with these kinds of feelings is considered to be a **transsexual**. Although the exact number of people who might identify themselves as transsexuals is unknown, there appear to be more men who feel like they are women than vice-versa (Carrera 1981).

Simply put, transsexuals do not like their bodies. They view their bodies as barriers to obtaining both sexual and emotional gratification. For example, a transsexual who is biologically a male is attracted, both sexually and emotionally, to other biological males. He may even have fantasies about having sexual relations with other men. Because he views himself as a woman, he will not have a homosexual relationship with a man; he sees himself as a woman having a heterosexual relationship with a man.

Transsexual James Morris, an English writer and mountain climber, resolved his conflict between biological gender and perceived sex through a sex-change operation. Now Jan Morris, she has written a book describing the transformation.

To render their bodies consistent with their emotional and sexual feelings, some transsexuals undergo sex-change surgery. Because physical alterations from sex-change surgery are irreversible, many physicians require their clients to undergo a trial period in which the transsexual adopts the opposite gender role: he or she begins living publicly as a member of the opposite sex. If the transsexual is a woman, she is treated with testosterone, which increases facial and body hair, deepens her voice, and inhibits menstruation. Male transsexuals are treated with estrogen, which softens their skin and stimulates breast growth. During the trial period, the transsexual periodically undergoes psychological evaluations. If the transsexual appears stable and has adjusted psychologically to adopting the lifestyle of the desired gender, he or she is given clearance for the surgery. How does sex-change surgery affect the life of the transsexual? The answer to this question is not clear. One study (Sorenson, 1981) showed that 20 percent of people who underwent the surgery regretted their decision. A more recent study (Lindemalm, Korlin, & Uddenberg, 1986) found that more than half of their 13 subjects showed no psychological improvement as a result of the surgery.

Theories of Gender Typing

Gender typing then, is usually, but not always, linked to a culture's expectations of male and female attitudes and behavior, that is, their gender roles.

In 1933, Sigmund Freud theorized that by the time a child reaches school age, he or she identifies with the same-gender parent. That is, the child begins to view the world and behave toward others from the perspective of the same-gender parent. Accordingly, girls want to grow up to be just like mom, and boys want to be just like dad. Modern-day psychologists have discovered, however, that children become gender typed long before they are off to school, and that children who grow up in single parent homes become appropriately gender typed although the same sex parent may not live with them. Since Freud, three other theories have been proposed to explain gender typing and the development of gender roles.

Social Learning Theory. According to social learning theory, femininity and masculinity are characteristics of our personalities that are learned through observation and reinforcement. Social learning theorists hold that children are rewarded for learning, usually through imitation, gender appropriate attitudes and behaviors. Likewise, behavior inappropriate to gender is punished. Other psychologists hold that children become gender typed based on the way they learn to think about describing their own behaviors. These psychologists subscribe to the cognitive-developmental theory of gender typing.

In social learning theory, it is believed that children learn gender-appropriate attitudes and behaviors by observation and reinforcement, such as boys observing men playing soccer.

Cognitive-Developmental Theory. Developmental theorists such as Lawrence Kohlberg (1966) maintain that children play an active role in gender typing themselves. Indeed, the language of most cultures requires children to know the difference between masculine and feminine pronouns. Children identify themselves and their actions according to their gender and begin to identify others as males or females and categorize their thoughts and actions on the same basis. Once their gender identity is firmly rooted in their personalities, children begin to relate to others solely within the context of that identity.

Critics of cognitive-developmental theory raise two questions. First, why do children choose gender to divide up their worlds—why not something else, such as body size or hair color (Bem, 1985)? Second, why do females tend to value male activities and events as well as their own and why do males tend to devalue female activities and events?

Gender Schema Theory. This theory, proposed by Sandra Bem (1985), represents a combination of both cognitive-developmental and social learning theories. According to this view, children actively develop concepts or schemas of their environments—a view consistent with cognitive-developmental theory. The substance of those schemas, in this case the attitudes and behaviors associated with gender, are learned through social interaction—a view consistent with social learning theory. However, gender schema theory differs from these two theories in that it holds that culture mandates which schemas are right and which are wrong. Thus, gender schema theory provides answers to the two questions posed by critics of cognitive-developmental theory. First, in some cultures such as in India, gender is not the schema that children use to organize their attitudes and actions. Rather, class and caste are. Who says so? The culture. How does the culture enforce its will? By rewarding culture-appropriate schemas and punishing inappropriate ones. Second, our own society has long tended to value male activities and events more than female ones. Thus, the gender schemas of both sexes generally follow suit.

Bem's research has also led her to the conclusion that not all gender schemas are exclusively male or female. Some people's schemas include both masculine and feminine qualities. Some women are not only emotionally warm and empathetic but they can also be ambitious and assertive. Likewise, males may possess characteristics traditionally described as feminine. Some men are not only kind and caring but they can also be competitive and independent. People who have both masculine and feminine schemas are said to be androgynous. Androgynous individuals are not any better psychologically adjusted than others who are more or less strongly masculine or feminine (Taylor & Hall, 1982). However, both males and females who possess traditionally masculine traits have positive self-concepts. This suggests that, in our culture anyway, having a positive self-concept may have its roots in the extent to which a person possesses traditionally masculine traits. Note, though, that there is no evidence to support the opposite: negative self-concepts are not likely to be based on the degree to which one possesses traditionally feminine traits. In fact, feminine qualities such as sensitivity and warmth are valuable, if not essential, to developing strong and satisfying interpersonal relationships (Kurdek & Schmitt, 1986).

In sum, we learn at a very early age to *identify* ourselves as males or females. As we interact with our social environments, we learn which attitudes and behaviors are appropriate to that identity. We come to judge or type our thoughts, feelings, and actions as more or less masculine or feminine. In essence, we view our sexuality in terms of how well our actual attitudes and behaviors mesh with our culture's expectations or gender roles. At birth we inherit a blueprint that outlines our biological sex and, to a certain extent, our physical development. But it is the culture in which we live that constructs the raw materials into final form. Biology provides the blueprint from which culture then fashions the behavioral patterns characteristic of a man or a woman.

Gender Differences

Our culture is filled with a plenitude of stereotypes about differences in personal qualities and abilities between males and females. A stereotype is a belief that people possess certain qualities and characteristics because of their membership in a particular group. A listing of common stereotypes of masculine and feminine characteristics and behaviors are given in Table 12.2. In general, these stereotypes are more flattering toward men than women: men are stereotyped to be more competent, independent, decisive, and logical (Broverman et al., 1972). Interestingly, the thousands of psychological studies that have examined gender differences do not confirm most stereotypes. In fact, the research shows that in terms of psychological characteristics, males and females are more alike than different. Psychological research has also uncovered two genuine differences between the sexes. The first concerns cognitive abilities and the second, social behaviors. Next, we take a closer look at these differences.

Cognitive Abilities. In terms of the kind of cognitive ability that intelligence tests are designed to measure, men and women do not differ. They do differ in terms of specific kinds of cognitive abilities such as mathematics, spatial relations, and verbal skills.

Starting during adolescence, males are more likely to outscore females on tests of mathematical ability (Holden, 1987). The difference is a small one and may reflect only achievement (Hogrebe, 1987). If differences in aptitude are slight, why then do boys tend to do better than girls on math tests? At least one researcher (Eccles, 1987) believes the answer is because gender roles influence academic interests and decisions: parents orient sons toward science-related classes and daughters toward humanities-related courses.

TABLE 12.2.   *Commonly held stereotypes of men and women.*

FEMININE CHARACTERISTIC BELIEVED TO BE BETTER:

Feminine	Masculine
Very tactful	Not very tactful
Very gentle	Very rough
Expresses feeling of warmth	Does not express feelings of warmth
Very quiet	Boisterous
Considerate of others' feelings	Not considerate of others' feelings

MASCULINE CHARACTERISTICS BELIEVED TO BE BETTER:

Feminine	Masculine
Not competitive	Very competitive
Dependent upon others	Very independent
Unambitious	Ambitious
Home-oriented; no business skills	Worldly; business skills
Passive and submissive	Active and aggressive

From Braverman et al., 1972.

Males also tend to outperform females on tests of spatial abilities, such as mentally representing objects and then manipulating those representations. Spatial abilities are tapped when we attempt to imagine how to get from one place in town to another or when we attempt to arrange neatly all of our belongings. Gender differences in spatial ability emerge during early adolescence and remain constant throughout adolescence and adulthood (Halpern, 1986).

Until recently, it was thought that females were superior to males on tests of verbal ability such as spelling, vocabulary, and reading comprehension. But, in their analysis of 165 studies on gender differences in verbal ability reported since 1973, Janet Shibley Hyde and Marcia Linn (1988) found no substantial differences in verbal ability between males and females. In their own words, ". . . the magnitude of gender difference in verbal ability is currently so small that it can effectively be considered to be zero" (p. 64).

Social Behavior. A social behavior that shows large gender differences is aggression; males are consistently reported to be more aggressive than females from childhood through adulthood (Hyde, 1984; 1986). Men also outnumber women in committing violent crimes. However, researchers are not sure if this gender difference is biologically based or is due to masculine gender role. There is evidence to support both interpretations. Boys are played with rougher than girls; they also are given more physical punishment than are girls (Maccoby & Jacklin, 1974). Recall, too, that Bandura's social learning research showed that aggression can be learned through observation, and in our culture, more men than women tend to model aggressive behavior. Yet, aggressiveness is a psychological characteristic for which there seems to be a strong genetic component.

Are males really better at math and spatially oriented tasks than females? Are males truly more aggressive than females? Perhaps. On the average (average is the key word here). We view gender differences in cognitive abilities and social behavior with a healthy dose of skepticism because studies of gender differences report their findings in terms of group averages rather than in terms of individuals. This means that on the average, gender differences exist in one of two directions: either males display a trait more often or in a greater quantity than women or vice versa. However, at the level of the individual, those differences may or may not exist or they may exist in the opposite direction. Whether they do exist or not depends upon the individual in question. On the average, do men tend to be more aggressive than women? Absolutely. At the individual level, are there certain women who tend to be more aggressive than particular men? Again, the answer is absolutely. Perhaps by focusing on the actual behavior of individual subjects instead of average behavior of large groups, the diversity (and similarity) would become more apparent and meaningful. So what can we conclude about gender differences? Just this: Gender differences do exist, but to be meaningful they must be interpreted at the level of the individual.

Studies reveal that males tend to be more aggressive than do females from childhood through adulthood. Whether this difference is biologically based or related to masculine gender role is still uncertain, although there is evidence to support both views.

GENDER AND SEXUAL BEHAVIOR

An individual's biological sex is defined according to whether one has the potential to produce ova, which are large gametes (the sex cells), or sperm, which are smaller gametes. Females, of course, produce the larger gametes (ova) whereas males produce the smaller gametes (sperm). *An individual's biological sex is defined solely on the basis of this distinction and nothing else, including physical appearance.*

According to evolutionary theory, whether one is an ova producer or sperm producer defines the gender-specific means by which one goes about choosing a mate and maximizing reproductive success. The fundamental asymmetry in gender-specific behavior between the sexes has been aptly expressed by sociobiologists Martin Daly and Margo Wilson:

> Although each parent contributes almost equally to the genetic resources of the new creature they create, not all contributions are equitable. The female provides the raw materials for the early differentiation and growth of their progeny. Here, at the very fundament of sexuality, is love's labor divided, and it is the female who contributes the most.
>
> (1978, p. 48)

As far as our own species is concerned, there can be little doubt that the costs associated with sexual behavior (and reproduction) are higher for women than for men. First, women have fewer opportunities than men to reproduce. Generally, women produce only one ovum every month whereas men produce vast quantities of sperm over substantially shorter time intervals. Second, women carry the fertilized ovum in their bodies for 9 months, continuously diverting a substantial portion of their own metabolic resources away from their own bodies to nourish the fetus. Women also assume all the risks that accompany pregnancy and childbirth, including considerable physical discomfort and possible illnesses that can stem from pregnancy. Third, after the child is born, they may continue to devote their metabolic resources to the infant through breast-feeding, and just as importantly, they usually devote more time and physical energy than fathers to caring for the newborn.

In addition, a woman can bear only so many children in a lifetime, regardless of the number of different men with whom she mates; but a man is limited in his reproductive success only by the number of females he impregnates. For example, if a woman became pregnant once a year for ten years, she would have 10 children, only a fraction of the number of children that a man is capable of fathering. Suppose that a man had intercourse with, and impregnated, a different woman every month for the same period—he would have fathered 120 children! This example is hardly an exaggeration. According to the *Guiness Book of World Records*, the largest number of live births credited to one woman is 69 (she had several sets of twins and triplets). In contrast, King Ismail of Morocco is reported to have fathered 1056 children!

It is little wonder that females generally tend to be more careful than males in selecting a mate, and that males generally tend to be more sexually promiscuous than females (Barash, 1982). Sociobiologists hold that such behavior is the cornerstone by which each sex maximizes its reproductive success, as measured in number of offspring produced (Barash, 1982; Daly & Wilson, 1978). Keep in mind, though, that most people neither court mates nor measure their reproductive success in terms of the total number of children they produce. Rather, they think of reproductive success in terms of rearing healthy, happy, and well-adjusted children. Although most people in our country have the biological capacity to produce a large number of children, many do not have the psychological and financial wherewithal to do so. Others fear that a large family would interfere with career goals and other life aspirations; still others simply do not wish to have any children at all. Sociobiologists refer to reproductive success in describing sexual aspects of our biological adaptiveness to the environment. In general, however, sociobiological theories do not consider the prevailing psychological and cultural factors that may influence the desire to have children.

There is no question, though, that in line with sociobiological theory, males and females differ with respect to sexual behavior. Men tend to

For most people, reproductive success is measured in terms of raising healthy, happy children, not by the biological capacity to produce many children.

*O*ur biological heritage endows us with the tendency to behave sexually in a gender-specific manner. How we actually behave, though, depends upon how the environment . . . interacts with that biological heritage.

engage in premarital sexual intercourse more often than do females (Kinsey, Pomeroy, & Martin, 1948; Kinsey, Pomeroy, Martin, & Gebhard, 1953; Hunt, 1974), although this gap seems to be decreasing (Wolfe, 1980). Men also tend to have more premarital sexual partners (Kinsey et al., 1953; Hunt, 1974; Sigusch & Schmidt, 1973) and more extramarital partners than do women (Symons, 1979; Hite, 1981). Unmarried women tend to desire long-term sexual relationships (Tavris & Sadd, 1977; Hite, 1974, 1976) while unmarried men tend to prefer more diversity and casualness in their sexual relationships (Schofield, 1965; Kinsey et al., 1953). Generally speaking, males show greater diversity in their number of sexual partners than do females.

Natural selection, then, seems to have favored different kinds of sexual behavior based solely on biological sex. In our evolutionary past, females who carefully selected a mate produced more offspring than those who were less choosy. Males who were successful in mating with a number of females produced more offspring than males who mated with fewer females. From an evolutionary perspective, females tend to be interested in the quality of their offspring, which, of course, will be influenced by the quality of their father, and in the resources he controls. Males, on the other hand, tend to be interested in sheer quantity of matings. Again keep in mind that human sexual behavior, although a product of natural selection, is also subject to strong control by cultural factors. For example, compare the sexual behavior of the average Mangaian with your own; it is surely different, but not due to a strict biological imperative. Evolutionary theory holds that our biological heritage endows us with the tendency to behave sexually in a gender-specific manner. How we actually behave, though, depends upon how the environment—important personal, social, and cultural factors—interacts with that biological heritage.

BIOLOGICAL BASES OF THE HUMAN SEXUAL RESPONSE

Despite differences in their reproductive systems and sex-related behavior, men and women have similar physiological responses during sexual arousal. Most of what we know about the physiology of the human sexual response is due to the pioneering research of William Masters and Virginia Johnson. Their research program began in 1954 at Washington University in St. Louis but did not attract widespread public attention until twelve years later when they published their best-selling book, *Human Sexual Response* (Masters & Johnson, 1966). The book reported the analysis of over 10,000 cycles of sexual arousal and orgasm in 694 people (312 males and 382 females). These volunteers were mostly married couples who were willing and able to produce orgasms, either through masturbation or intercourse, while attached to a battery of recording instruments and in full view of Masters and Johnson's research staff. Based on this research, Masters and Johnson have developed a biological model of sexual arousal that is widely accepted today. Let's take a close at their model.

The Masters and Johnson Model

Masters and Johnson identified two important physiological processes that occur in both sexes during sexual arousal, vasocongestion and myotonia. **Vasocongestion** is the flow of blood into a region of the body, in this case the genital area. **Myotonia** refers to muscle contractions. According to Masters and Johnson, vasocongestion and myotonia are the primary events

Virginia Johnson and William Masters

involved in the four stages of sexual arousal: excitement, plateau, orgasm, and resolution.

Excitement. Sexual excitement is generally accompanied by vasocongestion. In males, vasocongestion produces an erection or swelling of the penis. Erections occur rapidly, often after only a few seconds of sexual stimulation. In females, vasocongestion results in lubrication of the vagina and swelling of the clitoris. Vaginal lubrication may occur as quickly as 10 to 30 seconds after first being sexually stimulated. Both males and females experience a "sex flush," a reddening of the skin starting in the abdomen and gradually spreading over the chest and other body parts, as well as increases in heart rate, blood pressure, and breathing.

Plateau. During the plateau phase, vasocongestion produces a full erection in males and the testes swell to one and a half times their normal size. In females, swelling occurs in the breasts and in the outer third of the vagina. Breathing, heart rate, and blood pressure continue to increase in both men and women.

Orgasm. In both sexes, orgasm consists of rapid rhythmic contractions (every 0.8 of a second) in the pelvic region accompanied by still further increases in breathing, heart rate, and blood pressure. Myotonia occurs throughout the body. Women may have as few as three contractions in a mild orgasm or as many as ten or eleven in an intense one. The male orgasm occurs over two phases. First, myotonia of the internal genitalia produces the sensation that ejaculation is imminent and cannot be prevented. Second, myotonia results in ejaculation.

Men and women appear to experience similar physical sensations during orgasm. In one study (Vance & Wagner, 1976), male and female undergraduates were asked to provide written descriptions of what having an orgasm felt like. The descriptions were then handed to a panel of experts (clinical psychologists, medical students, and obstetrician-gynecologists) who were instructed to separate them according to whether they seemed to be descriptive of the male or the female orgasm. The results? The panel could not distinguish between the two.

Resolution. Following orgasm, the body returns to an unaroused state. Breathing, heart rate, and blood pressure return slowly to their normal levels. Men lose their erections and enter into a refractory period, a time in which they are incapable of having an erection and second orgasm. Males vary in their ability to become sexually rearoused. In some men, the refractory period may only last a few minutes and in others, an entire day. As men age, however, the refractory period tends to lengthen.

Females do not enter a refractory period after orgasm. Some women in fact, appear capable of having multiple orgasms, that is, two or more orgasms within a short period of time. Masters and Johnson discovered that through masturbation some women may experience as many as 5 to 20 orgasms within a brief time period.

Alternatives to the Masters and Johnson Model

Although Masters and Johnson established sexual behavior as a bona fide area of laboratory research, their work has not been accepted uncritically. In particular, two important alternative accounts of the human sexual arousal have arisen. Both models underscore the role of psychological factors in sexual arousal, a glaring omission in the Masters and Johnson model.

Kaplan's Biphasic Model. According to Helen Singer Kaplan (1974), the human sexual response does not progress through four stages as proposed by Masters and Johnson, but rather it has two distinct phases, vasocongestion of the genitalia and myotonia during orgasm. Her model is based on the observation that vasocongestion and myotonia involve different body structures, are controlled by different parts of the nervous system, are affected differently by age, and impairments specific to one but not to the other produce different sexual problems. Thus vasocongestion and muscle contractions represent independent phases of the sexual response. In her more recent work, Kaplan (1979) has added a psychological component, sexual desire, to her model. Sexual desire refers to an individual's interest in engaging in sexual activities. Kaplan considers sexual desire to constitute the first phase of sexual arousal because desire can affect the degree to which an individual can become sexually aroused. After all, if a person is not interested in engaging in sexual activity, he or she is not likely to experience sexual arousal.

Zilbergeld and Ellison's Five-Component Model. Bernie Zilbergeld and Carol Ellison's (1980) major criticism of the Masters and Johnson model is that it fails to take into account important psychological aspects of the sexual response such as sexual desire; arousal, the emotion of being excited during sexual activity; and satisfaction, the evaluation of the sexual experience in terms of its pleasure or "goodness." Combining these psychological aspects with the physiological components of the sexual response, in order, their model looks like this: sexual desire, arousal, physiological readiness (vasocongestion), orgasm (myotonia), and satisfaction. To Zilbergeld and Ellison, then, psychological variables are key elements of sexual arousal.

Sexual arousal involves the interaction of both physical and psychological factors.

These models have been useful in understanding sexual problems that are psychological in nature, while the Masters and Johnson model involves only physical factors. This difference is important to remember because sexual arousal involves the interaction of both physical and psychological factors. This fact is made especially clear in sexual dysfunctions, our next topic of discussion.

SEXUAL DYSFUNCTIONS

At one time or another, many of us are likely to experience **sexual dysfunction**, an impairment or difficulty in sexual arousal and orgasm. Sexual dysfunctions may be due to physical causes, but they are more likely due to psychological factors and can be either relatively short-lived or long-term in duration. Sexual dysfunctions can be embarrassing and disruptive to other aspects of our lives. For example, tension can develop between an otherwise happy couple because of sexual dysfunctions such as the man not being able to get or maintain an erection. Several sexual dysfunctions and their possible causes are discussed below.

Female Sexual Dysfunctions

A woman's inability to have an orgasm is called **orgasmic dysfunction**. There are three varieties of orgasmic dysfunctions: the woman has never had an orgasm; the woman has previously experienced orgasm, but now is no longer able to; and the woman is able to reach orgasm in some situations but not others.

Orgasmic dysfunctions are quite common. One survey (Hunt, 1974), found that only 53 percent of the female respondents regularly experienced orgasm. In many segments of today's society, there is a great deal of emphasis placed on the female orgasm. In a sense, it has become something of a prize (Hyde, 1986). For some couples, the goal is not to produce one female orgasm but several. Psychological pressures of this sort often create undue anxiety in women and impair their ability to experience orgasm. As a result, both partners may become frustrated and disappointed, creating even more pressure during their next attempt. Indirectly, the importance of psychological factors in orgasmic dysfunctions is underscored by the fact that hormonal factors do not seem to be involved since treatment with estrogens is ineffective (Marmor, 1976).

*S*exual dysfunctions may be due to physical causes, but they are more likely due to psychological factors . . .

Another female sexual dysfunction is **vaginismus**, or spastic contraction of the muscles surrounding the vagina. In many cases, the muscle contractions are so strong that intercourse is impossible. In all cases, attempted intercourse is extremely painful, further aggravating the vaginismic response.

Vaginismus appears to be a reflexive response much like other responses that become associated, through classical conditioning, with painful or fear-evoking stimuli. In some cases, women suffering from vaginismus have undergone a traumatic sexual experience such as rape. In others, merely being forewarned that sexual intercourse will be painful (Barbach, 1975) is enough to produce the vaginismic response. Vaginismus may also stem from physical problems that can cause sexual intercourse to be painful such as poor vaginal lubrication, vaginal infections, or damage to vaginal tissue from childbirth.

Male Sexual Dysfunctions

The inability to produce or maintain an erection is referred to as an **erectile dysfunction**. According to Masters and Johnson, there are two kinds of erectile dysfunctions: primary erectile dysfunction and secondary erectile dysfunction. Men who have never had an erection are said to suffer from primary erectile dysfunction, and men who have been able to have erections in the past, but now cannot at least 25 percent of the time, are said to experience secondary erectile dysfunction.

Erectile dysfunctions are common and may affect sexually active men of all ages. Erectile problems may stem from physical factors such as impairments of the circulatory system (recall that erections are caused by the penis becoming engorged with blood), diabetes (Jensen, 1981), damage to the lower part of the spinal cord, stress, fatigue, or the use of drugs and alcohol. Typically, however, erectile dysfunctions are caused by psychological factors. Performance anxiety (nervousness about having sexual intercourse or how well one's partner will enjoy it), guilt, or sexual apathy can each diminish a man's ability to develop and maintain an erection. That erectile dysfunctions are often psychological in nature is supported by Masters and Johnson's report (1970) that nearly 97 percent of the cases (213 in total) of secondary dysfunction they studied involved no physical impairments whatsoever. Indirect evidence for the role of psychological factors in erectile dysfunctions stems from the fact that hormones do not seem to be involved in erectile dysfunctions; treatment of erectile dysfunctions with testosterone is ineffective (Benkert, Witt, Adam, & Leitz, 1979).

Another very common sexual dysfunction in men is **premature ejaculation**, the inability to delay ejaculation. In some cases, ejaculation occurs before the penis is even inserted into the vagina; in others, ejaculation occurs before the man wishes it to or before his partner has an orgasm. Defining the boundaries of premature ejaculation has traditionally proved troublesome for sex researchers and sex therapists alike—how soon is too soon? Thirty seconds? Ten minutes? Anytime before the woman has had an orgasm? Presently, most sex experts let the couple define this dysfunction. If either partner believes poor ejaculatory control is diminishing the quality of their sexual experiences, then a problem exists (Hyde, 1986; Zilbergeld, 1978).

Premature ejaculation is also due primarily to psychological factors, particularly difficulties in learning to delay orgasm. For example, learning to hurry ejaculation in one situation, such as during masturbation (so as to prevent getting caught), may interfere with learning to delay ejaculation in other situations. As a result, some men have difficulty putting off ejaculation during sexual intercourse.

In sum, sexual dysfunctions are impairments in biological functioning that are often caused by psychological factors such as performance anxiety, guilt, or sexual apathy. That psychological variables can interfere with physiological responses to sexual stimulation reinforces the theme of this book: behavior is the result of the interaction of biology and experience.

PATTERNS OF SEXUAL BEHAVIOR

Studying patterns of human sexual behavior is a difficult task if only because it is not an area of research that lends itself well to rigorous experimentation. Most of our knowledge about the variety and frequency of sexual practices common to our culture has been derived from survey and interview analyses, particularly those of Alfred Kinsey and his colleagues (Kinsey et al., 1948, 1953), and more recently, Morton Hunt (1974). Unfortunately, people's descriptions of their behavior are not always accurate and candid. Imagine how you might respond to a questionnaire containing the following questions: (1) "What do you think about when you masturbate?" (2) "About how much time, on the average, do you spend in foreplay before intercourse begins?" (3) "When was the first time you had sex with an animal?" (Pomeroy, Flax, & Wheeler, 1982, pp. 108, 179, and 249, respectively).

Would your responses *honestly* reflect your behavior? Consider only a few of the possible biases that might color your answer:

- Would your answers be influenced by your perception of what constitutes "normal" sexual behavior in terms of its frequency and variety?
- Would you be willing to describe your most intimate sexual experiences and preferences to a stranger?
- Would you tend to boast of your sexual experiences, or exaggerate your account of your sexual history?
- Could you recall accurately the details of your early sexual experiences?

Despite the possibility of obtaining misleading, if not fictitious, accounts of sexual behavior using survey and interview methods, ethical considerations prevent researchers from eavesdropping on our sex lives in more obtrusive and objective ways. So, we must rely on the self-reports of people who consent to being interviewed. With this caveat in mind, let us proceed.

Heterosexuality

Sexual interaction between a man and a woman is probably the most common form of sexual behavior in our culture. Heterosexual behavior includes flirting, kissing, caressing, petting, sexual intercourse, oral-genital contact, and a variety of other types of sexual acts. The exact nature of these acts varies from couple to couple depending upon their personal preferences and previous sexual experiences. While the various forms of sexual interaction are interesting in and of themselves, our discussion of heterosexuality will be confined to the most common sexual behavior: sexual intercourse.

Because premarital sexual intercourse has traditionally been discouraged in our culture, the results from surveys of the actual sexual practices of unmarried men and women have surprised many people (see Figure 12.3). Kinsey's work (1948, 1953) revealed that by age 25, 71 percent of males and 33 percent of females in his survey had engaged in premarital sexual intercourse. Hunt's (1974) more recent survey indicated that these figures have increased dramatically: nearly all males (97 percent) and two-thirds (67 percent) of the females in his survey reported having premarital sexual intercourse by age 25. Zelnik and Kantner (1980) reported 56 percent of unmarried 17-year-old boys and 49 percent of unmarried 17-year-old girls have had sexual intercourse.

How do people typically react to their initial experiences with sexual intercourse? Both males and females react with less enthusiasm than one might expect. In one study, 20 percent of the males reported feelings of neutrality and unpleasantness and 33 percent felt guilty after their first experiences (Hunt, 1974). In the same study, over 50 percent of the females reported neutrality and unpleasantness and almost two-thirds regretted the experience. Guilt, concern over the value of the experience, and fears of becoming pregnant and of discovery by parents were among the major negative reactions voiced by females (Eastman, 1972; Hunt, 1974).

Teenagers and Unintended Pregnancy. One serious consequence of the large number of young people engaging in premarital sexual intercourse is the number of unintended pregnancies among teenage females. The frequency of teenage pregnancy in the United States is greater than that of other industrialized nations including Canada, Sweden, France, England, and Holland. Every year about 1,200,000 or 5 percent of unmarried American teenage females become pregnant (Adler, 1985).

The psychological consequences of pregnancy for the unmarried teenage female are difficult to overstate. Just the fact that she is pregnant may cause a considerable sense of regret, embarrassment, and worry. She is also faced with a series of important and stressful decisions—should she abort the baby or deliver it? If she chooses to deliver it, should she put it up for adoption or raise the baby herself? If she decides to rear the baby, should she quit school? How will she support her new family? Should she marry the baby's father? Here are some answers related to these questions.

- Each year in the United States about 400,000 teenage females have abortions (Zelnik, Kantner, & Ford, 1981).
- The majority of teenage females who become pregnant quit school and never return (McGee, 1982).
- Less than 5 percent of unmarried teenage mothers put their babies up for adoption (McGee, 1982).
- Most unwed pregnant teenagers receive little financial or emotional support from the teenage boys who made them pregnant (Masters, Johnson, & Kolodny, 1988).

FIGURE 12.3

The percentage of people who reported engaging in premarital sexual intercourse in both the Kinsey and Hunt reports.

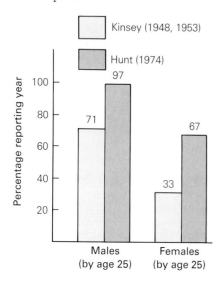

Right: Because sexual interaction is very personal, researchers must rely on couples' reports of their sexual experiences to gather data on sexual behavior. Far right: Teenage pregnancy is a serious problem in our country today. Lack of sex education and failure to use birth control contribute to the high incidence of unintended pregnancies.

The mere number of teenagers having sexual intercourse cannot alone explain the rate of teenage pregnancy. After all, we have a sophisticated technology that is aimed squarely at preventing pregnancy. Unfortunately, less than a third of sexually active teenagers regularly use contraception and about 25 percent never do (Morrison, 1985). Moreover, many teenagers are poorly informed about sexuality in general and contraception in particular. Why is this the case? Many experts agree that while premarital sex has become more prevalent, American attitudes toward it have remained intolerant. As a result, young people do not receive the kind of sex education and training that might prevent teenage pregnancies. In contrast, children and adolescents in many European countries with very low rates of teenage pregnancy such as Sweden and Holland, receive explicit training in reproductive physiology and biology as well as in the use of contraceptive devices.

Marriage and Sex. In most societies, including our own, marriage provides the context that officially sanctions interpersonal sexual behavior. The exact degree of sexual interaction varies from couple to couple over time, with couples in their 20s having sexual intercourse about two to three times a week and couples in their late 40s doing so about once a week (see Figure 12.4). As Figure 12.5 shows, however, these average frequencies vary considerably from couple to couple.

Advancing age does not necessarily signal the decline of sexual activity in marriage. Couples who establish strong sexual patterns in the early and middle years of their marriage often remain sexually active well into their later years (Kinsey et al., 1948, 1953; Masters & Johnson, 1966). However, compared to younger married men, married men over the age of 65 appear to masturbate more frequently than they engage in sexual intercourse (Weizman & Hart, 1987). Nonetheless, a couple may continue to have sexual intercourse well into their nineties! In one study (Starr & Weiner, 1982), only 15 percent of 80- to 90-year-old interviewees reported abstaining totally from sexual activity. When it does occur, sexual inactivity in older couples appears to be the result of boredom, concern over nonsexual issues, and the notion that an active sex life is inappropriate for older people (Griffitt, 1981). Thus, sexual inactivity among older people is not always due to biological malfunctions but to psychological ones.

Sexual activity is not only for the young. Older couples can also enjoy satisfying sex lives.

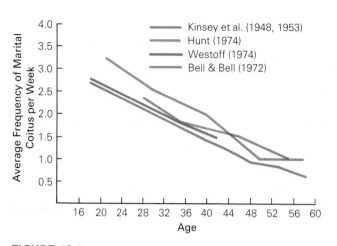

FIGURE 12.4

The average number of times per week that married couples have sexual intercourse. With age, the frequency of sexual intercourse decreases.

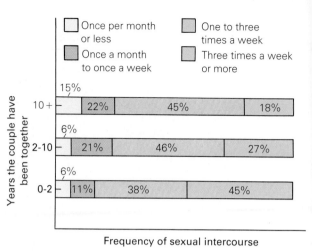

Frequency of sexual intercourse

FIGURE 12.5

Variety in sexual activity among married couples. Married couples vary tremendously in the frequency with which they have sexual intercourse.

Sexual satisfaction is one of the yardsticks by which marital happiness is measured, with the former being positively correlated with the latter (Tavris & Sadd, 1977). However, this does not mean that the more often a couple has sexual intercourse, the happier the marriage. Rather, marital happiness is related to the sexual compatibility of the people involved. A couple may only have intercourse once a month and yet be perfectly satisfied, sexually and maritally.

Although the majority of people in our society view extramarital sex or adultery with disapproval (over 80 percent of couples interviewed in the Hunt survey), it is nonetheless common. Kinsey (1948, 1953) estimated that about 50 percent of the husbands and about 25 percent of the wives in his sample had or would have sexual intercourse with someone other than their spouses during their marriage. Hunt estimated similar percentages from his 1974 sample. While the overall percentage of adulterous men and women has remained about the same over the past several decades, the number of younger women having affairs has increased. Hunt found that nearly 25 percent of wives under 25 years of age reported having an adulterous relationship while Kinsey had found only 8 percent for this age group.

Adulterous men tend to have more partners than their female counterparts. Husbands also are more likely than wives to have a casual affair, although spouses of both sexes may become involved in an affair when they are bored, unhappy, or otherwise dissatisfied with their marriages (Hunt, 1974; Tavris & Sadd, 1977). Spouses investing more time and emotional effort in their marriages than they are getting back are more likely to have affairs than those spouses whose contributions to, and returns from, their marriages are about equal (Walster, Traupmann, & Walster, 1978). According to Masters et al. (1988), for many spouses the psychologically distressing aspect of their partner's infidelity is not the fact that he or she had sex with someone else. Rather, it is the idea that the partner has developed an intimate relationship with someone else.

Divorce and Sex. In the past two decades the rate of divorce in the United States has doubled. What kinds of sex lives do divorced people lead? According to the Hunt survey, fairly active ones. Hunt found that 85 percent of divorced individuals had sexual intercourse within a year of their divorces, on the average of about twice a week. Divorced men, however, had about twice as many sexual partners (8) as divorced women (4). Both sexes reported their postmarital sexual relations to be generally enjoyable and pleasant.

Widowhood and Sex. What about widows? What is their reaction to the loss of their sexual partner? This is an especially interesting question in light of the fact that less than 5 percent of women widowed at age 55 or older remarry (Malatesta, Chambless, Pollack, & Cantor, 1988). Widows, of course, regret the loss of their lovers, but there are several other aspects of the loss that they regret even more. In one study, widows reported that not being able to converse or share emotional responsibilities with a man caused them the most unhappiness concerning the loss of their husbands (Malatesta et al., 1988). These women also reported that they missed touching, hugging, kissing, and even the actual presence of their husbands next to them in bed more than sexual intercourse itself. These findings support the idea that more goes into a successful marriage than just sex; companionship seems to be a more important ingredient in happy marriages.

Homosexuality

Homosexuality refers to sexual attraction to individuals of the same gender. Accurately characterizing a person's sexuality as either homosexual or heterosexual is a difficult task. In some cases, men and women may view themselves as homosexuals yet may only be involved in heterosexual relationships. And on the other hand, some people may identify themselves as heterosexuals yet may have had several homosexual experiences. Some people are bisexual, having a roughly equal number of homosexual and heterosexual experiences. And still other people may have had several homosexual contacts in the past but are presently involved in only heterosexual relationships.

To deal with the difficulty of defining his respondents' sexual orientation, Alfred Kinsey and his colleagues proposed that sexuality be viewed as a continuum with exclusive homosexual behavior and exclusive heterosexual behavior defining the end points and equal amounts of homosexual and heterosexual experiences anchoring the center point (see Table 12.3). Kinsey's major contribution in devising this scale was his focus on sexual behavior and not on sexual orientation. By focusing on the incidence of sexual acts between people of the same or different gender, he was able to describe accurately the magnitude of homosexual or heterosexual experiences of his respondents, thus sidestepping the thorny problem of defining their sexuality.

TABLE 12.3.	Kinsey's continuum of heterosexual-homosexual behavior.

RATING	HETEROSEXUAL-HOMOSEXUAL BALANCE
0	Exclusively heterosexual
1	Predominantly heterosexual, only incidentally homosexual
2	Predominantly heterosexual, but more than incidentally homosexual
3	Equally heterosexual and homosexual
4	Predominantly homosexual, but more than incidentally heterosexual
5	Predominantly homesexual, but incidentally heterosexual
6	Exclusively homosexual

Based on survey research such as the Kinsey et al. (1948, 1953) and Hunt (1974) reports, sex experts estimate that about 70 to 75 percent of men and 85 percent of women have exclusively heterosexual experiences. About 2 to 3 percent of men and less than 1 percent of women have exclusively homosexual experiences. The remaining men (about 25 percent) and women (about 15 percent) have bisexual experiences (Griffitt & Hatfield, 1985; Hyde, 1986).

Homosexual men and women tend to shy away from marriage, but when they do marry, the marriage is almost always to a heterosexual (Bell & Weinberg, 1978). In many cases the marriages are unhappy and short-lived. Marital unhappiness seems most often due to sexual problems, including the homosexual's disinterest in heterosexual activities and the spouse's discovery of his or her mate's homosexuality or bisexuality. About 50 percent of married homosexuals report fantasizing about homosexual acts during sexual intercourse with their heterosexual spouses (Bell & Weinberg, 1978).

There are also a number of interesting differences between homosexual men and women (also referred to as lesbians). Lesbians are more likely than homosexual men to become involved in intimate and enduring relationships. That is, compared to homosexual men, lesbians are more likely to feel affection and love for their partners and so be more intimate with them. Homosexual men generally have more sexual partners than lesbians and are more likely to have sex in public places and have more "one night stands" (Bell & Weinberg, 1978; Saghir & Robins, 1973). Note that these patterns are similar to those for heterosexual men and women in terms of gender-roles for sexual behavior discussed earlier.

Theories of Homosexual Development. There are several schools of thought as to the factors responsible for shaping our orientation for sexual partners. An early theory was espoused by Sigmund Freud (1962/1905) who held that as young children we have the capacity to develop either homosexual or heterosexual preferences, and depending upon early childhood experiences, a person might develop into either or both. According to Freud, a boy who fails to learn the "male role" either because his father did not permit a close father-son relationship or because his mother was more aggressive and domineering than his father, would grow up to be homosexual.

A second theory is that a hormone imbalance predisposes individuals to prefer same-gender sexual partners. For example, one study reported that homosexual men had lower levels of testosterone than a similar group of heterosexual males (Kolodny, Masters, Hendry & Toro, 1971). However, other studies have not found hormonal differences between adult homosexual and heterosexual men (Rose, 1975; Meyer-Bahlburg, 1980).

A third theory centers on the consequences of our early sexual experiences (Gagnon & Simon, 1973; Masters & Johnson, 1979). For instance, if a woman had positive heterosexual and/or negative homosexual experiences as a youth, she is likely to lean toward heterosexual relationships as an adult. On the other hand, if she had negative heterosexual and/or positive homosexual experiences as a youth, she is likely to lean toward lesbian relationships as an adult. According to this view, bisexuality would result from an individual having both positive heterosexual and homosexual experiences.

A fourth account holds that biological and environmental factors interact to determine sexual orientation. According to Michael Storms (1980, 1981), an individual's rate of sexual maturation combined with the gender of his or her circle of friends is the key factor. Young people are still moving in the same-gender social circles in early adolescence. Heterosexual activ-

In today's society, more homosexuals feel free to publicly display their sexual orientation.

ities generally do not begin to occur with any regularity until later in adolescence. Consequently, if a person becomes sexually mature while still a member of a same-gender social group, his or her sexual behavior may be directed toward same gender people, resulting in homosexual orientation. If an individual reaches sexual maturity later, while moving in largely heterosexual circles, heterosexual preference is likely to emerge. While Storms' theory remains largely untested, there is some evidence that lesbians tend to mature earlier than heterosexual women, as indicated by the age of first masturbation (Saghir & Robins, 1973).

So which theory best explains the development of sexual preferences? Apparently none of them. The extremely complicated nature of sexual orientation makes it unlikely that a single theory will be able to account for all cases of homosexuality. As we have already noted, the hormonal theory is plagued by inconsistent research findings and Storms' theory has yet to be thoroughly empirically validated. The other theories also have problems. For example, in an attempt to identify the role of early sexual experiences and parental influence in the development of sexual preferences, an interview of nearly 1000 homosexual men and women and 500 heterosexual men and women (Bell, Weinberg, & Hammersmith, 1981) found no support for the Freudian or experiential accounts. Bell and his colleagues also uncovered several other very interesting findings.

The factors that determine sexual orientation . . . exert their influence long before we reach adulthood.

1. Sexual orientation tends to be determined sometime between late childhood and early adolescence. Thus, whatever the factors that determine sexual orientation turn out to be, they exert their influence long before we reach adulthood.
2. In general, homosexual feelings developed in the homosexual respondents about three years prior to their first major homosexual experience.
3. The homosexuals in the study found their heterosexual experiences during their youth to be unrewarding.
4. For both homosexual men and women, negative relationships with their fathers appeared to be influential in the development of homosexual behavior.

Furthermore, sexual orientation, homosexual or otherwise, does not appear to be under direct genetic control—no gene for sexual orientation has yet been discovered. Some researchers hold, though, that sexual orientation is determined during the prenatal period. For example, in a review of biological and psychological variables influencing sexual orientation, Ellis and Ames (1987) proposed that sexual orientation is determined by "complex combinations of genetic, hormonal, neurological, and environmental factors although the orientation itself awaits the onset of puberty to be activated." In essence, they argue that during the second to fifth month of prenatal development, sexual orientation is determined by the extent to which the nervous system of the fetus is exposed to testosterone and other sex hormones. If the fetus is exposed to hormone levels typical of the female, the individual, whether male or female, will develop a sexual orientation toward males at puberty. On the other hand, if the fetus is exposed to hormone levels typical of the male, then he or she will develop a sexual orientation favoring females. In Ellis and Ames' view, then, sexual orientation is determined before we are born and learning appears to play only a role in determining the expression of the orientation. Is Ellis and Ames' theory supported by research? Yes, although most of the research is with nonhumans and involves exposure to unusually high or low levels of testosterone at a time in prenatal development when the nervous system is developing.

| | PERCENT OF SAMPLE | |
| TABLE 12.4. Comparison of American attitudes toward homosexuality, 1972–1982 and 1985. | | |
QUESTION AND RESPONSES	1972–1982	1985
Are sexual relations between two adults of the same sex:		
Always wrong	73	75
Almost always wrong	6	4
Wrong only sometimes	7	7
Not wrong at all	14	14

Although homosexuals today are able to be more open about their sexual orientation, homosexuality is still a controversial issue and is not totally accepted in our society.

Societal Attitudes Toward Homosexuality. Regardless of how homosexual preferences develop, homosexuals must deal with the consequences of those preferences, many of which are unpleasant. Unlike heterosexuals, homosexuals live within a society that by and large has extremely negative views of their sexuality.

Historically, society has characterized homosexual people as "sick" and "perverted." Judging by recent surveys, the efforts of homosexual rights organizations to change public attitudes about homosexuality has done little to change these kinds of views. Surveys conducted between 1972 and 1985 showed that homosexuality is viewed negatively by the majority of Americans (Davis & Smith, 1984). Nearly 75 percent of the respondents held that homosexual relations are always wrong while less than 15 percent held that there was nothing wrong at all with such relations (see Table 12.4). A more recent survey revealed that heterosexual people tend to view homosexuals as less happy and less in love in their relationships than heterosexuals (Testa, Kinder, & Ironson, 1987). Many college students have negative attitudes toward homosexuals. For example, in one study of 103 college students, 57 percent agreed that "Homosexual behavior is just plain wrong," 53 percent agreed that "Homosexuals are disgusting," and 70 percent agreed with the statement that they "would not like to have homosexual friends" (Kurdek, 1988). These attitudes persist despite the fact that the American Psychiatric Association officially changed its position on homosexuality by declassifying it as a psychiatric disorder. Furthermore, the American Psychological Association has urged its members to "take the lead in removing the stigma of mental illness that has long been associated with homosexual orientations" (Conger, 1975).

Regardless of how one views homosexuality and homosexual behavior, there seems to be little, if any, psychological evidence that homosexuality is either a sickness or a perversion. For example, Lawrence Kurdek, in his surveys of cohabitating homosexual men and women has found that homosexuals do not differ from heterosexuals in terms of psychological adjustment; that is, they suffer no more or less psychological distress with life events than do heterosexuals (Kurdek, 1987). However, lesbians do report greater satisfaction in their relationships than do homosexual men (Kurdek, 1988). We should note, though, that these findings may only hold for homosexual couples, not for homosexual individuals who are not involved in a stable relationship. Perhaps the support found in relationships influences the degree to which homosexuals are able to come to grips with the psychological pressures of their sexual orientation. Many homosexuals report being uncomfortable with their sexual orientation because of the negative outlook our culture at large has concerning that orientation. Psychologically, some homosexuals feel guilty or distressed about their sexual orientation and anxious about the pressure they experience from heterosexuals for attitudes and behavior that run contrary to the norm (Reiss, 1980).

In sum, homosexuality is a sexual attraction to individuals of the same gender. Theories of homosexual development are still in need of substantive empirical support. We do know, however, that sexual preferences are determined between childhood and adolescence. Homosexuals find heterosexual experiences unfulfilling, and in their youth, homosexuals tend to have poor relationships with their fathers. Although many people find homosexuality repugnant, there is no scientific evidence that homosexuality is either "sick" or "perverted."

Sexual Behavior and Sexually Transmitted Diseases

Sexually transmitted diseases (STDs) are diseases that are contracted through sexual contact with another person. Four common STDs, their symptoms and treatments are described in Table 12.5. Any kind of STD will negatively affect an afflicted individual's self-esteem and sexual behavior. Sexual relationships are difficult to initiate and sustain, and in many cases, individuals suffering from an STD come to view themselves with humiliation and disdain. Some STDs, such as syphilis and AIDS (acquired immune deficiency) can be killers. The threat of contracting AIDS has reduced the frequency of sexual behavior in both homosexual and heterosexual populations. For example, in one study of Chicago area homosexual men, over 90 percent said they have changed their sexual activities to reduce their risk of getting AIDS (Joseph et al., 1987). Another study of homosexual behavior has found similar results: a sample of homosexual men in the San Francisco area found that they had reduced the number of sexual partners over the period 1984–1986 (Winkelstein et al., 1987).

TABLE 12.5.   *Four STDs, their causes, symptomology, and treatment.*

STD	CAUSE	SYMPTOMS	TREATMENT
Gonorrhea	Gonococcus bacterium attacks cervix in females and urethra in males	Appear 3 to 5 days after sexual contact with afflicted person. In both sexes, discharges of pus. Urination accompanied by a burning sensation. If untreated, fevers, headaches, backaches, and abdominal pain develop.	Penicillin or other antibiotics
Genital herpes	Herpes simplex type I and II virus	Small blisters around point of sexual contact. Blisters burst causing pain. Symptoms recur every 1 to 2 weeks.	No cure, but an ointment called acyclovir speeds the healing process if applied early in the first episode of the disease
Syphilis	Treponema pallidum bacterium	Chancre or lesion where bacteria first entered body. If untreated, the bacteria penetrate body tissue, including the brain. May result in death.	Penicillin or other antibiotics
AIDS	Human immunodeficiency virus (HIV)	Destruction of body's immune system allowing diseases like cancer and pneumonia to infect the body.	Still in experimental stages

The increasing incidence of life-threatening sexually transmitted diseases like AIDS makes it vital that people practice safe sex.

Contracting an STD is not inevitable, but these diseases can be a consequence of our sexual behavior if we do not follow safe-sex practices. *In other words, STDs are preventable.* Typical guidelines to safeguard against contracting an STD include:

- Limiting the number of sexual partners. The risk of contracting an STD increases as the number of sexual partners increases. As long as two people have never had sexual contact with anyone but each other, there is virtually no risk of contracting a STD.
- Being discriminate in choosing sexual partners—finding out the sexual history of potential partners before having sexual relations.
- Using a condom during any sexual activity. Condoms not only reduce the risk of pregnancy, they also help prevent possible direct contact with the disease.

Following these few safe-sex practices does not guarantee that an individual will not contract a STD but it will reduce that likelihood.

SEXUAL AGGRESSION

For most of us, sexual behavior represents a wonderful, if not sublime, means of expressing love for another person. For others, though, sexual behavior represents a means of demonstrating strength and power, rather than love and tenderness. To these people, who are largely male, sex is a way of selfishly gratifying themselves at the expense of another person's dignity and esteem. To be sure, sexual aggression represents one of the darker sides of human nature. It is a side that begs for understanding simply because it is a problem that brings with it tremendous personal and psychological consequences. Two related issues are discussed next: pornography and rape.

Pornography and Sexual Aggression

Pornography is literature, art, and films "that depict erotic behavior with the intent of causing sexual excitement" (Masters, Johnson, & Kolodny, 1988). While conservative groups have always been concerned about the potentially damaging effects of pornography on the average citizen, an intensive study conducted by the President's Commission on Obscenity and Pornography in 1970 found no evidence that pornography deleteriously affected its subscribers. Shortly after publication of the Commission's report, the pornographic industry experienced a period of incredible growth and change. The number of pornographic magazines multiplied, as did full-length, sexually explicit cinematography. More recently, pornographic films have become available on videocassette and through cable television, allowing people to view them in the privacy of their homes.

In the late 1970s, feminists and many others began campaigning against pornography. Feminists leveled two charges against the porn industry. First, pornography typically degrades women: it portrays them as mere sex objects, naturally submissive to the sexual whims and fancies of men. Second, most pornography glorifies male violence toward women. Women are often depicted as sex slaves, who enjoy, and even desire, being physically forced to engage in any and every sexual act. In short, feminists argue that pornography often paints a blatantly false picture of female gender roles and female sexuality, thus, encouraging male violence toward women.

Research has shown that sexual violence depicted in pornographic literature and films increases males' feelings of aggressiveness toward females.

Social psychological research shows that these concerns are justified. In one study (Malamuth & Check, 1981), college men and women viewed one of two kinds of movies: 1) movies that showed women becoming sexually aroused by sexually violent males, or 2) movies that did not involve sexual violence. A few days later, the subjects responded to several attitude questionnaires. Males (but not females) who viewed the sexually violent movies showed greater acceptance of sexual violence against women and, to a lesser extent, acceptance of rape myths (such as the one that many women have secret desires to be raped), than did the students who viewed the neutral films.

Malamuth has also shown that reading literature that describes sexually violent acts increases the probability that males will respond aggressively toward females (Malamuth, 1984). In this study, male subjects read one of three illustrated stories. One involved rape, another involved nonviolent pornography, and the third involved a nonpornographic story. After reading one of the stories, each subject was insulted by a female confederate of the experimenter. Next, subjects were permitted to deliver electric shocks to her (of course, the shocks were not actually delivered). Males who read the sexually violent story showed significantly higher levels of aggression toward her than did males in the other two groups.

In a similar experiment, Dolf Zillmann and Jennings Bryant (1984) exposed male and female subjects to either three or six short pornographic movies a week for six weeks. Another group of men and women was shown neutral movies over the same time period. Several weeks later, all subjects read a newspaper article about a male awaiting sentencing for a rape conviction. Zillman and Bryant then asked subjects to recommend a suitable prison sentence for the rapist. The men and women who viewed the pornographic movies for six weeks recommended shorter prison sentences than subjects in the other two groups (see Figure 12.6). Interestingly, males, regardless of whether or not they were exposed to the sexually explicit movies, recommended shorter prison sentences than did females, indicating that men, in general, tend to view sexual violence toward women less harshly than do women.

Two experts on pornography and sexual violence, Edward Donnerstein and Daniel Linz, have argued that depictions of violence against women, whether or not they involve sexual themes, are a primary cause of negative attitudes about women and rape (Donnerstein & Linz, 1986). They base their argument on research in which men viewed one of three different film clips. One clip showed a sexually aggressive scene in which a female was bound, harassed with a gun, and raped. The second clip showed only the violent segment of the scene; the rape was not shown. The final version showed only the rape; the violence was omitted. The men who viewed the version containing only the violence scored the highest on measures that they would rape or use force against women. The men who viewed only the rape scene scored the lowest on these measures and the men who viewed the entire film clip scored in between the other two groups.

One does not need to be a porno enthusiast to view or read about violence toward women or to develop negative attitudes toward women. These attitudes may exist for other reasons. Thus, pornography should not receive all the credit for negative male attitudes toward women. As Donnerstein and Linz so aptly expressed it, "The most clear and present danger, well documented by the social science literature, is all violent material in our society, whether sexually explicit or not, promotes violence against women" (Donnerstein & Linz, 1986, p. 59).

In brief, the research on sexual violence against women indicates that exposure to pornography involving sexual violence contributes to (1) acceptance of sexual violence against women, (2) acceptance of myths regarding female sexuality and sexual desires, (3) increases of male aggression against females under laboratory conditions, and (4) any depiction of violence against women contributes to the development of negative attitudes about women by men. We now turn to a discussion of rape.

Rape

Sexual intercourse or other sexual acts that occur with threatened or actual coercion of one of the people involved is termed **rape**. Although most cases of rape go unreported due to its highly degrading and humiliating nature, researchers estimate that 26 out every 100 women will be raped during their lives (Russell & Howell, 1983).

Most rapes are planned and most occur in the neighborhood in which the rapist resides—usually in the home of the victim. About a third of all rapes involve more than one rapist and frequently involve aggression. In

FIGURE 12.6
Subjects in the Zillmann and Bryant study who were exposed to large amounts of pornography showed more tolerance of sexual aggression by males.

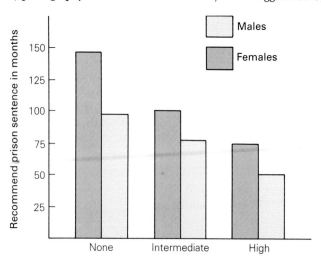

Researchers estimate that 26 out of every 100 women will be raped during their lives.

general, if the rapist and the victim know each other, the more severe and violent the rape.

Sexual gratification is not generally the motive for rape. In some cases, the intention of the rapist is to debase and shame the woman. In others, the goal may be a demonstration of power, anger, physical strength, or virility. That some rapists must masturbate to get an erection, while others urinate or smear their semen over their victims (Holmstrom & Burgess, 1980) is ample testimony to the fact that the causes of rape are often nonsexual. Based on reports of 133 convicted rapists and 92 rape victims, Groth, Burgess, & Holmstrom (1977) have devised a psychological typology or profile of rapists. They found that rapists could be classified according to two motives—power and anger— with two subtypes, bringing the total number of classes to four. None of the typologies involves purely sexual gratification. These classifications are listed below.

- Power-assertive type. For some rapists, rape represents a demonstration of power, control, and intimidation. Although power-oriented rapes may involve physical force or the threat of physical force, they do not usually involve brutal injury to the victim. The sexual act itself is viewed as a victory. Power-assertive rapists frequently fantasize that their victim(s), once subdued, will willingly submit to their control and become sexually aroused by their power. Of course, in actuality, the victim does not become excited. Of the 225 rapes studied, 44 percent of them involved power-assertive themes.
- Power-reassurance type. Twenty-one percent of the rape cases in the Groth et al. study involved rapists who, like power-assertive rapists, used intimidation to control their victims. But they did not rape to assert power. Rather they did it to reassure themselves, that they were in fact, "men." The researchers hypothesized that power-reassurance rapists have poor concepts of their own gender identity.
- Anger-retaliation type. Unlike power-oriented rapists, anger-motivated rapists are violent, often injuring their victims severely, sometime to the point of death. Anger-retaliation rapists hate women and are motivated in their acts by real or imagined threats to them from women. In other words, anger-retaliation rapists use sexual violence as a means of retribution against women for whatever "threats" the women may represent. Thirty percent of the rape cases studied by Groth et al. were motivated by anger-retaliation.
- Anger-excitation type. This kind of rapist, which comprised 5 percent of the Groth et al. sample, derives sexual pleasure from the suffering of their victims. That is, they become sexually excited by inflicting fear and pain (or the threat of pain) on their victims.

This research is important because it identified some important psychological characteristics of the rapists. Unfortunately, it is not so easy to identify these characteristics in potential rapists. Not all men who rape show these characteristics in a way that would clearly predict that they have the potential to become rapists; not all rapists, actual or potential, have obvious psychological problems. One example is date rape, which is common on college campuses. Two studies have identified the prevalence of this form of sexual aggression. Koss & Oros (1983) found that of 1846 male undergraduates interviewed, 15 percent said they had obtained sex by using coercive verbal pressure and about 2.5 percent said that they used threats or physical aggression. Likewise, Rapaport & Burkhart (1984) found that 15 percent of their subjects had sexual intercourse with a woman

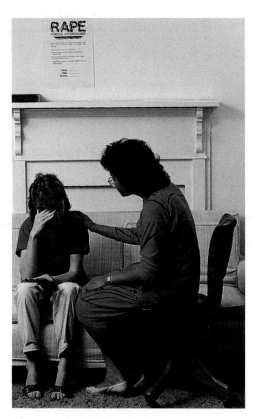

Counseling provided by rape crisis centers can often help rape victims deal with the emotional trauma they have experienced.

against her will. Perhaps an even more telling statistic about the degree of sexual aggression among college males was the finding that 71 percent of Rapaport and Burkhart's subjects admitted to using some form of sexual aggression with their dates. For example, 61 percent reported that they had fondled a woman's breast and 37 percent admitted that they had fondled a woman's genitals against her will. Date rapists hold rape belief myths (Koss, Leonard, Beezley, & Oros, 1985) and perceive women as adversaries (Rapaport & Burkhart, 1984).

Rape victims are left with emotional scars that often require considerable time to heal. Many rape victims experience a two-stage **rape trauma syndrome** (Burgess & Holmstrom, 1974). The first stage, or the acute phase, starts immediately after the rape and may last up to several weeks. A woman may first react with either an expressive reaction that involves crying, anxiety, and fear, or with a controlled reaction in which she reacts cooly to the rape and appears calm and collected. Physically, she may experience pain and discomfort from injuries incurred during the rape as well as headaches and anxiety from the psychological trauma of the experience. After her initial reaction to the incident, these reactions tend to give way to long-term feelings of humiliation, anxiety, and embarrassment. She may also experience strong feelings of self-blame, fretting over what she might have done to provoke or prevent the rape.

The second stage, or long-term reorganization phase, may last up to several months or even years. During this phase, it is not uncommon for the rape victim to quit her job, move several times, change her phone number, and develop strong, highly negative reactions to settings resembling that in which the rape occurred. Normal sexual routine between the rape victim and her boyfriend or husband may also be disrupted. In many cases, rape victims continue to suffer from psychological problems several years after the sexual assault (Cohen & Roth, 1987).

What can be done to hasten the rape victim's recovery? The extent to which a woman will experience serious psychological problems (anxiety, depression, impaired sexual functioning) as a consequence of being raped depends on her coping skills and on how psychologically well-adjusted she was before she was raped (Santiago et al., 1985). Rape crisis centers are helpful in providing individual and group support; they also can be very helpful in helping the victim deal with hospital, legal, and police issues. Emotional support from her husband or boyfriend, other friends, and parents would also seem to increase the victim's chances of successful adjustment.

BOUNDARIES AND FRONTIERS

The twentieth century has witnessed tremendous increases in scientific understanding of gender and sexual behavior. Scientists have, to a favorable degree, unravelled the mystery of gender development. We know the genetic, physiological, and psychological variables that appear to determine gender. We know how our sexual attitudes and behavior are affected by gender. We also have a solid understanding of the physiological and psychological variables involved in the sexual response, and we have the knowledge to treat several sexual dysfunctions. Thanks to the pioneering efforts of Alfred Kinsey and other modern demographers, we now know a good deal about historical and present trends in the ways people in our culture interact sexually.

So, what remains to be learned about sex? Plenty. A few specific topics stand out as particularly important areas in need of research.

- There remain a large number of unanswered questions about the causes of some kinds of sexual behavior, particularly those we often label "deviant." For example, we know little about the causes of rape, other than it is perpetrated by men who believe that women find force or aggression sexually exciting and who have, in general, condescending opinions of women. What would be useful to know, at least from the standpoint of understanding the motivation for rape, is why do rapists hold these ideas in the first place? Specifically, what kinds of social experiences lead rapists to such conclusions about women?

- Perhaps an even more important question is this: How can psychologists help women overcome the powerful and often devastating emotional impact of being raped? What types of counseling and postrape therapy will provide rape victims the best chances of experiencing full emotional recovery and leading fulfilling lives?

- Psychology is also still in search of an answer to the question of homosexual development. The work thus far is promising, but it falls short of what we need to know about homosexuality to fully understand its development. Knowledge gained from such research would, first of all, help all people better understand homosexuality and homosexual behavior regardless of their sexual orientation. Secondly, it would ostensibly allow homosexuals to deal more effectively with the psychological costs presently attached to identifying oneself as a homosexual.

- Finally, psychologists must also continue to seek answers to understand differences between men and women in terms of the interaction of biological and environmental events that shape their sexual attitudes and behavior. Although the physiology of the human reproductive system remains much the same generation after generation, our attitudes about the boundaries of sexually permissible behavior and gender roles change, not only from generation to generation, but from one region of the country to the next. How do these changes affect existing behavioral differences between males and females?

Let us leave you with two other questions. Suppose the western culture of the late 1990s was to reach the islands of Inis Beag and Mangaia. Would the sexual standards and mores of the western culture affect the sexual customs, practices, and gender roles of the natives? The second question: How might the sexual customs, practices, and gender roles of the natives affect those of the immigrants? Thinking about these questions will draw your imagination into the heart of many of the sex- and gender-related issues being addressed by psychologists today.

CONCEPT SUMMARY

- Why are the terms *gender* and *biological sex* not synonymous? What two factors contribute to gender? (pp. 422–423)

THE BIOLOGY OF GENDER DEVELOPMENT

- During the prenatal period, how does the development process differ between male and female fetuses? What role does androgen play in the sexual differentiation process? (pp. 423–424)

- What does the adrenogenital syndrome tell us about hormonal effects on behavior? (pp. 423–424)

- How is female gender development affected by puberty? How is male gender development affected by puberty? (pp. 424–427)

- What factors influence the onset of menarche? (pp. 425–426)

PSYCHOLOGICAL ASPECTS OF GENDER DEVELOPMENT

- What is the difference between gender identity and gender typing? How do we develop a gender identity? (pp. 429–432)
- How do socialization processes influence development of our gender roles? (pp. 429–430)
- Which of the four theories of gender typing and gender role development is the most plausible? What advantages does it have over the other theories? (pp. 432–434)
- In terms of their cognitive abilities and social behavior, do males and females really differ? If so, in what ways? (pp. 434–435)

GENDER AND SEXUAL BEHAVIOR

- How is an individual's biological sex defined? (p. 425)
- How do males and females differ with respect to sexual behavior? (pp. 436–437)

BIOLOGICAL BASES OF THE HUMAN SEXUAL RESPONSE

- What roles do vasocongestion and myotonia play in the Masters and Johnson model of sexual arousal? According to this model, how do the four stages of sexual arousal differ? (pp. 437–438)
- What important differences exist between the Kaplan and Zilbergeld and Ellison models of sexual arousal and the Masters and Johnson model? (pp. 437–439)

SEXUAL DYSFUNCTIONS

- What kinds of sexual dysfunctions are common in males? What are the symptoms of these dysfunctions? (pp. 439–440)
- What kinds of sexual dysfunctions are common in females? What are the symptoms of these dysfunctions? (pp. 440–441)
- What role do psychological factors play in sexual dysfunctions? (pp. 439–441)

PATTERNS OF SEXUAL BEHAVIOR

- What factors seem to contribute to the high rate of teenage pregnancies in the United States? (pp. 442–443)
- What is homosexuality? Why is it hard to define? (p. 445)
- According to psychological theory, what factors influence the determination of sexual orientation? (pp. 446–447)
- What is an STD? How do the symptoms of the various STDs differ? How can the chances of contracting an STD be reduced? (pp. 449–450)

SEXUAL AGGRESSION

- In what ways can pornographic materials influence a person's tendency to accept myths about female sexuality or to engage in sexual violence? (pp. 451–452)
- What are the stages and symptoms of the rape trauma syndrome? (p. 454)

KEY TERMS AND CONCEPTS

Gender The individual qualities of a person that a given culture uses to define that person as a male or female. (p. 422)

THE BIOLOGY OF GENDER DEVELOPMENT

Fertilization The union of a sperm and ovum resulting in conception. (p. 423)

Puberty The transitional period between childhood and adolescence in which each of us becomes sexually mature. (p. 424)

Follicle-stimulating Hormone (FSH) and luteinizing hormone (LH). In males, FSH stimulates the manufacture of sperm and LH stimulates production of testosterone by the testes. In females, FSH prepares the ovaries for ovulation and LH stimulates ovulation, the monthly release of mature ova from the ovaries. (p. 424)

Menarche A girl's first menstruation, which is usually experienced at about age 13. Menstruation is the result of monthly fluctuations of sex hormones that regulate ovulation. If an ovum is not fertilized, the tissues and substances lining the uterine wall that would support the developing fetus had fertilization occurred, are shed through the vagina. (p. 425)

Menopause The cessation of the menstrual cycle. (p. 427)

PSYCHOLOGICAL ASPECTS OF GENDER DEVELOPMENT

Gender Identity An individual's private sense of being a male or female. In most cases, one's gender identity matches one's biological gender. (p. 429)

Gender Typing The learning of the attitudes and behaviors appropriate to one's gender identity. (p. 429)

Gender Roles Cultural expectations that men and women should think and behave differently. (p. 429)

Transsexual An individual who does not develop a gender identity consistent with either his or her actual biological or assigned gender. For instance, a man may feel that he is actually a woman trapped in a man's body, or a woman may feel that she is actually a man trapped in a woman's body. (p. 431)

BIOLOGICAL BASES OF THE HUMAN SEXUAL RESPONSE

Vasocongestion The flow of blood during sexual arousal into a region of the body, in this case, the genital area. (p. 437)

Myotonia Muscle contractions that, in this case, occur during sexual arousal. (p. 437)

Masters and Johnson Model The theory that vasocongestion and myotonia are the primary processes involved in the four stages of sexual arousal: excitement, plateau, orgasm, and resolution. (p. 437)

SEXUAL DYSFUNCTIONS

Sexual Dysfunction An impairment or difficulty in achieving sexual arousal and orgasm. (p. 439)

Orgasmic Dysfunction A woman's inability to have an orgasm. Orgasmic dysfunctions are of three varieties: the woman has never had an orgasm; the woman has previously experienced orgasm, but now is no longer able to; and the woman is able to reach orgasm in some situations but not in others. (p. 439)

Vaginismus The spastic contraction of the muscles surrounding the vagina. In many cases, the muscle contractions are so strong that intercourse is impossible. (p. 440)

Erectile Dysfunction The inability to produce or maintain an erection. Men with primary erectile dysfunction have never had an erection; men with secondary erectile dysfunction have been able to have an erection but now cannot at least 25 percent of the time. (p. 440)

Premature Ejaculation The inability to delay ejaculation. (pp. 441)

PATTERNS OF SEXUAL BEHAVIOR

Homosexuality Sexual attraction to individuals of the same gender. Homosexual behavior involves any sexual contact with a member of one's own sex. (p. 445)

Sexually Transmitted Diseases (STDs) Diseases that are contracted through sexual contact with another person. Any kind of STD will negatively affect an afflicted individual's self-esteem and sexual behavior. (p. 449)

SEXUAL AGGRESSION

Pornography Sexually arousing literature, art, and films. (p. 450)

Rape Sexual intercourse or other sexual acts that occur without the willing consent of one of the people involved. (p. 452)

Rape Trauma Syndrome A two-stage emotional and physical reaction experienced by many rape victims. The first stage, the acute phase, starts immediately after the rape and may last up to several weeks. It involves anxiety, fear, humiliation, self-blame, and physical discomfort from injuries related to the rape. The second stage, the long-term reorganization phase, may last up to several months or even years. During this phase, it is not uncommon for the rape victim to quit her job, move several times, and change her phone number. (p. 454)

ADDITIONAL SOURCES OF INFORMATION

Griffitt, W., & Hatfield, E. (1985). *Human sexual behavior.* Glenview, IL: Scott, Foresman.

Hyde, J. S. (1986). *Understanding human sexuality.* New York: McGraw-Hill. Both of these books are well-written and provide complete introductions to the biology and psychology of human sexual behavior. Either book will provide a good start for exploring sexual behavior in more detail than presented here.

Malamuth, N. M., & Donnerstein, E. (Eds.). (1984). *Pornography and sexual aggression.* Orlando: Academic Press. This graduate-level text presents a wealth of data and theory on the relation between pornography and sexual violence.

Money, J. (1985). *The destroying angel.* Buffalo, NY: Prometheus Books. Written by one of the most prolific sex researchers in the 1980s, this book is an account of many myths that have surrounded sex and sexual behavior in history. This book is very interesting, informative, and, at times, entertaining.

13 Intelligence

WHAT IS INTELLIGENCE?
(461–463)

Achievement and Aptitude   General and Specific Intelligences

Intelligence is the capacity to acquire knowledge and the ability to use it in problem-solving situations. Achievement refers to knowledge that has already been acquired. Early researchers debated over whether intelligence was comprised of a single general factor or several specific factors.

A HISTORICAL OVERVIEW OF INTELLIGENCE TESTS
(463–468)

Sir Francis Galton   The Binet-Simon Test
Lewis Terman and the Stanford-Binet

Intelligence tests were first developed in a climate of racism. To many early researchers, the goal was to develop a screening device to encourage intelligent people to mate with one another in order to further the development of the species. Alfred Binet, the developer of the first truly useful intelligence test, was an exception. He was interested in intelligence testing as a means of identifying school children who needed special attention with their studies.

CONTEMPORARY INTELLIGENCE TESTS
(468–474)

The Stanford-Binet, 4th Edition   The Revised Wechsler Tests of Intelligence
Individual versus Group Tests

The primary individually administered intelligence tests are the fourth edition of the Stanford-Binet and the family of revised Wechsler tests. Each test defines a hierarchy of intelligence that is operationalized by a series of subtests. In addition to a score of general intelligence, each test provides more specific scores that distinguish among different kinds of intelligence. Intelligence tests are designed either to be administered to a single person or to a group of people at once.

CRITICAL ISSUES IN EVALUATING INTELLIGENCE TEST SCORES   *(475–479)*

Standard Scores and the Normal Curve   Reliability and Validity   Test Bias

The distribution of scores from intelligence tests, as well as the values of most psychological and physical variables, follow a normal distribution, which can be recognized by its bell-shaped pattern. Two key characteristics of a good test are that its results are consistent over repeated measurements and that it measures what it purports to measure. A special consideration that affects test validity is whether the test is biased in favor of one group over another.

HEREDITY, ENVIRONMENT, AND INTELLIGENCE
(479–483)

The Roots of Intelligence   Heredity, Intelligence, and Social Issues

Although intelligence is determined by both heredity and environmental variables, the relative contribution of each is debated among scientists. Those favoring the contribution of heredity over environment feel that differences in the genotypes play an influential role in explaining different levels of intelligence. Those favoring environment over heredity maintain that differences in mental ability result largely from environmental factors, such as different educational or cultural opportunities. Regardless of its roots, the level of intelligence in a culture influences and is influenced by social decisions.

MODERN THEORIES OF INTELLIGENCE
(484–489)

The Triarchic Theory of Intelligence   A Theory of Multiple Intelligences
Biological Measurements of Intelligence

Some psychologists are currently calling for an expanded definition of intelligence that goes well beyond that inherent in intelligence tests. The concept of intelligence has been broadened to include abilities such as music, athletics, and personal abilities, and some psychologists are currently studying specific cognitive processes that underlie intelligent behavior.

How smart are you? Obviously smart enough to attend a university or college. But are you smarter than the person sitting in front of you in class? Are you more intelligent than people who have never attended a university, or who have never attended school? After all, you can probably solve an algebraic equation or write an essay, or answer many questions on the SAT successfully. But could you survive for days alone in some of the harshest regions of the world such as the Kalahari desert in south-central Africa or in the Arctic? Without the benefit of formal schooling, an African bushman might manage quite well alone in the Kalahari, as would an Eskimo in the Arctic. So who is more intelligent?

The fact is that people differ widely in their abilities to solve different kinds of problems. The issue of interest to many is not the existence of these differences, but their meaning. Explaining why these differences exist and interpreting their meaning has often led to conflict and controversy involving not only psychologists but government officials, courts, the press, and the public. Probably no other topic studied by psychologists has led to more controversy (Weinberg, 1989). Do you like soap operas? A discussion of intelligence can include plenty of human drama: bodyguards to protect professors who advocate unpopular views, jail sentences for those who advocate the opposite view, forged data by professors who desperately want their research results to conform to their own hypotheses, forced sterilization of those who are thought to be intellectually dull, and sperm banks that store the frozen sperm from highly intelligent (and often athletic and otherwise talented) men.

To some psychologists, theories that specify the nature of intelligence and its development, and the tests devised to measure it, represent one of psychology's most important contributions to society. According to one proponent of intelligence testing, Richard Herrnstein (1973, pp. 53, 62),

> The heritability of IQ has doubtless become psychology's best proved, socially significant empirical finding. . . . The measurement of intelligence is psychology's most telling accomplishment to date.

To other psychologists, these same "contributions" represent some of psychology's most glaring embarrassments. As one critic, Leon Kamin (Eysenck & Kamin, 1981, p. 154) wrote,

> We can make no statement at all about how heritable intelligence . . . might be. We cannot measure such capacities and abilities.

Now *there* is a difference in opinion.

Intelligence is not always defined by formal schooling or by IQ. For people in different cultures, such as Eskimos in the Arctic or Bushmen in the African desert, intelligence may be defined in terms of a person's ability to function and survive in his or her environment.

Whether a person has a mechanical aptitude for fixing engines or an advanced education that prepares one to design buildings, one factor that defines intelligence is the ability to solve problems.

Why are these differences in capacities and abilities so important to so many people? How are they measured? To what extent are they influenced by heredity? By environment? How does the study of these differences affect society as a whole? How were the first intelligence tests developed? How is intelligence related to other cognitive processes?

These are the kinds of questions that we will address in this chapter. As we will see, the answers are not always clear, but their discussion has often been lively. But before we get ahead of ourselves, we need to define the concept of intelligence.

WHAT IS INTELLIGENCE?

Although intelligence has been defined in many different ways, most of the definitions share an underlying theme—problem solving ability—and it is around this theme that we define intelligence. **Intelligence** is the capacity to acquire knowledge and to use that knowledge to solve problems. This ability is demonstrated by providing a solution to a problem never before encountered, by providing with relative ease a solution to a problem previously solved, or by learning how to solve a problem. Simply put, intelligence is demonstrated when a problem is solved. The bushman who navigates through the desert and lives off of its resources, the executive who is promoted because of his or her leadership abilities, and the student who answers a test question correctly, are all demonstrating intelligence.

Simply put, intelligence is demonstrated when a problem is solved.

One way to characterize different approaches to understanding intelligence is by the type of the problems to be solved within a particular context. Intelligence, sometimes referred to as mental ability, has traditionally been studied only within the context of those problems that require various cognitive processes for their solution, processes of the type we discussed in Chapters 8 and 9 (Memory and Thinking and Language). An example of this type of problem is:

Square is to round as cube is to:
a) diamond b) spoon c) star d) ball

To solve this problem the problem solver must be able to reason from facts to conclusions, to recall information from long-term memory, to visualize geometric patterns, and to form and relate abstract concepts (Sternberg, 1985). Problem-solving abilities can also be studied from an even more general perspective in which the problems to be solved include playing a Mozart piano sonata, shooting a basketball through a hoop, or helping to transform an unhappy marriage into a mutually rewarding one (Gardener, 1983).

Achievement and Aptitude

Intelligence is demonstrated by solving problems, but the failure to solve a problem does not necessarily indicate a lack of intelligence. Instead, failure to solve a particular problem may simply mean that one lacks the required experience. For example, you would probably be unable to translate passages of text written in the Swahili language to English, but your inability to understand Swahili does not imply that you are not as intelligent as a native speaker of Swahili. Instead, you simply have not had the opportunity or the need to learn this language. Asking someone to understand a language with which he or she is not familiar would not be an indication of intelligence but of achievement. Intelligence refers to capacity for learning, whereas **achievement** refers to what has already been learned. That is, achievement refers to skills already acquired. An achievement test measures existing knowledge of facts, so your nonexistent knowledge of Swahili indicates a lack of achievement of Swahili language skills, not necessarily low intelligence.

A better indicator of intelligence than understanding Swahili would be how quickly and how well you could learn Swahili if you chose to do so. Within this context, intelligence is an **aptitude**, which refers to the potential for learning. A person with a good aptitude for language or desert navigation might learn these skills much faster than someone with only an average aptitude. And a person with a poor aptitude might never be able to learn Swahili or navigation skills, regardless of the amount of instruction he or she received.

General and Specific Intelligences

When intelligence tests were developed in the first few decades of the 1900s, the tests emphasized a single intelligence score called IQ. Each person was thought to be more or less intelligent, and the tests were designed to place an individual somewhere along the IQ continuum. An early intelligence theorist writing in 1904, Charles Spearman (1863–1945), referred to this general intelligence ability common to all intellectual tasks as **g**. (Spearman also believed that people possess intelligence for specific abilities, which he called s, but he focused his research on understanding the determinants of g.) To assess whether intelligence was comprised of general or specific abilities, Spearman developed a procedure known as **factor analysis**, which is a statistical technique used to determine whether different test questions are correlated with each other. According to Spearman's rationale, if all questions on an intelligence test require similar intellectual abilities, then intelligence may be viewed as a general capacity of individuals. On the other hand, if different questions on the test require different intellectual abilities, then intelligence may be viewed as a variety of specific kinds of capacities. So, to determine whether intelligence is a general or specific capacity, every question on an intelligence test is correlated, through factor analysis, with every other test question. Those that correlate highly with each other are hypothesized to tap the same intellectual capacity or factor of the individual being tested. Those that correlate weakly are believed to tap different intellectual capacities or factors. Spearman noted that questions on intelligence tests of his day were at least

TABLE 13.1.	*Thurstone's primary mental abilities.*
ABILITY	DESCRIPTION
Verbal comprehension	Word knowledge and usage
Word fluency	Generation of words quickly and accurately
Numerical calculation	Computational skills involving number problems
Spatial visualization	Discrimination of objects presented in varying spatial orientations
Memory	Recall of familiar items
Perceptual speed	Rapid recognition of objects in visual discrimination tasks
General reasoning	Deduction

moderately correlated. A person with high intelligence was seen to be able to solve a wide variety of problems from arithmetic to reading comprehension to learning how to navigate across the desert. Spearman argued that all people possess some degree of *g* (general intelligence), and therefore whether people perform well or poorly on an intelligence test depends upon the degree of *g* they possess.

A contemporary of Spearman's, Louis Thurstone (1938), disagreed. Using a different method of factor analysis, Thurstone derived seven primary mental abilities: verbal comprehension, word fluency, numerical calculation, spatial visualization, memory, perceptual speed, and reasoning (see Table 13.1). Although he denied Spearman's *g*, Thurstone himself found that the seven mental abilities were not wholly independent of each other; there was a moderate amount of correlation among the different abilities.

The views of both Spearman and Thurstone are represented among current intelligence researchers, although in an integrated, not dichotomous, form. Today, although not all psychologists have abandoned the concept of general ability, those who devise and administer intelligence tests are also now interested in specific kinds of abilities that people may have. For example, some people may be better at solving math problems than at comprehending passages of written text. As we will see, each major intelligence test now examines a hierarchy of abilities from something akin to Spearman's *g* to very specific abilities. One practical result of the emphasis on specific abilities is that intelligence tests provide a variety of information about specific as well as general intellectual abilities. A general intelligence score is provided, as well as scores on specific abilities such as reading comprehension and memory. We are now ready to look at the sociopolitical context under which intelligence testing and the concept of intelligence were developed.

A HISTORICAL OVERVIEW OF INTELLIGENCE TESTS

The meaning of intelligence and the interpretation of intelligence test scores has always been surrounded by controversy, and many current controversies in intelligence can be traced to the beginning of the mental testing movement. As we shall see, the first attempts to develop intelligence tests were motivated to support a particular sociopolitical viewpoint, initially under the leadership of one man, Sir Francis Galton. Reviewing the historical context of intelligence testing not only explains much of the content of today's tests, it allows us to introduce some general principles that continue to be important to intelligence testing.

Sir Francis Galton

Sir Francis Galton

The founding of the discipline of psychology and the first attempt at developing intelligence tests both occurred little more than a century ago. The first person to attempt to measure intelligence with a test was the Englishman and half cousin of Charles Darwin, Sir Francis Galton (1822–1911). Actually, Galton tried to measure just about everything in which he was interested. He explored and mapped previously uncharted regions of Southwest Africa, published some of the earliest weather maps, invented a system of cataloguing fingerprints, constructed a "beauty map" of Britain by counting the number of beautiful women in different towns, and observed whether religious people lived longer than nonreligious people to see if prayer contributed to longevity (Francher, 1985; Kevles, 1985).

Galton's ideological and political bias underlying his motivation to develop intelligence tests was clear: "The brains of the nation lie in the higher of our classes" (1909, p. 11). By "the higher of our classes," Galton was referring to the British upper class, whose members he believed were biologically superior to those who populated the lower classes, as well as to other "races." Today, Galton would be considered a racist, and his beliefs would be publicly and professionally scorned; but during the late 19th and early 20th centuries his beliefs were not only respectable, they were shared by many eminent psychologists and members of society in general.

Much of Galton's thinking was inspired by Darwin's (1859) book *On the Origin of Species*, which, as you recall from Chapter 3, proposed the theory of evolution by natural selection. Although Darwin emphasized the evolution of the physical characteristics of organisms, Galton applied the principles of natural selection to psychological characteristics, especially those regarding intelligence. Specifically, Galton reasoned that inherited differences in the physical structure of the brain might lead to differences in intellectual abilities. The first sentence of his influential book, *Hereditary Genius: An Inquiry into Its Laws and Consequences*, aptly captures Galton's intent:

> I propose to show in this book that a man's natural abilities are derived by inheritance, under exactly the same limitations as are the form and physical features of the whole organic world (the world of living things).
>
> (1870, p. 1)

Just as people differ regarding their physical abilities, Galton documented the large differences in the "mental powers" of different people, and he argued that these large differences were due in part to limits on the underlying capacities of how much can be learned by any one individual. Thus, one's mental powers were seen to be determined largely by one's biology. Galton's conclusion on this matter is to the point.

> I have no patience with the hypothesis . . . that babies are born pretty much alike, and that the sole agencies in creating differences between (people) are steady application and moral effort. It is in the most unqualified manner that I object to pretensions of natural equality.
>
> (1870, p. 14)

According to Galton, some people (mostly those of the lower classes) were born with inferior mental abilities, others were born with superior mental abilities, and most are born with average abilities.

Galton also attempted to apply his knowledge by developing social programs that would, in his opinion, improve the quality of life for future generations. Galton (1870, 1909) advocated that people should explicitly take control of the evolutionary process to improve the "human breed" by artificial breeding. He advocated nothing less than augmenting natural selection with artificial selection, so that "a highly gifted race" could be developed over several generations in the same way that dogs or horses are bred for specific traits.

Coining a word based on a Greek term for "well-bred," Galton used the term **eugenics** to describe the movement he founded to study and promote the principles of artificial selection. To implement his eugenics program, Galton needed to identify intelligent and otherwise talented and physically fit people before they had children. So he attempted to develop the intelligence test as a means of screening an individual's inherited intelligence.

Thus, Galton searched for a measure that could distinguish the intelligent from those who presumably were not. Because he believed that intelligence is an inherited trait, he measured primarily unlearned perceptual and physical responses. For example, he hypothesized that reaction time would be related to the efficiency of the nervous system; those with shorter reaction times might be biologically superior, and therefore, more intelligent. He believed that sensory acuity, including keenness of sight and hearing, was related to the quality of the nervous system. Similarly, Galton and some of his colleagues, including James McKeen Cattell (1860–1944), the person who originated the phrase, "mental test," measured the ability to discriminate between colors, the ability to bisect a line relying solely upon eyesight, the ability to distinguish among different weights in terms of just noticeable differences, the accuracy by which an interval of 10 seconds could be estimated, and the number of random consonants that could be memorized (Fancher, 1985).

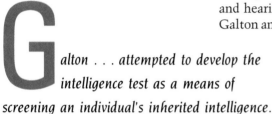

*G*alton . . . attempted to develop the intelligence test as a means of screening an individual's inherited intelligence.

In 1884 Galton established a testing laboratory at an international fair in London at which over 9000 people paid to be evaluated by Galton's tests (Johnson et al., 1985). Galton's extensive efforts were, however, in vain; he and his colleagues never succeeded in finding any meaningful biological difference among those he considered intelligent and those he did not. By the early 20th century, most psychologists had lost their enthusiasm for Galton's approach to mental testing, though as we shall see, Galton's rationale continued to influence the mental testing movement.

The Binet-Simon Test

Alfred Binet

Alfred Binet (1857–1911), the leading French psychologist at the beginning of the 20th century, constructed the first truly useful intelligence test. Binet, like Galton, was interested in studying individual differences in mental abilities, though from a much different perspective. First, Binet was not an advocate of eugenics, nor did he focus on measuring intellectual superiority. Unlike Galton, Binet assumed that intellectual performance was largely attributable to previous environmental experiences, and, in general, he was less concerned with the heredity-environment issue than with understanding the purely psychological nature of mental abilities as they existed (Fancher, 1985). Second, he believed that Galton and his colleagues emphasized sensory and physiological measures at the expense of cognitive processes such as problem solving and language comprehension.

Binet was also disappointed in the first intelligence tests he himself had devised. The event that finally led to success was when the French government invited him to measure the intelligence of children in the French school system. At the beginning of the 20th century a national law was passed that mandated compulsory education of all French children. To comply with the law, the authorities needed to identify those who required special educational efforts. In sharp contrast to Galton, Binet believed that with proper attention and educational opportunities, even those children doing poorly in school could increase their level of intelligence. Binet's job was to identify those children most in need of special assistance.

Binet, with his colleague Theodore Simon (1873–1961), developed a test to identify the slow learners. Published in 1905, the test consisted of only 30 items that were ordered according to difficulty, and that assessed abilities such as vocabulary, memory, and logical reasoning. The easiest item, which only required someone to follow a lighted match with his or her eyes, could be passed by very young normal children, but represented the upper limit of ability for severely learning disabled older children. More difficult items included memorizing a string of digits, defining various words, reproducing drawings from memory, and completing sentences. A sample of some of the items included in the Binet-Simon test is shown in Table 13.2.

Binet and Simon continued to refine this test with revisions in 1908 and 1911. Binet finished the later revision alone just before his death. Beginning with the 1908 version, the authors realized that the chronological age of the child should be considered in computing the overall test score; knowing just the number correct on a test is not enough information by which to gauge performance. To know only that a child was able to answer 35 out of 50 items correctly provides little information about the child's performance. What is needed is to compare a child's score of 35 to the scores of other children of the same age. To know that the average number correct for children of the same age is only 20, and that a score as high as 35 occurs less than once in every 100 children, provides much more information about the child's performance.

To account for the age of the child in the interpretation of his or her test score, Binet and Simon computed the average level of performance of the items on the test for each age group. In psychological testing, the average levels of performance on a test for different groups are called **norms.** When Binet and Simon developed their norms, they defined the different groups only for different age levels. For these early tests, other classifications such as ethnic group membership or sex were not considered.

To further enhance the comparison of the child's performance to that of other children on the test, Binet and Simon introduced the concept of the child's **mental age,** the age level of the normative performance the child was able to match. For example, a 7-year-old who could solve problems that usually were not solvable except by the average 9-year-old would have a mental age of 9. Today, consideration of age in the interpretation of a test score seems obvious, but this insight at the time was a genuine innovation

TABLE 13.2.   A *sample of items from the Binet-Simon test.*

AGE LEVEL	QUESTION
3	Repeat two digits.
4	Identify one's own sex.
5	Repeat a ten-syllable sentence.
6	Copy a picture of a diamond.
7	Show left ear and right hand.
8	Detect omissions from pictures of common objects.
9	Identify proper order of months of the year.
10	Arrange five blocks according to weight.
12	Interpret the meaning of a misarranged sentence.
15	Give three rhymes for a specific word in one minute.

(Herrnstein, 1973). Its consideration led to the first mental test with practical predictive value, a test that could successfully distinguish among children of normal intelligence and children of below or above average intelligence.

Binet's practice of interpreting intelligence test scores as measures of relative standing in a given reference group has become well established for intelligence tests and other tests as well. Each person's score is interpreted by comparing it to the norms of a group to which that person belongs, which is called the standardization group. The process of establishing the norms by testing hundreds or thousands of people in the group is called **standardization.** The relevant standardization group for an intelligence test used with American 9-year-olds would be American 9-year-olds.

Lewis Terman and the Stanford-Binet

Lewis Terman

In 1912, Lewis Terman (1877–1956) and several graduate students at Stanford University began the translation and modification of Binet's test into English. In 1916, Terman published the translated and revised test and gathered norms for it on over 2300 people. The result was the **Stanford-Binet** intelligence test, which was to become the most widely used intelligence test for many decades. The Stanford-Binet was revised in 1937, 1960, and 1986.

The Stanford-Binet was also the first test to report the standardized scores in the form of IQ scores. The **intelligence quotient** or **IQ** was suggested by the German psychologist William Stern (1871–1938) in 1914. The IQ score was originally an actual quotient—the ratio of a person's mental age (MA) to chronological age (CA) multiplied by 100. That is,

$$IQ = {}^{MA}\!/_{CA} \times 100$$

For example, an 8-year-old who answers the same number of items correctly as does the average 8-year-old would have an IQ of 100; the child's mental age would be the same as his or her chronological age. However, the 8-year-old who answers the same number of items correctly as does the typical 12-year-old would have a mental age of 12, so his or her IQ would be $^{12}\!/_8 \times 100 = 150$. However, as we shall see a bit later, intelligence test scores from today's tests are no longer computed in this manner, though some tests still use the term IQ.

The development of the Stanford-Binet, although inadvertent, also served the eugenics movement that had enjoyed a considerable level of support from both British and American citizens at that time. Organizations such as the American Eugenics Society and the Human Betterment Foundation were formed. Intelligence tests such as the Stanford-Binet were used to show "objectively" the supposed racial inferiority of several ethnic groups, and these test scores were used to limit immigration to America by Eastern Europeans (Kevles, 1985). Galton and his co-workers had been disappointed by their failure to find a test that discriminated among people in terms of their intelligence, but Terman's Stanford-Binet test provided eugenicists with renewed hope.

Terman himself agreed with many eugenics principles, and his racist opinions on this topic were clear. His belief that the Stanford-Binet measured "native intelligence" is particularly ironic since Binet, who died five years before the publication of the Stanford-Binet test, maintained just the opposite. Binet believed that his test did nothing more than identify those who had received poor educational training.

The eugenics movement, aided in part by the development of the Stanford-Binet, also advocated an increasingly ominous position. Galton wished to achieve a eugenically sound society through inducements such as monetary grants that would encourage intelligent people to marry other intelligent people. Increasingly, however, the emphasis shifted to a "negative eugenics" in which those deemed unfit were not allowed to reproduce. For example, the eugenics movement was partially responsible for the passage of laws in the United States that required sterilization of the "feebleminded" in 24 of the then 48 states (Popenoe, 1927). In all states between 1910 and 1930, 10,877 patients in state institutions were sterilized (Gosney, 1930).

It was not until the mid-1930s that the eugenics movement finally came to a halt (Kevles, 1985). In addition to a growing number of academics who questioned the scientific validity of its claims, two other events contributed to its growing unpopularity. First, the depression had begun, and many people suddenly found themselves poor. These people, many of whom had been well-off before the depression, were not willing to blame their misfortune on genetics. Second, the Nazis were growing in power, and the world was becoming aware of their atrocities, including their declaration of their racial superiority.

With a history like this, it's no wonder the subject of intelligence testing has remained controversial. Fortunately, academics and many other people are well aware of the shortcomings of contemporary intelligence tests, the topic of our next section.

CONTEMPORARY INTELLIGENCE TESTS

Because of the expense, time, and energy required to develop an intelligence test, as well as the difficulty of overcoming the inertia of well-established tests, new intelligence tests are not often published. Even so, it is surprising that in the history of intelligence testing only two individually administered intelligence tests have been widely used: the Stanford-Binet and the Wechsler tests. These tests can be used whenever an overall assessment of an individual's intellectual functioning is needed, though their most common use is similar to the application for which Binet originally designed his first test. They are most commonly used in schools to provide educators information regarding a student's abilities.

t is surprising that in the history of intelligence testing only two individually administered intelligence tests have been widely used . . .

As we will see, each of these tests is based on a theory of intelligence that defines a hierarchy of abilities, which means that the assessment of intellectual functioning provided by these tests is much more detailed than that provided by a single intelligence score (see Figure 13.1). In addition to a global score of general intelligence, each test provides more specific scores that distinguish, for example, between abilities that depend on a knowledge of a language such as English from those abilities that do not. Scores for the most specific levels of abilities are provided by performance on each of the individual subtests.

The Stanford-Binet, 4th Edition

The current version of the Stanford-Binet, the fourth edition, was published in 1986, and is used with people ranging from childhood through adulthood. Although the relation of this revision to the original Binet-Simon scales and the first edition of the Stanford-Binet is apparent, the fourth edition is a greater departure from these original tests than were any of the previous revisions (Thorndike, Hagen, & Sattler, 1986). For example, the fourth edition drops the term "IQ," and it now provides a variety of measures of intelligence in addition to a measure of *g*.

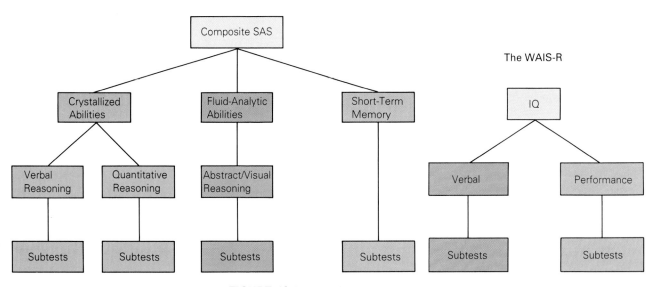

FIGURE 13.1
The hierarchy of intelligence as defined by the subtests of the Stanford-Binet, 4th edition and the WAIS-R.

The Stanford-Binet provides the psychologist with a variety of information regarding different kinds of intellectual abilities, and provides much more information than is provided by a single intelligence score. The most specific kind of information is provided by individual subtests. The items on each subtest all represent a particular kind of problem and are ordered according to increasing difficulty. Each subtest is administered and scored separately. These subtest scores are then summed together to form a score that represents a particular type of intellectual functioning, such as mathematical or verbal ability. Finally, the overall measure of general intelligence is computed from the mental functioning scores.

The overall intelligence score represented by Spearman's *g* on the Stanford-Binet is called the Composite Standard Age Score, sometimes abbreviated as Composite SAS. Underlying the Stanford-Binet measure of *g* are four second-level abilities: Verbal Crystallized Abilities, Quantitative Crystallized Abilities, Fluid-analytic Abilities, and Short-term Memory (see Table 13.3). The examinee receives a score on each of these second-level abilities, as well as scores on the 15 subtests, though not all examinees always take all 15 subtests (see Table 13.4). For example, only six of the subtests are appropriate for adults.

Crystallized abilities are those learned in school for solving verbal and quantitative problems. The subtests for these abilities are more dependent on school achievement than are the other subtests. Satisfactory performance on all of the crystallized abilities subtests require successful completion of schooling needed to solve the problems at the child's age level. The Verbal Reasoning score is based on four subtests that require knowing the meanings of words and situations (see Table 13.3). The Quantitative Reasoning score is computed on the basis of three subtest scores, all of which involve working with numbers or equations.

Fluid-analytic abilities are those that require the kind of abstract reasoning that is not dependent on language. Fluid-analytic abilities are also less dependent on schooling than are crystallized abilities. The subtests for fluid-analytic abilities use patterns that, for example, have to be copied as accurately as possible, or matched to another pattern within which they fit (such as fitting a round peg into a round hole).

TABLE 13.3. *The four second-level abilities of g in the Stanford-Binet, 4th ed.*

CRYSTALLIZED ABILITIES: VERBAL REASONING

Vocabulary	Define words, which are either presented as a picture of an object for the early age levels, or spoken by the examiner for later age levels.
Comprehension	Answer questions by giving reasons why and how abstract concepts fit into daily-life (e.g., What is a computer and how is it used?).
Absurdities	Identify what is absurd about a picture (e.g., a car might have square wheels).
Verbal relations	Explain the similarities and differences among four words, three of which are alike and one which is different.

CRYSTALLIZED ABILITIES: QUANTITATIVE REASONING

Quantitative	Do arithmetic operations ranging from counting to multiplication and division to solving more complex word problems.
Number series	Complete a series of numbers (e.g., 2, 4, 6, ?, ?)
Equation building	Create a balanced equation from a series of digits and algebraic signs (e.g., 2, 2, 4, +, =)

FLUID-ANALYTIC ABILITIES: ABSTRACT/VISUAL REASONING

Pattern analysis	Patterns are matched at young age levels by matching shapes to holes, and at older age levels by using blocks of various designs to copy patterns of increasing complexity.
Copying	Duplicate a series of geometric designs by drawing them on paper or building the design out of blocks, beginning at the earliest age levels with simple designs such as a square.
Matrices	Complete a series of pictures from a list of alternatives.
Paper folding & cutting	Fold and cut a sheet of paper to follow a specific pattern.

SHORT-TERM MEMORY

Bead memory	The task is to memorize from a photograph the position, shape, and color of a set of beads which are stacked on top of each other.
Memory for sentences	Memorize sentences that vary in complexity from just a few words for the early age levels to over 25 words for the later age levels.
Memory for digits	Memorize a string of digits, which is then recalled in forward or backward order. The number of digits ranges from two to nine.
Memory for objects	Pictures of several objects are presented one at a time. The task is to point out the objects in the order presented in a composite picture that contains not only all of the individual objects, but also other objects as well.

Short-term memory tests include tests of memory for a variety of different objects. One test is for memory of words, and another is for numbers. The two other subtests for memory do not use language. One tests for memory of objects, and the other tests for memory of a string of objects of different shapes and sizes. For each subtest, the examiner presents a sequence of words, numbers, or objects, and the examinee is asked to recall the sequence in which they were presented. An example of this is the Memory for Digits subtest. The child's task for the forward recall problems is to repeat the numbers in the same order as they are read by the examiner. The easiest problem has only two digits, while the hardest problem has nine digits.

The administration and scoring of the subtests requires specialized training, and even more training and experience is required for the interpretation of the test scores. Proper interpretation requires that the psychologist consider each of the scores in relation to each of the other scores, noting any pattern of specific strengths and weaknesses. These scores from different parts of the test are usually presented in the form of a **linear profile,** which graphically displays the scores of all the subtests to facilitate comparison among them (see Figure 13.2).

If all the scores indicate approximately the same level of intellectual performance, interpretation of the linear profile is straightforward. For example, a score of approximately 50 on each of the Stanford-Binet subtests implies an average score on the Crystallized Abilities, Fluid-analytic Abilities, and Short-term Memory scales as well as the Composite SAS. Not surprisingly, this person would be declared to be of average intelligence and achievement. The more interesting interpretative work occurs when different levels of scores are obtained on the subtests. For example, an individual with a high Verbal Reasoning score, average Quantitative Reasoning score and Short-term Memory scores, and a below average Abstract/Visual Reasoning score possesses more ability for verbal reasoning and less for visual reasoning.

The Revised Wechsler Tests of Intelligence

The version of the Stanford-Binet test used in the 1930s had several limitations. It could only be used with children, it relied more heavily on verbal skills than does the current version, and it provided only a single, global intelligence score. In 1939, David Wechsler addressed these issues by introducing the first test in his family of tests for different age ranges. The current adult version is called the Wechsler Adult Intelligence Scale, Revised, or **WAIS-R,** and the current version for children between the ages of 6 and 17 is called the **WISC-R,** for Wechsler Intelligence Scale for Children, Revised. Wechsler tests for younger children also exist. A brief description of the WAIS-R subscales is given in Table 13.5 (p. 474).

To lessen what he perceived in the Stanford-Binet as a bias toward verbal intelligence, Wechsler introduced the distinction between verbal and performance intelligence, and included subtests for measuring both types of intelligence. **Verbal intelligence** refers to the problem-solving capacity for language-oriented problems such as reading comprehension and vocab-

TABLE 13.4. *The 15 subtests of the 1986 edition of the Stanford-Binet Intelligence Scale.*

1. Vocabulary:	For ages 2–6, provide name and definition of picture of object; for older subjects, define words increasing in difficulty
2. Bead memory:	String a series of multicolored beads after seeing a picture of the required string
3. Quantitative:	Complete a series of arithmetic problems, from simple counting to complex word problems
4. Memory for sentences:	Repeat a series of sentences of increasing complexity
5. Pattern analysis:	At young ages, match shapes to holes; at older levels, use blocks of different designs to copy patterns of increasing complexity
6. Comprehension:	Answer questions like "Why does the government regulate radio and television broadcasts?"
7. Absurdities:	Identify what is wrong with picture; for example, a wagon with triangular wheels
8. Memory for digits:	Repeat a list of digits of increasing length; forward or backward
9. Copying:	Draw (duplicate) a series of geometric line drawings of increasing complexity
10. Memory for objects:	Recognize a series of pictures of simple objects presented one at a time from a larger picture displaying many objects
11. Matrices:	Shown a series of pictures, determine which of a number of alternatives comes next in the series
12. Number series:	Presented with a series of numbers, determine what number comes next in the series
13. Paper folding and cutting:	Fold and/or cut sheet of paper according to a prescribed pattern
14. Verbal relations:	Given three words that are alike and a fourth that is different, explain why the three are alike and the fourth is different
15. Equation building:	Given a series of digits and algebraic signs (+, ×, ÷), create a balanced equation

ulary. Individual subtests that contribute to the verbal intelligence score include comprehending questions, understanding vocabulary, recalling strings of digits (called Digit Span on the Wechsler tests), and doing arithmetic.

The second category of subtests was designed to measure what Wechsler called **performance** or nonverbal intelligence. Solving these types of problems does not require understanding a particular language. For example, in a performance subtest called Object Assembly, the task is to put the pieces of a puzzle together within a time limit. The WAIS-R has 11 specific subtests and each subtest is classified as either primarily a verbal subtest or a performance subtest.

The hierarchy of abilities defined by the theory of intelligence underlying the Wechsler tests—verbal and performance intelligence—is more complex than the simple g score provided by the first Stanford-Binet tests, but it is simpler than that of the fourth edition of the Stanford-Binet. Many of the subtests in the two intelligence tests are, however, almost identical. Subtests such as memorizing strings of digits or recalling vocabulary words have been part of intelligence tests since Binet's first test.

An analysis of the content of these subtests shows that the Wechsler Verbal subtests largely correspond to the Crystallized Abilities subtests of the Stanford-Binet, though the Stanford-Binet provides separate Verbal and Quantitative scores, and Short-term Memory subtests. Indeed, this similarity is demonstrated quantitatively by the high correlations between the WAIS-R Verbal score and the Stanford-Binet Verbal Reasoning and Quantitative Reasoning scores, which are .86 and .85, respectively (Thorndike,

FIGURE 13.2
A sample linear profile describing results from individual subtests of the Stanford-Binet, 4th edition.

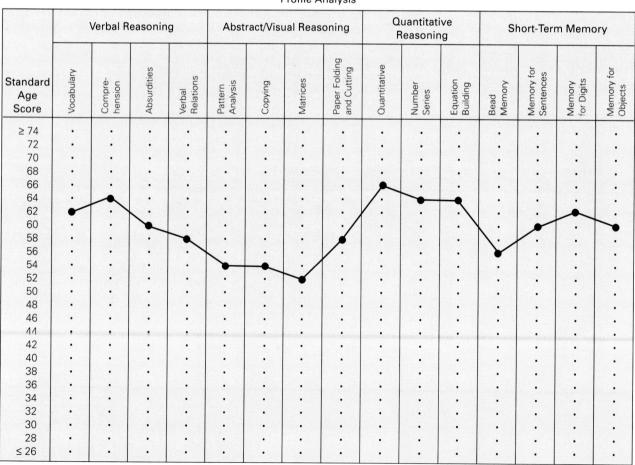

Standford-Binet, 4th ed.
Profile Analysis

The Weschler testing system has tests for both adults and children. The WAIS-R tests adult intelligence, while the WISC-R is the children's version.

Hagen, & Sattler, 1986). Similarly, the content of the Wechsler Performance scales corresponds to the content of the Stanford-Binet Abstract/Visual Reasoning subtests, which accounts for their high correlation of .81. The overall similarity of the two intelligence tests is shown by the very high correlation (.91) of their two estimates of g.

Individual versus Group Tests

Intelligence tests are designed either to be administered to a single person or to an entire group of people at once. Both the Stanford-Binet and the Wechsler tests are meant to be administered individually. For an individually administered intelligence test, a trained and experienced single examiner administers the test to a single person and records the examinee's responses. Depending on the test and the age of the person being tested, administration time of the test is usually about an hour. If cost were not a factor, individually administered tests would usually be preferred in place of group tests because of the individual attention given to the person being tested, and the greater variety of tasks that can be administered. The drawback is the additional time and money needed to administer the test to each examinee.

A less expensive and, therefore, more practical alternative in many situations is the group intelligence test in which a single examiner simultaneously administers the test to many people. Because the responses of a group test are usually restricted to paper and pencil problems (usually multiple-choice), the administrator of a group test requires little training. The administrator's primary responsibility is handing out the tests and answer forms and then timing each section of the test.

The first large-scale use of group intelligence tests was during World War I in which the U.S. Army used the tests to classify recruits for more specialized training (the Armed Forces continue to be large consumers of group intelligence tests). Another large-scale application of group tests is in educational selection, where test scores provide information that helps determine whether or not an individual is selected into an undergraduate, graduate, or professional program. Although these tests are not technically called intelligence tests, they are designed to measure broad aptitudes of intellectual performance.

Most of the group intelligence tests used for educational selection are administered by a single organization, the Educational Testing Service (ETS). These tests include the Scholastic Aptitude Test (SAT) and Ameri-

The first large-scale use of intelligence testing in the U.S. was during World War I, when the Army tested potential recruits.

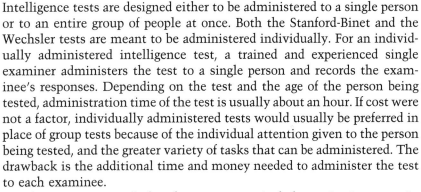

TABLE 13.5. *The subtests of the Wechsler Adult Intelligence Scale-Revised (WAIS-R)*

VERBAL SCALE

Information	(29 items) Questions designed to tap one's general knowledge about a variety of topics, e.g., "How many days in a week?"
Digit span	(7 series) Subject is read a series of 3 to 9 digits and is asked to repeat them; then a new series is to be repeated in reverse order.
Comprehension	(16 items) A test of the subject's judgment, common sense, and practical knowledge; e.g., "Why is it good to have schools?"
Similarities	(14 pairs) Subject must indicate the way(s) in which two things are alike; e.g., "In what way are an apple and a potato alike?"
Vocabulary	(35 words) Subject must provide an acceptable definition for the different words.
Arithmetic	(14 problems) Math problems must be solved without the use of paper and pencil; e.g., "Hamburgers cost 75 cents and hot dogs cost 60 cents. How much will it cost to buy 2 hamburgers and 3 hot dogs?"

PERFORMANCE SCALE

Picture completion	(20 pictures) Subject must identify the missing part or object in a drawing; e.g., a bird with one wing.
Picture arrangement	(10 series) A series of cartoonlike pictures must be arranged so that they tell a comprehensible story.
Block design	(9 items) Using blocks whose sides are either all red, all white, or diagonally red and white, subject must reproduce a designed picture or pattern shown on a card.
Object assembly	(4 objects) Jigsaw puzzles must be put together to form familiar objects.
Digit symbol	In a key, each of nine digits is paired with a symbol. When given a random series of digits, the subject must provide the paired symbol within a time limit.

can College Testing Program (ACT) for undergraduate admissions, as well as the Graduate Record Examination (GRE), Medical College Admissions Test (MCAT), Law School Admissions Test (LSAT), and Graduate Management Admissions Test (GMAT), used for admissions into graduate, medical, law, or business schools, respectively. Because ETS administers all of these tests, it has been called the "gatekeeper of the professions." Sufficiently high scores on all of these tests are now required for entry into many undergraduate and graduate schools and many of the most desirable professions.

The structure of all these tests is similar, so we will briefly discuss a representative group test that you might already have taken, the SAT. A multiple-choice test in use since 1926, the SAT yields two scores, the SAT-V and SAT-M, for verbal and mathematic abilities. The SAT-V contains problems on topics such as paragraph comprehension, sentence completion, and analogies. The SAT-M problems cover arithmetic, algebra, geometry, and story problems. When used in conjunction with high school grades, the SAT provides a reasonably accurate prediction of an applicant's eventual college GPA. The major weakness of the SAT when used for predicting college GPA is that GPA is determined by many factors other than intelligence, including interest and motivation for studying. Many instances can be found where a student was predicted not to do well in college but did well anyway, or vice versa.

Administering an intelligence test is one matter, evaluating the examinee's performance on it is another. What factors should be taken into consideration when devising a test? What do the scores provided by a intelligence test represent? The answers to those questions are provided in the next section, which looks at the issues involved in test construction and evaluation.

CRITICAL ISSUES IN EVALUATING INTELLIGENCE TEST SCORES

To understand contemporary intelligence tests, it helps to know something about the nature of testing in general and the meaning of test scores in particular. There are four critical aspects to constructing an intelligence test (or any other psychological test) and evaluating test scores: standard scores, reliability, validity, and test bias.

Standard Scores and the Normal Curve

Test scores from the earliest intelligence tests were reported as quotients of mental age to chronological age. The main problem with reporting the intelligence test score as a quotient is that after about age 16, people generally do not continue to answer more items correctly. That is, mental age does not continue to increase throughout a person's life. Accordingly, the practice of reporting the results of intelligence tests as a quotient was abandoned when the third edition of the Stanford-Binet appeared in 1960.

Today, psychological test scores are reported as standard scores. A **standard score** shows how far the score that represents the number of items answered correctly is from the mean (in units of standard deviation). In the language of psychological testing, the number of items answered correctly is called a "raw score." Before a psychologist interprets the results of the entire test or any of the subtests, he or she converts the raw score to a standard score by using a conversion table for the age of the person tested. For both the Stanford-Binet and the Wechsler tests, the average standard score of *g* for each age level is arbitrarily and conveniently defined to be 100. If the average 15-year-old gets 43 items correct, then a 15-year-old who has a raw score of 43 would have a standard score of 100. Although the method of computing intelligence test scores has changed from the original quotient, the logic underlying standard scores is the same as that underlying the quotient: performance on a test is interpreted according to the person's relative standing among his or her peers of the same age.

Performance on an intelligence test is interpreted according to the person's relative standing among his or her peers of the same age.

The distribution of scores from intelligence tests, as well as the values of most psychological and physical variables, follows a normal distribution, which can be recognized by a definite pattern. The **normal distribution** is the name for a frequency distribution of scores that is sometimes called the "bell-shaped curve" (see Figure 13.3). One characteristic of the normal curve is that there are as many scores above the mean as there are below the mean. Another characteristic is that most of the scores tend to cluster around the mean; that is, most scores are close to the average value of 100 for the standard scores from the intelligence tests. For the normal distribution, 95 percent of all scores fall within two standard deviations on either side of the mean, and 68 percent fall within one standard deviation on either side of the mean. The standard scores from intelligence tests are constructed so that they have a standard deviation of 15 or 16, depending on the test. So, with the mean of a test equal to 100 and a standard deviation equal to 15, 95 percent of the scores fall between 70 and 130 and 68 percent fall between 85 and 115.

According to the American Association on Mental Deficiency (AAMD), children are considered to be mentally retarded if their IQs fall below 70. In addition to low IQ, retarded individuals show deficits in adaptive behavior (Grossman, 1983). For example, a moderately retarded individual has an IQ that ranges from 36 to 51, can work if closely supervised, but has difficulty

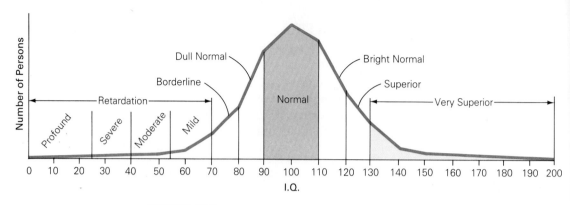

FIGURE 13.3
The expected distribution of IQ scores of a large sample population. (From Matarazzo, 1972).

in social situations. A severely retarded individual has an IQ that ranges from 20 to 35, is rarely employed, engages in little social interaction, and has few friends.

At the other end of the normal distribution are those people who are classified as gifted. These individuals have IQs that are equal to or higher than 130. Lewis Terman, whom you will remember as the individual who adapted the Binet test for use in the United States, also conducted a longitudinal study aimed at understanding the relationship between high IQ and success in life. Terman's original subject pool consisted of 1500 children and adolescents ranging in age from 3 to 19 years old. Every 5 to 10 years, Terman and his colleagues interviewed the subjects. As you might expect, people with IQs this high are generally considered by their peers to be bright; they generally graduate from college and are successful in their careers. However, the gifted appear no more or no less well adjusted to life than people of average intelligence (Terman & Oden, 1959).

Keep in mind that the evaluation of intelligence test scores is based on the principle that intelligence itself cannot be observed directly. Some things that we wish to measure can be observed directly. For instance, you can directly measure the weight of a rock because a rock is a specific physical object. Other things, such as motivation or intelligence, are abstract variables called **constructs** or **intervening variables,** and are variables that cannot be observed directly. Instead, the values of constructs like intelligence can only be estimated indirectly by their behavioral consequences, such as a score on an intelligence test. The score from an intelligence test is not intelligence, but it is supposed to reflect intelligence.

The point to remember here is that because intelligence is a construct, we understand that we can never estimate its value perfectly for any one person with any one test. Some tests, however, provide better estimates than do others. When a psychological test is developed, a question that must be answered is, "How good is it?" **Psychometrics** is the area of psychology that is devoted to psychological measurement, and psychometricians have devised a number of criteria for evaluating the worth of a test. Although many of the principles psychometricians use to evaluate a test are mathematically based, we can provide an overview of some of the criteria that every psychological test should satisfy.

Reliability and Validity

A key characteristic of a good test is the ability to repeat the measurement and obtain approximately the same result as that obtained for the first measurement. Suppose you weigh yourself in the morning right after waking up and your reading of the scale is 120 lbs. After stepping off of the scale, you wait a few moments and then step back on it, and now it reads 128 lbs. Guessing that you haven't gained 8 lbs. in ten seconds, you step back on the scale and now it reads 116 lbs! Your reaction would be either to believe the mid-range number, disregarding the others, or more appropriately, conclude that the scale is broken.

The problem with the scale is that it is unreliable. **Reliability** means that a test or other measure is consistent over repeated measurements. The measurements may be the same measures repeated at different times, or similar measures all administered on the same test. Although perfect reliability cannot be attained, the Stanford-Binet and Wechsler tests are among the most reliable tests that psychologists have devised. This means that a person's scores on repeated administrations of these tests are typically about the same. If the tests were perfectly reliable (and assuming that a person's intelligence did not change over the time between testings), then a person who scored 125 on a test on his or her sixteenth birthday would also score 125 on the same or very similar test at a later time. In practice, though, a person who scored 125 on the test might score 130 or 120 on a later test, but he or she would probably not score as high as 150 or as low as 100.

Test-retest reliability is gauged by comparing examinees' scores from two administrations of the same test. A numerical index of reliability, the **reliability coefficient,** is derived by computing a correlation coefficient for the two sets of scores. Like any correlation coefficient, the higher the reliability coefficient, the more consistent or reliable the intelligence test. Low reliability coefficients mean that the test is an unreliable measure of intelligence.

Whether the test measures what it is supposed to measure is called **validity.** More specifically, validity is a judgment of the extent to which theory and data support the "appropriateness of inferences . . . based on test scores" (Messick, 1989). In other words, a test is valid only to the extent that its results (the test scores) correlate with the behavior that the test was designed to measure. For example, some researchers in the nineteenth century held the false belief that a person with a bigger head had more brain, and therefore, more intelligence. On the basis of this belief, a corresponding intelligence test would consist of simply measuring the size of a person's head. Such a test would, however, be invalid, because in reality, head size does not necessarily reflect intelligence—head size is not correlated with intelligence or any of its actual behavioral consequences. Head size also does not correlate well with scores from intelligence tests.

Psychometricians who develop tests spend much of their time thinking about and evaluating the validity of their tests. Questions about whether the items on the test adequately represent the content of the particular area (verbal reasoning, memory, etc.) are questions of content validity. Questions about whether or not the items on the test appropriately measure the underlying construct of interest (in this case, intelligence) are questions of construct validity. As we shall see soon, many researchers have questioned the construct validity of all intelligence tests, claiming that the range of intellectual capacity addressed by these tests is too restrictive. Doing well on an intelligence test is by no means a guarantee of doing well in life in general, succeeding in such tasks as performing one's job, choosing a suitable marriage partner, or raising children. Conversely, many people who do not do well on the tests succeed admirably in life.

One way to assess the validity of a test is with the **validity coefficient,** the correlation between the score on the test and some other variable of interest. For example, correlations of .50 are typically obtained for intelligence test scores and school GPA, which means that as test scores increase, GPA also tends to increase. And, as we saw in Chapter 2, when two variables are correlated, the value of one (the test score) can be used to predict the value of the other (GPA). Using tests to predict performance on other tasks is an example of predictive validity. The correlations of intelligence test scores with other real life behaviors are, unfortunately, less impressive, which means that intelligence tests are reasonably valid predictors of school success, but that they have little predictive validity of success in life in general.

At one point in the history of intelligence testing, psychologists virtually ignored issues of validity. Instead, they arbitrarily defined intelligence as whatever an intelligence test measures (Boring, 1923). This meant that the study of intelligence was limited to intelligence testing. Defining something by the procedures used to measure it is called an operational definition. Can you see the problem with this approach to intelligence? Intelligence is too complex and abstract to be defined only in terms of a single test score. This particular operational definition, then, is too restrictive. For example, intelligence may have characteristics that a specific intelligence test does not measure. According to the view that intelligence is a construct, a score on an intelligence test is just one of many possible measures of intelligence. As we shall see later, psychologists have broadened their approach to the study of intelligence and other constructs to include other kinds of measures.

Test Bias

A special consideration that affects test validity is whether the test is biased in favor of a particular group because that group has had greater access to some kind of knowledge that helps test performance. **Test bias** is the discounting or favoring of an individual's test performance due to the particular experiences of that individual. If an intelligence test is a measure of innate capacity as Terman (1916) originally proposed, then a person should score the same on an intelligence test if he or she had been raised in an upper class household or in the midst of poverty. To the extent that the ability to answer test items correctly depends on previous learning, the intelligence test becomes less of a valid measure of capacity and more a measure of achievement. If success on a test depends on learning facts or other factors that are available only to a particular culture or subculture (such as white, middle, and upper class English speaking Americans), the test is biased in favor of individuals from that culture. In essence, this means that people who are raised in a specific environment have an unfair advantage on biased tests over those who were raised in other environments.

To reinforce this point, Robert Williams (1972) developed the Black Intelligence Scale for Cultural Homogeneity or BITCH. The BITCH test, which is not intended to actually serve as a real intelligence test, was written to show how a test could be biased to favor the experience of an African-American child raised in an urban environment. It asks questions such as, "What is a deuce-and-a-quarter." The answer? A Buick Electra 225, of course.

Obviously, knowledge of early 70s urban slang depends more on your past experiences than on any innate potential for problem solving. The BITCH test was deliberately written to be biased against those who were not familiar with this slang. However, real intelligence tests that show bias have, in fact, been administered to hundreds of thousands of people across the world. From the perspective of someone outside of the standard white, middle-class background, some of the questions on these tests appear to be just as biased as those on the BITCH test.

In sum, a reliable test is one that will yield similar results with each administration and a valid test is one that measures what it was designed to measure. A test is biased when it either discounts or favors a particular group of examinees because of their special experience. Bias is a variable that must be constantly considered when devising intelligence tests and interpreting their results. The attempts by psychologists to devise more "culture-fair" tests leads us to question the determinants of intelligence, which is the topic of our next section.

HEREDITY, ENVIRONMENT, AND INTELLIGENCE

As we have seen, the concepts of intelligence and intelligence testing have generated as much heat as they have light. In this section, we will focus on one of the most visible of these controversies: issues regarding the contribution of heredity and environment to intelligence.

The Roots of Intelligence

Our view regarding the determinants of intelligence reflects well the major theme of this book: intelligent behavior, like any behavior, is the result of the interaction of genetic and environmental variables. No behavior or trait is likely due 100 percent to either heredity or to environment, and no one can say exactly what proportion of any human behavioral phenotype is due to either factor. Be assured, though, that psychologists are still hotly debating the relative contribution of each to intelligence (as well as the contribution to other traits). According to the arguments that favor the contribution of heredity, differences in genotypes are hypothesized to play an influential role in explaining different levels of intelligence. Arguments that favor the contribution of environment over heredity maintain that differences in mental ability are believed to result largely from environmental factors, such as different educational or cultural opportunities.

How can we analyze the relative contributions of heredity and environment to intelligence? As we discussed in Chapter 2, the preferred method

The Colfax family of Boonville, California educated their four sons (two of whom are adopted) at home. The three oldest sons have been accepted at Harvard.

for analyzing cause and effect is the experiment. However, experimentation involving genetic and environmental variables with humans is obviously neither practical nor ethical. Parents cannot be randomly or deliberately selected and environments cannot be randomly assigned. Accordingly, researchers must use observational studies—studies in which existing relationships are observed without manipulation of the environment or genetics—to study the relative contributions of heredity and environment to intelligence. The standard statistic used in these studies is the correlation coefficient. (Remember that the correlation coefficient is computed from two matched sets of measurements. If the measurements are correlated, then a reasonably accurate prediction of the value of one measurement could be made from the value of the other measurement.)

Of the different kinds of correlational studies used to study intelligence, some of the most useful ones are based on the study of monozygotic twins (MZ). MZ twins develop from the same ovum, so they have the same genetic makeup. Of particular interest is the occasional pair of MZ twins who have been raised apart. These people are of special interest to researchers because they have the same genotype, yet they have been raised in different environments. Once enough of these pairs of twins are located, the correlation between their IQ scores is computed. At least to some extent this correlation reflects the genetic contribution to intelligence, because if the environments were truly distinct, then this correlation would reflect the contribution of the only common influence—genes.

Correlations of IQ based on MZ twins raised apart provide the cornerstone of heredity-environment studies, but the framework for the interpretation of these correlations is provided by correlations of intelligence for other family relationships. One comparison is the IQ correlation of MZ twins reared apart with the IQ correlation of MZ twins reared together. Twins reared together share similar environments and similar genetic structure, so any similarity in IQ is due to similar genetic structure, similar environment, or both. Similarly, a correlation that tends to reflect the influence of the environment only is the correlation of IQ based on unrelated children who are raised together, such as is found in families with two or more adopted children.

The results of many studies that compare these and other correlations lead to the conclusion that genetics and the environment both strongly influence the development of IQ (Plomin, 1989). The overall results are presented in Table 13.6. To begin to interpret the meaning of the numbers in this table, consider the typical correlation of IQ test scores of MZ twins

TABLE 13.6.	*Contributions of genetic and environmental factors to intelligence correlations.*	
RELATIONSHIP	*REARING*	*CORRELATION*
Same person	—	.87
MZ twins	together	.86
MZ twins	apart	.72
DZ twins	together	.60
Siblings	together	.47
Siblings	apart	.24
Unrelated children	together	.25
Cousins	apart	.15

Adapted from Bouchard & McGue, 1981.

reared together, which is very high—.86. To better understand the magnitude of this number, remember that because the reliability of the IQ tests is not perfect, even the correlation of IQ test scores at two different times for the same people will be less than a perfect 1.00. A correlation of .86, then, is extremely high.

What about the size of the correlation of MZ twins raised apart (.72) relative to that for MZ twins reared together (.86)? Environmental influence would be demonstrated if raising MZ twins together rather than apart results in a much higher correlation for IQ. As can be seen from Table 13.6, the IQ of MZ twins raised apart is .72, a high value that illustrates the strong influence of genetics on IQ.

The correlations reported in Table 13.6 also demonstrate the importance of the environment, however. The correlations of IQ scores for unrelated people who are raised together is .25. If a shared environment for each set of unrelated people had no effect on IQ, then this correlation would be zero. The influence of the environment is also demonstrated when comparing correlations such as those between MZ twins raised apart and those raised together. Although the large value of .72 for MZ twins raised apart demonstrates the influence of genetics, the fact that this value climbs to .86 for MZ twins raised together shows that environmental influences are also present.

A potential methodological problem with many of the twin studies may also mean that the high observed value of .72 for the correlation of MZ twins raised apart is somewhat inflated. The problem is that most twins raised apart were adopted, and adoption agencies do not randomly assign each of these twins to different families representative of the entire population. Instead, the children tend to be placed selectively in homes with comparable environments in terms of race, income, and education of the parents. The result is that the environments of twins raised apart are often more similar than would be expected if the twins had been randomly assigned to families.

Reducing all of this information to a single statement echoes the statement that was presented at the beginning of this section: Genetics and environment *both* exert an important effect on the development of intelligence. Another way to say this is that some people apparently are born brighter than others, but certain environments foster intellectual development more than others. So in brief, mental abilities are not fixed by genetic structure. The range by which the environment can modify IQ is rather substantial: 20 to 25 points (Zigler & Seitz, 1982).

Heredity, Intelligence, and Social Issues

Another avenue by which to approach the heredity-environment issue is in terms of the controversy over why intelligence appears to be distributed unequally among different social classes. Richard Herrnstein believes that differences in mental ability are inherited, and that only a relatively few people are highly intelligent. If Herrnstein is correct, what are the implications for society? In particular, what does this mean for a democratic society in which, at least to some extent, people are free to choose what to do with their lives? To answer this question, Herrnstein (1973, pp. 197, 198) presented the following argument:

- If differences in mental abilities are inherited, and
- if success requires those abilities, and
- if earnings and prestige depend on success,
- then social standing (which reflects earnings and prestige) will be based to some extent on inherited differences among people.

Most people in our country argue that a democratic, free society does not place artificial barriers, such as class membership, on the educational and occupational goals of its citizens. As our society removes more barriers to class mobility, people become freer to choose their professions, regardless of their economic or social backgrounds. Herrnstein argued that as barriers are removed, the United States is approaching a **meritocracy,** a society in which each person is rewarded according to his or her merit. Although few people would argue that our society has entirely achieved this goal, there is at least a reasonable amount of social mobility within our society, particularly when compared to other societies throughout the world and throughout history.

In a true meritocracy, inherited intelligence matters. The intelligent perform the most intellectually challenging and satisfying jobs. Because high intelligence is presumed to be in relatively short supply, these jobs would have the highest pay and the most prestige, yet they would be open to all people on a competitive basis, regardless of their religious and ethnic backgrounds, or the wealth of their parents. To see how the achievement of a true meritocracy might affect our society, consider the tendency of people to marry those most like themselves. Intelligent people tend to marry intelligent people, and people of below-average intelligence tend to marry people of below-average intelligence. It is not very often that someone with an IQ of 80 marries someone else with an IQ of 140.

If intelligence is inherited, then the irony of Herrnstein's argument is that society is likely to become more class oriented. Social classes will become ever more firmly established on inborn differences, so that "our society may be sorting itself willy-nilly into inherited classes" (1973, p. 215). According to Herrnstein, and reminiscent of Galton's observations, the upper-class segment of democratic societies will, over time, possess greater and greater levels of intelligence relative to lower classes.

As you probably expect, other scientists disagree with Herrnstein. Herrnstein's arguments regarding the meritocracy depend on his assumptions of the heritability of intelligence, and that success in life depends largely on this intelligence. Both of these assumptions have been questioned by other psychologists. Many theorists not only argue that intelligence is not inherited, but also that "cognitive ability is not a particularly scarce good" (Bowles & Gintis, 1974, p. 51). Instead, in what we may call a social distribution theory of intelligence, these theorists maintain that there is too much cognitive ability for our economic system to absorb; too many people have the capacity to be successful given an environment that provides technical training as well as social skills, expectations of success, and the right connections. That is, under the right circumstances, most people could learn just about any skill and could perform any of the jobs in our economic system.

How then should society allocate the good jobs? Who gets the prestigious, well-paying jobs and who gets the dreary, low-paying ones? In a meritocracy, native ability determines who does what. In a society with too many highly intelligent individuals, IQ is arbitrarily and unequally distributed by the opportunities afforded the individual by society. Those born into the "right" social class are placed into an environment that fosters performance in school and on IQ and related tests. Others are placed in an environment that suppresses test and school performance. Given IQ and related test performances, society justifies providing some people with the opportunity to become corporate executives, whereas for others, opportunities are more limited to jobs of considerably lesser status and money. Intelligence testing becomes a method used by one social class to justify the unequal distribution of wealth, privilege, and opportunity across all social classes.

C*homsky argues that not everyone is willing to define success in terms of wealth, prestige, and power . . .*

Parents who teach their children basic learning skills provide a nurturing environment that prepares the children for further learning.

The historian and linguist Noam Chomsky (1973), whose work we encountered in Chapter 9, advocates a position contrary to that maintained by Herrnstein. One reason our society is not moving towards a meritocracy is that intelligence may not be the primary determinant of occupational success. Chomsky argues that,

> One might speculate, rather plausibly, that wealth and power tend to accrue to those who are ruthless, cunning, avaricious, self-seeking, lacking in sympathy and compassion, subservient to authority, willing to abandon principle for material gain, and so on.
>
> (1973, p. 91)

Chomsky argues that not everyone is willing to define success in terms of wealth, prestige and power; not everyone will sit around and stagnate unless driven by money and power. To further underscore the wide discrepancy in opinion between himself and Herrnstein, Chomsky notes that

> The assumption that people will work only for gain in wealth and power is . . . quite probably false, except under extreme deprivation.
>
> (1973, p. 91)

Recently, Herrnstein has written about the social consequences of falling birth rates among intelligent American women (Herrnstein, 1989). According to Herrnstein, brighter women are having fewer children than less bright women. Assuming that intelligence has a strong genetic component, this appears to mean that the overall average IQ of Americans will drop about one point per generation. Herrnstein points out that this does not seem like much of a reduction until one considers how the lower and upper ends of the normal distribution for intelligence are affected (refer back to Figure 13.3). For example, a 5-point drop in the average national IQ would produce nearly a 60 percent reduction in the percentage of people scoring above 130 (gifted) and an equal increase in the percentage of people scoring lower than 70 (retarded). Because intelligence and aptitude tests are good predictors of job performance and productivity, these predictions are disconcerting. The point of this line of reasoning is that with less bright women having more babies, there will, in the not too distant future, be fewer individuals of high intelligence in the work force. Therefore, our economic productivity and performance may decrease.

Herrnstein offers two suggestions for remedying this situation. First, he suggests we use schools to teach intellectual skills that are related to occupational productivity and performance. His second suggestion is more delicate than the first. He feels that we need to become more aware of how public policy affects differential fertility rates among women of different intelligence. In Herrnstein's words:

> Nothing is more private than the decision to bear children, yet society has a vital interest in the aggregate effects of those decisions. The issue demands informed public consideration, and probably also public action to lessen the tension between parenthood and career. At the very least, we should stop telling bright young women that they make poor use of their lives by bearing and raising children. . . .
>
> (1989, p. 79)

The implications of the social distribution of intelligence go well beyond "mere academics." They touch the way we define ourselves and our capabilities, and ultimately the nature of society and governmental actions. Only time will tell how the level of intelligence in a culture really influences and is influenced by social decisions. We do know, though, that the way intelligence is viewed by psychologists is changing. We now turn to a look at contemporary views of intelligence.

Psychologists realize that our current knowledge of intelligence and intelligence testing is far from complete. They also realize that current and future research may continue to be as controversial and exciting as some of the earlier work in this area. In this section, we will explore some interesting new work that involves novel ways to define and measure intelligence, and, in a surprising twist, at least a partial affirmation of some of Galton's original attempts to measure intelligence with sensory and physiological measures.

The Triarchic Theory of Intelligence

Robert Sternberg (1985, 1988) is one psychologist who is developing a broad theory of intelligence that minimizes the importance of traditional intelligence tests. Ever since Binet developed a test to identify slow learners in the French school system, intelligence tests have focused on testing the kind of problems that relate generally to school performance. To permit a more complete understanding of intelligent behavior in everyday life, Sternberg has developed what he calls the **triarchic theory of intelligence.** This theory, as implied by its name, describes three components of intelligence:

- The cognitive component: the specific cognitive processes that underlie intelligent behavior,
- The experiential component: the way in which previous experience with a particular kind of problem affects the way that a problem is solved,
- The contextual component: the environmental context within which the problem solving occurs.

The first aspect of intelligence specified by the triarchic theory reflects the increasingly prominent role played by cognitive psychology and information processing in psychological theory. This emphasis on the cognitive component changes the focus of testing from a score on an intelligence test to an understanding of the cognitive processes of the examinee taking the intelligence test. For example, the first task of comprehending a written passage is to encode the passage. The written words must be perceived and translated into a conceptual representation in the person's cognitive system. Information from long-term memory may then be used to interpret the passage. Other aspects of the cognitive component would include reasoning abilities, vocabulary, language comprehension, general and specific knowledge, ability to plan, and so on.

According to Sternberg, the experiential component involves an individual's prior experience with the problem to be solved. Some problems that need solving may be ones we have never before encountered, and others we may have solved many times before. Consistent with many other theorists, Sternberg recognizes that the ability to apply existing knowledge to novel tasks and situations is an important element of intelligent behavior. Sternberg, however, also emphasizes the ability to "automate" a task that is frequently encountered. For example, as you read and comprehend the words on this page, you are not thinking about how to read or how to comprehend. Instead, these tasks are accomplished quickly and effortlessly, they are automatic. A child who is just learning to read, however, must concentrate on the steps involved in reading in order to comprehend the passage he or she is reading. To Sternberg, intelligence is illustrated by a continuum anchored on one end by the ability to solve novel problems and on the other end by the ability to automate frequently encountered tasks (see Figure 13.4).

FIGURE 13.4
Sternberg's continuum of intelligence. The continuum is anchored on one end by the ability to solve novel problems and on the other end by the ability to automate frequently encountered tasks. (After Sternberg, 1988).

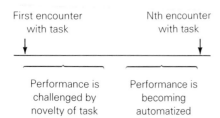

First encounter with task   Nth encounter with task

Performance is challenged by novelty of task   Performance is becoming automatized

Consequently, the key to understanding the experiential component is to understand that the assessment of intelligence requires consideration of both the traditional emphasis on solving novel problems and on how quickly familiar problems are solved. Both novelty and automatization work together to produce intelligent behavior. The more automatic the behavior, the more cognitive processing power is available to do other things such as solving novel problems. If, when traveling to a foreign country, you are continually concentrating on the exchange rate and learning the worth of a "ruble" or "lira" or "peso," then you will be less able to concentrate on other novel aspects of the environment, such as the merchandise that you would like to buy if you were not otherwise distracted (Sternberg, 1988).

The third aspect of the triarchic theory is the contextual component, which focuses on the environmental context within which intelligent behavior occurs—a context that can vary from the privileged one-on-one tutoring available to children whose parents are financially well-off to that involving high teacher-to-pupil ratios characteristic of the public school system. The contextual component also includes one's ability to change or adapt to different environments and to maximize skills and other resources. Traditional intelligence tests are useful to the extent that they predict real-world behavior, but the definition of such behavior depends on the environment in which the individual lives.

Traditional intelligence tests predict academic achievement well, but their validity decreases for more general considerations such as their usefulness in predicting one's annual salary at age 30. However, even for academic achievement the prediction is far from perfect because, according to Sternberg, intelligence is much more than what is measured by intelligence tests, and because there is more to school achievement than intelligence.

The triarchic theory represents an attempt not only to delineate the primary components of intelligence, but also to synthesize them. To understand general intelligence is to understand each of the three specific components of intelligence as they operate together. For example, we can attempt to understand intelligent behavior in terms of its underlying cognitive processes within given environmental contexts and given the previous experiences of the problem solver. By focusing on the context in which intelligent behavior occurs, we can attempt to consider situations other than traditional intelligence tests that can be used to assess intelligence. We might then analyze the underlying processes of intelligence in these new situations. Sternberg is developing his own intelligence test, the Sternberg Multidimensional Abilities Test, which will provide not only the traditional verbal, quantitative, and performance-based problems found on tests such as the Stanford-Binet, but will also provide scores for each of the three components of his triarchic theory.

A Theory of Multiple Intelligences

Howard Gardner (1983) has proposed a **theory of multiple intelligences** that generalizes the concept of intelligence away from the traditional focus on IQ even more broadly than does Sternberg's theory. Gardner's theory specifies seven distinct types of intelligence:

- linguistic intelligence—use and comprehension of language
- logical-mathematical intelligence—use and comprehension of logic and numbers
- spatial intelligence—ability to navigate through space and ability to manipulate mental images

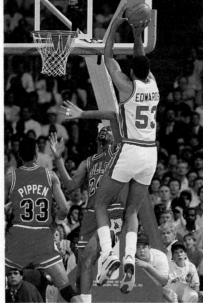

The theory of multiple intelligences proposes that there are intelligences other than those measured by IQ. People with musical aptitudes, athletic abilities, or excellent communication skills can excel in areas that cannot be measured by traditional intelligence tests.

- musical intelligence—ability to create and perceive pitch
- body-kinesthetic intelligence—athletic ability and motor coordination
- interpersonal intelligence—understanding and interacting with others
- intrapersonal intelligence—understanding one's own abilities.

The first three—verbal, logical-mathematical, and spatial intelligences—are well represented on standard intelligence tests. The remaining four—musical, body-kinesthetic, and interpersonal and intrapersonal intelligences—have not been traditionally considered part of intelligence, and are described briefly below.

People have been using language for thousands of years, but they have also been playing forms of music for probably at least as long. Those high in musical intelligence are able to analyze musical patterns and characteristics such as rhythm, as well as create and synthesize these patterns. They learn to play musical instruments easily, or they have a highly developed sense of pitch and rhythm and can compose music ranging from simple tunes to complex symphonies.

Body-kinesthetic intelligence is required to perform coordinated physical actions such as those that occur in athletics or dance. A professional ballerina or basketball player is using his or her body intelligently and at a level unachieved by most people. The two remaining kinds of intelligence in Gardner's theory involve the ability to understand both yourself and others. Successful salespeople, teachers, psychologists, and politicians are likely to possess a high degree of interpersonal intelligence. Can you recognize your own feelings and moods? Or do you often react inappropriately and then feel bad about your actions afterward? These two questions refer to the ability to understand yourself or the degree to which you possess intrapersonal intelligence.

By defining multiple intelligences, Gardner is encouraging psychologists who study intelligence to think of intelligence within a framework broader than that of the traditional intelligence test. In doing so, the accomplishments and potential of those who excel or could excel in areas other than those measured by an intelligence test are more easily recognized by educators, parents, and all of those who teach others to enhance psychological growth.

Biological Measurements of Intelligence

In the late 19th century, Galton tried but failed to measure intelligence with biological measures. Recently, several investigators have turned their attention to biological measurement. Using instrumentation unavailable to Galton a century ago, these investigators have provided support for some of Galton's hypotheses regarding the measurement of intelligence, though, once again, these results are not without controversy (Mackintosh, 1986). We will discuss two areas of particular interest from a biological perspective: reaction time and evoked potentials.

Reaction Time. One variable of interest to Galton was reaction time, the time it takes a person to react to a stimulus such as a light or a tone. In Galton's reaction time studies, a person hit a punching bag as quickly as possible after hearing a signal (Jensen, 1982). Reaction time was measured as the time from the onset of the auditory signal to the time that the punching bag was struck. Today we realize that this technique is too crude to obtain accurate results.

One problem with Galton's setup was that reaction time was not distinguished from movement time, the time it takes to move a hand to accomplish some activity such as punching a bag or pressing a button after hearing the signal. The person hears the tone and responds. The time it takes for this decision to be made is the reaction time. After deciding to react, the person then has to move his or her hand to hit the punching bag. Thus, Galton's reaction time measure was, in actuality, reaction time plus movement time. Jensen (1982) concluded that reaction time and movement time "involve different processes" (p. 102), and have no correlation over repeated trials for an individual. That is, a fast reaction time may be associated with a fast movement time or a slow movement time, so Galton's measure confounded movement with reaction time.

A second problem was that Galton limited his study to simple reaction time, a single response to a single stimulus. Another possibility is to study choice reaction time, in which one of several stimuli is presented at each trial, and the subject makes a different response to each stimulus. In such a study, the subject rests his or her hand on the button located at the bottom, middle of a response console, called the home button. One of several lights is turned on and the subject's task is to turn off the selected light as quickly as possible by pushing a button immediately below the light that was illuminated. Reaction time, which is distinguished from movement time in this setting, is measured as the time required for the subject to remove his or her finger from the home button after the onset of the stimulus. (Note that movement time would be the amount of time it takes for the person to move his or her finger from the home button to the button that is below the selected light.)

The general finding of this revised research program is that reaction time, particularly choice reaction time, is related to WISC-R or WAIS-R test scores. Within limits, this correlation increases as the number of available choices in the choice reaction time task increases. For example, given eight choices, Lally and Nettlebeck (1977) obtained a correlation of Choice Reaction Time and Wechsler Performance Scale scores of −.75, a fairly high correlation that indicates that the people who took longer to react tended to have lower WISC-R or WAIS-R scores. Vernon (1983) also obtained a high correlation between Choice Reaction Time and WISC-R scores. Thus, intelligent people tend to have faster reaction times than less intelligent people. This finding is potentially useful because it points to the possibility of using a quick, simple test, instead of a longer and more complex test to measure intelligence.

Evoked Potentials. Although Galton attempted to measure speed of mental processing indirectly by measuring reaction time, he did not have a method for measuring brain activity directly such as the EEG, which we discussed in Chapter 4. Pursuing this connection, Hendrickson (1982) has obtained results using EEGs that do link properties of brain wave activity with intelligence as measured by a standard intelligence test. The property that was measured is an evoked potential, a brain wave generated in response to the presentation of a specific stimulus. In Hendrickson's study, the evoked potentials were recorded with an EEG machine as the person listened to a tone that lasted for 30 milliseconds. He found that more intelligent people showed greater consistency in their EEG patterns.

Hendrickson (1982) presented an elaborate theory that explains the differences in the waveforms averaged over 100 or so tone presentations for those of high and low intelligence. The theory is concerned with errors of transmission as neurons communicate with each other. Basically, Hendrickson argues that the brains of more intelligent people work more efficiently in the sense that they have fewer transmission errors, which means that the EEG waveforms are more constant from trial to trial for more intelligent people. The key aspect of the EEG data that allows the theory to be tested is that the final waveform for each individual is the average waveform computed over many trials. The result is that the final, averaged waveform is jagged and complex for those with high intelligence and more smooth and rounded for those of lower intelligence.

Remarkably, this difference in the average evoked potential waveform was found empirically using the WAIS as a measure of IQ, as you can see from Figure 13.5. If you superimposed a string over an average waveform of a person with a high IQ, and then did the same with a waveform from a person with a low IQ, the string from the high IQ waveform would be longer. This difference in the length of the string reflects the greater complexity of the waveform from the subjects with the higher IQs.

In practice, the "string measure" was computed precisely from a formula that analyzed the value of the waveform every 2 milliseconds. The correlations obtained between the "string measure" and WAIS IQ for 219 15-year-olds was .72. Although these findings have been replicated (Federico, 1984), they are not unequivocal. Mackintosh (1986) suggests that more replication is needed before they should be accepted. He questions the meaning of the results, should they withstand replication. Mackintosh speculates that these findings may have less to do with the biological meaning of IQ than they do with "the ability to maintain concentration on a remarkably tedious task" (p. 11). On the other hand, part of being intelligent may be the ability to do well at "remarkably tedious" tasks.

R*egardless of what . . . intelligence tests measure, you will only know what you can accomplish once you have set goals for yourself and tried to achieve these goals.*

In sum, although intelligence is still measured using intelligence tests, the concept of intelligence is being studied by some contemporary psychologists in a broader light. The tools of modern cognitive psychology are being used to explore the specific computational processes that underlie intelligent behavior, and biological measures, such as choice reaction time and evoked potentials, have been shown to be related to intelligence test scores.

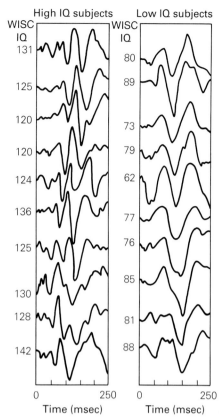

High IQ subjects   Low IQ subjects

WISC IQ: 131, 125, 120, 120, 124, 136, 125, 130, 128, 142

WISC IQ: 80, 89, 73, 79, 62, 77, 76, 85, 81, 88

0   250   0   250
Time (msec)   Time (msec)

FIGURE 13.5
Evoked potential EEG waveforms of ten high IQ subjects and ten low IQ subjects. (Ertl and Schafer, 1969).

In the final analysis, though, regardless of what it is that intelligence tests measure, you will only know what you can accomplish once you have set goals for yourself and tried to achieve these goals. As Robert Sternberg writes,

> To me, the whole point of testing is not to obtain an immutable score but rather to suggest strengths upon which the individual can capitalize and weaknesses that he can remediate.

(1988, p. 71)

The most general message of this chapter has been that although intelligence test scores can provide useful information regarding your intellectual abilities, your evaluation of this information should consider certain limitations. One limitation is our ignorance of defining and measuring intelligence, a problem that should be lessened as we await the outcome of further research.

BOUNDARIES AND FRONTIERS

Like any test, intelligence tests serve a variety of functions. For example, they can be used as screening devices. Just like performance on academic tests can be used to determine whether a student advances to a higher grade, intelligence tests can be used to assess an individual's potential to carry out intellectual tasks or to perform a particular job. Tests are also used to evaluate one's knowledge and to identify the need for remediation. Likewise, intelligence tests can be used to achieve one of Binet's original goals: to identify individuals who, if they received special tutoring, might become more intellectually adept.

Rightly or wrongly, tests are also used to make judgments about individuals or at least place them into categories that describe their intellectual performance. A student who gets an *A* on a test is considered smart; a student who gets an *F* is considered by some to be not so smart. Similarly, individuals who perform well on IQ tests (130 or above) are considered gifted, while those who perform poorly (70 or less) are considered mentally retarded.

This point brings us to a very important difference between IQ tests and other kinds of tests, namely, the kinds of social and political implications that performance on an IQ test carries with it. In short, the implications that arise from judgments about intellectual ability based on IQ tests can have far-reaching and often deleterious consequences. This has been especially true when comparisons in IQ have been made between different populations.

In the past several decades there has been considerable controversy over the finding that the average IQ score of African-Americans is about 15 points lower than that of the average score for white Americans. Few contend that this finding is not a genuine one. Rather, the melee begins when people try to interpret what this finding means.

Of course, it is utterly wrong to conclude from this finding that individual African-Americans are intellectually inferior to individual white Americans. Such a conclusion is wrong simply because it is derived from averaged data. Averaged IQ scores tell us very little about individual IQ scores. In fact, when we look at individual scores in both populations, we find a considerable degree of variability. This means that a substantial number of individual African-American scores are higher than the average white score (Shuey, 1966).

Is the difference between average African-American and white IQ scores due to hereditary or environmental causes? Some hereditarians, most notably Arthur Jensen (1969, 1973), have argued that because within-group differences in IQ are partially due to heredity, then so are between-group differences. But other scientists have pointed out that, logically, between-group differences may be caused by factors other than those producing within-group differences (Lewontin, 1976; Kamin, 1981). It is certainly wrong to argue that even if performance on IQ tests was genetically based, then IQ is immutable. As we have noted throughout the text, human phenotypes are the result of extensive interaction between genotype and experience. Intelligence is no exception.

One way to assess the relative contribution of heredity and environment to racial differences in intelligence is to equate children from various racial backgrounds in terms of important variables such as educational experiences, and their parents' education, occupational rank, and socioeconomic status. Studies that have matched subjects on these variables have shown that racial differences are dramatically reduced, although not eliminated completely (Loehlin, Lindzey, & Spuhler, 1975). In this case, the environment can account for some, but not all, of the difference in IQ levels. Another way to put the issue to a test is to compare the IQs of African-American children adopted by middle-class white couples to that of the average African-American child. One study (Scarr & Weinberg, 1976) found that the average IQ of African-American adoptees was 10—25 points above the national average for African-American children.

Studies such as these do not rule out the influence of genetic factors in determining intelligence; rather, they simply point up the fact that IQ scores can be modified by manipulating environmental variables. The problem is that we do not know much about how or why environmental variables cause IQ scores to change (and presumably academic performance as well). Although it is useful and important to engage in academic debates about the roots of intelligence, there is also research on more practical issues to be conducted. We must remember that sometime, preferably sooner than later, we must get about the business of extensively researching those environmental variables that can have significant impact on raising the intelligence levels of those who need the help. Hopefully, Sternberg's theory of intelligence will generate much needed research on the cognitive abilities that are related to intelligent behavior, and thus, will provide clues as to training practices that can be used to enhance those abilities. Community programs such as Project Head Start will also help us to understand better the effects of environment on intelligence. Research has already shown that children who have participated in such programs are less likely to need special assistance later in their education (Palmer & Anderson, 1979). They are also more likely to complete high school and attend college than are similarly disadvantaged children who were not involved in the program (Jordan et al., 1985). But we do not know which part of this early educational process accounts for the positive results. Maybe only one aspect is involved. Maybe it's the entire milieu. Perhaps there are other educational experiences that could produce even greater improvements in intellectual functioning. At this point, we simply don't know.

Eighty-five years ago Alfred Binet set out to develop a test to identify those individuals who would most benefit from special academic assistance. Psychology has had such tests for several decades, yet has failed to follow through in developing scientifically validated educational training for those individuals who require it to function effectively in our culture. What we need is more research on individual differences in intelligence and on intellectual development. This sort of research will provide fertile suggestions for how our schools can best enhance intellectual skills that accompany success later in life. In our view, that is both the boundary and the frontier encompassing research on intelligence.

CONCEPT SUMMARY

WHAT IS INTELLIGENCE?

- What is intelligence and how is it related to *g*? (pp. 461–463)
- What is the difference between achievement and aptitude? (p. 462)

A HISTORICAL OVERVIEW OF INTELLIGENCE TESTS

- How did eugenics influence the development of intelligence tests? (pp. 464–465)
- What are norms? (p. 466)
- What are mental age and IQ, and how are they related to norms? (p. 466–467)
- What is standardization? (p. 467)

CONTEMPORARY INTELLIGENCE TESTS

- What is the hierarchy of intelligence underlying the fourth edition of the Stanford-Binet? (pp. 468–469)
- What is the difference between verbal and nonverbal intelligence? Why is this distinction important? (pp. 471–472)
- Why is a linear profile important to interpreting intelligence tests? (pp. 470–472)

CRITICAL ISSUES IN EVALUATING INTELLIGENCE TEST SCORES

- What is a standard score and how is it related to the concept of norms? (pp. 475–476)
- What do we mean when we say that intelligence is a construct? (p. 476)
- How do constructs differ from variables that have been operationally defined? (p. 476)
- What are reliability and validity? Why is bias a form of invalidity? (pp. 476–479)

HEREDITY, ENVIRONMENT, AND INTELLIGENCE

- How does the view of society as a meritocracy differ from the view of society provided by the social distribution theory? (pp. 481–484)
- What assumptions do these views make regarding intelligence and intelligence tests? (pp. 481–484)

MODERN THEORIES OF INTELLIGENCE

- What are the three components of intelligence described by the triarchic theory? (pp. 484–485)
- How do these components relate to those tested for by traditional intelligence tests? (pp. 484–485)
- What are Gardner's multiple intelligences? (pp. 485–487)
- How is the recent research related to Galton's earlier attempt to construct intelligence tests? (pp. 487–489)

KEY TERMS AND CONCEPTS

WHAT IS INTELLIGENCE?

Intelligence The capacity to acquire knowledge and to use that knowledge to solve problems. (p. 461)

Achievement Skills that are already learned, such as having learned a foreign language. (p. 462)

Aptitude The capacity or potential for learning. (p. 462)

g The general ability that is purported by some theorists to be common to all intellectual tasks. (p. 462)

Factor Analysis A statistical technique developed by Spearman for determining the correlation of different test questions to each other. According to Spearman's rationale, if all questions on an intelligence test require similar intellectual abilities, then intelligence may be viewed as a general capacity of individuals. On the other hand, if different questions on the test require different intellectual abilities, then intelligence may be viewed as a variety of specific kinds of capacities. (p. 462)

A HISTORICAL OVERVIEW OF INTELLIGENCE TESTS

Eugenics A word based on a Greek term for "well-bred," that Galton used to describe the movement he founded to study and promote the principles of artificial selection in humans. (p. 465)

Norms In psychological testing, the average levels of performance on a test for different groups of people, such as 10-year-old Hispanic females or all 7-year-olds. (p. 466)

Mental Age The age level of the normative performance on an intelligence test that a child is able to match. This concept was introduced to enhance the comparison of the child's performance to the performance of other children on the test. (p. 466)

Standardization The process of establishing the norms of a test by testing hundreds or thousands of people in each group (age, sex, ethnicity) to which the test is to be administered. (p. 467)

Stanford-Binet The first widely used individually administered English intelligence test. (p. 467)

IQ The intelligence quotient—the ratio of a person's mental age to his or her chronological age multiplied by 100. The concept was established to facilitate the comparison of different people's scores. (p. 467)

CONTEMPORARY INTELLIGENCE TESTS

Linear Profile A graphical display of the scores from all of the subtests to facilitate comparison among them, with adjacent scores connected with straight lines. (p. 470)

WAIS-R The current version of Wechsler's individually administered adult intelligence test, called the Wechsler Adult Intelligence Scale, Revised. (p. 471)

WISC-R The current version of Wechsler's individually administered intelligence test for children, called the Wechsler Intelligence Scale for Children, Revised. (p. 471)

Verbal Intelligence The problem-solving capacity for language-oriented problems such as reading comprehension and vocabulary. (p. 471)

Performance (or nonverbal intelligence) The capacity for solving problems that does not depend on understanding language, but rather emphasizes some performance such as putting together a puzzle. (p. 472)

CRITICAL ISSUES IN EVALUATING INTELLIGENCE TEST SCORES

Standard Score The score that shows how far or how close a person's original responses are from the average level of responses on, for example, an intelligence test. Today virtually all psychological test scores are reported as standard scores. (p. 475)

Normal Distribution The mathematical name for a frequency distribution of scores that is sometimes called the "bell-shaped curve." (p. 475)

Constructs (or intervening variables) Abstract variables that cannot be observed directly, such as gravity and intelligence. The values of constructs can only be estimated by measuring their behavioral consequences. (p. 476)

Psychometrics The area of psychology that is devoted to psychological measurement. (p. 476)

Reliability A test is said to be reliable when it is consistent over repeated measurements. The measurements may be the same measures repeated at different times or similar measures all administered on the same test. (p. 477)

Reliability Coefficient A numerical index of the reliability of an intelligence test (or any other type of psychological test) derived by computing a correlation coefficient for the examinees' scores from two different administrations of the same test. Like any correlation coefficient, the higher the reliability coefficient, the more consistent or reliable the intelligence test. Low reliability coefficients mean that the test is an unreliable measure of intelligence. (p. 477)

Validity A test is said to be valid when it measures what it is supposed to measure. (p. 477)

Validity Coefficient The correlation between the score on a test and some other variable of interest. (p. 477)

Test Bias The discounting or favoring of an individual's test performance due to the particular experiences of that individual. To the extent that the ability to answer test items correctly depends on previous learning, the intelligence test becomes less of a valid measure of capacity and more a measure of achievement. (p. 478)

HEREDITY, ENVIRONMENT, AND INTELLIGENCE

Meritocracy A society in which each person is rewarded according to his or her merit. (p. 482)

MODERN THEORIES OF INTELLIGENCE

Triarchic Theory of Intelligence Robert Sternberg's theory that generalizes intelligence testing and the study of intelligence beyond that of IQ tests by accounting for three different aspects of intelligence: the specific cognitive processes that underlie intelligent behavior, the way in which previous experience with a particular kind of problem affects the way that a problem is solved, and the environmental context within which the problem solving occurs. (p. 484)

Theory of Multiple Intelligences Howard Gardner's theory of intelligence that generalizes the concept of intelligence away from the traditional focus on IQ by including problem solving in a wide variety of domains such as music and interpersonal competence. (p. 485)

ADDITIONAL SOURCES OF INFORMATION

Eysenck, H. J., & Kamin, L. (1981). *The intelligence controversy.* New York: Wiley. This book captures the liveliness of the heredity-environment debate. One advocate of each position debates the issues throughout the book.

Fancher, R. E. (1985). *The intelligence men: Makers of the IQ controversy.* New York: Norton. This book presents a readable historical survey of the psychological study of intelligence and intelligence tests.

Gould, S. J. (1981). *The mismeasure of man.* New York: Norton. This book is an engaging and highly critical review of the history of intelligence testing. It also outlines the ways in which intelligence tests have been abused.

Herrnstein, R. J. (1973). *IQ in the meritocracy.* Boston: Little, Brown. Herrnstein presents his argument for a meritocracy and his support for intelligence tests in this book.

Sternberg, R. J. (1988). *The triarchic mind.* New York: Viking. Sternberg's triarchic theory is described in this book in nontechnical language. The book is both readable and accessible, offering many real-life applications of different kinds of intelligence with suggestions for the reader for improving his or her own problem-solving skills.

14 Personality

The goal of personality psychologists is to study individual differences in thinking, emotion, and behavior. This goal has led to the development of both personality theories and methods to assess personality characteristics.

ASSESSING PERSONALITY

Objective Tests   Projective Tests   Behavior Assessment Techniques

Psychologists assess personality by using objective tests, projective tests, and behavior assessment. Objective tests include personality inventories such as the MMPI and the 16PF. Projective tests like the Rorschach and TAT require the individual to describe what he or she "sees" in an ambiguous stimulus. Behavior assessment focuses on what an individual actually does and not just on what he or she reports.

THE PSYCHODYNAMIC APPROACH

*Development of Freudian Theory   The Structure of Personality
Freud's Theory of Personality Development   Post-Freudian
Psychodynamic Theorists   Critique of Psychodynamic Approaches*

The psychodynamic approach to understanding personality stems from the work of Sigmund Freud. Freud maintained that personality is comprised of the id, ego, and superego, and that the ego uses defense mechanisms to prevent anxiety-provoking thoughts from becoming conscious. Freud also believed that personality development occurs largely during childhood and involves a series of predictable psychosexual stages. Several of Freud's followers accepted the idea that there are dynamic forces operating within the psyche but disagreed that sexual and aggressive instincts play an important role in determining personality. Criticisms of Freudian theory center on its weak research base.

THE TRAIT APPROACH

*Gordon Allport and the Trait Approach   Five-Factor Theory
Raymond Cattell's 16 Basic Traits   Hans Eysenck's Three Basic Traits
Critique of the Trait Approach*

Some personality researchers hold that an individual's personality is composed of relatively stable and observable characteristics referred to as traits. However, researchers do not agree on the number of personality traits that do exist. Critics of the trait approach maintain that traits alone do not determine personality. Rather, they say that personality is also the result of situational variables.

THE SOCIAL LEARNING APPROACH

*General Principles of Social Learning Theory
Critique of the Social Learning Approach*

The social learning approach holds that personality is the result of the interaction of behavioral, cognitive, and environmental variables. This approach is based on the idea that personality characteristics are learned through observation. Whether people act to produce changes in their environment is a matter of their self-efficacy, expectations, and personal variables. Critics of the social learning approach contend that it is narrow and descriptive rather than explanatory, and that it fails to account for developmental processes in personality.

THE HUMANISTIC APPROACH

*Maslow and Self-Actualization   Rogers and Conditions of Worth
Critique of the Humanistic Approach*

Humanistic psychologists are interested in personal growth, satisfaction with life, and positive human values. They believe that human beings are innately good and have an internal drive toward self-actualization. Maslow believed that people are free to pursue self-actualization only if their physiological, safety, love, and esteem needs were met first. Rogers maintained that self-actualization is best realized in circumstances characterized by unconditional positive regard. The humanistic approach is largely unsubstantiated empirically.

Every term, I ask students in my introductory psychology class to respond, anonymously and in writing, to different psychological questions. One of the questions I asked recently was, "Are you a happy person and why?" Consider two answers that I received to this question:

■ . . . I have always been a happy person. I don't really remember ever not being happy. Even as a kid I had lots of friends, nobody ever seemed to get mad at me. I like other people a lot. It seems the more I like people and the more I try to help them, the more they like me and the happier I am. There is no one thing that makes me happy. Even when things go wrong, like when I do lousy on a test or my boyfriend gets mad at me, I don't really become unhappy. I am bothered by things like this but not usually for long.

■ . . . I wouldn't say that I'm not happy. It's just that what makes me happiest doesn't usually seem to be the same kinds of things that make my parents or even some of my friends happy. I would rather stay home and read a novel or watch a movie by myself than go to a party or some other kind of social affair. I like people but I don't necessarily find my happiness in them.

How would you respond to this question—to which of these answers would your own response be most similar? It is likely that your response would not "match" either of the ones given above. Why? Simply because individuals differ so much. People have different styles of thinking, of relating to others, and of working, all of which reflect differences in personality—differences central to defining each of us as individuals. Common experience tells us that there is no one else who is just like us—individuals vary in the way they think and behave. Even between identical twins there can be considerable variability in personal characteristics.

Such everyday observations provide the starting point for psychology's study of personality. But unlike informal observations of people's personality, psychology's approach to studying personality is considerably more rigorous and calculated. For example, to many people, personality may be considered as "what makes people different from one another." To psychologists, though, the term is defined more precisely: **personality** is a particular pattern of behavior and thinking prevailing across time and situations that differentiates one individual from another. Psychologists are also not likely to draw inferences about personality on the basis of casual observations. Rather, their assessment of personality is derived from results of objective and projective tests designed to identify particular personality characteristics. For psychologists specializing in the study of personality, the goal is to discover the causes of individual differences in behavior.

This goal has led to two specific developments in the field of personality psychology: the development of methods by which individual patterns of behavior can be studied, classified, and manipulated, and the development of theories of personality that attempt to account for individual differences in behavior.

In this chapter, we will discuss what is presently known about personality. First, we will provide an overview of the methods used by personality researchers to assess individual differences. Next, we will discuss the major theories of personality.

ASSESSING PERSONALITY

Think for a moment of your best friend. What is he or she like? Outgoing? Impulsive? Thoughtful? Anxious? Moody? You can readily respond "yes" or "no" to these alternatives because you have spent enough time with your friend to know his or her personality quite well. After all, one of the

Psychologists use observation, testing, and a thorough analysis of the data collected to assess personality.

best ways to get to know a person—what he or she is like, things they enjoy doing, how they react in certain situations—is to spend time with them. For obvious reasons, a psychologist does not have the luxury of spending large amounts of time with each client, job candidate, or others in order to learn about their personalities. Rather, psychologists must assess the individual's personality within a limited time period. It is from this necessity that personality tests were first developed. **Personality tests** are tests designed to reveal the components of an individual's personality, or how one or more of the components interact with the other components, or how one person's personality differs from another's. The chief underlying assumption of any personality test is that personality characteristics can be measured. Personality tests come in two major varieties: objective tests (sometimes called inventories), which attempt to assess personality with fixed questions, and projective tests, which assess personality with open-ended questions.

Objective Tests

Objective tests for measuring personality are similar in structure to the ones given in the classroom to test your knowledge of different content areas: they may contain multiple choice or true-false items, although some allow examinees to indicate the extent to which they agree with an item. Objective tests are sometimes referred to as self-reports because they allow the person to respond to statements that describe aspects of their thoughts, emotions, and behavior. These inventories are scored by hand or by computer; the numbers they yield indicate the extent to which the individual's responses reflect a characteristic of personality (shyness, guilt, creativity). Two of the most widely used objective tests today are the Minnesota Multiphasic Personality Inventory and the 16 Personality Factor Questionnaire, both of which are discussed below.

The MMPI. The MMPI was first published in the early 1940s by a psychologist, Starke Hathaway, and a psychiatrist, J. C. McKinley, both from the University of Minnesota (Hathaway & McKinley, 1943). The original purpose of the test was to distinguish individuals with specific psychological problems from normal individuals. It has since become popular as a means of attempting to identify personality characteristics of people in a wide variety of everyday settings.

To devise the MMPI, Hathaway and McKinley constructed a large pool of statements to which individuals could respond "true," "false," or "cannot say." All of the items were then administered to several distinct groups of subjects: different groups of individuals known to have specific psychological problems, such as depression, schizophrenia, or extreme anxiety, and a single group of people considered to be normal (that is, these people were not diagnosed as suffering from any psychological disorders). The authors only retained items that discriminated among groups. In other words, if subjects in the different groups responded identically to a statement, that statement was discarded on the grounds that it was not differentially sensitive to subjects' characteristics. By using this procedure, Hathaway and McKinley hoped to develop a test that could be used to categorize individuals according to how similar their responses were to those individuals who have psychological problems.

The procedure eventually produced over 500 items, each of which belongs to one of ten clinical scales or one of four validity scales (see Figure 14.1). The higher a person scores on any one scale (each response is worth one point), the more likely he or she possesses the characteristics to which that scale is referenced. Clinical scales are those that identify aspects of

FIGURE 14.1
The MMPI scales and a summary of their functions.

CLINICAL SCALES

Scale 1	Hypochondriasis (Hs)	Measures excessive somatic concern and physical complaints.
Scale 2	Depression (D)	Measures symptomatic depression.
Scale 3	Hysteria (Hy)	Measures hysteroid personality features and the tendency to develop physical symptoms under stress.
Scale 4	Psychopathic deviate (Pd)	Measures antisocial tendencies.
Scale 5	Masculinity-femininity (Mf)	Measures sex-role conflict.
Scale 6	Paranoia (Pa)	Measures suspicious, paranoid ideation.
Scale 7	Psychasthenia (Pt)	Measures anxiety and obsessive behavior.
Scale 8	Schizophrenia (Sc)	Measures bizarre thoughts and disordered affect accompanying schizophrenia.
Scale 9	Hypomania (Ma)	Measures behavior found in manic affective disorder.
Scale 10	Social introversion (Si)	Measures social anxiety, withdrawal, and overcontrol.

VALIDITY SCALES

Cannot say scale (?)	Measures the total number of unanswered items.
Lie scale (L)	Measures the tendency to claim excessive virtue or to try to present an overall favorable image.
Infrequency scale (F)	Measures a tendency to falsely claim psychological problems.
Defensiveness scale (K)	Measures the tendency to see oneself in an unrealistically positive way.

Based on Aiken, 1970.

specific psychological characteristics. For example, the hypochondriasis or *Hs* scale measures excessive concern about physical illness and one's body; the Psychasthenia or *Pt* scale measures anxiety and obsessive behavior. Validity scales estimate the truthfulness of the individual's responses; they are included as a check for specific factors that may potentially interfere with the test's validity. The Cannot Say scale simply counts the number of unanswered questions. Although leaving a few questions blank will not invalidate the test, leaving too many will. The Lie scale measures the tendency of individuals to present themselves in an overly flattering manner. For example, responding "yes" to too many statements like "I am always happy" would lead to a high score on the Lie scale.

An individual's performance on the MMPI is generally interpreted in one of two ways. First, the performance on any scale may be compared, either by hand or by computer, against statistical norms for that scale. Second, performance on each scale is interpreted by the examiner. Obviously, the first method is more objective, but the second takes into consideration valuable insights that the examiner may have gained through his or her personal experiences in helping individuals with psychological disorders. A sample profile with an interpretation is provided in Figure 14.2.

In 1989, the University of Minnesota published the second edition of the MMPI, the MMPI-2 (Butcher et al., 1989). The MMPI-2 has been standardized on a larger, more heterogeneous group of people, and so is more representative of ethnic and socioeconomic differences. The original MMPI was standardized on 730 rural Minnesotans who were mostly white people with an average of an eighth-grade education. The MMPI-2 was standardized on a group of 2600 people from 7 states who had diverse educational, employment, and cultural backgrounds. In addition, a number of sexist, outdated, and other objectionable items have been deleted, and other more appropriate items added. In general, the MMPI-2 was developed to better reflect the cultural milieu of the 1990s. The MMPI-2 also contains more questions (over 700 items) and has four new scales that measure anxiety, repression, ego strength, and alcoholism.

The 16PF. Another widely used personality inventory, especially among marriage and vocational counselors, is the **16 Personality Factor (16PF)** inventory. The 16PF was developed in 1950 by Raymond B. Cattell (b. 1905). The test items on the 16PF refer to such characteristics as intelligence, sensitivity, shrewdness, and trust. Once the test is completed and analyzed, scores for each of the 16 traits are plotted in a linear profile, such as the one shown in Figure 14.3. This profile compares the average scores of airline pilots, creative artists, and writers (Cattell, 1973). As you might

FIGURE 14.2
An example of a profile and evaluation of an individual's performance on the MMPI.

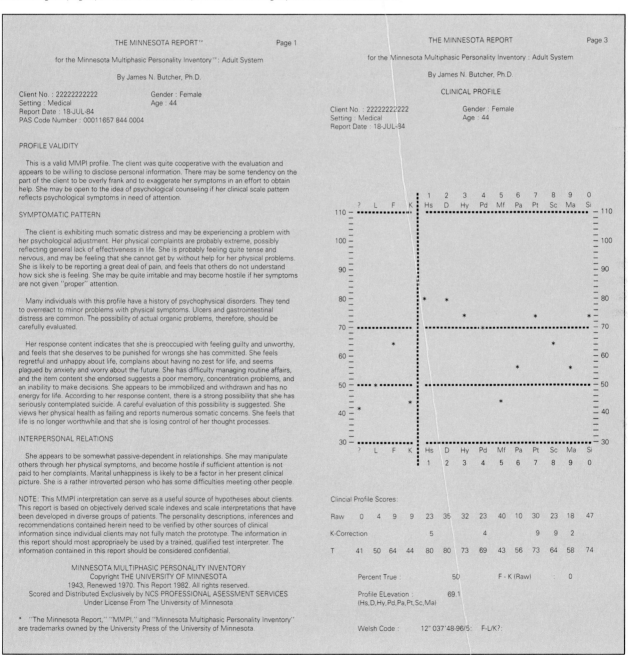

suspect, the personality characteristics, on average, of the writers and creative artists are similar; both differ from those of airline pilots. Regardless of the scores on any particular trait, a psychologist skilled in the use of the 16PF could use the information provided by the linear profile of the 16 scores, in addition to other test scores and demographic information, to develop a detailed psychological analysis of any individual or group of people, be they airline pilots or college students. Skilled interpretation of these profiles often requires years of practice because the meaning of each score must be considered as part of the overall configuration of scores. Focusing on the relations among individual traits provides insights into the dynamic nature of personality (Ahadi & Diener, 1989).

For example, to know someone as an introvert is not, by itself, sufficient to know if the person is well-adjusted or not. Many introverts prefer to spend much of their time alone, but they also interact with others, and may have few problems making friends. Other introverts, however, are very shy, have low self-esteem, and are anxious. The result is a person who has psychological problems and difficulties in adjusting to life in general. What is defined as a good score and what is defined as a bad score on any dimension of the 16PF depends on the pattern of the complete set of scale scores, interpreted within the context of the person's values and behavior relative to the organization or society as a whole.

Both the MMPI and the 16PF (as well as a variety of other objective tests) are widely used because they each possess good reliability and validity, have been standardized properly, are easy to administer and score, and are useful as indices of specific personality characteristics. For that reason, they often work well as screening devices for administrators and employers. Nonetheless, objective tests such as these have been criticized, namely because they serve as only one sample of an individual's behavior, and cannot capture the true overall nature of an individual's personality. Objective tests place rigid limits on the kinds of responses that subjects may provide. They also provide no opportunity for the examinee to elaborate on his or her answers. At the very least, other samples of an individual's behavior, preferably involving responses to a variety of real-life situations, need to be considered before making judgments about that person's personality. Although they do not capture real-life experiences of people, projective tests, our next topic, do provide the opportunity for the individual to elaborate upon his or her responses.

FIGURE 14.3
A comparison of personality profiles of airline pilots, creative artists, and writers on the 16PF.

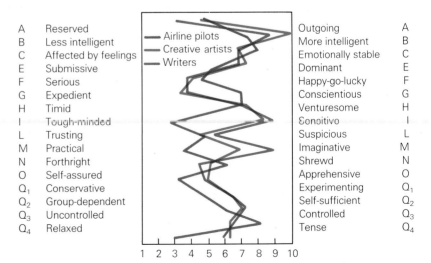

A	Reserved	Outgoing	A
B	Less intelligent	More intelligent	B
C	Affected by feelings	Emotionally stable	C
E	Submissive	Dominant	E
F	Serious	Happy-go-lucky	F
G	Expedient	Conscientious	G
H	Timid	Venturesome	H
I	Tough-minded	Sensitive	I
L	Trusting	Suspicious	L
M	Practical	Imaginative	M
N	Forthright	Shrewd	N
O	Self-assured	Apprehensive	O
Q_1	Conservative	Experimenting	Q_1
Q_2	Group-dependent	Self-sufficient	Q_2
Q_3	Uncontrolled	Controlled	Q_3
Q_4	Relaxed	Tense	Q_4

— Airline pilots
— Creative artists
— Writers

1 2 3 4 5 6 7 8 9 10

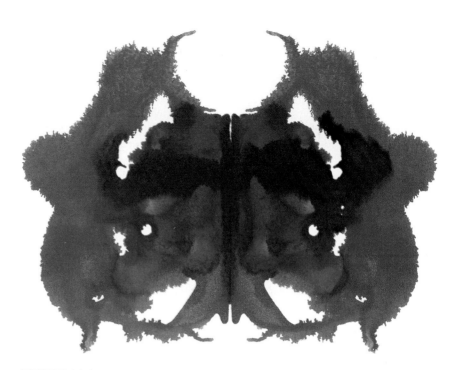

FIGURE 14.4
A Rorschach-like inkblot. The individual is asked what he or she sees in the inkblot.

Projective Tests

Objective tests are structured: they contain a fixed number of questions, and the possible alternative answers to those questions are spelled out unambiguously. However, some psychologists, especially those influenced by psychodynamic approaches, use *unstructured* personality measures called **projective tests,** in which a person is shown a series of ambiguous stimuli, such as pictures, inkblots, or incomplete drawings. The person is asked to describe what he or she "sees" in each stimulus or to create stories that reflect the theme of the drawing or picture. Because the stimuli are ambiguous, the person will presumably project his or her ideas, feelings, or thoughts onto the stimulus via their interpretation of it. These projections are believed by some personality psychologists to reflect the individual's personality. Two widely used projective tests are the Rorschach inkblot test and the Thematic Apperception Test.

The Rorschach Inkblot Test.   The **Rorschach inkblot test** was developed in 1921 by the Swiss psychologist Hermann Rorschach (1884–1922). In this test, the person is shown a series of symmetrical inkblots, like the one shown in Figure 14.4. Rorschach created 10 symmetrical inkblots, half of them in color (Rorschach, 1921). He also devised a scoring system and a method to interpret the scores. Here is how the test might go: The examiner asks the person to look at the inkblots, one at a time. Upon presentation of each inkblot, the person is asked to report what he or she sees in the stimulus (the person is also told that there are no right or wrong responses). The test examiner records each response, the response latency, and the total time required for each response. Later in the test, the person is asked to review and elaborate on his or her answers. The scoring and interpretation of the individual's responses depends on whether he or she responded to the entire inkblot or only part of it, the type of thing seen in the inkblot, and the aspects of the inkblot that determined the responses (color or shading).

FIGURE 14.5
A representative card from the TAT. Individuals are shown cards like this one and are asked to create stories about the people and events shown on each card. The stories are then evaluated for their thematic content.

B *ehavior assessment techniques focus on what an individual actually does, not just on what he or she reports.*

The Thematic Apperception Test. The **Thematic Apperception Test** or **TAT** was developed in 1938 by the American psychologist Henry Murray (1938). The TAT consists of 29 cards plus 1 blank card. Each of the 30 cards, such as the one shown in Figure 14.5, contains a black-and-white drawing of a person or persons in an ambiguous situation. For each card the examinee is shown, he or she is asked to make up a story about what the people are doing or thinking. The test examiner evaluates each response according to its content or theme. These themes are believed to reflect the examinee's primary personality characteristics. As you may recall from Chapter 10, motivation theorist David McClelland used TAT-like drawings to study the need for achievement and affiliation in his subjects.

The utility of projective tests has been debated vigorously among psychologists for decades. The main criticism of the tests is that they are subjective—the interpretation of test scores depends wholly on the expertise of the examiner. In addition, these tests have been criticized because of their low reliability and validity. In support of projective tests, many psychodynamic and clinical psychologists argue that the tests are valuable for discovering and evaluating inner determinants of personality. However, on the basis of poor reliability and validity, projective tests are questionable barometers of personality and its determinants.

Behavior Assessment Techniques

Unlike either objective or projective tests, **behavior assessment** techniques focus on what an individual actually does, not only just what he or she reports. This difference is due to the perspective and theoretical orientation of the people who develop and use different personality assessment strategies. Objective and projective tests were developed by people who view personality as being composed of a variety of constructs—unobservable and hypothetical variables. Psychologists who develop behavior assessment techniques, however, place less emphasis on constructs; rather, they view personality as being determined by behavior that is maintained by its consequences. To them, there are no underlying psychological forces that comprise personality; rather what counts is observable behavior and how it is influenced by its consequences.

There are several behavior assessment techniques. One way is to observe and note the behavior of an individual interacting with others at home, school, work, or other natural settings. Another is to develop a structured situation in which important variables can be manipulated. A third technique permits the individual to keep a diary of his or her activities, including when, where, and how often they occurred. In addition to the diary technique, a number of self-report inventories have been developed that focus on overt behavior and its consequences.

The actual assessment of personality is made by counting the frequency of particular behaviors as they occur under different conditions. For example, an individual is only categorized as fearful if, in fact, he or she demonstrates fear. Likewise, he or she is classified as submissive only if observed to show submissive behavior. One advantage of behavior assessment is that the conditions causing the fear or the submissive behavior can be identified and possibly even controlled. Perhaps the individual is fearful only when he or she is in confined spaces, such as elevators and hallways (claustrophobia). Using this rationale, it is not only possible to assess behavior but also how responsive it is to therapy. For example, observation of the frequency of behavior prior to therapy serves as a baseline against which the effects of therapy can later be assessed. If, for example, the frequency with which an individual shows fear of closed spaces after therapy decreases relative to the frequency before therapy, we know that therapy has likely been effective.

In conclusion, any attempt to measure personality, regardless of its objectivity or ability to sample real-life experiences, is bound at best, to be only an approximation. There is no one best measure or index of personality. Personality is too complex to be wholly reducible to answers on a personality inventory or a sample of observations of actual behavior. This does not mean, though, that we cannot make valid statements about aspects of an individual's personality or make accurate predictions about how he or she will behave in specific situations. Clearly, we can. Rather, it means that we must exercise caution in the inferences we draw from such statements and observations. Remember this: the more data and information we collect about an individual the better assessment we can make of his or her personality. For that reason, psychologists generally prefer to use information from a variety of tests, and where possible, from behavior assessment, before rendering definitive statements about an individual's personality.

THE PSYCHODYNAMIC APPROACH

The first and probably the most famous person to develop a comprehensive theory of personality was Sigmund Freud (1856–1939), a medical doctor whose primary interest was the study and treatment of neurological disorders. Freud spent almost his entire life of 83 years in Vienna. Because he was Jewish, he became the object of Nazi torment in the 1930s. His books were burned in public and his family was harassed by the Nazis. The Nazis eventually permitted Freud to emigrate to England, where he continued to work until his death in 1939. Freud's theory is rich in its description and detail of human life, and although many of its details are almost surely wrong by current reckoning, it represents one of the great attempts of humanity to understand its individual members.

Development of Freudian Theory

While earning his medical degree at the University of Vienna, which he received in 1881, he became interested in researching the nervous system. Not intending to practice medicine, Freud wished to obtain a university appointment as an academic scientist to pursue his research on the nervous system. As a medical student his career had a promising start, culminating in several publications on the invertebrate nervous system.

Although Freud enjoyed his laboratory work as much as he disliked the practice of medicine, academic salaries were meager, certainly not enough to support himself and his wife in the manner that their families expected. Soon, Freud established a private practice in neurology, in which he worked primarily with neurotic patients. (Neurosis is a family of psychological disorders typically classified today as either anxiety, somatoform, or dissociative disorders; we will formally discuss these in Chapter 15. For now, it is important that you remember that these disorders are marked by extreme and inappropriate anxiety.) As a practicing physician, hospital laboratories were available for research, providing him the opportunity to publish several more research papers in the years immediately following graduation from medical school. Freud was able to pursue his work "with gratifying success" (Freud, 1900, p. 170).

Josef Breuer

But Freud's contributions to psychology were not inspired directly by his research; rather it was his attempt to deal with the problems of his patients that led him to break new theoretical ground in the study of personality. At the beginning of his career Freud became friends with Josef Breuer, an older physician who also practiced in Vienna. Breuer related to Freud his experiences with Anna O., who suffered from hysteria. Although the symptoms of hysteria include paralysis of the limbs, loss of memory, blindness, deafness, and other physical problems, the underlying causes are psychological, not organic. (Today these symptoms, although less common, are involved in conversion disorders, which are discussed in the next chapter.) Anna O.'s symptoms, which first appeared when she was 21, included paralysis of her right arm and leg, visual difficulties, inability to drink fluids, occasional lapses of memory, and failure to speak or understand her native language.

Breuer treated Anna O. with hypnosis. Hypnosis is a clinical procedure for inducing a mental state characterized by deep relaxation and susceptibility to suggestion. Under such conditions, people may recall events that may have triggered certain emotional reactions that are involved in neuroses. While under hypnosis, Anna O. began to tell Breuer about her problems, which seemed to first appear while she was taking care of her dying father. Once Anna began talking to Breuer about her father, the severity of her symptoms decreased and later disappeared completely. Anna referred to Breuer's therapy as the "talking cure," because talking about her problems seemed to help them diminish.

Soon, Freud began using a nonhypnotic form of "the talking cure" with his own patients. Freud and Breuer worked together closely and in 1895 published a book, *Studies on Hysteria*, which described their new method. Shortly thereafter, Freud and Breuer had a falling out. Freud went on to develop the methods and the theory that eventually became the core of psychoanalysis, the name by which psychodynamic psychology was first known. Freud, however, gave Breuer total credit for discovering the psychoanalytic method.

Freud pondered the reasons for the talking cure's success. Why would just talking about the problem relieve the symptoms? He also questioned the basis of those symptoms—how can a traumatic event, in which no actual physical injury occurs, lead to the physical impairments observed in people suffering hysteria? Freud's answers to these sorts of questions led him to develop the following ideas:

- During the traumatic event, the individual is forced to hide strong emotion.
- Because it cannot be expressed normally, the emotion seeks other outlets, resulting in the neurotic symptoms.
- The individual cannot recall the emotions or the events that produced it because they are embedded in the **unconscious,** the inaccessible part of the mind.
- Those unconscious memories and emotions exert control over conscious thoughts and actions, causing the symptoms to linger and the emotions experienced during the original traumatic event to stay secret.

As Freud continued to work with his patients, he further developed his theory. One point that struck him was that therapy was a long process. Freud surmised that this was because two forces within the mind actively prevent conscious awareness of traumatic events. Freud referred to those forces that first relegate memories of past events into unconsciousness as **resistance.** The second force, which he called **repression,** is responsible for actively keeping those memories, most of which are potentially threatening or anxiety-provoking, from being consciously discovered. Freud used the idea of an iceberg as a metaphor to describe the mind. Only the tip of the iceberg is visible above water; the much larger and important part of the iceberg is submerged. Likewise, the conscious mind hides a larger and more important part of the mind—the unconscious. To understand a person's personality, then, we must tap his or her unconscious. To Freud, "the unconscious is the true psychical reality" (Freud, 1900, p. 651).

Freud argued that occasionally thoughts and ideas normally confined to the unconscious find their way into consciousness. For example, Freud theorized in what many consider to be his greatest work, *The Interpretation of Dreams*, that, "The interpretation of dreams is the royal road to a knowledge of the unconscious activities of the mind" (Freud, 1900, p. 647). The dream is like a mystery. The successful detective of the psyche unravels the mystery so as to understand the repressed wishes and urges that motivated the dream. By analyzing dreams, Freud thought repressed wishes and memories could be rediscovered. We will have more to say regarding the interpretation of dreams in Chapter 15; for now the important point is that Freud believed that repressed memories surface in dreams.

In the *Psychopathology of Everyday Life*, Freud gave examples of a second avenue by which normally repressed ideas enter consciousness (Freud, 1914). He referred to these examples as "faulty actions." What appear to be common mistakes instead often follow "lawful and rational paths" (p. 7) according to the underlying unconscious motivations. The most common of these faulty actions is probably familiar to you—mistakes of speech now referred to as **Freudian slips.** An example of such a slip comes from a soldier who had an affair while stationed far from home. He closed a letter to his wife by writing "I wish you could be her."

Freud, then, argued that our personalities are determined by both conscious and unconscious powers, with the unconscious exerting considerable influence on the conscious. Specifically, repressed ideas, thoughts, and wishes covertly influence how we consciously think and behave. Occasionally, these repressed entities surface in dreams and mistakes of speech. To fully understand how the unconscious exerts its control over conscious thought and action, we need to explore Freud's theory regarding the structure of personality.

The Structure of Personality

Freud believed that personality is composed of three primary interactive and often competing components: the id, ego, and superego. These components do not actually correspond to physical parts of the brain; instead they represent basic principles regarding how the mind works in shaping our personalities. The basic theme of Freudian theory is that the mind, especially the unconscious mind, is a perpetual battleground in which the id, ego, and superego are engaged in unending conflict. This inner conflict, which may take different forms in different people, is reflected in one's personality.

As can be seen in Figure 14.6, the id, superego, and ego occupy different levels of conscious awareness. The id is completely unconscious; its contents are normally inaccessible to the conscious mind. The influence of the superego can be exerted at both the level of the unconscious and conscious, as well as the preconscious, which is the level of the mind that contains ideas, memories, and so on that can be brought into consciousness through attention. The ego, like the superego, transcends all three levels of consciousness, although it does not penetrate the unconscious to the extent that the superego does. The unconscious portion of the ego houses the ego-defense mechanisms, which protect the ego from threatening ideas,

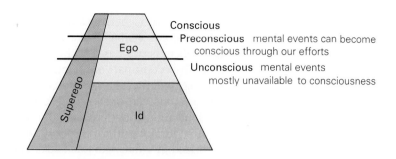

perceptions, emotions, and instincts. We shall learn more about the ego-defense mechanism shortly. In the meantime, we will discuss the properties of the id, superego, and ego.

The Id. The **id** is the personality structure that is the unconscious reservoir of libido, the psychic energy that fuels our inherited biological instincts. We have two primary instincts: those for food and sexual pleasure and those for aggression. Freud referred to these as *Eros*, representing life and love. Those instincts for aggression or those that lead to self-destructive behavior, he called *Thanatos*, representing a death wish. The id is our most primitive personality structure and is the source of energy for the entire personality system. The id follows one and only one rule, to obtain immediate gratification, whatever form it may take. This is known as the **pleasure principle**; if hungry then eat; if angry, then strike or seek revenge or destroy something. Freud conceived of the id as

> . . . the dark, inaccessible part of our personality. . . . We approach the id with analogies: we call it a chaos, a cauldron full of seething excitations . . . . It is filled with energy reaching it from the instincts, but it has no organization, produces no collective will, but only a striving to bring about the satisfaction of the instinctual needs subject to the observance of the pleasure principle.
>
> (1933, p. 65)

The id has an utter disregard for societal rules and values. It is held in partial check by Freud's second component of personality, the superego.

The Superego. The **superego** is the repository of an individual's moral values; it is stocked with the laws, mores, and sanctions of the society in which one lives. Although the id is complete and functioning at birth, the superego develops later. The superego is the personality structure in opposition to the id; when the id urges "do it now," the superego counters with "don't do it if it's morally wrong."

The superego is composed of two parts, the conscience and the ego-ideal. In the conscience moral sanctions reside that the superego uses to counter the aggressive and sexual promptings of the id. The conscience is a sort of substitute parent. The young child who begins to reach for a cookie before dinner, but then begins to feel guilty and withdraws her hand, is being influenced by her superego.

The superego also houses the ego-ideal, the standards of goodness and virtue that an individual strives to achieve. While the id prompts us to seek gratification via the pleasure principle, the superego is directing us toward our ego-ideal.

The Ego. The **ego** is the structure of personality that involves cognitive processes, such as thinking and reasoning, that the mind uses to process information about the environment. The ego serves as the interface between the individual and the environment; it is responsible for our self-awareness. The ego also serves as the general manager of personality; it makes the decisions regarding the pleasures that will be pursued at the urging of the id and the moral dictates of the superego that will be followed. In addition, the ego must also deal with the limitations imposed by external reality—not everything desired can be obtained immediately, if at all; some moral dictates cannot be followed or are simply impractical. The ego works according to the **reality principle,** or the tendency to satisfy the id's demands realistically, yielding to and accounting for the demands of reality, sometimes delaying the gratification of desires springing forth from the id, and sometimes softening the rules and regulations offered by the superego.

> *As the general manager, the ego must constantly juggle the competing demands of the id, superego, and reality. Hence Freud's metaphor of the ego as a battleground, the scene of perpetual conflict.*

As the general manager of personality, the ego must constantly juggle the competing demands of the id, superego, and reality to maintain an equilibrium in which neither the id nor the superego dominate; hence Freud's metaphor of the ego as a battleground, the scene of perpetual conflict. According to Freud,

> The poor ego . . . feels hemmed in on three sides, threatened by three kinds of danger, to which, if it is hard pressed, it reacts by generating anxiety. . . . Thus the ego, driven by the id, confined by the superego, repulsed by reality, struggles to master its economic task of bringing about harmony among the forces and influences working in and upon it; and we can understand how it is that so often we cannot suppress a cry: 'Life is not easy!'
>
> (1933, p. 69)

How does the ego deal with these competing forces? One of its primary strategies is to use defense mechanisms.

Defense Mechanisms. As you recall, Freud's patients all seemed to have one symptom in common—anxiety or an intense emotion apparently caused by a repressed internal conflict. What anxiety signals is that repression alone is not enough to keep the conflict unconscious. The conflict is beginning to emerge into consciousness, which, of course, will threaten the ego. In this case, the ego invokes its second line of protection: **defense mechanisms,** unconscious mental tactics that the ego uses to insulate itself from threatening ideas, perceptions, emotions, and instincts.

The most fundamental defense mechanism is repression. As a reminder, repression involves obstructing from awareness the instincts of the id and the emotions entailing guilt and regret of the superego. Traumatic experiences on the battlefield, for example, may result in a kind of amnesia. A soldier may survive a battle but cannot remember watching friends die. Although repressed feelings are not conscious, they continue to be active in the unconscious mind, shaping and influencing behavior many years after they occurred.

■ **Denial** works similarly to repression, except that it blocks from consciousness threatening perceptions of the real world. For example, an obese person may refuse to admit that she is overweight or that her diet is out of control. Likewise, an alcoholic may deny that there are dangers inherent in drinking.

- **Rationalization** is the justification of an unacceptable action by a more acceptable, but false, excuse. For example, the student who gets a D in a course may rationalize that the teacher was a poor one when, in fact, the teacher was a very good one. Whenever you do something that may generate anxiety, it is relatively easy to find all sorts of reasons to explain your action. Unfortunately, many of these reasons may be fabricated to reduce anxiety, and constructed simply so as to view ourselves in a more favorable light.

Two related examples of rationalization are the phenomena of sour grapes and sweet lemons. *Sour grapes* occurs when we falsely devalue something we really like, but can't have. Remember the fox from *Aesop's Fables* who wanted the grapes but couldn't jump high enough to reach them? Instead of facing the fact that he couldn't have what he wanted, he decided instead that the grapes were probably sour. *Sweet lemons* is overvaluing something you already have. After spending many thousands of dollars for what turns out to be a klunker of a car, it is difficult to admit your mistake. It is easier instead to distort reality by overlooking the faults—and, at least at the conscious level, feeling better for doing it.

- **Projection** occurs when one's own unacceptable behaviors or thoughts are attributed to someone else. For example, a person who cheats on exams may feel guilty, but to avoid her own guilt distorts her perception of reality by falsely accusing someone else of cheating. Or, a person may feel anger toward another person, and then falsely accuse the other person of being angry. In projection, the faults of one person are projected onto other people. The person sees in others that which he does not want to see in himself.

- **Reaction-formation** involves behaving in a way that is the opposite of how one really feels because the true feelings produce anxiety. An example is the strident "anti-sex" campaigner who vociferously protests issues such as sex education, planned parenthood for teenagers, and pornography—because he or she cannot deal with his or her own strong sexual urges.

- **Displacement** channels feelings of hostility and aggressive tendencies toward acceptable or less threatening persons or objects. For instance, a husband may be angry with his wife, but is afraid to express his true feelings to her. Instead, he yells at the dog or treats his children harshly.

- **Sublimation** entails redirecting pleasure-seeking or aggressive instincts toward socially acceptable goals. For example, instead of verbally or physically abusing the people around you, you participate in contact sports. Instead of seeking immediate gratification of one's sexual urges, one writes erotic stories. Sublimation, then, allows the whims of the id to be partially satisfied while also permitting the superego to exercise its moral imperatives.

Freud also theorized that there were a number of other defense mechanisms. These are listed and described in Table 14.1.

Freud's Theory of Personality Development

Freud believed that one's personality is basically formed during childhood. It is during this period when unconscious forces exert influences that will characterize an individual's thought and behavior patterns for the rest of his or her life. In general, Freud argued that personality develops across five psychosexual stages that span the period from birth until adolescence. Each of the **psychosexual stages** refers to the developmental stages that are defined by the part of the body or erogenous zone from which sexual gratification is primarily derived. Each stage is characterized by a particular psychosexual conflict that requires resolution (Freud, 1905). Freud also believed that an individual's failure to resolve the conflict associated with each stage results in **fixation,** or an unconscious obsession with the erogenous zone involved in that stage. Let's take a closer look at each psychosexual stage.

TABLE 14.1. *Additional defense mechanisms.*

DEFENSE MECHANISM	CHARACTERISTICS
Compartmentalization	Categorizing inconsistent beliefs into separate and mutually exclusive compartments to reduce anxiety produced by holding such beliefs simultaneously
Compensation	Masking anxiety by focusing on desirable qualities
Emotional insulation	Withdrawing into docility to prevent becoming emotionally hurt
Fantasy	Creating fictitious achievements to satisfy blocked desires
Identification	Identifying with famous people or institutions to increase feelings of self-esteem
Regression	Retreating to earlier stages of development that are less threatening
Undoing	Attempting to make up or compensate for unacceptable wishes and impulses

During the oral stage, infants up to 18 months of age not only use their mouths for eating and drinking but also for exploration. Freud theorized that oral gratification at this stage is crucial; however, too much or too little could result in personality disorders later on in life.

The Oral Stage. Freud referred to a child's first 18 months of life as the **oral stage,** because during this time the mouth is the major active erogenous zone. The id compels the infant to use its mouth not only for eating and drinking, but for exploration as well. Almost any object a baby of this age range can grasp ends up in or around the mouth. According to Freud, failure to obtain enough oral gratification or obtaining too much gratification causes fixation at this stage, which will eventually result in personality problems later in life. For example, fixation may cause an adolescent or adult to overeat, talk too much, become an alcoholic, or smoke.

The Anal Stage. From about 18 months to the age of 3 or 4, children pass through the **anal stage** during which the primary erogenous zone is the anal region. Freud argued that it is during this time that children take pleasure in retaining or expelling feces. However, it is also during this time that parents attempt to toilet train their children, which often leads to conflict between parent and child. If parents begin toilet training too early or too late, or are impatient with their child's progress in learning to use the toilet, Freud believed that fixation may result. Fixation during this stage may produce one of two types of adult personalities. Children who become fixated on retaining their feces develop into adults who are stingy, controlling, stubborn, and orderly. Children who become fixated on expelling their feces develop into adults who are impulsive, sloppy, disorganized, and always late.

The Phallic Stage. The next stage, which lasts from age 3 or 4 to between the ages of 5 and 6, is called the **phallic stage,** because during this period the genital area is the most sensitive erogenous zone. The primary conflict during this stage again involves parents. Children, driven by the promptings of the id, wish to touch their genitalia, but parents attempt to stop them. However, children wish to do more than manually stimulate their genitalia, they also have an unconscious yearning to become sexually involved with the opposite-sex parent. Freud referred to the boy's desire for his mother as the Oedipus complex (after the Greek tragedy Oedipus Rex, in which a man unwittingly kills his father and marries his mother). The girl's desire for her father is called the Electra complex (after another Greek tragedy in which Electra kills her mother). The gist of the Oedipus complex is this. The boy is unconsciously driven by the id to lust after his mother and he realizes (also unconsciously) that he must kill his father in order to have his mother to himself. He also fears that his father knows about his plans and so, will attempt to castrate him. (Freud referred to this emotion in the young boy as castration anxiety.) The boy's ego understands the problems that would result from the lustful feelings reaching consciousness and so, it must ensure that the instinct is not acted upon. It does so by reaching a compromise with the id, which motivates the boy to identify with his father, his arch rival. That is, the ego prompts the boy to become as much like his father as possible, and in that way, the id can vicariously enjoy the affection that mother shows to father. Of course, repression ensures that the adult male will remember none of this drama!

The resolution of the Oedipus complex is a prominent factor in the development of the superego. By assimilating the values of the father, the superego emerges as the third mental force, one that will be juxtaposed against the id. In Freud's view the Oedipus complex represents one of the most important milestones for the boy's developing personality, including the development of later psychological problems in adulthood if the Oedipus complex is not sufficiently resolved. If the boy continues his sexual attachment to mother, and never identifies with his father, his sexuality (and personality) will become self-centered and fail to mature into the interpersonal sexuality characteristic of the final stage of psychosexual development.

At the phallic stage, children experience an unconscious desire for the opposite-sex parent. Boys will desire their mothers, a stage Freud called the Oedipus complex.

Freud was not certain of how the Electra complex developed, so he did not describe it as clearly as he did the Oedipus complex. The Electra complex is convoluted and includes such "insights" as girls blaming their mothers for their own castration (Freud, 1933). The Electra complex is ultimately resolved by sublimation in which the girl wishes for a baby, especially a male baby, instead of a penis, which will briefly provide her with the long sought after organ.

Or so Freud's account goes. As you might suppose, it is an understatement to say that this theory is not substantiated. Freud himself asserted that he did not understand female sexuality very well (1933). Unfortunately, Freud's admitted ignorance on this issue did not prevent him or many of his followers from making sweeping, incorrect, and often sexist generalizations about women.

The Latency Stage. The phallic stage is followed by a period called the **latency stage**, which lasts from about age 5 or 6 to puberty. During this stage, the unconscious forces of the psyche are relatively dormant. That is, the developing child experiences no unconscious conflicts; the latency stage is a period of unconscious peace. The major events in the latency stage are all conscious: going to school, playing out-of-doors, and developing personal interests.

The Genital Stage. The final stage of psychosexual development, the **genital stage** is heralded by the onset of puberty and is marked by adult sexual desires. The id and superego once again become active, forcing the ego to find socially acceptable solutions to sexual (or aggressive) urges.

Like the caterpillar escaping its cocoon, it is also during this stage that the adult personality begins to emerge. The nature of adult personality and the quality of interpersonal relationships rest on two factors: first, whether the ego was successful in resolving crises that appeared in the first three stages; and second, the ability of the ego to meet the demands of the sexual promptings of the id, the morality of the superego, and the constraints of reality on a day-to-day basis during adulthood.

Post-Freudian Psychodynamic Theorists

As you might imagine, Freud's theory created quite a controversy in its day. Its emphasis on childhood sexuality and seething internal conflicts seemed preposterous to some. Yet, the theory's proposal that our thoughts and behavior as adults stem from unconscious forces as well as from our early childhood experiences were revolutionary and recognized by many scholars as genuinely original and profoundly important ideas. Freud attracted a number of followers who studied his work closely but who did not accept it completely. Each of these people accepted Freud's view regarding the dynamic forces operating within the psyche. Each of them disagreed with Freud, though, on how much importance to place on the role of unconscious sexual and aggressive instincts in shaping personality. We turn now to a discussion of three other psychodynamic theorists: Carl Jung, Alfred Adler, and Karen Horney.

Carl Jung

Carl Jung. Beginning in the first decade of the twentieth century, several students of psychoanalysis met with Freud to further the development of psychoanalytic theory and practice. One of these was Carl Jung (1875–1961), who many believe ranks only behind Freud in terms of productivity and influence in the development of psychoanalytic theory. Freud called Jung "his adopted eldest son, his crown prince and successor" (Hall & Nordby, 1973, p. 23). Jung was an established scholar and successful psychiatrist in Zurich before he first met Freud in 1907. Jung played an increasingly important role in the development of psychoanalysis, a role that included organizing the first public recognition of Freud's work, an international conference in 1908, and serving as the first president of the International Association of Psychoanalysis, founded in 1910 (Jones, 1961). However, Jung developed his own version of psychodynamic theory that de-emphasized the importance of sexuality in personality development. As we shall see, Jung also disagreed with his mentor with respect to the structure of the unconscious. Unfortunately, Freud had little tolerance of others changing his theory. After 1913, they never saw each other again. Jung continued to develop his theory of personality after the split by drawing ideas from a wide range of interests in mythology, anthropology, history, and religion, as well as an active clinical practice in which he saw people with psychological disorders.

To Jung, libido was not sexual energy; rather, it was a creative force that propels people toward personal growth. Likewise, he disagreed with Freud over the structures that define personality. Rather than the interaction of the id, ego, and superego, Jung believed other forces, such as the personal unconscious and the collective unconscious, form the core of personality. To Jung, the ego was totally conscious; it is comprised of ideas, perceptions, emotions, thoughts, and memories of which we are aware. The personal unconscious contains similar information, although we may not be consciously aware of its contents. It is similar to Freud's idea of preconscious; with a little effort, the information stored here can be brought into consciousness. One of Jung's more important contributions to psychodynamic theory was his notion of the **collective unconscious**, which contains memories and ideas inherited from our ancestors over the course of evolution. In Jung's words (1928), it is the "echo of the prehistoric world events to which each century adds an infinitesimally small amount of variation and differentiation" (p. 162). Stored in the collective unconscious are **archetypes**, universal thought forms and patterns. From the dawn of our species, all humans have roughly similar experiences with things such as mothers, evilness, masculinity, and femininity. Each one of these is represented by an archetype. For example, consider the shadow, the archetype that represents our evil, carnal side. It not only accounts for our immorality during our time, but throughout history as well. Archetypes are not stored images or ideas—we are not born with a picture of evil stored somewhere in our brain—but we are born with an inherited disposition to behave, perceive, and think in certain ways. Archetypes are "forms without content" (Jung, 1954, p. 48).

Jung developed the ideas of collective unconscious and archetypes through the study of dreaming and mythology. When interpreting dreams, Jung was struck by the similarity of the dream with cultural myths, from ancient civilizations of which the dreamer was certainly unaware. He also identified common themes in the myths of different cultures, and he attributed the similarity of the themes that underlie dreams and myths to the collective unconscious.

Jung believed that the mind has two different "attitudes" that prepare people to approach the world in one of two ways: either through introversion, an interest primarily in one's inner experiences, or extroversion, an orientation toward objects, people, and events in the environment. According to Jung, people tend to be either introverted or extroverted, but not both. This means that, in Jung's view, an individual's personality can become lopsided: too introverted or too extroverted; in such cases, Jung recommended therapy to restore balance and harmony to the psyche.

Alfred Adler. Like Jung, Alfred Adler (1870–1937) studied with Freud. Also like Jung, Adler felt that Freud overemphasized the role of sexuality in personality development. Instead, Adler theorized that feelings of inferiority play a key role in personality development. Upon birth, we are dependent on others for our survival. As we mature, we encounter people who are more gifted than us in almost every aspect of life. The inferiority we feel may be social, intellectual, physical, or athletic in nature. These feelings create tension that motivates us to compensate for the deficiency. Emerging from this need to compensate is a **striving for superiority**, a force that Adler believed to be the major motivational force in life.

According to Adler (1939), striving for superiority is affected by another force, **social interest**, which is an innate desire to make contributions to society. Social interest is not wholly instinctual, though, because it can be influenced to no small extent by family relationships and the experiences

According to Alfred Adler, a student of Freud, we have an innate desire to contribute to society. Helping others by working in a volunteer organization is an example of this social interest.

of youth. An individual's striving for superiority, then, is subordinate to social interest. Although individuals have a need to seek personal superiority, they have a greater desire to sacrifice for causes that benefit the society as whole. To Adler, social interest meant that humanity as a whole has an innate desire to work toward building better, perhaps perfect, societies. Thus, while Freud believed that people act in their own self-interest, as motivated by the id, Adler believed that people desire to help others, as directed by social interest.

However, Adler believed that society is comprised of individuals (Adler, 1924), and each individual is unique in how he or she strives for superiority and is influenced by social interest. He referred to this uniqueness as style of life. In other words, on our way to superiority we each travel different paths, and we each make different kinds of contributions to society. Style of life is influenced primarily by our conscious experiences, not by unconscious forces. Here, then, is a second way that Adler's views differed from those of Freud: Adler emphasized the role of learning and its effects on personality development more so than did Freud.

Karen Horney

Karen Horney. Karen Horney (1885–1952), like other Freudian dissenters, did not believe that sex and aggression are the primary themes of personality. She did agree with Freud, however, that anxiety is a basic problem in life that people must address and overcome. Unlike Freud, Horney did not believe that anxiety is a product of society.

According to Horney, individuals suffer from basic anxiety caused by insecurities in our relationships with others. People often feel alone, helpless, or uncomfortable in their interactions with friends, family, and colleagues. For example, a new person on the job is often unsure of how to perform his or her duties, whom to ask for help, and how to approach his or her new coworkers. Such situations give rise to basic anxiety. To deal with basic anxiety, Horney theorized that the individual may follow one of three general courses of action (Horney, 1942, 1945, 1950):

- *Moving toward others.* Accept the situation and become dependent on others. This strategy may entail an exaggerated desire for approval or affection.
- *Moving against others.* Resist the situation and become aggressive. This strategy may involve an exaggerated need for power, exploitation of others, recognition, or achievement.
- *Moving away from others.* Withdraw from others and become isolated. This strategy may involve an exaggerated need for self-sufficiency, privacy, or independence.

Horney believed that these three strategies corresponded to three **basic orientations** with which people approach their lives. These basic orientations reflect different personality characteristics. The *self-effacing solution* corresponds to the moving toward others strategy and involves the desire to be loved. The *self-expansive solution* corresponds to the moving against others strategy and involves the desire to master one's self. The *resignation solution* corresponds to the moving away strategy and involves the striving to be independent of others.

Horney maintained that personality is a mixture of the three strategies and basic orientations. They arise from the need to deal with basic anxiety; as the source of anxiety varies from one situation to the next, so may the strategy and basic orientation that is used to cope with it. Problems such as neurotic behavior result when an individual's personality is monopolized by one strategy or basic orientation. Such neurotic behavior leads to more anxiety and prevents the individual from achieving his or her potential.

As you can see, Horney, like Adler, considered the role of the environment as a determinant of personality development. Unlike Freud, she viewed personality to be just as much a product of present environmental circumstances as past experiences in life. From her view, to understand personality, one must not only consider psychodynamic forces within the mind, but the environmental conditions to which those forces are reacting.

Critique of Psychodynamic Approaches

The mark that Freud left on western thought rivals that left by Charles Darwin (Hall & Lindzey, 1978). Similar to the way Darwin's theory of evolution revolutionized the way we view the origin of life, Sigmund Freud's theory of the unconscious revolutionized the way we view personality and the human mind. Like Darwin, Freud was not a psychologist. And like Darwin's work, Freud's work continues to influence the way many psychologists approach their own work.

But unlike Darwin, Freud did not amass a large database from which to launch his theory. Darwin, as you recall, spent five years collecting specimens and studying the flora and fauna of numerous countries before beginning to theorize seriously about the origin of species. Freud never conducted any research in garnering support for his theory other than to work with his clients. Almost all criticisms of Freud's work are related to this point. Several criticisms of Freud's work are discussed below.

One important criticism of Freud's theory is that it is not based on empirical research. Because concepts like the id, ego, superego, fixation, and so on, are fuzzy, they are difficult, if not impossible, to study through experimentation. As a result, Freud's approach is almost entirely subjective, leaving little room for objective validation of psychodynamic constructs.

Another criticism involves the fact that Freud's theory is retrospective; it basically involves reconstruction of one particular way that the adult personality may develop. It is a post-hoc explanation of personality. Unlike theories that generate research, Freud's does not permit prediction. It does not, for example, allow us to explain in advance when or under what circumstances a particular defense mechanism will be invoked, nor will it permit us to predict the strength of the defense mechanism in protecting the ego. Almost anybody can explain things after the fact, but that is hardly scientific or useful. The major goal of psychology is to understand actions before they occur; that way, the effects of those actions can be controlled. For example, we might say that the reason one person attacked and killed another is because of the instinctual prompting of the id *(Thanatos)*. This is an explanation, but it is of no value in helping us understand the immediate causes of the murder or in helping us identify aspects of the murderer's behavior that would indicate that he might kill again.

Because Freud's theory is reconstructive, it also offers nothing in the way of explanation for how current environmental conditions may function as independent variables that affect personality. As we learned earlier, both Adler and Horney criticized Freud for failing to take into consideration the role of the environment in personality development.

Current psychodynamic theory emphasizes the social environment of the child as an important factor in personality development. That is, other people, particularly family and close friends, respond to the social needs of the young child. The child, in turn, learns how to interact with others and forms an idea of his or her relationship to the main characters of the social world. This view of personality development is known today as object relations.

In sum, there is little scientific credibility to the psychodynamic explanation of personality. Experimentation has played virtually no role in the development and testing of psychodynamic theory. Why then has Freud's work played such an important role in the history of psychology? The answer to that question is timing and substance. Freud's theory was developed at a time when few others had conscientiously explored the realm of human behavior to the depth and breadth that Freud did. Freud, in essence, was the first to explore the frontiers of the mind. That he was among the first to chart the mind, though, is overshadowed by the significance of the broad sweep of his theory and the power of his observations. His theory of personality is broader than any other theories of personality, and his ideas affected the way in which many early twentieth century scholars viewed humanity. But perhaps the greatest attraction to his theory is the recognition that behavior is sometimes caused by variables of which we are unaware and that one's sexuality can have profound effects on his or her behavior.

Psychodynamic theorists are primarily concerned with peering inside personality to explore its underlying dynamics. A very different tack to studying personality is the trait approach, our next topic.

THE TRAIT APPROACH

Instead of focusing on underlying dynamics, trait theorists are interested in determining the personality characteristics of an individual that are stable over long periods of time. For example, trait theorists believe that one such characteristic is described by the dimension Shy-Socially Venturesome. Some people are characteristically shy, others are very outgoing, but most are located somewhere between these two extremes. A relatively stable, measurable characteristic of a person is called a **trait**.

Gordon Allport and the Trait Approach

Gordon Allport (1897–1967), one of the first psychologists to search systematically for a basic core of personality traits, began his work by searching for all of the words in an unabridged dictionary of the English language that describe aspects of human personality (Allport & Odbert, 1936). He found approximately 18,000 words, which he then further analyzed for those that described only stable personality characteristics. Words that represented temporary states such as "flustered" or evaluations such as "admirable" were eliminated. This still left him with over 4000 words.

The key question for Allport was how many traits are needed to describe personality, and exactly what are these traits? For example, many of those 4000 words, such as shy and bashful, are synonyms. Although each synonym presumably makes some sort of distinction about personality, together a group of synonyms might be used to describe the same underlying trait. Most trait theorists believe that the most basic set of personality traits ranges from 3 to 20 traits.

Allport's research led him to believe that personality traits fall into different classes or categories of central traits that describe likely tendencies of people, for example, honest, hardworking, thrifty, or pessimistic. Secondary traits occur less frequently than central traits, and only in particular situations. Your psychology professor may be outgoing in front of class, but rather reserved in faculty meetings.

A common trait is one that is shared by many people and is often specific to certain environments. For example, salespersons generally have in common a degree of assertiveness, and athletes have in common a certain

Gordon Allport

A common trait, as defined by Gordon Allport, is one that many people share and is often specific to a certain environment. The competitiveness that swimmers and other athletes share is a type of common trait.

degree of competitiveness. To Allport, unique traits, those that distinguish one individual from another, were more interesting and important. He felt that way because it is these particular traits, a particular tack, a peculiar sense of humor, a biting sarcasm, that make people interesting.

Allport's ideas stimulated other psychologists to think about personality in terms of traits or dispositions that characterize people's thought and behavior patterns. In fact, most modern trait theories can be traced back to Allport's earlier theoretical work. Today's trait theorists maintain, as did Allport, that only when we know how to describe an individual's personality will we be better able to explain it. To describe a person's personality, trait theorists have devised objective personality inventories that can be completed in usually an hour or less. As you know, subjects' responses on the inventory are evaluated by the test examiner, producing a score for each of the traits measured by the inventory. These scores can then be related to a multitude of other personality variables or behaviors of interest. To the extent that these questionnaires provide meaningful information about an individual's personality, trait theorists have provided us with an inexpensive, straightforward method for measuring key aspects of personality. However, different trait theorists are often interested in only measuring certain traits, and, as a result, have developed specific inventories for specific traits. Only a few inventories, like the MMPI and 16PF, are designed to measure a broad mixture of personality traits. We turn now to an overview of three influential trait theories and the inventories used to test them.

M ost modern trait theories can be traced back to Allport's earlier theoretical work.

Five-Factor Theory

After several decades of work, a number of researchers (for example, Digman & Takemoto-Chock, 1981; Digman & Inouye, 1986; McCrae & Costa, 1985, 1987) have concluded that personality is best described by five broad traits: Extroversion, Emotional Stability (also called Neuroticism or Anxiety), Openness, Agreeableness, and Conscientiousness. This is known as the **five-factor theory**. These five factors were uncovered by giving subjects an inventory known as the NEO-PI (Costa & McCrae, 1985) and analyzing subjects' responses with factor analysis. In the last chapter, we described how factor analysis was used by Spearman to study intelligence. Let us refresh your memory for this procedure by showing you how it works for studying personality traits. Factor analysis is a statistical technique used to determine if different test questions are correlated with each other. To determine the number of specific traits of which personality is composed, every question on a personality inventory is correlated, through factor analysis, with every other test question. Those that correlate highly with each other are hypothesized to tap the same personality trait or factor of the individual being tested. Those that correlate weakly are believed to tap different personality traits or factors. Factor analyzing subjects' responses on the NEO-PI has shown that the personality of those subjects may be described using the five traits listed above.

Other trait theorists, using other personality inventories and factor analysis, have turned up a different number of traits that they believe are representative of personality. One such theorist is Raymond B. Cattell, to whom you were briefly introduced at the beginning of the chapter (Cattell, 1946, 1950).

Raymond Cattell's 16 Basic Traits

Using his 16PF inventory, Raymond Cattell has described personality in terms of 16 different traits, which means that his traits are more specific than those of the five-factor theory. Cattell's 16-trait theory is reasonably consistent with the five-factor theory, such that these broader traits can be directly related to the more specific 16 traits from Cattell's questionnaire (Gerbing & Tuley, 1990).

Cattell began his search for a relatively small number of basic personality traits with Allport and Odbert's (1936) list of thousands of adjectives describing human personality. In addition, he collected data about people's personality characteristics from interviews, records describing their life histories, and from observing people behave in particular situations. From this list, Cattell began to construct preliminary versions of the 16PF. Then, using factor analysis, he analyzed responses from thousands of people to whom the inventory had been administered. (Reviewing Figure 14.3 will help you recall the 16 traits or factors common to the responses of his subjects. Although Cattell gave these traits technical names, we have listed them according to their everyday names.) Each trait varies along a continuum, which means that it has two dimensions, high and low. If a person scores high on one dimension (say, outgoing), he or she has a low score on the other dimension (in this case, reserved).

Cattell referred to these 16 traits as source traits because in his view they are the cornerstones upon which personality is built. That is, they are the primary factors underlying overt expression of behavior. He termed groups of similar types of overt behavior as surface traits, such as kindness, honesty, and friendliness, because they are visible to others: they represent the surface of personality and spring forth from source traits, which lie deeper within the personality.

Hans Eysenck's Three Basic Traits

While Cattell has focused on 16 relatively specific personality traits, Hans Eysenck (b. 1916) has developed a personality theory that is based on three basic trait dimensions, *introversion-extroversion, stability-instability,* and *psychoticism* (see Figure 14.7). Introversion-extroversion refers to the tendencies of people to be more or less active, outgoing, or gregarious. Introverts are not very active, outgoing, or gregarious; extroverts are just the opposite. Stability-instability, often called neuroticism, refers to the tendencies of people to be more or less calm, even-tempered, or reliable. Unstable individuals show anxious, moody, and unreliable behavior; stable individuals behave oppositely. Psychoticism (not shown in Figure 14.7) is a characteristic of someone who is solitary, does not care for people, is

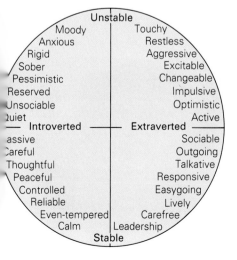

FIGURE 14.7
The dimensions of personality according to Eysenck.

generally troublesome, and not sensitive to the feelings of others. Of course, an individual's personality is not likely to reflect pure extroversion, pure stability, or pure psychoticism. Eysenck, like Cattell, believes that traits vary along dimensions. For example, an individual's personality can be described in terms of the degree to which he or she shows introversion or extroversion and stability or instability in behavior.

More than most other trait theorists, Eysenck emphasizes the biological nature of his basic traits. For example, consider the introversion-extroversion dimension, which is biologically based, according to Eysenck, on an optimum arousal level of the brain. Eysenck believes that the functioning of the reticular activating system, the brain nucleus involved in sleep and arousal, produces different levels of arousal of the cerebral cortex of introverts and extroverts. Introverts have a relatively high level of cortical excitation while extroverts have a relatively low level of excitation. Thus, in order to maintain the optimum arousal level, the extrovert requires more external stimulation than the introvert. The extrovert seeks stimulation from external sources by interacting with others, or pursuing novel and highly stimulating experiences. The introvert avoids external stimulation in order to maintain his or her lower arousal level at an optimal state. Thus different states of arousal are hypothesized to lead to different values of the extroversion trait for different people.

Eysenck has supported his theory using laboratory studies of human personality based on the Eysenck Personality Questionnaire (EPQ), an inventory he designed to study his three basic traits. For example, to the extent that extroversion is a biologically based personality trait, then certain laboratory tasks should differentiate high scorers on the EPQ extroversion scale from low scorers. Many experimental studies of both biological and psychological processes such as physiology, conditioning, memory, learning, and social behavior have demonstrated differences in behavior for extroverts and introverts (Eysenck, 1981; Eysenck & Eysenck, 1985).

One example of a laboratory investigation is a test of the following hypothesis: if introverts receive higher levels of cortical arousal than extroverts, then they should react more strongly than extroverts to external stimulation. Corcoran (1964) and Eysenck and Eysenck (1967) demonstrated this increased reaction to 4 drops of lemon juice dropped on the tongue. The dependent variable was the amount of saliva produced in response to the lemon juice. Eysenck and Eysenck (1967) reported a correlation of −.71 for the EPQ extroversion score with the amount of salivation, which indicates that the more extroverted subjects showed less of a reaction to the lemon juice. This is an important finding because it points up the possibility of developing biologically based measures of personality.

Introverts are generally quiet and not very active or outgoing, while extroverts are very gregarious and outgoing.

Critique of the Trait Approach

According to trait theory, an individual's disposition is more important in determining behavior than are the circumstances under which behavior occurs. Allport claimed that traits render situations "functionally equivalent," which in his view, means that people express the same traits across different situations. Do traits determine behavior? Do traits influence behavior more than situational or environmental variables?

To critics of the trait approach the answer to both questions is no. They contend that traits do not explain or predict behavior, but instead, only describe it. In this view, traits are merely labels. Labeling a person as calm or collected (emotionally stable according to the five-factor theory, more relaxed than tense on Cattell's scale, and stable on Eysenck's scale) may not allow us to predict accurately that he or she will show this trait in all situations. Will this person be calm and collected if attacked by a mugger? If accused of tax evasion by the IRS? If fired from his or her job? If he or she wins a million dollars in a lottery? In all these cases, the person is likely to deviate at least a modicum from his or her usual show of calmness. The point of the trait theory critics, of course, is that when explaining or predicting behavior, situational factors must also be taken into consideration.

Over the past two decades, an outspoken critic of the trait approach has been Stanford University psychologist Walter Mischel (1968, 1984). In his 1968 book, *Personality and Assessment*, he challenged the utility of the concept of trait by showing that people's behavior often varies widely from situation to situation. In Mischel's view, traits are not as important as cognitive and situational variables in determining personality. Mischel has also noted that a score on a personality inventory may paint a general picture of an individual's personality characteristics but it will not yield an accurate prediction of how he or she will behave in specific situations.

Mischel's criticisms have caused other researchers to view the trait approach with caution but not to abandon it completely. Some of these researchers contend that personality is a blending of dispositional and situational factors. In other words, in order to understand personality, both an individual's traits as well as environmental demands must be considered (Sarason, Smith, & Diener, 1975). Three factors seem to be particularly important when attempting to make predictions about any one individual's behavior (Bem & Funder, 1978; Kenrick & Funder, 1988):

- The traits of the individual: generally stable personality characteristics.
- Social perception: how different situations are perceived.
- Differences in trait expression in a given situation within individuals.

For example, although a person may be assertive, she may exhibit this trait in different forms depending on how she perceives different social environments. She may be more assertive in some situations than others. In some situations, she may not be assertive at all. She may choose not to keep pressing her point with her supervisor even though she is right. In this case, she may perceive that being too assertive could have negative consequences—denial of promotion, pay raises, or a strained interpersonal relationship.

Up to this point we have studied personality from the perspectives of psychodynamic theory and trait theory. Psychodynamic theory is a theory of how the unconscious mind influences conscious actions derived primarily from the analysis of case histories. Trait theory isolates the basic characteristics of human personality, and provides the personality questionnaires useful for measuring these traits. Both theories have been criticized on the grounds that they ignore environmental variables in accounting for personality development. Our next topic, the social learning approach, was formulated specifically to take into consideration the effects of environmental factors on personality.

THE SOCIAL LEARNING APPROACH

Both the psychodynamic and trait approaches focus on relatively stable aspects of an individual's personality. An assumption underlying both of these theories is that once personality develops, it remains consistent over long periods. From this view, to say that an individual is introverted is to imply that he or she is shy or reserved across a variety of settings and situations and from one time to the next. Our everyday experience shows us, though, that a person's personality can change. The shy high school senior may, over several years, become a successful and outgoing salesperson. The "life of the party" may at other times be quite pensive and placid. How can personality psychologists account for such changes? Such a question is not easily answered by psychodynamic and trait approaches, if only because they both attempt to explain personality based on internal constructs. Social learning theory, however, has a ready answer. Characteristics of personality change because the environmental contingencies—reinforcers and punishers—change from situation to situation. Just as importantly, our cognitions and perceptions about the relationship of our behavior to the environment change, which in turn, influence how we act in future situations.

General Principles of Social Learning Theory

Social learning theory may be defined as the notion that both consequences of behavior and the individual's beliefs about those consequences determine personality and behavior. Social learning theory stems partially from the work of B. F. Skinner's experimental analysis of behavior, which we discussed in Chapter 7. Although Skinner's work has influenced contemporary personality theory, he should not be mistaken for a personality theorist. He is definitely not one.

Recall that Skinner is concerned with the analysis of how contingencies of reinforcement affect behavior. For Skinner, behavior is explained entirely in terms of its consequences, which may be either reinforcing or punishing. Behavior is consistent from one situation to the next because it is maintained by similar kinds of consequences across those situations. Behavior changes only when the consequences for behaving change. Skinner's ideas have attracted the attention of some personality researchers because they are experimentally based and provide clear, testable hypotheses for predicting an individual's behavior within and across situations. Social learning theorists have modified and applied Skinner's ideas to their own work. One such researcher is Albert Bandura (b. 1925), who borrowed Skinner's ideas about behavioral consequences and blended them with his own ideas about how cognitive factors can influence behavior.

Expectancies and Observational Learning. Bandura has long argued that both environmental and cognitive events influence behavior (Bandura, 1973, 1986). Cognitive processing, including the individual's interpretation and understanding of the situation, is central to social learning theory. An important aspect of cognition for Bandura and other social learning theorists is **expectancy,** the individual's belief or perception that a specific consequence will follow a specific action (Rotter, Chance, & Phares, 1972). Expectancy refers to how someone perceives the contingencies of rein-

In observational learning, we learn by observing the consequences others experience as a result of their behavior. The more complex the behavior, the more times it must be observed before it is learned, such as learning to play a short tune on the xylophone, as these students are doing.

Albert Bandura

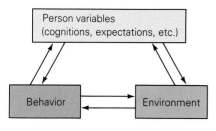

FIGURE 14.8
Patterns of interaction in reciprocal determinism. According to Bandura, person variables such as cognitions, expectations, behavior, and environment interact to determine personality.

forcement for his or her own behavior. If a person does something, it may be because he or she may expect to be rewarded or punished. Moreover, in different situations expectancies may vary. For example, a child may learn that he can get what he wants from his younger sister by behaving aggressively toward her. However, on one occasion his parents may "catch" him hitting his sister and punish him. Now his expectancy has changed and so may his behavior. His expectancy now holds that he may still get what he wants by behaving aggressively, but if he is caught being aggressive, he will be punished. This new expectancy may influence how he behaves toward his sister in the future (especially in the presence of his parents).

Expectancies also permit people to learn actions vicariously, that is, without those actions being directly reinforced. The vicarious nature of some learning experiences is obvious in children as they imitate the actions of their parents and others. A 3-year-old who applies deodorant to his underarms does so not because this behavior has been reinforced in the past, but rather because after watching his mother do it, he thinks it would be "fun" for him to do, too.

Vicarious learning is better known as **observational learning,** which we defined in an earlier chapter as learning through observing the kinds of consequences others (called models) experience as a result of their behavior. In other words, observational learning is a form of learning in which an expectancy about reinforcement is formed merely by observing another's behavior and the consequences it produces. Your own experience is no doubt filled with examples of observational learning—learning to dance, making a paper airplane, writing in cursive, doing jumping jacks, and hundreds of other activities. The more complex the behavior, the more times we must observe it being executed before we can learn it. Learning to tie a bow knot requires more attention to details than learning to roll a ball across the floor.

Bandura's Reciprocal Determinism and Self-Efficacy. Unlike many personality researchers, Bandura does not believe that either personal characteristics (dispositions) or the environment alone determines personality. Rather, he argues for **reciprocal determinism,** the idea that behavior, environmental variables, and person variables, such as cognitions and perceptions, interact to determine personality (Bandura, 1978). This pattern of interaction is diagrammed in Figure 14.8. We know that our actions can affect the environment. We also know that the environment can affect our behavior. Likewise, our thoughts can affect the ways in which we behave to change the environment, and in turn, those changes can influence our thoughts. People are generally kind to us when we are kind to them, and often rude to us when we are rude to them. When acts of kindness are met with kindness in return, we perceive the environment as friendly and are apt to show kindness under other similar circumstances. Likewise, when we are treated rudely, we perceive the environment as unfriendly (perhaps hostile) and will likely attempt to avoid similar environments in the future.

According to Bandura (1982), **self-efficacy,** or one's expectations of success, is an important determinant of whether people will attempt to make changes in their environment. Each day, we make many decisions based on our perception of the extent to which our actions will be successful in producing reinforcement. That is, our actions are based on our evaluation of our competency. Moreover, self-efficacy determines not only whether people will engage in a particular behavior, it also determines the extent to which they will maintain that behavior in the face of adversity. For example, if you believe you are unqualified for a job, although you really desire it, you are apt not to apply for an interview for it. However, if you are

B*ehavior, environmental variables, and person variables . . . interact to determine personality.*

confident of your qualifications for the job, you will surely attempt the interview. Even if you are turned down for that job though, you may interview for a similar position, because you are sure of your abilities. In other words, low self-efficacy can hamper both the frequency and quality of behavior-environment interactions and high self-efficacy can facilitate both.

Mischel and Person Variables. Like Bandura, Walter Mischel believes that much of our personality is learned through our interactions with the environment. Also like Bandura, Mischel emphasizes the role of cognition in determining how people learn the relationship between their behavior and its consequences. Mischel also argues that individual differences in cognition, or person variables as he refers to them, account for differences in personality. Mischel (1984) has proposed that there are five person variables that figure significantly in social learning:

■ *Competencies.* We each have different skills, abilities, and capacities. What we know and the kinds of behaviors that have been reinforced in the past influence the kinds of actions in which we will likely engage in the future.

■ *Encoding Strategies and Personal Constructs.* We also differ in our ability to process information. The way we process information determines how we perceive different situations. One person may perceive going on a date as fun, and so look forward to it; another person may perceive going on a date as potentially boring, and so dread it.

■ *Expectancies.* On the basis of our past behavior and our knowledge of current situations, we form expectancies about the effects our behavior will have on the environment. Expecting our behavior to affect the environment positively leads to one course of action; expecting our behavior to affect the environment negatively leads to another.

■ *Subjective Values.* The degree to which we value certain reinforcers over others influences our behavior. In short, we seek those outcomes we value most.

■ *Self-regulatory Systems and Plans.* We monitor our progress toward achieving goals and subject ourselves to either self-punishment or self-reinforcement, depending on our progress. We also modify and formulate plans regarding how we feel a goal can be best achieved.

Mischel's view of personality is a dynamic one. People's thoughts and behaviors are undergoing constant change as they interact with environmental variables. New plans are made and old ones reformulated; people adjust their actions in accordance with their competencies, subjective values, and their perceptions and expectancies of behavior-environment interactions. We look now at one final consideration in understanding personality from the social learning perspective, locus of control.

Julian Rotter

Rotter and Locus of Control. **Locus of control** refers to whether people believe that the consequences of their actions are controlled by either internal, person variables or external, environmental variables (Rotter, 1954, 1966). People who expect to control their own fate, or, more technically, people who perceive that rewards are dependent upon their own behavior, have an internal locus of control. Those who see their lives as being controlled by external forces outside of their control have an external locus of control.

Julian Rotter, the social learning theorist who is given credit for first making the internal-external locus of control distinction, devised a personality inventory, known as the I-E Scale. This scale assesses the degree to which people perceive the consequences of their behavior to be under the control of internal or external variables (see Figure 14.9). The I-E Scale

Internal locus of control

Poor performance on test	Good performance on test
It's my own fault. I should have spent more time studying.	Great! I knew all that studying would pay off.

External locus of control

Poor performance on test	Good performance on test
These tests are just too hard. The questions are impossible.	Did I get lucky or what? The teacher must really have graded this test easy.

FIGURE 14.9

Examples of the kinds of causal attributions related to perceptions of internal and external loci of control. The result depends on whether the situation involves positive or negative outcomes of one's behavior.

contains 29 pairs of statements to which the person indicates his or her degree of agreement. A typical item on the scale might look something like this:

> The grades that I get depend on my abilities and how hard I work to get those grades.

> The grades that I get depend mostly on the teachers of my classes and how hard the teachers' tests are.

The scale is scored by counting the number of choices consistent with either the internal or external locus of control orientation. Scores may range from 0 to 23, with higher scores indicative of greater external locus of control. Of all the populations Rotter has assessed with the I-E Scale, the group with the lowest average score was from a group of Peace Corps volunteers (Rotter, 1966).

Rotter's scale has been used in hundreds of studies concerning social behavior ranging from achievement motivation to resistance to persuasive attempts to change one's beliefs. What kinds of other personality differences exist among people with different locus of control orientations? Consider these findings:

■ People with an internal orientation will work harder to obtain a goal if they believe that they can control the outcome in a specific situation. Even when told that a goal could be obtained with their own skill and effort, those with an external orientation tended not to try as hard as those with an internal orientation (Davis & Phares, 1967).

■ People with an internal orientation are also more likely to be aware of good health practices and implement them in their daily lives. They are more apt to take preventive medicines, exercise regularly, and quit smoking than people with the external orientation (Strickland, 1978, 1979). They are, however, also more likely to blame themselves when they fail, even when the failure is not entirely their fault (Phares, 1984).

■ People with external orientation are more likely to attribute failure to bad luck or to environmental sources (Lefcourt, 1976).

In sum, social learning theorists view personality as an interactive process, in which person variables, behavior, and environment interact reciprocally to influence particular courses of action. Because these factors differ from person to person, individual differences in personality are often found. Social learning theorists argue that cognition is the critical person variable. However, Bandura, Mischel, and Rotter each emphasize different aspects of cognition as being important. Bandura emphasized self-efficacy, Mischel emphasized competencies, encoding strategies and personal constructs, expectancies, subjective values and self-regulatory systems and plans, and Rotter emphasized locus of control.

Critique of the Social Learning Approach

Social learning theorists have stressed the benefits of rigorous research in the construction and evaluation of psychological theory, and more so than other kinds of personality theorists, they have emphasized the direct study of behavior. But like the psychodynamic and trait approaches, the social learning approach is not without its flaws. We shall briefly discuss three criticisms of the social learning approach: its narrowness, its descriptive nature, and its failure to explain personality development (Phares, 1984).

To some psychologists, personality is ultimately much more than just behavior or the way one thinks or the result of a learning history: genetic and other biological variables must also somehow be involved. Physical variables such as the ebb and flow of hormones and activity of particular neurotransmitters in the brain would seem to influence personality in a wide variety of situations. For example, an individual who suffers from major depression, which can be traced to both heredity and deficiencies in synaptic transmission, will typically show an external locus of control. This appears to be a case where biological influences in personality cannot be ignored.

A second criticism of social learning theory is that it describes rather than explains personality. Bandura, particularly, has been criticized for failing to account for the processes underlying observational learning. For example, why do people observe in the first place? Is observation subject to reinforcement? If so, the reason why people observe others is because in the past doing so has been reinforced. And if that is the case, reinforcement would seem to be necessary for learning to occur.

Critics also charge that social learning theory neglects the development of personality. Social learning theorists can describe how situational variables influence changes in personality characteristics, but cannot explain how those personality characteristics developed in the first place. Are all personality characteristics attributable to social learning? And if so, how? For these two questions, social learning theorists do not have a definitive answer.

THE HUMANISTIC APPROACH

Early in this century, both the behavioral and psychodynamic perspectives were formed, beginning a period of dominance in psychology that has lasted for many decades. Although these perspectives differ dramatically in a number of ways, some psychologists reacted to what they considered a commonality in both theories: the same mechanistic and sterile view of humanity. Behavior analysts, for the most part, are environmental determinists—the causes for what we do are explained by our past reinforcement history and current circumstances. Psychodynamic psychologists are psychic determinists—the underlying causes of our behavior are explained by biological urges that can never be entirely fulfilled, and by the perpetual conflict among structures of the unconscious mind. Moreover, the bases for both approaches were derived from a rather restricted subject pool— much of behavioral theory was originally based on studies with white rats and pigeons, and much of psychodynamic theory originated from the study of people with symptoms of neurosis.

In contrast, the **humanistic approach** to personality seeks to emphasize the positive, fulfilling elements of life. Humanistic psychologists are interested in nurturing personal growth, satisfaction with life, and in general, positive human values. They believe that human beings are innately good and have an internal drive toward **self-actualization,** which as you may recall, is the realization of one's true intellectual and emotional potential. More so than the other approaches to personality, the humanistic approach addresses questions that concern people's thoughts, feelings, and perceptions about themselves and the world around them. The two most influential humanistic theorists who have grappled with these questions are Abraham Maslow and Carl Rogers.

Maslow and Self-Actualization

For both Freud and Abraham Maslow (1908–1970), motivation is one of the central concepts of personality. However, where Freud saw strong instinctual urges that had to be constantly kept in check, generating tensions that could not be completely resolved, Maslow saw positive impulses, such as a drive for psychological health and fulfillment, that could easily be overwhelmed by negative forces within one's culture. According to Maslow (1970), human motivation is organized according to a hierarchy of needs. This forms the idea that our motivation for different activities passes through several hierarchical levels, with entrance to subsequent levels depending upon satisfying the needs in previous stages. In Maslow's view, understanding personality requires understanding this hierarchy. Our most basic needs are physiological, the need for food, water, oxygen, rest, and so on. Until these needs are met, we cannot be motivated by needs found in the next (or any other) stage. If our physiological needs are met, we find ourselves motivated by safety needs, including the need for security and comfort, as well as for peace and freedom from fear. Once the basic survival and safety needs are met, we can become motivated by attachment needs, the need to love and be loved, to have friends and be a friend. If we are able to lead a life in which we have been able to provide ourselves with food and shelter and surround ourselves with loved ones and peace, we are free to pursue self-actualization, achievement of our greatest potential as a human being, whatever that might be. Self-actualization represents the pinnacle of psychological growth and fulfillment.

Mark Wellman, pictured here, aided by his climbing partner, fulfilled his self-actualization needs when he climbed to the top of El Capitan in Yosemite National Park despite being paralyzed.

Maslow based his theory partially on his own assumptions about human potential and partially on his case studies of historical figures whom he believed to be self-actualized, including Albert Einstein, Eleanor Roosevelt, Henry David Thoreau, and Abraham Lincoln. Maslow examined the lives and works of these individuals in order to assess the common qualities that led each to become self-actualized. What personality characteristics did he find these people to have in common? In general, he found that these individuals:

- were very self-accepting of themselves and their life circumstances;
- focused on finding solutions to important cultural problems rather than being too concerned with personal problems;
- were open to others' opinions and ideas and were spontaneous in their emotional reaction to events in their lives;
- had a strong sense of privacy, autonomy, human values, and appreciation for life;
- had a few intimate friendships rather than many superficial ones.

As you might guess, many people never become self-actualized. People who are not physically secure, people who are not loved or who cannot love others, or who have no hope for security or achievement are driven by the needs lower in the hierarchy. Acts of violence, theft, selfishness, and so forth are instances of behavior consistent with these motivations. If individuals' basic needs are not fulfilled, they cannot scale the hierarchy, and so, will fail to attain their potential as human beings.

Maslow (1964) believed that the hierarchy of needs and the innate drive for self-actualization are not specific to any particular culture. He viewed both as being a fundamental part of human nature. In his words, "Man has a higher and transcendent nature, and this is part of his essence, . . . his biological nature as a member of a species which has evolved" (Maslow, 1964, p. xvi).

Rogers and Conditions of Worth

Carl Rogers (1902–1987) also believed that people are motivated to grow psychologically, aspiring to higher levels of fulfillment as they make progress toward self-actualization (Rogers, 1961). Like Maslow, Rogers believed that people are inherently good and possess an innate desire for becoming better. Rogers, though, did not view personality development in terms of satisfying a hierarchy of needs. Instead, he believed that personality development centers on the individual's **self-concept,** or one's opinion of one's self, and the way he or she is evaluated and treated by others.

Carl Rogers

Rogers argued that all people have a need for positive regard, or approval, warmth, love, respect, and affection from others. Young children, in particular, show this need when they seek approval for their actions from parents and siblings. In Rogers' view, children often want others to like them to the extent that gaining positive regard is the major focus of their daily routine. The key to developing a psychologically healthy personality, though, is to develop positive self-regard as well, that is, approval and respect of one's own self. How does an individual develop positive self-regard? The answer, according to Rogers, is often to look to others and their opinions and feelings toward us. We are often happy with ourselves if others, particularly the significant people in our lives, are first happy with us. Likewise, we are also unhappy with ourselves when others have become disappointed or dissatisfied with us.

Thus, our feelings toward ourselves are dependent to a large extent on what others think of us. As children, we learn that there exist certain conditions or criteria that must be met before others bestow positive regard on us. Rogers referred to these criteria as **conditions of worth.** In short, positive regard is often conditional. For example, parents may act warmly and with approval toward their young son when he helps in the kitchen or with the yard work, but not when he pinches his little sister or tells a fib about how many cookies he has taken from the cookie jar. In this case, the boy learns that what others think of him depends on his actions. Soon, he too, may come to view himself according to his behavior: "People react positively when I do something good and negatively when I do something bad." Although conditions of worth are a necessary part of the socialization process, that can have deleterious effects on personality development if satisfying them becomes the individual's major ambition. So long as the individual focuses chiefly on seeking positive regard from others, he or she may ignore other aspects of life, especially those that lead to personality growth. In Rogers' view, then, conditions of worth many stand in the way of self-actualization. An individual may devote his life to satisfying the expectations and demands of others in lieu of working toward realizing his potential. In this light, the need for positive regard may smother the individual's attempts at self-actualization.

As children, we learn conditions of worth, the conditions that must be met before others bestow positive regard on us. For example, a child may discover that helping out in the kitchen meets with a favorable response from his or her parents.

What can be done about this dilemma? According to Rogers, the solution rests with **unconditional positive regard,** or love and acceptance with no strings attached. In a family setting this means that parents may establish rules and expect their children to obey them, but not if doing so compromises the children's feelings of worth and self-respect. For example, if a child misbehaves, the parents should focus on the child's behavior and not on the child. (As many a parent will attest, this is easier said than done.) In this way, the child learns that her behavior is wrong, but that her parents still love and care for her. Freedom from conditional positive regard allows people to work toward realizing their potential unfettered by what others think of them. Positive self-regard then is best developed in an atmosphere of unconditional positive regard.

In developing his theory, Rogers used unstructured interviews in which the client, not the therapist, directed the course of the conversation. Rogers believed that by providing an atmosphere of unconditional positive regard, a client would eventually reveal her real self, the kind of person she now is, as well as her ideal self, the kind of person she would like to become. Rogers also gave the Q sort test to many of his clients. This test consists of a variety of cards each of which contain a statement such as "I am generally an optimistic person" or "I am generally an intolerant person." The client's task is to sort the cards into several piles that vary in degree from "least like me" to "most like me." The client sorts the cards twice, first on the basis of her real self and next on the basis of her ideal self. The difference between the arrangement of the cards in the piles is taken as an index of how close the client is to reaching her ideal self. Rogers' goal as a therapist was to facilitate achievement of the ideal self in each of his clients. We will discuss Rogers' approach to therapy in more detail in Chapter 16.

> *Freedom from conditional positive regard allows individuals to work toward realizing their potential, unfettered by what others think of them.*

Critique of the Humanistic Approach

The humanistic approach is impressive because of its emphasis on promoting psychological health and personal well-being. Indeed, the approach has wide appeal to those who seek an alternative view to the more mechanistic and strictly biologically or environmentally determined views of human nature. However, critics point up two closely related problems with the humanistic approach. First, many of the concepts used by humanistic psychologists are defined subjectively and so, are difficult to test empirically. For example, how is it that one might examine experimentally the nature of self-actualization? Few published studies have even attempted to answer that question. By now you know the hallmark of a good theory: the amount of research it generates. On this count, the humanistic perspective comes up short.

A second criticism of the humanistic approach is that it cannot account for the origins of personality; it describes them, but it does not explain them. Self-actualization is believed by humanistic psychologists to be an innate tendency, yet there is no research that shows it to be so. Conditions of worth are said to hamper the child's quest for self-actualization, and thus alter the course of personality development away from positive psychological growth; however, humanistic theory has provided no objective explanation for this process. Although the humanistic approach may offer a positive view of human nature and give apparent purpose to life, that view is largely an unsubstantiated one.

BOUNDARIES AND FRONTIERS

Explaining personality is no simple task. The goal of personality research and theory is not just to explain why a person does what he or she does in a particular situation. A good theory of personality should do much more than that. It should be able to predict behavior in specific situations. It should also account for a variety of behaviors occurring across a range of situations over relatively long periods. Obviously, no personality theory yet exists that has this much explanatory power. The challenge of developing one that does is both the boundary and frontier for personality psychologists.

One of the more enduring controversies in personality research, if not all psychology, is the extent to which personality is influenced by person variables alone or situational variables alone. Psychodynamic, trait, and humanistic theorists have long emphasized the role of person variables, although each in their own unique way. On the other hand, approaches that were influenced by findings from classical and operant conditioning experiments tended to emphasize situational variables. The social learning approach, for example, emerged from the recognition that situational variables may influence personality, but quickly evolved along other lines as Bandura and others started to focus on the role of cognition in social learning. As you may remember, they argued that what is important is not the effects of reinforcement on behavior per se, but rather, the individual's perception of how reinforcement and behavior are related.

Today many personality theorists accept the idea that personality is due to the interplay of person variables (such as cognition) and situational variables (such as environmental events), albeit exactly how remains a thorny question. Although Henry Murray proposed the idea of person-situation interaction in his 1938 text, *Explorations in Personality*, it was not until the mid-1970s that theorists began to explore seriously its ramifications for research and theory. Interactionism, as this idea is often called, is exemplified by Bandura's reciprocal determinism: as both the person and situation influence behavior, so do the consequences of that behavior in turn affect both the person and the situation.

As we have seen, though, both person-oriented and situation-oriented approaches to personality have been criticized for their failure to explain personality: what each approach appears to offer is merely a different description of personality. Because it represents a blending of these approaches, the same criticism can be levied against interactionism. Simply combining descriptive approaches does not produce a new one that has increased explanatory power. Fully aware of this point, personality theorists have sought to borrow even more terms and ideas from modern cognitive psychology. Personality theory is now expressed in the language of information processing (Cantor & Kihlstrom, 1987) and personality research conducted within the cognitive paradigm, rather than, for example, merely appealing to social learning or traits. Some theorists are optimistic that the marriage of personality psychology with cognitive psychology will provide a clearer and more compelling explanation of personality (Kihlstrom, 1988). However, the honeymoon is not over yet, and it may be too early to predict whether the marriage will be long lasting and fertile in terms of the research and theory it produces.

We are cautious on this issue because personality theorists have generally overlooked another possible marriage partner, heredity, in their courting of explanations for their subject matter. As you know, complete explanations of human behavior require an understanding of both ultimate and proximate causes, that is, an account of both genetic and psychological causes. We learned in the last chapter, for example, that both factors influence intelligence, which is itself a characteristic of personality. We also know from Chapter 3 that social behavior such as altruism, aggression, and courtship is influenced by both hereditary and psychological factors. It seems likely that personality theory might also benefit from a serious consideration of how heredity, person variables, and situational factors jointly influence personality. There is no doubt that genetic factors influence human behavior. The question, of course, is to what extent are genetic factors involved and which personality characteristics do they influence? Until this question is answered, personality psychologists have only partially explored their theoretical and empirical frontiers.

CONCEPT SUMMARY

ASSESSING PERSONALITY

- What are objective tests? Describe the rationale underlying the use of the MMPI and the 16PF in personality assessment. (pp. 497–500)

- What are projective tests? Describe how the Rorschach and TAT are used in personality assessment. (pp. 501–502)

- What is behavioral assessment? How do behavioral assessment techniques differ from objective and projective tests? (pp. 502–503)

THE PSYCHODYNAMIC APPROACH

- What did Freud learn from Breuer that was to change his career? Describe the circumstances involved in the Anna O. case. (pp. 504–505)

- According to Freud, what is the unconscious? What is resistance and repression? (pp. 504–505)

- What is the role of the id, ego, and superego in determining personality? Explain how the ego uses defense mechanisms. Give examples. (pp. 505–508)

- What are the five stages of psychosexual development and what important psychodynamic processes occur within each? (pp. 508–510)

- On what issues did Jung, Adler, and Horney differ from Freud? Explain each of their theories of personality development. (pp. 511–514)

- What are the major criticisms of the psychodynamic approach? (pp. 514–515)

THE TRAIT APPROACH

- What is a trait? What is the trait approach to the study of personality? Why was Allport's early research important to the development of the trait approach? (pp. 515–516)

- What traits are emphasized in five-factor theory? Explain. (pp. 516–517)

- Explain Cattell's rationale for arguing that personality is made of 16 basic traits. What is the difference between source and surface traits? (p. 517)

- Along what kind of dimensions does Eysenck believe personality to be based? What role does arousal play in his theory? (pp. 517–518)

- What are the major criticisms of the trait approach? (pp. 519–520)

THE SOCIAL LEARNING APPROACH

- What was Skinner's influence on the social learning approach? What role do expectancy and other cognitive variables play in social learning? (pp. 520–521)

- What is learned in observational learning? Explain how reciprocal determinism and self-efficacy influence personality and behavior. (pp. 520–522)

- According to Mischel, what person variables figure significantly in social learning? (p. 522)

- How does the idea of locus of control account for individual differences in personality? (pp. 522–523)

- What are the major criticisms of the social learning approach? (p. 524)

THE HUMANISTIC APPROACH

- How does the humanistic approach differ from psychodynamic, trait, and social learning approaches? (pp. 524–525)

- How did Maslow explain personality? What factors prevent people from becoming self-actualized? (pp. 525–526)

- According to Rogers, how is one's self-concept affected by conditions of worth? How can unconditional positive regard facilitate growth of a healthy self-concept? (pp. 526–527)

- What are the major criticisms of the humanistic approach? (p. 527)

KEY TERMS AND CONCEPTS

Personality A particular pattern of behavior prevailing across time and situations that differentiates one individual from another. For psychologists specializing in the study of personality, the goal is to discover the causes of individual differences in behavior. (p. 496)

ASSESSING PERSONALITY

Personality Tests Tests designed to reveal the components of an individual's personality, how one or more of the components interact with the other components, and how one person's personality differs from another's. (p. 497)

Objective Tests Tests for measuring personality that are similar in structure to the ones given in the classroom to test knowledge of different content areas: they may contain multiple choice or true-false items, although some allow examinees to indicate the extent to which they agree with an item. Objective tests are sometimes referred to as self-reports because they allow examinees to respond to statements that describe aspects of their thoughts, emotions, and behavior. (p. 497)

MMPI An objective test originally designed to distinguish individuals with different psychological disturbances from normal individuals. It has since become popular as a means of attempting to identify personality characteristics of people in a wide variety of everyday settings. (p. 497)

16PF A personality inventory widely used among marriage and vocational counselors. The test items on the 16PF refer to such characteristics as intelligence, sensitivity, shrewdness, and trust. (p. 499)

Projective Tests Unstructured personality measures in which a person is shown a series of ambiguous stimuli such as pictures, inkblots, or incomplete drawings. The person is asked to describe what he or she "sees" in each stimulus or to create stories that reflect the theme of the drawing or picture. Because the stimuli are ambiguous, the person will presumably project his or her ideas, feelings, or thoughts onto the stimulus via their interpretation of it. (p. 501)

Rorschach Inkblot Test A projective test in which the examinee is shown a series of symmetrical inkblots and asked to describe what he or she thinks they represent. (p. 501)

TAT A projective test in which a person is shown a series of ambiguous pictures that involve people. The examinee is asked to make up a story about what the people are doing or thinking. The test examiner evaluates each response according to its content or theme. These themes are believed to reflect the examinee's primary personality characteristics. (p. 502)

Behavior Assessment Techniques for assessing personality that focus on what an individual actually does, not just what he or she reports. (p. 502)

THE PSYCHODYNAMIC APPROACH

Unconscious The inaccessible part of the mind. (p. 504)

Resistance Mental forces that relegate memories of past events into unconsciousness. (p. 504)

Repression The mental force responsible for actively keeping those memories, most of which are potentially threatening or anxiety-provoking, from being consciously discovered. (p. 504)

Freudian Slips Mistakes in speech that reflect unconscious motivations and wishes. (p. 505)

Id The personality structure that is the unconscious reservoir of libido, psychic energy that fuels our inherited biological instincts. (p. 506)

Pleasure Principle The rule that the id obeys: obtain immediate gratification, whatever form it may take. (p. 506)

Superego The repository of an individual's moral values that is stocked with the laws, mores, and sanctions of the society in which one lives. The superego is the personality structure in opposition to the id; when the id urges "Do it now," the superego counters with "Don't do it if it's morally wrong." (p. 506)

Ego The personality structure that contains cognitive processes, such as thinking and reasoning, that the mind uses to process information about the environment. The ego serves as the interface between the individual and the environment; it is responsible for the capacity for our self-awareness. The ego also serves as the general manager of personality; it makes the decisions regarding the pleasures that will be pursued at the urging of the id and the moral dictates of the superego that will be followed. (p. 507)

Reality Principle The rule of the ego to satisfy the demands of the id realistically, yielding to and accounting for the demands of reality, sometimes delaying the gratification of desires springing forth from the id, and sometimes softening the rules and reasons offered by the superego. (p. 507)

Defense Mechanisms Mental tactics that the ego uses to insulate itself from threatening ideas, perceptions, emotions, and instincts. (p. 507)

Denial A defense mechanism that works similarly to repression except that it blocks from consciousness threatening perceptions of the real world. (p. 507)

Rationalization A defense mechanism that justifies an unacceptable action by a more acceptable, but false, excuse. (p. 508)

Projection A defense mechanism in which one's own unacceptable behaviors or thoughts are attributed to someone else. (p. 508)

Reaction-formation A defense mechanism that involves behaving in a way that is the opposite of how one really feels because the true feelings produce anxiety. (p. 508)

Displacement A defense mechanism in which feelings of hostility and aggression are channeled toward acceptable or less threatening persons or objects. (p. 508)

Sublimation Redirecting pleasure-seeking or aggressive instincts toward socially acceptable goals. (p. 508)

Psychosexual Stages Developmental stages that are defined by the part of the body or erogenous zone from which sexual gratification is derived. (p. 508)

Fixation An unconscious obsession with the erogenous zone resulting from failure to resolve the crisis associated with the corresponding stage of psychosexual development. (p. 508)

Oral Stage The first psychosexual stage (the first 18 months of life). During this period, the mouth is the major active erogenous zone, and the id impels the infant to use its mouth not only for eating and drinking, but for exploration as well. (p. 509)

Anal Stage The second psychosexual stage (from about 18 months to 3 to 4 years). During this stage, the primary erogenous zone is the anal region. Freud argued that it is during this time that children take pleasure in retaining or expelling feces. (p. 509)

Phallic Stage The third psychosexual stage (about 3 to 4 years to between 5 and 6 years). During this stage, the primary erogenous zone is the genital area. At this time children not only wish to stimulate their genitalia, they also wish to become sexually involved with the opposite-sex parent (referred to by Freud as the Oedipus complex and Electra complex). (p. 509)

Latency Stage The fourth psychosexual stage (from about 5 or 6 years to puberty). During this stage, there are no unconscious conflicts. (p. 510)

Genital Stage The fifth and final psychosexual stage stage (from puberty through adolescence). During this stage, the adolescent experiences adult sexual desires. The id and superego once again become active, forcing the ego to find socially acceptable solutions to sexual (or aggressive) urges. (p. 510)

Collective Unconscious According to Jung, the part of the unconscious that contains memories and ideas inherited from our ancestors over the course of evolution. (The other part of the unconscious is the personal unconscious, which is roughly equivalent to Freud's idea of the preconscious.) (p. 512)

Archetypes Universal thought forms and patterns that Jung believed resided in the collective unconscious. From the dawn of our species, all humans have roughly similar experiences with things such as mothers, evilness, masculinity, and femininity. Each one of these is represented by an archetype. (p. 512)

Striving for Superiority The motivation to seek superiority. Adler felt that striving for superiority is born from our need to compensate for our inferiorities. According to Adler, it is the major motivational force in life. (p. 512)

Social Interest An innate desire to make contributions to society. (p. 512)

Basic Orientations Different sets of personality characteristics that correspond to the strategies of moving toward others, moving against others, and moving away from others. The self-effacing solution corresponds to the moving toward others strategy and involves the desire to be loved. The self-expansive solution corresponds to the moving against others strategy and involves the desire to master one's self. The resignation solution corresponds to the moving away strategy and involves the striving to be independent of others. (p. 513)

THE TRAIT APPROACH

Trait A relatively stable, measurable characteristic of a person. (p. 515)

Five-factor Theory The trait theory that specifies five basic personality traits: Extroversion, Emotional Stability (also called Neuroticism or Anxiety), Openness, Agreeableness, and Conscientiousness. (p. 516)

THE SOCIAL LEARNING APPROACH

Social Learning Theory The idea that both consequences of behavior and the individual's beliefs about those consequences determine personality and behavior. (p. 520)

Expectancy The individual's belief or perception that a specific consequence will follow a specific action. (p. 520)

Observational Learning Learning through observing the kinds of consequences others (called models) experience as a result of their behavior. (p. 521)

Reciprocal Determinism The idea that behavior, environment, and person variables, such as cognitions and perceptions, interact to determine personality. (p. 521)

Self-efficacy One's expectations of success are a primary influence in determining whether people will attempt to effect changes in their environment. (p. 521)

Locus of Control People's expectancies regarding the source of control of their reinforcements. People who expect to control their own fate have an internal locus of control, whereas those who view their lives as being controlled by external forces outside of their control have an external locus of control. (p. 522)

THE HUMANISTIC APPROACH

Humanistic Approach An approach to personality that seeks to emphasize the positive, fulfilling elements of life that are uniquely human. (p. 524)

Self-actualization The achievement of our greatest potential as a human being, whatever that might be. Self-actualization represents the pinnacle of psychological growth and fulfillment. (p. 524)

Self-concept One's opinion of one's self. According to Rogers, our self-concept is affected by the way we are evaluated and treated by others. (p. 526)

Conditions of Worth Our perception of the criteria we must meet in order to be worthy of positive regard from others. In Rogers' view, conditions of worth may stand in the way of self-actualization: an individual may devote his life to satisfying the expectations and demands of others in lieu of working toward realizing his potential. (p. 526)

Unconditional Positive Regard Love and acceptance with no strings attached. To Rogers, unconditional positive regard is the key factor in promoting personal growth. (p. 526)

ADDITIONAL SOURCES OF INFORMATION

Bandura, A. (1986). *Social foundations of thought and action. A social-cognitive theory.* Englewood Cliffs, NJ: Prentice-Hall. Written by the founder of social learning theory, this excellent text provides a thoughtful overview of the critical features of the social-cognitive account of personality.

Hall, C. S., Lindzey, G., Loehlin, J. C., & Manosevitz, M. (1985). *Introduction to theories of personality.* New York: Wiley. This book is a revision of the classic text written by the late Calvin Hall and Gardner Lindzey. It provides a thorough and critical introduction to the personality theories discussed in this chapter.

Phares, E. J. (1984). *Introduction to personality.* Glenview, IL: Scott, Foresman. A solid, comprehensive introduction to personality theory and research.

Rogers, C. R. (1961). *On becoming a person.* Boston: Houghton Mifflin. Perhaps Rogers' most noted work, this book is a sensitive overview of humanistic theory of personality development and how people can achieve healthy psychological growth.

15 Psychological Disorders

Psychological disorders are maladaptive in so far as they impair an individual's behaviors, thoughts, and feelings. However, we must take into consideration social and culture contexts and the extent to which the disorder causes that individual distress or discomfort.

The DSM-III-R   Some Problems with DSM-III-R Classification

The DSM-III-R is a classification system that describes an individual's psychological condition based on five different types of information called axes. The axes specify criteria that must be met before an individual should be diagnosed as having a psychological disorder. These criteria focus on behavioral, cognitive and affective symptoms, physical health, current and recent environmental stressors, and general level of functioning.

Anxiety Disorders   Somatoform Disorders   Dissociative Disorders
Etiology of Anxiety-Based Disorders

Anxiety-based disorders involve unrealistic and excessive anxiety that diminishes some aspect of an individual's life. These disorders may include anxiety that has no apparent cause, intense fear of specific objects, intrusive thoughts, compelling urges to engage in repetitive ritual-like behavior, physical problems for which there is no physiological basis, and sudden disruptions in consciousness that affect one's sense of identity. Although both hereditary and physiological factors have been implicated in anxiety-based disorders, learning factors appear to play a larger role in at least some of the disorders.

Major Depression   Bipolar Disorder   Etiology of Mood Disorders

Mood disorders involve either extreme depression or swings between depression and euphoria. Major depression, which is characterized by apathy and feelings of worthlessness and despair, appears strongly related to both heredity and brain biochemistry. Bipolar disorder also seems to have a genetic basis.

Symptoms of Schizophrenia   Types of Schizophrenia
Etiology of Schizophrenia

The symptoms of schizophrenia include disorganized thought, disturbances of affect, distorted perception, and disturbances of motor activity. Each of the four types of schizophrenia is diagnosed according to a specific set of criteria based upon these symptoms. Many researchers subscribe to the diathesis stress model of schizophrenia, which holds that the disorder is due to the interaction of both a genetic predisposition toward schizophrenia and environmental factors. However, biochemical factors may also play a causal role in schizophrenia.

Personality disorders are marked by rigid personality traits that impair functioning in personal, social, and occupational settings. These disorders may involve an exaggerated sense of self-worth, extreme suspicion and distrust of others, or a lack of guilt and anxiety, as well as other debilitating symptoms. The etiology of personality disorders is not well understood, but what is known suggests that the antisocial personality disorder is influenced by genetic variables, family problems, and underarousal of the autonomic nervous system.

The distinguishing feature of individuals with a paraphilia is that they cannot become sexually aroused or achieve orgasm without a particular stimulus object or situation present. Paraphilias include behaviors that involve the following: the use of inanimate objects, exposure of one's genitalia in public, secretly viewing nude members of the opposite sex, and inflicting or receiving pain. Learning is believed to play a central role in the development of paraphilias.

At one time or another, many of us have experienced feelings and thoughts of intense sadness or depression. Fortunately, most of us remain sad or depressed for only a short while; with time and perhaps some help from friends, we go about our normal lives. Some people, though, become depressed for longer periods and to the point that they begin to lose their sense of enjoying life. They soon view themselves in extremely negative ways, show a chronic inability to perform even routine tasks, and develop physical symptoms such as weight loss and insomnia. Often they cannot explain why they have become so depressed.

Another common experience for most of us is feeling anxious or nervous about something we have done or about an event in our lives that will soon occur. Perhaps we have done something we shouldn't have, or haven't done something we should have, and soon the consequences of our behavior are going to catch up with us and we know it. Usually, our anxiety does not interfere dramatically with day-to-day life and the source of our anxiety can be identified: an upcoming test, a date, or a play or athletic event in which we will participate. For many people, though, sources of anxiety can not be identified so easily. Can you imagine feeling anxious—extremely, distressingly anxious—for no apparent reason? Can you imagine spending hours or days anxiety-free only to be overwhelmed suddenly by attacks of heart-pounding, palm-sweating, mind-racing anxiety for which you can attribute no cause?

Many of us have also had the experience of an idea or a thought intruding uninvited into our consciousness. Perhaps a particularly vivid scene from a movie or a catchy jingle from a TV advertisement may have popped into our heads from time to time over the course of a day. We often treat these mental intrusions as random thoughts that have little to do with how we behave. For some people, however, such intrusions occur constantly and have profound effects on their behavior. Consider the following account from Carol North, now a practicing psychiatrist, in which she describes how she felt intruding thoughts were controlling her behavior:

> More and more, my thoughts escaped my control, diffusing out from my brain for others to hear. I increased my efforts to police the contents of my thoughts at all times. It wasn't easy trying to not think thoughts, but it was something I absolutely had to do. Most of all, I wanted to keep my mother from hearing my thoughts. Whenever it seemed that she was tuning in on my thought waves, I purposely substituted nonsense words for my true thoughts, or intentionally scrambled the words as they came to me. But in the process, my thoughts sometimes got so hopelessly jumbled that I needed to write them down to straighten them out for my own comprehension. To keep anyone from being able to read the thoughts I was writing, I invented a private code of original characters symbolizing letters, words, phrases, and tenses all mixed up in such a way that no one could possibly break it. On paper it looked like endless columns of nonsensical symbols. . . .
>
> My thoughts were not the only thing giving me trouble. My perceptions had changed. I had become vaguely aware of colored patterns decorating the air. When I first noticed them, I realized I had actually been seeing them for a long time, yet never paid attention to them before. . . .
>
> I decided I must have done something to evoke a leak from other planes of existence, allowing Cosmic Interference Patterns to spill into this world. But I could discover no connections. I was baffled. I would have to accept the interference as another of life's mysteries. . . .
>
> My distant stare became so habitual that when I talked to people, I would stare at them, unblinking, not moving or glancing away every few seconds as people normally do. At those moments, I felt that I penetrated

the inner spirit of the other person and connected with the greater reality of the universe. Then the Interference Patterns would sweep across my visual screen and break everything up.

My classmates whispered about me. "She's weird," they said. "Like, wow, you know she's intense."

(1987, pp. 60–63)

In this chapter we turn our attention to **psychological disorders,** which are persistent maladaptive patterns of behaving, thinking, and/or feeling that lead to distress or disability. This definition, while concise, only approximates the kinds of extraordinary behavior and thought patterns typical of individuals who are said to suffer from a psychological disorder. Below we look more closely at what psychologists mean when they refer to psychological disorders.

"Why doesn't he just snap out of it."

Mental illness is a disease that affects many of us in some form or degree of severity at some point in our lives.

THE NATURE OF PSYCHOLOGICAL DISORDERS

Even the very small sampling of examples we cited above should suggest to you that psychological disorders vary enormously (Figure 15.1 shows incidence rates for several types of disorders). Some people develop an inability to think coherent thoughts; some experience extreme mood swings with no apparent stimulus to trigger them; some seem despondent and unable to act in any way, while others seem uncontrollably energetic; some come to believe that others are plotting to harm them; some develop irresistible sexual attachments to inanimate objects; and some fear the very thought of leaving their home to venture out, while others fear being left alone. Some people are totally devastated by a psychological disorder and need constant care and attention, while others manage to get by on a day-to-day basis. One observation we can make is that psychological disorders may involve a wide range of psychological functioning, including a person's behaviors, thoughts (cognitions), and/or feelings (affect).

Another important characteristic of psychological disorders is that they are maladaptive. This implies that psychological disorders interfere with the individual's normal functioning either directly or indirectly. The individual may not be able to concentrate on his or her work, form meaningful relationships, or tend to basic needs, such as nutrition or personal hygiene. It also follows that the disruption in routine and the quality of one's life will cause a sense of distress and discomfort. In a way, this observation is obvious: Psychological disorders are painful; they are unpleasant; they hurt.

Throughout our discussion so far there has been a tacit assumption that we must now state explicitly: Whether behaviors or thoughts or feelings are judged to be disordered or maladjusted depends on the social or cultural context in which they occur. You shouldn't have to ponder too long to think of all sorts of behaviors of people in different cultures which, if practiced regularly in our culture, would be judged to be maladjusted and maladaptive at best. Even within our own culture, behaviors that are appropriate and even expected in some situations would be quite inappropriate in others. Singing your favorite song loudly in the shower is one thing; doing so in a bank lobby is another.

W*hether behaviors or thoughts or feelings are judged to be disordered or maladjusted depends on the social or cultural context in which they occur.*

One final observation: Psychological disorders are abnormal in a statistical sense, too. They are not normal, not average; they deviate from the standard practice of a culture or a social situation. Of course, behavior that is unlikely or unusual statistically is not necessarily indicative of a psy-

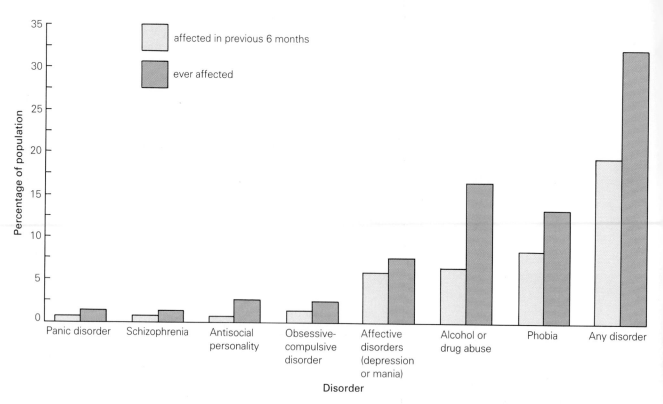

FIGURE 15.1

Prevalence of psychological disorders in the U.S. population. This graph shows the estimated percentages of Americans living in three major cities who experienced a psychological disorder either within the previous 6 months (Meyers et al., 1984) or at some time (Robins et al., 1984). The total percentage for all psychological disorders is less than the sum of the individual percentages because some individuals had more than one disorder.

chological disorder. Superior musical, artistic, intellectual, and athletic abilities are statistically infrequent, but we do not refer to these abilities as disordered. To qualify as disordered, they must be maladaptive and cause distress. And, sadly enough, psychological disorders are not rare. Mental health professionals conservatively estimate that nearly 20 percent of adult North Americans experience some sort of psychological disorder within any 6-month period (Locke & Regier, 1985; Offord et al., 1987).

Even momentary reflection on these observations tells us that the issues and concepts we examine in this chapter are not simple or unidimensional. Mirroring this complexity is the fact that as we study a number of specific examples of psychological disorders, we will encounter many variants of the major perspectives of psychological research and theory that were introduced in Chapter 1.

We will see that psychologists who work from the behavioral perspective tend to view psychological disorders as involving maladaptive behaviors—behaviors that have been learned in the same way that any other behavior is learned—largely through operant or classical conditioning. In contrast, those working from the psychodynamic perspective focus on unconscious conflicts and motives that lead to distress and anxiety. The cognitive perspective focuses on an analysis of the nature of one's thought processes. Becoming depressed, for example, may be due in large part to the development of inappropriate cognitions about one's self and one's self-worth. These cognitions influence and are influenced by inaccurate perceptions of one's actions and social interactions. Some psychologists approach psychological disorders from the humanistic perspective. This point of view claims that psychological disorders arise when one's personal growth and development become hindered or stunted. When that individual can be brought more in touch with his or her true self, growth and fulfillment can replace maladaptive responding and distress. Finally, the biological perspective traditionally derives from a medical model in which psychological disorders are seen as analogous to a physical disorder. In this case, the underlying problem is viewed as essentially biological, usually involving problems of brain functioning. It is from this point of view that we get the terminology that refers to someone in treatment for a psychological disorder as being a "patient" who is suffering from a "mental illness" that can be "diagnosed" on the basis of a set of recognizable "symptoms."

Regardless of one's perspective, however, the study of psychological disorders can be organized around three related topics—their description, their causes, and their treatment. The remainder of this chapter involves the description of the wide range of psychological disorders that people can experience, as well as a discussion of their causes. **Etiology** is the term commonly used to refer to the causes of a disorder. The next chapter addresses issues related to the treatment of psychological disorders. We turn now to a discussion of how psychological disorders are classified.

CLASSIFYING PSYCHOLOGICAL DISORDERS

To understand, discuss, diagnose, and treat psychological disorders, some rational basis for their classification is needed. Although it is true that no two people with the same disorder are exactly alike any more than are any two people without a disorder, there are recognizable categories that we can use to organize our thoughts regarding psychological disorders.

The need for a comprehensive classification system of psychological disorders was first recognized by Emil Kraepelin (1856–1926) who provided his version in a textbook of psychiatry published in 1883. The Association of Medical Superintendents of American Institutions for the Insane, a forerunner of the American Psychiatric Association, later incorporated Kraepelin's ideas into a classification system of their own. And the classification most widely used today, DSM-III-R, still retains a number of Kraepelin's original categories.

Emil Kraepelin

The DSM-III-R

The current source for classifying psychological disorders is a reference book of more than 500 pages called the ***Diagnostic and Statistical Manual of Mental Disorders,*** or **DSM.** The DSM is published by the American Psychiatric Association, the national professional organization of psychiatrists. First published in 1952, it has been updated periodically. In its third and revised edition, the current manual is referred to as the DSM-III-R, published in 1987. The DSM-IV is scheduled to be published in the early 1990s.

The DSM-III-R describes an individual's psychological condition based on five different types of information, called axes. A summary of the axes is shown in Table 15.1. Individuals undergoing evaluation are assessed on each of the five axes; that is, they are evaluated according to whether their particular patterns of behavior, thinking, and emotion meet the diagnostic criteria specified by each of the five different axes. The first two axes describe the variety of psychological disorders. Axis I contains information on 16 major disorders. Developmental disorders, such as mental retardation, autism, and personality disorders are all found on Axis II.

TABLE 15.1. *Summary of the five axes of the DSM-III-R.*

Individuals undergoing psychological evaluation are assessed on each of the five axes.

AXIS I *Major clinical disorders*

Psychological disorders whose symptoms impair functioning in school, employment, family, and social settings and/or that produce psychological distress in the individual.

AXIS II *Personality and development disorders*

Personality disorders are long-term, maladaptive, and rigid personality traits that impair normal functioning and involve psychological distress. Developmental disorders include psychological disorders that may appear during mental retardation and autism and other disorders that impair an individual's ability to read, write, speak or otherwise communicate. Developmental disorders typically occur in children and adolescents.

AXIS III *Physical disorders and conditions*

Physical disorders and conditions are those that relate to diagnosing and treating psychological disorders.

AXIS IV *Severity of psychosocial stressors*

The extent to which particular stressors involved in the psychological disorder are evaluated on a scale ranging from 1 (little or no stressors) to 6 (extremely potent stressors).

AXIS V *Global assessment of functioning*

The extent to which the individual is able to function in social, employment, and leisure activity settings is evaluated on a scale of 10 (extremely poor functioning) to 90 (normal or near normal functioning).

Diagnoses can be made that include both Axis I and Axis II disorders, and multiple diagnoses can occur on either axis alone. For example, major depression and alcohol dependence are both Axis I disorders, and both disorders may characterize one individual at any one period of time. A person's psychological condition may be due to several different psychological disorders described in the DSM-III-R, just as one person may suffer simultaneously from several different physical disorders, and this may complicate treatment.

Axes III through V of the DSM-III-R provide information about the life of the individual in addition to the basic classification provided by Axes I and II. Axis III is used to indicate and describe any physical disorders, such as skin rashes or heightened blood pressure, that accompany the psychological disorder. Axis IV information specifies the severity of stress that the person has experienced (usually within the last year). The axis details the source of stress (for example, is it family or work-related?), and indicates its severity and approximate duration. The severity of the stressors is rated on a 6-point scale with "1" meaning that stressors are virtually absent or only minimal, "3" meaning that stressors are moderate, such as those experienced when someone becomes unemployed suddenly, and "6" meaning that stressors are extremely severe, such as those experienced when someone is in an earthquake or plane crash. Axis V describes the person's overall level of functioning, be it psychological, social, or occupational. The purpose of Axis V is to provide the means to estimate the extent to which the individual's quality of life has been diminished by the disorder. Ratings are made on a 90-point "Global Assessment of Functioning" (GAF) with 90 representing the absence or near absence of impaired functioning in social, employment, or school settings, 50 representing serious problems in functioning, and 10 representing impairment that may result in injury to the individual or to others.

The DSM-III-R provides a systematic means of providing and evaluating a variety of personal and psychological information about any one specific individual. The interrelationship among the five axes can be illustrated by an example. Alcohol dependence (Axis I) leads to marital problems, problems that may also be partially associated with an antisocial personality disorder (Axis II). Marital problems, of course, may lead to a divorce. Marital problems and the divorce are themselves stressors (Axis IV) that subsequently may contribute to an episode of major depression (Axis I). Alcohol dependence may eventually lead to physical problems, such as cirrhosis of the liver (Axis III). These problems, now acting in concert, are likely to lead to an increased impairment in overall life functioning (Axis V) so that the individual has only a few friends, none of them close, and is unable to keep a job. The evaluation of this person might be summarized as follows:

Axis I: Alcohol Dependence
Axis II: Antisocial Personality Disorder
Axis III: Alcoholic cirrhosis of the liver
Axis IV: 4; Severe—divorce, loss of job
Axis V: GAF evaluation = 47; highest GAF in past year = 51.

Some Problems with DSM-III-R Classification

Although the DSM-III-R is our most widely referenced classification system for psychological disorders, it is not without its problems. Reflecting the fact that the DSM-III-R has been strongly influenced by psychiatrists, it tends to be more consistent with a medical approach to disorders. This means that diagnosis and treatment of psychological disorders based on the DSM-III-R emphasize biological factors, which, in turn, means that potential environmental determinants may be overlooked.

Another potential problem with the DSM-III-R (and perhaps with any such classification scheme) is its questionable reliability. Reliability in this context means what it did in the context of psychological testing— consistency across applications. If the DSM-III-R allowed for perfect reliability, users would be able to diagnose each case in the same way. Unfortunately, evaluating psychological disorders is not so easy. It is not like following a recipe; it is more like navigating your way through an unfamiliar city with only a crude map—you may or may not reach your ultimate destination. And if you do reach it, you may not have taken the most direct route. Although the DSM-III-R is much improved over previous versions, its reliability is still far from perfect (Robins & Helzer, 1986).

Diagnosing a psychological disorder only describes the symptoms of the disorder; it does not explain its origins.

You should also recognize the potential problems that are inherent in any system that ultimately results in applying a label to human beings. Sometimes it is easy to remember that the names of psychological disorders (the labels) are only that: words we have chosen to describe a given state of affairs at a particular moment. The alternative, of course, is to lapse into the mistaken belief that somehow or another, labeling a disorder, much less labeling a person, *explains* anything. Diagnosing a psychological disorder only describes the symptoms of the disorder; it does not explain its origins. To say that someone did something, "because he's schizophrenic" does not explain his behavior at all. We need to be constantly on guard against associating the names of disorders with people, rather than with their behaviors, thoughts, and feelings. By that we mean that it is more appropriate to talk about "someone who displays the characteristics of schizophrenia," than to say that "he is a schizophrenic."

Gladys Burr is a tragic example of the dangers of labeling. In 1936, Burr's mother had her committed to an institution because of "personality problems." Burr was diagnosed as psychotic, and later, was declared mentally retarded. Even though IQ tests given to Burr between 1946 and 1961 showed that she had normal intelligence and numerous doctors recommended that she be released, she was confined in the institution until 1978. She was then released and awarded financial compensation for her 42 years of unnecessary commitment.

It is also true that labels can be used to support political or social agendas rather than to promote genuine understanding of a psychological problem (Schact, 1985). For example, a century ago the term *drapetomania* was used to describe "the psychopathology of the slave possessed of the uncontrollable urge to run away from slavery" (Boxer, 1987). Saying that someone was suffering from drapetomania implied that the basic problem with a slave seeking freedom was with the slave, and not with the system that allowed the slavery.

In sum, psychological disorders are persistent, maladaptive behaviors, cognitions, or emotions, that ultimately lead to distress and discomfort. We have seen that there may be some inherent problems in systematically classifying the wide range of psychological disorders, but we have also seen the advantages. Consistent with general practice, we will use the terminology presented in the DSM-III-R in our discussion.

Sometimes the terms neurosis and psychosis are used to distinguish between the symptoms of psychological disorders. Neurosis is used to refer to symptoms such as anxiety or phobias while psychosis is used to describe more debilitating symptoms: severe mental deterioration and withdrawal from reality. What follows is only a sample of the more than 200 disorders listed in the DSM-III-R. We will begin with the anxiety-based disorders, which often require psychological intervention for their resolution, but which are seldom so debilitating as to require hospitalization. Then we will examine mood disorders, schizophrenia, personality disorders, and psychosexual disorders.

ANXIETY-BASED DISORDERS

Defining anxiety is tricky if only because it is characterized by so many symptoms. For our purposes, we define **anxiety** as a sense of apprehension or doom that is accompanied by a number of physiological reactions, such as accelerated heart rate, sweaty palms, and tightness in the stomach. We have all experienced anxiety. Its sources are virtually limitless. Our first date, having to give a speech, an upcoming visit to the dentist, and next week's exam may all be anxiety-producing. We have all experienced the dry mouth, sweaty palms, trembling, shortness of breath, the "knot" in the pit of our stomachs just before big events in our lives. Unfortunately, what for most people is experienced as mild distress becomes for others the basis of an **anxiety-based disorder** in which unrealistic and excessive anxiety diminishes some aspect of the person's life. The emphasis here is on the words *excessive* and *unrealistic*. There are times when anxiety may be appropriate, but there are also times when anxiety can be maladaptive and debilitating.

Anxiety Disorders

In this section, we will look at three broad categories of anxiety-based disorders: anxiety disorders, somatoform disorders, and dissociative disorders. In Chapter 18, we will examine another category of anxiety disorders, posttraumatic stress disorder.

Generalized Anxiety Disorder. An individual with a **generalized anxiety disorder** experiences chronically high levels of anxiety that are not specific to any one source. He or she experiences anxiety across many different situations but cannot identify its source. In addition to the usual physical symptoms of anxiety, individuals experiencing generalized anxiety show a wide range of behavioral and cognitive symptoms (see Table 15.2).

Situations that would cause most people to experience mild distress may cause unrealistic and excessive anxiety for people with anxiety-based disorders.

Because generalized anxiety disorder seems to come and go, and because it is not tied to any particular stimulus, it is often referred to as "free-floating" anxiety. As you might guess, people with generalized anxiety disorder are often restless, irritable, and "on edge" much of the time, and have difficulty sleeping well. As we shall see, unlike the generalized anxiety disorder, all other anxiety-based disorders have identifiable sources of anxiety.

Phobic Disorders. A **phobic disorder** involves an unrealistic, excessive fear of a specific class of stimuli. Unlike generalized anxiety disorder, the object of the anxiety is readily identifiable: It may be a snake, an insect, plastics, the out-of-doors, closed spaces, or any stimulus that has become associated with fear. The nature of a phobic disorder is illustrated in the following case report.

> A 28-year-old housewife complained that she was afraid she could no longer care for her three children. Over the past year, she has had recurring episodes of nervousness, lightheadedness, rapid breathing, trembling, and dizziness, during which things around her suddenly feel strange and unreal. Over the past 6 months she has become afraid to leave home unless in the company of her husband or mother. She now avoids supermarkets and department stores. She says that being in a crowded place makes her uneasy. When unable to avoid such situations, she tries to get near doorways and always checks for windows and exits. She is concerned that her nervous episodes will prevent her from helping her children in case of an emergency.
>
> (Spitzer, Skodol, Gibbon, & Williams, 1981, pp. 268–269)

The woman in this case is suffering from **agoraphobia,** the fear of being away from a safe place or a safe person. It is one of the most common phobias and is one in which fear can be expressed in many ways. Some people avoid public transportation, others avoid eating in restaurants, and others avoid grocery stores and malls.

Other types of phobic disorders are not so pervasive. Agoraphobia is considered to be a complex phobia because it can be so incapacitating

TABLE 15.2.	*Frequency of symptoms in 100 cases of generalized anxiety disorder.*		
AFFECTIVE/SOMATIC	%	*COGNITIVE/BEHAVIORAL*	%
Unable to relax	97	Difficulty concentrating	86
Tense	86	Fear losing control	76
Frightened	79	Fear being rejected	72
Jumpy	72	Unable to control thoughts	72
Unsteady	62	Confusion	69
Weakness all over	59	Mind blurred	66
Hands (only) sweating	52	Inability to recall	55
Terrified	52	Sentences disconnected	45
Heart racing	48	Blocking in speech	45
Face flushed	48	Fear of being attacked	35
Wobbly	45	Fear of dying	35
Sweating all over	38	Hands trembling	31
Difficult breathing	35	Body swaying	31
Urgent need to urinate	35	Stuttering	24
Nausea	31		
Diarrhea	31		
Faint/dizzy feeling	28		
Face is pale	24		
Feeling of choking	14		
Actual fainting	3		

Adapted from Beck & Emery, 1985, pp. 87–88

People suffering from agoraphobia fear being away from the safety of their homes and may avoid being in a crowd or in public places.

(becoming a prisoner in your own home drastically limits the kinds of activities in which you can participate). Some phobias, such as a fear of bees or spiders, are considered to be simple phobias because avoiding contact with them does not impair normal functioning so markedly. Many, if not most, individuals with phobic disorders are aware of their fear, and they are usually also aware that it is an irrational fear. Nevertheless, they are unable to subdue their anxiety when face-to-face with the fear-eliciting stimulus. Table 15.3 describes several different phobias.

Obsessive-Compulsive Disorder. An anxiety-based disorder in which an individual is beset by recurrent, unwanted thoughts or ideas and compelling urges to engage in repetitive ritual-like behavior is referred to as an **obsessive-compulsive disorder.** An **obsession** is an involuntary recurring thought, idea, or image. Examples of obsessions include repeated thoughts of doing something violent, fear of dying during a nuclear explosion, or wondering if you locked the door before leaving the house. Obsessive thoughts can easily become a preoccupation that eventually interferes with other, more important aspects of life. For example, no matter what the person does—whether eating, walking or talking—he or she is continually thinking about the object of the obsession.

A **compulsion** is an irresistible impulse to repeat some action over and over even though it serves no useful purpose. Compulsions are often behavioral responses to a specific obsession. Performing the compulsive act often requires a great deal of time and usually follows a precise agenda. Consider the case of Beth, a young woman who had become obsessed with cleanliness.

> Beth's concern for cleanliness gradually evolved into a thorough cleansing ritual, which was usually set off by her touching of her genital or anal area. In this ritual, Beth would first remove all of her clothing in a pre-established sequence. She would lay out each article of clothing at specific spots on her bed and examine each for any evidence of "contamination." She would thoroughly scrub her body, starting at her feet and working meticulously up to the top of her head, using certain washcloths for certain areas of her body. Any articles of clothing that appeared to have been "contaminated" were thrown into the laundry. Clean clothing was put on spots that were vacant. She would then dress herself in the opposite order from which she took the clothes off. If there were any deviations from this order, or if Beth began to wonder if she might have missed some contamination, she would go through the entire sequence again. It was not rare for her to do this four or five times in a row on certain evenings.
>
> (Meyer & Osborne, 1982, p. 158)

TABLE 15.3. *Examples of phobias.*

PHOBIA	DEFINITION
Acrophobia	Fear of heights
Aviophobia	Fear of flying
Claustrophobia	Fear of closed or cramped spaces
Hydrophobia	Fear of water
Lalophobia	Fear of speaking in public
Nyctophobia	Fear of the dark
Pathophobia	Fear of diseases
Phobophobia	Fear of fear
Thanatophobia	Fear of dying
Xenophobia	Fear of strangers

Mild obsessions and compulsive behavior can be quite adaptive. Many successful people attribute their success, in part, to their persistence. Despite continued rejections, a writer finally finds a publisher for his or her novel, which then becomes a best seller. Or, a computer programmer who refuses to quit thinking about a problem in a program finally figures out the error in the program. However, problems arise when the obsessions and compulsions become maladaptive, as in Beth's case. The person who has these maladaptive obsessions and compulsions may understand that his or her own behavior is silly or absurd, but understanding that there is a problem is not the same thing as being able to solve it. Because anxiety is reduced by engaging in obsessive thoughts and compulsive behaviors, the obsessive-compulsive pattern recurs.

Somatoform Disorders

"Soma" means body and a **somatoform disorder** involves a bodily or physical problem for which there is no physiological basis. Though the physical problems, such as blindness, paralysis of a limb, or numbness, do not have a physiological cause, the experience of the problem is nonetheless genuine to the individual. There are three types of somatoform disorders: somatization disorder, conversion disorder, and hypochondriasis.

In 1692, many of the young women were accused of being witches in the Salem witch trials because of their strange behavior. Today it is thought that many of these women may have been suffering from somatization disorders.

Somatization disorders, which occur mostly in women, involve complaints of wide ranging physical ailments for which there are no apparent biological causes. Over time, the nature of these complaints change. At one time, the complaints may focus on cardiovascular functioning, at another time, they may center on neurological functioning, and at still another time, they may concern respiratory functioning. In many cases, individuals with somatoform disorders undergo needless surgery. Soon, though, they begin complaining of other symptoms unrelated to the original complaint.

The somatoform disorder that involves the actual loss of bodily function such as blindness, paralysis, and numbness due to excessive anxiety is called a **conversion disorder** (formerly called hysteria). The degree to which actual physical symptoms can result is astonishing. Consider the following case.

> A woman described being overcome by feelings of extreme dizziness accompanied by slight nausea, four or five nights a week. Inexplicably, the attacks almost always occurred at about 4:00 p.m. She usually had to lie down on the couch and often did not feel better for three or four hours. When asked by a therapist about her marriage, she described her husband as a tyrant who was frequently demanding and verbally abusive of her and their four children. She admitted that she dreaded his arrival home from work each day, knowing that he would comment that the house was a mess and the dinner, if prepared, not to his liking. Recently, since the onset of her attacks, when she was unable to make dinner, he and the children would go out to eat.
>
> (Spitzer et al., 1981, pp. 92–93)

The key to understanding a conversion disorder is to understand how anxiety is reduced by the onset of the physical symptoms. Most of us would be concerned if we suddenly started experiencing dizzy spells or lost the use of a limb, but the individual with a conversion disorder feels relief from anxiety when the symptoms appear. The woman we just described escaped the anxiety produced by her nagging husband by feeling terribly ill just around the time he came home from work. Her "ailment" got her out of cooking dinner and listening to her husband's complaints and provided a logical reason for why she did not have the house in order.

Another somatoform disorder is **hypochondriasis,** which is a persistent and excessive worry about developing a serious illness or contracting a disease. People with hypochondriasis often misinterpret the appearance of normal physical aches and pains. A slight sore or occasional cough may be all that is needed to elicit fear and alarm. What could it be? Cancer? Tuberculosis? Heart disease? Convinced that they suffer from a serious ailment or disease, they will visit the doctor to obtain a second opinion. Not surprisingly, the physician usually fails to confirm the individual's diagnosis. As a result, the person may brand the doctor as incompetent. Individuals with this disorder may change physicians continually, always looking for that particularly skillful doctor who can recognize the "actual" underlying disease.

The diagnosis of any somatoform disorder is always accompanied by a thorough physical examination. Often the disorder is such that it is known for certain, at least by the physician, that the underlying cause is not physical. For example, some people whose legs are paralyzed by day, sleepwalk at night. Or some people lose the feeling in their hand, although if the nerves that provided feeling to the hand were actually damaged, the person would also lose feeling in parts of the arm.

The key to understanding a conversion disorder is to understand how anxiety is reduced by the onset of the . . . physical symptom.

Many Americans are preoccupied with their health, as this shelf full of over-the-counter medicines suggests. If taken to extremes, this preoccupation can lead to hypochondriasis.

Dissociative Disorders

In somatoform disorders, anxiety is avoided by developing the symptoms of a serious physical disorder. In a **dissociative disorder,** anxiety is reduced by a sudden disruption in consciousness, which in turn, produces changes in one's sense of identity. Three disorders of this type are psychogenic amnesia, psychogenic fugue, and multiple personality. Although all three disorders are relatively rare, their bizarreness has attracted widespread media attention, leading many people to believe that they are more common than they really are.

Psychogenic amnesia involves the inability to remember important events or vital personal information. The term *psychogenic* means that the underlying cause of the problem is psychological instead of biological; the term *amnesia* implies memory loss. The loss of memory in psychogenic amnesia is too extensive to be explained by common forgetfulness. For example, an individual would not be diagnosed as suffering from psychogenic amnesia if she simply could not remember the events of a family reunion 6 months ago, although that diagnosis might be made if she could not remember the names or recognize the faces of any of her relatives. The onset of psychogenic amnesia is usually accompanied by some stressful event, perhaps a divorce or death in the family. Not unexpectedly, the amnesia causes the individual to become disoriented and confused.

The duration and generality of memory loss varies greatly from case to case. In some cases, memory loss may endure for several hours, months, or even years, and in others, the amnesia may completely disappear as suddenly as it first appeared. In some cases, only selective events are forgotten, and in other cases, an entire life history is forgotten; the individual may not even recognize his or her spouse, friends, and parents.

Psychogenic amnesia is typified by a woman, known for a while only as "Jane Doe," who in 1980, was found near death in Florida. Her amnesia was so severe that she could not even remember her own name. She appeared on the "Good Morning America" television show with her doctor in a last attempt to find her identity. Even when reunited with her parents, she failed to recall her identity or aspects of her life prior to being found in Florida.

Psychogenic fugue involves amnesia but also is characterized by the individual deliberately leaving the area in which he or she lives, and then assuming a new identity in a new locale. In severe cases, the individual not only takes on a new name, new home, and a new occupation, but assumes different personality characteristics as well. Here is an example of an individual who experienced psychogenic fugue.

> Burt Tate was questioned by the police following an argument he had had with a customer in the diner where he worked as a short order cook. He had no identification, could not recall where he had lived prior to his arrival in town several weeks earlier, and could not describe his previous job. However, he did know the name of the town in which he now lived and the date. The police later identified Burt Tate as Gene Smith, who had been reported as a missing person in a city 200 miles away about a month earlier. He was identified positively by his wife, although he did not recognize her. His wife explained that he had been experiencing problems at work (as a manager in a manufacturing company), including being overlooked for a promotion, and that 2 days before his disappearance he had an argument with his son who referred to him as a "failure."
>
> (Spitzer et al., 1981, pp. 100–101)

Multiple personality disorder involves the emergence of two or more complete and independently functioning personalities in one person,

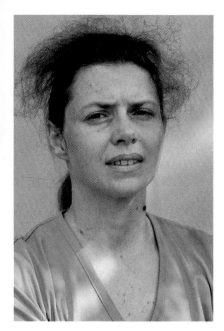

This woman, dubbed "Jane Doe," was found near death in Florida in 1980. She was suffering from a rare form of psychogenic amnesia and couldn't remember anything about herself, her past, or even how to read and write. After much publicity of her case, a couple identified the woman as their daughter. Despite the couple's certainty, Jane Doe was never able to remember her past.

though only one personality is dominant at any one time. The different personalities may have unique memories, behavior patterns, and social experiences, and the original personality is not usually conscious of the other personalities. However, the other personalities may be conscious of both the original personality and each other. There may be as few as two or as many as one hundred personalities, with about half of the reported cases having 10 or more distinct personalities. Each personality is generally comprised of traits that are not typical of the original personality. Sometimes one of the personalities may be reasonably "responsible," holding down a job and being socially adept. The other personalities, however, usually range from somewhat to very dysfunctional, perhaps exhibiting one or more psychological disorders (in addition to the multiple personality). How different can these personalities be? Not only might some be female and the others male, the personalities might be of people of different ages, and they can provide dramatically different scores on intelligence tests. The transition from one personality to another usually happens quickly, within several seconds to a few minutes.

An interesting instance of multiple personality is the case of Billy Milligan, as told in the book, *The Minds of Billy Milligan* (Keyes, 1981). Milligan was accused of rape and kidnapping when he was 22, but was deemed not guilty by reason of insanity. His psychiatric examination revealed him to have 24 different personalities. Two were women and one was a young girl. There was a Briton, an Australian, and a Yugoslavian who read, wrote, and spoke Serbo-Croatian. One woman, a lesbian, was a poet, while the Yugoslav was an expert on weapons and munitions and the Briton and Australian were minor criminals.

Multiple personality is extremely rare, with only several hundred known cases being reported in the last century. Some have argued, however, that it is not as rare as once thought since many cases of multiple personality may have been misdiagnosed as another disorder. For example, a diagnosis may be made on the basis of only one personality, without realizing that other personalities also exist (Greaves, 1980).

Billy Milligan, who was accused of committing several rapes, was acquitted of the crimes on the grounds that he was not responsible for his actions because he suffered from a multiple personality disorder.

Etiology of Anxiety-Based Disorders

As we shall see, uncovering the origins of psychological disorders is no easy task. It is complicated by the fact that many variables—genetic, physiological, behavioral, social, and cognitive—appear to interact to influence the onset of the disorder and the extent to which its symptoms are maladaptive. Some disorders seem to be influenced more by genetic factors and brain biochemistry than other disorders, some disorders are influenced more by environmental factors, and still others are influenced by all three factors. With this in mind, we will briefly examine possible causes of anxiety-based disorders.

Heredity and Physiological Factors. There is some evidence that anxiety-based disorders have a genetic basis. For example, the concordance rates for the disorder in MZ twins tends to be higher than that for DZ twins or any other two nontwin siblings (Slater & Shields, 1969; Eysenck, 1975). Although the gene segments that may predispose individuals to anxiety-based disorders have not been isolated, it is believed that the predisposition itself involves unusually low or unusually high autonomic reactivity to environmental stimulation. Such inherited differences in autonomic reactivity appear to involve either of two physiological factors. First, some individuals who experience attacks of intense anxiety have been shown to have elevated blood levels of lactic acid, which is produced by muscles in response to exercise (Klein & Rabkin, 1981; Fishman & Sheehan, 1985).

These two paintings by Sybil, another victim of multiple personality disorder, illustrate how different one personality can be from another. The painting on the left was done by Peggy, Sybil's angry, fearful personality, while the one on the right was painted by the home-loving Mary.

Other studies have shown that up to 40 or 50 percent of anxiety-sufferers have a defect in a major heart valve (the mitral valve) (Agras, 1985; Hafeiz, 1980).

Learning Factors. Whether or not anxiety-based disorders have a genetic basis, it is widely accepted that classical conditioning plays an important role in the actual development of some anxiety-based disorders, especially the acquisition of phobias (Seligman, 1971). Consider, for example, how a fear of bees and other stinging insects might develop. An individual is stung by a bee (at first a neutral stimulus), producing pain (the unconditional stimulus). The bee then becomes a conditional stimulus that elicits fear. The conditional fear response is highly generalizable: the buzzing of a bee, the sight of a bee's nest, or the sighting of an insect that looks like a bee, may elicit fear. The extent to which the conditional response developed may be related to a number of factors, such as the number of times an individual is stung by a bee, or learning that other individuals have died from bee stings. In fact, an individual never has to be stung by a bee to develop a bee phobia. Simply being warned that bees are dangerous and that a bee sting can hurt is enough to elicit conditional fear.

Avoidance or escape from anxiety-eliciting stimuli is also believed to be negatively reinforcing to individuals suffering from high levels of anxiety. Phobias, obsessive-compulsive disorders, somatoform disorders, and dissociative disorders each involve reduction of anxiety through expression of their respective symptoms. The housewife who wouldn't leave home unless in the company of her mother or husband, Beth, who felt compelled to go through a cleansing ritual after each time she touched her genitals, and Gene Smith, who left home, moved to another city under an assumed name after experiencing feelings of failure, each were successful in either avoiding or escaping anxiety-eliciting stimuli.

Such learning takes place in the broad context of family interactions. Many individuals with anxiety-based disorders have been found to have overprotective parents (Goodwin & Guze, 1984). Overprotective parents seem to either reinforce anxiety-reducing behaviors in their children by giving them comfort or by serving as models for such responses. For example, a child who observes her mother's fearful behavior in the presence of snakes may acquire the same responses when she, too, is confronted with snakes.

Other psychological disorders can, in many ways, be considered more debilitating than anxiety-based disorders. We say "more debilitating" not necessarily because the psychological pain and suffering are greater, but because they involve psychoses: the orientation to reality is more skewed. We turn now to a discussion of mood disorders, which involve severe impairment of meeting the demands of everyday life, and include drastic distortions of reality.

MOOD DISORDERS

Mood refers to the many emotional states that accompany our behavior, thoughts, and perceptions. Everyone experiences moods varying from sadness to feelings of incompetence to happiness to elation. We are excited when our team wins the big game, saddened to learn that a friend's father has had a heart attack, thrilled at news of a higher than expected raise at work, and devastated by the death of a loved one. Such are the emotions from which our lives are woven.

Some people, though, experience greater and more dramatic mood changes than these. Significant shifts or disturbances in mood that affect normal perception, thinking, and behavior are referred to as **mood disorders.** Mood disorders may be characterized by a deep, forboding depression, or a combination of depression and euphoria. In essence, the person with a mood disorder is either deeply depressed or alternates between periods of depression and elation. Mood disorders often accompany other disorders. In other instances, the shifts in mood are accompanied by bizarre perceptions and other distortions that effectively remove the person from contact with reality. We will discuss two types of mood disorders: major depression and bipolar disorder. People with major depression suffer only depression; people with bipolar disorder experience alternating periods of depression and **mania,** which is excessive emotional arousal and elation.

Major Depression

Persistent and severe feelings of sadness accompanied by changes in appetite, sleep, and behavior patterns is typical of **major depression,** sometimes referred to as unipolar disorder. Individuals with this disorder frequently describe themselves as worthless, incompetent, and no good. They often have inappropriate and excessive feelings of guilt and have difficulty concentrating on even the simplest tasks. Of course, losing a night's sleep or having a difficult time studying for an exam do not indicate major depression. Although the distinction between major depression and milder, less debilitating forms of depression is not always clear, an individual must experience depression daily for at least a 2-week period before he or she is considered to be suffering from major depression. Sometimes, severely depressed individuals have delusions, which are false beliefs maintained, often with deep commitment, in the face of no or contrary evidence. For example, an individual may mistakenly believe he or she is being punished by friends, family, and colleagues for some misdeed. Unfortunately, major depression is not uncommon. About 6 to 8 percent of all adults experience a bout of major depression during any 6-month period (Robins et al., 1984). Other figures indicate that about 10 percent of men and about 20 percent of women have had at least one episode of major depression during their lives

(Weissman & Myers, 1978). Many of the symptoms of major depression are illustrated in the following case example:

> Chris, a 55-year-old senior partner in a highly respected Wall Street agency was offered the presidency of a large company. Within a few days of the offer, he became severely depressed. His symptoms included weeping, suicidal threats, feelings of persecution, delusions that his insides were rotting, and expressions of guilt. He felt undeserving of his success and he complained that the offer was punishment for his incompetence. He often sat, in one position, for long periods. His appetite diminished and he refused to establish eye contact with others.
>
> (Schumer, 1983, p. 243)

For individuals with major depression, even the most common tasks seem laborious. Conversation, for example, becomes tedious. Individuals with major depression may fail to carry out habits of good personal hygiene such as changing clothes daily, washing and combing hair, and bathing. Hobbies that were once fun now hold little or no interest and provide no pleasure. Work becomes a burden with concentration becoming difficult, if not impossible. Even getting out of bed becomes a chore.

Severely depressed individuals, as you can imagine, are at risk for suicide. Half of all successful suicide attempts are carried out by people with major depression. The underlying motivations for suicide are varied and not well understood, but one contributing factor is apparently media exposure to other "successful" suicides. This factor perhaps exacerbates suicidal tendencies already present in depressed people. In one study (Phillips & Carstensen, 1986) researchers studied the relation between 38 nationally televised news or feature stories of teenage suicides from 1973 to 1979 and the incidence of suicide among American teenagers over the next week. A total of 1666 suicides occurred subsequent to the 38 stories, about 110 suicides more than would have been expected to have occurred without the effect of the television exposure.

Our ability to predict those most at risk for suicide is not impressive, although we do know that many cases of major depression are preceded by stressful events. For example, in a study involving 40 depressed people, Leff, Roatch, and Bunney (1970) discovered that each individual had experienced one or more stressful events in the month prior to becoming severely depressed. Figure 15.2 shows the ten stressors most often experienced by these people and the number of people who encountered them. What is needed is an increased understanding of how major depression, and environmental factors such as media exposure to other suicides, contribute to the act of suicide. This understanding will allow us to develop more effective ways to identify those most at risk and to prevent suicides that might otherwise occur.

Half of all successful suicide attempts are carried out by people with major depression.

Bipolar Disorder

Bipolar disorder is characterized by alternating states of depression and mania separated by relatively normal periods. During a manic episode, mood is elevated to euphoria with exaggerated self-esteem, unquestioned self-confidence, and nearly continuous rapid speech matched by a flight of ideas that often change abruptly from topic to topic. This disorder afflicts about 1 in every 100 people and is first apparent when the individual is between the ages of 15 and 35 (Wallis, 1987). The depression phase of a bipolar disorder differs in some ways from the depression of a major depressive disorder. For example, people with major depression typically sleep less than usual, whereas people suffering from bipolar depression typically sleep more than usual (DePue & Monroe, 1978).

Stressful event

Patients affected (from total of 40)

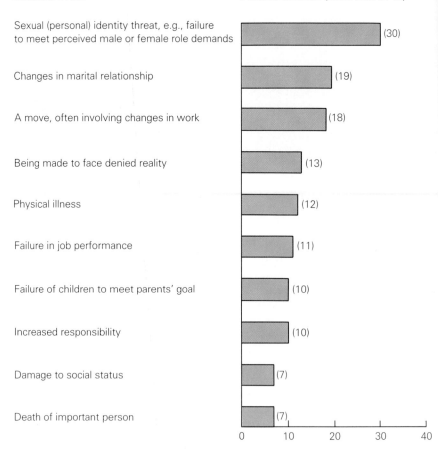

Sexual (personal) identity threat, e.g., failure to meet perceived male or female role demands (30)

Changes in marital relationship (19)

A move, often involving changes in work (18)

Being made to face denied reality (13)

Physical illness (12)

Failure in job performance (11)

Failure of children to meet parents' goal (10)

Increased responsibility (10)

Damage to social status (7)

Death of important person (7)

0   10   20   30   40

FIGURE 15.2

Deep depression is often preceded by one or more stressful events. Shown here are the 10 stressors that depressed people in the Leff et al., (1970) study most frequently experienced in the month just before becoming severely depressed. The numbers in parentheses represent the number of people who experienced that particular stressful event.

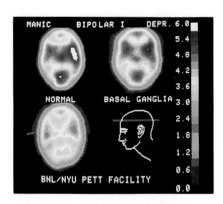

These PET scans compare a normal brain (bottom) with the brains of people suffering from manic/bipolar I and depression.

As an example of a manic episode that has reached psychotic proportions, consider the following statement made by a patient in response to his therapist's statement, "Well, you seem pretty happy today."

Happy! Happy! You certainly are a master of understatement, you rogue! (Shouting, literally jumping out of his seat.) Why I'm ecstatic. I'm leaving for the West coast today on my daughter's bicycle. Only 3100 miles. That's nothing you know. I could probably walk, but I want to get there by next week. And along the way I plan to contact a lot of people about investing in my fish equipment [believing that he had discovered a way to prevent tropical fish in aquaria from dying]. I'll get to know more people that way you know, Doc, "know" in the biblical sense (leering at the therapist seductively). Oh, God, how good it feels. It's almost like a nonstop orgasm.

(Davison & Neale, 1986, p. 196)

Etiology of Mood Disorders

Like the etiology of anxiety-based disorders, the etiology of mood disorders centers on three variables: heredity, physiological factors, and learning factors.

Heredity. There is considerable evidence that mood disorders tend to run in families. For example, Allen (1976) found a concordance rate for bipolar disorder of 72 percent in MZ twins but only 14 percent in DZ twins. In more recent research, Janet Egeland and her colleagues believe to have discovered a specific gene that appears to be related to bipolar mood disorder (Egeland et al., 1987). This research has centered on the occurrence of the disorder in a small number of Amish families. The Amish present an ideal community for this kind of study for two reasons. First, they have kept detailed genealogical records for the past 200 years. Second, they represent a relatively closed genetic pool: almost all 12,500 Amish in the county in which the study took place are descended from 20 or 30 couples who emigrated from Europe in the early 1700s and only a very few outsiders have ever married into these communities.

Researchers used the closed communities of the Amish to study bipolar mood disorders. Because they could trace the genetic history of all the community residents, researchers were able to find a link between bipolar mood disorder in present and past generations.

Thirty-two active cases of bipolar mood disorder were identified, and each had a history of the disorder through at least several generations. One group of 81 relatives, of which 14 had bipolar disorder, allowed Egeland and her associates to draw blood samples so that their DNA could be examined. When gene segments were compared across the normal and the bipolar mood cases, the genetic material on the 11th chromosome was found to be different for those with the disorder but not for the normal cases.

However, we should be cautious in interpreting the significance of this finding for two reasons. First, the finding probably does not mean that bipolar disorder itself is inherited; rather, it is more likely that a capacity for the disorder is inherited. This point is corroborated by the fact that a third of Egeland's subjects who possessed the aberrant genetic material did not exhibit symptoms of bipolar disorder. Second, Egeland's findings have not been corroborated using other groups of subjects (Hodgkinson et al., 1987). This, of course, does not mean that bipolar disorder does not have a genetic basis. It probably means that other genes in addition to gene 11 are related to the capacity to inherit bipolar disorder. One thing we do know for sure, though, is that other biological factors, particularly brain biochemistry, are involved in mood disorders. It is that topic to which we turn next.

Physiological Factors. Neuroscientists believe that two neurotransmitters, norepinephrine and serotonin, play an important role in mood disorders. Although the story is far from complete, here is basically what researchers know at present. When an individual with a mood disorder undergoes therapy involving antidepressant drugs, symptoms of the disorder are successfully, although temporarily, abated. These drugs, of which there are two classes, appear to work by increasing norepinephrine and serotonin levels. For example, tricyclic antidepressants, such as imipramine, likely block reuptake (reabsorption by the presynaptic membrane) of norepinephrine, leaving more of the neurotransmitter in the synaptic cleft to stimulate postsynaptic receptors. Monoamine oxydase inhibitors (MAO), the other class of antidepressant drugs, appear to render inactive the enzymes in the synaptic cleft that normally destroy molecules of norepinephrine. This process also leaves more norepinephrine in the synaptic cleft to stimulate postsynaptic receptors. That increased levels of neurotransmitters in the synaptic cleft lead to elevations in mood is corroborated by the effects of drugs that decrease neurotransmitter levels. For example, reserpine, a drug that may be prescribed for relief of high blood pressure, can induce depression by decreasing norepinephrine and serotonin levels in the brain.

Of course, the obvious question to ask is what factors cause levels of norepinephrine and serotonin to decrease in the first place. Many researchers addressing this question believe that environmental events can trigger biochemical changes in the brain that lead to mood alterations. For example, laboratory animals exposed to inescapable electric shock often show decreased levels of norepinephrine and changes in behavior that appear similar to those in depressed individuals: apathy, sluggishness, immobility, and failure to attempt to escape or avoid the aversive situation. The dogs just give up, a phenomena that Martin Seligman, the researcher who discovered this effect, has called learned helplessness.

What kinds of environmental events could lead to similar outcomes for people? For obvious ethical reasons, experiments to answer that question have not been conducted. Instead, psychologists have focused on people's cognitive reactions to stressful events. The rationale has been to study differences in how depressed individuals, relative to nondepressed people, draw inferences about the causes of the events that take place in their lives. We'll look at this issue more closely next.

Learning Factors. Individuals with mood disorders do not have the same outlook on the world as normal individuals. Specifically, they make negative statements about themselves and their abilities. "Nobody likes me." "I'm not any good at anything." "I feel useless." "What's the point in even trying, I'll just screw up anyway." These are all statements that individuals experiencing depression might make. Because they are so negative about themselves, depressed people are particularly unpleasant to be around. The problem is that the depressed individual is caught in a vicious circle: negative statements strain interpersonal relationships, which result in others withdrawing or failing to initiate social support, which in turn, reinforces the depressed individual's negative statements (Klerman & Weissman, 1986) (see Figure 15.3).

Aaron Beck, a well-known depression researcher, believes that the depressed individual's perspective is comprised of a highly integrated system of three negative beliefs concerning the self, the world, and the future. He refers to these three negative beliefs as the "cognitive triad" (Beck, 1974, 1976; Beck et al., 1979). These three beliefs stem from and are maintained by incorrect attributions about causal events. Relative to nondepressed people, depressed individuals tend to focus on internal, dispositional attributions to explain unpleasant events that happen to them and on external situational attributions to explain pleasant events.

Let's look at a specific example. How would a depressed individual explain getting turned down for a date? She might attribute the causes to a number of personal causes: "I'm ugly," "I'm no fun to be around," "People just don't like me," "People think I'm boring," and so on. Notice that she did not attribute the cause to external or situational factors: "It was just bad timing, he had already made plans with his friends," "He had to work," or "He's just playing hard to get."

On the other hand, suppose she did not get turned down for the date. How might she react then? Perhaps by thinking "He probably didn't have anything better to do," or "He's only going out with me so he can meet my roommate." Again, pay particular attention to the obvious—she never attributed her date to internal, dispositional factors. It never occurred to her to think, "He's going out with me because he likes me or because he finds me attractive or intelligent or fun."

Although it is well documented that depressed individuals endorse negative statements pertaining to themselves, it is not clear what role such statements play in the disorder. Are they a cause or an effect? It is likely that a third variable, perhaps changes in neurotransmitter substances, cause people to feel depressed and to think and say negative things about themselves. Beck's approach, then, may be more descriptive than explanatory.

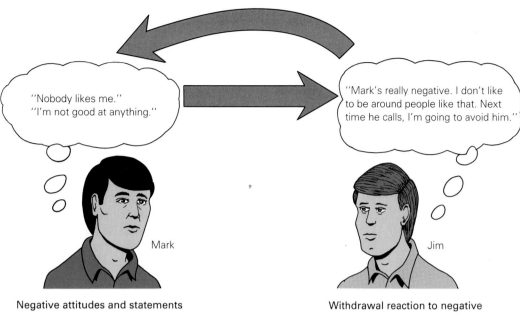

Jim's reaction to Mark's statements reinforce
Mark's feelings of worthlessness

"Nobody likes me."
"I'm not good at anything."

"Mark's really negative. I don't like
to be around people like that. Next
time he calls, I'm going to avoid him."

Mark

Jim

Negative attitudes and statements
of an individual with depression.

Withdrawal reaction to negative
attitudes and statements of others.

FIGURE 15.3

Depression and strained interpersonal relationships. Depressed individuals are often caught in a vicious circle. They make negative self-statements that cause others to withdraw or fail to initiate social support, which in turn, reinforces the depressed individual's low self-esteem and negative self-statements.

SCHIZOPHRENIA

Schizophrenia is the general term for a group of psychological disorders involving distortions of thought, perception and emotion, bizarre behavior, and social withdrawal. Any individual with schizophrenia may be characterized by symptoms such as one or all of the following: believing that he or she is Jesus Christ or that everyone else is a robot, hearing voices that no one else hears, laughing out loud for no apparent reason, or losing all interest in communicating with others. The different types of schizophrenic disorders that we will discuss are identified by the specific nature of the disordered cognitions and behavior, as well as by the way in which they develop.

Schizophrenia is a major health problem of enormous personal and financial cost. It afflicts an estimated 0.5 to 1.5 percent of the U.S. population, which means that at any one time, over 2 million Americans may be experiencing symptoms of schizophrenia (Gottesman & Shields, 1982). About 50,000 new cases of schizophrenia are diagnosed each year (Barnes, 1987). The cost for treating individuals with the disorder and lost job productivity is about $48 billion a year (Holden, 1987). In terms of the seriousness and prevalence of the disorder, schizophrenia may be considered the "cancer" of the psychological disorders.

The prognosis or estimate of likely outcome for schizophrenia is often described by what is called the "law of thirds." That is, approximately one-third of the people who are diagnosed as having this disorder will require institutionalization for the rest of their lives. About one-third respond to treatment or show "remission of symptoms" and, thus, may be said to be cured of the disorder. And the final third are occasionally symptom-free (sometimes for as long as periods of years) only to have the symptoms return, requiring another round of treatment and perhaps even institutionalization.

Symptoms of Schizophrenia

The symptoms of schizophrenia may develop suddenly (acute schizophrenia) or gradually over a long period (chronic schizophrenia). In most instances, the symptoms appear between middle adolescence and middle age. In general, the symptoms of schizophrenia alternate between two phases. In the active or psychotic phase, the individual experiences a break with reality, typified by disorganized thought, disturbances of affect, distorted perception, and disturbances of motor behavior. In the residual phase, these symptoms are still apparent but to a lesser degree. We turn now to a discussion of the symptoms.

At any one time, over 2 million Americans may be experiencing symptoms of schizophrenia.

Disorganized Thought. Individuals with schizophrenia do not think or reason in a way that would be considered rational or logical. They have difficulty organizing and retaining their ideas and have bizarre and inappropriate cognitions about the external world. Consider, for example, a schizophrenic's response to the question of "How do you feel today?"

> Yes, sir, it's a good day. Full of rainbows, you know. They go along on their merry way without concern for asphyxiation or impurities. Yes, sir, like unconcerned flappers of the cosmoblue. Big, yes, sir, big, blue, bottom, bright.
>
> (Excerpted from Sue, Sue, & Sue, 1981)

Schizophrenic thinking is also often characterized by **delusions,** which as you may recall, are false beliefs maintained in the face of no or contrary evidence. Common delusions among individuals with schizophrenia include:

- delusions of grandeur—the false belief that one is an important or powerful individual. This delusion may entail assuming the identity of that person, whether he or she is dead or alive. Common assumed identities include Jesus Christ and Napoleon.
- delusions of persecution—the false belief that other people are plotting against, abusing, or attempting to murder him or her.
- delusions of control—the false belief that other people, animals, or inanimate objects are attempting to control his or her mind.
- delusions of bodily disintegration—the false belief that one's body is decomposing.

Disturbances of Affect. Many of those suffering from schizophrenia also experience disturbances of affect, which are characterized by flat or inappropriate emotion. In flat affect, emotional intensity is greatly diminished or disappears altogether. Learning about the death of a parent might invoke the same lack of an emotional response that results from just discovering that you stepped on an ant. In inappropriate affect, the emotion may seem real, and may even be intense, but it is clearly out of place for the setting. When experiencing pain a schizophrenic may laugh, or when everyone else laughs at a joke, he or she may begin to cry.

Distorted Perception. Another set of prominent schizophrenic symptoms are disturbances of perception. Consider the description by Carol North, to whom you were introduced at the chapter's outset, of one of her perceptual experiences while she was a student:

> I began to notice things in a more sensitive way than I ever had before. Campus evergreens burst into the most intense contrasts of lights and darks and shades of greens that I had ever seen. I wandered around campus looking at everything I possibly could with great wonderment, as if I were seeing it all for the first time . . . . Weighted down with the burden of Pure Perception, I had to move slowly and carefully. I spent hours marveling at the texture of the bricks on the buildings, at the intricate moving patterns of the moonlight on the river . . . . I became so immersed in what I was doing that I didn't realize how ridiculous I must have looked bending down to examine and touch ordinary sidewalk cement. What no one else knew was that the cement had been secretly transformed into a wondrous substance, full of grains and lines, hieroglyphics, messages from worlds beyond, messages that I felt compelled to try to understand . . . .
>
> (1987, p. 84)

Often schizophrenic perceptions take the form of **hallucinations,** which are sensory experiences that occur in the absence of external stimulation of the corresponding sensory organ. For example, the individual may see objects that appear to be real but are not. Individuals with schizophrenia commonly report auditory hallucinations and to a lessor extent visual hallucinations, but the hallucinations may involve any sensory organ.

Sometimes those with schizophrenia may also hear a voice that keeps a running commentary on their behavior, or they hear two or more voices conversing. Here is how one man with schizophrenia described these voices:

> The voices are silent when I'm talking and so far they are silent while writing you. They take a type of being another person and sometimes two or three. The voices are rapid and are almost instantly forgotten by me. The other characteristic of them is that they are mostly constant. What they do is interrupt the train of thought—block some memory—fatigue— that's it.

Disturbances of Motor Behavior. Disturbances of motor behavior also characterize schizophrenic behavior. Sometimes a schizophrenic's actions are highly ritualized and precise and are performed repetitiously; sometimes the actions are excited and agitated. The schizophrenic may thrash his or her arms in all directions and kick. And sometimes there are no actions at all—the individual becomes catatonic, completely still, almost as if he or she had become a statue. In less extreme catatonic states, movement may occur, but it is slow and halting.

These general symptoms appear more or less in each of the four major categories of schizophrenia, which we will look at next.

Types of Schizophrenia

The systematic study of schizophrenia began late in the nineteenth century with the emergence of the discipline of psychiatry. One early and influential researcher, Emil Kraepelin, proposed a classification system for diagnosing major types of schizophrenia that continues to be used to this day as represented, for example, by the DSM-III-R, though the system has, of course, been greatly refined and expanded. The types of schizophrenia here include disorganized, catatonic, paranoid, and undifferentiated. Each type of schizophrenia is diagnosed according to a specific set of characteristics based on the symptoms we just discussed.

Sirhan Sirhan, who was convicted of assassinating Senator Robert F. Kennedy, was diagnosed as having chronic paranoid schizophrenia.

The key symptoms of **disorganized schizophrenia** are disturbances of thought and a flattened or silly affect. Behavior is often inappropriate and absurd, and language is incoherent. An individual with disorganized schizophrenia will make up new words or use words in strange and bizarre ways, as in "The umaloo is going to umbrella the newspaper guy tomorrow morning." Hallucinations and delusions may also be present. The delusions are, however, fragmentary. Today the individual may falsely believe that he or she has special insight into the nature of the universe, but tomorrow the belief may be replaced with a different delusion. Disorganized schizophrenia can be severely debilitating, and the individual suffering from it may require institutionalization.

Catatonic schizophrenia, not surprisingly, is characterized primarily by disorders of motor behavior. The affected individual alternates between uncontrolled excitement and immobility, with one or the other of the extremes dominating. The catatonic individual can move from wild activity to complete stillness, or vice versa, with startling speed. Individuals with catatonic schizophrenia often need supervision to prevent them from injuring themselves by banging into walls, or to avoid malnutrition and other problems resulting from maintaining fixed poses for long periods.

Systematic, well-developed, and persistent delusions are characteristic of **paranoid schizophrenia.** In particular, these delusions follow the specific theme of persecution or grandeur. Even in the presence of these delusions, however, the incoherence typical of disorganized schizophrenia is absent, and the individual can remain emotionally responsive and alert.

Undifferentiated schizophrenia is a category of schizophrenia for individuals whose symptoms do not fall neatly into any of the other categories. Thus, undifferentiated schizophrenia is characterized by fragments of the different symptoms. Often the beginning phases of schizophrenia are marked by a multitude of problems, and only later does a stable pattern characteristic of one of the other types emerge, though undifferentiated schizophrenia may itself remain over a long period of time.

Individuals who have experienced at least one episode of schizophrenia but are currently not exhibiting major symptoms of the disorder are often diagnosed as having **residual schizophrenia.** That is, these individuals either are not exhibiting symptoms or are exhibiting them weakly.

Although these types of schizophrenia continue to be recognized by many psychiatrists and psychologists, a growing number of them are arguing that dividing schizophrenia into different types is not very useful in terms of understanding its etiology and prescribing treatment (Pfohl & Andreasen, 1986). Some researchers, in particular, Nancy Andreasen, have suggested that schizophrenia be classified into only two categories based on the kind of symptoms, positive or negative, present in the individual being diagnosed (Andreasen & Olsen, 1982). Positive symptoms include disordered perception and bizarre cognitions and language. Negative symptoms include inappropriate affect, social withdrawal, incoherent language, and attention deficits. Whether or not this new classification scheme will be helpful in better understanding the nature of schizophrenia, however, remains an empirical question.

Etiology of Schizophrenia

Research into the etiology of schizophrenia throughout this century reflects the challenge that psychologists face in attempting to understand how psychological and biological factors interact to influence behavior. However, our understanding of the etiology of schizophrenia, though not complete, is progressing. Schizophrenia appears to result from one or more inherited, biological predispositions that are activated by environmental stress.

Heredity. Although many schizophrenics come from families with no history of schizophrenia, and many nonschizophrenics come from families with a high incidence of schizophrenia, the probability of developing schizophrenia increases as the number of close family members with schizophrenia increases. The evidence for this inheritability comes primarily from studies of MZ and DZ twins and adopted children.

Twin studies of schizophrenia, like those of intelligence, compare the concordance rates of MZ twins with those in which siblings of different genetic relatedness were reared either together or apart. According to Gottesman & Shields (1982), concordance rates for MZ twins are approximately 46 percent but only about 14 percent for DZ twins (see Figure 15.4).

The study of adopted children also provides an important source of evidence regarding inheritability. One researcher (Heston, 1966) identified 47 individuals born to hospitalized schizophrenic mothers, who were then adopted by another family. These children were compared later in life to 50 children of nonschizophrenic mothers who were placed through the same adoption agencies that had placed them. More of those adopted children of schizophrenic mothers developed schizophrenia than those of nonschizophrenic mothers. Just as important, Heston found that the adopted children of schizophrenic mothers developed other psychological disorders more often than did those of nonschizophrenic mothers.

The safest conclusion to draw from twin and adoption studies of schizophrenia is that the genotype for schizophrenia does not contain the code for the disorder itself, rather it predisposes individuals to becoming susceptible to the disorder. This means that factors in addition to genotype must be involved in schizophrenia. One such factor is brain biochemistry.

Physiological Factors. The most compelling evidence suggesting that biochemical factors are involved in schizophrenia stems from a series of discoveries over the past 40 years that particular drugs affect the occurrence of the disorder's symptoms. The one thing that these drugs have in common is that they appear to exert their influence on one particular neurotransmitter, dopamine. The idea that dopamine plays a central role in schizophrenia has come to be called the dopamine hypothesis.

FIGURE 15.4
Genetic relatedness and schizophrenia. As the degree of relatedness between an individual with schizophrenia and another person increases, so does the likelihood that the other person will be at risk for the disorder.

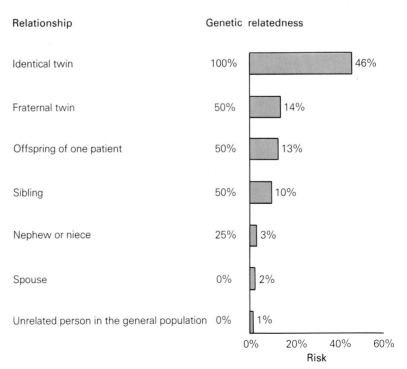

Relationship	Genetic relatedness	Risk
Identical twin	100%	46%
Fraternal twin	50%	14%
Offspring of one patient	50%	13%
Sibling	50%	10%
Nephew or niece	25%	3%
Spouse	0%	2%
Unrelated person in the general population	0%	1%

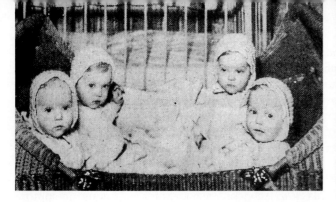

The Genain quadruplets, shown here as infants and celebrating their 51st birthday, enabled researchers to study the role of genetics in schizophrenia. Genetically identical, each of the quadruplets was diagnosed as schizophrenic before the age of 25.

According to the dopamine hypothesis, schizophrenia is due to excessive dopamine activity at particular receptor sites in the brain. Such overactivity may be due to either the presence of too many postsynaptic receptors or hypersensitivity of the receptors to dopamine. Drugs generally affect dopamine like they would any neurotransmitter system by either inhibiting or enhancing its interaction with postsynaptic receptors, which, in turn, correspond to temporary behavior changes. For example, if an individual with schizophrenia is given amphetamine, a stimulant that increases dopamine activity, the severity of his or her symptoms increases (Snyder, 1978). Drugs that belong to a family of chemical compounds called phenothiazines, which are often used in the treatment of schizophrenia, decrease dopamine activity by blocking postsynaptic receptors, thereby reducing the severity of the symptoms. Administration of phenothiazines, then, may directly alleviate schizophrenic symptoms, if only temporarily, presumably by redressing a chemical imbalance in the brain. Although this does not prove that the cause of schizophrenic symptoms is due to biochemical factors, it does suggest that they are likely involved in the expression of those symptoms (Davis, 1978).

The possibility that biological factors other than dopamine may be involved in the etiology of schizophrenia comes from research that has focused on brain anatomy. In particular, brain scans such as MRI, and postmortem studies have shown that the ventricles in the brains of some chronic schizophrenics are enlarged (Andreasen et al., 1986; Brown et al., 1986). Since the brain occupies the entire area between the skull and spinal cord, an enlarged ventricle suggests a decrease in brain mass. However, the implications of these findings are tempered by the fact that many nonschizophrenic individuals also have enlarged ventricles.

Although schizophrenia appears to have both a genetic and biochemical basis, we also know that social-cognitive factors are involved in schizophrenia. We will turn to this issue next.

Learning Factors. That the concordance rate for schizophrenia in MZ twins is less than 100 percent suggests that environmental factors also play a role in the development of schizophrenia. In fact, many researchers subscribe to the **diathesis-stress model** of schizophrenia, which proposes that the disorder is due to the interaction of both a genetic predisposition (diathesis) toward schizophrenia and environmental factors (stress).

We have already reviewed evidence of genetic involvement in schizophrenia and concluded that an individual's genotype is positively related to development of schizophrenic symptoms later in life. What evidence is there that environmental factors are also involved? Most researchers interested in seeking answers to this question have focused on family dynamics; that is, the social interaction between parents and children who later develop schizophrenic symptoms.

One important factor appears to be the personality and communicative abilities of either or both of the parents. Several studies have shown that children raised by parents who are dominating, overprotective, rigid, and insensitive to the needs of others later develop schizophrenia (Roff & Knight, 1981). In many cases, a parent may be verbally accepting of the child, yet in other ways reject him or her, which establishes a conflict for the child referred to by researchers as a **double-bind**. For example, a mother may encourage her son to become dependent upon her emotionally yet continually reject him when he tries to hug her or sit on her lap or play with her.

Schizophrenia also seems to occur at a higher than average rate among children who were reared in families wrought with discord. For example, in a study of 14 schizophrenic individuals, Lidz and his colleagues found that each of them had families that underwent either chronic discord in which the integrity of marriage was perpetually threatened, or marital skew in which the bizarre behavior of one family member is tolerated by the other members (Lidz et al., 1965).

In sum, one way to view the etiology of schizophrenia might be to include genetic, biochemical, and environmental factors as causal agents. In this way, schizophrenia would be seen as an inherited predisposition whose expression is triggered by environmental stressors, such as double-binds, and mediated by changes in the levels of particular neurotransmitters. In other words, neurotransmitters represent something of an interface between genotype and environment. Although researchers know that none of these factors, alone, seems to be involved in schizophrenia, they are not sure of the exact degree to which they interact. Obviously, more research is needed before we will have a clear understanding of the etiology of schizophrenia.

PERSONALITY DISORDERS

Personality disorders are a class of disorders characterized by extremely rigid personality traits that impair functioning in those settings. In this section, we will discuss briefly three personality disorders: narcissistic, paranoid, and antisocial.

Individuals with **narcissistic personality disorder** have an exaggerated sense of self-worth and are obsessed with success fantasies. We might characterize the actions of these people as egotistical. Individuals with this disorder often demand special treatment and favors and seek to be the center of attention regardless of the situation. Ironically, in private, they experience feelings of low self-esteem. They are overly sensitive to criticism, are prone to jealousy, and show little empathy for others. The following case illlustrates these traits:

> A graduate student believes that his dissertation may contribute significantly to his field of English literature. However, he has not made much progress with it. He blames his major professor for his lack of progress and thinks he deserves more credit for his ideas. He brags about his creativity and argues that other people are jealous of his brilliance. He considers his fellow graduate students as being brown-nosers and dull. He fantasizes that one day he will become an influential professor. His friendships with both men and women are to him very unsatisfying and none of his relationships are long-term.
>
> (Spitzer et al., 1981)

People diagnosed as having **paranoid personality disorder** show an exaggerated and unwarranted mistrust and suspicion of others. These symptoms are extremely rigid and unchanging even in the face of disconfirming evidence. People with paranoid personality disorder differ from people with paranoid schizophrenia in that their paranoia seems less disturbed and exaggerated.

The primary symptoms of **antisocial personality disorder** include a failure to conform to standards of decency, repeated lying and stealing, a failure to sustain lasting, loving relationships, low tolerance of boredom, and a complete lack of guilt and anxiety. Individuals with this disorder have been traditionally referred to as psychopaths or sociopaths, though neither of these terms are used in the DSM-III-R. A well-known individual with antisocial personality disorder is Charles Manson, who in the late 1960s, became the leader of a small band of men and women in Southern California. He led his "family," as the group came to be called, in a variety of crimes, including the murder of five people, among them pregnant movie actress Sharon Tate. After these people were murdered, he instructed the others to mutilate the bodies.

Individuals with antisocial personality disorder can be incredibly skilled manipulators, using people for their own selfish purposes, swindling, stealing, and all the while maintaining a superficial smoothness and charm. Although the crimes of only a few such people are propelled into the national news, this disorder is, unfortunately, not as rare as we would wish. According to the DSM-III-R, it is found in about 3 percent of American males and slightly fewer than 1 percent of American females.

ndividuals with antisocial personality disorder can be skilled manipulators, using people for their own selfish purposes . . . while maintaining a superficial smoothness and charm.

Researchers know less about the etiology of personality disorders than they do about that of other psychological disorders. This is partly due to the fact that researchers do not have as great an access to populations with personality disorders because these people seek treatment less often than people with more debilitating psychological disorders. What research has been conducted has focused largely on the antisocial personality disorder.

Like schizophrenia, the antisocial personality disorder may be described reasonably well by the diathesis-stress model. For example, twin studies suggest that some individuals may inherit a predisposition for the disorder (Crowe, 1983). Other studies have shown that family problems such as emotional stress, parental rejection, and rigidity may be a factor (Carson, Butcher, & Coleman, 1988). Still other studies suggest that underarousal of the autonomic nervous system causes the disorder (Lykken, 1957). This last suggestion is an interesting one because it lends itself to laboratory experimentation, which as you may recall, represents the optimal condition for making statements about cause and effect relationships. We will discuss briefly two such studies.

Lykken (1957) hypothesized what can be called the underarousal hypothesis for the disorder: individuals with an antisocial personality have underaroused autonomic nervous systems, which lead to unusually low levels of anxiety and a lack of concern about punishment. To test this idea, Lykken placed normal subjects and those with the disorder in an avoidance-learning situation. This experiment involved two conditions: one in which shock was delivered as a consequence of making an error and one in which error making did not result in shock. Lykken hypothesized that subjects with antisocial disorder would not reduce the number of errors in the experimental conditions relative to normal subjects. Lykken's idea was confirmed. Both types of subjects made about the same number of errors when shock was not a part of the learning situation. However, when shock was involved, the antisocial subjects made more errors than the control subjects.

Antisocial personalities exhibit a lack of conscience, seldom show any loyalty to others, and can be skilled manipulators. Giovanni Vigliotto, who suffers from the disorder, was convicted of defrauding one of his 105 wives. Vigliotto allegedly married lonely, middle-aged women, got control of their assets, and then disappeared. Several of his wives described him as charming, friendly, and warm.

Several years later, Schachter and Latané (1964) devised a more direct test of this hypothesis. They repeated Lykken's task with one difference: Adrenalin was administered to both the individuals with the disorder and the controls to stimulate their autonomic nervous systems. They were also, at a different time, administered a placebo that had no effect on their arousal levels. When injected with adrenaline, subjects with the antisocial personality disorder performed much better at avoiding shocks than when injected with the placebo, suggesting that the additional arousal led to increased responsiveness to the shocks. (Unexpectedly, the control subjects made more errors with the additional arousal, though this result was not reproduced in a follow-up study.)

Can we conclude from these studies that antisocial personality disorder is caused by biological factors? The answer is, "Only with some reservation." The reason for this answer is simple: Subjects in these studies entered the experiments with a long learning history, which means, of course, that it is possible that antisocial individuals have learned to respond to situations with low anxiety and diminished affect. It may be that they are not all that underaroused relative to normal individuals, but rather, that they are much better at tolerating punishing consequences (Vaillant, 1975).

PSYCHOSEXUAL DISORDERS

There are two classes of psychosexual disorders: sexual dysfunctions, which are impairments of the sexual response that interfere with achieving sexual satisfaction, and **paraphilias,** behaviors in which stimulation from unusual objects or events results in sexual satisfaction. Since we have discussed sexual dysfunctions already, we will discuss only paraphilias here. If you wish to refresh your memory about sexual dysfunctions refer to the chapter on Gender Development and Sexual Behavior.

The distinguishing feature of an individual with a paraphilia is that he or she cannot become sexually aroused or achieve orgasm without a particular stimulus object or situation present. Many people become aroused by unusual stimuli that have become associated with sexual pleasure, but those objects do not become the focus of sexual activity. For paraphiliac individuals, though, those objects become a powerful source of sexual motivation and reinforcement. We will discuss five paraphilias: fetishism, exhibitionism, voyeurism, sexual sadism, and sexual masochism.

Fetishism is the use of inanimate objects, such as shoes, fur, underwear, or hats, to obtain sexual pleasure. Such people are said to have a fetish for these objects. In fact, fetish objects become the center of sexual interest.

Fetishes are classified as either media or form fetishes. Media fetishes are those in which the fetish object is anything made from a particular substance, such as leather, rubber, or silk. Form fetishes are those in which the shape of the fetish object is arousing, such as shoes, boots, and lingerie. Fetishes are usually formed during childhood and most people who develop a fetish are male.

Exhibitionism is displaying one's genitalia to a stranger in a public place to achieve sexual gratification. The majority of people who engage in this kind of sexual behavior are males with poor social skills and an inability to obtain sexual satisfaction through heterosexual activities. Typically, these individuals will expose their erect penis to an unfamiliar woman, expecting to surprise, embarrass, frighten, or otherwise alarm her. They derive sexual gratification purely from the reaction this act elicits and generally, they do not sexually attack their victims. In fact, they are disappointed if their victims show little or no reaction, and typically will make haste in leaving the scene if women express a sexual interest!

Voyeurism involves achieving sexual gratification by secretly viewing nude members of the opposite sex. Like exhibitionism, voyeurism typically involves young men who have difficulty establishing satisfying sexual relationships with women. A voyeur views his subject without her consent, and the secrecy and risk involved in the act enhances his sexual arousal. Some voyeurs go as far as to masturbate while peering at their subject.

Most voyeurs pose no harm to the women they watch. Those that do seem to deviate from normal patterns of peeping in two ways: First, they are willing to enter a building to spy on their subject. Second, they will deliberately attract their subject's attention.

Sexual sadism involves obtaining sexual gratification from inflicting real or imagined physical pain and psychological distress on others. **Sexual masochism** involves obtaining sexual gratification by suffering real or imagined physical pain or psychological distress.

While psychologists are not entirely sure how paraphilias develop, one plausible explanation is that a person learns to associate a particular object with sexual arousal through classical conditioning. For example, in fetishism, a young boy may first become sexually aroused while seeing or touching his mother's lingerie. He may later masturbate while thinking about or touching the lingerie. Eventually, touching or rubbing lingerie is necessary for him to become sexually aroused. The lingerie gains power in eliciting the sexual response, until finally, it is the only stimulus that influences the response. Paraphilias also seem to be part of a larger personality problem. Often, those with the disorder are emotionally immature, and in some cases, more impulsive than normal individuals.

BOUNDARIES AND FRONTIERS

Few emerge from a psychological disorder without paying a stiff personal price. One may recover from a psychological disorder but never recoup the losses that occurred along the way.

Psychological disorders, regardless of the form they assume, alter the course of people's lives and seldom for the better. They can be both insidious and destructive. Few emerge from a psychological disorder without paying a stiff personal cost. One may recover from a psychological disorder but never recoup the losses that occurred along the way. Families can be torn apart. Careers, no matter how promising, can be ruined. Efforts to achieve personal goals and aspirations can be sidetracked forever. One individual who has shown symptoms of paranoid schizophrenia for nearly three decades summarized his life this way: "Twenty-eight years of my life down the drain."

Although psychology, psychiatry, and biomedicine have provided and continue to refine diagnostic criteria for assessment of psychological disorders, these disciplines have yet to provide well-established causal explanations for these disorders. As should have been obvious from your reading of the chapter, the overarching boundary facing our understanding of psychological disorders is that we really don't understand them very well. As one researcher who recently summarized our current state of knowledge about schizophrenia said, "The causes of schizophrenia are unknown . . ." (Barnes, 1987, p. 235). That remark aptly and sadly captures the essence of our knowledge about the causes of almost all psychological disorders.

Granted, the causes of psychological disorders are complex, perhaps even more complicated than those underlying most topics of scientific inquiry. But causal complexity is not a good reason for not understanding something. It may be an impediment to knowledge but not, ultimately, a dead end. There are other reasons for our lack of understanding of psychological disorders. One is the fact that many, if not most, people trained in clinical psychology and psychiatry eventually become practitioners, not researchers. We lack researchers and research support. Well-trained practitioners are vital to the treatment of psychological disorders, and we need them, but we also need proportionately more researchers. Without more well-trained researchers, who address thoughtful questions about psychological disorders, the pace at which etiological discoveries are made is likely to remain slow.

You may wonder why there aren't more etiologically oriented researchers. The answer to the question is partly an economic one. Etiological research is expensive, and governmental and other agencies have been slow to fund research aimed at uncovering the basis for psychological disorders. Without more research money, it is unlikely there will be more researchers and more hard data on the etiology of psychological disorders.

Why be so concerned with etiology? After all, we do have a battery of treatments that appear to be effective in abating, if only temporarily, the symptoms of many disorders. The answer is because better understanding of the etiology of a disorder will move us closer to predicting accurately those individuals who are likely to be "at risk" for the disorder. And once we can better predict the kinds circumstances—both biological and environmental—that place people at risk, we can offer prevention as well as intervention. When all is said and done, that is the frontier upon whose threshold we can cross if and when research efforts are intensified.

CONCEPT SUMMARY

THE NATURE OF PSYCHOLOGICAL DISORDERS

- In what sense are psychological disorders maladaptive? (pp. 535–536)
- What role do social and cultural contexts play in defining which behaviors are maladaptive and which are not? (pp. 535–537)

CLASSIFYING PSYCHOLOGICAL DISORDERS

- What is the DSM-III-R? What do each of its axes describe? (pp. 537–539)
- What are the problems with DSM-III-R classification? (pp. 539–540)

ANXIETY-BASED DISORDERS

- What is generalized anxiety disorder? How does it differ from a phobic disorder? (pp. 540–542)
- In what ways can obsessive-compulsive disorder be maladaptive? (pp. 542–543)
- What are three kinds of somatoform disorders and how do they differ from each other? (pp. 543–544)
- Why are psychogenic amnesia, psychogenic fugue, and multiple personality disorder considered to be dissociative disorders? Give specific examples in each case. (pp. 545–546)
- What are the major causal factors that have been implicated in the anxiety-based disorders? (pp. 546–548)

MOOD DISORDERS

- How does major depression differ from bipolar disorder? (pp. 548–550)
- Do the mood disorders have a biological basis or are they determined more by learning? Explain. (pp. 550–553)

SCHIZOPHRENIA

- What are the major symptoms of schizophrenia? (pp. 554–555)
- What are delusions? Describe the different kinds of delusions. (p. 554)
- How do hallucinations differ from delusions? (pp. 554–555)
- How do the four types of schizophrenia differ from each other? What is residual schizophrenia? (pp. 555–556)
- What factors have been implicated in the etiology of schizophrenia? Explain. (pp. 556–559)

PERSONALITY DISORDERS

- What are personality disorders? What are the symptoms of narcissistic, paranoid, and antisocial personality disorders? (pp. 559–560)
- What do researchers know about the causes of antisocial personality disorder? (pp. 560–561)

PSYCHOSEXUAL DISORDERS

- What are paraphilias? Describe them. (pp. 561–562)
- How might paraphilias be acquired? (p. 562)

KEY TERMS AND CONCEPTS

Psychological Disorders Persistent, maladaptive patterns of behaving, thinking, and/or feeling that lead to distress or disability. (p. 535)

THE NATURE OF PSYCHOLOGICAL DISORDERS

Etiology A general term for describing the causes of a disorder. (p. 537)

CLASSIFYING PSYCHOLOGICAL DISORDERS

Diagnostic and Statistical Manual of Mental Disorders (DSM) The current and most widely used manual for classifying psychological disorders. The DSM-III-R is a classification system that describes an individual's psychological condition based on five different types of information, which are called axes. (p. 537)

ANXIETY-BASED DISORDERS

Anxiety A sense of apprehension or doom that is accompanied by a number of physiological reactions, such as accelerated heart rate, sweaty palms, and tightness in the stomach. (p. 540)

Anxiety-based Disorder An unrealistic and excessive anxiety that diminishes some aspect of a person's life. (p. 540)

Generalized Anxiety Disorder Chronically high levels of anxiety that are not specific to any one source. An individual with this disorder experiences anxiety across many different situations but cannot identify its cause. In addition to the usual symptoms of physical anxiety, individuals experiencing generalized anxiety are particularly susceptible to restlessness, irritability, and tension, realizing that at any time, and for no apparent reason, they may be overcome by feelings of overwhelming anxiety. (p. 540)

Phobic Disorder The unrealistic, excessive fear of a specific class of stimuli. Unlike generalized anxiety disorder, the object of the anxiety is readily identifiable: it may be a snake, an insect, plastics, the out-of-doors, closed spaces. (p. 541)

Agoraphobia The fear of being away from a safe place or a safe person. (p. 541)

Obsessive-compulsive Disorder An anxiety-based disorder in which an individual is beset by recurrent, unwanted thoughts or ideas and compelling urges to engage in repetitive ritual-like behavior. (p. 542)

Obsession An involuntary recurring thought, idea, or image. (p. 542)

Compulsion An irresistible impulse to repeat some action over and over even though it serves no useful purpose. Compulsions are often behavioral responses to a specific obsession. (p. 542)

Somatoform Disorder An anxiety-based disorder involving a bodily or physical problem for which there is no physiological basis. Though the physical problems, such as blindness, paralysis of a limb, or numbness do not have a physiological cause, the experience of the problem is nonetheless genuine to the individual. (p. 543)

Somatization Disorders A class of somatoform disorder, which occurs mostly in women, and involves complaints of wide ranging physical ailments for which there is no apparent biological cause. Over time, the nature of these complaints changes. At one time, the complaints may focus on cardiovascular functioning, at another time, they may concern respiratory functioning. (p. 544)

Conversion Disorder The somatoform disorder that involves the actual loss of bodily function such as blindness, paralysis, and numbness due to excessive anxiety. Serious physical (somatic) disabilities can appear—without voluntary control—and are due entirely to anxiety. (p. 544)

Hypochondriasis A persistent and excessive worry of developing a serious illness or disease. People with this disorder often misinterpret the appearance of normal physical aches and pains. (p. 544)

Dissociative Disorder A class of disorders in which anxiety is reduced by a sudden disruption in consciousness, which in turn, produces changes in one's sense of identity. (p. 545)

Psychogenic Amnesia A dissociative disorder characterized by the inability to remember important events or vital personal information. (p. 545)

Psychogenic Fugue A dissociative disorder involving amnesia but which is also characterized by the individual deliberately leaving the area in which he or she lives, and then assuming a new identity in a new locale. In severe cases, the individual not only takes on a new name, new home, and a new occupation, but assumes new personality characteristics as well. (p. 545)

Multiple Personality Disorder A dissociative disorder involving the emergence of two or more complete and independently functioning personalities in one person, though only one is dominant at any given time. The different personalities may have unique memories, behavior patterns, and social experiences. The original personality is not usually conscious of the other personalities. However, the other personalities may be conscious of the original personalities as well as each other. (p. 545)

MOOD DISORDERS

Mania Excessive emotional arousal and elation. (p. 548)

Mood Disorders Significant shifts or disturbances in mood that affect normal perception, thinking, and behavior. The mood disorders may be characterized by a deep, forboding depression, a euphoria and elation, or a combination of the two. (p. 548)

Major Depression Persistent and severe feelings of sadness and worthlessness accompanied by changes in appetite, sleeping, and behavior patterns. (p. 548)

Bipolar Disorder Alternating states of depression and mania separated by relatively normal periods. During a manic episode, mood is elevated to euphoria, with exaggerated self-esteem, unquestioned self-confidence, and nearly continuous, rapid speech matched by a flight of ideas that often change abruptly from topic to topic. (p. 549)

SCHIZOPHRENIA

Schizophrenia A general term for a group of psychological disorders involving distortions of thought, perception, emotion, bizarre behavior, and social withdrawal. (p. 553)

Delusions False beliefs maintained in the face of no or contrary evidence. (p. 554)

Hallucinations Sensory experiences that occur in the absence of external stimulation of the corresponding sensory organ. (p. 555)

Disorganized Schizophrenia A type of schizophrenia characterized primarily by disturbances of thought and a flattened or silly affect. Behavior is often inappropriate and absurd; language is incoherent. An individual with disorganized schizophrenia will make up new words or use words in strange and bizarre ways. (p. 556)

Catatonic Schizophrenia A type of schizophrenia characterized primarily by disorders of motor behavior, including behavior alternating between uncontrolled excitement and immobility, with one or the other extreme dominating. (p. 556)

Paranoid Schizophrenia A type of schizophrenia characterized primarily by systematic, well-developed, and persistent delusions. In particular, these delusions follow themes of either persecution or grandeur. (p. 556)

Undifferentiated Schizophrenia A type of schizophrenia whose symptoms do not fall neatly into any of the other categories. Undifferentiated schizophrenia is characterized by fragments of the different symptoms. (p. 556)

Residual Schizophrenia The diagnosis for individuals who have experienced at least one episode of schizophrenia but who are currently not exhibiting major symptoms of the disorder. (p. 556)

Diathesis-stress Model The idea that psychological disorders, particularly schizophrenia, are due to the interaction of both a genetic disposition (diathesis) and environmental factors (stress). (p. 558)

Double-bind The conflict caused for a child when he or she is given inconsistent messages or cues from a parent. (p. 559)

PERSONALITY DISORDERS

Personality Disorders A class of disorders characterized by extremely rigid personality traits that impair functioning in personal, social, and occupational settings. (p. 559)

Narcissistic Personality Disorder A disorder characterized by an exaggerated public sense of self-worth and obsessions with success fantasies. Individuals with narcissistic personality disorder often demand special treatment and favors, and seek to be the center of attention regardless of the situation. Ironically, privately, they also experience feelings of low self-esteem. (p. 559)

Paranoid Personality Disorder A disorder characterized by an exaggerated and unwarranted mistrust and suspicion of others. These symptoms are extremely rigid and unchangeable, even in the face of disconfirming evidence. (p. 560)

Antisocial Personality Disorder A disorder characterized by a failure to conform to standards of decency, repeated lying and stealing, a failure to sustain lasting, loving relationships, low tolerance of boredom, and a complete lack of guilt and anxiety. (p. 560)

PSYCHOSEXUAL DISORDERS

Paraphilias Behaviors in which stimulation from unusual objects or events results in sexual satisfaction. (p. 561)

Fetishism The use of inanimate objects to obtain sexual pleasure. (p. 561)

Exhibitionism The displaying of one's genitalia to a stranger in a public place to achieve sexual gratification. (p. 561)

Voyeurism The achieving of sexual gratification by secretly viewing nude members of the opposite sex. (p. 562)

Sadism and Masochism Sadism involves obtaining sexual gratification from inflicting real or imagined physical pain and psychological distress on others. Masochism involves obtaining sexual gratification by suffering real or imagined physical pain or psychological distress. (p. 562)

ADDITIONAL SOURCES OF INFORMATION

Carson, R. C., Butcher, J. N., & Coleman, J. C. (1988). *Abnormal psychology and modern life* (8th ed.). Glenview, IL: Scott, Foresman. A highly readable upper-division undergraduate text about psychological disorders, including their etiology and treatment.

Neale, J. M., Oltmann, T. F., & Davison, G. C. (1986). *Case studies in abnormal psychology* (2nd ed.). New York: Wiley. This book provides a description of the development, symptoms, and treatment of a variety of psychological disorders on a case-by-case basis.

Andreasen, N. C. (1984). *The broken brain: The biological revolution in psychiatry.* New York: Harper & Row. A factual and highly readable account of how neuroscientific research is reshaping our ideas about the biological basis of psychological disorders.

North, C. N. (1987). *Welcome, silence.* New York: Simon & Schuster.

Vonnegut, M. (1975). *The Eden express: A personal account of schizophrenia.* New York: Praeger. Both of these books are excellent first-hand accounts of what it is like to suffer from schizophrenia.

16 Therapy

BIOMEDICAL APPROACHES
(570–575)

Electroconvulsive Therapy   Psychosurgery   Drug Therapy

Advances in treatment often follow from research on brain functioning and its relationship to psychological functioning. Biomedical therapies are based on such research, and in the case of drug therapies, have revolutionized the treatment of psychological disorders during the 1950s.

PSYCHODYNAMIC APPROACHES *(575–579)*

Psychodynamic Techniques   Psychodynamic Therapy and the Neo-Freudians

Freud's emphasis on bringing unconscious impulses and conflicts to conscious awareness remains the hallmark of insight-oriented psychodynamic therapies. Modern forms of psychodynamic therapy emphasize social factors in development as well as recent experiences in the origin of psychological disorders.

BEHAVIORAL APPROACHES
(579–584)

Behavior Therapy Based on Classical Conditioning
Behavior Therapy Based on Operant Conditioning

Using methods based on classical and operant conditioning principles, behavior therapists have focused on alleviating maladaptive behavior. Unlike psychodynamic therapists, behavior therapists consider the behavior to be the problem, not just a symptom of the underlying problem.

COGNITIVE BEHAVIORAL APPROACHES *(584–586)*

Rational-Emotive Therapy   Cognitive Therapy for Depression

For cognitive behavioral therapies such as RET and therapy for depression, the client's thoughts and perceptions are related directly to maladaptive behavior. The objective of cognitive behavioral treatment is to restructure the client's irrational or illogical patterns of thinking into more constructive patterns.

HUMANISTIC APPROACHES
(587–588)

Person-Centered Therapy   Gestalt Therapy

Humanistic approaches to therapy emphasize the potential each person has for positive growth and personal self-awareness and self-actualization.

GROUP AND COMMUNITY APPROACHES *(589–593)*

Group Therapy   Community Psychology

Group, marital, family, and community approaches to therapy all assume that maladaptive behavior develops within a complex sociocultural context. Therapy can be successful only if this context is taken into consideration.

THE EFFECTIVENESS OF PSYCHOTHERAPY *(593–594)*

More than 30 years of research on psychotherapy effectiveness has yet to produce conclusive findings. Predicting the success of any therapeutic effort requires specific information about the therapist, client characteristics, and the type of therapy employed.

ETHICAL AND LEGAL ISSUES IN PSYCHOTHERAPY
(594–596)

Because the therapeutic relationship can be exploited and abused, a detailed set of ethical standards has evolved to guide therapists in their practice. These guidelines often create situations in which therapists must make difficult ethical decisions.

As members of our present culture, we may often fail to appreciate that not all societies possess the same customs and institutions. Nor, for that matter, does any culture remain unchanged over time. Witness the tremendous alteration in values and behavior brought about by the sexual revolution in our own country. More recently, we have begun to challenge traditional notions about gender roles and the proper place of the family in modern society. In fact, we would be hard put to describe any contemporary custom or ethic that has not undergone some cultural evolution.

So it is with the treatment of psychological disorders. We live in a period of time in which any psychological disorder is commonly viewed as an illness, in much the same way that a physical disease, like cancer, is an illness. Although this is not a position held by all psychologists, there is generally a consensus that maladaptive behavior, whether it springs from underlying disease processes or not, should be dealt with in a humane and understanding manner. The person whose behavior is "abnormal" is believed to be in need of help, and the emergence of techniques to provide such help has become a multi-million dollar enterprise.

Behavior that is maladaptive or that deviates from acknowledged social norms has not always met with humane compassion and empathy. In fact, the history of humankind's ignorance and maltreatment of psychological disorders is a sobering one. At different time periods, people suffering from emotional or behavioral problems were believed to be possessed by demons or were accused of being witches (Zilboorg & Henry, 1941). Those whose misfortune it was to be so labeled frequently were subjected to unspeakable torture, including the procedure of trephining, in which a small hole was punctured in the skull of the afflicted person to allow demonic spirits to escape. Even if not being physically harmed, mental patients in 16th and 17th century asylums encountered abject humiliation. Prominent citizens in London could actually purchase tickets of admission to Bethlehem hospital for the purpose of viewing the bizarre and often violent behavior of such patients (Davison & Neale, 1986)!

Humane treatment of mental patients may have been influenced by a number of factors, but it was a French physician, Phillipe Pinel (1745–1826), who is often credited with bringing about significant changes in the asylum environment during the French Revolution. Having been put in charge of a large asylum in Paris, Pinel freed patients of their iron shackles and allowed light into their previously dark chambers. Pinel contended that the patients were sick and in need of attention and understanding, not humiliation and isolation. Patients were encouraged to exercise and were allowed to interact with one another and with staff members. A general atmosphere of tolerance and hope soon replaced that of despair. Pinel's reform eventually spread, though gradually and often with resistance, throughout much of Europe.

Today, a substantial range of practices exists for the purpose of helping those suffering from emotional or behavioral problems. Certainly, such options would not be available were it not for the contemporary view that people should be given opportunities to improve their level of functioning, not ridiculed, incarcerated, or even put to death for having psychological problems. Generally, any attempt to use known psychological principles to bring about improved emotional, cognitive, or social adjustment may be referred to as **psychotherapy**. As we shall see, psychotherapy is an extremely broad term, and there are many differences not only in the form that therapy takes, but also in the practitioners who provide therapy. In this chapter, we will discuss the various forms of therapy encompassed by the major theoretical orientations in psychology, what research has shown us about the effectiveness of therapy, and some of the more intriguing legal and ethical issues that arise within the practice of therapy. Before we begin,

Phillipe Pinel

Society's treatment of people with mental disorders has not always been compassionate or humane. For example, in the seventeenth century, it was common for people to visit Bethlehem Royal Hospital, from which the word bedlam *is derived, and view the disturbed patients for entertainment.*

however, let's take a brief look at some of the reasons people may seek therapy and what types of professionals are available to provide it.

There are many reasons why people choose to contact therapists. You might be surprised to learn that therapeutic assistance is commonly sought by people whose behavior is neither psychotic, dangerous, nor in other ways gravely disturbed. In fact, most people see therapists for problems that may seem quite ordinary, but are nevertheless bothersome to the individual, such as difficulties relating to friends, parents or one's spouse, feelings of worthlessness, anxiety about taking college exams, poor sleeping or eating habits, work-related stress, or just feeling generally unfulfilled. Therapy is reserved not only for those who are suffering from a severe disorder, but for anyone interested in enhancing the quality of their lives including, perhaps, a more complete understanding of themselves. In fact, psychiatrist Thomas Szaz (1960) has suggested that the term "mental illness" is misleading and should be removed from our language. Instead, we should recognize that ordinary people encounter problems in living, and that therapy provides one means by which to deal effectively with such problems.

M

ost people see therapists for problems that may seem quite ordinary . . .

When a person has decided to seek therapy, he or she is likely to face a broad choice of practitioners. Many professionals trained to assist people with various types and degrees of problems are available. Table 16.1 describes some of the more common types of therapists, training backgrounds and degree credentials, and the general types of responsibilities each assumes. As you can see, the nature of training and the types of professional duties assumed by therapists can vary considerably. In addition, therapists often conduct therapy from particular theoretical orientations, usually those in which they were trained. Interestingly, however, research seems to suggest that the orientation (for example, psychodynamic, cognitive, behavioral) of the therapist may not be a very important factor to consider in choosing a therapist, as each orientation boasts both advantages and limitations (Smith & Glass, 1977).

We have seen throughout this book that psychologists adopt very different perspectives or world views of their subject matter. Psychoanalytic and behavioral psychologists, for example, are in considerable disagreement as to what is important about human behavior. You will recall that

TABLE 16.1. *Types of therapists, their degree credentials and training and professional responsibilities.*

TITLE	DEGREE	TRAINING BACKGROUND AND PROFESSIONAL DUTIES
Clinical Psychologist	Ph.D. or Psy.D.	Graduate training in research, diagnosis, and therapy plus one year clinical internship. Conducts assessment, therapy, clinical research, and teaching in college or university setting.
Counseling Psychologist	Ph.D., Psy.D. or Ed.D.	Graduate training in counseling. Conducts educational, vocational, and personal counseling.
Psychoanalyst	M.D.	Medical training plus specialized training in psychoanalysis. Conducts psychoanalytic therapy.
Psychiatrist	M.D.	Medical training plus psychiatry residency. Conducts diagnosis and biomedical therapy and psychotherapy.
Social Worker	M.S.W.	Graduate work in counseling and community psychology. Conducts psychotherapy; helps patients return to community.

the psychoanalytic orientation views behavior as merely symptomatic or representative of more important but frequently hidden unconscious impulses or motivations. To the behaviorist, it is the behavior and not some hypothesized underlying conflict that matters. As you might expect, differences in perspective have led to similar variations in the themes and practices of therapy. We will begin our discussion of therapy approaches by introducing methods of intervention that borrow heavily from medicine; the explicit assumption guiding such therapies is that our thoughts, emotions, and behaviors are inevitably dependent upon our biology, especially the functioning of the brain.

BIOMEDICAL APPROACHES

Biomedical therapies involve the treatment of psychological problems by directly altering the physical functioning of the brain. Biomedical therapies are distinguished from psychotherapies by the method of treatment and by who administers the treatment. Psychotherapy is often administered by physicians, psychologists, counselors, and others. Biomedical therapies, however, can only be legally administered by a medical doctor. Treatment of the body itself is the province of medicine, even when the treatment is intended to bring about psychological change. This issue is a controversial one, however, and recently psychologists have begun to argue that they should, under certain circumstances, be allowed to provide some biomedical treatment, such as drugs, for psychological problems. This plea, however, has been strongly contested by physicians (Buie, 1989).

As we discuss the various forms of biomedical therapy, keep in mind that this therapy is provided by medical practitioners, many of whom adopt the position that psychological problems are the result of some underlying disease process. As a result, the physician is likely to use such terms as "symptoms of the disease" rather than "maladaptive behavior and cognition" to describe the particular problem. The psychologist is more likely to look at the client's life experiences to explain and treat psychological problems, whereas the medical doctor is likely to treat the problem by directly changing brain functioning. As we shall see, the differences in perspectives are quite noteworthy in those situations in which treatment could be provided either through a psychological or a biomedical approach, because the consumer must choose between these two quite different, sometimes competing, perspectives. Let's now look more closely at the biomedical therapies, which include electroconvulsive therapy, psychosurgery, and drug therapy.

Electroconvulsive Therapy

Few forms of therapy are as visually dramatic or as controversial as is **electroconvulsive therapy** or **ECT,** which involves passing small amounts of electric current through the brain to produce seizure activity. ECT has been predominantly used to treat major depression in hospitalized patients. Although its controversial nature and the advent of psychoactive drugs in the 1950s and 1960s led to a decline in its popularity, ECT has recently re-emerged as a viable treatment option for some forms of depression (Sackeim, 1985). In ECT, electrodes are attached to that part of the patient's head corresponding to the temporal lobes of the brain, and the patient is given anesthesia and several drugs to reduce the likelihood of injury from the convulsions that result from the seizure. The patient receives a brief (approximately 1 second) electric current, which produces a 30 to 60 second seizure, often followed by a lapse into unconsciousness. This treatment is usually repeated several times over the course of a few weeks.

ECT's origin as a treatment can be traced to the mid-1930s when psychiatrists recognized that the condition of some hospitalized patients often suddenly improved after they experienced spontaneous seizures. In 1934 a Hungarian psychiatrist, Ladislas Meduna, treated a person with schizophrenia by deliberately inducing convulsions with drugs. Upon hearing of this work, two Italian psychiatrists who were studying epilepsy realized from their work with animals that the most straightforward way to induce brain seizures was with electric current (Cerletti & Bini, 1938). Their first attempt to apply the procedure to a schizophrenic patient met with impressive success. They reported that after nine treatments the patient recovered, and was able to live a normal life and hold a skilled job.

ECT began to be used in the United States in the 1940s, though its use was not closely regulated and many abuses occurred as patients exhibiting "incorrigible" behavior were often subjected to the procedure against their will. Today, the procedure is used only with the patient's consent, and much more care is taken to insure that the patient is not harmed by the convulsions produced by the therapy. In addition, researchers are beginning to understand more fully than they did in the 1940s how ECT might produce its therapeutic effect.

One apparent fact about ECT is that it is the seizures produced by the electric shock and not the shock itself that is therapeutic. The seizures are believed to cause the brain to release higher than normal amounts of an inhibitory neurotransmitter called gamma aminobutyric acid (GABA). GABA sharply decreases activity in the brain, including the previously overactive areas associated with depression. Thus, all of us might be susceptible to episodes of depression if, for some reason, the amount of GABA in the brain were to become depressed suddenly (Sackeim, 1985). We must note, however, that theories concerning ECT's effect on brain biochemistry are as yet inconclusive (Frankel, 1984).

Despite its reported effectiveness in treating major depression, some concerns over ECT should be noted. First, and of extreme importance, ECT is considered to be a treatment of last resort; that is, its use is justified only *after* other forms of treatment—psychotherapy or use of anti-depressant drugs—have proved ineffective. Second, a number of side effects to ECT treatment have been reported, including headaches, general disorientation, and memory loss. The extent of these side effects is still being debated. For example, while some researchers contend that memory loss is usually

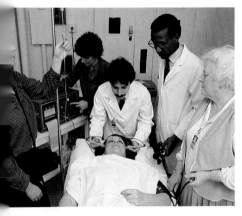

In electroconvulsive therapy, or ECT, small amounts of electric current are administered to the patient. The current induces a seizure followed by a period of unconsciousness. This type of therapy is usually given for several weeks.

slight and temporary (Martin, 1986), others argue that memory deficits are substantial and often permanent (Breggin, 1979). Because these issues are not yet settled, many psychiatrists either avoid the use of ECT altogether or use modified forms of the procedure that are believed to minimize memory loss (Squire, 1982).

Psychosurgery

Psychosurgery is unalterable brain surgery designed to relieve the symptoms of psychological disorders. The most widely practiced psychosurgery has been prefrontal lobotomy, the severing of the neurological connections between the thalamus and the frontal lobes. The first prefrontal lobotomy was performed by two Portuguese physicians, Antonio de Egas Moniz and Almeida Lima, in 1935, at almost the same time that ECT therapy was developed. Psychosurgery was adopted by physicians in the United States in the 1950s, and was most frequently performed on schizophrenic, depressed, and even occasionally on anxious patients. Although the treatment often produces a "calming effect" interpreted as therapeutic in nature, there seems to be little else to recommend it. In a follow-up study of 1000 lobotomy patients, Barahal (1958) reported a disturbingly high rate of negative side effects, including emotional listlessness, cognitive deficits, and even death.

The era of the prefrontal lobotomy in American psychiatry is something of an embarrassment to the profession and a tragedy to many thousands of patients. Not only did no one know precisely how the procedure was supposed to cure psychological disorders, but the few studies addressing its effectiveness cast much doubt on whether it worked at all. The technique was often used on virtually any patient whose behavior was problematic or irritating to the hospital staff. There was no real effort made to delineate the specific symptoms that might be alleviated by psychosurgery.

Several hundred lobotomies are still performed each year in the United States, though the operation today is only performed under stringent and highly controlled medical conditions. The early assembly-line procedures have been abandoned, and full consent from the patient and family are now first obtained. Also, as with ECT, psychosurgical procedures are employed only under rare circumstances, as when psychotherapy or drug therapy has proven ineffective.

Drug Therapy

Up to this point we have discussed two biomedical therapies—ECT and psychosurgery—both of which have declined drastically in use since the 1950s. This decline is due not only to their negative side effects, distastefulness, and questionable effectiveness, but also because of the rise of a generally more effective biomedical technique. **Drug therapy,** the treatment of psychological problems with chemical agents, is by far the most widely used form of biomedical therapy. Although abuses have also occurred, drug therapy heralded a revolution in the treatment of psychological problems.

Table 16.2 lists some of the more common drugs used to alter psychological functioning, their generic names, and their more recognizable trade names. Each of these drugs chemically alters brain function, resulting in a reduction of symptoms pertaining to the relevant problem, whether it be schizophrenia, depression, or anxiety. Drugs used to treat psychological problems fall into four general classes: antipsychotic drugs, antidepressant drugs, antianxiety drugs, and antimanic drugs. Next, we will examine each class of drugs.

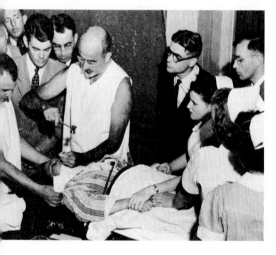

Psychosurgery was widely performed in the United States in the 1950s. Pictured here is a demonstration of a transorbital lobotomy being performed after ECT was administered to the patient. Tragically, this procedure caused negative side effects in many patients.

TABLE 16.2.	Common drugs used to treat psychological problems.		
THERAPEUTIC FUNCTION	CLASS OF DRUGS	GENERIC NAME	TRADE NAME
Antipsychotic	Soporific Nonsoporific Phenothiazines	*Chlorpromazine* Acetophenazine Thioridazine Fluphenazine Trifluoperazine Perphenazine	Thorazine Tindal Mellaril Permitil Stelazine Trilafon
Antidepressant	Butyrophenones Tricyclics Monoamine oxidase inhibitors	Haloperidol Imipramine Amitryptiline Phenelzine Tranylcypromine	Haldol Tofranil Elavil Nardil Parnate
Antianxiety	Propanediols Benzodiazepines	Meprobamate Chlordiazepoxide Diazepam	Miltown Librium Valium
Antimanic	Lithium salts	*Lithium carbonate*	Eskalith Lithane

Antipsychotic Drugs. Chemicals referred to as antipsychotic drugs are used to treat the cognitive and emotional disturbances and perceptual hallucinations of schizophrenia and other psychotic disorders. Used since the mid-1950s, antipsychotic medications drastically altered the deplorable conditions previously characterizing many psychiatric institutions, as seen in the writings of a hospital superintendent.

> The atmosphere of disturbed wards has been completely revolutionized. Patients now remain clothed; they are quiet, they do not annoy each other; they conform to the conventions, take an interest in their personal appearance and in the appearance of the ward. (Overholser, 1956, p. 199)

The drug that began this revolution in psychiatry is *chlorpromazine*, a member of the class of drugs referred to as phenothiazines. The chemical was first synthesized by a German chemist in 1883 while conducting research for the emerging artificial dye industry (Swazey, 1974). The dramatic effect of chlorpromazine on hospitalized patients soon silenced the skeptical voices of practitioners who had remained loyal to ECT and psychosurgery. Including the phenothiazines, several other major families of antipsychotic drugs are used today, which is fortunate because some patients who respond to drugs from one family may not respond to drugs from other families (Torrey, 1988).

Drugs tend to keep the major symptoms of the problem in check, but they do not in any sense "cure" the patient.

Despite their obvious advantages, the antipsychotic drugs have their own shortcomings. First, not everyone responds positively to the drugs. Second, the drugs tend to keep the major symptoms of the problem in check, but they do not in any sense "cure" the patient. In the words of one psychiatrist, "Drugs do not cure, but rather control, the symptoms of schizophrenia" (Torrey, 1988, pp. 186–187).

Further, as with most drugs, undesirable side effects are often associated with the use of antipsychotic drugs. For example, approximately 20 percent of older patients develop untreatable and irreversible muscle tremors, resulting in continual involuntary lip smacking, and grimacing and drooling, a condition known as tardive dyskinesia (APA Task Force, 1980). The cause of this side effect is known to be related to the biochemistry of the antipsychotics. As we saw in a previous chapter, the phenothiazines work by blocking dopamine receptors in the brain. After years of exposure to the drugs, however, the dopamine receptors in the patient's brain that help to control bodily movement begin to overcompensate for the blockage by becoming more sensitive to dopamine. The symptoms of tardive dyskinesia unfortunately may remain even if the drugs are no longer administered, though they seldom worsen if the drugs continue to be taken.

Antidepressant Drugs. Also discovered by accident was a class of drugs used to treat the symptoms of major depression, the antidepressants. The most widely used antidepressant drugs come from the family of chemicals known as tricyclics (Lickey & Gordon, 1983). Because their chemical structure is similar to that of the phenothiazines, tricyclics were used on the hunch that they might provide an effective treatment for schizophrenia. Although their use as an antipsychotic was quickly dismissed, researchers observed that they did tend to elevate mood, suggesting their potential use as an antidepressant.

Although the biology of depression is not yet completely understood, the most widely accepted theory is that depression may result from a deficiency of one or two neurotransmitters in the brain: norepinephrine or serotonin. Not surprisingly, the antidepressants are believed to work by interfering with the function of these neurotransmitters. The tricyclics seem to slow down the reuptake or reabsorption of these neurotransmitters by presynaptic axons. The outcome of these biochemical processes can be rather dramatic. Though they do not work for all people, many whose deep depression has brought despair and little joy or purpose to life, gradually return to normal after having been placed on tricyclics for several weeks (Prien, 1984).

Antianxiety Drugs. Antianxiety drugs are used in the treatment of phobias, obsessions, compulsions, panic attacks, and other anxiety related problems. The extreme popularity of antianxiety drugs, or minor tranquilizers as they are sometimes called, such as Librium, Valium, or other benzodiazepines, is indicated by large numbers of prescriptions filled for these drugs in the United States and Europe. In 1978 Valium was the most frequently prescribed of any drug, and Librium was third (Rickels, 1978).

Before the benzodiazepines were synthesized in the early 1960s, the only existing effective antianxiety drugs had been the barbiturates, which are addicting. The immediate success of Valium and Librium was due in part to the belief that these newer drugs were not addictive (Lickey & Gordon, 1983). Unfortunately, though they are the safest of antianxiety drugs available, researchers have found that the benzodiazepines can also be addictive (Winokur, 1980). Taken in low dosages and for short periods of time, however, benzodiazepines can be effective means of reducing anxiety without much risk of addiction.

Antimanic Drugs. The antimanic drugs are those used to reduce manic behaviors, including excessive levels of activity, racing thoughts, and rapid and often incoherent speech. The most commonly prescribed drug of this type is *lithium carbonate,* an inorganic salt whose sedating effect was first discovered in guinea pigs in the 1940s (Cade, 1949). Its main clinical application is not in reducing manic symptoms. Instead, lithium alleviates the rapid mood swings characteristic of a bipolar disorder (Prien, Kupfer, Mansky, Small, Tuason, Voss, & Johnson, 1984).

As is true of many of the other drugs discussed so far, researchers are not yet certain of how lithium produces its therapeutic effect. One suggestion has been that the drug alters the release of certain amino acid neurotransmitters (Fieve, 1979), while other researchers believe that the drug simply compensates for deficient supplies of lithium in the cell membranes of people suffering from bipolar disorder (Dorus, Pandey, Shaughnessy, Gaviria, Val, Ericksen, & Davis, 1979). We do know that lithium is a drug whose dosage must be very carefully monitored. Symptoms such as loss of appetite, nausea, vomiting, diarrhea, dizziness, tremors, and blurred vision are signals that the patient's blood lithium level is too high and must be adjusted (Honigfeld & Howard, 1978).

Taken together, the biomedical therapies represent one means by which to reduce the symptoms of psychological disorders. Of course, each type of therapy entails some potential risks, as our discussions have demonstrated. Consequently, biomedical therapies should in general be viewed as methods to employ only after less intrusive therapies have been attempted. We now turn to a discussion of the psychotherapies, which are based not upon medical or biological knowledge but on basic psychological principles. We will begin by examining the psychodynamic approach, perhaps most responsible for establishing psychotherapy as an institution of importance and influence in American culture (Albee, 1977).

PSYCHODYNAMIC APPROACHES

In the late 1800s, the Austrian physician Joseph Breuer consulted with a younger medical colleague on the unusual case of a female who reported a number of bizarre, disabling symptoms, including a violent repulsion of water. While under hypnosis, the woman revealed to Breuer an episode in which she had encountered her governess's dog drinking water from a bowl. She eventually admitted a disliking not only for the dog, but for its owner, though she had never expressed her feelings prior to her session with Breuer. After coming out of the trance, she reported no repulsion of water and was able to drink it without incident. She referred to this rather amazing occurrence as "the talking cure," though Breuer preferred to call it "the cathartic method," meaning a purging or purification.

The younger colleague to whom Breuer related this incident was a promising young Viennese physician, Sigmund Freud. Freud was fascinated by the account of the "talking cure," for he had recently returned from the University of Paris where he had attended lectures by the noted pathologist Jean Charcot. Charcot's lectures had concerned hypnosis, a trance-like state induced by the physician for the purpose of treating patients who exhibited physical symptoms but no underlying organic

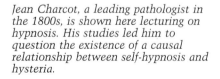

Jean Charcot, a leading pathologist in the 1800s, is shown here lecturing on hypnosis. His studies led him to question the existence of a causal relationship between self-hypnosis and hysteria.

pathology. Out of Breuer's and Freud's friendship and collaboration was born the practice of **psychoanalysis,** a therapy aimed at providing the client insight into unconscious motivations and impulses. Ironically, to hear Freud tell it, he was hardly the person responsible for the founding of psychoanalysis:

> Granted that it is a merit to have created psychoanalysis, it is not my merit. I was a student, busy with the passing of my last examinations, when another physician of Vienna, Dr. Joseph Breuer, made the first application of this method to the case of a hysterical girl.

(1910, p. 1)

It was Freud, however, who would develop the practice of psychoanalysis and forever change the way we look at the unconscious. Freud's contribution to psychology and to modern thought has been immense, if also controversial. Recall that his theory of personality suggests that unconscious conflicts based on the competing demands of the id (representing biological urges), the superego (representing the moral dictates of society), and the ego (representing reality) often lead to anxiety. The source of this conflict, according to Freud, can usually be traced back to unacceptable, often sexually-based urges from early childhood—impulses and feelings whose explicit memory has been repressed but which lead to conscious anxiety.

Psychoanalysis is referred to as an insight therapy because its goal is to provide the client with insight into unconscious conflicts. The individual may, for example, come to understand that his belittling of a colleague is based on jealously of the colleague's accomplishments, accompanied by his own feelings of inadequacy—feelings that were previously denied and repressed. As Freud explained,

> One of the tasks of psychoanalysis . . . is to lift the veil of amnesia which hides the earliest years of childhood and to bring to conscious memory the manifestations of early infantile sexual life which are contained in them.

(1933, p. 26)

This "veil" is not easily lifted in the early stages of therapy because both the analyst and the client are unaware of the underlying conflicts. The repression of these conflicts is seldom complete, however, and they frequently intrude into consciousness in ways that are often subtle or obscure; thus their meaning may not be obvious. By encouraging the client to talk, the analyst tries to bring certain conflicting themes and hidden meanings into view. The obscurity of the conflicts, however, requires the analyst to interpret them in order to uncover their true meaning, gradually weaving together a complete picture of the unconscious—much like Sherlock Holmes gradually piecing together the clues of a mystery until, at last, he reveals who committed the crime.

Psychodynamic Techniques

Although Freud was originally quite enthusiastic about hypnosis as a therapeutic aid, he eventually came to realize that it played neither a necessary nor always a desirable role in the psychoanalytic process. Instead, Freud felt that the client should be able to speak freely, without censoring possibly embarrassing or socially unacceptable thoughts or ideas. This process is called **free association.** Freud achieved this goal in two ways. First, the client was encouraged to report any thoughts or images that came to mind, without worrying about their content or meaning. Second, Freud attempted to minimize any authoritative influence over the client's disclosures, usually by sitting in a chair at the head of a couch and having the client recline on the couch in such a way as to eliminate eye contact.

Among the topics clients are encouraged to discuss are their dreams. **Dream interpretation,** the evaluation of the underlying meaning of dream content is a hallmark of psychoanalysis (Freud, 1900). But even dream content is subject to some censoring according to Freud, so that the analyst must be able to distinguish between the dream's manifest and latent content. The **manifest content** of a dream is the actual images and events occurring within the dream, whereas the **latent content** is the hidden meaning or underlying significance of the dream. The analyst must be especially skilled in recognizing the symbolic nature of dreams, for things are not always as they appear. For example, the client may relate the image of a growling, vicious dog chasing him or her down the street. The dog may actually symbolize an angry parent or spouse, though this idea may be so painful to the client that it has been disguised within the dream. The practice of bringing the client to an appreciation of the latent content of the dream is an important step toward insight.

Of course, insight is not achieved quickly, nor do clients always find it easy to disclose private aspects of their personal lives. In fact, there is something of a dilemma involved in achieving insight, for the often painful or threatening knowledge resulting from insight is precisely what led to its repression in the first place. For example, the client may have to confront the reality of being abused as a child, or of being unloved, or of feeling peculiar, inferior, or out of place. Though the client wishes to be cured, he or she does not look forward to the anxiety and apprehension that may result from painful memories brought to conscious awareness. So the client often becomes defensive at some point during the therapy, unconsciously attempting to halt further insight by censoring his or her true feelings, a process Freud called **resistance.**

Resistance may be indicated when the client tries to change the topic, begins to miss appointments for therapy, or suddenly forgets what he or she was about to say. The client may even act cured, and perhaps believes in the "cure," just to avoid getting closer to the real truth. The skilled therapist, who is not burdened by the client's resistances and defenses, recognizes such diversions and redirects the discussion to the sensitive topics while minimizing the pain of discovery.

Over a period of months or even years of therapy as often as several times a week, the client gradually becomes less inhibited, and the discussion begins to drift away from recent events to the more distant but crucial shores of early childhood. As the client relives aspects of childhood, he or she may begin to project powerful attitudes and emotions onto the therapist, a process called **transference.** The client may come to love or hate the therapist with the same intensity of the powerful emotions experienced in childhood toward parents or siblings.

Originally, Freud thought of transference as an impediment to therapy, a distraction from the real issues at hand. But he soon realized that the experience of transference was essential to the success of therapy (Erdelyi, 1985). Where free association uncovers many of the relevant events and facts of the client's life, transference provides the means for reliving the significant early experiences. The therapist contributes to these relived experiences by becoming a substitute for the real players in the drama of the client's life, and thus becomes a tool for illuminating the conflicts of the unconscious mind.

Interestingly, Freud reasoned that the analyst, being human too, could just as easily project his or her emotions onto the client, a process he called **countertransference.** Unlike transference, Freud believed countertransference to be an unhealthy and undesirable development during analysis. To be effective, the analyst must remain emotionally detached and objective in his or her appraisal of the client's disclosures. For this reason, he argued that the analyst, in order to understand his or her own unconscious conflicts, should undergo complete analysis at the hands of another therapist. This recommendation was to become a standard requirement among physicians who wished to become psychoanalysts.

Although Freud was not the first to talk about the unconscious mind (Whyte, 1979), he was the first to develop a significant theory of abnormal behavior and an equally influential therapy designed to uncover its complexities. Through the processes of free association and dream interpretation, the psychoanalyst takes the patient through a slow and sometimes painful process of discovery. The ultimate objective is to offer the client insight into the unconscious motives that underlie behavior and to demonstrate how these motives contribute to psychological functioning. Psychoanalysis remains a force among contemporary therapeutic practices even a century after its founding, though, as we shall see in the next section, its practice has undergone and continues to undergo substantial modification.

Psychoanalysis remains a force among contemporary therapeutic practices even a century after its founding . . .

Psychodynamic Therapy and the Neo-Freudians

Despite the controversial nature of Freud's theories, he eventually developed a devoted following of physicians and scholars who would oversee the establishment of psychoanalysis as an internationally recognized method of treatment. However, psychoanalysis underwent considerable change at the hands of Freud's followers. Two particularly important colleagues of Freud, Carl Jung and Alfred Adler, would go on to found separate schools of psychology which, though borrowing many concepts from psychoanalytic theory, broke much new theoretical ground.

This second generation of psychoanalysts, called Neo-Freudians, gradually departed more and more from classic psychoanalytic theory, though even modern forms of psychodynamic therapies still focus on achieving insight into unconscious conflicts. The methods by which insight is obtained, however, are often quite different from those of traditional psychoanalysis. For example, modern psychodynamic therapy tends to place less emphasis on sexual factors during development and more upon social or interpersonal experience. Second, contemporary therapists are more likely to address concerns and issues in the client's present life as opposed to examining childhood experiences exclusively. Finally, although Freud considered analysis to be an extremely involved and demanding process, often requiring years to complete, today's therapists feel much can be gained by shortening the process, for example, minimizing the client's over-dependence on the therapist. For this reason, psychodynamic therapy as presently practiced does not always take years to complete.

All forms of psychodynamic therapies share in common an interest in unconscious processes, and there is an important corollary that attaches itself to this emphasis: Behavior or overt action is seldom important by itself. Rather, behavior is only important to the extent that it serves as a manifestation or representation of the real, underlying motive or conflict. But not all professionals who conduct therapy would agree with this claim. We look next at a therapeutic orientation that views behavior change by itself to be the only appropriate objective of therapy.

BEHAVIORAL APPROACHES

As we have seen in earlier chapters, behavior analysis is the psychological perspective that focuses on the study of overt behavior, particularly on how this behavior is learned as a consequence of contingencies of reinforcement in the environment. According to Franks and Wilson, **behavior therapy**

> involves primarily the application of principles derived from research in experimental and social psychology for the alleviation of human suffering and the enhancement of human functioning.
>
> (1975, p. 1)

The fundamental assumption made by the behavior therapist is that maladaptive or self-defeating behavior is learned in the same way as are more adaptive behaviors. Solving the behavior problem is a matter of eliminating the undesirable behavior and bringing about, through conditioning, new and constructive ways of behaving. For the behavior therapist, the undesirable behavior is the problem, not just a reflection of the problem. The methods that behavior therapists use to bring about behavior change are extensions of the conditioning principles we discussed in Chapter 7, namely classical and operant conditioning. Quite literally, Pavlov's study of the conditional salivary reflex in dogs and Skinner's research on operant behavior in pigeons and rats have resulted in effective techniques for improving the quality of life for many people.

Behavior Therapy Based on Classical Conditioning

Remember that in classical conditioning, a previously neutral stimulus (ultimately the CS) comes to elicit the same response as a stimulus that naturally elicits the response (UCS) because the CS reliably predicts the UCS. How might this process be relevant to human behavior, especially abnormal behavior? According to Joseph Wolpe (1958), one of the founders of behavior therapy, many of our everyday fears and anxieties become associated with neutral stimuli through coincidence. Here's an illustration of how this might happen. Suppose you are involved in a serious car accident and although you aren't hurt seriously, you are emotionally upset for some time afterwards. In climbing back into a car for the first time after the accident, a sudden feeling of sheer terror comes over you. You begin to perspire and breathe heavily, you feel like you are about to pass out, and it's all you can do to get out of the car without screaming for help. In fact, you find that even approaching a car produces a sense of panic. Your anxiety in response to anything having to do with cars may be due to a classical conditioning process in which the pain and fear associated with the wreck (the UCS) is associated with cars (CS).

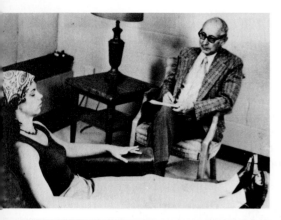

Joseph Wolpe, shown here with a patient, found that certain fears and anxieties could be treated using systematic desensitization, in which a person is trained to relax in the presence of increasingly fearful stimuli.

Systematic Desensitization. Even though research has shown that most anxieties and phobias are not the result of any noticeable traumatic episodes (Murray & Foote, 1979), the process of classical conditioning provides the foundation on which treatment of such problems rests (Ollendick & Francis, 1988). In **systematic desensitization,** for example, the subject is trained to relax in the presence of increasingly fear-evoking stimuli. The procedure begins with the development of a hierarchy of fear, a list of stimuli rank ordered from least to most anxiety-evoking. Table 16.3 shows a representative hierarchy of fear for our example of the car accident. Next, the client is taught to relax various muscle groups throughout the body systematically, a technique known as progressive muscle relaxation. The final step in treatment is to pair the relaxation with a gradual exposure to the hierarchy of fear. Learning to relax in the presence of anxiety-evoking stimuli is incompatible with a fear response, thus a new and more adaptive response has taken the place of the undesirable anxiety reaction.

Aversion Therapy. In systematic desensitization, the client is taught to respond positively to the presence of stimuli that originally produced fear and anxiety. In **aversion therapy,** just the opposite occurs: a negative reaction to a neutral stimulus is brought about by pairing it with an aversive stimulus (UCS). One of aversion therapy's first applications was in the treatment of alcoholism. The first such treatments used nausea-inducing chemicals such as emetine paired with the social and behavioral cues that accompany drinking. The initial results seemed promising (Lemere & Voegtlin, 1950; Raymond, 1964); however, the procedure often included presentation of the nausea-inducing chemical first, then the drinking cues. This is an example of a backward conditioning method, and researchers eventually questioned its effectiveness (Rachman & Teasdale, 1969; Farrar, Powell, & Martin, 1968).

In an improvement on the aversive conditioning method, clients are required to ingest a chemical called antabuse which, when mixed with alcohol, produces nausea and vomiting. The pairing of the aversive or noxious stimulus with drinking cues does not occur, of course, unless the client actually takes a drink after ingesting the antabuse. This method stems largely from research on taste aversion in animals (Garcia & Koelling, 1966), in which avoidance of a nausea-inducing chemical develops even when the nausea follows ingestion of the chemical by several hours. Although this procedure has advantages over the earlier aversive conditioning methods, it is not without shortcomings. The major limitation of the antabuse procedure is that some clients may have medical conditions, such as heart disease, that make use of the nausea-inducing chemical potentially dangerous (O'Brien & Chafetz, 1982). On an optimistic note, one study has shown that in conjunction with other forms of treatment, 63

TABLE 16.3. *Hierarchy of fear for car stimuli.*

Lowest fear evoking stimuli
1. Reading word *car* in magazine article.
2. Seeing picture of car in advertisement.
3. Imagining riding in car.
4. Seeing other person drive car.
5. Physically approaching car.
6. Opening door of car to get in.
7. Getting behind wheel of car to start engine.
8. Driving car and entering traffic.
Highest fear evoking stimuli

percent of clients who underwent aversion therapy for alcoholism were still abstaining from alcohol three years later (Wiens & Menustik, 1983).

Quite obviously, aversive therapy represents a dramatic and sometimes quite intrusive form of treatment. For this reason, it is often used as a last resort when other less extreme therapies have failed. At the same time, however, its merits should not be ignored, especially when dealing with certain problematic behaviors like alcoholism.

Behavior Therapy Based on Operant Conditioning

You will remember that in Chapter 7 we defined operant behavior as behavior that is acquired and maintained because of its consequences. **Behavior modification,** a general term describing therapy based on operant conditioning principles, involves altering maladaptive behavior by rearranging the contingencies between behavior and its consequences. Increases in desirable behavior can be brought about either through positive or negative reinforcement, and reduction of undesirable behavior can be achieved either through extinction or punishment.

In its infancy behavior modification was applied to rather restricted client populations and behavior problems, including schizophrenic patients and the mentally retarded (Lindsley, 1956; Ayllon & Azrin, 1968; Neisworth & Madle, 1982). In the past two decades, however, use of operant principles has been extended to a wide array of behaviors and circumstances, not just those indicating maladaptive functioning. Contemporary behavior modification, for example, has addressed such diverse concerns as educational curricula and teaching methods, proper fire escape behavior in children, promotion of seat belt use by drivers, energy conservation, weight management, smoking cessation, and compliance to important medical regimens (Kazdin, 1988). In fact, there are few facets of our behavior and everyday experiences that have not received attention by behavioral researchers and therapists. Next, we take a closer look at some of the behavior modification procedures that have been used to bring about more adaptive forms of behavior.

Reinforcement. Reinforcement, as you may recall, is a process by which behavior is strengthened because of its consequences. Almost all behavior modification efforts depend in large part on the process of reinforcing appropriate or adaptive behavior. A classic example of a behavior modification program utilizing reinforcement is the **token economy,** a setting in which clients—often psychiatric patients or delinquents or inmates in correctional facilities—are allowed to earn tokens through appropriate behavior. These tokens are conditioned reinforcers and can be exchanged for individually valued items or privileges, such as special foods, candies, or recreational activities. The first token economy was established in the early 1960s at Anna State Hospital in Illinois (Ayllon & Azrin, 1968). Special care was taken to teach the institutional staff how to attend and properly respond to appropriate and inappropriate behavior in patients. Through careful monitoring and consistent reinforcement of socially desirable and adaptive behavior, significant improvement in daily functioning was obtained. Token economies have since been widely used within institutional settings, though ironically, it is the institutional setting itself which represents the token economy's major limitation. Research has shown that change reliably produced within the institutional setting frequently does not transfer to noninstitutional settings, most likely because the consequences of behavior differ in the natural environment (Kazdin, 1977).

Modifying behavior requires the use of reinforcement. In a token economy, clients earn tokens for appropriate behavior. The tokens, in turn, may be exchanged for some other valued item or privilege. Here, a patient displays her record showing the tokens she's earned.

Extinction. Recall that extinction is the process through which behavior is eliminated by removing previously available reinforcers. While it is seldom used by itself to combat undesirable behavior, extinction is often combined with other methods in behavior modification programs. For example, extinction might be used to eliminate the tantrum behavior of a child in a supermarket. If it is likely that this behavior has met with frequent reinforcement—parents or others attending to the child and perhaps giving in to his or her wishes—extinction might include ignoring this undesirable behavior. In fact, extinction has been used to reduce a number of maladaptive behaviors, including the delusional speech of psychiatric patients (Liberman, Teigen, Patterson, & Baker, 1973), inappropriately "feminine" play in a male child (Rekers & Lovaas, 1974), and even aggressive behavior in preschool classrooms (Pinkston, Reese, LeBlanc, & Baer, 1973).

There are two potential problems that confront behavior therapists when using extinction. One is that of extinction burst. When a reinforcer that has previously followed a behavior is no longer forthcoming, the behavior will often intensify. You can imagine, for example, how the child whose tantrum behavior usually meets with social attention will likely increase his or her efforts to obtain these reinforcers during the early stages of extinction. Fortunately, extinction burst is temporary and if the extinction procedure is carried out, behavior generally diminishes. The other limitation to using extinction is that it isn't always possible to eliminate the reinforcer that maintains undesirable behavior. For example, aggressive behavior in the classroom may meet with reinforcement through the peer group, so attempts by a teacher to extinguish aggression may be only minimally effective.

Punishment. Another means of reducing or eliminating undesirable or maladaptive behavior is through punishment, which involves presentation of an aversive stimulus immediately following the undesirable behavior. Punishing stimuli can range from physically aversive events like electric shock, loud noises, or a puff of air blown into the face, to the more frequently used conditioned punishers of verbal reprimands, looks of disapproval, or the use of fines and penalties. When used properly, punishment can bring about rapid reductions in undesirable behavior, making it preferable to extinction under some circumstances which often takes much longer. However, several negative side effects have been associated with punishment, including emotional reactions in the client, attempts by the client to avoid the punishing person, and physical aggression in response to punishment (Kazdin, 1988).

The use of punishment in any form is quite controversial and is opposed by many people. The controversy surrounding the use of aversive stimuli involves not only psychologists, but political involvement by government agencies, Congress, and state legislatures. Bills have been introduced and sometimes passed at the state level that explicitly prohibit their use. As an assistant secretary of education and an assistant attorney general wrote, "We ask, as a number of behavioral psychologists have asked us, whether society can sanction for use with disabled citizens forms of punishment, such as electric shock, that would never be tolerated for use with nonhandicapped children and adults" (Will & Reynolds, 1988).

Some psychologists, however, including the person most responsible for the development of operant conditioning techniques, B. F. Skinner, support the judicious use of punishment in some situations. In Skinner's words:

> Punishment is usually used to the advantage of the punisher, but there are exceptions, and they can sometimes be justified. Some autistic children, for example, will seriously injure themselves unless drugged or restrained,

and other treatment is then virtually impossible. If brief and harmless aversive stimuli, made precisely contingent on self-destructive behavior, suppress the behavior and leave the children to develop in other ways, I believe it can be justified. When taken out of context, such stimuli may seem less than humane, but they are not to be distinguished from the much more painful stimuli sometimes needed in dentistry and various medical practices. To remain satisfied with punishment without exploring nonpunitive alternatives is the real mistake.

(1988, p. 2)

Also supporting Skinner's position is Ivar Lovaas (Lovaas, 1987; Lovaas, Koegel, Simmons, & Long, 1973; Lovaas & Simmons, 1969), who has for more than two decades applied behavior therapy, including punishment to one of the more bizarre and misunderstood of behavior problems, autism. Autism is a severe childhood disorder characterized by extreme social isolation, repetitive and stereotyped movements and often, self-injurious behaviors such as scratching, biting, gouging of the eyes, and head banging. We are not yet sure of its causes, and traditional therapy techniques have proved virtually useless in alleviating autistic symptoms. Lovaas, though, has demonstrated that an intensive behavioral program including social reinforcement and punishment of self-injurious behavior can bring about behavioral improvements once thought impossible in autistic children. Frequently, therapy entails use of electric shock as a punisher for self-injurious behavior, though patients do not receive large numbers of shocks.

*S*ocial learning theory argues that . . . we acquire a good deal of behavior merely by observing others . . .

In fact, if the technique is not almost immediately effective, it is usually discarded and other methods are employed. In deciding for yourself whether such therapy is justifiable, keep in mind the alternative ways of dealing with self-injurious behavior mentioned above by Skinner. What options would you exercise if you were the therapist?

Modeling. A recent development in behavior therapy has emerged from social learning theory, particularly as described in the writings of Albert Bandura (1977). Social learning theory argues that not all of our behavior occurs as the direct result of reinforcing or punishing consequences. Instead, we acquire a good deal of behavior merely by observing others, a phenomenon, which you may recall, is known as observational learning. Observational learning can be used by a therapist in a procedure called **modeling,** in which the client observes another person, the model, engaging in the appropriate behavior and then imitates this same behavior. Frequently, modeling involves reinforcing consequences for the model's behavior, and the client learns that appropriate behavior can result in reinforcement. For example, administering praise to handicapped children for

Bandura's theory of modeling can be used to help people suffering from phobias. By observing people handling snakes, those who once feared snakes overcome that fear.

engaging in social interaction in a classroom led to increases in social interaction in children who observed others being praised, but were not themselves praised (Strain, Shores, & Kerr, 1976). This tendency to engage in behaviors because we have seen the behavior of others reinforced for the same behavior is referred to as vicarious reinforcement.

Bandura's (1977) work was in part responsible for changing the emphasis of contemporary psychology from analyzing only behavior to also considering the person's cognitive interpretations of a situation. Observational learning can occur, after all, only if someone is an active observer of the situation, cognitively applying elements of the observed situation to himself or herself. In fact, the major elements of social learning theory have recently been combined with traditional cognitive research to bring about a therapeutic orientation enthusiastically adopted by many contemporary practitioners.

COGNITIVE BEHAVIORAL APPROACHES

Albert Ellis

All therapy has as its objective a change in the behavior of the client. The behavior therapist, of course, believes that behavior change is related to changes in the environment and altering the environmental variables related to behavior is both a necessary and sufficient treatment method. Practitioners of **cognitive behavior therapy,** however, believe that often a change in behavior is best brought about by altering the client's thoughts, beliefs, and perceptions about the environment rather than focusing exclusively on the external environment per se. The cognitive behavior therapist believes that thoughts lead directly to behavior; specifically, maladaptive behavior results from self-defeating thoughts. Behavior change is accomplished by what is called **cognitive restructuring**; negative thoughts are replaced with more constructive ways of thinking. That is, the client learns new, more effective ways of thinking that lead directly to more appropriate behavior.

Just as there are many types of psychodynamic therapy, cognitive behavior therapy takes many forms, each differing in accordance with the orientation of the therapist. We will discuss two of the more prominent forms of cognitive behavior therapy: Ellis's rational-emotive therapy and Beck's cognitive therapy for depression.

Rational-Emotive Therapy

While a practicing therapist in the early 1950s, Albert Ellis's disenchantment with psychoanalysis led him to develop a new method of therapy called rational-emotive therapy. **Rational-emotive therapy (RET)** is based on the belief that psychological distress such as anxiety and depression is not caused by upsetting events, but rather by how people think about such events. For example, after losing his or her job, the person might become depressed. The reason for the depression is not the job loss per se—but the irrational conclusion formed after losing the job that, for example, "I am worthless." Curing the depression hinges on replacing these inappropriate thoughts with more adaptive and realistic thoughts.

According to Ellis (1962, 1984), irrational thoughts and ideas are responsible for much of the unhappiness that leads many to therapy. He has referred to specific problem-causing thoughts as irrational beliefs. He tries to show his clients that beliefs such as the following (Ellis, 1973, pp. 152–153) are impossible to satisfy, that they make little logical sense, and that adhering to these beliefs creates needless anxiety, self-blame, and self-doubt.

- The idea that it is a necessity for an adult to be loved or approved by virtually every significant person in the community.
- The idea that one should be thoroughly competent, adequate, and goal oriented in all possible respects if one is to consider oneself as having worth.
- The idea that human unhappiness is externally caused and that people have little or no ability to control their sorrows and disturbances.
- The idea that one's past history is an all-important determinant of one's present behavior . . .
- The idea that there is invariably a right, precise, and perfect solution to human problems and that it is catastrophic if this perfect solution is not found . . .

The central tenet of RET is that it is these irrational beliefs that cause people to feel and behave badly. In RET, the therapist is quite likely to confront the client in order to demonstrate the irrationality of the client's beliefs. This may include requiring the client to examine basic assumptions about him or herself. The therapist then attempts to convince the client to realize the irrational and often impossible demands that such beliefs make on the person.

One client, for example, complained that his wife accused him of unfaithfulness, which led the client to feel angry and hurt because the accusations were "untrue and so unfair." Ellis (1973) then tried to show the client how it was not the accusations that led to his anger and hurt. Ellis directly confronted the client with the question, "How could her false accusations do anything whatever to you?" He reminded the client that his not liking the accusations had nothing to do with his wife's decision to make them. In other words, Ellis wanted his client to understand that other people do not act so as to satisfy someone else's likes or dislikes. The client was then led to see what really upset him was his own irrational premise, not the accusations. Once the beliefs or thoughts have been restructured, more effective patterns of behavior can be established.

Cognitive Therapy for Depression

Aaron Beck (1967) has developed a therapy for depression that shares with Ellis's RET therapy the emphasis on the client's beliefs, interpretations, and perceptions. Beck's cognitive therapy, however, focuses more on the faulty logic than on the beliefs themselves; the negative beliefs are seen as conclusions based on faulty logic. A depressed person concludes that he or she is "deprived, frustrated, humiliated, rejected or punished ('losers,' in the vernacular)" (Beck & Shaw, 1977, p. 120). As you may recall from the last chapter, Beck describes the cognitions of the depressed individual in terms of a "cognitive triad": a negative view of the self ("I am worthless"), of the outside world ("The world makes impossible demands on me"), and of the future ("Things are never going to get better").

Even when confronted with evidence that contradicts their negative beliefs, depressed individuals often find an illogical means of interpreting good news as bad news.

How does a depressed person maintain these negative beliefs over a long period of time? After all, occasionally he or she must do something right. Even when confronted with evidence that contradicts their negative beliefs, however, depressed individuals often find an illogical means of interpreting good news as bad news (Lewinsohn, Mischel, Chaplin, & Barton, 1980). For example, a student who receives an A on an exam might

Aaron Beck, pictured here with a client, uses cognitive therapy to reverse the negative attitudes people suffering from depression place on themselves. By showing the faulty logic that leads to a client's negative beliefs, the therapist can then work toward reversing those beliefs.

attribute the high grade to an easy, unchallenging exam, rather than to his or her own mastery of the material. The fact that few other people in the class received *A*s does little to convince the depressed person that he or she deserves congratulations for having done well. The depressed student goes on believing, against evidence to the contrary, that the good grade was a mistake and not really deserved.

In cognitive therapy, the therapist tries to convince the depressed individual that his or her misconceptions are illogical. Once the faulty logic is recognized for what it is, therapy entails exploring means for correcting the distortions. Consider the following example from an actual therapy session.

A woman who complained of severe headache and other somatic disturbances was found to [be very depressed]. When asked about the cognitions that seemed to make her unhappy, she said, "My family doesn't appreciate me;" "Nobody appreciates me, they take me for granted"; "I am worthless."

As an example she stated that her adolescent children no longer wanted to do things with her. Although this particular statement could very well have been accurate, the therapist decided to determine its authenticity. He pursued the "evidence" for the statement in the following interchange:

Patient: My son doesn't like to go to the theatre or to the movies with me anymore.

Therapist: How do you know he doesn't want to go with you?

P: Teenagers don't actually like to do things with their parents.

T: Have you actually asked him to go with you?

P: No, as a matter of fact, he did ask me a few times if I wanted him to take me . . . but I didn't think he really wanted to go.

T: How about testing it out by asking him to give you a straight answer?

P: I guess so.

T: The important thing is not whether or not he goes with you but whether you are deciding for him what he thinks instead of letting him tell you.

P: I guess you are right but he does seem to be inconsiderate. For example, he is always late for dinner.

T: How often has that happened?

P: Oh, once or twice . . . I guess that's really not all that often.

T: Is he coming late for dinner due to his being inconsiderate?

P: Well, come to think of it, he did say that he had been working late those two nights. Also, he has been considerate in a lot of other ways.

Actually as the patient later found, her son was willing to go to the movies with her.

(Beck et al., 1979, pp. 155–156)

This example shows the therapist does not accept the client's conclusions and inferences at their face value. Instead, those conclusions that result from faulty logic are reviewed and discussed so that the client may understand them from another perspective, changing his or her behavior in the future as a result.

In sum, cognitive behavior therapies seek to bring about behavior change by restructuring the thoughts, beliefs, and perceptions that lead to maladaptive behavior. By convincing clients to see the sometimes irrational and impossible demands that such thoughts often make on them, the therapist is able to lay the foundation for more realistic thoughts and beliefs, and ultimately to more adaptive and fulfilling behavior. As we will see next, though, some therapists prefer to allow their clients to reach that conclusion on their own.

HUMANISTIC APPROACHES

Whether the client's behavior or thoughts are considered to be maladaptive or irrational is an interpretation usually made by the therapist. To the client, however, the concern is more personal; it is, after all, the client who has sought help in the first place. Perhaps life has become boring and unfulfilling, work and family pressures have become apparently insurmountable, or maybe dreams and aspirations have fallen away as the dreary, mundane practicalities of day-to-day living take precedence. Jerome Frank (1972) believes that there is a common theme behind the psychological suffering that leads people to seek therapy. Frank argues that demoralization occurs whenever people begin to lose their ability to cope with circumstances that they and others believe should be manageable. From the standpoint of the humanistic psychologist, demoralization represents an obstacle to psychological growth and fulfillment. The aim of **humanistic therapy** is to provide the client with a greater understanding of his or her motivations and needs by focusing on the person's unique potential for growth and self-actualization. Humanistic therapies proceed from the assumption of the innate goodness of human nature; psychological problems reflect some type of blocking of the client's potential for self-understanding and self-awareness. Humanistic therapy is aimed at unblocking this potential. The two major forms of humanistic therapy are person-centered therapy and gestalt therapy.

Person-Centered Therapy

In the 1940s Carl Rogers founded the first humanistic therapy, creating a major alternative to psychoanalysis. Rogers had found the formalism of psychoanalysis too confining and its emphasis on psychological illness too pessimistic. Rogers's **person-centered therapy** is so named because of the respect afforded the client during therapy; the client decides what to talk about without direction and judgment from the therapist. The client takes ultimate responsibility for resolving his or her problems. In other words, it is the client who is the focus of the therapy, and not a method or theory.

Rogers believed that the cause of many psychological problems can be traced to people whose perceptions of themselves as they actually are (or their real selves) differs from the people they would like to be (or their ideal selves). Rogers called this discrepancy between the real and the ideal perceptions of the self **incongruence.** The goal of person-centered therapy is to reduce this incongruence by fostering experiences that will make attainment of the ideal self possible. Several techniques are commonly used by person-centered therapists to achieve this end, some of which we will discuss next.

Because it is the client's and not the therapist's thoughts that direct the course of therapy, the therapist strives to make those thoughts, perceptions, and feelings more noticeable to the client. This is frequently done through sensitive rephrasing or mirroring of the client's statements, a process known as **reflection.** The following is an example of how reflection might work within a therapy session to heighten the client's awareness of his feelings:

> Client: I get so frustrated at my parents. They just don't understand how I feel. They don't know what it's like to be me.
>
> Therapist: You seem to be saying that the things that are important to you aren't very important to your parents. You'd like them now and then to see things from your perspective.

By reflecting concerns of the client, the therapist demonstrates empathy, or the ability to perceive the world from another person's viewpoint. The establishment of empathy is an important ingredient in encouraging the client to deal with the incongruence between the real and the ideal self.

For Rogers (1951, p. 20), the "worth and significance of the individual" is a basic ground rule of therapy. This theme is represented in therapy through unconditional positive regard, in which the therapist tries to convey to the client that his or her worth as a human being is not dependent on anything they think, do, or feel. The person-centered therapist strives to show complete acceptance of the client during therapy, regardless of what is said or done during the session.

Through reflection and unconditional positive regard, the person-centered therapist tries to create an atmosphere in which the client can come to identify possible strategies for dealing with the problem of incongruence. The process, ideally, is one of self-guidance, as the therapist acts not as a director but as a facilitator in the client's self-discovery and healing.

For Rogers, the "worth and significance of the individual" is a basic ground rule of therapy.

Gestalt Therapy

As we have seen, the development of client-centered therapy owes much to its founder's disenchantment with classic psychoanalysis. For many of the same reasons, Fritz Perls (1893–1970), though trained in Freudian techniques, was to largely disengage himself from orthodox psychoanalysis in the process of founding gestalt therapy (Perls, 1969). In keeping with the primary philosophy of the gestalt school in psychology, **gestalt therapy** emphasizes the unity of mind and body by teaching clients to "get in touch" with bodily sensations and emotional feelings long since hidden from awareness. In a major departure from psychoanalytic theory, gestalt therapy places exclusive emphasis upon present experience rather than events in the past. Gestalt therapy also differs from person-centered therapy in that the gestalt therapist will often be quite confrontive, challenging the client to deal honestly with material of a highly emotional nature.

Fritz Perls

Perls, like Freud, believed that dreams are a rich source of information, though one must be able to deal with their symbolic content. In gestalt therapy, the therapist will often have the client adopt the perspective of some person or even some object in the dream in an empathic manner. In addition, the therapist often uses the **empty chair technique,** in which the client imagines that he or she is talking to someone sitting in the chair beside him or her. For example, a woman may be asked to say the things that she always wanted to say to her deceased father, but was never able to while he was alive. The empty chair technique allows her to experience in the here and now the feelings and perceptions that she may have learned to suppress while her father was alive. This technique is derived from Perls's belief that all of us carry around a good deal of emotional baggage in life and that these memories, fears, and feelings of guilt affect our relationships with others and our general sense of happiness. The gestalt therapist tries to guide the client toward an honest confrontation with these persistent emotional issues. Perls (1967, p. 331) argued that "In the safe emergency of the therapeutic situation, the neurotic discovers that the world does not fall to pieces if he or she gets angry, sexy, joyous, mournful."

In sum, the purpose of both person-centered therapy and gestalt therapy is to promote individual self-awareness and growth. Next, we will see that group and community approaches to therapy have the same goal, but attempt to achieve this by taking into consideration particular social contexts.

Understanding human behavior requires acknowledging our social nature and that it makes little sense to conceptualize behavior as an isolated, individual phenomenon. This recognition is the cornerstone of a number of relatively modern developments in therapy, all of which place some degree of emphasis upon understanding how maladaptive behavior may stem from ordinary social processes and how, importantly, therapy must take similar advantage of these processes. Three kinds of therapy adopt this approach: marital therapy, family therapy, and community psychology.

Group Therapy

Research on social influence effects has shown unequivocally how powerful groups can be in affecting individual behavior. This observation leads to some interesting implications for therapy. In **group therapy,** two or more clients meet simultaneously with a therapist, sharing and discussing problems within a supportive and understanding environment. There are a number of advantages that group procedures may have over individual psychotherapy. For instance, it is often helpful for individuals to learn that they are not alone in experiencing their particular problem. Second, the group environment allows for potential modeling of appropriate behaviors. Third, group therapy is usually less expensive than individual therapy and it is an efficient way for the therapist to help several people at once. There are several forms of therapy that group procedures may take, ranging from encounter groups to family and marital therapy.

Marital Therapy. As the name implies, **marital therapy,** or what is now sometimes called couple counseling to emphasize that the partners need not be husband and wife, involves identifying and alleviating problems that have developed in the partners' relationship. Although efforts to deal with problematic relationships are subject to the same difficulties as therapy applied to individuals, one ingredient stands out as being a prominent objective among marital therapists: the development of mutual empathy. An important theme in marital therapy is getting each partner to be able to view situations not only from their own perspective but from that of their

One of the major goals of marital therapy is to help couples develop a sense of empathy so they can see their partner's perspective in problem situations.

partner as well. This goal is not easily achieved, however, largely due to the development of inadequate communication patterns. Sager, for instance, has observed that

> . . . each partner in a marriage brings to it an individual, unwritten 'contract,' a set of expectations and promises, conscious and unconscious. . . . In a sense, the work of therapy can be seen as helping a couple arrive at one functioning contract the terms of which both partners are aware of and can subscribe to.
>
> (1981, pp. 86-87)

To assist each partner in stepping back from their own limited perspective, the couple may be videotaped interacting with each other. One partner may realize, for example, how he or she attempts to dominate the interaction by cutting off the other at crucial points in the conversation. This pattern is illustrated in the following excerpt from a marital therapy session in which the wife recognizes a particular pattern in her husband's interpersonal behavior (Carson, Butcher, & Coleman, 1988):

> See! There it is—loud and clear! As usual you didn't let me express my feelings or opinions, you just interrupted me with your own. You're always telling me what I think without asking me what I think. And I can see what I've been doing in response—withdrawing into silence. I feel like, what's the use of talking.

Sharing these sorts of insights often provides the perspective that leads to genuine change in the way that the partners interact. Such insight, however, may not have been obtained through individual psychotherapy.

Family Therapy.   There is probably no more important social group than the family, and recent years have brought an astonishing increase in the number of therapists and therapeutic organizations devoted to the treatment of family problems. For example, Gurman and Kniskern (1981) report that membership in the American Association for Marriage and Family Therapy increased by more than 700 percent from 1970 to 1979 and that while only one professional journal devoted to family issues existed in 1973, there are more than a dozen today. **Family therapy** focuses on the entire family as the unit of analysis; in essence, it is the family that is the client, not any particular family member.

An important conceptual stance taken by many family therapists is that a family is a system, characterized by considerable interdependence between its individual members, a position referred to as a family systems approach. According to this perspective, dealing with family problems, even if they are apparently due to the maladaptive behavior of just one family member, requires an appreciation of this interdependence and of the idea that the family, not the individual, has the problem. For example, a couple may initially consult a therapist with the complaint that an adolescent son refuses to obey family rules and regulations. The therapist operating from a family systems perspective may recommend that therapy include not just the son, but the parents and any other family members as well. In fact, family therapists often find that the real "problem" is not necessarily attributable to the individual identified by the family as in need of help. Instead one member of the family is being singled out for blame (Boszormenyi-Nagy & Ulrich, 1981).

D*ealing with family problems . . . requires an appreciation of the idea that the family, not the individual, has the problem.*

You can appreciate how difficult the family therapist's job is. How does one go about sifting through the complexity of family dynamics, hoping to find the source of problematic relationships and subjecting them to anal-

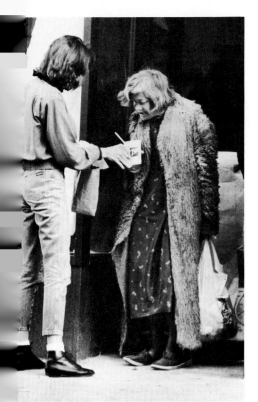

Although deinstitutionalization is viewed as a positive advancement by psychologists, patient homelessness has unfortunately resulted. This problem occurs because the deinstitutionalization process proceeds more quickly than the funding and development of community programs.

ysis and modification? The task is a formidable one, as was recognized by Freud (1912) himself who stated "When it comes to the treatment of relationships I must confess myself utterly at a loss and I have altogether little faith in any individual therapy of them." Of course, the modern therapist enjoys the benefit of several decades of research, theory, and practice not available to Freud, justifying some degree of optimism concerning the current status of family therapy.

Community Psychology

Until the last few decades, those with serious psychological disorders, particularly those without many financial resources, were hospitalized in large, state institutions. The stated goal of these institutions was treatment that would provide the skills to allow the patient to return to as close to a normal life as possible. More often than not, however, patients received only custodial care in understaffed hospitals, rather than constructive therapy aimed at improving their level of functioning. The goal of **community psychology** is to address psychological problems through an assessment of the sociocultural context in which the problems develop. Smith has aptly characterized the nature of the community movement in psychology:

> The first mental health revolution unshackled the insane. By calling them sick, it managed to treat them as humans. Its monuments and symbols are the great, usually isolated state hospitals. The second revolution came from the spread of dynamic psychiatry (mainly Freud's) and was characterized by individual, one-to-one psychotherapy. Now the third revolution throws off the constraints of the doctor-patient medical model—the idea that mental disorder is a private misery—and relates the trouble, and the cure, to the entire web of social and personal relationships in which the individual is caught.
>
> (1968, p. 19)

As an alternative to long-term hospitalization, several different kinds of community treatment programs have been developed. One example is the community mental health center, a form of treatment sponsored by Congress in the early 1960s, designed to supplement mental hospitals. Instead of confining patients to an institution, community mental health centers provide outpatient care within the client's home community. Some centers also provide inpatient care, meaning the client may receive treatment while living full time on the premises for a short time period.

A related type of community treatment program is the halfway house, a place where patients discharged from mental hospitals may receive outpatient care as they gradually begin to reintegrate themselves into the community. Using the halfway house as their base, clients may take on a part-time job, return to school, or just spend more time with their families and friends, while living and eating at the halfway house. The halfway house, then, represents something of a transition from complete supervision and care to complete independence.

The process of allowing previously hospitalized patients to return to their communities for treatment is called deinstitutionalization, and for the most part this movement has been viewed as an important advance by community psychologists. However, the deinstitutionalization process has often proceeded more rapidly than has the funding and development of adequate community care programs and facilities. One unfortunate consequence of this is that many patients with severe psychotic behavior problems are now living on the streets of many of our cities. In fact, one estimate is that about 130,000 schizophrenic individuals live on the streets or in public shelters, and only about 60,000 remain in traditional mental hospitals (Torrey, 1987). Of course, community psychologists would argue that the resolution to this problem is not to return such patients to mental hospitals, but to increase funding and development of community efforts.

Increasingly, community psychologists have begun to advocate treatment strategies aimed at forestalling the development of psychological problems; that is, targeting the root causes of the problem for intervention (Felner, Jason, Moritsugu, & Farber, 1983). This type of emphasis upon treating the sociocultural variables predictive of psychological distress is sometimes referred to as **preventive psychology.** A useful metaphor for describing preventive psychology is that individual therapy for psychological problems can be seen as similar to rescuing people from a river (Rappaport, 1977). Each person rescued is a life saved, but a more effective solution would be to go upstream and correct the problem that is causing people to fall into the water in the first place.

Community psychologists distinguish between two kinds of prevention, primary and secondary. Primary prevention refers to any efforts to eliminate the conditions responsible for psychological problems and simultaneously bring about conditions that contribute to psychological health and adaptive behavior. For example, providing children educational materials concerning the dangers of taking drugs while at the same time encouraging healthy recreational and exercise routines represents an attempt to prevent experimentation with drugs. Secondary prevention, on the other hand, refers to prompt identification of the problem and immediate attempts to intervene to minimize development of the problem. Suicide hotlines, which are staffed 24 hours a day by trained volunteers, are examples of secondary prevention measures.

We have seen that the community psychology approach explicitly acknowledges that psychological problems develop within a sociocultural context. It is to society's advantage that intervention strategies be developed to address the larger social and environmental issues that ultimately give rise to maladaptive functioning in the individual. Although the prevention of conditions known to lead to poor psychological adjustment would seem to be a herculean task, it is also one likely to pay considerable long-term dividends.

FIGURE 16.1
How effective is psychotherapy? The answer depends on which type of psychotherapy is being discussed. Consider the results of Smith et al.'s (1980) review of 475 studies comparing the outcome effectiveness of the psychotherapies shown in this figure to that of untreated control groups. The bars represent the percentile ranks that the average person undergoing psychotherapy achieved on outcome evaluations compared to that for control subjects for each type of psychotherapy. Each of the psychotherapies indicated above was more effective than no therapy. People undergoing cognitive behavior or systematic desensitization therapies scored the highest on outcome measures.

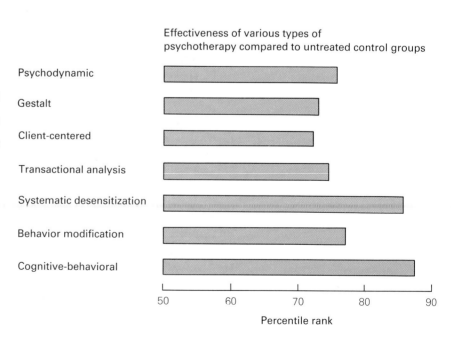

Effectiveness of various types of psychotherapy compared to untreated control groups

Remember that we began our discussion of therapy with the claim that the term "psychotherapy" itself refers to an extremely large and variegated collection of principles, techniques, and objectives. From biomedical manipulations of brain functioning to psychoanalytic interpretations of hidden dream content to person-centered therapy's provision of unconditional positive regard, there persists, nonetheless, a single purpose uniting all of these varied practices: to alleviate the demoralization about which Jerome Frank spoke. This brings us to a question of immeasurable importance. Does psychotherapy work? As we shall soon see, there are few matters on which psychologists disagree more than on the issue of psychotherapy effectiveness.

THE EFFECTIVENESS OF PSYCHOTHERAPY

The scientific evaluation of the effects of therapy is a surprisingly complex task that requires a working knowledge of statistics and a detailed reading of hundreds of studies across a variety of disciplines. Even then, conclusive answers rarely emerge. Some of the problems, such as how to measure change both before and after therapy, are technical. Other problems are largely ethical, such as how best to obtain informed consent from patients without disrupting the research (Imber et al., 1986).

In 1952 Hans Eysenck published the first major empirical article describing the relative success of psychotherapy in bringing about improved functioning in clients. Eysenck's rather unpromising conclusion was that psychodynamic therapy appeared to be no more effective than no intervention at all. Needless to say, this finding did not remain unchallenged for long, as researchers and therapists came quickly to the defense of psychotherapy, suggesting that Eysenck's study was flawed on methodological grounds (Bergin, 1971). Although his conclusions may indeed have been refutable, Eysenck's study was important as it served as the catalyst for what would soon become a major research concern among psychologists.

n considering how effective psychotherapy is as a treatment for psychological problems, there is one particularly important rule of thumb: Beware of generalities!

In considering how effective psychotherapy is as a treatment for psychological problems, there is one particularly important rule of thumb: Beware of generalities! Researchers studying therapy outcome have come to realize that universal statements about therapy's effectiveness are not possible. How effective therapy is depends on the specific form of therapy employed and the particular psychological problem to which it is applied. In addition, the competence of the therapist makes no small contribution to the therapy process. Nor should client characteristics be ignored. For example, certain types of psychological problems may render some forms of therapy irrelevant. It is not likely, for instance, that any form of therapy involving verbal interaction between client and therapist, be it psychodynamic or cognitive, will be of much help to a client who is socially withdrawn or incapable of interpersonal interaction. In this vein, it is natural to expect that an autistic child would be targeted for something other than psychodynamic or cognitive therapy (Lovaas et al., 1973).

Researchers have been especially interested in comparing various forms of therapy to discover which might be most effective. One of the more recent developments in outcome research is a complex quantitative procedure called meta-analysis, which entails sophisticated statistical analyses of hundreds of separate studies. Figure 16.1 summarizes one of these meta-analyses in which various therapeutic techniques were compared. As you can see, behavioral and cognitive therapies tended to exceed others in effectiveness, though these differences were often quite small (Smith &

Glass, 1977; Smith et al., 1980; Kazdin & Wilson, 1978). Keep in mind that these data reflect hundreds of studies and thousands of clients. No conclusions can be drawn from studies like this as to the effectiveness of a particular therapy for a particular client.

So, what conclusions can we draw from research on psychotherapy outcome? The answer seems to be, only tentative ones. The many methodological problems associated with this research do not presently warrant sweeping statements about psychotherapy's effectiveness. At the same time, there is no question that the combination of certain factors such as therapist competence, and an adequate match between the psychological problem being presented and the type of therapy employed, can bring about significant improvement. We simply do not have at this time a formula to determine which therapy will best assist which client. Like so many other questions confronting psychology, a suitable answer awaits further research. As we will see next, more than just questions about therapy effectiveness confronts therapists, for they must also deal with special ethical and legal issues.

ETHICAL AND LEGAL ISSUES IN PSYCHOTHERAPY

The special relationship that exists between the therapist and the client is duplicated in few other places in society. With the possible exception of the traditional role of many ministers and priests, few people earn their living by listening to others describe the deeply personal and intimate details of their lives. Unfortunately, the same characteristics that provide the therapeutic relationship its healing potential may also lead to abuses. For this reason, psychologists have developed a set of ethical standards to guide their professional activities, and legislatures and courts have provided additional regulations concerning the practice of therapy.

The same characteristics that provide the therapeutic relationship its healing potential may also lead to abuses.

The ethical standards for psychologists are formally defined by the publication of the Ethical Standards of the American Psychological Association (1979). One important standard, for example, is the sexuality restraint, which specifies that sexual intimacies with clients are unethical. A therapist who suggests such intimacy to a client or who allows himself or herself to be approached sexually by the client, is unquestionably violating this standard. In some states, this matter has actually gone beyond ethical considerations to become a matter of law—sexual intimacies with a client, even with consent, can be considered a felony (APA, 1988). Nonetheless, the problem of sexual relations between therapist and client remains a pervasive issue in psychotherapy (Pope, Tabachnick, & Keith-Spiegel, 1987).

Another ethical standard is the confidentiality restraint, which states that any information obtained about the client during therapy is considered privileged information and must remain confidential. This confidentiality extends not only to casual acquaintances of the therapist, but also to members of the client's family. The only exception to this rule is that a psychologist may consult with another professional about an individual case.

Because ethical principles are stated in absolute terms, problems and inconsistencies often arise in their application. For example, the confidentiality restraint sometimes leads to an ethical dilemma in which any course of action leads to a violation of an ethical principle. The event that initially brought this dilemma to the public's and psychology's attention is

Unlike in the past, numerous attempts at rehabilitation for patients in mental health facilities is standard procedure. Consequently, there has been a major drop in the number of hospitalized patients since the 1950s.

the 1969 Tarasoff case. A male student at the University of California at Berkeley began dating a fellow student, Tatiana Tarasoff. He fell in love with her, but she preferred casual dating. Being upset by her rebuff, he entered therapy, where he explicitly stated to the therapist his intentions to purchase a gun and injure or kill Tatiana. The therapist then faced the dilemma of deciding whether to breach confidentiality and report the threat to the police, or to respect confidentiality, but allow for the possibility of harm.

The therapist contacted the campus police, who interviewed the student and released him. Shortly thereafter, the student went to Tatiana's home, shot her with a pellet gun, and then repeatedly and fatally stabbed her. Tatiana's parents sued the university, the campus police, and the therapist—and won. The California Supreme Court ruled in 1974 that the therapist, in addition to informing the police, should have further breached confidentiality and warned the likely victim, in this case Tatiana Tarasoff. Further rulings in other cases have since established that the therapist can be liable for the violent behavior of a client even if the client does not specifically threaten anyone.

The resolution of this dilemma for therapists is particularly difficult given that no method exists for accurately predicting violent behavior. To avoid legal liability, the therapist would have to warn a variety of people of potential danger every time violence was even remotely probable. Given the impracticality of applying these court rulings literally, it is likely that further legislation will be required to clarify the therapist's legal responsibilities. In the interim, there is evidence that some therapists are simply not discussing aspects of violence with their clients to minimize liability (Wise, 1978).

Another dilemma that therapists encounter concerns the rights of hospitalized patients. In an effort to avoid the abuses of the past, patients are now afforded many rights not available to them earlier in the century. One of the advantages of these rights is that patients are not usually confined unnecessarily, and frequent attempts are made at rehabilitation. As we saw in the section on community psychology, the result of this movement has been a substantial drop in the number of hospitalized patients since the mid-1950s.

The combination of fewer patients being confined for long periods in mental hospitals and our current inadequacies in predicting violent behavior, however, makes for an extremely volatile social problem. For example, a potentially dangerous patient may be released too early because the therapist may be worried about liability for retaining the patient too long. Of course, the therapist and his or her institution can also be held liable if the patient later commits acts of violence. Thus the therapist would seem to be enmeshed in a no-win situation, having to be concerned about protecting himself or herself, the patient, and the general public—all without the means to predict accurately violence or the means to control factors in the patient's environment that might trigger the violence.

These and other legal and ethical issues make the practice of therapy a delicate balancing act. Not only do therapists assume responsibility for bringing effective methods of treatment to bear on the problems of the client, but he or she must also weigh the potential consequences of therapy for the family and friends of the client and for society in general.

BOUNDARIES AND FRONTIERS

In 1979 psychology celebrated its formal centennial as a scientific discipline, as marked by the founding of Wundt's laboratory in Leipzig in 1879. As we approach the end of this century, and psychology moves well into its second hundred years, it's tempting to wonder just how far we have come and whether the first 100 years produced more answers or more questions regarding psychological functioning. This is an issue of special relevance to the institution of psychotherapy. There would seem to be no contesting the claim that the practice of therapy has undergone immense change over time, since most current forms of therapy did not exist early in the previous century. Considering this fact, what might the future of therapy hold and what will be the major issues confronting the psychotherapist?

One issue is that of professional identity. As we saw in this chapter, therapists trained in psychology graduate programs are increasingly demanding more authority in traditional medical settings (Buie, 1989). These matters are currently being addressed through legislative actions at the state level. In addition, there are a number of problems associated with distinguishing among those who provide therapy, especially with respect to professional training and treatment credentials. For example, the title "clinical psychologist" is protected in most states, meaning only those who have completed the Ph.D. requirements in an accredited graduate program in clinical psychology plus a one year postdoctoral internship may refer to themselves as clinical psychologists. Others with somewhat less or different training in psychology or counseling may, however, refer to themselves as psychologists, therapists, or counselors. The important issue here is that despite similar titles, these individuals may have received extremely different amounts, quality, and types of training. The future will likely see further efforts to make more meaningful distinctions among these titles and the relative expertise each implies.

We can be fairly certain that the process of therapy itself will continue to evolve, reflected both in refinement of current practices and development of new treatment methods. Advances in biomedical therapy, for example, will likely parallel basic research findings in the behavioral neurosciences. This development is particularly important in view of current theories giving primacy to the relationship between brain chemistry and psychological functioning. Similar growth might be predicted for cognitive behavioral therapy, most notably as applied to the treatment of depression. Perhaps the most rapidly growing approaches to therapy are the many forms of marital and family therapy, both of which may owe their recent ascendance to the regrettably epidemic rise in marriage and family dissolution.

But if there is one concern that would seem to assume precedence among the therapeutic community, it would have to be the issue of the effectiveness of therapy. As we have already seen, this is a contentious issue whose resolution has so far been impeded by persistant methodological complications in outcome research. Although most recent studies seem to favor the position that therapy can indeed be effective, we are a long way from understanding which therapies are the most effective and under what circumstances. Assuming that answers to these questions will be forthcoming, other equally important issues arise. For example, can we expect that therapeutic methods that ultimately prove ineffective will be abandoned by loyal practitioners? Is it reasonable to predict that some day consumers of therapy will be able to make an intelligent choice as to which therapy or which practitioner would be most helpful in treating their problem? Of course, there exists no cookbook from which to select treatment strategies for particular psychological problems. Is there one in psychotherapy's future, and if so, would this be considered an advance or a hindrance? These are some of the issues with which members of the psychological community, and therapists in particular, will likely grapple with in the years to come.

CONCEPT SUMMARY

BIOMEDICAL APPROACHES

- What is electroconvulsive therapy? What aspect of this therapy is believed to be responsible for its effectiveness? (pp. 571–572)
- What is the rationale behind psychosurgery? What drawbacks does it have? (p. 572)
- Is drug therapy effective? Discuss the kinds of drugs used in this kind of therapy. (pp. 572–574)

PSYCHODYNAMIC APPROACHES

- What is the rationale underlying Freud's approach to therapy? (pp. 575–576)
- According to Freud, which aspects of a dream reveal its true meaning? Explain. (p. 577)
- What role do resistance and transference play in psychodynamic therapy? (pp. 577–578)

BEHAVIORAL APPROACHES

- How is systematic desensitization different from aversion therapy? (pp. 580–581)
- How are the concepts of reinforcement, extinction, and punishment used in behavioral therapy? (pp. 581–583)
- How is modeling used as a therapeutic technique? (pp. 583–584)

COGNITIVE BEHAVIORAL APPROACHES

- What is the logic underlying rational-emotive therapy? (pp. 584–585)
- According to Beck, what is the "cognitive triad"? Upon which aspects of the client's symptoms of depression is cognitive therapy generally focused? (pp. 585–586)

HUMANISTIC APPROACHES

- What are the key features of person-centered therapy? (pp. 587–588)
- What is gestalt therapy? Explain the empty chair technique. (p. 588)

GROUP AND COMMUNITY APPROACHES

- What are the goals of marital and family therapy? What is the basis for these kinds of therapies? (pp. 589–591)

THE EFFECTIVENESS OF THERAPY

- How effective is psychotherapy? Explain the results of research concerning the outcome of therapy. (pp. 593–594)

ETHICAL AND LEGAL ISSUES IN THERAPY

- What are the ethical responsibilities of psychotherapists? (pp. 594–595)
- What legal issues face psychotherapists? (pp. 594–595)

KEY TERMS AND CONCEPTS

Psychotherapy Any attempt to use known psychological principles to bring about improved emotional, cognitive, or social adjustment. (p. 568)

BIOMEDICAL APPROACHES

Biomedical Therapy Treatment of psychological problems by directly altering the physical functioning of the brain. (p. 570)

Electroconvulsive Therapy (ECT) A form of treatment that involves passing small amounts of electric current through the brain to produce seizure activity. (p. 571)

Psychosurgery Unalterable brain surgery designed to relieve the symptoms of psychological disorders. (p. 572)

Drug Therapy The treatment of psychological problems with chemical agents. (p. 572)

PSYCHODYNAMIC APPROACHES

Psychoanalysis A form of therapy aimed at providing the client insight into unconscious motivations and impulses. (p. 576)

Free-association A psychoanalytic procedure in which the client is encouraged to speak freely, without censoring possibly embarrassing or socially unacceptable thoughts or ideas. (p. 576)

Dream Interpretation The evaluation of the underlying meaning of dream content. (p. 577)

Manifest Content The actual images or events occurring within a dream. (p. 577)

Latent Content The hidden meaning or underlying significance of a dream. (p. 577)

Resistance A development during therapy in which the client becomes defensive, unconsciously attempting to halt further insight by censoring his or her true feelings. (p. 577)

Transference The process by which a client begins to project powerful attitudes and emotions onto the therapist. (p. 577)

Countertransference The process by which the therapist projects his or her emotions onto the client. (p. 578)

BEHAVIORAL APPROACHES

Behavior Therapy The application of principles derived from experimental research for the alleviation of psychological problems. (p. 579)

Systematic Desensitization A method of treatment in which the client is trained to relax in the presence of increasingly fearful stimuli. (p. 580)

Aversion Therapy A form of treatment in which the client is trained to respond negatively to a neutral stimulus that has been paired with an aversive stimulus. (p. 580)

Behavior Modification A form of behavior therapy based on operant conditioning principles. (p. 581)

Token Economy A therapeutic setting in which clients are taught to engage in appropriate behavior in order to earn tokens that can be exchanged for personally valued items or privileges. (p. 581)

Modeling A treatment method in which the client observes another person engaging in appropriate behavior and then imitates this same behavior. (p. 583)

COGNITIVE BEHAVIORAL APPROACHES

Cognitive Behavior Therapy Treatment method that focuses on altering the client's thoughts, beliefs, and perceptions. (p. 584)

Cognitive Restructuring The process of replacing the client's negative thoughts with more constructive ways of thinking. (p. 584)

Rational-Emotive Therapy (RET) Therapy based on the belief that psychological problems are caused not by upsetting events, but how people think about such events. (p. 584)

HUMANISTIC APPROACHES

Humanistic Therapy A form of therapy in which the aim is to provide the client with a greater understanding of his or her motivations and needs by focusing on the person's unique potential for growth and self-actualization. (p. 587)

Person-centered Therapy A form of therapy in which the client is allowed to decide what to talk about without direction and judgment from the therapist. (p. 587)

Incongruence A discrepancy between a client's real and ideal selves. (p. 587)

Reflection The therapist's sensitive rephrasing or mirroring of the client's statements during therapy. (p. 587)

Gestalt Therapy A form of therapy that emphasizes the unity of mind and body by teaching the client to "get in touch" with bodily sensations and emotional feelings long since hidden from awareness. (p. 588)

Empty-chair Technique A procedure in which clients imagine that they are talking to someone sitting in the empty chair beside them. (p. 588)

GROUP AND COMMUNITY APPROACHES

Group Therapy Therapy in which two or more clients meet simultaneously with a therapist, sharing and discussing problems within a supportive and understanding environment. (p. 589)

Marital Therapy Therapy aimed at identifying and alleviating problems that have developed within a marital or other intimate partnership. (p. 589)

Family Therapy Therapy in which the family, rather than any particular family member, is viewed as the client. (p. 590)

Community Psychology A form of therapy whose goal is to address psychological problems through an assessment of the sociocultural context in which the problems develop. (p. 591)

Preventive Psychology Any attempt to forestall the development of psychological problems by altering the sociocultural variables predictive of psychological distress. (p. 592)

ADDITIONAL SOURCES OF INFORMATION

Corsini, R. J. (1984). *Current psychotherapies* (3rd ed.). Itasca, IL: Peacock. This book provides a very thoughtful overview and comparison of the various forms of psychotherapy, its uses, and methods.

Freud, S. (1900). *The interpretation of dreams*. London: Allen & Unwin. This classic book is recommended to those who wish to understand better Freud's emphasis on dreams as the "royal road to consciousness."

Kazdin, A. E. (1978). *History of behavior modification: Experimental foundations of contemporary research*. Baltimore: University Park Press. This text provides an excellent summary of the development of behavior modification.

Perls, F. S. (1969). *Gestalt therapy verbatim*. Lafayette, CA: Real People Press. In this book, Perls demonstrates the ways and means of Gestalt therapy through actual transcripts of therapy sessions.

Rappaport, J. (1977). *Community psychology: Values, research and action*. New York: Holt, Rinehart, & Winston. This book contains a thorough presentation of community psychology's basic aims and methods.

Rogers, C. R. (1951). *Client-centered therapy*. New York: Houghton-Mifflin. Written by the founder of the humanistic movement in psychology, this book outlines all of the major features of client-centered therapy.

17 Social Psychology

SOCIAL COGNITION
(602–615)

Schemata and Social Perception   Attribution
Attitude and Attitude Development   Attitude Change and Persuasion
Attitude-Behavior Correspondence   Cognitive Dissonance Theory

Social psychologists study how people process information about their social world, including how we form impressions of others and how we explain our own and other people's behavior. Social cognition also entails research on attitude development and change and how behavior may or may not correspond to stated attitudes.

SOCIAL INFLUENCE
(615–629)

Social Facilitation   Social Norms and Conformity   Compliance
Obedience to Authority   Bystander Intervention and Helping
Interpersonal Attraction

People influence one another in an extraordinary number of ways, both intentionally and unintentionally. The nature of this influence can be quite subtle, as when we unwittingly conform to group norms, or very dramatic, as when we obey the demands of an authority figure or become intimately involved with another person.

SOCIOBIOLOGY AND SOCIAL INFLUENCE
(629–632)

In addition to the proximate or situational variables most often examined by social psychologists, several genetic factors may play a role in determining social influence. Sociobiologists have offered their own provocative account of how evolutionary forces have molded humankind's affiliative nature.

In the introduction to this book, we defined psychology as being focused on individual organisms. Although this focus helps us clarify the important differences between psychology and other social sciences, it is equally important to acknowledge that human behavior cannot be fully understood as an isolated phenomenon. Just as we appreciate that environmental pressures play a critical role in "selecting" for various characteristics in the evolution of species, we must also recognize the role of the social environment in the explanation of individual behavior.

Whatever else seems uncertain about human beings, there is no denying our social nature. Indeed, the pleasures and the pains that we derive from others provide the basis for much of the meaning of our lives; we need look no further than the joy of falling in love, or, on the flip side, the agony of a failed romance. Lovers, friends, parents, teachers, supervisors, and even strangers standing next to us in an elevator, are all examples of people with whom we interact.

Social psychology has been defined by Gordon Allport (1968) as that branch of psychology that studies "how the thought, feeling, and behavior of individuals are influenced by the actual, imagined, or implied presence of others" (p. 3). The number of ways in which we can influence and are influenced by others is enormous. Even the simplest, most routine activities in which we engage derive in some way from social interaction. Why do we dress the way we do? Why don't I paint my house purple if purple is my favorite color? Why is it that some of us like the Beatles, but find it difficult to appreciate Ozzy Osborne or Twisted Sister? On a perhaps more substantive note, why do we align ourselves with a particular political party or worship a particular deity? What are our beliefs and attitudes about child rearing? Needless to say, none of these actions, beliefs, or attitudes can be considered part of our innate endowment. To understand them requires an examination of the unique and continuing interaction between ourselves and our social environment.

We begin this chapter with a consideration of the cognitive factors that affect how individuals perceive and respond to other individuals. In particular, we will discuss how we form impressions of others and how we go about explaining behavior, both our own and others. We will then describe how psychologists study attitudes, their formation and change, and their correspondence to behavior. Next, we will discuss the many ways in which our behavior is influenced by others. The strength and pervasiveness of these influences will become apparent in our study of conformity, compliance, obedience, helping behavior, and interpersonal attraction.

SOCIAL COGNITION

Each person brings to his or her social world a unique constellation of personality, intellectual, and emotional characteristics. Understanding social behavior requires giving considerable attention to these qualities, for they determine how individuals perceive and subsequently respond to the social environment. For example, if you think the person walking down the sidewalk toward you means you harm, you are likely to act quite differently toward that person than if you think he or she is a friend.

Sizing up a social situation depends on a host of cognitive processes, including memory for people, places, and events, concept formation skills, and, more fundamentally, sensory and perceptual abilities. In recent years, social psychologists have begun to apply our knowledge of these basic processes to understand better how people process social information. This processing of social information is referred to as **social cognition**. Social cognition includes the topics of social perception, attribution, attitude, persuasion, the correspondence between attitudes and behavior, and cognitive dissonance.

Schemata and Social Perception

One of the first questions typically asked of a college roommate returning from her first date with someone is, "What is he like?" All of us form impressions not only of the people we date, but of friends, neighbors, supervisors, or teachers—virtually everyone whom we meet. And we seldom are reluctant to assign all sorts of characteristics to other people. We may, for example, think of someone else as friendly or hostile, helpful or selfish, trustworthy or cynical.

One of the major tasks of social psychology is to understand how we arrive at this knowledge. In Solomon Asch's words, "How do the perceptions, thoughts, and motives of one person become known to other persons? In what way is the gap that separates one person from another bridged?" (1952, p. 143). To answer questions like these, psychologists study **impression formation**, the way in which we form impressions of others and attribute specific characteristics and traits to them.

One general conclusion of the research on impression formation is that our impressions follow the general dictum of Gestalt psychology that we discussed in Chapter 5 on sensation and perception: The whole is greater than the sum of the parts. As noted by Asch over four decades ago, our impressions of others are formed from more complex rules than a simple sum of the characteristics that we use to describe the person. This point will be illustrated by our discussions of central traits and the primacy effect. Our starting point, however, will be the concept of schemata.

Schemata. As we saw in Chapter 9, the central organizing theme of much of cognitive psychology is the concept of schemata. **Schemata** provide an overall framework for processing information about people, objects, and situations. The first time you visited your psychology professor in his or her office, for example, there were probably few surprises. The schema that you have of "professor" guided your interactions with him or her. However, you would probably be quite surprised to see that your professor's office was spacious, and furnished with expensive furniture and rare art. Such interior decorating is inconsistent with the expectations that were dictated by your schema of "professor."

By serving as organizational frameworks for interpreting new information, schemata provide a much needed means for reducing an otherwise unmanageable complex social world to something within which we can function. As an example of how schemata guide our interpretations, try to understand the following passage:

> The procedure is actually quite simple. First you arrange things into different groups. Of course, one pile may be sufficient depending on how much there is to do. . . . It is important not to overdo things. That is, it is better to do too few things at once than too many. In the short run this may not seem important, but complications can easily arise. A mistake can be expensive as well. At first the whole procedure will seem complicated. Soon, however, it will become just another facet of life.
>
> (Bransford & Johnson, 1972, p. 722)

Does this passage make much sense to you? What if you are told that the title of the passage is "Washing Clothes?" The passage is now interpreted easily, for the sentences make perfect sense within the context of your schema for washing clothes. Not surprisingly, research has demonstrated that understanding is greater when the title of the passage is known before

Social cognition enables us to process all of the information that confronts us in a social situation, such as meeting a friend while walking on campus. Our behavior changes given all of the elements in a particular social environment.

the passage is read (Bransford & Johnson, 1972). According to social psychologists, we construct schemata not only for activities and events, but for people as well. For example, we often construct schemata about central characteristics of specific people.

Central Traits. If you were asked to describe a friend, you would probably list a few very general attributes that, in your opinion, best portray what that person is like. You might, for example, use the terms "caring" or "warm" to refer to those features that seem most enduring or representative of your friend's personality. When we are trying to describe personality attributes that seem to be the most representative of a person, we are describing what psychologists refer to as **central traits.** A central trait is a schema because it helps us process or summarize a large amount of information gathered through our interactions with that person. When we are meeting someone for the first time, prior information about that person's central traits may be the only context we have for forming an impression of that person. Although his research predated the modern emphasis on cognitive processing and schemata in social psychology, Solomon Asch (1946) demonstrated that central traits could be powerful tools for developing initial impressions of others. Asch provided subjects with a list of traits describing a hypothetical person. Some subjects received a list which included the trait "warm," while others received a list of traits that was identical, except the trait "warm" was replaced by "cold." Subjects receiving the list including "warm" were more likely to see the person as generous, happy, and altruistic. But, not all traits seemed to be so important in shaping one's perception of another person. When the words "polite" and "blunt" were substituted for "warm" and "cold" no discrepancies in subjects' perceptions were observed. In other words, the trait of "warmth" is somehow interpreted as being more central to the personality than is "politeness." Our perception of others, then, is based partially on the schemata we have regarding others' central traits.

The Primacy Effect. Getting to know someone in real life is a prolonged process, usually requiring frequent interaction. What happens when your impressions of a person over time contradict the initial impressions of that person? Perhaps the first time you saw someone was at a party when he was loud and boisterous, "having a good time" with his friends. But later, you learn that he is a math major with a 4.0 GPA, who is actually generally reserved. To determine whether first impressions might overpower later impressions in the development of schemata, Asch (1946) presented the following lists of words to two groups of subjects.

- Intelligent, industrious, impulsive, critical, stubborn, envious
- Envious, stubborn, critical, impulsive, industrious, intelligent

Notice that these lists contain the same words, but in reverse order. People who heard list A thought of the person as someone who was able and productive, but who possessed some shortcomings. The person described by list B, however, was seen as someone who had serious problems. The tendency to form an impression of a person based on the first information we receive about them is called the **primacy effect.** The first impression we receive of a person seems to be the most persistent. Later information may violate our schema of the person and is consequently given less consideration when forming perceptions of others. More recent work, which has involved developing mathematical equations of social cognition, has been able to predict the primacy effect with reasonable accuracy, indicating that social perception follows predictable rules (Anderson, 1974).

Schemata simplify the world around us by organizing information along specific themes.

Stereotypes. As we have seen, schemata simplify the world around us by organizing information along specific themes. For example, schemata allow us to categorize people into groups organized along one or more attributes such as profession (manager, school teacher), age (young, senior citizen), ethnicity (Caucasian, African American), or size (tall, short). Although these organizational structures allow us to function in a complex world, sometimes schemata can be misleading. Not everyone fits into our schemata, nor are all people who are classified into a particular group exactly alike.

One glaring example of the negative aspects of schemata are **stereotypes,** oversimplified schemata that are applied to an entire group of people. Even without spiteful intentions, most people misperceive members of other social groups. The groups could be students at a neighboring college, people from another region of the country, or members of another ethnic group. These misperceptions often occur in specific ways. For example, people who are members of other groups are often seen as more similar to one another than they actually are (Wilder, 1981; Quattrone, 1986). The oft-heard statement "They all look the same to me" is illustrative of people's tendency to view members of other groups as being so similar to one another.

Stereotyping has both cognitive and behavioral consequences. **Prejudice,** which literally means to "prejudge," refers to a negative evaluation of an individual based on his or her membership in a specific group. Prejudice involves forming expectations of an individual's behavior based on a stereotype of that person's membership in a particular group. **Discrimination,** which is the behavioral expression of prejudice, is treating someone differently because of his or her membership in a particular group. Stereotypes form the cornerstone on which both prejudice and discrimination rest.

Stereotypes are often extremely resistant to change. One reason for this may be the very nature of our cognitive systems. As we saw earlier, once a schema is established, subsequent information is interpreted within the context of that schema. Accordingly, information that appears to contradict the schema is discounted.

Despite their resistance to change, stereotypes and their expression in prejudice and discrimination can under certain circumstances be reduced. The case of Gerard Vaders is an especially interesting example. Through unfortunate circumstances, Vaders was taken hostage by a group of political terrorists in the Netherlands. The terrorists had decided to execute Vaders as a sign of their conviction, but first allowed him to dictate a final letter to his loved ones at home. In the letter, Vaders spoke of his life in very personal terms, referring to his successes and failures, his aspirations, and the dreams he held for his family. Amazingly, after having learned so much about Vaders, coming to see him as an individual with the same hopes and fears as themselves, the terrorists decided not to kill him.

A practice commonly employed under less extraordinary social circumstances is to substitute cooperation for competition between groups. In the jigsaw classroom, for instance, students from different ethnic backgrounds are placed in mixed-ethnic groups and provided with academic assignments. The grade a student receives is based upon the performance of the entire group, thus encouraging cooperation among the group's members. Such cooperation leads not only to improved academic performance among individuals, but to social interactions that are not dictated by previously held stereotypes (Aronson, Stephen, Sikes, Blaney, & Snapp, 1978). These two examples illustrate how personal interaction may reduce the negative stereotypes we have regarding other people.

Anti-racist demonstrations illustrate the presence of prejudice and discrimination that continue to prevail in our society and the difficulty that is encountered when we try to eliminate stereotypes.

Attribution

Social psychologists develop scientific theories that explain social behavior. All of us, however, have our own common-sense theories and explanations of social behavior—all of us in our daily lives try to explain both our own behavior and the behavior of others. Why was John late? Does the politician mean to keep her campaign promise, or is she just trying to get elected? Why did your best friend get such a good grade on the last psychology test when you did so poorly?

Answers to questions like these are important to our own lives and they contribute to an understanding of our behavior. To help explain how people infer the causes of their own and others' behavior, social psychologists have developed **attribution theories** (Kelley, 1967).

One attribution task that we face almost daily is deciding whether someone's behavior is due primarily to personality characteristics of that person, or to characteristics of the situation or environment in which the behavior occurred. You may, for example, see your favorite athlete in a TV ad promoting a soft drink. In real life does this person prefer that soft drink to others, or is the endorsement simply due to a large monetary inducement?

According to Fritz Heider

> Behavior can be ascribed primarily to the person or the environment; that is, behavior can be accounted for by relatively stable traits of the personality or by factors within the environment. Failure, for instance, can be attributed to lack of ability, a personal characteristic, or to the supposition that the task is very difficult, an environmental condition.
>
> (1958, p. 56)

Attributions to the person are called dispositional, and those directed toward the environment are called situational. Dispositional and situational attributions are made according to specific kinds of rules. Two important attributional rules are covariation and discounting.

Covariation.   People infer cause and effect from systematic and predictable patterns of relationships. To illustrate how this inference often occurs, consider a scenario in which a new friend tells you that she really likes you. Why did she say that to you? Did she say it because there is something special about you as a person that pleases her (situational), or is it because in general she likes everyone—and tells them so (dispositional)?

The **covariation rule** states that when we observe a particular event covarying with a response at different times, we conclude that that event is the cause for the response. Covariation is similar to correlation. Two events covary if, when one is present so is the other, and when one is not present neither is the other. Over a series of observations, a person can often judge whether or not the two events of interest covary. If you overhear your friend tell others that she really likes them, you might then (and rightfully so) attribute her remarks to you as being dispositional.

According to attribution theory, before you would attribute cause to your friend's comment to you, you would make a covariance assessment to see whether situational or dispositional causes covaried with that comment. According to Harold Kelley (1967), such an assessment is based on three different principles, the validity of which has been demonstrated experimentally (McArthur, 1972). The first principle is **distinctiveness,** the extent to which behavior occurs to a particular stimulus but not to others. Is your friend enthusiastic about only you and maybe a few others, or does she react that way to everyone? If her remark was limited to you then you would have evidence for a situational attribution—she likes you because

FIGURE 17.1

Kelley's theory of causal attribution is based on the principles of distinctiveness, consensus, and consistency. The theory predicts that people usually attribute another's behavior to external causes under conditions of high distinctiveness, consensus, and consistency and to internal causes under conditions of low distinctiveness and consensus, and high consistency.

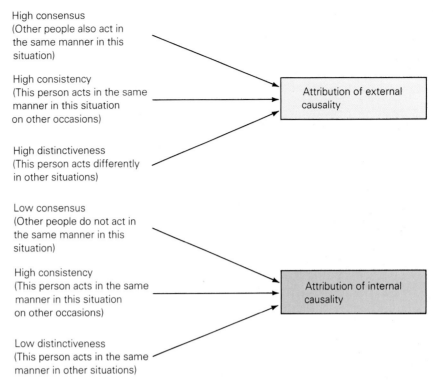

High consensus
(Other people also act in the same manner in this situation)

High consistency
(This person acts in the same manner in this situation on other occasions)

High distinctiveness
(This person acts differently in other situations)

Attribution of external causality

Low consensus
(Other people do not act in the same manner in this situation)

High consistency
(This person acts in the same manner in this situation on other occasions)

Low distinctiveness
(This person acts in the same manner in other situations)

Attribution of internal causality

of your personal qualities. If your friend likes everyone and tells them so, your attribution would be dispositional. (See Figure 17.1.)

A second covariation principle is **consensus,** the extent to which one person's behavior is consistent with that of others. How do other people respond to you? Do other people provide consensus, that is, do they also agree with your new friend that you are a likeable person, or do they have an opinion that differs from hers? To the extent that there is consensus, your attribution would be situational. To the extent that other people disagree with your friend, your attribution would be dispositional.

Consistency, or the extent to which one person's behavior is consistent across time and/or settings is the third covariation principle. How consistent is your friend's reaction to you? Does she like you one day, but not the next? If she consistently likes you, then your attribution about situational or dispositional causes made from the distinctiveness and the consensus rules would be strengthened. If her feelings toward you vary from week to week, however, then you might conclude that her response is due less to your personal qualities than to her disposition.

Discounting. In Chapter 2, we presented the concept of plausible rival hypotheses, which refers to the existence of multiple explanations of the same event. These multiple explanations not only exist for psychologists explaining the results of their studies, but also for the typical person making attributions in everyday life. Let's return to our example of your new friend. Does she genuinely like you, or does she have ulterior motives for saying that she likes you? Did her remark stem from the fact that she wants something from you—money, enhanced social status, tutoring, or so on? According to the **discounting rule,** the presence of several competing but reasonable attributions means that the judged probability of any one attribution being correct is reduced. That is, if you feel it is likely that she told you she liked you because she wants you to help her study, your confidence in the attribution that she likes you for your personal qualities is reduced.

Two Attributional Errors. The ability to make attributions regarding others is crucial to our ability to interact with others. Yet, as is true of most cognitive processes, mistakes can happen. Two common ones are the fundamental attribution error and the actor-observer effect.

Attribution theory describes the rather logical manner in which attributions are made. However, people do not always make logical attributions. One particular kind of error has been observed in so many different settings that it is called the **fundamental attribution error.** All too often people overestimate the influence of dispositional and underestimate the influence of the situational variables in other people's behavior (Ross, 1977).

The fundamental attribution error has received considerable experimental support. One study (Ross, Amabile, & Steinmetz, 1977) set up the scenario of a television quiz show in which college students were randomly assigned to be either the questioner or the contestant. The questioner wrote some reasonably difficult but easily scored items. An example of such a question might be, "Who won the 1969 World Series?" In essence, the questioner asked other people detailed questions that he or she could answer but that they probably could not. Yet, despite the fact that the contestants knew the unfair advantage of the questioner in this situation, contestants tended to rate the questioners as being generally more knowledgeable than themselves.

Another example of the fundamental attribution error is called the **belief in a just world,** the belief that people get what they deserve in life (Lerner, 1966). According to the just world hypothesis, when misfortune or tragedy strike, people tend to blame the victim instead of attributing the source of the problem to situational factors outside the victim's control. As a result, an innocent victim may be blamed for circumstances over which he or she had no control, and any suffering is seen as deserved.

Support for this tendency has been provided both by experimentation (Lerner & Matthews, 1967) and by interviewing victims. For example, the emotional trauma of rape is often compounded by the sometimes callous reactions of even friends and family who, instead of providing comfort and sympathy, grill the victim with questions such as, "How could you have gotten yourself into such a situation?" or "Why were you wearing such tight pants?" (Symonds, 1975). In addition, victims often mistakenly blame themselves for being raped (Janoff-Bulman, 1979).

Most often, though, the fundamental attribution error usually involves attributions we make about other people's behavior, not our own. Do we make the same error of attributing our own behavior more to dispositional than to situational factors? The answer appears to be no (Jones & Nisbett, 1972). Curiously, when trying to explain our own behavior, we are much more likely to attribute it to characteristics of the situation than to our own disposition, a phenomenon known as the **actor-observer effect.** In other words, we tend to see our own behavior as relatively variable and strongly influenced by the situation, while the behavior of others is seen as more stable, due to personal dispositions (Sande, Goethals, & Radloff, 1988).

A provocative study of college age male-female couples supports the actor-observer effect (Orvis, Kelley, & Butler, 1976). Each partner was asked separately to describe disagreements in the relationship, such as fighting, arguments, and criticism. Each partner was also asked to explain his or her attribution of the underlying causes of the disagreements. When describing his or her own behavior, each person tended to refer to environmental circumstances, such as financial problems or not getting enough sleep. However, when describing their partner's behavior, subjects often made reference to specific negative personality characteristics and attitudes, such as selfishness or low commitment to the relationship. The process of inferring the causes of behavior is a complicated one, and attribution research has helped to describe some of the mistakes and biases of which we are all occasionally guilty.

Attitude and Attitude Development

As we have already learned, social cognition involves how people construct impressions of themselves, of others, and of the social environment. Social cognition also involves our evaluation of people as well as social events or circumstances. An evaluative response to a person, event, or circumstance is referred to as an **attitude.** Oftentimes attitudes convey our feelings or emotions. A statement such as "I like you" implies both an evaluation and an emotion. The study of attitude formation and change commands the attention of many social psychologists, probably because of the intuitive belief that attitude and behavior are closely linked. How well does this common-sense assumption meet with experimental support? Answering this question requires first that we discuss some of the thorny issues confronted by social psychologists in trying to understand the concept of attitude.

Frequently, social psychologists think of an attitude as a concept entailing three separate components. The first component, beliefs, are cognitions that make a factual claim about the world. Examples of beliefs are:

- George Washington was the first president of the United States.
- The Detroit Pistons won the 1989 NBA championship.

Affect, on the other hand, represents our emotional reaction to a particular object, where "object" refers to almost anything including inanimate objects, specific places, social policies, and people. Affective responses are generally evaluative responses that involve terms such as good-bad, like-dislike, satisfied-dissatisfied, and approval-disapproval. Examples of affective responses are:

- My psychology professor is a good teacher.
- I like you.

Behavior, of course, is what an individual actually does. Examples include:

- Henry is talking on the phone.
- You are reading your psychology text.

For example, in describing Henry's attitude toward the Detroit Pistons, we may be interested in all three components of an attitude. Henry may believe that the Pistons have the most effective fast break in basketball, he feels good when the Pistons win, and he often watches them play on TV.

Keep in mind, however, that the social psychologist studying Henry's attitude is usually going to have information of only one type available, namely Henry's behavior. Henry may believe something to be true and he may feel a certain way about a person or event, but the only way the researcher has of discovering Henry's thoughts and feelings—with the exception of hooking him up to elaborate physiological recording devices in a laboratory—is through Henry's verbal reports or actions, both of which are behavioral in nature. This points up an important assumption many researchers make regarding attitudes, namely, that behavior is a reflection of underlying cognitive and affective components. For this reason, attitude research is frequently complicated by the problem of definition, because it is often unclear which of the components is being investigated.

We can identify the three components of the concept of attitude using many situations, such as a political convention. The belief or factual statement in this case would be that Michael Dukakis was a presidential candidate in 1988. Affective responses from his supporters were positive and approving. Their behavior, the third component, is to show support for their candidate, as they are doing here, with a convention.

Assuming that we can reach an agreeable definition of attitudes, how do we explain their origin? Why do you like one type of ice cream but not another? Why do you belong to one political party instead of another? Social psychologists have traced the development of attitudes to at least two likely factors, mere exposure and conditioning.

Mere Exposure. Surprisingly, simply being exposed repeatedly to an otherwise neutral object over a period of time may lead to a positive attitude toward that object. This attraction for the familiar is called the **mere exposure effect.** One of the first studies to demonstrate this effect used a variety of neutral stimuli—toward which there were no positive or negative feelings—such as nonsense words, photographs of the faces of unknown people, and Chinese characters (Zajonc, 1968). The more the subjects saw the stimuli, the more the stimuli were liked at a later point in time. Even stimuli that were seen only once were liked more than things never before seen. Even when the stimuli were flashed so briefly that they could not be recognized, subjects usually preferred a stimulus that had been previously presented to a novel one that they could recognize (Kunst-Wilson & Zajonc, 1980).

Conditioning. Conditioned attitudes are learned responses to the attitude object. For example, in classical conditioning, the attitude object (CS) becomes associated in some way with positive or aversive stimuli (UCS). Attitude formation through classical conditioning follows the basic process demonstrated by Pavlov in his studies of the conditional salivary reflex in dogs. In the case of attitude formation, the neutral stimulus (ultimately the CS) becomes associated with either positive or negative feelings. For example, you might be attracted to the person sitting next to you in psychology class—this person serves as an unconditional stimulus, producing positive feelings. As a result of being exposed to this person over a period of time in your psychology class, the class itself (the originally neutral stimulus) becomes a conditional stimulus. Consequently, you develop a positive attitude or a favorable response to being in psychology class.

The range of objects to which we may develop positive or negative attitudes through classical conditioning is extraordinary. Research has shown, for example, that even our emotional reactions to certain words may be due to conditioning of this sort (Staats, 1975). Consider how this might happen. When a toddler reaches for a potentially dangerous object in the environment, say an electrical outlet, a parent will likely respond both by firmly stating "No!" and by punishing the child, perhaps by restraining the child's movement. As a result of a classical conditioning process, the word "No," which, of course, has no innate meaning to the infant, becomes a conditional stimulus that leads to the sort of emotional responses originally provoked only by the physical restraint. Is it any wonder that such verbal reprimands often produce considerable emotional reactions in children?

Attitude Change and Persuasion

Another important source of our attitudes is the deliberate attempt by others to persuade us to change our attitudes. For example, billions of dollars are spent each year in advertising in the effort to affect our attitude toward a product. The psychological study of attitude change is based on the information processing model in the sense that attitudes change as a result of new information. Two aspects of the persuasion process have been given special attention by researchers, the source of the message and the message itself.

The Source. A message tends to be more persuasive if its source is either credible or attractive. Source credibility is high when the source is perceived as knowledgeable and is trusted to communicate accurately this knowledge. For example, in one study (Horland & Weiss, 1951), people developed a more favorable attitude towards different types of medicine when the information appeared in the prestigious medical journal, *New England Journal of Medicine*, than when it appeared in a mass-circulation tabloid (Hovland & Weiss, 1951).

As anyone who watches television realizes, attractiveness also can influence attitude formation. Messages seem to have more impact when the source is physically attractive. For example, physically attractive people are more likely than physically unattractive people to persuade others to sign a petition (Chaiken, 1979).

The Message. As you would expect, aspects of the message itself may be important in determining its persuasive appeal. For example, is an argument that provides only one side of an issue more effective than one that presents both sides? The answer, it seems, depends upon the prior attitudes and knowledge of the audience. If the audience either knows very little about the issue, or already holds a strong position with respect to the issue, one-sided arguments tend to be most effective. If the audience is well informed about the issue, however, the two-sided argument tends to be most persuasive (McAlister, Perry, Killen, Slinkard, & Maccoby, 1980).

How effective are scare tactics embedded in the message in changing someone's attitude? This question arose several years ago when a program entitled "Scared Straight" was implemented in New Jersey to persuade youthful offenders to abandon delinquent life-styles. The program entailed an afternoon visit to Rahway state prison, and a very distressing, intimidating encounter with a group of prison inmates. In quite graphic and often disturbing terms, the inmates described the horror and humiliation of prison life, suggesting that it would be a mistake for the youngsters to

Changing attitudes through scare tactics is effective only when it is combined with specific instructions that explain how to change a certain behavior. This conclusion was illustrated after a program called "Scared Straight" was implemented. In the program, prison inmates described the horror of prison life to delinquent youths in an attempt to discourage their negative behavior. Later studies showed that many of the youths who participated in the program returned to lives of crime.

continue their present lifestyles. Although the program initially appeared successful, and was certainly appealing at an emotional level, recent research has indicated that the majority of the offenders exposed to the "Scared Straight" program eventually returned to delinquent activities (Hagan, 1982). Additional research has shown that scare tactics may be effective in bringing about change, but only when combined with instructive information about how to actually go about changing one's behavior (Cialdini, Petty, & Cacioppo, 1981). In other words, messages are effective in changing attitude when they contain both emotional and informative components.

The Elaboration Likelihood Model. Petty and Cacioppo (1986) have proposed the elaboration likelihood model to account for attitude change or persuasion. According to this model, persuasion can take either a central or a peripheral route. The central route requires the person to think critically about the argument or arguments being presented, weighing their relative strengths and weaknesses and elaborating on the relevant themes. At issue is the actual substance of the argument, not its emotional or superficial appeal. The peripheral route, on the other hand, refers to attempts at persuasion in which the behavior or attitude to be changed is associated with something positive—a professional athlete, a millionaire, or an attractive female model—that actually may have nothing to do with the issue of importance. Selling products by associating them with attractive people or implying that buying the product will result in emotional, social, or financial benefits are examples of the use of peripheral attitude change techniques.

Attitude-Behavior Correspondence

Given that attitudes consist of cognitive, affective, and behavioral components, how interrelated are these components to one another? That behavior may or may not correspond to the other components of attitude was demonstrated by Richard LaPiere (1934) who, accompanied by two Chinese friends, visited many hotels and restaurants in the United States. Only once during their travels were they refused service. Following their travels, LaPiere wrote letters to the same hotels and restaurants they actually visited, requesting whether they would serve a Chinese couple. More than half of the establishments replied, and of these, 92 percent said that they would not serve Chinese customers! These stated attitudes, presumably reflecting the beliefs and feelings of the owners and managers toward Chinese people, were markedly inconsistent with their establishments' actual treatment of LaPiere and his Chinese friends.

LaPiere's study stimulated a great deal of research on the matter of attitude-behavior correspondence, and while we do not yet have a complete picture, some aspects of this complex relationship have been identified. For example, general attitude measures collected by questionnaire or interview can predict general classes of behavior quite successfully. Predicting specific behaviors, however, requires a specific attitude measure (Fishbein & Azjen, 1975). For example, if you wanted to predict whether a friend might volunteer to assist an elderly person to go shopping or to help supervise a group of disadvantaged youths at a local playground, you might find out whether he or she is generally in favor of community-based projects. If, however, you wished to predict only whether your friend would volunteer to assist the elderly person, you would need to ask specific questions about your friend's attitude toward the elderly.

Often attitude and behavior do not correspond when there are negative social consequences for acting in a manner consistent with the attitude

(Fishbein, 1980). Suppose, for example, that you have just finished watching a play and as you begin to leave your seat the entire theater audience stands to applaud the play. Even though you were not overly impressed by the play—your attitude is not as positive toward the play as was that of the majority of the audience—you nonetheless join along in the ovation, thereby avoiding the looks of disapproval that might otherwise be directed your way.

Finally, poor attitude-behavior correspondence may occur when the behavior is habitual, that is, when it occurs with considerable frequency. Many such behaviors may fit into this category. The cigarette smoker, for instance, may think or even know of the harmful effects of smoking and may have negative feelings about the habit. The behavioral habit may persist, however, despite the negative cognitive and affective components of the attitude.

Cognitive Dissonance Theory

In the example of the play, remember that your standing and applauding was not consistent with your actual emotional response to the play. In thinking about your behavior on the way home from the theater, how do you explain your actions? In other words, how do you reconcile the obvious discrepancy between your feelings toward the play and your applause for it? Leon Festinger (1957) proposed the **theory of cognitive dissonance**, that states that people are motivated to reduce anxiety produced when their cognitions and behavior are inconsistent. Cognitive dissonance theory has been tremendously influential, stimulating much social psychological research.

The central theme of cognitive dissonance theory is that people wish to avoid inconsistent thoughts and behaviors. For example, the thought "I need to study tonight" is inconsistent with the behavior of going to dinner and a movie tonight. When a person confronts his or her dissonant cognitions or behaviors, an unpleasant, uncomfortable internal state called dissonance results. According to the theory, a person is then motivated to reduce the dissonance.

One means of achieving dissonance reduction is to alter the cognition or somehow justify the behavior. An interesting example of this tactic is provided by a study of a group whose leader predicted the world would end with a massive flood (Festinger, Riecken, & Schacter, 1956). Only the true believers (who else?) of this particular faith were to be saved. A squadron of flying saucers was prophesied to fly in and rescue them from the rising waters. Of course, this did not happen. How did the leader reconcile, to both himself and others, the mismatch of prophecy and reality? How did those people reconcile their belief in the leader's prophecy with what actually happened? As it became apparent that there was going to be no flood that evening, the group leader announced that to reward the faithful, the world was to be saved. Not only was the dissonance eliminated, but joy broke out.

From the perspective of the followers, the dissonance resulting from the false prediction of the world's end could have been reduced by devaluing the leader of the group. These people could not admit to themselves that they had acted on a false and foolish belief. Eliminating the original dissonance by attacking their own beliefs would simply introduce a new source of dissonance—"I do not like to appear foolish" and "I just did a very silly thing." Instead, the leader's solution is much more elegant. Instead of feeling foolish, these people can believe that they just saved the world! Instead of admitting to themselves that they were wrong, their initial beliefs were reinforced.

FIGURE 17.2

Study of attitude change following counterattitudinal behavior. Festinger and Carlsmith found that subjects offered $1 to tell another subject that a boring task was interesting reported that the task was more interesting than did subjects offered $20.

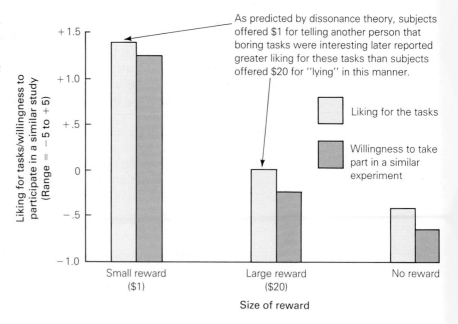

As predicted by dissonance theory, subjects offered $1 for telling another person that boring tasks were interesting later reported greater liking for these tasks than subjects offered $20 for "lying" in this manner.

Liking for the tasks

Willingness to take part in a similar experiment

Much of the experimental research on cognitive dissonance has focused on the discrepancy between public behavior and private attitudes. Public behavior that is discrepant with private attitudes is called **counterattitudinal behavior.** The theoretical significance of counterattitudinal behavior is that it could serve as a vehicle for attitude change—changing one's private attitude to be consistent with public behavior would reduce the resulting dissonance.

An early, well-known study (Festinger & Carlsmith, 1959) that evaluated attitude change following counterattitudinal behavior provided support for cognitive dissonance theory. Imagine yourself as a subject in the following study. The stated purpose of the study was to explore the effect of directions on task performance. Subjects performed a task that was designed to be extremely boring: turning each of many pegs on a board exactly one-quarter turn to the right, and when all the pegs were turned, beginning again by turning the first peg. After 20 minutes, the subject was instructed to stop. Before leaving, however, the experimenter told the subject that his assistant had called in sick, and he needed some help. The next subject, waiting his turn in an adjoining room, was to be told that the task was interesting and enjoyable. With a little embarrassment, the experimenter asked the real subject if he would mind filling in for the missing assistant and deliver the instructions. Although the choice of whether to do this or not was left to the subject, only 3 of the 51 subjects refused to lie. What would you have done?

The crux of the study is that the subject was asked to engage in counterattitudinal behavior, to say something that he did not believe. The independent variable was the amount of money the experimenter offered the subject to lie. Half of the subjects were offered $1 and the other half were offered $20. The true purpose of the study, of course, was to learn what effect this payment had on the subject's attitude toward the task. The interesting result was that subjects who were paid $1 to say that a boring task was interesting reported that the task was more interesting than did subjects who were paid $20 (see Figure 17.2). That is, subjects who were paid very little tended to change their attitude both toward the desirability of the task and their willingness to participate in further experiments.

Why would these subjects change their attitude? According to cognitive dissonance theory, the counterattitudinal behavior created dissonance—the subject feels uncomfortable for having lied about the task. Those paid $20 could easily justify their behavior for the money, thereby reducing their dissonance. The $1 payment, however, was insufficient justification; it did not provide ample reason for subjects to lie. To reduce this dissonance, the subjects were motivated to change their attitude toward the task. Subjects told themselves something like "The study wasn't all that bad after all," or , "Participating in a scientific study is interesting in and of itself."

Although the theoretical interpretation of results from dissonance experiments has often been the subject of intense debate among social psychologists (Bem, 1970; Gerard, Conolley, & Wilhelmy, 1974), results supporting dissonance theory such as those presented here have been replicated successfully across a wide range of situations and subjects.

SOCIAL INFLUENCE

We began this chapter by making the claim that human beings are unmistakably social creatures, that a good deal of our lives are spent in the company of other people. By itself this is not an especially profound or insightful observation, but it leads to some interesting implications, particularly for the social psychologist. We do not merely occupy physical space with other people. The very cognitions, emotions, and behaviors that define each of us as an individual are strongly influenced, oftentimes without our awareness, by those with whom we interact. Not only are we often unaware of the influence that others have on our lives, but quite frequently this influence is entirely unintentional, meaning other people may be equally unaware of how they are influencing us. In this section we will consider the means by which we influence and are influenced by other people, social facilitation, conformity, compliance, obedience to authority, and bystander intervention. We will also consider a type of mutual influence that gives special accent to humankind's social nature, that of interpersonal attraction.

Social Facilitation

Suppose you are jogging down a lonely country road at a leisurely pace. As you come around a bend, you spot a distant farm house and you can just barely make out the presence of a family gathered on the front porch. As you approach the house, you notice that your pace has quickened and by the time you pass in front of the house, you are moving at more of a sprint than a jog. By the time you have crested a hill, beyond sight of the family, you begin to slow down, eventually reaching the leisurely pace with which your run started. How would you explain this? According to social psychologists, your behavior would be described as an example of **social facilitation,** a change in task performance due to the presence of others. Though there was clearly no attempt made by the family members to cheer you on or in any other way influence your running, their very presence did, in fact, have an effect on your behavior, specifically the speed of your running.

As you can imagine, because we are so often in the presence of other people, social facilitation is a pervasive social phenomenon. Social psychologists have studied social facilitation in a variety of settings, such as college students doing multiplication problems (Allport, 1920), memorizing lists of words (Cottrell, Rittle, & Wack, 1967), playing pool (Michaels, Blommel, Brocato, Linkous, & Rowe, 1982), and remarkably enough, in a

In social facilitation, the presence of others changes our performance. We can see this phenomenon occurring in all types of sports where competitive forces are at work to make us outperform other athletes.

wide variety of different species ranging from monkeys to chickens to even ants. For example, individual ants were found to dig more than three times as much sand when working in groups than when working alone (Chen, 1937)! Importantly, other people (or animals) do not have to be actually engaged in the same task; their mere presence can lead to social facilitation in the person who is engaged in another task (Dashiell, 1930).

Facilitation of the response, however, does not inevitably occur when others are present. Robert Zajonc (1965) observed that performance on a very simple task or a more complex task mastered previously with repeated practice "is facilitated by the presence of spectators, while the acquisition of new responses is impaired" (p. 270). Zajonc hypothesized that the presence of others is arousing; their presence energizes the individual. For a task that the individual can perform very well, performance is enhanced by the presence of others. However, if the individual cannot perform the task very well, even when by himself or herself, the presence of others leads to an impairment in performance.

Social Norms and Conformity

Many of the rules that govern our social behavior are formally codified as laws and regulations that we are legally obligated to follow. Some of these laws are made and enforced by various levels of government, others by organizations to which we belong, such as our place of employment, schools, and churches. However, many other rules that influence our social behavior are not formally codified as law, but are, instead, unwritten agreements. These informal rules that define the expected and appropriate behavior in specific situations are called **social norms,** or, when applied to members of a particular group, group norms.

How we look at strangers, the way we talk to our friends or our supervisors at work, and the kind of food that we eat, are all influenced, at least in part, by the norms of the society in which we live. American men do not generally wear Scottish kilts, and most of us do not eat spiders—not because people in different parts of the world do not do these things, but because these types of behavior are not included in our social norms. Despite the fact that they do not develop from a conspicuous formal or legal process, norms are very powerful sources of social influence, as we shall see next.

An important social psychological study by Muzafer Sherif (1936) provided an empirical demonstration of the power of social influence in the establishment of group norms. Sherif's study was based on a perceptual illusion, originally discovered by astronomers, called the autokinetic effect: A small stationary light, when projected in an otherwise completely darkened room, appears to move. The illusion is so strong that even if someone is aware of the effect, the apparent movement often still persists.

Sherif at first placed a single person in the room, and asked how far the light was moving at different times. Each person tended to answer within a certain range. One person's answers might be between 6 centimeters and 12 centimeters, and another person's answers might be between 2 meters and 3 meters. Next, Sherif had groups of three people make a joint decision as to the extent of the movement. The most interesting result of the study was that the group would define a norm establishing the distance of the judged movement, and each person in the group would then adopt that norm as his or her own when later making individual judgments about the movement of the light. That is, the group established what Sherif (1936)

After disagreeing with the confederates in Asch's study, the subject begins to doubt his judgment and looks again at the card, even though the correct answer is obvious.

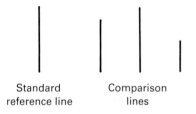

Standard reference line   Comparison lines

FIGURE 17.3

The Asch conformity experiment stimuli. Subjects in the experiment were asked to match a reference line to one of three other vertical lines. The correct match was always obvious. When the confederates in the experiment gave an obviously incorrect answer, the subject also conformed and gave that incorrect answer about one-third of the time.

called a collective frame of reference. This act of changing one's thoughts or behavior to be similar to those of a social group is called **conformity.**

Even when tested by themselves on a different day, the group members still tended to follow this frame of reference. Other researchers found that even a year later the group's norm continued to be adopted by the individual (Rohrer, Baron, Hoffman, & Swander, 1954). Thus, Sherif and others concluded that people's perceptions of ambiguous stimuli tend to conform to social norms.

In many ways, Sherif's (1936) findings are not too surprising if you consider that the subjects found themselves in an uncertain or ambiguous situation. It makes sense to use other people's opinions or judgments as a frame of reference when you are not too sure how to judge the situation. How strongly do group norms influence individual behavior, though, when the situation is not ambiguous, that is, when we are quite certain that we perceive things as they really are? The answer to this question was provided in a series of elegant studies conducted by Solomon Asch (1952, 1955).

Before we begin a specific discussion of Asch's work, we first need to discuss a technique sometimes used in social psychological experiments. The technique involves the use of deception, in which another person appears to be a subject in the experiment, when in fact he or she is really an assistant, or **confederate** of the experimenter. The confederate usually carries out prespecified instructions as defined by the experimenter. To the actual subject, though, the confederate appears to be acting spontaneously. The confederate is used so that the experimenter can exert some control over the social factors that may influence the behavior of the actual subject.

Asch's initial set of studies involved one real subject and six confederates, all of whom were seated around a table. All seven people were told that they were participating in an investigation of visual judgment in which they would be matching the lengths of three vertical lines to that of a standard reference line (see Figure 17.3). On a given trial, the subject's task was to choose the one comparison line that was the same length as the reference line. The line lengths were sufficiently different, and subjects were seated sufficiently close to the lines so that the correct answer was almost always given by the subject when judgments were made alone in the presence of the experimenter. A different result, though, emerged when the real subject was seated among the confederates and asked to make a judgment.

When seated with the confederates, the real subject was always placed one seat from the end, with five people to his right and one person to his left. The experimenter began on the subject's right by asking each person to call out the number of the correct comparison line. Each of the first five subjects called out the obvious answer, and the real subject mundanely provided the same answer. The group was unanimous in its judgment.

This procedure was followed for the first two trials, but on the third trial something remarkable from the subject's point of view occurred. For the third set of lines, the first subject called out what appeared to be an obviously wrong answer. Unknown to the real subject, all the confederates had been instructed to give the same wrong answer on the third trial. After the first five "subjects" had given the same wrong answer on this trial, the real subject had to choose one of two opposing alternatives: Does he remain independent and choose the evidence from his own eyes, or does he conform and provide the answer given by the first five members of the group? For each subject there were 18 trials; for 12, the confederates all provided the same wrong answer.

Asch found that the real subject conformed to the group's norm by providing incorrect answers on 36.8 percent of the trials (Asch, 1952, 1955). Approximately one quarter of the subjects, however, maintained complete independence in their responses, always giving the correct answer. Most people alternated between conforming on one trial and then giving the correct answer on another.

When asked to explain why they conformed, subjects provided different kinds of answers, clues that perhaps different underlying psychological processes may produce the same conforming behavior. Some conforming subjects continued to believe that their responses were incorrect, they conformed even though they believed that they were wrong—they simply did not want to appear different. This type of conformity is called public conformity. Other subjects apparently managed to convince themselves that, in fact, their responses were wrong and the group's answers were correct. This kind of conformity may be explained by cognitive dissonance theory (Festinger, 1957). Remember that according to this theory people are motivated to reduce dissonance. In the Asch studies, dissonance is created between a private perception and an obviously incorrect public (group) perception. Perhaps the real subjects conformed to the group answer because they started to doubt the accuracy of their original perception, just as Festinger and Carlsmith's (1959) subjects may have decided that the monotonous peg-turning task wasn't really so monotonous.

One of the advantages of Asch's experimental setup was that it could be modified to allow for an analysis of a number of other independent variable's effects that might influence the tendency to conform to group norms. One important independent variable has been group size. Interestingly, one other subject (actually a confederate) does not seem to result in high rates of conformity. Three additional subjects seems to be the minimum number to produce conformity to the group, but adding more than four does not seem to enhance the conformity effect (see Figure 17.4). In addition, the presence of just one other nonconforming subject—a confederate who was instructed to provide the correct answer, even though other confederates provided incorrect answers—significantly reduced conformity among actual subjects. In Asch's (1952) words, "The presence of a single voice pointing to the true state of affairs had an unmistakable liberating effect" (p. 479).

FIGURE 17.4
The relationship between group size and conformity on Asch's line matching task. Asch found that three other subjects usually need to be present in the experiment for conformity to occur.

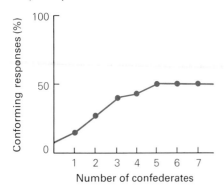

Compliance

In our discussion of conformity, we saw that people often behave in a manner consistent with a reference group even when there is no conscious attempt by members of that group to influence the individual's behavior. There are, of course, many times when other people openly and with obvious intent try to persuade us to act in certain ways. Automobile salesmen, insurance agents, politicians, and most certainly, college professors, are all people whose very livelihood depends upon their ability to influence the behavior of others. **Compliance** refers to a change in one's behavior or beliefs as the result of an explicit request or attempt made by another person.

Automobile salespeople are compliance professionals in that they are skilled in the ability to influence others' behavior.

All of us are asked to do things by those with no special authority, and all of us make such requests of others. We may, for example, want other people's money, companionship, or affection; we may want to cut in line at the grocery store or at a movie; or we may want our neighbor to turn down his or her stereo or television. Because most of us do not make a living intentionally trying to get others to comply with our wishes, we may be unaware of the very effective techniques that many professionals use to encourage our compliance (Cialdini, 1988). In our discussion of the foot-in-the-door, low-balling and door-in-the-face techniques, however, you will undoubtedly recognize some compliance games in which you have certainly participated, if only as an unwitting victim.

Foot-In-The-Door. The **foot-in-the-door technique,** often used very effectively by professional sales people, is employed to make an initial small request followed by a larger request. Of course, the ultimate goal is to gain compliance with the larger request, but the person begins by getting his or her foot in the door by first asking for something small.

The effectiveness of the foot-in-the-door technique was demonstrated experimentally in a field study (Freedman & Fraser, 1966). Posing as a volunteer worker, the experimenter simply asked homeowners to comply with a rather outlandish request; he asked them, in the name of public service, to install a large sign reading *Drive carefully* in their front yard. Not surprisingly, only 17 percent of subjects complied by agreeing to display the sign.

In another experimental condition, however, this same request was made of subjects who two weeks earlier had agreed to display a small sign reading *Be a safe driver.* Interestingly, having complied with the more reasonable request resulted in a marked increase in the probability of complying with the later, large request. Seventy-six percent of subjects in this condition agreed to the larger request. Though later research has not always provided such ample support for the foot-in-the-door technique (Foss & Dempsey, 1979), its success as a compliance technique is well accepted.

Why does the foot-in-the-door technique work? The most widely cited explanation is based on Daryl Bem's (1967) self-perception theory. According to the **self-perception theory,** we learn much about our own attitudes and behavior by observing our own actions. Bem suggests that if you ask a person why he or she likes to eat a particular food, that person might say, "Because I like it." Bem argues instead that at least part of the reason is "Because I eat it." (1970, p.54). In other words, we use our own actions as an important clue in explaining our attitudes and behavior.

For example, you may generally agree with the importance of safe driving, but you may not be so emotionally involved in the issue to post a large sign on your lawn. However, as a result of agreeing to display the smaller sign, you begin to see yourself as being considerably involved in the safe driving issue (DeJong, 1979). Now when the second, though more demanding request is made, you are more likely to agree to display the large sign, for doing so would be consistent with the emerging perception you have of yourself as an involved citizen. According to self-perception theory, the foot-in-the-door technique effectively changes your self-perception.

Low-Balling. Another often used compliance technique, called **low-balling technique,** occurs when something desirable is offered and then, after commitment is obtained, the desirable object or condition is withdrawn. Low-balling is sometimes used by unscrupulous car salespersons who may offer a price for a car that is indeed too good to be true. After the car has been test driven, after the customer has decided to purchase the car, and after the financing has been arranged, suddenly an "error" is discovered and the price is raised to the going market price. But after all, if you are already spending over $10,000 and you really like the car, what's another few hundred dollars? Not much, except it was the extra low price that originally attracted you to the dealer.

That low-balling is not a technique peculiar to the automobile salesperson was demonstrated in a study of Introductory Psychology students who were asked to do something that they would not ordinarily do: come to the psychology laboratory at 7A.M. to serve as subjects in a study of "thinking processes" (Cialdini, Cacioppo, Bassett, & Miller, 1978). Subjects in the control group were asked up front whether they would come to the laboratory at that hour, and, not surprisingly, only 24 percent agreed to participate. Students in the experimental group, however, were first asked only if they would participate in a study. Fifty-six percent agreed to participate. Only after agreeing to participate were the subjects told of the early morning hour of the experiment. Despite being given the opportunity to withdraw at this time, no subject did so.

Door-In-The-Face. In a sense, the **door-in-the-face technique** (Cialdini, Vincent, Lewis, Catalan, Wheeler, & Darby, 1975) is the opposite of the foot-in-the-door technique. This technique is a compliance procedure in which an unreasonable request is followed by a more reasonable request. A key aspect of this technique is that the same person makes both requests. By asking for something smaller the second time, a concession has been made, to which the person is obligated by the norm of reciprocity to return. If a different person makes the second request, then this norm need not apply, no concession is made, and compliance generally does not occur (Cialdini, 1988).

In a study by Cialdini et al. (1975), the goal was to get college students to agree to chaperone juvenile delinquents on a trip to the zoo. Posing as employees of the County Youth Counseling Program, the experimenters asked individual students who were walking across campus if they would serve as chaperones. Almost all (83 percent) subjects refused. Other subjects, however, were first asked to serve as voluntary counselors for two hours a week at a juvenile detention center for two years. As expected, subjects in this group also refused this rather formidable request, effectively slamming the door in the face of the person making the request.

The key aspect of this experiment is that, following the outlandish request, subjects in the latter condition were then asked to comply with the much less overwhelming request of chaperoning the juvenile delinquents on a trip to the zoo. The results? Simply making the initial request increased the rate of acceptance by more than three times that of subjects in the first group who were asked directly to be chaperones.

One explanation for the effects of the door-in-the-face technique is the **norm of reciprocity,** the idea that what one person does to you, you should do in return. In essence, a favor from someone else should be returned. The norm of reciprocity creates an obligation for repayment, usually resulting in a feeling of indebtedness on the part of the person receiving a gift. Slamming the door in the face of the requestor creates in the other person an obligation to do something to amend his or her refusal of the request.

The norm of reciprocity is pervasive (Gouldner, 1960). It establishes a basic guideline for behavior in a wide range of situations, and its emergence in evolutionary history is considered to be crucial to the development of social life. One person could give resources to another person without actually giving them away, making possible "sophisticated and coordinated systems of aid, gift giving, defense, and trade . . . bringing immense benefit to the societies that possessed them" (Cialdini, 1988, p. 22).

Note that the norm of reciprocity does not require that the "favor" be initially requested or even wanted. The norm is more general than this—if you have received something, then your obligation is to return the favor— period. The debt of obligation can be so strong that the norm of reciprocity can be exploited by those who want us to comply with their requests when we would otherwise not do so.

Obedience to Authority

All of us, regardless of how free-spirited or independent we are, have learned to obey others and follow rules to some extent. When driving a car we stop at red lights, and when shopping for groceries we pay for our items. **Obedience to authority** is defined as the following of orders issued by a legitimate authority such as a teacher, a parent, a police officer, or even an usher at a theater. The legitimate authority is someone who is perceived as having the proper right to give the orders.

The psychological study of obedience has focused on the problem of choosing between following the dictates of our own conscience versus obeying the commands of others.

The psychological study of obedience has focused on the problem of choosing between following the dictates of our own conscience versus obeying the commands of others. For some, such as the well-known 19th-century American writer, Henry David Thoreau (1849), the choice between conscience and obedience was straightforward, as he explained in his essay, "On the Duty of Civil Disobedience."

Why has every man a conscience then? I think that we should be men first, and subjects afterward. It is not desirable to cultivate a respect for the law, so much as for the right. The only obligation which I have a right to assume is to do at any time what I think right.

(1849/1960, p. 223)

Most people, however, find the prospect of everyone simply following their own conscience (or lack thereof) without regard for laws somewhat frightening. Yet the answer to the conscience versus obedience issue is also not easily answered at the other extreme in which obedience is always chosen. Obedience has manifested its ominous forms many times throughout human history, including one of the profound tragedies of modern history: World War II. The millions of military and civilian losses that resulted directly or indirectly from combat are startling in and of themselves. Particularly grotesque, however, was the systematic mass murder of millions of Jews by the Nazis. Entire families were killed with machine gun fire, or were sent en masse to gas chambers or ovens to be killed. After the war, many of the higher ranking Nazis who participated in the mass

The tragedy of the holocaust that occurred during World War II brings to light the powerful effects that obedience to authority has when taken to extremes. Pictured here is Franz Hoessler whose obedience to Hitler's commands resulted in the death of millions of innocent people.

murders were captured and put on trial. Time and time again the central theme of each of their defenses was obedience—they had simply been following orders. As military men they claimed that their primary obligation had been to carry out the commands of their superiors.

One of the more disturbing results of these war crime trials was that it became apparent that those on trial were not by their nature sadistic executioners; they were not psychopaths who had lived on the fringe of society before the war. On the contrary, many of them, before becoming Nazis just a few years earlier, were ordinary citizens who held respectable jobs in their communities and who had families of their own.

How was it possible, then, for otherwise reasonably normal people to become capable of the systematic and calculated mass murder of millions of people? Seeking an answer to this question, social psychologist Stanley Milgram (1933–1984) explored the situational variables that might influence obedience to authority. Milgram's research was unique in that it differed from more traditional studies that focused on dispositional traits.

To study obedience in the psychological laboratory, Milgram constructed a task in which subjects were told to carry out an action that would seem to violate a basic moral principle.

The Milgram Procedure. Subjects, who were paid for their efforts, were adult males recruited from the general community around Yale University where the initial experiments were conducted. The subject and another person, who also appeared to be a subject but was in fact a confederate, were told by the experimenter that the study concerned the effect of punishment on learning. Either the subject or the confederate would be the Teacher and the other would be the Learner, according to the outcome of a purportedly random drawing. In fact, the drawing was rigged, so that the true subject was always assigned the role of Teacher.

After the drawing, the experimenter strapped the Learner into his seat and attached electrodes to his arms, through which electrical shock was to be delivered when the Learner performed poorly at the task. Before the Teacher and Experimenter left the room, the Teacher was given a low-intensity shock of only 45 volts so that he could gauge the intensity of the shocks he was apparently to administer. The Learner was told that "although the shocks can be extremely painful, they cause no permanent tissue damage."

The Learner was then left alone in the small room. The Teacher and Experimenter went to an adjoining room that contained the shock generator. As you can see in Figure 17.5, the front panel of this machine had 30 switches. Each switch was labeled with a corresponding voltage, ranging from 15 to 450 volts. Labels such as "Slight Shock," "Danger: Severe Shock," and finally, "XXX" were provided alongside some of the switches in a progression from lower to higher intensity shock.

Under the watchful supervision of the Experimenter, the Teacher's job was to present to the Learner a standard paired-associate learning task. The Teacher read pairs of words such as green-toy, good-day, fast-horse, and small-lamp. Then, after a brief pause, the Teacher would read, for example, fast, car, toy, horse, jet. The Learner then responded by choosing the word paired with "fast." In actuality, the Learner always followed a predetermined sequence of responses, committing about three wrong answers for every correct answer.

When the Learner's response was wrong, the Experimenter instructed the Teacher to flip a switch on the shock generator to punish the Learner's response. Moreover, every time that the Learner missed a question, the Teacher was instructed by the experimenter to "move one level higher on the shock generator," and to announce the voltage level before administering the shock. If the last switch (450 volts—XXX) was reached, the Experimenter told the Teacher to continue using that level, though after two additional trials of this level, the experiment was terminated.

Throughout the procedure, the Learner emitted increasingly intense cries of pain that could be heard clearly through the wall separating the Learner and Teacher. At 315 volts, the confederate emitted a prolonged, violent scream. After 330 volts there was nothing but complete silence, and the Learner made no responses to further questions.

If the Teacher questioned the Experimenter about the wisdom of administering increasingly intense shocks, the Experimenter responded with a prearranged set of instructions that ranged from "Please continue." to "You have no other choice, you must go on." If the Teacher asked about any potential permanent injury to the Learner, the Experimenter responded with, "Although the shocks may be painful, there is no permanent tissue damage, so please go on." In reality, no electric shock was delivered to the Learner; subjects were only led to believe that they were administering shocks.

Results Predicted. The main dependent variable in which Milgram was interested was the highest level of shock that the Teacher was willing to administer before disobeying the Experimenter and quitting the experi-

FIGURE 17.5
Diagram of the shock generator control panel used in Milgram's obedience to authority experiment.

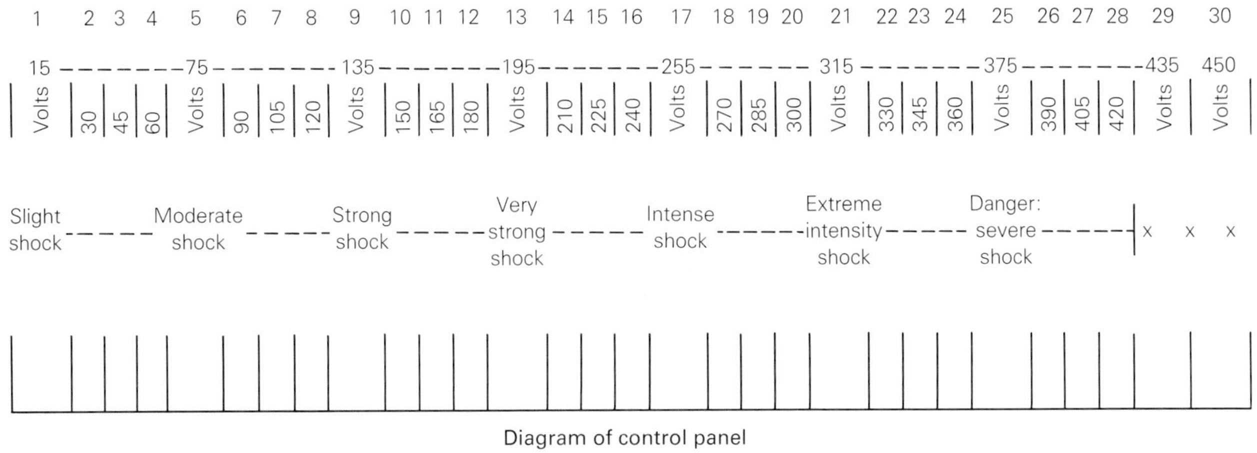

Diagram of control panel

ment. This measure could vary from 0, indicating no shocks administered, to 30, which corresponded to the 30th switch marked 450 volts—XXX.

Before beginning the study, Milgram asked 110 people from different groups—psychiatrists, college students, and middle-class adults—what they would do if placed in the role of the Teacher in this experiment. As shown in Table 17.1, their responses were unequivocal: all respondents predicted that they would disobey the experimenter before administering the most intense shocks. The mean predicted maximum shock levels for the three groups, respectively, were only 8.20, 9.35, and 9.15. These same respondents made similar predictions about other people's behavior: they believed that only a small, pathological fringe of about one in a thousand people would go as far as the maximum shock level.

Milgram observed that these respondents implicitly adopted a set of assumptions consistent with these predictions.

> These subjects see their reactions flowing from empathy, compassion, and a sense of justice . . . [They assume] that people are by and large decent and do not readily hurt the innocent. Second, that unless coerced by physical force or threat, the individual is preeminently the source of his own behavior. A person acts in a particular way because he has decided to do so. . . . The behavior itself flows from an inner core of the person. . . .
> With this view, they are likely to expect few subjects to go along with the experiment's orders.
>
> (1974, pp. 30-31)

As we shall see, these expectations were quite different from the actual results.

Results Obtained. To the surprise of everyone, including Milgram himself, the mean maximum shock level actually administered by Teachers was 24.5 on the 0-30 point scale, with 62.5 percent of the Teachers following the experimenter's orders to use 450 volts. Although many subjects were noticeably agitated, their voices cracked, they laughed nervously, or they continually touched and rubbed their faces—they nevertheless "administered" increasing intensities of shock to the Learner.

Milgram had succeeded, probably beyond his expectations, in creating a moral dilemma for his subjects, that is, a situation in which no matter what the subject did, a moral principle the subject held was violated. The subject experienced conflict, while simultaneously attempting to satisfy the competing demands of obedience to authority and personal conscience.

You might wonder, however, what factors in the experimental situation may have so strongly encouraged obedience and, conversely, what factors, if manipulated, might serve to decrease such obedience? Some answers were in fact provided by Milgram (1974) in a series of more than a dozen experiments in which variations of his obedience procedure were explored.

For example, the presence of the Experimenter in the room with the Teacher was found to produce more obedience than when the Experimenter simply gave the Teacher his instructions and then left the room. In a similar variation, when Teachers were required to have visual and physical contact with the Learner, even holding the Learner's hand down on a shock plate, the degree to which subjects obeyed the experimenter declined. However, when the Learner was in a separate room and could neither be seen nor heard, obedience was maximal. Some psychologists believe that this particular condition may be reflected in many real world situations; for example, when a pilot drops bombs on a city, he cannot see the death and destruction occurring on the ground below. Finally, the prestige associated with an institution like Yale University may have provided

TABLE 17.1. *Individuals predict their own breakoff points in Milgram's shock experiment.*

SHOCK LEVEL	VERBAL DESIGNATION AND VOLTAGE LEVEL	PSYCHIATRISTS (n = 39)*	COLLEGE STUDENTS (n = 31)	MIDDLE-CLASS ADULTS (n = 40)
	Slight shock	2*		3*
1	15	1		
2	30			
3	45			1
4	60	1		1
	Moderate shock			
5	75	6	4	7
6	90	1	3	1
7	105	4		1
8	120	4	1	3
	Strong shock			
9	135	1	3	2
10	150	14	12	9
11	165		1	2
12	180	2	6	3
	Very strong shock			
13	195	2		1
14	210		1	
15	225			1
16	240			1
	Intense shock			
17	255			1
18	270			
19	285			
20	300	1		3
	Extreme intensity shock			
21	315			
22	330			
23	345			
24	360			
	Danger: Severe shock			
25	375			
26	390			
27	405			
28	420			
	XXX			
29	435			
30	450			
	Mean maximum shock level	8.20	9.35	9.15
	Percentage predicting defiance	100.00%	100.00%	100.00%

*n refers to the number of subjects in the experimental condition.

subjects additional reason for obeying the instructions of the experimenter, himself attired in an authoritative looking white lab coat. Indeed, when the experiment was conducted in a rundown office building in Rockport, Connecticut and when the experimenter wore no distinguishing lab coat, obedience dropped to 48 percent.

Ethical Issues. Understandably, much of the attention given to Milgram's studies of obedience focused on their considerable ethical implications. Many people, psychologists and nonpsychologists alike, have attacked Milgram's studies on the grounds that they involved deception and they placed too much emotional strain on the Teachers—the real subjects in the studies. Indeed, the requirements for experimentation with human subjects have subsequently been greatly modified and expanded, in part as a reaction to these studies, so that today studies like Milgram's may not be approved by ethics review boards.

In his defense, however, Milgram conducted an extensive debriefing after the end of each experimental session in which the true purpose of the experiment was explained to the subject. The Teacher learned that he was not really administering electric shocks to the Learner. In addition, Teachers were told that their behavior was normal and quite typical. Finally, Teachers were later sent a detailed written report of the experimental procedure and results along with a follow-up questionnaire asking them about their feelings and thoughts regarding their participation. Eighty-four percent of the subjects said that they were glad to have participated in the experiment, and only 1.3 percent indicated that they wished they had not participated.

Many of Milgram's critics believe that an additional objection to the study is that people may have had to confront an uncomfortable and disturbing aspect of their own behavior—the self-realization that they are capable of actions they find reprehensible. Milgram replied that at least some of his subjects considered their enhanced insight into their own behavior and the general nature of obedience to have been very beneficial, having strongly justified their participation. Of course, Milgram could not guarantee that somebody, somewhere, who had participated in his study was not deeply hurt and troubled as a result of their participation. And therein lies another moral dilemma. To what extent is knowledge about behavior in general, and insight about oneself in particular, to be avoided in case some people may find this knowledge and insight upsetting? What do you think—at what costs should psychological research of this nature be conducted? That is not an easy question to answer.

Bystander Intervention and Helping

In the early hours of a March morning in 1964, a New York city resident named Kitty Genovese was attacked and stabbed by a stranger. Her screams alerted her neighbors, and the attacker jumped in his car and fled, leaving Ms. Genovese lying on her doorstep incapacitated and bleeding. Yet, no one came to her aid, or even called the police or an ambulance. Circling the block, her attacker returned. More stabbing, more screams, and once again the attacker fled. Still, no help. Finally, the man returned for a third time. This time the stabbings were fatal. The attack of Kitty Genovese lasted for more than 30 minutes and was witnessed by 38 people, yet no one came to her aid. Many psychologists and much of the general public blamed her death on the callousness and apathy of the big city (Rosenthal, 1964).

Despite the bystander effect, some bystanders will choose to intervene as the people pictured here did when they pulled this car accident victim away from his burning car.

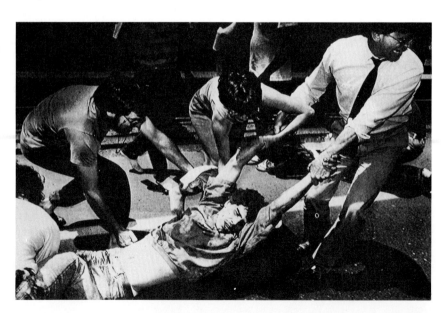

The Bystander Effect. As social psychologists are wont to do, Bibb Latané and John Darley (1970) wondered if perhaps the structure of the social situation—instead of personality characteristics of people who lived in large metropolitan areas—might provide the clues for understanding this appalling lack of help. They wondered, for instance, whether the presence of bystanders, or witnesses to such an event, might decrease, rather than increase the likelihood of receiving help. In other words, they questioned the common-sense assumption that there is "safety in numbers." The **bystander effect** refers to the finding that the larger the number of bystanders, the lower the probability that any one bystander will help.

To test the bystander effect experimentally, Latané and Darley (1968) devised an experiment in which subjects were asked to fill out questionnaires either by themselves or in a group with two others. Shortly after subjects began filling out the questionnaires, smoke was pumped into the room through a wall vent. Gradually the room filled with smoke so thick that it became difficult to see, and some subjects began coughing and rubbing their eyes. The results of the study supported the bystander effect. Of the subjects who were alone, 75 percent left the room to report the smoke to the experimenter, but only 13 percent of the subjects in groups did so. The presence of other people significantly reduced the likelihood that the smoke would be reported.

When subjects are questioned following participation in such an experiment, they frequently report not having viewed the situation as an emergency. Thus, it seems that whether a bystander will intervene in a particular circumstance depends, at least in part, on how they perceive the situation—their social perception of the event. Latané and Darley (1970) have proposed a model describing a chain of cognitive decisions the bystander faces when confronted with a potential emergency:

- The event must come to their attention or be noticed.
- The person must assume some responsibility for helping the victim.
- The possible courses of action must be considered and compared.
- Finally, the person must actually implement the chosen course of action.

Of course, this decision sequence takes place quite rapidly, and without much awareness on the bystander's part, as is true of many situations to which we respond on a daily basis.

Unfortunately, at least from the perspective of the person needing help, obstacles may arise at any one stage in this decision-making process that make it unlikely that the bystander will intervene. In many cases, the bystander who is aware that others are available to help, may not feel any personal responsibility to do so, a phenomenon referred to as **diffusion of responsibility**. It is this factor that is considered to be responsible for the finding that help is less likely to be offered when there are several bystanders present. In addition, the bystander may not feel competent to intervene or may be fearful of doing so; consequently, no course of action is decided on. Research has in fact shown that bystanders are more likely to intervene if they feel confident in their ability to help (Peterson, 1983).

Increasing Helping Behavior. Research into the bystander effect has attempted to discover how helping behavior might be encouraged. One particularly promising line of research has pointed to the importance of modeling in the enhancement of helping behavior. For instance, subjects who viewed a man helping a woman change a flat tire were twice as likely to offer similar assistance than subjects who did not view the model (Bryan & Test, 1967). This modeling effect has since been demonstrated in a wide variety of situations, including aiding in a search (Ross, 1970) and donating to a charity (Rushton, 1975).

Interpersonal Attraction

Most of the forms of social influence we have discussed so far have primarily been examples of unidirectional influence. When an individual conforms to a group norm, it is the individual, not the group, who is being influenced. When you comply with the request of a car salesperson or obey the dictates of an authority figure, the influence seems quite obviously to be in one direction; it is your behavior that is being influenced by the other person. Many cases of social influence, however, are reciprocal in nature. This is most certainly true of interpersonal attraction, in which the behaviors of two individuals may have mutual, although not necessarily equal positive influences on each other. Social psychologists have uncovered a number of factors that seem to play a role in the dynamics of interpersonal attraction. These include proximity, similarity, and physical attractiveness.

Keep in mind that the social psychologist takes a different perspective on interpersonal attraction than does the poet or romance novelist. On a personal level, the scientist is just as capable of appreciating the wonders and mysteries of interpersonal attraction and love, but research into interpersonal attraction requires the same kind of attention to definitional and measurement rigor as does any other phenomenon. As a result, some of the findings concerning interpersonal attraction may appear only as cold facts. Remember, though, that it is possible to subject a rose to a microscopic analysis of its elementary structural makeup, yet still appreciate its beauty.

Proximity. One factor that seems undeniably predictable of who will become attracted to whom, is physical proximity. We are simply more likely to have ample opportunities to interact with others in our immediate environment—the classroom, the workplace, the neighborhood—than with people from whom we are physically distanced. Growing up to marry the girl (or guy) next door doesn't seem all that unlikely an event after all. In fact, a good deal of research supports this notion. Even in a world in which mobility is common, and people are frequently moving from one geographical location to another, marriages still tend to occur between people who live near one another (Ineichen, 1979).

Similarity. We are also, not surprisingly, attracted to those with whom we share similar beliefs, attitudes, and opinions (Byrne, Clore, & Smeaton, 1986). Both close friends and marriage partners are likely to share educational and career goals, and political and religious beliefs (Brehm, 1985; Kandel, 1978). These similarities are probably responsible both for initiating and maintaining interpersonal relationships. For example, you are likely to attend a social function, such as a political rally or a religious service, in which others in attendance share your particular beliefs or opinions. Having initially been acquainted with someone at such a meeting, your common interests and aspirations are likely to become part of the glue that maintains the relationship.

Physical Attractiveness. Research has also demonstrated that physical attractiveness plays an important role in interpersonal attraction. An early study by Walster, Aronson, Abrahams, and Rottman (1966) recorded whether college students who met at a dance would be willing to date their dance partner at a later time. Although the researchers collected data on several subject characteristics, including intelligence and personality, only physical attractiveness appeared to influence overall expressed willingness for a later date. It may be, however, that physical attractiveness plays an

Above: Similarity of beliefs, attitudes, and opinions is one of the factors involved in interpersonal attraction. For example, the common beliefs held among anti-apartheid demonstrators brings them together for their cause and will likely strengthen their relationships with one another. Right: Studies also reveal that physical attractiveness plays a role in interpersonal attraction—at least initially.

important role in initial attraction, but that personality, intelligence, and attitudinal similarities determine whether the relationship will endure.

The complexities of interpersonal relationships have only begun to surrender themselves to social psychological study. Progress has been made both by recognizing that these phenomena are characterized by mutual or bi-directional influences, and by the development of an adequate vocabulary for objectively describing important concepts. Most importantly, social psychologists maintain that a complete understanding of interpersonal relationships can be brought about only through the research contributions of a host of disciplines related to psychology, including sociology and biology (Berscheid & Peplau, 1983). We turn now to a discussion of how one of these disciplines might contribute to our knowledge of interpersonal attraction and social influence in general: sociobiology.

SOCIOBIOLOGY AND SOCIAL INFLUENCE

Social conformity, compliance, obedience, helping, and interpersonal attraction are all common examples of how we influence and are influenced by others. Researchers have in some cases developed special theories for explaining particular phenomena—Bem's theory of self-perception to explain compliance, or Latané and Darley's model of bystander intervention. Is there any theory, though, that might be relevant to all kinds of social influence? If so, this would be an important advancement in psychology, for the maturity of a science is often measured by how well any one theory can integrate or unify a large number of experimental findings (Kuhn, 1962).

Remember that in Chapter 3 we discussed a theory that concerns itself with the genetic bases of social behavior. This theory, **sociobiology,** deals with ultimate causes of behavior, or the evolutionary roots of our present social customs and institutions. In reading this section, keep in mind both the criticisms that have been leveled at sociobiological theory and the equally important reply by sociobiologists that they are simply attempting to explain the "whys" and not the "ought to be's" of social behavior. What sort of ultimate causes might explain humankind's undeniably social nature?

The family structure allows for a division of labor. The caregiver attends to the newborn while the spouse or other family members provide food and other necessities.

There are a number of potential variables that might serve as evolutionary causes of our social nature. One clear example is sexual reproduction. We are a species whose survival requires sexual reproduction. Reproduction has historically required some minimal social contact between males and females—test tube babies and the modern revolution in genetic engineering notwithstanding. Thus, genotypes that code for tendencies to affiliate with others, particularly with members of the opposite sex, would be expected to persist, or be maintained by selective pressures.

The act of mating, however, is not the only component of the reproductive process that would seem to benefit from affiliation. As we saw in Chapter 11, the human newborn is among one of nature's most fragile creatures, requiring constant care and attention. Because humans, unlike many other species, produce a very limited number of offspring, tremendous parental investment must be made in protecting and rearing each child, which, of course, perpetuates the family gene pool. For this reason, a social arrangement that allowed for one individual to care exclusively for the young would be advantageous. This is precisely what the family unit, with its traditional division of labor, allows. The caregiver is able to provide exclusive and undivided attention to the newborn, while the spouse or other family members secure food and other necessities. Thus, part of our social disposition may be due to the advantages that such an arrangement provides in caring for children.

Recall that complying with another's request is often explained by what psychologists call the norm of reciprocity. This presumably universal social norm suggests that we feel compelled to return favors we receive from others. From an evolutionary standpoint, there may be many benefits that derive from such social interdependence. In fact, the norm of reciprocity may help to explain several types of social influence, including not only compliance and obedience, but altruistic behavior as well. Let's look at some specific predictions that sociobiology would make concerning altruistic behavior.

Sociobiologists argue that we are most likely to behave altruistically toward those individuals with whom we share genes, a phenomenon known as kin selection. An interesting prediction that follows from this concept is that in small towns, where there is a greater likelihood that any two people may be related, altruistic behavior should be greater than in large metropolitan areas where the chances are less likely that any two

f we can help another person in trouble, and there is little effort involved on our part and some likelihood that the favor will be returned, the chances are good that we will provide help.

people share genes. In support of this prediction, a study by Takooshian, Haber, and Lucido (1977) found that 72 percent of subjects approached by a lost child in a small town offered help to the child, but only 46 percent of subjects in a large city did so. This finding is consistent with a wealth of studies demonstrating kin selection in many social species other than humans (Wilson, 1975).

Of course, there are many examples of human altruism that clearly do not involve biological relatives. These acts may not operate according to the notion of kin selection, but according to reciprocal altruism. According to sociobiology, altruistic acts are most likely to occur when 1) there is low risk of injury to the helper, 2) there is considerable benefit to the recipient, 3) there is high expectation that the situation will be reversed, and 4) there is a high probability that the helper and recipient will recognize one another in the future (Barash, 1982). Social psychological research has indeed demonstrated that reciprocal altruism is more likely when these factors, which represent a low cost-benefit ratio, are present (Weyant, 1978). In other words, if we can help another person in trouble, and there is little effort involved on our part and some likelihood that the favor will be returned, the chances are good that we will provide help.

The issue of interpersonal attraction and human sexual behavior has surrounded sociobiology with intense controversy. Among the predictions offered by sociobiologists for interpersonal attraction is that males will, more often than not, prefer younger females. Why would sociobiology make this prediction? Compared to the male, the female can pass her genes on to only a small number of offspring, due in part to the limited time span within which she is reproductively fertile. Consequently, it is to the advantage of the male, particularly in predominantly monogamous cultures, to secure a young mate who has many years of child-bearing ahead of her. Research supports this prediction, even suggesting that males who remarry in their later years still prefer younger females (Bureau of the Census, 1975).

What do you think sociobiologists would say about factors influencing the females' selection of a mate? Do females find younger males attractive or are other characteristics more likely to be the basis of the female's choice? The female makes a much larger investment in the development of her child, certainly during the gestational period and frequently even after birth, so she is likely to be quite selective in choosing a mate. She needn't, however, select a mate based on youthful appearance, for male reproductive capacity is not strongly correlated with age. Berscheid and Walster (1974) demonstrated that females are much more likely than males to choose dating partners based on particular personality characteristics such as intelligence, competence, and social abilities. Rosenblatt (1974) has also shown that although males evaluate females on the basis of their physical attractiveness, females evaluate males more according to social status and competence. As you can see, each of these findings can be interpreted

According to the theories of sociobiology, males are more likely to choose younger females for mates partly because they will have more childbearing years ahead of them. Females, on the other hand, will choose males based more on intelligence, competence, and social abilities.

within sociobiology's framework, as the theory claims that natural selection has resulted in differing expressions of attraction and sexual behavior in males and females.

In considering the arguments of the sociobiologist, though, remember that ultimate and proximate causes of behavior are not mutually exclusive. Even sociobiologists admit that culture has to some degree altered the relationship between genes and behavior. As pointed out by the biologist Stephen Jay Gould (1981), it would be a mistake to give center stage entirely to the genes in the explanation of human behavior:

> To a biologist, heritability refers to the passage of traits or tendencies along family lines as a result of genetic transmission. It says little about the range of environmental modification to which these traits are subject. In our vernacular, "inherited" often means "inevitable." But not to a biologist. Genes do not make specific bits and pieces of a body; they code for a range of forms under an array of environmental conditions. Moreover, even when a trait has been built and set, environmental intervention may still modify inherited defects. Millions of Americans see normally through lenses that correct innate deficiencies of vision.
>
> (1981, pp. 156)

Likewise, our social behavior is not likely to be due entirely to our evolutionary history. As we have seen in this chapter, specific aspects of the environment play a crucial role in determining social behavior.

BOUNDARIES AND FRONTIERS

Social behavior may very well be psychology's richest subject matter. One needn't be a psychologist to appreciate the complex processes by which we form impressions of others, conform to group norms or obey the dictates of authority, decide whether to assist a person in need of help, or develop an intimate relationship with another person. But our everyday observations of behavior, made under rather casual conditions, may often contradict those made by the scientist who views behavior under more systematic circumstances. Indeed, as we saw in our examination of obedience, cognitive dissonance, and bystander intervention, our intuitions about human behavior frequently miss the mark. Consequently, to whatever extent social psychology can show us a clear, if occasionally unflattering, view of our social peculiarities, it has gone that far in illustrating the potential benefits of a science of behavior. And what of future benefits?

It is hard to say precisely what the future holds for social psychology, as the discipline draws so heavily from other sciences outside of psychology and addresses such a diverse range of behavioral phenomena. There is little question, however, that social psychology will continue to benefit from the cognitive revolution in psychology. In order to understand why this "marriage" of cognitive and social psychology is important, recall our discussion of learning, cognition, and memory in earlier chapters. The cognitive psychologist views the human being as an information processor. In basic cognitive research, the information processing characteristics of a subject are examined typically through memory experiments in which the subject is asked to recall such stimuli as numbers, letters, words, or sometimes combinations of these. The contributions made by the social psychologist to this basic research paradigm is in recognizing that in the real world we are likely to be processing information about people, their physical attributes or personality traits, or specific locations or events that in some way have been associated with other people. The schemata we develop are similarly social, in that they apply to generalized settings or types of interactions, or to groups of people. In other words, the normal duties performed by our cognitive processes apply to a broader range of information than was customarily examined in traditional cognitive experiments.

Do we process social information in a different way than we process the kinds of artificial information presented in traditional studies of cognition? The answer appears to be "yes." Even the human newborn, it seems, appears to respond in a different manner to a stimulus resembling a human face than one made up of the same basic features, but presented in a nonsensical or random pattern (Fantz, 1961). This finding, and others like it, suggest that further efforts by social psychologists to investigate the peculiarities of social cognition will prove fruitful.

As illustrated in the classic research on group norms and conformity (Asch, 1946, 1952, 1955; Sherif, 1961), social influence has always commanded considerable attention by social psychologists. For a number of reasons, research on how we influence and are influenced by others is likely to continue to receive such attention in the future. A persistent theme emerging from this research is that the individual person is undoubtedly immersed, for good or for bad, in a sea of humanity—no man, nor woman for that matter, is an island! Our very thoughts, feelings, and behavior are not only extraordinarily sensitive to the social environment, but make very little sense outside of that context.

The practical benefits likely to derive from an understanding of the dynamics of social influence are immense. For example, as the divorce rate in this country approaches 50 percent, comprehending the nature of interpersonal conflict becomes an imperative goal for family and marital therapists. There is, in fact, probably no other form of interpersonal behavior that serves so unmistakably as an example of interdependence than that of an intimate relationship. Of course, the implications of conflict resolution extend far beyond the intimate couple, to relations between ethnic groups, business corporations, and even nations. What insights might social psychology bring to the bargaining table when representatives from separate nations come to discuss their differences—differences which, though often substantial, do not change the fact that the modern world is characterized by unprecedented social, economic, and sometimes political, interdependence? The nuclear arms race provides an especially dramatic illustration. What techniques do negotiators employ to produce compliance to proposed treaties when weapon disarmament is at issue? Are the consequences of compliance always beneficial to both sides? These are types of questions that social psychologists will be addressing in the future.

Just as psychologists continue to examine the proximate causes of social behavior, sociobiologists further their efforts to describe relevant evolutionary factors. These efforts, of course, will be tempered by researchers who believe culture to be critical in molding or shaping the expression of underlying genetic structures. Is our aggressive behavior instinctive, and if so, is it nonetheless subject to change through learning? Do men and women act differently, especially in matters of courtship and sexual behavior, because of differing selective pressures in our evolutionary history? If so, should we expect these differences to persist, or, again, does culture offer us a means of transcending, at least in part, our biological heritage?

These and other complex questions constitute just a part of the upcoming research agenda for social psychology. As you can see, the future holds great promise and no small measure of challenge.

CONCEPT SUMMARY

SOCIAL COGNITION

- What primary role is played by schemata in the process of social perception? What is a stereotype, and how does it function as a schema? (pp. 603–605)
- What is the primacy effect, and how does it influence social perception? (p. 605)
- Describe the attributional errors we may make when trying to explain our own and other's behavior. (pp. 606–609)
- According to social psychologists, what are the three major components of an attitude? (p. 609)
- When might we expect to see inconsistencies between behaviors and attitudes? (pp. 612–613)
- What is meant by the term "dissonance" and what is cognitive dissonance theory? (p. 613)
- How does Bem's self-perception theory explain dissonance reduction? (pp. 613–615 & 619–620)

SOCIAL INFLUENCE

- If you are just learning to play the piano, would the presence of an audience make you play your best or play poorly? What would research on social facilitation predict? (pp. 615–616)
- How do social conformity, compliance, and obedience to authority differ from one another? (pp. 616–626)
- Describe an example of the foot-in-the-door technique. Who would be likely to use such a strategy? (pp. 619–620)
- What is the bystander effect, and in what way does this phenomena contradict common sense expectations? (pp. 626–627)
- What is "diffusion of responsibility," and how might it contribute to bystander apathy? (pp. 626–627)
- According to research, which factors seem to best predict interpersonal attraction? (pp. 628–629)

SOCIOBIOLOGY AND SOCIAL INFLUENCE

- According to sociobiologists, what advantages do humans receive from being social creatures? (pp. 629–630)
- What is the importance of kin selection in the sociobiologist's explanation of altruism? (pp. 630–632)

KEY TERMS AND CONCEPTS

Social Psychology The branch of psychology that studies how the thoughts, feelings, and behaviors of individuals are influenced by the actual, imagined, or implied presence of others. (p. 602)

SOCIAL COGNITION

Social Cognition The processing of information about other people and social situations. (p. 602)

Impression Formation The process of attributing characteristics and traits to other people. (p. 603)

Schemata An overall framework for processing information about people, objects, and situations. (p. 603)

Central Traits Personality attributes that seem to be the most representative of an individual. (p. 604)

Primacy Effect The tendency to form impressions about people based on the first information we receive about them. (p. 604)

Stereotypes Oversimplified schemata that are applied to entire groups of people. (p. 605)

Prejudice A negative evaluation of an individual based on his or her membership in a particular group. (p. 605)

Discrimination The differential treatment of people based on their membership in a particular group; the behavioral expression of prejudice. (p. 605)

Attribution Theory The theory that attempts to explain how people infer the causes of their own and other people's behavior. (p. 606)

Covariation Rule The attributional rule in which certain events are seen as occurring together in time. (p. 606)

Distinctiveness The principle of the covariation rule concerning the extent to which a behavior is a response to a specific stimulus but not to others. (p. 606)

Consensus The principle of the covariance rule concerning the extent to which one person's behavior is consistent with that of other people. (p. 607)

Consistency The principle of the covariance rule concerning the extent to which one person's behavior is consistent across time and/or settings. (p. 607)

Discounting Rule The presence of several competing attributions for the same behavior. (p. 607)

Fundamental Attribution Error The tendency to apply dispositional rather than situational attributions to other people's behavior. (p. 608)

Belief in a Just World The tendency to believe that people generally get what they deserve in life. This tendency is an example of a fundamental attribution error. (p. 608)

Actor-observer Effect. The tendency to attribute one's own behavior as being situationally determined, but other's behavior as being dispositionally caused. (p. 608)

Attitude An evaluative response to any person, object, or situation. (p. 609)

Mere Exposure Effect Attitude development based on continued or repeated presentation of an attitude object. (p. 610)

Theory of Cognitive Dissonance A theory that proposes that people are motivated to reduce the anxiety produced by inconsistent cognitions and behaviors. (p. 613)

Counterattitudinal Behavior Public behavior that is discrepant with private attitudes. (p. 614)

SOCIAL INFLUENCE

Social Facilitation A change in task performance due to the presence of others. (p. 615)

Social Norms Informal rules defining the expected and appropriate behavior in specific situations. (p. 616)

Conformity Thinking or behaving in a manner that is consistent with the norms of a social group. (p. 617)

Confederate A person acting as a subject in an experiment, but who is really an assistant of the researcher. (p. 617)

Compliance A change in one's behavior or beliefs as the result of an explicit request made by a nonauthoritative individual. (p. 619)

Foot-in-the-door Technique A compliance technique in which a small, reasonable request is followed by a larger, burdensome request. (p. 619)

Self-perception Theory A theory claiming that we come to understand our own attitudes by observing our own behavior. (p. 619)

Low-balling Technique A compliance technique in which a very attractive offer is made, but is then withdrawn after compliance with the original offer has occurred. (p. 620)

Door-in-the-Face Technique Compliance technique in which an unreasonable request is followed by a more reasonable request. (p. 620)

Norm of Reciprocity Social norm dictating that favors should be returned. (p. 621)

Obedience to Authority The following of orders issued by a legitimate authority. (p. 621)

Bystander Effect The finding that the larger the number of bystanders, the lower the probability that any one bystander would help in an emergency. (p. 627)

Diffusion of Responsibility An explanation of the bystander effect stating that when several bystanders are present, no one individual assumes responsibility for helping. (p. 627)

Sociobiology Theory attributing social behavior to the ultimate causes of genetic variation and the process of evolution. (p. 629)

ADDITIONAL SOURCES OF INFORMATION

Cialdini, R. B. (1988). *Influence: Science and practice* (2nd ed.). Glenview, IL: Scott, Foresman. A wonderfully written and authoritative narrative of the most effective strategies of social influence and persuasion found at large in our culture today. This book's strength is found in its real life examples of influence.

Milgram, S. (1974). *Obedience to authority.* New York: Harper & Row. In this book, Milgram explains his rationale for conducting his controversial obedience research, describes in detail the research itself, and finally, ponders its significance in light of moral and ethical considerations.

Myers, D. G. (1989). *Social psychology* (2nd ed.). New York: McGraw-Hill. A clearly written and thorough overview of the major areas of research, past and present, within social psychology. This book represents a good starting point for the reader interested in learning more about social psychology.

Zimbardo, P. G. (1989). Social psychology. In E. R. Hilgard (Ed.), *Fifty years of Psychology: Essays in honor of Floyd Ruch.* Glenview, IL: Scott, Foresman. This brief chapter provides a conceptual overview of important developments of social psychology in the last 50 years. In addition to providing a well-written and frank account of social psychology's past, the author also provides his view of what the future holds for this area.

18 Life-Style, Health, and Survival

LIFE-STYLE: CHOICES AND CONSEQUENCES *(639–648)*

Diet   Physical Fitness   Cigarette Smoking   Alcohol and Drug Abuse   Sexually Transmitted Diseases and AIDS   Personal Safety: Using Seat Belts   Unhealthy Life-Styles are Preventable

Our life-styles have been shaped by environmental changes brought about by cultural evolution and our biology. Life-styles impact significantly on individual survival. In the long run, behaviors that promote health tend to affect our lives positively by enhancing longevity and quality of life. Unhealthy behaviors tend to affect our lives negatively in the long run but positively in the short run. Such negative aspects are acquired and maintained because of their immediately reinforcing effects.

STRESS AND HEALTH *(648–654)*

The Biological Basis of Stress   The General Adaptation Syndrome   Cognitive Appraisal and Stress   Stressful Life-Styles and Impaired Health   Stressors and Their Sources   Coping with Stress

Life-styles that involve prolonged and severe stress can impair both the individual's psychological and physical well-being. Stress is controlled by the autonomic nervous system, which when stimulated by stressors, produces changes in the normal activities of many organs. Selye's General Adaptation Syndrome is a model of how the body responds to long-term stress. Lazarus' notion of cognitive appraisal explains how our perceptions of the threat posed by a stressor determine the experience of stress. Stressors are classified according to whether they are catastrophic and involve significant life changes or whether they are everyday conflicts. Stress can be controlled by implementing specific coping strategies.

LIFE-STYLE AND ENVIRONMENT *(655–663)*

Overpopulation   Environmental Pollution   You and the Environment

An important way that our actions can affect others is by diminishing critical aspects of the environment that we share, such as air, water, and land. The wastes produced by any one individual and his or her demand for natural resources are relatively insignificant, but when these are multiplied by the number of people in the world, very serious environmental problems result. Pollution is the product of particular human behaviors, and solving the pollution problem requires that we change those behaviors.

Your formal study of psychology will soon come to an end, at least as far as this particular class is concerned. The time is at hand to take stock of what you have learned about psychology. You have been inundated with information such as "neurons relay information to and from the brain via neurotransmitters," "our ability to retrieve information stored in memory is influenced by how we encode it in the first place," and "intelligence is the capacity to acquire knowledge and use that knowledge to solve problems." Facts such as these are important because they provide you with a close look at the substance of psychology. They have helped you gain an appreciation for the depth of our understanding of human thought and action. Realistically, though, you will forget many of these facts in the months to come. Unless you become a psychology major, there will be no more tests or quizzes or class discussions about what you learned here in introductory psychology. The important thing is that you come away from this course with the proverbial "big picture" of psychology.

At the risk of oversimplification, we will highlight here seven key principles that, we hope, have been evident throughout this text. These principles will help you not only to evaluate and appreciate what you've learned so far but also to understand better the content of this chapter, which, broadly speaking, is the role of psychology in the western culture of the 1990s. These principles follow.

1. Psychology is an interdisciplinary science whose goal is to acquire greater understanding of human behavior and to apply it to improving our quality of life. There are few fields of scientific inquiry that are genuinely unrelated to psychology and there are few, if any, aspects of our lives to which psychological principles do not apply.

2. Our capacity for learning and adapting to environmental changes is a product of our evolution in general and our genetic heritage in particular. Our capacity for learning has resulted in cultural evolution, which involves technological inventions, and the transmission of information across and within generations via language.

3. The capacity of our nervous systems to process information about the environment serves as the foundation for higher cognitive processes. Central to efficient functioning of higher cognitive processes is memory: the encoding, storage, and retrieval of information.

4. All behaviors have consequences; those consequences affect both the environment and the organism that produced them. Not all behaviors are equal in terms of the consequences they produce; some behaviors are more significant than others because their consequences have a greater impact on both the individual and his or her environment.

5. Our cognitive abilities influence how behavior is affected by its consequences. Our cognitive abilities allow us to think about and understand the relationship between our behavior and its consequences. They also serve as the basis for our ability to form expectancies about the kinds of consequences that our behavior may produce.

6. Behavior is mediated by the brain and nervous system; what alters brain and nervous system functioning also alters behavior. Nuclei in the brain oversee the autonomic functions of the body, process information from the senses, and regulate higher mental processes and motor actions. Impairments in both cognitive and motor functions can often be linked to specific physical problems.

As you shall see, this chapter adds another critical principle to the picture:

7. Behavioral solutions, not just technological ones, are required to solve human problems. Devising technological solutions to remedy human problems is one thing; getting people to implement those solutions is another.

An important goal of this chapter is to show you the relevance of these seven principles to everyday life in the 1990s. (Throughout this chapter we will note specific instances when these principles apply.) Admittedly, the picture we paint may be speculative, but that is because we are only now beginning to understand many of the real life consequences of our actions. The central theme of this chapter is that the particular behaviors that comprise an individual's life-style have tremendous consequences for his or her quality of life. Moreover, these consequences go beyond the individual; they also affect the lives of others by changing the environment in which they live. To further complicate things, the environmental changes that are a consequence of our actions can and do, in turn, influence our behavior and our life-styles.

The particular behaviors that comprise an individual's life-style have tremendous consequences for his or her quality of life.

We will look first at some of the personal choices reflected in our life-style. We will focus primarily on health and safety issues. Next, we will discuss stress, its biological and psychological effects, and how to cope with it. Finally, we will discuss how aspects of our life-styles affect the environment and how, in turn, our environment affects us.

LIFE-STYLE: CHOICES AND CONSEQUENCES

The world in which we live is a radically different world from the one in which our ancient ancestors lived. Changes in the environment are inevitable; they result from natural forces such as floods, erosion, wind, and so forth. In our case, changes in our ecological niche stem not just from natural forces but from cultural ones as well. **Cultural evolution**, as you may recall, involves the adaptive changes of cultures to recurrent environmental pressures; it is a product of human intellect and physical capacity (both of which have strong genetic components). For our species, cultural evolution has been a primary agent involved in shaping our habitat *(Principle 2)*. But cultural evolution has changed more than our habitat; it has also changed the manner in which we live, that is, our life-style.

Life-style has become something of a buzz word these days. Physicians use the word to refer to factors that put their patients at risk for disease and illness; reporters use it to describe the differences between the "rich and famous" and the rest of us. We will define the word more generally: **life-style** is the aggregate behavior of an individual; it is the way a person leads his or her life. Life-style may be thought of as a catch-all term that encompasses the choices we make within the context of particular biological and environmental pressures. The ways that we interact with others, the kinds of work we pursue, the hobbies and personal interests we enjoy, the habits we develop, and whether we marry and raise a family or remain single are examples of acts that reflect our life-styles. The unique ways in which people think and act mirror the rather idiosyncratic nature of life-style. In many ways, our life-styles represent the sum of psychological study because they are the sum of individual behavior. Our plan is to focus on several prevalent life-style behaviors and show how they have important consequences for us and for our environment. Specifically, we will look at aspects of life-style that can affect our physical health and, ultimately, our psychological well-being.

For our ancient ancestors, life-style was fairly homogeneous; that is, it was pretty much the same for everyone. When our ancestors were hungry,

Our environment is shaped not only by natural forces, but also by changes in our culture. Many technological developments that have advanced our culture have had a detrimental effect on our environment.

Because of the cultural evolution, we can choose among many life-style alternatives. We can choose whether to hunt for food or buy it. And unlike our ancient ancestors, we don't have to worry about survival. Instead, we worry about our jobs and how to spend our free time.

they hunted and gathered their food; they walked or ran to get from one place to another; they worked hard to stay alive. Options about how to accomplish these things arose only later as the pace of cultural evolution increased. Today, there is no predominant life-style: cultural evolution has afforded us the luxury of choosing from among many life-style alternatives. We can hunt or gather food if we want, but we can also buy it in grocery stores or go to a restaurant. When we want to go somewhere, we can walk or run, but more often we ride on bicycles or boats or in planes, trains, or automobiles. We no longer worry about only how to stay alive; we now worry about working for a living and how to spend our spare time. Grocery stores, transportation, working for a living, and leisure time are conceptual and technological innovations resulting from cultural evolution.

Often the consequences that result from particular aspects of life-style impact significantly on an individual's survival *(Principle 4)*. A healthy life-style can be viewed as one that ensures the individual's physical and psychological well-being. Typically, it includes, among other things, a balanced diet, regular exercise, no use of tobacco or psychoactive substances, and even the use of seat belts in automobiles. An unhealthy life-style tends to diminish an individual's physical and psychological well-being *(Principle 6)*. An important question to raise, then, is how and why are unhealthy life-styles acquired and maintained? After all, they appear to work against personal fitness. The answer to this question is a very complicated one, so we will only offer a general response here. In general, we can say that although the consequences of these life-style behaviors have obvious biological implications, the behaviors themselves are acquired and maintained by psychological factors.

According to evolutionary theory, those individuals with unhealthy life-styles should eventually become extinct. Unlike biological evolution, though, cultural evolution does not have a mechanism like natural selection that culls the weak and the unfit from the existing population. On the surface, you might think that the law of effect might play the role of natural selection in cultural evolution. The law of effect, as you may recall, holds that behaviors that produce favorable consequences tend to be repeated and those that produce aversive consequences tend not to be repeated. The problem here is that many of the behaviors involved in unhealthy life-styles have reinforcing consequences in the short run and damaging consequences only in the long run. Many unhealthy behaviors are maintained because they tend to be available on a pseudoversion of revolving credit. But instead of a "buy now, pay later" plan, it takes the form of "enjoy now, suffer later." The teenager who puffs on a cigarette is receiving immediate rewards (physiological and psychological pleasure), and he may also perceive that he is "cool" because he smokes. It is only many years later when he is in his 40s or 50s that the life-threatening effects of smoking may appear *(Principles 3, 5, & 6)*. In the meantime, he has become physiologically addicted to the nicotine contained in the cigarette smoke.

As you can see, the law of effect actually works to our disadvantage in this case and partially accounts for why cultural evolution shows a large degree of tolerance for those who adopt unhealthy life-styles. "Survival of the fittest" is no longer an appropriate description of evolution, at least for the majority of our species. Fortunately, our culture has become increasingly knowledgeable about both healthy and unhealthy life-styles and has attempted to put that knowledge to work to promote healthier ones *(Principles 1 & 5)*. We turn now to a discussion of six aspects of life-style: diet, physical fitness, cigarette smoking, alcohol abuse, sexual practices, and seat belt usage.

Diet

Until very recently, our species lived on a diet that was low in fat and high in fiber. Our biological predecessors lived mainly on a fare of fruits, vegetables, nuts, and lean meats. In the last 100 years or so, though, our diets have changed; they are now considerably higher in fats and lower in fiber, due largely to the consumption of fried foods and confections. Although foods like bananas, broccoli, and lean beef may be part of our diets, we may also consume hot fudge sundaes, doughnuts, and fried chicken. For some people, the latter kinds of foods may represent the bulk of their diet. Diets too high in saturated fats (that is, those fats found in animal products and a few vegetable oils) and too low in fiber have been linked with specific health disorders, such as **coronary heart disease (CHD)**, the narrowing of blood vessels that supply nutrients to the heart, and **cancer**, a malignant and intrusive tumor that can destroy body organs and tissue.

The chief culprit in CHD is **serum cholesterol**, a chemical that occurs naturally in the bloodstream where it serves as a detoxifier. Cholesterol has two important forms: LDL (low-density lipoprotein) and HDL (high-density lipoprotein). HDL is sometimes referred to as "good" cholesterol because high levels are inversely associated with CHD. It is believed that HDL may play a protective role in the bloodstream. LDL is often called "bad" cholesterol because high levels of it are associated with the formation of arteriosclerotic plaques, which clog the arteries. Fiber is an important dietary component because it helps reduce blood cholesterol levels.

In a recent *Scientific American* paper, L. A. Cohen (1987) showed that cultures with the highest death rates due to breast cancer are those whose citizens tend to consume relatively large amounts of fats. Figure 18.1 shows the correlation between cancerous death and daily fat consumption for forty countries. As you can see, the United States has both a relatively high fat intake and a relatively high death rate due to breast cancer.

On the basis of what we have learned so far, it is obvious that our diet plays an important role in good health and so is pivotal to a healthy life-style. We decrease our risk for both CHD and cancer by choosing to eat low fat, high fiber foods *(Principles 4 & 5)*. However, many of our favorite foods are high fat, low fiber foods. The immediate effect of eating these foods may be to delight the palate, but in the long run, a more serious consequence may occur: poor health, obesity, and possibly even death. Of course, it is those immediately reinforcing effects of eating certain foods

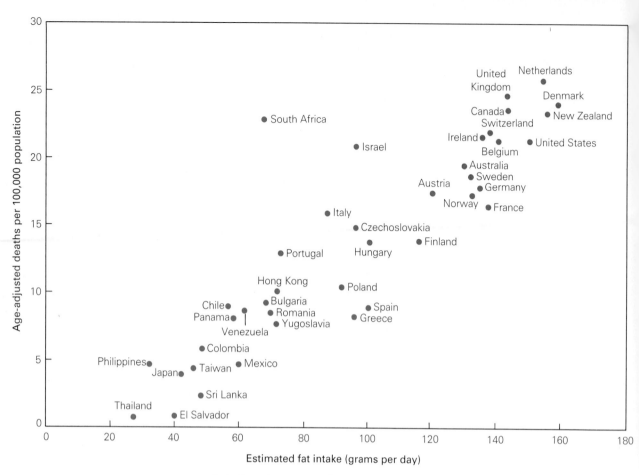

FIGURE 18.1
The correlation between diet and cancer. Nations whose citizens live on diets rich in fats face increased risk of death due to breast cancer.

Today many people lead sedentary lives and have unhealthy eating habits. These two factors can greatly increase the risk of coronary heart disease and cancer.

that contributes significantly to our continued eating of them. The question to ask here is which foods are low in fat but high in fiber? Figure 18.2 provides the answer by listing the classes of foods in increasing order of the health risk they pose.

Physical Fitness

Not only did our ancestors generally have healthier diets, but they were probably also in better physical shape than the typical person alive today. Hunting, gathering, and a nomadic existence ensured that they had plenty of exercise. Many people today lead rather sedentary lives. What exercise they get may consist of walking to and from their car several times a day. Like high fat, low fiber diets, lack of exercise is correlated with increased risk of CHD (Peters et al., 1983; Powell et al., 1987). According to Ralph Paffenbarger, a noted epidemiologist who has devoted his career to studying CHD and cancer, people who exercise regularly are likely to live longer (Paffenbarger et al., 1986). Paffenbarger's evidence comes from a long-term longitudinal study of the life-styles of 17,000 Harvard University alumni. Paffenbarger periodically questioned his subjects, inquiring about their exercise patterns (type of exercise, frequency, and so on) and physical health. Here is a sample of his results:

- Between 1962 and 1978, 1413 of the original 17,000 subjects had died, 45 percent from CHD and 32 percent from cancer. Significantly more of these deaths occurred in subjects who had led sedentary lives.

- Alumni who reported that they exercised the equivalent of 30 to 35 miles of running or walking per week faced half the risk of dying that those who reported exercising the equivalent of 5 or less miles per week faced.
- On average, those who exercised moderately (an equivalent of 20 miles running or walking per week) lived about 2 years longer than those who exercised less than the equivalent of 5 miles.

Of course, these results do not mean that everyone who exercises regularly will live an extra 2 years. However, because regular exercise reduces high blood pressure, increases lung capacity, and decreases the ratio of bad (LDL) cholesterol to good (HDL) cholesterol, Paffenbarger's results strongly suggest that regular exercise engenders good health. That is important because good health is considered by many people to be a cornerstone of life satisfaction *(Principles 4 & 5)*.

What kind of exercise produces the most positive health results? According to Kenneth Cooper, aerobic exercises such as running, walking, bicycling, and swimming are superior to others for improving the cardiovascular system (Cooper, 1968, 1970, 1985). **Aerobic exercises** stimulate and strengthen the heart and lungs, which in turn increase the body's efficiency in using oxygen. What is the minimum amount of aerobic exercise necessary to produce positive health benefits? Again, according to Cooper, running at least 2 miles in less than 20 minutes four times a week (or any equivalent aerobic exercise) produces a significant increase in cardiovascular health (Cooper, 1985).

Largely due to Cooper's research, aerobics has become a common lifestyle activity for millions of people throughout the world. During the early 1970s, jogging and swimming were favorite aerobic exercises for many people; during the 1980s, many other people took up bicycling, walking, and aerobic dance as alternatives to running and swimming. That Cooper's work could have such a profound effect on the everyday activities of people testifies to the power of scientific research in producing favorable changes in life-style. In the next section, we will see similar results: Recent research on the hazards of cigarette smoking has helped to reduce the number of people who smoke.

FIGURE 18.2

Fat, fiber, and health. Consuming foods low in fat but high in fiber contribute to a healthy life-style.

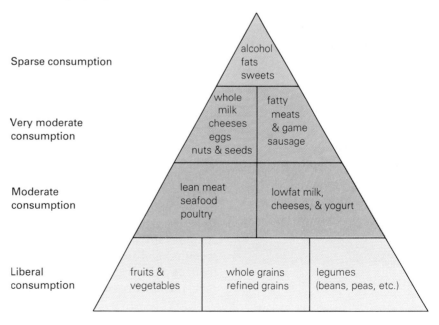

Cigarette Smoking

Although tobacco products have been used in one form or another for hundreds of years, we have only recently discovered how harmful they can be to one's health. The Centers for Disease Control (1987) reports that about 350,000 deaths in the United States each year are related to the use of tobacco. Smoking cigarettes has been found to be a particularly unhealthy behavior—in 1983, 30 percent of people who died from cancer and an equal number of those who died from CHD were cigarette smokers (Surgeon General, 1983). In addition to these health risks, cigarette smokers also face increased risks of bronchitis, emphysema, strokes, and ulcers. We know that the severity of these risks is directly correlated with the amount of carbon monoxide and tars contained in cigarette smoke. Given the strong albeit correlational link between cigarette smoking and increased health risks, plus the fact that people today are more knowledgeable about these risks *(Principle 5)*, it is surprising that smoking is still as popular a habit as it is today. Granted, the number of cigarette smokers is waning: a 1986 Gallup poll showed cigarette smoking to be at its lowest level in 40 years. However, according to the 1988 Surgeon General's report, there are still about 51 million cigarette smokers in the United States today.

iven the strong albeit correlational link between cigarette smoking and increased health risks, . . . it is surprising that smoking is still as popular a habit as it is today.

As we learned in Chapter 4, the nicotine contained in cigarette smoke exerts powerful effects on the central nervous system and heart by stimulating post-synaptic surfaces receptive to acetylcholine *(Principle 6)*. Such stimulation results in temporary increases in heart rate and blood pressure, decreases in body temperature, changes in hormones released by the pituitary gland, and the release of adrenalin from the adrenal glands. Such physiological arousal is reinforcing, and it is precisely these effects that contribute to the acquisition and maintenance of cigarette smoking. We also know that nicotine is an addictive drug that involves both physiological and psychological dependence. Cigarette smoking, then, is also maintained by negative reinforcement: people who attempt to quit smoking often suffer from such withdrawal symptoms as headaches, insomnia, anxiety, and irritability *(Principles 4 & 6)*. These symptoms can be relieved by smoking another cigarette. Such negative reinforcement appears to be extremely powerful: over 60 percent of all smokers have tried to quit smoking at least once.

Quitting smoking has both immediate and long-term positive effects, even if the individual has been smoking as long as 25 years. Table 18.1 shows the timeframe of the body's recovery from cigarette smoking. As you can see, even after as little as 20 minutes have passed since smoking a cigarette, the body begins showing recovery including a return to normal blood pressure, pulse rate, and body temperature in the extremities. After 72 hours, breathing becomes easier, partially due to increased lung capacity. After five years, the risk of death by lung cancer is reduced by almost 50 percent.

Although quitting smoking is a positive change in life-style, it is, of course, better never to have started in the first place. Psychologists and other health researchers are therefore not only interested in designing treatment programs to help people quit smoking, they are also interested in developing prevention programs to help people, especially adolescents, resist the temptation to start smoking *(Principle 1)*. Prevention programs are generally aimed at mitigating social factors, such as imitation, peer pressure, and influence from advertisements, that can induce people to light up initially (for example, Evans, Raines, & Hanselka, 1984). Such programs involve educating adolescents both about the health risks related

Smoking prevention programs try to help people, especially adolescents, resist the temptation to start smoking.

TABLE 18.1. *The body's response to stopping cigarette smoking.*

Within 20 minutes of last puff

Blood pressure and pulse decrease to normal levels.
Body temperature of extremities increases to normal levels.

Within 1 day

Risk of heart attacks decreases.

Within 2 days

Nerve endings begin regenerating.
Taste and smell acuity increases.

Within 3 days

Breathing becomes easier due to relaxing of bronchial tubes.
Lung capacity increases.

From 2 weeks to 3 months

Blood circulation improves.
Walking and other exercises begin to seem easier.
Lung efficiency increases as much as 30 percent.

After 5 years

Risk of death due to lung cancer decreases by 47 percent.

to cigarette smoking as well as how to respond negatively to those people who encourage them to smoke.

Alcohol and Drug Abuse

The psychological effects of alcohol and other drugs have been known to humanity longer than those of nicotine. Alcohol and opium, for example, have been used for hundreds of years for their euphoria-inducing properties. We discussed the physiological basis of drug effects and drug addiction in Chapter 4, so here we will focus on the ways in which alcohol and drug abuse can impair quality of life (*Principle 6*).

Referred to as *aqua vitae* or "water of life" during medieval times, alcohol is a widely abused substance today (Furnas, 1965). To abuse a substance means to use it in a way that poses a threat to the safety and well-being of either the user, society, or both. Not all people who use alcohol abuse it, and not all people who abuse alcohol are suffering from alcoholism. For example, the individual who drives under the influence of alcohol poses a serious threat to both herself and others, but she may not suffer from alcoholism. **Alcoholism** is an addiction to ethanol, which is the psychoactive agent in alcohol. In the United States today there are about 6 million people who are alcoholics and another 14 million who are considered to be problem drinkers. Male alcoholics outnumber female alcoholics by a ratio of about 4 or 5 to 1 (Lauer, 1989). Table 18.2 describes some of the physical and psychological consequences of alcohol abuse. The abuse of other drugs, such as cocaine or heroin, produces similar effects.

We do not yet understand why so many people abuse alcohol and drugs. The causal factors appear to be extremely complex and represent an intermingling of biological, psychological, and cultural variables. The best, though not perfect, predictor of who will use drugs and who will not is whether an individual's circle of friends are drug users (Schulz & Wilson, 1973). If an individual's friends use drugs, the chances are high that that individual also uses drugs. Of course, once the individual starts using drugs regularly, physiological and psychological dependence motivate him or her to maintain this aspect of life-style.

TABLE 18.2.	*The negative physical, psychological, and cultural consequences of alcohol abuse.*

Physical

Cirrhosis of the liver, which results in death
Poor nutrition
Impaired sexual functioning

Psychological

Gradual deterioration of cognitive functioning
Increased feelings of anxiety and irritability
Aggressive behavior

Cultural

Impaired social skills and interpersonal function
Divorce
Employee absenteeism and decreased productivity
Approximately 25,000 people a year die in alcohol-related traffic accidents

Because AIDS is a life-threatening disease, it is essential that people are informed about the dangers of the disease and about methods of prevention.

Sexually Transmitted Diseases and AIDS

Sex is an important factor in our lives, and for most, if not all of us, sex enhances our quality of life. In the context of a loving relationship, sexual activity represents the highest form of intimacy. In other contexts, though, especially in casual sexual relationships, sexual activity may have consequences other than intimacy; it may also result in contracting a sexually transmitted disease (STD). As we discussed in Chapter 12, individuals who contract an STD may find that their life-style is drastically affected (*Principle 4*). Typically these individuals experience a loss of self-esteem and often they lose their ability to initiate or maintain sexual relationships. (See Table 12.5 if you wish to review STDs and their symptoms.)

Without a doubt, the most life-threatening illness that may be transmitted sexually is AIDS (acquired immune deficiency syndrome), which can also be transmitted through the sharing of hypodermic needles among drug users and blood transfusions. Once prevalent only among homosexuals, AIDS is spreading among heterosexuals as well. The number of reported AIDS cases has nearly doubled between 1987 and 1988. Certain changes in life-style, referred to today as safe sex practices, can reduce one's risk of contracting an STD or AIDS. As you may recall, safe sex practices include limiting the number of sexual partners, finding out the sexual history of partners before engaging in sexual relations, and using a condom during sexual activity. In the case of AIDS, these changes must not only involve safe sex practices, but also behaviors that will prevent nonsexual transmission of the AIDS virus, such as refusal to share hypodermic needles.

If everyone engaged in safe sex practices and if intravenous drug users refused to share hypodermic needles, the AIDS threat would be reduced significantly. The problem, of course, is that it is one thing to talk about these behaviors but another thing to actually do them. Why? For the intravenous drug user, the answer is clear: The only thing in life that is important is getting high. Nothing else matters. For the couple about to engage in casual sex, the issue is less clear. Although each individual's behavior is motivated by sexual gratification, the social awkwardness involved in discussing each other's sexual history may lead to a failure to engage in safe sex behaviors (*Principles 4 & 5*). One way to reduce this problem may be to establish intervention programs in which people role play safe sex practices in an attempt to help them overcome the feelings of uneasiness involved in asking another person about his or her sexual history (Bosarge, 1989).

Personal Safety: Using Seat Belts

To our ancient ancestors, personal safety likely involved such things as avoiding sharp objects, dangerous animals, and burning themselves with fire. Although successfully avoiding these things is in our own best interest as well, our present culture represents a much more complex environment, with far more threats to personal safety than our ancient ancestors experienced *(Principle 2)*. A good example is traffic: only our very recent ancestors faced the possibility of being killed in a traffic accident. Today, traffic accidents result in hundreds of thousands of injuries and deaths each year. About 30 years ago, automobile manufacturers began installing seat belts in vehicles. The rationale was that staying put in a crash would result in fewer deaths and injuries than would result from being tossed about or from the vehicle. Their logic, of course, was sound, but there was a hitch in implementing the seat-belt program: getting people to buckle up in the first place. Recently, several states have passed mandatory seat-belt laws requiring that both driver and passengers wear a seat belt at all times while riding in a vehicle. How effective these laws will be in promoting seat-belt usage remains to be seen, although we can safely say that—based on estimates from foreign countries that have similar laws—compliance with the law will be less than 100 percent.

Why don't more people buckle up? According to E. Scott Geller (1985), a psychologist who specializes in applied behavior analysis, the reasons are twofold: First, people often travel safely in their vehicles without wearing their seat belts, which leads them to believe that riding in a car is not dangerous, and so there is no need to wear a seat belt. Geller believes that in these cases, people are essentially rewarded for not wearing their seat belts. Second, as we have seen, children and adolescents often imitate the behaviors of their parents *(Principles 3, 4, & 5)*. Young people may learn whether to wear seat belts or not simply by observing whether their parents wear seat belts. In addition, many television characters do not use seat belts in scenes involving moving vehicles (Geller's research has shown that less than 5 percent of actors in movies and TV shows are shown wearing their seat belts).

In an effort to change "seat-belt behavior," Geller has tried to alter environmental influences by developing community-based programs to promote seat-belt usage. One of his approaches has been to reward individuals with inexpensive items such as food coupons and lottery tickets for wearing their seat belts. The rewards are delivered to seat-belt wearers by police officers and people staffing drive-up windows of banks and fast-food restaurants. Geller's results: a more than doubling of seat-belt usage rates. Although usage rates drop when the reward program is removed, they do not generally reach previous levels of nonusage. When seat-belt programs are reinstituted intermittently, rates of usage increase.

Unhealthy Life-Styles Are Preventable

It is important to remember that the behaviors that make up our life-style are partially the consequence of the environmental conditions created by cultural evolution and partially the result of our genetic and physiological constitution *(Principle 2)*. Life-styles are not always wholly adaptive; some aspects of our life-styles are detrimental to both our longevity and quality of life. We have seen that unhealthy aspects of our life-styles include poor nutrition, physical inactivity, cigarette smoking, alcohol and drug abuse, failure to use safe sex practices, and not using seat belts while riding in automobiles.

Ironically, each of the negative aspects of life-style as well as their harmful consequences can be avoided. We now have the technological expertise to produce more nutritious foods than ever before; to develop the capacities of heart, lungs, and skeletal muscles to their optimal potential; to understand the detrimental effects of cigarette smoking, alcohol, and drug abuse on health; to prevent sexually transmitted diseases and AIDS; and to be safer while riding in moving vehicles.

The problem, of course, is getting people to apply that technical expertise in their personal lives *(Principle 7)*. For example, most people who smoke cigarettes are well aware of the health risks they face, but they continue to smoke anyway. Why? In our view, the answer to this question is because technological solutions to human problems are not aimed at the motivational and psychological causes of the problem; rather, they are aimed at only the problem itself. In short, the technological knowledge for actually solving problems is far ahead of our knowledge of the human motivation underlying those problems. What advances in technology have afforded us is choices: to use a condom or not, to eat foods enriched with vitamins and minerals or not; to wear seat belts or not, and so forth. What is sorely needed is a method to encourage people to make choices that benefit rather than impair their life-styles *(Principles 3, 4, & 5)*. Developing such a method or methods is a preeminent goal of **health psychology**, the branch of psychology concerned with the promotion and maintenance of sound health practices. One of the tasks that health psychologists face is understanding and helping people cope with stress, another aspect of life-style that can impair our quality of life. It is to this topic that we turn next.

STRESS AND HEALTH

Stress is a pattern of physiological, behavioral, and cognitive responses to real or imagined environmental stimuli that are perceived as endangering or otherwise threatening our well-being or personal abilities. These environmental stimuli are referred to as **stressors**. Stress is not a product of cultural evolution, although the changes in the environment wrought by that process have helped make stress commonplace in our culture today. Rather, stress is a product of natural selection *(Principle 2)*. It is a behavioral adaptation that helped our ancestors fight or flee from wild animals and enemies. Likewise, stress often helps us confront or escape threatening situations.

Stressors come in a variety of forms. They may be catastrophic—such as hurricanes and tornados—or they may be relatively trivial, such as being stuck in traffic when you are already late for an appointment. Stressors, though, are not always bad things. Some stressors, like athletic competition, class exams, and finding yourself attracted to another person can motivate behavior in positive ways *(Principles 4 & 5)*. However, life-styles in which stress is extended over long periods can have deleterious effects on both the individual's psychological and physical health.

The Biological Basis of Stress

Our physical response to stressors is governed by the autonomic nervous system which, as you may recall from Chapter 4, is controlled by the hypothalamus. Stress is a biological response that is experienced as an emotion, although the form it takes varies depending on the nature of the stressor. In some situations, we may feel scared or frightened, and in others we may feel inspired or exhilarated *(Principles 3 & 6)*.

Even minor situations such as being stuck in traffic can be a source of great negative stress for many people.

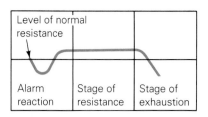

FIGURE 18.3
The General Adaptation Syndrome. When first exposed to a stressor, the organism's resistance to the stressor temporarily drops below normal. With continued exposure to the stressor, the organism enters the stage of resistance during which resistance to the stressor increases and eventually plateaus at above normal levels. With continued exposure to the stressor, the organism enters the stage of exhaustion during which the ability to adapt is decreased and resistance plummets to below normal levels, leaving it susceptible to illness and even death.

When an individual perceives a stressor, the hypothalamus sends signals to the autonomic nervous system and to the pituitary gland, both of which respond jointly by stimulating body organs to change their normal activities:

- Heart rate increases, blood pressure rises, blood vessels constrict, blood sugar levels rise, and blood flow is directed away from the extremities and toward major organs;
- Breathing becomes deeper and faster and air passages dilate, which permits more air into the lungs; digestion stops and perspiration increases;
- The adrenal glands secrete adrenalin, which, in addition to stimulating the heart also activates other organs; and
- Digestion stops; perspiration begins.

It is easy to see why these changes are adaptive; they each prepare the body to deal with the stressor. Whether we confront the stressor or run from it, the biological response is generally the same. Likewise, regardless of the nature of the stressor, the biological response is the same. Whether you find yourself in a dark alley confronted by a man with a gun, or facing your next psychology examination, the autonomic nervous system and the pituitary gland stimulate the viscera to respond to the stressor.

There are two cases in which such responses can be maladaptive. In the first case, stress can produce anxiety, and, as we learned in Chapter 15, anxiety can sometimes impair one's ability to perform a task. As you may have experienced for yourself, anxiety can, for example, hinder performance on class tests, speaking in public, "choking" during athletic competition, and forgetting lines in a play.

The second case involves the effects of prolonged and severe stress. The nature of many people's life-styles places them in situations in which they are confronted with stressors daily. As we will see shortly, such situations place those people at increased risk of illness. First, though, let's look closely at how the body responds to the presence of long-term serious stressors.

The General Adaptation Syndrome

Much of what we know about the effects of dealing with prolonged and severe stressors on the body stems from the efforts of Canadian endocrinologist, Hans Selye *(Principles 1 & 6)*. Through his work with laboratory animals, he found that chronic exposure to severe stressors produces a sequence of three physiological stages: the alarm stage, the stage of resistance, and the stage of exhaustion (see Figure 18.3). Selye (1956) referred collectively to these stages as the **General Adaptation Syndrome (GAS)**.

The responses in the alarm stage involve arousal of the autonomic nervous system as described above and occur when the individual is first confronted with a stressor. During this stage, the organism's resistance to the stressor temporarily drops below normal and the organism may experience shock. With continued exposure to the stressor, the organism enters the stage of resistance, during which its autonomic nervous system returns to normal levels of functioning. Resistance to the stressor increases and eventually plateaus at above normal levels. The stage of resistance, then, reflects the organism's adaptation to environmental stressors. However, with continued exposure to the stressor, the organism enters the stage of exhaustion. During this stage, the organism loses its ability to adapt, and resistance plummets to below normal levels, leaving it susceptible to illness and even death.

Biologically speaking, we are only able to adapt to the presence of environmental stressors for so long before we become susceptible to exhaus-

Hans Selye

tion and illness. The extent to which people can adapt varies across individuals and depends, as we will see in a moment, on how the stressor is perceived. The important point to remember is that there is a point beyond which our bodies are unable to tolerate stressful stimulation.

Cognitive Appraisal and Stress

Selye's model has been useful for understanding the biological components involved in stress, but it does not explain the role of psychological components in stress. Some psychologists argue that the psychological components in stress may influence the degree to which stressors arouse the autonomic nervous system *(Principle 6).* One such psychologist is Richard Lazarus, who argues that our perception of the stressor will, to a large extent, determine the stress we experience (Lazarus & Folkman, 1984). According to Lazarus, an individual's stress levels are affected by his or her **cognitive appraisal** or perception of the stressful situation *(Principles 3 & 5).* Cognitive appraisal is a two-stage process. In the first stage, we evaluate the nature of the threat: we attempt to address the seriousness of the perceived threat posed by the stressor. If we decide that the threat is real, we pass to the second stage, during which we assess whether we have the resources necessary to cope adequately with the threat. The extent to which we believe both that the stressor is a serious one and that we *don't* have the resources necessary to deal with it determines the level of stress that will be experienced. The belief that we cannot deal effectively with a stressor perceived as being extremely dangerous leads to the highest levels of stress. Because people may evaluate differently both the stressor and their ability to cope with it, they are likely to show different levels of stress when faced with the same stressor. We know from common experience that this is true. For example, how people react to snakes varies tremendously: a harmless garter snake will arouse intense fear in some people, and little, if any, in others.

O *ur perception of the stressor will, to a large extent, determine the stress we experience.*

Stressful Life-Styles and Impaired Health

Although Selye underestimated the role of psychological factors in stress, he was surely right about one thing, namely, that prolonged exposure to severe stressors appears to increase vulnerability to illness. Selye's research involved exposing laboratory animals to chronic and intense stressors under controlled laboratory conditions. In addition to showing that resistance to stressors appears to involve three stages, his results also showed that animals become seriously ill during the stage of exhaustion. Can prolonged exposure to severe stressors produce similar consequences in humans? Many studies investigating the relationship of life-style to health have shown that the answer to this question is, unfortunately, yes. Specifically, stressful life-styles have been shown to be related to increased risk of CHD, cancer, and impaired immune system functioning, ulcers, high blood pressure, and hypertension *(Principle 4).*

That stressful life-styles are related to CHD was first suggested by two cardiologists, Meyer Friedman and Ray Rosenman (1959, 1974), whose 9-year research program involved interviews with over 3000 males. Friedman and Rosenman found that men who were highly competitive, aggressive, time-conscious, and hardworking tended to suffer heart attacks more often than men whose life-styles were slower paced and less demanding. More recent research has shown, though, that the critical aspects of a stressful life-style that contribute to increased vulnerability to CHD involve negative emotions, for example, hostility, anger, and selfishness (Booth-Kewley & Friedman, 1987; Scherwitz, Graham, & Ornish, 1985).

Men who are highly competitive, aggressive, and hardworking tend to be more prone to heart attacks than men with less demanding life-styles.

There is also mounting evidence that prolonged stress also impairs the body's immune system (Jemmott & Locke, 1984). The **immune system** is a network of organs and cells that protect the body from invading bacteria, viruses, and other foreign substances. The different cells of the immune system are specialized to combat particular types of invaders. B-cells produce antibodies in response to bacterial infection and other foreign substances such as pollen; T-cells protect the body against cancer cells and viruses. B- and T-cells are often jointly referred to as lymphocytes.

As we learned earlier, when faced with a stressor, the autonomic nervous system reacts by stimulating various viscera to secrete hormones. Some of these hormones compromise the immune system's ability to ward off attacking agents, thus leaving the body susceptible to illnesses such as cancer. Support for the relationship between stress and impairment of the immune system comes from research with both animals and humans. Consider first two studies that were conducted with mice (Riley, 1981). In the first study, mice were subjected to a chronic and intense stressor: they were placed on a spinning turntable for 10 minutes per hour for 5 consecutive hours. The results: lymphocyte activity in these animal's immune system was below normal. In the second study, cancer cells were implanted in two groups of mice. The experimental group was exposed to the rotation stressor, but the control group was not. The cancer cells implanted in the experimental animals showed more rapid growth than those in the control animals.

Now consider similar evidence found with human subjects. Cancer and other illnesses have been observed to occur at higher than average rates among people who are widowed. To investigate the possibility that bereavement suppresses the immune system, Schleifer and several other researchers (1983) drew blood samples from 15 men whose wives were dying of terminal breast cancer. Two blood samples were drawn, the first before the spouse's death, and the second within two months afterward. Both times, an agent that normally stimulates blood lymphocyte activity was mixed with the lymphocytes and the resultant level of activity was measured. On average, the activity level of blood lymphocytes after the spouse's death was less than before her death, which meant that the bereaved spouses were more susceptible to illness. Taken together, the results of these studies (and many other similar studies) suggest a strong link between impaired immune system functioning triggered by stressors and vulnerability to ill health.

We also know that exposure to stressors can produce other illnesses that can vary from person to person. For some people, prolonged stress results in ulcers, which are caused by chronically high levels of digestive fluids in the stomach or small intestine. Other people's stress reactions are characterized by high blood pressure, which is due partially to constriction of the arteries near the heart, and partially to excessive amounts of sodium (which is why physicians encourage patients with high blood pressure to avoid high salt diets). High blood pressure, as you may know, is the cornerstone of hypertension, which can cause CHD.

Stressors and Their Sources

Stress is a fact of everyday life regardless of one's life-style. The degree to which we experience stress and the extent to which stress impairs our life-style depends to a large extent on our perception of the threat posed by the stressor *(Principles 3 & 5)*. How many different kinds of stressors are there? The number is seemingly infinite; depending on the individual, almost any aspect of the environment can be perceived as a stressor. For convenience, we can put stressors into one of three categories: catastrophes, life changes, and everyday conflict.

Catastrophes are natural or human-produced disasters that disrupt and often permanently change one's life. Earthquakes, tornados, floods, war, and nuclear accidents are just a few of the many kinds of catastrophes that may befall us. One kind of stress experienced as the result of severe (or prolonged) stress that is often related to catastrophe is called **posttraumatic stress disorder**, an anxiety disorder in which the individual has feelings of social withdrawal accompanied by untypically low levels of emotion. In many cases people suffering posttraumatic stress disorder may re-experience, through dreams and flashbacks, the feelings of terror and shock felt during the actual catastrophe. Posttraumatic stress disorder does not usually appear immediately following the catastrophic event; rather, it is delayed, usually beginning several days later.

Stress is also induced by changes that threaten or otherwise complicate life-style *(Principles 3, 4, & 5)*. Death of a spouse, being promoted at work, changes in social activities, getting married, and sustaining a personal injury or illness are significant life changes that cause stress and represent disruptions in life-style (Holmes & Rahe, 1967). Some evidence has accumulated that suggests that if an individual experiences enough changes in life-style over a short time period, he or she is likely to develop a physical illness within the next two years (Rahe & Arthur, 1978). Other research suggests that not all people who encounter a series of significant stressors over a short period are at risk for illness (DuPue & Monroe, 1986). Why? Apparently because of the way in which they perceive the stressor. Recall Lazarus' idea of cognitive appraisal: The amount of stress induced by any stressor is determined by how significant we believe its threat is and whether we feel competent in coping with that threat.

Stressors do not have to be catastrophic or cause significant changes in life-style to induce stress. Often the everyday hassles we experience are enough to leave us feeling "stressed out." Locking our keys in the car, being late for an appointment, or disagreements with friends are examples of everyday events that can induce stress.

A common source of daily stress comes from simply making routine choices regarding what to do, how to do it, or when to do it. Consider, for example, a choice between studying tonight for a test you have tomorrow or going to a party with some good friends. You want to do both, but you can only do one. Psychologists refer to this as an approach-approach conflict because the choice involves two desirable outcomes. Other choices involve approach-avoidance conflicts because one outcome is desirable and the other is not. For example, you want to visit England but are afraid of flying. To travel by ship is also not a viable option for you because you get seasick. Still other choices involve avoidance-avoidance conflicts. With these choices, both outcomes are undesirable. For instance, choosing between having a root canal or tooth extracted creates stress because you don't want to do either one of them, yet one needs to be done.

Coping with Stress

So far, we have concentrated on discussing the bad news about stress—its damaging effects on the body and mind. Now, for the good news—each of us can learn to control stress *(Principles 2, 4, & 5)*. We may not always be able to predict when and where we will encounter stressors or control their intensity, but we can mitigate their damaging effects by adopting a coping strategy that is consistent with our life-style. A coping strategy is simply a plan of action that we follow either in anticipation of encountering a stressor or as a direct response to stress as it occurs. Although each of us may have our own idiosyncratic way of dealing with stress, we will discuss briefly four general coping strategies that health psychologists have shown

Catastrophic events such as Hurricane Hugo in 1989 not only leave behind a path of physical destruction but also bring on posttraumatic stress disorder for many victims. The disorder usually occurs several days after the event; individuals become socially withdrawn and experience untypically low levels of emotion.

Studies have revealed that in addition to the physical benefits of regular aerobic workouts, doing some kind of aerobic exercise routinely helps reduce stress.

to be effective in controlling stress, namely aerobic exercise, cognitive reappraisal, progressive relaxation training, and social support.

We have already seen that people who engage regularly in aerobic exercise are likely to live longer than people who don't exercise regularly (Paffenbarger et al., 1986). Another important benefit also accrues to those who consistently take time for aerobic workouts, and that is stress reduction. Consider the results of an experiment involving mildly depressed female college students (McCann & Holmes, 1984). The students were assigned to one of three groups: a control group involving no treatment for depression, a group who received relaxation training, and a group who engaged in aerobic exercises (jogging and dancing). The students rated their depression levels at the beginning of the experiment and then again 10 weeks later. The results were impressive. As expected, self-reported levels of depression for control subjects showed no change. Subjects given relaxation training showed a slight decrease in depression. Those who participated in aerobic exercises, though, showed a dramatic decrease in depression.

Although we know that aerobic exercise is effective in reducing stress, we don't yet know exactly how it reduces stress. One possibility is that increased heart and lung efficiency coupled with lower blood pressure that results from aerobic exercise simply makes people feel better. Another possibility is that people who can adjust their schedules to make room for regular workouts have a sense of control that those who can't find the time for exercise don't have. People who make exercise a priority in their schedules have to control other aspects of their lives to ensure that they do, indeed, exercise. As we saw in Chapter 14, people who have an internal locus of control take responsibility for the course of their lives, which means that they enjoy taking credit for their successes. Credit and success make for a happier life.

Of course, aerobic exercise is not for everyone. Some people find that simply altering their perceptions of the threat posed by stressors reduces stress. This coping strategy is called **cognitive reappraisal** and is an extension of Lazarus' idea of cognitive appraisal *(Principles 3 & 5).* The rationale underlying this strategy is easy to grasp: If our cognitive appraisal of a stressor is a determining factor in producing stress, then by reappraising that stressor as being less threatening, stress should be reduced. Sometimes simply learning to substitute positive statements for negative ones is sufficient to reduce stress (Lazarus, 1971; Meichenbaum, 1977). For example, students who suffer from test anxiety perceive tests as extremely threatening. They may say to themselves, "I am going to flunk that test tomorrow," or "That test is going to be so hard. . . ." To reappraise the stressor in this case would involve replacing these statements with ones such as "I am going to pass that test tomorrow," or "Sure, that test will be hard, but I'm ready for it."

Cognitive reappraisal is an effective coping strategy because it is often a more realistic approach to interpreting the threat posed by stressors than the original appraisal. We have good reason to appraise a charging bear as a real threat, but not a college examination. After all, we may not be able to deal well with the bear, but we can always learn how to take tests and improve our study habits. An additional benefit of cognitive reappraisal is that it teaches the individual that he or she can take control of stressful situations.

A third coping strategy is simply learning to relax when confronted with a stressor. Relaxing is based on the same general principle as cognitive reappraisal: substitute an incompatible response for the stress reaction. Consider the following example. You are anxious to get home, but you are caught in rush hour traffic. Your blood pressure rises, you begin to perspire, and you feel a knot in your stomach. What would happen if you were to relax? First, these physical responses would gradually recede, and second, you would feel less stress.

One procedure for producing relaxation is the progressive relaxation technique. It involves three steps: (1) recognizing your body's signals informing you that you are experiencing stress; (2) using those signals as a cue to begin relaxing; and (3) relaxing by focusing your attention on different groups of muscles, beginning with those in the head and neck and then those in the arms and legs. Here is an example of how relaxation may be used to reduce feelings of stress. Suppose that when confronted by a stressor, say a test, you respond by tensing certain muscles: those in your hand and fingers that you use to hold your pen or pencil and those around your mouth that you use to clench your teeth. Once you become aware of these responses, you can use them as cues to relax the muscle groups involved.

Although all of us experience stress, the experience itself is a subjective and private matter *(Principles 3 & 6)*. Nobody else can know what we feel inside. However, being confronted by a stressor and coping with stress is often a social matter. We learn as children to seek others, parents, brothers and sisters, friends, when we are in trouble or need help. This is a pattern of coping that continues over the life-span. Social support, the help that we receive from others in times of stress is an important coping strategy for many people for two reasons. First, we can benefit from experience of others in dealing with the same or similar stressors. Other people can, in essence, show us how to cope, perhaps by teaching us how to reappraise the situation. Second, other people can provide encouragement and incentives to overcome the stressor when we may otherwise fail to cope with the stressful situation.

In sum, stress is an inevitable consequence of environmental change. Both large changes, such as a natural disaster or changing jobs, and small changes, like remembering that you have a quiz tomorrow, contribute to the overall level of stress that we can experience at any one time. Whether stress impairs our health depends upon three variables: the extent to which we appraise the stressor as threatening, whether we engage in good health practices, and the extent to which we use coping strategies effectively. The combined effects of these variables on the relationship between stress and health are summarized in Figure 18.4.

Participating in support groups such as the mother's group shown here, is a very effective way to cope with stress. One of the main reasons is that people benefit from each other's experiences in a similar situation. People can also provide encouragement to someone who alone was unable to cope with the stress of a certain situation.

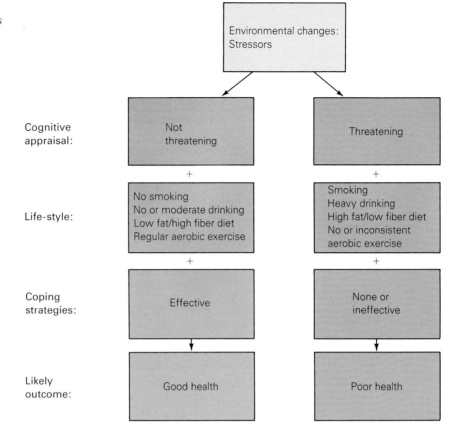

LIFE-STYLE AND ENVIRONMENT

There can be little doubt that the behaviors that comprise an individual's life-style have important consequences for his or her health and well-being. But the consequences of those behaviors are not merely personal. They are far-reaching and can affect the health and well-being of other people through their effects on the environment. Our actions affect others if we impact critical aspects of the environment: the air we breathe, the water we drink, and the land from which our food comes.

As we shall see, many of the environmental problems facing us today are related to specific behaviors in our life-styles, and the only way to solve these problems involves changing our behaviors. In this section, we will be considering life-styles within the broad context of an **ecosystem**, a system of interdependent relationships between organisms and between organisms and their physical environment. Changing one aspect of the ecosystem affects all other aspects of the system. Our focus will be on two major issues: overpopulation and environmental pollution.

> **M**any of the environmental problems facing us today are related to specific behaviors in our life-styles, and the only way to solve these problems involves changing our behavior.

Overpopulation

As ecologist Garrett Hardin pointed out over 20 years ago, individual self-interests can work to diminish the quality of environmental resources shared by the members of a community—be it a city, state, nation, or an entire planet. In his now classic 1968 paper, Hardin described "the tragedy of the commons." "Commons" is a term that was once used to refer to land that was shared by ranchers for grazing their cattle. To derive optimal use of the commons, the ranchers collectively must limit the number of cattle living off the commons; otherwise, the commons would be unable to support all the cattle adequately. However, it is in the interest of any one rancher to place more than his or her share of cattle on the commons in order to increase milk or beef production while distributing the costs of raising extra cattle across all the other ranchers. The tragedy unfolds when all of the ranchers, or at least a large percentage of them, place extra cattle on the commons. Soon the commons is overgrazed, all the cattle starve, and the ranchers go broke.

Hardin's point is that the natural environment is a commons shared by humanity. If it is overexploited by selfish individuals, we all lose. Expressed in psychological terms, the tragedy of the commons takes the following form:

> I perceive that my actions alone will not noticeably affect the quality of the environment; the cost of using natural resources and polluting is less than not using natural resources and not polluting. Therefore, I will consume natural resources and pollute.

When large numbers of people or corporations use the same reasoning, the environmental effects can be staggering *(Principles 4 & 5)*. Here are three real-life examples:

- An individual reasons that it is more convenient and less expensive to buy disposable products (diapers, razors, cameras, and so on) than nondisposable products and that recycling used products is too much work. "Besides," she reasons, "I don't really create that much waste by myself anyway." But because so many people have adopted the same logic, landfills are overflowing with refuse, and natural resources to create more products are becoming scarce, which pushes product prices up.
- The skipper of a tuna boat finds it easier and cheaper to let dolphins and other kinds of marine life caught in his fishing nets die rather than try to save them or use other methods of fishing that are not so harmful. When most or many skippers of tuna boats adopt the same strategy, as is true in many tuna fleets, the result is widespread destruction of marine species, some of which are already endangered.
- I find it useful and inexpensive to use my car for all sorts of purposes: to run errands, to get to and from work, to transport "stuff," and to just go for recreational drives. My individual contribution to air pollution and demand for oil is not, by itself, significant. Most people in industralized nations think the same way. The net result of this logic has been health-impairing air pollution and a tremendous demand for oil and oil derivatives. Our collective demand for oil is also indirectly responsible for oil spills, such as the one that took place in Prince William Sound, Alaska, in 1989.

As made obvious from our consideration of the tragedy of the commons, the effects of our behavior on the environment are multiplied by the number of people in the world, which at present numbers over 5 billion and is growing at the phenomenal pace of over 220,000 people per day (see Figure 18.5). Increasing world population poses two general threats to the environment. The first concerns the demand for natural resources, and the second the production of wastes. The demand for natural resources and the waste produced by any one individual is relatively insignificant, but when the demand for natural resources and the amount of waste is multiplied by 5 billion, serious problems result. Simply put, poisonous gases released into the air and toxic chemicals dumped onto the ground and into rivers and lakes has compromised the quality of the environment to the point that it threatens life, and not just the lives of our species but those of other species as well.

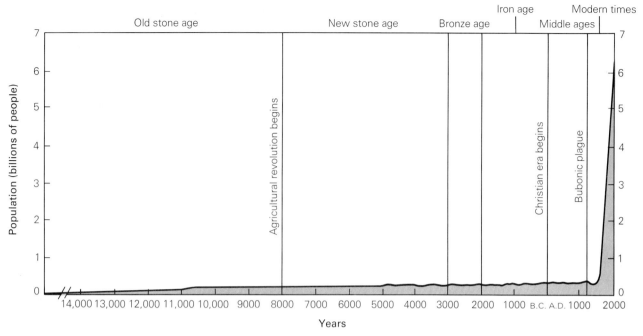

FIGURE 18.5

Human population growth during the last half million years. In the history of humankind, it is only relatively recently that the population has increased significantly. Because the population has increased so rapidly, we have not yet been able to adapt to many of its negative effects that may threaten our very existence.

The demand that 5 billion people place on the environment for food, water, fuel, and land is rapidly approaching the upper limits of the environment's capacity to support life. Not all of the world's people have the same demand for natural resources, and not all of us produce the same amount of waste. Industrialized nations by far demand and consume more natural resources than underdeveloped nations. For example, the average demand for water for each American citizen, calculated across both residential and industrial uses, is about 2000 gallons a day (just to produce one pound of beef requires about 2500 gallons). In contrast, citizens of an underdeveloped country use only an average of 12 gallons a day (Wallace, 1987).

Overpopulation also has a number of specific effects on our quality of life and on the quality of the environment. Consider just a few of them (Brown, McGrath, & Stokes, 1976):

- Hunger. The world's food supply and delivery system is inadequate to prevent starvation in many places of the world.
- Inadequate water supplies. Increased population size in combination with pollution has reduced the amount of water available for drinking and industrial uses.
- Inadequate housing. There simply is not enough adequate housing to shelter 5 billion people.
- Increased pollution. As the population increases, so does the amount of waste it generates, both in the form of sewage and industrial wastes.
- Inadequate health services. The population of many nations is growing faster than the ability to provide the necessary health services.
- Literacy. Because the greatest rate of population growth is occurring among underdeveloped nations and among the poverty-stricken, the number of uneducated and illiterate people is increasing.
- Overuse of recreation areas. Overuse causes deterioration of the aesthetic value in wilderness areas and parks.

The devastating effects of overpopulation throughout the world are many and include hunger, such as that caused by the famine in Ethiopia and deforestation of large areas, such as the rainforests of Brazil, shown at right.

- Deforestation. To feed and house larger populations, forests (particularly the world's rain forests) are being destroyed rapidly.
- Extinction of plant and wildlife. As land is developed for human use, natural habitats for both the world's flora and fauna are destroyed, thereby also destroying many plant and animal species.

It is ironic that although cultural evolution has allowed our species to proliferate so rapidly and so many of us to enjoy a high standard of living, it also threatens our very existence. Put differently, our life-styles—particularly our patterns of behavior related to production, consumption, and disposal of goods and services—are responsible for the rapidly deteriorating state of the environment (*Principle 4*). The primary cause of this deterioration is pollution, which we discuss next in terms of its behavioral causes. Our major point in focusing on environmental pollution echoes the one we made earlier when discussing the relationship between life-style and health: Environmental changes produced by our behavior in turn affect us and our quality of life. In this case, though, such changes affect the quality of life for millions of people. It is clear that a future challenge for psychologists is to develop ways to help society change people's behavior to better our environment. Assuming we won't be completely successful at this in the immediate future, it is likely that there will also be an increased demand for psychologists to aid people in adjusting to the new sources of stress created by changes in life quality due to environmental deterioration.

Environmental Pollution

A **pollutant** is any substance that has harmful or potentially harmful effects on the environment. Although some pollutants are natural, most are byproducts of human activity. Pollutants may be airborne, waterborne, or solid. Some pollutants have immediate toxic effects, like the gas that escaped from a pesticide manufacturing plant in India and killed over 2500 people in 1984. Other pollutants are not deadly until they have accumulated to a certain level. Another important problem with pollutants is that they also infringe upon the aesthetic value of our natural environment. Pollution comes in a variety of forms, of which we will discuss four: air, water, radioactive, and solid wastes. It is important to note that the harmful effects of pollution have been known for a long time, but people, businesses, and industries have nonetheless continued to pollute. Why? The answer is largely an economic one—it is simply cheaper and more convenient to dump wastes into the air, a river, or the ground than to dispose of them safely. In other words, improper disposal of wastes is maintained because it is believed to be cost effective from the point of view of the polluter (*Principles 4 & 5*).

Air pollution, such as the smog over the Los Angeles skyline, pictured here, prevents a certain amount of sunlight from reaching the earth and can contribute to illnesses such as bronchitis and emphysema.

Air Pollution. If you live in or have visited a large metropolitan area like New York or Los Angeles, you know firsthand about air pollution. Air pollution reduces the amount of sunlight reaching the earth, and can figure prominently in illnesses such as bronchitis and emphysema. Human activities responsible for the greatest quantities of air pollution are the use of internal combustion engines in our vehicles and industrial manufacturing, and to a lesser extent heating buildings. Table 18.3 summarizes the major types of air pollutants, their sources, and their harmful effects on the environment. Because of the threat it poses to both plant and animal life, one consequence of air pollution is particularly worrisome: the greenhouse effect.

The **greenhouse effect** involves the trapping of heat reflected from the earth by gases in the upper atmosphere. It is a natural process that owes its name to the fact that the windows in a greenhouse let sunlight through but prevent its heat from escaping. The greenhouse effect has been magnified by the huge amounts of carbon dioxide released into the air when gasoline and other fossil fuels are burned. Chlorofluorocarbons or CFCs—gases which are given off by refrigerators, air conditioners, aerosol spray cans, and polysterene food containers—also contribute to the greenhouse effect. Together, these gases collect in the upper atmosphere where they trap heat that would otherwise rise into outer space. The result is a global warming trend that, if left unchecked, will dramatically alter the earth's climate to the point that many life forms would become endangered, if not extinct. The greenhouse effect is aggravated by the rapid rate by which the world's forests are being destroyed. Trees absorb large quantities of carbon dioxide. Fewer trees means that more carbon dioxide is finding its way to the upper atmosphere.

The greenhouse effect is a threat to life for several reasons. First, even a slight increase in global temperature can produce changes in rainfall patterns. Some areas of the planet now lush with vegetation would become barren deserts; other areas that are now deserts would become lush. The greenhouse effect would also produce increases in the sea level due to melting of the polar ice caps. The rise in water level would permanently submerge many coastal cities and island nations, producing a migration of millions of refugees. It would also decrease our supply of fresh water. Although salt water would be more abundant, many inland sources of fresh water would disappear.

TABLE 18.3 *Major air pollutants and their sources.*

TYPES OF AIR POLLUTANTS	MAJOR HUMAN SOURCE	COMMENTS
Carbon monoxide	Vehicle exhaust	Most common type of air pollutant. Reduces oxygen supply to body tissues. Can cause headaches, nausea, and cramping. Particularly stressful on people with respiratory ailments.
Nitrogen oxide	Gasoline engines, power plants, and industry	Irritates lungs and eyes. Combines with hydrocarbons in sunlight to form smog.
Sulfur oxides	Coal burning	When combined with water, sulfuric acid is produced. Damages plants, trees, and marble, iron, and steel structures. Implicated in bronchitis, asthma, and emphysema.
Hydrocarbons	Incomplete combustion of fossil fuels	Implicated in development of respiratory disease and some cancers.
Particulate matter	Released from industry; includes dusts, minerals, plant products, and metals	Can aggravate lung and heart problems and cause cancer.

Source: Adapted from Wallace, R. A. (1987). *Biology: The world of life.* Glenview, IL: Scott-Foresman/Little, Brown, pp. 559–561.

The CFCs that contribute to the greenhouse effect also contribute to a related problem: depletion of ozone in the upper layers of the atmosphere. Ozone is a chemical that absorbs most of the ultraviolet radiation present in sunlight, preventing it from reaching earth, where its effects would be deadly. Ultraviolet radiation has two harmful effects on humans. First, it causes skin cancer and significantly impairs the human immune system, causing increased vulnerability to infectious diseases. Second, it destroys farm crops and interferes with photosynthesis of plankton, which is the foundation of the oceanic food chain. If plankton is destroyed or diminished significantly, every animal in that food chain, including humans, is adversely affected.

In sum, air pollution is a direct result of human activity and poses a threat to the quality of life for all living things. In particular, the greenhouse effect is changing the nature of the environment in which we live. This means that at some point we will have to alter our life-style patterns to either adapt to new and less healthy environments or take measures to keep our environment clean *(Principles 4, 5, & 7)*. The greenhouse effect, like all consequences of pollution, is a direct product of the technology and life-style changes wrought by cultural evolution. As one writer has put it: "The greenhouse crisis represents the final bill, come due, for the Industrial Age" (Rifkin & Howard, 1989).

Water Pollution. Another form of pollution is water pollution. Water pollution is a problem of epidemic proportions today because so much of the nation's water supply has been contaminated by sewage and chemicals (see Table 18.4). The problem stems from both private citizens and industries dumping untreated or partially treated waste into our waterways and soils. Water pollution not only makes water unsafe for drinking but also for recreational purposes such as swimming and fishing. Moreover, in the last two decades, massive fish kills have been traced to chemical effluents.

A common form of water pollution is caused by heat and not by organic wastes or chemicals. Many industries draw water from a natural source, say a river, use it for cooling purposes, and then return it to the source several degrees warmer than it was originally. The warmer water disrupts the local ecosystem of the river by hastening the rate at which fish and other aquatic species use oxygen while simultaneously reducing the oxygen-carrying capacity of the water. Some forms of aquatic life cannot adapt to the new living conditions and die.

Radioactive Pollution. We are surrounded by radiation, both natural and synthetic. Natural radiation stems from three sources: the earth's crust,

The effects of water pollution are not only harmful but fatal to some delicate ecosystems and aquatic life. For example, thousands of seals along the coast of the North Sea, such as the one pictured here, have died as a direct result of water pollution, which weakens their immune systems and makes them unable to overcome the pneumonia that eventually kills them.

TABLE 18.4. *Major water pollutants.*

TYPES OF WATER POLLUTANTS	MAJOR HUMAN SOURCE	COMMENTS
Oxygen-demanding	Sewage, natural run-off, and industrial wastes	Depletes oxygen in water, kills plants, fish, threatens land animals, creates foul odors
Disease-causing	Sewage and animal waste	Causes diseases such as typhoid, infectious hepatitis, cholera, and dysentery
Acidic	Industrial wastes and mining, especially coal	Kills plants, fish, and threatens land animals

Source: Adapted from Wallace, R. A. (1987). *Biology: The world of life.* Glenview, IL: Scott-Foresman/Little, Brown, p. 563.

Solid wastes are another form of pollution that threatens our health. The city of Love Canal, pictured above left, for example, was built on a toxic waste dumping site in the 1950s. It was not until 20 years later that the adverse effects on residents began to appear. These included higher incidence of cancer, nervous system disorders, and miscarriages. Garbage barges, such as the one shown above right arriving in Brooklyn are also a growing pollution problem, as more landfills reach capacity and barges are used to transport garbage to the ocean. The pollution problem arises when the waste that's been dumped washes up on shore.

atomic particles from space, and that which is a part of living systems. We do not know the health hazards posed by radiation from these sources, but we do know that birth defects, cancer, and other illnesses are caused by radiation that comes from human-generated sources, such as medical and dental radiation from x-rays, testing of nuclear weapons, nuclear power plants and nuclear accidents.

Although many people fear nuclear accidents such as those that occurred at the Three Mile Island nuclear plant in the United States and the Chernobyl nuclear power plant in the Soviet Union, radioactive pollution can also be produced by less sensational means including the mining and refining of radioactive fuels, transportation of the fuels, and storage of radioactive wastes. Regardless of the source of radioactive pollution, exposure to radioactivity can produce mutations in DNA, cause various cancers, impair the immune system, and produce other illnesses (see Figure 18.6).

Solid Wastes. A fourth form of pollution is solid wastes that are dumped at specific locations such as landfills and toxic waste sites. Often these wastes seep into the soil and contaminate underground water reservoirs. These reservoirs are tapped by wells that supply water for drinking and crop irrigation. The fumes from toxic wastes also seep into the atmosphere. Whether consumed in the food we eat, the water we drink, or the air we breathe, toxic wastes can have serious and long lasting effects on our health. Consider for example, the plight of the residents of Love Canal, a city located close to Niagara Falls. The land upon which the city was built was once owned by a chemical company that used it as a dumping site. The company covered the site with large amounts of soil and gave the land to the community in the early 1950s. Homes and schools were soon built on the property. Then in the late 1970s, the people living there noticed aversive odors in their homes. They also began to develop cancer and nervous system disorders at unusually high rates. The incidence of miscarriage

FIGURE 18.6

The effects of radiation pollution on the human body. Prolonged exposure to radiation pollution can cause abnormalities in the human body, several of which are indicated in the figure.

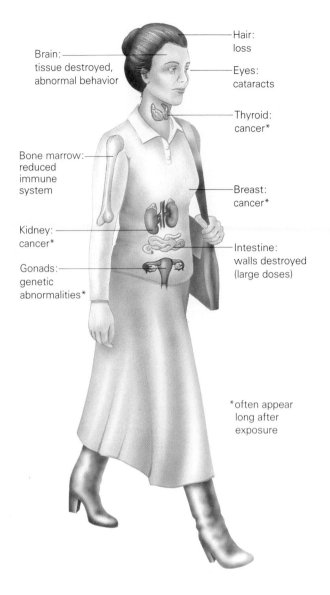

Brain:
tissue destroyed,
abnormal behavior

Hair:
loss

Eyes:
cataracts

Thyroid:
cancer*

Bone marrow:
reduced
immune
system

Breast:
cancer*

Kidney:
cancer*

Intestine:
walls destroyed
(large doses)

Gonads:
genetic
abnormalities*

*often appear
long after
exposure

among pregnant women soared. Several Love Canal residents were even discovered to have chromosomal damage.

Probably the most common type of pollution is garbage. Landfills are rapidly reaching capacity, and many cities are running out of places to put their garbage. But disposal of garbage is not restricted to landfills. Some companies have been known to load large barges with waste, take it out into the ocean, and dump it overboard. But, as the saying goes, what goes around comes around: the garbage returns. It washes up on shorelines, which, in addition to being unsightly, also poses a serious health hazard.

The garbage problem is obviously related to increasing population size. More and more people are generating more and more garbage with fewer and fewer locations to dispose of it. Much of what we call garbage, though, is recyclable. Many items that we put in our garbage cans—such as paper, plastic, glass, wood, metal, and so forth—can be used over again. Recycling has three specific benefits: it reduces the landfill space required for waste disposal; it reduces the demand for some natural resources; and it reduces pollution because recycling some used goods, like aluminum, creates less waste than producing new goods.

Several states (for example, Oregon, Vermont, Maine, Michigan, Connecticut, Delaware, Iowa, New York, and Massachusetts) as well as nations (for example, Canada), have established deposit laws requiring consumers to pay a deposit for beverage containers *(Principle 4)*. This encourages people to redeem their containers. How effective are beverage container laws? Very. Apparently, the reduction in container litter ranges from about 76 to 86 percent, depending on the state (Environmental Action Foundation, 1988).

You and the Environment

In the early 1970s, an often heard (and overused) comment was "If you are not part of the solution, then you are part of the problem." Although this statement is an oversimplification because it is possible to be part of neither the solution nor the problem, it carries with it a grain of truth in the case of our behavior and the environment. Each of us contributes in many ways to the environmental problems that currently beset our planet. When we drive our cars we contribute to air pollution and depletion of natural resources; using electricity when we don't need to means that more coal must be burned (or nuclear power generated), which contributes to air pollution. When we throw bottles, aluminum cans, plastic containers, and paper products into the garbage, we are wasting materials that could be recycled into new products. Collectively, our seemingly insatiable need for products—from video games to jewelry to cars—creates a demand for energy and excess waste. When these behaviors and their effects are multiplied, in the case of the United States over 200 million times, the collective effect is enormously negative. However, the opposite is also true: If each of us changed our life-style to incorporate more ecologically sound behaviors, the collective effect on the environment could be enormously positive *(Principles 4 & 5)*. Table 18.5 lists a variety of such behaviors and describes how they affect the environment and in turn the quality of our lives.

TABLE 18.5. *A sample of personal behaviors that have ecologically sound consequences on the environment.*

BEHAVIOR	CONSEQUENCES
Recycle used goods, including beverage containers, glass and paper products.	Reduces amount of land used as "dumps" and reduces pollution levels.
Use paper plates and cups instead of styrofoam ones.	Styrofoam products are made with ozone destroying CFCs.
Avoid using polystyrene products.	Reduces air pollution.
Drive less; walk or bicycle instead.	Reduces air pollution and decreases demand for fossil fuels.
Drive high mileage (fuel efficient) vehicles.	High mileage cars emit less carbon dioxide into the atmosphere.
Use public transportation where possible.	Reduces the amount of carbon dioxide emitted into the atmosphere.
Plant trees.	Absorbs carbon dioxide, reduces potential threat of greenhouse effect.
Replace incandescent light bulbs with fluorescent ones.	Uses less electricity, which may mean less coal is burned, which reduces air pollution.
Use rechargeable batteries instead of regular ones.	Reduces toxic seepage at dumps, which in turn, reduces pollution of ground water.

These behaviors by themselves may seem relatively inconsequential, but when their effects are multiplied across millions of people, the results can be extremely beneficial to our environment.

BOUNDARIES AND FRONTIERS

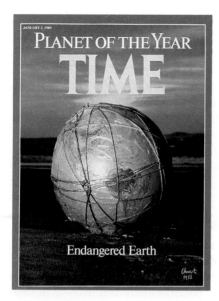

Even though psychologists possess great knowledge about the relationship between behavior and environment, their actual involvement in these areas is not as strong as that of other disciplines. The January 2, 1989 issue of Time, which was devoted to the environmental crisis, illustrates this point. Only other scientists, administrators, and political leaders were consulted to prepare the issue.

The September 1989 edition of *Scientific American* was a special issue ("Managing planet earth") devoted to the environmental crisis that now besets life on earth. The issue contains 11 articles on topics ranging from changes in the earth's atmosphere and climate to water pollution and overpopulation. The issue is a significant one because it summarizes our current state of knowledge about environmental pollution, depletion of natural resources, and suggests some ideas for how we might arrest environmental deterioration before our quality of life is diminished further. None of these articles, however, was written by a psychologist.

The January 2, 1989 issue of *Time* magazine (Planet of the Year) also contained special features devoted to the environmental crisis. To prepare for their special issue, "*Time* invited 33 scientists, administrators, and political leaders from 10 countries to a three-day conference held in Boulder" (Sancton, 1989, p. 28). No psychologists appear to have figured prominently in the information that *Time* reported in that issue.

Why were there no articles authored by psychologists in the special issue of *Scientific American*? Why was psychological research not cited in the special issue of *Time*? After all, psychologists are experts on the relationship between behavior and the environment. And since the environmental crisis we now face is a product of our behavior, one would think that psychology would be playing a central role, if not a predominant role, in addressing environmental problems.

The plain truth is that psychology is playing neither a large nor critical role in helping solve environmental problems. That is why psychologists probably were not invited to contribute to the *Scientific American* or *Time* special issues. There are a small number of psychologists interested in issues related to the quality of the environment, but generally speaking, their work so far has not attracted the attention of the press or other disciplines.

But psychology's failure to make significant contributions to environmental issues is not all its own fault. Part of the responsibility lies with our society, which views environmental problems as being largely solvable through technological innovations rather than changes in human behavior. As we have seen, though, our human problems, whether they are personal or global, cannot be solved using technological means alone. Technology is only effective to the extent that people use it *(Principle 7)*. And that is a behavioral matter and nothing else *(Principles 4 & 5)*. For example, birth control devices can be effective in helping curb increasing population only if people use them (and use them properly). Recycling prevents depletion of natural resources and decreases pollution, but only if people actually recycle their used goods. We know, too, that some measures that people can take to improve the quality of the environment involve reducing or eliminating the use of some technological products. For instance, driving our cars less would mean that fewer pollutants would be spewed into the atmosphere and that the rate of depleting oil reserves would be reduced.

Our society has also looked to government to establish policies regarding air and water quality standards, recycling, waste disposal, and so forth. Policies such as The Clean Air and Water Acts are a step in the right direction, but they are only effective to the extent that they influence our behavior. Policies that have no "teeth" in them are not sufficient to promote ecologically sound behavior. And as is obvious from the current state of our environment, the existing statutes and laws regarding pollution are not working.

In short, addressing environmental problems has been left to chemists, physicists, engineers, technicians, and politicians—none of whom are experts on human behavior. Perhaps part of the reason why technology has failed to solve so many environmental problems is that it ignores the human factors involved: the motivational and psychological causes of the problems. Although psychology has not played a significant role in addressing the environmental problems, can it do so in the future? Does psychology have the data-base and expertise to effect changes in people's ecological attitudes and behavior? We believe the answer to these questions is yes. But it is an answer that is based on faith and not on empirical evidence. We know that psychological research and theory have helped change attitudes and behavior relating to other aspects of life-style. Just as diet, smoking, and physical fitness are aspects of life-style that can be changed so, too, are ecologically sound (or unsound) behaviors. The task for psychologists is to apply their knowledge of human thought and action to engendering ecologically sound behavior.

Granted, it is our entire culture and the culture of many other nations that must change before the quality of the environment is improved significantly. But cultures are made up of individuals like you and me, and the way cultures change is through changes in the ideas and actions of their individual members. That is where the efforts of psychologists could have their greatest effects.

The important question to ask about the relationship between our behavior and its effects on the environment is how can we encourage people to make choices that have positive ecological consequences? We already know a good deal about how to persuade people to make choices that have positive outcomes. In order to encourage people to behave in an ecologically sound manner, we must first understand why they are not behaving that way in the first place. Or, at the very least, we must understand the kinds of contingencies that will change behavior from ecologically unsound to ecologically sound. Until psychologists join forces with scientists already studying environmental problems, specific agendas for psychological research remain unexplored *(Principle 1)*.

The bottom line is this: The environment in which we now live is a threat to our quality of life. That environment is a result of unsound ecological behaviors practiced by both us and our recent ancestors. If our behavior does not change—and soon—we, like so many other species, risk becoming endangered. Helping prevent that fate could be psychology's most important frontier.

CONCEPT SUMMARY

- What are the key principles that have been presented in this book? Give a brief description of each. (pp. 638–639)

LIFE-STYLE: CHOICES AND CONSEQUENCES

- What are some ways that cultural evolution has affected the life-style and environment of our species? (pp. 639–640)
- What kinds of consequences do our life-styles hold for us? (pp. 640–641)

- What factors contribute to the origin and maintenance of unhealthy life-styles? What role does the law of effect play? (pp. 640–641)
- What is the relationship between diet and coronary heart disease and cancer? (pp. 641–642)
- Why is physical fitness an important component of life-style? (pp. 642–643)
- In what ways can cigarette smoking and alcohol and drug abuse impair quality of life? What factors contrib-

ute to the maintenance of such unhealthy aspects of life-style? (pp. 644–646)

- What life-style changes can reduce the risks of contracting sexually transmitted diseases and AIDS? (p. 646)
- What factors influence seat-belt usage? Describe Geller's work in promoting seat-belt usage. (p. 647)

STRESS AND HEALTH

- What is the difference between stress and stressors? (p. 648)
- What is the role of the autonomic nervous system in stress? (pp. 648–650)
- In what ways can stress be maladaptive? (pp. 648–649)
- What are the stages of the General Adaptation Syndrome? Briefly explain each. (pp. 649–650)
- What is the role of cognitive appraisal in stress? (p. 650)
- In what ways might stressful life-styles impair health? (pp. 650–651)
- How are stressors classified? Briefly explain the differences in those classifications. (pp. 651–652)
- What is a coping strategy? Briefly explain the four coping strategies discussed in the chapter. (pp. 652–654)

LIFE-STYLE AND ENVIRONMENT

- What are two general threats that overpopulation poses to the environment? (pp. 655–657)
- What are some of the more specific effects that overpopulation has on our quality of life and on the quality of the environment? (pp. 657–658)
- What human activities contribute to air pollution? (pp. 659–660)
- What are the major chemicals involved in air pollution? Identify their sources and their effects on health. (p. 659)
- What is the greenhouse effect? What human activities contribute to this type of air pollution? (pp. 659–660)
- What human activities contribute to water pollution? (p. 660)
- What are the major chemicals involved in water pollution? Identify their sources and their effects on health. (p. 660)
- What are the effects of radioactive pollution on health? (pp. 660–661)
- What are the types of health and environmental problems caused by accumulating quantities of solid wastes? (pp. 661–663)
- How can recycling help diminish the solid waste problem? (pp. 661–663)
- What are some ecologically sound behaviors? How can they improve the quality of our lives? (p. 663)

KEY TERMS AND CONCEPTS

LIFE-STYLE: CHOICES AND CONSEQUENCES

Cultural Evolution The adaptive changes of cultures to recurrent environmental pressures. Cultural evolution has been a primary force involved in shaping our habitat. (p. 639)

Life-style The aggregate behavior of an individual. Simply, life-style is the way a person leads his or her life. (p. 639)

Coronary Heart Disease (CHD) The narrowing of blood vessels that supply nutrients to the heart. Unhealthy life-styles, especially frequent consumption of foods high in saturated fat and low in fiber, cigarette smoking, and heavy consumption of alcoholic beverages, contribute significantly to the risk of CHD. (p. 641)

Cancer A malignant and intrusive tumor that can destroy body organs and tissue. Unhealthy life-styles, especially diets high in fat and low in fiber and cigarette smoking contribute significantly to the risk of death due to cancer. (p. 641)

Serum Cholesterol A chemical that occurs naturally in all tissues and in the bloodstream where it serves as a detoxifier. Serum cholesterol has two important forms: LDL and HDL. LDL is often called bad cholesterol because high levels of it are associated with the formation of arteriosclerotic plaques that clog the arteries. HDL is sometimes referred to as good cholesterol because high levels

are inversely associated with CHD. It is believed that HDL may play a protective role in the bloodstream. (p. 641)

Aerobic Exercises Those exercises, such as running, walking, bicycling, and swimming that stimulate and strengthen the heart and lungs, which in turn, increases the body's efficiency in using oxygen. (p. 643)

Alcoholism An addiction to ethanol, which is the psychoactive agent in alcohol. (p. 645)

Health Psychology The branch of psychology involved in the promotion and maintenance of sound health practices. (p. 648)

STRESS AND HEALTH

Stress A pattern of physiological, behavioral, and cognitive responses to real or imagined environmental stimuli that are perceived as endangering or otherwise threatening our well being or personal abilities. (p. 648)

Stressors Environmental stimuli that are perceived as endangering or otherwise threatening our well-being or personal abilities. (p. 648)

General Adaptation Syndrome (GAS) The model proposed by Hans Selye to describe the body's adaptation to chronic exposure to severe stressors. Basically, the body passes through an orderly sequence of three physiological stages: the alarm stage, the stage of resistance, and the stage of exhaustion. (p. 649)

Cognitive Appraisal Our perception of the stressful situation. Cognitive appraisal is a two-stage process. In the first stage, we evaluate the nature of the threat in an attempt to address the seriousness of the perceived threat posed by the stressor. If we decide that the threat is real, we pass to the second stage, during which we assess whether we have the resources necessary to cope adequately with the stressor. The extent to which we believe both that the stressor is a serious one and that we *don't* have the resources necessary to deal with it influences the level of stress that will be experienced. (p. 650)

Immune System A network of organs and cells that protect the body from invading bacteria, viruses, and other foreign substances. The different cells of the immune system are specialized to combat particular types of invaders. B-cells produce antibodies in response to bacterial infection and other foreign substances, such as pollen. T-cells protect the body against cancer cells and viruses. B- and T-cells are often jointly referred to as lymphocytes. (p. 651)

Posttraumatic Stress Disorder An anxiety disorder in which the individual experiences feelings of social withdrawal accompanied by untypically low levels of emotion toward routine events. In many cases, people suffering posttraumatic stress disorder may re-experience through dreams and flashbacks the feelings of terror and shock experienced during the actual catastrophe. Posttraumatic stress disorder does not usually appear immediately following the catastrophic event; rather, it is delayed and usually begins several days later. (p. 652)

Cognitive Reappraisal A coping strategy in which the individual alters his or her perception of the threat posed by a stressor to reduce stress. The rationale underlying this strategy is easy to grasp: If our cognitive appraisal of stressors is a determining factor in producing stress, then by reappraising that stressor as being less threatening, stress should be reduced. (p. 653)

LIFE-STYLE AND ENVIRONMENT

Ecosystem A system of interdependent relationships between organisms and between organisms and their physical environment. (p. 655)

Pollutant Any substance that has harmful or potentially harmful effects on the environment. Although some pollutants are natural, most are produced by humans. Pollutants may be airborne, waterborne, or solid. (p. 658)

Greenhouse Effect The trapping of heat reflected from the earth by gases in the upper atmosphere. It is a natural process that owes its name to the fact that the windows in a greenhouse let sunlight through but prevent its heat from escaping. The greenhouse effect has been magnified by the huge amounts of carbon dioxide released into the air when gasoline and other fossil fuels are burned. Chlorofluorocarbons or CFCs—gases which are found in refrigerators, air conditioners, aerosol spray cans, and polysterene food containers—also contribute to the greenhouse effect. (p. 659)

ADDITIONAL SOURCES OF INFORMATION

Rifkin, J., & Howard, T. (1989). *Entrophy: Into the greenhouse world.* New York: Bantam Books. A captivating explanation of the greenhouse effect, its causes, and the steps we can take to mitigate its potential as a destructive force.

Skjel, E. W., & Whorton, M. D. (1983). *Of mice and molecules: Technology and human survival.* New York: Dial Press. An engaging overview of the health risks posed by human-made or altered environments. The central theme of this book is that environmental changes wrought by cultural evolution threaten our existence.

Scientific American (Special Issue, September, 1989). *Managing planet earth.* This special issue of *Scientific American* is devoted to a thoughtful analysis of current environmental problems ranging from population to pollution to extinction of plant and animal life. The time necessary to read each of the 11 articles in this issue represents a worthwhile investment toward better understanding the interaction of behavior, biology, and the environment on a global scale.

Taylor, S. E. (1986). *Introduction to health psychology.* New York: Random House. An excellent introduction to research on stress and aspects of life-style that contribute to and combat stress and stress-related illnesses.

Troyer, R. J., & Markle, G. E. (1983). *Cigarettes: The battle over smoking.* New Brunswick, N. J.: Rutgers University Press. A well-written and informative account of the controversies surrounding cigarette smoking.

Glossary

Absolute Threshold The value at which a stimulus is detected 50 percent of the time. (p. 151)

Accommodation In developmental psychology, the process by which existing schemes are modified or changed by new experiences. (p. 383). In sensory psychology, accommodation is the process by which the lens focuses light on the retina: as muscles contract (when viewing objects close up) or relax (when viewing distant objects), the lens bulges or narrows, respectively. (p. 158)

Acetylcholine A neurotransmitter found in the brain, where it is involved in learning and memory, and in the spinal cord and body, where it is involved in the control of the skeletal muscles and organs. (p. 103)

Achievement Skills that are already learned, such as having learned a foreign language. (p. 462)

Acquisition The portion of a classical conditioning experiment in which a conditional response first appears and then increases in frequency or strength. (p. 236)

Actor-observer Effect The tendency to attribute one's own behavior as being situationally determined, but others' behavior as being dispositionally caused. (p. 608)

Acupuncture A procedure of pain reduction developed by the Chinese in which small needles are inserted into the body at strategic spots. (p. 210)

Adolescence The period of life beginning with puberty and ending with the establishment of emotional and social independence from parents. (p. 405)

Aerial Perspective The monocular cue in which objects far off in the distance appear hazy and less distinct than nearby objects. (p. 174)

Aerobic Exercises Those exercises such as running, walking, bicycling, and swimming that stimulate and strengthen the heart and lungs, which in turn, increases the body's efficiency in using oxygen. (p. 643)

Aggression Any action, verbal or physical, that is intended to harm another individual. (p. 353)

Agoraphobia The fear of being away from a safe place or a safe person. (p. 541)

Alcoholism An addiction to ethanol, which is the psychoactive agent in alcohol. (p. 645)

Algorithm A completely specified, step-by-step set of rules for solving a problem. (p. 308)

Altruism The unselfish concern of one individual for the welfare of another. (p. 81)

Alzheimer's Disease A form of dementia or loss of intellectual ability that affects many people later in life. Typically, thinking, language skills, and memory deteriorate as the disease progresses. (p. 409)

Amnesia The profound loss of once-demonstrated memory skills. It occurs in two major forms, retrograde amnesia and anterograde amnesia. (p. 289)

Amplitude In vision, amplitude is the height of each light wave. The amplitude of a light wave determines a psychological property of brightness. (p. 157). In audition, amplitude is the difference between the high and low pressure levels of a sound wave. Graphically, amplitude is represented by the height of the wave. (p. 193)

Amygdala The structure in the limbic system that is involved with the control of aggression. (p. 125)

Anal Stage The second psychosexual stage (from about 18 months to 3 to 4 years). During the stage, the primary erogenous zone is the anal region. (p. 509)

Anorexia Nervosa An eating disorder, characterized by a pathological fear of weight gain, an obsession with not eating food, and a refusal to eat. (p. 351)

Anterograde Amnesia A condition in which an individual can remember events from before a certain time but has difficulty forming memories of events that occur after that time. (p. 289)

Antisocial Personality Disorder A disorder characterized by a failure to conform to standards of decency, repeated lying and stealing, a failure to sustain lasting, loving relationships, low tolerance of boredom, and a complete lack of guilt and anxiety. (p. 560)

Anxiety A sense of apprehension or doom that is accompanied by a number of physiological reactions, such as accelerated heart rate, sweaty palms, and tightness in the stomach. (p. 540)

Anxiety-based Disorder An unrealistic and excessive anxiety that diminishes some aspect of a person's life. (p. 540)

Aptitude The capacity or potential for learning.

Archetypes Universal thought forms and patterns that Jung believed resided in the collective unconscious. (p. 512)

Artificial Selection A procedure in which animals are deliberately mated to produce offspring that possess particularly desirable characteristics. (p. 63)

Assimilation The process by which new information about the world is modified to fit existing schemes. (p. 383)

Association Areas The portion of the cerebral cortex that is devoted to higher mental processes including planning and decision making. (p. 132)

Association Neuron A neuron found only in the brain and spinal cord that receives nerve impulses from sensory neurons and conveys these impulses to other association neurons or to motor neurons. (p. 96)

Associative Strength The correlation between the CS and UCS, or the degree to which the CS reliably predicts the UCS. (p. 242)

Astigmatism A visual disorder caused by defects in the spherical shape of the cornea. When the cornea is misshaped, visual images are not focused equally on different parts of the retina. (p. 160)

Attachment A social and emotional bond between infant and caregiver that spans both time and space. (p. 400)

Attitude An evaluative response to any person, object, or situation. (p. 609)

Attribution Theory The theory that attempts to explain how people infer the causes of their own and other people's behavior. (p. 606)

Auditory Canal The tubelike structure connecting the pinna with the tympanic membrane, and through which sound waves enter the ear. (p. 196)

Auditory Nerve The bundle of neurons along which nerve impulses carrying auditory information from the hair cells to the brain are channeled. (p. 198)

Authoritarian Parents Those who establish firm rules for their children and expect them to be obeyed without question. Disobedience is met with punishment rather than understanding or reasoning. (p. 404)

Authoritative Parents Those who establish rules and enforce them, but not through punishment alone. Authoritative parents seek to explain the relationship between rules and punishment to their children. (p. 404)

Automatic Processing The formation of memories without effort. (p. 279)

Autonomic Nervous System The part of the peripheral nervous system that controls bodily processes over which we generally exert no conscious control, such as heart rate, respiration, and digestion. (p. 95)

Availability Heuristic A heuristic for judging frequencies of events that relies primarily on the importance of the information that is most readily and easily available to the person solving the problem. (p. 313)

Aversion Therapy A form of treatment in which the client is trained to respond negatively to a neutral stimulus that has been paired with an aversive stimulus. (p. 580)

Axon The long pipelike fiber projecting from the cell body to the axon terminals that passes messages along to other neurons, glands, or muscles. (p. 95)

Axon Terminal The part of the neuron that connects the axon to the terminal buttons. (p. 95)

Backward Chaining A heuristic problem-solving procedure that begins with a potential solution called the hypothesis and searches for evidence that explains it. (p. 310)

Baseline Condition The part of a single-subject experiment in which the independent variable is not manipulated, but the independent variable is measured. (p. 38)

Basic Orientations Horney's idea that different sets of personality characteristics correspond to the strategies of moving toward others, moving against others, and moving away from others. (p. 513)

Basilar Membrane A structure that runs nearly the entire length of the cochlea and functionally divides the cochlea into upper and lower divisions. The hair cells are embedded in the basilar membrane. (p. 197)

Behavior The actions of organisms that can be observed directly by others. (p. 2)

Behavior Assessment Techniques for assessing personality that focus on what an individual actually does, not just what he or she reports. (p. 502)

Behavior Modification A form of behavior therapy based on operant conditioning principles. (p. 581)

Behavior Therapy The application of principles derived from experimental research for the alleviation of psychological problems. (p. 579)

Behavioral Perspective A current view in psychology holding that behavior is caused by environmental variables and their interaction with biological ones. (p. 7)

Behaviorism The school of psychology often associated with John B. Watson, who argued that observable and not mental processes were the proper subject matter of psychology. (p. 5)

Belief-bias Effect The improper evaluation of the validity of a conclusion on the basis of what is believed to exist beyond the known facts. (p. 306)

Belief in a Just World The tendency to believe that people generally get what they deserve in life. (p. 608)

Binocular Disparity A binocular cue produced because the eyes are positioned in slightly different locations, causing slightly different images of objects farther away. (p. 173)

Biological Evolution The theory that over time organisms originate and become adapted to their environment by biological means. (p. 60)

Biological Perspective A current view in psychology that behavior is influenced by genetic, physiological, and other biological processes. (p. 7)

Biomedical Therapy Treatment of psychological problems by directly altering the physical functioning of the brain. (p. 570)

Biopsychology The study of the nervous system and its relation to behavior. (p. 93)

Bipedalism The ability to move about the environment on two feet. (p. 70)

Bipolar Disorder Alternating states of depression and mania separated by relatively normal periods. (p. 549)

Blind Spot The point on the retina at which the optic nerve exits the back of the eye, creating a hole in our vision. (p. 161)

Blocking The ability of one CS to obstruct or block conditioning to a subsequent CS because of an organism's previous conditioning experience. (p. 242)

Bottom-up Processing Processing of a pattern that begins at the level of the receptors and proceeds in an orderly fashion through specialized cells in the visual cortex. (p. 185)

Brightness The psychological counterpart to a light wave's amplitude. (p. 157)

Brightness Contrast The phenomenon in which a color appears brighter as the background becomes darker. (p. 164)

Broca's Area The portion of the frontal lobe that is involved in the motor production of speech. (p. 131)

Bulimia An eating disorder in which people eat enormous quantities of food and then either force themselves to regurgitate or use laxatives to rid their bodies of the food. (p. 352)

Bystander Effect The reduced tendency of people to offer help in an emergency situation when other bystanders are present. (p. 627)

Cancer A malignant and intrusive tumor that can destroy body organs and tissue. (p. 641)

Cannon-Bard Theory The theory that the experiencing of emotion and the experiencing of physiological arousal are controlled by the brain and are independent of each other. (p. 366)

Case Study An intensive investigation of a single individual over an extended period of time based on the use of observational techniques. (p. 32)

Catatonic Schizophrenia A type of schizophrenia characterized primarily by disorders of motor behavior: alternation between uncontrolled excitement and immobility, with one or the other extreme dominating. (p. 556)

Category Clustering The recalling of words according to semantic categories. (p. 277)

Catharsis Freud's term to describe the process in which pent-up energy is released or purged. Displacement and sublimation may provide such an outlet. (p. 353)

Cell Body The part of the neuron that contains the nucleus and other structures that control the moment-to-moment functioning of the cell. (p. 95)

Central Core The portion of the brain comprised of the medulla, pons, cerebellum, thalamus, and reticular formation. (p. 123)

Central Nervous System The brain and spinal cord. (p. 95)

Central Traits Personality attributes that seem to be the most representative of an individual. (p. 604)

Cephalocaudal Principle The idea that growth of the body proceeds from head to torso to feet; control over the upper body takes place before control over the lower body. (p. 398)

Cerebellum A structure located just behind and slightly above the medulla that is involved in the regulation of coordinated movement. (p. 124)

Cerebral Cortex The large convoluted mass of brain tissue located just beneath the skull. This tissue, which is the most recent achievement of brain evolution, is involved in complex cognitive processes such as reasoning and decision-making. (p. 127)

Chromosomal Aberration The rearrangement of genes within or between cells or a change in the total number of chromosomes. (p. 74)

Chromosomes The rodlike structures found in the nuclei of living cells containing genes. (p. 72)

Chunk The representation in memory of a single, meaningful concept. (p. 270)

Circadian Rhythm The cycle of activities of the nervous system. Circadian rhythms wax and wane over the course of each 24-hour period. (p. 136)

Classical (or Pavlovian) Conditioning The form of learning in which one stimulus or event predicts another stimulus or event. (p. 234)

Clinical Psychologist A practitioner psychologist who specializes in therapy and/or therapy-related research. (p. 15)

Closure A principle of perceptual grouping in which an object tends to be perceived as a whole even though a part of it is missing. (p. 172)

Cochlea A bony, coiled fluid-filled chamber in the inner ear that houses the auditory receptors. (p. 197)

Cognition The full range of mental activities used to represent and process knowledge, including perception, memory, thought, and the use of language. (p. 296)

Cognitive Appraisal Our perception of a stressful situation. Cognitive appraisal is a two stage process. In the first stage we evaluate the nature of the threat. If we decide that the threat is real, we pass to the second stage, during which we assess whether we have the resources necessary to cope adequately with the stressor. (p. 650)

Cognitive Behavior Therapy A method of treatment that focuses on altering the client's thoughts, beliefs, and perceptions. (p. 584)

Cognitive Dissonance Theory A theory that proposes people are motivated to reduce the anxiety produced by inconsistent cognitions and behaviors. (p. 613)

Cognitive Economy The minimization of the amount of effort and time required in the processing of stimuli. (p. 301)

Cognitive Perspective A current view in psychology that emphasizes the study of how organisms process information about their environment. (p. 8)

Cognitive Processes Unobservable mental activities such as thinking, sensing, and perceiving. (p. 2)

Cognitive Reappraisal A coping strategy in which the individual alters his or her perception of the threat posed by a stressor to reduce stress. (p. 653)

Cognitive Restructuring The process of replacing the client's negative thoughts with more constructive ways of thinking. (p. 584)

Cohorts The people born in the same year or time period. (p. 379)

Collective Unconscious According to Jung, the part of the unconscious that contains memories and ideas inherited from our ancestors over the course of evolution. (p. 512)

Commitment According to Marcia, a decision based on consideration of alternative goals and values that leads to a specific course of action—the teenager is "committed" to thinking and acting in a manner consistent with how the crisis has been resolved. (p. 406)

Community Psychology A form of therapy whose goal is to address psychological problems through an assessment of the sociocultural context in which the problems develop. (p. 591)

Competition A striving or vying with others, who share the same ecological niche, for food, mates, and territory. (p. 66)

Complementary Colors Pairs of primary colors (red and green or yellow and blue) that produce a white or gray when mixed together. (p. 167)

Compliance A change in one's behavior or beliefs as the result of an explicit request made by a nonauthoritative person. (p. 619)

Compulsion An irresistible impulse to repeat some action over and over even though it serves no useful purpose. Compulsions are often behavioral responses to a specific obsession. (p. 542)

Computational Metaphor The metaphor used by cognitive psychologists that likens human cognition to a computer program. (p. 297)

Concept A grouping of similar objects, events, or people into categories. (p. 298)

Concrete Operational Period Piaget's third stage of cognitive development (roughly ages 7 to 11), in which children develop the ability to understand the conservation principle and other logical concepts, such as categorization. (p. 386)

Conditional Response (CR) In classical conditioning, any neutral stimulus paired with the unconditional stimulus that eventually elicits a response. (p. 235)

Conditional Stimulus (CS) In classical conditioning, any neutral stimulus paired with the unconditional stimulus that eventually elicits a response. (p. 235)

Conditioned Reinforcers Stimuli and events that acquire their reinforcing properties through their association with primary reinforcers. (p. 255)

Conditions of Worth Our perception of the criteria we must meet in order to be worthy of positive regard from others. (p. 526)

Conduction Hearing Loss The obstruction or destruction of the conductive structures of the ear, specifically, the external auditory canal, tympanic membrane, and ossicles. (p. 203)

Cones Color-sensitive receptors found primarily in the fovea, although some may be found in the retina's outer region or periphery. (p. 159)

Confederate A person acting as a subject in an experiment, but who is really an assistant of the researcher. (p. 617)

Confidentiality The privacy of the subject's participation in research. (p. 54)

Confirmation Bias People's tendency to search for instances that confirm their beliefs rather than to search for evidence that falsifies those beliefs. (p. 307)

Conformity Thinking or behaving in a manner that is consistent with the norms of a social group. (p. 617)

Confounding Variables Variables other than the independent variable that can influence the value of the dependent variable. (p. 40)

Consensus The extent to which one person's behavior is consistent with that of other people. (p. 607)

Conservation The understanding that specific properties of objects (height, weight, etc.) remain the same despite apparent changes in the shape or arrangement of those objects. (p. 385)

Consistency The extent to which one person's behavior is consistent across time and/or settings. (p. 607)

Constructs (intervening variables) Abstract variables that cannot be observed directly, such as gravity and intelligence. (p. 476)

Continuous Reinforcement Schedule A reinforcement schedule in which a reinforcer is arranged for each response. (p. 252)

Control Group The group of subjects in an experiment that is either not exposed to the independent variable or is exposed to a lesser value of the independent variable relative to the experimental group. (p. 36)

Conventional Level The second level in Kohlberg's theory of moral development during which children's moral reasoning becomes subject to conformity. (p. 389)

Convergence The binocular cue in which the eyes tend to turn inward when viewing nearby objects. (p. 173)

Conversion Disorder The somatoform disorder that involves the actual loss of bodily functions such as blindness, paralysis, and numbness due to excessive anxiety. (p. 544)

Cornea The transparent fluid-filled cover at the front of the eye through which light enters. (p. 157)

Coronary Heart Disease (CHD) The narrowing of blood vessels that supply nutrients to the heart. (p. 641)

Corpus Callosum A large cable of axons that connects the two hemispheres of the brain. (p. 134)

Correlation The statistical term used to describe the degree of relationship between two or more variables. (p. 26)

Correlation Coefficient A statistical expression of the amount of correlation between two variables, with a value that ranges from -1 to $+1$. (p. 48)

Counterattitudinal Behavior Public behavior that is inconsistent with private attitudes. (p. 614)

Countertransference The process by which the therapist projects his or her emotional issues onto the client. (p. 578)

Covariation Rule The attributional rule in which certain events are seen as occurring together in time. (p. 606)

Creativity The generation of novel and useful solutions to problems. (p. 316)

Crisis According to Marcia, a period during which the adolescent struggles intellectually to resolve issues related to personal values and goals. (p. 406)

Critical Period The period of time during which imprinting can occur. (p. 231)

Cross-adaptation The decrease in sensitivity to one odor because of exposure to a different odor. (p. 215)

Cross-sectional Approach A research design used to test or observe different individuals of various ages at the same point in time. (p. 379)

Crystallized Intelligence A kind of intelligence that reflects both formal education and the "seat of the pants" learning that comes in everyday life. (p. 411)

Cultural Evolution The adaptive changes of cultures to recurrent environmental pressures over time. (p. 71)

Dark Adaptation The process of our eyes adapting to decreasing levels of illumination. (p. 164)

Data Scientific information usually obtained by numeric measurement. (p. 23)

Debriefing A procedure of informing subjects of the true nature and purpose of the research after all data have been collected. (p. 54)

Decibel (dB) The unit of measurement for studying a sound wave's amplitude and loudness. (p. 194)

Deductive Reasoning A form of reasoning in which a conclusion is implied by two or more statements. (p. 304)

Deep Structure The structure underlying a sentence that is directly related to the meaning of the sentence. (p. 321)

Defense Mechanisms Mental tactics that the ego uses to insulate itself from threatening ideas, perceptions, emotions, and instincts. (p. 507)

Deferred Imitation The result of the child's new ability to form mental representations of actions that he or she has observed, which then may be recalled at a later point to direct particular imitative actions. (p. 384)

Degradation The process by which neurotransmitters are destroyed by enzymes in the synaptic cleft. (p. 102)

Delay Conditioning The relationship between the CS and UCS in which the CS begins shortly before the UCS. Specifically, the UCS begins while the CS is still present and both stimuli terminate at the same time. (p. 238)

Delusions False beliefs maintained in the face of no or contrary evidence. (p. 554)

Demand Characteristics Factors in an experiment that cause subjects to behave in a manner consistent with what they believe the study is about. (p. 44)

Dendrites Tiny, treelike projections jutting out from the cell body that receive nerve impulses from neighboring neurons or receptors. (p. 95)

Denial A defense mechanism that works similarly to repression except that it blocks from consciousness threatening perceptions of the real world. (p. 507)

Dependent Variable The variable that is measured in an experiment. In psychological research, the dependent variable is always behavior. (p. 34)

Depressants Psychoactive drugs that slow down the nervous system's activities, producing drowsiness and sedation. (p. 110)

Depth Cues Those aspects of any stimulus situation that indicate how far an object is from the observer or other objects. (p. 173)

Depth Perception The ability to judge the distance of objects from us or other objects. (p. 173)

Descriptive Statistics Statistics used to describe a particular set of data such as the mean or median. (p. 42)

Diagnostic and Statistical Manual of Mental Disorders (DSM) The current and most widely used manual for classifying psychological disorders. The DSM-III-R is a classification system that describes an individual's psychological condition based on five different types of information, which are called axes. (p. 537)

Diathesis-stress Model The idea that psychological disorders, particularly schizophrenia, are due to the interaction of both a genetic disposition (diathesis) and environmental factors (stress). (p. 558)

Difference Threshold The minimal change in stimulation that can be reliably detected 50 percent of the time. (p. 154)

Diffusion of Responsibility An explanation of the bystander effect stating that when several bystanders are present, no one individual assumes responsibility for helping the victim(s). (p. 627)

Discounting Rule The presence of several competing attributions for the same behavior. (p. 607)

Discrimination In classical conditioning, distinguishing one stimulus from another. (p. 239). In operant conditioning, discrimination means that responding occurs in the presence of only certain kinds of discriminative stimuli—those associated with reinforcement. (p. 250)

Discrimination The differential treatment of people based on their membership in a particular group. (p. 605)

Discriminative Stimulus In operant conditioning, the preceding event or stimulus that sets the occasion for responding because in the past that behavior has produced certain consequences in the presence of that particular stimulus. (p. 249)

Disorganized Schizophrenia A type of schizophrenia characterized primarily by disturbances of thought and a flattened or silly affect. Behavior is often inappropriate and absurd; language is incoherent. (p. 556)

Displacement A defense mechanism in which feelings of hostility and aggression are channeled toward acceptable or less threatening persons or objects. (p. 508)

Dissociative Disorder A class of disorders in which anxiety is reduced by a sudden disruption in consciousness, which in turn, produces changes in one's sense of identity. (p. 545)

Distal Stimulus Any object in the environment that can be known to us only through its image on the retina, the proximal stimulus. (p. 170)

Distinctiveness In social psychology, the extent to which a behavior is a response to a specific stimulus but not to others. (p. 606)

Dizygotic Twins Fraternal twins. Dizygotic twins develop from the separate fertilization of two ova. (p. 77)

DNA Deoxyribonucleic acid. Genetic material found in the cells of most living things. (p. 72)

Door-in-the-face Technique A compliance technique in which an unreasonable offer is followed by a more reasonable offer. (p. 620)

Dopamine A neurotransmitter that plays a role in brain regulation of movement, cognition, and emotion. Extremely high levels of dopamine produce symptoms of schizophrenia; extremely low levels produce symptoms of Parkinson's disease. (p. 104)

Doppler Effect The changes in pitch emanating from a sound-emitting object moving relative to a listener. (p. 200)

Double-bind The conflict caused for a child when he or she is given inconsistent messages or cues from a parent. (p. 559)

Double-blind An experimental procedure for controlling experimenter expectancy in which neither the person conducting the experiment nor the subjects know the purpose of the study or to which group subjects have been assigned. (p. 41)

Down's Syndrome A genetic disorder caused by a chromosomal aberration resulting in an extra 21st chromosome. (p. 79)

Dream Interpretation The evaluation of the underlying meaning of dream content. (p. 577)

Drive A state of internal tension or arousal caused by an unsatisfied need. (p. 336)

Drug Therapy The treatment of psychological problems with chemical agents. (p. 572)

Dual Center Theory of Eating The idea that the lateral hypothalamus and ventromedial hypothalamus work in concert to control eating. (p. 347)

Ecosystem A system of interdependent relationships among organisms and between organisms and their physical environment. (p. 655)

Effortful Processing Practicing or rehearsing information. (p. 278)

Ego The ego serves as the general manager of personality; it makes the decisions regarding the pleasures that will be pursued at the urging of the id and the moral dictates of the superego that will be followed. (p. 507)

Egocentric Self-centeredness, which is a characteristic of preoperational children: they are unable to see the world from any point of view but their own. (p. 385)

Elaborative Rehearsal The processing of information on a deeper or more meaningful level than mere repetition. (p. 273)

Electroconvulsive Therapy (ECT) A form of treatment that involves passing small amounts of electric current through the brain to produce seizure activity. (p. 571)

Electroencephalogram (EEG) An amplified tracing or recording of the brain's electrical activity. (p. 121)

Embryonic Stage The second stage of prenatal development, during which the heart begins to beat, the brain starts to function, and most of the major body structures begin to form. (p. 394)

Emotions Moods or feelings. Felt internal conditions that change from time to time largely as a function of things that happen to us. (p. 353)

Empirical Knowledge Knowledge that is obtained from carefully observing and measuring behavior under highly controlled conditions. (p. 23)

Empty Chair Technique A procedure in which the client imagines that he or she is talking to someone sitting in an empty chair close by. (p. 588)

Encephalization Increases in brain size. (p. 70)

Encoding The active process of putting stimuli into a form that can be used by our memory system. Encoding is simply a matter of placing information into memory. (p. 266)

Encoding Specificity The principle that how we encode information may determine our ability to retrieve it later. (p. 279)

Endocrine System A slow acting communication network composed of endocrine glands. These glands stimulate other glands and organs via hormones. (p. 116)

Enkephalins A class of neurotransmitters that appear to be involved in the body's ability to tolerate and mediate pain. (p. 105)

Epigenetic Principle The idea that human development proceeds according to a biologically determined agenda based on two factors, biology and culture. Biological factors exert their influence at critical points (conflicts) during the individual's maturation; the culture in which one lives provides the context in which the individual resolves the conflict. (p. 391)

Episodic Memory A type of memory found in long-term store that serves as a record of our life's experiences. Events stored there are quite literally autobiographical. (p. 272)

Erectile Dysfunction The inability to produce or maintain an erection. (p. 440)

Etiology A general term for describing the causes of a disorder. (p. 537)

Eugenics A word based on a Greek term for "well-bred," that Galton used to describe the movement he founded to study and promote the principles of artificial selection in humans. (p. 465)

Exhibitionism The displaying of one's genitalia to a stranger in a public place to achieve sexual gratification. (p. 561)

Expectancy The individual's belief or perception that a specific consequence will follow a specific action. (p. 520)

Expectancy Theory The theory that an individual's anticipation or expectancy of the reward motivates his or her behavior. (p. 344)

Experiment A research method in which the investigator manipulates independent variables and measures their effects on dependent variables. (p. 34)

Experimental Group The group or groups of subjects in an experiment that is exposed to the independent variable. (p. 36)

Experimenter Expectancy An experimenter's inadvertent communication of his or her expectations to the subject that may influence the subject's behavior. (p. 38)

Expert System A computer program that, like a human expert, uses heuristics and knowledge about the world to solve problems. (p. 310)

Extinction In classical conditioning, the procedure of no longer presenting the UCS after the CS to the subject after conditioning of a response. In operant conditioning, extinction is any procedure in which a reinforcer is no longer presented following a response. (p. 238)

Facial Feedback Hypothesis The idea that feedback from our facial muscles helps us experience emotion by providing us with information about the emotion. (p. 363)

Factor Analysis A statistical technique developed by Spearman for determining the correlation of different test questions to each other. (p. 462)

Falsifiability The ability to prove that a statement of inference is false. (p. 25)

Family Therapy Therapy in which the family, rather than any particular family member, is viewed as the client. (p. 590)

Feature Analysis The recognition of an object based on the distinctive characteristics or components that, because of the specific manner in which they are arranged, define that object. (p. 180)

Feature Detectors Neurons in the visual cortex are excited by particular patterns of light, such as lines and angles of different sizes and shapes. (p. 163)

Fertilization The union of a sperm and ovum resulting in conception. (p. 423)

Fetal Alcohol Syndrome (FAS) The several serious side-effects produced by a pregnant woman's heavy consumption of alcohol on her fetus. These effects include: both pre- and postnatal growth deficits, deformations of the eyes and mouth, brain and central nervous system abnormalities and deformation of the heart. (p. 396)

Fetal Stage The third and final stage of prenatal development. It begins with the appearance of bone and ends with birth. (p. 394)

Fetishism The use of inanimate objects to obtain sexual pleasure. (p. 561)

Figure-ground Relationship An organizational principle of Gestalt psychology describing our tendency to perceive some objects, called figures, as standing out from their surroundings, called the ground. (p. 171)

Five-factor Theory The trait theory that specifies five basic personality traits: Extraversion, Emotional Stability (also called Neuroticism or Anxiety), Openness, Agreeableness, and Conscientiousness. (p. 516)

Fixation An unconscious obsession with an erogenous zone resulting from failure to resolve the crisis associated with the corresponding stage of psychosexual development. (p. 508)

Fixation The tendency to view a problem solely in one particular way. (p. 315)

Fixed-action Pattern A species-typical behavior characterized by highly stereotyped pattern of responses. (p. 229)

Fixed-interval (FI) Schedules These schedules require that reinforcement be delivered only if a response occurs after a fixed amount of time has elapsed since delivery of the previous reinforcer. (p. 253)

Fixed-ratio (FR) Schedules These schedules require that reinforcement be delivered only after the organism has emitted a fixed number of responses. (p. 253)

Flavor A food or drink's taste, consistency, temperature, texture, and smell. (p. 216)

Fluid Intelligence A kind of intelligence that reflects our native capacity for reasoning, problem solving, and remembering. (p. 411)

Follicle-stimulating Hormone (FSH) In males, FSH stimulates the manufacture of sperm and in females FSH prepares the ovaries for ovulation. (p. 424)

Foot-in-the-door Technique A compliance technique in which a small, reasonable request is followed by a larger, burdensome request. (p. 619)

Formal Operational Period The fourth and final of Piaget's stages, which begins roughly at about age 11. During this stage, individuals first become capable of more formal kinds of abstract thinking and hypothetical reasoning. (p. 387)

Forward Chaining A heuristic problem-solving procedure that involves selecting the best out of many possible actions, observing what happens, and then, depending on the result, repeating the process by taking another action. (p. 310)

Fovea A tiny area (about one square millimeter) in the center of the retina, containing only cones. (p. 160)

Free-association The psychoanalytic procedure in which the client is encouraged to speak freely, without censoring possibly embarrassing or socially unacceptable thoughts or ideas. (p. 576)

Frequency Distribution A listing or graph of all the possible values of a variable, and how many subjects actually obtained each of these values. (p. 43)

Frequency Theory The theory of pitch that proposes that the entire basilar membrane vibrates in synchrony with the frequency of sound waves striking the ear. These vibrations are then transduced to an equivalent number of neural impulses that are channeled to the brain. (p. 198)

Freudian Slips Mistakes in speech that reflect unconscious motivations and wishes. (p. 505)

Functional Fixedness An example of a fixation. The tendency to limit possible solutions by using objects only in the way that they have been traditionally used. (p. 315)

Functionalism The school of psychology that studied the mind's role in helping organisms adapt to their environment. (p. 4)

Fundamental Attribution Error The tendency to apply dispositional rather than situational attributions to other people's behavior. (p. 608)

g The general ability that is purported by some theorists to be common to all intellectual tasks. (p. 462)

GABA (gamma-amino butyric acid) The main inhibitory neurotransmitter found in the brain. Without GABA the brain would be overrun with excitatory neural impulses, which would lead to convulsions and seizures. (p. 104)

Gambler's Fallacy A mistaken belief that the outcome of the next chance event is predicted on the basis of representativeness. (p. 314)

Gate-control Theory A theory stating that our perception of pain is determined by the interplay of the nerve fibers that carry information about pain to the brain. Large, fast fibers close a neural gate through which nerve impulses carrying information about pain must pass on their way to the brain. Small, slow fibers open the gate. (p. 208)

Gender The individual qualities of a person that a given culture uses to define that person as a male or female. (p. 422)

Gender Identity An individual's private sense of being a male or female. In most cases, one's gender identity matches one's biological gender. (p. 429)

Gender Roles Cultural expectations that men and women should think and behave differently. (p. 429)

Gender Typing The learning of the attitudes and behaviors appropriate to one's gender identity. (p. 429)

General Adaptation Syndrome (GAS) The model proposed by Hans Selye to describe the body's adaptation to chronic exposure to severe stressors. Basically, the body passes through an orderly sequence of three physiological stages: the alarm stage, the stage of resistance, and the stage of exhaustion. (p. 649)

Generalization In classical conditioning, conditional responses elicited by stimuli that resemble the CS used in training. (p. 238). In operant conditioning, generalization means something slightly different. Once a response has been reinforced in the presence of a discriminative stimulus, other similar stimuli may also serve as discriminative stimuli for the same response. (p. 250)

Generalized Anxiety Disorder Chronically high levels of anxiety that are not specific to any one source. (p. 540)

Genes The small units of DNA that are located on chromosomes. (p. 72)

Genetic Program The genetic instructions an organism inherits at birth. (p. 228)

Genital Stage The fifth and final psychosexual stage (from puberty through adolescence). During this stage, the adolescent experiences adult sexual desires. The id and superego once again become active, forcing the ego to find socially acceptable solutions to sexual or aggressive urges. (p. 510)

Genotype An organism's genetic make up. (p. 66)

Gestalt Psychology The school of psychology that studied the organization of cognitive processes, particularly perceptual processes. (p. 5)

Gestalt Therapy A form of therapy that emphasizes the unity of mind and body by teaching the client to "get in touch" with bodily sensations and emotions long since hidden from awareness. (p. 588)

Glial Cell A cell in the nervous system that binds neurons together, although not so close that they actually touch one another. (p. 94)

Good Continuation A principle of perceptual grouping in which objects are perceived to be constructed of smooth continuous features rather than discontinuous ones. (p. 172)

Greenhouse Effect The trapping of heat reflected from the earth by gases in the upper atmosphere. It is a natural process that owes its name to the fact that the windows in a greenhouse let sunlight through but prevent its heat from escaping. (p. 659)

Group Therapy Therapy in which two or more clients meet simultaneously with a therapist, sharing and discussing problems within a supportive and understanding environment. (p. 589)

Hair Cells The auditory receptors. Whenever the basilar membrane vibrates, it forces the hair cells upward against another membrane, bending them in a shearing motion. Deformations of the hair cells in this manner produce neural impulses that are sent to the brain. (p. 197)

Hallucinations Sensory experiences that occur in the absence of external stimulation of the corresponding sensory organ. (p. 555)

Health Psychology The branch of psychology dealing with the promotion and maintenance of sound health practices. (p. 648)

Heritability The amount of variability in a trait due to genetic factors in a given population at a given time. (p. 76)

Hertz (Hz) The unit of measurement for studying a sound wave's frequency and pitch. (p. 194)

Heuristics Intuitive strategies for solving problems that use simple and informal rules of thumb or general guidelines. (p. 309)

Hippocampus The structure in the limbic system that plays a crucial role in memory. (p. 127)

Homeostasis The tendency for all animals to strive to maintain internal bodily states at a constant level. (p. 336)

Homosexuality Sexual attraction to individuals of the same gender. (p. 445)

Hormones Chemical substances such as adrenalin that are secreted directly into the bloodstream by endocrine glands. (p. 116)

Hue The psychological counterpart of a wavelength, often called color. (p. 157)

Humanistic Approach An approach to personality that emphasizes the positive, fulfilling elements of life that are uniquely human. (p. 524)

Humanistic Therapy A form of therapy in which the aim is to provide the client with a greater understanding of his or her motivations and needs by focusing on the person's unique potential for growth and self-actualization. (p. 587)

Huntington's Chorea A genetic disorder caused by a dominant lethal gene in which a person experiences slow but progressive mental and physical deterioration. (p. 79)

Hyperopia A visual disorder, also called farsightedness, in which the distance between the lens and retina is shorter than normal, causing light to be focused behind the retina. Farsighted people can see distant objects clearly, but close objects appear fuzzy. (p. 160)

Hypochondriasis A persistent and excessive worry of developing a serious illness or disease. People with this disorder often misinterpret the appearance of normal physical aches and pains. (p. 544)

Hypothalamus The structure in the limbic system located directly below the thalamus. Different parts of the hypothalamus are involved in the control of hunger, thirst, body temperature, and sexual arousal. In essence the hypothalamus manages the body's internal state. (p. 126)

Hypothesis A proposed relationship between two or more variables that can be tested empirically. (p. 29)

Id The personality structure that is the unconscious reservoir of libido, or the psychic energy that fuels our inherited biological instincts. (p. 506)

Illusions Misperceptions of real objects or events. (p. 177)

Immune System A network of organs and cells that protect the body from invading bacteria, viruses, and other foreign substances. (p. 651)

Impression Formation The process of attributing characteristics and attributes to other people. (p. 603)

Imprinting A form of learning that occurs only during some restricted period in an organism's life. (p. 231)

Incentive Theory The theory that external events, such as goals or incentives, motivate or "pull" us to behave. (p. 343)

Inclusive Fitness The reproductive success of all those who share common genes. (p. 82)

Incongruence A discrepancy between a client's real and ideal perceptions of self. (p. 587)

Incubation The development of insight into a problem only after a person has stopped consciously thinking about potential solutions. (p. 316)

Independent Variable The variable that is manipulated in an experiment. In psychological research, the independent variable is always a variable hypothesized to influence behavior. (p. 34)

Inferential Statistics The kind of statistical analyses that allow the researcher to make informed estimates about characteristics of the complete population from the values of statistics computed from a single sample of data. (p. 50)

Information Processing The way that knowledge is represented and processed. (p. 297)

Informed Consent A written statement provided to potential subjects by the researcher that discloses those aspects of the research that might affect their willingness to participate in the study. In essence, informed consent constitutes a contract between subject and researcher. (p. 53)

Insecure Attachment A kind of attachment in which an infant is reluctant to explore a new environment, and is likely to cling to the mother in the presence of strangers. (p. 402)

Insight The sudden flash of understanding, where all of the pieces of a problem suddenly fit together and the solution becomes clear. (p. 316)

Instinct Inborn or genetically determined factors, which, in the earlier days of psychology, were believed by some to be the major determinants of behavior. (p. 227)

Instinct Theory The view, popular at the turn of the century, that all behavior is motivated by instinct, innate or genetically determined tendencies to perform certain acts or respond in particular ways. (p. 335)

Intelligence The capacity to acquire knowledge and to use that knowledge to solve problems. (p. 461)

Intermittent Reinforcement Schedules Reinforcement schedules in which responses are occasionally reinforced. (p. 252)

Interposition The monocular cue produced when one object partially blocks our view of another object, causing the first object to appear closer. (p. 174)

Intervening Variable Any hypothetical variable believed to cause behavior. (p. 333)

Interview A self-report procedure in which the researcher requires subjects to respond verbally to questions. The researcher then records the subject's answers either in written form or on video. (p. 30)

Intrinsic Motivation The need for competence and self-determination. (p. 344)

Introspection The method used by structuralists for the self-analysis of one's conscious experiences. The method involves learning how to describe precisely sensations, images, and emotions caused by simple stimuli such as lights and sound. (p. 4)

IQ The intelligence quotient—the ratio of a person's mental age to his or her chronological age multiplied by 100. (p. 467)

Iris A small muscle that contracts or relaxes in response to the amount of light passing through the cornea. (p. 157)

James-Lange Theory The idea that physiological arousal precedes the experiencing of an emotion. (p. 365)

Just Noticeable Difference (jnd) The exact point at which an observer can recognize two stimuli as being different 50 percent of the time. The jnd is the unit of measurement for studying difference thresholds. (p. 154)

Kin Selection A type of selection process that favors altruistic acts aimed at individuals who share some of the altruist's genes. (p. 82)

Kinesthetic System Our sense of the location, movement, and posture of the skeletal joints and muscles. (p. 211)

Language A written or spoken system of symbol manipulation that is used to represent and communicate our thoughts to others. (p. 317)

Latency Stage The fourth psychosexual stage (from about 5 or 6 years to puberty). During this stage, there are no unconscious conflicts. (p. 510)

Latent Content The hidden meaning or underlying significance of a dream. (p. 577)

Lateral Hypothalamus The brain region believed to function as the "on switch" for feeding, because when stimulated chemically or electrically, it induces foraging and eating. (p. 347)

Law of Effect Thorndike's description of operant conditioning: The effects that behavior has on the environment determine whether or not that behavior is likely to be repeated. Responses with positive effects tend to be repeated; those with negative effects tend not to be repeated. (p. 247)

Learning A relatively permanent change in behavior based on experience. (p. 227)

Lens A transparent structure within the eye that changes shape depending on whether we are viewing objects close up or far away, permitting light to be focused on the retina. (p. 157)

Lesion A cut produced with pinpoint accuracy by surgically removing or severing brain tissue or by chemically or electrically destroying brain tissue. (p. 120)

Levels of Processing Model A model of memory based on the work of Craik and Lockhart, which holds that memory is information processing. This model proposes that memory has a boundless capacity and that it can hold information indefinitely. (p. 272)

Life-span Developmental Psychology The study of the processes and patterns of change that occur within individuals over the life-span. (p. 377)

Life-style The aggregate behavior of an individual; simply, life-style is the way a person leads his or her life. (p. 639)

Light Adaptation The process of our eyes adapting to increasing levels of illumination. (p. 164)

Limbic System A group of structures, including the amygdala, the hypothalamus, and the hippocampus, which envelop the central core and are involved primarily with motivation, emotion, and memory. (p. 125)

Linear Perspective The monocular cue produced by receding parallel lines, which gives the appearance that the lines converge on a vanishing point somewhere in the distance, creating the perception of depth. (p. 174)

Linear Profile A graphical display of the scores from all of the subtests of a test to facilitate comparison among them, with adjacent scores connected with straight lines. (p. 470)

Locus of Control People's expectancies regarding the source of control of their reinforcements. People who expect to control their own fate have an internal locus of control, whereas those who view their lives as being controlled by external forces outside of their control have an external locus of control. (p. 522)

Long-term Store The third component of the three-component model in which information is represented on a permanent or nearly permanent basis. (p. 271)

Longitudinal Approach A research design involving repeated observation or testing of the same group of people over an extended period of time. (p. 380)

Loudness The psychological counterpart to a sound's amplitude. The more intense the vibration, the greater the amplitude, and to some extent, the louder the psychological experience of the sound. (p. 193)

Low-balling Technique A compliance technique in which a very attractive offer is made, but is then withdrawn after compliance with the original offer has occurred. (p. 620)

Luteinizing Hormone (LH) In males, LH stimulates production of testosterone by the testes and in females, LH stimulates ovulation. (p. 424)

Maintenance Rehearsal The rote repetition of a given rehearsal strategy, perhaps just by rehearsing a given item over and over again. (p. 273)

Major Depression Persistent and severe feelings of sadness and worthlessness accompanied by changes in appetite, sleeping, and behavior patterns. (p. 548)

Mania Excessive emotional arousal and elation. (p. 548)

Manifest Content The actual images or events occurring within a dream. (p. 577)

Marital Therapy Therapy aimed at identifying and alleviating problems that have developed with a marital or another intimate partnership. (p. 589)

Maslow's Hierarchy Maslow's idea that our motivation for different activities passes through several hierarchical stages, with entrance to subsequent stages depending upon satisfying the needs in previous stages. (p. 337)

Masochism The obtaining of sexual gratification by suffering real or imagined physical pain or psychological distress. (p. 562)

Mass to Specific Principle The idea that control over large groups of muscles that are used in gross body movements develop faster than control over smaller groups of muscles that are used in finer movements. (p. 398)

Masters and Johnson Model The theory that vasocongestion and myotonia are the primary processes involved in the four stages of sexual arousal: excitement, plateau, orgasm, and resolution. (p. 437)

Mean The average score of a distribution of scores. (p. 44)

Median The number above and below which 50 percent of the scores in a distribution fall. (p. 45)

Medulla A structure positioned at the very bottom of the brain that is involved with the control of autonomic processes such as breathing, swallowing, digestion, and heartbeat. (p. 123)

Memory The cognitive processes of encoding, storing, and retrieving information. (p. 266)

Menarche A girl's first menstruation, which is usually experienced at about age 13. (p. 425)

Menopause The cessation of the menstrual cycle. (p. 427)

Mental Age The age level of the normative performance on an intelligence test that a child is able to match. (p. 466)

Mere Exposure Effect Attitude development based on continued or repeated presentation of an attitude object. (p. 610)

Meritocracy A society in which each person is rewarded according to his or her merit. (p. 482)

Metacognition Self-awareness of one's cognitive processes. (p. 400)

MMPI An objective test originally designed to distinguish individuals with different psychological disturbances from normal individuals. (p. 497)

Mnemonic Devices Special techniques or strategies consciously employed in an attempt to improve memory. (p. 280)

Modeling A treatment method in which the client observes another person engaging in appropriate behavior and then imitates this same behavior. (p. 583)

Monozygotic Twins Identical twins. Monozygotic twins develop from a single fertilized ovum (egg), which has split into two genetically identical cells. (p. 77)

Mood Disorders Significant shifts or disturbances in mood that affect normal perception, thinking, and behavior. (p. 548)

Moral Development The development of a person's thoughts and actions regarding right and wrong. (p. 388)

Morpheme The smallest unit of meaning in language. (p. 319)

Motion Parallax The monocular cue in which nearby objects appear to race by while distant objects appear to move slowly. (p. 174)

Motion Sickness The nausea and dizziness caused by some kinds of stimulation of the vestibular system, such as that sometimes experienced by flying in turbulence or by being onboard a ship in rough waters. (p. 212)

Motivation The causes of behavior, particularly as they influence the initiation and cessation of behavior and the intensity or strength of behavior. (p. 332)

Motor Area The region of the cerebral cortex located in the portion of the frontal lobe closest to the central fissure that controls voluntary movement by sending nerve impulses to skeletal muscles. (p. 129)

Motor Neuron A neuron that transmits signals from the brain or spinal cord to the body's muscles and glands. (p. 96)

Multiple Personality Disorder A dissociative disorder involving the emergence of two or more complete and independently functioning personalities in one person, though only one is dominant at any given time. (p. 545)

Mutation An accidental alteration in the DNA code within a single gene. (p. 74)

Myelin Sheath A fatty substance that insulates and protects the neuron. (p. 95)

Myopia A visual disorder, also known as nearsightedness, in which the distance between the lens and retina is longer than normal, causing light to be focused in front of the retina. People who are nearsighted can see close objects well but distant objects appear fuzzy. (p. 160)

Myotonia Muscle contractions that, in this case, occur during sexual arousal. (p. 437)

Narcissistic Personality Disorder A disorder characterized by an exaggerated public sense of self-worth and obsessions with success fantasies. (p. 559)

Narcotics Psychoactive drugs that produce analgesia or pain reduction. (p. 114)

Nasal Cavity The hollow portion of each nostril. (p. 213)

Natural Selection The tendency of organisms to reproduce differentially, which is caused by differences among them. (p. 64)

Naturalistic Observation A type of research in which data are gathered by observing behavior as it occurs naturally. (p. 31)

Need for Achievement (nAch) The motivation to meet or surpass performance standards or to accomplish difficult tasks. (p. 339)

Need for Affiliation The motivation to form friendships and association with others. (p. 340)

Need for Power The motivation to be in control of events, resources, or other people, usually for one's own advantage. (p. 340)

Negative Reinforcer Any stimulus or event that, when removed, reduced, or prevented following a response, increases the frequency of that response over time. (p. 251)

Nerve Hearing Loss Decreases in hearing ability resulting from damage to the neural structures involved in transmitting auditory information from the cochlea to the brain, including the hair cells, basilar membrane, and the auditory nerve. (p. 203)

Nerve Impulse or **Action Potential** The electrochemical code that provides the means for neurons to exchange information within the nervous system. (p. 97)

Neurons The basic unit of the nervous system. Neurons relay information to and from the brain by chemical and electrical means. (p. 94)

Neurotransmitters Chemical substances released from the presynaptic neuron that stimulate postsynaptic neurons. (p. 100)

Norepinephrine A neurotransmitter that is involved in the regulation of mood. Decreases in norepinephrine are related to depression; increases of it are related to feelings of vigor and self-confidence. (p. 104)

Norm of Reciprocity A social norm dictating that favors should be returned. (p. 621)

Normal Distribution The mathematical name for a frequency distribution of scores that is sometimes called the "bell-shaped curve." (p. 475)

Norms In psychological testing, the average levels of performance on a test of different groups of people, such as 10-year-old Hispanic females or all 7-year-olds. (p. 466)

Obedience to Authority The following of orders issued by a legitimate authority. (p. 621)

Obesity A body weight 20 percent in excess of that considered average for a given height. (p. 348)

Object Permanence The idea that objects do not disappear when they are removed from sight. (p. 384)

Objective Tests Tests for measuring personality that are similar in structure to the ones given in the classroom to test knowledge of different content areas: they may contain multiple choice or true-false items, although some allow examinees to indicate the extent to which they agree with an item. (p. 497)

Observational Learning Learning by observing the consequences others experience as a result of their behavior. (p. 521)

Observational Research Research in which the variables of interest are observed without attempting to influence the values of the variables or to intervene in any other way. (p. 29)

Obsession An involuntary recurring thought, idea, or image. (p. 542)

Obsessive-compulsive Disorder An anxiety-based disorder in which an individual is beset by recurrent, unwanted thoughts or ideas and compelling urges to engage in repetitive ritual-like behavior. (p. 542)

Olfactory Bulb An enlarged bundle of neural tissue, located in the brain just above the bone separating the brain from the olfactory mucosa, that sends neural information about smell to various regions of the brain. (p. 213)

Olfactory Mucosa The part of the nose, located at the top of the nasal cavity just beneath the base of the brain, that contains odor receptors. (p. 213)

Operant (or Instrumental) Conditioning A form of learning in which behavior is affected by the consequences it produces. (p. 245)

Operant Chamber An apparatus in which an animal's operant behavior can be easily observed, manipulated, and automatically recorded. (p. 247)

Opponent-process Theory In vision, Hering's theory that there are three sets of color-sensitive receptors in the visual system: one set for red and green, another for blue and yellow and the third for black and white. Members of each set work in opposition to each other through neural inhibition. (p. 168). In the study of motivation and emotion, opponent process theory is also the name for Richard Solomon's theory that for every emotional experience there is an opposite emotional experience that maintains our emotional and motivational levels at some homeostatic level. (p. 342)

Optic Nerve The bundle of nerve fibers (the axons of ganglion cells) that make up the pathway leading from the retina to structures in the brain that react to neural impulses laden with visual information. (p. 161)

Optimal-arousal Theory The view that all organisms are motivated to maintain an optimal level of arousal. (p. 341)

Oral Stage The first psychosexual stage (the first 18 months of life). During this period, the mouth is the major active erogenous zone and, the id impels the infant to use its mouth not only for eating and drinking, but for exploration as well. (p. 509)

Orgasmic Dysfunction A woman's inability to have an orgasm. (p. 439)

Ossicles Three bones (the malleus, incus and stapes) that amplify and transmit the vibrations of the tympanic membrane to the oval window. (p. 196)

Oval Window The membrane dividing the inner and middle ears that vibrates when stimulated by the ossicles. (p. 196)

Ovum Stage The first of the three stages of prenatal development during which the zygote divides many times and the internal organs begin to form. (p. 394)

Pacinian Corpuscle A nerve ending that responds to touch and vibration. (p. 205)

Pain Threshold The lowest level of stimulation at which pain is sensed. (p. 207)

Papillae The tiny bumps on the tongue that are lined with taste buds. (p. 217)

Paranoid Personality Disorder A disorder charcterized by an exaggerated and unwarranted mistrust and suspicion of others. These symptoms are extremely rigid and unchangeable, even in the face of disconfirming evidence. (p. 560)

Paranoid Schizophrenia A type of schizophrenia characterized primarily by systematic, well-developed, and persistent delusions. In particular, these delusions follow themes of either persecution or grandeur. (p. 556)

Paraphilias Behaviors in which stimulation from unusual objects or events results in sexual satisfaction. (p. 561)

Parasympathetic Nervous System The part of the autonomic nervous system that functions to slow down nervous system activities after stressful emergency situations are over. (p. 95)

Perception The processes by which the brain organizes and interprets sensations. (p. 149)

Perceptual Constancy Our ability to perceive objects as possessing certain stable features, including lightness, size, and shape, despite changes in the condition under which we view those objects. (p. 177)

Perceptual Grouping An organizational principle of Gestalt psychology that describes our ability to organize a figure into a meaningful pattern or shape. (p. 172)

Perceptual Learning Increases in a person's expectations to influence his or her perception. (p. 184)

Performance (nonverbal intelligence) The capacity for solving problems that does not depend on understanding language, but rather emphasizes performance such as putting together a puzzle. (p. 472)

Peripheral Nervous System The network of neurons that connect the central nervous system to other parts of the body. (p. 95)

Permissive Parents Those who establish few rules and who do little to influence the behavior of their children. (p. 404)

Person-centered Therapy A form of therapy in which the client is allowed to decide what to talk about without direction and judgment from the therapist. (p. 587)

Personal Fable The belief that what one thinks and feels is completely new and unique and never before experienced by anyone else. (p. 405)

Personal Fitness The relative ability of an individual to produce offspring. (p. 65)

Personality A particular pattern of behavior prevailing across time and situations that differentiates one individual from another. (p. 496)

Personality Disorders A class of disorders characterized by extremely rigid personality traits that impair functioning in personal, social, and occupational settings. (p. 559)

Personality Tests Tests designed to reveal the components of an individual's personality, how one or more of the components interact with the other components, and how one person's personality differs from another's. (p. 497)

Phallic Stage The third psychosexual stage (about 3 to 4 years to between 5 and 6 years). During this stage, the primary erogenous zone is the genital area. (p. 509)

Phenotype The outward expression of an organism's genotype; an organism's physical appearance and behavior. (p. 66)

Phenylketonuria (PKU) A genetic disorder characterized by the inability to break down phenylalanine, an amino acid found in many high protein foods. (p. 79)

Phobic Disorder The unrealistic, excessive fear of a specific class of stimuli. (p. 541)

Phoneme The smallest unit of sound that can be heard. (p. 319)

Physical Dependence The phenomenon in which the neurons in the nervous system require the drug to function adequately. Without the drug, the individual will experience withdrawal symptoms, which may include trembling, perspiration, nausea, headaches, and depending on the drug, even death. (p. 106)

Pinna The visible part of the ear. (p. 196)

Pitch The psychological quality of sound corresponding to wave frequency. (p. 194)

Place Theory The theory proposed by von Helmholtz stating that the basilar membrane is composed of independent nerve fibers, each sensitive to a different sound frequency, and so also sensitive to pitch. (p. 198)

Placebo Any substance that an individual believes to contain pain-relieving ingredients, when in fact, it does not. (p. 210)

Pleasure Principle The rule that the id obeys: obtain immediate gratification, whatever form it may take. (p. 506)

Pollutant Any substance that has harmful or potentially harmful effects on the environment. Although some pollutants are natural, most are produced by humans. Pollutants may be airborne, waterborne, or solid. (p. 658)

Pons A structure just above the medulla that is involved with arousal and dreaming. (p. 124)

Population A large group of individuals to which researchers generalize their results. (p. 49)

Pornography Sexually arousing literature, art, and films. (p. 450)

Positive Reinforcer Any stimulus or event, that when it follows a response, increases the frequency of that response over time. (p. 251)

Postconventional Level The last level of moral development in Kohlberg's theory. This level is concerned mainly with the development of personal values of morality. (p. 389)

Posttraumatic Stress Disorder An anxiety disorder in which the individual experiences feelings of social withdrawal accompanied by untypically low levels of emotion toward routine events. In many cases, people suffering posttraumatic stress disorder may reexperience, through dreams and flashbacks, the feelings of terror and shock experienced during the actual catastrophe. Posttraumatic stress disorder does not usually appear immediately following the catastrophic event; rather, it is delayed, usually beginning several days later. (p. 652)

Practitioner Psychologist A psychologist who provides psychological services, such as counseling or therapy, to the public. (p. 12)

Preconventional Level The first level in Kohlberg's theory of moral development during which children tend to think solely in terms of the immediate consequences of their behavior. (p. 388)

Prediction The ability to foretell the value of one variable from the value of another variable. (p. 26)

Prejudice A negative evaluation of an individual based on his or her membership in a particular group. (p. 605)

Premature Ejaculation The inability to delay ejaculation. (p. 441)

Prenatal Period The 9 months between conception and birth. (p. 394)

Preoperational Period The second of Piaget's four stages, which represents a 4- to 5-year period of transition (from age 2 to about 6 or 7) between first being able to think symbolically and being able to think logically. (p. 385)

Preventive Psychology Any attempt to forestall the development of psychological problems by altering the sociocultural variables predictive of psychological distress. (p. 592)

Primacy Effect The tendency to form impressions about people based on the first information we receive. (p. 604)

Primary Drives Drives that arise from physiological needs and do not involve learning. Primary drives serve as the motivations that impel us to seek food when hungry, to drink when thirsty, and to seek warmth when cold. (p. 336)

Proactive Interference The kind of interference in recall that is caused when previously learned information disrupts our ability to remember newer information. (p. 287)

Problem A situation in which there is a goal that is not immediately obtainable. Problem solving involves processing information about that situation. (p. 308)

Procedural Memory The portion of long-term store where our knowledge of simple learned associations and our knowledge of how to perform well-learned habits is stored. (p. 272)

Projection A defense mechanism in which one's own unacceptable behaviors or thoughts are attributed to someone else. (p. 508)

Projective Tests Unstructured personality measures in which a person is shown a series of ambiguous stimuli such as pictures, inkblots, or incomplete drawings. The person is asked to describe what he or she "sees" in each stimulus or to create stories that reflect the theme of the drawing or picture. (p. 501)

Prototypes A set of characteristics that apply to the most representative or typical member of the category but not necessarily to all instances. (p. 302)

Proximal Stimulus The two-dimensional and ever-changing image of the distal stimulus as it appears on the retina. (p. 170)

Proximate Causes Events and conditions in the immediate environment that affect behavior. (p. 60)

Proximity A principle of perceptual grouping in which objects near one another tend to be perceived as a group. (p. 172)

Proximodistal Principle The idea that development of the internal organs and torso occurs faster than development of the hands and feet. (p. 398)

Psychedelics Psychoactive drugs that produce dramatic changes in consciousness including hallucinations and enhanced perception. (p. 112)

Psychiatrist A person with an M.D. degree who treats individuals with psychological problems. (p. 15)

Psychoactive Drugs Those drugs that affect our behavior, perceptions, arousal level, emotional status, and ability to think clearly. (p. 105)

Psychoanalysis The school of psychology founded by Sigmund Freud that portrays human behavior and personality development as due primarily to unconscious motivations and desires. (p. 6). Psychoanalysis is also a contemporary form of therapy aimed at providing the client insight into his or her unconscious motivations and impulses. (p. 576)

Psychodynamic Perspective A current view in psychology that focuses on the unconscious determinants of behavior and mental processes. (p. 9)

Psychogenic Amnesia A dissociative disorder characterized by the inability to remember important events or vital personal information. (p. 545)

Psychogenic Fugue A dissociative disorder involving amnesia but which is also characterized by the individual deliberately leaving the area in which he or she lives, and then assuming a new identity in a new locale. (p. 545)

Psychological Dependence An all-consuming craving to use a psychoactive drug for its euphoric effects. (p. 106)

Psychological Disorders Persistent, maladaptive patterns of behaving, thinking, and/or feeling that lead to distress or disability. (p. 535)

Psychology The scientific study of the behavior and cognitive processes of individual organisms. (p. 2)

Psychometrics The area of psychology that is devoted to psychological measurement. (p. 476)

Psychosexual Stages Developmental stages that are defined by the part of the body or erogenous zone from which sexual gratification is derived. (p. 508)

Psychosurgery Unalterable brain surgery designed to relieve the symptoms of psychological disorders. (p. 572)

Psychotherapy Any attempt to use known psychological principles to bring about improved emotional, cognitive, or social adjustment. (p. 568)

Puberty The sudden maturation of the genitalia that endows each of us with the capacity for sexual reproduction. (pp. 405, 424)

Punisher Any stimulus or event that, when it occurs following a response, decreases the frequency of that response. The delivery of a punisher following a response is called punishment. (p. 251)

Pupil The opening, surrounded by the iris, that controls the amount of light entering the eye. (p. 157)

Purity The mixture of sound waves that makes up a sound. (p. 194)

Purity The number of wavelengths that constitute a light. Psychologically, the purity of a light determines its colorfulness or saturation. (p. 157).

Questionnaire A self-report technique in which a series of written questions, specifically designed to address a particular topic, are given to a subject to answer. (p. 30)

Random Assignment An experimental procedure in which each subject is assigned to a group on the basis of chance alone. (p. 36)

Rape Sexual intercourse or other sexual acts that occur without the willing consent of one of the people involved. (p. 452)

Rape Trauma Syndrome A two-stage emotional and physical reaction experienced by many rape victims. The first stage starts immediately after the rape and involves anxiety, fear, humiliation, self-blame, and physical discomfort from injuries related to the rape. The second stage may last up to several months or even years. During this phase, it is not uncommon for the rape victim to quit her job, move several times, and change her phone number. (p. 454)

Rational Emotive Therapy (RET) Therapy based on the belief that psychological problems are caused not by upsetting events, but by how people think about such events. (p. 584)

Rationalization A defense mechanism that justifies an unacceptable action by a more acceptable, but false, excuse. (p. 508)

Reaction-formation A defense mechanism that involves behaving in a manner that is the opposite of how one really feels because the true feelings produce anxiety. (p. 508)

Reality Principle The rule used by the ego to satisfy the demands of the id realistically, yielding to and accounting for the demands of reality, sometimes delaying the gratification of desires springing forth from the id, and sometimes softening the rules and reasons offered by the superego. (p. 507)

Reasoning The process of drawing conclusions from a set of facts. (p. 304)

Reciprocal Altruism A kind of altruism in which people behave altruistically toward each other because they are confident that such acts will be reciprocated toward either them or their kin. (p. 83)

Reciprocal Determinism The idea that behavior, environment, and person variables, such as cognitions and perceptions, interact to determine personality. (p. 521)

Reflection The therapist's sensitive rephrasing or mirroring of the client's statements during therapy. (p. 587)

Refractory Period A very brief recovery period just after the neuron has stimulated another neuron, in which its membrane cannot be stimulated to generate another nerve impulse. (p. 98)

Regression Line The line drawn through the points in a scatter plot that allows researchers to predict the value of one variable when given the value of the other variable. (p. 47)

Relational Hypotheses Hypotheses that specify that two or more variables are related, but none of the variables can be specified to cause the other variable(s). (p. 29)

Relative Size The monocular cue in which large objects appear closer than small objects because they cast larger images on the retina. (p. 174)

Reliability A test is said to be reliable when it is consistent over repeated measurements. The measurements may be the same measures repeated at different times or similar measures all administered on the same test. (p. 477)

Reliability Coefficient A numerical index of the reliability of an intelligence test (or any other type of psychological test) derived by computing a correlation coefficient for the examinees' scores from two different administrations of the same test. (p. 477)

REM Sleep The stage of sleep characterized by rapid eye movements and dreaming. (p. 137)

Representativeness Heuristic A heuristic in which people classify an object into the category to which it appears to be the most similar. (p. 314)

Repression The mental force responsible for actively keeping an individual from consciously discovering their potentially threatening or anxiety-provoking memories. (p. 504)

Reproductive Success The number of viable offspring one produces relative to the number of viable offspring produced by other individuals of the same species. (p. 65)

Rescorla-Wagner Model A current and widely held view of classical conditioning that is based on two assumptions. First, classical conditioning produces changes in the associative strength between a given CS and a given UCS. Second, a given UCS can support only a certain amount of conditioning. (p. 242)

Research Psychologist A psychologist, generally a Ph.D., who conducts psychological research. (p. 12)

Residual Schizophrenia The diagnosis for individuals who have experienced at least one episode of schizophrenia but who are currently not exhibiting major symptoms of the disorder. (p. 556)

Resistance Mental forces that relegate memories of past events into unconsciousness (p. 504). Also, resistance refers to a development during therapy in which the client becomes defensive, unconsciously attempting to halt further insight by censoring his or her true feelings. (p. 577)

Response Bias The tendency of an individual to detect or report the presence or absence of a stimulus whether or not he or she was actually stimulated. (p. 152)

Response Criterion In a signal detection experiment, the level of sensation above which an individual will report detecting a stimulus and below which he or she will report not detecting a stimulus. (p. 153)

Resting Potential The electrical potential (−70 millivolts) of the neuron when it is not generating a nerve impulse. (p. 97)

Reticular Formation A fingerlike network of neurons found in the central core that extends from the lower tip of the medulla through the thalamus and that plays a role in sleep and arousal. (p. 124)

Retina The thin layer of receptors, the rods and cones, that lines the interior of the back of the eye. (p. 157)

Retrieval The active processes of locating and using stored information. (p. 266)

Retroactive Interference The kind of interference in recall that is caused when recently learned information disrupts our ability to remember older information. (p. 287)

Retrograde Amnesia The loss of the ability to retrieve memories of one's past, particularly episodic memories or memories involving personal experiences. (p. 289)

Reuptake The absorption of neurotransmitter molecules by terminal buttons of the presynaptic neuron. (p. 102)

Rods Light-sensitive receptors that are found throughout the retina except in the fovea. (p. 159)

Rorschach Inkblot Test A projective test in which the examinee is shown a series of symmetrical inkblots and then is asked to describe what he or she thinks they represent. (p. 501)

Sadism The obtaining of sexual gratification from inflicting real or imagined physical pain and psychological distress on others. (p. 562)

Sample A representative subset of a population. (p. 49)

Saturation The psychological counterpart to purity. As the number of wavelengths in light increases, its saturation decreases. (p. 157)

Scatter Plot A two-dimensional graph used to display the degree of correlation between two variables. (p. 46)

Schema Overall frameworks for processing information about people, objects, or situations. (p. 603)

Schemes Mental representations of the world based on previous experiences. (p. 382)

Schizophrenia A general term for a group of psychological disorders involving distortions of thought, perception, emotion, bizarre behavior, and social withdrawal. (p. 553)

Secondary Drives Drives that are brought about through experience. They are learned drives believed to underlie psychological motives such as acquiring wealth, desiring affiliation, seeking approval from parents and significant others, and so on. (p. 336)

Secure Attachment A kind of attachment in which infants will use their mother as a "base" for exploring a new environment. They will venture out from her to explore a strange situation but return periodically. (p. 402)

Selective Listening The ability to perceive only one auditory stimulus while ignoring others. (p. 202)

Selective Looking The ability to perceive only one visual stimulus while ignoring others. (p. 180)

Self-actualization The achievement of our greatest potential as human beings, whatever that might be. (p. 338)

Self-concept One's opinion of one's self. According to Rogers, our self-concept is affected by the way we are evaluated and treated by others. (p. 526)

Self-efficacy Bandura's notion that one's expectations of success are a primary influence in determining whether people will attempt to change their environment. (p. 521)

Self-perception Theory A theory claiming that we come to understand our own attitudes by observing our own behavior. (p. 619)

Self-report A technique in which people provide subjective information about themselves—feelings, beliefs, evaluations, or interests—to the researcher. (p. 29)

Semantic Memory A type of memory found in long-term store that houses data, facts, and other information, including your vocabulary. (p. 272)

Semicircular Canals The structure in the inner ear that contains receptors sensitive to changes in body orientation. (p. 211)

Sensation Immediate and simple experiences caused by stimuli. (p. 149)

Sensorimotor Period This stage, the first in Piaget's theory of cognitive development, is marked by an orderly progression of increasingly complex cognitive development: reflexive behavior, object permanence, a rough approximation of cause and effect, imitating the actions of others, symbolic thinking (p. 383)

Sensory Neuron A neuron that transmits nerve impulses from the receptors to the brain and spinal cord. (p. 95)

Sensory Register The first component of the three-component model of memory in which the physical features of a stimulus are stored for extremely brief durations. (p. 268)

Separation Anxiety A set of fearful responses in infants, such as crying and clinging to their caregiver when the caregiver attempts to leave the infant's presence. (p. 400)

Serotonin An inhibitory neurotransmitter found in the brain and spinal cord that plays an important role in the brain's control of sleep and arousal, body temperature, and sensory and perceptual functions. (p. 105)

Serum Cholesterol A chemical that occurs naturally in all tissues and in the bloodstream where it serves as a detoxifier. Serum cholesterol has two important forms: LDL and HDL. LDL is often called bad cholesterol because high levels of it are associated with the formation of arteriosclerotic plaques, which clog arteries. HDL is sometimes referred to as good cholesterol because high levels are inversely associated with CHD. (p. 641)

Set Point The idea that the hypothalamus, functioning as a homeostatic mechanism, sets a level, probably based on the combination of body weight, blood sugar levels, and metabolism, that determines when and how much an animal will eat. (p. 347)

Sex Chromosomes The chromosomes containing the instructional code for the development of male or female sex characteristics. (p. 72)

Sexual Dysfunction An impairment or difficulty in achieving sexual arousal and orgasm. (p. 439)

Sexually Transmitted Diseases (STDs) Diseases that are contracted through sexual contact with another person. (p. 449)

Shaping Reinforcing any behavior that successfully approximates the desired response until that response is acquired. (p. 249)

Short-term Store The second component of the three-component model. This store has a limited capacity (7 +/−2 chunks of information), limited duration (less than 20 seconds), and is encoded acoustically. (p. 269)

Sign Stimulus Stimuli that elicit fixed-action patterns. (p. 229)

Signal Detection Theory The theory that detection of any stimulus is a matter of distinguishing that stimulus from all other stimuli in the sensory world. (p. 153)

Similarity A principle of perceptual grouping in which objects that look alike tend to be perceived as a group. (p. 172)

Single-subject Research A type of research in which experiments are conducted using only one or a few subjects. (p. 38)

16PF A personality inventory widely used among marriage and vocational counselors. The test items on the 16PF refer to such characteristics as intelligence, sensitivity, shrewdness, and trust. (p. 499)

Social Cognition The processing of information about other people and social situations. (p. 602)

Social Facilitation A change in task performance due to the presence of others. (p. 615)

Social Interest According to Adler, an innate desire to make contributions to society. (p. 512)

Social Learning Theory The idea that both consequences of behavior and the individual's beliefs about those consequences determine personality and behavior. (p. 520)

Social Norms Informal rules defining the expected and appropriate behavior in specific situations. (p. 616)

Social Perspective A current view in psychology emphasizing the role that our social environment plays in shaping our behavior, attitudes, and thinking. (p. 10)

Social Psychology The branch of psychology that studies how thought, feeling, and behavior of individuals are influenced by the actual, imagined, or implied presence of others. (p. 602)

Sociobiology The study of the genetic bases of social behavior. (p. 81)

Somatic Nervous System The part of the peripheral nervous system that controls the actions of the skeletal muscles (p. 95)

Somatization Disorders A class of somatoform disorder, which occurs mostly in women, and involves complaints of wide ranging physical ailments for which there is no apparent biological cause. Over time, the nature of these complaints changes. (p. 544)

Somatoform Disorders An anxiety-based disorder involving a bodily or physical problem for which there is no physiological basis. (p. 543)

Somatosensory Areas The region of the cerebral cortex lying in the parietal lobes just behind the central fissure that is involved in the ability to sense warmth, cold, pain, touch, and bodily movement. (p. 130)

Somatosensory System Our sense of pressure, temperature, pain, balance, and equilibrium. (p. 204)

Sound Wave An alternating pattern of high and low air pressure caused by vibrating objects. (p. 193)

Species-typical Behavior Behavior that is common among the members in a given species. (p. 229)

Spontaneous Recovery The reemergence of the conditional response after it has been extinguished. (p. 238)

Standard Deviation A descriptive statistic that expresses the amount of variability among scores in a frequency distribution. (p. 45)

Standard Score The score that shows how far or how close a person's original responses are from the average level of responses on, for example, an intelligence test. (p. 475)

Standardization The process of establishing the norms of a test across hundreds or thousands of peoples in each group (age, sex, ethnicity) to which the test is later to be administered. (p. 467)

Stanford-Binet The first widely used individually administered English intelligence test. (p. 467)

State-dependent Memory The tendency to recall information better when the subject's mental or emotional state at retrieval matches that during encoding. (p. 285)

Statistically Significant. A term used in inferential statistics to indicate that results from a study are generalizable to an entire population of individuals. (p. 51)

Stereotypes Oversimplified schemata that are applied to entire groups of people. (p. 605)

Stimulants Psychoactive drugs that speed up the nervous system's activities, producing increases in arousal and mood. (p. 107)

Storage The process of maintaining information in memory for future use. (p. 266)

Stranger Anxiety A set of fearful responses in infants, such as crying and clinging to their caregiver in the presence of strangers. (p. 400)

Stress A pattern of physiological, behavioral, and cognitive responses to real or imagined environmental stimuli that are perceived as endangering or otherwise threatening our well-being or personal abilities. (p. 648)

Stressors Environmental stimuli that are perceived as endangering or otherwise threatening our well-being or personal abilities. (p. 648)

Striving for Superiority According to Adler, the motivation to seek superiority. (p. 512)

Stroboscopic Movement A form of apparent movement that can be produced by flashing a light in darkness and then several milliseconds later, flashing an identical light in a slightly different location. (p. 175)

Structuralism The school of psychology (founded by Wilhelm Wundt) that emphasized the structure of the mind as being the appropriate subject matter for psychology. (p. 4)

Sublimation Redirecting pleasure-seeking or aggressive instincts toward socially acceptable goals. (p. 508)

Superego The repository of an individual's moral values that is stocked with laws, mores, and sanctions of the society in which one lives. (p. 506)

Surface Structure The organization of a sentence in terms of its component phrases as it is actually spoken or read. (p. 320)

Symbols A mental construction that stands for or represents something else. (p. 298)

Sympathetic Nervous System The part of the autonomic nervous system that speeds up nervous system activities in stressful or emergency situations. (p. 95)

Synapse Junctions where two neurons meet but do not actually establish contact with one another. (p. 99)

Synaptic Cleft The very small fluid-filled gap that separates the terminal buttons of one neuron from the adjacent surface of a cell body or dendrite. (p. 99)

Synaptic Transmission The electrochemical process by which one neuron stimulates another. (p. 100)

Synaptic Vesicles Tiny saclike structures found in the terminal buttons that contain neurotransmitters. (p. 100)

Syntax The well-defined rules that specify how the words of a sentence should be arranged. (p. 319)

Systematic Desensitization A method of treatment in which the client is trained to relax in the presence of increasingly fearful stimuli. (p. 580)

Taste The sensation produced by chemical molecules stimulating receptor cells found in the mouth. (p. 216)

Taste Buds The parts of the papillae that house the receptors for taste. (p. 217)

TAT (Thematic Apperception Test) A projective test in which a person is first shown a series of ambiguous pictures that involve people. Then he or she is asked to make up a story about what the people are doing or thinking. These themes are believed to reflect the examinee's primary personality characteristics. (p. 502)

Telegraphic Speech A form of early speech in which a young child uses short, two-word phrases resembling those sent in a telegram. (p. 323)

Terminal Button The part of the neuron that releases neurotransmitters. (p. 95)

Test Bias The discounting or favoring of an individual's test performance due to the particular experiences of that individual. To the extent that the ability to answer test items correctly depends on previous learning, the intelligence test becomes less of a valid measure of capacity and more a measure of achievement. (p. 478)

Texture Gradient The monocular cue in which objects that are larger and coarser appear closer than objects that are smaller and smoother. (p. 174)

Thalamus The structure of the central core that relays sensory information to the cerebral cortex. (p. 124)

Theory A set of statements attempting to explain relationships that may exist between behavior and other variables. (p. 28)

Theory of Multiple Intelligences Howard Gardner's theory of intelligence that generalizes the concent of intelligence away from the traditional focus on IQ by including problem solving in a wide variety of domains such as music and interpersonal competence. (p. 485)

Thinking The manipulation or construction and modification of internal symbolic presentations. (p. 304)

Three-component Model The model of memory proposed by Atkinson and Shiffrin, which postulates a sensory register (or store) that "picks up" and briefly holds stimuli from the environment, a short-term store of limited capacity and a long-term store where information is kept with some permanency. (p. 267)

Three-term Contingency The relationship among discriminative stimuli, behavior, and the consequences of that behavior. (p. 249)

Timbre The psychological quality corresponding to a sound's clarity. (p. 194)

Token Economy A system involving tokens of some kind, which are later exchangeable for different goods and services, and are used to reinforce desired behavior. (p. 255)

Tolerance A physical condition in which neurons in the central nervous system respond progressively less and less to a drug. Larger doses of the drug are required to produce the same effects on the nervous system that smaller doses produced earlier. (p. 106)

Top-down Processing Processing of a pattern that begins with the higher brain centers directing receptors to attend to particular features of the pattern. (p. 185)

Trait A relatively stable, measurable characteristic of a person. (p. 515)

Transduction The conversion of physical energy into nerve impulses. (p. 150)

Transference The process by which a client begins to project powerful attitudes and emotions onto the therapist. (p. 577)

Transsexual An individual who does not develop a gender identity consistent with either his or her actual biological or assigned gender. (p. 431)

Treatment Condition The part of an experiment in which the independent variable is manipulated and its effect on the subject's behavior is measured. (p. 38)

Triarchic Theory of Intelligence Robert Sternberg's theory that generalizes intelligence testing and the study of intelligence beyond that of IQ tests by accounting for three different aspects of intelligence: the specific cognitive processes that underlie intelligent behavior, the way in which previous experience with a particular kind of problem affects the way that a problem is solved, and the environmental context within which the problem solving occurs. (p. 484)

Trichromatic Theory The theory proposed by Young and Helmholtz that the typical human eye has color receptors sensitive to the primary colors of red, green, and blue. (p. 167)

Two-factor Theory of Emotion The theory that two factors are involved in emotion: physiological arousal and cognition. (p. 367)

Tympanic Membrane A thin, conically shaped membrane separating the outer and middle ears that vibrates when struck by sound waves. This membrane is also known as the ear drum. (p. 196)

Ultimate Causes Evolutionary conditions and processes that have slowly shaped behavior of our species over generations. (p. 60)

Unconditional Positive Regard Love and acceptance with no strings attached. To Rogers, unconditional positive regard is the key to promoting personal growth. (p. 526)

Unconditional Response (UCR) In classical conditioning, the response, such as salivation that is naturally elicited by the unconditional stimulus. (p. 235)

Unconditional Stimulus (UCS) In classical conditioning, any stimulus, such as food that naturally elicits a reflexive response such as salivation. (p. 235)

Unconscious The inaccessible part of the mind. (p. 504)

Undifferentiated Schizophrenia A type of schizophrenia whose symptoms do not fall neatly into any of the other categories of schizophrenia. Undifferentiated schizophrenia is characterized by fragments of the different symptoms. (p. 556)

Vaginismus The spastic contraction of the muscles surrounding the vagina. In many cases, the muscle contractions are so strong that intercourse is impossible. (p. 440)

Validity A test is said to be valid when it measures what it is supposed to measure. (p. 477)

Validity Coefficient The correlation between the score on a test and some other variable of interest. (p. 477)

Value The level or degree of a variable. (p. 26)

Variable-interval (VI) Schedules These schedules require that responses be reinforced only after varying amounts of time have elapsed between reinforcer deliveries. (p. 253)

Variable-ratio (VR) Schedules Reinforcement schedules in which the response requirement for reinforcement varies from one reinforcer delivery to the next. (p. 253)

Variables Any characteristics of organisms or the environment that may vary from one instance to the next. (p. 26)

Variation The differences found across individuals of any given species in terms of their biological characteristics and psychological characteristics. (p. 66)

Vasocongestion The flow of blood during sexual arousal into a region of the body, in this case, the genital area. (p. 437)

Ventromedial Hypothalamus (VMH) The brain region thought to be the "off switch" for eating because, when stimulated, eating stops. (p. 347)

Verbal Intelligence The problem-solving capacity for language-oriented problems such as reading comprehension and vocabulary. (p. 471)

Vestibular Sacs A set of receptors located just below the semi-circular canals, that plays a critical role in maintaining the head in its proper upright orientation. (p. 212)

Vestibular System Our sense of equilibrium or balance. (p. 211)

Visual Acuity Keenness of vision. Visual acuity is greatest for images that are focused on the fovea. (p. 160)

Volley Principle The idea that the hair cells in the cochlea alternately fire and rest. This principle was developed to account for hearing sound wave frequencies above 1000 Hz. (p. 198)

Voyeurism The achieving of sexual gratification by secretly viewing nude members of the opposite sex. (p. 562)

WIAS-R The current version of Wechsler's individually administered adult intelligence test, called the Wechsler Adult Intelligence Scale, Revised. (p. 471)

Wave Frequency The speed with which variations (from high to low) in air pressure occur. (p. 194)

Wavelength The distance from one wave crest to the next. Different wavelengths of light are seen as distinct hues or colors. (p. 157)

Weber's Law The size of the value, expressed as a constant, of the ratio of jnd to the reference stimulus. (p. 154)

Wernicke's Area The portion of the temporal lobe that is involved in the motor production of speech. (p. 131)

WISC-R The current version of Wechsler's individually administered intelligence test for children, called the Wechsler Intelligence Scale for Children, Revised. (p. 471)

XYY Syndrome A genetic disorder in which an individual has an extra Y chromosome. (p. 79)

Yerkes-Dodson Law The inverted U-shaped relationship between performance and arousal: for any task to be performed there is an optional level of arousal necessary for optimal performance. Too little or too much arousal interferes with performance. (p. 342)

References

A

Abeles, N. (1985) Proceedings of the American Psychological Association, 1985. *American Psychologist, 41,* 633–663.

Abramson, H. A. (Ed.). (1959). *Neuropharmacology: Transactions of the Fourth Macy Conference.* Madison, NJ: Madison Printing Co.

Ahadi, S. A., & Diener, E. (1989). Multiple determinants and effect size. *Journal of Personality and Social Psychology, 56,* 398–406.

Atkinson, R. C., & Shiffrin, R. M. (1968). Human memory: A proposed system and its control processes. In W. K. Spence & J. T. Spence (Eds.), *The psychology of learning and motivation: Vol. 1. Advances in research and theory.* New York: Academic Press, 89–195.

Atkinson, R. C., & Shiffrin, R. M. (1971). The control of short-term memory. *Scientific American, 225,* 82–90.

Adler, A. (1939). *Social interest: A challenge to mankind.* New York: Putnam.

Ahadi, S. A., & Diener, E. (1989). Multiple determinants and effect size. *Journal of Personality and Social Psychology, 56,* 398–406.

Adler, A. (1924). *The practice and theory of individual psychology.* New York: Harcourt, Brace.

Adler, J. (1985, March 25). The teen pregnancy epidemic. *Newsweek,* 90.

Agras, W. S. (1985). *Stress, panic, and the cardiovascular system.* In A. H. Tuma & J. Maser (Eds.), Anxiety and anxiety disorders. Hillsdale, NJ: Erlbaum.

Ainsworth, M. D. S. (1974). The development of infant–mother attachment. In B. Caldwell & H. Riciutti (Eds.), *Review of child development* (Vol 3). Chicago: University of Chicago Press.

Ainsworth, M. D. S. (1979). Infant–mother attachment. *American Psychologist, 34,* 932–937.

Ainsworth, M. D. S., Bell, S. M., & Slayton, D. J. (1971). Individual differences in the strange situation behavior of one-year-olds. In H. R. Schaffer (Ed.), *The origins of human social relations.* London: Academic Press.

Ainsworth, M. D. S., & Wittig, B. A. (1969). Attachment and the exploratory behavior of one-year-olds in strange situations. In B. M. Foss (Ed.), *Determinants of infant behavior* (Vol. 4). London: Methuen.

Albee, G. W. (1977). The Protestant ethic, sex, and psychotherapy. *American Psychologist, 32,* 150–161.

Allen, M. G. (1976). Twin studies of affective illness. *Archives of General Psychiatry, 33,* 1476–1478.

Allport, F. H. (1920). The influence of the group upon association and thought. *Journal of Experimental Psychology, 3,* 159–182.

Allport, G. W. (1968). The historical background of modern social psychology. In G. Lindzey & E. Aronson (Eds.), *The handbook of social psychology* (Vol. 1). Reading, MA: Addison-Wesley.

Allport, G. W., & Odbert, H. S. (1936). Trait-names, a psycho-lexical study. *Psychological Monographs, 47* (1, Whole No. 211).

American Psychological Association. (1979). *Ethical standards of psychologists.* Washington, DC: author.

American Psychological Association (1981). Ethical Principles of Psychologists. *American Psychologist, 36,* 633–638.

American Psychological Association. (1988). Trends in ethics cases, common pitfalls, and published resources. *American Psychologist, 43,* 564–572.

Amoore, J. E. (1970). *Molecular basis of odor.* Springfield, IL: Thomas.

Anderson, J. A. (1983). Cognitive and psychological computation with neural models. *IEEE Transactions on Systems, Man, and Cybernetics, 13,* 799–815.

Anderson, N. H. (1974). Cognitive algebra: Integration theory applied to social attribution. In L. Berkowitz (Ed.), *Advances in experimental social psychology* (Vol. 7, pp. 1–102). New York: Academic Press.

Anderson, R. C., & Myrow, D. L. (1971). Retroactive inhibition of meaningful discourse. *Journal of Educational Psychology, 77,* 171–179.

Andreasen, N. C., Nasrallah, H. A., Dunn, V., Olsen, S. A., & Grove, W. M. (1986). Structural abnormalities in the frontal system in schizophrenia: A magnetic resonance. *Archives of General Psychiatry, 43,* 136–144.

Andreasen, N. C., & Olsen, S. A. (1982). Negative versus positive schizophrenia: Definition and validation. *Archives of General Psychiatry, 36,* 1325–1330.

Annau, Z., & Kamin, L. J. (1961). The conditioned emotional response as a function of intensity of the UCS. *Journal of Comparative and Physiological Psychology, 54,* 428–432.

APA Council of Representatives Report (1987).

Aronson, E., Stephan, C., Sikes, J., Blaney, N., & Snapp, M. (1978). *The jigsaw classroom.* Beverly Hills, CA: Sage.

Asch, S. E. (1946). Forming impressions of personality. *Journal of Abnormal and Social Psychology, 41,* 258–290.

Asch, S. E. (1952). *Social psychology.* New York: Prentice-Hall.

Asch, S. E. (1955). Opinions and social pressure. *Scientific American, 193,* 31–35.

Aserinsky, E., & Kleitman, N. (1953). Regularly occurring periods of eye mobility and concomitant phenomena during sleep. *Science, 118,* 273–274.

Ashcraft, M. H. (1989). *Human memory and cognition.* Glenview, IL: Scott, Foresman.

Astin, A. W., Green, K. C., & Korn, W. S. (1987). The American freshman: Twenty year trends. (A report of the Cooperative Institutional Research Program Sponsored by the American Council on Education.) Los Angeles: Higher Education Research Institute, University of California–Los Angeles.

Averbach, E., & Corriell, A. S. (1961). Short-term memory in vision. *Bell System Technical Journal, 40,* 302–328.

Averbach, E., & Sperling, G. (1961). Short-term storage and information in vision. In C. Cherry (Ed.), *Information theory.* London: Butterworths, 196–211.

Ayllon, T., & Azrin, N. H. (1968). *The token economy: A motivational system for therapy and rehabilitation.* New York: Appleton-Century-Crofts.

B

Babkin, B. P. (1949). *Pavlov: A biography.* Chicago: University of Chicago Press.

Baddeley, A. D. (1966). Short-term memory for word sequences as a function of acoustic, semantic and formal similarity. *Quarterly Journal of Experimental Psychology, 18,* 362–365.

Baddeley, A. D., & Dale, H. C. (1966). The effect of semantic similarity on retroactive interference in long- and short-term memory. *Journal of Verbal Learning and Verbal Behavior, 5,* 417–420.

Bahrick, H. P. (1983). The cognitive map of a city—50 years of learning and memory. In G. Bower (Ed.), *The psychology of learning and memory.* New York: Academic Press.

Bahrick, H. P. (1984a). *Semantic memory content in permastore: Fifty years of memory for Spanish learned in school. Journal of Experimental Psychology: General, 113,* 1–29.

Bahrick, H. P. (1984b). Long-term memories: How durable, and how enduring? *Physiological Psychology, 12,* 53–58.

Bahrick, H. P., Bahrick, P. O., & Wittlinger, R. P. (1975). Fifty years of memory for names and faces: A cross-sectional approach. *Journal of Experimental Psychology: General, 104*, 54–75.

Bandura, A. (1965). Influence of a model's reinforcement contingencies on the acquisition of imitative responses. *Journal of Personality and Social Psychology, 1*, 589–595.

Bandura, A. (1973). *Aggression: A social learning analysis.* Englewood Cliffs, NJ: Prentice-Hall.

Bandura, A. (1977). *Social learning theory.* Englewood Cliffs, NJ: Prentice-Hall.

Bandura, A. (1978). The self system in reciprocal determinism. *American Psychologist, 33*, 344–358.

Bandura, A. (1982). Self-efficacy mechanism in human agency. *American Psychologist, 37*, 122–147.

Bandura, A. (1986). *Social foundations of thought and action: A social-cognitive theory.* Englewood Cliffs, NJ: Prentice-Hall.

Bandura, A., Ross, D., & Ross, S. A. (1963). Imitation of film-mediated aggressive models. *Journal of Abnormal and Social Psychology, 66*, 3–11.

Barahal, H. S. (1958). 1000 prefrontal lobotomies: Five-to-ten-year follow-up study. *Psychiatric Quarterly, 32*, 653–678.

Barash, D. P. (1979). *The whisperings within.* New York: Harper & Row.

Barash, D. P. (1982). *Sociobiology and behavior.* New York: Elsevier.

Barbach, L. G. (1975). *For yourself: The fulfillment of female sexuality.* Garden City, NY: Anchor Press/Doubleday.

Bard, P. (1928). A diencephalic mechanism for the expression of rage with special reference to the sympathetic nervous system. *American Journal of Physiology, 84*, 490–515.

Barker, R., Dembo, T., & Lewin, K. (1941). Frustration and regression: An experiment with young children. *University of Iowa Studies in Child Welfare, 18*, 1–314.

Barkow, J. H. (1980). Sociobiology: Is this the new theory of human nature? In A. Montagu (Ed.), *Sociobiology examined.* New York: Oxford University Press, 171–197.

Barnes, D. (1987). Biological issues in schizophrenia. *Science, 235*, 430–433.

Baron, A., & Galizio, M. (1983). Instructional control of human operant behavior. *Psychological Record, 33*, 495–520.

Barrera, M. E., & Maurer, D. (1981). Recognition of mother's photographed face by the three-month-old infant. *Child Development, 52*, 714–716.

Bartlett, F. C. (1932). *Remembering: A study in experimental and social psychology.* London: Cambridge University Press.

Baumrind, D. (1967). Child care practices anteceding three patterns of preschool behavior. *Genetic Psychology Monographs, 75*, 43–88.

Baumrind, D. (1983). Rejoinder to Lewis' reinterpretation of parental firm control effects: Are authoritative families really harmonious? *Psychological Bulletin, 94*, 132–142.

Bebeau, M., & Brabeck, M. (1987). Integrating care and justice issues in professional moral education. *Journal of Moral Education, 16*, 189–203.

Beck, A. T. (1967). *Depression: Clinical, experimental and theoretical aspects.* New York: Harper and Row.

Beck, A. T. (1974). The development of depression: A cognitive model. In R. J. Friedman & M. M. Katz (Eds.), *The psychology of depression: Contemporary theory and research.* New York: Wiley.

Beck, A. T. (1976). *Cognitive therapy and the emotional disorders.* New York: International Universities Press.

Beck, A. T., Rush, A. J., Shaw, B. F., & Emery, G. (1979). *Cognitive therapy of depression.* New York: Guilford Press.

Becklen, R., & Cervone, D. (1983). Selective looking and the noticing of unexpected events. *Memory and Cognition, 11*, 601–608.

Beidler, L. M. (1978). Biophysics and chemistry of taste. In E. C. Carterette & M. P. Friedman (Eds.), *Handbook of perception,* (Vol. 6A, pp. 21–49). New York: Academic Press.

Beidler, L. M., & Smallman, R. L. (1965). Renewal of cells within taste buds. *Journal of Cell Biology, 27*, 263–272.

Bell, A. P., & Weinberg, M. S. (1978). *Homosexualities: A study of diversity among men and women.* New York: Simon & Schuster.

Bell, A. P., Weinberg, M. S., & Hammersmith, S. K. (1981). *Sexual preference: Its development in men and women.* Bloomington, IN: Indiana University Press.

Bem, D. J. (1967). Self-perception: An alternative interpretation of cognitive dissonance phenomena. *Psychological Review, 74*, 183–200.

Bem, D. J. (1970). *Beliefs, attitudes, and human affairs.* Belmont, CA: Brooks/Cole.

Bem, D. J., & Funder, D. C. (1978). Predicting more of the people more of the time: Assessing the personality of situations. *Psychological Review, 85*, 485–501.

Bem, S. L. (1985). Androgeny and gender schema theory: A conceptual and empirical integration. *Nebraska Symposium on Motivation, 32*, 179–226.

Benkert, O., Witt, W., Adam, W., & Leitz, A. (1979). Effects of testosterone undecanoate on sexual potency and the hypothalamic-pituitary-gonadal axis of impotent males. *Archives of Sexual Behavior, 8*, 471–480.

Bergin, A. E. (1971). The evaluation of therapeutic outcomes. In A. E. Bergin & S. L. Garfield (Eds.), *Handbook of psychotherapy and behavior change: An empirical analysis.* New York: Wiley.

Berkowitz, L. (1980). *A survey of social psychology.* New York: McGraw-Hill.

Berlin, B., & Kay, P. (1969) *Basic color terms.* Berkeley: University of California Press.

Berlyne, D. E. (1971). *Aesthetics and psychology.* New York: Appleton-Century-Crofts.

Berndt, T. J. (1979). Developmental changes in conformity to peers and parents. *Developmental Psychology, 15*, 608–616.

Berscheid, E., & Peplau, L. A. (1983). The emerging science of relationships. In H. H. Kelley, E. Berscheid, A. Christensen, J. H. Harvey, T. L. Huston, G. Levinger, E. McClintock, L. A. Peplau, & D. Peterson, *Close Relationships.* New York: Freeman.

Berscheid, E., & Walster, E. (1974). Physical attractiveness. In L. Berkowitz (Ed.), *Advances in experimental social psychology.* New York: Academic Press.

Biederman, I. (1981). On the semantics of a glance at a scene. In M. Kubovy & J. Pomerantz (Eds.), *Perceptual organization.* Hillsdale, NJ: Erlbaum.

Bird, G., Bird, G., & Scruggs, M. (1984). Determinants of family task sharing: A study of husbands and wives. *Journal of Marriage and the Family, 46*, 345–355.

Bischof, N. (1975). Comparative ethology of incest avoidance. In R. Fox (Ed.), *Biosocial anthropology.* London: Malaby.

Blakemore, C., & Cooper, G. F. (1970). Development of the brain depends on the visual environment. *Nature, 228*, 477–478.

Blasi, A. (1980). Bridging moral cognition and moral action: A critical review of the literature. *Psychological Bulletin, 88*, 1–45.

Blumstein, P., & Schwartz, P. (1983). *American couples.* New York: William Morrow.

Boden, M. A. (1988). *Computer models of the mind.* New York: Cambridge University Press.

Bogen, J. E., & Vogel, P. J. (1962). Cerebral commissurotomy in man: preliminary case report. *Bulletin of the Los Angeles Neurological Society, 27*, 169.

Bohannon, J. N., III, & Warren-Leubecker, A. (1985). Theoretical approaches to language acquisition. In J. Berko Gleason (Ed.), *The development of language.* Columbus, OH: Merrill Publishing.

Bolles, R. C. (1979). *Learning theory.* New York: Holt, Rinehart and Winston.

Booth Kewely, S., & Friedman, H. S. (1987). Psychological predictors of heart disease: A quantitative review. *Psychological Bulletin, 101*, 343-362.

Boring, E. G. (1923). Intelligence as the tests test it. *New Republic, 35*, 35–37.

Bower, G. H. & Clark, M. C. (1969). Narrative stories as mediators for serial learning. *Psychonomic Science, 14*, 181–182.

Bowles, S., & Gintis, H. (1974). IQ in the United States class structure. In A. Gartner, C. Greer, & F. Riessman (Eds.), *The new assault on equality.* New York: Harper & Row. pp. 7–84.

Bosarge, L. (1989). Educating college students about sexually transmitted diseases, AIDS, and safe-sex practices. Unpublished masters thesis, Auburn University.

Boszormenyi-Nagy, I., & Ulrich, D. N. (1981). Contextual family therapy. In A. S. Gurman & D. P. Kniskern (Eds.), *Handbook of family therapy*. New York: Brunner/Mazel.

Bouchard, T. J., Jr. (1981). Separated identical twins: Preliminary findings. Invited address, annual meeting of the American Psychological Society, Los Angeles.

Bouchard, T. J., Jr., & McGue, M. (1981). Familial studies of intelligence: A review. *Science, 212*, 1055–1059.

Bousfield, W. A. (1953). The occurrence of clustering in the recall of randomly arranged associates. *Journal of General Psychology, 49*, 229–240.

Bower, G. H. (1981). Mood and memory. *American Psychologist, 36*, 129–148.

Bowlby, J. (1969). *Attachment and loss, Vol. 1*. London: Hogarth Press.

Bowlby, J. (1973). *Attachment and loss, Vol. 2*. New York: Basic Books.

Bowlby, J. (1982). Attachment and loss: Retrospect and prospect. *American Journal of Orthopsychiatry, 52*, 664–678.

Bradley, R. M. (1979). Effects of aging on the sense of taste: Anatomical considerations. In S. S. Hans & D. H. Coons (Eds.), *Special senses in aging: A current biological assessment*. Ann Arbor, MI: Institute of Gerontology, University of Michigan.

Bransford, J. D., & Johnson, M. K. (1972). Contextual prerequisites for understanding: Some investigations of comprehension and recall. *Journal of Verbal Learning and Verbal Behavior, 11*, 717–726.

Breggin, P. R. (1979). *Electroshock: Its brain-disabling effects*. New York: Springer.

Brehm, S. S. (1985). *Intimate relationships*. New York: Random House.

Breuer, J., & Freud, S. (1955). *Studies on hysteria*. In J. Strachey (Ed. & Trans.) London: Hogarth Press. (Originally published 1895).

British Psychological Society. (1986). Report of the working group on the use of polygraph in criminal investigation and personal screening. *Bulletin of the British Psychological Society, 39*, 81–94.

Brittain, C. V. (1963). Adolescent choices and parent-peer cross-pressures. *American Sociological Review, 28*, 385–391.

Brittain, C. V. (1966). Age and sex of siblings and conformity toward parents versus peers in adolescence. *Child Development, 37*, 709–714.

Broadbent, D. D. (1958). *Perception and communication*. New York: Pergamon.

Brody, L. R. (1981). Visual short-term recall memory in infancy. *Child Development, 52*, 242–250.

Broverman, I. K., Vogel, S. R., Broverman, D. M., Clarkson, F. E., & Rosenkrantz, P. S. (1972). Sex role stereotypes. A current appraisal. *Journal of Social Issues, 28*, 59–78.

Brown, G. L., Ebert, M. H., Goyer, P. F., Jimerson, D. C., Klein, W. J., Bunney, W. E., & Goodwin, F. K. (1982). Aggression, suicide, serotonin. Relationships of CSF amine metabolites. *American Journal of Psychiatry, 139*, 741–746.

Brown, L. R., McGrath, P. L., & Stokes, B. (1976). The population problem in 22 dimensions. *The Futurist* (October), 238-244.

Brown, R. (1973). *A first language: The early stages*. Cambridge, MA: Harvard University Press.

Brown, R., Colter, N., Corsellis, J. A. N., Crow, T. J., & Frith, C. D. (1986). Postmortem evidence of structural brain changes in schizophrenia: Differences in brain weight, temporal horn area, and para hippocampal gyrus compared with average data. *Archives of General Psychiatry, 43*, 36–42.

Bryan, J. H., & Test, M. A. (1967). Models and helping: Naturalistic studies in aiding behavior. *Journal of Personality and Social Psychology, 6*, 400–407.

Buie, J. (1989). Scope of practice debated in 12 states. *The APA monitor, 20*, 22.

Bureau of the Census, Current Population Reports, Series P-20, No. 312. Washington, D.C.: Government Printing Office.

Bureau of the Census (1987). *Statistical Abstract of the U.S.* Washington, DC: U.S. Government Printing Office.

Burgess, A. W., & Holmstrom, L. L. (1974). Rape trauma syndrome. *American Journal of Psychiatry, 131*, 981–986.

Buri, J. R., Louiselle, P. A., Misukanis, T. M., & Mueller, R. A. (1988). Effects of parental authoritarianism and authoritativeness on self-esteem. *Personality and Social Psychology Bulletin, 14*, 271–282.

Bush, K. M., Sidman, M., & de Rose, T. (1989). Contextual control of emergent relations. *Journal of the Experimental Analysis of Behavior, 51*, 29–45.

Buskist, W., & Miller, H. L., Jr., (1986). Interaction between rules and contingencies in the control of human fixed-interval performance. *Psychological Record, 36*, 109–116.

Butcher, J. N., Dahlstrom, W. G., Graham, J. R., Tellegren, A., & Kaemmer, B. (1989). *Manual for the restandardized Minnesota Multiphasic Personality Inventory: MMPI-2. An administrative and interpretive guide*. Minneapolis, MN: University of Minnesota Press.

Butler, R. N., & Lewis, M. I. (1982). *Aging and mental health*. (3rd ed.). St. Louis: Mosby.

Butterfield, E. C., & Siperstein, G. N. (1972). Influence of contingent auditory stimulation upon non-nutritional suckle. In J. F. Bosma (Ed.), *Third symposium on oral sensation and perception: The mouth of the infant*. Springfield, IL: Thomas.

Byrne, D., Clore, G. L., & Smeaton, G. (1986). The attraction hypothesis: Do similar attitudes affect anything? *Journal of Personality and Social Psychology, 51*, 1167–1170.

C

Cade, J. F. J. (1949). Lithium salts in the treatment of psychotic excitement. *Medical Journal of Australia, 36*, 349–352.

Cain, W. S. (1977). Differential sensitivity for smell. "Noise" at the nose. *Science, 195*, 796–798.

Cain, W. S. (1978). The odoriferous environment and the application of olfactory research. In E. C. Carterette & M. P. Friedman (Eds.), *Handbook of perception*, (Vol. 7 pp. 277–304). New York: Academic Press.

Cain, W. S. (1982). Odor identification by males and females: Predictions versus performance. *Chemical Senses, 7*, 129–142.

Campbell, D. T., & Stanley, J. C. (1963). *Experimental and quasi-experimental designs for research*. Chicago: Rand McNally.

Cannon, W. B. (1927). The James-Lange theory of emotion: A critical examination and an alternative theory. *American Journal of Psychology, 39*, 106–124.

Cannon, W. B. (1932). *The wisdom of the body*. New York: Norton.

Cannon, W. B., & Washburn, A. (1912). An explanation of hunger. *American Journal of Physiology, 29*, 441–454.

Cantor, N., & Kihlstrom, J. F. (1987). *Personality and social intelligence*. Englewood Cliffs, NJ: Prentice-Hall.

Carrera, M. (1981). *Sex: The facts, the acts, and your feelings*. New York: Crown.

Carson, R. C., Butcher, J. N., & Coleman, J. C. (1988). *Abnormal psychology and modern life* (8th ed.). Glenview, IL: Scott, Foresman.

Cartwright, R. D. (1974). The influence of a conscious wish on dreams: A methodological study of dream meaning and function. *Journal of Abnormal Psychology, 83*, 387–393.

Cattell, R. B. (1946). *Description and measurement of personality*. Yonkers, NY: World Book Co.

Cattell, R. B. (1950). *Personality*. New York: McGraw-Hill Book Company, Inc.

Cattell, R. B. (1973). Personality pinned down. *Psychology Today, 7*, 40–46.

The Centers for Disease Control. (1987). *Smoking, tobacco and health: A fact book*. Washington, DC: U.S. Government Printing Office.

Cermak, L. S., & Craik, F. I. M. (1979). *Levels of processing in human memory*. Hillsdale, NJ: Erlbaum.

Chaiken, S. (1979). Communicator's physical attractiveness and persuasion. *Journal of Personality and Social Psychology, 37*, 1387–1397.

Chapman, C. R., Wilson, M. E., & Gehrig, J. D. (1976). Comparative effects of acupuncture and transcutaneous stimulation of the perception of painful dental stimuli. *Pain, 2,* 265–283.

Chen, S. C. (1937). Social modification of the activity of ants in nest-building. *Physiological Zoology, 10,* 420–436.

Cherry, E. C. (1953). Some experiments on the recognition of speech with one and two ears. *Journal of the Acoustical Society of America, 25,* 975–979.

Cherry, E. C., & Taylor, W. K. (1954). Some further experiments on the recognition of speech with one and two ears. *Journal of the Acoustical Society of America, 26,* 554–559.

Chomsky, N. (1957). *Syntactic structures.* The Hague: Mouton.

Chomsky, N. (1965). *Aspects of a theory of syntax.* Cambridge, MA: MIT Press.

Chomsky, N. (1972). *Language and mind.* New York: Harcourt Brace Jovanovich.

Chomsky, N. (1973). The fallacy of Richard Herrnstein's IQ. In A. Gartner, C. Greer, & F. Riessman (Eds.), *The new assault on equality.* New York: Harper & Row, pp. 85–101.

Cialdini, R. B. (1988). *Influence: Science and practice* (2nd ed). Glenview, IL: Scott, Foresman.

Cialdini, R. B., Cacioppo, J. T., Bassett, R., & Miller, J. A. (1978). Low-ball procedure for producing compliance: Commitment then cost. *Journal of Personality and Social Psychology, 36,* 463–476.

Cialdini, R. B, Petty, R. E., & Cacioppo, J. T. (1981). Attitude and attitude change. *Annual Review of Psychology, 32,* 357–404.

Cialdini, R. B., Vincent, J. E., Lewis, S. K., Catalan, J., Wheeler, D., & Darby, B. L. (1975). Reciprocal concessions procedure for inducing compliance. The door-in-the-face technique. *Journal of Personality and Social Psychology, 31,* 206–215.

Clarren, S. K., & Smith, D. W. (1978). The fetal alcohol syndrome. *New England Journal of Medicine, 298,* 1063–1067.

Cloninger, C. R. (1987). A systematic method for clinical observation and classification of personality variants. *Archives of General Psychiatry, 44,* 573–588.

Cohen, L. A. (1987). Diet and cancer. *Scientific American,* 42-48.

Cohen, L. J., & Roth, S. (1987). The psychological aftermath of rape: Longterm effects and individual differences in recovery. *Journal of Social and Clinical Psychology, 5,* 525–534.

Cohen, N. J. (1984). Preserved capacity in amnesia: Evidence for multiple memory systems. In N. Butters & L. Squires (Eds.), *The neuropsychology of memory.* New York: Guilford Press.

Cohen, N. J., & L. Squires, L. (1980). Preserved learning and retention of pattern analyzing skill in amnesia: Dissociation of knowing how and knowing that. *Science, 210,* 207–210.

Cohen, S. (1981). Adverse effects of marijuana: Selected issues. Research developments in drug and alcohol use. *Annals of the New York Academy of Sciences, 362,* 123.

Colby, A., Kohlberg, L., Gibbs, J., & Lieberman, M. (1983). A longitudinal study of moral development. *Monographs of the Society for Research in Child Development, 48* (Serial No. 200).

Collings, V. B. (1974). Human taste response as a function of locus on the tongue and soft palate. *Perception & Psychophysics, 16,* 169–174.

Collins, A. M., & Loftus, E. F. (1975). A spreading-activation theory of semantic processing. *Psychological Review, 82,* 407–428.

Collins, A. M., & Quillian, M. R. (1969). Retrieval time from semantic memory. *Journal of Verbal Learning and Verbal Behavior, 8,* 240–247.

Collip, P. J. (1980). Obesity in childhood. In A. J. Strunkard, (Ed.), *Obesity.* Philadelphia: Saunders.

Colt, W. D., Wardlaw, S., & Frantz, A. (1981). The effect of running on plasma beta-endorphin. *Life Science, 28,* 1637–1640.

Conger, J. J. (1975). Proceedings of the American Psychological Association, Incorporated for 1974: Minutes of the annual meeting of the Council of Representatives. *American Psychologist, 30,* 620–651.

Conrad, C. (1972). Cognitive economy in semantic memory. *Journal of Experimental Psychology, 92,* 149–154.

Conrad, R. (1964). Acoustic confusions in immediate memory. *British Journal of Psychology, 55,* 75–84.

Cook, T. D., & Campbell, D. T. (1979). *Quasi-Experimentation: Design analysis issues for field settings.* Boston: Houghton Mifflin.

Cooper, K. (March, 1985). Running without risk. *Runner's World, 20,* 61–64.

Cooper, K. H. (1968). *Aerobics.* New York: Evans and Company.

Cooper, K. H. (1970). *The new aerobics.* New York: Evans and Company.

Corcoran, D. W. J. (1964). The relation between introversion and salivation. *American Journal of Psychology, 77,* 298–300.

Corkin, S. (1984). Lasting consequences of bilateral medial temporal lobectomy: Clinical course and experimental findings in H. M. *Seminars in Neurology, 4,* 249–259.

Costa, P. T., & McRae, R. R (1985). *The NEO Personality Inventory.* Odessa, FL: Psychological Assessment Resources, Inc.

Cottrell, N. B., Rittle, R. H., & Wack, D. L. (1967). The presence of an audience and list type (competitional or noncompetitional) as joint determinants of performance in paired-associate learning. *Journal of Personality, 35,* 425–433.

Cowan, N. (1984). On short and long auditory stores. *Psychological Bulletin, 96,* 341–370.

Cowart, B. J. (1981). Development of taste perception in humans: Sensitivity and preference throughout the life span. *Psychological Bulletin, 90,* 43–73.

Craik, F. I. M. (1970). The fate of primary memory in terms of free recall. *Journal of Verbal Learning and Verbal Behavior, 9,* 143–148.

Craik, F. I. M., & Lockhart, R. S. (1972). Levels of processing: A framework for memory research. *Journal of Verbal Learning and Verbal Behavior, 11,* 671–684.

Craik, F. I. M., & Tulving, E. (1975). Depth of processing and the retention of words in episodic memory. *Journal of Experimental Psychology: General, 104,* 268–294.

Craik, F. I. M., & Watkins, M. J. (1973). The role of rehearsal in short-term memory. *Journal of Verbal Learning and Verbal Behavior, 12,* 599–607.

Cravey, R. H., Reed, D., & Ragle, J. L. (1979). Phencyclidine-related deaths: A report of nine fatal cases. *Journal of Analytical Toxicology, 23,* 199–201.

Crossman, E. K. (1983). Las Vegas knows better. *The Behavior Analyst, 6,* 109–110.

Crowder, R. G. (1971). The sound of vowels and consonants in immediate memory. *Journal of Verbal Learning and Verbal Behavior, 10,* 587–596.

Cumberbatch, G., Jones, I., & Lee, M. (1988). Measuring violence on television. *Current Psychology: Research & Reviews, 7,* 10–25.

D

Dallenbach, K. M. (1927). The temperature spots and end organs. *American Journal of Psychology, 39,* 402–427.

Daly, M., & Wilson, M. (1978). *Sex, evolution, and behavior.* North Scituate, MA: Duxbury Press.

Daniels, P., & Weingarten, K. (1982) *Sooner or later: The timing of parenthood in adult lives.* New York: Norton.

Dartnell, H. J. A., Bowmaker, J. K., & Mollon, J. D. (1983). Microspectrometry of human photoreceptors. In J. D. Mollon & L. T. Sharpe, (Eds.), *Colour vision: Physiology and psychophysics.* New York: Academic Press.

Darwin, C. (1859). *The origin of species.* London: John Murray.

Darwin, C. (1872). *The expression of the emotions in man and animals.* New York: Philosophical Library.

Darwin, C. J., Turvey, M. T., & Crowder, R. G. (1972). The auditory analogue of the Sperling partial report procedure: Evidence for a brief auditory storage. *Cognitive Psychology, 3,* 225–267.

Darwin, F. (Ed.). (1950/1887). *Charles Darwin's autobiography.* New York: Henry Schuman.

Dashiell, J. F. (1930). An experimental analysis of some group effects. *Journal of Abnormal and Social Psychology, 25,* 290–299.

Davis, J. A., & Smith, T. (1984). *General social surveys, 1972–1984: Cumulative data.* New Haven, CT: Yale University, Roper Center for Public Opinion Research.

Davis, J. M. (1978). Dopamine theory of schizophrenia: A two-factor theory. In L. C. Wynne, R. L. Cromwell, & S. Matthysse (Eds.), *The nature of schizophrenia: New approaches to research and treatment.* New York: Wiley.

Davis, R. (1986). Assessing the eating disorders. *The Clinical Psychologist, 39,* 33–36.

Davis, W. L., & Phares, E. J. (1967). Internal-external control as a determinant of information-seeking in a social influence situation. *Journal of Personality, 35,* 547–561.

Davison, G. C., & Neale, J. M. (1986). *Abnormal psychology: An experimental clinical approach* (4th ed.). New York: Wiley.

Dawkins, R. (1976). *The selfish gene.* London: Oxford University Press.

Deaux, K., & Major, B. (1987). Putting gender into context: An interactive model of gender-related behavior. *Psychological Review, 94:* 369–389.

Deci, E. L., & Ryan, R. M. (1980). The empirical exploration of intrinsic motivational processes. *Advances in Experimental Social Psychology, 13,* 39–80.

de Groot, A. D. (1965). *Thought and choice in chess.* The Hague: Morton.

DeJong, W. (1979). An examination of self-perception mediation of the foot-in-the-door effect. *Journal of Personality and Social Psychology, 37,* 2221–2239.

Dement, W. C. (1960). The effect of dream deprivation. *Science, 131,* 1705–1707.

Dement, W. C. (1969). The biological role of REM sleep. In A. Kales (Ed.), *Sleep physiology and pathology.* Philadelphia: Lippincott.

Dement, W. C. (1978). *Some must watch while some must sleep. Exploring the world of sleep.* New York: Norton.

Dement, W. C., & Wolpert, E. (1958). The relation of eye movements, bodily motility, and external stimuli to dream content. *Journal of Experimental Psychology, 55,* 543–553.

Depue, R. A., & Monroe, S. M. (1978). The unipolar-bipolar distinction in the depressive disorders. *Psychological Bulletin, 85,* 1001–29.

DePue, R. A., & Monroe, S. M. (1986). Conceptualization and measurement of human disorder in life-stress research: The problem of chronic disturbance. *Psychological Bulletin, 99,* 36–51.

Desor, J. A., & Beauchamp, G. K. (1974). The human capacity to transmit olfactory information. *Perception & Psychophysics, 16,* 551–556.

Deutscher, I. (1968). The quality of postparental life. In B. L. Neugarten (Ed.), *Middle age and aging.* Chicago: University of Chicago Press.

DeValois, R. L., & DeValois, K. K. (1975). Neural coding of color. In E. C. Carterette & M. P. Friedman (Eds.), *Handbook of Perception.* San Diego: Academic Press.

DeValois, R. L., & Jacobs, G. H. (1984). Neural mechanisms of color vision. In I. Darian-Smith (Ed.), *Handbook of physiology, the nervous system.* Bethesda, MD: American Physiological Society.

Digman, J. M., & Inouye, J. (1986). Further specifications of the five robust factors of personality. *Journal of Personality and Social Psychology, 50,* 116–123.

Digman, J. M., & Takemoto-Chock, N. K. (1981). Factors in the neural language of personality: Re-analysis, comparison, and interpretation of six major studies. *Multivariate Behavioral Research, 16,* 149–170.

Dollard, J., Doob, L. W., Miller, N., Mowrer, O. H., & Sears, R. R. (1939). *Frustration and aggression.* New Haven, CT: Yale University Press.

Donnerstein, E. I., & Linz, D. (1986). The question of pornography. *Psychology Today,* 56–59.

Donovan, W. L., Leavitt, L. A., & Balling, J. D. (1978). Maternal physiological response to infant signals. *Psychophysiology, 15,* 68–74.

Dooling, D. J., & Lachman, R. (1971). Effects of comprehension on retention of prose. *Journal of Experimental Psychology, 88,* 216–222.

Dorus, E., Pandey, G. N., Shaughnessy, R., Gaviria, M., Val, E., Ericksen, S., & Davis, J. M. (1979). Lithium transport across red cell membrane: A cell membrane abnormality in manic-depressive illness. *Science, 205,* 932–933.

Doyle, J. (1985). *Sex and gender.* Dubuque, IA: Wm. C. Brown.

Drabman, R. S., & Thomas, M. H. (1974). Does media violence increase children's tolerance of real-life aggression? *Developmental Psychology, 10,* 418–421.

Duncker, K. (1945). On problem-solving. (L. S. Lees, Trans.). *Psychological Monographs, 58* (whole no. 270). (Original work published 1935.)

Dunn, J. (1981). Studying temperament and parent-child interaction: Comparison of interview and direct observation. In S. Chess & A. Thomas (Eds.), *Annual progress in child psychiatry and child development.* (pp. 415–430). New York: Bruner/Mazel.

Durrant, J., & Lovrinic, J. (1977). *Bases of hearing science.* Baltimore: Williams & Wilkins.

E

Eastman, W. F (1972). First intercourse. *Sexual Behavior, 2,* 22–27.

Ebbinghaus, H. (1885/1913). *Memory: A contribution to experimental psychology.* (Translated by H. A. Ruger & C. E. Bussenius). New York: Teachers College, Columbia University.

Eccles, J. S. (1987). Gender roles and women's achievement-related decisions. *Psychology of Women Quarterly, 11,* 135–172.

Egeland, J. A., Gerhard, D. S., Pauls, D. L., Sussex, J. N. Kidd, K. K, Allen, C. R., Hostetter, A. M., & Houseman, D. E. (1987). Bipolar affective disorder linked to DNA markers on chromosome 11. *Nature, 325,* 783–787.

Ehrhardt, A., & Meyer-Bahlburg, H. (1981). Effects of prenatal sex hormones on gender-related behavior. *Science, 448,* 1312–1313.

Ehrhardt, A., & Money, J. (1967). Progestin-induced hermaphroditism: IQ and psychosexual identity in a study of ten girls. *Journal of Sex Research, 3,* 83–100.

Eich, J., Weingartner, H., Stillman, R., & Gillin, J. (1975). State-dependent accessibility of retrieval cues and retention of a categorized list. *Journal of Verbal Learning and Verbal Behavior, 14,* 408–417.

Eichorn, D. H., Hunt, J. V., & Honzik, M. P. (1981). Experience, personality, and IQ: Adolescence to middle age. In D. Eichorn, J. Clausen, N. Haan, M. Honzik, & P. Mussen (Eds.), *Present and past in middle age.* New York: Academic Press.

Eisner, J., Roberts, W., Heynsfield, S., & Yeager, J. (1985). Anorexia nervosa and sudden death. *Annals of Internal Medicine, 102,* 49–52.

Ekman, P. (1980). Biological and cultural contributions to body and facial movement in the expression of emotions. In A. Rorty (Ed.), *Explaining emotions.* Berkeley: University of California Press.

Ekman, P., & Friesen, W. V. (1971). Constants across cultures in the fact and emotion. *Journal of Personality and Social Psychology, 17,* 124–129.

Ekman, P., Levensen, R. W., & Friesen, W. V. (1983). Autonomic nervous system activity distinguishes among emotions. *Science, 221,* 1208–1210.

Ekman, P., Sorenson, E. R., & Friesen, W. V. (1969). Pancultural elements in facial displays in emotions. *Science, 764,* 86–88.

Elkind, D., & Bowen, R. (1979). Imaginary audience behavior in children and adolescents. *Developmental Psychology, 15,* 38–44.

Ellis, A. (1962). *Reason and emotion in psychotherapy.* New York: Lyle Stuart.

Ellis, A. (1984). Rational-emotive therapy. In R. J. Corsini (Ed.), *Current psychotherapies* (3rd ed.). Itasca, IL: Peacock Press.

Ellis, L., & Ames, M. A. (1987). Neurohormonal functioning and sexual orientation: A theory of homosexuality-heterosexuality. *Psychological Bulletin, 101,* 233–258.

Engel, L. (1962). Darwin and the Beagle. In L. Engel (Ed.), *The voyage of the Beagle.* Garden City, NY: Doubleday.

Environmental Action Foundation. (1988). *Briefing papers: Beverage container deposit laws.* Washington, D.C.: Environmental Action Foundation.

Epling, W. F., & Pierce, W. D. (1988). Applied behavior analysis: New directions from the laboratory. In G. Davey & C. Cullen (Eds.) *Human operant conditioning and behavior modification.* Chichester, England: Wiley.

Epstein, L. H., & Wing, R. R. (1987). Behavioral treatment of adult obesity. *Psychological Bulletin, 101,* 331–342.

Erdelyi, M. H. (1985). *Psychoanalysis: Freud's cognitive psychology.* San Francisco: W. H. Freeman.

Erickson, R. P. (1982). Studies on the perception of taste: Do primaries exist? *Physiology & Behavior, 28,* 57–62.

Erikson, E. (1963). *Childhood and society* (2nd ed.). New York: Norton.

Eron, L. D., & Huesmann, L. R. (1985). The role of television in the development of prosocial and antisocial behavior. In D. Olweus, M. Radke-Yarrow, & J. Block (Eds.), *Development of antisocial and prosocial behavior.* Orlando, FL: Academic Press.

Essman, W. B., & Essman, E. J. (1986). Drug effects and receptor changes in aggressive behavior. In C. Shagrass, R. C. Josiassen, W. H. Bridger, K. J. Weiss, D. Stoff, & G. M. Simpson (Eds.), *Biological psychiatry, 1985* New York: Elsevier.

Evans, R. I., Raines, B. E., & Hanselka, L. (1984). Developing data-based communications in social psychological research: Adolescent smoking prevention. *Journal of Applied Social Psychology, 14,* 289–295.

Eysenck, H. J. (1952). The effects of psychotherapy: An evaluation. *Journal of Consulting Psychology, 16,* 319–324.

Eysenck, H. J. (1975). A genetic model of anxiety. In L. G. Sarason & C. D. Spielberger (Eds.), *Stress and anxiety: Vol. 2.* New York: Wiley.

Eysenck, H. J. (1981). General features of the model. In H. J. Eysenck (Ed.), *A model for personality.* New York: Springer-Verlag.

Eysenck, H. J., & Eysenck, M. W. (1985). *Personality and individual differences.* New York: Plenum Press.

Eysenck, H. J., & Kamin, L. (1981). *The intelligence controversy.* New York: Wiley.

Eysenck, S. B. G., & Eysenck, H. J. (1967). *Perceptual and Motor Skills, 24,* 1047–1053.

F

Fagan, J. F. (1973). Infants' delayed recognition memory and forgetting. *Journal of Experimental Child Psychology, 16,* 424–450.

Fancher, R. E. (1979). *Pioneers of psychology.* New York: Norton.

Fancher, R. E. (1985). *The intelligence men: Makers of the IQ controversy.* New York: Norton.

Fantino, E., & Logan, C. A. (1979). *The experimental analysis of behavior: A biological perspective.* San Francisco: Freeman.

Fantz, R. L. (1961). The origin of form perception. *Scientific American, 204,* 66–72.

Fantz, R. L. (1970). Visual perception and experience in infancy: Issues and approaches. In National Academy of Science, *Early experience and visual information processing in perceptual and reading disorders,* 351–381. New York: National Academy of Science.

Farrar, C. H., Powell, B. J., & Martin, L. K. (1968). Punishment of alcohol consumption by apneic paralysis. *Behavior Research and Therapy, 6,* 13–16.

Federico, P. A. (1984). Event-related potentials (ERP) correlates of cognitive styles, abilities and aptitudes. *Personality and Individual Differences, 5,* 575–585.

Feiner, R. D., Jason, L. A., Moritsugu, J. M., & Farber, S. S. (1983). *Preventive psychology:* Theory, research and practice. New York: Pergamon Press.

Ferguson, D. M., Horwood, L. J., & Shannon, F. T. (1987). Breastfeeding and subsequent social adjustment in six-to eight-year-old children. *Journal of Child Psychology & Psychiatry & Allied Disciplines, 28,* 379–386.

Ferster, C. B. & Skinner, B. F. (1957). *Schedules of reinforcement.* New York: Appleton-Century-Crofts.

Festinger, L. (1957). *A theory of cognitive dissonance.* Stanford, CA: Stanford University Press.

Festinger, L., & Carlsmith, J. M. (1959). Cognitive consequences of forced compliance. *Journal of Abnormal and Social Psychology, 58,* 203–210.

Festinger, L., Riecken, H., & Schacter, S. (1956). *When prophecy fails.* Minneapolis: University of Minnesota Press.

Fieve, R. R. (1979). The clinical effects of lithium treatment. *Trends in Neurosciences, 2,* 66-68.

Fishbein, M. (1980). A theory of reasoned action: Some applications and implications. *Nebraska symposium on motivation, 27,* 65–116.

Fishbein, M., & Azjen, I. (1975). *Belief, attitude, intention and behavior: An introduction to theory and research.* Reading, MA: Addison-Wesley.

Fisher, R. A. (1925). *Statistical methods for research workers.* Edinburgh: Oliver & Boyd.

Fishman, J. (1960). Fatness, puberty, and ovulation. *New England Journal of Medicine, 303,* 424–43.

Fishman, S. M., & Sheehan, D. V. (1985, April). Anxiety and Panic: Their cause and treatment. *Psychology Today,* 26–32.

Flexser, A. J., & Tulving, E. (1978). Retrieval independence in recognition and recall. *Psychological Review, 85,* 153–171.

Flynn, J. P., Vanegas, H., Foote, W., & Edwards, S. (1970). Neural mechanisms involved in a cat's attack on a rat. In R. E. Whalen, R. F. Thompson, M. Verzeano, & N. M. Weinberger (Eds.), *The neural control of behavior.* New York: Academic Press.

Flynn, J. R. (1984). The mean IQ of Americans: Massive gains 1932 to 1978. *Psychological Bulletin, 95,* 29–51.

Fodor, J. A., & Bever, J. G. (1965). The psychological reality of linguistic segments. *Journal of Verbal Learning and Verbal Behavior, 4,* 414–420.

Foss, R. D., & Dempsey, C. B. (1979). Blood donation and the foot-in-the-door technique: A limiting case. *Journal of Personality and Social Psychology, 37,* 580–590.

Fouts, R. S. (1973). Acquisition and testing of gestural signs in four young chimpanzees. *Science, 180,* 978–980.

Fouts, R. S., Hirsch, A. D., & Fouts, D. H. (1982). Cultural transmission of human language in a chimpanzee mother/infant relationship. In H. E. Fitzgerald, J. A. Mullins, & P. Page (Eds.), *Psychological perspectives: Child nuterance series,* Vol 4. New York: Plenum.

Frank, J. D. (1972). The bewildering world of psychotherapy. *Journal of Social Issues, 28,* 27–43.

Frankel, F. H. (1984). Electroconvulsive therapies. In T. B. Karasu (Ed.), *The psychiatric therapies.* Washington, D.C.: American Psychological Association.

Franks, C. M., & Wilson, G. T. (1975). *Annual review of behavior therapy: Theory and practice* (Vols. 1–7). New York: Brunner/Mazel.

Frederickson, R. C. A., & Geary, L. E. (1982). Endogenous opioid peptides: Review of physiological, pharmacological, and clinical aspects. *Progress in Neurobiology, 19,* 19–69.

Freedman, J. L., & Fraser, S. (1966). Compliance without pressure: The foot-in-the-door technique. *Journal of Personality and Social Psychology, 4,* 195–202.

Freud, S. (1900). *The interpretation of dreams.* London: George Allen & Unwin Ltd.

Freud, S. (1910/1939). The origin and development of psycho-analysis. In *The Major Works of Sigmund Freud*. Chicago: Encyclopedia Britannica.

Freud, S. (1912). Recommendations for physicians on the psychoanalytic method of treatment. (J. Riviere, Trans.), *Zentral-blatt*, Bd. II. Reprinted in Sammlung, Vierte Folge.

Freud, S. (1913). *The interpretation of dreams*. (3rd ed.) (A. A. Brill, Trans.) New York: Macmillan.

Freud, S. (1914). *The psychopathology of everyday life*. New York: Macmillan.

Freud, S. (1933) *New introductory lectures on psychoanalysis* (J. Strachey, Trans.). New York: Norton.

Freud, S. (1957). The essays on the theory of sexuality. In J. Strachey (Ed. and Trans.), *The standard edition of the complete works of Sigmund Freud. Vol. 7*. London: Hogarth Press. (Originally published 1905.)

Freud, S. (1962/1905). *Three essays on the theory of sexuality*. Translated and ideated by J. Strachey. New York: Basic Books.

Freud, S. (1964). New introductory lectures on psycho-analysis. In J. Strachey (Ed. and Trans.), *The standard edition of the complete works of Sigmund Freud. Vol. 22*. London: Hogarth Press. (Originally published 1933.)

Freud, S. (1965). The interpretation of dreams. In J. Strachey (Ed. and Trans.), *The standard edition of the complete works of Sigmund Freud. Vols. 4 and 5*. London: Hogarth Press. (Originally published 1900.)

Friedman, M., & Rosenman, H. S. (1974). *Type A behavior and your heart*. New York: Knopf.

Friedman, M., & Rosenman, R. H. (1959). Association of overt behavior patterns with blood and cardiovascular findings: Blood cholesterol level, blood clotting time, incidence of arcus senilis, and clinical coronary heart disease. *Journal of the American Medical Association, 169*, 1286–1296.

Friedman, M. I., & Stricker, E. M. (1976). The physiological psychology of hunger: A physiological perspective. *Psychological Review, 88*, 409–431.

Frijda, N. H. (1988). The laws of emotion. *American Psychologist, 43*, 349–358.

Frisch, R. E., & McArthur, J. W. (1974). Menstrual cycles: Fatness as a determinant of minimum weight for height necessary for their maintenance or onset. *Science, 185*, 949–951.

Fritsch, G., & Hitzig, E. (1870). Uber die elektrische Erregbarkeit des Grosshirns. *Archive Anatomie und Physiologie*, 300–322.

Fromkin, V., & Rodman, R. (1983). *An introduction to language* (3rd ed.). New York: Holt, Rinehart & Winston.

Furnas, J. C. (1965). *The life and times of the late demon rum*. New York: Capricorn Books.

G

Gagnon, J. H., & Simon, W. (1973). *Sexual conduct: The social origins of human sexuality*. Chicago: Aldine.

Galanter, E. (1962). Contemporary psychophysics. In R. Brown, E. Galanter, E. H. Hess, & G. Mandler (Eds.), *New directions in psychology*. New York: Holt, Rinehart, & Winston.

Galizio, M. (1979). Contingency-shaped and rule-governed behavior: Instructional control of human loss avoidance. *Journal of the Experimental Analysis of Behavior, 31*, 53–70.

Galizio, M., & Buskist, W. (1988). Laboratory lore and research practices in the experimental analysis of behavior: Selecting reinforcers and arranging contingencies. *The Behavior Analyst, 11*, 65–69.

Gallatin, J. (1980). Political thinking in adolescence. In J. Adelson (Ed.), *Handbook of adolescent psychology*. New York: Wiley.

Gallup Organization. (June, 1986). Cigarette smoking audit. *Gallup Report*, No. 249, 3.

Galton, F. (1870). *Hereditary genius: An inquiry into its laws and consequences*. New York: D. Appleton & Co.

Galton, F. (1909). *Essays in eugenics*. London: The Eugenics Education Society.

Garcia, J., & Koelling, R. (1966). Relation of cue to consequence in avoidance learning. *Psychonomic Science, 4*, 123–124.

Gardner, B. T., & Gardner, R. A. (1971). Two-way communication with an infant chimpanzee. In A. M. Schrier and F. Stollnitz (Eds.), *Behavior of nonhuman primates, Vol. 4*, 117–184. New York: Academic Press.

Gardner, H. (1983). *Frames of mind: The theory of multiple intelligences*. New York: Basic Books.

Gardner, R. A., & Gardner, B. T (1969). Teaching sign language to a chimpanzee. *Science, 165*, 664–672.

Gazzaniga, M. S. (1967). The split brain in man. *Scientific American, 156*, 24–29.

Geller, E. S. (May, 1985). Seat belt psychology. *Psychology Today, 19*, 12–13.

Gelman, R. (1969). Conservation acquisition: A problem of learning to attend to relevant attributes. *Journal of Experimental Child Psychology, 7*, 167–187.

Gelman, R., & Baillargeon, R. (1983). A review of Piagetian concepts. In J. H. Flavell & E. M. Markman (Eds.), *Handbook of child psychology. Vol. 3: Cognitive development*. New York: Wiley.

Gentry, W. D. (1970). Effects of frustration, attack, and prior aggressive training on overt aggression and vascular processes. *Journal of Personality and Social Psychology, 16*, 718–725.

Gerard, H. B., Connolley, E. S., & Wilhelmy, R. A. (1974). Compliance, justification, and cognitive change. In L. Berkowitz (Ed.), *Advances in experimental social psychology (Vol. 7)*. pp. 217–248. New York: Academic Press.

Gerbing, D. W., & Tuley, M. R. (in press). The 16PF related to the five-factor model of personality: Multiple-indicator measurement versus the a priori scales. *Multivariate Behavioral Research*.

Geschwind, N. (1979). Specializations of the human brain. *Scientific American, 241*, 180–199.

Gibson, E. J. (1969). *Principles of perceptual learning and development*. New York: Appleton-Century-Crofts.

Gibson, J. J. (1966). *The senses considered as perceptual systems*. Boston: Houghton-Mifflin.

Gillam, B. (1980). Geometrical illusions. *Scientific American, 242*, 102–111.

Gilligan, C. (1982). *In a different voice: Psychological theory and women's development*. Cambridge, MA: Harvard University Press.

Gluck, M. A., & Thompson, R. F. (1987). Modeling the neural substrates of associative learning and memory: A computational approach. *Psychological Review, 94*, 176–191.

Glucksberg, S. (1988). Language and thought. In R. J. Sternberg and E. Smith, *The psychology of human thought*. New York: Cambridge University Press.

Godden, D. R., & Baddeley, A. D. (1975). Context-dependent memory in two natural environments: On land and under water. *British Journal of Psychology, 66*, 325–331.

Goldstein, E. B. (1989). *Sensation and Perception* (3rd ed.). Belmont, CA: Wadsworth.

Goodall, J. (1971). *In the shadow of man*. Boston: Houghton Mifflin.

Goodwin, D. W., & Guze, S. B. (1984). *Psychiatric Diagnosis* (3rd Ed.). New York: Oxford University Press.

Gosney, E. S. (1930). *Collected papers on eugenic sterilization in California*. Pasadena, California: The Human Betterment Foundation.

Gottesman, I. I., & Shields, J. (1982). *Schizophrenia: The epigenetic puzzle*. Cambridge, MA: Cambridge University Press.

Gottfries, C. G. (1985). Alzheimer's disease and senile dementia: Biochemical characteristics and aspects of treatment. *Psychopharmacology, 86,*.

Gould, S. J. (1976). Biological potential versus biological determinism. *Natural History, 85*, 12–22.

Gould, S. J. (1977). *Ever since Darwin*. New York: Norton.

Gould, S. J. (1981). *The mismeasure of man*. New York: Norton.

Gould, S. J. (1982). *The Panda's thumb*. New York: Norton.

Gould, S. J. (1985). *The Flamingo's smile*. New York: Norton.

Gould, S. J., & Eldridge, N. (1977). Punctuated equilibria: The tempo and mode of evolution reconsidered. *Paleobiology, 3,* 115–151.

Gouldner, A. W. (1960). The notion of reciprocity: A preliminary statement. *American Sociological Review, 25,* 161–178.

Granneman, J., & Friedman, M. J. (1980). Hepatic modulation of insulin-induced gastric acid secretion and EMG activity in rats. *American Journal of Physiology, 238,* R346–R352.

Greaves, G. B. (1980). Multiple personality 165 years after Mary Reynolds. *Journal of Nervous and Mental Disease, 168,* 577–595.

Green, D. M. (1976). *Introduction to hearing.* New York: Academic Press.

Green, D. M., & Swets, J. A. (1966). *Signal detection theory and psychophysics.* New York: Wiley.

Gregory, R. L. (1978). *Eye and brain. The psychology of seeing.* (3rd ed.). New York: McGraw-Hill.

Greif, E. B., & Ulman, K. J. (1982). The psychological impact of menarche on early adolescent females. A review of the literature. *Child Development, 53,* 1413–1430.

Griffitt, W. (1981). Sexual intimacy in aging marital partners. In J. Marsh & S. Kiesler (Eds.), *Aging: Stability and change in the family.* New York: Academic Press.

Griffitt, W., & Hatfield, E. (1985). *Human sexual behavior.* Glenview, IL: Scott, Foresman & Co.

Grossman, H. J. (1983). *Manual of terminology and classification in mental retardation.* Washington, DC: American Association on Mental Deficiency.

Grossman, S. P. (1979). The biology of motivation. *Annual Review of Psychology, 30,* 209–242.

Grotevant, H. D., & Cooper, C. R. (1985). Patterns of interaction in family relationships and the development of identity exploration in adolescence. *Child Development, 56,* 415–428.

Groth, A. N., Burgess, A. W., & Holmstrom, L. (1977). Rape: Power, anger, and sexuality. *American Journal of Psychiatry, 134,* 1239–1243.

Grove, R., & Thompson, T. (1970). Effects of pentobarbital on performance maintained by an interlocking fixed-ratio fixed-interval reinforcement schedule. In T. Thompson, R. Pickens, & R. Meisch, (Eds.), *Readings in behavior pharmacology.* Englewood Cliffs, NJ: Prentice-Hall.

Groves, P. M., & Rebec, G. V. (1988). *Introduction to biological psychology.* Dubuque, IA: Brown.

Gulevich, G., Dement, W. C., & Johnson, L. (1966). Psychiatric and EEG observations on a case of prolonged wakefulness. *Archives of General Psychiatry, 15,* 29–35.

Gurman, A. S., & Kniskern, D. P. (1981). Preface. In A. S. Gurman & D. P. Kniskern (Eds.), *Handbook of Family Therapy.* New York: Brunner/Mazel.

Gustavson, C., Garcia, J., Hankins, W. M., & Rusinak, K. Coyote predation by aversive conditioning. *Science, 184,* 581–583.

H

Haber, R. N., & Standing, L. G. (1969). Direct measures of short-term visual storage. *Quarterly Journal of Experimental Psychology, 21,* 43–54.

Hafeiz, H. B. (1980). Hysterical conversion: A prognostic study. *British Journal of Psychiatry, 136,* 548–551.

Hagan, F. E. (1982). *Research methods in criminal justice and criminology.* NY: Macmillan.

Haith, M. (1980). *Rules newborns look by.* Hillsdale, NJ: Erlbaum.

Hake, D. F. (1982). The basic-applied continuum and the possible evolution of human operant social and verbal research. *The Behavior Analyst, 5,* 21–28.

Hall, C. S., & Lindzey, G. (1978). *Theories of personality,* (3rd ed.). New York: Wiley.

Hall, C. S., & Nordby, V. J. (1973). *A primer of Jungian psychology.* New York: New American Library.

Hallstrom, T. (1979). Sexuality of women in middle age: The Goteberg study. *Journal of Biosocial Sciences, 6,* 165–175.

Halpern, D. F. (1986). *Sex differences in cognitive abilities.* Hillsdale, NJ: Erlbaum

Hamilton, W. D. (1964). The genetical evolution of social behaviour: I & II. *Journal of Theoretical Biology, 7,* 1–52.

Hamilton, W. D. (1970). Selfish and spiteful behavior in an evolutionary model. *Nature, 228,* 1218–1220.

Hanson, J. W., Jones, K. L., & Smith, D. W. (1976). Fetal alcohol syndrome: Experience with 41 patients. *Journal of the American Medical Association, 235,* 1458–1466.

Hardin, G. (1968). The tragedy of the commons. *Science, 162,* 1243–1248.

Harlow, H. F. (1958). The nature of love. *American Psychologist, 13,* 673–685.

Harlow, H. F., & Harlow, M. K. (1962). Social deprivation in monkeys. *Scientific American, 207,* 136–146.

Harlow, H. F., & Suomi, S. J. (1970). The nature of love—simplified. *American Psychologist, 25,* 161–168.

Harrity, R., & Martin, R. G. (1962). *The three lives of Helen Keller.* Garden City, NY: Doubleday.

Hartup, W. W. (1979). The social worlds of children. *American Psychologist, 34,* 944–951.

Hasher, L., & Zacks, R. T. (1979). Automatic and effortful processes in memory. *Journal of Experimental Psychology: General, 108,* 356–388.

Hathaway, S. R., & McKinley, J. C. (1943). *MMPI manual.* New York: The Psychological Corp.

Hayes, C. (1952). *The ape in our house.* New York: Macmillan.

Hayes, S. C. (Ed.) (1989). Rule-governed behavior: Cognition, contingencies, and instructional control. New York: Plenum.

Heath, R. G., Martens, S., Leach, B. E., Cohen, M., & Angel, C. (1957). Effect on behavior in humans with administration of taraxin. *American Journal of Psychiatry, 114,* 14–24.

Heath, R. G., Martens, S., Leach, B. E., Cohen, M., & Feigley, C. A. (1959). Behavioral changes in nonpsychotic volunteers following administration of taraxin, the substance obtained from serum of schizophrenic patients. *American Journal of Psychiatry, 114,* 917–919.

Hebb, D. O. (1949). *The organization of behavior.* New York: Wiley.

Heider, E. R. (1972). Universals in color naming and memory. *Journal of Experimental Psychology, 93,* 10–20.

Heider, F. (1958). *The psychology of interpersonal relations.* New York: John Wiley & Sons.

Hendrickson, D. E. (1982). The biological basis of intelligence, Part II: Measurement. In H. J. Eysenck (Ed.), *A model for intelligence.* New York: Springer-Verlag Berlin Heidelberg, pp. 197–226.

Henning, H. (1916). *Der geruch.* Leipzig: Barth.

Herman, H. C., & Mack, D. (1975). Restrained and unrestrained eaters. *Journal of Personality, 43,* 647–660.

Herrnstein, R. J. (1973). *IQ in the meritocracy.* Boston: Little, Brown.

Herrnstein, R. J. (1989, May.) IQ testing and falling birth rates. *The Atlantic Monthly,* 73–79.

Hess, E. H. (1959). The relationship between imprinting and motivation. In M. R. Jones (Ed.), *Nebraska symposium on motivation* (pp. 4–77). Lincoln: University of Nebraska Press.

Heston, L. L. (1966). Psychiatric disorders in foster home reared children of schizophrenic mothers. *British Journal of Psychiatry, 143,* 148–152.

Hilgard, E. R. (1987). *Psychology in America: A historical survey.* San Diego: Harcourt Brace Jovanovich.

Hinde, R. A. (1984). Why do the sexes behave differently in close relationships? *Journal of Social and Personal Relationships, 1,* 471–501.

Hirsch, J., & Knittle, J. L. (1970). Cellularity of obese and nonobese human adipose tissue. *Federation of American Societies for Experimental Biology: Federation Proceedings, 29,* 1516–1521.

Hite, S. (1974). *Sexual honesty: For women by women.* New York: Warner Paperback Library.

Hite, S. (1976). *The Hite report*. New York: Macmillan.

Hite, S. (1981). *The Hite report on male sexuality*. New York: Alfred A. Knopf

Hochberg, J. (1971). Perception II: Space and movement. In J. W. Kling & L. A. Riggs (Eds.), *Woodworth and Schlosberg's experimental psychology* (3rd ed.). New York: Holt, Rinehart and Winston.

Hodgkinson, S., Sherrington, R., Gurling, H., Marchbancks, R., Reeders, S., Mallet, J., McInnis, M., Petursson, H., & Brynjolfsson. (1987). Molecular genetic evidence for heterogeneity in manic depression. *Nature, 325,* 805–806.

Hogrebe, M. C. (1987). Gender differences in mathematics. *American Psychologist, 42,* 265–266.

Hohmann, G. W. (1966). Some effect of spinal cord lesions on experienced emotional feelings. *Psychophysiology, 3,* 143–156.

Holden, C. (1987). Female math anxiety on the wane. *Science, 236,* 660–661.

Holmes, T. H., & Rahe, R. H. (1967). The social readjustment rating scale. *Journal of Psychosomatic Research, 11,* 213–218.

Holmstrom, L. L., & Burgess, A. W. (1980). Sexual behavior of assailants during reported rapes. *Archives of Sexual Behavior, 9,* 427–440.

Honigfeld, G., & Howard, A. (1978). Psychiatric Drugs: A desk reference (2nd ed.). New York: Academic Press.

Horland, C. I., & Weiss, W. (1951). The influence of source credibility on communication effectiveness. *Public Opinion Quarterly, 15,* 635–650.

Hormann, H. (1986). *Meaning and context: An introduction to psycholinguistics.* New York: Plenum.

Horn, J. L. (1970). Organization of data on life-span development of human abilities. In L. R. Goulet and P. B. Baltes (Eds.), *Life-span developmental psychology: Research and theory.* New York: Academic Press.

Horn, J. L. (1982). The aging of human abilities. In J. Wolman (Ed.), *Handbook of developmental psychology.* Englewood Cliffs, NJ: Prentice-Hall.

Horney, K. (1942). *Self-analysis.* New York: Norton.

Horney, K. (1945). *Our inner conflicts.* New York: Norton.

Horney, K. (1950). *Neurosis and human growth.* New York: Norton.

Horowitz, M. J. (1988). *Introduction to psychodynamics: A new synthesis.* New York: Basic Books.

Hovland, C. I. (1937). The generalization of conditioned responses: I. The sensory generalization of conditioned responses with varying frequencies of tone. *Journal of General Psychology, 17,* 125–148.

Hubel, D. H., & Weisel, T. N. (1959). Receptive fields of single neurons in the cat's striate cortex. *Journal of Physiology, 148,* 574–591.

Hubel, D. H., & Weisel, T. N. (1963). Receptive fields of cells in striate cortex of very young, visually inexperienced kittens. *Journal of Neurophysiology, 26,* 994–1002.

Hubel, D. H., & Weisel, T. N. (1968). Receptive fields and functional architecture of monkey striate cortex. *Journal of Physiology, 195,* 215–243.

Hull, C. L. (1943). *Principles of behavior.* New York: Appleton-Century-Crofts.

Hunt, E. (1982). *The universe within: A new science explores the human mind.* New York: Simon and Schuster.

Hunt, M. (1974). *Sexual behavior in the 1970s.* Chicago: Playboy.

Hurvich, L. M. (1981). *Color vision.* Sunderland, MA: Sinauer Associates.

Hurvich, L. M., & Jameson, D. (1957). An opponent-process theory of color vision. *Psychological Review, 64,* 384–404.

Hurvich, L. M., & Jameson, D. (1974). Opponent processes as a model of neural organization. *American Psychologist, 29,* 88–102.

Huxley, J. S. (1923). Courtship activities in the red-throated diver (*Colymbus stellatus*); together with a discussion of the evolution of courtship in birds. *Journal of the Linnaen Society of London, Zoology, 35,* 253–292.

Hyde, J. S. (1984). How large are gender differences in aggression? A developmental meta-analysis. *Developmental Psychology, 20,* 722–736.

Hyde, J. S. (1986). Gender differences in aggression. In J. S. Hyde & M. C. Linn (Eds.), The psychology of gender: Advances through meta-analyses. Baltimore: Johns Hopkins University Press.

Hyde, J. S. (1986). *Understanding human sexuality.* New York: McGraw-Hill.

Hyde, J. S., & Linn, M. C. (1988). Gender differences in verbal ability: A meta-analysis. *Psychological Bulletin, 104,* 53–69.

I

Imber, S. D., Glanz, L. M., Elkin, I., Sotsky, S. M., Boyer, J. L., & Weber, W. R. (1986). Ethical issues in psychotherapy research. *American Psychologist, 41,* 137–146.

Ineichen, B. (1979). The social geography of marriage. In M. Cook & G. Wilson (Eds.), *Love and attraction.* New York: Pergamon Press.

Inglefinger, F. J. (1944). The late effects of total and subtotal gastrectomy. *New England Journal of Medicine, 231,* 321–327.

Istomina, Z. M. (1975). The development of voluntary memory in preschool age children. *Soviet Psychology, 13,* 5–64.

Izard, C. E. (1971). *The face of emotion.* New York: Appleton-Century-Crofts.

Izard, C. E. (1977). *Human emotions.* New York: Plenum.

J

Jacobson, J. L., & Wille, D. E. (1986). The influence of attachment pattern on developmental changes in peer interaction from the toddler to the preschool period. *Child Development, 57,* 338–347.

Jaffe, J. H. (1985). Drug addiction and abuse. In A. G. GIlman, L. S. Goodman, T. W. Rall, & F. Murad (Eds.), *Goodman and Gilman's The Pharmacological Basis of Therapeutics.* New York: Macmillan.

James, W. (1890). *Principles of psychology* (Vols. 1–2). New York: Holt.

Janoff-Bulman, R. (1979). Characterological versus behavioral self-blame: Inquiries into depression and rape. *Journal of Personality and Social Psychology, 37,* 1798–1809.

Janowitz, H. D., & Grossman, M. I. (1950). Hunger and appetite: Some definitions and concepts. *Journal of the Mount Sinai Hospital, 16,* 231–240.

Jemmott, J. B., & Locke, S. E. (1984B). Psychosocial factors, immunologic mediation, and human susceptibility to infectious diseases: How much do we know? *Psychological Bulletin, 95,* 78–108.

Jenkins, J. G., & Dallenbach, K. M. (1924). Oblivescence during sleep and waking. *American Journal of Psychology, 35,* 605–612.

Jensen, A. R. (1969). How much can we boost IQ and scholastic achievement? *Harvard Educational Review, 39,* 1–123.

Jensen, A. R. (1973). *Educability and group differences.* New York: Harper & Row.

Jensen, A. R. (1982). Reaction time and Psychometric g. In H. J. Eysenck (Ed.), *A model for intelligence.* New York: Springer-Verlag Berlin Heidelberg, pp. 93–132.

Jensen, S. B. (1981). Diabetic sexual dysfunction. *Archives of Sexual Behavior, 10,* 493–504.

Johnson, D., & Drenick, E. J. (1977). Therapeutic fasting in morbid obesity: Long-term follow up. *Archives of Internal Medicine, 137,* 1381–1382.

Johnson, R. C., McClearn, G. E., Yuen, S., Nagoshi, C. T., Ahern, F. M., & Cole, R. E. (1985). Galton's data a century later. *American Psychologist, 40,* 875–892.

Johnston, J. M., & Pennypacker, H. S. (1980). *Strategies and tactics of human behavioral research.* Hillsdale, NJ: Erlbaum.

Jones, E. E., & Nisbett, R. E. (1972). The actor and the observer: Divergent perceptions of the causes of behavior. In E. E. Jones, D. E. Kanouse, H. H. Kelley, R. E. Nisbett, S. Valins, & B.

Weiner (Eds.), *Attribution: Perceiving the causes of behavior* (pp. 79–94). Morristown, NJ: General Learning Press.

Jordan, T. G., Grallo, R., Deutch, M., & Deutch, C. P. (1985). Long-term effects of enrichment: A 20-year perspective on persistence and change. *American Journal of Community Psychology, 13,* 393–414.

Joseph, J. G., Montgomery, S. B., Emmons, C. A., Kirscht, J. P., Kersler, R. C., Ostrow, D. G., Wartman, C. B., O'Brien, K., Eller, M., & Eshleman, S. (1987). Perceived risk of AIDS: Assessing the behavioral and psychosocial consequences in a cohort of gay men. *Journal of Applied Social Psychology, 17,* 231–250.

Julien, R. M. (1988). *A primer of drug action.* New York: Freeman.

Jung, C. G. (1928). *Contributions to analytical psychology.* New York: Harcourt, Brace.

K

Kalish, R. A. (1976). Death and dying in a social context. In R. H. Binstock and E. Shanas (Eds.), *Handbook of aging and the social sciences.* New York: Van Nostrand Reinhold.

Kamin, L. J. (1969). Predictability, surprise, attention, and conditioning. In B. A. Campbell & R. M. Church (Eds.), *Punishment and aversive behavior,* (pp. 279–296). New York: Appleton-Century-Crofts.

Kamin, L. J. (1981). Some historical facts about IQ testing. In H. J. Eysenck versus L. Kamin, *The intelligence controversy.* New York: Wiley.

Kandel, D. B. (1978). Similarity in real-life adolescent friendship pairs. *Journal of Personality and Social Psychology, 36,* 306–312.

Kandel, E. R., & Schwartz, J. H. (1982). Molecular biology of learning: Modulation of transmitter release. *Science, 218,* 433–443.

Kaplan, H. S. (1974). *The new sex therapy.* New York: Brunner/Mazel.

Kaplan, H. S. (1979). *Disorders of sexual desire.* New York: Simon & Schuster.

Kaplan, P. S. (1988). *The human odyssey: Life-span development.* New York: West.

Kastenbaum, R. (1981). *Death, society, and human experience* (2nd ed.). St. Louis: Mosby.

Kazdin, A. E. (1977). *The token economy: A review and evaluation.* New York: Plenum Press.

Kazdin, A. E. (1983). The token economy: A decade later. *Journal of Applied Behavior Analysis, 15,* 431–445.

Kazdin, A. E. (1988). *Behavior modification in applied settings* (4th ed.). Pacific Grove, CA: Brooks/Cole.

Kazdin, A. E., & Wilson, G. T. (1978). Criteria for evaluating psychotherapy. *Archives of General Psychiatry, 35,* 407–416.

Keesey, R. E., & Powley, T. L. (1986). Hypothalamic regulation of body weight. *American Scientist, 63,* 558–565.

Keesey, R. E., & Powley, T. L. (1986). The regulation of body weight. *Annual Review of Psychology, 37,* 109–133.

Keller, H. (1904). *The story of my life.* New York: Grosset & Dunlap.

Kelley, H. H. (1967). Attribution theory in social psychology. In D. Levine (Ed.), *Nebraska symposium on motivation* (Vol. 15). Lincoln, NE: University of Nebraska Press.

Kellog, W. N., & Kellog, L. A. (1933). *The ape and child: A study of environmental influence on early behavior.* New York: Whittlesey House.

Kenrick, D. T., & Funder, D. C. (1988). Profiting from controversy: Lessons from the person-situation debate. *American Psychologist, 43,* 23–34.

Kenshalo, D. R. (1971). Biophysics and psychophysics of feeling. In E. C. Carterette & M. P. Friedman (Eds.), *Handbook of perception* (Vol. 6B). New York: Academic Press.

Kevles, D. J. (1985). *In the name of eugenics: Genetics and the uses of human heredity.* New York: Alfred A. Knopf.

Keyes, D. (1981). *The minds of Billy Milligan.* New York: Bantam.

Kinsey, A., Pomeroy, W. B., & Martin, C. E. (1948). *Sexual behavior in the human male.* Philadelphia: Saunders.

Kinsey, A. C., Pomeroy, C. E., Martin, C. E., & Gebhard, P. H. (1953). *Sexual behavior in the human female.* Philadelphia: W. B. Saunders.

Klein, D. F., & Rabkin, J. G. (1981). *Anxiety: New research and changing concepts.* New York: Raven Press.

Klerman, G. L., & Weissman, M. M. (1986). The interpersonal approach to understanding depression. In T. Millon & G. L. Klerman (Eds.), *Contemporary directions in psychopathology: Toward the DMS-IV.* New York: Guilford Press.

Kline, D., & Schieber, F. (1985). Vision and aging. In J. E. Birren, & K. W. Schaie (Eds.), *Handbook of the psychology of aging.* New York: Van Nostrand Reinhold.

Kling, A. (1972). Effects of amygdalectomy on social-affective behavior of non-human primates. In B. E. Eleftheriou (Ed.), *The neurobiology of the amygdala.* New York: Plenum.

Klug, W. S., & Cummings, M. R. (1986). *Concepts of Genetics* (2nd ed.). Glenview, IL: Scott, Foresman and Company.

Kluver, H. & Bucy, P. C. (1937). "Psychic blindness" and other symptoms following bilateral lobectomy in rhesus monkeys. *American Journal of Physiology, 119,* 352–353.

Kohlberg, L. (1966). A cognitive-developmental analysis of children's sex-role concepts and attitudes. In E. E. Maccoby (Ed.), *The development of sex differences.* Stanford, CA: Stanford University Press.

Kohlberg, L. (1981). *The philosophy of moral development: Essays on moral development* (Vol. 1). San Francisco: Harper & Row.

Kohlberg, L. (1984). *The philosophy of moral development: Essays on moral development* (Vol. 2). San Francisco: Harper & Row.

Kohler, W. (1925). *The mentality of apes.* London: Routledge & Kegan-Paul.

Kolata, G. (1985). Obesity declared a disease. *Science, 227,* 1019–1020.

Kolb, L. C., & Brody, H. K. (1982). *Modern clinical psychology.* Philadelphia: Saunders.

Kolodny, R. C., Masters, W. H., Hendry, B. F., & Toro, G. (1971). Plasma testosterone and semen analysis in male homosexuals. *New England Journal of Medicine, 285,* 1170–1174.

Koss, M. P., Leonard, K. E., Beezley, D. A., & Oros, C. J. (1985). Nonstranger sexual aggression: A discriminant analysis of the psychological characteristics of undetected offenders. *Sex roles, 12,* 981–992.

Koss, M. P., & Oros, C. J. (1983). Sexual experiences survey: A research instrument investigating sexual aggression and victimization. *Journal of Consulting and Clinical Psychology, 50,* 455–457.

Koulack, D., & Goodenough, D. R. (1976). Dream recall and dream recall failure: An arousal-retrieval model. *Psychological Bulletin, 83,* 975–984.

Krebs, R. L., & Kohlberg, L. (1973). *Moral judgment and ego controls as determinants of resistance to cheating.* Unpublished manuscript, Center for Moral Education, Harvard University, Cambridge University.

Kübler-Ross, E. (1969). *On death and dying.* New York: Macmillan.

Kübler-Ross, E. (1981). *Living with death and dying.* New York: Macmillan.

Kuhn, T. S. (1962). *The structure of scientific revolutions.* Chicago: University of Chicago Press.

Kunst-Wilson, W. R., & Zajonc, R. B. (1980). Affective discrimination of stimuli that cannot be recognized. *Science, 207,* 557–558.

Kurdek, L. A. (1987). Sex role self-schema and psychological adjustment in coupled homosexual and heterosexual men and women. *Sex Roles, 17,* 549–562.

Kurdek, L. A. (1988). Correlates of negative attitudes toward homosexuals in heterosexual college students. *Sex Roles, 18,* 727–738.

Kurdek, L. A. (1988). Relationship quality of gay and lesbian cohabiting couples. *Journal of Homosexuality, 15,* 93–118.

Kurdek, L. A., & Schmitt, J. P. (1986). Interaction of sex-role self-concept with relationship quality and relationship beliefs in married, heterosexual cohabiting, gay, and lesbian couples. *Journal of Personality and Social Psychology, 51,* 365–370.

L

Lachman, R., Lachman, J. L., & Butterfield, E. C. (1979). *Cognitive psychology and information processing: An introduction.* Hillsdale, NJ: Erlbaum.

Lagerspetz, K. (1979). Modification of aggressiveness in mice. In S. Feshbach & A. Fraczek (Eds.), *Aggression and behavior change: Biological and social processes.* New York: Praeger.

Lally, M., & Nettlebeck, T. (1977). Intelligence, reaction time and inspection time. *American Journal of Mental Deficiency, 82,* 271–281.

Lamb, M. E. (1979). Paternal influences and the father's role: A personal perspective. *American Psychologist, 34,* 938–943.

Lamb, M. E. (1987). Predictive implications of individual differences in attachment. *Journal of Clinical and Consulting Psychology, 55,* 817–824.

Lamb, M. E., Thompson, R. A., Gardner, W. P., Charnov, E. L., & Estes, D. (1984). Security of infantile attachment as assessed in the "strange situation": Its study and biological interpretation. *Behavioral and Brain Sciences, 7,* 127–171.

LaPiere, R. T. (1934). Attitudes versus actions. *Social Forces, 13,* 230–237.

Lashley, K. S. (1950). In search of the engram. *Society for Experimental Biology Symposium, 4,* 454–482.

Latané, B., & Darley, J. M. (1968). Group inhibition of bystander intervention in emergencies. *Journal of Personality and Social Psychology, 10,* 215–221.

Latané, B., & Darley, J. M. (1970). *The unresponsive bystander: Why doesn't he help?* New York: Appleton-Century-Crofts.

Lauer, R. H. (1989). *Social problems and the quality of life.* Dubuque, IA: Wm. C. Brown.

Lawless, H. T., & Engen, T. (1977). Association to odors: Interference, memories, and verbal labeling. *Journal of Experimental Psychology, 3,* 52–59.

Lazarus, A. A. (1971). *Behavior therapy and beyond.* New York: McGraw-Hill.

Lazarus, R. S. (1982). Thoughts on the relations between emotion and cognition. *American Psychologist, 37,* 1019–1024.

Lazarus, R. S. (1984). On the primacy of cognition. *American Psychologist, 39,* 124–129.

Lazarus, R. S., & Folkman, S. (1984). *Stress, appraisal, and coping.* New York: Springer.

LeBoeuf, B. J. (1974). Male–male competition and reproductive success in elephant seals. *American Zoologist, 14,* 163–176.

Lefcourt, H. (1976). *Locus of control: Current trends in theory and research.* Hillsdale, NJ: Erlbaum.

Leff, M. J., Roatch, J. F., & Bunney, V. E. Jr. (1970). Environmental factors preceding the onset of severe depressions. *Psychiatry, 33, (3),* 298–311.

Lemere, F., & Voegtlin, W. L. (1950). An evaluation of the aversion treatment of alcoholism. *Quarterly Journal of Studies on Alcohol, 11,* 199–204.

Lepper, M. R., & Greene, D. (Eds.). (1978). *The hidden costs of reward.* Hillsdale, NJ: Erlbaum.

Lepper, M. R., Greene, D., & Nisbett, R. E. (1973). Undermining children's intrinsic interest with extrinsic rewards: A test of the overjustification hypothesis. *Journal of Personality and Social Psychology, 28,* 129–137.

Lerner, M. J. (1966, September). *The unjust consequences of the need to believe in a just world.* Paper presented at the meeting of the American Psychological Association.

Lerner, M. J., & Matthews, G. (1967). Reactions to suffering of others under conditions of indirect responsibility. *Journal of Personality and Social Psychology, 5,* 319–325.

Lesgold, A. (1988). Problem solving. In R. J. Sternberg and E. E. Smith, *The psychology of human thought.* New York: Cambridge University Press.

Levinson, D. J. (1978). *The seasons of a man's life.* New York: Ballantine.

Lewin, R. (1984). *Human Evolution.* New York: Freeman.

Lewinsohn, P. M., Mischel, W., Chaplin, W., & Barton, R. (1980). Social competence and depression: The role of illusory self-perceptions. *Journal of Abnormal Psychology, 89,* 194–202.

Lewis, M., & Brooks-Gunn, J. (1972). The reactions of infants to people in J. Belsky (Ed.), *In the beginning* (pp. 167–177). New York: Columbia University Press.

Lewontin, R. C. (1976). Race and intelligence. In N. J. Block & G. Dworkin (Eds.), *The IQ controversy.* New York: Pantheon.

Leyens, J. P., Camino, L., Parke, R. D., & Berkowitz, L. (1975). The effects of movie violence on aggression in a field setting as a function of group dominance and cohesion. *Journal of Personality and Social Psychology, 32,* 346–360.

Liberman, R. P., Teigen, J., Patterson, R., & Baker, V. (1973). Reducing delusional speech in chronic, paranoid schizophrenics. *Journal of Applied Behavior Analysis, 6,* 57–64.

Lickey, M. E., & Gordon, B. (1983). *Drugs for mental illness.* New York: W. H. Freeman.

Lidz, T., Fleck, S., & Cornelison, A. R. (1965). *Schizophrenia and the family.* New York: International Universities Press.

Liebert, R. M., & Baron, R. A. (1972). Some immediate effects of televised violence on children's behavior. *Developmental Psychology, 6,* 469–475.

Liebert, R. M., & Poulos, R. W. (1975). Television and personality development. The socializing effects of the entertainment medium in A. Davids (Ed.), *Child personality and psychopathology: Current topics. Vol. 2.* New York: Wiley.

Liebert, R. M., & Sprafkin, J. (1988). *The early window: Effects of television on children and youth.* New York: Pergamon Press.

Lindemalm, G., Korlin, D., & Uddenberg, N. Long-term follow-up of "sex change" in 13 male-to-female transsexuals. *Archives of Sexual Behavior, 15,* 187–210.

Lindsay, P. N., & Norman, D. A. (1977). *Human information processing.* New York: Academic Press.

Lindsley, O. R. (1956). Operant conditioning methods applied to research in chronic schizophrenia. *Psychiatric Research Reports, 24,* 289–291.

Lipsitt, L. P., & Kaye, H. (1964). Conditioned sucking in the newborn. *Psychonomic Science, 1,* 29–30.

Locke, B. Z., & Regier, D. A. (1985). Prevalence of selected mental disorders. *Mental Health, United States, 1985.* Washington, DC: U.S. Government Printing Office, 1–6.

Loeb, G. E. (1985). The functional replacement of the ear. *Scientific American, 252,* 104–111.

Loehlin, J. C., Lindzey, G., & Spuhler, J. N. (1975). *Race difference in intelligence.* San Francisco: Freeman.

Loftus, E. F., & Loftus, G. R. (1980). On the permanence of stored information in the human brain. *American Psychologist, 35,* 409–420.

Loftus, E. F., Miller, D. G., & Burns, H. J. (1978). Semantic integration of verbal information into visual memory. *Journal of Experimental Psychology: Human Learning and Memory, 4,* 19–31.

Loftus, E. F., & Palmer, J. C. (1973). Reconstruction of automobile destruction. An example of the interaction between language and memory. *Journal of Verbal Learning and Verbal Behavior, 13,* 585, 589.

Londerville, S., & Main, M. (1981). Security, compliance, and maternal training methods in the second year of life. *Developmental Psychology, 17,* 289–299.

Lorenz, K. (1966). *On aggression.* London: Methuen.

Lorenz, K., & Tinbergen, N. (1938). Taxis und instinkthandlung in der eirollbewegung der graugans I. *Zeitschrift fur Tierpsychologie, 2,* 1–29.

Lorenz, K. Z. (1952). *King Solomon's ring.* New York: T. Y. Crowell.

Lorenz, K. Z. (1970). Companions as factors in the bird's environment. In K. Z. Lorenz (Ed.), *Studies on animal and human behavior.* Cambridge, MA: Harvard University Press.

Lovaas, O. I. (1987). Behavioral treatment and normal educational/intellectual functioning in young autistic children. *Journal of Consulting and Clinical Psychology, 55,* 3–9.

Lovaas, O. I., Koegel, R., Simmons, J. Q., & Long, J. S. (1973). Some generalization and follow-up measures on autistic children in behavior therapy. *Journal of Applied Behavior Analysis, 6,* 131–166.

Lovaas, O. I., & Simmons, J. Q. (1969). Manipulation of self-destruction in three retarded children. *Journal of Applied Behavior Analysis, 2,* 143–157.

Lowe, C. F. (1979). Determinants of human operant behavior. In M. D. Zeiler & P. Harzem (Eds.), *Advances in the analysis of* behavior: Vol. 1: Reinforcement and the organization of behaviour (pp. 159–192). Chichester, England: Wiley.

Lowe, C. F., Beasty, A., & Bentall, R. P. (1983). The role of verbal behavior in human learning: Infant performance on fixed-interval schedules. *Journal of the Experimental Analysis of Behavior, 39,* 157–164.

Luce, G. G. (1971). *Body time.* New York: Random House.

Lutkenhaus, P., Grossmann, K. E., & Grosmann, K. (1985). Infant-mother attachment at twelve months and style of interaction with a stranger at the age of three years. *Child Development, 56,* 1538–1542.

Lykken, D. T. (1957). A study of anxiety in the sociopathic personality. *Journal of Abnormal and Social Psychology, 55,* 6–10.

Lykken, D. T. (1979). The detection of deception. *Psychological Bulletin, 86,* 47–53.

Lynch, G., & Baudry, M. (1984). The biochemistry of memory: A new and specific hypothesis. *Science, 224,* 1057–1063.

M

Maccoby, E. E. (1980). *Social development: Psychological growth and the parent-child relationship.* New York: Harcourt Brace Jovanovich.

Maccoby, E. E., & Jacklin, C. N. (1974). *The psychology of sex differences.* Stanford, CA: Stanford University Press.

Maccoby, E. E., & Martin, J. A. (1983). Socialization in the context of the family: Parent-child interaction. In P. H. Mussen (Ed.), *Handbook of child development* (4th ed.), (pp. 1–103). New York: Wiley.

MacIntosh, N. J. (1986). The biology of intelligence? *British Journal, 77,* 1–18.

Malamuth, N. M. (1984). Aggression against women: Cultural and indivdual causes. In N. M. Malamuth & E. Donnerstein (Eds.), *Pornography and sexual aggression.* Orlando: Academic Press.

Malamuth, N. M., & Check, J. V. P. (1981). The effects of mass media exposure on acceptance of violence against women: A field experiment. *Journal of Research in Personality, 15,* 436–446.

Malatesta, V. J., Chambless, D. L., Pollack, M., & Cantor, A. (1988). Widowhood, sexuality, and aging: A life span analysis. *Journal of Sex and Marital Therapy, 14,* 49–62.

Malt, B. C., & Smith, E. E. (1984). Correlated properties in natural categories. *Journals of Verbal Learning and Verbal Behavior, 23,* 250–269.

Malthus, T. (1798). *An essay on the principle of population as it affects the future improvement of society, with remarks on the speculations of Mr. Goodwin, M. Condorcet, and other writers.*

Marcia, J. E. (1967). Ego identity crisis: Relationship to change in self-esteem, "general maladjustment," and authoritarianism. *Journal of Personality, 25,* 118–133.

Marcia, J. E. (1980). Identity in adolescence. In J. Adelson (Ed.), *Handbook of adolescent psychology.* New York: Wiley.

Mark, V. H., & Ervin, F. R. (1970). *Violence and the brain.* New York: Harper and Row.

Markus, H. (1977). Self-schemata and processing information about the self. *Journal of Personality and Social Psychology, 35,* 63–78.

Marmor, J. (1976). Frigidity, dyspareunia, and vaginismus. In B. J. Sadock, et al. (Eds.), *The sexual experience.* Baltimore: Williams & Wilkins.

Marshack, A. (1976). Some implications of the Paleolithic symbolic evidence for the origin of language. *Current Anthropology, 17,* 274–282.

Marshall, D. S. (1972). Sexual behavior on Mangaia. In D. S. Marshall & R. C. Suggs (Eds.), *Human sexual behavior: Variations in the ethnographic spectrum.* Englewood Cliffs, NJ: Prentice-Hall.

Marshall, G. D., & Zimbardo, P. G. (1979). Affective consequences of inadequately explained physiological arousal. *Journal of Personality and Social Psychology, 37,* 970–988.

Marshark, M., Richman, C. L., Yuille, J. C., & Hunt, R. R. (1987). The role of imagery in memory: On shared and distinctive information. *Psychological Bulletin, 102,* 28–41.

Martin, B. A. (1986). Electroconvulsive therapy: Contemporary standards of practice. *Canadian Journal of Psychiatry, 31,* 759–771.

Maslow, A. H. (1943). A theory of human motivation. *Psychological Review, 50,* 370–396.

Maslow, A. H. (1964). *Religions, values, and peak-experiences.* New York: Viking Press, Inc.

Maslow, A. H. (1970). *Motivation and personality.* (2nd ed.). New York: Harper and Row.

Masters, W. H., & Johnson, V. (1966). *Human sexual response.* Boston: Little, Brown.

Masters, W. H., & Johnson, V. (1970). *Human sexual inadequacy.* Boston: Little, Brown.

Masters, W. H., & Johnson, V. (1979). *Homosexuality in perspective.* Boston: Little, Brown.

Masters, W. H., & Johnson, V. E., & Kolodny, R. C. (1988). *Human sexuality.* Glenview, IL: Scott, Foresman.

Matlin, M. W. (1983). *Perception.* Newton, MA: Allyn & Bacon.

Matthews, B. A., Catania, A. C., & Shimoff, E. (1985). Effects of uninstructed verbal behavior on nonverbal responding: Contingency descriptions versus performance descriptions. *Journal of the Experimental Analysis of Behavior, 43,* 155–164.

Mayer, D. M., Price, D. D., & Rafii, A. (1977). Antagonism of acupuncture analgesia in man by the narcotic antagonist nalaxone. *Brain Research, 121,* 368–372.

Mayer, J. (1955). Regulation of energy intake and body weight: The glucostatic theory and the lipostatic hypothesis. *Annals of the New York Academy of Sciences, 63,* 15–43.

Maynard Smith, J. (1964). Group selection and kin selection. *Nature, 210,* 1145–1147.

Mayr, E. (1974). Behavior programs and evolutionary strategies. *American Scientist,* 650–659.

Mayr, E. (1978). Evolution. *Scientific American, 239,* 46–55.

Mazur, J. E. (1986). *Learning and behavior,* Englewood Cliffs, NJ: Prentice-Hall.

McAlister, A., Perry, C., Killen, L. A., Slinkard, L. A., & Maccoby, N. (1980). Pilot study of smoking, alcohol, and drug abuse prevention. *American Journal of Public Health, 70,* 719–721.

McArthur, L. A. (1972). The how and what of why: Some determinants and consequences of causal attribution. *Journal of Personality and Social Psychology, 22,* 171–193.

McBurney, D. H. (1978). Psychological dimensions and perceptual analyses of taste. In E. C. Carterette & M. P. Friedman (Eds.), *Handbook of perception* (Vol. 6a. pp. 125–155). New York: Academic Press.

McCann, I. L., & Holmes, D. S. (1984). Influence of aerobic exercise on depression. *Journal of Personality and Social Psychology, 46,* 1142–1147.

McCary, J. L. (1978). *McCary's human sexuality* (3rd ed.). New York: Van Nostrand.

McClelland, D. C. (1985). *Human motivation.* Glenview, IL: Scott, Foresman.

McClelland, D. C., Atkinson, J. W., Clark, R. A., & Lowell, E. L. (1976). *The achievement motive* (2nd ed.). New York: Irvington.

McCrae, R. R., & Costa, P. T. (1985). Updating Norman's "adequate taxonomy": Intelligence and personality dimensions in natural language and in questionnaires. *Journal of Personality and Social Psychology, 49,* 710–721.

McCrae, R. R., & Costa, P. T. (1987). Validation of the five-factor model of personality across instruments and observers. *Journal of Personality and Social Psychology, 52,* 81–90.

McDougall, W. (1908). *An introduction to social psychology.* London: Methuen.

McDougall, W. (1908). *Social psychology.* New York: Putnam.

McGee, E. A. (1982). *Too little, too late: Services for teenage parents.* New York: Ford Foundation.

McIntire, K. D., Cleary, J., & Thompson, T. (1987). Conditioned relations by monkeys: Reflexivity, symmetry, and transivity. *Journal of the Experimental Analysis of Behavior, 47,* 279–285.

McIntire, K. D., Cleary, J., & Thompson, T. Reply to Saunders and Hayes. *Journal of the Experimental Analysis of Behavior, 51,* 393–396.

Meichenbaum, D. (1977). *Cognitive behavior modification: An integrative approach.* New York: Plenum Press.

Meiselman, H. L., & Dzendolet, E. (1967). Variability in gustatory quality identification. *Perception & Psychophysics, 2,* 496–498.

Meltzoff, A. N., & Moore, M. K. (1983). Newborn infants imitate adult facial gestures. *Child Development, 54,* 702–709.

Melzack, R. (1973). *The puzzle of pain.* New York: Basic Books.

Melzack, R., & Wall, P. D. (1962). On the nature of cutaneous sensory mechanisms. *Brain, 85,* 331–352.

Melzack, R., & Wall, P. D. (1965). Pain mechanisms: A new theory. *Science, 150,* 971–979.

Merikle, P. M. (1980). Selection from visual persistence by perceptual groups and category membership. *Journal of Experimental Psychology: General, 109,* 279–295.

Messenger, J. C. (1972). Sex and repression in the Irish folk community. In D. S. Marshall & R. C. Suggs (Eds.), *Human sexual behavior: Variations in the ethnocentric spectrum.* Englewood Cliffs, NJ: Prentice-Hall.

Meyer, R. G., & Osborne, Y. V. (1982). *Case studies in abnormal behavior.* Boston: Allyn and Bacon.

Meyer-Bahlburg, H. F. L. (1980). Homosexual orientation in men and women: A hormonal basis? In J. E. Parsons (Ed.), *The psychobiology of sex differences and sex roles.* New York: McGraw-Hill.

Michaels, J. W., Blommel, J. M., Brocato, R. M., Linkous, R. A., & Rowex, J. S. (1982). Social facilitation and inhibition in a natural setting. *Replications in Social Psychology, 2,* 21–24.

Milgram, S. (1974). *Obedience to authority: An experimental view.* New York: Harper & Row.

Miller, G. A. (1956). The magical number seven, plus or minus two: Some limits on our capacity for processing information. *Psychological Review, 63,* 81–97.

Miller, G. A., Galanter, E., & Pribram, K. (1960). *Plans and the structure of behavior.* New York: Holt, Rinehart, and Winston.

Milner, B. (1966). Amnesia following operation on the temporal lobes. In C. W. M. Whitty & O. L. Zangwill (Eds.), *Amnesia.* London: Butterworths, 109–133.

Milner, B. (1970). Memory and medial temporal regions of the brain. In K. H. Pribram & D. E. Broadbent (Eds.), *Biology of memory.* Orlando, FL: Academic Press, 29–50.

Mischel, W. (1968). *Personality and assessment.* New York: Wiley.

Mischel, W. (1984). Convergences and challenges in the search for consistency. *American Psychologist, 39,* 351–364.

Mishkin, M., & Appenzeller, J. H. (1987). The anatomy of memory. *Scientific American, 256,* 80–89.

Mitchell, P. B. (1988). The pharmacological management of bulima nervosa: A critical review. *International Journal of Eating Disorders, 7,* 29–41.

Money, J. (1985). *The destroying angel.* Buffalo, NY: Prometheus Books.

Money, J., & Erhardt, A. A. (1972). *Man and woman, boy and girl: Differentiation and dimorphism of gender identity.* Baltimore: Johns Hopkins Press.

Montagu, A. (Ed.). (1980). *Sociobiology examined.* New York: Oxford University Press.

Moore, H. T. (1922). Further data concerning sex differences. *Journal of Abnormal and Social Psychology, 17,* 210–214.

Moore, T. E. (1985). Subliminal delusion. *Psychology Today,* 10–11.

Moray, N. (1959). Attention in dichotic listening: Affective cues and the influence of instructions. *Quarterly Journal of Experimental Psychology, 12,* 214–220.

Morrison, D. M. (1985). Adolescent contraceptive behavior: A review. *Psychological Review, 98,* 538–568.

Mozel, M. M., Smith, B., Smith, P., Sullivan, R., & Swender, P. (1969). Nasal chemoreceptors in flavor identification. *Archives of Otolaryngology, 90,* 367–393.

Murray, E. J., & Foote, F. (1979). The origins of fear of snakes. *Behavior Research and Therapy, 17,* 489–493.

Murray, H. A. (1938). *Explorations in personality.* New York: Oxford.

Mussen, P. H., & Eisenberg-Berg, N. (1977). *The roots of caring.* New York: Freeman.

Myers, R. E., & Sperry, R. W. (1958). Interhemispheric communication through the corpus callosum: Mnemonic carryover between hemispheres. *Archives of Neurology and Psychiatry, 80,* 298–303.

Mynatt, C. R., Doherty, M. E., & Tweney, R. D. (1978). Consequences of confirmation and disconfirmation in a simulated research environment. *Quarterly Journal of Experimental Psychology, 30,* 395–406.

N

Neisser, U. (1967). *Cognitive psychology.* New York: Appleton-Century-Crofts.

Neisser, U. (1976). *Cognition and reality.* New York: Appleton.

Neisser, U. (1979). The control of information pickup in selective looking. In A. D. Pick (Ed.), *Perception and its development: A tribute to Eleanor J. Gibson.* Hillsdale, NJ: Lawrence Erlbaum Associates.

Neisser, U., & Becklen, R. (1975). Selective looking: Attending to visually significant events. *Cognitive Psychology, 7,* 480–494.

Neisworth, J. T., & Madle, R. A. (1982). Retardation. In A. S. Bellack, M. Hersen, & A. E. Kazdin (Eds.), *International Handbook of Behavior Modification and Therapy.* New York: Plenum Press.

Nelson, D. A., & McEvoy, C. L. (1979). Encoding context and set size. *Journal of Experimental Psychology: Human Learning and Memory, 5,* 292–314.

Neugarten, B. L. (1974). The roles we play. In American Medical Association, *Quality of life: The middle years.* Acton, MA: Publishing Sciences Group.

Newell, A., Shaw, J. C., & Simon, H. A. (1958). Elements of a theory of human problem solving. *Psychological Review, 65,* 151–166.

Newell, A., & Simon, H. A. (1972). *Human problem solving.* Englewood Cliffs, NJ: Prentice-Hall.

Nisbett, R. E. (1968). Taste, deprivation, and weight determination of eating behavior. *Journal of Personality and Social Psychology, 10,* 107–116.

Nisbett, R. E. (1972). Eating behavior and obesity in man and animals. *Advances in Psychosomatic Medicine, 7,* 173–193.

North, C. N. (1987). *Welcome, silence.* New York: Simon & Schuster.

O

O'Brien, R., & Chafetz, M. (1982). *The encyclopedia of alcoholism.* New York: Facts on File Publications.

Offord, D. R., Boyle, M. H., Szatmari, P., Rae-Grant, N. I., Links, P. S., Cadman, D. T., Byles, J. A., Crawford, J. W., Blum, H. M., Byrne, C., Thomas, H., & Woodward, C. A. (1987). Ontario child health study. *Archives of General Psychiatry, 44,* 832–836.

Olds, J. M. (1958). Self-stimulation experiments and differentiated reward systems. In H. H. Jasper, L. D. Proctor, R. S. Knighton, W. C. Noshay, & R. T. Costello (Eds.), *Reticular formation of the brain.* Boston: Little, Brown.

Olds, J. M., & Milner, P. M. (1954). Positive Reinforcement produced by electrical stimulation of the septal area and other areas of the brain. *Journal of Comparative and Physiological Psychology, 47,* 419–427.

Olds, M. E., & Forbes, J. L. (1981). The central basis of motivation: Intracranial self-stimulation studies. *Annual Review of Psychology, 32,* 523–574.

Ollendick, T. H., & Francis, G. (1988). Behavioral assessment and treatment of childhood phobias. *Behavior modification, 12,* 165–204.

Oller, D. K., Wieman, L. A., Doyle, W. J., & Ross, C. (1976). Infant babbling and speech. *Journal of Child Language, 3*, 1–11.

Orvis, B. R., Kelley, H. H., & Butler, D. (1976). Attributional conflict in young couples. In J. H. Harvey, W. J. Ickes, & R. F. Kidd (Eds.), *New directions in attribution research*, (Vol. 1, pp. 353–386). Hillsdale, NJ: Erlbaum.

Overholser, W. (1956). Has *chlorpromazine* inaugurated a new era in mental hospitals? *Journal of Clinical Experimental Psychopathology, 17*, 197–201.

P

Paffenbarger, R. S., Jr., Hyde, J. T., Wing, A. L., & Hsieh, C. C. (1986). Physical activity, all-cause mortality, and longevity of college alumni. *New England Journal of Medicine, 314*, 605–612.

Paivio, A. (1969). Mental imagery in associative learning and memory. *Psychological Review, 76*, 241–263.

Paivio, A. (1986). *Mental representations: A dual coding approach*. New York: Oxford University Press.

Palmer, F. H., & Anderson, L. W. (1979). Long term gains from early intervention: Findings from longitudinal studies. In E. Zigler & J. Valentine (Eds.), *Project Head Start: A legacy on the war on poverty*. New York: Free Press.

Parke, R. D., & Tinsley, B. R. (1981). The father's role in infancy: Determinants of involvement in caregiving and play. In M. E. Lamb (Ed.), *The role of father in child development.* (2nd ed.) New York: Wiley.

Pastor, D. L. (1981). The quality of the mother-infant attachment and its relationship to toddler's initial sociability with peers. *Developmental Psychology, 17*, 326–335.

Patterson, F., & Linden, E. (1981). *The education of Koko.* New York: Holt, Rinehart and Winston.

Pavlov, I. P. (1927). *Conditioned reflexes.* Oxford, England: Oxford University Press.

Penfield, W. (1975). *The mystery of the mind.* Princeton: Princeton University Press.

Perlmutter, M., & Hall, E. (1985). *Adult development and aging.* New York: Wiley.

Perls, F. S. (1967). Group vs. individual therapy. *ETC: A review of general semantics, 34*, 306–312.

Perls, F. S. (1969). *Gestalt therapy verbatim.* Lafayette, CA: Real People Press.

Peskin, J. (1982). Measuring household production for GNP. *Family Economics Review, 3*, 16–25.

Peters, R. K., Cady, L. D., Jr., Bischoff, D. P., Bernstein, L., & Pile, M. C. (1983). Physical fitness and subsequent myocardial infarction in healthy workers. *Journal of the American Medical Association, 249*, 3052–3056.

Peterson, L. (1983). Role of donor competence, donor age, and peer presence on helping in an emergency. *Developmental Psychology, 19*, 873–880.

Peterson, L. R., & Peterson, M. J. (1959). Short-term retention of individual verbal items. *Journal of Experimental Psychology, 58*, 193–198.

Petty, R. E., & Cacioppo, J. T. (1986). The elaboration likelihood model of persuasion. In L. Berkowitz (Ed.), *Advances in Experimental Social Psychology, 19*, 123–205.

Pfaffman, C. (1955). Gustatory nerve impulses in rat, cat, and rabbit. *Journal of Neurophysiology, 18*, 429–440.

Pfohl, B., & Andreasen, N. C. (1986). Schizophrenia: Diagnosis and classification. In A. J. Frances & R. E. Hales (Eds.), *Psychiatry update: Annual Review* (Vol. 5). Washington, DC: American Psychiatric Association.

Phares, E. J. (1984). *Introduction to personality.* Columbus, OH: Merrill.

Piaget, J. (1952). *The origins of intelligence in children.* New York: International Universities Press.

Piaget, J. (1972). Intellectual evolution from adolescence to adulthood. *Human Development, 15*, 1–12.

Piaget, J., & Inhelder, B. (1969). *The child's concept of space.* New York: Basic Books.

Pinkston, E. M., Reese, N. M., LeBlanc, J. M., & Baer, D. M. (1973). Independent control of a preschool child's ag-

gression and peer interaction by contingent teacher attention. *Journal of Applied Behavior Analysis, 6*, 115–124.

Platt, S. A., & Sanislow, C. A. (1988). Norm-of-reaction: Definition and misinterpretation of animal research. *Journal of Comparative Psychology, 102*, 254–261.

Pleck, J. H. (1987). The contemporary man. In M. Scher (Ed.), *Handbook of counseling and psychology with men.* Beverly Hills: Sage.

Pleck, J. H., & Staines, G. L. (1982). Work schedules and work-family conflict in two earner couples. In J. Aldous (Ed.), *Two paychecks: Life in dual-earner families.* Beverly Hills, CA: Sage.

Plomin, R. *Nature, nurture, and human development.* Paper presented at a Science and Public Policy Seminar, March 27, 1987, Federation of Behavioral, Psychological, and Cognitive Sciences.

Plomin, R. (1989). Environment and genes. *American Psychologist, 44*, 105–111.

Plutchick, R. (1980). *Emotion: A psycho-evolutionary synthesis.* New York: Harper & Row.

Plutchick, R. (1984). A psycho-evolutionary theory of emotions. *Social Science Information, 21*, 529–553.

Polivy, J., & Herman, C. P. (1985). Dieting and binging: A causal analysis. *American Psychologist, 40*, 193–201.

Pomeroy, W. B., Flax, C. C., & Wheeler, C. C. (1982). *Taking a sex history: Interviewing and recording.* New York: The Free Press.

Poon, L. (1985). Differences in human memory with aging: Nature, causes, and clinical implications. In J. E. Birren & K. W. Schaie (Eds.), *Handbook of the psychology of aging* (2nd ed.). New York: Van Nostrand Reinhold.

Pope, K. S., Tabachnick, B. G., & Keith-Spiegel, P. (1987). Ethics of practice: The beliefs and behaviors of psychologists as therapists. *American Psychologist, 42*, 993–1006.

Popenoe, P. (1929). *Sterilization for human betterment.* New York: Macmillan.

Popper, D. R. (1959). *The logic of scientific discovery.* New York: Basic Books.

Posner, M. I., & Snyder, C. R. R. (1975). Facilitation and inhibition in the processing of signals. In P. M. A. Rabbitt & S. Dornic (Eds.), *Attention and performance V.* New York: Academic Press, 669–682.

Powell, K. E., Thompson, P. D., Caspersen, C. J., & Kendrick, J. S. (1987). Physical activity and the incidence of coronary heart disease. *Annual Review of Public Health, 8*, 253–287.

Q

Quattrone, G. A. (1986). On the perception of a group's variability. In S. Worschel & W. G. Austin (Eds.), *Psychology of intergroup relations.* Chicago: Nelson-Hall.

R

Rachman, S., & Teasdale, J. (1969). *Aversion therapy and behavior disorders.* Coral Gables: University of Miami Press.

Rader, N., Spiro, D. J., & Firestone, P. B. (1979). Performance on a Stage 4 object-permanence task with standard and nonstandard covers. *Child Development, 50*, 905–910.

Rahe, R. H., & Arthur, R. J. (1978). Life changes and illness reports. In K. E. Gunderson & R. H. Rahe (Eds.), *Life stress and illness.* Springfield, IL: Thomas.

Rapaport, K., & Burkhart, B. R. (1984). Personality and attitudinal characteristics of sexually coercive college males. *Journal of Abnormal Behavior, 93*, 216–221.

Rapoport, R., & Rapoport, R. N. (1980). Three generations of dual-career family research. In F. Pepitone-Rockwell (Ed.), *Dual career couples.* Beverly Hills, CA: Sage.

Rappaport, J. (1977). *Community psychology: Values, research and action.* New York: Holt, Rinehart, and Winston.

Raskin, D. C., & Podlesny, J. A. (1979). Truth and deception: A reply to Lykken. *Psychological Bulletin, 86*, 54–59.

Raymond, M. (1964). The treatment of addiction by aversion conditioning with apomorphine. *Behaviour Research and Therapy, 1*, 287–291.

Reisenzein, R. (1983). The Schachter theory of emotion: Two decades later: *Psychological Bulletin, 94*, 239–264.

Reiss, B. F. (1980). Psychological tests in homosexuality. In J. Marmor (Ed.), *Homosexual behavior.* New York: Basic Books.

Rekers, G. A., & Lovass, O. I. (1974). Behavioral treatment of deviant sex role behaviors in a male child. *Journal of Applied Behavior Analysis, 7*, 173–190.

Repetti, R. L. (1984). Determinants of children's sex-stereotyping: Parental sex-role traits and television viewing. *Personality and Social Psychology Bulletin, 10*, 457–468.

Rescorla, R. A. (1966). Predictability and number of pairings in Pavlovian fear conditioning. *Psychonomic Science, 4*, 383–384.

Rescorla, R. A., & Wagner, A. R. (1972). A theory of Pavlovian conditioning: Variations in the effectiveness of reinforcement and nonreinforcement. In A. H. Black & W. F. Prokasy (Eds.), *Classical conditioning II: Current research and theory.* New York: Appleton-Century-Crofts.

Rheingold, H. L. (1985). Development as the acquisition of familiarity. *Annual Review of Psychology, 36*, 1–17.

Rheingold, H. L., & Eckerman, C. O. (1973). Fear of the stranger: A critical examination. In H. W. Reese (Ed.), *Advances in child development and behavior,* Vol. 8. New York: Academic Press.

Rice, M. L. (1989). Children's language acquisition. *American Psychologist, 44*, 149–156.

Rickels, K. (1978). Use of antianxiety agents in anxious outpatients. *Psychopharmacology, 58*, 1–17.

Riley, V. (1981). Psychoneuroendocrine influences on immunocompetence and neoplasia. *Science, 212*, 1100–1109.

Rips, L. J. (1988). Deduction. In R. J. Sternberg and E. E. Smith, *The psychology of human thought.* New York: Cambridge University Press.

Robins, L. N., & Helzer, J. E. (1986). Diagnosis and clinical assessment: The current state of psychiatric diagnosis. In M. R. Rosenzweig & L. W. Porter (Eds.), *Annual review of psychology: 1986.* Palo Alto, CA: Annual Reviews.

Robins, L. N., Helzer, J. E., Weissman, M. M., Orvaschel, H., Gruenberg, E., Burke, J. D., & Regier, D. A. (1984). Lifetime prevalence of specific psychiatric disorders in three sites. *Archives of General Psychiatry, 41*, 949–958.

Robinson, William J. (1912). *Practical eugenics.* New York: The Critic and Guide Company.

Rodin, J. (1973). Effects of distraction on the performance of obese and normal subjects. *Journal of Comparative and Physiological Psychology, 83*, 68–78.

Rodin, J. (1980). The externality theory today. In A. J. Strunkard, (Ed.), *Obesity,* pp. 226–239. Philadelphia: Saunders.

Rodin, J. (1984, December). A sense of control. *Psychology Today,* 38–45.

Rodin, J. (1985). Insulin levels, hunger, and food intake: An example of feedback loops in body weight regulation. *Health Psychology, 4*, 1–18.

Rodin, J. (1987). The determinants of successful aging. Edited transcript of a paper presented at a Science and Public Policy seminar sponsored by the Federation of Behavior, Psychological, and Cognitive Sciences, October 30, 1987.

Roff, J. D., & Knight, R. (1981). Family characteristics, childhood symptoms, and adult outcome in schizophrenia. *Journal of Abnormal Psychology, 90*, 510–520.

Rogers, C. R. (1961). *On becoming a person.* Boston: Houghton Mifflin.

Rohrer, J. H., Baron, S. H., Hoffman, E. L., & Swander, D. V. (1954). The stability of autokinetic judgments. *Journal of Abnormal and Social Psychology, 49*, 595–597.

Roitblat, H. L. (1987). *Introduction to comparative cognition.* New York: W. H. Freeman.

Rollins, B. C., & Feldman, H. (1970). Marital satisfaction over the life cycle. *Journal of Marriage and the Family, 32*, 20–28.

Rorschach, H. (1921). *Psychodiagnostics: A diagnostic test based on perception.* New York: Grune & Stratton.

Rosch, E. (1973). Natural categories. *Cognitive Psychology, 4*, 328–350.

Rosch, E. (1977). Classification of real-world objects: Origins and representations in cognition. In P. N. Johnson-Laird and P. C. Wason (Eds.), *Thinking: Readings in cognitive science,* 212–222. New York: Cambridge University Press.

Rosch, E. H., Mervis, C. B., Gray, W. D., Johnson, D. M., & Boyes-Braem, P. (1976). Basic objects in natural categories. *Cognitive Psychology, 8*, 382–439.

Rose, R. M. (1975). Testosterone, aggression, and homosexuality. A review of the literature and implications for future research. In E. J. Sachar (Ed.), *Topics in psychoendocrinology.* New York: Grune & Stratton.

Rosenblatt, P. C. (1974). Cross-cultural perspective on attraction. In T. L. Huston (Ed.), *Foundations of interpersonal attraction.* New York: Academic Press.

Rosenthal, A. M. (1964). Thirty-eight witnesses. New York: McGraw-Hill.

Rosenthal, R. (1966). *Experimenter effects in behavioral research.* New York: Appleton-Century-Crofts.

Rosenthal, R., & Fode, K. L. (1963). The effect of experimental bias on the performance of the albino rat. *Behavioral Science, 8*, 183–187.

Ross, A. S. (1970). The effect of observing a helpful model on helping behavior. *Journal of Social Psychology, 81*, 131–132.

Ross, L. (1977). The intuitive psychologist and his shortcomings: Distortions in the attribution process. In L. Berkowitz (Ed.), *Advances in experimental social psychology (Vol. 10).* New York: Academic Press.

Ross, L., Amabile, T. M., & Steinmetz, J. L. (1977). Social roles, social control, and biases in social-perception processes. *Journal of Personality and Social Psychology, 35*, 485–494.

Rossman, I. (1980). Bodily changes with aging. In E. W. Busse & D. G. Blazer (Eds.), *Handbook of geriatric psychiatry.* New York: Von Nostrand Reinhold.

Rosvold, H. E., Mirsky, A. F., & Pribram, K. H. (1954). Influence of amygdalectomy on social behavior in monkeys. *Journal of Comparative and Physiological Psychology, 47*, 173–178.

Rothenberg, A. M. (1979). *The emerging goddess: The creative process in art, science, and other fields.* Chicago: The University of Chicago Press.

Rotter, J., Chance, J., & Phares, E. (1972). *Applications of a social learning theory to personality.* New York: Holt, Rinehart and Winston, Inc.

Rotter, J. B. (1954). *Social learning and clinical psychology.* Englewood Cliffs, NJ: Prentice-Hall.

Rotter, J. B. (1966). Generalized expectancies for internal versus external control of reinforcement. *Psychological monographs, 80*, (1, Whole No. 609).

Rubin, Z. (1980). *Children's friendships.* Cambridge, MA: Harvard University Press.

Rumelhart, D. E. (1970). A multicomponent theory of perception of briefly exposed stimulus displays. *Journal of Mathematical Psychology, 7*, 191–218.

Rushton, J. P. (1975). Generosity in children: Immediate and long-term effects of modeling, preaching and moral judgment. *Journal of Personality and Social Psychology, 31*, 459–466.

Russell, D. E. H., & Howell, N. (1983). The prevalence of rape in the United States revisited. *Signs, 8*, 688–695.

Russell, M. J. (1976). Human olfactory communication. *Nature, 260*, 520–522.

Rutherford, W. (1886). The sense of hearing. *Journal of Anatomy and Physiology, 21*, 166–168.

S

Sachs, J. S. (1967). Recognition memory of syntactic and semantic aspects of connected discourse. *Perception and Psychophysics, 2*, 437–442.

Sackeim, H. A. (1985, June). *Psychology today,* 36–40.

Sackett, G. P. (1966). Monkeys reared in isolation with pictures of visual input: Evidence for an innate releasing mechanism. *Science, 154*, 1468–1473.

Sager, C. J. (1981). Couples therapy and marriage contracts. In A. S. Gurman & D. P. Kniskern (Eds.), *Handbook of Family Therapy.* New York: Brunner/Mazel.

Saghir, M. T., & Robins, E. (1973). *Male and female homosexuality: A comprehensive investigation.* Baltimore: Williams & Wilkins.

Salthe, S. N. (1972). *Evolutionary biology.* New York: Holt, Rinehart & Winston.

Sancton, T. (1989, January). What on earth are we doing? *Time,* 24–30.

Sande, G. N., Goethals, G. R., & Radloff, C. E. (1988). Perceiving one's own traits and others: The multifaceted self. *Journal of Personality and Social Psychology, 54,* 13–20.

Santiago, J. M., McCall-Perez, F., Gorcey, M., & Beigel, A. (1985). Long-term psychological effects of rape in 35 rape victims. *American Journal of Psychiatry, 142,* 1338–1340.

Sarason, I. G., Smith, R. E., & Diener, E. (1975). Personality research: Components of variance attributed to the person and the situation. *Journal of Personality and Social Psychology, 32,* 199–204.

Scarr, S., & Weinberg, R. A. (1976). IQ test performance of black children adopted by white families. *American Psychologist, 31,* 726–729.

Scarr, S., & Weinberg, R. A. (1986). The early childhood enterprise: Care and education of the young. *American Psychologist, 41,* 1140–1146.

Schachter, S. (1959). *The psychology of affiliation.* Stanford, CA: Stanford.

Schachter, S. (1975). Cognition and the peripheralist-centralist controversies in motivation and emotion. In M. S. Gazzaniga & C. Blakemore (Eds.), *Handbook of psychobiology.* New York: Academic Press.

Schachter, S., & Friedman, L. N. (1974). The effects of work and cue prominence on eating behavior. In S. Schachter & J. Rodin, (Eds.), *Obese humans and rats.* Washington, DC: Erlbaum-Halstead.

Schachter, S., & Latane, B. (1964). Crime, cognition, and the autonomic nervous system. In D. Levine (Ed.), *Nebraska symposium on motivation,* Vol. 12. Lincoln, NE: University of Nebraska Press.

Schachter, S., & Rodin, J. (1974). *Obese humans and rats.* Washington, DC: Erlbaum-Halstead.

Schachter, S., & Singer, J. A. (1962). Cognitive, social, and psychological determinants of emotional state. *Psychological Review, 69,* 379–399.

Schact, T. E. (1985). DSM-III and the politics of truth. *American Psychologist, 40,* 513–520.

Schaie, K. W. (1975). Age changes in intelligence. In D. S. Woodruff & J. E. Birren (Eds.), *Aging: Scientific perspectives and social issues.* New York: Van Nostrand.

Schaie, K. W. (1980). Cognitive development in aging. In L. K. Obler & M. L. Martin (Eds.), *Language and communication in the elderly.* Lexington, MA: Heath.

Schaie, K. W., & Hertzog, C. (1982). Longitudinal methods. In B. B. Wolman (Ed.), *Handbook of developmental psychology.* Englewood Cliffs, NJ: Prentice-Hall.

Schaie, K. W., & Willis, S. L. (1986). *Adult development and aging.* Boston: Little, Brown.

Scherwitz, L., Graham, L. E., & Ornish, D. (1985). Self-involvement and the risk factors for coronary heart disease. *Advances, 2,* 6–18.

Schiffman, H. R. (1976). *Sensation and perception: An integrated approach.* New York: Wiley.

Schiffman, S. S. (1974). Physiochemical correlates of olfactory quality. *Science, 185,* 112–117.

Schiffman, S. S. (1983). Taste and smell in disease. *New England Journal of Medicine, 308,* 1275–1279.

Schiffman, S. S., & Dackis, C. (1975). Taste of nutrients: Amino acids, vitamins, and fatty acids. *Perception & Psychophysics, 17,* 140–146.

Schleifer, S. J., Keller, S. E., Camerino, M., Thornton, J. C., & Stein, M. (1983). Suppression of lymphocyte stimulation following bereavement. *Journal of the American Medical Association, 250,* 364–377.

Schmeck, H. M., Jr. (1984, March 27). Implant brings sound to deaf and spurs debate over its use. *The New York Times,* pp. C1+.

Schmitt, D. R. (1976). Some conditions affecting the choice to cooperate and compete. *Journal of the Experimental Analysis of Behavior, 25,* 165–178.

Schofield, M. (1965). *The sexual behavior of young people.* Boston: Little, Brown.

Schreiner, L., & Kling, A. (1953). Behavioral changes following rhinencephalic injury in the cat. *Journal of Neurophysiology, 16,* 643–659.

Schulz, D. A., & Wilson, R. A. (1973). Some traditional family variables and their correlations with drug use among high school students. *Journal of Marriage and the Family, 35,* 628–631.

Schumer, F. (1983). *Abnormal psychology.* Lexington, MA: Heath.

Schwartz, G. E., Weinberger, D. A., & Singer, J. A. (1981). Cardiovascular differentiation of happiness, sadness, anger, and fear following imagery and exercise. *Psychosomatic Medicine, 43,* 343–364.

Scoville, W. B., & Miller, B. (1957). Loss of recent memory after bilateral hippocampal lesions. *Journal of Neurology, Neurosurgery, and Psychiatry, 20,* 11–21.

Seamon, J. G., Brody, N., & Kauff, D. M. (1983). Affective discrimination of stimuli that are not recognized: Effects of shadowing, masking, and cerebral laterality. *Journal of Experimental Psychology: Learning Memory and Cognition, 9,* 544–555.

Sekuler, R., & Blake, R. (1985). *Perception.* New York: Knopf.

Seligman, M. E. P. (1970). On the generality of the laws of learning. *Psychological Review, 77,* 406–418.

Seligman, M. E. P. (1971). Phobias and preparedness. *Behavior Therapy, 2,* 307–321.

Selkoe, D. J. (1989). Biochemistry of altered brain proteins in Alzheimer's disease. *Annual Review of Neuroscience, 12,* 463–490.

Selye, H. (1956). *The stress of life.* New York: McGraw-Hill.

Shapley, R., & Lennie, P. (1985). Spatial frequency analysis in the visual system. *Annual Review of Neuroscience, 8,* 547–583.

Sheffield, F. D., & Roby, T. B. (1950). Reward value of a nonnutritive sweet taste. *Journal of Comparative and Physiological Psychology, 43,* 471–481.

Sheffield, F. D., Wulff, J. J., & Backer, R. (1951). Reward value of copulation without sex drive reduction. *Journal of Comparative and Physiological Psychology, 44,* 3–8.

Sherif, M. (1936). *The psychology of social norms.* New York: Harper.

Sherif, M., Harvey, O. J., White, B. J., Hood, W. R., & Sherif, C. W. (1961). *Intergroup conflict and cooperation: The Robber's Cave experiment.* Norman, OK: University of Oklahoma Institute of Intergroup Relations.

Sherrick, C. E., & Cholewiak, R. W. (1986). Cutaneous activity. In K. R. Boff, L. Kaufman, & J. P. Thomas (Eds.), *Handbook of perception and human performance.* New York: Wiley.

Shiffrin, R. M., & Schneider, W. (1977). Controlled and automatic human information processing: II. Perceptual learning, automatic attending, and a general theory. *Psychological Review, 84,* 127–190.

Shuey, A. (1966). *The testing of Negro intelligence.* New York: Social Science Press.

Shulman, H. G. (1971). Similarity effects in short-term memory. *Psychological Bulletin, 75,* 399–415.

Shulman, H. G. (1972). Semantic confusion errors in short-term memory. *Journal of Verbal Learning and Verbal Behavior, 11,* 221–227.

Sidman, M. (1960). *Tactics of scientific research.* New York: Basic Books.

Sidman, M., & Tailby, W. (1982). Conditional discrimination versus matching to sample: An expansion of the testing paradigm. *Journal of the Experimental Analysis of Behavior, 37,* 5–22.

Siegal, M. G., Niswander, G. D., Sach, E., Jr., & Stavros, D. (1959). Taraxin: Fact or artifact? *American Journal of Psychiatry, 115:* 819–822.

Sigusch, V., & Schmidt, G. (1971). Lower-class sexuality: Some emotional and social aspects in West German males and females. *Archives of Sexual Behavior, 1,* 29–44.

Simon, H. (1980). Cognitive science: The newest science of the artificial. *Cognitive Science, 4,* 33–46.

Sjostrom, L. (1980). Fat cells and body weight. In A. J. Strunkard, (Ed.), *Obesity.* Philadelphia: Saunders.

Skarin, K. (1977). Cognitive and contextual determinants of stranger fear in six- and eleven-month-old infants. *Child Development, 48,* 537–544.

Skeels, H. M. (1966). Adult status of children with contrasting early life experiences. *Monographs of the Society for Research and Child Development.* (Vol. 31).

Skinner, B. F. (1938). *The behavior of organisms.* New York: Appleton-Century-Crofts.

Skinner, B. F. (1948). *Walden Two.* New York: Macmillan.

Skinner, B. F. (1953). *Science and human behavior.* New York: Macmillan.

Skinner, B. F. (1956). A case history in the scientific method. *American Psychologist, 11,* 221–233.

Skinner, B. F. (1957). *Verbal behavior.* New York: Appleton-Century-Crofts.

Skinner, B. F. (1971). *Beyond freedom and dignity.* New York: Vantage.

Skinner, B. F. (1974). *About behaviorism.* New York: Knopf.

Skinner, B. F. (1978). Why I am not a cognitive psychologist. *Behaviorism, 5,* 1–10.

Skinner, B. F. (1981). Selection by consequences. *Science, 213,* 501–504.

Skinner, B. F. (1986). The evolution of verbal behavior. *Journal of the Experimental Analysis of Behavior, 45,* 115–122.

Skinner, B. F. (1987). *Upon further reflection.* Englewood Cliffs, NJ: Prentice-Hall.

Skinner, B. F. (1988, June). A statement on punishment. *APA Monitor,* p. 22.

Skyrms, B. (1966). *Choice & chance.* Belmont, California: Dickenson Publishing Company.

Slater, B., & Shields, J. (1969). Genetic aspects of anxiety. *British Journal of Psychiatry Special Publication No. 3. Studies of Anxiety.* Ashford, Kent: Headley Bros.

Slobin, D. I. (1985). *The cross-linguistic study of language acquisition,* Vols. 1 & 2. Hillsdale, NJ: Erlbaum.

Slochower, J. (1976). Emotional labeling of overeating in obese and normal weight individuals. *Psychosomatic Medicine, 38,* 131–139.

Smith, E. E. (1988). Concepts and thought. In R. J. Sternberg and E. E. Smith, *The psychology of human thought.* New York: Cambridge University Press.

Smith, E. E., Shoben, E. J., & Rips, L. J. (1974). Structure and process in semantic memory: A featural model for semantic decisions. *Psychological Review, 81,* 214–241.

Smith, M. B. (1968). The revolution in mental health care: A bold new approach? *Trans-action, 5,* 19–23.

Smith, M. L., & Glass, G. V. (1977). Meta-analysis of psychotherapy outcome studies. *American Psychologist, 32,* 752–760.

Smith, M. L., Glass, G. V., & Miller, T. I. (1980). *The benefits of psychotherapy.* Baltimore: Johns Hopkins University Press.

Snyder, S. H. (1978). Dopamine and schizophrenia. In L. C. Wynne, R. L. Cromwell, & S. Matthysse (Eds.), *The nature of schizophrenia: New approaches to research and treatment.* New York: Wiley.

Snyder, S. H. (1984). Drug and neurotransmitter receptors in the brain. *Science, 224,* 22–31.

Solomon, R. L. (1980). The opponent-process theory of motivation. *American Psychologist, 35,* 691–712.

Solomon, R. L., & Corbitt, J. D. (1974). An opponent-process theory of motivation. I. Temporal dynamics of affect. *Psychological Review, 81,* 119–145.

Sorenson, T. (1981). A follow-up study of operated transsexual males. *Acta Psychiatrica Scandinavia, 63,* 486–503.

Spearman, C. E. (1904). "General intelligence": Objectively determined and measured. *American Journal of Psychology, 15,* 201–292.

Sperling, G. (1960). The information available in brief visual presentations. *Psychological Monographs, 74,* 1–29.

Sperling, G. (1963). A model for visual memory tasks. *Human Factors, 5,* 9–31.

Sperry, R. W. (1968). Hemisphere deconnection and unity in conscious awareness. *American Psychologist, 23,* 723–733.

Sperry, R. W. (1982). Some effects of disconnecting the cerebral hemispheres. *Science, 217,* 1223–1226.

Spiro, R. L. (1980). Accommodative reconstruction in prose recall. *Journal of Verbal Learning and Verbal Behavior, 19,* 84–95.

Spitzer, R. L., Skodol, A. E., Gibbon, M., & Williams, J. B. W. (1981). *Diagnostic and statistical manual of mental disorders case book.* Washington, DC: American Psychiatric Association.

Springer, J.P., & Deutsch, G. (1985). *Left brain, right brain.* San Francisco: Freeman.

Squire, L. R. (1982). Neuropsychological effects of ECT. In R. Abrams and W. B. Essman (Eds.), *Electroconvulsive therapy: Biological foundations and clinical applications.* New York: SP Medical and Scientific Books.

Squire, L. R. (1982). The neuropsychology of human memory. *Annual Review of Neuroscience, 5,* 241–273.

Squire, L. R. (1987). *Memory and brain.* New York: Oxford University Press.

Sroufe, L. A. (1978). Attachment and the roots of competence. *Human Nature, 1,* 50–57.

Sroufe, L. A., Fox, N. E., & Pancake, V. R. (1983). Attachment and dependency in developmental perspective. *Child Development, 54,* 1615–1627.

Staats, A. W. (1975). *Social behaviorism.* Homewood, IL: The Dorsey Press.

Stanislaw H., & Rice, F. J. (1988). Correlation between sexual desire and menstrual cycle characteristics. *Archives of Sexual Behavior, 17,* 499–508.

Stapp, J., & Fulcher, R. (1981). The employment of APA members. *American Psychologist, 36,* 1263–1314.

Stapp, J., Tucker, A. M., & VandenBos, G. R. (1985). Census of psychological personnel: 1983. *American Psychologist, 40,* 1317–1351.

Starr, B. D., & Weiner, M. B. (1981). *The Starr-Weiner report on sex and sexuality in the mature years.* New York: Stein & Day.

Steinberg, L. (1987). Born to bicker. *Psychology Today,* 36–39.

Sternbach, R. A. (1978). Psychological dimensions and perceptual analyses, including pathologies of pain. In E. C. Carterette & M. P. Friedman (Eds.), *Handbook of perception* (Vol. 6B). New York: Academic Press.

Sternberg, R. J. (1985). *Beyond IQ.* New York: Cambridge University Press.

Sternberg, R. J. (1988). *The Triarchic Mind.* New York: Viking.

Stevens, S. S. (1955). The measurement of loudness. *Journal of the Acoustical Society of America, 27,* 815–819.

Stipp, H., & Milvasky, J. R. (1988). U. S. Television programming's effects on aggressive behavior of children and adolescents. *Current Psychology: Research and reviews, 7,* 76–92.

Storms, M. D. (1980). Theories of sexual orientation. *Journal of Personality and Social Psychology, 38,* 783–792.

Storms, M. D. (1981). A theory of erotic orientation development. *Psychological Review, 88,* 340–353.

Strain, P. S., Shores, R. E., & Kerr, M. M. (1976). An experimental analysis of "spillover" effects on the social interaction of behaviorally handicapped preschool children. *Journal of Applied Behavior Analysis, 9,* 31–40.

Stratton, G. W. (1897). Vision without inversion of the retinal image. *Psychological Review, 4,* 341–360.

Stricker, E. M., & Zigmond, M. J. (1976). Recovery of function after damage to catecholamine-containing neurons: A neurochemical model for the lateral hypothalamic syndrome. In J. Sprague & A. N. Epstein, (Eds.), *Progress in psychobiology and physiological psychology, 6,* pp. 121–188. New York: Academic Press.

Strickland, B. R. (1978). Internal-external expectancies of health-related behaviors. *Journal of Consulting and Clinical Psychology, 46,* 1192–1211.

Strickland, B. R. (1979). Internal-external expectancies and cardiovascular functioning. In L. C. Perlmutter, & R. A. Monty

(Eds.), *Choice and perceived control.* Hillsdale, NJ: Erlbaum.

Strunkard, A. J., Sorensen, T. I. A., Hanis, C., Teasdale, T. W., Chakraborty, R., Shull, W. J., Schulsinger, F. (1986). An adoption study of human obesity. *New England Journal of Medicine, 314,* 193–198.

Sue, D., Sue, D. W., & Sue, S. (1981). *Understanding abnormal behavior.* Boston: Houghton Mifflin.

Surgeon General. (1983). *The health consequences of smoking: Cardiovascular disease.* Washington, DC: U. S. Government Printing Office.

Surgeon General. (1988). *The health consequences of smoking: Nicotine addiction.* Washington, DC: U. S. Government Printing Office.

Swazey, J. P. (1974). *Chlorpromazine in psychiatry: A study of therapeutic innovation.* Cambridge, MA: MIT Press.

Symonds, M. (1975). Victims of violence: Psychological effects and aftereffects. *American Journal of Pscyhoanalysis, 35,* 19–26.

Symons, D. (1979). *The evolution of human sexuality.* New York: Oxford University Press.

Szaz, T. S. (1960). The myth of mental illness. *American Psychologist, 15,* 113–118.

T

Takooshian, H., Habers, S., & Lucido, D. J. (1977). Who wouldn't help a lost child? *Psychology Today, 10,* 67–88.

Tanner, W. P., Jr., & Swets, J. A. (1954). A decision-making theory of visual detection. *Psychological Review, 61,* 401–409.

Tavris, C., & Sadd, S. (1977). *The Redbook report on female sexuality.* New York: Delacorte Press.

Taylor, M. C., & Hall, J. A. (1982). Psychological androgeny: Theories, methods, and conclusions. *Psychological Bulletin, 92,* 347–366.

Teghtsoonian, R., Teghtsoonian, M., Berglund, B., & Berglund, U. (1978). Invariance of odor strength with sniff vigor: An olfactory analogue to size constancy. *Journal of Experimental Psychology: Human Perception and Performance, 4,* 144–152.

Teitelbaum, P. (1955). Sensory control of hypothalamic hyperphagia. *Journal of Comparative and Physiological Psychology, 48,* 156–163.

Teitelbaum, P., & Epstein, A. N. (1962). The lateral hypothalamic syndrome: Recovery of feeding and drinking after lateral hypothalamic lesions. *Psychological Review, 69,* 74–90.

Teitelbaum, P., & Stellar, E. (1954). Recovery from failure to eat produced by hypothalamic lesions. *Science, 120,* 894–895.

Terman, L. M., & Oden, M. H. (1959). *The gifted child at midlife.* Stanford, CA: Stanford University Press.

Testa, R. J., Kinder, B. N., & Ironson, G. (1987). Heterosexual bias in the perception of loving relationships of gay males and lesbians. *The Journal of Sex Research, 23,* 163–172.

Thompson, T., & Sturm, T. (1965). Classical conditioning of aggressive display in male Siamese fighting fish. *Journal of the Experimental Analysis of Behavior, 8,* 397–403.

Thoreau, H. D. (1849/1960). On civil disobedience. New York: NAL Penguin, Inc.

Thorndike, E. L. (1898). Animal intelligence: An experimental study of the associative processes in animals. *Psychological Monographs 2* (Whole No. 8).

Thorndike, E. L. (1899). The associative processes in animals. *Biological lectures from the Marine Biological Laboratory at Woods Hole.* Boston: Atheneum.

Thorndike, E. L. (1911). *Animal intelligence: Experimental studies.* New York: Macmillan.

Thorndike, R. L., Hagen, E. P., & Sattler, J. M. (1986). *Technical Manual, Stanford-Binet intelligence scale: 4th edition.* Chicago: The Riverside Publishing Co.

Thurstone, L. L. (1938). *Primary mental abilities.* Chicago: University of Chicago Press.

Tierney, J., Wright, L., & Springen, K. (1988). The search for Adam and Eve. *Newsweek* (January 11, 1988), 46–52.

Torrey, E. F. (1988). *Surviving schizophrenia: A family manual.* New York: Harper & Row.

Treichel, J. A. (1982). Anorexia Nervosa: A brain shrinker? *Science News, 122,* 262–263.

Trivers, R. L. (1971). The biology of reciprocal altruism. *Quarterly Review of Biology, 46,* 35–57.

Tucker, O. M. (1981). Lateral brain functions, emotion, and conceptualization. *Psychological Bulletin, 89,* 19–46.

Tulving, E. (1972). Episodic and semantic memory. In E. Tulving and W. Donaldson (Eds.), *Organization of memory.* New York: Academic Press.

Tulving, E. (1983). *Elements of episodic memory.* London: Oxford University Press.

Tulving, E. (1985). How many memory systems are there? *American Psychologist, 40,* 385–398.

Tulving, E. (1986). What kind of hypothesis is the distinction between episodic and semantic memory? *Journal of Experimental Psychology: Learning, Memory, and Cognition, 12,* 307–311.

Tulving, E., & Osler, S. (1968). Effectiveness of retrieval cues in memory for words. *Journal of Experimental Psychology, 77,* 593–601.

Tversky, A., & Kahneman, D. (1971). Belief in the law of small numbers. *Psychological Bulletin, 75,* 105–110.

Tversky, A., & Kahneman, D. (1973). Availability: A heuristic for judging frequency and probability. *Cognitive Psychology, 5,* 207–232.

Tversky, A., & Kahneman, D. (1982). Judgments of and by representativeness. In D. Kahneman, P. Slovic, & A. Tversky (Eds.), *Judgment under uncertainty: Heuristics and biases.* New York: Cambridge University Press.

U

Udry, J. R. (1974). *The social context of marriage* (3rd ed.). New York: Lippincott.

U. S. Bureau of the Census. (1982). Projections of the population of the United States (Current Population Reports, Series P-25, No. 922). Washington, DC: U. S. Government Printing Office.

V

Vaillant, G. E. (1975). Sociopathy as a human process: A viewpoint. *Archives of General Psychiatry, 32,* 178–183.

Vaillant, G. E., & Milofsky, E. S. (1982). The etiology of alcoholism. *American Psychologist, 37,* 494–503.

Valzelli, L. (1981). Aggression and violence: A biological essay of the distinction. In L. Valzelli & L. Morgese (Eds.), *Aggression and violence.* Milano, Italy: Edizioni Saint Vincent.

Valzelli, L., Bernasconi, S., & Garattini, S. (1981). p-Chlorophenylalanine-induced muricidal aggression in male and female laboratory rats. *Neuropsychobiology, 7,* 315–320.

Van Horn, M. (1986). *Understanding expert systems.* New York: Bantam Books.

Van Wagener, W., & Herren, R. (1940). Surgical division of commisural pathways in the corpus callosum. *Archives of Neurology and Psychiatry, 44,* 740–759.

Vance, E. B., & Wagner, N. B. (1976). Written descriptions of orgasm: A study of sex differences. *Archives of Sexual Behavior, 5,* 87–98.

Vernon, P. A. (1983). Speed of information processing and general intelligence. *Intelligence, 7,* 53–70.

Vokey, J. R., & Read, J. D. (1985). Subliminal messages: Between the devil and the media. *American Psychologist, 40,* 1231–1239.

von Bekesy, G. (1960). *Experiments in hearing.* New York: McGraw-Hill.

von Helmholtz, H. (1863). On the sensations of a tone as physiological basis for the theory of music. (A. J. Ellis, Trans.). New York: Dover.

W

Wadden, T. A., & Stunkard, A. J. (1985). Adverse social and psychological consequences of obesity. *Annals of Internal Medicine, 103,* 10,620–10,670.

Wagner, A. R., Siegal, S., Thomas, E., & Ellison, G. D. (1964). Reinforcement history and the extinction of a conditioned salivary response. *Journal of Comparative and Physiological Psychology, 58,* 354–358.

Walk, R. D., & Gibson, E. J. (1961). A comparative and analytical study of visual depth perception. *Psychological Monographs, 75* (Whole No. 519).

Wallace, P. (1977). Individual discrimination of humans by odor. *Physiology & Behavior, 19,* 577–599.

Wallace, R. A. (1987). Biology: The world of life. Glenview, IL: Scott, Foresman/Little, Brown.

Walster, E., Aronson, E., Abrahams, D., & Rottman, L. (1966). Importance of physical attractiveness in dating behavior. *Journal of Personality and Social Psychology, 4,* 508–516.

Walster, E., Traupmann, J., & Walster, G. W. (1978). Equity and extramarital sexuality. *Archives of Sexual Behavior, 7,* 127–142.

Wason, P. C. (1968). On the failure to eliminate hypotheses—a second look. In P. C. Wason, & P. N. Johnson-Laird (Eds.), *Thinking and reasoning.* Baltimore: Penguin.

Watkins, L. R., & Mayer, D. J. (1982). Organization of endogenous opiate and nonopiate pain control systems. *Science, 216,* 1185–1192.

Watson, J. B. (1913). Psychology as the behaviorist views it. *Physiological Review, 20,* 158–177.

Watson, J. B., & McDougall, W. (1929). *The battle of behaviorism.* New York: Norton.

Waugh, N. C., & Norman, D. A. (1965). Primary memory. *Psychological Review, 72,* 89–104.

Webb, W. B. (1975). *Sleep the gentle tyrant.* Englewood Cliffs, NJ: Prentice-Hall.

Webb, W. B. (1982). Sleep and biological rhythms. In W. B. Webb (Ed.), *Biological rhythms, sleep, and performance.* Chichester, England: Wiley.

Weinberg, R. A. (1989). Intelligence and IQ: Landmark issues and great debates. *American Psychologist, 44,* 98–104.

Weingarten, H. P. (1982). Diet palatability modulates sham feeding in VMH-lesioned rats and normal rats: implications for finickiness and evaluation of sham feeding data. *Journal of Comparative and Physiological Psychology, 96,* 223–233.

Weissman, M. M., & Myers, J. K. (1978). Affective disorders in a U.S. urban community. *Archives of General Psychiatry, 35,* 1304–1310.

Weizman, R., & Hart, J. (1987). Sexual behavior in healthy married elderly men. *Archives of Sexual Behavior, 16,* 39–44.

Wells, G. L., & Loftus, E. F. (1986). *Eyewitness testimony: Psychological perspectives.* London: Cambridge University Press.

Wever, E. G., & Bray, C. W. (1937). The perception of low tones and the resonance-volley theory. *Journal of Psychology, 3,* 101–114.

Weyant, J. M. (1978). The effects of mood states, costs and benefits on helping. *Journal of Personality and Social Psychology, 36,* 1169–1176.

Whalen, R. E. (1971). The concept of instinct. In J. L. McGaugh (Ed.), *Psychobiology: Behavior from a biological perspective.* New York: Academic Press.

Whorf, B. L. (1956). *Language, thought and reality.* Boston: MIT Press.

Whyte, L. L. (1979). *The unconscious before Freud.* New York: St. Martin's Press.

Wickelgren, W. A. (1965). Size of rehearsal group and short-term memory. *Journal of Experimental Psychology, 68,* 413–419.

Wilcoxin, H., Dragoin, W. & Kral, P. (1971). Illness-induced aversions in the rat and quail: Relative salience of visual and gustatory cues. *Science, 171,* 826–828.

Wilder, D. A. (1981). Perceiving persons as a group: Categorization and intergroup relations. In D. L. Hamilton (Ed.), *Cognitive processes in stereotyping and intergroup behavior.* Hillsdale, NJ: Erlbaum.

Wilding, J. M. (1983). *Perception: From sense to object.* New York: St. Martin's Press.

Will, M., & Reynolds, W. B. (1988). Letter to the editor of *The Washington Post,* cited in *APA Monitor,* June, 1988, p. 22.

Williams, R. L. (1972). *The BITCH Test (Black Intelligence Test of Cultural Homogeneity.* St. Louis: Williams and Associates.

Wilson, E. O. (1975). *Sociobiology: The new synthesis.* Cambridge, MA: Harvard University Press.

Wilson, E. O. (1978). *On human nature.* Cambridge, MA: Harvard University Press.

Wilson, W. R. (1979). Feeling more than we can know: Exposure effects without learning. *Journal of Personality and Social Psychology, 37,* 811–821.

Winchester, A. M. (1972). *Genetics: A survey of the principles of heredity.* Boston: Houghton Mifflin.

Winklestein, W., Jr., Samuel, M., Radian, N. S., & Wiley, J. A. (1987). Selected sexual practices of San Francisco heterosexual men and risk of infection by the human immunodeficiency virus. *Journal of the American Medical Association, 257,* 1470.

Winokur, A., et al. (1980). Withdrawal reaction from long-term, low dosage administration of diazepam: A double-blind, placebo-controlled study. *Archives of General Psychiatry, 37,* 101–105.

Wise, R. (1978). Where the public peril begins: A survey of psychotherapists to determine the effects of Tarasoff. *Stanford I Review, 31,* 165–190.

Wise, S., & Grossman, F. K. (1980). Adolescent mothers and their infants: Psychological factors in early attachment and interaction. *American Journal of Orthopsychiatry, 50,* 454–468.

Wolfe, J. B. (1936). Effectiveness of token rewards for chimpanzees. *Comparative Psychology Monographs, 12,* 1–72.

Wolfe, L. (September, 1980). The sexual profile of that cosmopolitan girl. *Cosmopolitan,* 254–265.

Wolpe, J. (1958). *Psychotherapy by reciprocal inhibition.* Stanford, CA: Stanford University Press.

Wolpoff, M. H. (1980). *Paleoanthropology. New York:* Knopf.

Women on Words and Images. (1972). *Dick and Jane as victims: Sex-stereotyping in children's readers.* Princeton, NJ: Women on Words and Images.

Woods, J. W. (1956). Taming of the wild Norway rat by rhinencephalic lesions. *Nature, 170,* 869.

Woods, N. F., Dery, G. K., & Most, A. (1983). Recollections of menarche, current menstrual attitudes, and premenstrual symptoms. In S. Golub (Ed.), *Menarche: The transition from girl to woman.* Lexington, MA: Lexington Books.

Y

Yerkes, R. M., & Dodson, J. D. (1908). The relation of strength of stimulus to rapidity of habit-formation. *Journal of Comparative Neurology and Psychology, 18,* 459–482.

Z

Zadeh, L. (1965). Fuzzy sets. *Information and control, 8,* 338–353.

Zajonc, R. B. (1965). Social facilitation. *Science, 149,* 269–274.

Zajonc, R. B. (1968). Attitudinal effects of mere exposure. *Journal of Personality and Social Psychology, Monograph Supplement, 9,* 1–27.

Zajonc, R. B. (1980). Feeling and thinking: Preferences need no inferences. *American Psychologist, 35,* 151–175.

Zajonc, R. B. (1984). On the primacy of affect. *American Psychologist, 39,* 117–123.

Zanna, M. P., & Pack, S. J. (1975). On the self-fulfilling nature of apparent sex differences in behavior. *Journal of Experimental Social Psychology, 11,* 583–591.

Zelnik, M., & Kantner, J. F. (1980). Sexual activity, contraceptive use, and pregnancy among metropolitan area teenagers. *Family Planning Perspectives, 1971–1979. 12*, 230–237.

Zelnik, M., Kantner, J. F., & Ford, K. (1981). *Sex and pregnancy in adolescence.* Beverly Hills: Sage.

Zigler, E., & Seitz, V. (1982). Social policy and intelligence. In R. J. Sternberg (Ed.), *Handbook of human intelligence.* Cambridge: Cambridge University Press.

Zilbergeld, B. (1978). *Male sexuality.* Boston: Little, Brown.

Zilbergeld, B., & Ellison, C. R. (1980). Desire discrepancies and arousal problems in sex therapy. In S. R. Leiblum & L. A. Pervin (Eds.), *Principles and practice of sex therapy.* New York: Guilford Press.

Zilboorg, G., & Henry, G. W. (1941). *A history of medical psychology.* New York: Norton.

Zillmann, D. (1978). Attribution and misattribution of excitatory reactions. In J. H. Harvey, W. J. Ickes, & R. F. Kidd (Eds.), *New directions in attribution research. Vol. 2.* Hillsdale, NJ: Erlbaum.

Zillmann, D. (1982). Transfer of excitation in emotional behavior. In J. T. Cacioppo & R. E. Petty (Eds.), *Social psychophysiology: A sourcebook.* New York: Guilford Press.

Zillmann, D. (1988). Cognition-excitation interdependencies in aggressive behavior. *Aggressive Behavior, 14*, 51–64.

Zillmann, D., & Bryant, J. (1984). Effects of massive exposure to pornography. In N. Malamuth & E. Donnerstein (Eds.), *Pornography and sexual aggression.* Orlando: Academic Press.

Zillmann, D., Katcher, A. H., & Milavsky, B. (1972). Excitation from physical exercise to subsequent aggressive behavior. *Journal of Experimental Social Psychology, 8*, 247—259.

Zuckerman, M., Buchsbaum, M. S., & Murphy, D. L. (1980). Sensation seeking and its biological correlates. *Psychological Bulletin, 88*, 187–214.

Zukin, R. S., & Zukin, S. R. (1983). A common receptor for phencyclidine and the sigma opiates. In J. M. Kamenka, E. F. Domino, & P. Geneste (Eds.), *Phencyclidine and related arylcyclohexylamines: Present and future applications.* Ann Arbor, MI: NPP Books.

ADDITIONAL REFERENCES

Cerletti, U., & Bini, L. (1938). Electroshock therapy. *Bulletin Accademia Medica di Roma, 64*, 136–138.

Devany, J. M., Hayes, S. C., & Nelson, R. O. (1986). Equivalence class formation in language-able and language-disabled children. *Journal of the Experimental Analysis of Behavior, 46*, 243–257.

Evans, J., Barston, J. L., & Pollard, P. (1983). On the conflict between logic and belief in syllogistic reasoning. *Memory and Cognition, 11*, 295–306.

Jones, E. (1969). *The life and work of Sigmund Freud.* New York: Basic Books.

Phillips, D. P., & Carstensen, L. L. (1986). Clustering of teenage suicides after television news stories about suicide. *New England Journal of Medicine, 315*, 685–689.

Acknowledgments

Credits for photographs, illustrations, and quoted material not given on the page where they appear are listed below.

ILLUSTRATION CREDITS

Patrice Rossi: Figures 4.8, 4.9, 4.17, 4.18, 4.21, 4.22, 4.24, 4.26, 4.27, 5.5, 5.6, 5.10, 6.16, 6.17, 8.1, 18.6
Ron Ervin: Figures 4.4, 4.5, 4.6, 4.7, 4.11, 4.16, 6.5a & b, 6.6, 6.12, 6.15
May Cheney: Figure 6.14
Lou Calver: Figure 4.2
Sara Woodward: Figure 4.20
Sandra McMahen: Figure 4.10
Precision Graphics: Mechanical and Illustrative Art Program

PHOTO CREDITS

Positions of photographs are indicated in the abbreviated form as follows: top (t), bottom (b), center (c), left (l), right (r). All photographs not credited are the property of Scott, Foresman.

Cover: Galen Rowell/Mountain Light; background photo: Michael Stuckey/COMSTOCK

Table of Contents
xiv Michael S. Grecco/Stock, Boston
xv Martha Bates/Stock, Boston
xvii (b) NASA
xviii Edith G. Haun/Stock, Boston
xix Walter Hodges/West Light
xx (t) Carol Palmer/The Picture Cube; (b) Warren Garst/Tom Stack & Associates
xxii Stacy Pickerell/TSW-Click/Chicago
xxiii NASA

Chapter 1
xxvi-1 Manfred Kage/Peter Arnold, Inc.
xxvi Robert Llewellyn
2 Ellis Herwig/The Picture Cube
4 Archives of the History of American Psychology, University of Akron, Akron, Ohio
5 (t l) The Bettmann Archive; (t r) Historical Pictures Service, Chicago; (c) The Ferdinand Hamburger, Jr. Archives, The Johns Hopkins University, Baltimore, Maryland; (b) Library of Congress
6 The Bettmann Archive
7 (l) Courtesy Michael S. Gazzaniga; (r) Joe McNally
8 (l) Benno Friedman; (r) John Bowden/© 1984 Discover Publications
9 Historical Pictures Service, Chicago
10 Alan Carey/The Image Works
13 Mark Antman/The Image Works
15 Bob Daemmrich

Chapter 2
20–21 Manfred Kage/Peter Arnold, Inc.
20 Sharon Beals for *Insight* magazine
23 (l) Charles Gupton/Stock, Boston; (r) Joseph Nettis/Stock, Boston
24 Ira Wyman/© 1984 Discover Publications
28 (both) Michael S. Grecco/Stock, Boston

30 Bohdan Hrynewych/Stock, Boston
31 Baron Hugo Van Lawick © 1965 National Geographic Society
32 Rick Friedman/Black Star
35 Courtesy Columbia University Office of Public Information
42 Alfred Wolf/Explorer/Pasteur Institute, Paris/Photo Researchers
49 (l) Barth Falkenberg/Stock, Boston; (r) Bob Daemmrich/Stock, Boston
52 Robert Maass/Photoreporters

Chapter 3
58–59 Manfred Kage/Peter Arnold, Inc.
58 © Michel Tcherevkoff for National Geographic Society
61 (l) By permission of the Darwin Museum, Down House; (r) National Maritime Museum, London
63 Fig. 3.1 *Biological Science* by William T. Keeton. Copyright © 1967 by W. W. Norton & Company, Inc. Based on photographs in W. W. Levi, *The Pigeon*, Levi Publishing Company, 1957.
64 The Granger Collection, New York
72 (both) Howard Sochurek
74 Lawrence Migdale/Photo Researchers
76 Fig. 3.8 *Genetics: A Survey of the Principles of Heredity,* Fourth Edition, by A. M. Winchester. Copyright © 1972 by Houghton Mifflin Company, Boston.
78 Martha Bates/Stock, Boston
80 Mousson/Gamma-Liaison
82 (l) Erwin & Peggy Bauer/Bruce Coleman Inc.; (r) AP/Wide World

Chapter 4
90–91 Manfred Kage/Peter Arnold, Inc.
90 Biophoto Associates/Science Source/Photo Researchers; (inset) Chris Harvey/TSW-Click/Chicago
92 Guy Gillette/Photo Researchers
105 Neal Graham/Taurus Photos
109 (l) Jay Foreman/Taurus Photos; (r) Joseph Rodriguez/Black Star
111 Campbell & Boulanger/West Light
112 Collection Ronald K. Siegel
118 Fig. 4.12 Martin M. Rotker/Taurus Photos; (l) Martin M. Rotker/Taurus Photos; (r) Custom Medical Stock Photo
119 Fig. 4.13 The Bettmann Archive
121 Charles Gupton/Picturesque
123 Fig. 4.15 (t l, b l) Dan McCoy/Rainbow; (r) Courtesy Steven E. Petersen, Washington University School of Medicine, St. Louis
127 Fig. 4.19 Dr. James Olds
133 Fig. 4.25 *The Excitable Cortex in Conscious Man* by Wilder Penfield. Liverpool University Press, 1958. Second impression 1967.
134 (l) The Granger Collection, New York; (r) Courtesy California Institute of Technology
136 Fig. 4.28 "The Split Brain in Man" by Michael S. Gazzaniga in *Scientific American*, August 1967. Copyright © 1967 by Scientific American, Inc. Reprinted by permission of the author.
138 Christopher Springmann
139 Courtesy Stanford University News and Publications Service
141 Allan Hobson/Science Source/Photo Researchers

Chapter 5

146–147 Biophoto Associates/Science Source/Photo Researchers
146 Ralph C. Eagle, M. D./Science Source/Photo Researchers
148 Photograph by George Grantham Bain. Courtesy *Vanity Fair*. Copyright © 1919 (renewed 1947) by Conde Nast Publications, Inc.
150 The Bettmann Archive
154 The Granger Collection, New York
159 Ralph Eagle, Jr., M. D./Science Source/Photo Researchers
163 (both) Courtesy Harvard University News Office
165 Bodleian Library, Oxford, MS New College 361/2, fol. 45v
167 Fig. 5.13 Macmillan Science Co., Inc.
168 The Granger Collection, New York
170 Fig. 5.16, Fig. 5.17 Ron James
171 Courtesy David Linton
174 (interposition, relative size) Tony Freeman/PhotoEdit; (texture gradient) Francis De Richemond/The Image Works; (aerial perspective) John Lemker/Earth Scenes
175 (1) Enrico Ferorelli; (r) *Ascending and Descending* by M. C. Escher. © 1990 M. C. Escher Heirs/Cordon Art—Baarn—Holland. Collection Haags Gemeentemuseum—The Hague
178 Fig. 5.28 (t) Charles Palek/Earth Scenes, (b) Stouffer Productions Ltd./Earth Scenes
179 Fig. 5.30 (both) David Wells/The Image Works
180 Fig. 5.32 U. Neisser, "The control of information pickup in selective looking." In A. D. Pick (Ed.), *Perception and its development: A tribute to Eleanor J. Gibson.* Copyright © 1979 by Laurence Erlbaum Associates, Inc. Hillsdale, NJ.; Fig. 5.33 (both) AP/Wide World
182 Fig. 5.36 I. Biederman, "On the semantics of a glance at a scene." In *Perceptual organization,* M. Kubovy and J. Pomerantz (Eds.). Copyright © 1981 by Laurence Erlbaum Associates, Inc. Hillsdale, NJ.; Fig. 5.37 E. G. Boring (1930) "A new ambiguous figure." *American Journal of Psychology, 42,* 109–116.
184 (t) Karen R. Preuss/Taurus Photos; (b) Margo Granitsas/The Image Works

Chapter 6

190–191 Biophoto Associates/Science Source/Photo Researchers
190 G. Adams/Stock Imagery
199, 219 From Margaret W. Matlin, *Perception.* Copyright © 1983 by Allyn and Bacon. Reprinted with permission.
202 Ellis Herwig/The Picture Cube
203 IBM
205 (1) Paula M. Lerner/The Picture Cube; (r) Focus On Sports
206 Stephen Frisch/Stock, Boston
208 Bob Daemmrich
210 Fig. 6.13 the Bettmann Archive
212 Focus On Sports
213 Fay Torresyap/Stock, Boston

Chapter 7

224–225 TSW-Click/Chicago
224 Joseph Schuyler/Stock, Boston
226 (1) Gary W. Griffen/Animals Animals; (r) Kojo Tanaka
228 The Granger Collection, New York
232 Thomas McAvoy, *Life* Magazine © 1955 Time Inc.
234 Fig. 7.4 I. P. Pavlov, *Conditioned reflexes* (G. V. Anrep, Trans.). Copyright © 1927 by Oxford University Press, New York.
236 (t) Courtesy Professor Benjamin Harris, University of Wisconsin—Parkside. From Watson's 1919 film, *Experimental Investigation of Babies;* (b) Martin Rogers/Stock, Boston
248 Fig. 7.16 (1) Courtesy Pfizer Inc., (r) Courtesy B. F. Skinner; Fig. 7.17 Courtesy Ralph Gerbrands Co., Inc.
250 James Pozarik/Gamma-Liaison
251 Brain Seed/TSW-Click/Chicago
254 Thomas K. Wanstall/The Image Works
255 Fig. 7.20 Yerkes Regional Primate Research Center of Emory University
256 Bob Daemmrich/The Image Works

Chapter 8

264–265 TSW-Click/Chicago
264 Tim Olive/SharpShooters
270 (1) Mary Kate Denny/PhotoEdit; (r) Richard Pasley/Stock, Boston
273 (1) Charles Gupton/Stock, Boston; (r) John Coletti/The Picture Cube
279 Bob Daemmrich/The Image Works
282 The Bettmann Archive
283 (both) NASA
284 Jim Harrison/Stock, Boston
289 Rick Browne/Stock, Boston

Chapter 9

294–295 TSW-Click/Chicago
294 © 1988 Clayton J. Price
297 Courtesy On-Line Software International
304 Charles Gupton
309 Jeffrey Mark Dunn/Stock, Boston
311 John Griffin/The Image Works
313 Courtesy Ministry of the Attorney General, Ontario, Canada
314 John Coletti/Stock, Boston
317 Fig. 9.7 (both) *The Mentality of Apes* by Wolfgang Köhler. Routledge & Kegan Paul Ltd., London, 1927. (Reprinted 1948, 1973).
319 David Wells/The Image Works
322 Bruce Plotkin/The Image Works
325 Dr. Ronald H. Cohn/The Gorilla Foundation

Chapter 10

330–331 TSW-Click/Chicago
330 Michael Freeman
333 (1) Richard Fukuhara/West Light; (r) Warren Morgan/West Light
336 (r) Herb Snitzer/Stock, Boston
338 (t) The Bettmann Archive; (b 1) Library of Congress; (b r) Courtesy Co-Workers of Mother Teresa
340 Fig. 10.6 Courtesy Dr. David C. McClelland, from *Motivation Workshops* by D. C. McClelland and R. S. Steele. New York: General Learning Press, 1972.
341 Alan Carey/The Image Works
342 Edith G. Haun/Stock, Boston
345 The Bettmann Archive
347 Fig. 10.9 Courtesy Dr. Neal Miller
348 Bob Daemmrich/Stock, Boston
351 (1) Steve Schapiro/Gamma-Liaison; (r) Bonnie Schiffman/Gamma-Liaison
352 Dion Ogust/The Image Works
353 Jim Brandenburg
355 Charles Biasiny Rivera
356 AP/Wide World
357 Fig. 10.11 Courtesy Albert Bandura
360 (1) Bob Daemmrich/The Image Works; (r) Lawrence Manning/West Light
362 Fig. 10.13 *Darwin and Facial Expression: A Century of Research in Review,* edited by Paul Ekman. Academic Press, 1973. By Permission of Dr. Paul Ekman, Ed Gallob, and Dr. Silvan Tomkins.
365 Brian Seed/TSW-Click/Chicago

Chapter 11

374–375 Guy Motil/West Light
374 Walter Hodges/West Light
376 Adamsmith Productions/West Light
382 (t) Yves De Braine/Black Star; (b 1) Carol Palmer/The Picture Cube; (b r) Sally Cassidy/The Picture Cube
384 (t) Cary Wolinsky/Stock, Boston; (b-all) George Zimbel/Monkmeyer
385 Walter Hodges/West Light
388 Lawrence Manning/West Light

389 (l) Franklin D. Roosevelt Library; (r) The Granger Collection, New York
391 (t) Jon Erikson; (b) Erika Stone
395 (t l, t r) Carlo Bevilacqua/CEDRI; (b) Courtesy American Cancer Society
396 Dr. Sterling K. Clarren, *New England Journal of Medicine,* 298; 1063–1067, 1978.
398 (l) Alan Carey/The Image Works; (r) Peter Vandermark/Stock, Boston
401 Fig. 11.8 Harlow Primate Laboratory, University of Wisconsin
404 Mark Antman/The Image Works
407 (l) Kindra Clineff/The Picture Cube; (r) Jeffry W. Myers/Stock, Boston
409 (l) Walter Hodges/West Light; (r) Ira Wyman/Sygma
412 Walter Hodges/West Light

Chapter 12

420–421 Guy Motil/West Light
420 D. Luria/Stock Imagery
422 Ellis Herwig/Taurus Photos
423 Lennart Nilsson from *The Incredible Machine.* Copyright © 1986 National Geographic Society
424 Stacy Pick/Stock, Boston
428 Fig. 12.2 Pam Hasegawa/Taurus Photos
429 (l) Doug Menuez/Stock, Boston; (r) Arnie Feinberg/The Picture Cube
431 (l) Carol Palmer/The Picture Cube; (r) Bob Daemmrich/Stock, Boston
432 (t l) Derek Bayes, *Life* Magazine © Time Inc.; (t r) Henry Grossman; (b) George Mars Cassidy/The Picture Cube
435 George J. Caspar/Taurus Photos
436 Richard Wood/The Picture Cube
438 Robert J. Levin/Black Star
443 (t l) Walter Hodges/West Light; (t r) Jeff Albertson/Stock, Boston; (b) Stephen R. Swinburne/Stock, Boston
446 Dagmar Fabricius/Stock, Boston
448 Owen Franken/Stock, Boston
450 Charles Gatewood/The Image Works
451 Charles Gatewood/The Image Works
454 Billy E. Carnes/Southern Light

Chapter 13

458–459 Guy Motil/West Light
458 Joe Baraban/The Stock Market; (inset) Jeff Zaruba/The Stock Market
460 (l) Warren Garst/Tom Stack & Associates; (r) Jim Brandenburg
461 (l) Mark Antman/The Image Works
464 National Portrait Gallery, London
465 Historical Pictures Service, Chicago
467 Courtesy Stanford University News and Publications Service
473 (t l) Reprinted with permission from PSYCHOLOGY TODAY MAGAZINE. Copyright © 1985 (PT Partners, L. P.); (t r) Ray Stott/The Image Works; (b) Courtesy Library of the National Academy of Sciences
479 James D. Wilson/Woodfin Camp & Associates
483 Robert Brenner/PhotoEdit
486 (l) Mark Antman/The Image Works; (c) Focus On Sports; (r) Dennis Brack/Black Star

Chapter 14

494–495 Guy Motil/West Light
494 Robert Landau/West Light
502 Fig. 14.5 Reprinted by permission of the publishers from THEMATIC APPERCEPTION TEST by Henry A. Murray, Cambridge, Mass.: Harvard University Press, Copyright © 1943 by the President and Fellows of Harvard College; © 1971 by Henry A. Murray.
504 Culver Pictures
509 Bruce Plotkin/The Image Works

510 MacDonald/The Picture Cube
511 (b) The Bettmann Archive
512 Bob Daemmrich/The Image Works
513 Association for the Advancement of Psychoanalysis of the Karen Horney Psychoanalytic Institute and Center, New York
516 (l) Courtesy Harvard University News Office; (r) Focus On Sports
518 (l) Gale Zucker/Stock, Boston; (r) Jeff Dunn/The Picture Cube
520 (t) Gregg Mancuso/Stock, Boston; (b) Courtesy Albert Bandura
522 Courtesy Julian Rotter
525 S. Anger/Gamma-Liaison
526 (t) The Bettmann Archive

Chapter 15

532–533 Cradoc Bagshaw/West Light
532 Steve Elmore/Tom Stack & Associates
535 Courtesy The Advertising Council Inc. and the American Mental Health Fund
537 Historical Pictures Service, Chicago
540 AP/Wide World
541 Dave Schaefer/The Picture Cube
542 Patt Blue
543 Courtesy Essex Institute, Salem, MA
545 Susan Greenwood/Gamma-Liaison
546 AP/Wide World
547 (both) Courtesy Cornelia B. Wilbur, M.D.
550 Brookhaven National Laboratory and New York University Medical Center
551 David S. Strickler/The Picture Cube
556 AP/Wide World
558 (both) NIMH
561 AP/Wide World

Chapter 16

566–567 Cradoc Bagshaw/West Light
566 Tom Casalini/SharpShooters
568 Culver Pictures
569 By Courtesy of the Trustees of Sir John Soane's Museum, London
571 Andy Freeberg
572 UPI/Bettmann Newsphotos
575 The Granger Collection, New York
577 Ann Chwatsky/The Picture Cube
580 Courtesy Dr. Joseph Wolpe
581 Courtesy California Department of Mental Health
583 Courtesy Albert Bandura
584 UPI/Bettmann Newsphotos
586 Reprinted with permission from PSYCHOLOGY TODAY MAGAZINE. Copyright © 1985 (PT Partners, L. P.)
588 Hugh Wilkerson
589 Stacy Pickerell/TSW-Click/Chicago
591 Fred R. Conrad/NYT Pictures
595 Mike Douglas/The Image Works

Chapter 17

600–601 Cradoc Bagshaw/West Light
600 Wally McNamee/Woodfin Camp & Associates; (inset) Christopher Morris/Black Star
603 Walter Hodges/West Light
605 Carl Andon/Black Star
609 Dirck Halstead/Gamma-Liaison
611 Neal Boenzi/NYT Pictures
615 Focus On Sports
617 William Vandivert
619 Mark Antman/The Image Works
622 Courtesy World Federation of Bergen-Belsen Associations
626 AP/Wide World
629 (l) Lawrence Migdale/Stock, Boston; (r) Adamsmith Productions/West Light
630 Brian Leng/West Light
631 Willie Hill, Jr./The Image Works

Chapter 18

636–637 Cradoc Bagshaw/West Light
636 Michael Baytoff/Black Star; (inset) © Tony Dawson
639 NASA
640 (1) Jim Pickerell/TSW-Click/Chicago; (r) Walter Hodges/ West Light
642 Gale Zucker/Stock, Boston
644 Courtesy American Cancer Society
646 Bob Daemmrich/The Image Works
648 John Coletti/The Picture Cube
649 © Laszlo
651 Jeffry W. Myers/Stock, Boston
652 AP/Wide World
653 John Coletti/TSW-Click/Chicago
654 Alan Carey/The Image Works
658 (1) Chiasson/Gamma-Liaison; (r) Herve Collart/Gamma-Liaison
659 L. L. T. Rhodes/TSW-Click/Chicago
660 DPA/Photoreporters
661 (1) Fred Ward/Black Star; (r) Stephen Ferry/Gamma-Liaison
664 Copyright 1988 The Time Inc. Magazine Company. Reprinted by permission.

LITERARY CREDITS

Chapter 1

14 Table 1.5 From "Census of Psychological Personnel: 1983" by Joy Stapp, Anthony M. Tucker, and Gary R. VandenBos, *American Psychologist*, December 1985. Copyright © 1985 by the American Psychological Association, Inc. Reprinted by permission of Joy Stapp.

Chapter 3

65, 67, 68, 70 Figs. 3.2, 3.3, 3.4, 3.5 Adapted figures from *Human Evolution: An Illustrated Introduction* by Roger Lewin. Copyright © 1984 by Blackwell Scientific Publications Ltd. Reprinted by permission of W. H. Freeman and Company.
74, 77 Tables 3.1, 3.2 From *Concepts of Genetics*, Second Edition by William S. Klug and Michael R. Cummings. Copyright © 1986 Scott, Foresman and Company.
78 Fig. 3.9 Adaptation of figure from "Familial Studies of Intelligence: A Review" by T. J. Bouchard, Jr., and M. McGue, *Science*, May 29, 1981. Copyright © 1981 by the American Association for the Advancement of Science. Reprinted by permission.

Chapter 4

101 Fig. 4.8 From "Action Potentials Recorded from Inside a Nerve Fiber" by A. L. Hodgkin and A. F. Huxley. Reprinted by permission from *Nature*, Vol. 144, No. 3651, October 21, 1939. Copyright 1939 Macmillan Magazines Ltd.
107 Table 4.1 From *A Primer of Drug Action*, Fifth Edition by Robert M. Julien. Copyright © 1975, 1978, 1981, 1985, 1988 by W. H. Freeman and Company. Reprinted by permission.
131 Fig. 4.23 Adapted from *Seeing: Illusion, Brain and Mind* by John P. Frisby (New York: Oxford University Press, 1980). Reprinted by permission of Roxby Press, London.
138 Fig. 4.30 From *A Primer On Sleep and Dreaming* by Rosalind Dymond Cartwright (Reading, MA: Addison-Wesley Publishing Company, 1978). Reprinted by permission of the author.
139 Fig. 4.31 From "Ontogenetic Development of the Human Sleep-Dream Cycle" by Howard P. Roffwarg, Joseph H. Muzio, and William C. Dement, *Science*, April 1966, 152 (9). Copyright © 1966 by the American Association for the Advancement of Science. Reprinted by permission of the American Association for the Advancement of Science and Howard P. Roffwarg.

Chapter 5

155 Table 5.1 From *Fundamentals of Psychology* by F. A. Geldard. Copyright © 1962 by John Wiley & Sons. Reprinted by permission.
162 Fig. 5.10 Adapted from *Seeing: Illusion, Brain and Mind* by John P. Frisby (New York: Oxford University Press, 1980). Reprinted by permission of Roxby Press, London.
164 Fig. 5.11 From "Adaptometer for Measuring Human Dark Adaptation" by Selig Hecht and Simon Shlaer, *Journal of the Optical Society of America*, Vol. 28, No. 7, July 1938. Reprinted by permission of the Optical Society of America.
166, 179, 181 Table 5.2, Figs. 5.31, 5.34 From *Sensation and Perception*, Second Edition by E. Bruce Goldstein. Copyright © 1984 by Wadsworth, Inc. Reprinted by permission of the publisher.
173 Fig. 5.22 From "Organizational Determinants of Subjective Contour" by D. R. Bradley and H. M. Petry, *American Journal of Psychology*, Vol. 90, 1977. Copyright © 1977 by the American Journal of Psychology. Reprinted by permission of the University of Illinois Press.

Chapter 6

195 Fig. 6.4 From *Perception* by Robert Sekuler and Randolph Blake. Copyright © 1985 by McGraw-Hill Publishing Company. Reprinted by permission.
199, 219 Figs. 6.6, 6.18 Adapted figures from *Perception* by Margaret W. Matlin. Copyright © 1983 by Allyn & Bacon, Inc. Reprinted by permission.

Chapter 7

230 Fig. 7.2 From *Psychology* by Roger Brown and Richard J. Herrnstein (Glenview, Illinois: Scott, Foresman/Little, Brown, 1975). Reprinted by permission of Roger Brown.
237 Fig. 7.6 Adapted from "Performance Changes in Eyelid Conditioning as Related to the Motivational and Reinforcing Properties of the UCS" by M. A. Trapold and K. W. Spence, *Journal of Experimental Psychology*, Vol. 59, No. 4, April 1960, p. 212. Reprinted by permission of Milton A. Trapold.
238 Fig. 7.8 From "The Generalization of Conditioned Responses: I. The Sensory Generalization of Conditioned Responses with Varying Frequencies of Tone" by Carl Iver Horland, *Journal of General Psychology*, 17:125–148, July 1937. Reprinted with permission of the Helen Dwight Reid Educational Foundation. Published by Heldref Publications, 4000 Albemarle St., N.W. Washington, DC 20016. Copyright 1937.
240 Fig. 7.9 From "Traumatic Avoidance Learning: Acquisition in Normal Dogs" by Richard L. Solomon and Lyman C. Wynne, *Psychological Monographs*, Vol. 67, No. 4, 1953. Reprinted by permission of Richard L. Solomon.
241 Fig. 7.10 From "Predictability and number of pairings in Pavlovian fear conditioning" by Robert A. Rescorla, *Psychonomic Science*, 1966, Vol. 4 (11). Reprinted by permission of the author.
243 Fig. 7.12 Adapted from *Behavior and Learning* by Howard Rachlin. Copyright © 1976 by W. H. Freeman and Company. Reprinted by permission.
244 Fig. 7.14 From "Learned Association over Long Delays" by Sam Revusky and John Garcia in *The Psychology of Learning and Motivation*, Vol. IV, edited by Gordon H. Bower. Copyright © 1970 by Academic Press, Inc. Reprinted by permission of Academic Press, Inc. and John Garcia.

Chapter 8

268 Fig. 8.3 Adapted from "The Control of Short-Term Memory" by Richard C. Atkinson and Richard M. Shiffrin, *Scientific American*, August 1971. Reprinted by permission.
269 Fig. 8.5 From "The Information Available in Brief Visual Presentations" by George Sperling, *Psychological Monographs*, Vol. 74, No. 11, 1960. Copyright © 1960 by the American Psychological Association. Reprinted by permission of the author.
269 Fig. 8.6 From "Short-Term Retention of Individual Verbal Items" by Lloyd R. Peterson and Margaret Jean Peterson,

Journal of Experimental Psychology, September 1959. Reprinted by permission of the author.

275 Fig. 8.9 From "The Role of Rehearsal in Short-Term Memory" by Fergus I. M. Craik and Michael J. Watkins, *Journal of Verbal Learning and Verbal Behavior*, Vol. 12, No. 6, December 1973. Copyright © 1973 by Academic Press, Inc. Reprinted by permission of Academic Press, Inc. and Fergus I. M. Craik.

282 Fig. 8.12 From *Memory: A Contribution to Experimental Psychology* by Hermann Ebbinghaus. Copyright © 1964 by Dover Publications, Inc. Reprinted by permission.

282 Fig. 8.13 From "Semantic Memory Content in Permastore: Fifty Years of Memory for Spanish Learned in School" by Harry P. Bahrick, *Journal of Experimental Psychology: General*, Vol. 113, No. 1, March 1984. Copyright © 1984 by the American Psychological Association. Adapted by permission of the author.

290 Fig. 8.16 From *Cellular Basis of Behavior: An Introduction to Behavioral Neurobiology* by Eric R. Kandel. Copyright © 1976 by W. H. Freeman and Company. Reprinted by permission.

Chapter 9

299, 300 Figs. 9.1, 9.2 From "Retrieval Time from Semantic Memory" by Allan M. Collins and M. Ross Quillian, *Journal of Verbal Learning and Verbal Behavior*, Vol. 8, No. 2, April 1969. Copyright © 1969 by Academic Press, Inc. Reprinted by permission of Academic Press, Inc. and Allan M. Collins.

302 Table 9.1 From "Correlated Properties in Natural Categories" by Barbara C. Malt and Edward E. Smith, *Journal of Verbal Learning and Verbal Behavior*, Vol. 23, No. 2, April 1984. Copyright © 1984 by Academic Press, Inc. Reprinted by permission of Academic Press, Inc. and Barbara C. Malt.

303 Fig. 9.3 From *New Ways of Analyzing Variations in English* by Charles-James N. Bailey and Roger W. Shuy, Editors. Copyright © 1973 by Georgetown University. Reprinted by permission.

315, 316 Fig. 9.4 From "Problem-Solving" by Martin Scheerer, from *Scientific American*, Vol. 208, 1963.

Chapter 10

335 Fig. 10.3 From Fig. 47, "The mating behavior of the three-spined stickleback" in *The Study of Instinct* by N. Tinbergen. Reprinted by permission of Oxford University Press.

339 Table 10.1 From *Explorations in Personality* edited by Henry A. Murray. Copyright © 1938 by Oxford University Press, Inc.; renewed by Henry A. Murray. Reprinted by permission of the publisher.

350 Fig. 10.10 Adaptation of table, "Number of grams of ice cream consumed" from "Restrained and unrestrained eating" by C. Peter Herman and Deborah Mack, *Journal of Personality*, Vol. 43, No. 1, March 1975. Copyright © 1975 by Duke University Press. Reprinted by permission.

361 From *Emotion: A Psychoevolutionary Synthesis* by Robert Plutchik. Copyright © 1980 by Individual Dynamics, Inc. Reprinted by permission of Harper & Row Publishers, Inc.

362 Fig. 10.13 From "Cross-Cultural Studies of Facial Expressions" from *Darwin and Facial Expression: A Century of Research in Review* edited by Paul Ekman. Copyright © 1973 by Academic Press, Inc. Reprinted by permission of Academic Press, Inc. and the author.

369 Fig. 10.17 From "Cognition and Peripheralist-Centralist Controversies in Motivation and Emotion" by Stanley Schacter in *Handbook of Psychobiology*, edited by Michael S. Gazzaniga and Colin Blakemore. Copyright © 1975 by Academic Press, Inc. Reprinted by permission of Academic Press, Inc. and Stanley Schacter.

Chapter 11

393 Fig. 11.5 From P. B. Baltes, "Life-span development psychology: Some converging observations on history and theory" in P. B. Baltes and O. G. Brim, Jr., eds., *Life-Span*

Development and Behavior, Vol. 2. Copyright © 1979 by Academic Press, Inc. Reprinted by permission of Academic Press, Inc. and Paul B. Baltes.

399 Fig. 11.6 Adapted from Table IV, Frankenburg and Dodds, *The Journal of Pediatrics*, vol. 71, no. 2, p. 186, 1967. Reprinted by permission.

410 Fig. 11.10 From "Cognitive Development in Aging" by K. Warner Schaie in *Language and Communication in the Elderly*, edited by Loraine K. Obler and Martin L. Albert. Copyright © 1980 by D. C. Heath and Company. Reprinted by permission.

410 Fig. 11.11 From "A Cross-Sequential Study of Age Changes in Cognitive Behavior" by K. Warner Schaie and Charles R. Strother, *Psychological Bulletin*, Vol. 70, 1968, p. 675. Copyright © 1968 by the American Psychological Association. Reprinted by permission of K. Warner Schaie.

411 Fig. 11.12 From "Organization of Data on Life-Span Development of Human Abilities" by John L. Horn in *Life Span Developmental Psychology: Research and Theory*, edited by L. R. Goulet and Paul B. Baltes. Copyright © 1970 by Academic Press, Inc. Reprinted by permission of Academic Press, Inc. and John L. Horn.

Chapter 12

425, 442 Table 12.1, Fig. 12.3 From tables, "Summary of the Changes of Puberty and Their Sequence" and "Percentages of People Who Had Engaged in Premarital Intercourse, According to the Kinsey Report and the Hunt Report" from *Understanding Human Sexuality*, 3rd edition by Janet Shibley Hyde. Copyright © 1986, 1982, 1979 by McGraw-Hill, Inc. Reprinted by permission.

426 Fig. 12.1 From "Standards from Birth to Maturity for Height, Weight, Height Velocity, and Weight Velocity: British Children, 1965" by J. M. Tanner, R. H. Whitehouse, and M. Takaishi, *Archives of Disease in Childhood*, Vol. 41, October 1966. Reprinted by permission of the British Medical Journal.

434 Table 12.2 Adapted from "Sex-Role Stereotypes: A Current Appraisal" by Inge K. Broverman, Susan Raymond Vogel, Frank E. Clarkson, Donald M. Broverman, and Paul S. Rosenkrantz, *Journal of Social Issues*, Vol. 28, No. 2, 1972. Copyright © 1972 by The Society for the Psychological Study of Social Issues. Reprinted by permission of the SPSSI and Inge K. Broverman.

444 Fig. 12.4 From *Human Sexual Behavior* by William Griffitt and Elaine Hatfield. Copyright © 1985 Scott, Foresman and Company.

444 Fig. 12.5 From *American Couples* by Philip Blumstein and Pepper Schwartz. Copyright © 1983 by Philip Blumstein and Pepper Schwartz. Reprinted by permission of William Morrow & Company, Inc.

445 Table 12.3 Based on data from *Sexual Behavior in the Human Male*, 1948 and *Sexual Behavior in the Human Female*, 1935 by Alfred C. Kinsey et al. Reprinted by permission of The Kinsey Institute for Research in Sex, Gender and Reproduction.

448 Table 12.4 From Davis, James Allan and Smith, Tom W.: *General Social Surveys, 1972–1985*. Principal Investigator, James A. Davis; Senior Study Directory, Tom W. Smith. NORC ed. Chicago: National Opinion Research Center, producer, 1985. Reprinted by permission.

452 Fig. 12.6 From "Effects of Massive Exposure to Pornography" by Dolf Zillmann and Jennings Bryant in *Pornography and Sexual Aggression*, edited by Neil M. Malamuth and Edward Donnerstein. Copyright © 1984 by Academic Press, Inc. Reprinted by permission of Academic Press, Inc. and Dolf Zillman.

Chapter 13

469 Fig. 13.1 (top) Reprinted with permission of The Riverside Publishing Company from page four of the *Stanford-Binet Intelligence Scale Guide for Administering and Scoring the Fourth Edition* by R. L. Thorndike, E. P. Hage, and J. M. Sattler. THE RIVERSIDE PUBLISHING COMPANY, 8420 W. Bryn Mawr Avenue, Chicago, IL 60631. Copyright © 1986.

471 Table 13.4 Reprinted with permission of The Riverside

Publishing Company from the *Stanford-Binet Intelligence Scale Guide for Administering and Scoring the Fourth Edition* by R. L. Thorndike, E. P. Hagen, and J. M. Sattler. The Riverside Publishing Company, 8420 W. Bryn Mawr Avenue, Chicago, IL 60631. Copyright © 1986.

472 Fig. 13.2 Reprinted with permission of The Riverside Publishing Company from the *Stanford-Binet Intelligence Booklet: Fourth Edition* Record Booklet by R. L. Thorndike, E. P. Hage, and J. M. Sattler. THE RIVERSIDE PUBLISHING COMPANY, 8420 W. Bryn Mawr Avenue, Chicago, IL 60631. Copyright © 1986.

474 Table 13.5 From *Wechsler Adult Intelligence Scale-Revised*. Copyright © 1981, 1955 by The Psychological Corporation. Reproduced by permission. All rights reserved.
From *Psychology: An Introduction*, Second Edition, by Josh R. Gerow. Copyright © 1989, 1986 Scott, Foresman and Company.

476 Fig. 13.3 From *Wechsler's Measurement and Appraisal of Adult Intelligence*, Fifth Edition by Joseph D. Matarazzo. Copyright © 1972 by Oxford University Press, Inc. Reprinted by permission.

480 Table 13.6 Adaptation from "Familial Studies of Intelligence: A Review" by T. J. Bouchard, Jr., and M. McGue, *Science*, May 29, 1981. Copyright © 1981 by the American Association for the Advancement of Science. Reprinted by permission.

484 Fig. 13.4 From *The Triarchic Mind: A New Theory of Human Intelligence* by Robert J. Sternberg. Copyright © 1989 by Robert J. Sternberg. Reprinted by permission of Viking Penguin, a division of Penguin Books USA Inc.

489 Fig. 13.5 From "Brain Response Correlates of Psychometric Intelligence" by John P. Ertl and Edward W. P. Schaefer, *Nature*, Vol. 223, July 26, 1969. Copyright © 1969 by Macmillan Magazines Ltd. Reprinted by permission.

Chapter 14

498 Fig. 14.1 Table, "Description of MMPI scales and simulated items" from *Psychological Testing and Assessment* by Lewis R. Aiken. Copyright 1943, renewed © 1970 by the University of Minnesota. Reprinted by permission.

499 Fig. 14.2 From *Minnesota Multiphasic Personality Inventory*. Copyright 1943, renewed © 1970 by The University of Minnesota. Reprinted by permission.

500 Fig. 14.3 From *Handbook for the 16PF*. Copyright © 1970, 1968 by the Institute for Personality and Ability Testing, Inc. All rights reserved. Reproduced by permission.

506 Fig. 14.6 From *Personality: Strategies and Issues*, 6th ed. by R. M. Liebert and M. D. Spiegler. Copyright © 1990 by Wadsworth, Inc. Copyright © 1987, 1982, 1978, 1974, 1970 by The Dorsey Press. Reprinted by permission of Brooks/Cole Publishing Co., Pacific Grove, CA 94950.

517 Fig. 14.7 From "Principles and methods of personality, description, classification and diagnosis" by H. J. Eysenck, *British Journal of Psychology*, Vol. 55, 1964. Copyright © 1964 by The British Psychological Society. Reprinted by permission of The British Psychological Society and the author.

Chapter 15

536 Fig. 15.1 From "Six-Month Prevalance of Psychiatric Disorders in Three Communities" by J. K. Myers, et al., *Archives of General Psychiatry*, Vol. 41, October 1984. Copyright ©

1984 by the American Medical Association. Reprinted by permission of the American Medical Association and Jerome K. Myers.

541 Table 15.2 Adapted from *Anxiety Disorders and Phobias: A Cognitive Approach*, by Aaron T. Beck and Gary Emery. Copyright © 1985 by Aaron T. Beck, M.D., and Gary Emery, Ph.D. Reprinted by permission of Basic Books, Inc., Publishers, New York.

550 Fig. 15.2 From "Environmental Factors Preceding the Onset of Severe Depression" by Melitta J. Leff, John F. Roatch, and William E. Bunney, Jr., *Psychiatry*, Vol. 33, No. 3, August 1970. Reprinted by permission.

557 Fig. 15.4 From "Clue to the Genetics and Neurobiology of Schizophrenia" by Susan E. Nicol and Irving I. Gottesman, *American Scientist*, Vol. 71, No. 4, July–August 1983. Reprinted by permission.

Chapter 16

573 Table 16.2 From *Abnormal Psychology: Patterns, Issues, Interventions* by Frank Costin and Juris G. Draguns. Copyright © 1989 by John Wiley & Sons, Inc. Reprinted by permission.

592 Fig. 16.1 From figure, "Effectiveness of Various Types of Psychotherapy Compared to Untreated Control Groups" from *Abnormal Psychology: Current Perspectives* by Richard R. Bootzin and Joan Ross Acocella. Copyright © 1972, 1977, 1980, 1984, 1988 by Random House, Inc. Reprinted by permission.

Chapter 17

607, 614 Figs. 17.1, 17.2 From Robert A. Baron and Donn Byrne, *Exploring Social Psychology*. Copyright © 1979 by Allyn and Bacon. Reprinted with permission.

618 Fig. 17.4 Adapted from figure "Number of Opponents" from "Opinions and Social Pressure" by Solomon E. Asch, *Scientific American*, November 1955, p. 35. Reprinted by permission.

623, 625 Fig. 17.5, Table 17.1 From *Obedience to Authority* by Stanley Milgram. Copyright © 1974 by Stanley Milgram. Reprinted by permission of Harper & Row, Publishers, Inc.

Chapter 18

642 Fig. 18.1 Adapted from "Diet and Cancer" by Leonard A. Cohen, *Scientific American*, November 1987. Copyright © 1987 by Scientific American, Inc. All rights reserved. Reprinted by permission.

643 Fig. 18.2 From "Considerations for a New Food Guide" by Jean A. T. Pennington, *Journal of Nutrition Education*, Vol. 12, No. 2, June 1981, p. 53. Copyright © 1981 Society for Nutrition Education. Reprinted by permission.

645 Table 18.1 "It's never too late to quit" from *Living Well*, Vol. IX, No. 4, Spring 1989. Copyright © 1989 the Bob Hope International Heart Research Institute. Reprinted by permission, HOPE Health Letter, Kalamazoo, Michigan.

649 Fig. 18.3 From *Stress Without Distress* by Hans Selye M.D. Copyright © 1974 by Hans Selye. Reprinted by permission of Harper & Row, Publishers, Inc.

657, 659, 660, 662 Fig. 18.5, Tables 18.3, 18.4, Fig. 18.6 From *Biology: The World of Life*, Fourth Edition by Robert A. Wallace. Copyright © 1987, 1981 Scott, Foresman and Company.

Name Index

Crossman, E. K., 254
Crow, T. J., 558
Crowder, R. G., 269
Crowe, 560
Cumberbath, G., 358
Cummings, M. R., 78, 80

D

Dackis, C., 217
Dahlstrom, W. G., 498
Dale, H. C., 271
Dallenbach, K. M., 207, 287
Daly, M., 436
Daniels, P., 412
Darby, B. L., 620
Darley, J. M., 627
Dartnell, H. J. A., 168
Darwin, C. J., 269
Darwin, C., 4, 60, 64, 362
Darwin, F., 60, 62, 63, 64
Dashiell, J. F., 616
Davis, J. A., 448
Davis, J. M., 558, 575
Davis, R., 351
Davis, W. L., 523
Davison, G. C., 550, 568
Dawkins, R., 83
de Groot, A. D., 309
de Rose, T., 258
Deaux, K., 430
Deci, E. L., 344
DeJong, W., 620
Dement, W. C., 138, 139, 140, 141
Demo, T., 355
Dempsey, C. B., 619
DePue, R. A., 549
Dery, G. K., 425
Desor, J. A., 215
Deutch, C. P., 490
Deutch, M., 490
Deutsch, G., 135
Deutscher, I., 412
DeValois, K. K., 163
DeValois, R. L., 163, 169
Devany, J. M., 258
Diener, E., 500, 519
Digman, J. M., 516
Dodson, J. D., 342
Doherty, M. E., 307
Dollard, J., 355
Donnerstein, E. I., 451, 452
Donovan, W. L., 403
Doob, L. W., 355
Dooling, D. J., 280
Dorus, E., 575
Doyle, J., 430
Doyle, W. J., 322
Dragoin, W., 244
Drenick, E. J., 349
Duncker, K., 315–16
Dunn, J., 403
Dunn, V., 558
DuPue, R. A., 652
Durrant, J., 197
Dzendolet, E., 219

E

Eastman, W. F., 442
Ebbinghaus, H., 282
Ebert, M. H., 355
Eccles, J. S., 434
Eckerman, C. O., 400

Edwards, S., 364
Egeland, J. A., 551
Eich, J., 285
Eichorn, D. H., 381
Eisenberg, N., 357
Eisner, J., 351
Ekman, P., 362, 363, 366
Eldridge, N., 65
Elkind, D., 405
Eller, M., 449
Ellis, A., 584, 585
Ellis, L., 447
Ellison, C. R., 439
Ellison, G. D., 237
Emery, G., 552, 586
Emmons, C. A., 449
Engel, L., 62
Engen, T., 215
Environmental Action Foundation, 63
Epling, W. F., 248
Epstein, A. N., 347
Epstein, L. H., 348
Erdelyi, M. H., 578
Erhardt, A. A., 423, 424, 430, 431
Ericksen, S., 575
Erickson, R. P., 217
Erikson, E., 391
Eron, L. D., 358
Ervin, F. R., 354
Eshleman, S., 449
Essman, E. J., 355
Essman, W. B., 355
Evans, 305
Evans, R. I., 644
Eysenck, H. J., 460, 518, 546, 593
Eysenck, M. W., 518
Eysenck, S. B. G., 518

F

Fagan, J. F., 399
Fancher, R. E., 4, 8, 464, 465
Fantino, E., 228
Fantz, R. L., 171, 633
Farber, S. S., 592
Farrar, C. H., 580
Feigley, C. A., 25–26
Feldman, N., 412
Felner, R. D., 592
Ferguson, D. M., 402
Ferster, C. B., 252
Festinger, L., 613, 618
Fieve, R. R., 574
Firestone, P. B., 388
Fishbein, M., 612, 613
Fishman, J., 426
Fishman, S. M., 546
Flattau, P. E., 12, 14, 16
Flax, C. C., 441
Fleck, S., 559
Flynn, J. P., 364
Flynn, J. R., 380
Fode, K. L., 40–41
Fodor, J. A., 320
Folkman, S., 650
Foote, F., 580
Foote, W., 364
Forbes, J. L., 127
Ford, K., 442
Foss, R. D., 619
Fouts, D. H., 325
Fouts, R. S., 325

Fox, N. E., 402
Francis, G., 580
Frank, J. D., 587
Frankel, F. H., 571
Franks, C. M., 579
Frantz, A., 105
Fraser, S., 619
Frederickson, R. C. A., 210
Freedman, J. L., 619
Freud, S., 6, 9, 33, 108, 446, 503, 505, 506, 507, 508, 510, 576, 577, 591
Friedman, H. S., 650
Friedman, L. N., 348
Friedman, M. I., 346
Friedman, M., 650
Friesen, W. V., 362, 363, 366
Frijda, N. H., 359
Frisch, R. E., 426
Frith, C. D., 558
Fritsch, G., 129
Fromkin, V., 322
Fulcher, R., 12
Funder, D. C., 519
Furnas, J. C., 645

G

Gagnon, J. H., 446
Galanter, E., 151, 281
Galizio, M., 247, 257
Gallatin, J., 407
Galton, F., 464
Garattini, S., 355
Garcia, J., 244, 245, 580
Gardner, B. T., 324
Gardner, H., 462, 485
Gardner, R. A., 324
Gaviria, M., 575
Gazzaniga, M. S., 7, 134
Geary, L. E., 210
Gebhard, P. H., 437, 441, 442, 443, 444, 446
Gehring, J. D., 210
Geller, E. S., 647
Gelman, R., 388
Gentry, W. D., 355
Gerard, H. B., 615
Gerbing, D. W., 517
Gerhard, D. S., 551
Geschwind, N., 131, 132
Gibbon, M., 541, 544, 545, 559
Gibbs, J., 391
Gibson, E. J., 174–75, 184–85
Gibson, J. J., 216
Gillam, B., 178
Gilligan, C., 390, 407
Gillin, J., 285
Gintis, H., 482
Glanz, L. M., 593
Glass, G. V., 569
Gluck, M. A., 327
Godden, D. R., 285
Goethals, G. R., 608
Goldstein, B., 425
Goldstein, E. B., 166, 197
Goltesman, I. I., 553, 557
Goodall, J., 31
Goodenough, D. R., 141
Goodwin, D. W., 547
Goodwin, F. K., 355
Gorcey, M., 454
Gordon, B., 574
Gosney, E. S., 468

Gottfredson, G. D., 12, 14, 16
Gottfries, C. G., 409
Gould, S. J., 62, 63, 65, 84, 632
Gouldner, A. W., 621
Goyer, P. F., 355
Graham, J. R., 498
Graham, L. E., 650
Grallo, R., 490
Granneman, J., 346
Gray, W. D., 301
Greaves, G. B., 546
Green, D., 344
Green, D. M., 153, 200
Green, K. C., 429
Gregory, R. L., 183
Greif, E. B., 425
Griffitt, W., 443, 446
Grossman, F. K., 403
Grossman, H. J., 475
Grossman, K., 402
Grossman, K. E., 402
Grossman, M. I., 345
Grossman, S. P., 347
Grotevant, H. D., 407
Groth, A. N., 453
Grove, R., 254–55
Grove, W. M., 558
Groves, P. M., 194
Gruenberg, E., 548
Gulevich, G., 138
Gurling, H., 551
Gurman, A. S., 590
Gustavson, C., 244
Guze, S. B., 547

H

Haber, R. N., 269, 276
Haber, S., 630
Hafeiz, H. B., 547
Hagan, F. E., 612
Hagen, E. P., 468, 472–73
Haith, M., 171
Hake, D. F., 257
Hall, C. S., 141, 511, 514
Hall, E., 408
Hall, J. A., 433
Hallstrom, T., 428
Halpern, D. F., 435
Hamilton, W. D., 82
Hammersmith, S. K., 447
Hanis, C., 349
Hankins, W. M., 244
Hanselka, L., 644
Hanson, J. W., 396
Harlow, H. F., 401, 402
Harlow, M. K., 402
Harrity, R., 148
Hart, J., 443
Hartup, W. W., 404
Hasher, L., 279
Hatfield, E., 446
Hathaway, S. R., 497
Hayes, C., 324
Hayes, S. C., 258
Heath, R. G., 25–26
Hebb, D. O., 267
Heider, F., 606
Helzer, J. E., 539, 548
Hendrickson, D. E., 488
Hendry, B. F., 446
Henning, H., 213
Henry, G. W., 568
Herman, C. P., 351

Herman, H. C., 350
Hernstein, R. J., 460, 467, 481, 482, 483
Hess, E. H., 231–32
Heynsfield, S., 351
Hilgard, E. R., 16, 339
Hirsch, A. D., 325
Hirsch, J., 349
Hite, S., 437
Hitzig, E., 129
Hochberg, J., 173
Hodgkinson, S., 551
Hoffman, E. L., 617
Hofmann, A., 112–13
Hogrebe, M. C., 434
Hohmann, G. W., 367
Holden, C., 434, 553
Holmes, D. S., 653
Holmes, T. H., 652
Holmstrom, L., 453, 454
Honigfeld, G., 575
Honzik, M. P., 381
Hopefield, J., 326
Horland, C. I., 611
Hormann, H., 318
Horn, J. L., 411
Horney, K., 513
Horowitz, M. J., 9
Horwood, L. J., 402
Hostetter, A. M., 51
Housman, D. E., 551
Hovland, C. I., 238
Howard, T., 660
Howard, A., 12, 14, 16, 575
Howell, N., 452
Hsieh, C. C., 642, 653
Hubel, D. H., 163
Huesmann, L. R., 358
Hull, C. L., 336
Hunt, E., 306, 311
Hunt, J. V., 381
Hunt, M., 30, 437, 440, 442, 444, 446
Hunt, R. R., 281
Hurvich, L. M., 169
Huxley, J. S., 362
Hyde, J. T., 652, 653
Hyde, J. S., 435, 440, 441, 446

I

Imber, S. D., 593
Ineichen, B., 628
Inglefinger, F. J., 345
Inhelder, B., 382
Inouye, J., 516
Ironson, G., 448
Istomina, Z. M., 399
Izard, C. E., 363

J

Jacklin, C. N., 435
Jacobs, G. H., 169
Jacobson, J. L., 402
Jaffe, J. H., 114
James, W., 4, 335, 366
Jameson, D., 168
Janoff-Bulman, R., 608
Janowitz, H. D., 345
Jason, L. A., 592
Jemmott, J. B., 651
Jenkins, J. G., 287
Jensen, A. R., 487, 490
Jensen, S. B., 440

Jimerson, D. C., 355
Johnson, D., 349
Johnson, D. M., 301
Johnson, L., 138
Johnson, M. K., 280, 603, 604
Johnson, R. C., 465
Johnson, V. E., 427, 428, 437, 440, 443, 450
Johnson, W. E., 574
Johnston, J. M., 38
Jones, E. E., 511, 608
Jones, I., 358
Jones, K. L., 396
Jordan, T. G., 490
Joseph, J. G., 449
Julien, R. M., 107, 109, 110, 113
Jung, C. G., 512

K

Kaemmer, B., 498
Kalish, R. A., 413
Kamin, L. J., 237, 239, 241–42, 460, 490
Kandel, D. B., 628
Kandel, E. R., 290, 291
Kantner, J. F., 442
Kaplan, H. S., 439
Kaplan, P. S., 403
Karl, P., 244
Kastenbaum, R., 414
Katcher, A. H., 356
Kauff, D. M., 152
Kaye, H., 397
Kazdin, A. E., 255, 581, 582
Keesey, R. E., 347, 349
Keith-Spiegle, P., 594
Keller, H., 148–49
Keller, S. E., 651
Kellogg, L. A., 324
Kellogg, W. N., 324
Kely, H. H., 606, 608
Kendrick, J. S., 642
Kenrick, D. T., 519
Kenshalo, D. R., 207
Kerr, M. M., 584
Kersler, R. C., 449
Kevles, D. J., 464, 467, 468
Keyes, D., 546
Khahneman, D., 313, 314
Kihlstrom, J. F., 528
Killen, L. A., 611
Kinder, B. N., 448
Kinsey, A., 30
Kinsey, A. C., 437, 441, 442, 443, 444, 446
Kirscht, J. P., 449
Klein, D. F., 235
Klein, W. J., 355
Kleitman, N., 137
Klerman, G. L., 552
Kline, D., 161
Kling, A., 125, 354
Klug, W. S., 78, 80
Kluver, H., 125
Knight, R., 559
Kniskern, D. P., 590
Knittle, J. L., 349
Koegel, R., 583, 593
Koelling, R. A., 244, 245, 580
Kohlberg, L., 388, 390, 391, 433
Köhler, W., 5, 316
Kolata, G., 348

Kolb, L. C., 113
Kolodny, R. C., 47, 442, 444, 446, 450
Korlin, D., 432
Korn, W. S., 429
Koss, M. P., 453, 454
Koulack, D., 141
Kraines, R. J., 428
Krebs, R. L., 390
Kübler-Ross, E., 413
Kuhn, T. S., 629
Kunst-Wilson, W. R., 152, 369, 610
Kupfer, D. J., 574
Kurdek, L. A., 433, 448

L

Lachman, J. L., 297
Lachman, R., 280, 297
Lagerspetz, K., 354
Lally, M., 487
Lamb, M. E., 402
Lashley, K. S., 133
Latané, B., 561, 627
Lauer, R. H., 645
Lawless, H. T., 215
Lazarus, A. A., 653
Lazarus, R. S., 369
Le Boeuf, B. J., 65
Leach, B. E., 25–26
Leber, W. R., 593
LeBlanc, J. M., 582
Lee, M., 358
Lefcourt, H., 523
Leff, M. J., 549
Leitz, A., 440
Lemere, F., 580
Lennie, P., 163
Leonard, K. E., 454
LePiere, G. T., 612
Lepper, M. R., 344
Lerner, M. J., 608
Lesgold, A., 311, 315
Levensen, R. W., 363, 366
Levinson, D. J., 393
Levitt, L. A., 403
Lewin, K., 355
Lewin, R., 69
Lewsinson, P. M., 585
Lewis, M., 400
Lewis, M. I., 409
Lewis, S. K., 620
Lewontin, R. C., 490
Leyens, J. P., 358
Liberman, R. P., 582
Lickey, M. E., 574
Lidz, T., 559
Lieberman, M., 391
Liebert, R. M., 357, 358
Likous, R. A., 615
Lindemalm, G., 432
Linden, E., 325
Lindsay, P. N., 180
Lindsley, O. R., 581
Lindzey, G., 490, 514
Links, P. S., 536
Linn, M. C., 435
Linz, D., 451, 452
Lipsitt, L. P., 397
Locke, B. Z., 536
Locke, S. E., 651
Lockhart, R. S., 272, 273
Loeb, G. E., 203
Loehlin, J. C., 490

Loftus, E. F., 282, 285–86, 300
Loftus, G. R., 282
Logan, C. A., 228
Londorville, S., 402
Long, J. S., 583, 593
Lorenz, K. 230, 231, 353
Louiselle, P. A., 403
Lovaas, O. I., 582, 583, 593
Lovrinic, J., 197
Lowe, C. F., 257, 258
Lowell, E. L., 340
Luce, G. G., 140
Lucido, D. J., 630
Lutkenhaus, P., 402
Lykken, D. T., 364, 560
Lynch, G., 290
Lzars, R. S., 650

M

Maccoby, E. E., 390, 401, 403, 435
Maccoby, N., 611
MacIntosh, N. J., 487
Mack, D., 350
Madle, R. A., 581
Main, M., 402
Major, B., 430
Malamuth, N. M., 451
Malatesta, V. J., 445
Mallet, J., 551
Malt, B. C., 302
Malthus, T., 64
Mansky, P. A., 574
Marchbancks, R., 551
Marcia, J. E., 393, 406
Mark, V. H., 354
Marmor, J., 440
Marshack, A., 70
Marshall, D. S., 422
Marshall, G. D., 368
Marshark, M., 281
Martens, S., 25–26
Martin, B. A., 572
Martin, C. E., 437, 441, 442, 443, 444, 446
Martin, J. A., 403
Martin, L. K., 580
Martin, R. G., 148
Maslow, A. H., 337, 525, 526
Masters, W. H., 427, 428, 437, 440, 443, 446, 450
Matlin, M. W., 214
Matthews, B. A., 257
Matthews, G., 608
Mauer, D., 399
Mayer, D. J., 105, 210
Mayer, D. M., 105
Mayer, J., 345
Mayr, E., 60, 64, 228
Mazur, J. E., 247
McAlister, A., 611
McArthur, J. W., 426
McArthur, L. A., 606
McBurney, D. H., 219
McCall-Perez, F., 454
McCann, I. L., 653
McClearn, G. E., 465
McClelland, D. C., 340, 341
McCrae, R. R., 516
McDougall, W., 228, 232, 335
McEvoy, C. L., 277
McGee, E. A., 442
McGrath, P. L., 657
McGue, M., 77, 78

McInnis, M., 551
McIntyre, K. D., 258
McKinley, J. C., 497
Meichenbaum, D., 653
Meiselman, H. L., 219
Meltzoff, A. N., 397
Melzack, R., 204, 208, 209
Menustik, C. E., 581
Merikle, P. M., 275–76
Mervis, C. B., 301
Messenger, J. C., 422
Messick, S., 477
Meyer, R. G., 542
Meyer-Bahlburg, H. F. L., 430, 446
Michaels, J. W., 615
Milavsky, B., 356
Milavsky, J. R., 358
Milgram, S., 624
Miller, G. A., 267, 270, 281
Miller, H. L., Jr., 257
Miller, J. A., 620
Miller, N., 355
Milner, B., 266, 289
Milner, P. M., 126–27, 365
Milofsky, E. S., 111
Mirsky, A. F., 354
Mischel, W., 519, 522, 585
Mishkin, M., 289
Misukanis, T. M., 403
Mitchell, P. B., 352
Mollen, J. D., 168
Money, J., 423, 424, 431
Monroe, 549
Monroe, S. M., 652
Montagu, A., 85
Montgomery, S. B., 449
Moore, M. K., 397
Moore, T. E., 152
Moray, N., 202
Morrison, D. M., 443
Mortisugu, J. M., 592
Most, A., 425
Mower, O. H., 355
Mozel, M. M., 213, 219
Mueller, R. A., 403
Murphy, D. L., 342
Murray, E. J., 580
Murray, H. A., 339, 502, 528
Mussen, P. H., 357
Mynatt, C. R., 307
Myrow, D. L., 288

N

Nagoshi, C. T., 465
Nasrallah, H. A., 558
Neale, J. M., 550, 568
Neisser, U., 178, 179, 259, 275
Neisworth, J. T., 581
Nelson, D. A., 277
Nelson, R. O., 258
Nettlebeck, T., 487
Neugarten, B. L., 412, 428
Newell, A., 297, 310
Nisbett, R. E., 344, 347, 348, 349, 608
Niswander, G. D., 25
Nordby, V. J., 141, 511
Norman, D. A., 180, 267
North, C. N., 534–35

O

O'Brien, K., 449
O'Brien, R., 580

Odbert, H. S., 515, 517
Oden, M. H., 476
Offord, D. R., 536
Olds, J. M., 126–27
Ollendick, T. H., 580
Oller, D. K., 322
Olsen, S. A., 58, 556
Ornish, D., 650
Oros, C. J., 453, 454
Orvashel, H., 548
Orvis, B. R., 608
Osborne, Y. V., 542
Oskamp, S., 12, 14, 16
Osler, S., 285
Ostrow, D. G., 449
Overhoser, W., 573

P

Pack, S. J., 429
Paffenbarger, R. S., Jr., 642, 653
Paivio, A., 280
Palmar, F. H., 490
Palmer, J. C., 286
Pancake, V. R., 402
Pandey, G. N., 575
Parke, R. D., 358, 412
Pastor, D. L., 402
Patterson, F., 325
Patterson, R., 582
Pauls, D. L., 551
Pavlov, I. P., 233, 236, 239
Penfiela, W., 129
Pennypacker, H. S., 38
Peplau, L. A., 629
Perlmutter, M., 408
Perls, F. S., 588
Perry, C., 611
Peskin, J., 412
Peters, R. K., 642
Peterson, L., 627
Peterson, L. R., 269
Peterson, M. J., 269
Petty, R. E., 612
Petursson, H., 551
Pfafflin, S. M., 12, 14, 16
Pfaffman, C., 218
Pfohl, B., 556
Phares, E. J., 520, 523, 524
Phillips, D. P., 549
Piaget, J., 33, 382, 387
Pierce, W. D., 248
Pile, M. C., 642
Pinkston, E. M., 582
Pion, G. M., 12, 14, 16
Platt, S. A., 378
Pleck, J. H., 413, 429
Plomin, R., 378, 480
Plutchik, R., 361
Podlesny, J. A., 364
Polivy, J., 351
Pollack, M., 445
Pollard, P., 305
Pomeroy, C. E., 437, 441, 442, 443, 444, 446
Pomeroy, W. B., 441
Poon, L., 410
Pope, K. S., 594
Popenoe, P., 468
Popper, D. R., 25
Posner, M. I., 279
Poulos, R. W., 57
Powell, B. J., 580
Powell, K. E., 642
Powley, T. L., 347, 349

Premack, A. J., 325
Premack, D., 325
Pribram, K. H., 281, 354
Price, D. D., 105
Prien, R. F., 574
Pylyshyn, Z. W., 296

Q

Quattrone, G. A., 605
Quillian, M. R. 299, 300

R

Rabkin, J. G., 546
Rachman, S., 580
Rader, N., 388
Radian, N. S., 449
Radloff, C. E., 608
Rae-Grant, N. I., 536
Rafii, A., 105
Ragle, J. L., 113
Rahe, R. H., 652
Raines, B. E., 644
Rapaport, K., 453, 454
Rapoport, R., 413
Rapoport, R. N., 413
Rappaport, J., 592
Raskin, C. E., 364
Raymond, M., 580
Read, J. D., 152
Rebec, G. V., 194
Reed, D., 113
Reeders, S., 551
Reese, N. M., 582
Regier, D. A., 536, 548
Reisenzein, R., 368
Reiss, B. F., 449
Rekers, G. A., 582
Repetti, R. L., 431
Rescorla, R. A., 239–43
Reynolds, W. B., 582
Rheingold, H. L., 400, 401
Rice, F. J., 426
Rice, M. L., 323
Richman, C. L., 281
Rickels, K., 574
Ridd, K. K., 551
Riecken, H., 613
Rifkin, J., 660
Riley, V., 651
Rittle, R. H., 615
Rips, L. J., 303, 305
Roatch, J. F., 549
Roberts, W., 351
Robins, E., 446, 447
Robins, L. N., 539, 548
Roby, T. B., 337
Rodin, J., 346, 348, 349, 415
Rodman, R., 322
Roff, J. D., 559
Rogers, C. R., 526, 588
Rohrer, J. H., 617
Roitblat, H. L., 324
Rollins, B. C., 412
Rorschach, H., 501
Rosch, E. H., 301, 302
Rose, R. M., 446
Rosenblatt, P. C., 631
Rosenkrantz, P. S., 434
Rosenman, R. H., 650
Rosenthal, R., 40–41
Ross, A. S., 627
Ross, C., 322
Ross, D., 357
Ross, L., 608

Ross, S. A., 357
Rossman, I., 428
Rosvold, H. E., 354
Roth, S., 454
Rothenberg, A. M., 316
Rotter, J., 520, 522–23
Rottman, L., 628
Rowe, J. S., 615
Rubin, Z., 404
Rumelhart, D. E., 269
Rush, A. J., 552, 586
Rushton, J. P., 627
Rusinak, K., 244
Russell, D. E. H., 452
Russell, M. J., 216
Rutherford, W., 199
Ryan, R. M., 344

S

Sach, E. Jr., 25
Sachs, J. S., 271
Sackeim, H. A., 571
Sadd, S., 437, 444
Sager, C. J., 590
Saghir, M. T., 446, 447
Salthe, S. N., 67
Samuel, M., 449
Sancton, T., 664
Sande, G. N., 608
Sanislow, C. A., 378
Santiago, J. M., 454
Sarason, I. G., 519
Satmari, P., 536
Sattler, J. M., 468, 472–73
Scarr, S., 403, 490
Schachter, S., 21, 35, 36, 38, 40, 50–51, 348, 367–68, 561
Schact, T. E., 540
Schacter, S., 613
Schaie, K. W., 380, 409–10, 413
Scherwitz, L., 650
Schieber, F., 161
Schiffman, H. R., 155, 204, 212, 213, 217
Schiffrin, R. M., 267, 268, 271, 279
Schleifer, S. J., 651
Schmeck, H. M., Jr., 203
Schmidt, G., 437
Schmitt, J. P., 433
Schneider, W., 279
Schofield, M., 437
Schreiner, L., 125, 354
Schulz, D. A., 645
Schumer, F., 549
Schwartz, G. E., 366
Schwartz, J. H., 290, 291
Scoville, W. B., 266
Scruggs, M., 413
Seamon, J. G., 152
Sears, R. R., 355
Seitz, V. R., 481
Sekuler, R., 215, 217
Selfridge, O., 180
Selkoe, D. J., 409
Selye, H., 649
Shannon, F. T., 402
Shapley, R., 163
Shaughnessy, R., 575
Shaw, B. F., 552, 585, 586
Sheehan, D. V., 546
Sheffield, F. D., 337
Sherif, M., 616, 617, 633
Sherrick, C. E., 209

Subject Index

Brain: definition of, 93, 143; endocrine system and, 116–17; frontiers of, 141–42; nervous system and, 94–105
Bipedalism in human evolution, 70, 88
Bipolar disorder, 549–50, 564
Blind spot, 161, 187
Blindness, color, 166
Blocking, classical conditioning and, 241–42, 262
Bottom-up processing in pattern recognition, 185, 189
Brain, 118–41; central core of, 123–24, 145; from cochlea to, 198; consciousness and, 133–41; damage/injury to, 119–20; development of, in infancy and childhood, 397; eating and, 347–48; electrical recording and stimulation in study of, 120–22; emotion and, 364–65; functions of, 122–33; lesions of, 20, 144; limbic system of, 125–27, 145; from retina to, 161–62; scans of, 122; sleeping, 136–41; split, 133–35; structures of, 122–33; study of, 118–22
Brightness contrast, 164, 188
Brightness of light, 157, 187
Broca's area, 131, 145
Broca's speech center, 119
Bulimia, 352, 372
Bystander intervention, helping and, 626–27, 635

C

Caffeine, 109
Cancer, diet and, 641–42, 666
Cannon-Bard theory of emotion, 366–67, 373
Case studies in observation research, 32–33, 56
CAT (computed axial tomography) scan of brain, 122, 123
Catatonic schizophrenia, 556, 565
Category clustering in memory, 277
Catharsis, aggression as, 353, 372
Cattell, Raymond, source traits of personality and, 517
Causal hypothesis, definition of, 56
Causes: proximate, of behavior in evolution, 60, 88; ultimate, of behavior in evolution, 60, 88
Cell body of neuron, 95, 143
Central core of brain, 123–24, 145
Central nervous system (CNS), 95, 143
Central traits in social perception, 604, 634
Cephalocaudal principle of motor development, 398, 418
Cerebellum, 124, 145
Cerebral cortex, 127–33, 145
Chemical senses, 212–20
Child and parent, interaction between, attachment and, 403
Childbearing, approaches to, social development of child and, 403–5
Childhood: brain development in, 397; cognitive development in, 399–400; motor development in, 398–99; physical development in, 397–99; psychosocial development in, 391–92; social development in, 400–5
Cholesterol, serum, coronary heart disease and, 641, 666
Chorea, Huntington's, 79, 88; symptoms and neuronal base of, 120
Chromosomal aberration, 74–75, 88

Chromosomes, 72, 88
Chunk in memory, 270, 292
Cigarette smoking, 644–45
Circadian rhythm, 136–37, 145
Classical conditioning, 233–45, 261; acquisition in, 236–38, 262; behavior therapy based on, 579–81; blocking and, 241–42, 262; contingency and, 239–41; continuity and, 239–41; discovery of, 234–35; discrimination in, 239, 262; extinction in, 238, 262; importance of, 235–36; principles of, 236–39; Rescorla-Wagner model of, 242–43, 262; spontaneous recovery in, 238, 262; stimulus generalization in, 238–39, 262; taste-aversion learning and, 243–45
Clinical psychologist, 15, 19
Closure in perceptual grouping, 172–73, 188
Cocaine, 108–9
Cochlea, 197, 222; to brain, 198
Cognition: computational metaphor for, 297–98, 328; emotion and, 369–70; social, 602–15. See also Social cognition
Cognitive, definition of, 296, 328
Cognitive abilities, gender differences in, 434–35
Cognitive appraisal, stress and, 650, 667
Cognitive behavior therapy, 584, 598
Cognitive behavioral approaches to therapy, 584–86, 598
Cognitive development: in adolescence, 405–6; in adulthood and old age, 409–11; in infancy and childhood, 399–400; Piaget's theory of, 382–88
Cognitive-developmental theory of gender typing, 433
Cognitive dissonance theory of social cognition, 613–15, 635
Cognitive economy, 301
Cognitive perspective on psychology, 8–9, 19
Cognitive processes, definition of, 2, 19
Cognitive reappraisal in coping with stress, 653–54, 667
Cognitive restructuring, 584, 598
Cognitive therapy for depression, 585–86
Cohorts in life-span studies, 379–80
Collective unconscious, 512, 531
Color(s): complementary, 167; seeing, 165
Color blindness, 166
Color circle, 166–67
Color vision, 165–69; theories of, 167–69
Commitment in adolescence, 406, 419
Communication, 317–25. See also Language; nonhuman, 324–25
Community psychology, 591–93, 598
Competition in natural selection, 66–67, 88
Complementary colors, 167
Compliance, social influence and, 619–21, 635
Compulsion, 542, 564
Computational metaphor for cognition, 297–98, 328
Concept(s): definition of, 298–99, 328; meaning of, 301–4; organization of, 299–301; organizing knowledge with, 298–304
Concrete operational period in cognitive development, 386–87
Conditional response (CR) in classical conditioning, 235, 261
Conditional stimulus (CS) in classical conditioning, 235, 261

Conditioned reinforcement in operant conditioning, 255, 263
Conditioning: of attitudes, 610; classical, 233–45. See also Classical conditioning; delay, 238; operant, 245–59. See also Operant conditioning
Conditions of worth in personality, 526–27, 531
Conduction hearing loss, 202, 222
Cones in retina, 159–60, 187
Confederate in social psychological experiment, 617, 635
Confidentiality in psychological research, 54, 57
Confirmation bias, 307–8, 328
Conformity, social influence and, 616–18, 635
Confounding variables in experimental research, 40, 57
Conscious experience, drugs and, 105–16
Consciousness, brain and, 133–41
Consensus in covariance assessment, 607, 634
Consent, informed, for participation in psychological research, 53–54, 57
Conservation in preoperational thinking, 385–86, 417
Consistency in covariance assessment, 607, 634
Constructs, intelligence test scores and, 476, 492
Consumer psychologists, 15
Context in pattern recognition, 181–82
Contingency: classical conditioning and, 239–41; three-term, in operant conditioning, 248–50
Continuity, classical conditioning and, 239–41
Continuous reinforcement schedule in operant conditioning, 252, 262
Control group in experiment, 36–38, 56–57
Conventional level in moral development, 389, 418
Convergence in depth perception, 173, 188
Conversion disorders, 544, 564
Cornea of eye, 157, 187
Coronary heart disease (CHD), diet and, 641–42, 666
Corpus callosum, 134–35, 145
Correlation: statistical, 46; of variables, 26–27, 56
Correlation coefficient, 48, 57
Counseling, genetic, 80
Counterattitudinal behavior, cognitive dissonance and, 614–15, 635
Countertransference in psychoanalysis, 578, 598
Covariation rule in attribution, 606–7, 634
Crack, 109
Creativity in problem solving, 316, 328
Crisis in adolescence, 406, 419
Critical period for imprinting, 231–32
Cross-adaptation, olfactory, 215, 223
Cross-sectional approach to study of life-span changes, 379–80
Crystallized intelligence, 411, 419
Cultural evolution, 71, 88, 639, 666

D

Dark adaptation of eyes, 164, 188
Darwin, Charles: biography of, 61–64; theory of, development of, 62–64

Data, definition of, 56
Data analysis, 42–51, 57; correlation and, 46–49; descriptive statistics in, 42, 43–46; inferential statistics in, 49–51; prediction and, 46–49
Death in social development, 413–14
Debriefing in psychological research, 54, 57
Decibel (dB), 194
Deductive reasoning, 304–6, 328
Deep structure of sentence, 321–22
Defense mechanisms, 507–8, 530
Deferred imitation in sensorimotor period of cognitive development, 384
Degradation in synaptic transmission, 102, 144
Delay conditioning, 238
Delirium tremens (DTs), 111
Delusions in schizophrenia, 554
Demand characteristics in experimental research, 41–42, 57
Dendrites, 95, 143
Denial: in coping with death, 413; as defense mechanism, 507, 530
Dependence: physical, 106, 115, 144; psychological, 106, 144
Depressants, 110–12, 144
Depression: cognitive therapy for, 585–86; in coping with death, 413; drugs for, 574; major, 548–49, 564
Depth cues, 174–75, 188
Depth perception, 173–75, 188
Descriptive statistics in data analysis, 42, 43–46, 57
Desensitization, systematic, in psychotherapy, 580, 598
Determinism, reciprocal, in personality, 521, 531
Development, theories of, 381–93; Erikson's, 391–93; Kohlberg's, 388–91; Piaget's, 382–88
Deviation, standard, 45–46, 57
Diathesis-stress model: of personality disorder, 560; of schizophrenia, 558, 565
Diet, 641–42
Difference thresholds in sensation, 154–55, 187
Diffusion of responsibility, bystander effect and, 627, 635
Discounting rule in attribution, 607, 634
Discrimination, 64, 605; in classical conditioning, 239, 262; in operant conditioning, 250
Discriminative stimulus in operant conditioning, 249
Disinhibition, obesity and, 350
Disorganized schizophrenia, 556, 565
Disorganized thought in schizophrenia, 554
Displacement: as cathartic outlet, 353; as defense mechanism, 508, 530
Dissociative disorders, 545–46, 564
Distal stimulus in visual perception, 170, 188
Distinctiveness in covariance assessment, 606–7, 634
Divorce, sex and, 444–45
Dizygotic (DZ) twins, 72–78, 88
DNA (deoxyribonucleic acid), 72, 88
Door-in-the-face technique to gain compliance, 620–21, 635
Dopamine (DA) as neurotransmitter, 104
Doppler effect in locating sound, 200–1, 222
Double-bind, schizophrenia and, 559, 565
Double-blind study, 41, 57

Down's syndrome, 79, 88
Dream interpretation in psychoanalysis, 577, 598
Drive, 336, 372
Drive theory of motivation, 36–37
Drug(s): abuse of, 645, 666; conscious experience and, 105–16; psychoactive, 105, 107–16; therapy with, 572–75, 598
Drunkenness, 111
DSM-III-R (Diagnostic and Statistical Manual of Mental Disorders) in psychological disorder classification, 537–40, 564; problems with, 539–40
Dual center theory of eating, 347, 372

E
Ear, 195–98; inner, 197–98; middle, 196–97; outer, 196
Eardrum, 196
Eating: aggression and motivation and, 359; brain and, 347–48; disorders of, 351–53; dual center theory of, 347, 372; motivation for, 345–53. See also Hunger
Ecosystem, 655, 667
Educational psychologists, 15–16
Effortful processing of information in memory, 278–79, 293
Ego, 507, 530
Egocentric nature of preoperational children, 385, 417
Ejaculation, premature, 441, 457
Elaboration likelihood model of attitude change/persuasion, 612
Elaborative rehearsal in levels of processing model of memory, 273
Electrical recording of brain activity, 120–22
Electrical stimulation of brain activity, 121–22
Electroconvulsive therapy (ECT), 571–72, 598
Electroencephalogram (EEG), 121, 145
Embryonic stage, 394, 418
Emotion, 359–70; autonomic nervous system and, 363–64; boundaries of, 370–71; brain and, 364–65; Cannon-Bard theory of, 366–67, 373; classifying, 360–62; cognition and, 369–70; definition of, 59, 372; facial expressions of, 362–63; facial feedback hypothesis of, 363, 373; frontiers of, 370–71; James-Lange theory of, 365–66, 373; physiology of, 363–65; theories of, 365–70; two-factor theory of, 367–69, 373
Empirical knowledge: definition of, 56; falsifiability and, 25–26; scientific knowledge as, 22–26; variables and, 26–27
Empty chair technique in Gestalt therapy, 588, 598
Encephalization in human evolution, 70, 88
Encoding, 266, 278–81, 292; automatic versus effortful processing in, 279, 293; improving memory by, 280–81; meaningful elaboration in, 279–80; specificity, 279, 293
Endocrine system, 116–17, 144
Engineering psychologists, 15
Enkephalins as neurotransmitters, 105
Environment: and genes, interaction of, 76; life-style and, 655–63; overpopulation and, 655–58; pollution of, 658–63; you and, 663

Epigenetic principle in psychosocial development, 391
Episodic memory, 272, 292
Equilibrium, 211–12, 223
Erectile dysfunction, 440, 457
Erikson, Erik, theory of psychosocial development of, 391–93
Ethical issues: in Milgram's studies of obedience, 625–26; in psychotherapy, 594–96
Ethics in psychological research, 51–54, 57; on animal use, 51–52; on human subject use, 52–54
Etiology, 537, 564; of anxiety-based disorders, 546–48; of mood disorders, 550–52; of schizophrenia, 556–59
Eugenics, 465, 492
"Eve theory," 69
Evoked potentials as measure of intelligence, 488
Evolution: biological, 60, 88; cultural, 71, 88, 639, 666; selective pressures in, 70–71; sketch of, 68–69
Excitement phase in sexual arousal, 438
Exercises, aerobic, 643, 666; in coping with stress, 653
Exhibitionism, 561, 565
Expectancy in personality, 520–21, 531
Expectancy theory of motivation, 344–45, 372
Experiment: control group in, 36–38, 56–57; definition of, 56; experimental group in, 36–38, 56; variables in, 34–36, 56
Experimental group in experiment, 36–38, 56
Experimental research, 34–42, 56–57; confounding variables in, 40–57; demand characteristics in, 41–42, 57; experiment in, 34–38; experimenter expectancy in, 40–41, 57; potential pitfalls of, 40–42; single-subject, 38–39; variables in, 34–36
Experimenter expectancy in experimental research, 40–41, 57
Expert system, 312, 328
External cues to eating, obesity and, 349
Extinction: in behavior therapy, 582; in classical conditioning, 238, 262; in operant conditioning, 251
Eye, 157–61; cornea of, 157, 187; functions of, 157–59; iris of, 157, 187; lens of, 157–58, 187; pupil of, 157, 187; retina of, 157, 159–61, 187; structures of, 157–59
Eysenck, Hans, personality theory of, 517–18

F
Facial expressions of emotion, 362–63
Facial feedback hypothesis of emotion, 363, 373
Facilitation, social, 615–16, 635
Factor analysis in intelligence testing, 462–63
Falsifiability: definition of, 56; empirical knowledge and, 25–26
Family in social development, 412
Family therapy, 590, 598
Farsightedness, 160
Fat cells, obesity and, 349
Feature analysis in pattern recognition, 180–81, 188
Feature detectors, 163, 187
Fertilization, 423, 456; in vitro, 80
Fetal alcohol syndrome (FAS), 111–12, 396

Fetal stage, 394–95, 418
Fetishism, 561, 565
Figure-ground relationship, 171, 188
Fitness: inclusive, 82, 89; personal, in natural selection, 65–66, 88
Five-factor theory of personality, 516–17
Fixation: in personality development, 508, 530; thinking and, 315–17
Fixed-action pattern of behavior, 229–31, 261
Fixed-interval (FI) schedule of reinforcement, 253, 262–63
Fixed-ratio (FR) schedule of reinforcement, 253, 262
Flavor, 216–17, 223
Fluid intelligence, 411, 419
Follicle-stimulating hormone (FSH), 424, 456
Foot-in-the-door technique to gain compliance, 619, 635
Foreclosure, 406
Form perception, 171–73
Formal operational period in cognitive development, 387
Forward chaining, 310, 328
Fovea in retina, 159–60, 187
Free association in psychoanalysis, 576, 598
Frequency distribution in statistics, 43–44, 57
Frequency theory of pitch, 199–200
Freud, Sigmund, approach of, to personality, 503–10
Freudian slips, 505, 530
Frustration, aggression and, 355–56
Fugue, psychogenic, 545, 564
Functional fixedness, 315, 328
Functionalism, 4, 19
Fundamental attribution error, 608, 634

G

GABA (gamma-amino butyric acid) as neurotransmitter, 104
Galton, Sir Francis, intelligence tests and, 464–65
Gambler's fallacy, 314, 328
Gate-control theory of pain perception, 208–10, 223
Gender, 422–23, 456; sexual behavior and, 435–37
Gender development, 420–35; biology of, 423–28; prenatal contributions to, 423–24; psychological aspects of, 428–35; in puberty, 424–27
Gender differences, 434–35
Gender identity, 429, 430–31, 456
Gender perspective, biology and, 428
Gender roles, 429–30, 456
Gender schema theory of gender typing, 433–34
Gender typing, 429, 431, 456; gender schema theory of, 433–34; social learning theory of, 432; theories of, 432–34
Gene therapy, 80–81
General adaptation syndrome (GAS), 649–50, 666–67
Generalization: in classical conditioning, 238–39, 262; in operant conditioning, 250
Generalized anxiety disorder, 540–41, 564
Genes, 72, 88; and environment, interaction of, 76
Genetic counseling, 80
Genetic disorders, 79–81

Genetic engineering, 80–81
Genetic influences, assessing, 77–78
Genetic material, organization of, 72
Genetic program for behavior, 228–29, 261
Genetics, 71; learning and, 227–32; principles of, 72–75
Genital herpes, 449
Genital stage in personality development, 510, 530–31
Genotype in natural selection, 66, 88
Gestalt psychology, 5, 19
Gestalt therapy, 588, 598
Gland(s): adrenal, 116–17; pituitary, 116; sex, 117
Glial cell, 94, 143
Gonorrhea, 449
Good continuation in perceptual grouping, 172, 188
Greenhouse effect, 659–60, 667
Group therapy, 589–91, 598

H

Hair cells, 197, 222
Hallucinations in schizophrenia, 555
Health, stress and, 648–54
Health psychology, 648, 666
Hearing impairment, 202–3
Helping behavior, increasing, 627
Heredity, 71–72, 75–81. See also Genetics; anxiety-based disorders and, 546–47; intelligence and, 479–81; mood disorders and, 551; schizophrenia and, 557; sex influences on, 74
Heritability, 76–77, 88
Heroin, 114
Herpes, genital, 449
Hertz (Hz), 194, 222
Heterosexuality, 442–45
Heuristic(s), 309–14, 328; availability, 313, 328; biases in use of, 312–14; expertise and, 311–12; representativeness, 313–14, 328
Heuristic strategies based on induction, 309–11
Hippocampus, 127, 145
Homeostasis, drive theory and, 336
Homo eretus, 68–69
Homo habilis, 68
Homo sapiens, 69
Homosexuality, 445–49; development of, theories of, 446–47; societal attitudes toward, 448–49
Hormones, 116–17, 144
Horney, Karen, personality theory of, 513
Hues, 157, 187
Humanistic approach to personality, 524–27; conditions of worth in, 526–37, 531; critique of, 527; self-actualization and, 525–26, 531
Humanistic therapy, 587–88, 598
Humans as subjects in psychological research, ethics of, 52–54
Hunger: external signals for, 346–47; internal signals for, 345–46
Huntington's chorea, 79, 88; symptoms and neuronal base of, 120
Hyperopia, 160, 187
Hypochondriasis, 544, 564
Hypothalamus, 126–27, 145; lateral, feeding and, 347, 372; ventromedial, feeding and, 347, 372
Hypothesis(es): causal, definition of, 56; relational, 29, 56; in scientific knowledge, 27–29, 56

I

Id, 506, 530
Identity achievers, 406
Identity diffusions, 406
Illusions, 177–78, 188
Imitation, deferred, in sensorimotor period of cognitive development, 384
Immune system, 651, 667; impairment of, by stressful life-style, 651
Impression formation in social perception, 603, 634
Imprinting, 231–33
In vitro fertilization, 80
Incentive theory of motivation, 343–44, 372
Inclusive fitness, 82, 89
Incongruence in person-centered therapy, 587, 598
Incubation in problem solving, 316–17, 328
Induction, heuristic strategies based on, 309–11
Inductive reasoning, 306–8, 328
Industrial/organizational (I/O) psychologists, 15
Infancy, 396–405; brain development in, 397; cognitive development in, 399–400; motor development in, 398–99; physical development in, 397–99; social development in, 400–5
Inferential statistics in data analysis, 49–51, 57
Information processing, 297, 328; computational metaphor for, 297–98, 328; in memory, 278–88, 293; automatic versus effortful, 278–79, 293
Informed consent for participation in psychological research, 53–54, 57
Insight in problem solving, 316, 328
Instinct, behavior and, 227–28, 261
Instinct theory of motivation, 335, 372
Instrumental conditioning, 245–59, 262. See also Operant conditioning
Intelligence(s), 458–93; biological measurements of, 487–89; boundaries of, 489; crystallized, 411, 419; definition of, 461–63, 491; fluid, 411, 419; frontiers of, 489; general, 462–63; heredity and, 479–81; modern theories of, 484–89; multiple, theory of, 485–87, 492; roots of, 479–81; social issues and, 481–83; specific, 462–63; tests of, 463–79. See also Intelligence tests; triarchic theory of, 484–85, 492; verbal, measurement of, 471–72, 492
Intelligence quotient (IQ), 467
Intelligence tests: bias of, 478–79, 492; Binet-Simon, 465–67; contemporary, 468–74; Galton's, 464–65; historical overview of, 463–68; individual versus group, 473–74; reliability of, 476–78, 492; scores of, evaluating, critical issues in, 475–79; Stanford-Binet, 467–71; validity of, 477–78, 492; Wechsler, revised, 471–73
Interference, retrieval and, 287–88
Intermittent reinforcement schedule in operant conditioning, 252–54, 262
Interpersonal attraction, social influence and, 628–29
Interposition in depth perception, 174, 188
Intervening variable(s), 333, 372; intelligence test scores and, 476, 492; motivation as, 333
Interview for self-reporting, 30, 56

Intrinsic motivation, 344, 372
Introspection in structuralism, 4, 19
Iris of eye, 157, 187

J

James-Lange theory of emotion, 365–66, 373
Jung, Carl, personality theory of, 511–12
Just noticeable difference (jnd), 154, 187

K

Kaplan's biphasic model of human sexual response, 439
Kin selection, 82, 89
Kinesthetic system, 211, 223
Knowledge: organizing, with concepts, 298–99, 328; scientific, 21–29. See also Scientific knowledge; types of, 21–22
Kohlberg, Lawrence, theory of moral development of, 388–91; conventional level in, 389, 418; postconventional level in, 389–90, 418; preconventional level in, 388, 418; reactions to, 390–91

L

Language, 317–24, 328; development, 322–24; structure of, 319–22
Latency stage in personality development, 510, 530
Latent content in psychoanalysis, 577, 598
Lateral hypothalamus (LH), feeding and, 347, 372
Law of effect, 246–47, 262
Learning, 224–63; behavior and, 227; behavioral analysis and, 232–33; boundaries of, 259–60; classical conditioning and, 233–45. See also Classical conditioning; definition of, 27, 261; frontiers of, 259–60; genetics and, 227–32; observational, in personality, 521, 531; operant conditioning and, 245–59. See also Operant conditioning; perceptual, 184–85, 189; taste-aversion, classical conditioning and, 243–45
Learning factors: anxiety-based disorders and, 547–48; mood disorders and, 552; schizophrenia and, 558–59
Legal issues in psychotherapy, 594–96
Lens of eye, 157–58, 187
Levels of processing model of memory, 272–75, 292–93; modification of, 277
Life-span development, 374–419; adolescence in, 405–8; adulthood in, 408–14; approaches to study of, 379–81; boundaries of, 414–16; childhood in, 396–405; frontiers of, 414–16; infancy in, 396–405; old age in, 408–14; prenatal period in, 394–96; questions in, 378–79; theories of, 381–93
Life-span developmental psychology, 377
Life-span perspective, 377–81
Life-style, 636–67; AIDS in, 646; alcohol/drug abuse in, 645; boundaries of, 664–65; choices and consequences of, 639–48; cigarette smoking in, 644–45; definition of, 639, 666; diet in, 641–42; environment and, 655–63; frontiers of, 664–65; personal safety in, 647; physical fitness in, 642–43; sexually trans-

mitted diseases in, 646; stressful, impaired health and, 650–51; unhealthy, prevention of, 647–68
Light, nature of, 156–57
Light adaptation of eyes, 163–64, 188
Limbic system, 125–27, 145
Linear perspective in depth perception, 174, 188
Linear profile in Stanford-Binet, 470–71
Listening, selective, in auditory perception, 202, 222
Lithium carbonate as antimanic drug, 574–75
Locus of control in personality, 522–23, 531
Long-term store in three-component model of memory, 271–72, 292
Longitudinal approach to study of life-span changes, 380–81
Loudness, 193–94, 222
Low-balling technique to gain compliance, 620, 635
LSD (lysergic acid diethylamide), 112–13
Luteinizing hormone (LH), 424, 456

M

Maintenance rehearsal in levels of processing model of memory, 273
Mania, 548, 564; drugs for, 574–75
Manifest content in psychoanalysis, 577, 598
Marijuana, 113–14
Marital therapy, 589–90, 598
Marriage, 412; sex and, 443–44
Maslow, Abraham, on self-actualization, 525–26
Maslow's hierarchy of needs, 337–39, 372
Masochism, sexual, 562, 565
Mass to specific principle of motor development, 398, 418
Masters and Johnson model of human sexual response, 437–38, 457; alternatives to, 438–39
Mathematical knowledge, 21–22
Mean, statistical, 44–45, 57
Meaningful elaboration in encoding, 279–80
Median, statistical, 45, 57
Medulla, 45, 123
Memory, 264–93; amnesia and, 289–90; biological bases of, 288–90; boundaries of, 291; definition of, 266, 292; encoding in, 266, 278–81, 292. See also Encoding; episodic, 272, 292; frontiers of, 291; improving, encoding and, 280–81; information processing in, 278–88; insights on, at neural level, 290; levels of processing model of, 272–75, 292–93; procedural, 272, 292; psychologists' views of, 267–78; retrieval in, 266, 284–88, 292. See also Retrieval; semantic, 272, 292; state-dependent, 285, 293; storage in, 266, 282–83, 292; three-component model of, 267–72
Menarche, 425, 456
Mendel, Gregor, 72, 73
Menopause, 427–28, 456
Mental age in intelligence testing, 466, 492
Mental set, 315, 328
Mere exposure effect on attitude, 610, 635
Meritocracy, 482–83, 492

Metacognition in child development, 400, 418
Methadone for heroin addiction, 116
Milgram procedure for evaluation of obedience to authority, 622–23
Mischel, Walter, on person variables in personality, 522
MMPI (Minnesota Mutiphasic Personality Inventory), 497–99, 530
Mnemonic devices, 280–81, 293
Modeling in behavior therapy, 583–84, 598
Monaural cues in locating sound, 200–1
Monocular cues in depth perception, 174–75
Monozygotic (MZ) twins, 72–78, 88
Mood disorders, 548–52, 564
Moral development, 388, 418; Kohlberg's theory of, 388–91
Moratoriums, 406
Morpheme, 319, 328
Morphine, 115
Motion parallax in depth perception, 174, 188
Motion perception, 176
Motion sickness, 212, 223
Motivation, 330–59; for aggression, 353–58; boundaries of, 370–71; definition of, 332, 372; drive theory of, 336–37; for eating, 345–53. See also Hunger; eating and aggression and, 359; expectancy theory of, 344–45, 372; frontiers of, 370–71; incentive theory of, 343–44, 372; instinct theory of, 335, 372; intrinsic, 344, 372; need theories of, 337–41; opponent-process theory of, 342–43, 372; optimal-arousal theory of, 341–42, 372; theories of, 335–45
Motor area of cerebral cortex, 129, 145
Motor behavior, disturbances of, in schizophrenia, 555
Motor development in infancy and childhood, 398–99
Motor neurons, 96, 144
MRI (magnetic resonance imaging) scan of brain, 123
Multiple intelligences, theory of, 485–87, 492
Multiple personality disorder, 545–46
Multiple sclerosis, symptoms and neuronal base of, 120
Mutations, 74, 88
Myelin sheath, 95, 144
Myopia, 160, 187
Myotonia in human sexual response, 437–39, 457

N

Narcissistic personality disorder, 559, 565
Narcotics, 114–16
Nasal cavity, 213, 223
Natural selection, 65–67, 88
Naturalistic observation in observational research, 31–32, 56
Nearsightedness, 160
Need(s): for achievement (n Ach), 339–40, 372; for affiliation, 340, 372; Maslow's hierarchy of, 337–39, 372; for power, 340–41, 372
Need theories of motivation, 337–41
Negative reinforcer in operant conditioning, 251, 262
Neo-Freudians, psychodynamic theory and, 578–79

11; heuristics in, 309–14. See also Heuristic(s); thinking in, 315–17

Procedural memory, 272, 292

Projection as defense mechanism, 508, 530

Projective tests in personality measurement, 501–2, 530

Prototypes in concept representation, 302–3, 328

Proximal stimulus in visual perception, 170, 188

Proximate causes of behavior in evolution, 60, 88

Proximity: interpersonal attraction and, 628; in perceptual grouping, 172, 188

Proximodistal principle of motor development, 398, 418

Psychedelics, 112–14

Psychiatrist, 15, 19

Psychoactive drugs, 105; classes of, 107–16

Psychoanalysis, early, 6, 19

Psychodynamic approach to personality, 503–15; Adler's theory in, 512–13; Freud's theory in, 503–10; Horney's theory in, 513–14; Jung's theory in, 511–12

Psychodynamic approaches to therapy, 575–79

Psychodynamic perspective on psychology, 9, 19

Psychogenic amnesia, 545, 564

Psychogenic fugue, 545, 564

Psychological aspects of gender development, 428–35

Psychological dependence, 106, 144

Psychological disorders, 532–65; anxiety-based, 540–48; boundaries of, 562–63; classifying, 537–40; definition of, 535, 564; frontiers of, 562–63; mood, 548–52; nature of, 535–37; personality, 559–61; psychosexual, 561–62; schizophrenia as, 553–59

Psychological research: boundaries of, 54–55; data analysis in, 42–51. See also Data analysis; ethics in, 51–54; experimental, 34–42. See also Experimental research; frontiers of, 54–55; observational, 29–34. See also Observational research; scientific knowledge and, 21–29

Psychologists: clinical, 15, 19; practitioner, 14–17, 19; research, 12–13, 19; in school, 15–16; in workplace, 15

Psychology: beginnings of, 3–6; behavioral perspective on, 7, 19; behavioral school of, 5; biological perspective on, 7–8, 19; boundaries of, 17–18; clinical, 15; cognitive perspective on, 8–9, 19; community, 591–93, 598; comparing perspectives on, 10–11; current perspectives in, 6–11; definition of, 2, 19; developmental, life-span, 377; educational, 15–16; frontiers in, 17–18; functionalist theory of, 4; Gestalt, 5, 19; health, 648, 666; industrial, 15; introduction to, 1–19; practice in, 14–17; preventive, 592, 598; psychodynamic perspective on, 9, 19; research methods in, 12–13; research methods in, 20–57. See also Research, psychological; science and practice in, 16–17; scope of, 2–3; social, 600–35; social perspective on, 9–10, 19; structuralist theory of, 4

Psychometrics, 476, 492

Psychosexual disorders, 561–62

Psychosexual stages in personality development, 508, 530

Psychosis, drugs for, 573–74

Psychosocial development, Erikson's theory of, 391–93

Psychosurgery, 572, 598

Psychotherapy, 566–99; behavioral approaches to, 579–84; biomedical approaches to, 570–75; boundaries of, 596–97; cognitive behavioral approaches to, 584–86; community approaches to, 591–93; definition of, 568, 598; effectiveness of, 593–94; ethical issues in, 594–96; frontiers of, 596–97; group approaches to, 589–91; humanistic approaches to, 587–88; legal issues in, 594–96; psychodynamic approaches to, 575–79

Puberty, 405, 419; female development in, 424–27; gender development in, 424–27; male development in, 417

Punisher in operant conditioning, 251–52, 262

Punishment: in behavior therapy, 582–83; in operant conditioning, 250–51, 255–56

Pupil of eye, 157, 187

Purity: of light, 157, 187; of sound, 194, 222

Pychodynamic approach to personality, critique of, 514–15

Q

Questionnaire for self-reporting, 30, 56

R

Radioactive pollution, 660–61

Random assignment, definition of, 56

Rape, 452–54; trauma syndrome, 454

Rational-emotive therapy (RET), 584–85, 598

Rationalization as defense mechanism, 508, 530

Reaction formation as defense mechanism, 508, 530

Reaction time as measure of intelligence, 487–88

Reality principle, 507, 530

Reappraisal, cognitive, in coping with stress, 653–54, 667

Reasoning, 304–8; deductive, 304–6, 328; definition of, 304, 328

Reciprocal altruism, 83–85, 89

Reciprocal determinism in personality, 521, 531

Recovery, spontaneous, in classical conditioning, 238, 262

Reflection in person-centered therapy, 587–88, 598

Reflexes in infancy, 396–97

Refractory period, 98, 144

Regression line, 47–48, 57

Reinforcement: in behavior therapy, 581; in operant conditioning, 250–55

Reinforcers in operant conditioning, 251, 262

Relational hypothesis, 29; definition of, 56

Relative size in depth perception, 174, 188

Relaxation in coping with stress, 654

Reliability coefficient for intelligence tests, 477, 492

Reliability of intelligence tests, 476–78, 492

Religious knowledge, 22

REM (rapid eye movement) sleep, 137, 145; mysteries of, 139–40; as paradoxical sleep, 140–41

Representativeness heuristic, 313–14, 328

Repression in Freudian theory, 504–5, 530

Reproductive success in natural selection, 65–66, 88

Rescorla-Wagner model of classical conditioning, 242–43, 262

Research: experimental, 34–42, 56–57; observational, 29–34

Research psychological. See Psychological research

Research psychologists, 12–13, 19

Residual schizophrenia, 556, 565

Resistance: in Freudian theory, 504, 530; in psychoanalysis, 577, 598

Resolution phase in sexual arousal, 438

Response acquiring in operant conditioning, 245–50

Response bias in stimulus detection, 152, 187

Response criterion in signal detection experiment, 153, 187

Responsibility, diffusion of, bystander effect and, 627, 635

Resting potential, 97

Reticular formation, 124, 145

Retina, 157, 159–61, 187; to brain, 161–62; visual acuity and, 160–61, 187

Retrieval, 266, 284–88, 292; cues for, 284–85; interference and, 287–88; as reconstructive process, 285–87

Retroactive interference, retrieval and, 287, 293

Retrograde amnesia, 289

Reuptake in synaptic transmission, 102, 144

Rods of retina, 159, 187

Rogers, Carl, on conditions of worth, 526–27

Rorschach inkblot test in personality assessment, 501

Rotter, Julian, on locus of control, 522–23

S

Sadism, sexual, 562, 565

Safety, personal, 647

Sample in inferential statistics, 49–50, 57

Saturation of light, 157, 187

Scatter plot, 46–47, 57

Schemata in social perception, 603–4, 634

Schemes in cognitive development, 382–83, 417

Schizophrenia, 553–59; catatonic, 556, 565; definition of, 553, 565; disorganized, 556, 565; etiology of, 556–59; paranoid, 556, 565; residual, 556, 565; symptoms of, 554–55; and treatment of, 120; types of, 555–56; undifferentiated, 556, 565

School, psychologists in, 15–16

Scientific knowledge: as empirical knowledge, 2–26; hypotheses and, 27–29; nature of, 21–29; theory and, 28–29; variables and, 26–27

Scores, standard, on intelligence tests, 475, 492
Seat belts, use of, 647
Secondary drives, 336, 372
Selection: artificial, 63, 88, 465; kin, 82, 89; natural, 65–67, 88
Selective attention in auditory perception, 202
Selective listening in auditory perception, 202, 222
Selective looking in perception, 178, 188
Self-actualization: need for, 338, 372; in personality, 525–26
Self-concept, 56, 531
Self-efficacy in personality, 521–22, 531
Self-perception theory, 619–20, 635
Self-report in observational research, 29–30, 56
Semantic memory, 272, 292
Semicircular canals, 211, 223
Sensation, 146–69; absolute thresholds in, 150–52, 187; auditory, 192–203. See also Audition; definition of, 149, 187; difference thresholds in, 154–55, 187; principles of, 150–55; signal detection theory of, 152–54, 187
Sense(s): of smell, 212–16; of taste, 216–20, 223
Sensorimotor period in cognitive development, 383–85
Sensory neurons, 95–96, 144
Sensory register in three-component model of memory, 268–69, 292
Separation anxiety, 400–1, 408
Serotonin as neurotransmitter, 105
Set point, eating, 347, 372; obesity and, 349
Sex: divorce and, 444–45; influences of, on heredity, 74; marriage and, 443–44; widowhood and, 445
Sex chromosomes, 72, 88
Sexual aggression, 450–54; pornography and, 450–52; rape as, 452–54
Sexual behavior, 435–37, 435–55. See also Sexual behavior; boundaries of, 454–55; frontiers of, 454–55; patterns of, 441–50; sexually transmitted diseases and, 449–50
Sexual dysfunctions, 439–41, 457; female, 439–40; male, 440–41
Sexual response, human: biological bases of, 437–39; Kaplan's biphasic model of, 439; Masters and Johnson model of, 437–38, 457; Zilbergeld and Ellison's five-compartment model of, 439
Sexually transmitted diseases (STDs), 646; sexual behavioral and, 449–50
Shaping in operant conditioning, 249–50
Short-term store in three-component model of memory, 269–71, 292
Sign stimulus, behavior and, 229–30, 261
Signal detection theory of sensation, 152–54, 187
Similarity: interpersonal attraction and, 628; in perceptual grouping, 172, 188
Single-subject research, 38–39, 57
Sixteen Personality Factor Questionnaire (16PF), 499–500, 530
Skin senses, 204–10
Skinner, Burrhus Frederic, operant behavior and, 247–48
Sleep: brain in, 136–41; circadian rhythms and, 136–37, 145; need for, 138–39; REM, 137, 145. See also REM (rapid eye movement) sleep; stages of, 137

Smell: nature of, 213; sense of, 212–16
Smoking, cigarette, 644–45
Social behavior, gender differences in, 435
Social cognition: attitude in, 609–13, 635; attribution in, 606–9, 634; cognition dissonance theory of, 613–15; definition of, 602–3, 634; schemata for, 603–4, 634
Social development: in adolescence, 406–8; in adulthood and old age, 411–14; in infancy and childhood, 400–5
Social facilitation, 615–16, 635
Social influence, 615–32; bystander intervention and, 626–27; compliance and, 619–21, 635; conformity and, 616–18, 635; helping behavior and, 627; interpersonal attraction and, 628–29; obedience to authority and, 621–26, 635; social facilitation and, 615–16, 635; social norms and, 616, 635; sociobiology and, 629–32, 635
Social interest in personality development, 512–13, 531
Social issues, intelligence and, 481–83
Social learning of aggression, 356–58
Social learning theory of gender typing, 432
Social learning theory of personality, 520–24, 531; expectancy and, 520–21, 531; locus of control and, 522–23, 531; observational learning and, 520–21, 531; person variables and, 522; reciprocal determinism and, 521, 531; self-efficacy and, 521–22, 531
Social norms, 616, 635
Social perspective on psychology, 9–10
Social psychology, 600–5; boundaries of, 632–33; definition of, 602, 634; frontiers of, 632–33; social cognition in, 602–15; sociobiology of social influence in, 629–32
Social support in coping with stress, 654
Society, attitudes of, toward homosexuality, 448–49
Sociobiology, 81–86, 86; criticisms of, 85–86; social influence and, 629–32, 635
Solid waste pollution, 661–63
Somatic nervous system, 94, 143
Somatization disorders, 544, 564
Somatoform disorders, 543–44, 564
Somatosensory areas of cerebral cortex, 130
Somatosensory system, 204–12, 223
Sound: locating, 200–1; nature of, 193–95; neural processing of, 198–200
Sound wave, 193–95, 222
Species-typical behavior, 229, 261
Speech, telegraphic, 323, 328
Split brain, 133–35
Spontaneous recovery in classical conditioning, 238, 262
Standard deviation, 45–46, 57
Standard scores on intelligence tests, 475, 492
Standardization in intelligence testing, 467, 492
Stanford-Binet: 4th edition, 468–71; Lewis Terman and, 467–68
State-dependent memory, 285, 293
Statistically significant, 57
Statistics in data analysis, 42–51; descriptive, 42, 43–46, 57; inferential, 49–51, 57
Stereotypes in social perception, 605, 634
Stimulants, 107–10

Stimulation, electrical, of brain activity, 121–22
Stimulus generalization in classical conditioning, 238–39, 262
Storage in memory, 266, 282–83, 292
Stranger anxiety, 400, 418
Stress, 648, 666; biological basis of, 648–49; cognitive appraisal and, 650, 667; coping with, 652–54; health and, 648–54; obesity and, 350
Stressors, 648, 666
Striving for superiority in personality development, 512–13, 531
Stroboscopic movement, 176, 188
Structuralism, 4, 19
Sublimation: as cathartic outlet, 353; as defense mechanism, 508, 530
Suicide, depression and, 549
Superego, 506, 530
Symbols in information processing, 298, 328
Sympathetic nervous system, 95, 143, 144
Synapses, neuronal, 99, 144
Synaptic cleft, 99, 144
Synaptic transmission, 99–102, 144
Synaptic vesicles, 100, 114
Syntax of language, 319–20
Syphilis, 449
Systematic desensitization in psychotherapy, 580, 598

T

Taste: adaptation to, 220; nature of, 217; sense of, 216–20, 223; thresholds for, 29–30
Taste-aversion learning, classical conditioning and, 243–45
Taste buds, 217–18, 223
Teenagers, unwanted pregnancy and, 442–43
Telegraphic speech, 323, 328
Temperature, sense of, 206–7
Terminal button of neuron, 95, 144
Test bias of intelligence tests, 478–79
Texture gradient in depth perception, 174, 188
Thalamus, 124, 145
Thematic Apperception Test (TAT) in personality assessment, 502
Theory in scientific knowledge, 28–29, 56
Therapy, 566–99. See also Psychotherapy
Therman, Lewis, Stanford-Binet test and, 467–68
Thinking, 294–329; boundaries of, 326–27; definition of, 304, 328; fixation and, 315–17; frontiers of, 326–27; language and, 317–24. See also Language; problem solving and, 308–17; reasoning and, 304–8. See also Reasoning
Thought, disorganized, in schizophrenia, 554
Three-component model of memory, 267–72; long-term store in, 271–72, 292; modification of, 275–77; sensory register in, 268–69, 292; short-term store in, 269–71, 292
Three-term contingency in operant conditioning, 248–50
Thresholds: absolute, in sensation, 150–52, 187; difference, in sensation, 154–55, 187; olfactory, 214–15; pain, 207–8, 223; taste, 219–20

Timbre, 194, 222
Token economy, 255; in behavior therapy, 581, 594
Tolerance, 106, 144; to narcotics, 115
Top-down processing in pattern recognition, 185, 189
Trait, 515, 531
Trait approach to personality, 515–20; Allport and, 515–16; Cattell and, 517; critique of, 519–20; Eysenck and, 517–18; five-factor theory and, 516–17
Traits, central, in social perception, 604, 634
Transduction sensation, 150, 187
Transference in psychoanalysis, 577–78, 598
Transsexual, 431–32, 456
Treatment condition, definition of, 57
Triarchic theory of intelligence, 484–85, 492
Trichromatic theory of color vision, 167–68, 169
Twins: dizygotic, 77–78, 88; monozygotic, 77–78, 88
Two-factor theory of emotion, 367–69, 373
Two-point discrimination threshold, 205
Tympanic membrane, 196, 222

U

Ultimate causes of behavior in evolution, 60, 88
Unconditional positive regard, 526–27, 531
Unconditonal response (UCR) in classical conditioning, 235, 261
Unconditional stimulus (UCS) in classical conditioning, 235, 261

Unconscious, 504, 530; collective, 512, 531; memories in, personality in, 504–5
Underarousal hypothesis for personality disorder, 560–61
Undifferentiated schizophrenia, 556, 565

V

Vaginismus, 440, 457
Validity coefficient for intelligence tests, 477–78, 492
Validity of intelligence tests, 476–78, 492
Value of variable, 26, 56
Variable-interval (VI) schedule of reinforcement, 253–54, 263
Variable-ratio (VR) schedule of reinforcement, 253, 262
Variable(s): confounding, in experimental research, 40, 57; correlation of, 26–27, 56; definition of, 56; dependent, 34, 37, 56; empirical knowledge and, 26; in experimental research, 34–36; independent, 34, 37, 56; intervening, 333, 372; intelligence test scores and, 476, 492; motivation as, 333; manipulating, 35–36, 37; person, in personality, 522; prediction from, 26–27; relationships among, 26–27
Variation in natural selection, 66, 88
Vasocongestion in human sexual response, 437–39, 456
Ventromedial hypothalamus (VMH), feeding and, 347, 372
Verbal intelligence, measurement of, 471–72, 492
Vestibular sacs, 212, 223
Vestibular system, 211–12, 223

Vision, 146–89; color, 165–69; as perceptual process, 170–85; as sensory process, 155–69
Visual acuity: age and, 161; retina and, 160–61, 187
Visual information, neural processing of, 163
Volley principle of sound, 199–200, 222
Voyeurism, 562, 565

W

WAIS-R (Wechsler Adult Intelligence Scale, Revised), 471, 492
Water pollution, 660
Wave frequency, 194, 222
Wavelength of light, 157, 187
Weber's fraction, 154–55, 187
Weber's law, 154, 187
Wechsler tests of intelligence, revised, 471–73
Wernicke's area, 131–32, 145
Widowhood, sex and, 445
WISC-R (Wechsler Intelligence Scale for Children, Revised), 471, 492
Work in social development, 413
Workplace, psychologists in, 15

X

XYY syndrome, 79, 89

Y

Yerkes-Dodson law, 342, 372

Z

Zilbergeld and Ellison's five compartment model of human sexual response, 439